KU-093-450

STREET ATLAS
Surrey

Contents

III	Key to map symbols
IV-V	Key to map pages
VI-VII	Route planning
VIII	Administrative and post code boundaries
1	Street maps
219	Extra-large-scale maps of town centres

219 Dorking
219 Epsom
220 Guildford
220 Kingston upon Thames
221 Leatherhead
221 Woking

222 Index of hospitals, industrial estates, railway stations, schools, shopping centres, street names and universities

First published 1996 by

George Philip Ltd, a division of
Octopus Publishing Group Ltd
2-4 Heron Quays, London E14 4JP

Second colour edition 2000
Third impression 2001

ISBN 0-540-07796-8 (pocket)

 Ordnance
Survey®

Printed and bound in Spain by Cayfosa-Quebecor

Digital Data

The exceptionally high-quality mapping
found in this book is available as
digital data in TIFF format, which is
easily convertible to other bit-mapped
(raster) image formats.

The index is also available in digital
form as a standard database table.
It contains all the details found in the
printed index together with the
National Grid reference for the map
square in which each entry is named
and feature codes for places of
interest in eight categories such as
education and health.

For further information and to discuss
your requirements, please contact
Philip's on 020 7531 8440 or
george.philip@philips-maps.co.uk

Motorway (with junction number)	**Railway station**
Primary route (dual carriageway and single)	**London Underground station**
A road (dual carriageway and single)	**Croydon Tramlink**
B road (dual carriageway and single)	**Private railway station**
Minor road (dual carriageway and single)	**Bus, coach station**
Other minor road (dual carriageway and single)	**Ambulance station**
Road under construction	**Coastguard station**
Pedestrianised area	**Fire station**
DY7 Postcode boundaries	**Police station**
County and Unitary Authority boundaries	**Accident and Emergency entrance to hospital**
Railway	**Hospital**
Tramway, miniature railway	**Places of worship**
Rural track, private road or narrow road in urban area	**Information Centre** (open all year)
Gate or obstruction to traffic (restrictions may not apply at all times or to all vehicles)	**Parking, Park and Ride**
Path, bridleway, byway open to all traffic, road used as a public path	**Post Office**
The representation in this atlas of a road, track or path is no evidence of the existence right of way	**Important buildings, schools, colleges, universities and hospitals**
	River Medway **Water name**
Adjoining page indicators	**Stream**
	River or canal (minor and major)
The map area within the pink band is shown at a larger scale on the page indicated by the red block and arrow	**Water**
	Tidal water
	Woods
	Houses
	House **Non-Roman antiquity**
	VILLA **Roman antiquity**

■ The dark grey border on the inside edge of some pages indicates that the mapping does not continue onto the adjacent page
■ The small numbers around the edges of the maps identify the 1 kilometre National Grid lines

Acad	**Academy**	Ent	**Enterprise**	LC	**Level Crossing**	Obsy	**Observatory**	Sch	**School**
Crem	**Crematorium**	Ex H	**Exhibition Hall**	Liby	**Library**	Pal	**Royal Palace**	Sh Ctr	**Shopping Centre**
Cemy	**Cemetery**	Ind Est	**Industrial Estate**	Mkt	**Market**	PH	**Public House**	TH	**Town Hall/House**
C Ctr	**Civic Centre**	Inst	**Institute**	Meml	**Memorial**	Recn Gd	**Recreation Ground**	Trad Est	**Trading Estate**
CH	**Club House**	Ct	**Law Court**	Mon	**Monument**	Resr	**Reservoir**	Univ	**University**
Coll	**College**	L Ctr	**Leisure Centre**	Mus	**Museum**	Ret Pk	**Retail Park**	YH	**Youth Hostel**

The scale of the maps is 3.92 cm to 1 km (2½ inches to 1 mile)	0 ¼ ½ ¾ 1 mile 0 250m 500m 750m 1 kilometre
The scale of the maps on pages numbered in red is 7.84 cm to 1 km (5 inches to 1 mile)	0 220 yards 440 yards 660 yards ½ mile 0 125m 250m 375m ½ kilometre

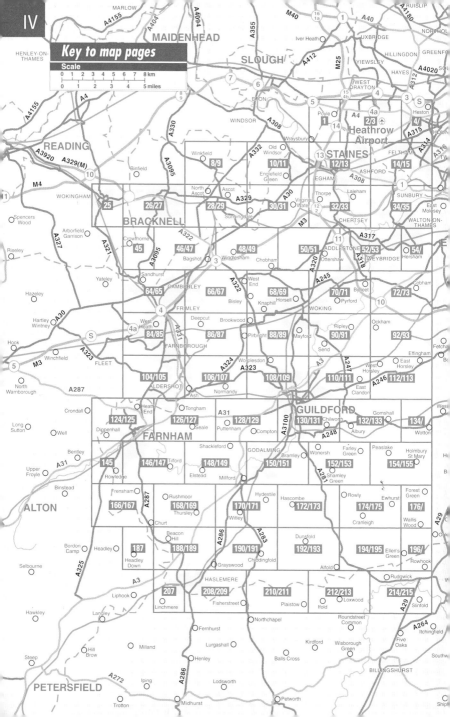

IV

Key to map pages

Scale
0 1 2 3 4 5 6 7 8 km
0 1 2 3 4 5 miles

MARLOW
A4155
A404
A4094
M40
16 1a
1
A40
RUISLIP
A4180
NORTHOL

MAIDENHEAD
A355
Iver Heath
UXBRIDGE
HILLINGDON
GREENF

HENLEY-ON-THAMES
A4155
SLOUGH
A412
M25
YIEWSLEY
HAYES
A4020
SOU

WEST DRAYTON
15 4b
4
3
S
Heston

A4
4a
4/

READING
A3920
A329(M)
A330
A3095
WINDSOR
A308
Wraysbury
Poyle
1
14
Heathrow Airport
2/3
A315
HOUN

M4
10
Binfield
Winkfield
8/9
Old Windsor
10/11
Englefield Green
13
STAINES
12/13
14/15
FELTHAM
A314
TW
A316

WOKINGHAM
North Ascot
Ascot
28/29
A329
30/31
A30
Virginia Water
32/33
34/35
Laleham
SUNBURY
East Molesey

Spencers Wood
25
26/27
BRACKNELL
Sunningdale
Thorpe
12
EGHAM
A308
ASHFORD
1
WALTON-ON-THAMES

Arborfield Garrison
A327
A322
A3095
Crowthorne
45
46/47
Windlesham
48/49
Chobham
50/51
ADDLESTONE
52/53
WEYBRIDGE
54/
Hersham

Riseley
A321
Sandhurst
Bagshot
3
Ottershaw
A318
CHERTSEY
11
A317

Yateley
64/65
CAMBERLEY
66/67
Bisley
West End
68/69
Horsell
70/71
Byfleet
Pyrford
72/73
Cobham

Hazeley
A30
FRIMLEY
Deepcut
Brookwood
Knaphill
WOKING
10

Hartley Wintney
West Heath
4
4a
84/85
86/87
88/89
Pirbright
Mayford
90/91
Ripley
Send
Ockham
92/93
Fetcha

Hook
M3
A323
A341
FARNBOROUGH
A324
A323
Worplesdon
108/109
A3
West Horsley
East Horsley
112/113
A246
Bo

North Warnborough
5
FLEET
104/105
ALDERSHOT
Ash
106/107
Normandy
110/111
East Clandon
Effingham

A287
A31
Tongham
Seale
128/129
Puttenham
Compton
A3100
130/131
Chilworth
A248
Albury
132/133
Gomshall
134/
Wotton
Wess

Crondall
Heath End
124/125
126/127
GUILDFORD

Long Sutton
Well
Dippenhall
FARNHAM
Shackleford
GODALMING
Bramley
Wonersh
Farley Green
Peaslake
Holmbury St Mary
154/155
He

Bentley
145
146/147
Tilford
148/149
Elstead
Millford
150/151
152/153
Shamley Green
A281
174/175
Ewhurst
Forest Green
176/

Upper Froyle
A31
Rowledge
Frensham
Rushmoor
Thursley
Hydestile
Hascombe
Rowly
Cranleigh
Wallis Wood
Osk

Binstead
A287
166/167
168/169
170/171
Witley
172/173

ALTON
Churt
Beacon Hill
A286
A283
Dunsfold
194/195
Ellen's Green
196/
Rowhook

Bordon Camp
Headley
187
188/189
190/191
Chiddingfold
192/193
Alfold
Rudgwick
W

Selbourne
A325
Headley Down
Grayswood
HASLEMERE

A3
Liphook
207
208/209
Fisherstreet
210/211
Plaistow
Ifold
212/213
Loxwood
214/215
Slinfold
A29

Hawkley
Langley
Linchmere
Fernhurst
Northchapel
Roundstreet Common
A264
Itchingfield

Steep
Hill Brow
Milland
Lurgashall
Henley
Kirdford
Wisborough Green
Five Oaks
Southw

PETERSFIELD
A272
Iping
Trotton
Midhurst
Lodsworth
Balls Cross
Petworth
BILLINGSHURST
Ship

Major administrative and Postcode boundaries

County and unitary authority boundaries
District boundaries
Postcode boundaries
Area covered by this atlas

Scale

0   5   10   15 km
0   5   10 miles

1 Hammersmith and Fulham
2 Royal Borough of Kensington and Chelsea
3 City of Westminster
4 County of the City of London
5 Wandsworth
6 Kingston upon Thames

Bucks
SU | TQ
Slough
Bracknell Forest
Windsor and Maidenhead
Hillingdon
Ealing
Hounslow
Richmond upon Thames
Tower Hamlets
Southwark
Lambeth
Merton
Sutton
Croydon
Bromley
Lewisham
Greenwich
Bexley
Kent
East Sussex
West Sussex
Hampshire
Wokingham

Surrey
Spelthorne
Runnymede
Woking
Guildford
Elmbridge
Epsom and Ewell
Mole Valley
Reigate and Banstead
Tandridge
Waverley
Surrey Heath

Chiswick
SW13
SW14
SW15
Putney
SW11
SW12
SW18
SW19
SW20
SW4
SW2
SW16
SW17
Wimbledon
Mitcham
Carshalton
Sutton
Banstead
Tadworth
Epsom
Ewell
Kingston upon Thames
Esher
East Molesey
Walton-on-Thames
Cobham
Oxshott
Leatherhead
Fetcham
Bookham
Dorking
Wotton
Ockley
Capel
Newdigate
Brockham
Reigate
Redhill
Horley
Gatwick
South Nutfield
Godstone
Oxted
Crowhurst
Lingfield
Newchapel
East Grinstead
Worth Abbey
Crawley
Horsham
Slinfold
Rudgwick
Cranleigh
Ewhurst
Peaslake
Gomshall
Chilworth
West Clandon
West Horsley
Effingham
Ockham
Byfleet
Addlestone
Ottershaw
Chobham
Bisley
Chertsey
Virginia Water
Egham
Staines
Poyle
Wraysbury
Old Windsor
Ascot
Sunningdale
Bagshot
Camberley
Frimley
Farnborough
Aldershot
Ash
Pirbright
Worplesdon
Compton
Godalming
Witley
Dunsfold
Chiddingfold
Haslemere
Hindhead
Rushmoor
Farnham
Sandhurst
Crowthorne
Wokingham
Bracknell
Crondall
Plaistow
Fisherstreet

SL3 SL4 SL5
RG11 RG12
UB3 UB7 UB6
TW5 TW7 TW8 TW9 TW3 TW4 TW14 TW13 TW1 TW2 TW12 TW11 TW16 TW15 TW18 TW17 TW19 TW20
SW
SE12 SE13 SE6 SE4 SE23 SE26 SE25 SE19 SE20 SE21 SE22 SE24 SE27 SE
BR6 BR1 BR3 BR2 BR4
CR0 CR2 CR3 CR5 CR6 CR7 CR8 CR4
SM1 SM2 SM3 SM4 SM5 SM6 SM7
KT1 KT2 KT3 KT4 KT5 KT6 KT7 KT8 KT9 KT10 KT11 KT12 KT13 KT14 KT15 KT16 KT17 KT18 KT19 KT20 KT21 KT22 KT23 KT24
GU1 GU2 GU3 GU4 GU5 GU6 GU7 GU8 GU9 GU10 GU11 GU12 GU13 GU14 GU15 GU16 GU17 GU18 GU19 GU20 GU21 GU22 GU23 GU24 GU25 GU26 GU27 GU28 GU30 GU34 GU35
RH1 RH2 RH3 RH4 RH5 RH6 RH7 RH8 RH9 RH10 RH11 RH12 RH13 RH14 RH16 RH18 RH19
TN8 TN16

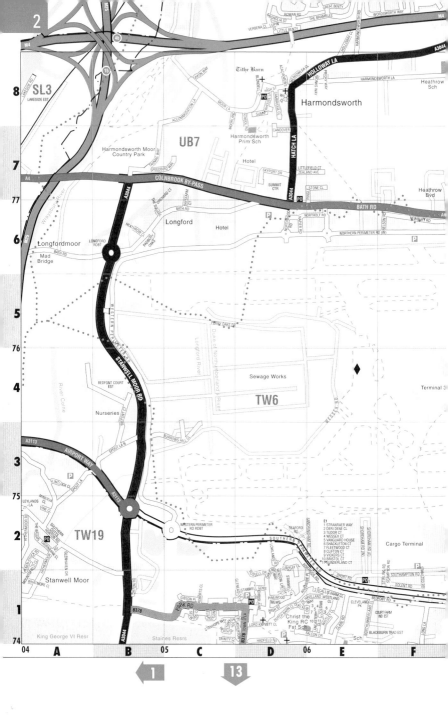

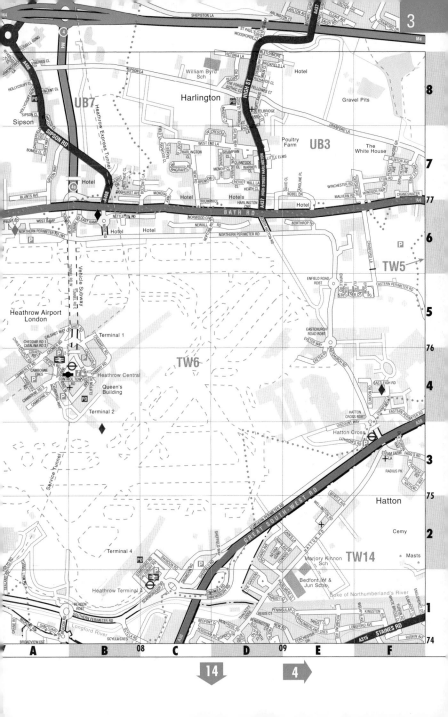

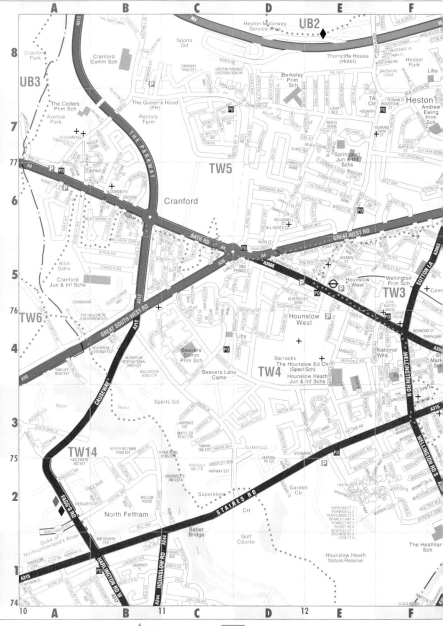

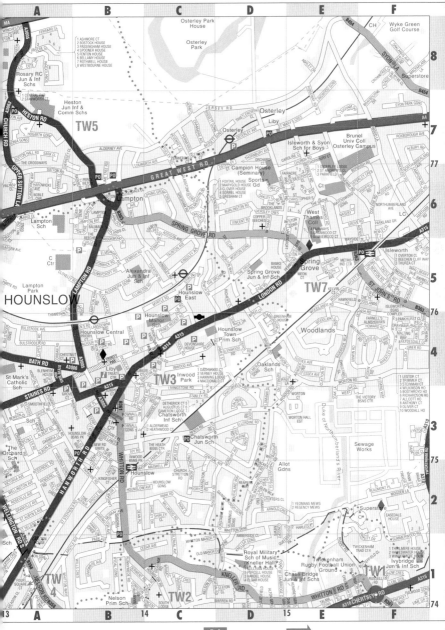

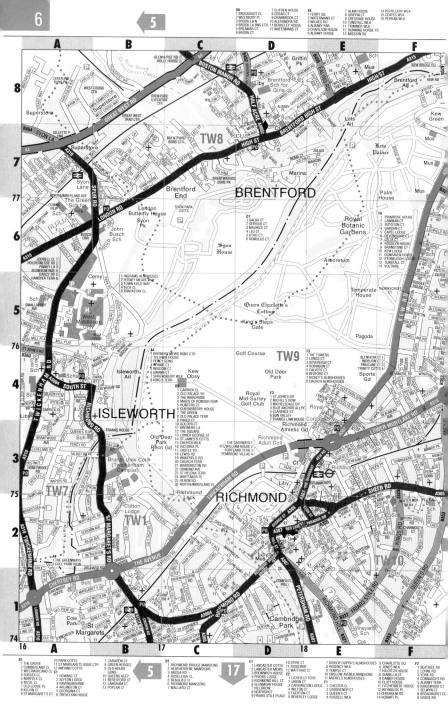

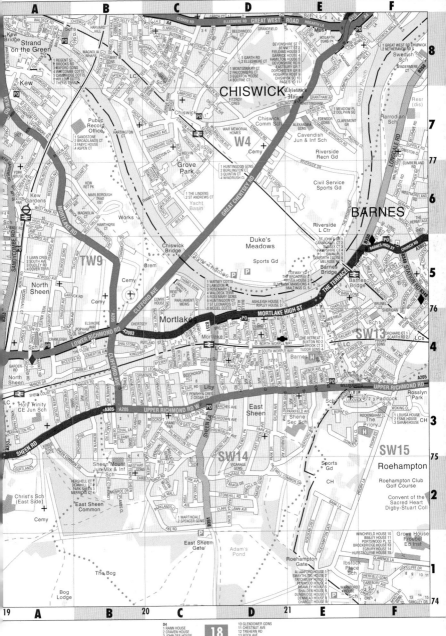

A6
1 CLARENDON CT
2 QUINTOCK HOUSE
3 BROOME CT
4 LONSDALE MEWS
5 ELIZABETH COTTS
6 SANDWAYS
7 VICTORIA COTTS
8 NORTH AVE
9 GROVEWOOD
10 HAMILTON HOUSE
11 MELVIN CT

GREAT WEST ROAD

CHISWICK

Chiswick House

W4

Grove Park

BARNES

Public Record Office

TW9

Chiswick Bridge

River Thames

Duke's Meadows

North Sheen

Mortlake

SW13

Barnes Bridge

Barnes

North Sheen

UPPER RICHMOND RD

East Sheen

SW14

SW15

Roehampton

Roehampton Club Golf Course

Sheen Rd

Christ's Sch (East Side)

East Sheen Common

Convent of the Sacred Heart Digby-Stuart Coll

Grove House Froebel Ed Inst

Ibstock Place Sch

East Sheen Gate

Adam's Pond

Roehampton Gate

The Bog

Bog Lodge

D4
1 RANN HOUSE
2 CRAVEN HOUSE
3 JOHN DEE HOUSE
4 KINDELL HOUSE
5 MONTGOMERY HOUSE
6 AVONDALE HOUSE
7 ADDINGTON CT
8 DOVECOTE GDNS
9 FIRMSTON HOUSE
10 GLENDOWER GDNS
11 CHESTNUT AVE
12 TREHERN RD
13 ROCK AVE

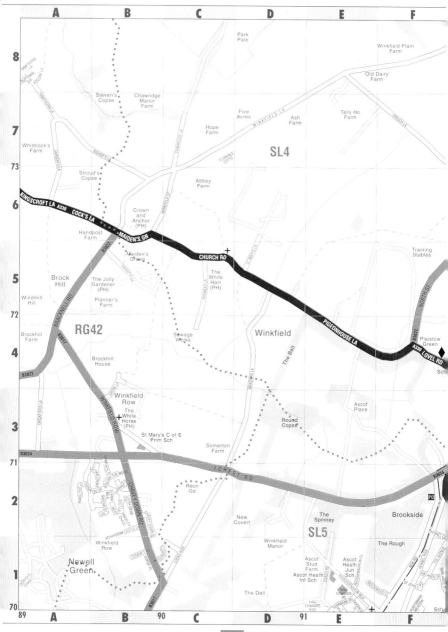

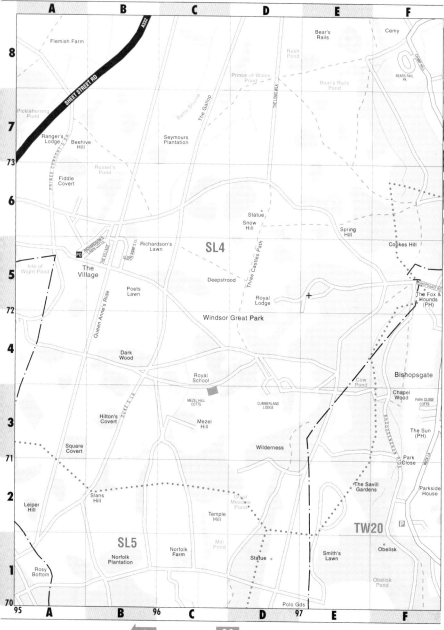

8

Flemish Farm

Bear's
Rails

Cemy

Rush
Pond

BEARS RAIL
PK

Pickleherring
Pond

Prince of Wales
Pond

Bear's Rails
Pond

7

SHEET STREET RD

Ranger's
Lodge

Beehive
Hill

Seymours
Plantation

The Gallop

Battle Bourne

THE LONG WALK

73

PRINCE CONSORT DR

Russel's
Pond

Fiddle
Covert

6

Statue

Snow
Hill

Spring
Hill

Cookes Hill

Richardson's
Lawn

SL4

Three Castles Path

THE VILLAGE

QUEEN ANNE'S CL

PO

Isle of
Wight Pond

The
Village

5

Deepstrood

BISHOPSGATE RD

The Fox &
Hounds
(PH)

72

Poets
Lawn

Royal
Lodge

+

QUEEN ANNE'S RIDE

Windsor Great Park

4

Dark
Wood

Cow
Pond

Bishopsgate

Royal
School

Chapel
Wood

PARK CLOSE
COTTS

DUKE'S LA

MEZEL HILL
COTTS

CUMBERLAND
LODGE

3

Hilton's
Covert

Mezel
Hill

Wilderness

The Sun
(PH)

BISHOPSGATE RD

WICK LA

Park
Close

71

Square
Covert

The Savill
Gardens

Parkside
House

2

Leiper
Hill

Slans
Hill

Great
Meadow
Pond

Temple
Hill

TW20

P

Parkside
House

SL5

Norfolk
Plantation

Norfolk
Farm

Mill
Pond

Statue

Smith's
Lawn

Obelisk

1

Rosy
Bottom

Obelisk
Pond

70

Polo Gds

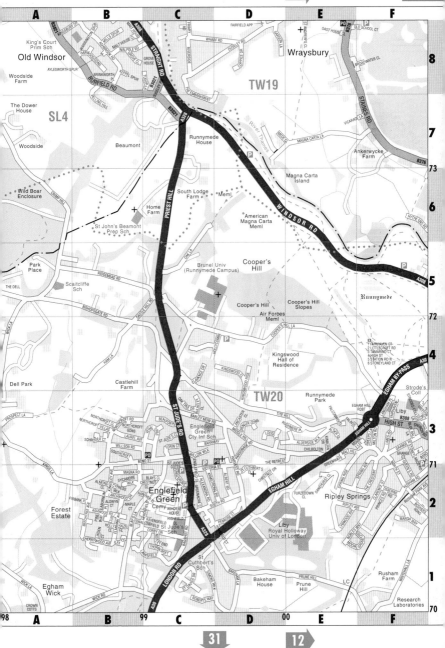

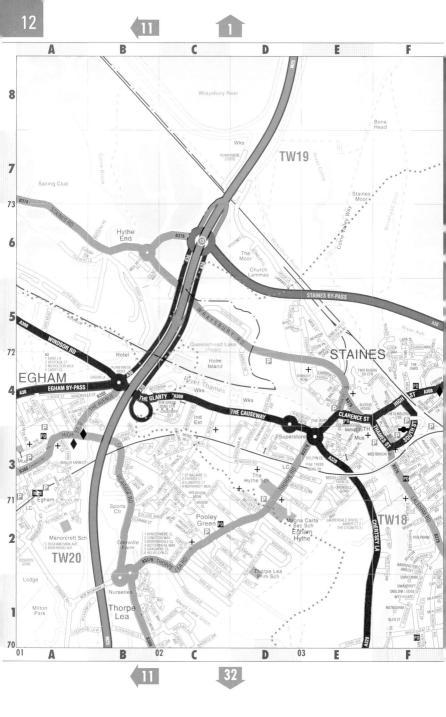

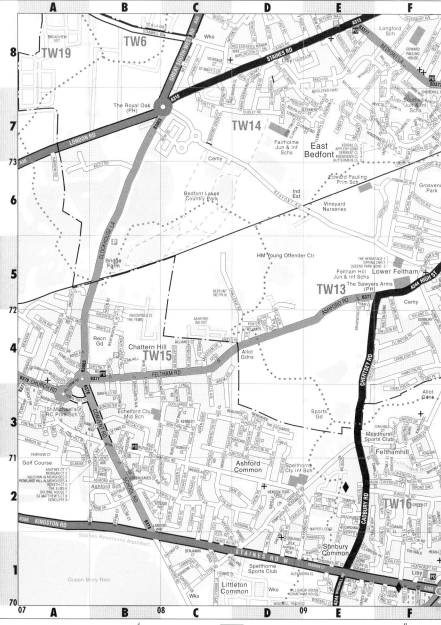

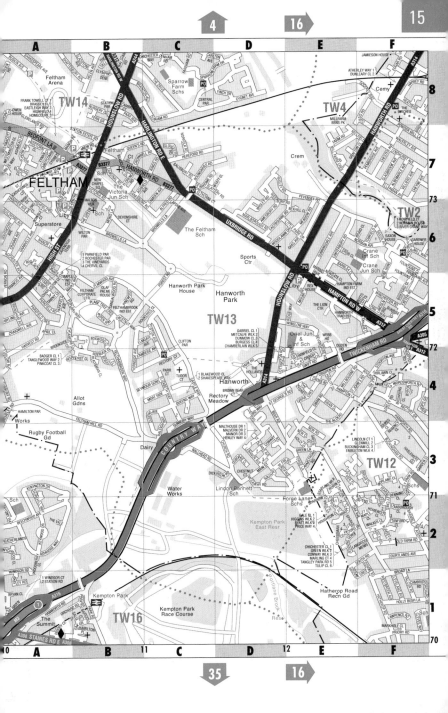

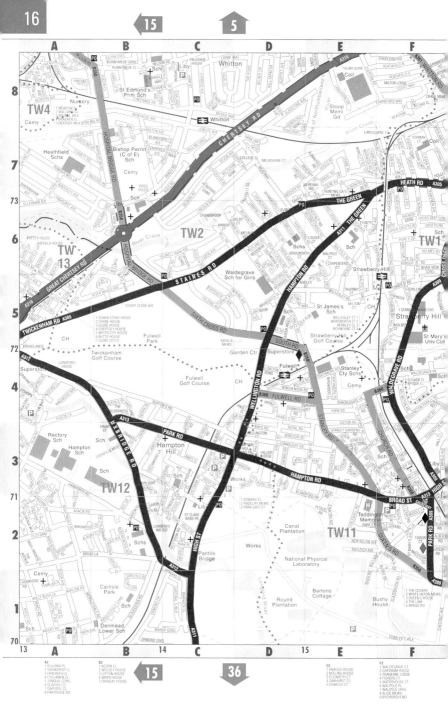

A7
1 KATHARINE RD
2 GARFIELD RD
3 ARRAGON RD
4 FLOOD LA
5 JOHN WESLEY CT
6 KING STREET PAR

A8
1 THAMES EYOT

6 MARCH RD
7 BERKLEY CT
8 COLE COURT LODGE
9 CHELTENHAM AVE
10 RAILWAY APP

B8
1 HARTINGTON RD
2 MELTON CT
3 AMYAND PARK GDNS
4 CROWN CT
5 BURRELL HOUSE
6 OWEN HOUSE

7 BRENTFORD HOUSE
8 LEESON HOUSE
9 WESTBOURNE HOUSE
10 ORLEANS CT
11 LEBANON CT

1 HOBART PL
2 SAYER'S WLK

A3
1 CHERRYWOOD CT
2 CAMBRIDGE HOUSE
3 GLENEAGLES CT
4 CHRISTCHURCH AVE
5 HALES CT
6 SPRINGFIELD RD

C1
1 BELGRAVIA HOUSE
2 HAYDON HOUSE
3 CRIEFF CT
4 THE MAPLES

D4
1 BYRON CT
2 COLERIDGE CT
3 TENNYSON CT
4 HERRICK CT
5 SPENSER CT
6 MARLOWE CT
7 BROOKE CT
8 GRAY CT
9 SHELLEY CT

10 POPE CT
11 DRYDEN CT

F1
1 McDONALD HOUSE
2 ELM HOUSE
3 DALE CT
4 YORK HOUSE
5 FLORENCE HOUSE
6 FLORENCE RD
7 ROUPELL HOUSE
8 CANBURY AVE

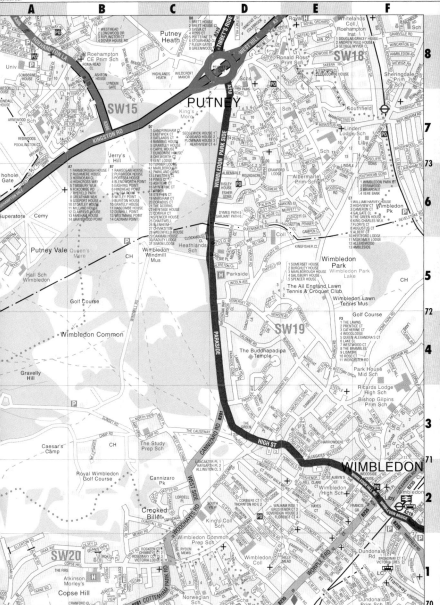

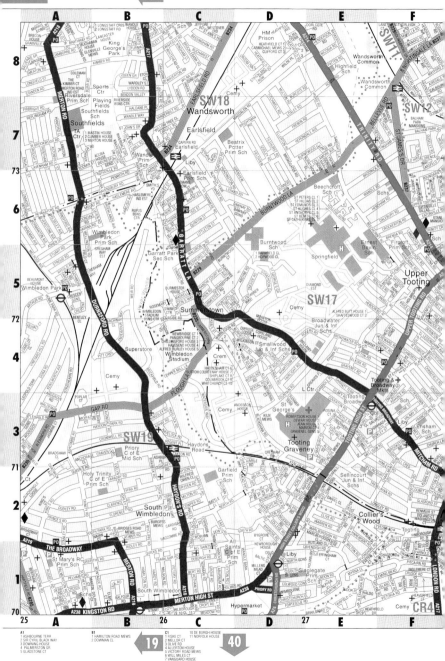

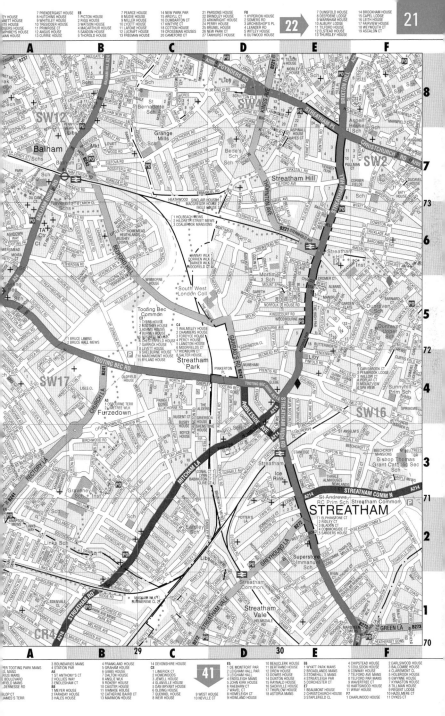

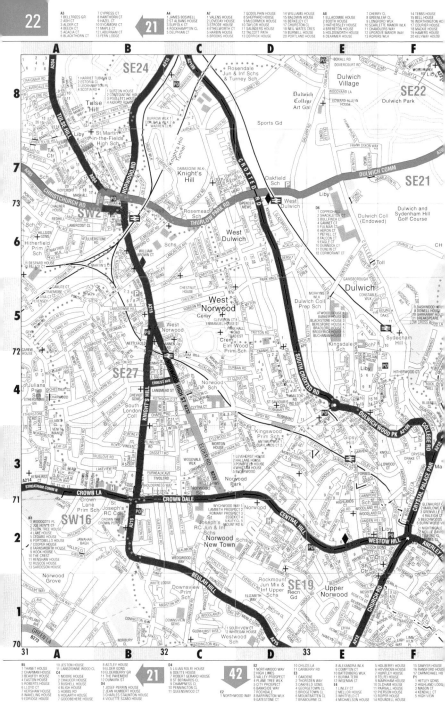

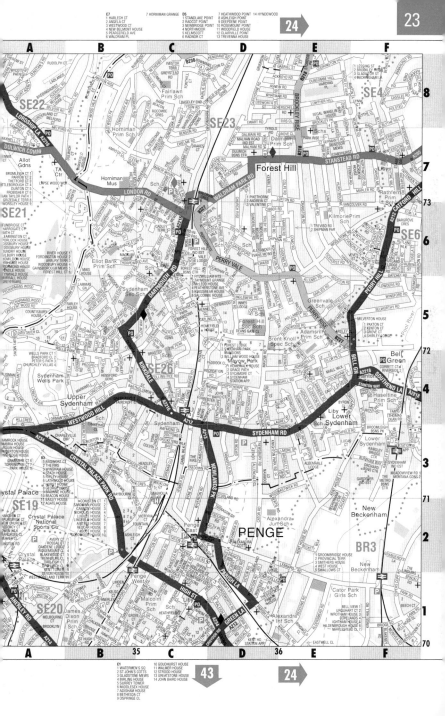

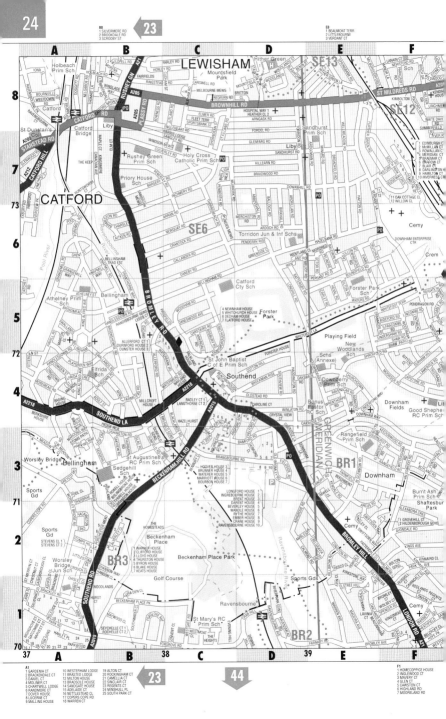

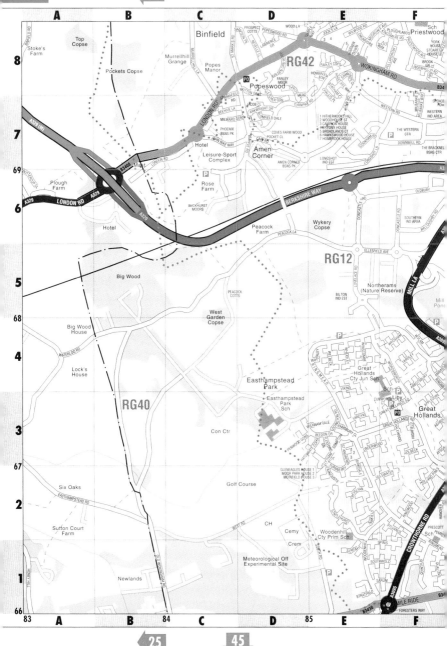

Binfield

RG42

WOKINGHAM RD

Popeswood

1 HITHERHOOKS HILL
2 WOODHOUSE ST
3 WARREN HOUSE
4 BROADLANDS CT
5 HAWKSWOOD HOUSE
6 HORNBROOK HOUSE

THE WESTERN CTR

WESTERN IND AREA

THE BRACKNELL BSNS CTR

Amen Corner

Hotel

Leisure-Sport Complex

LONGSHOT IND EST

Rose Farm

BERKSHIRE WAY

BICKHURST MOORS

Wykery Copse

Peacock Farm

RG12

Big Wood

PEACOCK COTTS

Northerams (Nature Reserve)

BILTON IND EST

West Garden Copse

Big Wood House

WATERLOO RD

Lock's House

RG40

Easthampstead Park

Easthampstead Park Sch

Great Hollands Cty Jun Sch

Sch Liby

Great Hollands

Con Ctr

Golf Course

GLENEAGLES HOUSE 1
MOOR PARK HOUSE 2
MUIRFIELD HOUSE 3

Six Oaks

EASTHAMPSTEAD RD

Sutton Court Farm

WEST RD

CH

Cemy

Crem

Woodenhill Cty Prim Sch

Meteorological Off Experimental Site

Newlands

CROWTHORNE RD

MILE RIDE

FORESTERS WAY

Stoke's Farm

Top Copse

Pockets Copse

Murrellhill Grange

Popes Manor

LONDON RD

A329(M)

Plough Farm

LONDON RD A329

Hotel

A329

Priestwood

Sch

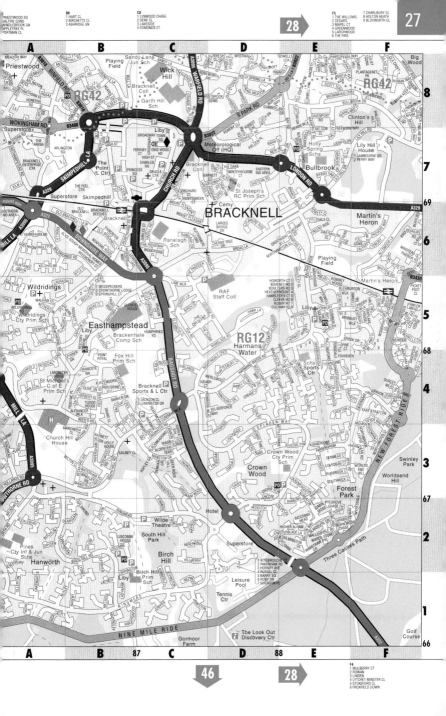

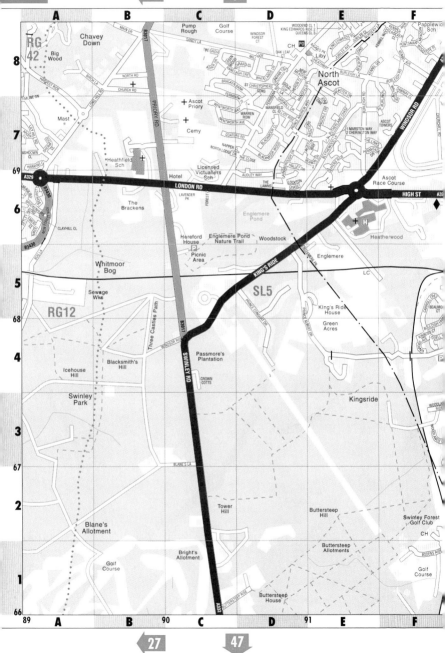

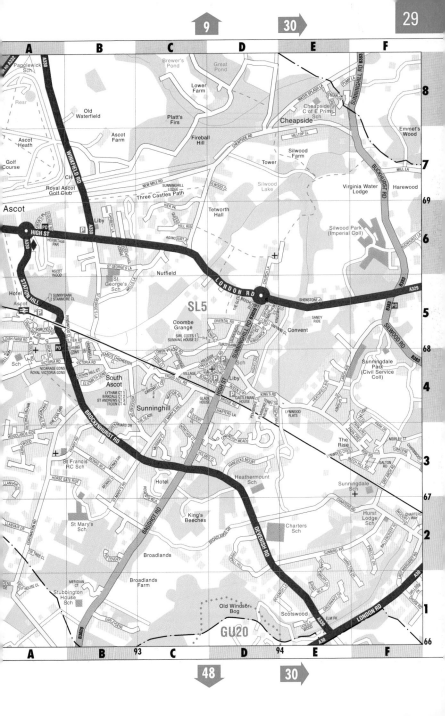

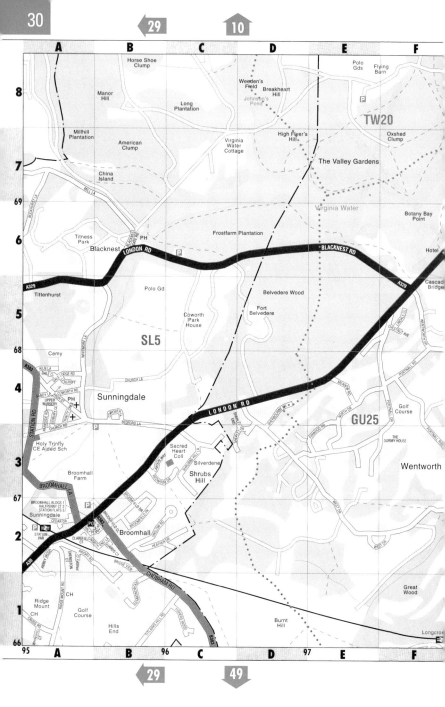

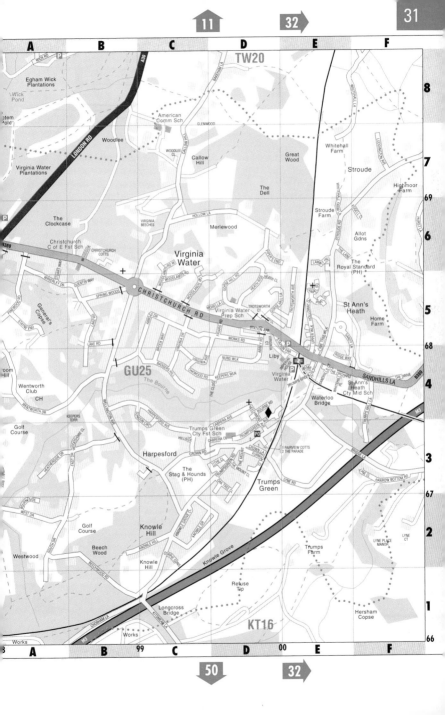

Milton Park
Great Fosters
BLACK LAKE CL
Nursery
Padd Farm
Longside Lake
Thorpe Green
GREEN RD
B389
GU 25
Redlands Farm
Lyne Farm
Lyne Hill Nursery
The Brooks
The Rough
Merrywood Farm
Little Almners
Almners Priory
Pantiles Farm
Lyne
Royal Marine (PH)
Fangrove Caravan Pk
Fan Grove

THORPE BY-PASS
THORPE LEA RD
Crabtree CNR
Crabtree Office Village
TW20
SKY BSNG PK
Thorpe C of E Fst Sch
PH
Thorpe
The Moat
MILL HOUSE LA
B389
BOURNE MEADOW
GREEN RD

THORPE IND PK
Green La
THORPE IND EST
Cemy
COLDHARBOUR LA
Coldharbour
VENTTREES
COTTAGE FARM WAY
The American Sch in Switzerland (English Branch)
St Ann's Lake
The Bourne

Green La
CHERTSEY LA
TW18
River Thames
TEMPLE GDNS
Sycamore Farm
Pento Hook Marin
Works
Fleet Lake
Manor Lake
Miniature Rly
Thorpe Park
Abbey Lake
STAINES RD

THORPE RD
St Ann's Hill
Monk's Grove
Hamperstone Bridge (PH)
STAINES RD
ST ANN'S RD
Sewage Wks
Ruxbury Farm
KT16
St Ann's Hill Rd
RUXBURY RD
PH
ST ANN'S RD
CHILSEY GREEN RD
B388
North GR
Pyrcroft Grange Prim Sch
Chilseygreen Farm
Freemantles Sch (Specl Sch)
Hillside Farm
LASSWADE CT
PYRCROFT RD
A320
Chertsey
CHARLES ST 1
FOX DRS 2
FLORAL HOUSE 3
RAILWAY APR 4
Sir William Perkin's Sch
LC
Great Cockcrow Rly
Barrsbrook Farm
GUILDFORD RD
Cockcrow Hill
A320
KNOLL PARK RD
HAMWORTH TRAD EST
CHERTSEY BVD
M25

LYNE CROSSING RD
FARM RD
LYNE LA
ALMNERS RD
ALMNERS RD

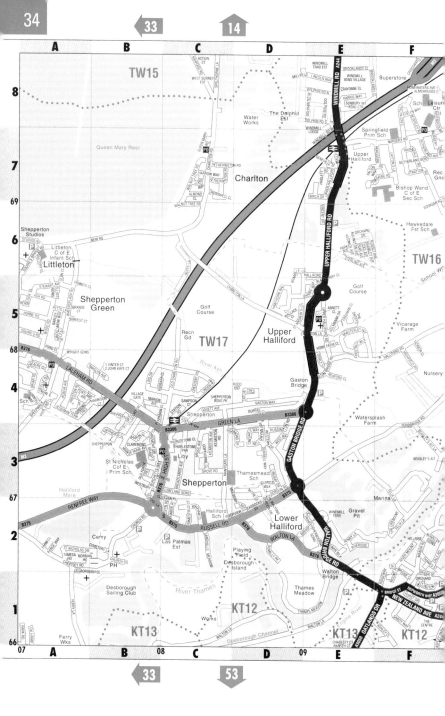

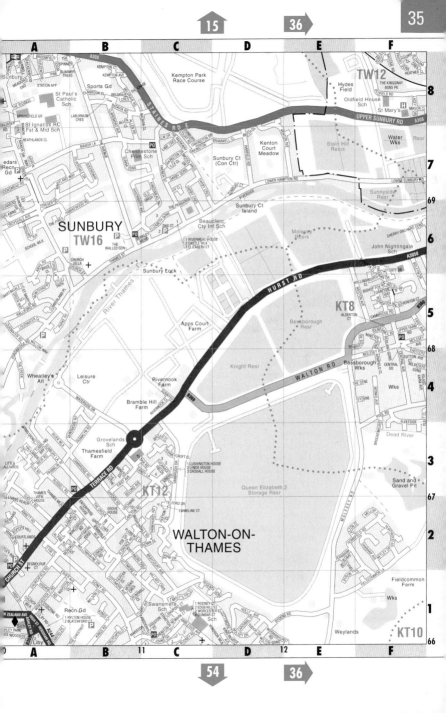

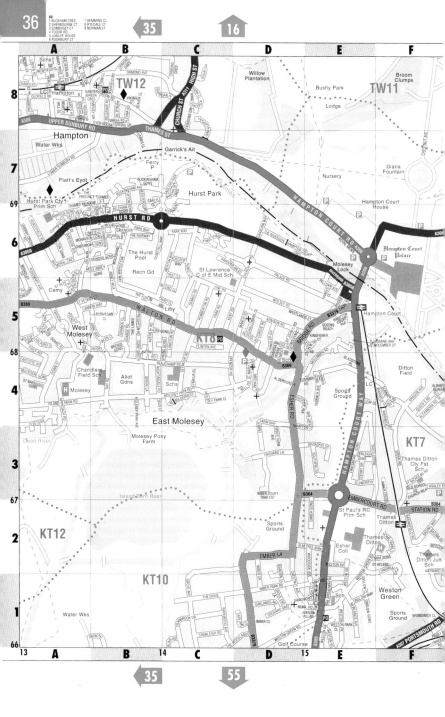

E6		E7				E8		F7		F8	
MARQUIS CT	1 COLLEGE RDBT	1 ST JAMES' CT	1 CLEAVE'S ALMSHOUSES	7 LADY BOOTH RD		1 REGENTS PL		1 VICARAGE HOUSE		1 ONSLOW HOUSE	
GARRICK HOUSE	2 EDINBURGH CT	8 GROVE CT	2 THE PARADE	8 CAVERSHAM HOUSE		2 WALTER ST		2 RAYLEIGH CT		2 DOWLER CT	
	3 WESTON CT	9 SPRINGFIELD CT	3 DROVERS CT	9 LITTLEFIELD CL		3 CANBURY BSNS PK		3 SCHOOL PAS			
	4 GREBE TERR	10 COLLEGE WLK	4 GOUGH HOUSE	10 THE BENTALL CTR		4 SIGRIST SQ		4 CHIPPENHAM			
	5 HERON CT		5 EDEN WLK	11 ADAMS WL		5 ASHWAY CT		5 CAMM GDNS			
	6 AGAR HOUSE		6 ALDERMAN JUDGE MALL	12 THE KINGFISHER SPORTS CTR		6 WARWICK HOUSE					

17   **38**   **37**

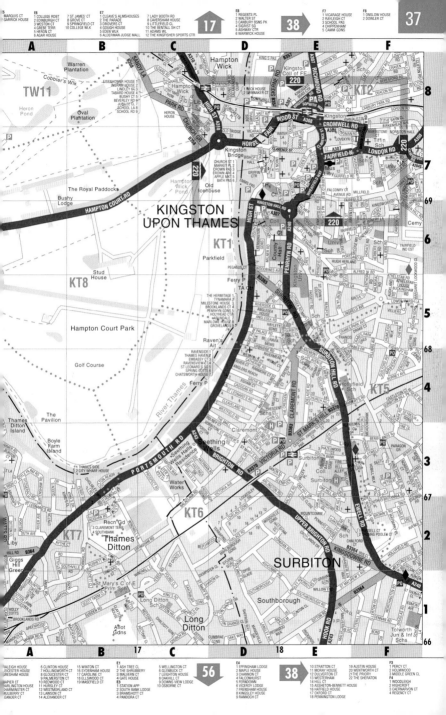

Bottom index

A

RALEIGH HOUSE
LEICESTER HOUSE
GRESHAM HOUSE

NAPIER CT
DARLINGTON HOUSE
CHARMINSTER CT
MULBERRY CT
LEANDER CT

6 CLINTON HOUSE
7 HOLLINGWORTH CT
8 GLOUCESTER CT
9 PALMERSTON CT
10 REDWOOD CT
11 HURSLEY CT
12 WESTMORLAND CT
13 LAWSON CT
14 ALEXANDER CT

15 WINTON CT
16 SYDENHAM HOUSE
17 CAROLINE CT
18 ELLSWOOD CT
19 MASEFIELD CT

B   **17**

E1
1 ASH TREE CL
2 THE SHRUBBERY
3 MALVERN CT
4 GATE HOUSE
E3
1 STATION APP
2 SOUTH BANK LODGE
3 BRAMSHOTT CT
4 PANDORA CT

C

5 WELLINGTON CT
6 GLENBUCK CT
7 LEIGHTON HOUSE
8 OAKHILL CT
9 DOWNS VIEW LODGE
10 OSBORNE CT

56

E4
1 EFFINGHAM LODGE
2 MAPLE HOUSE
3 CHANNON CT
4 FALCONHURST
5 FERNDOWN
6 VICEROY LODGE
7 FRENSHAM HOUSE
8 KINGSLEY HOUSE
9 RANNOCH CT

38

10 STRATTON CT
11 MORAY HOUSE
12 DULVERTON CT
13 WESTERHAM
14 HILL CT
15 ASSHETON-BENNETT HOUSE
16 HATFIELD HOUSE
17 OXFORD CT
18 PENNINGTON LODGE

19 AUSTIN HOUSE
20 WENTWORTH CT
21 THE PRIORY
22 THE SHERATON

F
1 PERCY CT
2 HOLMWOOD
3 MIDDLE GREEN CL
F4
1 WOODLEIGH
2 HIGHCROFT
3 CAERNARVON CT
4 REGENCY CT

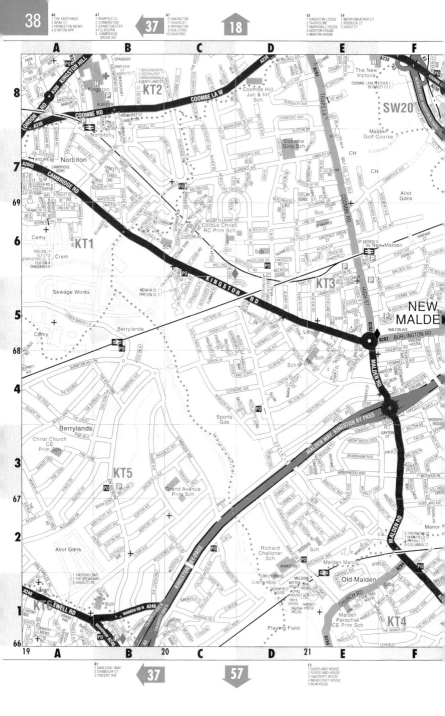

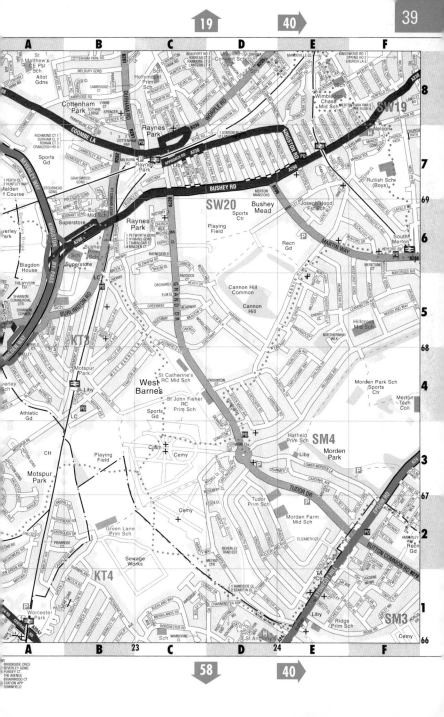

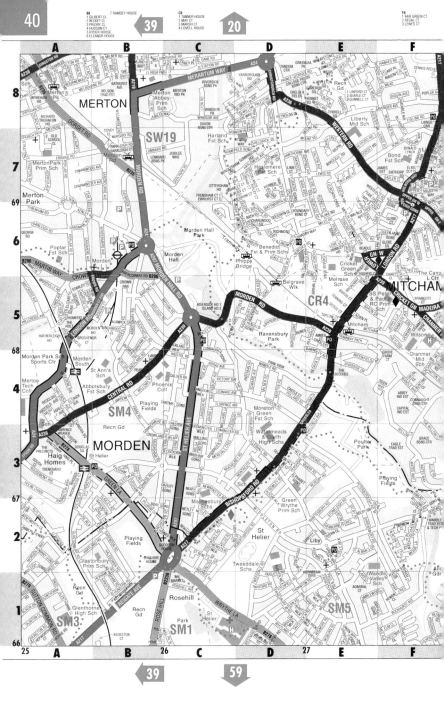

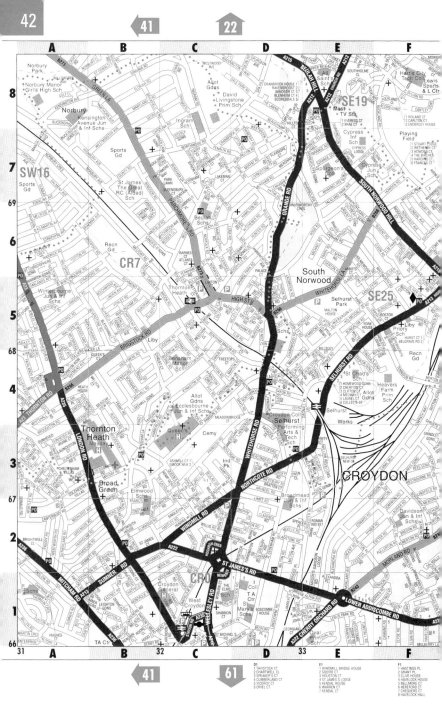

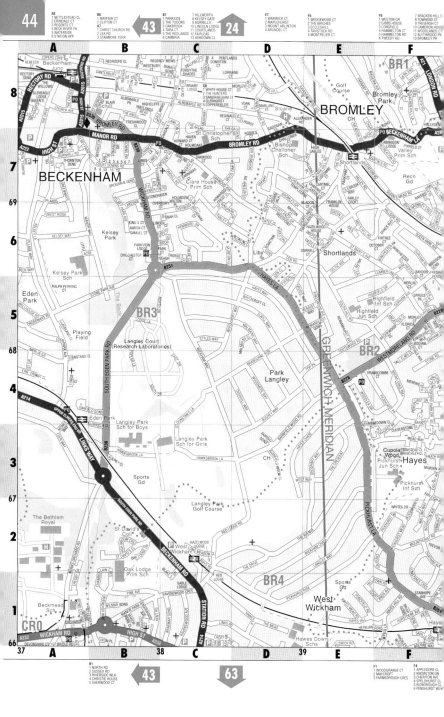

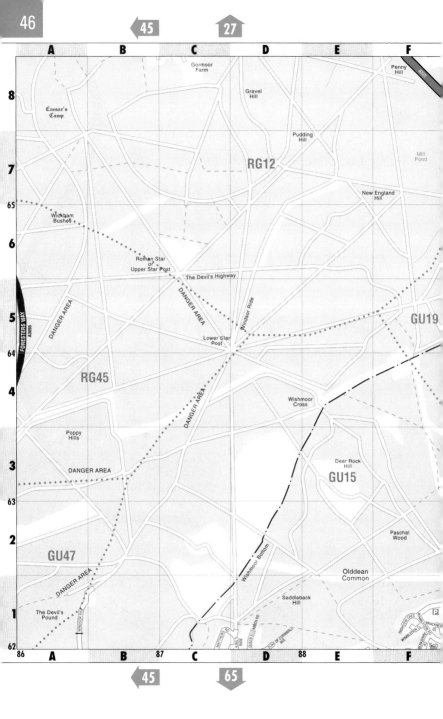

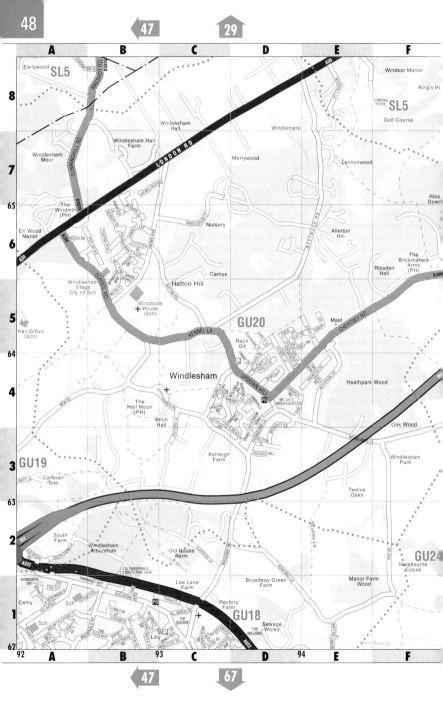

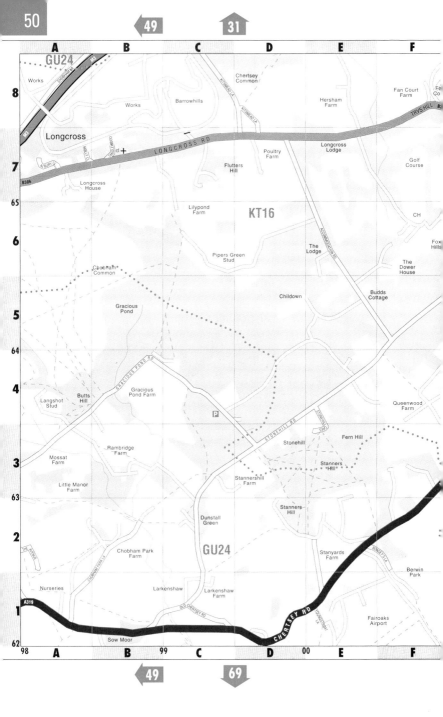

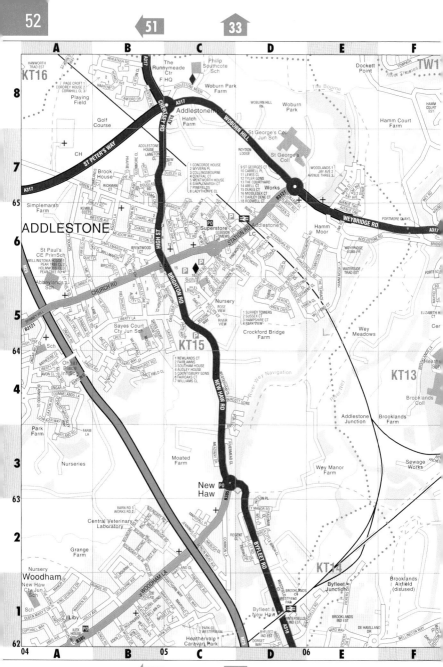

A B C D E F

8

WALTON-ON-THAMES

Red House La
Grange Ct
Rydens
Walton Common
Danesfield Sch

BRANKSOME CL

NORTH WEYLANDS IND EST

Sewage Works (dis)

MAITLAND RD

HERSHAM TRAD EST

EMBER LN

PO

7

Ashley Park

HERSHAM RD

Hersham

CH

Golf Course

1 RODWELL CT
2 OAKDENE CT

Cardinal Newman RC Sch

COLNE LODGE

South Weylands Equestrian Ctr

65

1 KINGSLEY CT
2 MOORLANDS
3 BEECHWOOD CT
4 COLLINGWOOD PL
5 RUSHMON GDNS

NOBLE ST

Rydens Sch

Playing Field

Bell Farm Jun Sch

Coronation Playing Fields

CHILTON CT
GAINSBOROUGH

Walton-on-Thames

P

FENNER HOUSE

6

A317 QUEENS RD

KILRUE LA

ROBINSWAY

HERSHAM RD

ALBANY RD

A244 QUEENSWAY N

Liby

ESHER RD

THE LEYS

MOLE HOUSE

RIVERSIDE RD

A317

THE FAIRINGS

QUEENSWAY

A317 QUEENSWAY S

KT12

LOWER

RIVERDENE IND EST

OLD ESHER RD

SURREY LODGE 1
CLARENCE HOUSE 2
WILLIAM LILLY HOUSE 3
HYLTON LODGE 4

5

BROADWATER RD

Broad Water

BROADWATER RD S

Burwood Park

GREEN LANE

THE MALL

PO

West End Recn Gd

THE HEREMITAGE

MARNCREST CT

LINFIELD GDNS

ASHTON CT

NEW BERRY LA

Hersham

Garson Farm

West End

64

POLICE STATION

Burhill Cty Inf Sch

PAUL VANSON CT

LARKHALL CL

VAUX CRES

River Mole

Winterhouse Farm

KT10

4

Cemy

BURWOOD RD

Golf Course

Southwood Manor Farm

West End Common

West End

STORY

Clare Lands Gd

3

Riverside Farm

SOUTH LODGE RD

BURHILL RD

RABBIT LA

P

63

Burhill

Burhill Park

CH

The Ledges

PORTSMOUTH RD

BLACKHILLS

2

KT11

American Comm Sch

Winterdown Wood

Blac Pond

1

Norwood Farm

Heywood

Fairmile Common

A307

TOWER COTTS

Upper Court

62

10 A B 11 C D 12 E F

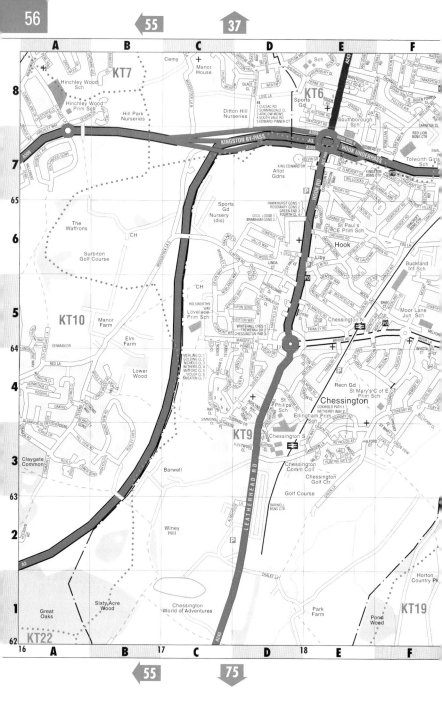

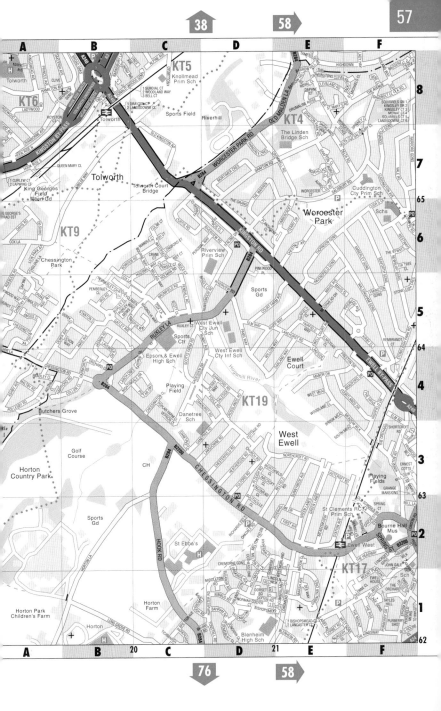

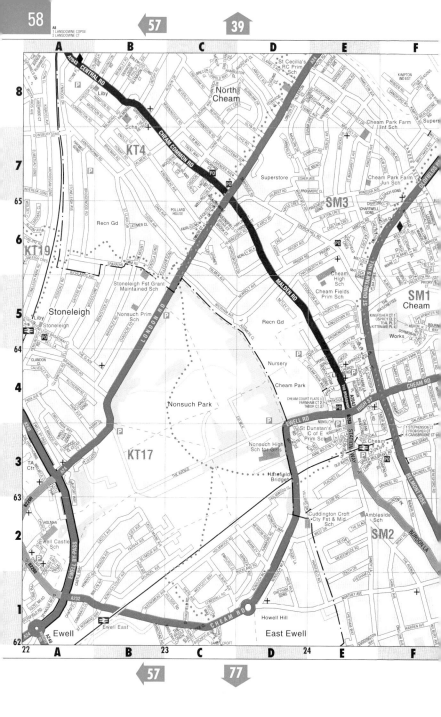

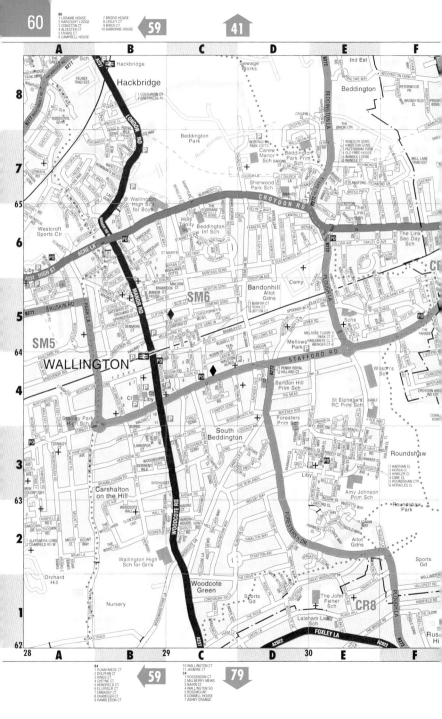

B6
1 LORAINE HOUSE
2 HARCOURT LODGE
3 CONISTON CT
4 ALCESTER CT
5 FRIARS CT
6 CAMPBELL HOUSE
7 BRODIE HOUSE
8 LESLEY CT
9 BIRCH CT
10 AIRBORNE HOUSE

B4
1 RUNNYMEDE CT
2 DOLPHIN CT
3 KINGS CT
4 CHEYNE CT
5 HENDFIELD CT
6 ELLERSLIE CT
7 EMBASSY CT
8 CHANDLER CT
9 HAMBLEDON CT
10 WALLINGTON CT
11 JASMINE CT
C4
1 ROSSENDON CT
2 MULBERRY MEWS
3 NAIRN CT
4 WALLINGTON SQ
5 ROSEMOUNT
6 CONNELL HOUSE
7 ASHBY GRANGE

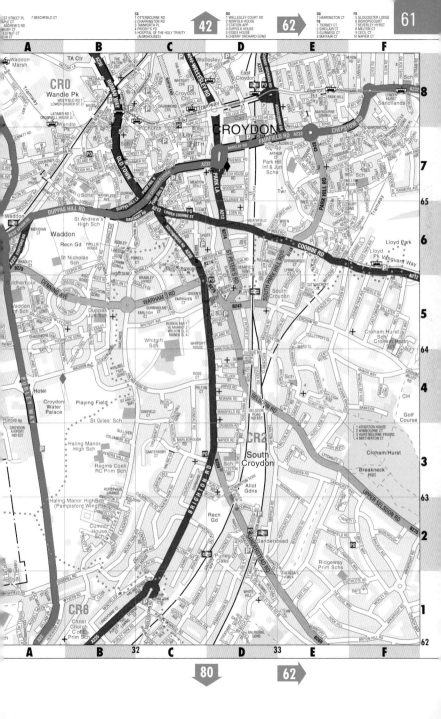

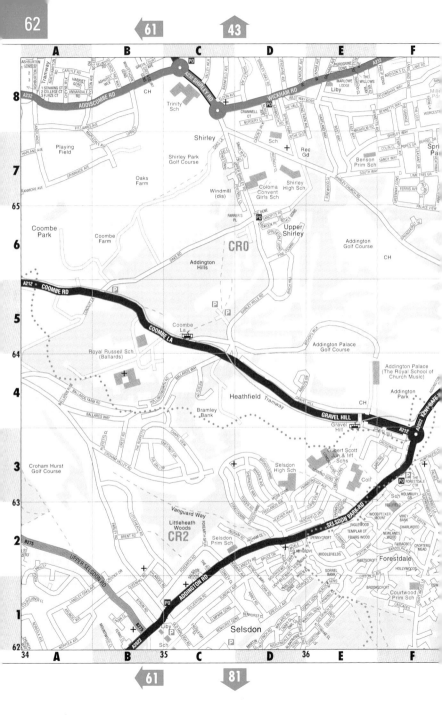

45

D8
1 MULBERRY CL
2 MAY CL
3 SHRIVENHAM CL
4 CENTURION CL
5 CHAFFINCH CL
6 TARBAT CT

7 ROCKFIELD WAY
8 BALINTORE CT

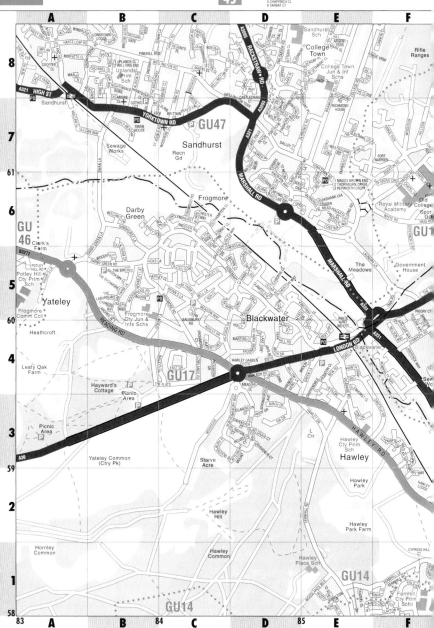

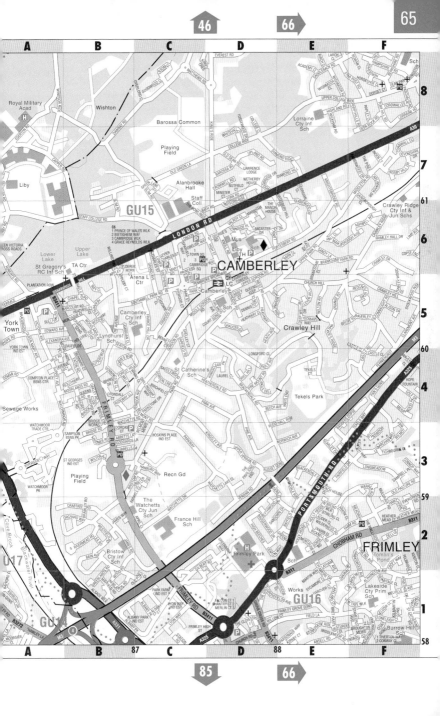

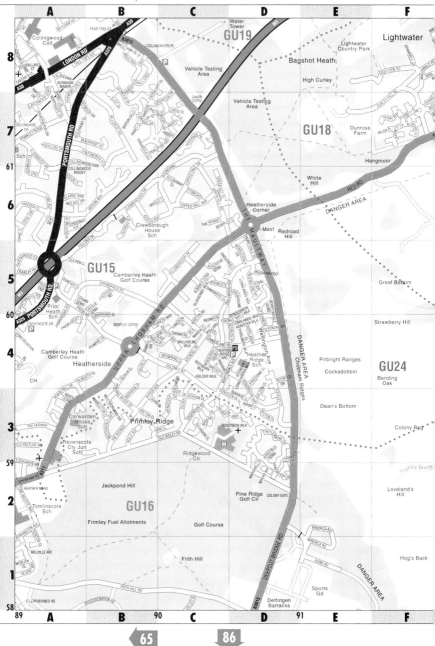

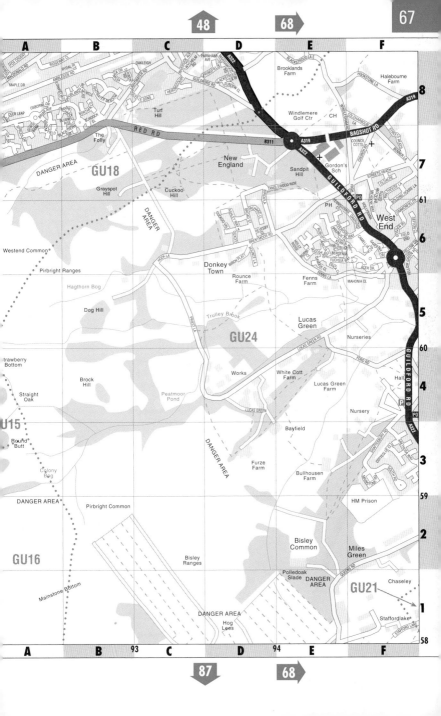

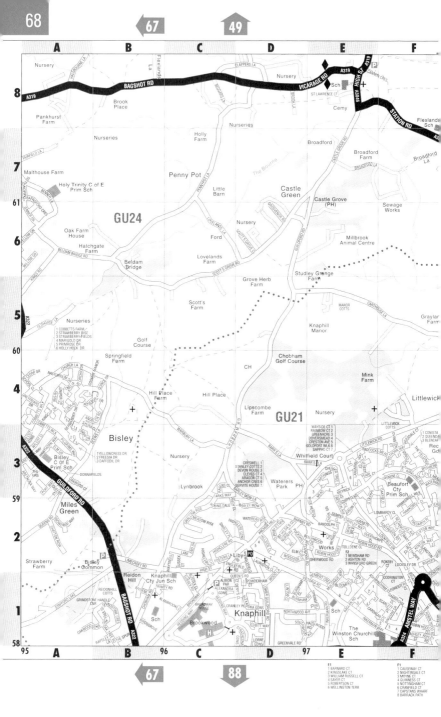

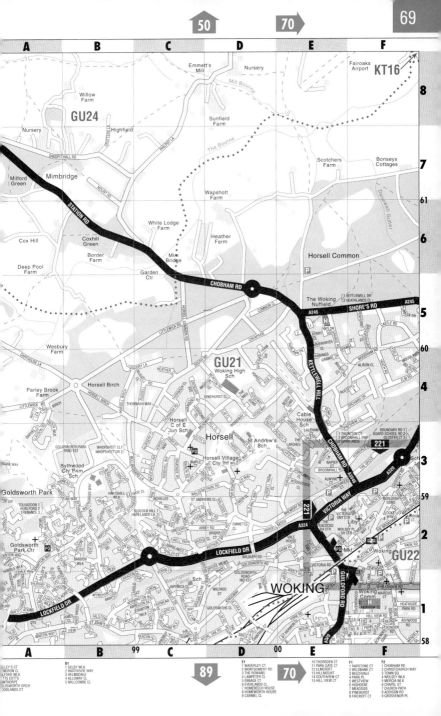

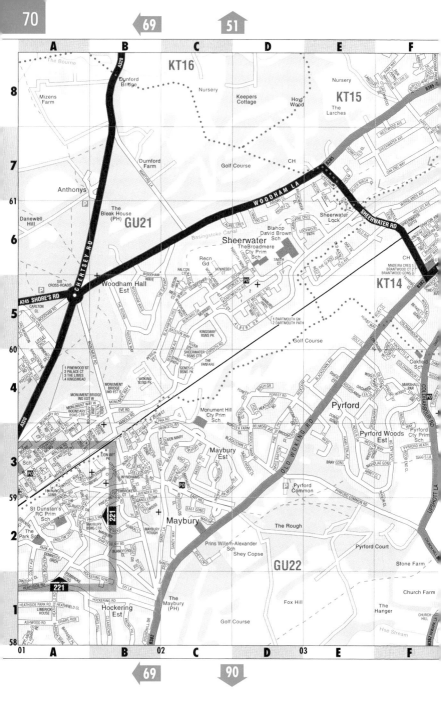

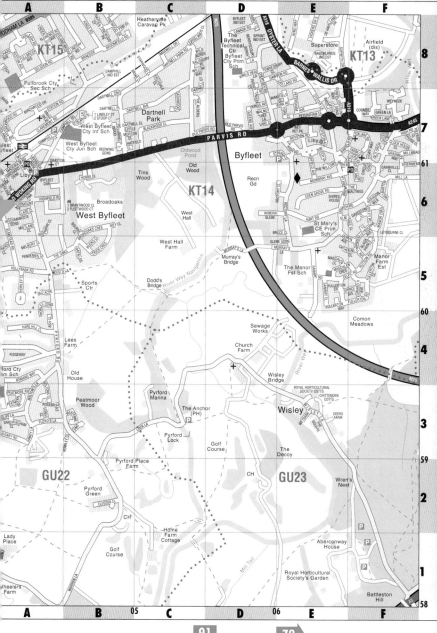

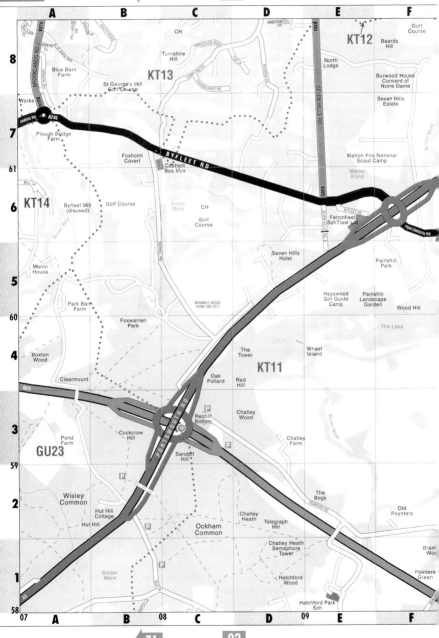

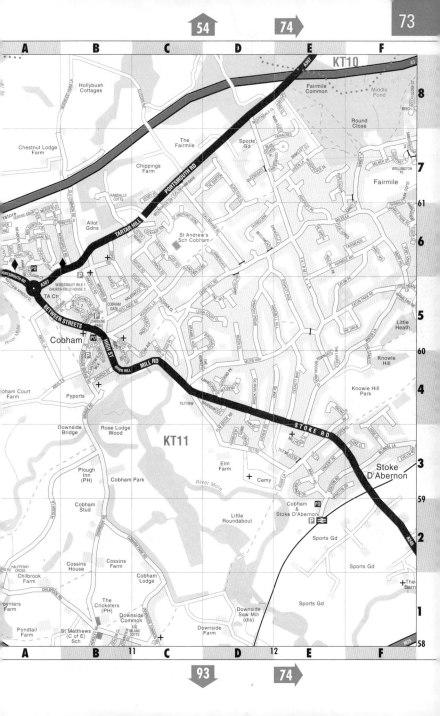

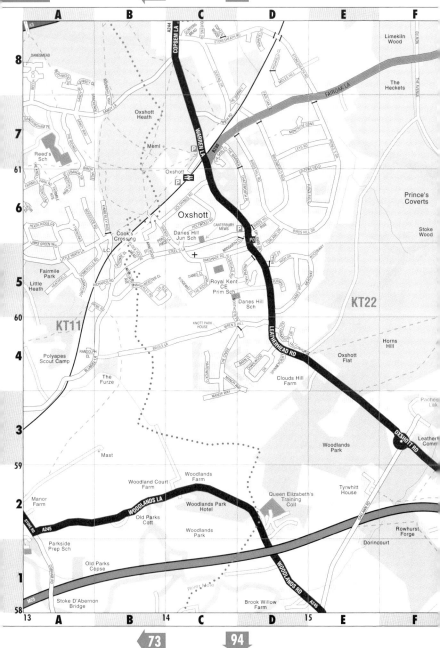

A B C D E F

8

7

61

6

5

60

4

3

59

2

1

58

13 A B 14 C D 15 E F

Limekiln Wood

The Heckets

The Avenue

FAIROAK LA

COPSEM LA

WARREN LA

STOKESHEATH RD

A244

Oxshott Heath

Meml

Prince's Coverts

Stoke Wood

Oxshott

P

P

Montrose Gdns

Leys Rd

Spicers Field

Reed's Sch

Danesmead

A3

Cook's Crossing

LC

Oxshott

Danes Hill Jun Sch

Canterbury Mews

P

PO

Danes Hill Sch

KT22

Royal Kent CE Prim Sch

Oakshade Rd

Danes Cl

Horns Hill

Oxshott Flat

KT11

Knott Park House

Wren's Hill

LEATHERHEAD RD

Fairmile Park

Little Heath

BRIDLE LA

Randolph Cl

The Chase

Polyapes Scout Camp

The Furze

Clouds Hill Farm

Paches Lake

Manor Way

OXSHOTT RD

Leather Comm

Mast

Woodlands Park

Woodlands Farm

Woodland Court Farm

Tyrwhitt House

59

Manor Farm

Old Parks Cott

WOODLANDS LA

A245

Woodlands Park Hotel

Queen Elizabeth's Training Coll

Rowhurst Forge

Parkside Prep Sch

Woodlands Park

Dorincourt

STOKE RD

Old Parks Copse

WOODLANDS RD

A245

River Mole

M25

Stoke D'Abernon Bridge

Brook Willow Farm

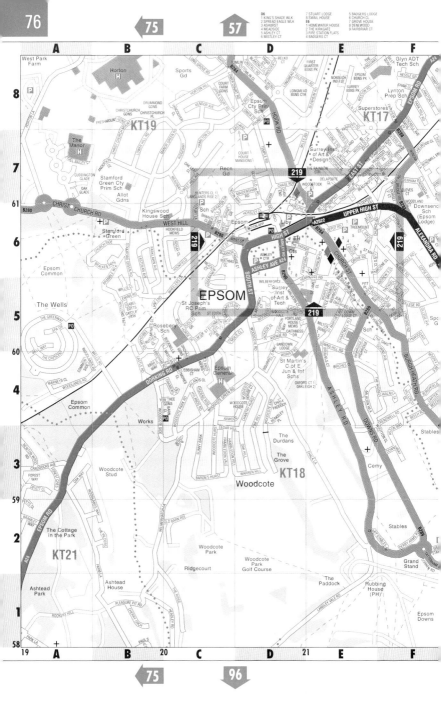

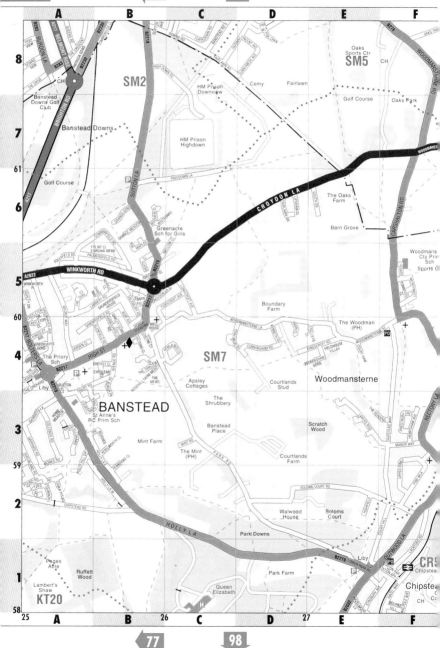

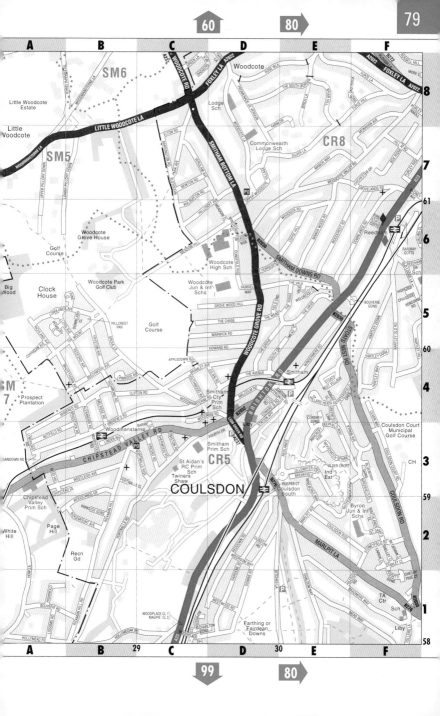

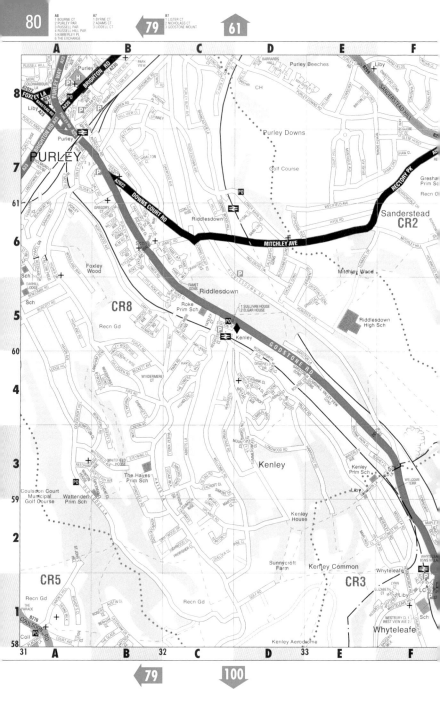

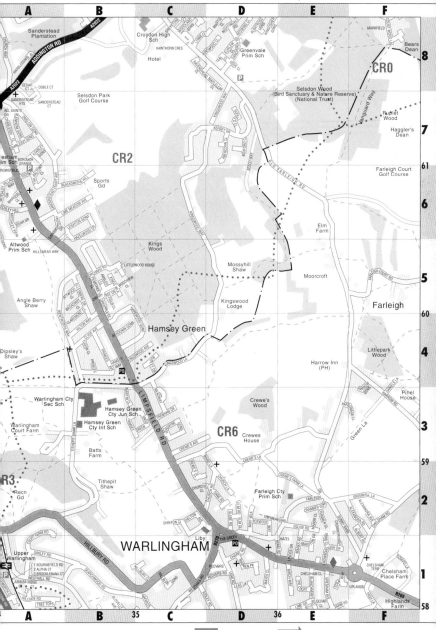

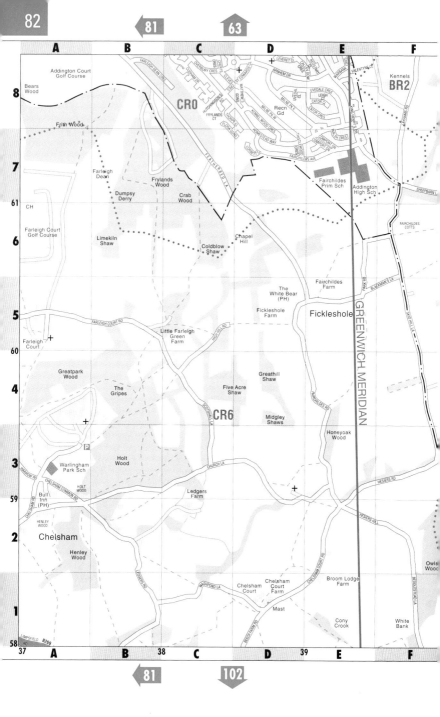

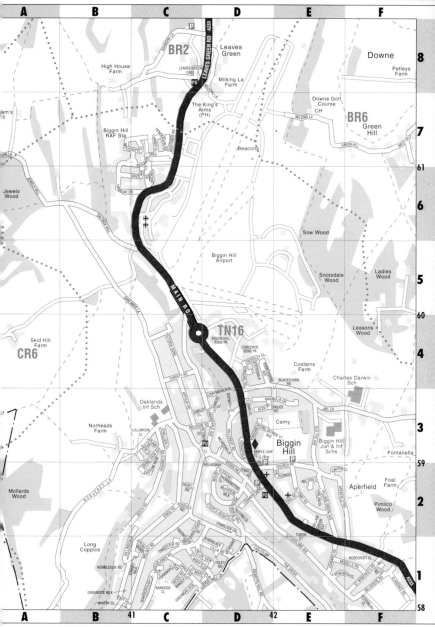

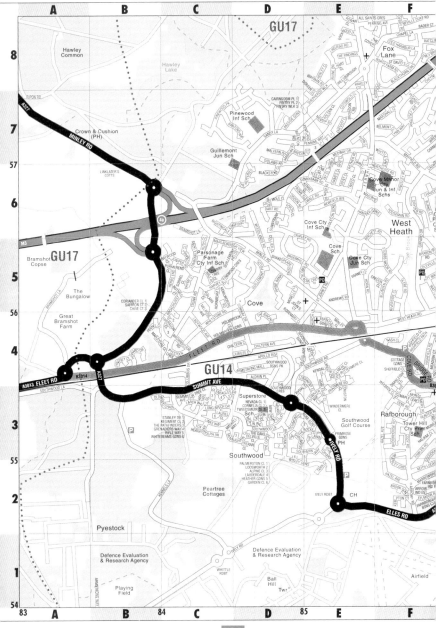

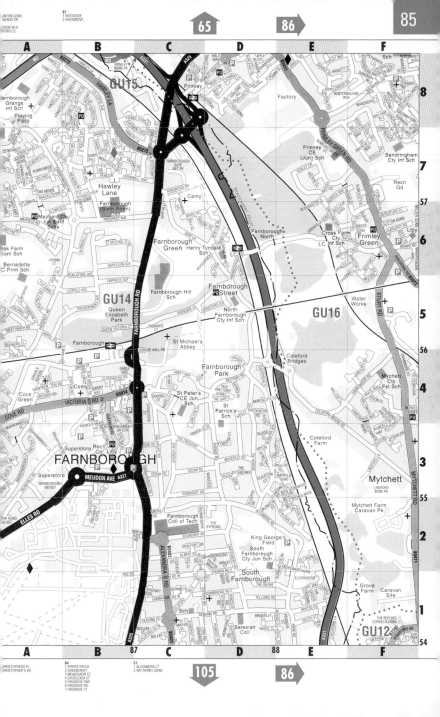

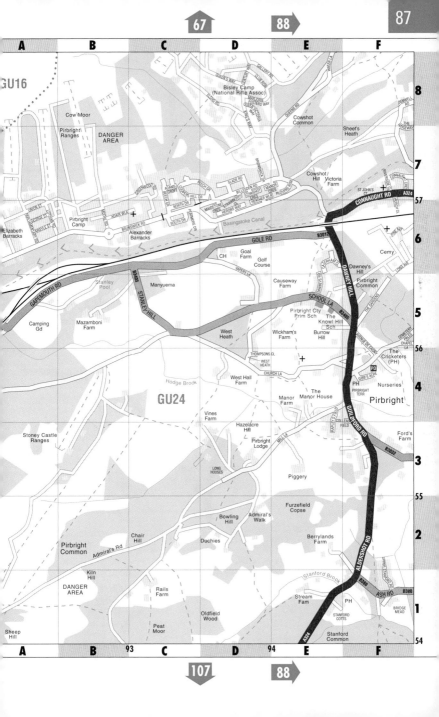

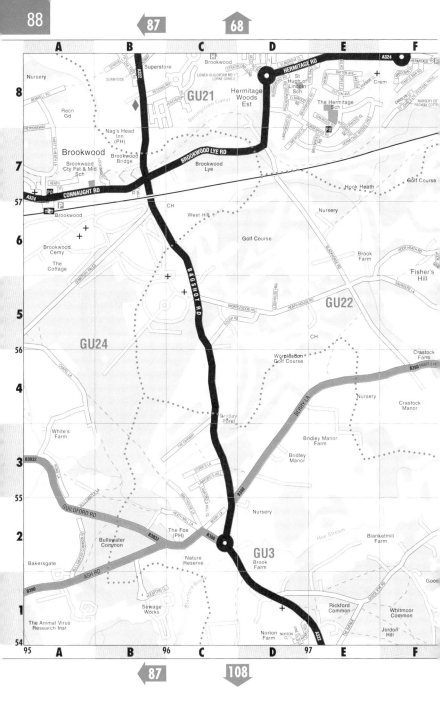

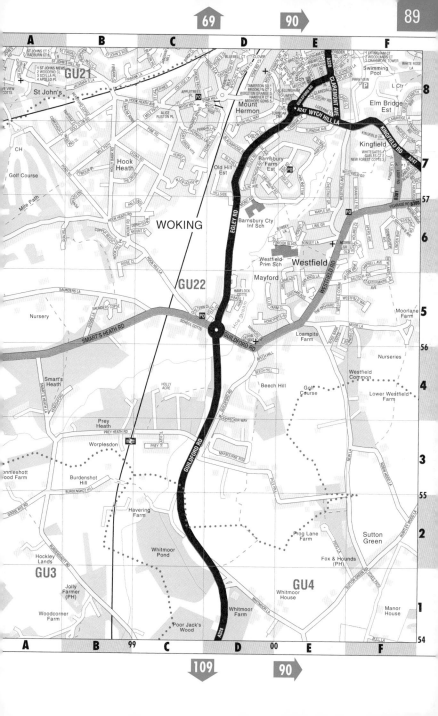

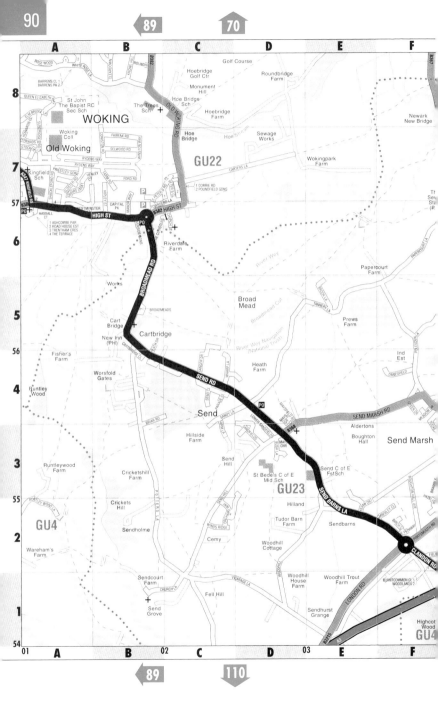

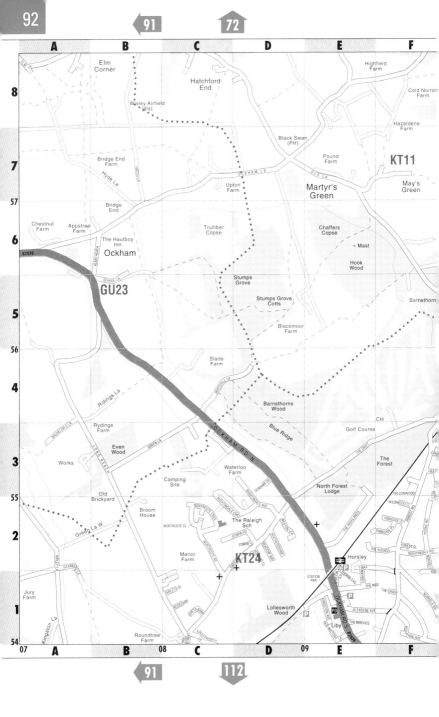

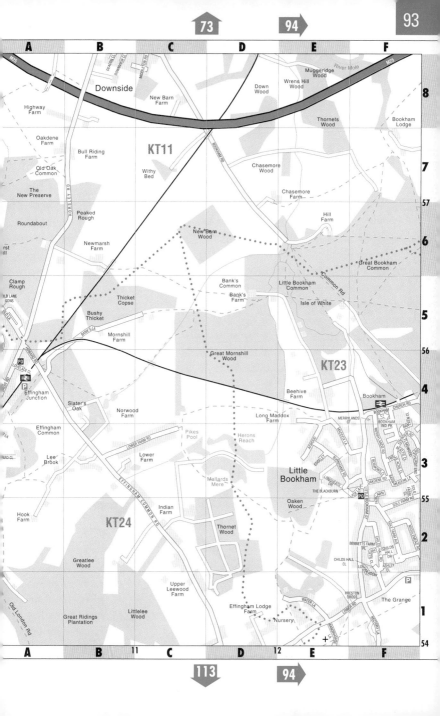

95
76

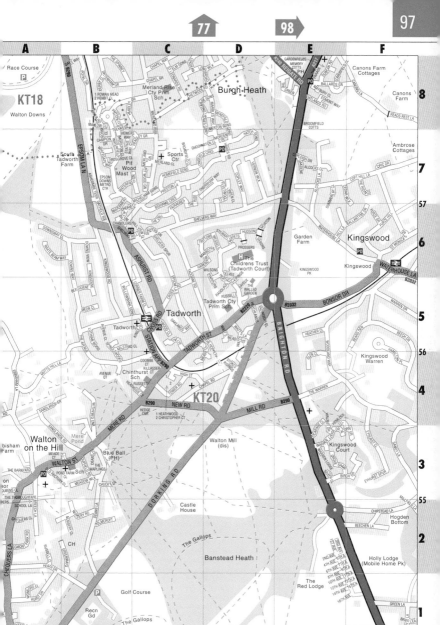

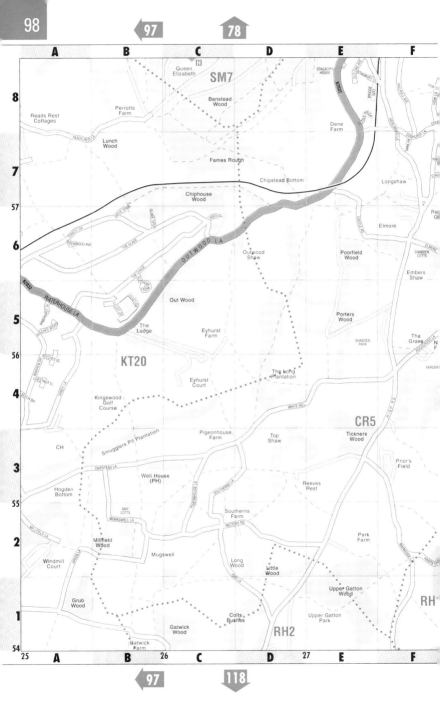

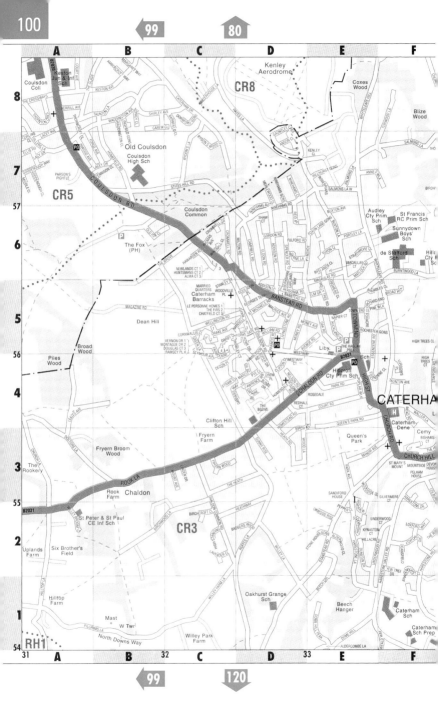

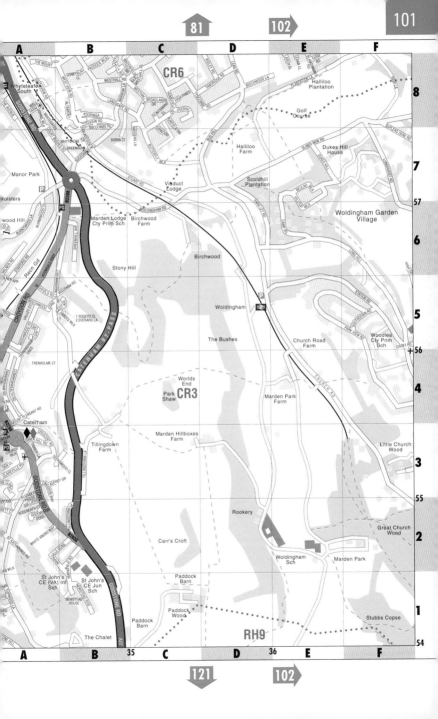

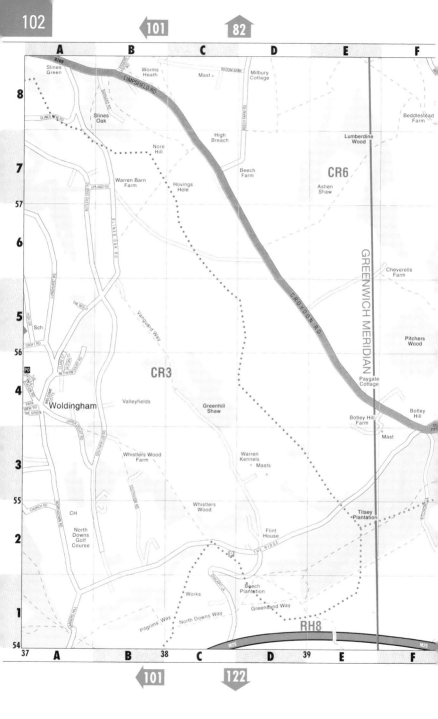

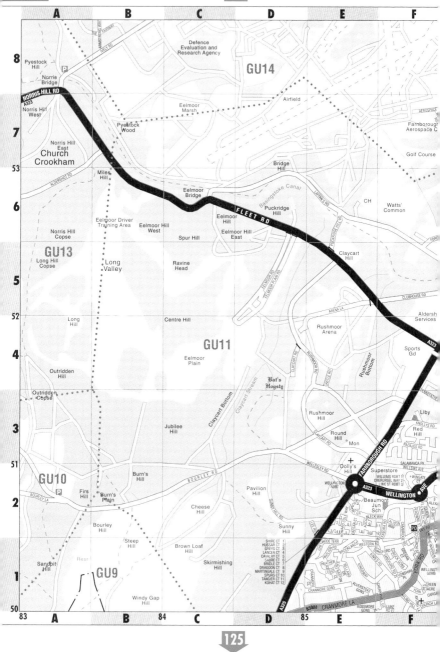

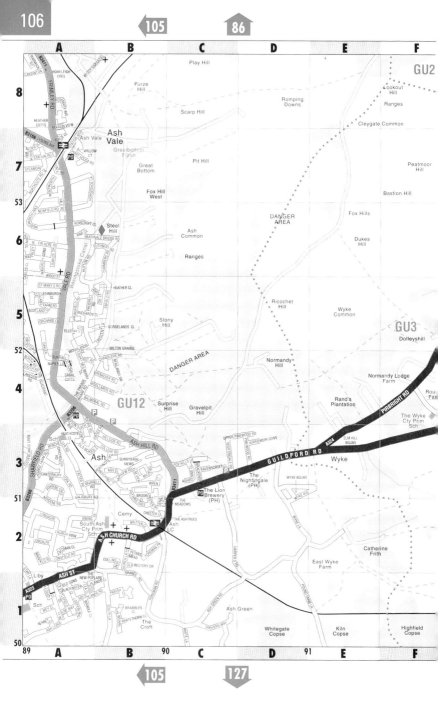

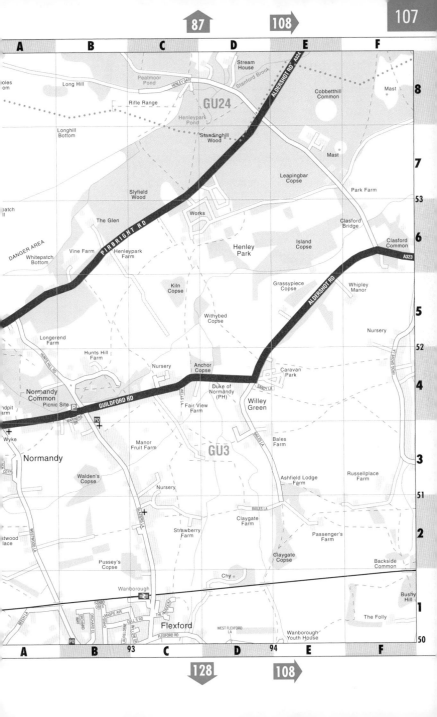

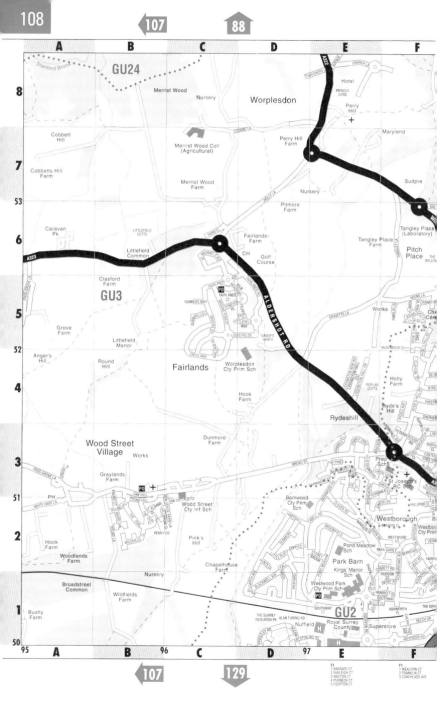

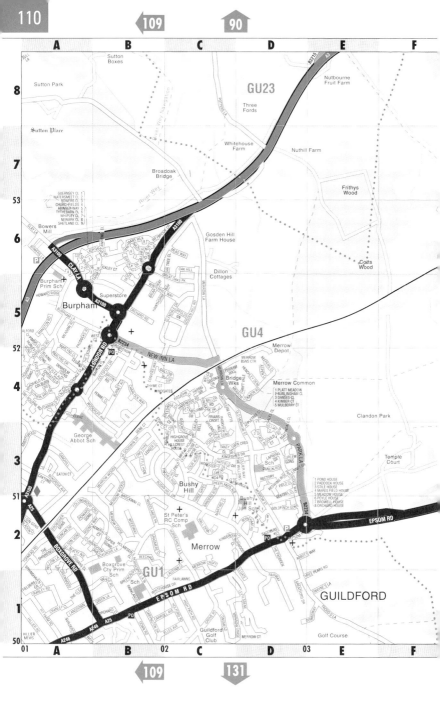

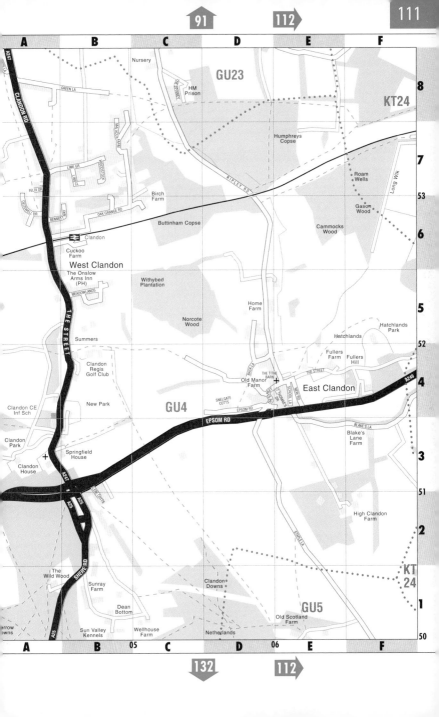

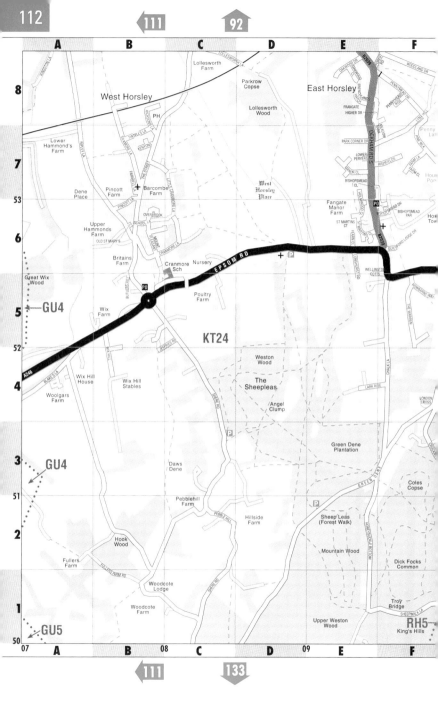

8

Lollesworth Farm

Parkrow Copse

West Horsley

Lollesworth Wood

East Horsley

WOODLAND DR

PENNYMEAD DR

Lower Hammond's Farm

7

PH

THE STREET

NIGHTINGALE LA

KINGSTON AV

FRANGATE

HIGHER DR

PARK CORNER DR

LOWER PERYERS

HIGHFIELDS

OAK CL

FARM CL

Penny Cl

53

Dene Place

Pincott Farm

Barcombe Farm

FAIRFIELD LA

LITTLE CRANMORE LA

West Horsley Place

Fangate Manor Farm

BISHOPSMEAD CL

St Martins Ct

PO

BISHOPSMEAD DR

House Pon

Hoo Tov

Upper Hammonds Farm

SCHOOL LA

OVERBROOK

ST MARTINS CT

FEARN CL

Bishopsmead Par

6

OLD ST MARY'S

MOUNT PLEASANT

CRANMORE LA

Cranmore Sch

Nursery

PO

BISHOPMEAD LODGE DR

Britains Farm

EPSOM RD

P

Wellington Cotts

WELLINGTON COTTS

Great Wix Wood

BUTLERS LA

Poultry Farm

LONGREACH RD

THE WARREN

GU4

PO

FERRIERS RD

5

Wix Farm

ROWBRANKS WAY

52

WIX HILL

REYNARD RD

KT24

Weston Wood

CHALK LA

A246

BLAKES LA

Wix Hill House

Wix Hill Stables

The Sheepleas

LARK RISE

4

Wooglars Farm

Angel Clump

LONDON CROSS

3

GU4

Daws Dene

Green Dene Plantation

GREEN DENE

Coles Copse

51

Pebblehill Farm

PEBBLE HILL

Hillside Farm

P

Sheep Leas (Forest Walk)

CROCKS

2

Hook Wood

HONEYSUCKLE BOTTOM

Mountain Wood

Dick Focks Common

Fullers Farm

FULLERS FARM RD

SHERE RD

1

Woodcote Lodge

Troy Bridge

SHEEPWALK LA

Woodcote Farm

Upper Weston Wood

RH5

King's Hills

GU5

50

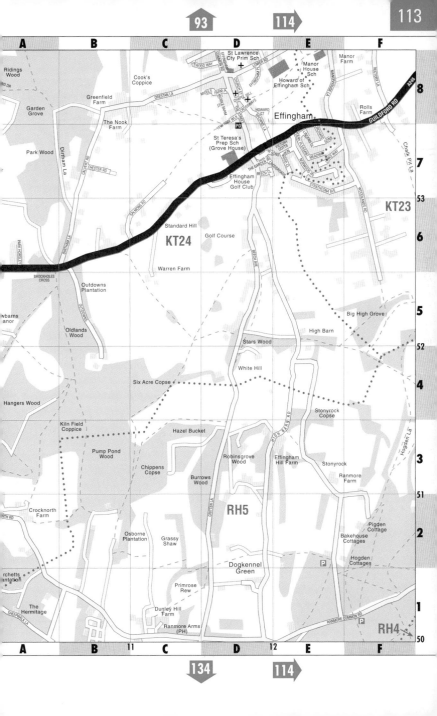

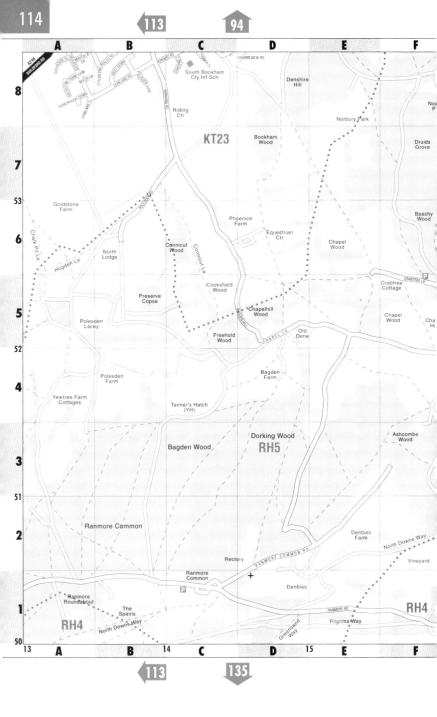

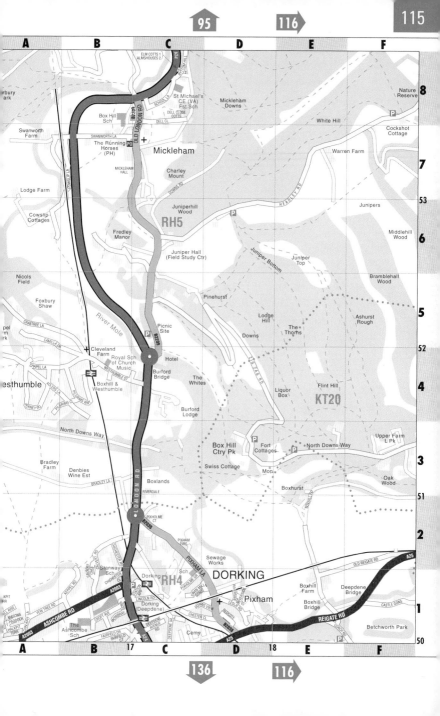

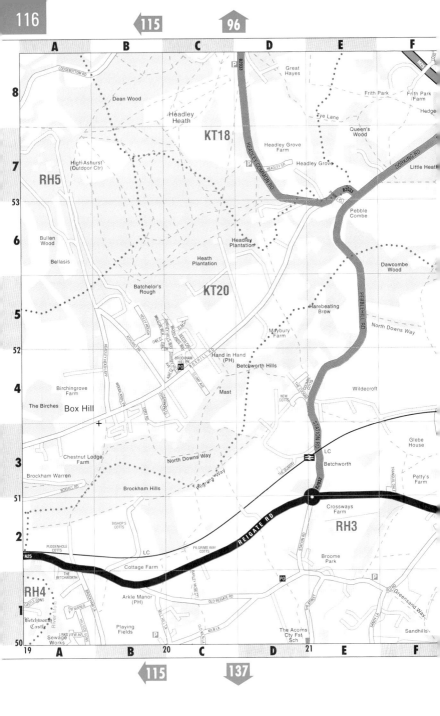

A B C D E F

Walton Heath
Chussex Plain
Golf Course
Lower Kingswood
KT20
Walton Oaks
The Gallops
Round Wood
Dewriding Plantation
Sportsman (PH)
Mogador Cotts
Mogador
Wayside Farm
Dent's Farm
Margery Wood
Kingswood Cty Prim Sch
Recn Gd
The Mint Arms (PH)
Freshfield
Thistle Hill
Buckland Hills
Mount Hill
Conybury Hill
North Downs Way
Juniper Hill
The Saddle Knob
Colley Hill
Merriwood Gr
M25
RH3
Kemps Farmyard
Underhill Farm
Buckland Green
Pilgrim's Way
Colleyland Shaw
Broadleas
Dowde's Farm
Colley Pit
Claypit Shaw
Clears Cotts
The Cleans
Colley Copse
Colley Wood
Greensand Way
Tap Wood
Reigate Rd
Buckland
Buckland Ct
The Jolly Farmers (PH)
Normanton
Buckland Cnr
Shagbrook
Buckland Rd
RH2
Park Pit
Dungate's Farm
Shag Brook
Reigate Heath
Golf Course
Reigate Heath Cotts
West St
A25
REIGATE
Green La
CH
Dorking Rd
Mogador Rd
Margery La
23 24
50 51 52 53
1 2 3 4 5 6 7 8

Gatwick Farm
Upper Gatton Park
Ashstead Hill
RH1
Old Mint House
Park Shaw
Crossways Farm
Kingswood Grange
Kingswood Hill
Gatton Bottom
Whitehall Farm
Kingswood Manor
Glebe Shaw
Gatton
KT20
Tower Wood
CHURCH SIDE
Margery
Margery Farm
North Downs Way
The Royal Alexandra & Albert Sch
The Lake
Hop Garden Pond
Engine Pond
The Serpentine
M25
Margery Hall
Gatton Park
Serpentine Wood
Bridge House (Hotel)
RH2
Nut Wood
Greenclump Hill
Temple Lodge
Reigate Hill
GATTON PARK RD
St Bede's Sch
Coles Meads Sch
REIGATE HILL
BRIGHTON RD
A217
Holmsdale Cty Inf Sch
Brooklands Sch
Wray Common
Micklefield Prep Sch
St David's (FHQ)
Wray Common Cty Prim Sch
St Joseph's RC Prim Sch
St Matthew C of E Pri Sch
CROYDON RD
REDHILL
TA Ctr
Donyngs Place Recn Ctr
REIGATE
Reigate Coll
LONDON RD
CASTLEFIELD RD
CHURCH ST
HIGH ST
STATION RD
Reigate Gram Sch
REIGATE RD
HATCHLANDS RD
Superstore
Reigate Sch of Art & Design
Reigate St Mary's Prep Sch
Cemy
Reigate Parish Church Inf Sch
East Surrey
GROVE HOUSE
Reigate Priory Cty Sch
BELL ST
A25
A23
A242
B2034
BLACKBOROUGH RD
25
26
27
50
51
52
53
A
B
C
D
E
F
1
2
3
4
5
6
7
8

A2
1 SOMERS PL
2 FLANCHFORD HOUSE
3 CLAYHALL HOUSE
4 LITTLETON HOUSE

C1
1 VICTORIA ALMSHOUSES
2 EVERSFIELD CT
3 HILLBROW

D1
1 CLAIRVILLE CT
2 HIGHVIEW CT
3 TREEVIEW CT
4 HARLOW CT
5 WRAYMILL CT

F1
1 CROMWELL WLK
2 EDGEHILL HOUSE
3 MORRISS CT
4 OBSERVATORY WLK
5 WAVENEY HOUSE
6 GROVE HOUSE
7 ELY HOUSE
8 MAPLE HO
9 CHRISTCHURCH HTS
10 GLAMIS HO
11 ATHOLL HOUSE
12 DUNVEGAN HOUSE
13 STIRLING HOUSE
14 MARKETFIELD RD

F2
1 CHILMEAD
2 COLNE HOUSE
3 TAVY HOUSE
4 ROTHER HOUSE
5 WANDLE HOUSE
6 KENNET HOUSE
7 ORWELL HOUSE
8 WINDRUSH HOUSE
9 AVON HOUSE
10 HILLARY HOUSE
11 DOUGLAS HOUGHTON HOUSE
12 SQUIRRELS GN
13 CHILWORTH CT

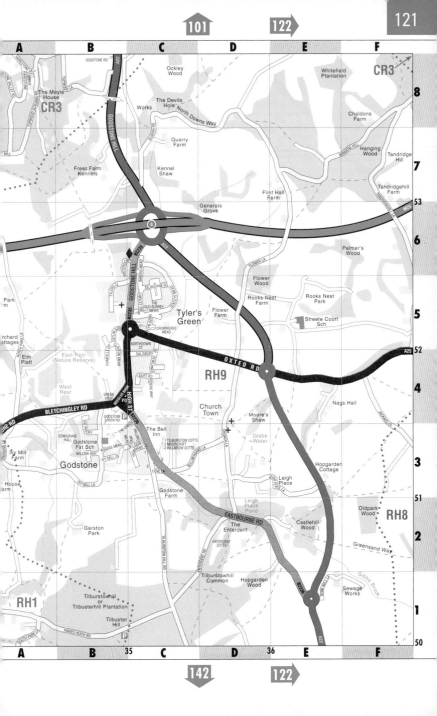

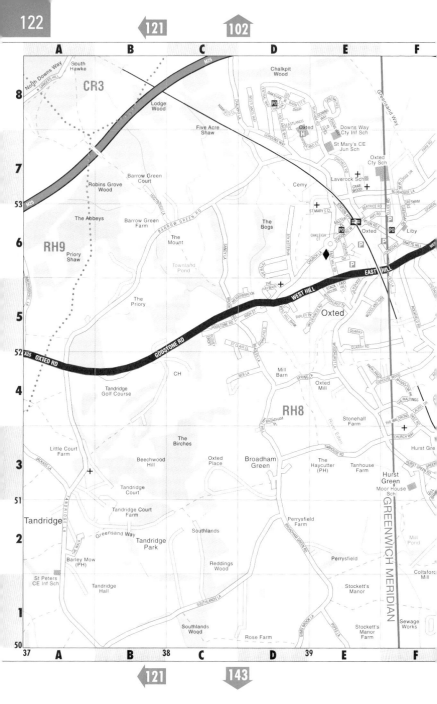

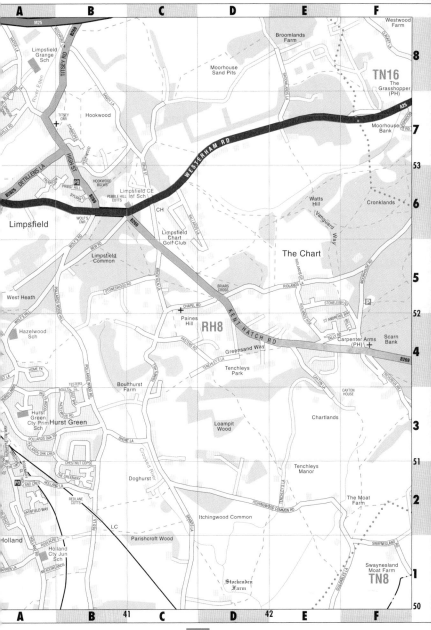

103

A **B** **C** **D** **E** **F**

Westwood
Farm

M25

Limpsfield
Grange
Sch

Broomlands
Farm

8

Moorhouse
Sand Pits

TN16

The
Grasshopper
(PH)

River Eden

Titsey
CNR

Hookwood

7

A25

Moorhouse
Bank

WESTERHAM RD

HIGH ST

DETILLENS LA

53

B2025

PO

Hookwood
BGLWS

Watts
Hill

Cronklands

6

PRIEST HILL

SYLMAI

Limpsfield CE
Inf Sch

PEBBLE HILL
COTTS

Vanguard Way

CH

WOLF'S
CNR

Limpsfield

Limpsfield
Chart
Golf-Club

The Chart

Limpsfield
Common

RIDLANDS

5

West Heath

STONEWOOD RD

BRIARS
CROSS

RIDLANDS

STONELEIGH

P

52

Hazelwood
Sch

Chapel Rd

Paines
Hill

ST ANDREWS DRV

KENT HATCH RD

RH8

Carpenter Arms
(PH)

Scarn
Bank

4

HOME PK

TESTERS

Greensand Way

TENCHLEYS LA

Tenchleys
Park

CAXTON
HOUSE

B269

Hurst
Green
Cty Prim
Sch

Hurst Green

Boulthurst
Farm

Chartlands

3

SHORT LA

Loampit
Wood

CHESTNUT COPSE

Crooked River

THE GREENWAY

HOLLAND LA

Doghurst

Tenchleys
Manor

51

REDLANE
COTTS

ITCHINGWOOD COMMON RD

TENCHLEYS LA

The Moat
Farm

2

RD LA

LC

Itchingwood Common

Parishcroft Wood

SWAYNESLAND RD

Holland

Holland
Cty Jun
Sch

MEADOWLANDS

Swaynesland
Moat Farm

TN8

1

Stockenden
Farm

50

A **B** 41 **C** **D** 42 **E** **F**

144

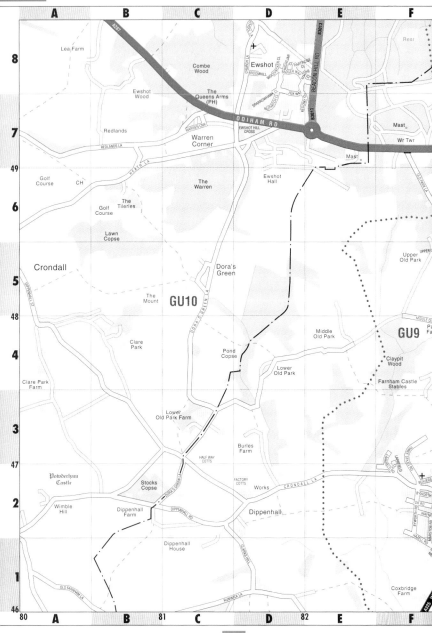

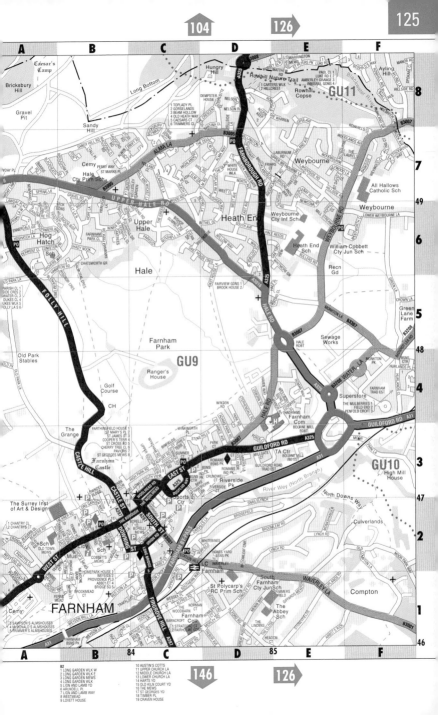

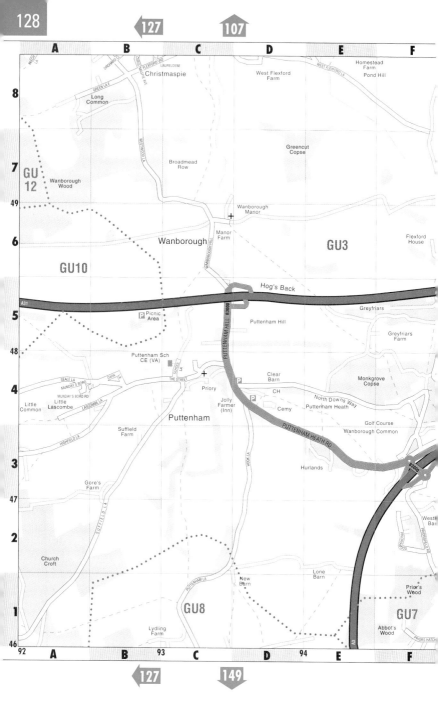

127
107

A   **B**   **C**   **D**   **E**   **F**

Homestead Farm
Pond Hill

WEST FLEXFORD LA

LAUREDENE
Christmaspie
West Flexford Farm

GREEN LA E
Long Common

WESTWOOD LA

Greencut Copse

8

GU 12

7

Wanborough Wood

Broadmead Row

49

Wanborough Manor

6

Wanborough

Manor Farm

GU3

Flexford House

GU10

WANBOROUGH HILL

Hog's Back

A31

Picnic Area

Greyfriars

5

Puttenham Hill

PUTTENHAM HILL B3000

Greyfriars Farm

48

Puttenham Sch CE (VA)

SCHOOL

THE STREET

Priory

Clear Barn

CH

North Downs Way
Puttenham Heath

Monkgrove Copse

4

SEALE LA

MUNDAY'S BORD
MUNDAY'S BORD RD

LARK LA

Jolly Farmer (Inn)

Cemy

Golf Course
Wanborough Common

Little Common

Little Lascombe

LASCOMBE LA

Puttenham

Suffield Farm

PUTTENHAM HEATH RD

B3000

HIGHFIELD LA

3

Gore's Farm

Hurlands

47

SUFFIELD LA

HIGH LA

2

Church Croft

PUTNAM LA

New Barn

Lone Barn

Prior's Wood

West Ba

PRIORS WOOD

1

GU8

GU7

Lydling Farm

Abbot's Wood

PRIORS HATCHE

46

92   **A**   **B**   93   **C**   **D**   94   **E**   **F**

127
149

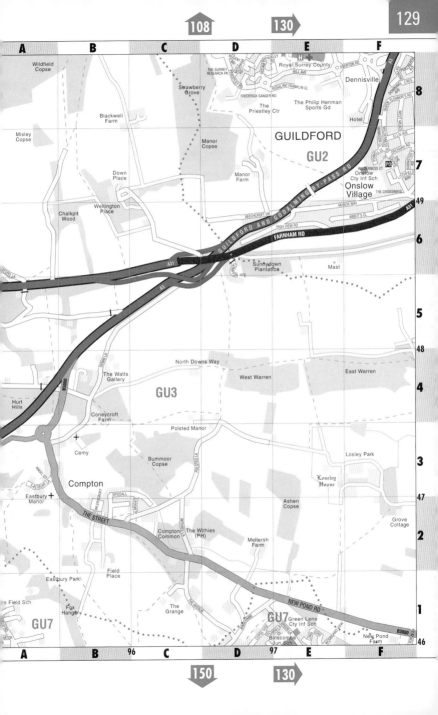

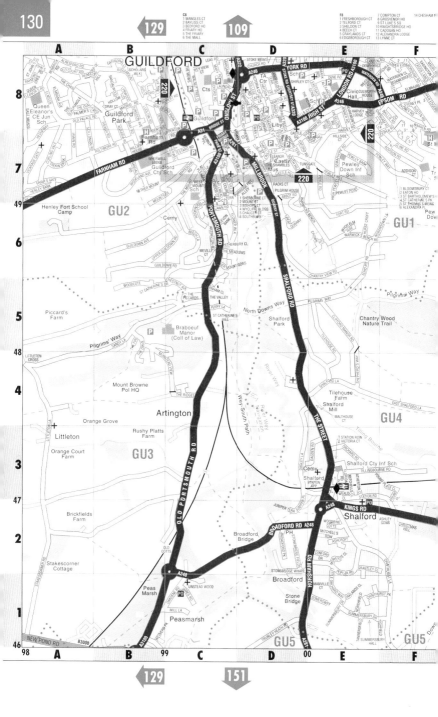

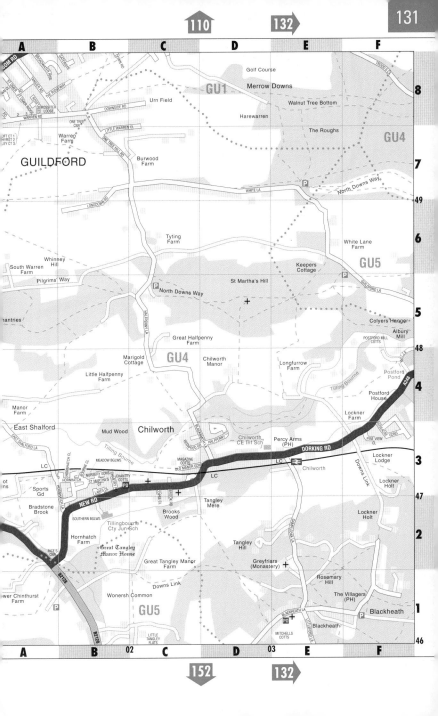

GUILDFORD

GU1
Merrow Downs
Golf Course
Walnut Tree Bottom
Urn Field
Harewarren
The Roughs
GU4

Warren Farm
Burwood Farm

WHITE LA
North Downs Way

Tyting Farm

Whinney Hill
South Warren Farm
Pilgrims' Way
Keepers Cottage
St Martha's Hill
White Lane Farm
GU5

Chantries
North Downs Way
Colyers Hanger
Albury Mill
POSTFORD MILL COTTS

Great Halfpenny Farm
Marigold Cottage
Chilworth Manor
Longfurrow Farm
GU4
Tilling Bourne
Postford Pond

Little Halfpenny Farm
Postford House

Manor Farm
Lockner Farm

East Shalford
Mud Wood
Chilworth
Tilling Bourne

EAST SHALFORD LA
Chilworth CE Inf Sch
Percy Arms (PH)
DORKING RD
Lockner Lodge

MAGAZINE COTTS
OLD MANOR GDNS
Chilworth
LC
Downs Link
Lockner Holt

LC
Sports Gd
NURSERY GDNS
ST MARTHA'S CT
CHANTRY COTTS
LAKES CL
Tangley Mere
Lockner Holt

Bradstone Brook
NEW RD
Brooks Wood
Greyfriars (Monastery)

Hornhatch Farm
Tillingbourne Cty Jun Sch
SOUTHERN BGLWS
Tangley Hill

RICE'S CNR
Great Tangley Manor House
Great Tangley Manor Farm
Rosemary Hill

ower Chinthurst Farm
Downs Link
The Villagers (PH)
Blackheath

Wonersh Common
GU5
Greyfriars
BLACKHEATH LA
Blackheath

LITTLE TANGLEY FLATS
MITCHELLS COTTS

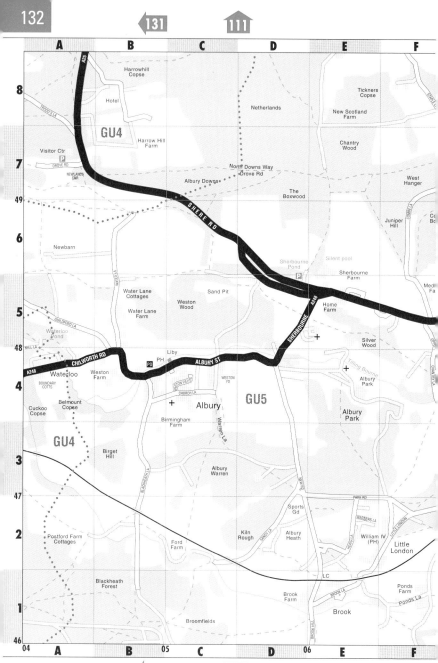

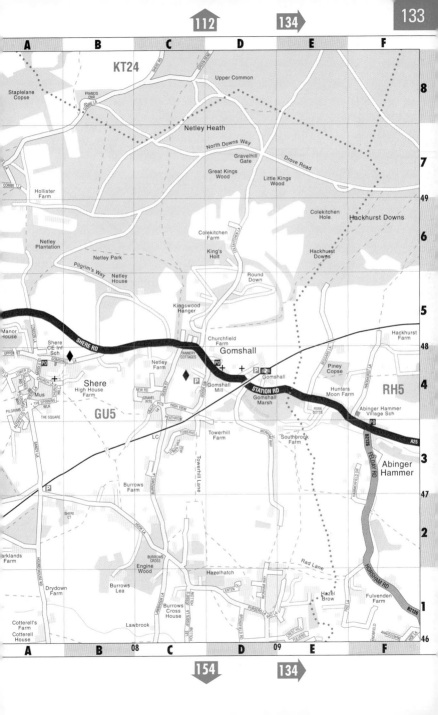

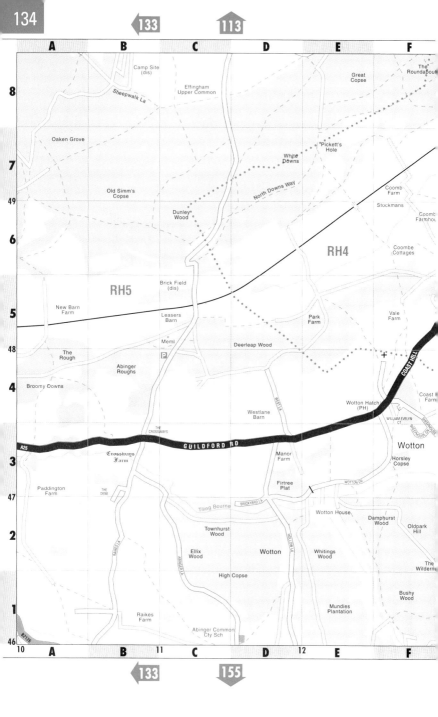

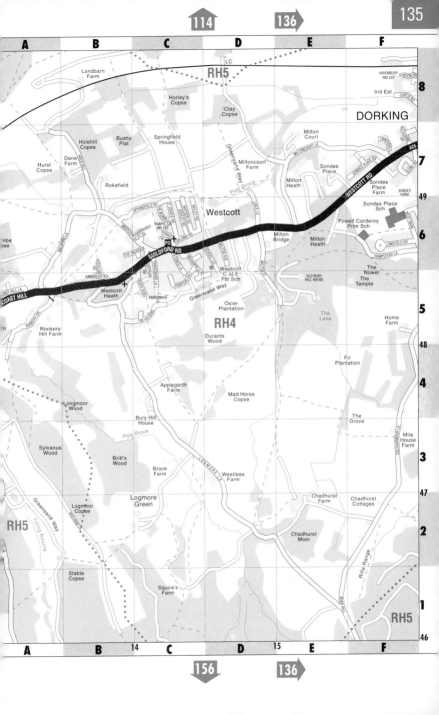

114
136
156
136

DORKING

Westcott

RH5

RH4

RH5

RH5

LC
Landbarn Farm
Horley's Copse
Clay Copse
HAVENBURY IND EST
STATION RD
CURTIS RD
Ind Est
Holehill Copse
Bushy Plat
Springfield House
Greensand Way
Miltoncourt Farm
Milton Court
MILTONCOURT LA
SONDES PLACE DR
Dene Farm
Hurst Copse
Rokefield
Pipp Brook
Milton Heath
Sondes Place
Sondes Place Farm
WESTCOTT RD
A25
Sondes Farm
Springfield Rd
IND EST
CHAPEL LA
CL
KILN LA
GUILDFORD RD
Milton Bridge
Milton Heath
Powell Corderoy Prim Sch
LONGFIELD RD
The Nower
The Temple
The Paddock
PO
PARSONAGE LA
Westcott C of E Fst Sch
Westcott Heath
GREENSAND WAY
Old Bury Hill House
HAMPSTEAD LA
The Lake
Home Farm
COAST HILL LA
ROOKERY DR
COAST HILL
Sandrock Rd
PARSONAGE LA
THE HEATH
Osier Plantation
Rookery Hill Farm
Durants Wood
Fir Plantation
The Grove
COLTHURST LA
Mile House Farm
Applegarth Farm
Mad Horse Copse
Longmoor Wood
Bury Hill House
Pipp Brook
Sylvanus Wood
Britt's Wood
LOGMORE LA
Brook Farm
Westlees Farm
Chadhurst Farm
Chadhurst Cottages
Greensand Way
Tilling Bourne
Logmoor Copse
Logmore Green
Chadhurst Moor
Rifle Range
Stable Copse
Squire's Farm
BOAR HILL

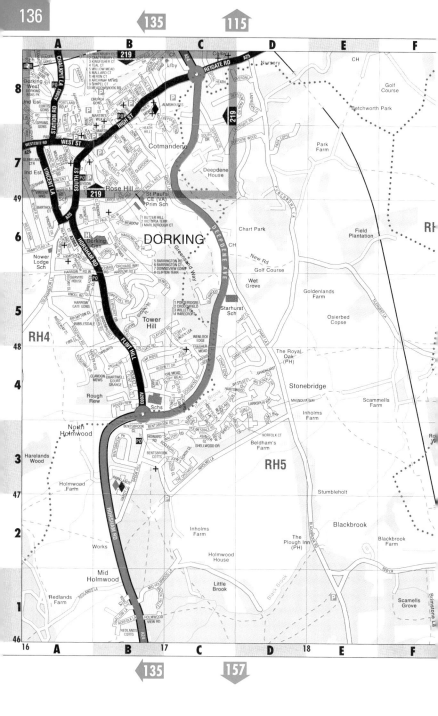

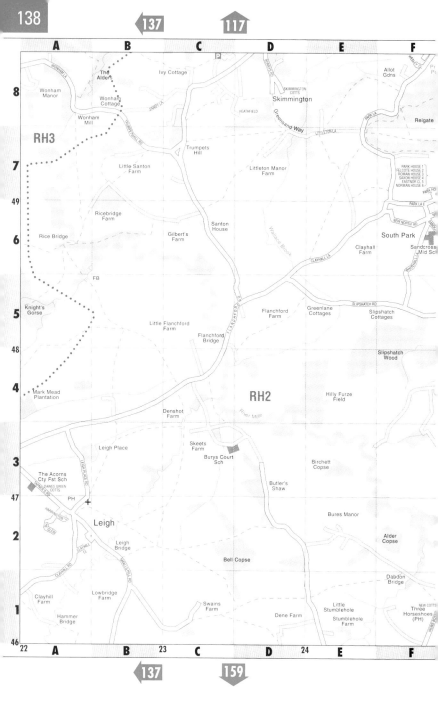

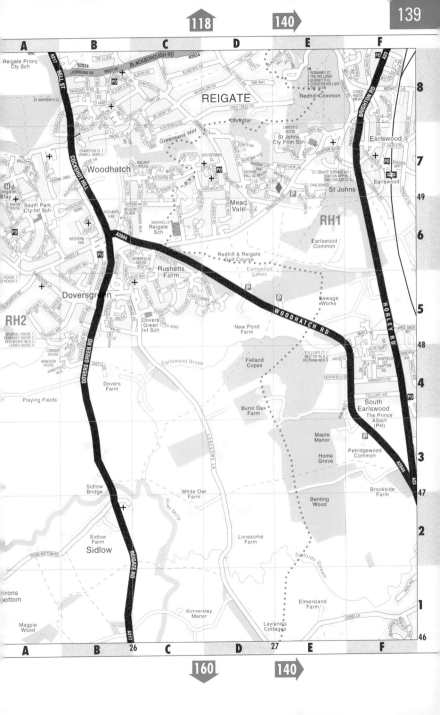

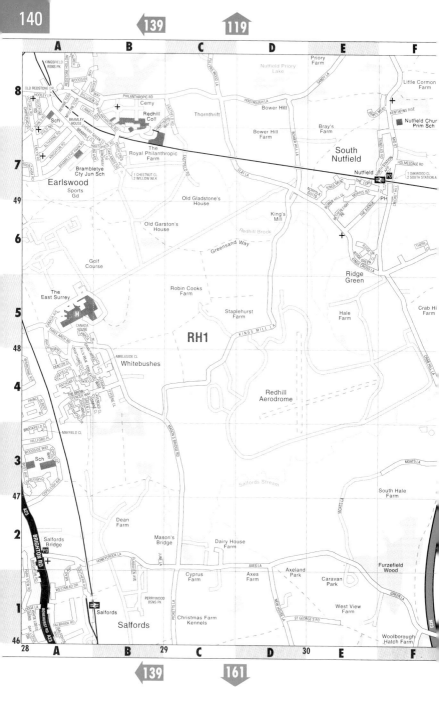

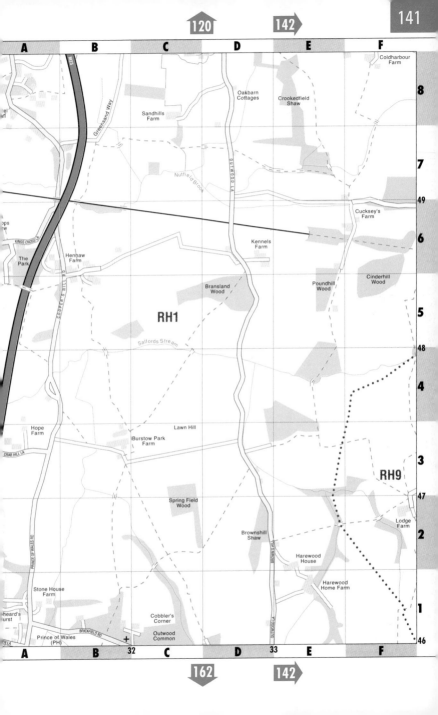

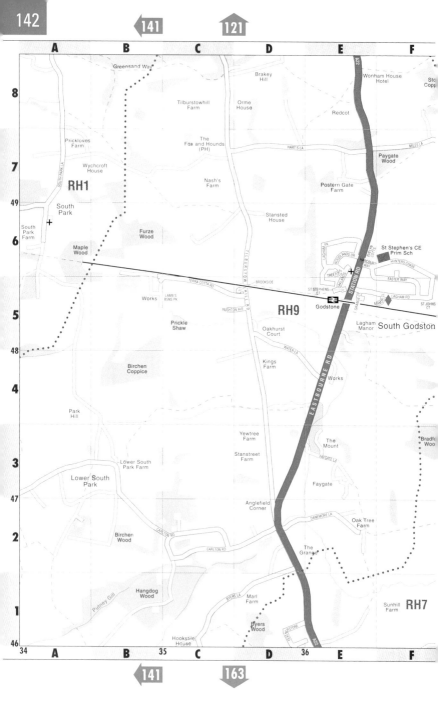

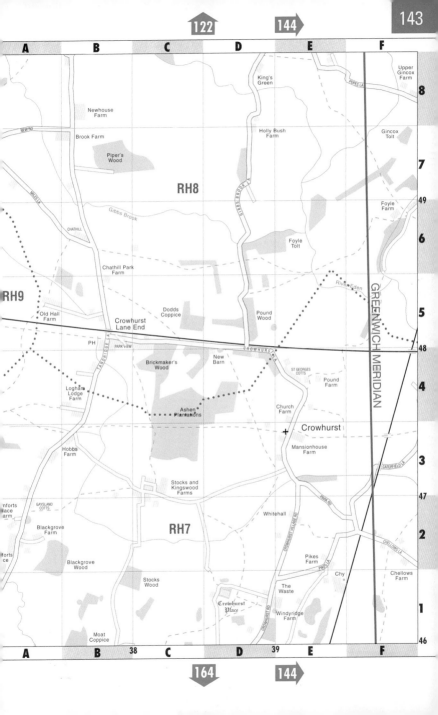

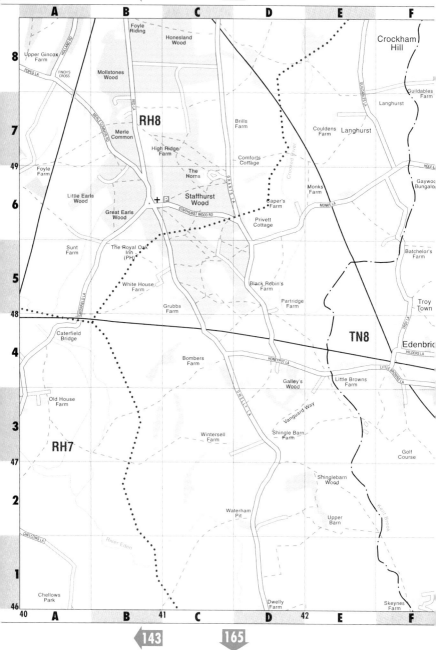

A B C D E F

8 Upper Gincox Farm
FINCH'S CROSS

Foyle Riding

Honesland Wood

Crockham Hill

Guildables Farm

Mollstones Wood

Langhurst

RH8

7 Merle Common

High Ridge Farm

Brills Farm

Couldens Farm Langhurst

Monks Farm

Gaywood Bungalow

49 Foyle Farm

The Horns

Comforts Cottage

Crooked River

Little Earls Wood

Staffhurst Wood

6 Great Earls Wood

STAFFHURST WOOD RD

Caper's Farm

MONKS LA

Privett Cottage

Sunt Farm

The Royal Oak Inn (PH)

Batchelor's Farm

5 White House Farm

Black Robin's Farm

Troy Town

Grubbs Farm

Partridge Farm

48 Caterfield Bridge
CATERFIELD LA

TN8

Edenbridge

HILDERS LA

4 Old House Farm

Bombers Farm

HONEYPOT LA

Little Browns Farm

LITTLE BROWNS LA

Galley's Wood

3 RH7

Wintersell Farm

Vanguard Way

Shingle Barn Farm

Golf Course

47

Shinglebarn Wood

2 CHELLOWS LA

River Eden

Waterham Pit

Upper Barn

Kent Brook

1 Chellows Park

Dwelly Farm

Skeynes Farm

46

40 A B 41 C D 42 E F

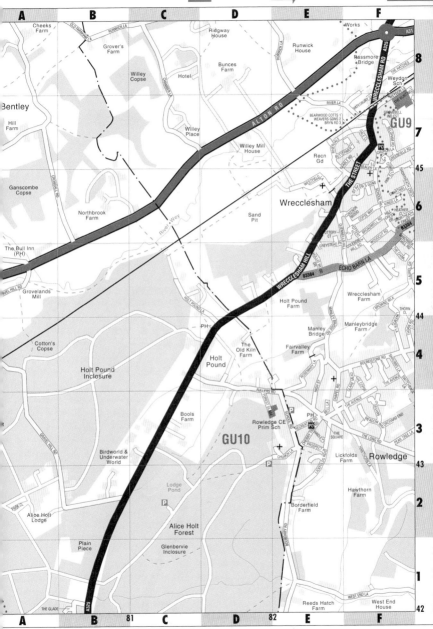

The Bull Inn
(PH)

Cheeks
Farm

Grover's
Farm

Runwick La

Old Farnham Rd

Ridgway
House

Runwick
House

Bunces
Farm

Works

A31

Rassmore
Bridge

Weydon
Sch

Willey
Copse

Hotel

Chamber La

ALTON RD

Willey
Place

Willey Mill
House

River Wey

RIVER LA

Waterside La

BEARWOOD COTTS 1
WEAVERS GDNS 2
BRYN RD 3

WRECCLESHAM RD

A325

GROVEBELL
IND EST

GU9

Bentley

Hill
Farm

Recn
Gd

Ganscombe
Copse

Northbrook
Farm

THE STREET

PO

Wrecclesham

45

6

Sand
Pit

WESTBURY LA

POTTERY LA

GREYSTEAD PK

WRECCLESHAM HILL

B3384

ECHO BARN LA

B3384

45

Grovelands
Mill

RIVER HILL RD

Cotton's
Copse

HOLT POUND LA

PH

Holt Pound
Farm

Manley
Bridge

Manleybridge
Farm

Wrecclesham
Farm

THORN CL

BROWNS WLK

44

5

The
Old Kiln
Farm

Holt
Pound

Fairvalley
Farm

ROSEMARY LA

BOUNDSTONE RD

THE AVENUE

4

Holt Pound
Inclosure

Bools
Farm

FULLERS RD

P

PH

GU10

Rowledge CE
Prim Sch

PO

MILL LA

THE LONG RD

THE SQUARE

MEADOW END

ORCHARD END

PEAK DELL LA

3

Birdworld &
Underwater
World

DEANE RD

CHURCH LA

Lickfolds
Farm

Rowledge

43

P

Lodge
Pond

P

Hawthorn
Farm

2

Alice Holt
Lodge

TASK CL

BEALE HILL RD

Alice Holt
Forest

Glenbervie
Inclosure

Borderfield
Farm

BUNDWAY RD

Plain
Piece

A325

THE GLADE

WEST END LA

Reeds Hatch
Farm

West End
House

1

42

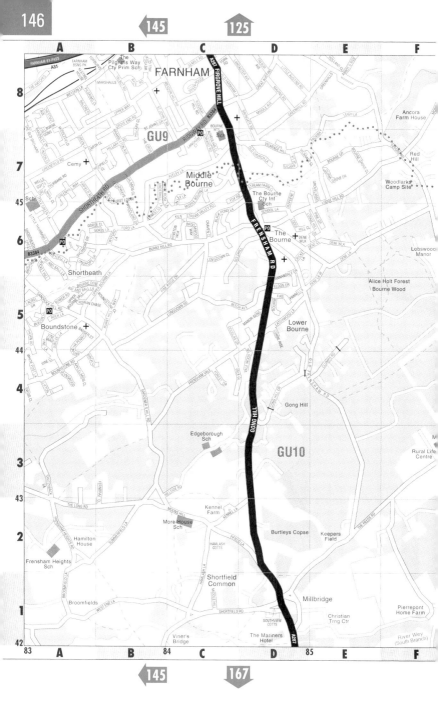

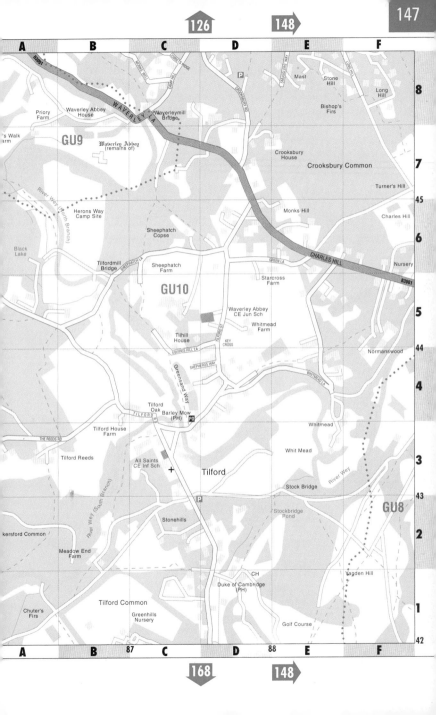

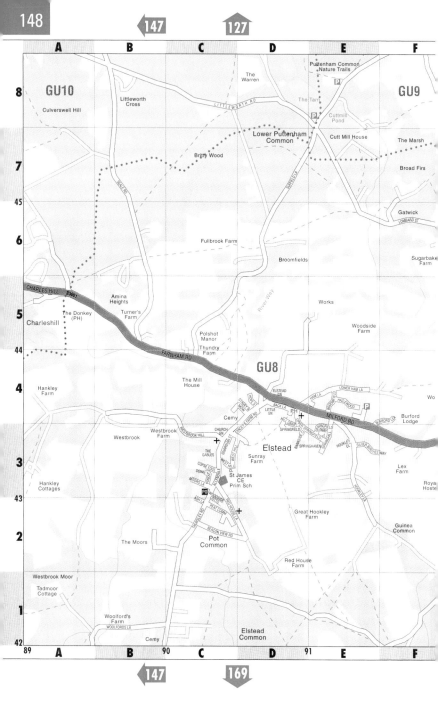

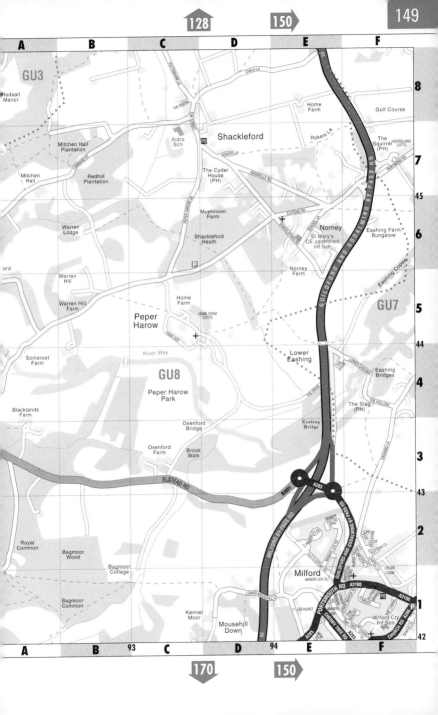

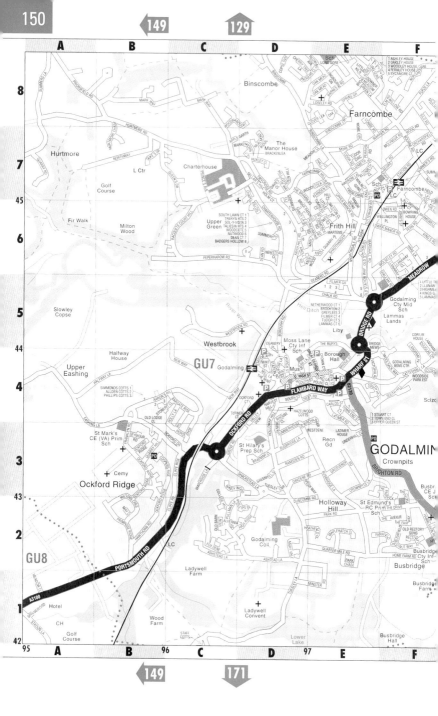

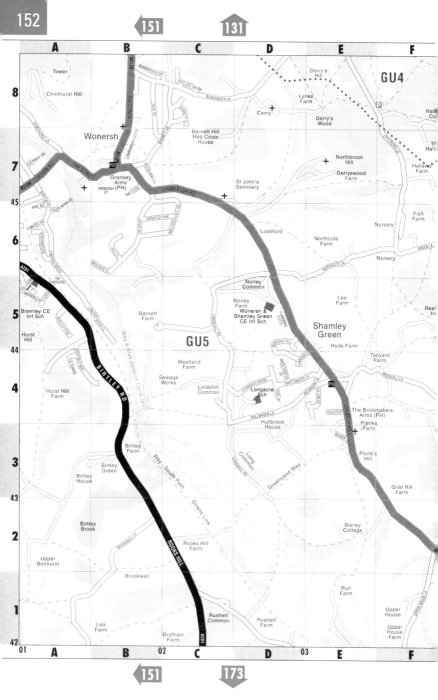

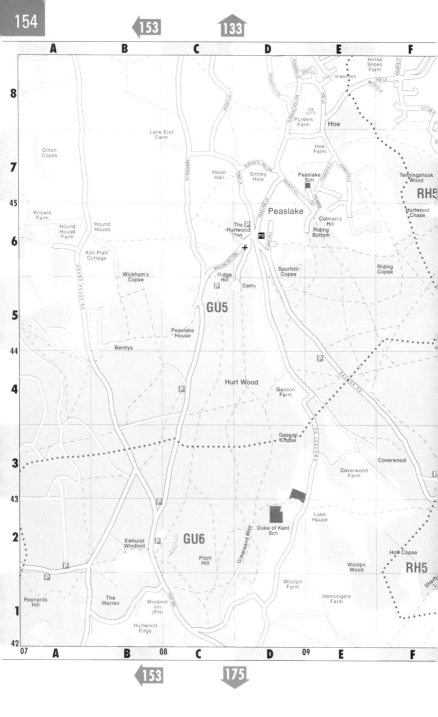

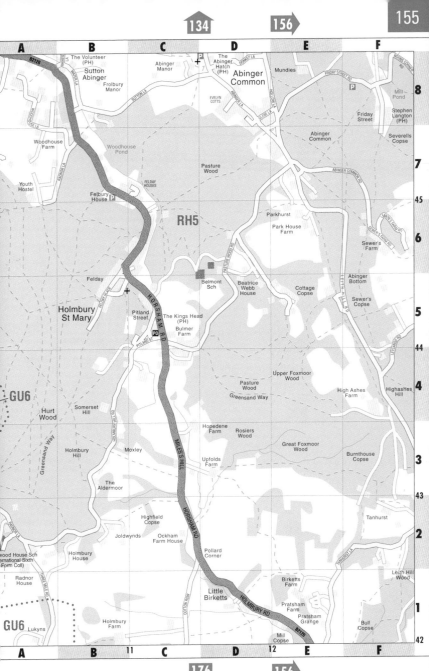

A B **C** D **E** F

8

B2126
The Volunteer (PH)
Sutton Abinger
Frolbury Manor
Abinger Manor
The Abinger Hatch (PH)
Abinger Common
Mundies
Friday Street

Woodhouse Farm
Woodhouse Pond
Evelyn Cotts
Friday Street
Stephen Langton (PH)

Youth Hostel
Felbury House
Felday Houses
Pasture Wood
Abinger Common
Severells Copse

7
ABINGER COMMON RD

45

RH5
Parkhurst
Park House Farm
Sewer's Farm

6

Felday
Belmont Sch
Beatrice Webb House
Cottage Copse
Abinger Bottom
Sewer's Copse

Holmbury St Mary
Pitland Street
The Kings Head (PH)
Bulmer Farm
HORSHAM RD

5

44

PITLAND ST
Upper Foxmoor Wood
Pasture Wood
Greensand Way
High Ashes Farm
Highashes Hill

4

GU6
Hurt Wood
Somerset Hill
Hopedene Farm
Rosiers Wood
Great Foxmoor Wood
Burnthouse Copse

Greensand Way
Holmbury Hill
Moxley
Upfolds Farm
MILES'S HILL

3

43

The Aldermoor
Highfield Copse
Joldwynds
Ockham Farm House
Pollard Corner
Tanhurst

HORSHAM RD
2

wood House Sch
International Sixth Form Coll)
Radnor House
Holmbury House
Birketts Farm
Leith Hill Wood

GU6 Lukyns
Holmbury Farm
Little Birketts
HOLMBURY RD
Pratsham Farm
Pratsham Grange
Bull Copse

1

Mill Copse
B2126

42

A B 11 **C** D 12 **E** F

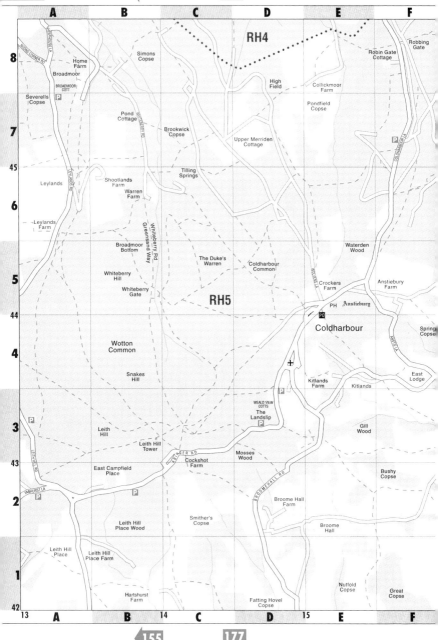

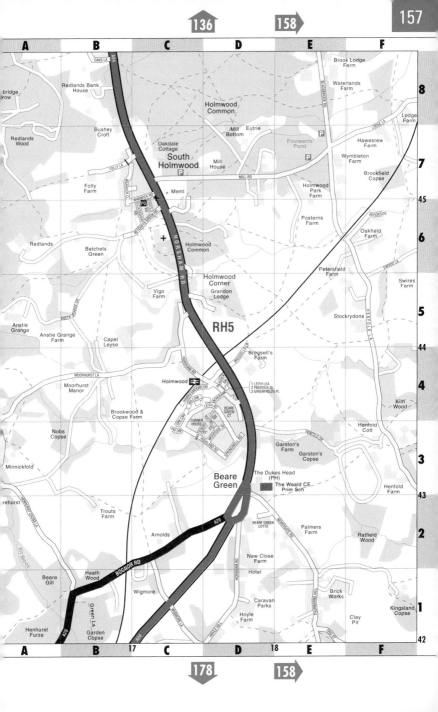

157
137

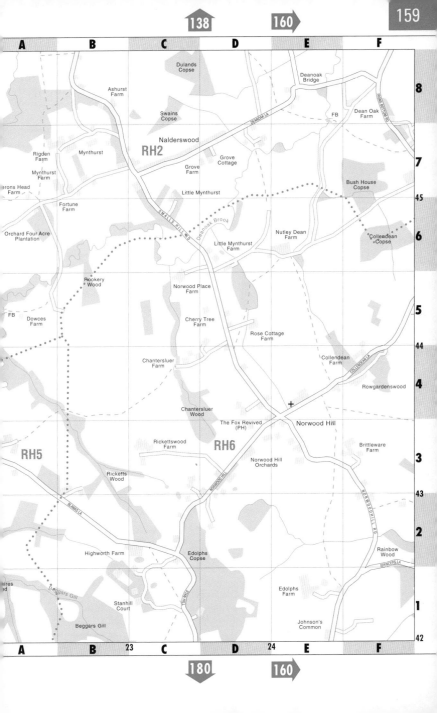

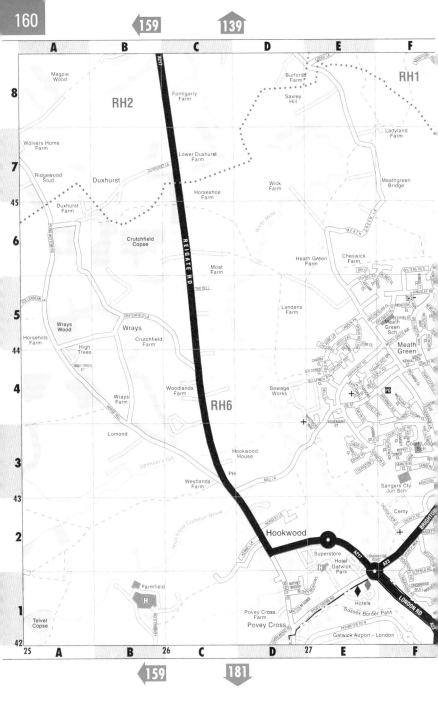

A   **B**   **C**   **D**   **E**   **F**

RH1

Magpie Wood

8

RH2

Fontigarry Farm

Burfords Farm

Saxley Hill

Wolvers Home Farm

Ladyland Farm

7

Ridgewood Stud

Duxhurst

Lower Duxhurst Farm

DUXHURST LA.

Wick Farm

Meathgreen Bridge

45

Duxhurst Farm

Horseshoe Farm

MEATH GREEN LA.

6

Crutchfield Copse

REIGATE RD

Moat Farm

THE DELL

Heath Green Farm

Cheswick Farm

BAY DR

POYNES RD

PALMER CL

BOLTERS RD S

KINGSLEY RD

COLLENDEAN LA.

5

Wrays Wood

CRUTCHFIELD LA.

Wrays

Landens Farm

LANDEN PK

Meath Green Sch

PEPPERFIELDS

MEADOWSIDE

MOSFORD CL

Meath Green

Horsehills Farm

High Trees

Crutchfield Farm

CHESTERS

Meath Green

44

HIGH TREES CT

CHARM

GOLDCREST CL

BULLFINCH CL

HORSHAM RD

4

Wrays Farm

Woodlands Farm

HORSE HILL

RH6

Sewage Works

LEE ST

ROSEMARY CT

Court Lodge Sch

Lomond

Hookwood House

3

Spencer's Gill

PH

MILL LA.

Sangers Cty Jun Sch

Westlands Farm

NURSERY LA.

43

Hookwood Common Brook

Cemy

BRIGHTON

2

Hookwood

Superstore

Hotel Gatwick Park

H

A217

LONGBRIDGE RDBT

A23

LONDON RD

Farmfield

H

WITHEY BROOK

Hotels

LONGBRIDGE RD

Telvet Copse

Povey Cross Farm

Povey Cross

Sussex Border Path

1

PERIMETER RD N

Gatwick Airport - London

42

25   **A**   **B**   **26**   **C**   **D**   **27**   **E**   **F**

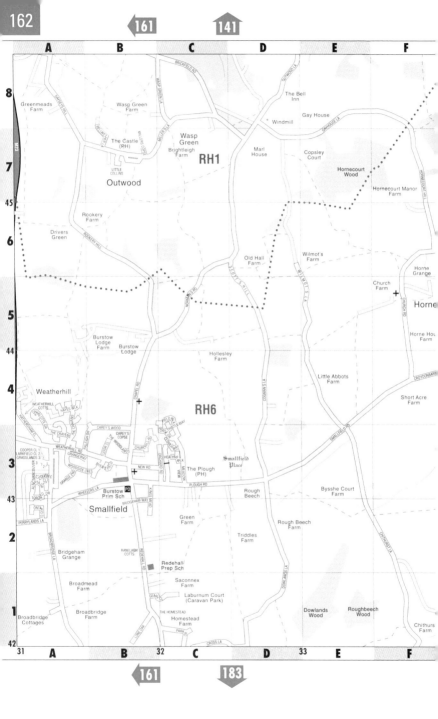

163
143

	A	B	C	D	E	F

8 Moat Farm

Bowerland Farm

ARDENRUN

ARDEN MEAD COTTS
ARDENRUN COTTS

BOWERLAND LA

Arden Green

7 The Red Barn (PH)

Waterside

B2029

RAY LA

GREENWICH MERIDIAN

45

Sugham Farm

Sewage Works

HAYTED RD

Ray Bridge

RAY LA

6 Ray Lodge Farm

Hare & Hounds (PH)

LINGFIELD COMMON RD

Rushford Farm

RAY DRV
RAY DR

Lingfield Common

5 Pond Farm

Lingfield

Park Farm

RH7

HAYWARDENS
SAURY LA
LITTLE LULLENDEN

PARK LA

44 Lyne House Farm

GLENSTONE RD

BAKER'S PAULS
ASH
SHALE'S
NEW PLACE GDNS
MEAD

Lingfield Prim Sch

STATION RD

4 Pollard Farm

HEADLAND WAY
OLD SCHOOL
CHURCH RD
TOWN HILL

Cemy

Lingfield

The Star (PH)

EDENBRIDGE

Notre D Sch

3 Meadhurst Farm

Oat Barns

NEWCHAPE RD

PARADISE
NATURE PL
JENNY LA

FLAGSTAFF
HIGH ST
STAMFORD PL
CAMDEN RD

RACECOURSE RD

Notre Dame Sch

STANWORTH COTTS

ORMUZ COTTS 1
THE ROW 2
BILLHURST COTTS 3
ST CHRISTOPHER'S 4

Rowlands Court

DEVERS MEAD

EAST GRINSTEAD RD

Lingfield House

43 Rowland's Farm

Jacksbridge Farm

CH

2 B2028

Devil's Den

Collier's Wood

Jacks Bridge

Lingfield Park Race Course

Golf Course

1 Long Acres Farm

RH19

Felcourt Wood

Green Wood

Felcourt Dairy Farm

FELCOURT RD

BLACKBERRY LA

Mill Wood

MILL LA

42

FELCOURT COTTS

Southernleigh

37	A	B	38	C	D	39	E	F

163
185

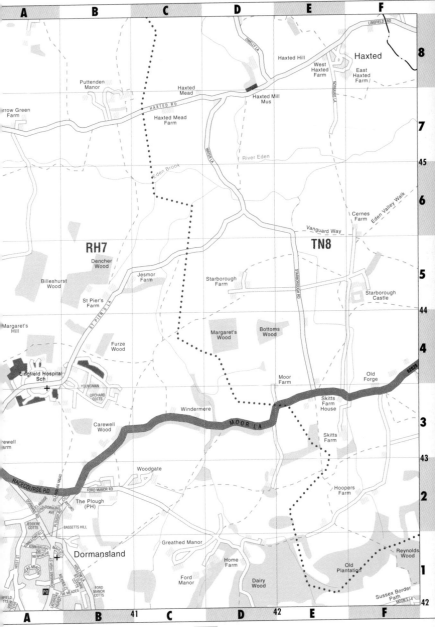

A B C D E F

8

Haxted

LINGFIELD RD

West
Haxted Hill Haxted
Farm East
Haxted
Farm

SHELLEY LA

Haxted
Mead

Haxted Mill
Mus

NORMANS LA

HAXTED RD

Haxted Mead
Farm

7

rrow Green
Farm

Puttenden
Manor

45

River Eden

Eden Brook

WELLS LA

6

Cernes
Farm

Eden Valley Walk

Vanguard Way

RH7 TN8

Dencher
Wood

5

Jesmor
Farm

Starborough
Farm

Starborough
Castle

STARBOROUGH RD

Billeshurst
Wood

St Pier's
Farm

44

ST PIER'S LA

Margaret's
Wood

Bottoms
Wood

Margaret's
Hill

Furze
Wood

4

Moor
Farm

Old
Forge

Skitts
Farm
House

B2028

Lingfield Hospital
Sch

YOUNGMAN

ORCHARD
COTTS

Windermere

MOOR LA

3

Carewell
Wood

Skitts
Farm

rewell
arm

43

RACECOURSE RD

Woodgate

Hoopers
Farm

2

FORD MANOR RD

The Plough
(PH)

JEDDERE
COTTS

BASSETTS HILL

Greathed Manor

Reynolds
Wood

1

Dormansland

Home
Farm

Old
Plantation

PO

Ford
Manor

Dairy
Wood

Sussex Border
Path

FORD MANOR
COTTS

THE MEADES

B2028 14

42

A B C D E F
41 42

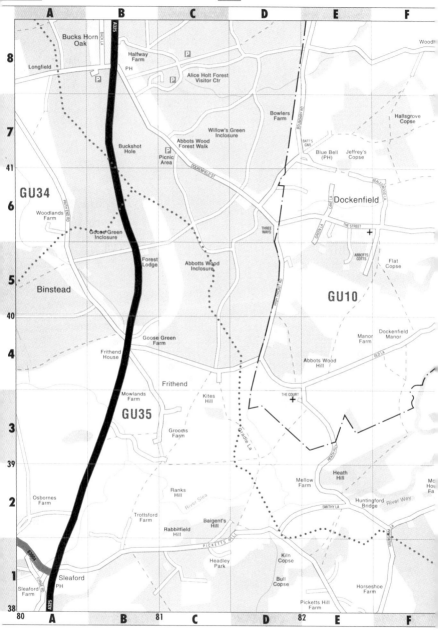

8

Longfield

Bucks Horn
Oak

Halfway
Farm

PH

P

P

Alice Holt Forest
Visitor Ctr

Bowlers
Farm

Woodl

Hallsgrove
Copse

7

Willow's Green
Inclosure

Abbots Wood
Forest Walk

Buckshot
Hole

P

Picnic
Area

BATT'S
CNR

Blue Bell
(PH)

Jeffrey's
Copse

41

DOCKENFIELD ST

GU34

Dockenfield

6

Woodlands
Farm

Goose Green
Inclosure

THREE
WAYS

THE STREET

ABBOTTS
COTTS

Flat
Copse

5

Binstead

Forest
Lodge

Abbotts Wood
Inclosure

GU10

40

4

Goose Green
Farm

Frithend
House

Manor
Farm

Dockenfield
Manor

Abbots Wood
Hill

OLD LA

Frithend

Mowlands
Farm

Kites
Hill

THE COURT

GU35

3

Grooms
Farm

Gadle La

39

Ranks
Hill

Mellow
Farm

Heath
Hill

Mc
Hou
Fa

2

Osbornes
Farm

River Slea

Trottsford
Farm

Baigent's
Hill

SMITHY LA

Huntingford
Bridge

River Wey

Rabbitfield
Hill

PICKETTS HILL

1

Sleaford

PH

Headley
Park

Kiln
Copse

Horseshoe
Farm

Sleaford
Farm

Bull
Copse

Picketts Hill
Farm

38

80   **A**   **B**   81   **C**   **D**   82   **E**   **F**

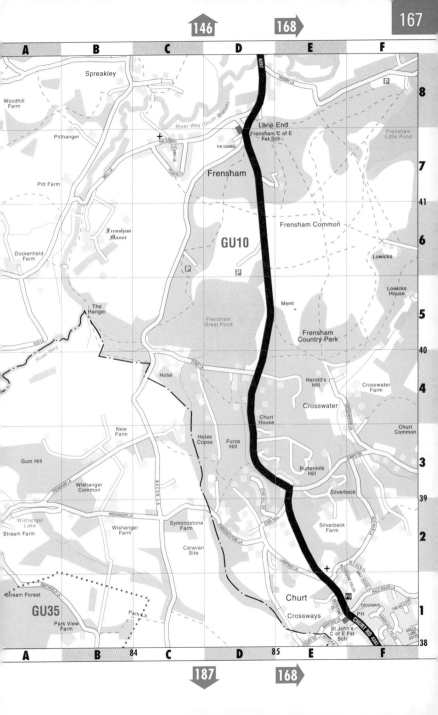

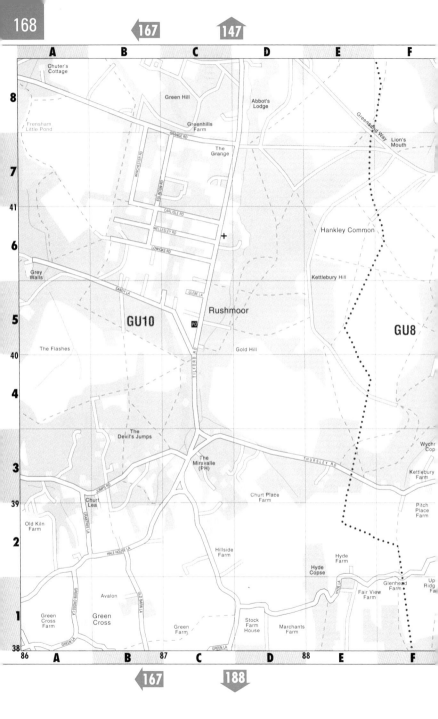

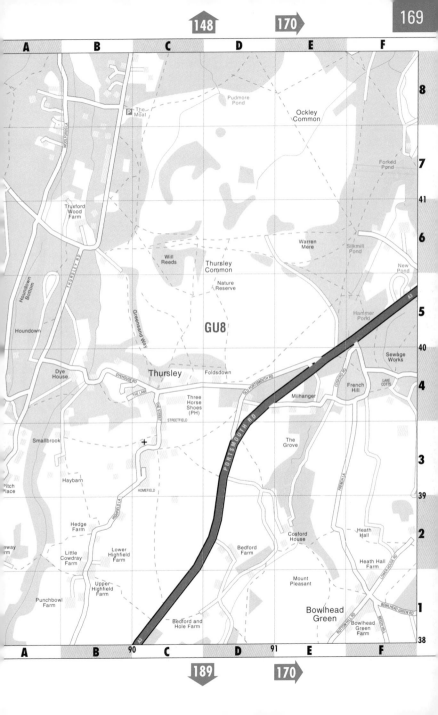

A   B   C   D   E   F

8

7

41

6

Pudmore Pond

Ockley Common

Forked Pond

Truxford Wood Farm

Will Reeds

Thursley Common

Warren Mere

Silkmill Pond

New Pond

Houndown Bottom

Houndown

Greensand Way

Nature Reserve

GU8

Hammer Pond

5

40

Dye House

Thursley

Foldsdown

French Hill

Sewage Works

LAKE COTTS

4

Three Horse Shoes (PH)

Milhanger

Smallbrook

STREETFIELD

The Grove

3

Haybarn

HOMEFIELD

39

Pitch Place

Hedge Farm

Cosford House

Heath Hall

2

eway rm

Little Cowdray Farm

Lower Highfield Farm

Bedford Farm

Heath Hall Farm

Upper Highfield Farm

Mount Pleasant

Punchbowl Farm

Bowlhead Green

1

Bedford and Hole Farm

Bowlhead Green Farm

38

A   B   90   C   D   91   E   F

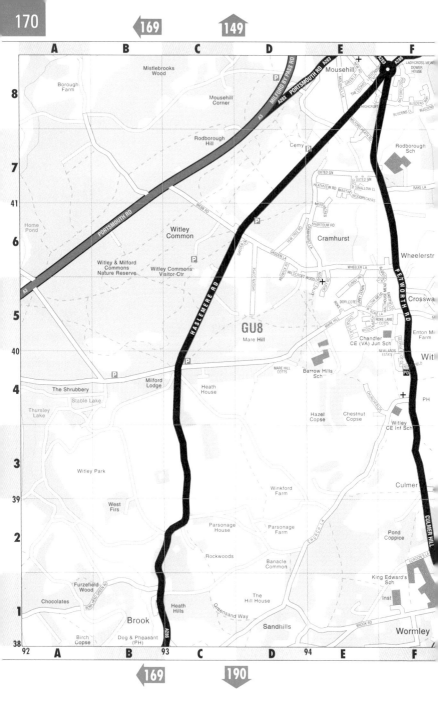

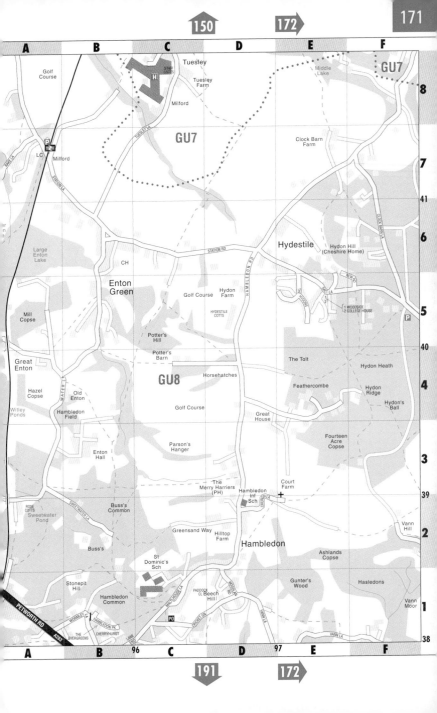

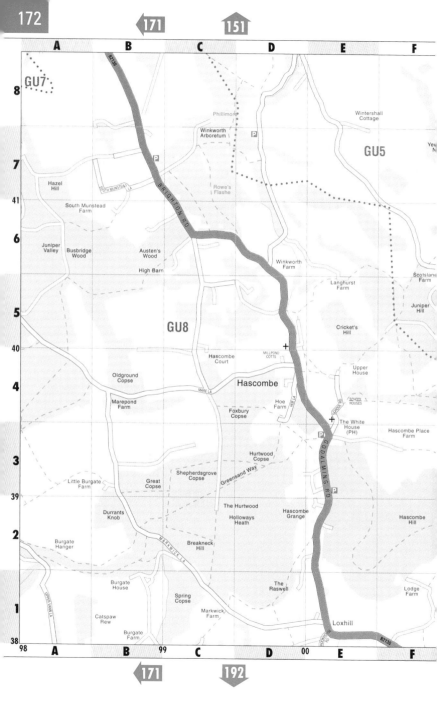

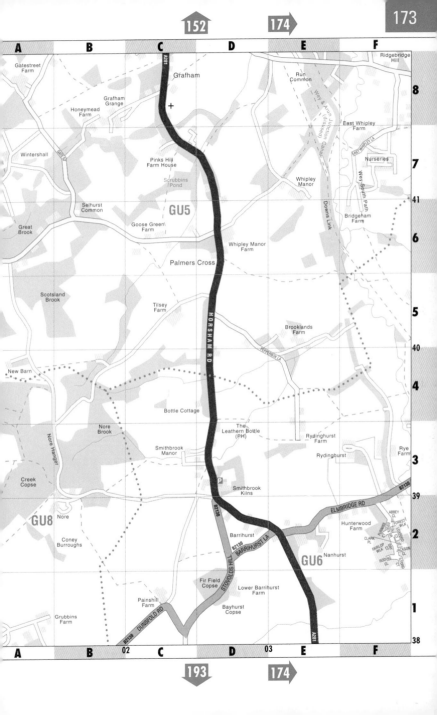

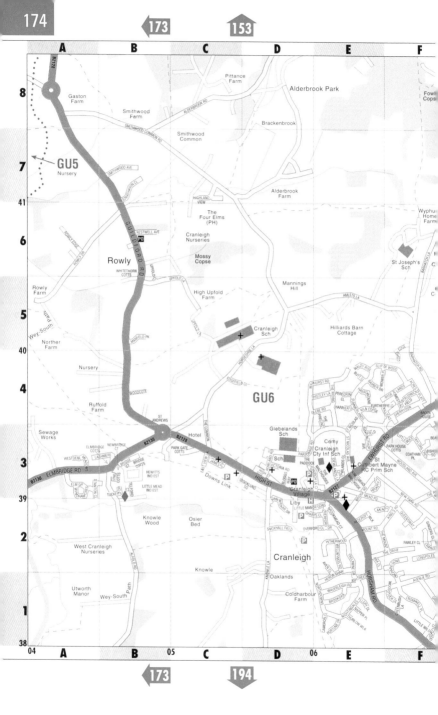

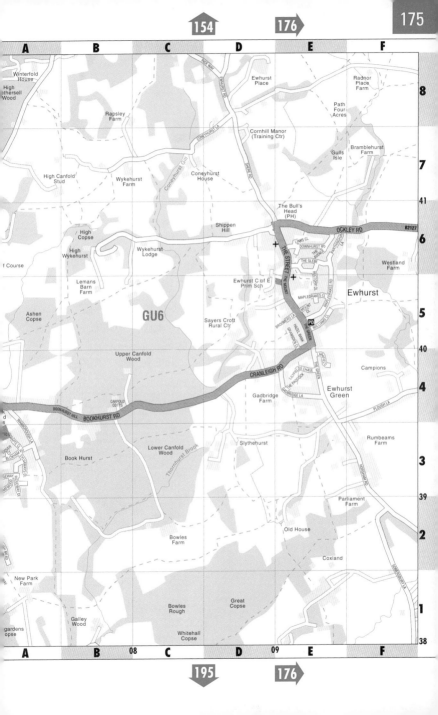

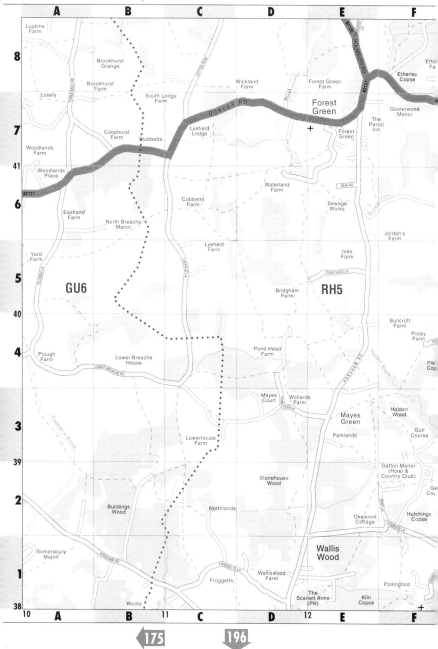

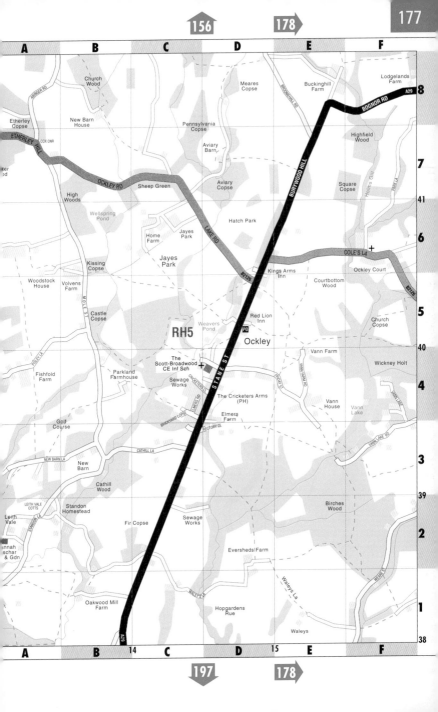

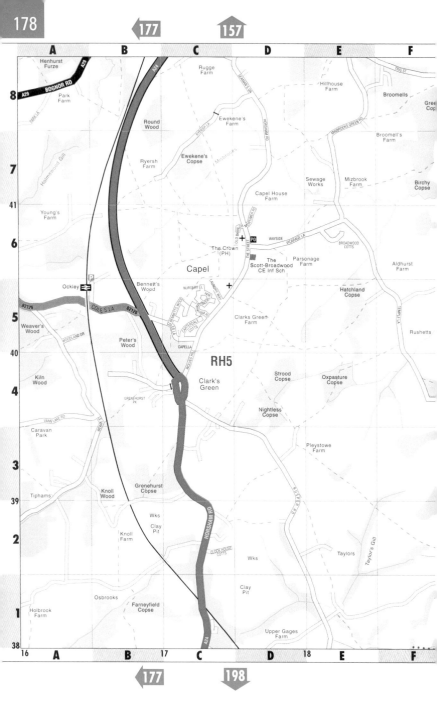

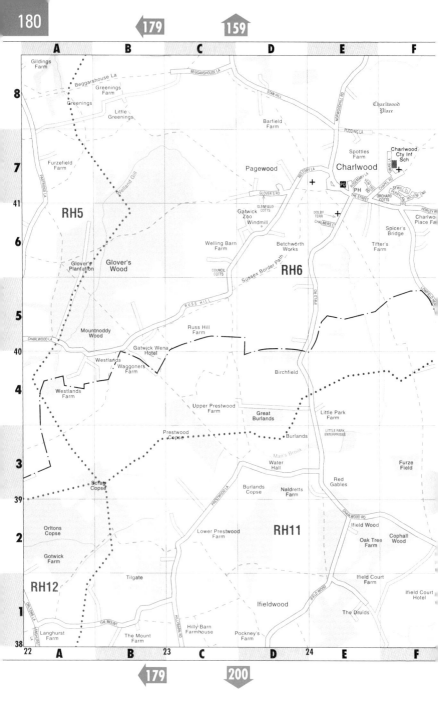

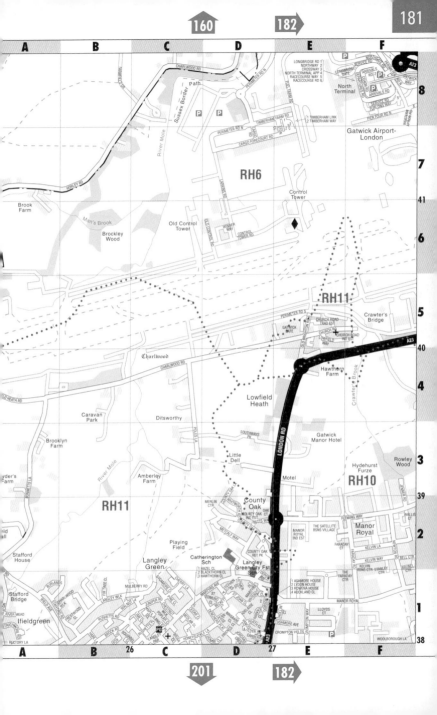

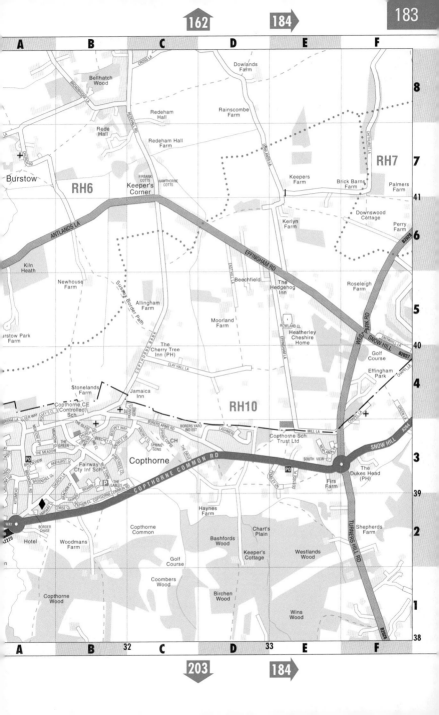

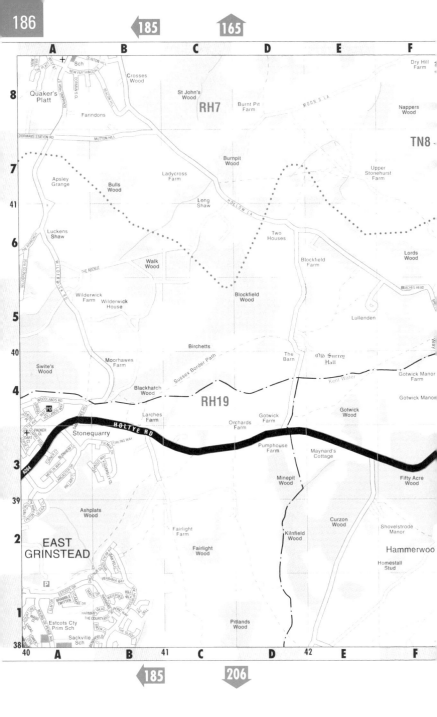

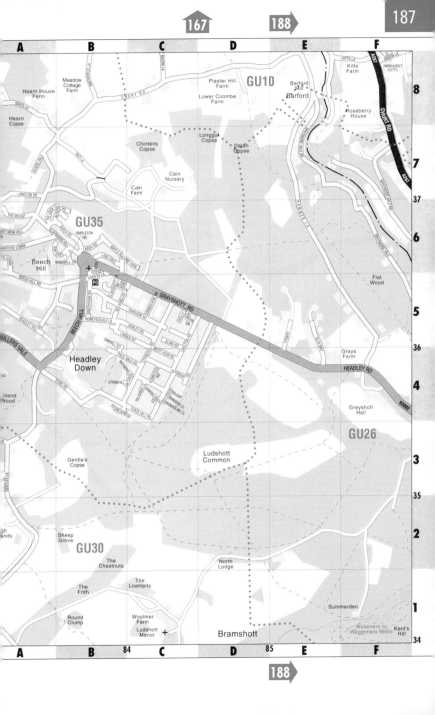

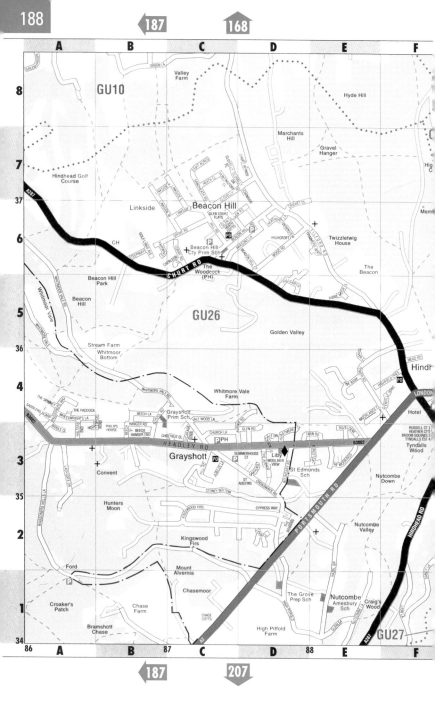

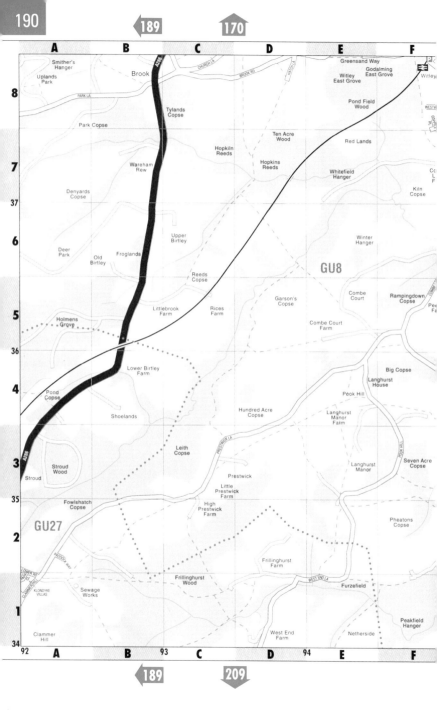

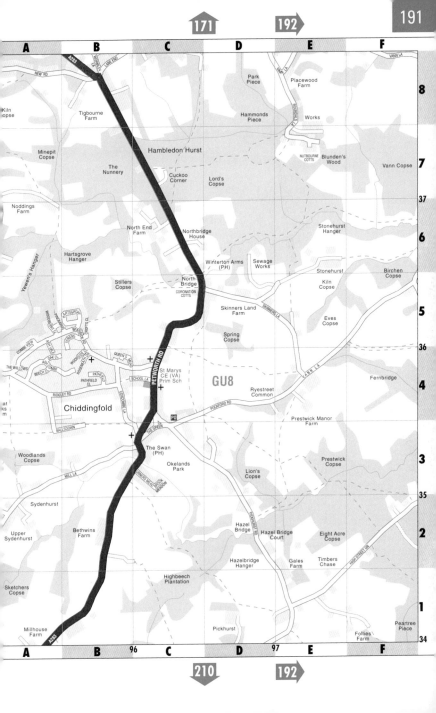

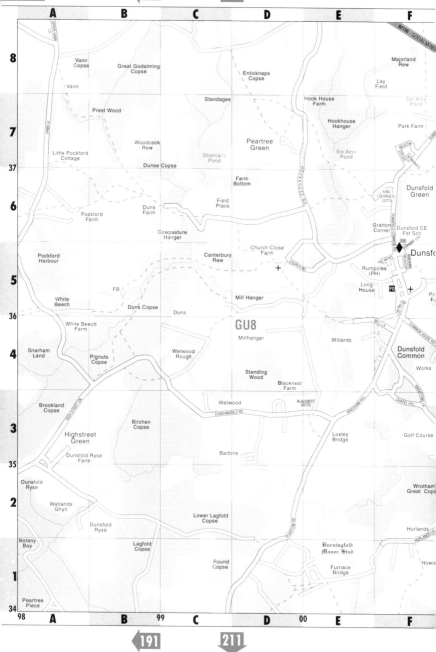

A   B   C   D   E   F

8

Vann
Copse

Great Godalming
Copse

Enticknaps
Copse

Majorland
Rew

Lay
Field

Ten Acre
Pond

Vann

Hook House
Farm

Standages

Prest Wood

7

Woodcock
Rew

Hookhouse
Hanger

Park Farm

Peartree
Green

Little Pockford
Cottage

Shernalls
Pond

Six Acre
Pond

37

Dunse Copse

Farm
Bottom

Dunsfold
Green

6

Pockford
Farm

Duns
Farm

Field
Place

KING
GEORGE'S
COTT'S

Gratton
Corner

Dunsfold CE
Fst Sch

Cowpasture
Hanger

Dunsf

Pockford
Harbour

Canterbury
Rew

Church Close
Farm

THE MEWS

Rumpoles
(PH)

5

FB

Mill Hanger

Long
House

PO

Po
F

White
Beech

Duns Copse

Duns

36

White Beech
Farm

GU8

Millhanger

Willards

Dunsfold
Common

Snarham
Land

Pignuts
Copse

Wetwood
Rough

4

Works

Standing
Wood

Blacknest
Farm

Brookland
Copse

Wetwood

CHIDDINGFOLD RD

BLACKNEST
COTTS

3

Birchen
Copse

Loxley
Bridge

Golf Course

Highstreet
Green

Dunsfold Ryse
Farm

Barbins

35

Dunsfold
Ryse

Watlands
Ghyll

Lower Lagfold
Copse

Wrotham
Great Cops

2

Dunsfold
Ryse

Hurlands

Botany
Bay

Lagfold
Copse

Round
Copse

Burningfold
Manor Stud

Howie

Furnace
Bridge

1

Peartree
Piece

34

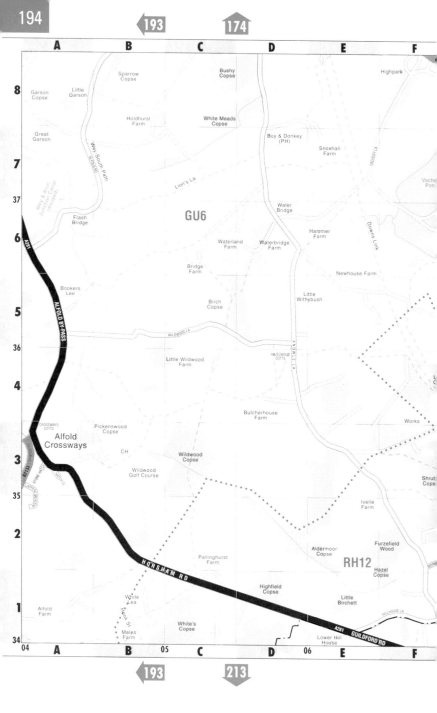

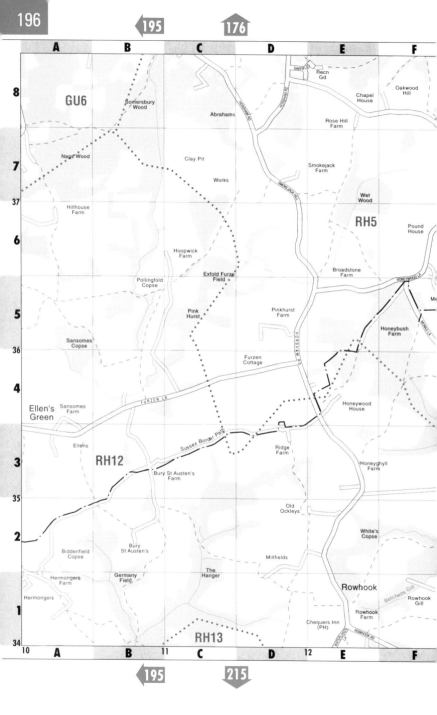

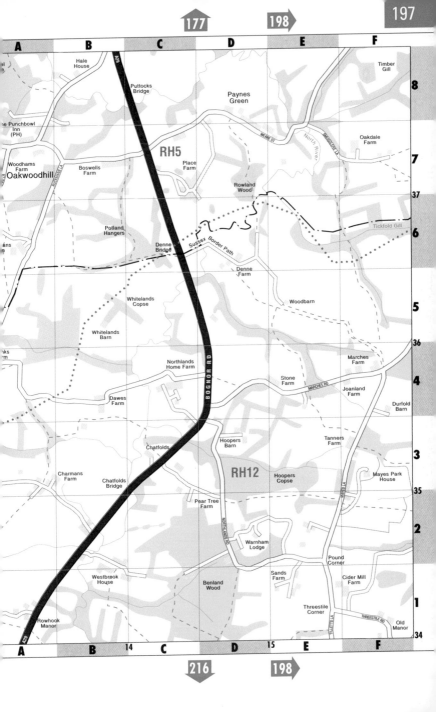

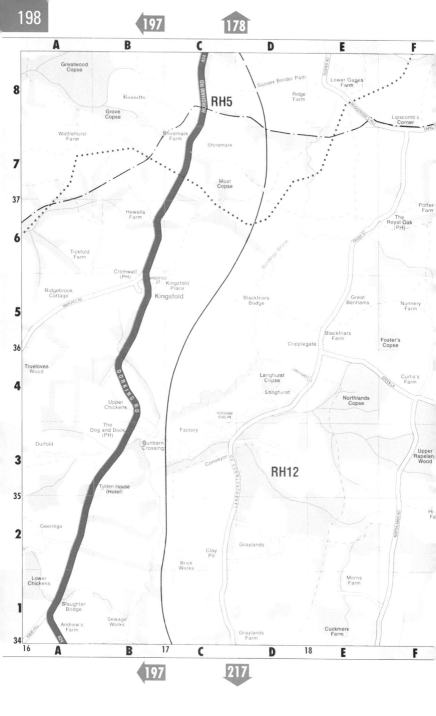

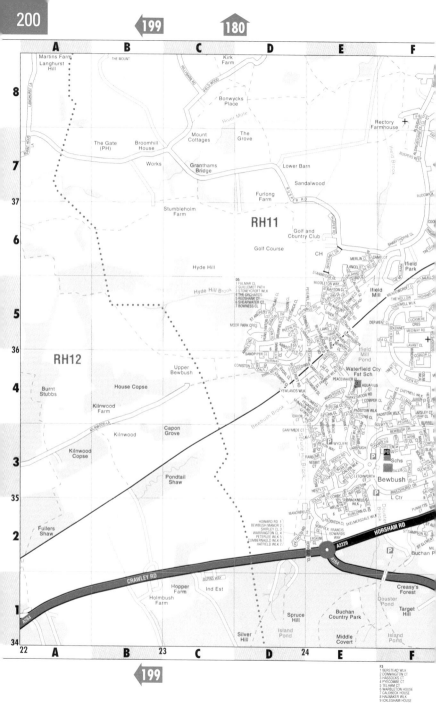

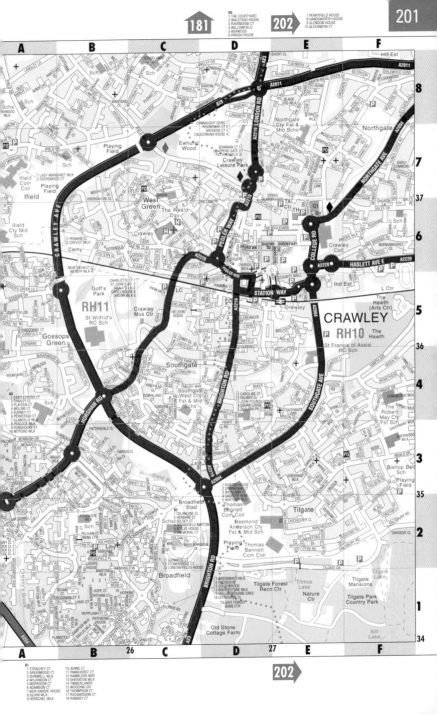

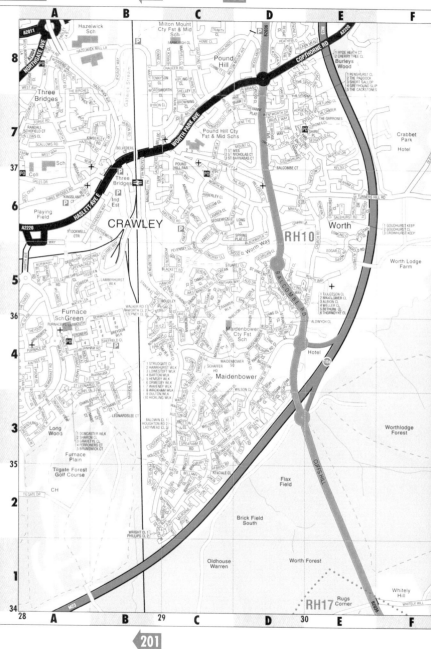

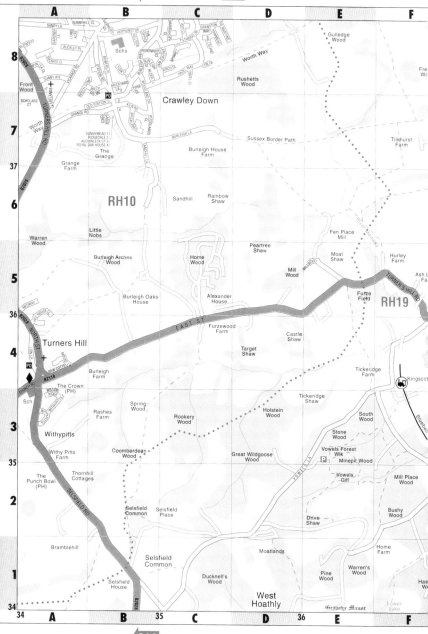

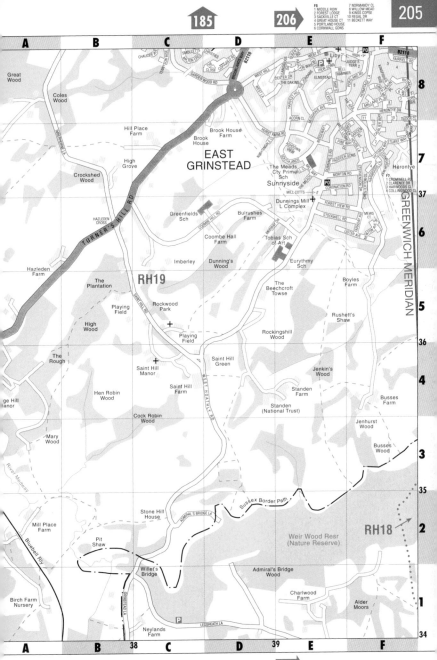

A B C D E F

8

Sackville Sch Beechfield Pk Great Well Farm
Warbleton Cl Oak Bank Farm Hse Cl
Martins Pl Woodbury Cl
St Gloucester Sandringham Cl Constantine Cl

Worsted Farm Wood Cottage Shovelstrode Farm Little Water Farm

Brockhurst Stoke Brunswick Sch

Truscott Manor Berry Wood Culver Farm

7

Home Farm Sussex Border Path

RH19

Luxford's Oakley Beeches Farm Thornhill Farm

37

Luxford's Farm Lewes Rd Box La Ashurstwood Cty Prim Sch

Wealden House Woods Hill La School La

6

The Three Crowns (PH) Hammerwood Rd Ashurstwood Abbey

Sewage Works Ashurst Wood

Ladder La Brambletye Sch

5

Horseshoe Farm Home Wood

Sussex Border Path

36

High Wood Wall Hill Rd

4

Botley Wood Forest Way Wallhill Farm London Rd

River Medway Vanguard

Water Works Brambletye House (remains of) Blenheim Fields Forest Row

Weir Wood Brambletye Manor Farm Kennard Ct Lower Sq Upper Sq Forest Row BSN9

3

Weir Wood Resr (Nature Reserve) Burnthouse Farm

35

Cemy Hartfield Rd Blackland Farm

RH18

South Park Farm Court-in-Holmes Kidbrooke Farm Kidbrooke Rise Hotel Oakwood Pl Forest Row C of E Inf Sch

2

Kidbrooke Park Lewes Rd Dale Rd Hotel Shales

1

Spring Hill Wildfowl Park Spring Hill Farm Newgate Farm Kidbrooke Park (Michael Hall Sch) South Lodge Highgate

Mudbrookes House Popular Farm Royal Ashdown Golf Course

34

GREENWICH MERIDIAN

Greenfields Sch Priors Hatch Farm

40 A B 41 C D 42 E F

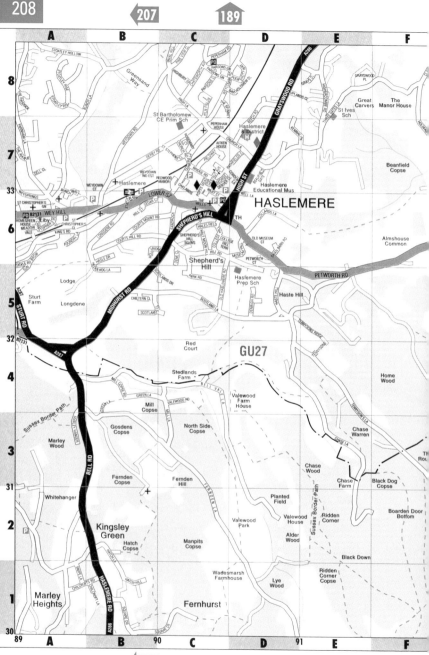

208

207

189

207

HASLEMERE

GU27

Fernhurst

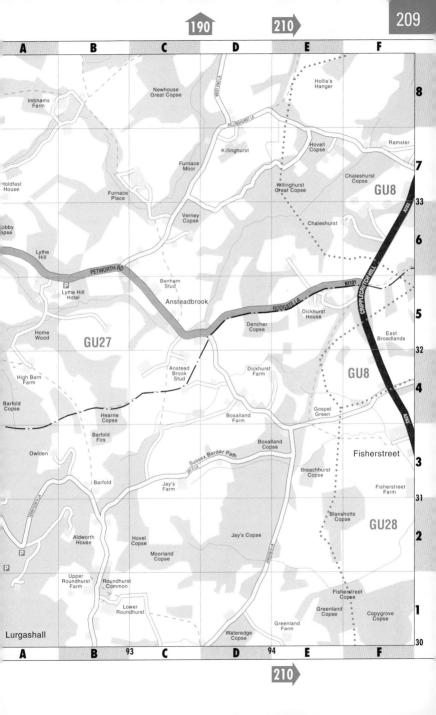

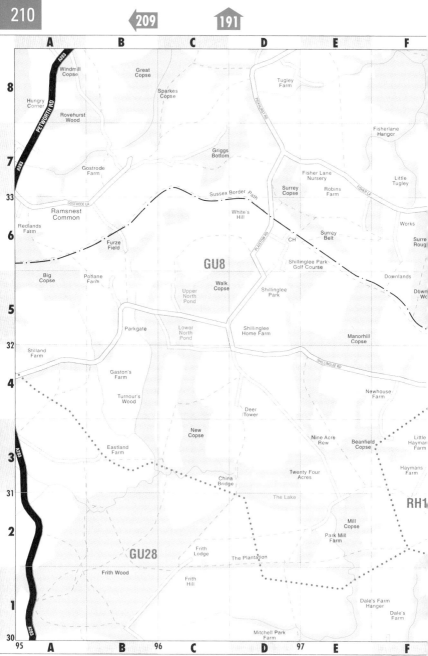

A   B   C   D   E   F

8

Windmill
Copse

Great
Copse

Tugley
Farm

Hungry
Corner

Sparkes
Copse

Fisherlane
Hanger

Rovehurst
Wood

7

Griggs
Bottom

Gostrode
Farm

Fisher Lane
Nursery

Little
Tugley

33

Sussex Border Path

Surrey
Copse

Robins
Farm

Works

Ramsnest
Common

White's
Hill

6

Redlands
Farm

Surrey
Belt

CH

Surre
Roug

Furze
Field

GU8

Shillinglee Park
Golf Course

Downlands

Dowl
Wo

Big
Copse

Potlane
Farm

Walk
Copse

Shillinglee
Park

5

Parkgate

Upper North
Pond

Lower
North
Pond

Shillinglee
Home Farm

Manorhill
Copse

32

Stilland
Farm

SHILLINGLEE RD

4

Gaston's
Farm

Newhouse
Farm

Turnour's
Wood

Deer
Tower

New
Copse

Nine Acre
Rew

Beanfield
Copse

Little
Hayman
Farm

3

Eastland
Farm

Haymans
Farm

China
Bridge

Twenty Four
Acres

31

The Lake

RH1

2

Mill
Copse

GU28

Park Mill
Farm

Frith
Lodge

The Plantation

Frith Wood

Frith
Hill

Dale's Farm
Hanger

1

Dale's
Farm

30

Mitchell Park
Farm

95   A   B   96   C   D   97   E   F

209

211
193

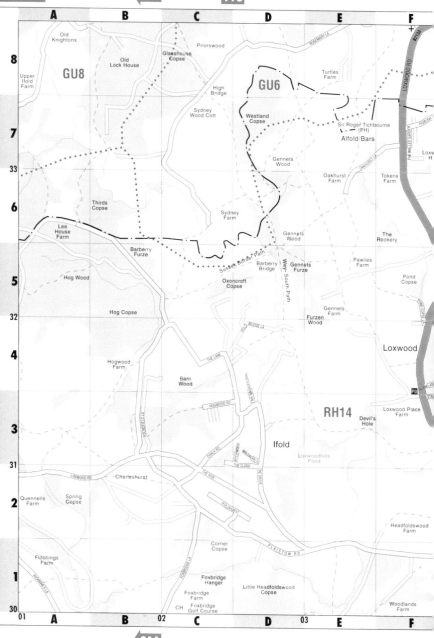

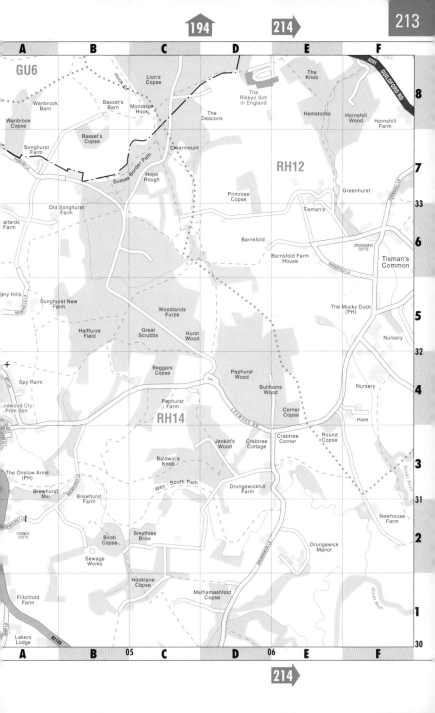

GU6

Wanbrook Barn

Wanbrook Copse

Lion's Copse

Basset's Barn

Monckton Hook

Hook St

The Deacons

The Rikkyo Sch in England

The Knob

Hemstocks

Hornshill Wood

Hornshill Farm

A281 GUILDFORD RD

Songhurst Farm

Basset's Copse

Clearmount

Sussex Border Path

Hope Rough

RH12

Primrose Copse

Greenhurst

Tisman's

HORNSHILL LA

Old Songhurst Farm

allards Farm

Barnsfold

Barnsfold Farm House

CROSSWAYS COTTS

Tisman's Common

BARNSFOLD LA

rry Hills

Songhurst New Farm

MERRY HILL LA

Woodlands Furze

The Mucky Duck (PH)

Halffurze Field

Great Scrubbs

Hurst Wood

Nursery

Beggars Copse

Pephurst Wood

Bullhams Wood

Nursery

Spy Farm

Pephurst Farm

RH14

LOXWOOD RD

Corner Copse

Hale

Loxwood Cty Prim Sch

Jenkin's Wood

Crabtree Cottage

Crabtree Corner

Round Copse

River Arun

The Onslow Arms (PH)

Baldwin's Knob

Wey South Path

Drungewickhill Farm

Newhouse Farm

Brewhurst Mill

Brewhurst Farm

BREWHURST LA

COUNCIL COTTS

Birch Copse

Smythies Brow

Drungewick Manor

BREWHURST LA

Sewage Works

Hooklane Copse

Malhamashfold Copse

River Arun

Flitchfold Farm

B2133

Lakers Lodge

8
7
33
6
5
32
4
3
31
2
1
30

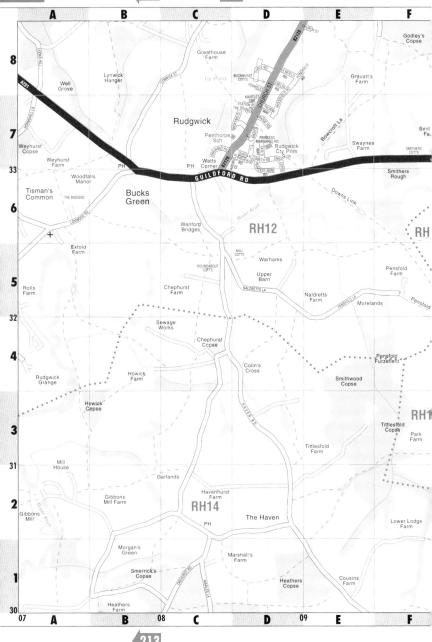

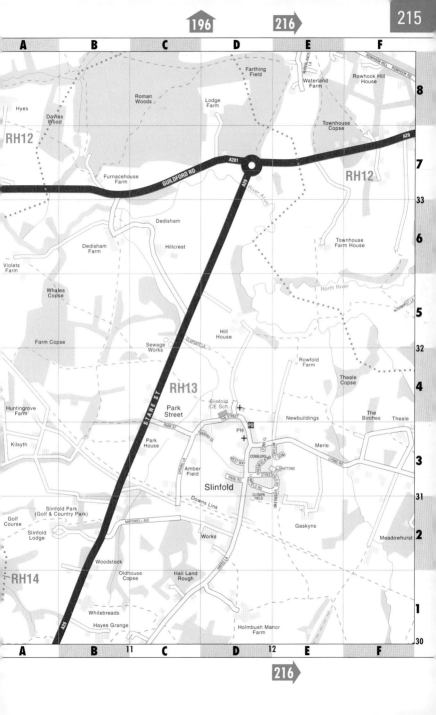

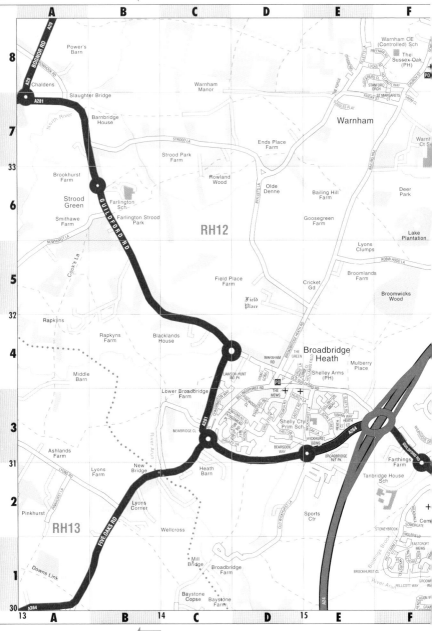

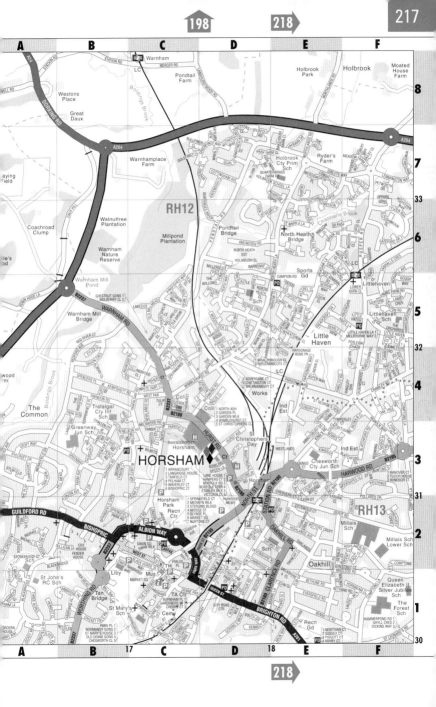

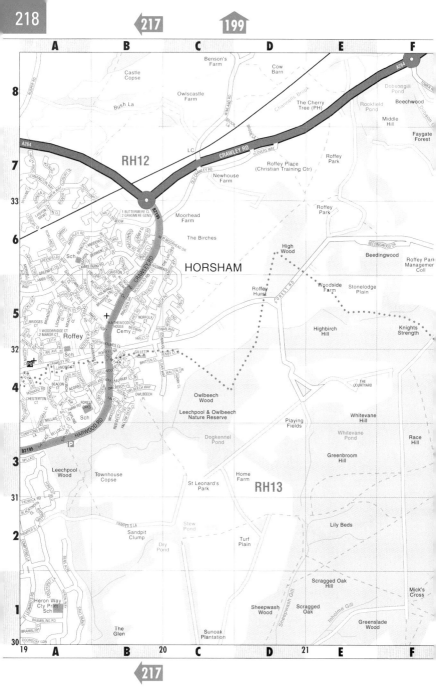

Scale: 5 inches to 1 mile

One-way Streets

House numbers

Dorking

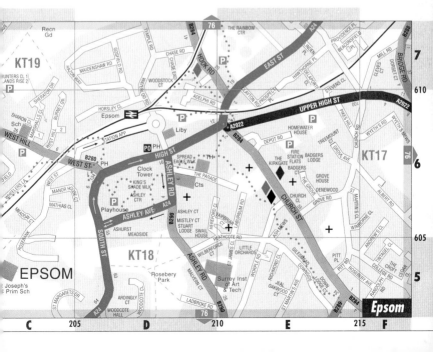

Epsom

Scale: 5 inches to 1 mile

GUILDFORD

GU1

GU2

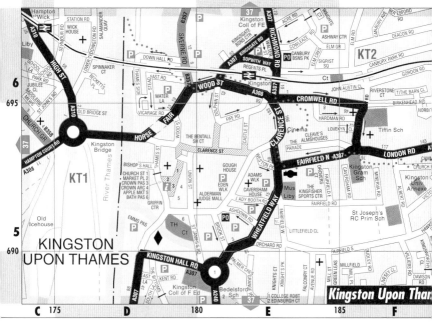

KINGSTON UPON THAMES

KT1

KT2

Kingston Upon Thames

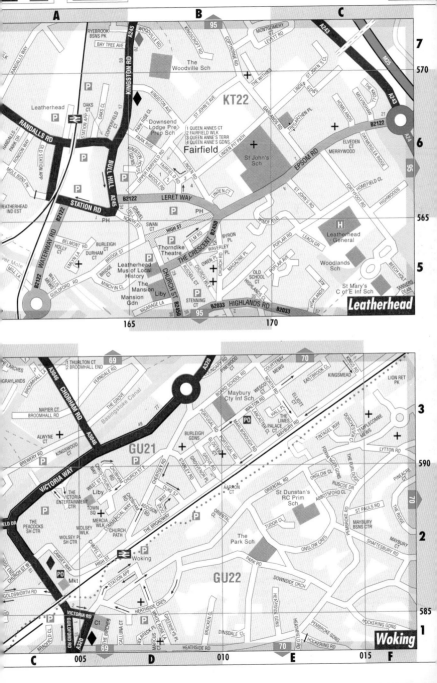

One-way Streets

House numbers
HIGH ST

Leatherhead (top map)

A245 KINGSTON RD

RYEBROOK BSNS PK
BAY TREE AVE
RANDALLS WAY
OAKS CL
Leatherhead
STATION APP
OLD STATION APP
RANDALLS RD
HAMMALLS CL
FORTYFOOT RD
RONSON WAY
MOLE BSNS PK
OAKS CT
CHAPERD CT
PARK RISE CL
PARK RISE
KINGSTON APP
BULL HILL
WATERWAY RD
B2122
STATION RD
A245
B2122
LEATHERHEAD IND EST
GRAVEL
NORTH ST
SWAN CT
PH
BELMONT RD
MOLLY CT
DURHAM CT
BURLEIGH CT
BRIDGE ST
EARLY LA
WALLIS MEWS
GUILDFORD RD
MINCYN LA
The Mansion
Mansion Gdn
Liby
Leatherhead Mus of Local History
BRIDGE ST
VICARAGE LA
B2450
STENNING CT
B2033 HIGHLANDS RD
B2033
KINGSCROFT RD
WOODVILLE RD
95
The Woodville Sch
MONTGOMERY RD
LEVETT RD
COPTHORNE RD
A243
M25
7
570
ST JOHN'S AVE
KT22
LINDEN GDNS
ST JOHN S CT
THE WITHIES
HOMELANDS
TREGARTHEN PL
A243
A24
B2122
21
95
6
1 QUEEN ANNES CT
2 FAIRFIELD WLK
3 QUEEN ANNE'S TERR
4 QUEEN ANNE S GDNS
Fairfield
LINDEN PIT PATH
UPPER FAIRFIELD RD
FAIRFIELD RD
GARLANDS RD
EPSOM RD
St John's Sch
ELVEDEN CL
MERRYWOOD
DAYMERSE LA RIDGE
HOMEFIELD CL
HIGHWOODS
LERET WAY
LINDEN CT
ST JOHN'S RD
KINFOLD
565
ELM RD
HIGH ST
B2450
Thorndike Theatre
WAVERLEY
BYRON PL
OWEN PL
MAGAZINE PL
POPLAR RD
LEACH GR
POPLAR AVE
H
Leatherhead General
BEECH HOLT
5
CHURCH ST
RUSSELL CT
CHURCH RD
HIGHLANDS CL
OLD SCHOOL LA
HIGHLANDS RD
LANE
Woodlands Sch
St Mary's C of E Inf Sch
TANNERS DEAN
B2450
95
B2033
2
57
Leatherhead

165   170

Woking (bottom map)

1 THURLTON CT
2 BROOMHALL END
69
THE LARCHES
GRAYLANDS
BROOMHALL LA
A3046 CHOBHAM RD
FERNDALE RD
Basingstoke Canal
PINEWOOD RD
BOARD SCHOOL RD
A320
70
COURTENAY MEWS
EASTBROOK CL
KINGSMEAD
LION RET PK
NAPIER CT
BROOMHALL RD
THE GROVE
77
49
PORTUGAL RD
WESCOTT RD
NORTH RD
HALL LA
MAYBURY CTY INF SCH
ELLIOTT RD
PO
LANCASTER CT
THE LIMES PALACE CT
MAYBURY RD
TINTAGEL WAY
FORMAN GROVE
THE FAIRLOOP
TEMPLECOMBE MEWS
3
590
ALWYNE CT
KINGSWOOD CT
A3046
GU21
BREWERY RD
VICTORIA WAY
CHOBHAM RD
CHRIST CHURCH WAY
WEST ST
CHURCH ST E
BURLEIGH GDNS
OATERSLEY RD
STANLEY RD
GROVE RD
DUKE ST
WAY
AARRON CT
ADDISON RD
ORIENTAL RD
St Dunstan's RC Prim Sch
ONSLOW RD
RUSCOE DR
BEDFORD CL
ONSLOW GDNS
PEMBROKE RD
THE RIDGE
LYTTON RD
PINEACRE CT
70
MAYBURY CT
SHAFTESBURY RD
590
THE VICTORIA ENTERTAINMENT CTR
Liby
TOWN SQ
MERCIA WLK
WOLSEY WLK
WOLSEY PL SH CTR
CHAPEL ST
CHURCH PATH
COMMERCIAL WAY
THE BROADWAY
THE PEACOCKS SH CTR
The Park Sch
TUDOR CT
ORIENTAL RD
MAYBURY BSNS CTR
ST PAULS RD
2
HIGH ST
Woking
STATION APP
PARK RD
GU22
DOWNSIDE ORCH
PO
Mkt
HEATHSIDE CRES
WHITE ROSE LA
GREENERS RD
BRACKEN CL
HEATHSIDE GDNS
HEATHFIELD RD
PEMBROKE GDNS
HOCKERING GDNS
585
VICTORIA RD
GUILDFORD RD
69
THE BIRCHES
CALLUNA CT
HO BROOK PL
DINSDALE CL
HEATHSIDE RD
70
HOCKERING RD
1
Woking

C   005   D   010   E   015   F

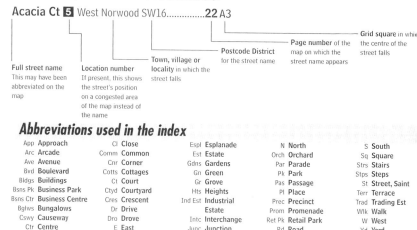
Abbreviations used in the index

App Approach	Cl Close	Espl Esplanade	N North	S South
Arc Arcade	Comm Common	Est Estate	Orch Orchard	Sq Square
Ave Avenue	Cnr Corner	Gdns Gardens	Par Parade	Strs Stairs
Bvd Boulevard	Cotts Cottages	Gn Green	Pk Park	Stps Steps
Bldgs Buildings	Ct Court	Gr Grove	Pas Passage	St Street, Saint
Bsns Pk Business Park	Ctyd Courtyard	Hts Heights	Pl Place	Terr Terrace
Bsns Ctr Business Centre	Cres Crescent	Ind Est Industrial Estate	Prec Precinct	Trad Trading Est
Bglws Bungalows	Dr Drive	Intc Interchange	Prom Promenade	Wlk Walk
Cswy Causeway	Dro Drove	Junc Junction	Ret Pk Retail Park	W West
Ctr Centre	E East	La Lane	Rd Road	Yd Yard
Cir Circus	Emb Embankment		Rdbt Roundabout	

Town and village index

...th Ave KT20 ....97 A1
...th Ave KT20 ....97 F1
...th Ave KT20 ....97 F1
...th Ave KT20 ....97 F1
...th Ave KT20 ....97 F1
...th Ave KT20 ....97 F1
...th Ave KT20 ....97 F1
t Ave KT20 ....97 E2

ad KT20 ....97 E2

d Ave KT20 ....97 E2

h Ave KT20 ....97 E2

h Ave KT20 ....97 F2

h Ave KT20 ....97 E2

h Ave KT20 ....97 E2

aron Ct BR3 ....44 B6
arron Ct GU12 ....150 B4
arron Cl GU2 ....69 F2
obess Cl SW2 ....22 B7
betts La GU15 ....65 B3
obey Church The RH10 ...203 B1
obey Cl Bracknell RG12 ...24 F2
Crawley GU6 ....173 F2
pyford GU22 ....70 E3
Wokingham RG40 ....25 C7
obey Ct
Camberley GU15 ....65 D5
Chertsey KT16 ....33 B2
obey Cres GU21 ....125 C2
obey Dr Laleham TW18 ...33 E5
pper Tooting SW17 ....21 A3
obey Gdns KT16 ....33 A1
obey Gn KT16 ....33 A2
obey Ind Est CR4 ....40 F4
obey La BR3 ....24 A1
obey Lodge TW18 ....12 F3
obey Par SW19 ....20 C1
obey Pk BR3 ....24 A1
obey Rd Chertsey KT16 ...33 B2
Croydon CR0, CR9 ....61 B7
.ower Halliford TW17 ...34 A1
Merton SW19 ....40 C8
.elsdon CR2 ....62 D1
/irginia Water GU25 ....31 D5
Woking GU21 ....69 E4
obey River Cotts KT16 ...33 C3
obey Sch The GU9 ...125 D1
obey St GU9 ....125 D2
obey Way GU14 ....85 C4
obey Wlk TW18 ....36 B5
obey Wood SL5 ....30 A2
obeylands Sch KT15 ...52 A5
obot Cl Byfleet KT14 ...71 D8
Staines TW18 ....13 D1
obot Rd GU1 ....130 D7
obot's Cl GU2 ....129 F6
obot's Way GU1, GU4 ...110 D2
obots Ct SE25 ....42 E6
obots Dr GU25 ....31 C5
obots Gn CR0, CR2 ...62 D4
obots La CR8 ....80 C3
obots Pk SW2 ....22 A7
obots Way BR3 ....43 E4
obots Wlk CR5 ....98 D5
obots Wood Forest Wlk
GU10 ....166 C7
obotsbury RG12 ....26 F4
obotsbury Ct RH13 ...217 E3
obotsbury Fst Sch SM4 ...40 B4
obotsbury Rd
.oney Hall BR2, BR4 ...63 F8
Morden SM4, SW19 ...40 B4
obotsfield Rd RH11 ...200 D4
obotsford Cl GU22 ...70 A2
obotshall Rd SE6 ....24 D6
obotsleigh Ct SM2 ...59 B3
obotsleigh Rd SW16 ...21 C3
obotsmede Cl TW1 ...16 F6

Abbotswood
Guildford GU1 ....109 F3
Walton-on-T KT13 ....53 F7
Abbotswood Cl GU1 ...109 F4
Abbotswood Dr KT13 ...53 D1
Abbotswood Rd SW16 ...21 C5
Abbott Ave SW20 ....39 D8
Abbott Cl TW12 ....15 E2
Abbott House SW12 ....20 F8
Abbotts Cotts GU10 ...166 E5
Abbotts Rd
Cheam SM1, SM3 ....58 E6
Mitcham CR4, SW16 ...41 C5
Abbotts Rise RH1 ....119 A3
Abbotts Tilt KT12 ....54 E6
Abelia Cl GU24 ....67 E6
Abell Ct KT15 ....52 C6
Abercairn Rd SW16 ...21 C1
Aberconway Rd SM4 ...40 B5
Abercorn Cl CR2 ....81 D7
Abercorn Way GU21 ...69 A1
Aberdare Cl BR4 ....63 C8
Aberdeen Rd CR0 ...61 D6
Aberdour KT20 ....77 F1
Aberfoyle Rd SW16 ...21 D2
Abingdon Cl Bracknell RG12 ...27 E4
Merton SW19 ....20 C2
Woking GU21 ....69 C1
Abingdon Lodge BR2 ...44 F7
Abingdon Rd
Sandhurst GU47 ....45 C1
Thornton Heath SW16 ...41 E8
Abinger Ave SM2 ....58 B3
Abinger Cl Dorking RH5 ...136 C3
Wallington SM6 ....60 E5
Abinger Common Cty Sch
RH5 ....134 D1
Abinger Common Rd
RH5 ....155 F7
Abinger Ct SM6 ....60 E5
Abinger La RH5 ....134 C2
Abinger Rd RH5 ....156 C3
Abinger Way GU4 ...110 B6
Aboyne Dr SW20 ....39 A7
Aboyne Rd SW17 ....20 D5
Abrahams Rd RH11 ....201 A2
Acacia Ave Brentford TW8 ...6 B7
Littleton TW17 ....34 A4
Sandhurst GU47 ....45 D1
Woking GU21 ....89 D7
Acacia Cl Penge SE20 ...43 A8
Woodham KT15 ....51 F1
Acacia Ct Bracknell RG12 ...27 B6
West Norwood SW16 ...22 A3
Acacia Dr Banstead KT17 ...77 D5
Cheam SM1 ....40 A1
Woodham KT15 ....51 F1
Acacia Gdns BR4 ....63 C8
Acacia Gr Dulwich SE21 ...22 D6
Kingston u T KT3 ....38 E6
Acacia House RH2 ...118 A3
Acacia Mews UB7 ....2 D8
Acacia Rd Beckenham BR3 ...43 F6
Guildford GU1 ....109 D1
Hampton TW12 ....16 A2
Mitcham CR4 ....41 B7
South Norwood SW16 ...41 B8
Staines TW18 ....13 B3
Academy Cl GU15 ....65 E8
Academy Gdns CR0 ...42 F1
Accommodation La UB7 ...2 D8
Accommodation Rd KT16 ...50 E6
Ace Par KT9 ....56 E6
Acer Dr GU24 ....67 F6
Acer Rd TN16 ....83 D3
Achelidian Cl GU9 ...146 C7
Achilles Pl GU21 ....69 C2
Ackroyd Rd SE23 ....23 E8
Acorn Cl
East Grinstead RH19 ...205 E8
Hampton TW12 ....16 B2
Horley RH6 ....161 C4
Acorn Dr RG40 ....25 E6
Acorn Gdns SE19 ....42 F8
Acorn Gr Harlington UB3 ...3 F7
Kingswood KT20 ....97 F3
Woking GU22 ....89 C5
Acorn Keep GU9 ...125 D8
Acorn Mews GU14 ...85 A7
Acorn Rd GU17 ....64 B5
Acorn Way SE23 ....23 D5
Acorns RH13 ....218 A4
Acorns Cty Fst Sch The
Betchworth RH3 ....116 D1
Leigh RH2 ....138 A3
Acorns Way KT10 ...55 D5
Acre La SM5 ....60 A6
Acre Rd Kingston u T KT2 ...37 E8
Mitcham SW19 ....20 D2
Acres Gdns KT20 ....97 D8
Acres Platt GU6 ....174 F4
Action Ct TW15 ....34 C8
Acuba House SW18 ....20 B6
Acuba Rd SW18 ....20 B6
Adair Cl SE25 ....43 B6
Adair Wlk GU24 ....49 E5
Adams Cl KT5 ....37 F3
Adams Croft GU24 ....87 C7
Adams Ct CR8 ....80 A7
Adams House SW19 ....21 C3
Adams Park Rd GU9 ...125 D3

Adams Rd BR3 ....43 E4
Adams Way SE25, CR0 ...43 A3
Adams Wlk KT1 ....37 E7
Adams Cl GU RH11 ...201 B1
Adamsrill Prim Sch SE26 ...23 E5
Adamsrill Rd SE23, SE26 ...23 E4
Adare Wlk SW16, SW2 ...21 F6
Addington Bsns Ctr CR7 ...42 A4
Addington Court Golf
Course CR0 ....63 A2
Addington Ct ⑦ SW14 ...7 D4
Addington Golf Course
CR0, CR9 ....62 E6
Addington Gr SE26 ....23 E4
Addington High Sch CR0 ...82 F7
Addington Palace Golf
Course CR0 ....62 E5
Addington Palace (the
Royal Sch of Church
Music) CR9 ....62 F4
Addington Rd
Sanderstead CR2 ....81 A8
Selsdon CR2 ....62 C1
Thornton Heath CR0 ...42 A1
West Wickham BR4, CR0 ...63 A6
West Wickham BR4 ....63 A8
Addington Village Rd CR0 ...63 A5
Addiscombe Ave CR0 ...43 A2
Addiscombe Court Rd
CR0, CR9 ....61 E8
Addiscombe Rd
Crowthorne RG45 ....45 C4
Croydon CR0, CR9 ....61 E8
South Croydon CR0 ....61 E8
Addison Ave TW3 ....5 C6
Addison Cl CR3 ....100 D5
Addison Ct GU1 ....130 F7
Addison Gdns KT5 ....37 F5
Addison Rd Caterham CR3 ...100 C6
Croydon SE25 ....43 A5
Farnborough GU16 ...85 E8
Guildford GU1 ....130 F7
Teddington TW11 ....17 B2
⑧ Woking GU21 ....69 F2
Addison's Cl CR0 ....62 F8
Addlestone House KT15 ...52 C8
Addlestone Moor KT15 ...52 C8
Addlestone Pk KT15 ...52 B5
Addlestone Rd KT13, KT15 ...52 E6
Addlestone Sta KT15 ...52 D6
Adecroft Way KT8 ....36 D6
Adela Ave KT3 ....39 B5
Adelaide Cl Crawley RH11 ...181 D1
Horsham RH12 ....217 F4
Adelaide Ct ⑮ BR3 ....24 A1
Adelaide Pl KT13 ....53 D6
Adelaide Rd Ashford TW15 ...13 D3
Heston TW5 ....4 C6
Kingston u T KT6 ....37 E4
Richmond TW9 ....6 F3
Teddington TW11 ....16 F3
Walton-on-T KT12 ...54 B7
Adelina Mews SW12 ...21 D7
Adelphi Cl RH10 ...202 D4
Adelphi Rd KT17 ....76 D6
Ademore Rd SE6 ....24 B8
Adisham House ⑦ SE26 ...23 C1
Adlers La RH5 ...115 A4
Adlington Pl GU14 ...85 E2
Admiral Ct SM5 ....40 E1
Admiral Rd RH11 ....201 A3
Admiral's Bridge La
RH19 ....205 D4
Admiral's Wlk The CR5 ...99 F7
Admirals Ct GU1 ...110 B2
Admiralty Rd TW11 ...16 F2
Admiralty Way GU15 ...64 F4
Adolf St SE6 ....24 B4
Adrian Ct RH11 ....201 B1
Advance Rd SE27 ....22 C4
Adversane Ct RH12 ...217 D4
Aerodrome Way TW5 ....4 C8
Aerospace Bvd GU14 ...105 A7
Agar Cl KT6 ....56 F8
Agar House ⑥ KT1 ....37 E6
Agate House
West Norwood SW16 ...38 E1
⑦ Penge SE26 ....23 B3
Agate La RH12 ....217 F5
Agates La KT21 ....95 D8
Agincourt Pl SL5 ....29 C6
Agnes Scott Ct ⑤ KT13 ...53 D8
Agnew Rd SE23 ....23 D8
Agraria Rd GU2 ....130 B7
Ailsa Ave TW1 ....6 B2
Ailsa Cl RH11 ....201 B3
Ailsa Rd TW1 ....6 B1
Ainger Cl GU12 ...105 D2
Ainslie Way GU21 ...69 A1
Ainsworth Rd CR0, CR9 ...61 B8
Aintree Cl SL3 ....1 A5
Aintree House SE26 ...23 B2
Aintree Rd RH10 ....202 A4
Air Forces Meml TW20 ...11 D4
Airborne House ⑩ SM6 ...60 B6
Airbourne Forces Mus
GU11 ....105 A5
Aircraft Espl GU14 ...85 C1
Airedale Rd SW12 ...20 F8
Airport Way Horley RH6 ...182 B8
Stanwell TW19 ....2 B1
Airport Way Rdbt W RH6 ...181 F8
Aisne Rd GU16 ....66 E1
Aitken Cl CR4 ....40 F2
Aitken House GU27 ...208 C7
Aitken Rd SE6 ....24 B6
Akabusi Cl SE25 ....43 A3
Akehurst Cl RH10 ....183 B3

Akehurst St SW15 ....19 A8
Akerman Rd KT6 ....37 C5
Alamein Rd GU1 ....105 B3
Alamein Rd GU1 ....51 D4
Alan Hilton Ct KT16 ...51 D4
Alan Rd SW19 ....19 E3
Alan Turing Rd GU2 ...108 D1
Alanbrooke Cl GU21 ...68 C1
Alanbrooke Rd GU11 ...105 D6
Alban Cres TW15 ...13 E6
Albans Cl SW16 ....21 E5
Albany Cl Esher KT10 ...55 A2
Mortlake SW14 ....7 B3
Albany Cres KT10 ....55 E4
Albany Ct Frimley GU16 ...65 C1
Kingston u T KT12 ....17 E2
Oatlands Park KT13 ...53 E8
Richmond TW10 ....17 B5
⑥ Weybridge KT13 ...53 B6
Albany Ho ⑧ TW8 ....6 E8
Albany Mews
Kingston u T KT2 ....17 D2
Sutton SM1 ....59 B5
Albany Par ⑷ TW8 ....6 E8
Albany Park Ind Est GU15 ...65 C1
Albany Pk Camberley GU15 ...65 C1
Frimley GU15 ....65 C1
Poyle SL3 ....1 D7
Albany Pl Brentford TW8 ...6 E8
Egham TW20 ....12 B4
Albany Rd Brentford TW8 ...6 E8
Crawley RH11 ....201 C6
Hersham KT12 ....54 D5
New Malden KT3 ....38 D5
Richmond TW10 ....6 E2
Wimbledon SW19 ....20 B3
Albany Reach KT7 ....36 F4
Albany Terr ⑥ TW10 ...6 F2
Albanys The RH2 ...118 A3
Albatross Gdns CR2 ...81 D8
Albemarle SW19 ....19 D6
Albemarle Ave TW2 ...15 F7
Albemarle Gdns KT3 ...38 D5
Albemarle Lodge SE26 ...23 E3
Albemarle Pk BR3 ...44 B8
Albemarle Rd BR2, BR3 ...44 C8
Albemarle Prim Sch
SW19 ....19 E6
Albemarle Prim Sch
(Annexe) SW19 ...19 E7
Albert Ave KT16 ....33 A4
Albert Carr Gdns SW16 ...21 A3
Albert Crane Ct RH11 ...201 A8
Albert Ct ⑻ SW19 ....19 E7
Albert Dr Putney SW19 ...19 E6
Sheerwater GU21, KT14 ...70 D5
Albert Gr SW20 ....39 D8
Albert Rd Addlestone KT15 ...52 D6
Aldershot GU11 ....105 C1
Ashford TW15 ....13 F3
Ashstead KT21 ....75 F1
Bagshot GU19 ....47 E1
Bracknell RG42 ....27 B8
Camberley GU15 ....65 C5
Carshalton SM1 ....59 C5
Crowthorne RG45 ...45 B5
Croydon CR0, SE25 ...43 B5
Englefield Green TW20 ...11 D2
Epsom KT17 ....76 E6
Farnborough GU14 ....85 C2
Hampton TW12 ....16 C3
Horley RH6 ....161 A3
Hounslow TW3 ....5 A3
Kingston u T KT1 ....37 F7
Merstham RH1 ....119 C6
Mitcham CR4 ....40 F6
New Malden KT3 ....38 F5
Penge SE20 ....23 D2
Richmond TW10 ....6 E2
Sutton SM1 ....59 D5
Teddington TW11 ....16 F2
Twickenham TW1 ....16 F7
Warlingham CR6 ....81 F2
Wokingham RG40 ....25 B6
Albert Road N RH2 ...117 F2
Albert Wlk RG45 ....45 B5
Alberta Ave SM1 ....58 F5
Alberta Dr RH6 ....162 A3
Albertine Cl KT17 ....77 B2
Albery Cl RH12 ....217 B4
Albion Cl RH10 ....202 D5
Albion Cotts SM3 ....59 D3
Albion Par GU21 ....68 C2
Albion Pl SE25 ....43 A6
Albion Rd Hounslow TW3 ...5 A3
Kingston u T KT2 ....18 B1
Reigate RH2 ....139 C8
Sandhurst GU47 ....64 B8
Sutton SM2 ....59 D3
Twickenham TW2 ....16 E7
Albion St SE16, CR0 ...42 B1
Albion Villas Rd
SE23, SE26 ....23 C5
Albion Way RH12 ....217 C2
Albury Ave East Ewell SM2 ...58 C1
Hounslow TW7 ....5 F7
Albury Cl Hampton TW12 ...16 B2
Longcross KT16 ....50 A7
Albury Ct ④ Croydon CR0 ...61 C6
Hampton TW12 ....16 B2
Sutton SM1 ....59 C6
Albury Keep RH6 ....161 B4
Albury Lodge ⑩ SW2 ...21 F8
Albury Pl RH1 ....119 C6
Albury Rd Chessington KT9 ...56 E5
Guildford GU1 ....131 A8

Albury Rd continued
Hersham KT12 ....53 F4
Merstham RH1 ....119 C6
Albury St GU5 ....132 C4
Alcester Ct ⑻ SM6 ....60 B6
Alcester Rd SM6 ....60 B6
Alcock Cl TW5 ....60 D3
Alcock Rd TW5 ....4 D7
Alcocks Cl KT20 ....97 E7
Alcocks La KT20 ....97 E7
Alcorn Cl SM3 ....59 A8
Alcot Cl RG45 ....45 B4
Alden Ct CR0 ....61 D7
Aldenham Terr RG12 ...27 C3
Aldenholme KT13 ....53 E4
Alder Cl Ash Vale GU12 ...106 A7
Crawley Down RH10 ...204 B8
Englefield Green TW20 ...11 E3
Alder Croft CR5 ....79 F3
Alder Ct ⑶ SW18 ....22 A3
Alder Rd
Headley Down GU35 ...187 B6
Mortlake SW14 ....7 D4
Alderbrook Prim Sch
SW12 ....21 B8
Aldermoor Rd
Balham SW12 ....21 B8
Cranleigh GU6 ....174 C8
Aldergrove Gdns TW4 ...4 E5
Alderman Judge Mall ⑻
KT1 ....37 E7
Alderman Willey Cl RG41 ...25 B6
Aldermead ⑦ SW3 ....5 B3
Aldermoor Rd SE6 ....23 F5
Alderney Ave TW5 ....5 B7
Alders Rd RH19 ....185 E3
Alders Rd RH2 ....118 B3
Alders The Feltham TW13 ...15 E4
Heston TW5 ....4 F8
Streatham SW16 ....21 C4
West Byfleet KT14 ....71 C7
West Wickham BR4 ....63 B8
Alders View Dr RH19 ...185 E3
Aldersbrook Dr KT2 ...17 F2
Aldersey Rd GU1 ....109 F1
Aldersgrove KT8 ....36 D4
Aldershot Military Mus
GU11 ....105 F1
Aldershot Rd Ash GU12 ...105 F1
Church Crookham GU13 ...104 A6
Fairlands GU3 ....108 D5
Guildford GU2, GU3 ....87 F2
Pirbright GU24, GU3 ....107 C5
Wood St V GU3 ....107 C5
Aldershot Sta GU11 ....105 B1
Alderside Wlk TW20 ....11 E3
Aldersmead Ave CR0 ...43 D3
Aldersmead Rd BR3 ...23 E1
Alderstead La RH1 ....99 D2
Alderton KT2 ....38 B8
Alderton Ct KT8 ....35 F5
Alderton Rd CR0 ....43 A2
Alderwick Dr TW3 ....5 D4
Alderwood Cl CR3 ....100 C2
Aldingbourne Cl RH11 ...200 F7
Aldis Mews SW17 ....20 E3
Aldis St SW17 ....20 E3
Aldous House SW18 ...12 E4
Alden Rd SW17 ....20 C5
Aldrich Cres CR0 ....63 C2
Aldrich Gdns SM3 ....58 F7
Aldrich House SW18 ...20 C6
Aldridge Rise KT3 ....38 E3
Aldrin Pl GU14 ....84 D4
Aldrington Rd SW16 ...21 C4
Aldro Sch GU8 ....149 C7
Aldwick Cl GU14 ....85 A6
Aldwick Rd CR0 ....60 F6
Aldworth Cl RG12 ....27 A5
Aldworth Gdns RG45 ...45 A5
Aldwych Cl RH10 ....202 C4
Aldwyn Ct TW20 ....11 B2
Alexa Ct SM7 ....59 A4
Alexander Cl TW2 ....16 E5
Alexander Ct
Beckenham BR3 ....44 D8
⑭ Surbiton KT6 ....37 D2
Alexander Evans Mews
SE23 ....23 D6
Alexander Godley Cl KT21 ...95 F8
Alexander Rd Coulsdon CR5 ...79 B4
Egham TW20 ....12 C3
Reigate RH2 ....139 A6
Alexander Wlk CR3 ...101 A1
Alexandra Ave
Camberley GU15 ....65 A5
Sutton SM1 ....59 A7
Warlingham CR6 ....81 F2
Alexandra Cl Ashford TW15 ...14 D1
Staines TW18 ....13 D2
Walton-on-T KT12 ...54 A8
Alexandra Cotts SE20 ...23 D2
Alexandra Cres BR1 ...24 F2
Alexandra Ct Ashford TW15 ...14 D2
⑩ Crawley RH10 ....201 D5
⑴ Farnborough GU14 ...85 C1
Alexandra Dr Surbiton KT5 ...38 A2
West Norwood SE19 ....22 E3
Alexandra Gdns Chiswick W4 ...7 E7
Hounslow TW3 ....5 B5
Knaphill GU21 ....68 D1
Wallington SM5 ....60 A2
Alexandra Inf Sch
Kingston u T KT2 ....18 A1

Alexandra Inf Sch continued
Penge BR3 .... 23 D1
Alexandra Jun & Inf Sch
TW3 .... 5 B5
Alexandra Jun Sch SE26 .. 23 D2
Alexandra Lodge
1 Guildford GU1 .... 130 F8
1 Weybridge KT13 .... 53 B6
Alexandra Pl Croydon CR0 .. 42 E1
Guildford GU1 .... 130 F7
South Norwood SE25 .... 42 D4
Alexandra Rd
Addlestone KT15 .... 52 D6
Aldershot GU11 .... 104 F2
Ash GU12 .... 105 F1
Ashford TW15 .... 14 D8
Biggin Hill TN16 .... 103 B8
10 Brentford TW8 .... 6 D8
Croydon CR0 .... 42 E2
Englefield Green TW20 ...... 11 C2
Epsom KT17 .... 76 F6
Farnborough GU14, GU11 .. 85 C1
Hounslow TW3 .... 5 B5
Kingston u T KT2 .... 18 A1
Mitcham SW19 .... 20 E1
Mortlake SW14 .... 7 D4
Penge SE26 .... 23 D2
Richmond TW9 .... 6 F5
Thames Ditton KT7 .... 36 F4
Twickenham TW1 .... 6 C1
Warlingham CR6 .... 81 F2
Wimbledon SW19 .... 20 A3
Alexandra Sq SM4 .... 40 A4
Alexandra Terr GU1 .... 130 E8
Alexandra Wlk 8 SE19 ..... 22 E3
Alfold By-Pass Alfold GU6 .193 F7
Alfold Crossways GU6 ...... 194 A5
Alfold Cotts GU6 .... 193 F2
Alfold La GU6 .... 194 A7
Alfold Rd Alfold GU8 .... 193 B7
Cranleigh GU6 .... 194 B7
Dunsfold GU8 .... 193 B3
Alfonso Cl GU12 .... 126 C8
Alford Cl GU4 .... 110 A4
Alford Ct 5 SM2 .... 59 B3
Alford Gn CR0 .... 63 D4
Alfred Butt House SW17 .. 20 F5
Alfred Cl RH10 .... 202 E5
Alfred Hurley House
SW17 .... 20 C4
Alfred Mizen Prim Sch The
CR4 .... 41 D6
Alfred Rd Croydon SE25 ... 43 A4
Farnham GU9 .... 125 C1
Feltham TW13 .... 15 C6
Kingston u T KT1 .... 37 F6
Sutton SM1 .... 59 C5
Alfreton Cl SW19 .... 19 D5
Alfriston KT5 .... 37 F3
Alfriston Ave CR0 .... 41 E2
Alfriston Cl KT5 .... 37 F3
Alfriston Rd GU16 .... 86 C7
Algar Cl TW7 .... 6 A4
Algar Rd TW7 .... 6 A4
Algarve Rd SW18 .... 20 B7
Alice Gough Memorial
Homes RG12 .... 27 B6
Alice Holt Forest Visitor
Ctr GU10 .... 166 C8
Alice Mews 8 TW11 .... 16 F3
Alice Rd GU11 .... 105 B2
Alice Ruston Pl GU22 ...... 89 C8
Alice Way TW3 .... 5 B3
Alicia Ave RH10 .... 202 C6
Alington Gr SM6 .... 60 D2
Alison Cl Croydon CR0 ...... 43 D1
Farnborough GU14 .... 84 F3
Woking GU21 .... 69 E4
Alison Dr GU15 .... 65 F5
Alison Way GU11 .... 104 F2
Alison's Rd GU11 .... 105 B4
All England Lawn Tennis
& Croquet Club The
SW19 .... 19 E5
All Hallows Catholic Sch
GU9 .... 125 F7
All Saint's Prim Sch SE19 .42 E8
All Saints' Benhilton C of
E Prim Sch SM1 .... 59 B7
All Saints C of E Prim Sch
SW19 .... 20 C1
All Saints Carshalton CE
Sch SM5 .... 60 A5
All Saints CE Inf Sch
GU10 .... 147 C3
All Saints Cl RG40 .... 25 C7
All Saints Cres GU14 .... 64 E1
All Saints Ct TW5 .... 4 D6
All Saints Dr CR2 .... 81 A7
All Saints Inf Sch KT22 ... 95 A8
All Saints Rd
Lightwater GU18 .... 48 C1
Merton SW19 .... 20 C1
Sutton SM1 .... 59 C7
All Souls' Rd SL5 .... 29 A5
Allan Cl KT3 .... 38 D4
Allbrook Cl TW11 .... 16 E3
Allbrook House 5 SW15 .. 19 A8
Allcard Cl RH12 .... 217 D4
Allcot Cl Crawley RH11 .. 200 E3
East Bedfont TW14 .... 14 F7
Allcott House The SW17 .. 14 F7
Allden Ave GU11, GU12 .. 126 D7
Allden Cotts GU7 .... 150 B4
Allden Gdns GU7 .... 126 D7

Alldens Hill GU5, GU8 ..... 151 D1
Alldens La GU8 .... 151 B1
Allen Cl Streatham CR4 ..... 41 C8
Sunbury TW16 .... 35 B8
Allen House Pk GU22 .... 89 C7
Allen Rd
Great Bookham KT23 .... 94 B1
Penge BR3 .... 43 D7
Sunbury TW16 .... 35 B7
Thornton Heath CR0 .... 42 A1
Allen's Cl RH19 .... 206 D6
Allenby Ave CR2 .... 61 C2
Allenby Rd Biggin Hill TN16 .83 E2
Forest Hill SE23 .... 23 E5
Sandhurst GU15 .... 65 A6
Allendale GU8 .... 148 C3
Allendale Cl
Forest Hill SE26 .... 23 D3
Sandhurst GU47 .... 45 A2
Allenford House SW15 .... 7 F1
Allenswood 12 SW19 .... 19 E7
Allerford Ct SE6 .... 24 B5
Allerford Rd SE6 .... 24 B4
Allerton Cl SM3 .... 58 D8
Allerton House 4 SW19 .. 20 C1
Alleyn Cres SE21 .... 22 D6
Alleyn Pk SE21 .... 22 E5
Alleyn Rd SE21 .... 22 E5
Allgood Cl SM4 .... 39 D3
Alliance Ct TW15 .... 14 C4
Allingham Ct GU7 .... 150 F7
Allingham Gdns RH12 ..... 218 B5
Allingham Rd RH2 .... 139 A6
Allington Ave TW17 .... 34 E6
Allington Cl SW19 .... 19 D3
Allison Gr SE21 .... 22 E7
Alloway Cl 4 GU21 .... 69 B1
Allsmoor La RG12 .... 27 F6
Allum Gr KT20 .... 97 B6
Allwood Cl SE26 .... 23 D4
Allyington Way RH10 ...... 202 D5
Alma Cl GU21 .... 68 E1
Alma Cres SM1 .... 58 E5
Alma Ct CR3 .... 100 C6
Alma Gdns GU16 .... 86 E8
Alma Ho 7 TW8 .... 6 E8
Alma La GU9 .... 125 C2
Alma Pl Penge SE19 .... 22 F1
Thornton Heath CR7 .... 42 A4
Alma Rd Carshalton SM5 .. 59 E5
Headley Down GU35 ...... 187 C5
Reigate RH2 .... 118 B3
Thames Ditton KT10, KT7 .. 36 E1
Alma Sq GU14 .... 105 C8
Alma Terr SW18 .... 20 D8
Alma Way GU9 .... 125 D7
Almer Rd SW20 .... 19 A1
Almners Rd Chertsey KT16 .. 32 C2
Lyne KT16 .... 32 B1
Almond Ave Carshalton SM5 .59 F8
Kingston u T 89 D6
Almond Cl Charlton TW17 .. 34 C7
Crawley RH11 .... 201 A5
Englefield Green TW20 ..... 11 B2
Guildford GU1 .... 109 D5
Almond Gr TW8 .... 6 B7
Almond Rd KT19 .... 76 D8
Almond Way CR4 .... 41 D5
Alms Heath GU23 .... 92 B6
Almsgate GU3 .... 129 C2
Almshouse La KT9 .... 56 D2
Almshouses Dorking RH4 .136 B8
Mickleham RH5 .... 115 C8
Tadworth KT20 .... 34 F8
Alnwick Gr SM4 .... 40 B5
Alpha Ct CR6 .... 81 A1
Alpha Rd Chobham GU24 .. 49 F1
Crawley RH11 .... 201 C6
Croydon CR0 .... 42 E1
Surbiton KT5 .... 38 A3
Teddington TW12 .... 16 D3
Woking GU22 .... 70 C4
Alpha Way TW20 .... 32 C8
Alphabet Gdns SM5 .... 40 D3
Alphea Cl SW19 .... 20 E1
Alphington Ave GU16 .... 65 F1
Alphington Gn GU16 .... 65 F1
Alpine Ave KT5 .... 57 C8
Alpine Cl Farnborough GU14 .84 D3
South Croydon CR0 .... 61 E7
Alpine Rd Redhill RH1 ..... 119 A4
Walton-on-T KT12 .... 35 A8
Alpine View SM1 .... 59 E5
Alresford Rd GU2 .... 130 A8
Alric Ave KT3 .... 38 E6
Alsace Wlk GU15 .... 65 B1
Alsford Cl GU18 .... 66 F7
Alston Cl KT7 .... 37 B2
Alston Rd SW17 .... 20 D4
Alt Gr SW19 .... 19 F1
Alterton Cl GU21 .... 69 A2
Althorne Rd RH1 .... 140 A7
Althorp Rd SW17 .... 20 E7
Alton Cl TW7 .... 5 F5
Alton Ct 11 Beckenham BR3 . 24 A1
Egham TW18 .... 32 E8
Alton Gdns Beckenham BR3 .24 A1
Twickenham TW2 .... 16 D8
Alton House 1 RH1 .... 119 A2
Alton Rd
South Croydon CR0, CR9 .. 61 A7
Farnham GU10, GU9 .... 145 D7
Richmond TW10, TW9 .... 6 E3
Roehampton SW15 .... 19 A7

Alton Ride GU17 .... 64 C6
Altwood Prim Sch CR2 ..... 81 A6
Altyre Cl BR3 .... 43 F4
Altyre Rd CR0, CR9 .... 61 D8
Altyre Way BR3 .... 43 F4
Alvernia Cl GU7 .... 150 C2
Alvernia Lodge SM1 .... 59 C8
Alverstoke Gdns GU11 .... 104 E1
Alverston Gdns SE25 .... 42 E4
Alverstone
Ave SW18, SW19 .... 20 A6
Alverstone Rd KT3 .... 38 F5
Alvia Gdns SM1 .... 59 C6
Alway Ave KT19 .... 57 D5
Alwin Pl GU9 .... 125 B7
Alwyn Cl CR0 .... 63 B3
Alwyne Ct GU21 .... 69 E3
Alwyne Rd SW19 .... 19 F2
Alwyns Cl KT16 .... 33 A3
Alwyns La KT16 .... 33 A3
Amalgamated Dr TW8 .... 6 B8
Amanda Ct TW15 .... 13 F6
Ambassador RG12 .... 26 F4
Ambassador Cl TW3 .... 4 E5
Amber Cl Aldershot GU12 .105 C2
Mitcham CR4 .... 40 E5
Staines TW18 .... 12 F3
Amber Hill GU15 .... 66 B4
Ambercroft Way CR5 ...... 100 B8
Amberley Cl
Crawley RH10 .... 202 C6
Horsham RH12 .... 218 A6
Send Marsh GU23 .... 90 F2
Amberley Ct SM2 .... 59 C3
Amberley Dr KT15 .... 70 F8
Amberley Gdns KT19 .... 57 F6
Amberley Gr Croydon CR0 .42 F2
Forest Hill SE26 .... 23 B3
Amberley Grange GU11 .. 125 F8
Amberley Rd
Horsham RH12 .... 218 A6
Milford GU8 .... 149 E2
Amberley Way Heston TW4 .. 4 C2
Morden SM4 .... 39 F2
Amberside Cl TW7 .... 5 D1
Amberwood Dr GU15 .... 65 F7
Amberwood Rise KT3 .... 38 E3
Amblecote KT11 .... 73 E7
Amblecote Catford BR1 ... 24 D2
Godalming GU7 .... 151 A5
11 Putney SW19 .... 19 E7
Ambleside Ave
Beckenham BR3 .... 43 E4
Streatham SW16 .... 21 D3
Walton-on-T KT12 .... 35 C1
Ambleside Cl
Farnborough GU14 .... 84 E3
Mytchett GU16 .... 86 A2
Redhill RH1 .... 140 A7
Ambleside Cres GU9 .... 125 A6
Ambleside Cty Jun Sch
KT12 .... 35 C1
Ambleside Dr TW14 .... 14 F7
Ambleside Gdns
Selsdon CR2 .... 62 D1
Streatham SW16 .... 21 D3
Sutton SM2 .... 59 C4
Ambleside Rd GU18 .... 67 B8
Ambleside Way TW20 ...... 12 B1
Ambrey Way CR8, SM6 ..... 60 D2
Amen Corner SW17 .... 20 F2
Amen Corner Bsns Pk
RG12 .... 26 F2
Amenity Way SM4 .... 39 C2
American Comm Sch
KT11 .... 54 C1
American Magna Carta
Meml TW20 .... 11 D6
American Sch in
Switzerland (English
Branch) The TW20 .... 32 C6
Amersham Rd CR0 .... 42 D3
Amesbury Ave SW2 .... 21 F6
Amesbury Cl KT4 .... 39 C1
Amesbury Dr E4 .... 15 D6
Amesbury Sch GU26 ...... 188 E1
Amey Dr KT23 .... 94 C3
Amhurst Gdns TW7 .... 6 A5
Amis Ave Chessington KT19 .57 B5
Woodham KT15 .... 52 A1
Amity Gr SW20 .... 39 C8
Amlets La GU6 .... 174 E5
Ampere Way CR0, CR9 ..... 41 F1
Amroth Cl SE23 .... 23 B7
Amstel Cl RH1 .... 119 A2
Amundsen Rd RH12 .... 217 D6
Amy Johnson Prim Sch
SM2 .... 59 B2
Amy Rd RH8 .... 122 E6
Amyand Cotts 12 TW1 ..... 17 B8
Amyand La TW1 .... 17 A8
Amyand Park Gdns 3
TW1 .... 17 B7
Amyand Park Rd TW1 ..... 17 A8
Anarth Ct KT13 .... 53 E7
Ancaster Cres KT3 .... 39 A3
Ancaster Dr SL5 .... 28 E8
Ancaster Rd BR3 .... 43 D6
Anchor Cotts RH7 .... 164 D3
Anchor Cres GU21 .... 68 D2
Anchor Hill GU21 .... 68 D2
Anchor Meadow GU14 ..... 84 F4
Anchorage Cl SW19 .... 20 A3
Anderson Ave GU2 .... 109 B5
Anderson Cl KT19 .... 76 B7

Anderson Dr TW15 .... 14 C4
Anderson House SW17 .... 20 D3
Anderson Pl GU19 .... 47 E4
Anderson Rd KT13 .... 53 D7
Anderson's Pl TW3 .... 5 B3
Andhurst Ct KT2 .... 38 B8
Andon Ct BR3 .... 43 D5
Andover Cl
East Bedfont TW14 .... 14 F7
Epsom KT19 .... 76 D8
Andover Ct TW19 .... 13 D8
Andover Rd
Blackwater GU17 .... 64 C6
Twickenham TW2 .... 16 D7
Andover Way GU11, GU9 .126 B7
Andrew Cl RG40 .... 25 C7
Andrew Ct RG40 .... 25 E5
Andrew Ewing Prim Sch
TW5 .... 4 F7
Andrew Reed House
SW18 .... 19 E8
Andrew's Cl KT17 .... 76 F6
Andrewartha Rd GU14 ..... 85 C2
Andrewes House SM1 ...... 59 A6
Andrews Cl KT4 .... 58 D8
Andrews Rd GU14 .... 84 E5
Andromeda Cl RH11 ...... 200 E4
Anerley Ct SE20 .... 23 B1
Anerley Gr SE19 .... 22 F1
Anerley Hill SE19 .... 22 F2
Anerley Park Rd SE20 ...... 23 B1
Anerley Pk SE20 .... 23 B1
Anerley Prim Sch SE20 ... 43 A8
Anerley Rd SE20, SE19 .... 43 B8
Anerley Sta SE20 .... 43 B8
Anerley Station Rd SE20 .. 43 B8
Anerley Vale SE19 .... 23 A1
Anfield Cl SW12 .... 21 C8
Angas Ct 4 KT13 .... 53 C5
Angel Ct GU3 .... 129 C3
Angel Gate GU1 .... 130 D8
Angel Hill SM1 .... 59 B7
Angel Hill Dr SM1 .... 59 B7
Angel Mews SW15 .... 19 A8
Angel Rd KT7 .... 37 A1
Angela Ct 3 SE23 .... 23 C7
Angelfield TW3 .... 5 B2
Angelica Gdns CR0 .... 43 D1
Angelica Rd Bisley GU24 .. 68 A4
Guildford GU2 .... 109 A5
Angell Cl RH10 .... 202 C5
Angers Cl GU15 .... 66 C7
Anglers Reach KT6 .... 37 D4
Angles Rd SW16 .... 21 E4
Anglesea House KT1 .... 37 D5
Anglesea Rd KT1 .... 37 D5
Anglesey Ave GU14 .... 84 F7
Anglesey Cl Ashford TW15 .14 A5
Crawley RH11 .... 201 C2
Anglesey Court Rd SM5 ... 60 A4
Anglesey Gdns SM5 .... 60 A4
Anglesey Rd GU12 .... 105 D1
Angus Cl Chessington KT9 .57 A5
Horsham RH12 .... 217 D4
Angus House 12 SW12 ..... 21 D8
Anlaby Rd TW11 .... 16 E3
Ann Parkes Ct TW5 .... 4 F4
Annandale Dr GU10 .... 146 D6
Annandale Rd Croydon CR0 .62 A8
Guildford GU2 .... 130 A8
Anne Armstrong Cl
GU11 .... 105 D5
Anne Boleyn's Wlk
Cheam SM2, SM3 .... 58 E3
Kingston u T KT2 .... 17 E3
Anne Way KT8 .... 36 B5
Anne's Wlk CR3 .... 100 E7
Annella Ct GU11 .... 105 D8
Anners Cl TW20 .... 32 C6
Annesley Dr CR0 .... 62 F7
Annett Cl TW17 .... 34 E5
Annett Rd KT12 .... 35 A2
Annie Brookes Cl TW18 ... 12 D5
Anningsley Pk KT16 .... 51 C1
Annisdowne RH5 .... 133 F1
Annsworthy Ave CR7, SE25 .42 D6
Annsworthy Cres SE25 .... 42 D7
Ansell Gr SM5 .... 41 A1
Ansell Rd Dorking RH4 ... 136 B8
Frimley GU16 .... 65 E1
Upper Tooting SW17 .... 20 F5
Anselm Cl CR0 .... 61 F7
Ansford Rd BR1, SE6 .... 24 D4
Ansley Cl CR2 .... 81 B5
Anslie Wlk 8 SW12 .... 21 B8
Anson Cl CR3, CR8 .... 100 D7
Anstice Cl W4 .... 7 E7
Anstie Grange Dr RH5 .... 157 B5
Anstie La RH5 .... 156 F4
Anstiebury CE Prim Sch
RH5 .... 157 D4
Anston Ct 3 GU2 .... 108 E1
Anthony Ct TW7 .... 5 F4
Anthony Rd CR0, SE25 ..... 43 A3
Anthony West
House 8 RH3 .... 137 B7
Antigua Wlk SE19 .... 22 D3
Antlands La Burstow RH6 .183 B6
Crawley RH6 .... 182 C5
Antlands La E RH6 .... 182 F5
Antlands La W RH6 .... 182 E6
Anton Cres SM1 .... 59 A7
Antrobus Cl SM1 .... 58 F5
Anvil Cl SW16 .... 21 C1
Anvil La KT11 .... 73 A5
Anvil Rd TW16 .... 35 A6
Anyards Rd KT11 .... 73 B5

Anzio Cl GU11 105
Apeldoorn Dr CR8, SM6 60
Aperdele Rd KT22 75
Aperfield Rd TN16 83
Apers Ave GU22 89
Apex Cl Beckenham BR3 44
Oatlands Park KT13 53
Apex Dr GU16 65
Apley Rd RH2 139
Aplin Way Hounslow TW7 5
Loughton Village SE18 48
Apollo Pl GU21 89
Apollo Rise GU14 84
Apple Garth GU7 150
Apple Gr KT9 56
Apple Mkt KT1 37
Apple Tree Cl KT13 94
Apple Tree Way GU47 45
Appleby Cl TW2 16
Appleby Ct GU15 65
Appleby Gdns TW14 14
Appledore RG12 26
Appledore Cl Hayes BR2 ... 44
Upper Tooting SW12, SW17 .20
Appledore Mews GU14 85
Appledown Rise CR5 79
Applefield RH10 201
Applegarth Claygate KT10 .. 55
New Addington CR0 63
Applegarth Ave GU2 108
Applegarth Inf & Jun Sch
CR0 63
Applelands Cl GU10 146
Appleton Gdns KT3 39
Appleton Sq CR4 40
Appletree Cl
Godalming GU7 150
6 Penge SE20 43
Appletree Ct GU4 110
Appletree Pl 4 RG42 27
Appletrees Pl GU22 89
Appley Dr GU15 65
Approach Rd Ashford TW15 .14
East Molesey KT8 36
Farnham GU9 125
Merton SW20 39
Purley CR8 80
Tatsfield CR6, TN16 103
Approach The RH19 185
April Cl Ashtead KT21 75
Camberley GU15 65
Feltham TW13 15
Horsham RH12 217
April Glen SE23 23
Aprilwood Cl KT15 70
Apsley Ct Crawley RH11 .. 200
Sutton SM2 59
Apsley Rd Croydon SE25 ... 43
Kingston u T KT3 38
Aquarius TW1 17
Aquarius Ct RH11 200
Aquila Cl KT21 95
Arabella Dr SW15 7
Aragon Ave Ewell KT17 58
Thames Ditton KT7 36
Aragon Cl Ashford TW16 ... 14
New Addington CR0 63
Aragon Ct Bracknell RG12 .. 27
Knaphill GU21 68
Aragon Rd Kingston u T KT2 .17
West Barnes SM4 39
Aram Ct GU22 70
Arbor Ct BR3 44
Arbour Cl KT22 95
Arbourfield Cl SW2 21
Arbrook La KT10 55
Arbury Terr SE26 23
Arbutus Cl RH1 139
Arbutus Rd RH1 139
Arcade The 11 GU11 105
Arch Rd KT12 54
Archbishop Lanfranc Sch
The CR0 41
Archbishop Tenison's Sch
CR0 61
Archbishop's Pl 3 SW2 21
Archdale Pl KT3 38
Archdeacon Cambridge's
Prim Sch C of E) TW2 16
Archer Cl KT2 17
Archer Rd SE25 43
Archers Ct RH10 201
Archway Cl Wallington SM6 .60
Wimbledon SW19 20
Archway Mews RH4 136
Archway Pl RH4 136
Archway St SW13, SW14 7
Arcturus Rd RH11 200
Arcus Rd BR1 24
Arden 3 SW19 19
Arden Cl Bracknell RG12 ... 28
Reigate RH2 139
Arden Mead Cotts RH7 ... 164
Arden Rd RH10 201
Ardenrun RH7 164
Ardenrun Cotts RH7 164
Ardent Cl SE25 42
Ardesley Wood KT13 53
Ardfern Ave SW16 41
Ardfillan Rd SE6 24
Ardgowan Rd SE6 24
Ardingly RG12 27
Ardingly Cl Crawley RH11 .201
South Croydon CR0 62
Ardingly Ct KT18 76
Ardleigh Gdns SM3 40
Ardley Cl SE23, SE6 23
Ardlui Rd SE27 22

dmay Gdns KT6 ....37 E4
dmore Ave GU2 ....109 B3
dmore House GU2 ......109 B3
dmore Way GU2 ....109 B3
doch Rd SE6 ....24 D6
drossan Ave GU15 .....64 A5
drossan Gdns KT4 .....58 A7
dshiel Dr RH1 ....139 E7
dwell Rd SW2 ....21 E6
e Gdns GU15 ....65 C6
ena La GU11 ....104 E5
ena Tne RG12 ....27 A7
enal Dr RG45 ....45 C3
ethusa Way GU24 ......67 F3
ford Comm GU35 ......187 A6
gent Terr GU47 ....64 E8
gosy Gdns TW18 ....12 F2
gosy La TW19 ....13 D8
gill Ct ⬛ SU24 ....21 E8
gyle Ave
gyle House SM2 ....59 C4
gyle Rd TW3 ....5 B2
gyle St SU24 ....87 A6
gill Ct ⬛ SU24 ....21 E8
kell Gr SW16 ....22 B1
kendale RH10 ....185 A4
kindale Rd SE6 ....24 C5
klow Mews ⬛ KT6 .....56 E8
kwright Dr RG42 ......26 D7
kwright House ⬛ SW27 .21 E7
kwright Rd Poyle SL3 ..1 E5
South Croydon CR2 ....61 F2
rlington Ct Bracknell RG42 ..27 A8
Sutton SM1 ....59 A8
Twickenham TW3 ....6 C1
rlington Ct Reigate RH2 ..118 A3
⬛ Twickenham TW1 .....6 B3
rlington Gr SW5 ......59 F8
rlington Lodge KT13 ..53 B6
rlington Rd Ashford TW15 .13 F3
Richmond TW10 ....37 D3
Teddington TW11 ....6 C1
rlington Sq RG12 .....37 D3
Surbiton KT6 ....37 D3
Teddington TW11 ....6 C1
rlington Terr GU11 ..104 F2
rmadale Rd Feltham TW14 ..4 A2
Woking GU21 ....69 A2
rmeston x3 RH13 ......38 D2
rmfield Ct KT8 ....35 F4
rmfield Cres CR4 ....40 F7
rmitage Ct SL5 ......29 C3
rmitage Dr GU16 .....65 F1
rmstrong Cl KT12 ....35 A3
rmstrong Mall GU14 ..84 D6
rmstrong Rd
Englefield Green TW20 ..11 C2
Feltham TW13 ....15 E3
rmytage Rd SW5 ......84 B1
rmytage Rd TW5 ......4 D7
rnal Cres SW18 ......19 E8
rncliffe RG12 ....27 A4
rne Cl RH11 ....200 F3
rne Gr RH6 ....160 E5
rnella Ct GU14 ....105 D8
rnewood Cl Oxshott KT22 ..74 B5
Roehampton SW15 ....19 A7
rney's La CR4 ....41 A1
rngask Rd SE6 ......200 E5
rngask Rd SE6 ....24 A7
rnhem Cl GU11 .....105 B2
rnhem Dr CR0 ....82 D8
rnison Rd KT8 ....36 B6
rnold Cres TW7 ....5 D7
rnold Dr KT9 ....56 D4
rnold Rd Mitcham SW17 ..20 F1
Sheerwater GU21 .....70 B4
Staines TW18 ....13 C1
rnull St SE6 ....24 C4
rnull's Rd SW16 ....22 B2
rrosa Rd ⬛ SW1 ......6 D1
rragon Gdns
Streatham SW16 .....21 E1
West Wickham BR4 ...63 A7
rragon Rd ⬛
⬛ Twickenham TW1 ....5 F1
Twickenham TW1 ......6 C1
Wandsworth SW18 ...20 A7
rragon Wlk KT14 ....71 F6
rragon St ⬛ GU11 ..105 B2
Wallington SM6 .....60 C6
rran Cl Crawley RH11 ..201 B3
rran Rd SE6 ....24 C6
rran Way SE6 ....24 C6
rrancourt RH12 ....217 B2
rras Ave SM4 ....40 C4
rrivals Rd RH6 ....181 F8
rrol Rd BR3 ....43 D6
rrow Ind Est GU14 ..84 F2
rrow Rd GU14 ....84 E1
rtel Croft RH10 ...202 A6
rterberry Rd SW20, SW19 ..39 D8
rthur Cl ⬛ Bagshot GU19 ..47 E1
Farnham GU9 ....125 B1
rthur Ct CR0 ....61 D7
rthur Rd Biggin Hill TN16 ..83 D3
Crawley RH12 ......200 E6
Farnham GU9 ....125 C1
Horsham RH13 ......217 D1
⬛ Kingston u T KT2 ..18 A1
West Barnes KT3 ....39 B4
Wimbledon SW19 ....20 A5
Wokingham RG41 ....25 A6
rthur St GU11 .....105 B2

Arthur's Bridge Rd GU21 ..69 D2
Artillery Rd
⬛ Aldershot GU11 ...105 B2
Farnborough GU11, GU14 ..105 D8
⬛ Guildford GU1 ....109 D1
Artillery Terr GU1 ..109 D1
Arun Wlk RH13 .....217 E1
Arundale 37 D5
Arundel Ave Ewell KT17 ..58 B1
Merton SM4 ....40 C4
South Croydon CR2 ..62 A1
Arundel Cl Crawley RH10 ..202 C6
Croydon CR0, CR9 ...61 B7
Hampton TW12 ......16 B3
Hampton Twr12 .....44 E7
Arundel House
Croydon CR0 ....61 D5
Reigate RH2 ....139 B5
Arundel Rd Belmont SM2 ..58 F3
Dorking RH4 ....136 A7
Frimley GU15 ......66 C4
Thornton Hth ⬛ CR0 ..42 D3
Wimbledon SW19 ...125 B2
Arunside RH12 ....217 A1
Arunside Cty Prim Sch
RH12 ....217 A2
Ascalon Ct ⬛ SW2 ..21 F8
Aschurch Rd GU10 ..23 F1
Ascot Ct GU11 .....105 A1
Ascot Heath Inf Sch SL5 ..8 E1
Ascot Heath Jun Sch SL5 ..8 E1
Ascot House SE26 ..23 B2
Ascot Mews SM6 ....60 C2
Ascot Race Course SL5 ..8 F6
Ascot Rd
East Bedfont TW14, TW15 ..14 B6
Mitcham SW17 ......21 A2
Ascot Sta SL5 ....9 A4
Ascot Towers SL5 ...28 F7
Ascot Way KT11 .....73 D3
Ash Church Rd GU12 ..106 B2
Ash Cl Ash GU12 ...106 B3
Blackwater GU17 ....64 C5
Box Hill KT20 .....116 C4
Carshalton SM5 ....59 F8
Crawley Down RH10 ..204 C8
Kingston u T KT3 ...164 E5
Lingfield RH7 .....164 E5
Merstham RH1 .....119 C5
Penge SE20 ....43 C7
Pyrford GU22 ......71 A4
Woking GU22 ....89 E7
Ash Combe GU8 ....191 A4
Ash Ct ⬛ Ottershaw KT16 ..51 C5
West Ewell KT19 ...57 C6
⬛ West Norwood SW16 ..22 A2
Ash Dr RH1 ....140 B7
Ash Gr East Bedfont TW14 ..14 E7
Guildford GU2 .....109 A2
Heston TW5 ....4 D7
Penge SE20 ....43 C7
Staines TW18 ......13 C2
West Wickham BR4 ..44 C1
Ash Grange Cty Prim Sch
GU12 ....106 B2
Ash Green La E GU12 ..127 C8
Ash Green La W
Ash GU12 ....126 F8
Ash, Ash Green GU12 ..127 C8
Ash Green Rd GU12 ..106 C1
Ash Hill Rd GU12 ..106 B3
Ash Keys RH10 ....201 E5
Ash La GU8 ....148 C2
Ash Lodge ⬛ TW16 ..14 F1
Ash Lodge Cl GU12 ..106 A1
Ash Lodge Dr GU12 ..106 A1
Ash Manor Sch GU12 ..126 F8
Ash Mews KT18 ....76 E6
Ash Rd Aldershot GU12 ..126 D8
Cheam SM3, SM4 ...39 F1
Crawley RH10 .....202 A8
Croydon CR0 ......63 A8
Littleton TW17 ....34 A5
Pirbright GU24, GU23 ..88 A1
Woking GU22 ......89 E7
Ash St GU12 ......106 A1
Ash Sta GU12 .....106 B2
Ash Tree Cl
Croydon BR3, CR0 ..43 E3
Farnborough GU14 ..84 F7
Graywood GU27 ...189 F1
⬛ Surbiton KT6 ....43 E3
Ash Tree Way CR0 ..43 E3
Ash Vale GU8 .....191 A4
Ash Vale Sta GU12 ..106 A7
Ashbourne GU12 ...26 F3
Ashbourne Cl
Coulsdon CR5 .....79 C1
Ashbourne Rd CR4, SW17 ..21 A1
Ashbourne Terr ⬛ SW19 ..20 A1
Ashbrook Rd SL4 ..11 B8
Ashburnham Pk KT10 ..55 C6
Ashburnham Rd
Crawley RH10 ....202 A4
Richmond TW10 ....17 C5
Ashburton Ave CR0 ..43 B1
Ashburton Cl CR0 ..43 A1
Ashburton Gdns CR0 ..62 A8
Ashburton Jun & Inf Sch
CR0 ....43 B3
Ashburton Rd CR0, CR9 ..62 A8
Ashburton Sch CR0 ..43 B3
Ashbury Cres GU4 ..110 C3
Ashbury Dr GU17 ..65 A1

Ashby Pl SW19 .....20 C2
Ashby Ave KT19, KT9 ..57 A4
Ashby Ct RH1 ......141 B5
Ashby Grange ⬛ SM6 ..60 C5
Ashby Way ⬛ UB7 ...3 A7
Ashby Wlk CR0 ....42 C3
Ashcombe Ave KT6 ..37 D2
Ashcombe Par GU22 ..90 A7
Ashcombe Rd
Dorking RH4 ....115 A1
Merstham RH1 .....119 C8
Wallington SM5 ....60 A4
Wimbledon SW19 ...20 A3
Ashcombe Sch The RH4 ..115 B3
Ashcombe Sq KT3 ..38 C6
Ashcombe Terr KT20 ..97 B7
Ashcroft GU4 .....130 E2
Ashcroft Pk KT11 ..73 E6
Ashcroft Rd KT9 ..56 E5
Ashcroft Rise CR5 ..79 E3
Ashdale Cl Stanwell TW19 ..13 E6
Twickenham TW2 ...16 C8
Ashdale Way TW2 ..16 B8
Ashdene Cl TW15 ..14 C1
Ashdene Cres GU12 ..106 A3
Ashdene House TW20 ..11 C2
Ashdene Rd GU12 ..106 A2
Ashdown Ave GU14 ..85 E2
Ashdown Cl
Beckenham BR3 ....44 B7
Bracknell RG12 .....28 A7
Reigate RH2 ......139 B5
Ashdown Gate RH19 ..185 D2
Ashdown Gdns CR2 ..81 B4
Ashdown Pl KT7 ...37 A2
Ashdown Rd Ewell KT17 ..77 A6
Forest Row RH18 ..206 F2
Kingston u T KT1 ...37 E7
Reigate RH2 ......139 B5
Ashdown View RH19 ..205 E7
Ashdown Way SW17 ..21 A6
Ashen Gr SW19 ....20 A6
Ashen Vale CR2 ...62 E2
Ashenden Rd GU2 ..108 F1
Ashfield Ave TW13 ..15 B7
Ashfield Cl Beckenham BR3 ..24 A1
Richmond TW10 ....17 E7
Ashfields RH2 ....118 A3
Ashford Ave TW15 ..14 B2
Ashford C of E Fst & Mid
Sch TW15 ....14 B2
Ashford Cres TW15 ..13 E4
Ashford High Sch
The TW15 ....13 E5
Ashford Hospl TW15 ..14 C4
Ashford Ind Est TW15 ..14 C4
Ashford Manor Golf Club
TW15 ....13 F2
Ashford Park Cty Prim Sch
TW15 ....13 D4
Ashford Rd
Feltham TW13, TW15 ..14 E4
Littleton TW15, TW17 ..14 C1
Staines TW18 ......33 D8
Ashford Sta TW15 ..13 E5
Ashgrove Rd Ashford TW15 ..14 C3
Catford BR1 ......24 D2
Ashlake Rd SW16 ..21 E4
Ashlea Ct CR6 .....81 A1
Ashleigh Ave TW20 ..12 C1
Ashleigh Cl RH6 ..160 F3
Ashleigh Gdns SE26 ..23 B2
Ashleigh House SW14 ..7 E3
Ashleigh Point ⬛ SE26 ..23 D5
Ashleigh Rd
Horsham RH12 ....217 C4
Mortlake SW14 .....7 E4
Penge SE20 ....43 C5
Ashley Ave Epsom KT18 ..76 D6
Morden SM4 ....40 A4
Ashley Cl Frimley GU16 ..86 A6
Little Bookham KT23 ..93 F2
Oatlands Park KT12, KT13 ..54 A7
Ashley Cres ⬛ Epsom KT18 ..76 D6
Knaphill GU21 ....68 F1
Ashley Ct KT18 ...76 C5
Ashley Dr Banstead SM7 ..78 A5
Blackwater GU17 ..64 C4
Hounslow TW7 ......5 E8
Twickenham TW2 ...16 B7
Walton-on-T KT12 ..54 A7
Ashley Gdns
Richmond TW10 ....17 D6
⬛ Shalford GU4 ...130 F2
Ashley House ⬛ GU7 ..150 E8
Ashley Inf Sch KT12 ..35 A1
Ashley La CR0 ....61 A6
Ashley Park Ave KT12 ..53 F8
Ashley Park Cres KT12 ..54 A7
Ashley Park Rd KT12 ..54 A7
Ashley Rd Epsom KT18 ..76 D6
Farnborough GU14 ..85 D4
Hampton TW12 .....36 A8
Knaphill GU21 ....68 F1
Richmond TW9 ......6 E3
Thames Ditton KT7 ..37 A3
Thornton Heath CR7 ..41 F5
Walton-on-T KT12 ..54 A8
Westcott RH4 .....135 C6
Wimbledon SW19 ...20 C2
Ashley Rise KT12 ..54 A6
Ashley Way GU24 ..67 D6
Ashling Rd CR0, CR9 ..43 A1
Ashlyn's Pk KT11 ..73 E6

Ashlyns Way KT9 ..56 D4
Ashmead Rd TW14 ..15 A7
Ashmere Ave BR3 ..44 D7
Ashmere Cl SM3 ...58 D5
Ashmill Ct CR0 ....42 C3
Ashmore Ct TW5 ....5 A8
Ashmore House RH1 ..181 D1
Ashmore La
Biggin Hill BR2, TN16 ..83 C8
Rusper RH12 ......199 C6
Ashridge GU14 ....84 F7
Ashridge Gn ⬛ RG42 ..27 B8
Ashridge Rd RG40 ..25 D8
Ashridge Way
Ashford TW15 .....15 A2
Merton SM4, SW20 ..39 F5
Ashstead La GU7 ..150 C2
Ashstead Sta KT21 ..75 E3
Ashtead Cl ⬛ SW19 ..19 D7
Ashtead Hospl The RH12 ..95 E8
Ashtead La GU7 ...150 C2
Ashtead Woods Rd KT21 ..75 C3
Ashton Cl Cheam SM1 ..59 A6
Hersham KT12 .....54 B4
Ashton Ct BR3 ....43 F8
Ashton Gdns SW14 ..4 F3
Ashton House SW15 ..19 B8
Ashton Rd ⬛ GU21 ..68 F2
Ashtree Ave CR4 ..40 D7
Ashtree Ct TW15 ..14 B3
Ashtrees GU6 ....174 E1
Ashtrees The GU12 ..106 B2
Ashurst ⬛ KT18 ...76 D6
Ashurst Cl Horsham RH12 ..218 A5
Kenley CR8 ....80 D4
Penge SE20 ....43 B8
Ashurst Dr Box Hill KT20 ..116 B5
Crawley RH10 ....202 D6
Littleton TW17 ....33 E5
Ashurst Rd Ash Vale GU12 ..105 F4
Tadworth KT20 ....97 C6
Ashurst Wlk CR0 ..62 B8
Ashurstwood Cty Prim Sch
RH19 ....206 E6
Ashvale Rd SW17 ..20 F3
Ashview Cl TW15 ..13 E3
Ashview Gdns TW15 ..13 E3
Ashville Way RG41 ..25 A5
Ashwell Ave GU15 ..47 F8
Ashwell Ave GU15 ..65 F6
Ashwell Ct TW15 ..13 E3
Ashwood ⬛ Crawley RH11 ..201 D5
Warlingham CR6 ..101 C7
Ashwood Gdns CR0 ..63 C4
Ashwood Pk
⬛ Belmont SM2 ...59 A3
Fetcham KT22 ....94 C4
Woking GU22 .....70 A1
Ashwood Rd
Englefield Green TW20 ..11 B2
Woking GU22 .....70 A1
Ashworth Pl GU2 ..108 F1
Aslett St ⬛ SW18 ..20 C8
Asmar Cl CR5 ....79 E3
Aspen Cl Guildford GU4 ..110 D4
Staines TW18 .....12 F5
Stoke D'Abernon KT11 ..73 E3
Aspen Ct TW9 ......6 F3
Aspen Gdns Ashford TW15 ..14 C3
Mitcham CR4 .....41 A4
Aspen House SW2 ..21 B8
Aspen Sq KT13 ....53 D7
Aspen Vale CR3 ..100 E6
Aspen Way Banstead KT17 ..77 D5
Feltham TW13 ....15 B5
Horsham RH12 ...217 E4
Aspin Way GU17 ..64 B5
Aspinall House ⬛ SW12 ..21 E7
Asprey Gr CR3 ...100 F4
Asquith House ⬛ SM4 ..77 F4
Assembly Wlk SM5 ..40 E2
Assher Rd KT12 ..54 E7
Assheton-Bennett House
⬛ 37 E4
Astelham Rd TW17 ..33 E4
Astley House ⬛ SE27 ..22 C4
Aston Cl KT21 ....75 C1
Aston Ct RH11 ...201 B1
Aston Gn TW5 .....4 D5
Aston Mead ⬛ SL4 ..9 B7
Aston Rd Claygate KT10 ..55 E5
Merton SW20 .....39 D7
Astonville St ⬛ SW18 ..20 A7
Astor Cl Addlestone KT15 ..52 D6
Kingston u T KT2 ..18 B2
Astoria Mansions ⬛ SW16 ..21 E5
Astoria Par SW16 ..21 E5
Astra Bsns Ctr RH1 ..161 A7
Astra Mead RG42 ...8 B2
Atalanta Cl CR8 ..61 A1
Atbara Ct TW11 ...17 B2
Atbara Rd TW11 ...17 B2
Atcham Rd TW3 ....5 C3
Atfield Gr GU20 ..48 D4
Atheldene Rd SW18 ..20 C7
Athelney Prim Sch SE6 ..24 A5
Athelney St SE6 ..24 A5
Athelstan Cl RH10 ..202 E6
Athelstan House Sch
TW12 ....36 A8
Athelstan Rd KT1 ..37 F5
Athena Cl KT1 ....37 F6
Atherfield House RH1 ..139 C6
Atherfield Rd RH2 ..139 C6
Atherley Way TW4 ..15 F7

Atherton Cl Shalford GU4 ..130 E3
Stanwell TW19 ....2 D1
Atherton Dr SW19 ..19 D4
Atherton House ⬛ GU14 ..61 E4
Athlone KT10 .....55 E4
Athlone Rd SW2 ..22 A8
Atholl House ⬛ RH1 ..118 F1
Atkins Cl GU21 ...69 A1
Atkins Dr BR4 ....63 D8
Atkins Rd SW4, SW12 ..22 B8
Atkinson Ct RH6 ..161 B2
Atkinson Morley's Hospl
SW20 ....19 B1
Atkinson Rd RH10 ..202 C4
Atlanta Ct CR7 ...42 C6
Atrebatti Rd GU47 ..45 C1
Attebrouche Ct RG12 ..27 D2
Attfield Cl GU12 ..105 F1
Attleborough Ct SE21 ..22 B5
Attlee Cl CR7 ....42 C4
Attlee House ⬛ RH11 ..202 B2
Attwood Cl CR2 ..81 B5
Atwater Cl SW2 ..22 A7
Atwood KT23 .....93 E3
Atwood Ave TW9 ..7 A5
Atwood House ⬛ SE21 ..22 E5
Aubyn Hill SE27 ..22 D4
Auchinleck Ct RH10 ..204 B7
Auchinleck Way GU11 ..104 C2
Auckland Cl
Crawley RH11 ....181 D1
South Norwood SE19 ..42 F8
Auckland Gdns SE19 ..42 F8
Auckland Hill SE27 ..22 C4
Auckland Rd
Caterham CR3 ....100 C5
Kingston u T KT1 ..37 F5
South Norwood SE19, SE25 ..42 F8
Auckland Rise SE19 ..42 F8
Audley Cl RH11 ...181 D1
Audley Ct Surbiton KT5 ..37 F3
Twickenham TW2 ...16 C5
Audley Cty Prim Sch CR3 ..100 F6
Audley Dr CR2, CR6 ..81 C4
Audley Firs KT12 ..54 C6
Audley House KT13 ..52 B5
Audley Pl SM2 ...59 B3
Audley Rd KT13 ..53 D6
Audley Way SL5 ..28 D6
Audrey Cl BR3 ...44 B3
Audric Cl KT2 ...38 A8
Augur Cl TW18 ..12 F3
August La GU5 ..153 D7
Augusta Rd TW2 ..16 C6
Augustus Cl TW8 ..6 D7
Augustus Ct Hounslow TW3 ..5 C3
⬛ Putney SW19 ....19 E1
South Norwood SE19 ..22 E1
Streatham SW16 ..21 D6
Augustus Gdns GU15 ..66 C5
Augustus Rd SW19 ..19 E6
Aultone Way
Carshalton SM5 ..59 F7
Sutton SM1 ......59 C8
Aurelia Gdns CR7 ..41 F3
Aurelia Rd CR0, CR7, CR9 ..41 F3
Auriol Cl KT19 ..57 C2
Auriol Cty Jun Sch KT19 ..57 C2
Auriol Park Rd KT19, KT4 ..57 E7
Aurum Cl RH6 ...161 B2
Austen Cl RH19 ..185 B1
Austen Rd
Farnborough GU14 ..85 A6
Guildford GU1 ...130 F8
Austin Cl Coulsdon CR8 ..80 B1
Forest Hill SE23, SE6 ..23 F8
Twickenham TW1 ..6 C2
Austin House ⬛ KT6 ..37 E4
Austin's Cotts ⬛ GU9 ..125 B2
Austyn Gdns KT5 ..38 B1
Autumn Cl SW19 ..20 C2
Autumn Dr SM2 ..59 B2
Avalon Cl SW20 ..39 E7
Avarn Rd SW17 ..20 F2
Avebury RG12 ...27 A3
Avebury Cl RH12 ..218 A7
Avebury Rd SW19 ..39 F8
Aveley La GU10, GU9 ..146 C2
Aveling Cl Crawley RH10 ..202 C4
Purley CR8 ......79 F6
Aven Cl GU6 ....174 E2
Avening Rd SW18 ..20 A8
Avening Terr SW18 ..20 A8
Avenue C KT15 ..52 E7
Avenue Cl Cranford TW5 ..4 B7
Avenue Cres TW5 ..4 B7
Avenue Ct Penge SE20 ..23 D1
Avenue De Cagny GU47 ..87 F5
Avenue Elmers KT6 ..37 E4
Avenue Gdns Cranford TW5 ..4 B7
Horley RH6 ......161 C2
Mortlake SW14 ...7 E4
South Norwood SE25 ..43 A2
Teddington TW11 ..16 F2
Avenue One KT15 ..52 E6
Avenue Park Rd
SE21, SE27 ......22 B6
Avenue Prim Sch The
SM2 ....59 A1
Avenue Rd Banstead SM7 ..78 B4
Belmont SM2 ....59 A1

Avenue Rd *continued*
Caterham CR3 . . . . 100 E5
Cobham KT11 . . . . 73 D3
Cranleigh GU6 . . . . 174 F1
Egham TW18 . . . . 12 D3
Epsom KT18 . . . . 76 D5
Farnborough GU14 . . . . 85 D3
Feltham TW13 . . . . 14 F5
Grayshott GU26 . . . . 188 C3
Hampton TW12 . . . . 36 B8
Hounslow TW7 . . . . 5 F6
Kingston u T KT1 . . . . 37 E6
Mitcham SW16 . . . . 41 D7
New Malden KT3 . . . . 38 E5
South Norwood,
Anneriley SE25 . . . . 43 A7
South Norwood, Elmers End
BR3, SE20 . . . . 43 D8
Tatsfield TN16 . . . . 103 E7
Teddington TW11 . . . . 17 A2
Wallington SM6 . . . . 60 C3
Wimbledon SW20 . . . . 39 B7
Avenue S KT5 . . . . 38 A2
Avenue Sucy GU15 . . . . 65 B4
Avenue Terr KT13 . . . . 38 C6
Avenue The
Aldershot GU11, GU12 . . . . 126 C7
Beckenham BR3 . . . . 44 C8
Belmont SM2 . . . . 58 F2
Biggin Hill TN16 . . . . 103 F5
Brockham RH3, RH5 . . . . . . 116 A1
Camberley GU15 . . . . 65 B5
Chobham GU24 . . . . 50 A2
Claygate KT10 . . . . 55 E5
Compton GU3, GU7 . . . . . . 129 C1
Coulsdon CR5 . . . . 79 D4
Cranford TW5 . . . . 4 A6
Crowthorne RG45 . . . . 45 B5
Dormansland RH19 . . . . . . 186 B6
Egham TW20 . . . . 12 B4
Ewhurst GU6 . . . . 175 E6
Godalming GU7 . . . . 150 F2
Grayshott GU26 . . . . 188 D3
Hampton TW12 . . . . 15 F2
Haslemere GU27 . . . . 207 F7
Horley RH6 . . . . 160 F2
Hounslow TW3 . . . . 5 B2
Isleworth TW1 . . . . 6 C2
Lightwater GU18 . . . . 48 A1
◀ New Malden KT4 . . . . 39 A1
North Ascot SL5 . . . . 8 F1
Oxshott KT10, KT22 . . . . . . 74 F8
Richmond TW9 . . . . 7 A6
Rowledge GU10 . . . . 145 F3
South Croydon CR0 . . . . 61 E7
South Nutfield RH1 . . . . . . 140 E6
Staines TW18 . . . . 33 B8
Stoneleigh KT17, SM3 . . . . . 58 C3
Sunbury TW16 . . . . 35 B7
Surbiton KT5 . . . . 37 F3
Tadworth KT20 . . . . 97 B5
Twickenham TW1 . . . . 6 B2
West Wickham BR4 . . . . 44 E2
Whyteleafe CR3 . . . . 101 A8
Woodham KT15 . . . . 52 A1
Worcester Park KT4 . . . . 57 F8
Worplesdon GU3 . . . . 88 E1
Avenue Three KT15 . . . . . 52 E7
Avenue Two KT15 . . . . . . 52 E6
Averil Gr SW16 . . . . 22 B2
Avern Gdns KT8 . . . . 36 B5
Avern Rd KT8 . . . . 36 B5
Avery Ct SE20 . . . . 23 B1
Aviary Rd GU22 . . . . 71 A3
Aviary Way RH10 . . . . 184 C1
Aviemore Cl BR3 . . . . 43 F4
Aviemore Way BR3 . . . . . . 43 E4
Avington Cl GU1 . . . . 109 E1
Avington Gr SE20 . . . . 23 C1
Avoca Rd SW17 . . . . 21 A4
Avocet Cres GU47 . . . . 64 E8
Avon Cl Addlestone KT15 . . . 52 A4
Ash GU12 . . . . 105 F1
Farnborough GU14 . . . . 84 E7
Sutton SM1 . . . . 59 C6
Worcester Park KT4 . . . . 58 A8
Avon Ct GU9 . . . . 125 C1
Avon House ❾ RH1 . . . . . 118 F2
Avon Rd Ashford TW16 . . . . 14 F1
Farnham GU9 . . . . 125 C1
Avon Wlk RH11 . . . . 200 F5
Avondale GU12 . . . . 105 F7
Avondale Ave
Hinchley Wood KT10 . . . . . . 56 A7
New Malden KT4 . . . . 38 F1
Staines TW18 . . . . 12 F1
◀ Staines TW18 . . . . 12 F1
Avondale Cl Hersham KT12 . 54 C5
Horley RH6 . . . . 161 A5
Avondale Ct SM2 . . . . 59 C3
Avondale Gdns TW4 . . . . . . 4 F2
Avondale High CR3 . . . . . 101 A6
Avondale House ❻ SW14 . . . 7 D4
Avondale Rd
Aldershot GU11 . . . . 126 B8
Ashford TW15, TW19 . . . . . . 13 D5
Bromley BR1 . . . . 24 F2
Catford BR1 . . . . 24 F2
Mortlake SW14 . . . . 7 D4
South Croydon CR2 . . . . 61 C4
Wimbledon SW19 . . . . 20 B3
Avonmore Ave GU1 . . . . . 109 F2
Avonwick Rd TW3 . . . . 5 B5
Avro Way Byfleet KT13 . . . . 52 E1
Wallington SM6 . . . . 60 E3
Axbridge RG12 . . . . 27 E4

Axes La RH1 . . . . 140 D2
Axford House SW2 . . . . 22 B7
Axwood KT18 . . . . 76 C4
Aycliffe Ct KT1 . . . . 38 A7
Ayebridges Ave TW20 . . . . . 12 C1
Ayjay Cl GU11 . . . . 126 A7
Aylesbury Ct SM1 . . . . 59 C7
Aylesford Ave BR3 . . . . 43 E4
Aylesworth Spur SL4 . . . . . 11 B8
Aylett Rd Croydon SE25 . . . 43 B5
Isleworth TW7 . . . . 5 E5
Ayling Ct GU9 . . . . 125 F7
Ayling Hill GU11 . . . . 104 F1
Ayling La GU11 . . . . 125 F8
Aylward Rd Forest Hill SE23 . 23 D6
Merton SW20 . . . . 39 F6
Aymer Cl TW18 . . . . 32 E8
Aymer Dr TW18 . . . . 32 E8
Aysgarth RG12 . . . . 27 A3
Aysgarth Ct SM1 . . . . 59 B7
Aysgarth Rd SE21 . . . . 22 E8
Ayshe Court Dr RH13 . . . . 217 E3
Azalea Cl GU22 . . . . 89 D8
Azalea Dr GU27 . . . . 207 F8
Azalea Way GU15 . . . . 66 A6
Azelea Ct CR8 . . . . 80 B8

B

Babbacombe Cl KT9 . . . . . . 56 D5
Babbs Mead GU9 . . . . 125 A1
Baber Dr TW14 . . . . 4 C1
Babington Ct SW16 . . . . . . 21 D3
Babington Rd SW16 . . . . . . 21 D3
Babylon La KT20, RH2 . . . 118 B8
Bachelor's La GU23 . . . . . . 92 A3
Back Gn KT12 . . . . 54 C4
Back La Binstead GU10 . . . 166 B8
Brentford TW8 . . . . 6 D8
Crawley RH10 . . . . 203 D1
East Clandon GU4 . . . . 111 D4
Elstead GU8 . . . . 148 D4
Plaistow RH14 . . . . 211 E2
Richmond TW9 . . . . 17 C6
Back Rd TW11 . . . . 16 E2
Bacon Cl GU47 . . . . 64 D6
Bacon La GU10 . . . . 145 E5
Badajos Rd GU11 . . . . 104 F3
Baden Cl TW18 . . . . 13 B1
Baden Dr RH6 . . . . 160 E4
Baden Powell Cl KT6 . . . . . 56 F8
Baden Rd GU2 . . . . 109 A3
Bader Cl CR8 . . . . 80 D4
Bader Ct GU14 . . . . 84 F8
Badger Cl Feltham TW13 . . . 15 B5
Guildford GU2 . . . . 109 B4
Hounslow TW4 . . . . 4 C4
Badger Cl GU10 . . . . 146 A5
Badger Dr GU18 . . . . 48 A1
Badger Way GU10 . . . . 124 D8
Badgers Cl Ashford TW15 . . . 13 F3
Farncombe GU7 . . . . 150 D8
Horsham RH12 . . . . 217 F6
Woking GU21 . . . . 69 C1
Badgers Copse
Frimley GU15 . . . . 65 E4
Worcester Park KT4 . . . . 57 F8
Badgers Cross GU48 . . . . . 149 E1
Badgers Ct ❹ KT17 . . . . . . 76 E6
Badgers Hollow GU7 . . . . 150 D6
Badgers La CR6 . . . . 101 C8
Badgers Lodge ❺ KT17 . . . 76 E6
Badgers Way
Bracknell RG12 . . . . 27 F7
East Grinstead RH19 . . . . . 185 F2
Loxwood RH14 . . . . 213 A4
Badgers Wlk
Kingston u T KT3 . . . . 38 E7
Purley CR8 . . . . 79 C8
Whyteleafe CR3 . . . . 80 F1
Badgers Wood CR3 . . . . . 100 D2
Badgerwood Dr GU16 . . . . 65 D2
Badingham Dr KT22 . . . . . . 94 E4
Badminton Rd SW12 . . . . . 21 A8
Badshot Lea Cty Inf Sch
GU9 . . . . 126 A6
Badshot Lea Rd
GU11, GU9 . . . . 126 A6
Badshot Pk GU9 . . . . 126 A6
Bagden Hill KT23 . . . . 114 D5
Bagot Cl KT21 . . . . 75 F3
Bagshot Cty Inf Sch GU19 . . 47 E2
Bagshot Gn GU19 . . . . 47 E3
Bagshot Rd Ascot SL5 . . . . . 29 C2
Bracknell RG12 . . . . 27 C4
Bracknell SL5 . . . . 48 A8
Brookwood GU21, GU22,
GU24, GU3 . . . . 88 C5
Englefield Green TW20 . . . . . 11 C2
Knaphill GU21, GU22,
GU24, GU3 . . . . 88 C5
Pirbright GU21, GU22,
GU24, GU3 . . . . 88 C5
West End GU24 . . . . 68 B8
Woking GU21, GU22,
GU24, GU3 . . . . 88 C5
Bagshot Sta GU19 . . . . 47 E4
Bahram Rd KT19 . . . . 57 D1
Baigents La GU20 . . . . 48 D4
Bailes La Flexford GU3 . . . 107 D2
Normandy GU3 . . . . 107 D3
Bailey Cl Frimley GU16 . . . . 85 D8
Horsham RH12 . . . . 217 E4
Bailey House ❶❶ SE26 . . . . 23 B3
Bailey Pl SE26 . . . . 23 D2
Bailey Rd RH4 . . . . 135 C6

Baileys Cl GU17 . . . . 64 C4
Bailing Hill RH12 . . . . 216 E7
Baillie Rd GU1 . . . . 130 F8
Bain Ave GU15 . . . . 65 B2
Bainbridge Cl KT2 . . . . 17 E3
Baines Cl CR0 . . . . 61 D5
Bainton Mead GU21 . . . . . . 69 A2
Baird Cl RH10 . . . . 182 A1
Baird Dr GU3 . . . . 108 B2
Baird Gdns SE19, SE21 . . . . 22 E4
Baird Rd GU14 . . . . 85 C2
Bakeham La TW20 . . . . 11 D1
Bakehouse Barn Cl RH12 . 217 E7
Bakehouse Rd RH6 . . . . . . 161 A5
Baker Cl RH10 . . . . 201 D4
Baker La CR4 . . . . 41 A7
Baker St KT13 . . . . 53 B6
Baker's Cl RH7 . . . . 164 E5
Baker's La RH7 . . . . 164 E4
Bakers Ct SE25 . . . . 42 E6
Bakers End SW20 . . . . 39 E7
Bakers Gdns SM5 . . . . 59 E8
Bakers Mead RH9 . . . . 121 C6
Bakers Way RH5 . . . . 178 C5
Bakery Mews KT6 . . . . 38 A1
Bakewell Dr KT3 . . . . 38 E7
Balaam House SM1 . . . . . . 59 A6
Balaclava Rd KT6 . . . . 37 C2
Balchins La RH4 . . . . 135 B6
Balcombe Ct RH10 . . . . . . 202 D7
Balcombe Gdns RH6 . . . . 161 C2
Balcombe House ❽ SW2 . . . 21 F7
Balcombe Rd Crawley,
Tinsley Green RH10, RH6 . . 182 D5
Crawley, Worth RH10 . . . . . 202 D5
Horley RH6 . . . . 161 B2
Baldreys GU9 . . . . 146 A8
Baldry Gdns SW16 . . . . 21 F2
Baldwin Cl RH10 . . . . 202 C3
Baldwin Cres GU4 . . . . . . 110 C3
Baldwin House ❶❺ SW2 . . . 22 A7
Baldwins Hill Cty Prim Sch
RH19 . . . . 185 D3
Balfont Cl CR2 . . . . 81 A6
Balfour Ave GU22 . . . . 89 F5
Balfour Cres RG12 . . . . 27 B4
Balfour Gdns RH18 . . . . . . 206 E1
Balfour Rd Croydon SE25 . . . 43 A5
Hounslow TW3 . . . . 5 B4
Merton SW19 . . . . 20 B1
Wallington SM5 . . . . 59 F3
Weybridge KT13 . . . . 53 A6
Balgowan Cl KT3 . . . . 38 E5
Balgowan Prim Sch BR3 . . . 43 E7
Balgowan Rd BR3 . . . . 43 E7
Balham Gr SW12 . . . . 21 A8
Balham High Rd
Balham SW12, SW17 . . . . . . 21 A7
Upper Tooting SW12 . . . . 21 A7
Balham Hill SW12 . . . . 21 B8
Balham New Rd SW12 . . . . 21 B8
Balham Park Mansions
SW12 . . . . 20 F7
Balham Park Rd
SW12, SW17 . . . . 20 F7
Balham Sta SW12 . . . . 21 B7
Balham Station Rd SW12 . . 21 B7
Balintore Ct ❽ GU47 . . . . . 64 D8
Ball and Wicket La GU9 . . 125 C7
Ballands N The KT22 . . . . . 94 E5
Ballands' S The KT22 . . . . . 94 E4
Ballantyne Dr KT20 . . . . . . 97 F6
Ballantyne Rd GU14 . . . . . . 85 A6
Ballard Cl KT2 . . . . 18 D1
Ballard Ct GU15 . . . . 66 A8
Ballard Rd GU15 . . . . 66 A8
Ballards Farm Rd CR2 . . . . 62 A4
Ballards Gn KT20 . . . . 97 E8
Ballards Rise CR2 . . . . 62 A4
Ballards Way CR0, CR2 . . . . 62 B4
Ballater Rd CR2 . . . . 61 F5
Ballencrieff Rd SL5 . . . . . . 29 F2
Ballfield Rd GU7 . . . . 150 E6
Ballina St SE23 . . . . 23 D8
Balliol Cl RH10 . . . . 182 D1
Balliol Way GU47 . . . . 45 E1
Balloch Rd SE6 . . . . 24 D6
Ballsdown GU8 . . . . 191 A3
Balmain Ct TW3 . . . . 5 B6
Balmoral RH19 . . . . 206 A8
Balmoral Ave BR3 . . . . 43 E5
Balmoral Cres
East Molesey KT8 . . . . 36 A6
Hale GU9 . . . . 125 B6
Balmoral Ct
❶❶ Belmont SM2 . . . . 59 A3
❻ Crawley RH11 . . . . 201 B2
North Cheam KT4 . . . . 58 B8
West Norwood SE27 . . . . 22 C4
Balmoral Dr Frimley GU16 . . 85 F8
Woking GU22 . . . . 70 C3
Balmoral Gdns CR2 . . . . . . 61 D1
Balmoral Grange TW11 . . . 33 A1
Balmoral Rd Ash GU12 . . . 106 B4
Kingston u T KT1 . . . . 37 F5
North Cheam KT4 . . . . 58 B8
Balmoral Way SM2 . . . . 59 A1
Balquhain Cl KT21 . . . . 75 D2
Baltic Cl SW19 . . . . 20 D1
Balvernie Gr SW18 . . . . 20 A8
Bamford Rd BR1 . . . . 24 D3
Bampfylde Cl SM6 . . . . 60 C7
Bampton Rd SE23 . . . . 23 D5
Bampton Way GU21 . . . . . . 69 A2
Banavie Gdns BR3 . . . . 44 C8
Banbury RG12 . . . . 27 E2
Banbury Cl GU16 . . . . 86 A7

Banbury Ct ❽ SM2 . . . . 59 A3
Bancroft Cl TW15 . . . . 14 A3
Bancroft Ct RH2 . . . . 118 B1
Bancroft Rd
Crawley RH10 . . . . 202 D5
Reigate RH2 . . . . 118 B1
Band La ❶ TW20 . . . . 12 A3
Banders Rise GU1 . . . . . . 110 C2
Bandon Hill Prim Sch
SM6 . . . . 60 D4
Bandon Rise SM6 . . . . 60 D5
Banfor Ct SM6 . . . . 60 C4
Bank Ave CR4 . . . . 40 D7
Bank La Crawley RH10 . . . . 201 D6
Kingston u T KT2 . . . . 17 E1
Roehampton SW15 . . . . 7 E2
Bank Mews SM1 . . . . 59 C4
Bank Rd GU11 . . . . 105 D1
Bank Willow TW10 . . . . 17 B5
Bank's La KT11, KT24 . . . . . 93 B5
Bankfoot Rd BR1 . . . . 24 E4
Bankhurst Rd SE4, SE6 . . . . 23 F8
Banks House TW7 . . . . 5 E5
Banks Rd RH10 . . . . 202 C5
Banks Way GU1 . . . . 109 F4
Bankside Heath End GU9 . . 125 F7
South Croydon CR2 . . . . 61 F4
Woking GU21 . . . . 69 B1
Bankside Cl Biggin Hill TN16 . 83 C1
Carshalton SM5 . . . . 59 E4
Elstead GU8 . . . . 148 D3
Isleworth TW7 . . . . 5 F3
Bankside Dr KT7 . . . . 56 B8
Bankside Way ❹ SE19 . . . . . 22 E2
Banning House ❹ SW19 . . . 19 D7
Bannister Cl
Streatham SW2 . . . . 22 A7
Witley GU8 . . . . 170 F6
Bannister's Rd GU2 . . . . . 129 F7
Banstead Cty Inf Sch SM7 . . 77 F4
Banstead Cty Jun Sch
SM7 . . . . 77 F4
Banstead Downs Golf Club
SM2 . . . . 78 A8
Banstead Rd Banstead SM7 . 77 D2
Belmont SM2 . . . . 77 D7
Caterham CR3 . . . . 100 A7
East Ewell KT17 . . . . 77 D7
Purley CR8 . . . . 80 A8
Sutton SM2, SM5 . . . . 59 E3
Banstead Rd S SM2 . . . . . . 59 D1
Banstead Sta SM7 . . . . 77 F5
Banstead Way SM6 . . . . 60 E5
Barbara Cl TW17 . . . . 34 B4
Barber Cl RH10 . . . . 202 C2
Barber Dr GU6 . . . . 174 E4
Barberry Way GU17 . . . . . . 64 F2
Barbon Cl GU15 . . . . 66 D3
Barclay Cl KT23 . . . . 94 B3
Barclay Rd CR0, CR9 . . . . . . 61 D7
Barcombe Ave SW2 . . . . . . 21 F6
Bardney Rd SM4 . . . . 40 B5
Bardolph Ave CR0 . . . . 62 F2
Bardolph Rd TW9 . . . . 6 F4
Bardon Wlk GU21 . . . . 69 B2
Bardsley Cl CR0 . . . . 61 F7
Bardsley Dr GU9 . . . . 146 A7
Barfield Ct ❽ RH1 . . . . . . 119 A3
Barfield Sch GU10 . . . . . . 126 B3
Barfields RH1 . . . . 120 C2
Barford La GU10 . . . . 167 E1
Barfreston Way SE20 . . . . . 43 B8
Bargate Cl KT3 . . . . 39 A2
Bargate Ct GU2 . . . . 108 E1
Bargate Rise GU7 . . . . 150 C4
Barge Cl GU11 . . . . 105 E5
Bargery Rd SE6 . . . . 24 B7
Bargrove Cl ❽ SE20 . . . . . . 23 A1
Bargrove Cres SE6 . . . . 23 F6
Barham Cl KT13 . . . . 53 C6
Barham Rd
Croydon CR0, CR9 . . . . 61 C5
Wimbledon SW20 . . . . 19 A1
Barhatch La GU6 . . . . 175 B6
Barhatch Rd GU6 . . . . 174 F4
Baring Rd CR0, CR9 . . . . . . 43 A1
Barker Gn RG12 . . . . 27 B4
Barker House SE21 . . . . 22 E5
Barker Rd KT16 . . . . 32 E2
Barker Wlk SW16 . . . . 21 D5
Barkham Rd RG40, RG41 . . . 25 A5
Barkhart Dr RG40 . . . . 25 C7
Barkhart Gdns RG40 . . . . . 25 C7
Barks Mead GU47 . . . . 45 E2
Barley Cl RH10 . . . . 201 D5
Barley Mow Cl GU21 . . . . . . 68 D2
Barley Mow Ct RH3 . . . . . . 116 C1
Barley Mow Hill GU35 . . . . 187 A6
Barley Mow La GU21 . . . . . . 68 D3
Barley Mow Rd TW20 . . . . . 11 C3
Barley Mow Way TW17 . . . . 34 A5
Barleymead RH6 . . . . 161 B4
Barlow Cl SM6 . . . . 60 E3
Barlow Rd Crawley RH11 . . 200 E3
Hampton TW12 . . . . 16 A1
Barmeston Rd SE6 . . . . 24 B6
Barmouth Rd CR0 . . . . 62 D8
Barn Cl Ashford TW15 . . . . . 14 B3
Bracknell RG12 . . . . 27 D7
Camberley GU15 . . . . 65 C6
Epsom KT18 . . . . 76 D5
Oxshott KT22 . . . . 74 D4
Woodmansterne SM7 . . . . . . 78 D4
Barn Cres CR8 . . . . 80 D6
Barn Field SM7 . . . . 78 B5
Barn Meadow La KT23 . . . . 93 F3
Barn Rd KT15 . . . . 52 B2

Barnard Cl Frimley GU16 . . . 85 [D]
Sunbury TW16 . . . . 15 [ ]
Wallington SM6 . . . . 60 [ ]
Barnard Ct ❶**1**
Knaphill GU21 . . . . 68 [ ]
Streatham SW16 . . . . 21 [ ]
Barnard Gdns KT3 . . . . 39 [ ]
Barnard Rd Chelsham CR6 . 102 [ ]
Mitcham CR4 . . . . 41 [ ]
Barnards Pl CR2 . . . . 61 [ ]
Barnato Cl KT14 . . . . 71 [ ]
Barnby Rd GU21 . . . . 68 [ ]
Barncroft GU9 . . . . 125 [ ]
Barnes Bridge Sta SW13 . . . 7 [ ]
Barnes Cl GU14 . . . . 85 [ ]
Barnes Ct CR7 . . . . 42 [ ]
Barnes End KT3 . . . . 39 [ ]
Barnes High St SW13 . . . . . . 7 [ ]
Barnes Hospl SW14 . . . . 7 [ ]
Barnes Rd Farncombe GU7 . 150 [ ]
Frimley GU16 . . . . 85 [ ]
Barnes Wallis Dr
KT13, KT14 . . . . 71 [ ]
Barnett Cl Leatherhead KT22 . 95 [ ]
Wonersh GU5 . . . . 152 [ ]
Barnett Ct RG12 . . . . 27 [ ]
Barnett Gr GU6 . . . . 174 [ ]
Barnett La Lightwater GU18 . 66 [ ]
Wonersh GU5 . . . . 152 [ ]
Barnett Row GU4 . . . . 109 [ ]
Barnett Wood La
Ashtead KT21, KT22 . . . . 75 [ ]
Leatherhead KT22 . . . . 95 [ ]
Barnett's Shaw RH8 . . . . . 122 [ ]
Barnfield Cranleigh GU6 . . 174 [ ]
New Malden KT3 . . . . 38 [ ]
Barnfield Ave Croydon CR0 . 62 [ ]
Kingston u T KT2 . . . . 17 [ ]
Mitcham CR4 . . . . 41 [ ]
Barnfield Cl Coulsdon CR5 . 100 [ ]
Wandsworth SW17 . . . . 20 [ ]
Barnfield Cotts RH7 . . . . . 165 [ ]
Barnfield Gdns KT2 . . . . . . 17 [ ]
Barnfield Rd
Crawley RH10, RH11 . . . . . 201 [ ]
South Croydon CR2 . . . . 61 [ ]
Tatsfield TN16 . . . . 103 [ ]
Barnfield Way RH8 . . . . . . 123 [ ]
Barnfield Wood Cl BR3 . . . . 44 [ ]
Barnfield Wood Rd BR3 . . . 44 [ ]
Barnhill Ave BR2 . . . . 44 [ ]
Barnlea Cl TW13 . . . . 15 [ ]
Barnmead GU24 . . . . 49 [ ]
Barnmead Rd BR3 . . . . 43 [ ]
Barns The GU8 . . . . 149 [ ]
Barnsbury Cl KT3 . . . . 38 [ ]
Barnsbury Cres KT5 . . . . . . 38 [ ]
Barnsbury Cty Inf & Jun
Schs GU27 . . . . 89 [ ]
Barnsbury La KT5 . . . . 38 [ ]
Barnscroft SW20 . . . . 39 [ ]
Barnsfold La RH12 . . . . . . 213 [ ]
Barnsford Cres GU24 . . . . . 68 [ ]
Barnsley Cl GU12 . . . . 86 [ ]
Barnsnap Cl RH12 . . . . . . 217 [ ]
Barnway TW20 . . . . 11 [ ]
Barnwood Cl
Crawley RH10 . . . . 202 [ ]
Guildford GU3 . . . . 108 [ ]
Barnwood Ct GU2, GU3 . . . 108 [ ]
Barnwood Cty Inf Sch
GU2, GU3 . . . . 108 [ ]
Barnwood Rd GU2, GU3 . . . 108 [ ]
Barnyard The KT20 . . . . 97 [ ]
Baron Cl SM2 . . . . 59 [ ]
Baron Ct CR4 . . . . 40 [ ]
Baron Gr CR4 . . . . 40 [ ]
Baron's Hurst KT18 . . . . . . 76 [ ]
Baron's Way RH2 . . . . 139 [ ]
Baron's Wlk CR0 . . . . 43 [ ]
Barons Cl SM5 . . . . 60 [ ]
Barons The TW1 . . . . 6 [ ]
Barons Way TW20 . . . . 12 [ ]
Baross Rd GU12 . . . . 90 [ ]
Barossa Rd GU15 . . . . 65 [ ]
Barr Beacon SE23 . . . . 23 [ ]
Barr's La GU21 . . . . 88 [ ]
Barracane Dr RG45 . . . . 45 [ ]
Barrack Path ❽ GU21 . . . . . 68 [ ]
Barrack Rd
Aldershot GU11 . . . . 105 [ ]
Guildford GU2 . . . . 109 [ ]
Hounslow TW4 . . . . 4 [ ]
Barracks Hall CR2 . . . . 80 [ ]
Barrens Brae GU22 . . . . 70 [ ]
Barrens Cl GU22 . . . . 90 [ ]
Barrens Pk GU22 . . . . 90 [ ]
Barrett Cres RG40 . . . . 25 [ ]
Barrett Rd KT22, KT23 . . . . 94 [ ]
Barrhill Rd SW2 . . . . 21 [ ]
Barricane GU21 . . . . 89 [ ]
Barrie Cl CR5 . . . . 79 [ ]
Barrie Rd GU9 . . . . 125 [ ]
Barrihurst La GU6 . . . . . . 173 [D]
Barringer Sq SW17 . . . . 21 [ ]
Barrington Ct
Dorking RH4 . . . . 136 [A]
Staines TW18 . . . . 12 [ ]
Barrington Lodge KT13 . . . 53 [ ]
Barrington Rd Cheam SM3 . . 40 [A]
Crawley RH10 . . . . 201 [ ]
Dorking RH4 . . . . 136 [A]
Horsham RH13 . . . . 217 [ ]
Purley CR8 . . . . 79 [ ]
Barrington Wlk ❻ SE19 . . . . 22 [ ]
Barrow Ave SM5 . . . . 59 [ ]

arrow Ct SE6 . . . . .24 F7
arrow Green Rd
  Ixted RH8 . . . . .122 C6
  Pandridge RH9 . . . . .122 C6
arrow Hedges Cl SM5 . . . . . .59 E3
arrow Hedges Prim Sch
  SM2, SM5 . . . . .59 E3
arrow Hedges Way
  SM2, SM5 . . . . .59 E3
arrow Hill K1 . . . . .57 E8
arrow Hill Ct KT4 . . . . .57 E8
arrow Hills Sch GU8 . .170 E4
arrow Rd Croydon CR0 . . . .61 A5
  treatham SW19 . . . . .21 D2
arrowsfield CR2 . . . . .81 A7
arry Cl RH10 . . . . .201 E3
arry Sq RG12 . . . . .27 D2
arry Terr TW15 . . . . .13 F6
arst The GU1 . . . . .130 D8
arsons Cl SE20 . . . . .23 C1
arston Rd SE27 . . . . .22 C5
arstowcres SW2 . . . . .21 F7
artholomew Cl GU27 . .208 D8
artholomew Ct RH4 . . . .136 A6
artholomew Way RH12 . .218 A7
artlett St CR0, CR2 . . . . . .61 D5
artlett Terr TW11 . . . . .34 B3
arten Cres RH19 . . . . . . .206 A8
arton Cl BR2 . . . . .44 D6
arton Gn KT3 . . . . .38 D7
arton Pl GU1 . . . . .110 B4
arton Rd GU5 . . . . .152 A7
arton The KT11 . . . . .73 D7
arton House WD19 . . . .202 B4
artons Way GU21 . . . . .70 C5
arwell Bsns Pk KT9 . . . . .56 D2
arwood Ave BR4 . . . . .44 B1
asden Gr TW13 . . . . .16 A6
asemoors RG12 . . . . .27 E7
ashford Way RH10 . . . . . .202 D8
asil Gdns Croydon CR0 . .43 D1
  West Norwood SE27 . . . . . . .22 C3
asildene Rd TW4, TW5 . . .4 D4
asildon Cl SM2 . . . . .59 B3
asildon Way RH11 . . . . .200 E2
asing Cl KT1 . . . . .37 D7
asing Dr GU11 . . . . .126 B7
asing House SE6 . . . . .24 A4
asing Rd SM7 . . . . .77 F4
asing Way KT7 . . . . .36 F2
asingfield Rd KT7 . . . . . . .37 A2
asinghall Gdns SM2 . . . .59 B1
askerville Rd SW18 . . . . .20 E8
asset C KT15 . . . . .52 C1
asset Ct Frimley GU16 . . .85 E8
  Sutton SM2 . . . . .59 B2
assett Gdns TW7 . . . . .5 C7
assett Rd Crawley RH10 . .202 D3
  Woking GU22 . . . . .70 C3
assetts Hill RH7 . . . . .165 A2
assingham Rd SW18 . . . .20 C8
ast and Ball La
  Rowledge GU10 . . . . .146 A5
  Wrecclesham GU10, GU9 . .146 A6
atavia Cl TW16 . . . . .35 C8
atavia Rd TW16 . . . . .15 A2
atcombe Mead RG12 . . . .27 E2
atford Gr GU12 . . . . .126 F8
atemans Ct RH10 . . . . . .202 A3
ates Cres Croydon CR0 . . .61 A5
  Streatham SW16 . . . . .21 C1
ates Wlk KT15 . . . . .52 C4
ateson Way GU21 . . . . . . .70 C5
ath Cl SE26 . . . . .23 A5
ath House Rd CR0, CR9 . .41 E1
ath Pas KT1 . . . . .37 D7
ath Rd Camberley GU15 . .65 D6
  Cranford TW3, TW4, TW5 . . .4 E5
  Harlington TW6, UB7, TW5 . .3 B6
  Harmondsworth TW6, UB7 . .2 E6
  Hounslow TW3, TW4, TW5 . .4 A5
  Mitcham CR4 . . . . .40 D6
  Poyle SL3, UB7, TW6 . . . . . .1 E6
athgate Rd SW19 . . . . . .19 D5
athurst Ave SW19 . . . . . .40 A8
atsworth Rd CR4 . . . . .40 D6
att's Cnr GU10 . . . . .166 E7
atten Ave GU21 . . . . .88 E8
attenburg Wlk ⑩ SE19 . .22 E3
attersby Rd SE20 . . . . .23 D1
attle Cl SW19 . . . . .20 C2
attlebridge House RH1 . .119 B5
attlebridge La RH1 . . . . .119 B3
atts Hill RH2 . . . . .118 E3
atty's Barn Ct RG40 . . . . .25 D5
ay House SW2 . . . . .21 F7
audwin Rd SE6 . . . . .24 E6
avant Rd SW16 . . . . .41 F7
awtree Cl SM2 . . . . .59 C7
ax Cl GU6 . . . . .174 E2
axter Ave RH1 . . . . .118 F1
axter Cl RH10 . . . . .202 B4
ay Cl RH6 . . . . .160 E6
ay Dr RG12 . . . . .27 E8
ay Rd RG12 . . . . .27 E8
ay Tree Ave KT22 . . . . .95 A2
ayards CR6 . . . . .81 C1
aycroft Ct BR2 . . . . .44 F6
ayeux KT20 . . . . .97 E5
ayfield Ave GU16 . . . . .65 E2
ayfield Rd BR3 . . . . .160 E4
ayford Cl GU17 . . . . .65 A1
ayham Rd SM4 . . . . .40 B5
ayhorne La RH6 . . . . .161 C1
ayleaf Cl TW12 . . . . .16 D3

Baylis Wlk RH11 . . . . .201 B1
Bayliss Ct ② GU1 . . . . . . .130 C8
Baynards Rd RH12 . . . . . .195 A2
Bays Cl SE26 . . . . .23 C3
Baysfarm Ct TW6, UB7 . . . .2 C6
Baywood Cl GU14 . . . . .84 C5
Bazalgette Cl KT3 . . . . .38 D4
Bazalgette Gdns KT3 . . . . .38 D4
Beach Gr TW13 . . . . .16 A6
Beachborough Rd BR1 . . .24 C4
Beachy Rd RH11 . . . . .201 A1
Beacon Cl Banstead SM7 . . .77 D3
  Rowledge GU10 . . . . .146 A5
Beacon Ct Colnbrook SW3 . . .1 C7
  Horsham RH13 . . . . .218 A4
Beacon Gr SM5 . . . . .60 A6
Beacon Hill
  Dormansland RH7 . . . . . . .186 B8
  Woking GU21 . . . . .89 C8
Beacon Hill Ct GU26 . . . .188 D6
  GU26 . . . . .188 C6
Beacon Hill Rd
  Beacon Hill GU26 . . . . . . .188 D6
  Crondall GU10 . . . . .124 E8
Beacon Hill Cty Prim Sch
  GU26 . . . . .188 C6
Beacon Hill Rd
  Beacon Hill GU26 . . . . . . .188 D6
Beacon Rd TW19, TW6 . . . .3 A1
Beacon Rdbt TW6 . . . . .3 A1
Beacon Sch The KT20 . . . .77 E2
Beacon View Rd GU8 . . . .148 C2
Beacon Way SM7 . . . . .77 E3
Beaconsfield Pl KT17 . . . . .76 F7
Beaconsfield Rd
  Claygate KT10 . . . . .55 E3
  Kingston u T KT3 . . . . .38 D7
  Langley Vale KT18 . . . . .96 E8
  Old Woking GU22 . . . . .89 F7
  Surbiton KT5 . . . . .37 F2
  Thornton Heath CR0 . . . . . .42 D3
  Twickenham TW1 . . . . .6 B1
Beaconshaw BR1 . . . . .24 F1
Beadle Ct CR4 . . . . .40 E6
Beadles La RH8 . . . . .122 D4
Beadlow Cl SM4 . . . . .40 D3
Beadman Pl SE27 . . . . .22 B4
Beadman St SE27 . . . . .22 B4
Beadnell Rd SE23 . . . . .23 D7
Beaford Gr SW20 . . . . .39 F6
Beagle Cl TW13 . . . . .15 B4
Beale Cl RG40 . . . . .25 E7
Beale Ct RH11 . . . . .201 A3
Beale's La KT14 . . . . .53 B7
Beales La GU10 . . . . .145 F7
Beales Rd KT23 . . . . .94 B1
Bealeswood La GU10 . . . .166 F6
Beam Hollow GU9 . . . . . .125 C7
Bean Oak Rd RG40 . . . . . . .25 F6
Bear La GU9 . . . . .125 C3
Bear Rd TW13 . . . . .15 D4
Beard Rd KT2 . . . . .17 F3
Beard's Hill TW12 . . . . . . .36 A8
Beard's Rd TW15, TW16 . .14 E2
Beardell St SE19 . . . . .22 F2
Beards Hill Cl TW12 . . . . .36 A8
Beare Green Cotts RH5 . .157 D4
Beare Green Ct RH5 . . . .157 D4
Bearfield Rd KT2 . . . . .17 E1
Bears Den KT20 . . . . .97 F5
Bears Rail Pk SL4 . . . . . . .10 F8
Bearsden Way RH12 . . . .216 D3
Bearwood Cl KT15 . . . . . . .52 A4
Bearwood Cotts GU10 . .145 F7
Beasley's Ait La
  TW16, TW17 . . . . .34 F3
Beatrice Ave SW16 . . . . . .41 F7
Beatrice Rd Oxted RH8 . .122 E6
  Richmond TW10 . . . . .6 F2
Beatrix Potter Prim Sch
  SW18 . . . . .20 C7
Beattie Cl
  East Bedfont TW14 . . . . . . .14 F7
  Little Bookham KT23 . . . . . .93 F3
Beatty Ave GU1 . . . . .110 A2
Beauchamp Rd
  East Molesey KT8 . . . . .36 C4
  South Norwood CR7, SE25 . .42 D8
  Sutton SM1 . . . . .59 A6
  Twickenham TW1 . . . . .17 A8
Beauclare Cl KT21 . . . . . . .95 D6
Beauclerc Cty Inf Sch
  TW16 . . . . .35 C6
Beauclere House SM2 . . . .59 C3
Beauclerk Cl TW13 . . . . . .15 B7
Beauclerk House ⑩ SW16 . .21 E5
Beaufield Gate GU27 . . . .208 D7
Beaufort Cl Putney SW15 . .19 B8
  Reigate RH2 . . . . .117 F2
  Woking GU22 . . . . .70 C3
Beaufort Cty Prim Sch
  GU21 . . . . .68 F3
Beaufort Gdns Heston TW5 . .5 A8
  North Ascot SL5 . . . . .28 E8
  South Norwood SW16 . . . . .21 F1
Beaufort House SW20 . . . .39 D8
Beaufort Rd Farnham GU9 . .125 C3
  Kingston u T KT1, KT5, KT6 . .37 E5
  Reigate RH2 . . . . .117 F2
  Richmond TW10 . . . . .17 C4
  Twickenham TW1 . . . . .17 B8
  Woking GU22 . . . . .70 C3
Beaufort Way KT17 . . . . . .58 A3
Beaufoy House ⑧ SE27 . . .22 B5
Beaufront Cl GU15 . . . . . . .66 A7
Beaufront Rd GU15 . . . . . .66 B7
Beaulieu Ave SE26 . . . . . . .23 B4
Beaulieu Cl Bracknell RG12 . .28 A6

Beaulieu Cl continued
  Hounslow TW4 . . . . .4 F2
  Mitcham CR4 . . . . .41 A8
  ③ Twickenham TW1 . . . . . . .6 D1
Beaulieu Gdns GU47 . . . . .64 C5
Beaulieu Pk RH10 . . . . . . .85 F8
Beaumaris Par GU16 . . . . .85 F8
Beaumont Ave TW9 . . . . . . .6 F4
Beaumont Cl RH11 . . . . . .200 E5
Beaumont Ct Ascot SL5 . . .28 F5
  Mitcham CR4 . . . . .41 A7
Beaumont Dr TW15 . . . . . .14 D3
Beaumont Gdns RG12 . . . .27 E4
Beaumont Gr GU11 . . . . . .104 E2
Beaumont House
  ① Streatham SW2 . . . . . . .21 E7
  Wimbledon SW19 . . . . .20 A5
Beaumont Jun Sch GU11 . .104 E2
Beaumont Pl[7] Iver 1 A2
Beaumont Prim Sch CR8 . .80 A5
Beaumont Rd Purley CR8 . .80 A6
  Putney SW15, SW19 . . . . . .19 E8
  South Norwood SE19 . . . . . .22 C2
Beaumont Sq GU6 . . . . . .174 F3
Beaumont Terr ① SE13 . .24 E8
Beaumonts RH1 . . . . .139 F1
Beaver Cl Hampton TW12 . .36 B8
  Horsham RH12 . . . . .217 F6
  ⑨ Penge SE20 . . . . .23 A1
  Wokingham RG41 . . . . .25 B3
Beaver Water World
  TN16 . . . . .103 B5
Beavers Comm Prim Sch
  TW4 .4 C4
Beavers Cres TW4 . . . . .4 C4
Beavers Hill GU9 . . . . .124 F2
Beavers La TW4 . . . . .4 C4
Beavers Rd GU9 . . . . .125 A2
Beck Cl BR3 . . . . .43 D6
Beck Gdns GU9 . . . . .125 A6
Beck Ind Est The GU12 . .126 D8
Beck La BR3 . . . . .43 D6
Beck River Pk BR3 . . . . . . .44 A8
Beck Way BR3 . . . . .44 A6
Beckenham Bsns Ctr BR3 . .23 E2
Beckenham Ct BR3 . . . . . .44 B7
Beckenham Gr BR2 . . . . . .44 D7
Beckenham Hill Rd
  BR3, SE6 . . . . .24 C3
Beckenham Hill Sta SE6 . .24 C3
Beckenham Hospl BR3 . . .44 A6
Beckenham Junction Sta
  BR3 . . . . .44 A8
Beckenham La BR1, BR2 . .44 F7
Beckenham Place Pk BR3 . .24 A1
Beckenham Rd
  Beckenham BR3 . . . . .43 E8
  Penge BR3 . . . . .44 A8
  West Wickham BR3, BR4 . . .44 C2
Beckenshaw Gdns SM7 . . .78 E4
Becket Cl Croydon SE25 . .43 A3
  ② Merton SW19 . . . . .40 B8
Becket Wood RH5 . . . . . .158 C4
Beckett Ave CR8 . . . . .80 B4
Beckett Cl Streatham SW16 . .21 D6
  Wokingham RG40 . . . . .25 E6
Beckett La RH11 . . . . .181 D1
Beckett Way ⑪ RH19 . . . .205 F8
Beckett Wlk BR3 . . . . .23 E2
Becketts Cl TW14 . . . . .4 B1
Becketts Pl KT1 . . . . .37 D8
Beckford Ave RG12 . . . . . .27 B3
Beckford Rd CR0, SE25 . . .42 F3
Beckford Way RH10 . . . . .202 B2
Beckingham Rd GU2 . . . .109 A2
Beckley Cotts KT23 . . . . . .94 C1
Beckmead Sch BR4 . . . . . .44 A1
Beckway Rd SW16 . . . . . . .41 D7
Beckworth Pl KT13 . . . . . .53 B6
Beclands Rd SW17 . . . . . . .21 A2
Becmead Ave SW16 . . . . . .21 D4
Becondale Rd SE19 . . . . . .22 E3
Bedale Cl RH11 . . . . .201 C4
Beddington Cross CR0 . . .41 E2
Beddington Farm Rd
  Croydon CR0 . . . . .41 F2
  Wallington CR0, CR9 . . . . . .41 E1
Beddington Gdns
  SM5, SM6 . . . . .60 A4
Beddington Gr SM6 . . . . . .60 D6
Beddington Inf Sch SM6 . .60 C6
Beddington La CR0 . . . . . .41 D4
Beddington Manor SM2 . .59 C4
Beddington Park Cotts
  CR0 . . . . .60 D7
Beddington Park Prim Sch
  CR0 . . . . .60 D7
Beddlestead La CR6 . . . .103 A6
Bedelsford Sch KT1 . . . . . .37 E6
Bedens Rd
  East Bedfont TW14 . . . . . . .14 F7
  Mitcham CR4 . . . . .41 A7
Bedfont Cl TW19 . . . . .2 B4
Bedfont Green Cl TW14 . .14 C7
Bedfont Ind Pk N TW15 . .14 E6
Bedfont Ind Pk TW14 . . . . .3 E1
Bedfont Jun Sch TW14 . . .14 F8
Bedfont La
  East Bedfont TW13, TW14 . .14 C6
  Feltham TW13, TW14 . . . . .14 D6
  Stanwell TW19 . . . . .2 F1
Bedfont Lane Sta TW14 . .14 E6
Bedfont Rd
  East Bedfont TW13, TW14 . .14 D6
  Feltham TW13, TW14 . . . . .14 C6
  Stanwell TW19 . . . . .2 E1
Bedford Ave GU16 . . . . . . .85 F6
Bedford Cl GU16 . . . . .85 F6
  ⑥ Richmond TW9 . . . . .6 F3
South Norwood SE19 . . . . . .42 F8
Bedford Hill Balham SW12 . .21 B6

Bedford Hill continued
  Streatham SW16 . . . . .21 B6
  Upper Tooting SW12,
  SW16, SW17 . . . . .21 B6
Bedford House ③ GU1 . .130 C8
Bedford La Frimley GU16 . .85 F6
  Sunningdale SL5 . . . . .30 A5
Bedford Pk CR0 . . . . .42 C1
Bedford Pl CR0 . . . . .42 D1
Bedford Rd Guildford GU1 . .130 D8
  Horsham RH13 . . . . .217 D1
  North Cheam KT4 . . . . .58 C8
  Twickenham TW2 . . . . .16 D5
Bedgebury Gdns SW19 . . .19 E6
Bedlow Way CR0 . . . . .60 F6
Bedser Cl CR7 . . . . .42 C6
Bedster Gdns KT8 . . . . . . .36 B6
Bedwardine Rd SE19 . . . . .22 E1
Beech Ave Brentford TW8 . . .6 B7
  Camberley GU15 . . . . .65 D4
  Effingham KT24 . . . . .113 D6
  Farnham GU10 . . . . .146 C5
  South Croydon CR2 . . . . . . .61 D1
  Tatsfield TN16 . . . . .103 D8
Beech Cl Ashford TW15 . . .14 D3
  Blindley Heath RH7 . . . . . .163 E8
  Byfleet KT14 . . . . .71 E7
  Carshalton SM5 . . . . .59 F8
  Chiddingfold GU8 . . . . . . .191 A4
  Cobham KT11 . . . . .74 A8
  Dorking RH4 . . . . .136 A8
  Effingham KT24 . . . . .113 D7
  Hersham KT12 . . . . .54 B5
  Putney SW15 . . . . .19 A8
  Stanwell TW19 . . . . .13 D8
  Sunbury TW16 . . . . .35 D7
  Wimbledon SW19 . . . . .19 C2
  Woking GU21 . . . . .69 C7
Beech Copse CR2 . . . . .61 E5
Beech Cres KT20 . . . . .116 C5
Beech Ct Beckenham BR3 . .23 F1
  ④ Guildford GU1 . . . . .130 E8
  ⑦ West Norwood SW16 . . .22 A3
Beech Dr Blackwater GU17 . .64 D4
  Kingswood KT20 . . . . .97 F5
  Reigate RH2 . . . . .118 D1
  Send Marsh GU23 . . . . .91 A3
Beech Farm Rd CR6 . . . . .102 D8
Beech Fields RH19 . . . . . .185 E3
Beech Gdns
  Crawley Down RH10 . . . . .204 A8
  Woking GU21 . . . . .69 E4
Beech Glen RG12 . . . . .27 B5
Beech Gr Addlestone KT15 . .52 B6
  Burgh Heath KT18 . . . . .77 B2
  Caterham CR3 . . . . .100 E1
  Great Bookham KT23 . . . .114 A8
  Guildford GU2 . . . . .108 F1
  Kingston u T KT3 . . . . .38 D6
  Mitcham CR4 . . . . .41 D5
  Pirbright GU24 . . . . .87 C7
  Pirbright GU24 . . . . .87 D7
  Wimbledon SW19 . . . . .19 D3
Beech Hanger End GU26 . .188 B3
Beech Hill
  Bowlhead Green GU8 . . . .189 F8
  Headley Down GU35 . . . . .187 B5
  Woking GU22 . . . . .89 D4
Beech Hill Rd
  Headley Down GU35 . . . . .187 A5
  Sunningdale SL5 . . . . .29 F3
Beech Holme RH10 . . . . . .204 B8
Beech Holt RH4 . . . . .136 B6
Beech House Heston TW5 . . .4 E7
  New Addington CR0 . . . . . .63 B4
Beech House Rd CR0, CR9 . .61 D7
Beech La Flexford GU3 . . .107 A1
  Grayshott GU26 . . . . .188 B4
  Guildford GU2 . . . . .130 C6
Beech Lodge TW18 . . . . . .12 E3
Beech Rd Biggin Hill TN16 . .83 D2
  East Bedfont TW14 . . . . . . .14 E8
  Epsom KT18 . . . . .76 F4
  Farnborough GU14 . . . . . . .85 F6
  Frimley GU16 . . . . .85 F6
  Haslemere GU27 . . . . .208 D8
  Horsham RH13 . . . . .218 B5
  Merstham RH1 . . . . .99 C1
  Oatlands Park KT13 . . . . . .53 D6
  Reigate RH2 . . . . .118 A4
  Thornton Heath SW16 . . . .41 F6
  Weybridge KT13 . . . . .53 A6
Beech Tree Cl RH10 . . . . .201 D7
Beech Tree Dr GU9 . . . . .126 A5
Beech Tree La TW18 . . . . .33 B7
Beech Tree Pl SM1 . . . . . . .59 B5
Beech Way Epsom KT17 . . .76 F4
  Godalming GU7 . . . . .150 D3
  Selsdon CR2 . . . . .81 D8
  Twickenham TW13 . . . . . . .16 A5
Beech Wlk KT17 . . . . .77 A8
Beech Wood CR3 . . . . .100 F3
Beechcroft Ashstead KT21 . .95 F8
  Kingston u T KT3 . . . . .38 B8
Beechcroft Ave Kenley CR8 . .80 D4
  Kingston u T KT1, KT3 . . . . .38 C7
Beechcroft Cl Ascot SL5 . .29 C3
  Heston TW5 . . . . .5 A8
  Streatham SW16 . . . . .21 F3
Beechcroft Dr GU2 . . . . . .129 D6
Beechcroft Lodge SM2 . . .59 C3
Beechcroft Manor KT13 . .53 D7
Beechcroft Mansions
  SW16 . . . . .21 F3
Beechcroft Rd
  Chessington KT9 . . . . .56 F7

Beechcroft Rd continued
  Mortlake SW14 . . . . .7 C4
  Upper Tooting SW17 . . . . . .20 E6
Beechcroft Sch SW17 . . . .20 E6
Beechdene KT20 . . . . .97 B5
Beechen Cliff Way ⑨ TW7 . .5 F5
Beechen La KT20 . . . . .97 F2
Beechen Pl SE23 . . . . .23 C6
Beeches Ave The SM5 . . . .59 E3
Beeches Cl Kingswood KT20 . .98 A4
  Penge SE20 . . . . .43 C8
Beeches Cres RH10 . . . . .201 E4
Beeches Head RH19 . . . . .186 F5
Beeches La RH19 . . . . . . .206 D6
Beeches Rd Cheam SM3 . . .39 E1
  Upper Tooting SW17 . . . . . .20 E5
Beeches The Ash Vale GU12 . .85 F1
  Banstead SM7 . . . . .78 B3
  Bramley GU5 . . . . .151 F6
  Fetcham KT22 . . . . .94 E3
  Hounslow TW3 . . . . .5 B6
  Mitcham CR4 . . . . .40 E4
  Staines TW18 . . . . .13 A3
  West End GU24 . . . . .68 A6
Beechey Cl RH10 . . . . .183 B3
Beechey Way RH10 . . . . . .183 B3
Beechfield SM7 . . . . .78 B6
Beechfield Ct ⑦ CR0 . . . . .61 C6
Beechfield Rd SE6 . . . . . . .23 F7
Beeching Cl GU12 . . . . . . .106 B3
Beeching Way RH19 . . . . .185 E1
Beechland Cotts RH5 . . . .117 F7
Beechlawn GU1 . . . . .130 F8
Beechmeads KT11 . . . . . . .73 D6
Beechmont Ave GU25 . . . .31 C4
Beechmont Cl BR1 . . . . . . .24 E3
Beechmore Gdns SM3 . . . .58 D8
Beechnut Ind Est ⑨
  GU12 . . . . .105 B1
Beechnut Rd ⑧ GU12 . . .105 B1
Beecholme KT17 . . . . .77 C5
Beecholme Ave CR4 . . . . . .41 B8
Beecholme Fst Sch CR4 . .41 B8
Beechover Rd SE9 . . . . . . .17 F4
Beechside RH10 . . . . .201 E5
Beechtree Ave TW20 . . . . .11 B2
Beechvale ③ GU22 . . . . . .69 F1
Beechway GU1 . . . . .110 B2
Beechwood Ave
  Ashford TW16 . . . . .15 A2
  Kingswood KT20 . . . . .98 A6
  Oatlands Park KT13 . . . . . .53 E6
  Richmond TW9 . . . . .7 A6
  Staines TW18 . . . . .13 B2
  Thornton Heath CR7 . . . . . .42 B5
  Wallington CR5 . . . . .79 B4
Beechwood Cl
  Knaphill GU21 . . . . .68 E2
  Long Ditton K6 . . . . .37 D2
  North Ascot SL5 . . . . .8 F1
  Oatlands Park KT13 . . . . . .53 E6
Beechwood Ct
  Carshalton SM5 . . . . .59 F6
  Chiswick W4 . . . . .7 D8
  Sutton SM1 . . . . .59 A5
  Walton-on-T KT12 . . . . .54 A7
Beechwood Dr KT11 . . . . . .74 A8
Beechwood Gdns CR3 . . .101 A5
Beechwood La CR6 . . . . . .101 D8
Beechwood Manor KT13 . .53 E6
Beechwood Pk KT22 . . . . . .95 C5
Beechwood Rd
  Caterham CR3 . . . . .101 A5
  Knaphill GU21 . . . . .68 D2
  South Croydon CR2 . . . . . . .61 E2
  Wentworth GU25 . . . . .31 B1
Beechwood Villas RH1 . . .161 A7
Beechwoods Ct SE19 . . . . .22 F3
Beecot La KT12 . . . . .54 C8
Beeding Cl RH12 . . . . .218 A5
Beedingwood Dr RH12 . .218 F6
Beedon Dr RG12 . . . . .26 E7
Beehive La RG12 . . . . .26 C7
Beehive Rd
  Bracknell RG42, RG40 . . . .26 D7
  Staines TW18 . . . . .12 F3
Beehive Ring Rd RH6 . . . .182 B4
Beehive Way RH2 . . . . . . .139 B5
Beeleigh Rd SM4 . . . . .40 B5
Beeston Way TW14 . . . . . . .4 C1
Beeton's Ave GU12 . . . . . .106 A4
Beggar's Roost La
  SM1, SM2 . . . . .59 A4
Beggars La Chobham GU24 . .68 C8
  Gomshall RH5 . . . . .133 E4
Beggarshouse La RH6 . . .180 C8
Begonia ⑩ ① TW12 . . . . . .16 A2
Behenna Cl RH11 . . . . . . .200 E5
Beira St SW12 . . . . .21 B8
Belcroft Cl BR1 . . . . .24 F1
Beldam Bridge Rd GU24 . .68 A8
Beldham Gdns KT8 . . . . . . .36 B6
Beldham Rd GU10, GU9 . .145 F7
Belenoyd Ct SE25 . . . . .43 B5
Belfast Rd SE25 . . . . .43 B5
Belfield Rd KT19 . . . . .57 E3
Belfry The RH1 . . . . .118 F2
Belgrade Rd TW12 . . . . . . .36 B8
Belgrave Ct KT12 . . . . .54 B8
Belgrave Cres TW16 . . . . .35 B8
Belgrave Ct GU17 . . . . .64 D3
Belgrave Manor GU22 . . . .89 E8
Belgrave Rd Barnes SW13 . .7 F7

Belgrave Rd *continued*
Hounslow TW4 4 F4
Mitcham CR4 40 D6
South Norwood SE25 42 F5
Sunbury TW16 35 B8
Belgrave Wlk CR4 40 D6
Belgravia Ct RH6 161 B3
Belgravia Gdns BR1 24 E2
Belgravia House 1 TW11 17 C1
Belgravia Mews KT1 37 D5
Bell Bridge Rd KT16 32 F1
Bell Cl GU14 85 C6
Bell Cnr KT16 32 F2
Bell Cres CR5 99 B6
Bell Ct KT5 57 B8
Bell Ctr RH10 181 F2
Bell Dr SW18 19 E8
Bell Farm Jun Sch KT12 54 C6
Bell Foundry La RG40 25 C8
Bell Gn SE6 23 F4
Bell Green La
BR3, SE26, SE6 23 F4
Bell Hammer RH19 205 E8
Bell House 16 SW2 22 A8
Bell House Gdns RG41 25 B6
Bell La Blackwater GU17 64 C5
Fetcham KT22 94 D4
Rowledge GU10 145 E3
Twickenham TW1 17 A7
Bell Lane Cl KT22 94 D4
Bell Meadow Dulwich SE19 22 E4
Godstone RH9 121 C3
Bell Pl GU19 47 F3
Bell Rd East Molesey KT8 36 D4
Hounslow TW3 5 B3
Kingsley Green GU27 208 B3
Warnham RH12 217 A8
Bell St RH2 139 B8
Bell Vale La
Haslemere GU27 208 C4
Lurgashall GU27 208 C4
Bell View BR3 23 F1
Bell Weir Cl TW19 12 B6
Bellamy House Heston TW5 5 A8
Upper Tooting SW17 20 D4
Bellamy Rd RH10 202 C2
Bellamy St SW12 21 B8
Belland Dr GU11 104 E1
Bellasis Ave SW2 21 E6
Belle Vue Cl
Aldershot GU12 105 D2
Staines TW18 33 A8
Belle Vue Ent Ctr GU12 105 E2
Belle Vue Inf Sch GU12 105 D2
Belle Vue Rd GU12 105 D2
Bellever Hill GU15 65 E5
Bellevue Pk CR7 42 C5
Bellevue Rd
Kingston u T KT1 37 E6
Upper Tooting SW17 20 E8
Bellew Rd GU16 86 B7
Bellew St SW17 20 C5
Bellfield CR0 62 F3
Bellfields Ct GU1 109 C5
Bellfields Rd GU1 109 D3
Bellingham Cl GU15 66 C4
Bellingham Gn SE6 24 A5
Bellingham Rd SE6 24 C5
Bellingham Sta SE6 24 B5
Bellingham Trad Est SE6 24 B6
Bellmarsh Rd KT15 52 B6
Bellmore Ct 5 CR0 42 F1
Bello Cl SE24, SW2 22 B7
Belloc Cl RH10 202 C7
Belloc Ct RH13 218 A3
Bells La SL3 1 B4
Belltrees Gr 1 SW16 22 A3
Bellwether La RH1 162 B7
Belmont KT13 53 C4
Belmont Ave
Guildford GU2 108 F4
West Barnes KT3 39 A5
Belmont Cl GU14 84 F7
Belmont Mews GU15 65 C3
Belmont Rd
Beckenham BR3 43 F7
Belmont SM2 59 A1
Camberley GU15 65 C4
Crowthorne RG45 45 B6
Croydon SE25 43 B4
Leatherhead KT22 95 A5
Reigate RH2 139 C8
Twickenham TW2 16 D6
Wallington SM6 60 C5
Belmont Rise SM1, SM2 58 F3
Belmont Sch RH5 155 D6
Belmont Sta SM2 59 B1
Belmore Ave GU22 70 D3
Belsize Gdns SM1 59 B6
Belstone Mews GU14 85 A7
Beltane Dr SW19 19 D5
Belthorn Cres SW12 21 C8
Belton Rd GU15 65 E5
Belvedere Ave SW19 19 E3
Belvedere Cl Esher KT10 55 B5
Guildford GU2 109 B3
Teddington TW11 16 E3
Weybridge KT13 53 A5
Belvedere Ct
Blackwater GU17 64 D3
Crawley RH10 202 B7
8 Kingston u T KT2 18 A1
Belvedere Dr SW19 19 E3
Belvedere Gdns KT8 36 A4
Belvedere Gr SW19 19 E3
Belvedere Rd
Biggin Hill TN16 83 F1
Farnborough GU14 85 C2
Penge SE19 22 F1
Belvedere Sq SW19 19 E3
Belvoir Cl GU16 65 F1
Belvoir Lodge SE22 23 A8
Belvoir Rd SE22 23 A8
Benbow La GU8 193 C4
Benbrick Rd GU2 130 A8
Benbury Cl BR1 24 C3
Bence The TW20 32 B6
Bench Field CR2 61 F5
Benchfield Cl RH19 186 B1
Bencombe Rd CR8 80 A5
Bencroft Rd SW16 21 C1
Bencurtis Pk BR4 63 D8
Bendon Valley SW18 20 B8
Benedict Dr TW14 14 D8
Benedict Fst Sch CR4 40 D6
Benedict Prim Sch CR4 40 D6
Benedict Rd CR4 40 D6
Benedict Wharf CR4 40 E6
Benen-Stock Rd TW19 2 A2
Benett Gdns SW16 41 E7
Benfleet Cl Cobham KT11 73 E7
Sutton SM1 59 C7
Benham Cl Chessington KT9 56 C4
Coulsdon CR5, CR8 80 B1
Benham Gdns TW3, TW4 4 F2
Benhams Cl RH6 161 A5
Benhams Dr RH6 161 A5
Benhill Ave SM1 59 C6
Benhill Rd SM1 59 D6
Benhill Wood Rd SM1 59 C6
Benhilton Gdns SM1 59 B7
Benhurst Cl CR2 62 D1
Benhurst Ct 13 Penge SE20 43 B8
Streatham SW16 22 A3
Benhurst Gdns CR2 62 C1
Benhurst La SW16 22 A3
Benin St SE13 24 D8
Benjamin Ct TW15 14 C1
Benjamin Rd RH10 202 D4
Benner La GU24 68 A7
Bennet Cl KT1 37 C8
Bennett Cl Cobham KT11 73 A6
Crawley RH10 202 B2
Bennett Ct GU15 65 C5
Bennett House 2 SW4 21 D8
Bennett St W4 7 E8
Bennett Way GU4 111 B6
Bennetts Ave CR0 62 E8
Bennetts Cl CR4, SW16 41 B8
Bennetts Farm Pl KT23 93 F2
Bennetts Rd RH13 217 E1
Bennetts Way CR0 62 F8
Bennetts Wood RH5 178 C5
Bens Acre RH13 218 A2
Bensbury Cl SW15 19 C8
Bensham Cl CR7 42 C5
Bensham Gr CR7 42 C7
Bensham La CR0, CR7 42 B3
Bensham Manor Rd
CR0, CR7 42 C5
Bensham Manor Sch CR7 42 C4
Bensington Ct TW14 3 D1
Benson Cl TW3 5 A3
Benson Prim sch CR0 62 E7
Benson Rd
Croydon CR0, CR9 61 A7
Forest Hill SE23 23 C7
Benson's La RH12 199 C1
Bentall Sh Ctr The 10 KT2 37 E7
Benthall Gdns CR8 80 C2
Bentham Ave GU21 70 C4
Bentley Cl SW19 20 A5
Bentley Copse GU15 66 B4
Bentley Dr KT13 53 A2
Benton's La SE27 22 C4
Benton's Rise SE27 22 D3
Bentsbrook Cl RH5 136 B3
Bentsbrook Cotts RH5 136 B3
Bentsbrook Pk RH5 136 B3
Bentsbrook Rd RH5 136 B3
Benwell Ct TW16 35 A8
Benwell Rd GU24 88 A8
Benwick Ct SE20 43 C8
Benwood Ct SM1 59 C7
Beomonds KT16 33 A2
Beomonds Row KT16 33 A2
Berberis Cl GU1 109 C3
Bere Rd RG12 27 E3
Beresford Ave
Tolworth KT5 38 C2
Twickenham TW1 6 C1
Beresford Cl GU16 85 F6
Beresford Ct 11 TW1 6 C1
Beresford Gdns TW4 4 F2
Beresford House SE21 22 E5
Beresford Rd Belmont SM2 58 F3
Dorking RH4 136 B7
Kingston u T KT2 37 F8
Kingston u T, Norbiton KT3 38 C5
Bergenia Ct GU24 67 E6
Berkeley Ave TW4 4 A5
Berkeley Cl Crawley RH11 200 E2
Stanwell TW19 12 D6
Berkeley Cres GU16 86 A8
Berkeley Ct Ashstead KT21 75 F1
Oatlands Park KT13 53 E8
16 Streatham SW2 22 A7
Wallington SM6 60 C6
Berkeley Dr
East Molesey KT8 36 A6
Winkfield SL4 9 B7
Berkeley Gdns
Claygate KT10 56 A4
Berkeley Gdns *continued*
Pyrford KT14 70 F5
Walton-on-T KT12 34 F2
Berkeley House 11 TW8 6 D8
Berkeley Pl Epsom KT18 76 D4
Wimbledon SW19 19 D2
Berkeley Prim Sch TW5 4 D7
Berkeley Waye TW5 4 D7
Berkeleys The KT22 94 E3
Berkley Cl TW2 16 E5
Berkley Ct Guildford GU1 109 E1
7 Twickenham TW1 17 A8
Berkley Mews TW16 35 C6
Berkshire Cl CR3 100 D5
Berkshire House SE6 24 A4
Berkshire Rd GU15 65 F8
Berkshire Sq CR4 41 E5
Berkshire Way
Bracknell RG12 26 D6
Mitcham CR4 41 E5
Bernard Ct GU15 65 B4
Bernard Gdns SW19 19 F3
Bernard Rd SM5, SM6 60 B6
Berne Rd CR7 42 C4
Bernel Dr CR0 62 F7
Bernersh Cl GU47 45 C1
Berney House BR3 43 E4
Berney Rd CR0 42 D2
Berridge Rd SE19 22 E3
Berrington Dr KT24 92 F3
Berry Ct TW4 4 F2
Berry La Pirbright GU3 88 C2
West Norwood SE21, SE27 22 D4
Woking GU22, GU3 88 D4
Berry Meade KT21 75 F2
Berry Wlk KT21 95 F8
Berry's La KT14 71 D8
Berrybank GU47 64 E6
Berrycroft RG12 27 D8
Berrylands Surbiton KT5 37 F3
West Barnes SW20 39 C5
Berrylands Ct 7 SM2 59 B3
Berrylands Rd KT5 37 F3
Berrylands Sta KT5 38 B5
Berryman's La SE26 23 D4
Berrymeade Wlk RH11 200 E5
Berryscourt KT14 71 D8
Berryscroft Ct TW18 13 C1
Berryscroft Rd TW18 13 C1
Berstead Wlk 1 RH11 200 F3
Bert Rd CR7 42 C4
Bertal Rd SW17 20 D4
Bertie Rd SE26 23 D2
Bertram Cotts SW19 20 A1
Bertram House Sch SW17 21 A6
Bertram Rd KT2 18 A1
Bertrand House 11 SW16 21 E5
Berwyn Ave TW3 5 B6
Berwyn Rd
Mortlake SW14, TW10 7 B3
Streatham SE24 22 B7
Beryl Harding House 3
SW19 19 D1
Berystede KT2 18 B1
Besley St SW16 21 C2
Bessant Dr TW9 7 B6
Bessborough Rd SW15 19 A7
Bessborough Wks KT8 35 F4
Beswick Gdns RG12 27 F8
Beta Rd Chobham GU24 49 F1
Farnborough GU14 85 A5
Woking GU22 70 B3
Beta Way TW20 32 C8
Betchets Green Rd RH5 157 C6
Betchley Cl RH19 185 E3
Betchworth Cl SM1 59 D5
Betchworth Sta RH3 116 E3
Betchworth The RH4 116 A1
Betchworth Way CR0 63 C2
Betchworth Works RH6 180 D6
Bethany Waye TW14 14 E8
Bethel Cl GU9 125 D6
Bethel La GU9 125 D6
Bethersden Cl BR3 23 F1
Bethesda Ct 8 SE20 23 C1
Bethlem Royal Hospl The
BR3 44 A2
Bethune Cl RH10 202 D5
Bethune Rd RH13 217 E1
Betjeman Cl CR5 79 F2
Betley Ct KT12 54 B7
Betony Cl CR0 43 D1
Betts Cl BR3 43 E7
Betts Way Crawley RH10 181 D2
Long Ditton KT6 37 B1
Penge SE20 43 B8
Bettswood Ct 16 SE20 43 B8
Betula Cl CR8 80 D4
Between Streets KT11 73 A5
Beulah Ave CR7 42 C7
Beulah Cres CR7 42 C7
Beulah Gr CR0 42 C3
Beulah Hill SE19, SW16 22 C1
Beulah Inf Sch CR7 42 C6
Beulah Jun Sch CR7 42 C6
Beulah Rd Merton SW19 19 F1
South Norwood CR7 42 C6
Sutton SM1 59 A6
Beulah Wlk CR3 101 E7
Bevan Ct Crawley RH11 201 B1
Croydon CR0 61 A5
Beverley Ave Hounslow TW4 4 F3
Wimbledon SW20 38 F8
Beverley Cl
Addlestone KT15 52 D5
Ash GU12 105 F1
Chessington KT9 56 C6
East Ewell KT17 77 C8
Beverley Cl *continued*
Frimley GU15 66 D6
Oatlands Park KT13 53 E8
Beverley Cotts SW15 18 E5
Beverley Cres GU14 84 F2
Beverley Ct Hounslow TW4 4 F3
Kingston u T SW20 38 F8
Beverley Gdns Barnes SW13 7 F4
2 North Cheam KT4 39 A1
Beverley House BR1 24 D3
Beverley Hts RH2 118 B3
Beverley Hyrst 7 CR0 61 F8
Beverley La KT2 18 E1
Beverley Lodge 6 TW10 6 E2
Beverley Mansions TW4 4 F3
Beverley Rd Barnes SW13 7 F4
Kenley CR3 80 F2
Mitcham CR4 41 D5
New Malden KT3 39 A5
North Cheam KT4 58 C8
Penge SE20 43 B7
Sunbury TW16 34 F8
Teddington KT1 37 C8
Beverley Sch KT3 39 A4
Beverley Trad Est SM4 39 D2
Beverley Way
Kingston u T KT3, SW20, KT2 38 F8
Wimbledon KT3, SW20 39 A6
Beverley Way (Kingston
By Pass) KT3, SW20 39 A6
Beverley Way Kingston
Bypass KT3 38 F8
Beverstone Rd CR7 42 B5
Bevill Allen Cl SW17 20 F3
Bevill Cl SE25 43 A6
Bevin Sq SW17 20 F5
Bevington Rd BR3 44 B7
Bew Ct SE21 23 A8
Bewbush Dr RH11 200 F3
Bewbush Fst Sch RH11 200 F3
Bewbush Manor RH11 200 E2
Bewbush Mid Sch RH11 200 F3
Bewlys Rd SE27 22 B3
Bexhill Cl TW13 15 E6
Bexhill Rd Forest Hill SE4 23 F8
Mortlake SW14 7 C4
Beynon Rd SM5 59 F5
Bglws The CR3 100 D4
Bicester Rd TW9 7 B4
Bickersteth Rd SW17 20 F2
Bickley Ct RH11 201 A3
Bickley St SW17 20 F3
Bicknell Rd GU16 65 E2
Bickney Way KT22 94 C5
Bicknoller Cl SM2 59 B1
Bidborough Cl BR2 44 F4
Biddulph Rd CR2 61 C2
Bideford Cl
Farnborough GU14 85 A7
Feltham TW13 15 F5
Bideford Rd BR1 24 F5
Bidhams Cres KT20 97 C6
Bidmead Ct KT6 56 E7
Bield The RH2 139 A7
Bietigheim Way 2 GU15 65 C6
Big Common La RH1 120 B3
Biggin Ave CR4 40 F8
Biggin Cl RH11 201 C4
Biggin Hill SE19, SW16 22 B1
Biggin Hill Airport TN16 83 D5
Biggin Hill Bsns Pk TN16 83 D4
Biggin Hill Cl KT2 17 C3
Biggin Hill Jun & Inf Schs
TN16 83 E3
Biggin Way
CR7, SE19, SW16 22 C1
Bigginwood Rd SW16 42 B8
Bignor Cl RH12 218 A7
Bilberry Cl RH11 201 B3
Bilbets RH12 217 C3
Billesden Rd GU24 87 D7
Billet Rd TW18, TW19 13 A5
Billhurst Cotts RH7 164 D4
Billingshurst Rd RH12 216 D3
Billinton Dr RH10 202 B5
Billockby Cl KT9 56 F4
Billsley Ct SE25 42 E5
Bilton Ind Est RG12 26 E5
Binbury Row TW18 12 E4
Binfield Rd
Bracknell, Dowlesgreen RG40 25 F7
Bracknell, Priestwood RG42 27 A8
Byfleet KT14 71 E7
South Croydon CR2 61 F5
Wokingham RG40 25 F7
Binfields GU9 125 C3
Bingham Cnr CR0 43 A1
Bingham Dr Knaphill GU21 68 F1
Staines TW18 13 D1
Bingham Rd CR0, CR9 43 B1
Bingley Rd TW16 15 A1
Binhams Lea GU8 192 F5
Binhams Meadow GU8 192 F5
Binley House SW15 7 F1
Binney Ct RH10 182 E1
Binscombe Cres GU7 150 E8
Binscombe Jun Sch GU7 129 E1
Binscombe La GU7 150 E7
Binstead Cl RH11 201 B8
Binsted Dr GU17 64 D5
Binton La GU10 126 E3
Birch Ave Caterham CR3 100 D3
Leatherhead KT22 94 F8
Birch Circ GU7 150 F8
Birch Cl Brentford TW8 6 B7
Camberley GU15 65 E8
Crawley Down RH10 204 C8
Hounslow TW3 5 D5
Birch Cl *continued*
New Haw KT15 52
Rowledge GU10 146
Send Marsh GU23 90
Teddington TW11 17
Woking GU21 89
Birch Ct Ashstead KT21 75
Sutton SM1 59
9 Wallington SM6 60
Birch Dr GU17 64
Birch Gn TW18 13
Birch Gr Bracknell RG12 27
Guildford GU1 109
Kingswood KT20 97
Lewisham SE12 24
Upper Halliford TW17 34
Woking GU22 70
Birch Hill CR0 62
Birch Hill Prim Sch RG12 27
Birch Hill Rd RG12 27
Birch La Purley CR8 79
West End GU24 67
Winkfield RG12, SL5 28
Birch Lea RH10 182
Birch Platt GU24 67
Birch Rd Farncombe GU7 151
Feltham TW13 15
Headley Down GU35 187
Windlesham GU20 48
Birch Side RG45 45
Birch Tree Ave BR4 63
Birch Tree View GU18 48
Birch Tree Way CR0 62
Birch Vale KT11 74
Birch Way Ash Vale GU12 106
Warlingham CR6 81
Birch Wlk CR4 41
Birchanger GU7 150
Birchanger Rd SE25 43
Birchcroft Cl CR3 100
Birchdale Cl KT14 71
Birchend Cl CR2 61
Birches Cl Epsom KT18 76
Mitcham CR4 40
Birches Ind Est RH19 185
Birches Rd RH12 218
Birches The
Beckenham BR2 44
Blackwater GU17 64
Crawley RH10 202
East Horsley KT24 92
Farnborough GU14 84
South Norwood SE25 42
Twickenham TW4 15
Woking GU22 69
Birchett Rd
Aldershot GU11 105
Farnborough GU14 84
Birchetts Cl 2 RG42 27
Birchfield Cl
Addlestone KT15 52
Coulsdon CR5 79
Birchfield Gr KT17 58
Birchfields GU15 65
Birchgrove KT11 73
Birchington Rd KT5 37
Birchlands GU47 45
Birchlands Ave SW12 20
Birchway RH1 140
Birchwood Ave
Beckenham BR3 43
Hackbridge SM5, SM6 60
Birchwood Cl
Crawley RH10 202
Horley RH6 161
Morden SM4 40
Birchwood Dr
Lightwater GU18 48
West Byfleet KT14 71
Birchwood Gr TW12 16
Birchwood La
Caterham CR3 100
Oxshott KT10, KT22 55
Birchwood Rd
Streatham SW17 21
West Byfleet KT14, KT15 71
Bird Mews RG40 25
Bird Wlk TW2 15
Bird-In-Hand Pas SE23 23
Birdham Cl RH11 201
Birdhaven GU10, GU9 146
Birdhurst CR3 100
Birdhurst Ave CR2 61
Birdhurst Ct SM6 60
Birdhurst Gdns CR2 61
Birdhurst Rd
Mitcham SW19 20
South Croydon CR2 61
Birdhurst Rise CR2 61
Birds Hill Dr KT22 74
Birds Hill Rd KT22 74
Birds Hill Rise KT22 74
Birdsgrove GU21 68
Birdswood Dr GU21 88
Birdwood Cl Selsdon CR2 81
Teddington TW11 16
Birdwood Rd GU15 64
Birdworld & Underwater
World
GU10 145
Birkbeck Hill SE21 22
Birkbeck Pl Sandhurst GU47 45
West Norwood SE21 22
Birkbeck Rd Penge BR3 43
Wimbledon SW19 20
Birkbeck Sta SE20 43
Birkdale RG12 26
Birkdale Ct SL5 29

rkdale Dr RH11 . . . . .200 D5
rkdale Gdns CR0 . . . . .62 D8
kenhead Ave KT2 . . . . . . .37 F8
kenholme CI SL03. . . . . .187 C4
khall Rd SE6 . . . . .24 D6
kheads Rd RH2 . . . . .118 A2
kwood CI TW2 . . . . .21 D8
rling House ■ SE20 . . . . . .23 C1
rnham CI GU23 . . . . .91 A3
rtley Rd GU5 . . . . .152 B4
tley Rise GU5 . . . . .152 A5
scoe CI TW5 . . . . .5 A8
senden Rd CR0 . . . . .61 E8
sham CI Carshalton CR4 . . .40 F1
shanley RH10 . . . . .202 D3
shams Ct CR3 . . . . .100 F3
shop Bell Sch RH10 . . . . .201 F3
shop Challoner Sch
    KT2 . . . . .44 D7
shop David Brown Sch
    U21 . . . . .70 D6
shop Duppa's
    almshouses ■ TW10 . . . .6 E2
shop Duppas Pk TW17 . . .34 E2
shop Fox Way KT6 . . . . . .35 F5
shop Gilpins Prim Sch
    W19 . . . . .19 F3
shop Perrin (C of E) Sch
    W2 . . . . .16 B7
shop Reindorp CE Sch
    U1 . . . . .109 C4
shop Sumner Dr GU3 . . .125 C6
shop's Dr
    ast Bedfont TW14 . . . . . .3 A1
    Wokingham RG40 . . . . . .25 C7
shops Gr Hampton TW12 . .15 F4
    Windlesham GU20 . . . . . .48 C4
shops Hill KT12 . . . . .35 A2
shops Park Rd SW16 . . . . .41 E8
shops Rd GU7 . . . . .150 D4
shops Sq GU6 . . . . .174 F3
shops Wlk CR0, CR9 . . . . .62 E5
shops Wood GU21 . . . . . . .69 D3
shopscourt ■ CR0 . . . . . . .61 F8
shopsford Rd SM4 . . . . . . .40 D3
shopsgate Rd SL4, TW20 . .11 B5
shopsmead CI
    pstm KT24 . . . . .112 E7
shopsmead Ct KT19 . . . . . .57 E1
shopsmead Dr KT24 . . . . .112 F6
shopsmead Par KT24 . . . .112 F6
shopsthorpe Rd SE26 . . . . .23 D4
shopstone Wlk RH11 . . . .201 C1
sley C of E Prim Sch
    KT4 . . . . .68 A3
sley CI KT4 . . . . .39 C1
sley House Sw19 . . . . .19 D6
tmead CI RH11 . . . . .200 E5
ttams La KT15, KT16 . . . . .51 E6
tterne Dr GU21 . . . . .69 A2
ttoms The KT1 . . . . .37 D6
ack Dog Wlk RH10 . . . . .201 E8
ack Horse Way RH12 . . . .217 C2
ack Lake CI TW20 . . . . . . .32 A8
ack Pond La GU10 . . . . . .146 C6
ack Prince CI KT14 . . . . . .71 F5
ackberry CI
    uildford GU1 . . . . .109 A4
    upper Halliford TW17 . . .34 E5
ackberry Farm CI TW5 . . . . .4 F7
ackberry La RH7 . . . . . . .185 E8
ackberry Rd RH19, RH7 . . .185 D8
ackbird CI GU47 . . . . .64 D8
ackborough CI RH2 . . . . .118 C1
ackborough Rd RH2 . . . . .118 C1
ackbridge La RH12 . . . . .217 A1
ackbridge Rd GU22 . . . . . .89 D7
ackbrook Rd
    Dorking RH5 . . . . .136 E2
    South Holmwood RH5 . . .157 E8
ackburn The KT23 . . . . . . .93 F3
ackburn Trad Est TW19 . . . .2 F1
ackburn Way GU7 . . . . . .151 A5
ackbush CI SM2 . . . . .59 B3
ackcap CI RH11 . . . . .201 C4
ackcap Rd GU47 . . . . .64 D8
ackdown Ave GU22 . . . . . .70 E4
ackdown CI GU22 . . . . . . .70 D3
ackdown Prim Sch
    SU16 . . . . .86 E8
ackdown Rd GU16 . . . . . . .86 C8
ackenham Rd SW17 . . . . .20 F4
ackett CI TW18, TW20 . . . .32 F7
ackett Rd RH10 . . . . .202 C5
ackfold Rd RH10 . . . . . . .202 A5
ackford CI CR2 . . . . .61 B2

Blackham House SW19 . . . . .19 E2
Blackheath RH10 . . . . .202 D8
Blackheath Gr GU5 . . . . . .152 B8
Blackheath La Albury GU5 .132 B3
    Wonersh GU5, GU4 . . . .152 C8
Blackheath Rd GU9 . . . . . .125 A7
Blackhills KT10 . . . . .54 E2
Blackhorse La Croydon CR0 . .43 A2
    Lower Kingswood
    KT20, RH2 . . . . .118 C7
Blackhorse Rd GU21, GU22 . .88 E6
Blacklands Cres RH18 . . . .206 F2
Blacklands Meadow RH1 . .119 E2
Blacklands Rd SE6 . . . . . . .24 C4
Blackman Gdns GU11 . . . .126 B8
Blackman's La CR6 . . . . . . .82 F5
Blackmeadows RG12 . . . . . .27 C3
Blackmoor CI SL5 . . . . .28 D7
Blackmoor Wood SL5 . . . . .28 D7
Blackmore Cres GU21 . . . . .70 C5
Blackmore House SE23 . . . .23 F7
Blackmore's Gr TW11 . . . . .17 A2
Blackness La GU22 . . . . . . .89 E8
Blackness Cotts GU6 . . . . .192 E3
Blackness Gate Rd SL5 . . . .30 A1
Blacknest Rd GU25, SL5 . . . .30 E6
Blackshaw Rd SW17 . . . . . .20 D3
Blacksmith CI KT21 . . . . . . .95 F8
Blacksmith's La GU4 . . . . .131 D3
Blacksmith's La TW18 . . . . .33 C6
Blacksmiths Hill CR2 . . . . . .81 B6
Blacksmiths La KT16 . . . . . .33 A2
Blackstone CI
    Farnborough GU14 . . . . .84 D6
    Reigate RH1 . . . . .139 B7
Blackstone Hill RH1, RH2 . .118 C1
Blackstone House SE21 . . . .22 E5
Blackstroud La
    E GU18, GU24 . . . . .67 E8
Blackstroud La W GU18 . . . .67 D8
Blackthorn CI
    Crawley RH11 . . . . .181 C1
    Horsham RH13 . . . . . . .218 A2
    Reigate RH2 . . . . .139 C7
Blackthorn Ct Heston TW5 . . .4 E7
    ■ West Norwood SW16 . . .22 A3
Blackthorn Dr GU18 . . . . . .67 B7
Blackthorn Rd
    Biggin Hill TN16 . . . . . . .83 E3
    Reigate RH2 . . . . .139 C7
Blackthorne Ave CR0 . . . . . .43 C1
Blackthorne Cres SL3 . . . . . .1 F5
Blackthorne Ind Pk SL3 . . . . .1 F5
Blackthorne Rd
    Great Bookham KT23 . . . .94 C1
    Poyle SL3 . . . . .1 F5
Blackwater CI GU12 . . . . . .106 A1
Blackwater La RH10 . . . . . .202 D6
Blackwater Sta GU17 . . . . . .64 E4
Blackwater Way Ind Est
    GU12 . . . . .126 D8
Blackwell Ave GU2 . . . . . . .108 E1
Blackwell Cty Prim Sch
    RH19 . . . . .185 E3
Blackwell Farm Rd RH19 . .185 F2
Blackwell Hollow RH19 . . .185 F2
Blackwell Rd RH19 . . . . . .185 F2
Blackwood CI KT14 . . . . . . .71 C7
Bladen CI CT13 . . . . .53 E4
Blades CI KT22 . . . . .95 D7
Bladon CI GU1 . . . . .110 A2
Bladon Dr Beckenham BR2 . .44 E7
    Streatham SW16 . . . . . . .21 E2
Blagdon Rd KT3 . . . . .38 E5
Blagdon Wlk TW11 . . . . . . .17 C2
Blair Ave KT10 . . . . .55 C8
Blair Ct Beckenham BR3 . . . .44 B8
    Catford SE6 . . . . .24 F7
Blairderry Rd SW2 . . . . . . .21 E6
Blaise CI GU14 . . . . .85 D3
Blake CI Carshalton SM5 . . .40 E1
    Crawley RH10 . . . . .201 F2
    Crowthorne RG45 . . . . . .45 C4
    Wokingham RG40 . . . . . .25 E8
Blake House BR3 . . . . .24 B2
Blake Rd Croydon CR0 . . . . .61 E8
    Mitcham CR4 . . . . .40 E6
Blake's Gn BR4 . . . . .44 C1
Blake's La
    East Clandon GU4 . . . . .111 F3
    West Horsley GU4 . . . . .111 F3
Blakeden Dr KT10 . . . . .55 F4
Blakehall Rd SM5 . . . . .59 F4
Blakemore Rd
    Streatham SW16 . . . . . . .21 E5
    Thornton Heath CR7 . . . .41 F4
Blakeney Ave BR3 . . . . .43 F8
Blakeney CI KT19 . . . . .76 D8
Blakeney Rd BR3 . . . . .43 F8
Blakes Ave KT3 . . . . .38 F4
Blakes La KT3 . . . . .38 F4
Blakes Terr KT3 . . . . .39 A4
Blakewood CI TW13 . . . . . .15 C4
Blanchards Hill GU4 . . . . . .89 F2
Blanchland Rd SM4 . . . . . . .40 B4
Blanchman's Rd CR6 . . . . . .81 E1
Blandfield Rd SW12 . . . . . .21 A8
Blandford Ave Penge BR3 . . .4 F3
    Twickenham TW2 . . . . . .16 B7
Blandford CI
    Wallington CR0 . . . . .60 E7
    Woking GU22 . . . . .70 B2
Blandford Rd Penge BR3 . . .43 D7
    Teddington TW11 . . . . . .16 E3
Blane's La SL5 . . . . .28 C3

Blanford Rd RH2 . . . . .139 C8
Blanks La
    Charlwood RH5, RH6 . . . .159 B2
    Cudworth RH5, RH6 . . . .159 B2
Blashford St SE13 . . . . .24 D8
Blatchford CI RH13 . . . . . .217 F3
Blatchford Ct KT12 . . . . . . .35 A1
Blatchford Rd RH13 . . . . . .217 F3
Blay's La TW20 . . . . .11 B2
Blays Ct TW20 . . . . .11 C2
Blean Gr SE20 . . . . .23 C1
Blegborough Rd SW16 . . . .21 C2
Blencarn CI GU21 . . . . .68 F3
Blendworth Point ■
    SW15 . . . . .19 B7
Blenheim ■ SW19 . . . . .19 D7
Blenheim Bsns Ctr CR4 . . . .40 F7
Blenheim CI
    Farnham RH10 . . . . . . .182 D1
    East Grinstead RH19 . . . .186 A3
    Tongham GU10 . . . . . . .126 F7
    Wallington SM6 . . . . . . .60 C3
    West Barnes SW20 . . . . .39 C6
    South Croydon CR2 . . . . .61 C3
Blenheim Cres Egham TW18 . .12 D4
    Farnborough GU13 . . . . . .6 E4
    Richmond TW9 . . . . .6 E2
    South Norwood SE19 . . . .42 E8
    Sutton SM2 . . . . .59 C4
Blenheim Fields RH18 . . . .206 E3
Blenheim Gdns
    Kingston u T KT2 . . . . . .18 B1
    Sanderstead CR2 . . . . . . .81 A7
    Wallington SM6 . . . . .60 C3
    Woking GU22 . . . . .89 B8
Blenheim High Sch KT19 . . .57 D1
Blenheim House TW3 . . . . . .5 A4
Blenheim Park Rd CR2 . . . . .61 C2
Blenheim Pk GU11 . . . . . . .105 C7
Blenheim Rd Epsom KT19 . . .76 E8
    Horsham RH12 . . . . . . .217 D4
    Penge SE20 . . . . .23 C1
    Sutton SM1 . . . . .59 B7
    West Barnes SW20 . . . . .39 C6
Blenheim Way TW7 . . . . .6 A6
Bleriot Rd TW5 . . . . .4 D7
Bletchingley CI RH1 . . . . . .119 C6
Bletchingley Golf Course
    RH1 . . . . .120 B8
Bletchingley Rd
    Bletchingley RH1, RH9 . .121 B4
    Godstone RH1, RH9 . . . .121 B4
    Merstham RH1 . . . . .119 C6
    Nutfield RH1 . . . . .120 A2
    Nutfield, South
    Merstham RH1 . . . . .119 B6
Bletchingly Ct ■ CR7 . . . . .42 B6
Bletchingly CI UB3 . . . . .3 D8
Blewburton Wlk RG12 . . . . .27 E5
Blewfield GU7 . . . . .150 F2
Bligh CI RH10 . . . . .201 F4
Bligh House ■ SE27 . . . . . .22 C4
Blighton La GU10 . . . . .126 E3
Blincoe CI SW19 . . . . .19 D6
Blind Cnr SE25 . . . . .43 B5
Blindley Ct RH7 . . . . .163 E8
Blindley Rd RH10 . . . . .182 C1
Bloggs CI SE19 . . . . .22 D2
Blomfield Dale GU14 . . . . . .84 C3
Blondell CI UB7 . . . . .2 D8
Bloom Gr SE27 . . . . .22 B5
Bloomfield CI GU21 . . . . . . .68 F2
Bloomfield Rd KT1 . . . . .37 E6
Bloomhall Rd SE19 . . . . . . .22 D3
Bloomsbury CI KT19 . . . . . .57 D1
Bloomsbury Ct Cranford TW5 . .4 F6
    Guildford GU1 . . . . .130 F7
Bloomsbury Way GU17 . . . . .64 D3
Blossom CI CR2 . . . . .61 E5
Blossom Waye TW5 . . . . .4 F7
Blount Ave RH19 . . . . .185 C1
Bloxham Cres TW12 . . . . . .35 F8
Bloxham Rd GU6 . . . . .175 A3
Bloxworth CI
    ■ Bracknell RG12 . . . . . .27 F5
    Wallington SM6 . . . . .60 C7
Blue Anchor Alley ■ TW9 . . .6 E3
Blue Ball La TW20 . . . . .11 F3
Blue Barn Way KT13 . . . . . .72 A8
Blue Cedars SM7 . . . . .77 D5
Blue Cedars PI KT11 . . . . . .73 D7
Blue Coat Wlk RG12 . . . . . .27 D4
Blue Sch The TW7 . . . . .6 A4
Bluebell CI Crawley RH11 . .201 B3
    East Grinstead RH19 . . . .185 C3
    Forest Hill SE19, SE26 . . .22 F4
    Horsham RH12 . . . . . . .217 E5
    Wallington CR4 . . . . .41 B1
Bluebell Ct GU22 . . . . .89 D8
Bluebell Hill RG12 . . . . .27 E7
Bluebell Rise GU18 . . . . . . .67 B8
Blueberry Gdns CR5 . . . . . .79 F3
Bluefield CI TW12 . . . . .16 A3
Bluegates Stoneleigh KT17 . .58 A3
    Wimbledon SW19 . . . . . .19 F3
Bluehouse Gdns RH8 . . . . .123 A7
Bluehouse La RH8 . . . . . . .122 F7
Bluethroat CI GU47 . . . . . . .64 E8
Bluff Cove AL11 . . . . .105 C3
Blundel La Oxshott KT11 . . . .74 B4
    Stoke D'Abernon KT11 . . .74 B4
Blundell Ave RH6 . . . . .160 F4
Blunden Rd GU14 . . . . .84 F5
Blunt Rd CR0 . . . . .61 D5

Blunts Ave UB7 . . . . .3 A7
Blunts Way RH12 . . . . .217 C3
Blyth CI TW1 . . . . .5 F1
Blyth Rd BR1, BR2 . . . . .44 F8
Blythe CI SE23 . . . . .23 F8
Blythe Hill SE23, SE6 . . . . . .23 F8
Blythe Hill La SE23, SE6 . . .23 F7
Blythe Vale SE23, SE6 . . . . .23 E7
Blythewood La SL5 . . . . . . .28 E7
Blythwood Dr GU16 . . . . . . .65 D2
Blythwood Pk BR1 . . . . .44 F8
Blytons The RH19 . . . . .185 B1
Boar Hill RH5 . . . . .135 E1
Board School Rd GU21 . . . . .69 F3
Bocketts Farm Pk KT22 . . . .94 F2
Bockhampton Rd KT2 . . . . . .17 F1
Boddicott CI SW19 . . . . .19 E6
Bodens Ride SL5 . . . . .28 F1
Bodiam CI RH10 . . . . .202 C6
Bodiam Ct BR2 . . . . .44 F5
Bodiam Rd SW16 . . . . .21 D1
Bodley CI KT3 . . . . .38 E4
Bodley Manor Way SE24 . . .22 A8
Bodley Rd KT3 . . . . .38 E4
Bodmin Gr SM4 . . . . .40 B4
Bodmin St SW18 . . . . .20 A7
Bodnant Gdns SW20 . . . . . .39 B6
Bog La RG12 . . . . .28 A5
Bognor Rd
    Beare Green RH5 . . . . . .157 B2
    Ockley RH5 . . . . .157 B2
    Warnham RH12, RH5 . . .197 D4
Bois Hall Rd KT15 . . . . .52 D5
Bolderwood Way BR4 . . . . . .63 B8
Bolding House La GU24 . . . .67 F7
Boleyn Ave KT17 . . . . .58 B1
Boleyn CI Crawley RH10 . . .202 D3
    Egham TW18 . . . . .12 E2
Boleyn Ct East Molesey KT8 . .36 D5
    ■ Redhill RH1 . . . . .119 A2
Boleyn Dr KT8 . . . . .35 F6
Boleyn Gdns BR4 . . . . .63 B8
Bolingbroke Gr SW11 . . . . .20 F8
Bolingbroke House BR3 . . . .24 B3
Bolney Ct Crawley RH11 . . .200 F3
    Kingston u T KT6 . . . . . . .37 C4
Bolsover Gr RH1 . . . . .119 E6
Bolstead Rd CR4 . . . . .41 B8
Bolters La SM7 . . . . .78 A4
Bolters Rd RH6 . . . . .161 A5
Bolters Rd S RH6 . . . . .160 F6
Bolton CI Chessington KT9 . . .56 E4
    Penge SE20 . . . . .43 A7
Bolton Gdns Bromley BR1 . . .24 F1
    Teddington TW11 . . . . . .17 A2
Bolton Rd Chessington KT9 . .56 E4
    Chiswick W4 . . . . .7 C7
    Crawley RH10 . . . . .202 C2
Bolton's La
    Harlington TW6, UB7 . . . . .3 C7
    Pyrford GU22 . . . . .71 A3
Boltons CI GU22 . . . . .71 A3
Bomer CI UB7 . . . . .3 A7
Boncharch CI SM2 . . . . .59 B3
Bond Fst Sch CR4 . . . . .40 F6
Bond Gdns SM6 . . . . .60 C6
Bond Rd Mitcham CR4 . . . . .40 E7
    Surbiton KT6 . . . . .56 F8
    Warlingham CR6 . . . . . . .81 E1
Bond St TW20 . . . . .11 C3
Bond's La RH5 . . . . .136 B1
Bone Mill La RH9 . . . . .121 E1
Bonehurst Rd RH1, RH6 . . .161 A1
Bones La RH6, RH7 . . . . . .163 B2
Boner Hill Rd KT1 . . . . .38 A7
Bonners CI GU22 . . . . .89 F5
Bonnetts La RH11, RH6 . . .181 A3
Bonnys Rd RH2 . . . . .138 D8
Bonser Rd TW1 . . . . .16 F6
Bonsey CI GU22 . . . . .89 E6
Bonsey La GU22 . . . . .89 E6
Bonsey's La GU24, KT16 . . .52 F2
Bonsor Dr KT20 . . . . .97 E4
Bonville Rd BR1 . . . . .24 F3
Bookham Ct
    Little Bookham KT23 . . . .93 F4
    Mitcham CR4 . . . . .40 D6
Bookham Gr KT23 . . . . .94 B1
Bookham Ind Pk KT23 . . . . .93 F4
Bookham Rd KT11 . . . . .93 D7
Bookham Sta KT23 . . . . . . .93 F4
Bookhurst Rd GU6 . . . . . . .175 B4
Booth Dr TW18 . . . . .13 E2
Booth House ■ SW2 . . . . . .22 A8
Booth Rd Crawley RH11 . . .200 E3
    Croydon CR0, CR9 . . . . .61 B8
Boothby House ■ SW16 . . . .21 C3
Boothroyd House TW7 . . . . . .5 F4
Borage CI RH11 . . . . .201 A3
Border Chase RH10 . . . . . .183 A2
Border Ct RH19 . . . . .185 B4
Border End GU27 . . . . .207 D6
Border Gate GU47 . . . . .64 C8
Border Gdns CR0 . . . . .63 B6
Border Rd Forest Hill SE26 . .23 B3
    Haslemere GU27 . . . . . .207 D6
Bordesley Rd SM4 . . . . .40 B5
Bordon Wlk ■ SW15 . . . . . .19 A8
Boreen The RH19 . . . . .185 C3
Borelli Mews GU9 . . . . .125 C2
Borelli Yd GU9 . . . . .125 C2
Borers Arms Rd RH10 . . . . .183 C3
Borers Yard Ind Est
    RH10 . . . . .183 C3
Borland Rd TW11 . . . . .17 B1

Borough Grange CR2 . . . . . .81 A7
Borough Hill CR0, CR9 . . . . .61 B7
Borough Rd
    Farncombe GU7 . . . . . . .150 D5
    Godalming GU7 . . . . . . .150 D5
    Hounslow TW7 . . . . .5 F6
    ■ Kingston u T KT2 . . . . .18 A1
    Mitcham CR4 . . . . .40 E7
    Tatsfield TN16 . . . . .103 D6
Borough The
    Brockham RH3 . . . . .137 A8
    Farnham GU9 . . . . .125 B2
Borrowdale CI
    Crawley RH11 . . . . .201 B4
    Sanderstead CR2 . . . . . . .80 E1
    Thorpe Lea TW20 . . . . . .12 B1
Borrowdale Dr CR2 . . . . . . .80 F1
Borrowdale Gdns GU15 . . . .66 D4
Bosbury Rd SE6 . . . . .24 C5
Boscombe CI TW20 . . . . . . .32 C8
Boscombe Gdns SW16 . . . .21 E2
Boscombe House CR0 . . . . .42 D1
Boscombe Rd
    Merton SW19 . . . . .40 B8
    Mitcham SW17 . . . . .20 D1
    North Cheam KT4 . . . . . .39 D1
Bosham Rd RH10 . . . . .202 C3
Boshers Gdns TW20 . . . . . .11 F2
Bosman Dr GU20 . . . . .48 B6
Bostock Ave RH12 . . . . . . .218 A5
Bostock House TW5 . . . . .5 A8
Boston CI
    South Norwood SE25 . . . .42 F5
    Sutton SM2 . . . . .59 C4
Boston Gdns W4 . . . . .7 E8
Boston Manor Rd TW8 . . . . . .6 C8
Boston Rd CR0 . . . . .42 A3
Boswell House ■ SW16 . . . .21 C3
Boswell Rd Crawley RH10 . .201 E3
    Thornton Heath CR7 . . . .42 C5
Bosward Ct TW4 . . . . .4 F4
Botany Hill GU10 . . . . .126 D1
Botery's Cross RH1 . . . . . .120 B2
Bothwell Rd CR0 . . . . .63 C1
Botsford Rd SW20 . . . . .39 E7
Boucher CI TW11 . . . . .16 F3
Boughton Ave BR2 . . . . .44 F2
Boughton Hall Ave GU23 . . .90 F3
Bouldish Farm Rd SL5 . . . . .29 A5
Boulevard The
    Crawley RH10, RH11 . . .201 E6
    ■ Upper Tooting SW17 . . .21 A6
Boullen Ct SM1 . . . . .59 C6
Boulogne Rd CR0 . . . . .42 C3
Boulters House RG12 . . . . . .27 E5
Boulters Rd ■
    GU11, GU12 . . . . .105 B2
Boulthurst Way RH8 . . . . . .123 B3
Boundaries
    Mansions ■ SW12 . . . . .21 A7
Boundaries Rd
    Balham SW12 . . . . .21 A7
    Feltham TW13 . . . . .15 C7
    Upper Tooting SW12, SW17 . .21 A7
Boundary Bsns Ct CR4 . . . . .40 D6
Boundary Bsns Ctr GU21 . . .70 A4
Boundary CI
    Crawley RH10 . . . . .201 E7
    Kingston u T KT1 . . . . . . .38 B6
    Penge SE20 . . . . .43 A7
Boundary Cotts GU4 . . . . . .132 A4
Boundary House TW1 . . . . . .6 B2
Boundary Rd
    Binstead GU10 . . . . .145 E2
    Crawley RH10 . . . . .201 E7
    Dockenfield GU10 . . . . . .166 D7
    Farnborough GU14 . . . . .85 C2
    Frensham GU10 . . . . . . .145 E2
    Grayshott GU26 . . . . . . .188 D3
    Mitcham SW19 . . . . .20 D2
    Staines TW15 . . . . .13 A3
    Wallington SM5, SM6 . . .60 A4
    Woking GU21 . . . . .70 A4
Boundary Rd E KT15 . . . . . .52 B2
Boundary Rd N KT15 . . . . . .52 B2
Boundary Rd W KT15 . . . . . .52 B2
Boundary Way
    Addington CR0 . . . . .63 A5
    Woking GU21 . . . . .70 A4
Boundfield Rd SE6 . . . . .24 E6
Boundstone CI GU10 . . . . .146 B5
Boundstone Rd GU10 . . . . .146 A4
Bourbon House SE6 . . . . . . .24 C3
Bourdon Rd SE20 . . . . .43 C7
Bourg-de-Peage Ave
    RH19 . . . . .186 A1
Bourke Hill CR5 . . . . .78 F1
Bourley La GU10 . . . . .104 A2
Bourley Rd
    Aldershot GU11 . . . . . . .104 C2
    Crondall GU10 . . . . .104 C2
Bourne Ave KT16 . . . . .33 A6
Bourne CI Chilworth GU4 . .131 B3
    West Byfleet KT14 . . . . . .71 A7
Bourne Ct Aldershot GU11 . .126 A8
    Chiswick W4 . . . . .7 C8
    ■ Purley CR8 . . . . .80 A8
Bourne Cty Inf Sch The
    GU10 . . . . .146 A5
Bourne Dene GU10 . . . . . . .146 A5
Bourne Dr CR4 . . . . .40 D7
Bourne Firs GU10 . . . . .146 D5
Bourne Gr Ashtead KT21 . . .95 D8
    Farnham GU10 . . . . .146 A5
Bourne Grove CI GU10 . . . .146 E7

Bourne Grove Dr GU10 ....146 E7
Bourne Hall Mus KT17 ......57 F2
Bourne House TW15 ....14 A3
Bourne Hts GU9 ....146 C8
Bourne La CR3 ....100 D6
Bourne Meadow
  KT16, TW20 ....32 B5
Bourne Mill Ind Est GU9 ...125 E3
Bourne Mill Rdbt
  GU10, GU9 ....125 E3
Bourne Park Cl CR8 ....80 E3
Bourne Rd Farncombe GU7 ..150 F7
  Merstham RH1 ....119 C5
  Wentworth GU25 ....31 D4
  Woodham KT15 ....52 B8
Bourne St CR0, CR9 ....61 B8
Bourne Vale BR2 ....44 F1
Bourne View CR8 ....80 D4
Bourne Way
  Addlestone KT15 ....52 C5
  Cheam SM1 ....58 F5
  Coney Hall BR2, BR4 ....63 F8
  West Ewell KT19 ....57 C6
  Woking GU22 ....89 D5
Bournefield Rd CR3 ....81 A1
Bournemouth Rd SW19 ....40 A8
Bourneside GU25 ....31 A2
Bourneside Gdns SE6 ....24 C3
Bourneside Rd KT15 ....52 D5
Bournes Ct RH13 ....217 E3
Bournville Rd SE13, SE6 .....24 A8
Bousley Rise KT16 ....51 D4
Bouverie Gdns CR8 ....79 F5
Bouverie Rd CR5 ....79 A1
Boveney House RG12 ....27 E5
Boveney Rd SE23 ....23 D8
Bovey House 3 RH1 ....119 A3
Bovill Rd SE23 ....23 D8
Bovingdon Sq CR4 ....41 E5
Bowater Rd RH10 ....202 C3
Bowater Ridge KT13 ....53 D1
Bowden Cl TW14 ....14 E7
Bowden Rd SL5 ....29 D4
Bowen Dr SE19, SE21 ....22 E5
Bower Cl GU22 ....70 B3
Bower Hill Cl RH1 ....140 E6
Bower Hill La RH1 ....140 D7
Bower Rd GU10 ....146 A5
Bowerland La RH7 ....164 E2
Bowers Cl GU4 ....110 A5
Bowers Farm Dr GU4 ......110 B5
Bowers La GU4 ....110 A6
Bowers Pl RH10 ....204 B8
Bowes Ct RH13 ....217 E3
Bowes Rd Egham TW18 .....12 E2
  Walton-on-T KT12 ....54 B8
Bowie Cl SW4 ....21 D8
Bowland Dr RG12 ....27 E2
Bowley Cl SE19 ....22 F2
Bowley La SE19 ....22 F3
Bowlhead Green Rd GU8 ...170 B1
Bowling Green Cl SW19 .....19 B8
Bowling Green Ct GU16 .....85 E7
Bowling Green La RH12 ....217 D3
Bowling Green Rd GU24 .....49 E2
Bowlings The GU15 ....65 C6
Bowman Ct RH10 ....201 D7
Bowman Mews SW18 ....19 F7
Bowman's Meadow SM6 .....60 B7
Bowmans Lea SE23 ....23 C8
Bowness Cl 7 RH11 ....200 D5
Bowness Cres KT2, SW15 ..18 E3
Bowness Dr TW4 ....4 E3
Bowness Rd SE6 ....24 B8
Bowring House GU7 ....150 F6
Bowsley Ct TW13 ....15 A6
Bowsprit The KT11 ....73 C4
Bowyer Cres RG40 ....25 C8
Bowyers Cl KT21 ....75 F1
Box Cl RH11 ....201 C1
Box Hill Ctry Pk RH4 ....115 D3
Box Hill Sch RH5 ....115 B8
Box La RH10 ....206 E6
Box Ridge Ave CR8 ....79 F7
Boxall Rd SE21 ....22 E8
Boxall Wlk RH13 ....217 D1
Boxall's La GU11 ....126 A8
Boxall's La GU11 ....126 B7
Boxford Cl CR2 ....81 D7
Boxford Ridge RG12 ....27 A4
Boxgrove Ave GU1 ....110 A3
Boxgrove Cty Prim Sch
  GU1 ....110 B2
Boxgrove La GU1 ....110 B2
Boxgrove Rd GU1 ....110 A2
Boxhill Rd RH4 ....115 E3
Boxhill Way RH3 ....115 A3
Boxhill & Westhumble
  Sta RH5 ....115 B4
Boxley Rd SM4, SW19 ....40 C5
Boxwood Way CR6 ....81 D2
Boyce House GU7 ....21 C3
Boyd Cl KT2 ....18 A1
Boyd Ct RG42 ....27 A8
Boyd Rd SW19 ....20 D2
Boyland Rd BR1 ....24 F3
Boyle Farm Rd KT7 ....37 A3
Brabazon Ave SM6 ....60 E3
Brabazon Rd TW5 ....4 D7
Braboeuf Manor (Coll
  of Law) GU2 ....130 C5
Brabon Rd GU14 ....84 F5
Brabourne Cl 7 SE19 ....22 E3
Brabourne Rise BR3 ....44 D4

Brabrook Ct SM6 ....60 B5
Bracebridge GU15 ....65 A5
Bracewood Gdns CR0 ....61 F7
Bracken Ave Balham SW12 ..21 A8
  West Wickham CR0 ....63 B7
Bracken Bank SL5 ....28 C8
Bracken Cl Ashford TW16 ...14 F2
  Copthorne RH10 ....183 B2
  Farnborough GU10 ....201 E8
  Little Bookham KT23 ....93 F3
  Twickenham TW4 ....16 A8
  Woking GU22 ....69 F1
  Wonersh GU5 ....152 B6
Bracken End TW7 ....5 D2
Bracken Gr RH12 ....218 B5
Bracken Hill Cl BR1 ....44 F8
Bracken Hill La BR1 ....44 F8
Bracken Path KT18 ....76 B6
Bracken Way
  Chobham GU24 ....48 F1
  Guildford GU3 ....108 E3
Brackendale KT1 ....38 B7
Brackendale Cl
  Frimley GU15 ....65 E3
  Hounslow TW5 ....5 B6
Brackendale Ct 8 BR3 ......24 A1
Brackendale Rd GU15 ....65 D4
Brackendene GU12 ....106 C3
Brackendene Cl GU21 ....70 A4
Brackenhale Comp Sch
  RG12 ....27 B5
Brackenhill KT11 ....74 B7
Brackenlea GU7 ....150 D7
Brackens The RG45 ....24 A1
Brackens The RG45 ....45 A7
Brackenside RH6 ....161 B4
Brackenwood
  Frimley GU15 ....66 D5
  Sunbury TW16 ....35 A8
Brackenwood Rd GU21 ......88 D8
Bracklesham Cl GU14 ....85 A7
Brackley KT13 ....53 D5
Brackley Cl SM6 ....60 E3
Brackley Rd BR3 ....24 A1
Bracknell Beeches RG12 ....27 B6
Bracknell Bsns Ctr The
  RG12 ....26 F7
Bracknell Cl GU15 ....46 F1
Bracknell Coll
  Bracknell RG12 ....27 C7
  Bracknell, Wick Hill RG12 ...27 C8
Bracknell Enterprise Ctr
  RG12 ....27 A7
Bracknell Rd
  Bracknell GU19 ....47 E5
  Camberley GU15 ....47 A1
  Crowthorne RG45 ....45 D6
  Winkfield RG42 ....8 A5
Bracknell Sports & L Ctr
  RG12 ....27 C4
Bracknell Sta RG12 ....27 B6
Bracknell Wlk RH11 ....200 E3
Bracondale KT10 ....55 C5
Bracondale Rd SE2 ....23 A8
Braddon Rd TW9 ....6 F4
Bradenhurst Cl CR3 ....100 F2
Bradfield Cl Guildford GU1 .110 A4
  Woking GU22 ....69 E1
Bradfields RG12 ....27 D4
Bradford Cl SE26 ....23 B4
Bradford Dr KT19 ....57 F4
Brading Rd Streatham SW2 .21 F8
  Thornton Heath CR0 ....41 F3
Bradley Cl SM2 ....59 B1
Bradley Ct CR0 ....61 A6
Bradley Dr RG40 ....25 A2
Bradley La RH4, RH5 ....115 B3
Bradley Mews SW12 ....20 F7
Bradley Rd SE19 ....22 C2
Bradmore Way CR5 ....79 F3
Bradshaw Cl SW19 ....20 A2
Bradshaws Cl SE25 ....43 A6
Bradsole House 1 SE16 .....24 A1
Brae Ct 2 Kingston u T KT2 .38 A8
  South Norwood SE25 ....42 E8
Braemar Ave
  South Croydon CR2 ....61 C2
  Thornton Heath CR7 ....42 B6
  Wimbledon SW18, SW19 ....20 A6
Braemar Ct 2 Frimley GU16 .85 F8
  Godalming GU7 ....150 D3
Braemar Cl
  5 Brentford TW8 ....6 D8
  Catford SE6 ....24 F7
Braemar Gdns BR4 ....44 C1
Braemar House TW11 ....17 B3
Braemar Rd Brentford TW8 ...6 D8
  North Cheam KT4 ....58 B7
Braes Mead RH1 ....140 E8
Braeside Beckenham BR3 ...24 B3
  Woodham KT15 ....71 B8
Braeside Ave SW19 ....39 E8
Braeside GU27 ....207 F8
Braeside Rd SW16 ....21 C1
Brafferton Rd CR0 ....61 C6
Braganza Ct GU1 ....109 E2
Bragg Rd TW11 ....16 F2
Braid Cl TW13 ....15 F6
Braidwood Rd SE6 ....24 D7
Brailsford Cl SW19 ....20 C8
Brakey Hill RH1 ....120 E1
Bramber Cl Crawley RH10 ..201 E8
  Horsham RH12 ....218 B5
Bramble Acres Cl SM2 ......59 A3
Bramble Bank GU16 ....86 A6

Bramble Banks SM5 ....60 A2
Bramble Cl
  Copthorne RH10 ....183 B3
  Croydon CR0 ....63 B6
  Guildford GU3 ....108 A3
  Redhill RH1 ....140 A7
  Upper Halliford TW17 ......34 D6
Bramble Hedge Farm
  (Ind Est) KT11 ....72 C5
Bramble La TW12 ....15 F2
Bramble Rise KT11 ....73 C5
Bramble Twitten RH19 .....186 A1
Bramble Way GU23 ....90 F3
Bramble Wlk KT18 ....76 B6
Brambledene Cl GU21 ....69 C1
Brambledown TW18 ....33 B8
Brambledown Rd
  South Croydon CR2 ....61 E3
  Wallington SM5, SM6 ....60 B3
Bramblegate RG45 ....45 A6
Brambles Cl Ash GU12 .....106 B1
  Brentford TW7, TW8 ....6 B7
  Caterham CR3 ....100 E5
Brambles Pk GU5 ....151 F6
Brambles The
  Farncombe GU7 ....150 D7
  8 Wimbledon SW19 ....19 F3
  Wimbledon SW19 ....19 F3
Brambleton Ave GU9 ....146 B7
Brambletye Cty Jun Sch
  RH1 ....140 A7
Brambletye La RH18 ....206 D4
Brambletye Park Rd RH1 ...140 A7
Brambletye Rd RH10 ....202 A5
Brambletye Sch RH19 ......206 C5
Bramblewood RH2 ....119 B6
Bramblewood Cl SM5 ....40 E1
Brambling Cl RH13 ....218 A1
Brambling Rd RH13 ....218 A1
Bramcote GU15 ....66 C5
Bramcote Ave CR4 ....40 F5
Bramcote Ct CR4 ....40 F5
Bramerton Rd BR3 ....43 F6
Bramham Gdns KT9 ....56 D6
Bramley Ave Coulsdon CR5 .79 C4
  Sunbury TW17 ....34 E6
Bramley CE Inf Sch GU5 ...152 A5
Bramley Cl Chertsey KT16 ...33 B1
  Crawley RH10 ....201 F6
  Croydon CR2 ....61 C5
  Staines TW18 ....13 C2
  Twickenham TW2 ....5 C1
Bramley Ct Mitcham CR4 ....40 D7
  Redhill RH1 ....118 E3
  Wallington SM6 ....60 C5
Bramley Hill CR0, CR2 ......61 C6
Bramley Ho 1 SW3 ....4 F3
Bramley House
  1 Kingston u T KT2 ....18 B1
  Roehampton SW15 ....7 F1
Bramley La GU17 ....64 B5
Bramley Park Ct GU5 ......151 F6
Bramley Rd
  Camberley GU15 ....65 B2
  Carshalton SM1 ....59 D5
  East Ewell SM2 ....58 D2
Bramley Way
  Ashstead KT21 ....75 F2
  Hounslow TW4 ....4 F2
  West Wickham BR4 ....63 B8
Bramley Wlk RH6 ....161 C3
Bramleyhyrst CR2 ....61 C5
Brampton Gdns KT12 ....54 C5
Brampton Rd CR0 ....42 F3
Bramshaw Rise KT3 ....38 E3
Bramshot La
  Blackwater GU17 ....64 A6
  Farnborough GU14 ....84 C6
Bramstott Ct 8 KT6 ....37 E3
Bramston Rd SW17 ....20 C5
Bramswell Rd GU7 ....150 F6
Bramwell Cl TW16 ....35 D7
Brancaster La CR8 ....80 C8
Brancaster Rd SW16 ....21 E5
Brancker Cl SM6 ....60 E3
Brandon Cl Crawley RH10 ..202 D4
  Frimley GU15 ....66 D5
Brandon House BR3 ....24 B3
Brandon Rd SM1 ....59 B6
Brandreth Rd SW17 ....21 B6
Brandries The SM6 ....60 D7
Brands Rd SL3 ....1 B8
Brandsland RH2 ....139 B6
Brandy Way SM2 ....59 A3
Brangbourne Rd BR1 ....24 C3
Brangwyn Cres SW19 ....40 D7
Branksome Cl
  Camberley GU15 ....65 E6
  Walton-on-T KT12 ....54 D8
Branksome Hill Rd GU47 ....64 E8
Branksome Park Rd GU15 ...65 E6
Branksome Rd SW19 ....40 A8
Branksome Way KT3 ....38 D8
Bransby Rd KT9 ....56 E4
Branscombe Ct BR2 ....44 E4
Branstone Ct 8 TW9 ....6 F6
Brantridge Rd RH10 ....202 A6
Brants Bridge RG12 ....27 E7
Brantwood Ave TW7 ....6 A4
Brantwood Cl 1 KT14 ....71 A6
Brantwood Ct KT14 ....70 F6
Brantwood Dr KT14 ....70 F6
Brantwood Gdns KT14 ......71 A6
Brantwood Rd CR2 ....61 D2
Brassey Cl TW14 ....15 A7
Brassey Rd RH8 ....123 A4

Brasted Cl Belmont SM2 .....59 A1
  Forest Hill SE26 ....23 C4
Brasted Lodge 1 BR3 ....24 A1
Brathway Rd SW18 ....20 A8
Bratten Ct CR0 ....42 D3
Bravington Cl TW17 ....33 F4
Braxted Pk SW16 ....21 F2
Bray Cl RH10 ....202 D4
Bray Ct KT9 ....56 F5
Bray Gdns GU22 ....70 E3
Bray Rd Guildford GU2 .....130 B8
  Stoke D'Abernon KT11 ......73 E3
Braybourne Dr TW7 ....5 F7
Braybrooke Gdns SE19 ......22 E1
Braycourt Ave KT12 ....35 C2
Braye Cl GU47 ....45 C1
Braywick Ct 9 KT2 ....18 A1
Braywood Ave TW20 ....12 A2
Braziers La SL4, SL5 ....8 D4
Breakfield CR5 ....79 E3
Breakspeare SE21 ....22 F5
Breamore Cl SW15 ....19 A7
Breamwater Gdns TW10 ....17 B5
Brecon Cl
  Farnborough GU14 ....84 D7
  Mitcham CR4 ....41 E6
  North Cheam KT4 ....58 C8
Brecon House SW18 ....20 A8
Bredhurst Cl SE20 ....23 C2
Bredinghurst SE22 ....23 A8
Bredon Rd CR0 ....42 F2
Bredune CR8 ....80 D4
Breech La KT20 ....97 A2
Breech The GU47 ....64 E7
Breezehurst Dr RH11 ......200 F3
Bregsells La RH5 ....157 D4
Bremans Row SW18 ....20 C6
Bremer Rd TW18, TW19 ....13 A5
Bremner Ave RH6 ....160 F4
Brenchley Cl BR2 ....44 F3
Brenda Rd SW17 ....20 F6
Brende Gdns KT8 ....36 B5
Brendon Cl Esher KT10 .....55 C4
  Harlington LB7 ....3 C7
Brendon Dr KT10 ....55 C4
Brendon House SM2 ....59 C4
Brendon Rd GU14 ....84 D7
Brenley Cl CR4 ....41 A6
Brent House 8 KT2 ....18 B1
Brent Knoll Spec Sch
  SE23 ....23 D5
Brent Lea TW8 ....6 C7
Brent Rd Brentford TW8 ......6 C7
  South Croydon CR2 ....62 B2
Brent Way TW8 ....6 D7
Brentford Bsns Ctr TW8 .....6 C7
Brentford High St TW8 ....6 C8
Brentford House 7 TW1 ....17 B8
Brentford Sch for Girls
  TW8 ....6 C8
Brentford Sta TW8 ....6 C8
Brentmoor Rd GU24 ....67 D6
Brentside TW8 ....6 C7
Brentside Executive Ctr
  TW8 ....6 B7
Brentwaters Bsns Pk TW8 ...6 C7
Brentwood Ct KT15 ....52 B6
Brereton House 4 SW2 .....22 A8
Breton Cross KT23 ....93 F1
Bret Harte Rd GU14 ....85 E1
Bretherton Ct CR2 ....62 A1
Bretlands Rd KT16 ....51 E8
Brett House 1 SW15 ....19 D8
Brett House Ct 2 SW15 .....19 D8
Brettgrave RH11 ....200 E2
Brettingham Cl RH11 ......200 E3
Brew House Rd RH3 ....137 B5
Brewer Rd RH10 ....201 E4
Brewer St RH1 ....120 C4
Brewers Cl GU14 ....85 A5
Brewers La 11 TW9 ....6 D2
Brewery La KT14 ....71 E6
Brewery Mews Bsns Ctr
  TW7 ....6 D4
Brewery Rd GU21 ....69 E2
Brewhurst La RH14 ....213 A2
Breydon Wlk RH10 ....202 B4
Brian Ave CR2 ....80 E7
Briane Rd KT19 ....57 C1
Briar Ave Lightwater GU18 ..67 A8
  South Norwood SW16 ....21 F1
Briar Banks SM5 ....60 A2
Briar Cl Crawley RH11 ......181 C1
  Hampton TW12 ....15 F3
  Isleworth TW7 ....5 F2
  West Byfleet KT14 ....71 A6
Briar Ct Cheam SM3 ....58 C6
  Hampton TW12 ....16 B3
Briar Gdns BR2 ....44 F1
Briar Gr CR2 ....80 E7
Briar Hill CR8 ....79 E8
Briar La Croydon CR0 ....63 B6
  Wallington SM5 ....60 A2
Briar Patch GU7 ....150 D6
Briar Rd Littleton TW17 ......34 A6
  Send GU23 ....90 B4
  Thornton Heath CR7, SW16 .42 A6
Briar Wlk KT14 ....71 A6
Briardale SW19 ....19 D7
Briars Cross RH8 ....123 D5
Briars Ct KT22 ....74 D5
Briars The Ash GU12 ....106 B1
  Stanwell TW7 ....19 F7
Briars Wood RH6 ....161 C4

Briarswood Cl RH10 ....202...
Briarwood Cl TW13 ....14 D7
Briarwood Ct 5 KT4 ....39...
Briarwood Rd
  Knaphill GU21 ....88...
  Stoneleigh KT17 ....58...
Briary Lodge BR3 ....44...
Briavels Ct KT18 ....76...
Brick Farm Cl TW9 ....7...
Brick Kiln La RH8 ....123...
Brickfield Cl TW8 ....6...
Brickfield La UB3 ....3...
Brickfield Rd
  Outwood RH1 ....162...
  South Norwood CR7, SW16 ..42...
  Wimbledon SW19 ....20...
Brickhouse La RH7, RH9 ...163...
Bricklands RH10 ....204...
Bricksbury Hill GU9 ....125...
Brickwood Cl SE26 ....23...
Brickwood Rd CR0 ....61...
Brickyard Copse RH5 ....177...
Brickyard La
  Crawley Down RH10 ....204...
  Shere GU5 ....134...
Brideake Cl RH11 ....201...
Bridge Barn La GU21 ....69...
Bridge Cl Byfleet KT14 ......71...
  Lower Halliford KT12 ....34...
  Staines TW18 ....13...
  Teddington TW11 ....16...
  Woking GU21 ....69...
Bridge Cotts GU6 ....174...
Bridge Ct Cranleigh GU6 ...174...
  Leatherhead KT22 ....95...
  2 Weybridge KT13 ....53...
  Woking GU21 ....69...
Bridge End GU15 ....65...
Bridge Gdns
  East Molesey KT8 ....36...
  Littleton TW15 ....14...
Bridge La GU25, KT16 ......31...
Bridge Mead GU24 ....87...
Bridge Mews
  Godalming GU7 ....150...
  Tongham GU10 ....126...
  Woking GU21 ....69...
Bridge Par CR8 ....80...
Bridge Pl CR0 ....42...
Bridge Rd Aldershot GU11 .126...
  Ascot SL5 ....29...
  Bagshot GU19 ....47...
  Beckenham BR3 ....23...
  Camberley GU15 ....65...
  Chertsey KT16 ....33...
  Chessington KT9 ....56...
  Cobham KT11 ....73...
  Cranleigh GU6 ....174...
  East Molesey KT8 ....36...
  Epsom KT17 ....76...
  Farnborough GU14 ....84...
  Farnham GU9 ....125...
  Haslemere GU27 ....208...
  Hounslow TW3 ....5...
  Isleworth TW3, TW7 ....5...
  Penge BR3 ....23...
  Rudgwick RH12 ....214...
  Sutton SM2 ....59...
  Twickenham TW1 ....16...
  Wallington SM6 ....60...
  Weybridge KT13 ....53...
  Bridge Row CR0 ....42...
  Bridge St GU9 ....125...
  Bridge St Colnbrook SL3 .....1...
  Godalming GU7 ....150...
  Guildford GU1 ....130...
  Leatherhead KT22 ....95...
  Richmond TW10 ....6...
  Staines TW18 ....12...
  Walton-on-T KT12 ....35...
  Bridge View SL5 ....30...
  Bridge Way Chipstead CR5 ..98...
  Twickenham TW2 ....16...
  Bridge Works GU15 ....65...
  Bridgefield GU9 ....125...
  Bridgefield Cl SM7 ....77...
  Bridgefield Rd SM1, SM2 ...59...
  Bridgeham Cl KT13 ....53...
  Bridgeham Way RH6 ....162...
  Bridgehill Cl GU2 ....109...
  Bridgelands RH10 ....183...
  Bridgeman Rd TW11 ....17...
  Bridgemead RG16 ....85...
  Bridges La CR0 ....60...
  Bridges Ct RH12 ....218...
  Bridges La CR0 ....60...
  Bridges Rd SW19 ....20...
  Bridges Road Mews SW19 ..20...
  Bridgetown Cl 6 SE19 ......22...
  Bridgewater Rd KT13 ....53...
  Bridgewood Cl
    North Cheam KT17, KT4 ....58...
    Streatham SW16 ....21...
  Bridge Cl SW17, SW18 ....20...
  Bridle Cl Grayshott GU26 ..188...
    Kingston u T KT1 ....37...
    Stoneleigh KT19 ....57...
    Sunbury TW16 ....35...
    West Ewell KT19 ....57...
  Bridle Ct GU11 ....104...
  Bridle La
    Oxshott KT11, KT22 ....74...
    Twickenham TW1 ....6...
  Bridle Path CR0 ....60...
  Bridle Path The KT17 ......58...
  Bridle Rd Addington CR0 ....63...
    Claygate KT10 ....56...
    Croydon CR0 ....63...

idle Rd continued
psom KT17 . . . . 76 F6
idle Rd The CR8 . . . . 89 A1
idle Way Crawley RH10 . . . 202 D7
Croydon CR0 . . . . 63 A6
idle Way The SW6 . . . . . . 60 C5
idlepath Way TW14 . . . . . 14 E8
estonary GU1 . . . . 58 C1
idlington Ct TN16 . . . . . . 103 B8
idport Rd CR7 . . . . 42 B6
ier Lea KT20 . . . . 97 F1
ierley Rd KT20 . . . . 97 B8
ierley CR0 . . . . 83 B9
ierley Ct SE25 . . . . 43 A5
ierley Rd SW12 . . . . 21 C6
ierley Cl GU22 . . . . 109 A3
iggs Cl CR4 . . . . 41 B8
ight Hill GU1 . . . . 130 E7
ighlands Rd RH2 . . . . . . 118 C3
ightman Rd SW18 . . . . . . 20 D7
ighton Cl KT15 . . . . 52 C5
ighton Rd
addlestone KT15 . . . . . . 52 C5
Aldershot GU11, GU12 . . . 126 C8
unstead SM2 . . . . 79 B5
iugh Heath KT20, SM2, SM7 77 F3
imshot Ca CR5, CR8 . . . . 79 D4
rawley RH11 . . . . 201 A4
reydon CR2, CR8 . . . . . . 61 C3
oodalming GU7 . . . . 151 A1
ooley CR5, RH1 . . . . 99 B6
orley RH6 . . . . 160 F2
orsham RH13 . . . . 217 C1
ingston u t KT8 . . . . 37 D3
ingswood KT20 . . . . 97 E5
ower Kingswood KT20 . . . 117 F8
urley CR8 . . . . 80 B8
edhill RH1 . . . . 139 F8
edhill RH1 . . . . 139 F1
alfords RH1 . . . . 140 A2
outh Croydon CR2 . . . . . 61 C3
utton SM2 . . . . 59 B2
ightside Ave TW18 . . . . . 13 C1
ightwell CF0 . . . . 42 A1
ightwall Cres SW17 . . . . 20 F3
ightwells Rd GU9 . . . . . . 125 C2
igstock Ra Coulsdon CR5 . 79 B3
hornton Heath CR7 . . . . . 42 B5
imshot La GU24 . . . . 49 E2
indle CI GU11 . . . . 126 C4
indles The SM7 . . . . 77 F2
indley House E2 SW12 . . 21 C8
ine Ct KT6 . . . . 37 D4
inkley Rd KT4 . . . . 58 B8
inkworth PI SL4 . . . . 11 B8
inn's La GU7 . . . . 64 C5
insworth Cl TW2 . . . . . . 16 B6
isbane Ave SW19 . . . . . . 40 B8
isbane Cl RH11 . . . . 181 D1
iscoe Rd SW19 . . . . 20 D2
isson Cl KT13 . . . . 54 E4
istol Cl Crawley RH10 . . . 182 D1
tanwell TW19 . . . . 2 E1
istol Ct 7 TW19 . . . . 2 E1
istol Rd SM4 . . . . 40 C4
istow Cty Inf Sch GU15 . . 65 B2
istow Rd
amberley GU15 . . . . 65 B3
ounslow TW3 . . . . 5 C4
vallington CR0 . . . . 60 F8
orset Norwood SE19 . . . . 22 E3
itannia Ind Est SL3 . . . . . 1 E5
itannia Rd KT5 . . . . 37 F2
itannia Way TW19 . . . . . 13 D8
itish Home & Hospl for
ncurables SE27 . . . . 22 B3
iton Ct CR2 . . . . 80 E8
iton Cres CR2 . . . . 80 E8
iton Hill Rd CR2 . . . . . . 61 F1
ittain Ct GU47 . . . . 64 C7
ittain Rd KT12 . . . . 54 D5
itten La Ash GU12 . . . . . 106 B2
rawley RH11 . . . . 200 F3
roadlands RH14 . . . . 218 B4
ittens Cl GU2, GU3 . . . . . 109 A6
itton Cl SE6 . . . . 24 D8
ixton Hill SW2 . . . . 21 E8
ixton Hill PI SW2 . . . . . . 21 E8
oad Acres GU7 . . . . 150 E8
oad Cl KT12 . . . . 54 E7
oad Green Ave CR0 . . . . . 42 B1
oad Ha'penny GU10 . . . . 146 A5
oad Highway KT11 . . . . . 73 D5
oad La Bracknell RG12 . . 27 D6
ampton TW12 . . . . 16 A2
arkgate RH2, RH5 . . . . . 158 E6
oad Oak TW16 . . . . 14 C7
oad Oak SW15 . . . . 57 B8
oad Oaks Way BR2 . . . . . 44 F4
oad St Guildford GU3 . . . 108 D3
eddington TW11 . . . . . . 16 F2
vest End GU24 . . . . 67 E6
Wokingham RG40 . . . . . . 25 C6
Wood St V GU3 . . . . 108 D3
oad St Wlk RG40 . . . . . . 25 C6
oad Wlk
urgh Heath KT18 . . . . . . 97 D8
aterham CR3 . . . . 100 F5
ranleigh GU6 . . . . 174 F1
rawley RH10 . . . . 201 D6
eddington TW5 . . . . 4 D6
rmley GU16 . . . . 65 E2
eston TW5 . . . . 4 B6
ower Kingswood CR5 . . . 99 A4
ichmond TW9 . . . . 6 F7
oadacre TW18 . . . . 13 A3
oadacres GU3 . . . . 108 E2
oadbridge Heath Rd
RH12 . . . . 216 D4

Broadbridge La
Burstow RH6 . . . . 183 B8
Smallfield RH6 . . . . 162 A2
Broadbridge Ret Pk
RH12 . . . . 216 E3
Broadcoombe CR2 . . . . . 62 D3
Broadfield Barton 4
RH11 . . . . 201 B2
Broadfield Cl
Burgh Heath KT20 . . . . . 97 C7
Croydon CR0 . . . . 60 F8
Broadfield Dr RH11 . . . . . 201 B3
Broadfield East Cty Fst Sch
RH11 . . . . 201 C2
Broadfield East Cty Mid
Sch RH11 . . . . 201 C2
Broadfield North Cty Fst
& Mid Sch RH11 . . . . . . 201 B2
Broadfield Pl RH11 . . . . . 201 B2
Broadfield Rd Catford SE6 . 24 E7
Peaslake GU5 . . . . 154 D8
Broadfields 36 E3
Broadford La GU24 . . . . . 68 E7
Broadford Pk GU4 . . . . . 130 D2
Broadford Rd GU4 . . . . . 130 D2
Broadgates Rd SW18 . . . . 20 D7
Broadham Green Rd
RH8 . . . . 122 D2
Broadham Pl RH8 . . . . . . 122 D4
Broadhurst Ashstead KT21 . 75 E3
Farnborough GU14 . . . . . 84 C5
Broadhurst Cl 8 RH2 . . . . 118 B1
Broadhurst Gdns RH2 . . . 139 B6
Broadlands
Farnborough GU14 . . . . . 85 E2
Feltham TW13 . . . . 16 A5
Frimley GU16 . . . . 85 F8
Horley RH6 . . . . 161 C4
Broadlands Ave
Shepperton SW17 . . . . . . 34 C3
Streatham SW16 . . . . 21 E6
Broadlands Ct SW16 . . . . 21 E6
Broadlands Ct
Bracknell RG42 . . . . 26 E8
Richmond TW9 . . . . 7 A7
Broadlands Dr
Sunningdale SL5 . . . . 29 D2
Warlingham CR6 . . . . 101 C8
Broadlands Mansions 2
SW16 . . . . 21 E6
Broadlands Way KT3 . . . . 38 F3
Broadley Gn GU20 . . . . . 48 C4
Broadmead Ashstead KT21 . 75 F2
Catford SE6 . . . . 24 A5
Horley RH6 . . . . 161 C4
Merstham RH1 . . . . 119 C6
Broadmead Ave KT4 . . . . 39 A2
Broadmead Cl TW12 . . . . 16 A2
Broadmead Inf Sch CR0 . . 42 D2
Broadmead Jun Sch CR0 . . 42 D3
Broadmead Rd GU22, GU23 . 90 B5
Broadmeads GU23 . . . . . . 90 B5
Broadmere Cty Prim Sch
The GU21 . . . . 70 C4
Broadmoor Cott RH5 . . . . 156 A8
Broadmoor Cty Prim Sch
RG45 . . . . 45 D4
Broadmoor Hospl RG45 . . 45 E5
Broadoaks Cres KT14 . . . . 71 B6
Broadview Est TW19 . . . . 14 A8
Broadview Rd SW16 . . . . 21 D1
Broadwater Cl
Hersham KT12 . . . . 54 A5
Sheerwater GU21 . . . . . . 70 D7
Wraysbury TW19 . . . . 11 F8
Broadwater House 1
KT13 . . . . 53 B7
Broadwater Inf Sch SW17 . 20 E4
Broadwater Jun Sch
SW17 . . . . 20 E4
Broadwater Rd SW17 . . . . 20 E4
Broadwater Rd N KT12 . . . 54 A5
Broadwater Rd S KT12 . . . 54 A5
Broadwater Rise GU1 . . . 131 A8
Broadway Bracknell RG12 . . 27 C7
Knaphill GU21 . . . . 68 C1
Staines TW18 . . . . 13 B2
Tolworth KT6 . . . . 38 B1
Winkfield SL4 . . . . 9 B7
Broadway Ave
Thornton Heath CR0 . . . . 42 D4
Twickenham TW1 . . . . . . 6 B1
Broadway Cl CR2 . . . . . . 81 B5
Broadway Ct
Beckenham BR3 . . . . 44 C6
Wimbledon SW19 . . . . . . 19 F2
Broadway Gdns CR4 . . . . 40 E5
Broadway House GU21 . . . 68 C1
Broadway Mkt SW17 . . . . 20 F4
Broadway Rd
Lightwater GU18 . . . . 48 C2
Windlesham GU18, GU20 . . 48 C2
Broadway The Cheam SM3 . 58 E4
Crawley RH10 . . . . 201 D6
Laleham TW18 . . . . 33 C7
Mortlake SW14 . . . . 7 E5
Sandhurst GU47 . . . . 64 B8
Sutton SM1 . . . . 59 C6
Thames Ditton KT10 . . . . 36 E1
Tolworth KT6 . . . . 38 B4
Wallington SM6 . . . . 60 B6
Wimbledon SW19 . . . . . . 19 E2
Woking GU21 . . . . 69 E2
Woodham KT15 . . . . 52 A1
Broadwell Ct TW5 . . . . . . 4 D6
Broadwell Rd GU10 . . . . . 145 F6

Broadwood Cl RH12 . . . . 218 A5
Broadwood Cotts RH5 . . . 178 E6
Broadwood Rise RH11 . . . 201 A2
Brock Rd RH11 . . . . 181 B1
Brock Way GU25 . . . . 31 C5
Brock's Cl GU7 . . . . 151 A5
Brockbridge House SW15 . 7 F1
Brockenhurst V19 . . . . . . 7 F1
Brockenhurst Ave KT4 . . . 38 E1
Brockenhurst Cl GU21 . . . 69 F5
Brockenhurst Rd
Aldershot GU11 . . . . 126 B8
Ascot SL5 . . . . 29 B3
Bracknell RG12 . . . . 28 A6
Croydon CR0 . . . . 43 B2
Brockenhurst Way SW16 . . 41 D7
Brockham Cl SW19 . . . . . 19 F3
Brockham Cres CR0 . . . . . 63 D3
Brockham Ct 4 SM2 . . . . 59 B3
Brockham Dr SW2 . . . . . . 21 F8
Brockham Dr SW2 . . . . . . 21 F8
Brockham Hill Pk KT20 . . 116 C4
Brockhamhurst Rd RH3 . . 137 A2
Brockham La RH3, RH4 . . 116 A1
Brockhurst CI RH12 . . . . . 216 F1
Brockhurst Cotts GU6 . . . 193 F4
Brockhurst Lodge GU9 . . . 146 B7
Brocklebank Ct CR6 . . . . 81 A1
Brocklebank Rd SW18 . . . 20 C8
Brocklesby Rd SE25 . . . . 43 B5
Brocks Dr Cheam SM3 . . . 58 E7
Fairlands GU3 . . . . 108 C5
Brockshot Cl 1 TW8 . . . . . 6 D8
Brockton GU7 . . . . 150 E5
Brockway Cl GU1 . . . . . . 110 A2
Brockwell Park Gdns SE24 . 22 B8
Broderick House SE21 . . . 22 E5
Brodie House 7 SM6 . . . . 60 B6
Brodie Rd GU1 . . . . 130 E8
Brodrick Gr KT23 . . . . . . 94 A1
Brodrick Rd SW17 . . . . . . 20 E6
Brograve Gdns BR3 . . . . . 44 B7
Broke Ct GU4 . . . . 110 C4
Brokes Cres RH2 . . . . 118 A3
Brokes Rd RH2 . . . . 118 A3
Bromford Ct RH8 . . . . . . 123 A2
Bromleigh Ct SE21, SE22 . 23 B6
Bromley Ave BR1 . . . . . . 24 E1
Bromley Cres BR1 . . . . . . 24 F1
Bromley Gdns BR2 . . . . . 44 F6
Bromley Gr BR2 . . . . 44 D7
Bromley Hill BR1 . . . . . . 24 E2
Bromley Pk BR1 . . . . 44 F8
Bromley Rd Beckenham BR3 . 44 B8
Beckenham BR2, BR3 . . . . 44 D7
Catford SE6, BR1 . . . . . . 24 C5
Bromley Road Infs Sch
BR3 . . . . 44 B8
Brompton Cl Hounslow TW4 . 4 F2
Penge SE20 . . . . 43 A7
Bromwich House 3 TW10 . . 6 E1
Bronson Rd SW20 . . . . . . 39 E7
Bronte Ct 14 RH1 . . . . . . 119 A2
Brontes The RH19 . . . . . . 185 D1
Brook Ave GU9 . . . . 125 F7
Brook Cl Ash GU12 . . . . . 106 B3
East Grinstead RH19 . . . . 186 B1
Epsom KT19 . . . . 57 E2
Sandhurst GU47 . . . . 45 E1
Stanwell TW19 . . . . 13 F8
West Barnes SW20 . . . . . 39 D6
Wokingham RG41 . . . . . . 25 A8
Brook Cl Bracknell BR3 . . . 44 E8
Brentford TW8 . . . . 6 D8
Cheam SM3 . . . . 58 E8
Mortlake SW14 . . . . 7 E4
Brook Dr Ashford TW16 . . 14 C7
Bracknell RG12 . . . . 27 E5
Brook Farm Rd KT11 . . . . 73 D4
Brook Gdns Barnes SW13 . . 7 F4
Farnborough GU14 . . . . . 84 E3
Kingston u T KT2 . . . . . . 38 C8
Brook Gn Bracknell RG42 . . 26 F8
Chobham GU24 . . . . 49 F1
Brook Hill
Farley Green GU5 . . . . . . 153 D8
Oxted RH8 . . . . 122 C5
Brook House
Cranleigh GU6 . . . . 174 F4
Heath End GU9 . . . . 125 D6
4 Twickenham TW1 . . . . . 17 A8
Brook La Chobham GU24 . . 68 D8
Farley Green GU5 . . . . . . 132 E1
Faygate RH12 . . . . 218 C8
Send GU23 . . . . 90 E5
Brook La Bns Ctr 4 TW8 . . 6 D8
Brook La N 8 TW8 . . . . . . 6 D8
Brook Mead KT19 . . . . . . 57 E4
Brook Meadow GU8 . . . . 191 C3
Brook Rd Bagshot GU19 . . 47 E3
Brook GU8 . . . . 190 D8
Camberley GU15 . . . . 65 B4
Chilworth GU4 . . . . 131 C3
Horsham RH12 . . . . 217 E6
Merstham RH1 . . . . 119 C7
Redhill RH1 . . . . 139 F8
Surbiton KT6 . . . . 56 E8
Thornton Heath CR7 . . . . 42 C5
Twickenham TW1 . . . . . . 6 A1

Brook Rd continued
Wormley GU8 . . . . 170 E1
Brook Rd S TW8 . . . . 6 D8
Brook St KT1 . . . . 37 E7
Brook Trad Est The GU12 . 105 E2
Brook Valley RH5 . . . . . . 136 B1
Brook Way KT22 . . . . 75 A1
Brookdale Rd Catford SE6 . 24 B8
2 Lewisham SE13 . . . . . . 24 B8
Brooke Ct 7 . . . . 17 D4
Brooke Forest GU3 . . . . . 108 C5
Brookehowse Rd SE6 . . . . 24 B5
Brookers Cl KT21 . . . . . . 75 D2
Brookers Cnr RG45 . . . . . 45 C5
Brookers Row RG45 . . . . 45 C6
Brookfield Farncombe GU7 . 151 A8
Brookfield Woking GU21 . . 69 A3
Brookfield Ave SM1, SM5 . . 59 E7
Brookfield Cl
Ottershaw KT16 . . . . 51 D4
Redhill RH1 . . . . 140 A3
Brookfield Gdns KT10 . . . 55 F4
Brookfield Gdns GU12 . . . 105 F3
Brookfield Rd GU12 . . . . . 105 F3
Brookfield Rd GU14 . . . . . 84 F6
Brookhill Cl RH10 . . . . . . 183 A3
Brookhill Rd RH10 . . . . . . 183 A3
Brookhouse Rd GU14 . . . . 84 F3
Brookhurst Rd KT15 . . . . 52 B4
Brooklands GU11 . . . . . . 104 E1
Brooklands Ave SW19 . . . 20 C2
Brooklands Cl
Charlton TW16 . . . . 34 E8
Cobham KT11 . . . . 73 E4
Heath End GU9 . . . . 125 D7
Brooklands Coll KT13 . . . 52 F4
Brooklands Ct
Kingston u T KT1 . . . . . . 37 D5
Mitcham CR4 . . . . 40 D7
New Haw KT15 . . . . 52 D1
Reigate RH2 . . . . 118 B3
Brooklands Ind Est KT13 . 52 E1
Brooklands La KT13 . . . . . 52 E1
Brooklands Mus KT13 . . . 53 A1
Brooklands Rd
Crawley RH11 . . . . 201 C1
Heath End GU9 . . . . 125 E7
Thames Ditton KT7 . . . . . 37 A1
Weybridge KT13 . . . . 53 B3
Weybridge KT13, KT14 . . . 72 A8
Brooklands Sch RH2 . . . . 118 B3
Brooklands The TW7 . . . . 5 D6
Brooklands Way
East Grinstead RH19 . . . . 205 D8
Heath End GU9 . . . . 125 E7
Redhill RH1 . . . . 118 E3
Brookley Cl GU10 . . . . . . 126 C3
Brookleys GU24 . . . . 49 F1
Brooklyn Ave SE20 . . . . . 23 A1
Brooklyn Cl Carshalton SM5 . 59 E8
Woking GU22 . . . . 89 E8
Brooklyn Ct GU22 . . . . . . 89 E8
Brooklyn Gr SE25 . . . . . . 43 B5
Brooklyn Rd Croydon SE25 . 43 B5
Woking GU22 . . . . 89 E8
Brookmead CR4 . . . . 41 C3
Brookmead Ct
Cranleigh GU6 . . . . 174 F2
Farnham GU9 . . . . 125 B1
Brookmead Rd CR0 . . . . . 41 C3
Brooks Cl KT13 . . . . 53 A1
Brooks House 6 SW2 . . . . 22 A7
Brooks La W4 . . . . 7 A8
Brooks Rd W4 . . . . 7 A8
Brooksby Cl GU17 . . . . . . 64 B5
Brookscroft CR0 . . . . 62 E1
Brookside
Beare Green RH5 . . . . 157 F6
Chertsey KT16 . . . . 32 E2
Colnbrook SL3 . . . . 1 C7
Copthorne RH10 . . . . 183 A3
Cranleigh GU6 . . . . 174 E3
Crawley RH10 . . . . 174 E3
Guildford GU4 . . . . 109 D6
Hale GU9 . . . . 125 D6
Sandhurst GU47 . . . . 64 C8
South Godstone RH9 . . . . 142 D5
Wallington SM5 . . . . 60 A3
Wokingham RG41 . . . . . . 25 A7
Brookside Ave TW15 . . . . 13 D3
Brookside Cl TW13 . . . . . 15 A5
Brookside Way CR0 . . . . . 43 D3
Brookside Cres KT4 . . . . . 39 A1
Brookview RH10 . . . . 183 A3
Brookview Rd SW16, SW17 . 21 C3
Brookwell La GU5 . . . . . . 152 B2
Brookwood RH6 . . . . 161 B4
Brookwood Ave SW13 . . . 7 F5
Brookwood CI BR2 . . . . . 44 F5
Brookwood Cty Fst & Mid
Sch GU24 . . . . 88 A7
Brookwood Hospl GU21 . . 88 D2
Brookwood Lye Rd
GU21, GU22 . . . . 88 C7
Brookwood Rd
Farnborough GU14 . . . . . 85 D4
Hounslow TW3 . . . . 5 B6
Wandsworth SW18 . . . . . 20 A7
Brookwood Sta GU24 . . . . 88 A6
Broom Acres GU47 . . . . . 45 B1
Broom Bank CR6 . . . . . . 102 C8
Broom Cl Blackwater GU17 . 64 E4
Esher KT10 . . . . 55 B5
Teddington TW11, TW11 . . 17 E2
Broom Field GU18 . . . . . . 67 A8

Broom Gdns CR0 . . . . . . 63 A7
Broom Hall GU22 . . . . . . 74 D5
Broom La GU24 . . . . 49 E3
Broom Lock TW11 . . . . . . 17 C2
Broom Pk KT1 . . . . 17 D1
Broom Rd Croydon CR0 . . 63 A7
Richmond TW11 . . . . 17 C3
Teddington KT1, TW11 . . . 17 C2
Broom Squires GU26 . . . . 188 E4
Broom Water TW11 . . . . . 17 C2
Broom Water W TW11 . . . 17 C2
Broom Way KT13 . . . . . . 53 E6
Broomcroft Cl GU22 . . . . 70 D3
Broomcroft Dr GU22 . . . . 70 D3
Broomdashers Rd RH10 . . 201 F7
Broome Cl RH12 . . . . 217 D5
Broome Ct 3 TW9 . . . . . . 7 A6
Broome Lodge TW12 . . . . 13 B3
Broome Rd TW12 . . . . . . 35 F8
Broome St KT18 . . . . 96 C1
Broomehall Rd
Coldharbour RH5 . . . . . . 156 D2
Ockley RH5 . . . . 177 E8
Broomers La GU6 . . . . . . 175 E5
Broomfield Ehstead GU8 . . 148 E4
Guildford GU2 . . . . 108 E2
Staines TW16 . . . . 13 A2
Sunbury TW16 . . . . 35 A8
Broomfield Cl
Guildford GU3 . . . . 108 E3
Sunningdale SL5 . . . . 30 B2
Broomfield Cotts RH2 . . . 97 E8
Broomfield Ct KT13 . . . . . 53 B4
Broomfield Dr SL5 . . . . . . 30 B3
Broomfield La GU10 . . . . . 146 A1
Broomfield Pk
Sunningdale SL5 . . . . 30 B2
Westcott RH4 . . . . 135 C6
Broomfield Rd
Beckenham BR3 . . . . 43 F6
Richmond TW9 . . . . 6 F6
Surbiton KT5 . . . . 37 F1
Teddington TW11 . . . . . . 17 C2
Woodham KT15 . . . . 71 B8
Broomfield Ride KT22 . . . 74 D7
Broomfields KT10 . . . . . . 55 C5
Broomhall Bldgs SL5 . . . . 30 B2
Broomhall End GU21 . . . . 69 E3
Broomhall La
Sunningdale SL5 . . . . 30 A3
Woking GU21 . . . . 69 E3
Broomhall Rd
South Croydon CR2 . . . . . 61 D2
Woking GU21 . . . . 69 E3
Broomhill GU10 . . . . 124 D8
Broomhill Rd GU14 . . . . . 84 D5
Broomhurst Ct RH4 . . . . . 136 B5
Broomlands La RH8 . . . . . 123 E8
Broomleaf Cnr GU9 . . . . . 125 E2
Broomleaf Rd GU9 . . . . . 125 E2
Broomleigh Bsns Pk SE26 . 23 E3
Broomloan La SM1 . . . . . 59 A8
Broomsquires Rd GU19 . . 47 F2
Broomwood Cl CR0 . . . . . 43 D4
Broomwood Way GU10 . . 146 C6
Broseley Gr SE26 . . . . . . 23 E3
Broster Gdns SE25 . . . . . 42 F6
Brough Cl KT2 . . . . 17 D3
Brougham Pl GU9 . . . . . . 125 B7
Broughton Ave TW10 . . . 17 C4
Broughton Gdns GU16 . . . 65 F1
Broughton Rd CR7 . . . . . 42 A3
Brow The RH1 . . . . 140 A4
Browell House GU4 . . . . . 110 D2
Browells La TW13 . . . . . . 15 B6
Brown Bear Ct TW13 . . . . 15 D4
Brown Cl SM6 . . . . 60 E3
Brown's Hill RH1 . . . . . . 141 D2
Brown's Rd KT5, KT6 . . . . 37 F2
Browne House 3 SE26 . . . 23 A4
Browngraves Rd UB7 . . . . 3 C7
Brownhill Rd SE6 . . . . . . 24 C8
Browning Ave
Carshalton SM1 . . . . 59 E6
North Cheam KT4 . . . . . . 39 B1
Browning Cl
Crawley RH10 . . . . 202 C7
Frimley GU15 . . . . 66 C4
Hampton TW12 . . . . 15 F4
Browning Rd KT22 . . . . . 94 D2
Browning Way TW5 . . . . . 4 D6
Brownings The 1 RH19 . . . 185 C1
Brownlow Rd redhill RH1 . 118 E1
South Croydon CR2 . . . . . 61 E6
Brownrigg Cres RG12 . . . 27 E8
Brownrigg Rd TW15 . . . . 14 A4
Browns La KT24 . . . . 113 D8
Browns Wlk GU10 . . . . . . 145 F5
Browns Wood RH19 . . . . 185 E4
Brownsover Rd GU14 . . . 84 C4
Brox La
Addlestone KT15, KT16 . . . 51 D2
Ottershaw KT15, KT16 . . . 51 D2
Woodham KT15, KT16 . . . 51 D2
Brox Rd KT16 . . . . 51 D3
Broxholm Rd SE27, SW16 . 22 A5
Broxted Rd SE23, SE6 . . . 23 F6
Bruce Ave TW17 . . . . 34 C3
Bruce Cl KT14 . . . . 71 E6
Bruce Dr CR2 . . . . 62 D2
Bruce Hall Mews SW17 . . 21 A4
Bruce Lawns SW17 . . . . . 21 A4
Bruce Rd Mitcham CR4 . . 21 A1
South Norwood SE25 . . . . 42 D5
Brudenell Rd SW17 . . . . . 21 A4

Brumana Cl KT13 . . . . .53 B4
Brumfield Rd KT19 . . . . .57 C5
Brunel Cl Cranford TW5 . . . . . . .4 B7
 South Norwood SE19 . . . . .22 F2
Brunel Ct SW13 . . . . .7 F5
Brunel Cir TW10 . . . . .181 F2
Brunel Dr RG45 . . . . .45 C8
Brunel House **25** SW2 . . . . . . .21 E8
Brunel Pl RH10 . . . . .201 E5
Brunel Univ Coll Osterley
 Campus TW7 . . . . .5 F7
Brunel Univ Coll
 (Twickenham Campus)
 TW1 .6 B3
Brunel Univ (Runnymede
 Campus) TW20 . . . . .11 C5
Brunel Wlk **5** TW4 . . . . .16 A8
Brunner Ct KT16 . . . . .51 C5
Brunner House SE6 . . . . .24 C4
Brunswick RG12 . . . . .27 A2
Brunswick Cl
 Crawley RH10 . . . . .202 A4
 Thames Ditton KT7 . . . . .36 F1
 Twickenham TW2 . . . . .16 D5
 Walton-on-T KT12 . . . . .54 C8
Brunswick Ct
 Crawley RH10 . . . . .202 A4
 Kingston u T KT2 . . . . .17 D2
 2 Penge SE19 . . . . .23 A1
Brunswick Dr GU24 . . . . .87 D7
Brunswick Gr KT11 . . . . .73 C6
Brunswick Mews SW16 . . . . . .21 D2
Brunswick Pl SE19 . . . . .23 A1
Brunswick Rd
 Kingston u T KT2 . . . . .38 A8
 Pirbright, Alexander
  Barracks GU24 . . . . .87 C6
 Pirbright, Blackdown
  Barracks GU16, GU24 . . . . . .86 E6
 Sutton SM1 . . . . .59 B6
Bruntile Cl GU14 . . . . .85 D1
Brushwood Rd RH12 . . . . . . .218 B6
Bruton Rd SM4 . . . . .40 C5
Bruton Way RG12 . . . . .27 E2
Bryan Cl TW16 . . . . .15 A1
Bryanston Ave TW2 . . . . .16 B7
Bryanstone Ave GU2 . . . . . . .109 A4
Bryanstone Cl GU2 . . . . .108 F4
Bryanstone Ct SM1 . . . . .59 C7
Bryanstone Gr GU2 . . . . .108 F5
Bryce Cl RH12 . . . . .218 A5
Bryce Gdns GU11 . . . . .126 C7
Bryden Cl SE26 . . . . .23 E3
Brympton Cl RH4 . . . . .136 A5
Bryn Rd GU10 . . . . .145 F7
Brynford Cl GU21 . . . . .69 E4
Bryony House RG42 . . . . .26 E8
Bryony Rd GU1 . . . . .110 B4
Bryony Way TW16 . . . . .15 A2
Buchan Country Park
 RH11 . . . . .200 E1
Buchan The GU15 . . . . .66 A8
Buchanan House
 Dulwich SE21 . . . . .22 E5
 Wandsworth SW18 . . . . .20 A8
Buchans Lawn RH11 . . . . . . .201 B2
Bucharest Rd SW18 . . . . .20 C8
Buckfast Rd SM4 . . . . .40 B5
Buckhurst Ave CR4, SM5 . . . . .40 F1
Buckhurst Cl
 East Grinstead RH19 . . . . . . .185 C3
 Redhill RH1 . . . . .118 F3
Buckhurst Cotts RH12 . . . . . .214 D8
Buckhurst Gr RG40 . . . . .25 F5
Buckhurst Hill RG12 . . . . .27 F5
Buckhurst La SL5 . . . . .30 A6
Buckhurst Mead RH19 . . . . . .185 C4
Buckhurst Moors RG12 . . . . . .26 C6
Buckhurst Rd Ascot SL5 . . . . .29 F7
 Frimley GU16 . . . . .85 F6
Buckhurst Way RH19 . . . . . . .185 C3
Buckingham Ave
 East Molesey KT8 . . . . .36 B7
 Feltham TW14 . . . . .4 B1
 South Norwood CR7 . . . . .42 A8
Buckingham Cl
 Guildford GU1 . . . . .109 F2
 Hampton TW12 . . . . .15 F3
Buckingham Ct
 Belmont SM2 . . . . .59 A4
 Crawley RH11 . . . . .201 B2
 Staines TW18 . . . . .13 A4
 Wokingham RG40 . . . . .25 C6
Buckingham Dr RH19 . . . . . . .206 A8
Buckingham Gate RH6 . . . . . .182 C7
Buckingham Gdns
 Hampton KT8 . . . . .36 B7
 South Norwood CR7 . . . . .42 A7
Buckingham La SE23 . . . . .23 E8
Buckingham Prim Sch
 TW12 . . . . .15 F3
Buckingham Rd
 Hampton TW12, TW13 . . . . . . .15 F3
 Kingston u T KT1 . . . . .37 F5
 Mitcham CR4 . . . . .41 A4
 Richmond TW10 . . . . .17 D6
 South Holmwood RH5 . . . . . .157 C6
Buckingham Way SM6 . . . . . . .60 C2
Buckland Cl GU14 . . . . .85 C7
Buckland Cnr RH2 . . . . .117 D2
Buckland Ct RH3 . . . . .117 B3
Buckland Cty Jun & Inf
 Sch TW18 . . . . .13 C1
Buckland Inf Sch KT9 . . . . .56 F6
Buckland La RH3 . . . . .117 B5

Buckland Rd
 Chessington KT9 . . . . .56 F5
 East Ewell SM2 . . . . .58 D2
 Lower Kingswood KT20 . . . . .117 F7
 Reigate RH2 . . . . .117 D2
Buckland Way KT4 . . . . .39 C1
Buckland Wlk SM4 . . . . .40 C5
Bucklands Rd TW11 . . . . .17 C2
Buckleberry RG12 . . . . .27 A2
Buckleigh Ave SW20 . . . . .39 F6
Buckleigh Rd SW16 . . . . .21 E1
Buckleigh Way SE19 . . . . .22 F1
Bucklers' Way SM5 . . . . .59 F7
Buckles Way SM7 . . . . .77 E3
Buckley Pl RH10 . . . . .204 A8
Buckmans Rd RH11 . . . . .201 D6
Bucknills Cl KT18 . . . . .76 C5
Bucks Cl KT14 . . . . .71 B5
Buckswood Dr RH11 . . . . . . .201 A4
Buckthorn Cl RG40 . . . . .25 E7
Buddhapadipa Temple The
 SW19 . . . . .19 D4
Budebury Rd TW18 . . . . .13 A3
Budge La CR4 . . . . .40 F2
Budge's Cotts RG40 . . . . .25 E8
Budge's Gdns RG40 . . . . .25 E7
Budge's Rd RG40 . . . . .25 D7
Budgen Dr RH10 . . . . .182 D1
Budgen Dr RH1 . . . . .119 A3
Budham Way RG12 . . . . .27 B3
Buff Ave SM7 . . . . .78 B4
Buffbeards La GU27 . . . . .207 E6
Buffers La KT22 . . . . .95 A8
Bug Hill CR6 . . . . .101 D7
Buckingham Way GU16 . . . . . .65 F1
Bulbrook Row RG12 . . . . .27 F7
Bulganak Rd CR7 . . . . .42 C5
Bulkeley Cl TW20 . . . . .11 C3
Bull Hill KT22 . . . . .95 A6
Bull La Bracknell RG42 . . . . . . .27 B8
 Woking GU4 . . . . .89 F1
Bullard Rd TW11 . . . . .16 F2
Bullbeggars La
 Godstone RH9 . . . . .121 C3
 Woking GU21 . . . . .69 B3
Bullbrook Dr RG12 . . . . .27 F8
Buller Cl GU14 . . . . .85 C1
Buller Rd CR7 . . . . .42 D6
Bullers Rd GU9 . . . . .125 E6
Bullfinch Cl Horley RH6 . . . . . .160 E4
 Horsham RH12 . . . . .217 C7
 Sandhurst GU47 . . . . .64 E8
Bullfinch Ct **3** SE21 . . . . .22 D6
Bullfinch Rd CR0 . . . . .62 D1
Bullrush Cl CR0 . . . . .42 E3
Bulls Alley SW14 . . . . .7 D4
Bullswater Common Rd
 GU24, GU3 . . . . .88 A2
Bullswater La GU24 . . . . .88 A2
Bulstrode Ave TW3 . . . . .5 A4
Bulstrode Gdns TW3 . . . . .5 A4
Bulstrode Rd TW3 . . . . .5 A4
Bunbury Way KT17 . . . . .77 B4
Bunce Common Rd
 RH2, RH3 . . . . .137 C2
Bunce Dr CR3 . . . . .100 D4
Bunch La GU27 . . . . .208 B8
Bunch Way GU27 . . . . .208 A6
Bundy's Way TW18 . . . . .12 F2
Bungalow Rd SE25 . . . . .42 E5
Bungalows The GU9 . . . . .146 B1
Bunting Cl Horsham RH13 . . . .217 F3
 Mitcham CR4 . . . . .40 F4
Buntings The GU9 . . . . .145 F8
Bunyan Cl RH11 . . . . .200 E3
Bunyard Dr GU21 . . . . .70 D6
Burbage Gn RG12 . . . . .27 F4
Burbage Rd SE21, SE24 . . . . . .22 D8
Burbeach Cl RH11 . . . . .201 B3
Burberry Cl KT3 . . . . .38 E7
Burbidge Rd TW17 . . . . .34 A5
Burchets Hollow GU5 . . . . . . .154 D7
Burchetts Way TW17 . . . . .34 B3
Burcote **6** KT15 . . . . .53 D4
Burcott Gdns KT15 . . . . .52 D4
Burcott Rd CR8 . . . . .80 A4
Burden Way GU2 . . . . .109 A5
Burdenshot Hill GU3, GU23 . . .89 B3
Burdenshott Ave TW10 . . . . . . .7 B3
Burdenshott Rd
 Guildford GU4 . . . . .109 C8
 Woking GU22, GU3, GU4 . . . . .89 A2
Burdett Ave SW20 . . . . .39 A8
Burdett Cl RH10 . . . . .202 D5
Burdett Rd Richmond TW9 . . . . .6 F4
 Thornton Heath CR0 . . . . .42 D3
Burdock Cl Crawley RH11 . . . .201 A2
 Croydon CR0 . . . . .43 D1
 Lightwater GU18 . . . . .67 B8
Burdon La SM2 . . . . .58 F2
Burdon Pk SM2 . . . . .58 F2
Burfield Cl SW17 . . . . .20 D4
Burfield Dr CR6 . . . . .101 C8
Burfield Rd SL4, TW19 . . . . . . .11 B8
Burford Ct RG40 . . . . .25 E5
Burford La KT17 . . . . .77 C8
Burford Lea GU8 . . . . .148 E4
Burford Rd Camberley GU15 . . .65 B4
 Forest Hill SE6 . . . . .23 F6
 Horsham RH13 . . . . .217 E2
 New Malden KT4 . . . . .39 A2
 Sutton SM1 . . . . .59 A8
Burford Way CR0 . . . . .63 C4
Burgess Way TW18 . . . . .13 A3
Burgess Cl TW13 . . . . .15 E4
Burgess Mews SW19 . . . . .20 B2
Burgess Rd SM1 . . . . .59 B6

Burgh Cl RH10 . . . . .182 D1
Burgh Heath Rd
 KT17, KT18 . . . . .76 F4
Burgh Mount SM7 . . . . .77 F4
Burgh Wood SM7 . . . . .77 F4
Burghead Cl GU47 . . . . .64 D7
Burghfield KT17 . . . . .76 F4
Burghill Rd SE26 . . . . .23 E4
Burghley Ave KT3 . . . . .38 D8
Burghley House SW19 . . . . . . .19 E5
Burghley Pl CR4 . . . . .40 F5
Burghley Rd SW19 . . . . .19 E4
Burgoyne Rd Ashford TW16 . . .14 F2
 Camberley GU15 . . . . .66 A6
 South Norwood SE25 . . . . .42 F5
Burham Cl SE20 . . . . .23 C1
Burhill Cty Inf Sch KT12 . . . . . .54 D4
Burhill Rd KT12 . . . . .54 C3
Burke Cl SW15 . . . . .7 E3
Burlands RH11 . . . . .181 A1
Burlea Cl KT12 . . . . .54 B5
Burleigh Ave SM6 . . . . .60 B7
Burleigh Cl
 Addlestone KT15 . . . . .52 B5
 Crawley Down RH10 . . . . . . .204 B8
Burleigh Ct GU22 . . . . .95 A5
Burleigh Cty Inf Sch
 RH10 . . . . .204 B8
Burleigh Gdns
 Ashford TW15 . . . . .14 C3
 Woking GU21 . . . . .69 F2
Burleigh La
 Crawley Down RH10 . . . . . . .204 C7
 North Ascot SL5 . . . . .28 E8
Burleigh Pk KT11 . . . . .73 E7
Burleigh Rd
 Addlestone KT15 . . . . .52 B5
 Cheam SM3, SM4 . . . . .39 E1
 Frimley GU16 . . . . .85 D8
 North Ascot SL5 . . . . .28 E7
Burleigh Way RH10 . . . . .204 B8
Burleigh Wlk SE6 . . . . .24 C7
Burley Cl Loxwood RH14 . . . . .213 A4
 Mitcham SW16 . . . . .41 D7
Burley Orchard KT16 . . . . .33 A3
Burley Way GU17 . . . . .64 C6
Burleys Rd RH10 . . . . .202 C6
Burlingham Cl GU4 . . . . .110 D3
Burlington Ave TW9 . . . . .7 A6
Burlington Cl TW14 . . . . .14 D8
Burlington Ct **6**
 Aldershot GU11 . . . . .105 A1
 Blackwater GU17 . . . . .64 D3
 Chiswick W4 . . . . .7 C7
Burlington Jun Sch KT3 . . . . . .38 F5
Burlington La W4 . . . . .7 E8
Burlington Rd
 Hounslow TW7 . . . . .5 D6
 New Malden KT3 . . . . .38 F5
 South Norwood SE25 . . . . .43 B6
Burlsdon Way RG12 . . . . .27 E8
Burma Rd KT16 . . . . .49 F8
Burma Terr **11** SE19 . . . . .22 E3
Burmarsh Ct SE20 . . . . .43 C8
Burmester House SW17 . . . . . .20 C5
Burmester Rd SW17 . . . . .20 C5
Burn Cl KT15 . . . . .52 D6
Burn Moor Chase RG12 . . . . . .27 E2
Burnaby Cres W4 . . . . .7 C8
Burnaby Gdns W4 . . . . .7 B8
Burnbury Rd SW12 . . . . .21 C7
Burne-Jones Dr GU47 . . . . . . .64 D6
Burnell Ave TW10 . . . . .17 C3
Burnell House SW2 . . . . .22 A7
Burnell Rd SM1 . . . . .59 B6
Burnet Ave GU1, GU4 . . . . . . .110 B4
Burnet Cl GU24 . . . . .67 E6
Burnet Gr KT19 . . . . .76 C6
Burney Ave KT5 . . . . .37 F4
Burney Cl KT23 . . . . .94 C2
Burney Ct **5** RH11 . . . . .201 A3
Burney House **4** SW16 . . . . .21 C3
Burney Rd RH5 . . . . .115 A4
Burnham Cl GU21 . . . . .68 D1
Burnham Dr
 North Cheam KT4 . . . . .58 D8
 Reigate RH2 . . . . .118 A2
Burnham Gdns
 Cranford TW5 . . . . .4 B6
 Croydon CR0 . . . . .42 F2
Burnham Manor GU15 . . . . . . .66 A8
Burnham Pl RH13 . . . . .217 D1
Burnham Rd Knaphill GU21 . . . .68 D1
 Morden SM4 . . . . .40 B5
Burnham St KT2 . . . . .38 A8
Burnham Way SE26 . . . . .23 F3
Burnhams Rd KT23 . . . . .93 E3
Burns Ave TW14 . . . . .4 A1
Burns Cl Farnborough GU14 . . .84 F6
 Horsham RH12 . . . . .217 E7
 Mitcham SW19 . . . . .20 E1
Burns Ct SM6 . . . . .60 B3
Burns Dr SM7 . . . . .77 E5
Burns Rd RH10 . . . . .202 C8
Burns Way Crawley RH12 . . . .200 C1
 East Grinstead RH19 . . . . . . .185 C1
 Heston TW5 . . . . .4 C5
Burnsall Cl GU14 . . . . .85 B6
Burnside KT21 . . . . .75 F1
Burnside Cl TW1 . . . . .6 A1
Burnt Ash Prim Sch SE12 . . . .24 F8
Burnt Ash Rd GU10, GU9 . . . .146 B6
Burnt Hill Rd GU10 . . . . .146 A6
Burnt Hill Way GU10 . . . . .146 B5
Burnt House La RH12 . . . . . . .200 A7
Burnt Pollard La GU24 . . . . . . .48 E1
Burntcommon Cl GU23 . . . . . . .90 F2

Burntcommon La GU23 . . . . . .91 A2
Burntwood Cl
 Caterham CR3 . . . . .101 A6
 Wandsworth SW18 . . . . .20 E7
Burntwood Ct SW17 . . . . .20 C5
Burntwood Grange Rd
 SW18 . . . . .20 E7
Burntwood La
 Caterham CR3 . . . . .101 A6
 Wandsworth SW17 . . . . .20 D6
Burntwood Sch SW17 . . . . . . .20 D6
Burntwood View SE19 . . . . . . .22 F3
Burnwood Park Rd KT12 . . . . .54 B6
Burpham Court Farm Park
 GU4 . . . . .109 F7
Burpham La GU4 . . . . .110 A5
Burpham Prim Sch GU4 . . . . .110 A5
Burr Hill La GU24 . . . . .49 F2
Burr Rd SW18 . . . . .20 A8
Burrell Cl CR0 . . . . .43 E3
Burrell Ct RH11 . . . . .200 E4
Burrell House **5** TW1 . . . . .17 B8
Burrell Rd GU16 . . . . .85 C8
Burrell Row BR3 . . . . .44 A7
Burrell The RH4 . . . . .135 C6
Burrells BR3 . . . . .44 B7
Burrow Hill Gn GU24 . . . . .49 E2
Burrow Hill Sch GU16 . . . . .65 F1
Burrow Wlk SE21 . . . . .22 C8
Burrows Cl Guildford GU2 . . . .108 F2
 Little Bookham KT23 . . . . .93 F3
Burrows Cross GU5 . . . . .133 C2
Burrows Hill Cl TW19, TW6 . . . .2 C3
Burrows La GU5 . . . . .133 C3
Burrwood Gdns GU12 . . . . . . .106 A4
Burstead Cl KT11 . . . . .73 D7
Burston Gdns RH19 . . . . .185 D4
Burstow House SE6 . . . . .24 B4
Burstow Prim Sch RH6 . . . . . .162 B3
Burstow Rd SW20 . . . . .39 E8
Burtenshaw Rd KT7 . . . . .37 A3
Burton Cl Chessington KT9 . . . .56 D3
 Horley RH6 . . . . .161 A2
 Windlesham GU20 . . . . .48 D4
Burton Ct KT17 . . . . .37 A3
Burton Gdns TW5 . . . . .4 F6
Burton House SE26 . . . . .23 B3
Burton Rd KT2 . . . . .17 E1
Burton's Rd TW12 . . . . .16 C1
Burtons Ct RH12 . . . . .217 C2
Burwash La SE21, SE27 . . . . . .22 D4
Burwash Rd RH10 . . . . .202 A5
Burway Cres KT16 . . . . .33 A5
Burwood Ave CR8 . . . . .80 B5
Burwood Cl Guildford GU1 . . . .110 D2
 Hersham KT12 . . . . .54 C4
 Reigate RH2 . . . . .118 D1
 Tolworth KT6 . . . . .38 A1
Burwood Park Sch KT12 . . . . .53 F5
Burwood Rd
 Hersham KT12, KT13 . . . . . . .54 B4
 Walton-on-T KT12 . . . . .54 D5
Bury Cl GU21 . . . . .69 D3
Bury Fields GU2 . . . . .130 C7
Bury Gr SM4 . . . . .40 B4
Bury St GU2 . . . . .130 C7
Burys Court Sch RH2 . . . . . . .138 C3
Burys The GU7 . . . . .150 E4
Burywood Hill RH5 . . . . .177 E7
Busbridge CE Jun Sch
 GU7 .150 F2
Busbridge Cty Inf Sch
 GU7 .150 F2
Busbridge La GU7 . . . . .150 E3
Busby House SW16 . . . . .21 C4
Busch Cl TW7 . . . . .6 B6
Busch Cnr TW7 . . . . .6 B6
Busdens Cl GU8 . . . . .170 F8
Busdens La GU8 . . . . .170 F8
Busdens Way GU8 . . . . .170 F8
Bush Cl KT15 . . . . .52 C5
Bush La GU23 . . . . .90 D3
Bush Rd Littleton TW17 . . . . . . .33 F4
 Richmond TW9 . . . . .6 F8
Bushbury La RG40 . . . . .25 C6
Bushbury La RH3 . . . . .137 A5
Bushell Cl SW2 . . . . .21 F6
Bushell House **3** SE27 . . . . . .22 C4
Bushetts Gr RH1, RH2 . . . . . .119 B6
Bushey Cl CR3, CR8 . . . . .80 F3
Bushey Croft RH8 . . . . .122 C5
Bushey Ct SW20 . . . . .39 B7
Bushey Down SW12 . . . . .21 B6
Bushey Fst Sch KT3 . . . . .39 B6
Bushey Mid Sch SW20 . . . . . . .39 B6
Bushey Rd Croydon CR0 . . . . .63 A8
 Merton SW20 . . . . .39 B6
 Sutton SM1 . . . . .59 A6
 West Barnes SW20 . . . . .39 D7
Bushey Way BR3 . . . . .44 C4
Bushfield RH14 . . . . .211 D2
Bushfield Dr RH1 . . . . .140 A4
Bushnell Rd SW17 . . . . .21 B6
Bushwood Rd TW9 . . . . .7 A8
Bushy Cl KT1 . . . . .37 C8
Bushy Hill Dr GU1 . . . . .110 C2
Bushy Hill Jun Sch GU1 . . . . .110 D2
Bushy Park Gdns TW12 . . . . . .16 F3
Bushy Park Rd TW11 . . . . .17 B1
Bushy Rd
 Fetcham KT22, KT23 . . . . .94 B5
 Teddington TW11 . . . . .16 F1
Bushy Shaw KT21 . . . . .75 C2

Business Ctr The RG41 . . . . . . .25 C4
Busk Cres GU14 . . . . .84 F3
Bute Ave TW10 . . . . .17 E6
Bute Ct SM6 . . . . .60 D5
Bute Gdns SM6 . . . . .60 D5
Bute Gdns W SM6 . . . . .60 D5
Bute Rd Thornton Heath CR0 . . .42 A1
 Wallington SM6 . . . . .60 D6
Butler Rd Bagshot GU19 . . . . . .47 C3
 Crowthorne RG45 . . . . .45 C4
Butlers Dene Rd CR3 . . . . . . .102 A3
Butlers Hill KT24 . . . . .112 C1
Butlers Rd RH13 . . . . .218 A5
Butt Cl GU6 . . . . .174 E3
Butter Hill Dorking RH4 . . . . . .136 C6
 Hackbridge SM5, SM6 . . . . . . .60 A6
Buttercup Cl RG40 . . . . .26 F1
Buttercup Sq TW19 . . . . .13 E7
Butterfield Camberley GU15 . . .65 C6
 East Grinstead RH19 . . . . . . .185 C1
Butterfield Cl TW1 . . . . .5 F1
Butterfly Wlk CR6 . . . . .101 C1
Buttermer Cl GU10 . . . . .145 C3
Buttermere Cl
 East Bedfont TW14 . . . . .14 C1
 Farnborough GU14 . . . . .84 E4
 West Barnes SM4 . . . . .39 E2
Buttermere Ct GU12 . . . . .105 D2
Buttermere Dr GU15 . . . . .66 C5
Buttermere Gdns
 Bracknell RG12 . . . . .27 C5
 Sanderstead CR8 . . . . .80 E8
Buttermere Way TW20 . . . . . . .12 C3
Buttersteep Rise
 GU20, SL5 . . . . .28 A1
Butterworth Ct SW16 . . . . .21 E5
Butts Cl RH11 . . . . .201 A5
Butts Cotts Feltham TW13 . . . .15 E5
4 Woking GU21 . . . . .69 E1
Butts Cres TW13 . . . . .16 A6
Butts House TW13 . . . . .16 A6
Butts Rd Catford BR1 . . . . .24 E4
 Woking GU21 . . . . .69 E2
Butts The TW8 . . . . .6 D8
Buxton Ave CR3 . . . . .100 E6
Buxton Cres SM3 . . . . .58 E6
Buxton Dr KT3 . . . . .38 E7
Buxton La CR3 . . . . .100 E7
Buxton Rd Ashford TW15 . . . . .13 D3
 Mortlake SW14 . . . . .7 E4
 Thornton Heath CR7 . . . . .42 A4
Byards Croft SW16 . . . . .41 D4
Bychurch End **9** TW11 . . . . . .16 F3
Bycroft St SE20 . . . . .23 D1
Bycroft Way RH10 . . . . .202 C8
Bye Ways TW2 . . . . .16 B5
Byerley Way RH10 . . . . .202 D8
Byers Lane RH9 . . . . .142 A3
Byeway The SW14 . . . . .7 C2
Byeways The KT5 . . . . .38 C6
Byfield Ct KT3 . . . . .39 A5
Byfield Rd TW7 . . . . .6 A4
Byfleet Cnr KT14 . . . . .71 C7
Byfleet Cty Prim Sch KT14 . . . .71 E7
Byfleet Ind Est KT14 . . . . .71 F6
Byfleet & New Haw Sta
 KT15 .52 C3
Byfleet Rd
 New Haw KT14, KT15 . . . . . . .52 D2
 Weybridge KT11, KT13, KT14 . .72 D8
Byfleet Tech Ctr The KT14 . . . .71 F7
Byfleets La RH12 . . . . .216 C4
Byfrons The GU14 . . . . .85 D1
Bygrove CR0 . . . . .63 B4
Bygrove Ct SW19 . . . . .20 D8
Bylands GU22 . . . . .70 B2
Byne Rd Carshalton SM5 . . . . . .59 F8
 Penge SE20, E26 . . . . .23 C3
Bynes Rd CR2 . . . . .61 D3
Byne Rd RH11 . . . . .200 F4
Byrefield Rd GU2 . . . . .108 F3
Byrne Ct **1** CR8 . . . . .80 A8
Byrne Rd SW12 . . . . .21 B6
Byron Ave Carshalton SM1 . . . .59 E6
 Coulsdon CR5 . . . . .79 C4
 Cranford TW4 . . . . .4 B5
 Frimley GU15 . . . . .66 C3
 West Barnes KT3 . . . . .39 A4
Byron Ave E SM1 . . . . .59 E6
Byron Cl Crawley RH10 . . . . . .202 F8
 Forest Hill SE26 . . . . .23 D4
 Hampton TW12 . . . . .15 F4
 Horsham RH12 . . . . .217 E5
 Knaphill GU21 . . . . .68 E1
 Mitcham SW19 . . . . .41 A8
Byron Ct Dulwich SE21 . . . . . . .22 E5
 1 Richmond TW10 . . . . .17 C4
Byron Dr RG45 . . . . .45 C3
Byron Gdns SM1 . . . . .59 E6
Byron Gr **2** RH19 . . . . .185 C1
Byron House BR3 . . . . .24 B2
Byron Inf Sch CR5 . . . . .79 E3
Byron Pl KT22 . . . . .95 B5
Byron Rd Addlestone KT15 . . . .52 D7
 South Croydon CR2 . . . . .62 A1
Byton Rd SW17 . . . . .20 F2
Byttom Hill RH5 . . . . .115 C7
Byward Ave TW14 . . . . .4 B2
Byway The SM2 . . . . .59 D2
Byways The Ashtead KT21 . . . .75 C2
 Worcester Park KT19 . . . . .57 C4
Bywood RG12 . . . . .27 A1
Bywood Ave CR0 . . . . .43 C3

Bywood Cl CR8 .....80 B4
Bywood Terr CR0 .....43 C3
Byworth Cl GU9 .....124 F2
Byworth Rd GU9 .....124 F2

C

Cabbell Pl KT15 .....52 C6
Cabell Rd GU2 .....108 E2
Cabin Moss RG12 .....27 E2
Cabin House Sch GU21 .....69 E4
Cabrera Ave GU25 .....31 D3
Cabrera Cl GU25 .....31 D3
Cabrol Rd GU14 .....85 A5
Caburn Cl RH11 .....201 C4
Caburn Hts RH11 .....201 C4
Cackstones The RH10 .....202 D7
Cadbury Cl Ashford TW16 .....14 E1
  Isleworth TW7 .....6 A6
Cadbury Rd TW16 .....14 E1
Caddy Cl ▣ TW20 .....12 A3
Cadley Terr SE23 .....23 C6
Cadmer Cl KT3 .....38 E5
Cadnam Cl GU11 .....126 C6
Cadnam Point ▣ SW15 .....19 B7
Cadogan Cl Beckenham BR3 .....44 D7
  Teddington TW11 .....16 E3
Cadogan Ct SM2 .....59 B4
Cadogan Ho ▣ GU1 .....130 FB
Cadogan Rd KT6 .....37 D4
Cadogen Rd GU11 .....105 D2
Caen Wood Rd KT13 .....75 C1
Caenshill Rd KT13 .....53 A3
Caenwood Hill KT13 .....53 A1
Caenwood Cl KT13 .....53 A1
Caerleon Cl GU26 .....188 C6
Caernarvon GU16 .....85 F8
Caernarvon Cl CR4 .....41 E6
Caernarvon Ct ▣ KT5 .....37 F4
Caesar's Camp Rd GU15 .....66 A8
Caesar's Cl GU15 .....66 A8
Caesar's Way TW17 .....34 D3
Caesars Ct GU9 .....125 C7
Caesar's Wlk CR4 .....40 F4
Caffins Cl RH10 .....201 E8
Caillard Rd KT14 .....71 E8
Cain Rd RG12, RG42 .....26 E7
Cain's La TW14 .....3 E2
Cairn Cl GU15 .....66 B3
Cairndale Cl BR1 .....24 F1
Cairngorm Pl GU14 .....84 E7
Cairo New Rd CR0, CR9 .....61 B8
Caister House ▣ SW12 .....21 B8
Caistor Mews SW12 .....21 B8
Caistor Rd SW12 .....21 B8
Caithness Dr KT18 .....76 D5
Caithness Rd CR4 .....21 B1
Calbourne Rd SW12 .....21 A8
Caldbeck Ave KT4 .....39 B1
Caldbeck House ▣ RH11 .....200 F3
Calder Rd SM4 .....40 C4
Calder Way SL3 .....1 E4
Calderdale Cl RH11 .....201 B4
Caldwell Rd GU20 .....48 D5
Caledon Pl GU11 .....110 A4
Caledon Rd SM5, SM6 .....60 A6
Caledonia Rd TW19 .....13 E7
Caledonian House RH6 .....182 B8
Calfridus Way RG12 .....27 F6
California Ct SM2 .....59 B1
California Rd KT3 .....38 C6
Callander Rd SE6 .....24 C6
alley Down Cres
  CR0, CR9 .....63 D1
Callis Farm Cl TW19 .....2 E1
Callisto Cl RH11 .....200 E3
Callow Field CR8 .....80 A6
Callow Hill GU25, TW20 .....31 C7
Calluna Ct GU22 .....69 F1
Calluna Dr RH10 .....183 A3
Calmont Rd BR1 .....24 E2
Calonne Rd SW19 .....19 D4
Calshot Rd TW6 .....3 B5
Calshot Way Frimley GU16 .....86 A7
  Harlington TW6 .....3 A5
Calthorpe Gdns SM1 .....59 C7
alton Gdns GU11 .....126 C7
alverley Cl BR3 .....24 B2
alverley Rd KT17 .....58 A4
alvert Cl GU21 .....105 D1
alvert Cres RH4 .....115 B1
alvert Ct ▣ TW9 .....6 F3
alvert Rd Dorking RH4 .....115 B1
  Effingham KT24 .....113 B7
alvin Cl GU15 .....66 B4
alvin Wlk RH11 .....200 E3
amac Rd TW11 .....16 D7
amberley Ave SW20 .....39 B7
amberley Cl SM3 .....58 D3
amberley Cl SM2 .....59 B3
amberley Cty Inf Sch
  GU15 .....65 C5
amberley Heath Golf
  Course GU15 .....66 B5
amberley Rd TW6 .....3 A4
amberley Sta GU15 .....65 D5
amberley Towers GU15 .....65 C5
ambisgate SW19 .....19 E3
amborne Rd SW6 .....3 B4
amborne Cres TW6 .....3 A4
amborne Rd Belmont SM2 .....59 B2
  Croydon CR0 .....43 A2
  Sutton SM2 .....59 B3
  Wandsworth SW18 .....20 A8

Camborne Rd continued
  West Barnes SM4 .....39 D4
Camborne Rd S TW6 .....3 A4
Camborne Way
  Harmondsworth TW6 .....3 A4
  Heston TW5 .....5 A6
Cambray Rd SW12 .....21 C7
Cambria BR3 .....44 B7
Cambria Cl TW3 .....5 A3
Cambria Ct Feltham TW14 .....15 B8
  Staines TW18 .....12 E4
Cambria Gdns TW19 .....13 E8
Cambria House SE26 .....23 A4
Cambrian Cl
  Camberley GU15 .....65 B5
  West Norwood SE27 .....22 B5
Cambrian Rd
  Farnborough GU14 .....84 D7
  Richmond TW10 .....6 F1
Cambridge Ave KT3 .....38 F7
Cambridge Cl
  Harmondsworth UB7 .....2 D8
  Hounslow TW4 .....4 E3
  Knaphill GU21 .....68 F1
  Wimbledon SW20 .....39 B8
Cambridge Cotts TW9 .....7 A8
Cambridge Cres TW11 .....17 A3
Cambridge Ct SW20 .....39 B8
Cambridge Gdns KT1 .....38 A7
Cambridge Gr SE20 .....43 B8
Cambridge Grove Rd
  Kingston u-t KT1 .....38 A6
  ▣ Kingston u-t KT1 .....38 A7
Cambridge House ▣
  TW11 .....17 A3
Cambridge House Sch
  SW20 .....39 C8
Cambridge Meadows
  GU9 .....125 A1
Cambridge Park Ct TW1 .....17 D8
Cambridge Pk TW1 .....6 C1
Cambridge Pl GU9 .....125 C2
Cambridge Rd
  Aldershot GU11 .....104 F2
  Barnes SW13 .....7 F5
  Carshalton SM5 .....59 E5
  Crowthorne RG45 .....45 C4
  Croydon SE20, SE25 .....43 A6
  East Molesey KT8 .....35 F5
  Hampton TW12 .....15 F1
  Horsham RH13 .....217 D2
  Hounslow TW4 .....4 E3
  Kingston u-t KT1 .....38 A7
  Littleton TW15, TW17 .....14 C1
  Mitcham CR4 .....41 C6
  New Malden KT3 .....38 E5
  Richmond TW9 .....7 A7
  Sandhurst GU47 .....45 E1
  Teddington TW11 .....17 A3
  Twickenham TW1 .....6 D1
  Walton-on-T KT12 .....35 B3
  Wimbledon SW20 .....39 B8
Cambridge Rd E GU14 .....85 C1
Cambridge Rd W GU14 .....85 C1
Cambridge Sq GU15 .....65 C6
Cambridge Wlk ▣ GU15 .....65 C6
Camden Ave TW13 .....15 C7
Camden Gdns
  South Norwood CR7 .....42 B6
  Sutton SM1 .....59 B5
Camden Hill Rd SE19 .....22 E2
Camden Jun Sch SM5 .....59 F6
Camden Rd Carshalton SM5 .....59 F6
  Lingfield RH7 .....164 E4
  Sutton SM1 .....59 B5
Camden Way CR7 .....42 B6
Cameford Ct ▣ SW12 .....21 B8
Camel Cl KT2 .....17 D3
Camellia Ct
  ▣ Beckenham BR3 .....24 A1
  West End GU24 .....67 F6
Camellia Pl TW2 .....16 B8
Camelot Cl Biggin Hill TN16 .....83 C3
  Wimbledon SW18 .....20 A6
Cameo Cl GU9 .....125 B1
Cameron Ct ▣ SW19 .....19 E7
Cameron House
  ▣ SW12 .....44 FB
Cameron Lodge TW3 .....5 C3
Cameron Rd
  Farnborough GU11 .....105 D7
  Forest Hill SE6 .....24 A5
  Thornton Heath CR0 .....42 B3
Cameron Sq CR4 .....40 E8
Camgate Est TW19 .....13 F8
Camilla Cl Ashford TW16 .....14 F1
  Great Bookham KT23 .....94 B2
Camilla Dr RH5 .....115 A5
Camille Cl SE25 .....43 A6
Camlan Rd BR1 .....24 F4
Camm Gdns
  ▣ Kingston u-t KT1 .....37 F2
  Thames Ditton KT7 .....37 F2
Camomile Ave CR4 .....40 F8
Camp End Rd KT11, KT13 .....72 C8
Camp Farm Rd GU11 .....105 D5
Camp Hill GU10, GU9 .....147 C8
Camp Rd
  Farnborough GU14 .....105 D7
  Wimbledon SW19 .....19 C3
  Woldingham CR3 .....101 E6
Camp View SW19 .....19 B3
Campbell Ave GU22 .....89 F6

Campbell Cl
  Aldershot GU11 .....126 C7
  Streatham SW16 .....21 D4
  Twickenham TW2 .....16 D7
Campbell Cres RH19 .....185 B1
Campbell Ct Dulwich SE21 .....23 A7
  Leatherhead KT22 .....95 B5
Campbell House ▣ SM6 .....60 B6
Campbell Rd GU21 .....65 F3
Campion Cl
  Blackwater GU17 .....64 F3
  South Croydon CR2 .....61 E6
Campion Dr KT20 .....97 B7
Campion House
  Bracknell RG42 .....26 E8
  Redhill RH1 .....119 A4
Campion House (Seminary)
  TW7 .....5 D6
Campion Rd
  Horsham RH12 .....217 C5
  Hounslow TW7 .....5 F6
Campion Way RG40 .....25 E7
Camrose Ave SW19 .....15 C4
Camrose Cl Croydon CR0 .....43 E2
  Morden SM4 .....40 A5
Can Hatch KT20 .....77 E1
Canada Ave RH1 .....140 A5
Canada Dr RH1 .....140 A5
Canada House RH1 .....140 A5
Canadian Ave SE6 .....24 B7
Canal Cl GU21 .....105 D5
Canal Cotts GU12 .....106 A4
Canal Wlk Croydon CR0 .....42 F3
  Forest Hill SE26 .....23 C3
Canberra Cl Crawley RH11 .....181 D1
  Horsham RH12 .....217 F4
Canberra Pl RH12 .....217 F5
Canberra Rd TW6 .....3 A4
Canbury Ave KT2 .....37 F8
Canbury Bsns Pk ▣ KT2 .....37 E8
Canbury Cl KT2 .....17 E1
Canbury Mews SE26 .....23 A5
Canbury Park Rd KT2 .....37 F8
Candlerush Cl GU22 .....70 B2
Candover Cl UB7 .....2 D8
Candy Croft KT23 .....94 B2
Cane Hill SM6 .....60 E3
Canewdon Cl GU22 .....89 E8
Canford Dr KT15 .....52 B8
Canford Gdns KT3 .....38 E3
Canham Rd SE25 .....42 E6
Canning Rd
  Aldershot GU12 .....105 D2
  Croydon CR0, CR9 .....61 F8
Cannizaro Rd SW19 .....19 D3
Cannon Cl Hampton TW12 .....16 B2
  Sandhurst GU47 .....45 E1
  West Barnes SW20 .....39 C5
Cannon Gr KT22 .....94 D3
Cannon Hill La
  Merton KT3, SM4, SW20 .....39 C5
  West Barnes KT3,
  SM4, SW20 .....39 C5
Cannon Side KT22 .....94 D3
Cannon Way
  East Molesey KT8 .....36 B5
  Fetcham KT22 .....94 D4
Canon's Hill CR5, CR8 .....80 A1
Canon's Wlk CR0 .....62 D7
Canonbie Rd SE23 .....23 C8
Canonbury Cotts RH12 .....199 F6
Canons Cl RH2 .....117 F2
Canons La KT20 .....97 F8
Canopus Way TW19 .....13 E8
Cansiron La RH19 .....206 F6
Cantelupe Rd RH19 .....185 F1
Canter The RH10 .....202 E7
Canterbury Cl BR3 .....44 B8
Canterbury Ct
  Ashford TW15 .....13 F4
  Dorking RH4 .....136 A8
  South Croydon CR2 .....61 C3
Canterbury Gr SE27, SW16 .....22 A5
Canterbury Mews KT22 .....74 C6
Canterbury Rd Ash GU12 .....106 A3
  Crawley RH10 .....201 E2
  Farnborough GU14 .....85 A6
  Feltham TW13 .....15 E6
  Guildford GU2 .....108 F2
  Morden SM4 .....40 C3
  Thornton Heath CR0, CR7 .....42 A2
Cantley Cres RG41 .....25 A8
Cantley Gdns SE19 .....42 E8
Canute Ct SW16 .....22 A5
Canvey Cl RH11 .....201 C3
Cape Copse RH12 .....214 D7
Capel KT5 .....37 F2
Capel Ave SM6 .....60 F5

Capel CE (VA) Fst Sch
  RH5 .....178 D6
Capel Ct SE20 .....43 C8
Capel La RH11 .....200 F5
Capel Lodge
  ▣ Richmond TW9 .....6 F6
  ▣ Streatham SW2 .....21 FB
Capel Rd RH12 .....199 A8
Capella House RH5 .....178 C5
Caperne Rd SW18 .....20 C7
Capital Ind Est CR4 .....40 F4
Capital Pk GU22 .....90 B6
Caplan Est CR4 .....41 C8
Capper Rd GU15 .....65 A7
Capri Rd CR0 .....42 F2
Capricorn Cl RH11 .....200 E4
Capsey Rd RH11 .....200 D6
Captains Wharf ▣ GU21 .....68 F1
Capstone Rd BR1 .....24 F4
Caradon Cl GU21 .....69 B1
Caradon Ct ▣ TW1 .....6 C1
Caraway Cl RH11 .....201 B2
Caraway Pl Guildford GU2 .....109 A6
  Hackbridge SM6 .....60 B7
Carberry Rd ▣ SE19 .....22 E2
Carbery La SL5 .....29 B6
Card Hill RH18 .....206 F1
Cardamom Cl GU2 .....109 A5
Cardigan Cl GU21 .....69 B1
Cardigan Rd Richmond TW10 .....6 E1
  Wimbledon SW19 .....20 C2
Cardinal Ave
  Kingston u-t KT2 .....17 E2
  West Barnes SM4 .....39 E3
Cardinal Cl
  West Barnes SM4 .....39 E3
  Worcester Pk KT19, KT4 .....58 A6
Cardinal Cres KT3 .....38 C7
Cardinal Dr KT12 .....35 D1
Cardinal Newman RC Sch
  KT12 .....54 D7
Cardinal Rd TW13 .....15 B7
Cardinal Road Inf Sch
  TW13 .....15 B7
Cardinal's Wlk
  Ashford TW16 .....14 E2
  Hampton TW12 .....16 C1
Cardingham GU21 .....69 B2
Cardington Sq TW4 .....4 D3
Cardwell Cres SL5 .....29 C4
Cardwells Keep GU2 .....109 A4
Carew Cl CR5 .....100 B8
Carew Ct SM2 .....59 B2
Carew House SW16 .....22 A5
Carew Manor Sch SM6 .....60 D7
Carew Rd Ashford TW15 .....14 C2
  Mitcham CR4 .....41 A7
  Thornton Heath CR7 .....42 B5
  Wallington SM6 .....60 C6
Carey House RH11 .....201 C6
Carey Rd RG40 .....25 C6
Carey's Copse RH6 .....162 B3
Carey's Wood RH6 .....162 B3
Carfax RH12 .....217 C2
Carfax Ave GU10 .....126 F8
Cargate Ave GU11 .....105 A1
Cargate Gr GU11 .....105 A1
Cargate Hill GU11 .....104 F1
Cargate Terr GU11 .....104 F1
Cargill Rd SW18 .....20 C7
Cargo Forecourt Rd RH6 .....181 D7
Cargo Rd RH6 .....181 D7
Cargreen Rd SE25 .....42 F5
Carisbrooke GU16 .....85 F8
Carisbrooke Cl TW4 .....4 B5
Carisbrooke Ct
  ▣ Cheam SM1, SM3 .....58 F5
  ▣ Penge SE20 .....43 B8
  South Norwood SE19 .....42 F8
Carleton Cl KT10 .....36 E1
Carlingford Gdns CR4 .....21 A1
Carlingford Rd SM4 .....39 D3
Carlinwark Dr GU15 .....65 F7
Carlisle Cl KT2 .....38 A8
Carlisle Inf Sch TW12 .....16 B2
Carlisle Rd Cheam SM1, SM3 .....58 F4
  Hampton TW12 .....16 B1
  Rushmoor GU10 .....168 C6
Carlos St GU7 .....150 E4
Carlton Ave Feltham TW14 .....4 C1
  South Croydon CR2 .....61 D3
Carlton Cl Chessington KT9 .....56 D4
  Frimley GU16 .....65 F1
  Woking GU21 .....70 A5
Carlton Cres SM3 .....58 E6
Carlton Ct Horley RH6 .....161 A3
  ▣ Penge SE20 .....43 B8
  South Norwood SE19 .....42 F8
Carlton Gn RH1 .....118 E4
Carlton House Cheam SM1 .....58 F4
  Hounslow TW4 .....5 B3
Carlton Park Ave SW20 .....39 D7
Carlton Rd Farnborough GU14 .....84 F4
  Headley Down GU35 .....187 C5
  Kingston u-t KT3 .....38 E7
  Mortlake SW14 .....7 C4
  Redhill RH1 .....118 E4
  South Croydon CR2 .....61 D3
  Walton-on-T KT12 .....35 B2
  Woking GU21 .....70 A5
Carlton Terr SE26 .....23 C5
Carlton Tye RH6 .....161 C3
Carlwell St SW17 .....20 E3
Carlyle Cl KT8 .....36 B7
Carlyle Ct RG45 .....45 C5

Carlyle Rd Croydon CR0 .....62 A8
  Staines TW18 .....13 A1
Carlyon Cl
  Farnborough GU14 .....85 C4
  Mytchett GU16 .....85 F4
Carlys Cl BR3 .....43 D7
Carmalt Gdns KT12 .....54 C5
Carman Wlk RH11 .....201 B1
Carmarthen Cl GU14 .....85 A7
Carmel Cl ▣ GU22 .....69 E1
Carmichael Ct SW13 .....7 F5
Carmichael House ▣
  SE21 .....22 E4
Carmichael Mews SW18 .....20 D8
Carmichael Rd SE25 .....43 A5
Carminia Rd SW17 .....21 B6
Carnac St SE21, SE27 .....22 D5
Carnation Dr RG42 .....8 B2
Carnegie Cl KT6 .....56 F8
Carnegie Pl SW19 .....19 D5
Carnforth Cl KT19 .....57 B4
Carnforth Rd SW16 .....21 D1
Carnoustie RG12 .....26 E2
Carole House SE20 .....43 B8
Carolina Rd CR7 .....42 C8
Caroline Cl Hounslow TW7 .....5 E7
  South Croydon CR0 .....61 E6
  Streatham SW16 .....21 F5
Caroline Ct Ashford TW15 .....14 B2
  Catford SE6 .....24 D4
  Crawley RH11 .....201 D4
  ▣ Surbiton KT6 .....37 D2
Caroline Dr RG41 .....25 A7
Caroline Pl UB3 .....3 E8
Caroline Rd SW19 .....19 F1
Carolyn Cl GU21 .....88 F8
Carpenter Cl KT17 .....57 F2
Carpenters Ct TW2 .....16 E6
Carrick Cl TW7 .....6 A4
Carrick Gate KT10 .....55 C7
Carrington Ave TW3 .....5 B2
Carrington Ct Croydon CR0 .....43 E2
  Redhill RH1 .....118 F2
Carrington Lodge ▣ TW10 .....6 E2
Carrington Pl KT10 .....55 B6
Carrington Rd TW10 .....7 A3
Carrinton La GU12 .....106 A6
Carroll Ave GU1 .....110 B1
Carroll Cres SL5 .....28 F5
Carrow Rd KT12 .....54 D7
Carshalton Beeches Sta
  SM5 .....59 F4
Carshalton Coll SM5 .....59 E7
Carshalton High Sch for
  Boys SM5 .....59 E8
Carshalton High Sch for
  Girls SM5 .....59 E7
Carshalton Lodge SM1 .....53 E2
Carshalton Park Rd SM5 .....59 F5
Carshalton Pl SM5 .....60 A5
Carshalton Rd
  Camberley GU15 .....47 A1
  Carshalton SM1, SM5 .....59 D5
  Mitcham CR4 .....41 A4
  Sutton SM1, SM5 .....59 D5
  Wallington SM7 .....78 F6
  Woodmansterne SM7 .....78 F6
Carshalton Sta SM5 .....59 F6
Carson Rd SE21 .....22 D6
Carstairs Rd SE6 .....24 C5
Carswell Rd SE6 .....24 C8
Cartbridge Cl GU23 .....90 B4
Carter Cl SM6 .....60 D3
Carter Rd Crawley RH10 .....202 D3
  Mitcham SW19 .....20 D2
Carter's Cotts RH1 .....139 E7
Carter's Rd KT17 .....76 F4
Carterdale Cotts RH5 .....178 C5
Carters Cl
  GU15 .....66 A3
Carters La GU22 .....90 D7
Cartersmead Cl RH6 .....161 B4
Carthouse Cotts GU4 .....110 C4
Carthouse La GU21 .....68 E5
Cartmel Cl RH2 .....118 D1
Cartmel Ct BR2 .....44 E7
Cartmel Gdns SM4 .....40 C4
Carwarden House Sch
  GU15 .....66 A3
Caryl House ▣ SW19 .....19 D7
Carylls Cotts RH12 .....199 F1
Cascades CR0 .....62 F1
Caselden Cl KT15 .....52 C5
Casewick Rd SE27 .....22 B4
Casher Rd RH10 .....202 C3
Cassel Hosp The TW10 .....17 D4
Cassilis Rd TW1 .....6 B1
Cassino Cl GU11 .....105 B2
Cassiobury Ave TW14 .....14 F8
Cassland Rd CR7 .....42 C5
Cassocks Sq TW17 .....34 D2
Castellane Cl GU47 .....64 D8
Castillon Rd SE6 .....24 F6
Castle Ave KT17 .....76 F4
Castle Cl Beckenham BR2 .....44 E6
  Bletchingley RH1 .....120 C2
  Charlton TW16 .....14 E1
  Frimley GU15 .....65 F4
  Reigate RH2 .....139 B5
  Wimbledon SW19 .....19 D5
Castle Ct Belmont SM2 .....59 A4
  Forest Hill SE26 .....23 E4
  Morden SM4 .....40 D4

Castle Dr Horley RH6 .... 161 C2
Reigate RH2 .... 139 B4
Castle Gdns RH4 .... 115 F1
Castle Gn KT13 .... 53 E7
Castle Grove Rd GU24 .... 68 E7
Castle Hill Farnham GU9 .... 125 B3
Guildford GU1 .... 130 D7
Castle Hill Ave CR0 .... 63 C2
Castle Hill Prim Sch CR0 ...... 63 C4
Castle Hill Rd TW20 .... 11 C5
Castle House **10** SM6 .... 59 A3
Castle Par KT17 .... 58 A3
Castle Rd Ald Aldershot GU11 .. 104 E4
Broadbridge Heath RH12 .... 216 D3
Camberley GU15 .... 65 F4
Epsom KT18 .... 76 B4
Isleworth TW7 .... 5 F5
Kingswood GR5 .... 98 E6
Oatlands Park KT13 .... 53 E7
Woking GU21 .... 69 F5
Castle Sq Bletchingley RH1 .... 120 C2
Castle St Bletchingley RH1 .... 120 C2
Farnham GU9 .... 125 B3
Guildford GU1 .... 130 D7
Kingston u T KT2 .... 37 E7
Castle Thw RH12 .... 217 E7
Castle View RH13 .... 76 B5
Castle View Rd KT13 .... 53 A6
Castle Way Ewell KT17 .... 58 A2
Feltham TW13 .... 15 C4
Wimbledon SW19 .... 19 D5
Castle Wlk TW16 .... 35 C6
Castle Yd **7** TW10 .... 6 D2
Castlecombe Dr SW19 .... 19 D8
Castlecraig Ct GU47 .... 64 D7
Castledine Ct GU47 .... 23 B1
Castlefield Rd RH2 .... 118 A1
Castlegate TW9 .... 6 F4
Castlemaine Ave
Ewell KT17 .... 58 B2
South Croydon CR0, CR2 .... 61 F5
Castleman House SL5 .... 29 D4
Castleton Cl Banstead SM7 .... 78 A4
Croydon CR0 .... 43 E3
Castleton Ct KT5 .... 37 F4
Castleton Dr SM7 .... 78 A5
Castleton Rd CR4 .... 41 D5
Caswell Cl GU14 .... 84 F6
Catalina Rd TW6 .... 3 A4
Catalpa Cl GU1 .... 109 C3
Catena Rise GU18 .... 48 B1
Cater Gdns GU3 .... 108 F3
Caterfield La
Crowhurst RH7 .... 143 F3
Oxted RH7, RH8 .... 144 A5
Caterham By-Pass CR3 .... 101 B4
Caterham Cl GU24 .... 87 F6
Caterham Dene Hospl
CR3 .... 100 F4
Caterham Dr
CR3, CR5, CR8 .... 100 C8
Caterham Sch CR3 .... 100 F1
Caterham Sch Prep CR3 .... 100 F1
Caterham Sta CR3 .... 101 A3
Caterways RH12 .... 217 A3
Catford Bridge Sta SE6 ...... 24 A8
Catford Broadway SE6 .... 24 B3
Catford Cty Sch SE6 .... 24 C5
Catford Cty Sch (Annexe)
BR1 .... 24 A4
Catford Hill SE6 .... 24 A4
Catford Rd SE6 .... 24 A8
Catford Sta SE6 .... 24 A8
Cathedral Cl GU2 .... 130 B8
Cathedral Hill Ind Est
GU2 .... 109 A2
Cathedral View GU2 .... 108 F1
Catherine Baird Ct **12**
SW12 .... 21 B8
Catherine Cl KT14 .... 71 F5
Catherine Ct **3** SW19 ..... 19 F3
Catherine Dr TW16 .... 14 F2
Catherine Drive TW9 .... 6 E3
Catherine Gdns TW3 .... 5 D3
Catherine Howard Ct **6**
KT13 .... 53 B7
Catherine Rd KT6 .... 37 D4
Catherine Wheel Rd TW8 ...... 6 D7
Catheringtom Sch RH11 .... 181 D2
Cathill La RH5 .... 177 C3
Cathles Rd SW12 .... 21 C8
Catlin Cres TW17 .... 34 D4
Catlin Gdns RH9 .... 121 B5
Catling Cl SE23 .... 23 C5
Caton Ct BR2 .... 44 F7
Cator Cl CR0 .... 82 E8
Cator Cres CR0 .... 82 E8
Cator La BR3 .... 43 F8
Cator Park Girls Sch BR3 .... 23 F1
Cator Rd Penge SE20, SE26 ... 23 D2
Wallington SM5 .... 59 F1
Catteshall Hatch GU7 .... 151 A6
Catteshall La GU7 .... 150 F4
Catteshall Rd GU7 .... 151 A5
Catteshall Terr GU7 .... 151 A5
Catteshall Wks GU7 .... 151 A6
Causeway TW14, TW4 .... 4 B3
Causeway Cl **1** GU21 ...... 68 F1
Causeway Est TW20 .... 12 C4
Causeway The
Carshalton SM5 .... 60 A8
Claygate KT10 .... 55 F3
Egham TW18, TW20 .... 12 D4
Horsham RH12 .... 217 C1

Causeway The continued
Sutton SM2 .... 59 C2
Teddington TW11 .... 16 F2
Wimbledon SW19 .... 19 C3
Cavalier Way RH19 .... 205 F7
Cavalry Cres TW4 .... 4 D3
Cavalry Ct GU11 .... 104 E2
Cavans Rd GU11 .... 105 C6
Cave Rd TW10 .... 17 C4
Cavell Rd RH10 .... 202 C5
Cavendish Ave KT3 .... 39 B5
Cavendish Cl Ashford TW16 ... 14 F2
Horsham RH12 .... 217 D7
Cavendish Ct Ashford TW16 ... 14 F2
Blackwater GU17 .... 64 D3
Poyle SL3 .... 1 E6
Cavendish Dr KT10 .... 55 E5
Cavendish Gdns RH11 .... 119 A2
Cavendish House TW1 .... 6 A1
Cavendish Jun & Inf Sch
W4 .... 7 E7
Cavendish Meads SL5 .... 29 D3
Cavendish Mews GU11 .... 105 A1
Cavendish Rd
Aldershot GU11 .... 105 A1
Ashford TW16 .... 14 F2
Balham SW12 .... 21 B8
Chiswick W4 .... 7 C6
Mitcham SW19 .... 20 E1
New Malden KT3 .... 38 F5
Redhill RH1 .... 119 A2
Sutton SM2 .... 59 C3
Thornton Heath CR0 .... 42 B1
Weybridge KT13 .... 53 A3
Woking GU22 .... 89 D8
Cavendish Terr **1** TW13 ... 15 A6
Cavendish Way BR4 .... 44 B1
Cavenham Cl GU22 .... 89 E8
Caverleigh Way KT4 .... 39 B2
Caversham Ave SM3 .... 39 E1
Caversham House **3** KT1 ... 37 E7
Caversham Rd KT1 .... 37 F7
Caves Farm Cl GU47 .... 64 A8
Cawnpore St SE19 .... 22 E3
Cawsey Way GU21 .... 69 E2
Cawston Ct BR1 .... 24 F1
Caxton Ave KT15 .... 52 A4
Caxton Cl RH10 .... 201 E3
Caxton Gdns GU2 .... 109 B2
Caxton House RH8 .... 123 E3
Caxton La RH8 .... 123 E4
Caxton Rd SW19 .... 20 C3
Caxton Rise RH1 .... 119 A2
Caxtons Ct GU1 .... 110 A3
Caygill Cl BR2 .... 44 F5
Cayley Cl SM6 .... 60 E3
Cearn Way CR5 .... 79 F4
Cecil Cl Ashford TW15 .... 14 C1
Chessington KT9 .... 56 D6
Cecil Ct **5** CR0 .... 61 F8
Cecil Lodge KT9 .... 56 D6
Cecil Mansions **2** SW17 ... 21 A6
Cecil Pl CR4 .... 40 F4
Cecil Rd Ashford TW15 .... 14 C2
Cheam SM1, SM2 .... 58 F4
Hounslow TW3 .... 5 C5
Merton SW19 .... 20 B1
Thornton Heath CR0 .... 41 F3
Cedar Ave Blackwater GU17 ... 64 D5
Cobham KT11 .... 73 C4
Twickenham TW2 .... 5 C1
Cedar Cl Aldershot GU12 ..... 126 E8
Bagshot GU19 .... 47 E3
Crawley RH11 .... 181 C1
Dorking RH4 .... 136 B7
East Molesey KT8 .... 36 E5
Epsom KT17 .... 76 F5
Esher KT10 .... 54 F3
Horsham RH12 .... 217 C3
Kingston u T KT2 .... 18 D4
Laleham TW18 .... 33 C6
Reigate RH2 .... 139 C7
Wallington SM5 .... 59 F4
Warlingham CR6 .... 101 E8
West Norwood SE21 .... 22 C6
Wokingham RG40 .... 25 C6
Cedar Ct **5** Brentford TW8 6 D8
Egham TW20 .... 12 A4
Haslemere GU27 .... 208 B6
Mortlake SW14 .... 7 C2
Ottershaw KT16 .... 51 C5
Sanderstead CR2 .... 81 A8
Stoneleigh KT17 .... 58 A3
Sutton SM2 .... 59 C4
Wimbledon SW19 .... 19 D5
Cedar Dr Fetcham KT22 .... 94 E4
Sunningdale SL5 .... 30 A2
Cedar Gdns Sutton SM2 .... 59 C4
Woking GU21 .... 69 B1
Cedar Gr Bisley GU24 .... 68 A4
Weybridge KT13 .... 53 A6
Cedar Hill KT18 .... 76 C3
Cedar House
New Addington CR0 .... 63 B4
Cedar Hts TW10 .... 17 D3
Cedar La GU16 .... 85 D8
Cedar Lodge
Crawley RH11 .... 201 D4
Milford GU8 .... 149 F2
Cedar Rd Cobham KT11 .... 73 B5
Cranford TW5 .... 4 C5
Croydon CR0, CR9 .... 61 E8
East Bedfont TW14 .... 14 D7
East Molesey KT8 .... 36 E5
Farnborough GU14 .... 85 C3
Sutton SM2 .... 59 C4
Teddington TW11 .... 17 A3

Cedar Rd continued
Weybridge KT13 .... 53 A6
Woking GU22 .... 89 C2
Cedar Terr **3** TW9 .... 6 E3
Cedar Tree Gr SE27 .... 22 B3
Cedar Way Charlton TW16 ..... 14 E1
Guildford GU1 .... 109 C4
Cedar Wlk Claygate KT10 ..... 55 F6
Kenley CR8 .... 80 C3
Kingswood KT20 .... 97 E7
Cedarcroft Rd KT9 .... 56 F6
Cedars **2** Bracknell RG12 . 27 F5
Woodmansterne SM7 .... 78 F5
Cedars Ave CR4 .... 40 F5
Cedars Ct GU1 .... 110 A4
Cedars House **5** SM7 ...... 22 B3
Cedars Prim Sch The TW5 .... 4 A7
Cedars Rd Barnes SW13 .... 7 F5
Beckenham BR3 .... 43 F7
Morden SM4 .... 40 A5
Teddington TW11 .... 37 C8
Wallington CR0 .... 60 E6
Cedars The
Ashstead KT21, KT22 .... 95 D6
Byfleet KT14 .... 71 F7
Guildford GU1 .... 110 A4
Milford GU8 .... 170 E8
Reigate RH2 .... 118 D1
Teddington TW11 .... 16 F2
Wallington SM6 .... 60 C6
Cedarville Gdns SW16 .... 21 F2
Cedarways GU9 .... 146 B7
Celandine Cl
1 Crawley RH11 .... 201 B2
Crowthorne RG45 .... 45 C6
Celandine Rd KT12 .... 54 E6
Celia Cres TW15 .... 13 D2
Celia Ct **7** TW9 .... 6 F6
Celtic Ave BR2 .... 44 E6
Celtic Rd KT14 .... 71 F5
Cemetery La TW17 .... 34 B2
Cemetery Pales
Brookwood GU24 .... 88 A6
Pirbright GU24 .... 87 F5
Centaurs Bsns Pk TW7 .... 6 A6
Central Ave
East Molesey KT8 .... 35 F4
Isleworth TW3, TW7 .... 5 C3
Wallington SM6 .... 60 E5
Central Ct KT15 .... 52 B7
Central Hill SE19, SE27 ..... 22 D2
Central La SL4 .... 9 B7
Central Par Feltham TW14 .... 15 C8
Heston TW5 .... 5 A7
Kingston u T KT6 .... 37 E4
New Addington CR0, CR9 ...... 63 C1
Penge SE20 .... 23 D1
Central Pk Est TW4 .... 4 D3
Central Rd Morden SM4 .... 40 B4
North Cheam KT4 .... 58 B8
Central Sq KT8 .... 35 F5
Central Terr BR3 .... 43 D6
Central Veterinary
Laboratory KT15 .... 52 B2
Central Way Feltham TW14 .... 4 A2
Oxted RH8 .... 122 D8
Sutton SM5 .... 59 C8
Winkfield SL4 .... 9 B7
Central Wlk RG40 .... 25 C6
Centre The Feltham TW13 ..... 15 B6
Walton-on-T KT12 .... 34 F1
Centurion Cl **4** GU47 ..... 64 D8
Centurion Ct SM6 .... 60 B8
Century Rd TW20 .... 12 C3
Century Way GU24 .... 87 F8
Cerne Rd SM4 .... 40 C3
Cerotus Pl KT16 .... 32 F2
Chadacre Rd KT17 .... 58 B5
Chadhurst Cl RH5 .... 136 D4
Chadwick Ave SW19 .... 20 A2
Chadwick Cl
Crawley RH11 .... 201 B1
Teddington TW11 .... 17 A2
Chadworth Way KT10 .... 55 D5
Chaffers Mead KT21 .... 75 F3
Chaffinch Ave CR0 .... 43 D3
Chaffinch Cl
Crawley RH11 .... 201 D8
Croydon CR0 .... 43 D3
Horsham RH12 .... 217 D7
5 Sandhurst GU47 .... 64 D8
Tolworth KT6 .... 57 A7
Chaffinch Rd BR3 .... 43 E8
Chaffinch Way RH6 .... 160 E4
Chagford St SW19 .... 20 E1
Chailey Cl
5 Crawley RH11 .... 201 A3
Heston TW5 .... 4 C6
Chailey Pl KT12 .... 54 D6
Chalcot Cl SM2 .... 59 A3
Chalcot Mews SW16 .... 21 E5
Chaldon Cl RH1 .... 139 E7
Chaldon Common Rd
CR3 .... 100 C2
Chaldon Rd Caterham CR3 .... 100 D4
Crawley RH11 .... 201 C1
Chaldon Way CR5 .... 79 E1
Chale Wlk SM2 .... 59 B1
Chalet Ct CR7 .... 42 B4
Chalfont Dr GU14 .... 85 C2
Chalfont Rd SE25 .... 42 F6
Chalford Cl KT8 .... 36 A5
Chalford Rd SE21 .... 22 D4
Chalgrove Ave SM4 .... 40 A4
Chalgrove Rd SM2 .... 59 D3
Chalice Cl SM6 .... 60 D4

Chalk La Ashstead KT21 ...... 96 A8
East Horsley KT24 .... 112 F4
Epsom KT18 .... 76 E3
Shackleford GU8 .... 149 D8
Chalk Paddock KT18 .... 76 D4
Chalk Pit Rd Banstead SM7 ... 78 A2
Langley Vale KT18, KT21 ..... 96 C8
Sutton SM1 .... 59 C5
Chalk Rd Farncombe GU7 ...... 150 E5
Ifold RH14 .... 212 C3
Chalkenden Cl SE20 .... 23 B1
Chalkley Cl CR4 .... 41 A7
Chalkpit La Dorking RH4 ..... 136 A8
Oxted RH8 .... 122 D8
Woldingham CR3, RH8 .... 102 C1
Chalkpit Terr RH4 .... 115 A1
Chalkpit Wood RH8 .... 122 D8
Chalky La KT9 .... 56 D6
Challen Ct RH12 .... 217 B3
Challenge Ct KT22 .... 95 B8
Challenge Rd TW15 .... 14 D5
Challice Way SW2 .... 21 F7
Challin St SE20 .... 43 C8
Challis Pl RG42 .... 26 E8
Challock Cl TN16 .... 83 C3
Challoner Ct BR2 .... 44 D7
Challoners Cl KT8 .... 36 D5
Chalmers Cl RH6 .... 180 E6
Chalmers Rd Ashford TW15 ... 14 B3
Banstead SM7 .... 78 C4
Chalmers Rd E TW15 .... 14 C3
Chalmers Way TW14 .... 4 B2
Chalner House **21** SW2 ... 22 A7
Chamber La GU10 .... 145 C4
Chamberlain Cres BR4 .... 44 B2
Chamberlain Way KT6 .... 37 E2
Chamberlain Wlk TW13 ...... 15 E4
Chambers House **2** SW16 .. 21 C4
Chambers Rd GU12 .... 106 B6
Chamomile Gdns GU14 .... 84 C5
Champion Cres SE26 .... 23 E4
Champion Rd SE26 .... 23 E4
Champness Cl **9** SE27 .... 22 D4
Champneys Cl SM2 .... 58 E3
Chancellor Gdns CR2 .... 61 B2
Chancellor Gr SE21 .... 22 C5
Chancery La BR3 .... 44 B7
Chanctonbury Chase
RH1 .... 119 A1
Chanctonbury Dr SL5 .... 29 E1
Chanctonbury Gdns SM2 ...... 59 B3
Chanctonbury Way RH11 ...... 201 C4
Chandler CE (VA) Jun Sch
GU8 .... 170 F5
Chandler Cl
Crawley RH10, RH11 .... 201 D4
Hampton TW12 .... 36 A8
Chandler Ct
2 Tolworth KT5 .... 38 B1
4 Wallington SM6 .... 60 B6
Chandlers KT20 .... 97 B6
Chandlers Cl TW14 .... 14 F8
Chandlers Field Sch KT8 .... 36 A4
Chandlers Rd GU12 .... 106 B4
Chandlers Way **11** SW2 ... 22 A8
Chandon Lodge SM2 .... 59 C3
Chandos Rd TW18 .... 12 D3
Channel Cl TW5 .... 5 A6
Channings GU21 .... 69 E4
Channon Ct **8** KT6 .... 37 E4
Chantlers Cl RH19 .... 185 C2
Chanton Dr SM2 .... 58 C1
Chantrey Cl KT21 .... 95 C8
Chantrey Rd RH10 .... 201 E3
Chantry Cl Farnham GU9 ..... 125 A2
Horley RH6 .... 160 F4
Chantry Cotts GU4 .... 131 B3
Chantry Ct GU16 .... 65 D1
Chantry Hurst KT18 .... 76 D4
Chantry La GU5 .... 152 E7
Chantry Rd Bagshot GU19 .... 47 D2
Chertsey KT16 .... 33 A2
Chessington KT9 .... 57 A5
Chilworth GU4 .... 131 B3
Chantry View Rd GU1 .... 130 E6
Chantry Way CR4 .... 40 D7
Chantry Wood Nature
Trail GU1 .... 130 E5
Chantrys Ct GU9 .... 125 A2
Chantrys The GU9 .... 125 A1
Chapel Ave KT15 .... 52 B6
Chapel Cl Bracknell RG12 ... 27 D6
Milford GU8 .... 149 F2
Chapel Ct RH4 .... 136 B7
Chapel Farm Park RH5 .... 115 A5
Chapel Fields GU7 .... 150 D7
Chapel Gdns GU8 .... 80 A6
Chapel Gr Addlestone KT15 .. 52 B6
Burgh Heath KT18 .... 97 F3
Chapel Hill Dunsfold GU8 ... 192 F3
Effingham KT24 .... 113 D8
Chapel La
Ashurst Wood RH19 .... 206 D6
Bagshot GU19 .... 47 F3
Copthorne RH10 .... 183 F4
Farnborough GU14 .... 84 F8
Forest Row RH18 .... 206 F2
Great Bookham KT23 .... 114 D5
Milford GU8 .... 149 F2
Pirbright GU24 .... 88 A4
Westcott RH4 .... 135 C6
Warlingham CR6 .... 80 A6
Chapel Lane Ind Est RH4 .... 135 C6
Chapel Park Rd KT15 .... 52 B6
Chapel Rd Camberley GU15 ... 65 B5
Charlwood RH6 .... 180 F7
Hounslow TW3 .... 5 B4
Limpsfield RH8 .... 123 C5

Chapel Rd continued
Redhill RH1 .... 118 F1
Rowledge GU10 .... 145 E3
Smallfield RH6 .... 162 B4
Tadworth KT20 .... 97 D4
Twickenham TW1 .... 17 B8
Warlingham CR6 .... 81 D1
West Norwood SE27 .... 22 B4
Chapel Sq Sandhurst GU15 .... 64 F6
Thorpe GU25 .... 31 E5
Chapel St
Farnborough GU14 .... 85 D6
Guildford GU1 .... 130 D7
6 Woking GU21 .... 69 F2
Chapel View CR2 .... 62 C3
Chapel Way KT18, KT20 ...... 77 C1
Chapelhouse Cl GU2 .... 108 E1
Chaplain's Hill RG45 .... 45 D4
Chaplin Cres TW16 .... 14 E2
Chapman Rd
Crawley RH10 .... 202 C2
Thornton Heath CR0 .... 42 A1
Chapman's La
East Grinstead RH19 .... 185 B3
East Grinstead RH19 .... 185 D3
Chapter Way TW12 .... 16 A4
Chara Pl W4 .... 7 D8
Charcot House SW15 .... 7 F8
Chargate Cl KT12 .... 54 A4
Charing Ct BR2 .... 44 E7
Charlbury Cl **7** RG12 .... 27 F5
Charlecombe Ct TW18 .... 13 B1
Charlecote Cl GU14 .... 85 D7
Charlecote Gr SE26 .... 23 B5
Charles Ct **5** TW11 ...... 16 E1
Charles Darwin Sch TN16 .... 83 F4
Charles Dickens Ct SE25 .... 43 A4
Charles Hill GU10 .... 148 E7
Charles Mills Ct SW16 ...... 21 E2
Charles Rd Merton SW19 ..... 40 A8
Staines TW18 .... 13 D2
Charles Sq RG12 .... 27 C3
Charles St Chertsey KT16 ... 32 F2
Croydon CR0, CR9 .... 61 C7
Hounslow TW3 .... 4 F5
Mortlake SW13, SW14 .... 7 E7
Charles Staunton House
SE27 .... 22 D3
Charlesfield Rd RH6 .... 160 F4
Charleston Cl TW13 .... 15 A4
Charleston Ct RH10 .... 202 A3
Charleville Cir SE19, SE26 . 23 A3
Charlmont Rd SW17 .... 20 F2
Charlock Cl RH11 .... 201 A2
Charlock Way GU1 .... 110 B4
Charlotte Cl GU9 .... 125 D7
Charlotte Ct RH11 .... 201 C1
Charlotte Gr RH6 .... 162 A4
Charlotte Mews **3** KT13 .. 55 B8
Charlotte Rd Barnes SW13 ... 7 F6
Wallington SM6 .... 60 C4
Charlton Ave KT12 .... 54 B6
Charlton Ct GU47 .... 45 D2
Charlton Dr TN16 .... 83 D3
Charlton Gdns CR5 .... 79 D2
Charlton Ho **5** TW8 ...... 6 E8
Charlton Kings KT13 .... 53 E6
Charlton La TW17 .... 34 C6
Charlton Rd TW17 .... 34 C5
Charlwood CR0 .... 62 F2
Charlwood Cl KT23 .... 94 B3
Charlwood Cty Inf Sch
RH6 .... 180 E7
Charlwood Dr KT22 .... 74 D7
Charlwood House **1** SW2 .. 21 E8
Charlwood La RH5 .... 180 A4
Charlwood Rd
Crawley RH6, RH11 .... 181 C1
Crawley RH6, RH11 .... 181 C1
Rusper RH11, RH6 .... 180 C1
Charlwood Sq CR4 .... 40 D6
Charlwood Wlk RH11 .... 181 C1
Chartwoods Bsns Ctr
RH19 .... 185 C1
Charlwoods Pl RH19 .... 185 D1
Charlwoods Rd RH19 .... 185 D2
Charm Cl RH6 .... 160 E4
Charman Rd RH1 .... 118 F1
Charmans Cl RH12 .... 218 B4
Charminster Ave SW19 .... 40 A6
Charminster Ct **3** KT6 ... 37 D2
Charminster Rd KT4 .... 39 B1
Charmouth Ct TW10 .... 6 F2
Charnwood SL5 .... 29 E1
Charnwood Ave SW19 .... 40 A6
Charnwood Cl KT3 .... 38 E5
Charnwood Rd SE25 .... 42 E4
Charrington Rd **2**
CR0, CR9 .... 61 C7
Charrington Way RH12 ...... 216 A4
Charsley Rd SE6 .... 24 B6
Chart Cl Bromley BR2 ...... 44 E7
Croydon CR0 .... 43 C3
Dorking RH5 .... 136 B8
Mitcham CR4 .... 40 F4
Chart Downs RH5 .... 136 C6
Chart Gdns RH5 .... 136 B8
Chart House Rd GU12 .... 106 B3
Chart La Dorking RH4, RH5 .. 136 B6
Reigate RH2 .... 139 C8
Chart La S RH5 .... 136 D5
Chart Rd RH8 .... 123 E4
Charta Rd E TW20 .... 12 C3
Charta Rd S TW20 .... 12 C3
Charta Rd W TW20 .... 12 C3
Charter Cres TW4 .... 4 E3

arter Ct KT3 . . . . .38 E6
arter Rd KT1 . . . . .38 B6
arter Sq KT1 . . . . .38 B7
arterhouse GU7 . . . . .150 C7
arterhouse CI RG12 . . . . .27 E4
arterhouse Rd GU7 . . . . .150 D6
arters CI SE19 . . . . .22 E3
arters La SL5 . . . . .29 D4
arters Rd SL5 . . . . .29 E2
arters Sch SL5 . . . . .29 D2
arters Way SL5 . . . . .29 F2
artfield Rd RH2 . . . . .139 C8
artham Gr SE27 . . . . .22 B5
artham Rd SE25 . . . . .43 B6
arts CI GU6 . . . . .174 E2
artway RH2 . . . . .118 B1
artwell Frimley GU16 . . . . .85 F6
Putney SW19 . . . . .19 F7
ecclesham GU9 . . . . .145 F6
artwell CI **2** CR0 . . . . .42 D1
artwell Court Grange
. . . . .136 B4
artwell Gdns
artwell CI SM3 . . . . .58 E6
artwell CI **2** CR0 . . . . .105 C7
artwell Lodge **5** BR3 . . . . . .24 A1
artwell Rd GU18 . . . . .76 E5
artwell Way **4** SE20 . . . . . . .43 B8
arwood SW16 . . . . .22 A4
arwood Rd RG40 . . . . .25 F7
ase Bridge Inf Sch TW2 . . . . . .5 E1
ase Bridge Jun Sch TW2 . . . . . .5 E1
ase Cotts GU26 . . . . .188 C1
ase Ct Isleworth TW7 . . . . .6 A5
erton SW20 . . . . .39 E7
ase End KT19 . . . . .76 D7
ase Gdns TW2 . . . . .16 D8
ase La GU27 . . . . .208 E3
ase Rd KT17, KT19 . . . . .76 D7
ase The Ashstead KT21 . . . . . . .75 C1
asecote Cotts SL5 . . . . .79 D5
awley RH10 . . . . .202 A5
owthorne RG45 . . . . .45 A6
st Horsley KT24 . . . . .92 F1
nborough GU14 . . . . .85 D6
ssifield GU2 . . . . .130 A8
ggswood KT20 . . . . .98 B6
chott KT22 . . . . .74 E2
gate RH2 . . . . .139 D8
sth Norwood SW16 . . . . .22 A1
nbury TW6 . . . . .35 B8
llington CR0, SM6 . . . . .60 F5
asefield CI SL4, GU4 . . . . .110 A4
asefield Ct GU14 . . . . .110 A4
aseley Ct KT13 . . . . .34 E1
asemore CI CR4 . . . . .40 F2
asemore Gdns GU27 . . . . .61 A5
aseside Ave SW20 . . . . .39 E7
aseside Gdns KT16 . . . . .33 B2
asewater CI **5** GU11 . . . . . .105 A1
atelet CI RH6 . . . . .161 B4
atfield CI GU14 . . . . .85 C2
atfield Ct CR3 . . . . .100 D5
atfield Dr GU4 . . . . .110 C3
atfield Rd CR0 . . . . .42 B1
atfields RH11 . . . . .201 B4
atham Ave BR2 . . . . .44 F2
atham CI SM3 . . . . .39 F2
atham Rd KT1, KT22 . . . . .38 A7
athill RH6 . . . . .143 B6
atley Heath
emaphore Tower KT11 . . . .72 D1
atley Rd KT17 . . . . .58 A1
atterton Ct TW9 . . . . .6 F5
ation Row GU24 . . . . .68 A2
East Ave Cranford TW4 . . . . . . .4 B5
East Grinstead RH19 . . . . .185 C1
hmond TW9 . . . . .7 A4
wbridge KT13 . . . . .53 A3
aucer CI Banstead SM7 . . . . . .77 E5
okingham RG40 . . . . .25 F6
aucer Ct GU2 . . . . .130 C7
aucer Gdns SM1 . . . . .59 A7
aucer Gn CR0 . . . . .43 C2
aucer Gr GU15 . . . . .65 D5
aucer House Sutton SM1 . . . . .59 A7
West Norwood SE27 . . . . .22 C4
aucer Rd Crowthorne RG45 . . .13 F4
arnham GU9 . . . . .202 C8
owthorne RG45 . . . . .45 A4
aucer Rd cont 84 F6
tton SM1 . . . . .59 A6
aucer Way KT15 . . . . .52 A4
vey Down Rd RG42 . . . . .9 A6
worth CI KT16 . . . . .51 C4

Chaworth Rd KT16 . . . . .51 C4
Chawridge La SL4 . . . . .8 C7
Cheam CI Bracknell RG12 . . . . .27 D4
Burgh Heath KT20 . . . . .97 B6
Cheam Common Inf Sch
KT4 . . . . .58 B8
Cheam Common Jun Sch
KT4 . . . . .58 B8
Cheam Common Rd KT4 . . . . . .58 C7
Cheam Court Flats SM3 . . . . . .58 E4
Cheam Fields Prim Sch
SM3 . . . . .58 E5
Cheam High Sch SM3 . . . . .58 E6
Cheam Mansions SM3 . . . . .58 E3
Cheam Park Farm Inf Sch
SM3 . . . . .58 E7
Cheam Park Farm Jun Sch
SM3 . . . . .58 E4
Cheam Park Way SM3 . . . . .58 E4
Cheam Rd Belmont SM2 . . . . . .58 C1
Cheam SM1 . . . . .59 A4
East Ewell KT17, SM2 . . . . .58 C1
Ewell SM2 . . . . .58 C1
Cheam Sta SM3 . . . . .58 E3
Cheapside SL5 . . . . .29 D5
Cheapside C of E Prim Sch
SL5 . . . . .29 E8
Cheapside Rd SL5 . . . . .29 D7
Cheddar Rd TW6 . . . . .3 A5
Cheeseman CI
Hampton TW12 . . . . .15 E2
Wokingham RG40 . . . . .25 D7
Chelford Rd BR1, E6 . . . . .24 D3
Chellows La RH7 . . . . .143 F2
Chelmsford CI SM2 . . . . .59 A2
Chelsea CI Hampton TW12 . . . .16 C3
New Malden KT4 . . . . .39 A2
Chelsea Fields SW19 . . . . .40 D8
Chelsea Gdns SM3 . . . . .58 E6
Chelsfield Gdns SE26 . . . . .23 C5
Chelsham Common Rd
CR6 . . . . .82 A3
Chelsham Court Rd CR6 . . . . . .82 C1
Chelsham Rd Croydon CR2 . . . .61 D4
Warlingham CR6 . . . . .81 F2
Chelsham Terr CR6 . . . . .81 F1
Cheltenham Ave **9** TW1 . . . .17 A8
Cheltenham CI KT3 . . . . .38 C6
Cheltenham Villas CR7 . . . . . . .42 A3
Chelwood CI
Crawley RH10 . . . . .201 F4
Ewell KT17 . . . . .76 F7
Chelwood Gdns TW9 . . . . .7 A5
Cheney Ct SE23 . . . . .23 D8
Cheniston CI KT14 . . . . .71 A6
Cheniston Ct SL5 . . . . .30 A2
Chennells Way RH12 . . . . .217 C5
Chennestone Cty Prim Sch
TW16 .35 B7
Chepstow CI RH10 . . . . .202 E6
Chepstow Rd CR0 . . . . .61 F8
Chequer Grange RH18 . . . . . . .206 E1
Chequer Rd RH19 . . . . .185 F1
Chequer Tree Ct GU21 . . . . . . .68 E3
Chequers Ct Horley RH6 . . . . .161 A4
Walton on t H RG40 . . . . .97 A2
Chequers Ct
7 Croydon CR0 . . . . .42 F1
Horsham RH13 . . . . .217 E2
Walton on t H KT20 . . . . .97 A2
Chequers Dr RH6 . . . . .161 A4
Chequers La KT20 . . . . .97 A2
Chequers PI RH4 . . . . .136 B7
Cherimoya Gdns KT8 . . . . .36 B6
Cherington Way SL5 . . . . .28 E7
Cheriton Ave BR2 . . . . .44 F4
Cheriton Ct
South Norwood SE25 . . . . .42 E4
Walton-on-T KT12 . . . . .35 C1
Cheriton Sq SW17 . . . . .21 A6
Cheriton Way GU17 . . . . .64 D5
Cherkley Hill KT22, RH5 . . . . . .95 D1
Cherrimans Orch GU27 . . . . . .207 F6
Cherry CI Banstead KT17 . . . . .77 C3
Carshalton SM5 . . . . .59 F8
Merton SM4 . . . . .39 E5
7 Streatham SW2 . . . . .22 A8
Cherry Cres TW8 . . . . .6 B7
Cherry Ct RH13 . . . . .217 D1
Cherry Green CI RH1 . . . . .140 B7
Cherry Hill Gdns CR0 . . . . .60 F6
Cherry La RH11 . . . . .181 C1
Cherry Lodge **2** GU21 . . . .105 B1
Cherry Orch Ashtead KT21 . . . .76 B1
Staines TW18 . . . . .13 B2
Cherry Orchard Gdns **6**
Croydon CR0 . . . . .61 D8
East Molesey KT8 . . . . .35 F6
Cherry Orchard Rd
Croydon CR0 . . . . .42 E1
East Molesey KT8 . . . . .36 A6
Cherry St GU21 . . . . .69 E1
Cherry Tree Ave
Guildford GU2 . . . . .108 F1
Haslemere GU27 . . . . .207 F7
Staines TW18 . . . . .13 B2
Cherry Tree CI
Crawley RH10 . . . . .202 D8
Farnborough GU14 . . . . .84 C5
Farnham GU9 . . . . .125 C3
Sandhurst GU47 . . . . .45 D1
Cherry Tree Ct CR5 . . . . .79 F1
Cherry Tree Dr
Bracknell RG12 . . . . .27 D6
2 Streatham SW16 . . . . . . .21 E5
Cherry Tree Gn CR2 . . . . .81 B5
Cherry Tree La GU7 . . . . .150 D8

Cherry Tree Rd
Milford GU8 . . . . .149 E1
Rowledge GU10 . . . . .145 E3
Cherry Tree Wlk
Beckenham BR3 . . . . .43 F5
Coney Hall BR4 . . . . .63 F6
Cherry Way Horton SL3 . . . . . . .1 C4
Upper Halliford KT17 . . . . .34 E5
West Ewell KT19 . . . . .57 D4
Cherrydale Rd GU15 . . . . .66 D5
Cherryhill Gr GU11 . . . . .104 F1
Cherrywood Ave TW20 . . . . . . .11 B1
Cherrywood CI KT2 . . . . .18 A1
Cherrywood Ct **1** TW11 . . . .17 A3
Cherrywood La SM4, SW20 . . . .39 E5
Cherrywood Rd GU14 . . . . .85 B7
Chersey Bridge Rd
KT16, TW18 . . . . .33 D2
Chertsey Bvd KT16 . . . . .32 F1
Chertsey Ct SW14 . . . . .7 B4
Chertsey Dr SM3 . . . . .58 E8
Chertsey House TW18 . . . . .16 A5
Chertsey La Staines TW18 . . . .12 F2
Chertsey Rd
Addlestone KT15 . . . . .52 B8
Ashford TW15
&TW16TWTW16 . . . . .14 D2
Burrowhill GU20, GU24 . . . . . . .49 C6
Byfleet KT14 . . . . .71 D8
Chertsey KT15 . . . . .52 B8
Chobham GU24, KT16, GU21 . .50 D1
Feltham TW13 &TW16 TW16 . .14 D4
Feltham, Ashford Common
TW13, TW16 . . . . .14 D2
Lower Halliford TW17 . . . . .34 A2
Shepperton TW17 . . . . .33 F2
Twickenham TW2 . . . . .16 D7
Windlesham GU20 . . . . .48 E5
Woking GU21 . . . . .69 F3
Chertsey St Guildford GU1 . . .130 D8
Upper Tooting SW17 . . . . .21 A3
Chertsey Sta KT16 . . . . .32 F1
Chertsey Wlk KT16 . . . . .33 A2
Chervil CI TW13 . . . . .15 A5
Cherwell CI SL3 . . . . .1 B8
Cherwell Ct Teddington KT1 . . .37 D1
West Ewell KT19 . . . . .57 C6
Cherwell Wlk RH11 . . . . .200 F5
Cheselden Rd GU1 . . . . .130 E8
Cheseman St SE26 . . . . .23 B5
Chesfield Rd KT2 . . . . .17 F1
Chesham CI SM2 . . . . .58 E1
Chesham Cres SE20 . . . . .43 C8
Chesham Ct SW18 . . . . .20 D8
Chesham Mews **18** GU1 . . .130 F8
Chesham Rd
Guildford GU1 . . . . .130 F8
Kingston u T KT1, KT2 . . . . . . .38 A7
Penge SE20 . . . . .43 C8
Cheshire CI
Mitcham CR4, SW16 . . . . .41 E6
Ottershaw KT16 . . . . .51 D4
Cheshire Gdns KT9 . . . . .56 D4
Cheshire House
Cheam SM4 . . . . .40 B2
Morden SM4 . . . . .40 B2
Chesney Cres CR0 . . . . .63 C3
Chessholme Ct TW16 . . . . .14 E1
Chessholme Rd TW15 . . . . .14 C2
Chessington CI KT19 . . . . .57 C4
Chessington Comm Coll
KT9 . . . . .56 D3
Chessington Hall Gdns
KT9 . . . . .56 D4
Chessington Hill Pk KT9 . . . . . .57 A5
Chessington North
Sta KT9 . . . . .56 E5
Chessington Par KT9 . . . . .56 D5
Chessington Park KT9 . . . . .57 A6
Chessington Rd Ewell KT19 . . .57 C3
West Ewell KT19 . . . . .57 D4
Chessington South Sta
KT9 . . . . .56 D3
Chessington Way BR4 . . . . .63 B8
Chessington World of
Adventures KT9 . . . . .56 C1
Chester Ave Richmond TW10 . . .6 F1
Twickenham TW2 . . . . .15 F7
Chester CI Ash GU12 . . . . .106 B2
Ashford TW15 . . . . .14 D3
Dorking RH4 . . . . .115 C1
Guildford GU2 . . . . .108 F3
1 Richmond TW10 . . . . .6 F1
Sutton SM1 . . . . .59 A8
Chester Gdns SM4 . . . . .40 C3
Chester House **7** 38 B7
Chester Rd Ash GU12 . . . . . . .106 B2
Effingham KT24 . . . . .113 B7
Harlington TW6 . . . . .3 C4
Hounslow TW4 . . . . .4 B4
Wimbledon SW19, SW20 . . . . . .19 C2
Chester Way GU10 . . . . .126 F6
Chesterblade La RG12 . . . . . . .27 E2
Chesterfield CI RH19 . . . . .184 C4
Chesterfield Ct KT6 . . . . .37 E4
Chesterfield Dr KT10 . . . . .56 A8
Chesterfield House **6**
SW16 .21 C3
Chesterfield Rd
Ashford TW15 . . . . .13 E3
Chiswick W4 . . . . .7 C8
West Ewell KT19 . . . . .57 D3
Chesterfield Sch
Ashford TW15 . . . . .13 E3
Chesters Rd GU15 . . . . .66 B5
Chesters The KT3 . . . . .38 E8

Chesterton CI RH19 . . . . .205 F7
Chesterton Ct RH13 . . . . .218 A4
Chesterton Dr
Merstham RH1 . . . . .119 E7
Stanwell TW19 . . . . .13 F7
Chesterton Terr KT1 . . . . .38 A7
Chestnut Ave
Aldershot GU12 . . . . .126 E8
Camberley GU15 . . . . .66 A6
Coney Hall BR4 . . . . .63 E6
Farnham GU9 . . . . .146 A8
Guildford GU2 . . . . .130 C5
Hampton TW12 . . . . .16 A1
Hampton, Hampton Court
KT8 &KT11 . . . . .36 F7
Haslemere GU27 . . . . .208 C7
West Norwood SE24 . . . . .7 D4
Tatsfield TN16 . . . . .103 E5
Thames Ditton KT10 . . . . .36 D1
Wentworth GU25 . . . . .30 F5
Weybridge KT13 . . . . .53 C3
Whiteley Village KT12 . . . . .53 E2
Worcester Park KT19 . . . . .57 E6
Chestnut CI
Addlestone KT15 . . . . .52 B8
Ashford, Chattern Hill TW15 . .14 B4
Ashford, Felthamhill TW16 . . . .14 B2
Blackwater GU17 . . . . .64 E4
Carshalton SM5 . . . . .40 F1
Catford SE6 . . . . .24 C4
East Grinstead RH19 . . . . .186 A1
Englefield Green TW20 . . . . . . .11 C2
Grayshott GU26 . . . . .188 C3
Hampton UB7 . . . . .3 B7
Kingswood KT20 . . . . .98 A4
Redhill RH1 . . . . .140 B7
West Norwood SE27 . . . . .22 C4
West Norwood SE27, SW16 . . . .22 A4
Chestnut Copse RH8 . . . . .123 B2
Chestnut Cres KT12 . . . . .53 E2
Chestnut Ct
Aldershot GU12 . . . . .105 D2
Beckenham BR3 . . . . .24 A1
5 Croydon CR0 . . . . .61 C6
Feltham TW13 . . . . .15 D3
Horsham RH13 . . . . .217 E2
Hounslow TW3 . . . . .5 A4
Kingston u T KT3 . . . . .38 E6
Chestnut Dr TW20 . . . . .11 D2
Chestnut End GU35 . . . . .187 A4
Chestnut Gdns RH12 . . . . .217 C5
Chestnut Gr Balham SW12 . . . .21 A7
Isleworth TW7 . . . . .6 A3
Kingston u T KT3 . . . . .38 D6
Mitcham CR4 . . . . .41 D5
South Croydon CR2 . . . . .62 C3
Staines TW18 . . . . .13 B2
Woking GU22 . . . . .89 E7
Chestnut Grove Sch SW12 . .21 A7
Chestnut House SE27 . . . . .22 C5
Chestnut La Chobham GU24 . . .49 C4
Weybridge KT13 . . . . .53 B5
Chestnut Manor CI TW18 . . . . .13 B3
Chestnut Mead RH1 . . . . .118 E2
Chestnut PI Ashtead KT21 . . . .95 E8
Ewell KT17 . . . . .77 A8
Chestnut Rd Ashford TW15 . . .14 B4
Farnborough GU14 . . . . .85 A5
Guildford GU1 . . . . .109 D2
Horley RH6 . . . . .161 B5
Kingston u T KT2 . . . . .17 E1
Merton SW20 . . . . .39 D7
Twickenham TW2 . . . . .16 E6
West Norwood SE21, SE27 . . . .22 C5
Chestnut Way
Bramley GU5 . . . . .152 A4
Feltham TW13 . . . . .15 B5
Godalming GU7 . . . . .150 F2
Chestnut Wlk
Crawley RH10 . . . . .181 C1
Felcourt RH19 . . . . .185 C8
Upper Halliford TW17 . . . . .34 E5
Whiteley Village KT12 . . . . .53 E2
Cheston Ave CR0 . . . . .43 F1
Cheswick CI SW18 . . . . .20 A1
Chesworth CI RH13 . . . . .217 C1
Chesworth Cres RH13 . . . . . . .217 C1
Chesworth Cty Jun Sch
RH13 .217 D3
Chesworth Gdns RH13 . . . . . . .217 C1
Chesworth La RH12, RH13 . . . .217 C1
Chesywcks Sch GU6 . . . . .86 B5
Chetwode Ct RG40 . . . . .25 F6
Chetwode PI GU11 . . . . .126 C7
Chetwode Rd
Burgh Heath KT20 . . . . .97 C8
Upper Tooting SW17 . . . . .20 F5
Chetwode Terr GU11 . . . . .104 E1
Chetwood Rd RH11 . . . . .200 D2
Chevening CI RH11 . . . . .201 C1
Chevening Rd SE19 . . . . .22 D2
Chevington Villas RH1 . . . . . . .120 F3
Cheviot CI Banstead SM7 . . . . .78 B4
Farnborough GU14 . . . . .84 E7
Frimley GU16 . . . . .66 C4
Harlington UB3 . . . . .3 D7
Sutton SM2 . . . . .59 D2
Cheviot Gdns SE27 . . . . .22 B4
Cheviot Rd SE27 . . . . .22 B3
Cheviot Wlk RH11 . . . . .201 B6
Chewter CI GU19 . . . . .47 F3
Chewter La GU20 . . . . .48 B6
Cheyham Gdns SM2 . . . . .58 D1
Cheyham Way SM2 . . . . .58 E1

Cheylesmore Dr GU16 . . . . . . .66 D3
Cheyne Ave TW2 . . . . .15 F7
Cheyne CI Banstead SM7 . . . . .78 B4
8 Wallington SM6 . . . . .60 B5
Cheyne Hill KT5 . . . . .37 F5
Cheyne Rd TW15 . . . . .14 D2
Cheyne Way GU14 . . . . .84 F8
Cheyne Wlk Croydon CR0 . . . . .62 A8
Horley RH6 . . . . .161 A1
Cheynell Wlk RH11 . . . . .200 F4
Chichele Gdns CR0 . . . . .61 E6
Chichele Rd RH8 . . . . .122 E7
Chichester CI
Crawley RH10 . . . . .201 E2
Dorking RH4 . . . . .115 B1
Hampton TW12 . . . . .15 F2
Witley GU8 . . . . .170 E5
Chichester Ct Ewell KT17 . . . . .57 F2
Stanwell TW19 . . . . .13 E7
Chichester Dr CR8 . . . . .79 F7
Chichester Mews SE27 . . . . . . .22 A4
Chichester Rd Ash GU12 . . . . .106 A3
Dorking RH4 . . . . .115 B2
Croydon CR0 . . . . .61 E7
Chichester Terr RH12 . . . . .217 D2
Chichester Way TW14 . . . . .15 C8
Chiddingfold Rd GU8 . . . . .192 C3
Chiddingly CI RH10 . . . . .202 B5
Chiddingstone CI SM2 . . . . . . .59 A1
Chilberton Dr RH1 . . . . .119 C5
Chilbolton TW20 . . . . .11 E3
Chilbrook Rd KT11 . . . . .73 A1
Chilchester Ct BR3 . . . . .44 B6
Chilcombe House **7**
SW15 .19 A8
Chilcroft La GU27 . . . . .208 B1
Chilcroft Rd GU27 . . . . .207 F2
Chilcrofts Rd GU27 . . . . .208 A1
Child CI RG40 . . . . .25 D8
Childebert Rd SW17 . . . . .21 B6
Childerly KT1 . . . . .38 A6
Childrens Trust
(Tadworth Court) The
KT20 .97 D6
Childs Hall CI KT23 . . . . .93 F2
Childs Hall Dr KT23 . . . . .93 F2
Childs Hall Rd KT23 . . . . .93 F2
Childs La **10** SE19 . . . . .22 E2
Chilham CI GU16 . . . . .85 F8
Chillerton Rd SW17 . . . . .21 B3
Chillingford House SW17 . . . . .20 C4
Chillingham Way GU15 . . . . . . .65 C4
Chillingworth Gdns TW1 . . . . . .16 F5
Chilmans Dr KT23 . . . . .94 B2
Chilmark Gdns
Merstham RH1 . . . . .119 E6
New Malden KT3 . . . . .39 A3
Chilmead **1** RH1 . . . . .118 F2
Chilmead La RH1 . . . . .119 D3
Chilsey Green Rd KT16 . . . . . . .32 E2
Chiltern GU22 . . . . .89 C5
Chiltern Ave
Farnborough GU14 . . . . .84 D4
Twickenham TW2 . . . . .16 A7
Chiltern CI Crawley RH11 . . . .201 B6
Farnborough GU14 . . . . .84 D4
Haslemere GU27 . . . . .208 B5
North Cheam KT4 . . . . .58 C8
South Croydon CR2 . . . . .61 E7
Chiltern Gdns BR2 . . . . .44 F5
Chiltern Rd Sandhurst GU47 . . .45 A1
Sutton SM2 . . . . .59 C1
Chilterns The SM2 . . . . .59 B2
Chilthorne CI SE6 . . . . .23 F8
Chiltington CI RH12 . . . . .217 D4
Chilton CI KT12 . . . . .54 A6
Chilton Rd TW9 . . . . .7 A4
Chiltons CI SM7 . . . . .78 B4
Chilworth CE Inf Sch GU4 . . .131 D3
Chilworth Ct
8 Putney SW19 . . . . .19 D7
15 Redhill RH1 . . . . .118 F2
Chilworth Gdns SM1 . . . . .59 C7
Chilworth Rd GU4, GU5 . . . . . .132 A4
Chilworth Sta GU4 . . . . .131 E3
Chimneys CI SW19 . . . . .19 C1
Chinchilla Dr TW4 . . . . .4 C5
Chine The GU10 . . . . .145 F5
Chingford Ave GU14 . . . . .85 D5
Chingley CI BR1 . . . . .24 E2
Chinthurst La
Shalford GU4, GU5 . . . . .130 F2
Wonersh GU5 . . . . .152 A7
Chinthurst Pk GU4 . . . . .152 A3
Chinthurst Sch KT20 . . . . .97 C4
Chippendale CI GU17 . . . . .64 E4
Chippendale Rd RH11 . . . . . . .201 B3
Chippenham **4** KT1 . . . . . . .37 F7
Chipstead Ave CR7 . . . . .42 B5
Chipstead CI Belmont SM2 . . . .59 B2
Coulsdon CR5 . . . . .79 A3
Penge SE19 . . . . .22 F1
Redhill RH1 . . . . .140 A7
Chipstead Ct GU21 . . . . .68 E2
Chipstead House **1** 22 A8
Chipstead La CR5, KT20 . . . . . .98 B3
Chipstead Sta CR5 . . . . .78 F1
Chipstead Valley Prim
Sch CR5 . . . . .79 A3
Chipstead CR5 . . . . .79 B3
Coulsdon CR5 . . . . .79 B3

Chipstead Way CR5, SM7 ....78 F3
Chirton Wlk GU21 ....69 A1
Chisbury CI RG22 ....27 E3
Chisholm Rd Croydon CR0 ...6 A8
  8 Richmond TW10 ....6 F1
Chislehurst Rd TW10 ....6 E2
Chislet CI BR3 ....24 A1
Chiswick CI CR0 ....60 F7
Chiswick Comm Sch W4 ....7 D7
Chiswick House W4 ....7 E7
Chiswick La S W4 ....7 F8
Chiswick Mall W4 ....7 F8
Chiswick Quay W4 ....7 C6
Chiswick Sq W4 ....7 F8
Chiswick Sta W4 ....7 C7
Chiswick Staithe W4 ....7 C6
Chiswick Village W4 ....7 B8
Chithurst La RH6, RH7 ....162 F2
Chittenden Cotts
  GU23, KT14 ....71 E3
Chitterfield Gate UB7 ....3 A7
Chitty's Wlk GU3 ....108 F5
Chive CI GU11 ....84 C4
Chivelston 27 SW19 ....19 D7
Chivenor Gr KT2 ....17 D3
Chobham CI KT16 ....51 B4
**Chobham Common
(Nature Reserve)** KT16 ....49 F6
Chobham Gdns SW19 ....19 D6
Chobham Golf Course
  GU21 ....68 C5
Chobham La KT16, GU24 ....50 A8
Chobham Park La GU24 .....50 B2
Chobham Rd
  Chobham GU21 ....69 E3
  Frimley GU16 ....66 A2
  Knaphill GU21 ....68 D3
  Ottershaw KT16 ....51 B4
  2 Woking GU21 ....69 F2
Chobham, Horsell Common
  GU21, GU24 ....69 D5
**Chobham St Lawrence C
of E Prim Sch** GU24 ....68 E8
Choir Gn GU21 ....68 E2
Cholmley Rd KT7 ....37 B3
Cholmondeley Wlk TW9 .....6 C2
Chrislaine CI TW19 ....2 D1
Chrismas Ave GU12 ....105 C1
Chrismas PI GU12 ....105 C1
**Christ Church C of E
Prim Sch** Purley CR8 ......61 B1
  Streatham SW2 ....21 F7
Christ Church C of E Sch
  KT16 ....51 D4
Christ Church CE Inf Sch
  KT3 ....38 E6
Christ Church CE Jun Sch
  KT3 ....38 D6
Christ Church CE Prim Sch
  KT5 ....38 A3
Christ Church Mount
  KT19 ....76 B7
Christ Church Prim Sch
  SE23 ....23 D6
Christ Church Rd
  Beckenham BR3 ....44 A7
  Epsom KT18 ....76 A6
  Surbiton KT5 ....37 F3
Christ the King RC Fst Sch
  TW19 ....2 E1
Christ's Sch (East Side)
  SW14 ....7 D4
Christ's Sch (West Side)
  TW10 ....7 C4
Christabel CI TW7 ....5 E4
Christchurch Ave 4 TW11 ..17 A3
Christchurch C of E Fst Sch
  GU25 ....31 B6
Christchurch CI SW19 ....20 D1
Christchurch Cotts GU25 ...31 B6
Christchurch Dr GU47 ....64 D6
Christchurch Gdns KT19 ...76 B8
Christchurch House 2
  SW2 ....21 E7
Christchurch Hts 9 RH2 ..118 F1
Christchurch Pk SM2 ....59 C3
Christchurch PI KT19 ....76 B8
Christchurch Rd
  Harlington TW6 ....3 A4
  Mitcham SW19 ....20 D1
  Mortlake SW14 ....7 C2
  Purley CR8 ....80 B8
  Streatham SW2 ....21 F7
  Virginia Water GU25 ....31 C5
Christchurch Way 2 GU21 ..69 F2
Christian Fields SW16 ......22 A1
Christie CI Guildford GU1 ..109 D4
  Lightwater GU18 ....48 C1
  Little Bookham KT23 ....93 F3
Christie Dr SE25 ....43 A4
Christie House BR4 ....44 B1
Christies RH19 ....100 D6
Christine CI GU12 ....105 F1
Christmas Hill GU4 ....130 F2
Christmaspie Ave GU3 .....107 B1
Christopher CI
  Ashford TW15 ....13 E3
  6 Croydon CR0 ....43 A1
  Tadworth KT20 ....97 C4
Christopher Rd RH19 ....185 E1
Christy Rd TN16 ....83 C4
Chrystie La KT23 ....94 B1
Chuck's La KT20 ....97 B3
Chudleigh CI 4 GU14 ....85 B4
Chudleigh Gdns SM1 ....59 C7

Chudleigh Rd TW1, TW2 .....16 F8
Chulsa Rd SE26 ....23 B3
Chumleigh Wlk KT5 ....37 F5
Church Almshouses 8 TW9 ..6 F3
Church App Dulwich SE21 ...22 D5
  Thorpe TW20 ....22 C6
Church Ave Beckenham BR3 ..44 A8
  Farnborough GU14 ....85 C3
  Mortlake SW14 ....7 D4
Church Circ GU14 ....85 C1
Church CI Addlestone KT15 ..52 B6
  8 Epsom KT17 ....76 E6
  Fetcham KT22 ....94 D3
  Grayswood GU27 ....189 F2
  Hounslow TW4 ....4 F5
  Laleham TW18 ....33 C6
  Lower Kingswood KT20 ...117 F8
  Milford GU8 ....149 F1
  Pirbright GU24 ....87 F6
  Woking GU21 ....69 E3
Church Ct Forest Hill SE26 ..23 E3
  Reigate RH2 ....118 B1
Church Dr BR4 ....63 E7
Church Farm La SM3 ....58 E4
Church Field House KT11 ...73 B5
Church Gdns Dorking RH4 ..136 B8
  Leatherhead KT22 ....95 B7
Church Gn Elstead GU8 .....148 C3
  Hersham KT12 ....54 C4
Church Gr KT1 ....37 C7
Church Hill
  Aldershot GU11, GU12 ....126 C8
  Camberley GU15 ....65 E5
  Caterham CR3 ....100 F3
  Merstham RH1 ....99 B1
  Nutfield RH1 ....119 F2
  Purley CR8 ....60 F1
  Shamley Green GU5 ....152 E4
  Shere GU5 ....133 A4
  Tatsfield TN16 ....103 D5
  Wallington SM5 ....59 F5
  Wimbledon SW19 ....19 F3
  Woking GU21 ....69 D3
Church Hill House Hospl
  RG12 ....27 A3
Church Hill Rd
  Cheam SM1, SM3 ....58 E6
  Kingston u T KT6 ....37 E4
Church La Albury GU5 ......132 C4
  Ascot SL5 ....29 D5
  Ash GU12 ....106 B2
  Binstead GU10 ....145 E3
  Bisley GU21, GU24 ....68 A4
  Bletchingley RH1 ....120 D3
  Broadbridge Heath RH12 ..216 D3
  Brook GU8 ....190 C8
  Burgh Heath KT18, SM7 ....77 E2
  Burstow RH6 ....182 F7
  Caterham CR3 ....100 A3
  Chelsham CR6 ....82 C3
  Chessington KT9 ....56 F4
  Copthorne RH10 ....183 B3
  Cranleigh GU6 ....174 E3
  Crawley RH10 ....201 F6
  Crondall GU10 ....124 D8
  East Grinstead RH19 .....185 F1
  Farnborough GU14 ....84 E4
  Godstone RH9 ....121 D3
  Grayshott GU26 ....188 C3
  Hambledon GU8 ....171 D2
  Haslemere GU27 ....208 D7
  Headley KT18 ....96 D2
  Hooley CR5 ....99 B5
  Merton SW19 ....20 B6
  Oxted RH8 ....122 E6
  Pirbright GU24 ....87 D4
  Send GU23 ....90 C1
  Shere GU5 ....133 A4
  Sunningdale SL5 ....30 A4
  Teddington TW11 ....16 F3
  Thames Ditton KT7 ....37 A3
  Twickenham TW1 ....17 A7
  Upper Tooting SW17 ....21 A3
  Upper Tooting,
  Furzedown SW17 ....21 B4
  Wallington SM6 ....60 D7
  Wallis Wood RH5 ....176 F1
  Warlingham CR6 ....81 D2
  Weybridge KT13 ....53 A6
  Witley GU8 ....170 G2
  Wormley GU8 ....170 E2
  Worplesdon GU3 ....108 E8
  Wrecclesham GU10 ....145 F7
Church La E GU11 ....126 B8
Church La W GU11 ....105 A1
Church Lane Ave CR5 ....99 B5
Church Lane Dr CR5 ....99 B5
Church Meadow KT6 ....56 C8
Church Mews KT15 ....52 C6
Church Par TW15 ....13 F4
Church Pas GU9 ....125 B2
Church Path
  Aldershot GU14 ....105 C8
  Ash GU12 ....106 A3
  Croydon CR0, CR9 ....61 C8
  Merton SW19 ....40 A7
  Mitcham CR4 ....40 E6
  5 Woking GU21 ....69 F2
Church PI CR4 ....40 E6
Church Rd Addlestone KT15 ..52 B5
  Aldershot GU11 ....104 F2
  Ascot SL5 ....29 A5
  Ashford TW15 ....13 F4
  Ashstead KT21 ....75 D1
  Bagshot GU19 ....47 D3
  Barnes SW13 ....7 F5
  Beckenham BR2 ....44 E6
  Biggin Hill TN16 ....83 E2

Church Rd *continued*
  Bracknell RG12 ....27 C7
  Broadbridge Heath RH12 ..216 D3
  Burstow RH6 ....183 A7
  Byfleet KT14 ....71 E6
  Caterham CR3 ....100 F3
  Cheam SM3 ....58 E4
  Claygate KT10 ....55 F3
  Copthorne RH10 ....183 B3
  Crawley, Lowfield
  Heath RH11 ....181 E5
  Crawley, Worth RH10 ....202 E6
  Croydon CR0, CR9 ....61 C7
  Dunsfold GU8 ....192 D5
  East Molesey KT8 ....36 D6
  Egham TW20 ....12 A3
  Epsom KT17 ....76 E6
  Feltham TW13 ....15 D3
  Fetcham KT23 ....94 A3
  Frimley GU16 ....65 D1
  Guildford GU1 ....130 D8
  Harlington UB7 ....208 C7
  Haslemere,
  Shottermill GU27 ....207 F6
  Heston TW5 ....4 B8
  Heston TW5 ....5 A7
  Horley RH6 ....160 F2
  Horley RH6 ....161 A3
  Horne RH6 ....162 F5
  Horsham RH12 ....218 B5
  Hounslow TW7 ....5 E7
  Kenley CR8 ....80 D4
  Kingston u T KT1 ....37 F7
  Leatherhead KT22 ....95 B5
  Lingfield RH7 ....164 D4
  Little Bookham KT23 ......93 F4
  Long Ditton KT6 ....37 C1
  Lower Halliford TW17 .....34 B2
  Milford GU8 ....149 F1
  Mitcham CR4, SW19 ....40 D7
  New Malden KT4 ....38 E1
  Purley CR8 ....60 E1
  Redhill RH1 ....139 E7
  Reigate RH2 ....139 A7
  Richmond TW10, TW9 ......6 E2
  Richmond, Ham Common
  TW10 ....17 E4
  Sandhurst GU47 ....64 F7
  Sandhurst, Owlsmoor GU47 ..45 E1
  South Norwood SE19 ......22 E1
  Sunningdale SL5 ....30 A3
  Teddington TW11 ....16 F3
  Turners Hill RH10 ....204 A5
  Wallington SM6 ....60 D7
  Warlingham CR6 ....81 D2
  West End GU24 ....67 F7
  West Ewell KT19 ....57 D3
  Whyteleafe CR3 ....100 F8
  Wimbledon SW19 ....19 F4
  Wimbledon GU20 ....48 C4
  Winkfield SL4 ....8 C5
  Winkfield, Chavey Down SL5 ..28 B8
  Woking, Horsell GU21 .....69 E4
  Woking, St John's GU21 ...89 A8
  Woldingham CR3 ....101 E4
Church Rd E
  Crowthorne RG45 ....45 B5
  Farnborough GU14 ....85 D2
  Sutford Wd GU14 ....85 C1
Church Rise
  Chessington KT9 ....56 F4
  Forest Hill SE23 ....23 D6
Church Road Ind Est
  RH11 ....181 E5
Church Road Trad Est
  RH11 ....181 E5
Church Row GU23 ....91 C6
Church Side Epsom KT18 ...76 B6
  Gatton RH2 ....118 F6
Church Sq TW17 ....34 B2
Church St
  Aldershot GU11 ....104 F2
  Betchworth RH3 ....137 E8
  Chiswick W4 ....7 B8
  Cobham KT11 ....73 B4
  Crawley RH11 ....201 C6
  Crowthorne RG45 ....45 B4
  Croydon CR0, CR9 ....61 C8
  Dorking RH4 ....136 A7
  Effingham KT24 ....113 D8
  Epsom KT17, KT18 ....76 E6
  Esher KT10 ....55 B6
  Ewell KT17 ....58 A2
  Godalming GU7 ....150 D4
  Hampton TW12 ....36 C8
  Isleworth TW7 ....6 B5
  Kingston u T KT1 ....37 D7
  Leatherhead KT22 ....95 B5
  Old Woking GU22 ....90 C6
  Reigate RH2 ....118 B1
  Rudgwick RH12 ....214 E8
  Rudgwick, Cox Green RH12 ..195 E1
  Staines TW18 ....12 E4
  Sunbury TW16 ....35 B6
  Twickenham TW1 ....17 A7
  Walton-on-T KT12 ....35 A2
  Warnham RH12 ....216 F8
  Weybridge KT13 ....53 A6
Church St E GU21 ....69 F2
Church St W GU21 ....69 E2
Church Stretton Rd TW3 .....5 C2
Church Terr 12 TW10 ....6 D2
Church Vale SE23 ....23 D6
Church View GU12 ....106 A2
Church View CI RH6 ....160 F2
Church Villa TW16 ....35 B6
Church Way Oxted RH8 ....122 F3
  South Croydon CR2 ....81 A8

Church Wlk
  Bletchingley RH1 ....120 D2
  Brentford TW8 ....6 C8
  Caterham CR3 ....101 A3
  Chertsey KT16 ....33 A3
  Crawley RH10 ....201 D6
  Horley RH6 ....160 F2
  Leatherhead KT22 ....95 B5
  Mitcham SW16 ....41 C7
  Reigate RH2 ....118 C1
  18 Richmond TW10 ....6 D2
  Thames Ditton KT7 ....36 F3
  Walton-on-T KT12 ....35 A1
  West Barnes SW20 ....39 C6
  Weybridge KT13 ....53 B8
Churchcroft CI SW12 ....21 A8
Churchdown BR1 ....24 E4
Churchfield Rd
  Reigate RH2 ....117 F2
  Walton-on-T KT12 ....35 A1
  Weybridge KT13 ....53 A6
Churchfields
  East Molesey KT8 ....36 A6
  Guildford GU4 ....110 A6
  Witley GU8 ....170 E4
  Woking GU21 ....69 E3
Churchfields Ave
  Feltham TW13 ....16 A5
  Weybridge KT13 ....53 B6
Churchfields Prim Sch
  BR3 ....43 D6
Churchfields Rd BR3 ....43 E7
Churchill Ave
  Aldershot GU12 ....126 C8
  Horsham RH12 ....217 B3
Churchill CI
  East Bedfont TW14 ....14 F7
  Farnborough GU14 ....85 B8
  Fetcham KT22 ....94 E4
  Warlingham CR6 ....81 D2
Churchill Cres GU14 ....85 B8
Churchill Ct Crawley RH10 .182 A1
  Staines TW18 ....13 C2
Churchill Dr KT13 ....53 C6
Churchill House SM7 ....77 F4
Churchill Rd
  Guildford GU1 ....130 F8
  North Ascot SL5 ....28 E7
  Smallfield RH6 ....162 B3
  South Croydon CR2 ....61 C3
Churchill Way TW16 ....15 A2
Churchley Rd SE26 ....23 B4
Churchley Villas SE26 ......23 B4
Churchmore Rd SW16 ....41 D8
Churchside CT TN16 ....83 C2
Churchview Rd TW2 ....16 D6
Churston CI 11 SW2 ....22 A7
Churston Dr SM4 ....39 E4
Churt Rd Beacon Hill GU26 .188 C6
  Headley Down GU10, SL5 ..187 C8
Churt Wynde GU26 ....188 D7
Chuters CI KT14 ....71 F7
Chuters Gr KT17 ....76 F7
Cibber Rd SE23 ....23 D6
Cinder Path GU22 ....89 C8
Cinderford Way BR1 ....24 E4
Cinnamon Gdns GU2 ....109 A6
Cintra Ct SE19 ....22 F2
Cintra Pk SE19 ....22 F1
Circle Gdns Byfleet KT14 ...71 F6
  Merton SW19 ....40 A7
Circle Hill Rd RG45 ....45 C5
Circle Rd KT12 ....53 E2
Circle The GU7 ....150 D6
Cissbury CI RH12 ....218 A6
Cissbury Hill RH11 ....201 C4
Cissbury House 8 SE26 .....23 A5
City Bsns Ctr RH13 ....217 D1
**City of London
Freemen's Sch** KT21 ......96 A8
City Prospect 5 SE19 ....22 E2
City Wharf House KT7 ....37 B3
Clacket La TN16 ....103 E2
Clairvale Rd TW5 ....4 C6
Clairview Rd SW16, SW17 ..21 B4
Clairville CI 3 RH2 ....118 D1
Clairville Point 12 SE23 .....23 D5
Clammer Hill GU27 ....189 F1
Clandon Ave TW20 ....12 C1
Clandon CE Inf Sch GU4 ..111 A4
Clandon CI KT17 ....58 A4
Clandon Ct GU14 ....85 D3
Clandon House 12 KT2 ......18 B2
Clandon Mews RH4 ....136 B4
Clandon Rd GU1 ....111 A3
Clandon Rd Guildford GU1 .130 E8
  Send Marsh GU4, GU23 .....91 A1
  West Clandon GU4, GU23 .111 A8
Clandon Regis Golf Club
  GU4 ....111 B4
Clandon Sta GU4 ....111 B6
Clanfield House 18 SW15 ...19 A7
Clanfield Ride GU17 ....64 D5
Clapgate La RH13 ....215 C5
Clappers Gate
  RH10, RH11 ....201 D7
Clappers La GU24 ....68 D8
Clappers Meadow GU6 .....194 A3
Clare Ave RG40 ....25 C7
Clare CI Crawley RH10 .....182 C1
  West Byfleet KT14 ....71 A6
Clare Cotts RH1 ....120 B3
Clare Cres KT22 ....75 B1
Clare Ct
  Wimbledon SW19 ....19 E2
  Woldingham CR3 ....102 A4
Clare Gdns TW20 ....12 A3

Clare Hill Golf Course
  KT10 ....55 [?]
Clare Hill (No 1) KT10 .....55 [?]
Clare Hill (No 2) KT10 .....55 [?]
**Clare House Prim
Sch** BR3 ....4[?]
Clare Lawn Ave SW14 ....7 [?]
Clare Mead GU10 ....14[?]
Clare Rd Hounslow TW4 .....[?]
  Stanwell TW19 ....[?]
Clare Wood KT22 ....7[?]
Claredale GU22 ....8[?]
Claredale Ct SM2 ....5[?]
Clarefield Ct SL5 ....3[?]
Claremont TW17 ....3[?]
Claremont Ave
  Camberley GU15 ....[?]
  Esher KT10 ....5[?]
  Hersham KT12 ....5[?]
  Sunbury TW16 ....3[?]
  West Barnes KT3 ....3[?]
  Woking GU22 ....8[?]
Claremont CI
  Hamsey Green CR2 ....8[?]
  Hersham KT12 ....5[?]
  4 Streatham SW2 ....2[?]
Claremont End KT10 ....5[?]
Claremont Dr Esher KT10 ...5[?]
  Shepperton TW17 ....3[?]
Claremont End KT10 ....5[?]
Claremont Fan Court Sch
  KT10 ....5[?]
Claremont Gdns KT6 ....3[?]
Claremont Gr W4 ....[?]
Claremont Hospl KT6 ....3[?]
Claremont La KT10 ....5[?]
Claremont Landscape Gdn
  KT10 ....5[?]
Claremont Park Rd KT10 ...5[?]
Claremont Rd
  Claygate KT10 ....5[?]
  Croydon CR0 ....4[?]
  Egham TW18 ....1[?]
  Kingston u T KT6 ....3[?]
  Redhill RH1 ....11[?]
  Teddington TW11 ....1[?]
  Twickenham TW1 ....[?]
Claremont Terr KT7 ....3[?]
Claremont CI KT18 ....7[?]
Claremont Gdns KT18 ......7[?]
Clarence Ave
  Kingston u T KT3 ....3[?]
  Streatham SW4 ....2[?]
Clarence CI
  Aldershot GU12 ....105[?]
  Hersham KT12 ....5[?]
Clarence Ct RH6 ....16[?]
Clarence Dr
  Camberley GU15 ....[?]
  2 East Grinstead RH19 ...20[?]
  Englefield Green TW20 ....1[?]
Clarence House KT12 ....5[?]
Clarence La SW15 ....[?]
Clarence Rd
  Biggin Hill TN16 ....8[?]
  Hersham KT12 ....5[?]
  Horsham RH13 ....21[?]
  Reigate RH1 ....11[?]
  Richmond TW9 ....[?]
  Sutton SM1 ....5[?]
  Teddington TW11 ....1[?]
  Thornton Heath CR0 ......4[?]
  Wallington SM6 ....6[?]
  Wimbledon SW19 ....[?]
Clarence St Egham TW20 .....1[?]
  Kingston u T KT1, KT2 ....3[?]
  4 Richmond TW9 ....[?]
  Staines TW18 ....1[?]
Clarence Terr TW3 ....[?]
Clarence Way RH6 ....16[?]
Clarence Wlk RH1 ....13[?]
Clarendon Cres TW2 ....1[?]
Clarendon Ct
  Blackwater GU17 ....6[?]
  4 Richmond TW9 ....[?]
Clarendon Cty Prim Sch
  TW15 ....1[?]
Clarendon Gate KT16 ....5[?]
Clarendon Gr CR4 ....4[?]
Clarendon Rd
  Ashford TW15 ....[?]
  Croydon CR0, CR9 ....6[?]
  Mitcham SW19 ....2[?]
  Redhill RH1 ....11[?]
  Wallington SM6 ....6[?]
Clarendon Sch TW12 ....1[?]
Clarens St SE6 ....2[?]
Clares The CR3 ....10[?]
Claret Gdns SE25 ....4[?]
Clareville Rd CR3 ....10[?]
Clarewood Dr GU15 ....6[?]
Clarice Way SM6 ....6[?]
Claridge Gdns RH7 ....16[?]
Claridges Mead RH7 ......160[?]
Clark PI GU6 ....17[?]
Clark Rd RH11 ....20[?]
Clark Way TW5 ....[?]
Clarke Cres GU15 ....6[?]
Clarke's Ave KT4, SM3 .....5[?]
Clarks Hill GU10 ....12[?]
Clarks La CR6, TN16 ....10[?]
Claudia PI SW19 ....[?]
Claverdale Rd SW2 ....2[?]
Claverdon RG12 ....2[?]
Clavering CI TW1 ....[?]
Claverton KT21 ....7[?]
Clay Ave CR4 ....4[?]

Clay Hall La RH10 . . . . .183 C4
Clay La
Guildford, Blackburn GU4 . .110 A5
Guildford, Jacobswell GU4 . .109 E7
Headley KT18 . . . . . . .96 B3
Horne RH7 . . . . .163 D3
Nutfield RH1 . . . . . . .140 D7
South Nutfield RH1 . . . .140 D7
Wokingham RG40 . . . . .25 F5
Claycart Rd
Aldershot GU11 . . . . .104 C4
Aldershot GU11 . . . . .104 E3
Claydon Ct TW18 . . . .13 A4
Claydon Dr CR0 . . . . .60 E6
Claydon Gdns GU17 . . .65 A1
Claydon Rd GU21 . . . .69 A3
Clayford RH7 . . . . . .165 B2
Claygate Cres CR0 . . . .63 D4
Claygate La
Hinchley Wood KT10 . . . .56 A8
Thames Ditton KT7 . . . . .56 A1
Claygate Lodge Cl KT10 . .55 E3
Claygate Prim Sch KT10 . .55 E3
Claygate Rd RH4 . . . . .136 B5
Claygate Sta KT10 . . . . .55 E8
Clayhall House ❸ RH2 . .118 A2
Clayhall La RH2 . . . . .138 E6
Clayhanger GU1, GU4 . . .110 C3
Clayhill Cl Bracknell RG12 . .28 A6
Leigh RH2 . . . . .138 A2
Clayhill Rd RH2 . . . . .137 F1
Claylands Cl SE19 . . . .22 D3
Claymore Cl SM3, SM4 . . .40 A2
Claypole Dr TW5 . . . . . .4 E6
Clays Cl EH19 . . . . . .205 E8
Clayton Dr GU2 . . . . .108 F4
Clayton Gr RG12 . . . . .27 E8
Clayton Hill RH11 . . . .201 C4
Clayton House KT7 . . . . .37 B1
Clayton Mead RH9 . . . .121 B4
Clayton Rd
Chessington KT10, KT9 . . . .56 D6
Ewell KT17 . . . . . . .76 F6
Farnborough GU14 . . . . .84 F1
Isleworth TW7 . . . . . . .5 E4
Clear Water Pl KT6 . . . .37 C3
Cleardene RH4 . . . . .136 B7
Cleardown GU22 . . . . .70 B2
Clears Cotts RH2 . . . . .117 E3
Clears The RH2 . . . . .117 E3
Clearsprings GU18 . . . . .67 A8
Cleave Prior CR5 . . . . .98 E8

Cleave's Almshouses ❶
KT2 . . . . .37 E7
Cleveland Rd KT6 . . . . .37 D4
Cleaverholme Cl SE25 . .43 B3
Cleeve Ct TW14 . . . . .14 E7
Cleeve Hill SE23 . . . . .23 B7
Cleeve House RG12 . . . .27 E5
Cleeve Rd KT22 . . . . . .95 A7
Cleeve The GU1 . . . . .110 A1
Cleeves Ct ❺ RH1 . . . .119 A2
Clement Ho ❷ KT6 . . . .37 D4
Clement Rd Penge BR3 . . .43 D7
Wimbledon SW19 . . . . .19 E3
Clements Ct TW4 . . . . . .4 D3
Clements House KT22 . . .95 A8
Clements Mead KT22 . . .95 A8
Clements Rd KT12 . . . . .54 B8
Clensham Ct SM1 . . . . .59 A8
Clensham La SM1 . . . . .59 A8
Clerics Wlk TW17 . . . . .34 D3
Clerks Croft RH1 . . . . .120 D2
Clevedon KT13 . . . . . .53 D5
Clevedon Ct
Farnborough GU14 . . . . .85 D3
Frimley GU16 . . . . . . .86 A8
West Norwood SE21 . . . .22 D5
Clevedon Gdns TW5 . . . .4 B6
Clevedon Rd
Kingston u T KT1 . . . . . .38 A7
Penge SE20 . . . . .43 D8
Twickenham TW1 . . . . . .6 D1
Cleveland Ave
Hampton TW12 . . . . . .15 F7
Merton SW20 . . . . . . .39 F7
Cleveland Cl KT12 . . . . .54 B7
Cleveland Dr TW18 . . . .33 B8
Cleveland Gdns
Barnes SW13 . . . . .7 F5
Worcester Park KT4 . . . . .57 F8
Cleveland Pk TW19 . . . . .2 E1
Cleveland Rd Barnes SW13 . .7 F5
Isleworth TW7 . . . . .6 A3
New Malden KT3 . . . . . .38 E5
Worcester Park KT4 . . . . .57 E8
Cleveland Rise SM4 . . . .39 D2
Cleves Ave KT17 . . . . . .58 B2
Cleves Cl KT11 . . . . . .73 B5
Cleves Cres CR0 . . . . . .82 C8
Cleves Ct Epsom KT17 . . .76 F7
Kingston u T KT2 . . . . . .17 E3
Knaphill GU21 . . . . . . .68 D2
Cleves Rd TW10 . . . . . .17 C5
Cleves Sch KT13 . . . . . .53 E6
Cleves Way Ashford TW16 . .14 F2
Hampton TW12 . . . . . . .15 F1
Cleves Wood KT13 . . . . .53 E6
Clewborough House Sch
GU15 . . . . .66 B6
Clews La GU24 . . . . . . .68 A3

Cliff End CR8 . . . . . . .80 B7
Cliffe Rd Croydon CR2 . . .61 D5
Cliffe La 150 C2
Cliffe Rise GU7 . . . . .150 C3
Cliffe Wlk ❷ SM1 . . . . .59 C5
Clifford Ave
Mortlake SW14, TW10, TW9 . .7 B4
Wallington SM6 . . . . . .60 C6
Clifford Ct TW18 . . . . . .20 D8
Clifford Gr TW15 . . . . . .14 A4
Clifford House BR3 . . . . .44 B8
Clifford Manor Rd GU4 . .130 E5
Clifford Rd Croydon SE25 . .43 A5
Hounslow TW4 . . . . .4 D4
Richmond TW10 . . . . . .17 D6
Clifton Av SM2 . . . . . .78 B8
Clifton Ave TW13 . . . . .15 C5
Clifton Cl Caterham CR3 . .100 D4
Chertsey KT15 . . . . . . .52 B8
Rowledge GU10 . . . . . .146 A4
Clifton Ct Beckenham BR3 . .44 B8
South Norwood SE25 . . . .42 E4
❸ Stanwell TW19 . . . . . .2 E1
Clifton Gdns GU16 . . . . .85 F6
Clifton Hill Sch CR3 . . . .100 D4
Clifton Lodge (Brunel Univ
Coll Twickenham Campus)
TW1 . . . . .6 B2
Clifton Mews SE25 . . . . .42 E5
Clifton Par TW13 . . . . . .15 C4
Clifton Park Ave SW20 . . .39 C7
Clifton Pl SM7 . . . . . . .78 A4
Clifton Rd Coulsdon CR5 . .79 D5
Crawley RH10 . . . . . .202 C5
Harlington TW6 . . . . . . .3 B4
Hounslow TW7 . . . . .5 E5
Kingston u T KT2 . . . . . .37 F8
South Norwood SE25 . . . .42 E5
Teddington TW11 . . . . . .16 A4
Wallington SM6 . . . . . .60 B5
Wimbledon SW19 . . . . . .19 D2
Wokingham RG41 . . . . . .25 A8
Clifton Terr ❹ RH1 . . . .136 B6
Clifton Way GU21 . . . . . .68 F2
Cliftons La RH2 . . . . . .117 D2
Cliftonville RH4 . . . . .136 B6
Climping Rd RH11 . . . .201 B8
Cline Rd GU1 . . . . . . .130 F7
Clinton Ave ❹ KT8 . . . . .36 C5
Clinton Cl GU21 . . . . . .68 D1
Clinton Hill RH7 . . . . .186 A8
Clinton House
New Malden KT3 . . . . . .38 D1
❻ Surbiton KT6 . . . . . .37 D2
Clinton Rd KT22 . . . . . .95 C4
Clintons Gr RG42 . . . . . .27 A8
Clippesby Cl KT9 . . . . . .56 F4
Clipstone Rd TW3 . . . . . .5 A4
Clive Ct Streatham SW16 . .21 D3
Tolworth KT6 . . . . .57 A8
Clive Gn RG12 . . . . . . .27 B4
Clive House ❸ Croydon CR0 . .42 F1
Redhill RH1 . . . . .118 E3
Clive Rd Aldershot GU12 . .105 D1
Esher KT10 . . . . .55 B3
Feltham TW14 . . . . .4 A1
Mitcham SW19 . . . . . . .20 E2
Teddington TW1 . . . . . .17 A4
West Norwood SE21, SE27 . .22 D5
Clive Way RH10 . . . . . .34 C3
Cliveden Pl TW17 . . . . . .34 C3
Cliveden Rd SW19 . . . . .39 F8
Clock Barn La GU8 . . . .171 F6
Clock House Ct KT14 . . . .71 F7
Clock House Cotts RH5 . .178 C2
Clock House Ct BR3 . . . .43 E7
Clock House Mead KT11 . .74 B5
Clock House Rd BR3 . . . .43 E7
Clock Tower Rd TW7 . . . . .5 F4
Clockhouse Cl SW19 . . . .19 C6
Clockhouse Ct GU1 . . . .109 C5
Clockhouse La
Ashford TW14, TW15 . . . .14 B5
Bramley GU5 . . . . . . .151 F7
East Bedfont TW14, TW15 . .14 B5
Clockhouse La E TW20 . . .12 B1
Clockhouse La W TW20 . . .12 A1
Clodhouse Hill GU22 . . . .88 D5
Cloister Cl TW11 . . . . . .17 B3
Cloister Gdns SE25 . . . .43 A3
Cloisters The Frimley GU16 . .65 D1
Old Woking GU22 . . . . . .90 B6
Clone The ❺ KT2 . . . . . .18 B1
Clonmel Rd
TW11, TW12, TW2 . . . . . .16 B4
Clonmore St SW18 . . . . .19 F7
Close The Beckenham BR3 . .43 E5
Bracknell RG12 . . . . . . .27 C5
Brockham RH3 . . . . . .137 B5
Cheam SM3 . . . . .58 E4
Croydon SE25 . . . . .43 A3
East Grinstead RH19 . . . .205 D8
Esher KT10 . . . . .55 B3
Godalming GU7 . . . . . .150 F3
Horley RH6 . . . . .161 C1
Hounslow TW7 . . . . .5 D5
Mitcham CR4 . . . . .40 F5
Mortlake TW9 . . . . .7 B4
North Ascot SL5 . . . . . .28 D7
Purley CR8 . . . . .61 B1
Purley, Russell Hill CR8 . . .60 F1

Close The continued
Reigate RH2 . . . . . . .139 B8
Sandhurst GU47 . . . . . .64 E8
Sutton KT6 . . . . .37 D4
Virginia Water GU25 . . . .31 D6
Wallington SM5 . . . . . . .59 E2
West Byfleet KT14 . . . . . .71 A6
Wonersh GU5 . . . . . . .152 B7
Closeworth Rd GU14 . . . .105 E8
Cloudesdale Rd SW17 . . .21 B6
Clouston Cl SM6 . . . . . .60 E5
Clouston Rd GU14 . . . . .84 F5
Clovelly Ave CR6 . . . . .101 B8
Clovelly Dr GU26 . . . . .188 D7
Clovelly Pl GU26 . . . . .188 E8
Clovelly Rd
Beacon Hill GU26 . . . . .188 C7
Hounslow TW3 . . . . .5 B4
Clover Cl RG40 . . . . . . .25 C7
Clover Ct GU22 . . . . . . .89 D8
Clover Field RH12 . . . . .215 D4
Clover Hill RH11 . . . . . .201 A1
Clover House RH13 . . . . . .5 C6
Clover Lea GU7 . . . . . .150 E8
Clover Rd GU2 . . . . . .108 E2
Clover Way Carshalton CR4 . .41 A1
Smallfield RH6 . . . . . .162 C3
Clovers Cotts RH12 . . . .199 F1
Clovers End RH12 . . . . .218 A5
Clovers Way RH12 . . . . .218 D7
Clowders Rd SE6 . . . . . .23 F5
Clowser Cl ❻ SM1 . . . . .59 C5
Club La RG45 . . . . .45 A6
Club Row GU24 . . . . . . .87 D8
Clubhouse Rd GU11 . . . .104 F5
Clump Ave KT20 . . . . . .116 C4
Clumps Rd GU10 . . . . . .146 E4
Clumps The TW15 . . . . . .14 C4
Clyde Ave CR2 . . . . . . .81 B4
Clyde Cl RH1 . . . . . . .119 A2
Clyde Ct RH1 . . . . . . .119 A2
Clyde Rd Croydon CR0 . . .61 F8
Stanwell TW19 . . . . . . .13 E7
Sutton SM1 . . . . .59 A5
Wallington SM6 . . . . . . .60 C4
Clyde Terr SE23 . . . . . .23 C6
Clyde Vale SE23 . . . . . .23 C6
Clydesdale Cl TW7 . . . . . .5 F4
Clydesdale Gdns TW10 . . . .7 B3
Clymping Dene TW14 . . . .15 B8
Clytha Ct SE27 . . . . . . .22 C4
Clyve Way TW18 . . . . . .32 E8
Coach House Cl GU16 . . . .65 E3
Coach House La SW19 . . .19 D5
Coach Rd Brockham RH3 . .137 A7
Brockham, Pixham RH4 . . .115 C1
Crawley, Norchard
Terminal RH6 . . . . . . .181 F8
North Ascot SL5 . . . . . . .8 E1
Ottershaw KT16 . . . . . . .51 C4
Coachlads Ave ❻ GU2 . .108 F1
Coachmans Dr RH11 . . . .201 B2
Coalbrook Mansions
SW12 . . . . .21 B7
Coaldale Wlk SE21 . . . . .22 C8
Coast Hill RH4, RH5 . . . .134 F4
Coast Hill La RH4 . . . . .135 A5
Coates Wlk ❻ TW8 . . . . . .6 E8
Coatham Pl GU6 . . . . . .174 F3
Cob Cl RH10 . . . . .204 C8
Cob Wlk RH11 . . . . . . .201 A6
Cobb's Rd TW4 . . . . .4 E3
Cobbets Ridge GU10 . . . .147 C8
Cobbett Cl RH10 . . . . . .202 C8
Cobbett Rd Guildford GU2 . .108 F1
Twickenham TW2 . . . . . .16 A7
Cobbets La GU47 . . . . . .64 E8
Cobbets Farm GU24 . . . .68 A4
Cobbetts Hill KT13 . . . . .53 B3
Cobbetts Way GU10, GU9 . .145 F6
Cobbetts Wlk GU24 . . . . .68 A4
Cobbler's Wlk TW11 . . . .16 F1
Cobbles Cres RH10 . . . . .201 E7
Cobden La GU27 . . . . . .208 D7
Cobden Mews SE26 . . . . .23 B3
Cobden Rd SE25 . . . . . .43 A4
Cobham Ave KT3 . . . . . .39 A4
Cobham Cl SM6 . . . . . . .60 E4
Cobham Gate KT11 . . . . .73 B5
Cobham Park Rd KT11 . . .73 C2
Cobham Rd
Fetcham KT11, KT22, KT23 . .94 C6
Heston TW5 . . . . .4 C7
Kingston u T KT1 . . . . . .38 A7
Cobham & Stoke
D'Abernon Sta KT11 . . . .73 E2
Cobham Way
Crawley RH10 . . . . . .182 B4
East Horsley KT24 . . . . .92 E1
Cobnor Cl RH11 . . . . . .200 F4
Cobs Way KT15 . . . . . . .52 C1
Coburg Cres SW2 . . . . . .22 A7
Cochrane Ct KT23 . . . . . .94 A2
Cochrane Pl GU20 . . . . . .48 D5
Cochrane Rd SW19 . . . . .19 F1
Cock La KT22 . . . . .94 C5
Cock's La Newell Green SL4 . .8 A6
Winkfield SL4 . . . . .8 A6
Cock-A-Dobby GU47 . . . . .45 A1
Cocks Cres KT3 . . . . . . .38 F5
Cockshot Hill RH2 . . . . .139 B7

Cockshot Rd RH2 . . . . .139 C8
Codrington Ct GU1 . . . . .68 F1
Codrington Hill SE23, SE4 . .23 E8
Cody Cl Ash Vale GU12 . . .105 F5
Wallington SM6 . . . . . . .60 D3
Cody Rd GU14 . . . . . . .84 D3
Coe Ave SE25 . . . . .43 A3
Coe Cl GU11 . . . . .105 A1
Cogman's La RH6 . . . . .162 D4
Cokenor Wood GU10 . . .145 F6
Cokers La SE21 . . . . . . .22 D7
Colborne Way KT4 . . . . .58 C8
Colburn Ave CR3 . . . . .100 E3
Colburn Cres GU1 . . . . .110 A4
Colburn Way SM1 . . . . .59 D7
Colby Rd Dulwich SE19 . . .22 E3
Walton-on-T KT12 . . . . . .35 A1
Colchester Vale RH18 . . .206 E2
Colchester Villas SE27 . . .42 A3
Colcokes Rd SM7 . . . . . .78 A3
Cold Harbour La GU14 . . .84 F8
Coldharbour Cl TW20 . . . .32 C6
Coldharbour La
Bletchingley RH1 . . . . . .120 F1
Dorking RH4, RH5 . . . . .135 F3
Egham TW20 . . . . .32 D6
Pyrford GU22 . . . . .61 A1
Pyrford GU22 . . . . .70 F4
South Holmwood RH5 . . .156 F6
West End GU24 . . . . . . .67 F8
Coldharbour Rd
Croydon CR0 . . . . .60 F5
Pyrford GU22, KT14 . . . . .70 F4
Coldharbour Sch CR9 . . . .61 A5
Coldharbour Way CR0 . . .61 A5
Coldshott RH8 . . . . . . .123 A2
Cole Cl RH11 . . . . .201 A3
Cole Court Lodge ❽ TW1 . .17 A8
Cole Gdns TW5 . . . . .4 A7
Cole Park Gdns TW1 . . . . .6 A1
Cole Park Rd TW1 . . . . . .6 A1
Cole Rd TW1 . . . . .6 A1
Cole's La RH5 . . . . . . .178 B5
Colebrook KT16 . . . . . . .51 D4
Colebrook Cl SW19 . . . . .19 D8
Colebrook Rd SW16 . . . . .41 E8
Colebrook Rise BR2 . . . . .44 E7
Colebrooke Pl KT16 . . . . .51 C3
Colebrooke Rd RH1 . . . .118 E3
Coleford Bridge Rd
Farnborough GU16 . . . . . .85 D4
Mytchett GU16 . . . . . . .85 E4
Coleford Cl GU16 . . . . . .85 E3
Coleford Paddocks GU16 . .85 F4
Colekitchen La GU5 . . . .133 D6
Coleman Cl SE25 . . . . . .43 A7
Coleman Rd GU12 . . . . .105 D1
Coleman Rd SW18 . . . . .20 A8
Coleridge Ave SM1 . . . . .59 E6
Coleridge Cl
Crowthorne RG45 . . . . . .45 C4
Horsham RH12 . . . . . . .217 E6
Coleridge Cres SL3 . . . . . .1 E6
Coleridge Ct ❷ TW10 . . . .17 D4
Coleridge Rd Ashford TW15 . .13 F4
Croydon CR0 . . . . .43 C2
Coles La RH5 . . . . . . .178 C5
Colesburg Rd BR3 . . . . .43 F7
Colescroft Hill CR8 . . . . .80 B4
Coleshill Rd TW11 . . . . .16 E2
Colesmead Rd RH1 . . . .118 E4
Coleson Hill Rd GU10 . . .145 F5
Colet Rd RH10 . . . . . . .201 D3
Coleville Rd GU14 . . . . . .84 F5
Coley Ave GU22 . . . . . . .70 A2
Colfe Rd SE23 . . . . .23 E7
Colgate Cl RH11 . . . . . .201 B8
Colin Cl Coney Hall BR4 . . .63 F7
Croydon CR0 . . . . .62 F7
Colin Ct SW16 . . . . . . .21 C6
Colin Rd CR3 . . . . . . .101 A4
Coliston Rd SW18 . . . . . .20 A8
Coll of Liberal Arts SM1 . . .59 B5
Coll of St Barnabas RH7 . .185 F8
Coll of Tech Three
Bridges Boppot RH10 . . . .202 A7
Collamore Ave SW18 . . . .20 E7
Collards La GU27 . . . . . .208 D6
College Ave Egham TW20 . .12 B2
Epsom KT17 . . . . .76 F5
College Cl Addlestone KT15 . .52 D7
Camberley GU15 . . . . . .65 D7
East Grinstead RH19 . . . .185 F1
Lingfield RH7 . . . . . . .164 D4
College Cres Redhill RH1 . .119 A4
Sandhurst GU47 . . . . . .64 E8
College Ct SE19 . . . . . . .22 F2
College Dr Ash GU12 . . . .106 B3
Thames Ditton KT7 . . . . .36 F2
College Fields Bsns Ctr
SW19 . . . . .40 E8
College Gdns Dulwich SE21 . .22 E7
Farnham GU9 . . . . . . .125 B2
New Malden KT3 . . . . . .38 F4
Upper Tooting SW17 . . . . .20 E6
College Gn SE19 . . . . . .22 E1
College Hill
Godalming GU7 . . . . . .150 C2
Haslemere GU27 . . . . . .208 C6
College Hill Terr GU27 . . .208 C6
College House GU8 . . . .171 E5
College La
East Grinstead RH19 . . . .185 F1
Wokingham RG40 . . . . . .89 C8
College Rd Ash GU12 . . . .106 B3
Bracknell RG12 . . . . . . .27 D5
Crawley RH10 . . . . . . .201 E6
Croydon CR0, CR9 . . . . . .61 D8

College Rd continued
Dulwich SE19, SE21 . . . . .22 E3
Epsom KT17 . . . . .76 F5
Ewell KT17 . . . . .77 B5
Guildford GU1 . . . . . . .130 D8
Hounslow TW7 . . . . .5 F6
Mitcham SW19 . . . . . . .20 D2
Sandhurst GU47 . . . . . .64 E8
Woking GU22 . . . . .70 B2
College Ride ❶ KT1 . . . . .37 E6
College Ride Bagshot GU19 . .47 C2
Camberley GU15 . . . . . .65 D7
College Town Inf Sch
GU47 . . . . .64 E8
College Town Jun Sch
GU47 . . . . .64 E8
College Way TW15 . . . . .13 F4
College Wlk KT1 . . . . . .37 E6
Collendean La RH6 . . . .159 F4
Collens Field GU24 . . . . .87 F4
Collette Ct SE25 . . . . . .42 F4
Colley La RH2 . . . . . . .117 E3
Colley Manor Dr RH2 . . .117 D2
Colley Way RH2 . . . . . .117 E4
Collier Cl Farnborough GU14 . .84 D5
West Ewell KT19 . . . . . . .57 B4
Collier Row RH10 . . . . .201 D4
Collier Way GU4 . . . . . .110 D3
Collier's Wood Sta SW19 . .20 D1
Colliers CI GU21 . . . . . . .69 B2
Colliers Ct CR0 . . . . . . .61 D8
Colliers Water La CR7 . . . .42 A4
Collingdon GU4 . . . . . .174 F1
Collingsbourne KT15 . . . .52 B6
Collingtree Rd SE26 . . . . .23 C4
Collingwood GU15 . . . . . .66 C6
❹ East Grinstead RH19 . . .205 F7
Horley RH6 . . . . .161 B4
Horsham RH12 . . . . . . .217 C4
❸ Penge SE20 . . . . .43 B8
Twickenham TW2, TW4 . . . .16 A8
Collingwood Cl Horley RH6 . .161 B4
Collingwood Cres GU1 . . .110 A2
Collingwood Mount GU15 . .66 A7
Collingwood Pl
Camberley GU15 . . . . . .66 B8
Walton-on-T KT12 . . . . . .54 B7
Collingwood Rd
Crawley RH10 . . . . . . .202 D5
Horsham RH12 . . . . . . .217 B4
Mitcham CR4 . . . . .40 E6
Sutton SM1 . . . . .59 A6
Collingwood Rise GU15 . . .66 A7
Collins Gdns GU12 . . . . .106 B2
Collins Path TW12 . . . . .15 F2
Collins Prim Sch TW11 . . .17 B2
Collyer Ave CR0 . . . . . . .60 E6
Collyer Rd CR0 . . . . . . .60 E6
Collyer's Sixth Form Coll
RH12 . . . . .217 D4
Colman Cl KT18 . . . . . . .77 C2
Colman House RH1 . . . .118 F3
Colman Rd RH1 . . . . . .118 E4
Colmans Hill GU5 . . . . .154 E7
Colmer Rd SW16 . . . . . .21 E1
Coln Trad Est SL3 . . . . . .1 F6
Colnbrook By-Pass
Brands Hill SL3, UB7 . . . . .1 D7
Colnbrook SL3, UB7 . . . . .1 D7
Harmondsworth UB7 . . . . .2 C7
Colnbrook C of E Comb Sch
SL3 . . . . .1 D7
Colnbrook Ct Poyle SL3 . . . .1 F6
Upper Tooting SW17 . . . . .20 D4
Colndale Rd SL3 . . . . . . .1 E5
Colne Bank SL3, TW19 . . . .1 C4
Colne Ct KT19 . . . . .57 C6
Colne Dr KT12 . . . . .54 D7
Colne House ❷ RH1 . . . .118 F2
Colne Lodge KT12 . . . . . .54 D7
Colne Rd TW1, TW2 . . . . .16 F7
Colne Reach TW19 . . . . . .1 F2
Colne Way Ash GU12 . . . .106 A1
Wraysbury TW19 . . . . . .12 B6
Colne Wlk RH11 . . . . . .200 F5
Colnebridge Cl TW18 . . . .12 E3
Colona Convent Girls Sch
CR9 . . . . .62 D7
Colonel's La KT16 . . . . . .33 A3
Colonial Ave TW2 . . . . . .5 C1
Colonial Rd TW14 . . . . . .14 E8
Colonsay Rd RH11 . . . . .201 B3
Colony Gate GU16 . . . . . .66 C2
Colson Rd CR0, CR9 . . . . .61 E8
Colson Way SW16 . . . . . .21 C4
Colston Ave SM1, SM5 . . .59 E6
Colston Ct SM5 . . . . . . .59 F6
Colston Rd SW14 . . . . . . .7 C3
Coltash Rd RH10 . . . . . .202 A5
Coltsfoot Dr
Guildford GU1, GU4 . . . .110 B4
Horsham RH12 . . . . . . .217 E5
Coltsfoot La RH8 . . . . . .123 A2
Columbia Ave KT4 . . . . . .38 E2
Columbia Ct ❻ KT4 . . . . .38 F2
Columbine Ave CR2 . . . . .61 B3
Columbus Dr GU14 . . . . .84 C4
Colville Gdns GU18 . . . . .67 C8
Colvin Cl SE26 . . . . .23 C3
Colvin Rd CR7 . . . . .42 A4
Colwood Gdns SW19 . . . .20 D1
Colworth Rd CR0 . . . . . .43 A1
Colwyn Cl Crawley RH11 . .200 F4

Colwyn Cl continued
Streatham SW16 . . . . 21 C3
Colwyn Cres TW1 . . . . 5 C6
Colyton Cl GU21 . . . . 69 C1
Combe House SW14 . . . . 7 C5
Combe Hurst KT2 . . . . 18 C3
Combe La
Bramley GU5, GU8 . . . . 151 D2
Chiddingfold GU8 . . . . 191 A7
Farnborough GU14 . . . . 85 A6
Shere KT24, GU4 . . . . 133 B8
Whiteley Village KT12 . . . . . . 53 F2
Wormley GU8 . . . . 170 F1
Combe Martin Coll KT2 . . . . . 18 C3
Combe Rd GU7 . . . . 150 E8
Combe Rise GU10 . . . . 146 D5
Combe View GU10 . . . . 191 A5
Combemartin Rd SW18 . . . . . 19 E7
Combemere Rd SM4 . . . . 40 B4
Comeragh Cl GU22 . . . . 89 A7
Comet Rd TW19 . . . . 13 D8
Comforts Farm Ave RH8 . . . 123 A3
Comfrey Cl
Farnborough GU14 . . . . 84 C5
Wokingham RG40 . . . . 25 E8
Commerce Rd TW8 . . . . 6 C7
Commerce Way CR0 . . . . . . 60 F8
Commercial Rd
Aldershot GU12 . . . . 126 C8
Guildford GU1 . . . . 130 D8
Staines TW18 . . . . 13 A2
Commercial Way GU21 . . . . . 69 F2
Commodore Ct GU4 . . . . . . 105 B8
Common Cl GU21 . . . . 69 D5
Common House Rd GU8 . . . . 192 H4
Common La Claygate KT10 . . . 56 A3
New Haw KT15 . . . . 52 C2
Common Rd Claygate KT10 . . . 56 A3
Redhill RH1 . . . . 139 F7
Common Side KT18 . . . . 76 A4
Common The GU6 . . . . 174 C3
Commonfield Rd SM7 . . . . . . 78 B6
Commonfields GU24 . . . . . . 67 F6
Commonside KT22, KT23 . . . . 94 A5
Commonside Cl SM2 . . . . 78 B8
Commonside Ct SW16 . . . . . 21 E2
Commonside E CR4 . . . . 41 B6
Commonwealth Lodge Sch
CR8 . . . . 79 D7
Commonwealth Rd CR3 . . . . 101 A4
Community Cl TW5 . . . . 4 A6
Como Rd SE23 . . . . 23 E6
Compass Hill TW10 . . . . 6 D1
Compasses Mobile Home
Pk GU6 . . . . 193 F5
Compassion Cl RH11 . . . . . 200 E5
Comper Cl RH11 . . . . 200 E4
Comport Gn CR0 . . . . 82 E8
Compton Cl Bracknell RG12 . . 26 E3
Esher KT10 . . . . 55 D5
Sandhurst GU47 . . . . 45 C1
Compton Cres
Chessington KT9 . . . . 56 E4
Chiswick W4 . . . . 7 C8
Compton Ct
☐ Guildford GU1 . . . . 130 F8
Sutton SM1 . . . . 59 C6
☑ West Norwood SE19 . . . . 22 E3
Compton Hts GU3 . . . . 129 D6
Compton Place Bsns Ctr
GU21 . . . . 65 A4
Compton Rd Croydon CR0 . . . 43 B1
Wimbledon SW19 . . . . 19 F2
Compton Way GU10 . . . . . . 126 B3
Comptons Brow La RH13 . . . 218 A13
Comptons La RH12, RH13 . . . 217 F3
Comsaye Wlk RG12 . . . . 27 C4
Conal Ct SW16 . . . . 21 D3
Conaways Cl KT17 . . . . 58 A1
Concorde Bsns Pk TN16 . . . . 83 D4
Concorde Cl TW3 . . . . 5 B4
Concorde House KT15 . . . . . . 52 B6
Condor Cl GU22 . . . . 89 B8
Condor Rd TW18 . . . . 33 C6
Conduit La CR0 . . . . 62 A5
Conduit The RH1 . . . . 120 E5
Coney Acre SE21 . . . . 22 C7
Coney Cl RH11 . . . . 201 B8
Coney Croft RH12 . . . . 218 B5
Coney Hall Par BR4 . . . . 63 E7
Coney Hill Rd BR4 . . . . 63 F7
Coney Hill Sch GU22 . . . . . . 63 F7
Coneyberry RH2 . . . . 139 D5
Coneybury RH1 . . . . 120 E1
Coneybury Cl CR6 . . . . 101 B8
Coneyhurst La GU6 . . . . 175 E6
Conford Dr GU4 . . . . 130 E2
Coniers Way GU1, GU4 . . . . 110 B4
Conifer Cl RH2 . . . . 118 A3
Conifer Ct ☐ SW19 . . . . . . 19 D7
Conifer Dr GU15 . . . . 66 A6
Conifer Gdns
Streatham SW16 . . . . 21 F6
Sutton SM1 . . . . 59 B8
Conifer La TW20 . . . . 12 C3
Conifers KT13 . . . . 53 F6
Conifers Cl Horsham RH12 . . 218B6
Teddington TW11 . . . . 17 C1
Conifers The RG45 . . . . 45 A7
Coningsby RG12 . . . . 27 C3
Coningsby Ct CR4 . . . . 41 A2
Coningsby Rd CR2 . . . . 61 C2
Conisborough Cres SE6 . . . . 24 C5
Conista Ct GU21 . . . . 68 F3
Coniston Cl Barnes SW13 . . . . 7 F7

Coniston Cl continued
Chiswick W4 . . . . 7 C7
Crawley RH11 . . . . 200 D4
Farnborough GU14 . . . . 84 E3
Frimley GU15 . . . . 66 C3
Horsham RH12 . . . . 218 B6
West Barnes SM4 . . . . 39 D3
Coniston Ct
Beckenham BR3 . . . . 44 C8
Chessington KT9 . . . . 56 E5
Lightwater GU18 . . . . 48 B1
Penge SE26 . . . . 23 B2
☑ Wallington SM6 . . . . 60 B6
Weybridge KT13 . . . . 53 B4
Coniston Dr GU9 . . . . 125 A6
Coniston Gdns SM2 . . . . 59 D4
Coniston Rd Catford BR1 . . . . 24 E2
Coulsdon CR5 . . . . 79 C3
Croydon CR0 . . . . 43 A2
Old Woking GU22 . . . . 90 B7
Twickenham TW2 . . . . 16 B8
Coniston Way
Chessington KT9 . . . . 56 E7
Redhill RH2 . . . . 118 E2
Thorpe Lea TW20 . . . . 12 B1
Connaught Ave
Ashford TW15 . . . . 13 E4
Hounslow TW4 . . . . 4 E3
Mortlake SW14 . . . . 7 C3
Connaught Bsns Ctr
Mitcham CR4 . . . . 40 F4
Wallington CR9 . . . . 60 F4
Connaught Cl SM1 . . . . 59 D8
Connaught Cres GU24 . . . . . 87 F7
Connaught Gdns
Crawley RH10 . . . . 201 D8
Morden SM4 . . . . 40 C5
Connaught Rd
Aldershot GU12 . . . . 105 D2
Bagshot GU19 . . . . 47 C3
Brookwood GU24 . . . . 87 F7
Camberley GU15 . . . . 65 F5
Carshalton SM1 . . . . 59 D8
New Malden KT3 . . . . 38 E5
☑ Richmond TW10 . . . . 7 A2
Teddington TW11, TW12 . . . . 16 D3
Connaught Sch The
GU12 . . . . 126 E7
Connell House ☐ SM6 . . . . . 60 C4
Connington ☑ KT1 . . . . 38 A7
Connop Way GU16 . . . . 65 F3
Conquest Rd KT15 . . . . 52 A5
Conrad Dr KT4 . . . . 39 D1
Consfield Ave KT3 . . . . 39 A4
Consort Dr GU15 . . . . 66 C7
Consort Mews TW7 . . . . 5 D2
Consort Way RH6 . . . . 161 B2
Constable Gdns TW7 . . . . 5 D2
Constable Rd RH10 . . . . . . 201 F2
Constable Way GU47 . . . . . . 64 E6
Constable Wlk SE21 . . . . . . 22 E5
Constance Ct Catford 44 F1
Constance Rd Sutton SM1 . . . 59 C6
Thornton Heath CR0 . . . . . . 42 B2
Twickenham TW2 . . . . 16 B8
Constantine House SW2 . . . . 22 B7
Constitution Hill GU22 . . . . 89 E8
Contley House Hotel RG40 . . 25 B8
Control Tower Rd
Crawley RH6 . . . . 181 D6
Harlington TW6 . . . . 3 C3
Convent Cl BR3 . . . . 24 C1
Convent Hill SE19 . . . . 22 C2
Convent of the Sacred
Heart Digby-Stuart Coll
SW15 . . . . 7 F2
Convent Rd TW15 . . . . 14 B3
Conway Cl GU16 . . . . 65 C1
Conway Dr Ashford TW15 . . . 14 C2
Farnborough GU14 . . . . 84 D4
Sutton SM2 . . . . 59 B4
Conway Gdns CR4 . . . . 41 E5
Conway House
Reigate RH2 . . . . 139 A4
☐ Streatham SW2 . . . . 21 E7
Conway Rd Feltham TW13 . . . 15 D3
Harlington TW6 . . . . 3 C3
Twickenham TW4 . . . . 16 A8
Wimbledon SW20 . . . . 39 C8
Conway Wlk TW12 . . . . 15 F2
Conyer's Rd SW16 . . . . 21 D3
Conyers Cl KT12 . . . . 54 D5
Cook Rd Crawley RH10 . . . . . 201 F4
Horsham RH12 . . . . 217 D6
Cookes La SM3 . . . . 58 E4
Cookham Cl GU47 . . . . 45 C1
Cookham Rd RG12 . . . . 26 E7
Cooks Hill RH12 . . . . 214 A8
Cooks Mead RH12 . . . . 199 D7
Colarne Rise GU15 . . . . 66 A6
Coolgardie Rd TW15 . . . . . . 14 C3
Coolham Ct RH11 . . . . 200 F6
Coolhurst La RH13 . . . . 218 A1
Coombe Ave CR0 . . . . 61 E6
Coombe Bank KT2, KT3 . . . . 38 E8
Coombe Cl Crawley RH11 . . . 181 D1
Frimley GU16 . . . . 85 D8
Hounslow TW3 . . . . 5 A3
Coombe Cotts RH11 . . . . . . 116 D4
Coombe Cres TW12 . . . . 15 E1
Coombe Ct Beckenham BR3 . . 43 F8
Tadworth KT20 . . . . 97 C4
Coombe Dr KT15 . . . . 51 F4
Coombe End KT2 . . . . 18 D1
Coombe Gdns
New Malden KT3 . . . . 38 F5
Wimbledon SW20 . . . . 39 A8

Coombe Girls Sch KT3 . . . . . 38 D7
Coombe Hill Glade KT2 . . . . 18 E1
Coombe Hill Golf Course
KT2 . . . . 18 E1
Coombe Hill Inf Sch KT3 . . . 38 D8
Coombe Hill Jun Sch KT3 . . 38 D8
Coombe Hill Rd
East Grinstead RH19 . . . . . 205 D6
Kingston u T KT2 . . . . 18 E1
Coombe House Chase
KT3 . . . . 38 D8
Coombe La
South Croydon CR0 . . . . . . 62 B5
Wimbledon SW20 . . . . 39 B7
Worplesdon GU3 . . . . 108 D7
Coombe La W KT2 . . . . 18 E1
Coombe Lane Flyover
SW20 . . . . 38 F8
Coombe Manor GU24 . . . . . . 68 B4
Coombe Neville KT2 . . . . . . 18 D1
Coombe Pine RG12 . . . . 27 D3
Coombe Pk KT2 . . . . 18 D3
Coombe Rd Croydon CR0 . . . . 61 E6
Forest Hill SE26 . . . . 23 B4
Hampton TW12 . . . . 15 F2
Kingston u T KT3 . . . . 38 E6
Kingston u T, Norbiton KT2 . . 38 A8
South Croydon CR0, CR2 . . . 61 E6
Coombe Ridings KT2 . . . . . . 18 C3
Coombe Rise KT2 . . . . 38 C8
Coombe The CR4 . . . . 15 F6
Coombe Way KT14 . . . . 71 F7
Coombe Wlk SM1 . . . . 59 B7
Coombe Wood Golf Course
KT2 . . . . 18 C1
Coombe Wood Hill CR5 . . . . 80 C6
Coombe Wood Rd KT2 . . . . . 18 C3
Coombefield Cl KT3 . . . . 38 E4
Coombelands La KT15 . . . . . 52 A4
Coomber Way CR0, CR4 . . . . 41 D2
Coombes The GU5 . . . . 152 A5
Cooper Cl RH6 . . . . 162 A3
Cooper Cres SM5 . . . . 59 F7
Cooper Ct GU14 . . . . 85 C4
Cooper House
Hounslow TW4 . . . . 4 F4
☑ West Norwood SW27 . . . . 22 B3
Cooper Rd
Croydon CR0, CR9 . . . . 61 B6
Guildford GU1 . . . . 130 F8
Windlesham GU20 . . . . 48 D4
Cooper's Hill La TW20 . . . . . 11 D4
Cooper's Hill La TW20 . . . . . 11 D4
Cooper's Hill Rd
Nutfield RH1 . . . . 120 A1
South Nutfield RH1 . . . . . . 141 B5
Cooper's Terr GU9 . . . . 125 C3
Cooper's Yd SE19 . . . . 22 E2
Coopers Cl TW18 . . . . 12 E3
Coopers Hill Dr GU24 . . . . . 87 C7
Coopers Rise GU7 . . . . 150 C3
Cootes Ave RH12 . . . . 217 A3
Copeland House SW17 . . . . . 20 D4
Copelands BR3 . . . . 23 F1
Copelands Cl GU15 . . . . 66 D4
Copeman Cl SE26 . . . . 23 C3
Copenhagen Way KT12 . . . . . 54 B7
Copenhagen Wlk RG45 . . . . 45 B4
Copers Cope Rd BR3 . . . . . . 23 F1
Copleigh Dr KT20 . . . . 97 E7
Copley Cl Knaphill GU21 . . . . 88 E8
Redhill RH1 . . . . 118 E3
Copley Pk SW16 . . . . 21 F2
Copley Way KT20 . . . . 97 D7
Copnall Way RH12 . . . . 217 C2
Coppard Gdns KT9 . . . . 56 C4
Copped Hall Dr GU15 . . . . . . 66 C6
Copped Hall Way GU15 . . . . 66 C6
Coppedhall ☐ SE21 . . . . . . 22 D6
Copper Beech Cl GU22 . . . . . 89 C4
Copper Beeches TW7 . . . . . . 5 D6
Copper Cl SE19 . . . . 22 F1
Copper Mill Dr TW7 . . . . 5 F5
Copper Mill La SW17 . . . . . . 20 C4
Copperfield Ave GU47 . . . . . 45 E2
Copperfield Cl CR2, CR8 . . . . 80 C8
Copperfield Ct KT22 . . . . . . 95 A6
Copperfield Pl RH12 . . . . . 217 B4
Copperfield Rise KT15 . . . . . 51 F4
Copperfields
Beckenham BR3 . . . . 44 C8
Fetcham KT22 . . . . 94 C5
Coppermill Rd TW19 . . . . . . 2 A8
Coppice Cl Guildford GU2 . . 108 D2
Heath End GU9 . . . . 125 E6
West Barnes SW20 . . . . 39 C6
Coppice Dr TW19 . . . . 11 D8
Coppice La RH2 . . . . 117 F3
Coppice Pl GU8 . . . . 170 E6
Coppice Rd RG12 . . . . 218 A5
Coppice The Ashford TW15 . . 14 B2
Crawley Down RH10 . . . . . 204 B8
Coppice Wlk RH10 . . . . 202 A7
Coppin House SW2 . . . . 22 B7
Copping Cl CR0 . . . . 61 E6
Coppins The CR0 . . . . 63 A4
Coppsfield KT8 . . . . 36 A6
Copse Ave Heath End GU9 . . 125 E8
West Wickham BR4 . . . . 63 B8
Copse Cl Chilworth GU4 . . . . 131 C3
Crawley Down RH10 . . . . . 204 B8
East Grinstead RH19 . . . . . 186 A3
Horsham RH12 . . . . 217 F4
Teddington TW11 . . . . 201 C7
Copse Dr RG41 . . . . 25 A6
Copse Edge Cranleigh GU6 . . 174 F4
Elstead GU8 . . . . 148 C3

Copse Edge Ave KT17 . . . . . 76 F6
Copse End GU15 . . . . 66 A6
Copse Glade KT6 . . . . 37 D1
Copse Hill Purley CR8 . . . . . 79 E6
Sutton SM2 . . . . 59 B3
Wimbledon SW20 . . . . 19 B1
Copse La RH6 . . . . 161 D4
Copse Rd Cobham KT11 . . . . . 73 B6
Knaphill GU21 . . . . 68 E2
Linchmere GU27 . . . . 207 D5
Reigate RH1 . . . . 139 D7
Copse Side GU7 . . . . 129 D1
Copse The Caterham CR3 . . . 101 A1
Farnborough GU14 . . . . 84 D3
Fetcham KT22, KT23 . . . . . . 94 B4
Rowledge GU10 . . . . 145 F4
South Nutfield RH1 . . . . . . 140 E7
Copse View CR2 . . . . 62 E2
Copse Way GU10 . . . . 145 F6
Copse Wood Ct RH1 . . . . . . 118 E3
Copsem Dr KT10 . . . . 55 A4
Copsem La Esher KT10 . . . . . 55 C3
Oxshott KT22 . . . . 55 C1
Copsem Way KT10 . . . . 55 C4
Copsen Wood KT22 . . . . 74 C8
Copsleigh Ave RH1 . . . . . . 140 A3
Copsleigh Cl RH1 . . . . 140 A3
Copsleigh Way RH1 . . . . . . 140 A3
Copt Hill La KT20 . . . . 97 F7
Copthall Gdns TW1 . . . . 16 F7
Copthall Way KT15 . . . . 52 A1
Copthorne Ave SW12 . . . . . . 21 D8
Copthorne Bank
RH10, RH6 . . . . 183 C3
Copthorne CE (Controlled)
Sch RH10 . . . . 183 B3
Copthorne Chase TW15 . . . . 13 F4
Copthorne Cl TW17 . . . . 34 C3
Copthorne Common Rd
RH10 . . . . 183 C3
Copthorne Dr GU18 . . . . 48 B1
Copthorne Rd
Copthorne RH10 . . . . 182 F1
Crawley RH10 . . . . 202 E8
Domewood RH10, RH10, RH6 184 D4
Felbridge RH10, RH19 . . . . 184 D4
Leatherhead KT22 . . . . 95 B7
Copthorne Rise CR8 . . . . . . 80 D6
Copthorne Sch Trust Ltd
RH10 . . . . 183 E3
Copthorne Way RH10 . . . . . 182 F2
Copyhold Rd RH19 . . . . 205 D8
Corban Rd TW3 . . . . 5 A4
Corbet Cl CR4, SM6 . . . . 60 A8
Corbet Rd KT17 . . . . 57 E1
Corbett Cl CR0 . . . . 82 D7
Corbett Ct SE6 . . . . 23 F4
Corbett Dr GU18 . . . . 66 F7
Corbiere Ct SW19 . . . . 19 D2
Corby Cl RH11 . . . . 200 E3
Corby Dr TW20 . . . . 11 C2
Cordelia Croft RG42 . . . . . . 27 E8
Cordelia Gdns
Ash Vale GU12 . . . . 85 F1
Stanwell TW19 . . . . 13 E8
Cordelia Rd TW19 . . . . 13 E8
Corderoy Pl KT16 . . . . 32 F3
Cordrey Gdns CR5 . . . . 79 E4
Cordrey House KT15 . . . . . . 52 B8
Cordwalles Cty Jun Sch
GU15 . . . . 65 F8
Corfe Cl KT21 . . . . 75 C1
Corfe Gdns GU16 . . . . 65 F1
Corfe Way GU14 . . . . 85 E1
Coriander Cl GU14 . . . . 84 C4
Coriander Cres GU2 . . . . . . 109 A6
Corium House GU7 . . . . 150 D5
Cork Tree House ☑ SW27 . . . 22 B3
Corkran Rd KT6 . . . . 37 E2
Corkscrew Hill BR4 . . . . 63 D7
Cormongers La RH1 . . . . . . 119 D2
Cormorant Ct ☐ SM1 . . . . . 58 F5
Cormorant Ct ☑ SE21 . . . . . 22 D6
Cormorant Pl GU47 . . . . 64 E7
Cornbunting Cl GU47 . . . . . 64 D8
Cornelia Cl GU14 . . . . 84 D3
Corner Farm Cl KT20 . . . . . . 97 C5
Corner Fielde SW2 . . . . 21 F7
Cornerside TW15 . . . . 14 C1
Cornerstone Sch The
KT18 . . . . 76 C6
Corney Rd W4 . . . . 7 E8
Cornfield Rd RH2 . . . . 139 C8
Cornfields GU7 . . . . 151 A8
Cornflower La CR0 . . . . 43 D1
Cornford Gr SW12 . . . . 21 B6
Cornhill Cl KT15 . . . . 52 B8
Cornish Gr SE20 . . . . 43 B8
Cornwall Ave Byfleet KT14 . . 71 F5
Claygate KT10 . . . . 55 E3
Cornwall Cl GU15 . . . . 65 F7
Cornwall Gdns ☐ RH19 . . . 205 F8
Cornwall Rd Belmont SM2 . . . 59 A2
Thornton Heath CR0, CR9 . . 61 B8
Twickenham TW1 . . . . 17 A8
Cornwall Way TW18 . . . . 12 E2
Cornwallis Cl CR3 . . . . 100 C5
Coronation Cotts GU8 . . . . . 191 C5
Coronation Rd
Aldershot GU11 . . . . 126 B7
Ascot SL5 . . . . 29 A2
Bracknell SL5 . . . . 28 A2
East Grinstead RH19 . . . . . 205 D7
Coronation Sq RG40 . . . . . . 25 D7
Coronet Cl RH10 . . . . 202 E7
Coronet The RH6 . . . . 161 C1
Corporation Ave TW4 . . . . . . 4 E3

Corpus Christi RC Prim Sch
KT3 . . . . 38 C6
Corrib Dr SM1 . . . . 59 E5
Corrie Gdns GU25 . . . . 31 C2
Corrie Rd Addlestone KT15 . . 52 D6
Old Woking GU22 . . . . 90 C4
Corrigan Ave CR5 . . . . 79 A4
Corry Rd GU26 . . . . 188 C4
Corsair Cl TW19 . . . . 13 E8
Corsair Rd TW19 . . . . 13 E8
Corscombe Cl KT2 . . . . 18 C3
Corsehill St SW16 . . . . 21 C1
Corsham Way RG45 . . . . 45 B7
Corsletts Ave RH12 . . . . . . 216 D3
Corsten Hollow ☑ RH1 . . . . 139 F8
Corunna Dr RH13 . . . . 217 F1
Cosdach Ave SM6 . . . . 60 D3
Cosedge Cres CR0, CR9 . . . . 61 B5
Cosford Rd GU8 . . . . 169 E4
Coteford St SW17 . . . . 21 A4
Cotelands CR0 . . . . 61 E7
Cotford Rd CR7 . . . . 42 C5
Cotherstone KT19 . . . . 57 D1
Cotherstone Rd SW2 . . . . . . 21 F7
Cotland Acres RH1 . . . . 139 D1
Cotsford Ave KT3 . . . . 38 D3
Cotswold Cl Crawley RH11 . . 201 B6
Farnborough GU14 . . . . 84 E3
Hinchley Wood KT10 . . . . . . 55 F7
Kingston u T KT2 . . . . 18 C1
Staines TW18 . . . . 13 A
Cotswold Ct RH13 . . . . 217 E
Cotswold Rd
Hampton TW12 . . . . 16 A
Sutton SM2 . . . . 59 B4
Cotswold St SE27 . . . . 22 B4
Cotswold Way KT4 . . . . 58 C
Cottage Cl Horsham RH12 . . 218 B
Ottershaw KT16 . . . . 51 C
Cottage Farm Way TW20 . . . 32 C
Cottage Gdns GU14 . . . . 84 E3
Cottage Gr KT6 . . . . 37 D
Cottage Pl RH10 . . . . 183 E
Cottage Rd KT19 . . . . 57 D8
Cottenham Dr SW20 . . . . . . 19 B
Cottenham Par SW20 . . . . . . 39 B
Cottenham Park Rd SW20 . . . 39 B
Cottenham Pl SW20 . . . . . . 19 B
Cottenhams RH7 . . . . 163 E
Cotterill Rd KT6 . . . . 37 F
Cottesbrooke Cl SL3 . . . . 1 D
Cottesloe Cl GU24 . . . . 67 F
Cottesmore RG12 . . . . 27 A
Cottimore Ave KT12 . . . . . . 35 B
Cottimore Cres KT12 . . . . . . 35 B
Cottimore La
Walton-on-T KT12 . . . . 35 B
Walton-on-T KT12 . . . . 35 D
Cottimore Terr KT12 . . . . . . 35 B
Cottingham Ave RH12 . . . . . 217 D
Cottingham Rd SE20 . . . . . . 23 D
Cottington Rd TW13 . . . . . . 15 D
Cotton Hill BR1 . . . . 24 D
Cotton House ☑ SW12 . . . . . 21 E
Cotton Row RH5 . . . . 176 C
Cotton Wlk RH11 . . . . 201 A
Cottongrass Cl CR0 . . . . 43 D
Cottrell Flats GU14 . . . . . . 105 C
Cotts Wood Dr GU4 . . . . . . 110 A
Couchmore Ave KT10 . . . . . . 55 E
Coulsdon C of E Prim Sch
CR5 . . . . 100 A
Coulsdon Court Municipal
Golf Course
CR5 . . . . 79 F
Coulsdon Court Rd CR5 . . . . 79 F
Coulsdon High Sch CR5 . . . 100 B
Coulsdon House ☑ SW2 . . . . 21 E
Coulsdon La CR5 . . . . 99 A
Coulsdon Pl CR3 . . . . 100 C
Coulsdon Rd
Caterham CR3, CR5 . . . . . . 100 E
Coulsdon CR3, CR5 . . . . . . 100 B
Coulsdon Rise CR5 . . . . 79 E
Coulsdon South Sta CR5 . . . . 79 D
Coulthurst Ct SW16 . . . . 21 E
Council Cotts
Charlwood RH6 . . . . 180 C
Loxwood RH14 . . . . 213 A
Plaistow RH14 . . . . 211 L
West End GU24 . . . . 67 F
Countisbury Gdns KT15 . . . . 52 B
Countisbury House SE26 . . . 23 A
Country Way TW13, TW16 . . . 15 C
Countryways
Experience The** GU6 . . . . 193 H
County Hall RH1 . . . . 201 H
County Oak Ind Est RH10 . . 181 L
County Oak La RH11 . . . . . . 181 C
County Oak Ret Pk RH11 . . 181 L
County Oak
Way RH10, RH11 . . . . 181 C
Courier House ☐ SW2 . . . . . 22 A
Courland Rd KT15 . . . . 52 A
Course Rd SL5 . . . . 29 A
Court Ave CR5 . . . . 100 A
Court Bushes Rd CR3 . . . . . 101 A
Court Cl
East Grinstead RH19 . . . . . 186 C
Twickenham TW13, TW2 . . . . 16 B
Court Close Ave
TW13, TW2 . . . . 16 B
Court Cres Chessington KT9 . . 56 E
East Grinstead RH19 . . . . . 185 L
Court Downs Rd BR3 . . . . . . 44 B
Court Dr Carshalton SM1 . . . . 59 E

Court Dr continued
Croydon CR0 ....60 F6
Court Farm Ave KT19 .....57 D5
Court Farm Gdns KT19 ....76 C8
Court Farm Ind Est TW9 ...2 F1
Court Farm Rd CR6 ....81 A2
Court Gdns GU15 ....65 D5
Court Green Hts GU22 ....89 C7
Court Haw SM7 ....78 E4
Court La Dulwich SE21 ....22 E2
 Epsom KT19 ....76 C6
Court Lodge Ct SE21 .....22 E8
Court Lodge Cty Inf Sch
 RH6 ....160 F3
Court Lodge Rd RH6 .....160 F3
Court Rd
 Dockenfield GU10 ......166 D3
 Guildford GU1 ....130 C7
 Warlingham CR6 ....81 E1
Court Way TW1,TW2 ....16 F8
Court Wood La CR0 ....62 F1
Courtenay Ave SM2 ....59 A2
Courtenay Dr BR3 ....44 D7
Courtenay Mews TW20 ....70 A3
Courtenay Rd
 Heath End GU9 ....125 E7
 North Cheam KT4, SM3 ...58 C7
 Penge BR3, SE20 ....23 D2
 Woking GU21 ....70 A3
Courtfield Rd TW15 ......14 B2
Courtfield Rise BR4 .....63 D7
Courthope Rd SW19 ....19 E3
Courthope Villas SW19 ...19 E1
Courtland Ave SW16 .....21 F1
Courtlands Beckenham BR3 ..44 B7
 Richmond TW10 ....7 A2
 [2] Sutton SM2 ....59 B3
 Walton-on-t KT12 ......35 A2
Courtlands Ave Esher KT10 .55 A4
 Hampton TW12 ....15 F2
 Richmond TW9 ....7 B5
Courtlands Cl SM2 ....44 F1
Courtlands Cl CR2 ....62 A1
Courtlands Cres SM7 .....78 A3
Courtlands Dr KT19 ......57 F4
Courtlands Rd KT5 ....38 A2
Courtleas KT11 ....14 A6
Courtney Cl SE19 ....22 E2
Courtney Cres SM5 ......59 F2
Courtney Pl Cobham KT11 ..73 F7
 Croydon CR0 ....61 A7
Courtney Rd
 Croydon CR0, CR9 ....61 A7
 Harlington TW6 ....3 A4
 Mitcham SW19 ....20 E1
Courts Hill Rd GU27 ....208 B6
Courts Mount Rd GU27 ...208 B6
Courts The Isleworth 21 E1
Courtside SE23 ....23 C5
Courtwood Prim Sch CR0 ..62 F1
Courtyard The
 Addlestone KT15 ....52 C6
 Cranleigh GU6 ....153 E1
 [1] Crawley RH10 ......201 D5
 Crawley, Whitewane
 Hill RH13 ....218 E4
Court Grained RH19 .....186 B2
Couts Ave KT9 ....56 E5
Cove Rd GU14 ....84 F4
Cove Sch GU14 ....84 E5
Coveham Cres KT11 ......73 A6
Coventry Rd SE25 ....43 A5
Coverack Cl CR0 ....43 E2
Coverdale Ct KT19 ......61 F7
Coverdale Gdns CR0 .....61 F7
Covert Cl RH10 ....201 E7
Covert La RG12 ....27 C5
Covert The Ascot SL5 ....29 B2
 Farnborough GU14 ......84 D7
Coverton Rd SW17 ....20 E3
Coverts Cl GU9 ....125 E4
Coverts Rd KT10 ....55 F3
Coves Farm Wood RG42 ...26 D7
Covey Cl Farnborough GU14 .85 A8
 Merton SW19 ....40 B7
Covey The RH10 ....202 E8
Covington Gdns SW16 ...22 B1
Covington Way
 South Norwood SW16 ....22 A1
 South Norwood SW16 ....22 B2
Cowden St SE6 ....24 A4
Cowdray Cl RH10 ....202 C5
Cowdray Rd SW19 ....20 C3
Cowfold Cl RH11 ....200 F3
Cowick Rd SW17 ....20 F4
Cowleaze Rd KT2 ....37 E8
Cowley Ave TW16 ....32 F2

Cowley Cl CR2 ....62 C2
Cowley Cres KT12 ....54 C6
Cowley La GU46 ....64 D1
Cowley Rd SW14 ....7 E4
Coworth Cl SL5 ....30 B4
Coworth Park Sch GU24 ..49 B6
Coworth Rd SL5 ....30 A4
Cowper Ave SM1 ....59 D6
Cowper Cl KT16 ....32 E3
Cowper Gdns SM6 ....60 C4
Cowper Rd Kingston u T ...17 F3
 Wimbledon SW19 ....20 C2
Cowshot Cres GU24 .....87 D7
Cowslip La RH5 ....115 B7
Cox Cnr RH5 ....177 A7
Cox Green Rd
 Cranleigh RH12 ....195 C2
 Ewhurst RH12 ....195 C2
Cox House RH12 ....217 B2
Cox La Chessington KT9 ..56 F6
 West Ewell KT19 ......57 C5
Coxbridge GU9 ....124 F1
Coxcomb Wlk RH11 .....201 A4
Coxcombe La GU8 ......191 B4
Coxdean KT18 ....97 C8
Coxgreen GU47 ....64 D6
Coxley Rise CR8 ....80 C6
Coxs Ave TW17 ....34 E6
Coxwell Rd SE19 ....22 E1
Crab Hill BR3 ....24 D1
Crab La KT16 ....140 F4
Crabbet Rd RH10 ......202 B7
Crabtree Cl KT23 ....94 C1
Crabtree Cnr TW20 .....32 B8
Crabtree Dr KT22 ....95 C2
Crabtree La Churt GU10 ..168 A2
 Great Bookham KT23 ....94 C1
 Headley KT22 ....96 C1
 Westhumble RH5 ....115 A5
Crabtree Office Village
 TW20 ....32 C8
Crabwood RH8 ....122 E7
Craddocks Ave KT21 ....75 F3
Craddocks Par KT21 ....75 E2
Cradhurst Cl RH4 ......135 C6
Crag Rd TW10 ....17 C4
Craigans RH11 ....201 A5
Craigen Ave CR0 ....43 B1
Craignore Tower GU22 ..89 E8
Craignair Rd SW2 ......22 A8
Craignish Ave SW16 ...41 F7
Craigside Kingston u T KT2 .38 B8
 Purley CR8 ....79 F5
Craigwell Ave TW13 ....15 A5
Craigwell Cl TW18 .....32 E8
Crail Cl RG41 ....25 A3
Crake Pl GU47 ....64 D8
Crakell Rd RH2 ....139 C8
Cramhurst La GU8 .....170 E6
Cramond Ct TW14 ......14 E7
Crampshaw La KT21 ....95 F7
Crampton Rd SE20 .....23 C2
Cranbourne Ave KT6 ...57 A7
Cranborne Wlk RH10 ...201 F4
Cranbourne Cl
 Horley RH6 ....161 B5
 Thornton Heath SW16 ..41 E6
Cranbourne Cotts SL4 ...9 B5
Cranbourne Sch SL4 .....9 A4
Cranbrook Ct [1] RH8 ....6 D8
Cranbrook Dr
 Thames Ditton KT10 ....36 C1
 Twickenham TW2 ....16 C6
Cranbrook House SE13 ..42 D8
Cranbrook Rd Houn TW4 ...4 F3
 South Norwood CR7 ....42 C7
 Wimbledon SW19 ....19 E1
Cranbrook Terr GU6 ...174 F3
Crane Ave TW7 ....6 A2
Crane Ct Sandhurst GU47 ..64 D8
 West Ewell KT19 ......57 C6
Crane House Catford BR1 ..24 D3
 Feltham TW13 ....15 F4
Crane Inf Sch TW13 ....15 F6
Crane Jun Sch TW13 ....15 F6
Crane Lodge Rd TW5 .....4 B8
Crane Park Rd TW2 .....16 B6
Crane Rd Stanwell TW19 ...3 A1
 Twickenham TW2 ....16 E7
Cranebank Mews TW1 ....6 B2
Cranebrook TW2 ....16 C6
Craneford Cl TW2 ......16 F8
Craneford Way TW2 ....16 C8
Cranes Dr KT5 ....37 F5
Cranes Park Ave KT5, KT6 .37 F5
Cranes Park Cres KT5 ..37 F5
Cranes Pk KT5, KT6 ....37 E4
Craneswater TW5 ....5 A8
Cranfield Ct [3] GU21 ..68 F1
Cranfield Rd E SM5 ....60 A2
Cranfield Rd W SM5 ....60 A2
Cranford Ave TW19 .....13 F8
Cranford Cl Purley CR8 ..80 C6
 Stanwell TW19 ....13 E8
 Wimbledon SW19 ....19 B1
Cranford Comm Sch TW5 ..4 B8
Cranford Ct SM1 ....59 C6
Cranford Jun & Inf Schs
 TW4 ....4 B5
Cranford La Cranford UB3 ..4 A7
 Harlington UB3 ....3 E7
 Hatton TW6 ....3 F6
 Heston, Hatton Cross TW6 .3 F4

Cranford La continued
 Heston TW5 ....4 D7
Cranford Lodge SW19 ...19 E6
Cranford Rise KT10 ....55 C5
Cranleigh Ct
 Farnborough GU14 .....84 F4
 Mitcham CR4 ....40 D6
 Richmond TW9 ....7 A4
Cranleigh Cty Inf Sch
 GU6 ....174 E3
Cranleigh Gdns
 South Croydon CR2 ....61 D3
 Sanderstead CR2 ......42 E6
 Sutton SM1 ....59 B8
Cranleigh House SW20 ..39 B7
Cranleigh Mead GU6 ...174 F2
Cranleigh Rd
 Ewhurst GU6 ....175 D4
 Feltham TW13 ....14 F4
 Merton SW19 ....40 A6
 Thames Ditton KT10 ...36 C1
 Wonersh GU5 ....152 C7
Cranleigh Sch GU6 ....173 D8
Cranleigh Village Hospl
 GU6 ....174 D3
Cranley Cl GU1 ....110 A1
Cranley Gdns SM6 .....60 C3
Cranley Pl GU21 ......68 D1
Cranley Rd Guildford GU1 ..109 F1
 Hersham KT12 ....53 F5
Cranmer Cl
 Warlingham CR6 ......81 E2
 West Barnes SM4 .....39 E3
 Weybridge KT13 ......53 C3
Cranmer Ct Hampton TW12 .16 B3
Cranmer Gdns CR6 ....81 E2
Cranmer Mid Sch CR4 ..40 F5
Cranmer Rd
 Croydon CR0, CR9 ....61 C7
 Hampton TW12 ....16 B3
 Kingston u T KT2 ....17 E3
 Mitcham CR4 ....40 F5
Cranmer Terr SW17 ...20 D3
Cranmer Wlk RH10 ....202 C5
Cranmore Ave TW7 .....5 C7
Cranmore Cl GU11 ....104 E1
Cranmore Ct GU16 ....85 F4
Cranmore Gdns GU11 ..104 E1
Cranmore La
 Aldershot GU11 ......104 E1
 West Horsley KT24 ...112 C6
Cranmore Rd Catford BR1 ..24 F5
 Mytchett GU16 ....86 A4
Cranmore Sch KT24 ...112 C6
Cranston Cl
 Hounslow TW3, TW4 ....4 E5
 Reigate RH2 ....139 B8
Cranston Rd
 East Grinstead RH19 ..185 F2
 Forest Hill SE23 .....23 E6
Cranstoun Cl GU3 ....108 F5
Crantock Rd SE6 ......24 C6
Cranwell Ct CR0 ......62 D8
Cranwell Gr
 Lightwater GU18 .....66 F8
 Littleton TW17 ....33 F5
Cranwell Rd TW6 ....3 B5
Craster Rd SW2 ....21 F8
Cravan Ave TW13 .....15 A6
Craven Cl GU10 ......146 C6
Craven Gdns SW19 ....20 A3
Craven House
 [2] Farnham GU9 .....125 B2
 [2] Mortlake SW14 .....7 C4
Craven Rd Crawley RH10 ..202 B5
 Croydon CR0 ....43 B1
 Kingston u T KT2 .....18 A1
 Ravens The RH6 ......162 A3
Crawford Cl TW7 ....5 E5
Crawford Gdns
 Camberley GU15 ......65 B5
 Hampton TW12 ....36 A8
Crawford Way RH19 ...185 F3
Crawley Ave
 Crawley RH10 ....182 C1
 Crawley, Ifield RH10, RH11 .201 A6
Crawley Chase RG42 ....8 B2
Crawley Coll
 RH10 ....201 E6
 Crawley, Three
 Bridges RH10 ....202 A6
Crawley Coll (West
 Green Annexe) RH11 ..201 C7
Crawley Down Rd
 East Grinstead RH19 ..184 F4
 Felbridge RH19 ......184 F4
Crawley Dr GU15 .....65 F6
Crawley Hill GU15 ....65 F6
Crawley Hospl RH11 ..201 C6
Crawley La RH10 .....202 C7
Crawley Leisure Pk
 RH11 ....201 D6
Crawley Mus Ctr RH11 ..201 C5
Crawley Rd Crawley RH12 .208 D1
 Faygate RH12 ....218 D7
 Horsham RH12 ....217 D4
Crawley Ridge GU15 ..65 F6
Crawley Ridge Cty Inf Sch
 GU15 ....65 F6
Crawley Ridge Cty Jun Sch
 GU15 ....65 F7

Crawley Sta RH10 ....201 E5
Crawley Wood Cl GU15 ..65 F5
Crawshaw Rd KT16 ....51 D4
Crawters Cl RH10 ....201 F7
Cray Ave KT21 ....75 F2
Crayke Hill KT9 ......56 E3
Crayonne Cl TW16 ....34 F8
Crealock St SW18 ....20 B8
Creasys Dr RH11 ....201 B1
Credenhill St SW16 ..21 C2
Crediton Way KT10 ...56 A5
Credon Cl GU14 .....85 A8
Cree's Meadow GU20 ..48 D3
Creek Rd KT8 ....36 E5
Creek The TW16 .....35 A4
Creeland Gr SE6 .....23 F7
Cremorne Gdns KT19 ..57 D1
Crerar Cl GU14 .....84 D3
Crescent Ct KT6 ....37 D2
Crescent Day Hospl CR0 .63 C4
Crescent Gdns SW19 ..20 A5
Crescent Gr CR4 ....40 E5
Crescent La GU12 ...106 B5
Crescent Rd
 Beckenham BR3 ......44 B7
 Bletchingley RH1 ...120 D6
 Caterham CR3 ....101 A3
 East Grinstead RH19 ..185 D1
 Kingston u T KT2 ...18 A1
 Reigate RH2 ....139 A2
 Shepperton TW17 ...34 C4
 Wimbledon SW20 ....39 D8
 Wokingham RG40 ....25 C5
Crescent The
 Ashford TW15 ....13 F3
 Barnes SW13 ....7 F5
 Beckenham BR3 ......44 A7
 Belmont SM2 ....78 A8
 Bracknell RG12 .....27 B6
 Carshalton SM1 .....59 D6
 Chertsey KT16 ......33 A6
 East Molesey KT8 ...36 A6
 Egham TW20 ....11 F2
 Epsom KT18 ....76 E6
 Farnborough GU14 ..105 C1
 Felcourt RH19 .....185 C8
 Guildford GU2 ......109 A3
 Harlington UB7 ......3 D7
 Heath End GU9 .....125 D8
 Horsham RH12 ......217 A2
 Kingston u T KT6 ...37 D3
 Kingston u T, Norbiton KT3 .38 C7
 Leatherhead KT22 ...95 B5
 Lower Halliford TW17 .34 C4
 Reigate RH2 ....118 B1
 Thornton Heath CR0, SE25 .42 D3
 West Wickham BR4 ...44 E3
 Weybridge KT13 .....53 A7
 Wimbledon SW19 ....19 D3
 Wimbledon SW20 ....39 D8
Crescent Way Horley RH6 .161 A1
 South Norwood SW16 ..22 A1

Crescent Wood Rd
 SE21, SE26 ....23 A5
Cressage Ho [10] TW8 ...6 E8
Cressall Cl KT22 ....95 B7
Cressall Mead KT22 ..95 B7
Cressingham Gr SM1 ..59 C6
Cresswell Rd Croydon SE25 .43 A5
 Feltham TW13 ......15 B7
 Twickenham TW1 ......6 B1
Crest Hill GU5 .....133 E1
Crest Rd South Croydon CR2 .62 B3
 West Wickham BR2 ...44 F2
Crest The Surbiton KT5 ..38 A4
 [2] West Norwood SW27 .22 B3
Cresta Dr KT15 .....51 F1
Creston Ave GU21 ...68 E3
Creston Way KT4 ....39 D1
Crestwood Way TW4 ...4 E2
Creswell GU21 ......68 D2
Crewdson Rd RH6 ...161 B3
Crewe's Ave CR6 ....81 C2
Crewe's Cl CR6 .....81 C2
Crewe's Farm La CR6 ..81 D2
Crewe's La CR6 .....81 D3
Crichton Ave SM6 ...60 D5
Crichton Rd SM5 ....59 F3
Cricket Cl GU26 ...188 D6
Cricket Ct RH19 ...185 E3
Cricket Field Gr RH12 .217 B1
Cricket Gn
 Hambledon GU8 ....171 C1
 Mitcham CR4 ....40 F5
Cricket Green Sch CR4 .40 E6
Cricket Hill RH1 ..140 F7
Cricket La BR3 ....23 D1
Cricketers Cl
 Chessington KT9 ...56 D6
 Ockley RH5 ....177 C4
Cricketers La
 Windlesham GU20 ...48 D4
 Winkfield RG42 ......8 A3
Cricketers Terr [2] SM5 .59 E7
Cricketers Wlk SE26 ..23 C3
Cricklade Ave SW2 ..21 F6
Crieff Ct [3] TW11, KT8 .17 C1
Criffel Ave SW2 ....21 D7
Crimea Rd Aldershot GU11 .105 B2
 Frimley GU16 ....66 D3
Crimp Hill
 Englefield Green SL4, TW20 .11 A4
 Old Windsor SL4, TW20 ..11 B6
Cripley Rd GU14 ...84 D6

Cripplecrutch Hill
 Chiddingfold GU27 ..209 F5
 Fisherstreet GU27 ..209 F5
Cripps House RH11 ..201 B2
Crispen Rd TW13 ...15 E3
Crispin Cl Ashstead KT21 .75 F1
 Wallington SM6 ....60 E8
Crispin Cres CR0 ...60 D8
Critchmere Hill GU27 .207 E7
Critchmere La GU27 ..207 E6
Critchmere Vale GU27 .207 E6
Critten La KT24, RH5 .113 D2
Crittenden Lodge BR4 ..44 A1
Crocker Cl SL5 ....28 F8
Crockers La RH7 ...163 D4
Crockerton Rd SW17 ..20 F6
Crockford Cl KT15 ..52 C6
Crockford Park Rd KT15 .52 C5
Crockham Cl RH11 ..201 C4
Crocknorth Rd KT24 .113 D2
Crocus Cl CR0 .....43 D1
Crofters KT20 .....97 D6
Croft Ave Dorking RH4 .115 B1
 West Wickham BR4 ..44 C1
Croft Cl Harlington UB7 ..3 C7
 Wokingham RG41 ....25 A2
Croft End Aldershot GU12 ..126 B8
 Carshalton SM1 ....59 E5
 Godalming GU7 ....150 E4
 Merton SW19 ......20 C1
 South Norwood SW16 ..22 A1
 Witley GU8 ....170 C5
 Wokingham RG40 ...25 A5
 Woldingham CR3 ..102 A5
Croft The Crawley RH11 .201 A6
 Epsom KT17 ....76 F7
 Heston TW5 ....4 F7
Croft Way Frimley GU16 .65 F2
 Horsham RH12 .....217 A3
 Richmond TW10 ....17 B5
Crofter's Cl GU47 ..64 A8
Crofters Cl TW7 ...5 D2
Crofters Mead CR0 ..62 F2
Croftleigh Ave CR8 ..80 B3
Crofton KT21 ......75 E1
Crofton Ave Chiswick W4 ..7 D7
 Walton-on-t KT12 ...54 C7
Crofton Cl Bracknell RG12 .27 E4
 Ottershaw KT16 ...51 C3
Crofton Terr TW9 ...6 F3
Crofts Cl GU8 ....191 B5
Crofts The TW17 ..34 E5
Croftside The SE25 ..43 A6
Crogman Cl CR2 ...61 E4
Croham Hurst Golf Course
 CR2 ....62 A3
Croham Manor Rd CR2 .61 E4
Croham Mount CR2 ..61 E3
Croham Park Ave CR0, CR2 .61 F5
Croham Rd
 South Croydon CR0, CR2 .61 F5
Croham Valley Rd CR2 .62 B3
Croindene Rd SW16 .41 E8
Cromer Ct SW16 ...21 C3
Cromer Rd Croydon SE25 .43 B6
 Harlington TW6 .....3 A5
 Thornton Heath SW16 .41 A2
Cromford Way KT3 ..38 D8
Crompton Fields RH10 .181 E1
Crompton Way RH10 .181 E1
Cromwell Ave KT3 ..38 F4
Cromwell Cl KT12 ..35 B1
Cromwell Ct [1] KT2 .18 A1
Cromwell Gr CR3 ..100 C6
Cromwell House CR0 .61 B7
Cromwell Pl
 [1] East Grinstead RH19 .205 F7
 Mortlake SW14 .....7 C4
Cromwell Rd Ascot SL5 .29 B4
 Beckenham BR3 ....43 E6
 Camberley GU15 ...65 D7
 Caterham CR3 .....100 C6
 Feltham TW13 .....15 B7
 Hounslow TW3 ......5 B3
 Kingston u T KT2 ..37 E8
 Redhill RH1 ......118 F1
 Teddington TW11 ..17 A2
 Thornton Heath CR0 .42 B1
 Wimbledon SW19 ...20 B3
 Worcester Park KT19, KT4 .57 A7
Cromwell St TW3 ...5 A3
Cromwell Way GU14 .85 C7
 Mortlake SW14 .....7 C4
Cromwell Wlk [1] RH1 .118 F1
Crondace Rd GU10 ..65 B4
Crondall House SW15 .19 A7
Crondall La GU10 ..124 D2
Crondall Rd GU10 ..145 A6
Cronks Hill RH1, RH2 .139 D7
Cronks Hill Cl RH1 .139 D7
Cronks Hill Rd RH1 .139 D7
Crooksbury Rd
 Farnham GU10 .....126 C2
 Tilford GU10 .....147 D8
Crosby Hill Dr GU15 .15 E4
Crosby Way GU9 ...125 A3
Cross Deep TW1 ...17 A6
Cross Deep Gdns TW1 .17 A6
Cross Farm Cty Inf Sch
 GU16 ....85 E6
Cross Fell RG12 ...27 A5

Cross Gates Cl RG12 ..... 27 F6
Cross Gdns GU16 ..... 85 F6
Cross Keys RH10 ..... 201 D6
Cross La Burstow RH6 ..... 162 C1
Frimley GU16 ..... 85 F6
Ottershaw K14 ..... 51 C4
Cross Lances Rd TW3 ..... 5 B3
Cross Lanes GU1 ..... 130 F8
Cross Oak La RH1, RH6 ..... 161 C7
Cross Rd Ash GU12 ..... 106 B3
Belmont SM2 ..... 59 A1
Carshalton SM1 ..... 59 D5
Croydon CR0 ..... 42 D1
Feltham TW13 ..... 15 E4
Kingston u T KT2 ..... 17 F1
Merton SW19 ..... 20 A1
Oatlands Park KT13 ..... 53 D7
Purley CR8 ..... 80 B6
Tadworth KT20 ..... 97 C5
Wentworth SL5 ..... 30 A1
Cross St
⬛ Aldershot GU11 ..... 105 A2
Farnborough GU14 ..... 105 C8
Hampton TW12 ..... 16 C3
Mortlake SW13 ..... 7 E4
Wokingham RG40 ..... 25 C6
Crossacres GU22 ..... 70 E4
Crossfield Pl KT13 ..... 53 B3
Crossland Rd Redhill RH1 ..... 119 A1
Thornton Heath CR7 ..... 42 B3
Crosslands KT16 ..... 51 E6
Crosslands Rd KT19 ..... 57 D4
Crossley Cl TN16 ..... 83 D4
Crossman Ct RH11 ..... 201 B1
Crossman Houses 19
SW12 ..... 21 E8
Crosspath RH10 ..... 201 E7
Crossroads The KT24 ..... 113 D7
Crosswater La GU10 ..... 167 F4
Crossway Bracknell RG12 ..... 27 C7
Crawley RH6 ..... 181 F8
Walton-on-T KT12 ..... 54 B8
West Barnes KT3, SW20 ..... 39 C5
Crossways Aldershot GU12 ..... 105 C1
Charlton TW16 ..... 14 F1
Churt GU10 ..... 167 F1
Crawley RH10 ..... 202 A7
Effingham KT24 ..... 113 D8
Egham TW20 ..... 12 D2
South Croydon CR0, CR2 ..... 62 F3
Sutton SM2 ..... 59 D6
Tatsfield TN16 ..... 103 C7
Crossways Ave RH19 ..... 185 C1
Crossways Cl RH10 ..... 201 F7
Crossways Cotts
Alfold Crossways GU6 ..... 194 A3
Rudgwick RH12 ..... 213 F6
Crossways Ct TN16 ..... 103 C7
Crossways La RH2 ..... 118 D7
Crossways Rd
Beckenham BR3 ..... 44 A5
Grayshott GU26 ..... 188 D3
Mitcham CR4 ..... 41 B6
Crossways The
Abinger Hammer RH5 ..... 134 B3
Coulsdon CR5 ..... 100 A8
Guildford GU2 ..... 129 F7
Heston TW5 ..... 4 F7
Lower Kingswood RH2 ..... 118 C7
Merstham RH1 ..... 119 C6
Crosswell Cl TW17 ..... 34 C7
Crouch Cl BR3 ..... 24 A3
Crouch La SL4 ..... 8 F7
Crouch Oak La KT15 ..... 52 C6
Crouchfield RH4 ..... 136 C4
Crouchmans Cl SE21, SE26 ..... 23 A5
Crowberry Cl RH11 ..... 201 A2
Crowborough Cl CR6 ..... 81 E1
Crowborough Dr CR6 ..... 81 E1
Crowborough Rd SW17 ..... 21 A3
Crowhurst SE25 ..... 43 A6
Crowhurst Cl RH10 ..... 202 E6
Crowhurst Keep RH10 ..... 202 E6
Crowhurst La
Crowhurst RH7, RH8 ..... 143 D4
Tandridge RH7 ..... 143 D5
Crowhurst Mead RH9 ..... 121 C5
Crowhurst Rd
Crowhurst RH7 ..... 164 D7
Lingfield RH7 ..... 164 D7
Crowhurst Village Rd
RH7 ..... 143 E2
Crowland Rd CR7 ..... 42 D5
Crowland Wlk SM4 ..... 40 C3
Crowley Cres CR0 ..... 61 A5
Crowmarsh Gdns SE23 ..... 23 C8
Crown Arc KT1 ..... 37 D7
Crown La Farnham GU9 ..... 126 A5
Merton SM4, SW19 ..... 40 A6
South Norwood SE19, SW16 ..... 22 A3
Wentworth GU25 ..... 31 D3
Crown Lane Gdns SE27 ..... 22 D5
Crown Lane Prim Sch
SE27 ..... 22 B3
Crown Meadow SL3 ..... 1 B7

Crown Par Morden SM4 ..... 40 A5
South Norwood SE19 ..... 22 B2
Crown Pas KT1 ..... 37 D7
Crown Pl GU47 ..... 45 E1
Crown Point SE19 ..... 22 B2
Crown Rd Kingston u T KT3 ..... 38 C8
Morden SM4, SW19 ..... 40 B5
Sutton SM1 ..... 59 B6
Twickenham TW1 ..... 6 B1
Wentworth GU25 ..... 31 C3
Crown Rise KT16 ..... 32 F1
Crown Row RG12 ..... 27 D3
Crown Sq TW20 ..... 12 A4
Crown Terr TW9 ..... 6 F3
Crown Wood Cty Prim Sch
RG12 ..... 27 E3
Crown Yard TW3 ..... 5 C4
Crownbourne Ct SM1 ..... 59 B6
Crownpits La GU7 ..... 150 E3
Crowntree Cl TW7 ..... 5 F8
Crowther Rd SE25 ..... 43 A5
Crowthorne C of E
Sch RG45 ..... 45 C5
Crowthorne Cl SW18 ..... 19 F7
Crowthorne Lodge RG12 ..... 27 B5
Crowthorne Rd
Bracknell RG40, RG12 ..... 26 F2
Bracknell,
Easthampstead RG12 ..... 27 A5
Sandhurst GU47 ..... 45 B2
Crowthorne Rd N RG12 ..... 27 B6
Croxall House GU2 ..... 35 C3
Croxden Wlk SM4 ..... 40 C3
Croxted Cl SE21 ..... 22 C8
Croydc Cl GU14 ..... 85 A7
Croydon Airport Ind Est
CR9 ..... 60 F4
Croydon Coll CR9 ..... 61 D8
Croydon Coll Annexe CR0 ..... 42 D1
Croydon Coll (Selhurst
Tertiary Ctr) SE25 ..... 42 D4
Croydon Flyover The
CR0, CR9 ..... 61 C7
Croydon General Hospl
CR9 ..... 42 C1
Croydon Gr CR0 ..... 42 B1
Croydon High Sch CR2 ..... 62 E1
Croydon La Banstead SM7 ..... 78 D6
Wallington SM7 ..... 78 B5
Croydon La S SM7 ..... 78 B5
Croydon Rd Beckenham BR3 ..... 43 E6
Caterham CR3 ..... 101 A5
Chelsham CR6 ..... 102 D5
Coney Hall BR2, BR4 ..... 63 F7
Croydon CR0 ..... 60 D7
Harrington TW6 ..... 3 B4
Mitcham CR0, CR4, CR9 ..... 41 C4
Penge SE20 ..... 43 C8
Reigate RH2 ..... 118 C2
Tatsfield TN16 ..... 103 F7
Titsey CR6 ..... 102 D5
Wallington CR0, SM6, SM5 ..... 60 E6
Croydon Rd Ind Est BR3 ..... 43 D5
Croydon Water Palace
CR9 ..... 61 A4
Croydonbarn La
RH6, RH9 ..... 163 B4
Croylands Dr KT6 ..... 37 E2
Croysdale Ave TW16 ..... 35 A6
Crozier Dr CR2 ..... 62 A1
Cruikshank Lea GU47 ..... 64 E6
Crunden Rd CR2 ..... 61 D3
Crundwell Ct GU9 ..... 125 D3
Crusader Gdns CR0 ..... 61 E7
Crusoe Rd CR4 ..... 20 F1
Crutchfield La Sidlow RH6 ..... 160 B5
Walton-on-T KT12 ..... 54 B8
Crutchley Rd Catford SE6 ..... 24 E6
Wokingham RG40 ..... 25 D7
Crystal Ct SE19 ..... 22 F3
Crystal Palace National
Sports Ctr SE19 ..... 23 A2
Crystal Palace Par SE19 ..... 22 F3
Crystal Palace Park Rd
SE19, SE26 ..... 23 B3
Crystal Palace Sta SE19 ..... 23 A2
Crystal Palace Station Rd
SE19 ..... 23 A2
Crystal Terr SE19 ..... 22 D2
Crystal View Ct BR1 ..... 24 D4
Cubitt St CR0 ..... 60 F5
Cubitt Way GU21 ..... 68 D1
Cuckfield Cl RH11 ..... 200 F3
Cuckmere Cres RH11 ..... 200 F5
Cuckoo La GU24 ..... 67 D6
Cuckoo Vale GU24 ..... 67 D6
Cuda's Cl KT19 ..... 57 F6
Cuddington Ave KT19, KT4 ..... 57 F7
Cuddington Cl KT20 ..... 97 D7
Cuddington Croft Cty Fst
& Mid Sch SM2 ..... 58 D2
Cuddington Cty Prim Sch
KT4 ..... 57 F7
Cuddington Glade KT19 ..... 76 A7
Cuddington Golf Course
SM7 ..... 77 F6
Cuddington Park Cl SM7 ..... 77 F6
Cuddington Way
SM2, SM7 ..... 77 D8
Cudham Dr CR0 ..... 82 C8
Cudham La N TN16 ..... 103 E8
Cudham St SE6 ..... 24 C8
Cudworth La RH5 ..... 179 E8
Cuffs Hill RH10 ..... 202 E2
Culham Ho RG12 ..... 27 E5
Culham House RG12 ..... 27 E5
Cull's Rd GU3 ..... 107 B1
Cullens Mews ⬛ GU11 ..... 105 A1

Cullerne Cl KT17 ..... 57 F1
Cullesden Rd CR8 ..... 80 B4
Culmer Hill GU8 ..... 170 F2
Culmington Rd CR2 ..... 61 C2
Culsac Rd ⬛ KT6 ..... 56 E8
Culver Dr RH8 ..... 122 E5
Culver Rd GU47 ..... 45 D1
Culverden Ct ⬛ KT13 ..... 53 D7
Culverden Rd SW12 ..... 21 C6
Culverden Terr KT13 ..... 53 D7
Culverhay KT1 ..... 75 E3
Culverhouse Gdns SW16 ..... 21 F5
Culverlands Cres GU2 ..... 106 A3
Culverley Rd SE6 ..... 24 C7
Culvers Ave SM5, CR4 ..... 59 F8
Culvers Retreat SM5 ..... 41 A1
Culvers Way SM5 ..... 59 F8
Culverstone Cl BR2 ..... 44 F4
Culworth House ⬛ SM1 ..... 130 E8
Cumber House SM1 ..... 20 A7
Cumberland Ave
GU2, GU3 ..... 109 A6
Cumberland Cl Epsom KT19 ..... 57 E1
⬛ Twickenham TW1 ..... 6 B1
⬛ Wimbledon SW20 ..... 19 D1
Cumberland Ct ⬛ CR0 ..... 42 D1
Cumberland Dr
Bracknell RG12 ..... 27 E8
Chessington KT9 ..... 56 F7
Hinchley Wood KT10 ..... 56 A8
Cumberland House GU1 ..... 18 B1
Cumberland Lodge SL4 ..... 10 C8
Cumberland Pl Catford SE6 ..... 24 F7
Sunbury TW16 ..... 35 A5
Cumberland Rd
Ashford TW15 ..... 13 D5
Barnes SW13 ..... 7 F6
Beckenham BR2 ..... 44 F6
Croydon SE25 ..... 43 B3
Frimley GU15 ..... 66 C4
Richmond TW9 ..... 7 A7
Cumberland St TW18 ..... 12 D3
Cumberlands CR8 ..... 80 D4
Cumberlow Ave SE25 ..... 43 A6
Cumbernauld Gdns TW16 ..... 14 F3
Cumbernauld Wlk RH11 ..... 200 E2
Cumbrae Gdns KT6 ..... 56 D8
Cumbria Ct GU14 ..... 85 E1
Cunnor Gdns KT17 ..... 58 A4
Cumnor House Sch CR2 ..... 61 B2
Cumnor Rd SM2 ..... 59 C4
Cumnor Rise CR8 ..... 80 C2
Cumnor Way RG12 ..... 27 E5
Cunliffe Cl KT18 ..... 96 B3
Cunliffe Rd KT19 ..... 57 F6
Cunliffe St SW16 ..... 21 C2
Cunningham Ave GU1 ..... 110 B2
Cunningham Cl BR4 ..... 63 B8
Cunningham Rd SM7 ..... 78 D4
Cunnington Rd GU14 ..... 85 E2
Cunworth Ct RG12 ..... 26 F3
Curfew Bell Rd KT16 ..... 32 F2
Curl Way RG41 ..... 25 A5
Curlew Cl CR2 ..... 81 D8
Curlew Ct KT6 ..... 57 A7
Curlew Gdns GU4 ..... 110 D3
Curley Hill Rd GU18 ..... 66 F7
Curling Cl CR5 ..... 100 A7
Curling Vale GU2 ..... 130 A7
Curly Bridge Cl GU14 ..... 84 F8
Curnick's La SE27 ..... 22 C4
Curran Ave SM6 ..... 60 A7
Currie Hill Cl SW19 ..... 19 F4
Currie House ⬛ SW12 ..... 21 D8
Curteys Wlk RH11 ..... 201 A3
Curtis Cl GU15 ..... 66 C7
Curtis Field Rd SW16 ..... 22 A4
Curtis Gdns RH4 ..... 136 A8
Curtis Rd Dorking RH4 ..... 136 A8
Hounslow TW4 ..... 15 F8
Curvan Cl KT17 ..... 57 F1
Curzon Ave RH12 ..... 217 B3
Curzon Cl KT13 ..... 53 A6
Curzon Rd
Thornton Heath CR7 ..... 42 A3
Weybridge KT13 ..... 53 A5
Cusack Cl TW1 ..... 16 F4
Cuthbert Gdns SE25 ..... 42 E6
Cuthbert Rd Ash GU12 ..... 106 B6
Thornton Heath CR7 ..... 61 B8
Cuttinglye La RH10 ..... 184 A1
Cuttinglye Rd RH10 ..... 184 C2
Cutts Rd GU11 ..... 105 D7
Cyclamen Cl ⬛ TW12 ..... 16 A2
Cyclamen Way KT19 ..... 57 C5
Cygnet Ave TW14 ..... 15 D7
Cygnet Cl GU21 ..... 69 B3
Cygnets Cl RH1 ..... 119 A3
Cygnets The Feltham TW13 ..... 15 E4
Staines TW18 ..... 12 F5
Cypress Ave TW2 ..... 16 C8
Cypress Ct ⬛ SM1 ..... 59 A4
West Norwood SW16 ..... 22 A3
Cypress Gr GU17 ..... 55 C3
Cypress Hill Ct GU14 ..... 64 F1
Cypress Inf Sch SE25 ..... 42 E7
Cypress Jun Sch SE25 ..... 42 E7
Cypress Lodge SE25 ..... 42 E7
Cypress Rd Guildford GU1 ..... 109 C4
South Norwood SE25 ..... 42 E7
Cypress Way
Banstead KT17 ..... 77 D5
Blackwater GU17 ..... 64 B5
Grayshott GU26 ..... 188 C3
Cypress Wlk TW20 ..... 11 B2

Cyprus Rd GU16 ..... 86 D8

D

D'abernon Cl KT10 ..... 55 A6
D'Abernon Dr KT11 ..... 73 E3
D'arcy Rd SM3 ..... 58 D6
Dacre Rd CR0 ..... 41 E2
Dacres Rd SE23 ..... 23 D5
Daffodil Cl Croydon CR0 ..... 43 D1
⬛ Hampton TW12 ..... 16 A2
Daffodil Dr GU24 ..... 68 A3
Daffin Rd SW17 ..... 21 A5
Dagden Rd GU4 ..... 130 E3
Dagley La GU4 ..... 130 D3
Dagmar Rd
⬛ Kingston u T KT2 ..... 18 A1
Kingston u T KT2 ..... 42 E4
Dagnall Pk CR0, SE25 ..... 42 E4
Dagnall Rd SE25 ..... 42 E4
Dagnan Rd SW12 ..... 21 C8
Dahlia Gdns CR4 ..... 41 D5
Dahomey Rd SW16 ..... 21 C2
Daimler Way SM6 ..... 60 E3
Dainford Cl BR1 ..... 24 D3
Dairy Cl CR7 ..... 42 C7
Dairyfields RH11 ..... 201 A5
Dairymans Wlk GU4 ..... 110 B6
Daisy Cl CR0 ..... 43 D1
Dakin Cl RH10 ..... 202 C2
Dakins The RH19 ..... 205 E8
Dalcross RG12 ..... 27 E3
Dalcross Rd TW4, TW5 ..... 4 F5
Dale Ave TW4 ..... 4 E4
Dale Cl Addlestone KT15 ..... 52 B5
Horsham RH12 ..... 217 F5
Sunningdale SL5 ..... 30 A4
Wrecclesham GU10 ..... 145 F7
Dale Ct ⬛ KT2 ..... 17 F1
Dale Gdns GU47 ..... 64 A8
Dale Lodge Rd SL5 ..... 30 A4
Dale Park Ave SM5 ..... 59 F8
Dale Park Rd SE19 ..... 42 C8
Dale Rd Ashford IW16 ..... 14 F1
Cheam SM1 ..... 58 F6
Forest Row RH18 ..... 206 F1
Purley CR8 ..... 80 B7
Walton-on-T KT12 ..... 34 F2
Dale View
Haslemere GU27 ..... 207 F5
Headley KT18 ..... 96 B4
Woking GU21 ..... 69 B1
Dalebury Rd SW17 ..... 20 F6
Dalegarth Gdns CR8 ..... 80 D6
Daleham Ave TW20 ..... 12 A2
Daleside Rd
Streatham SW17 ..... 21 B3
West Ewell KT19 ..... 57 D4
Dalewood Gdns
Crawley RH10 ..... 201 F8
North Cheam KT4 ..... 58 B8
Dalkeith Rd SE21 ..... 22 C8
Dallas Rd Cheam SM3 ..... 58 E4
Forest Hill SE26 ..... 23 B5
Dallaway Gdns RH19 ..... 185 E1
Dalley Ct GU47 ..... 64 D7
Dallington Cl KT12 ..... 54 C4
Dalmain Prim Sch SE23 ..... 23 E7
Dalmain Rd SE23 ..... 23 D7
Dalmally Rd CR0 ..... 43 A2
Dalmeny Ave SW16 ..... 42 A2
Dalmeny Cres TW3 ..... 5 D3
Dalmeny Rd
North Cheam KT4 ..... 58 B7
Wallington SM5 ..... 60 A3
Dalmore Ave KT10 ..... 55 F4
Dalmore Rd SE21 ..... 22 C6
Dalston Cl GU15 ..... 66 D3
Dalton Ave CR4 ..... 40 E7
Dalton Cl RH11 ..... 201 B1
Dalton House ⬛ SW12 ..... 21 B8
Dalton St SE27 ..... 22 B5
Damascene Wlk SE21 ..... 22 C7
Damask Cl GU24 ..... 67 E6
Damer House ⬛ TW10 ..... 6 F1
Dampier Wlk RH11 ..... 201 B1
Dan Bryant House ⬛
SW12 ..... 21 C8
Danbrook Rd SW16 ..... 21 E1
Danbury Mews SM5, SM6 ..... 60 B6
Dancer Rd TW9 ..... 7 A4
Dane Ct GU22 ..... 70 F4
Dane Rd Ashford TW15 ..... 14 D2
Merton SW19 ..... 40 C8
Warlingham CR6 ..... 81 C1
Danbury CR0 ..... 63 B4
Danbury Prim Sch SW16 ..... 18 F8
Danbury Wlk GU16 ..... 85 F8
Daneby Rd SE6 ..... 24 C6
Danecourt Gdns CR0 ..... 61 F7
Danehurst Cl SE27 ..... 22 C4
Danehurst TW8 ..... 6 C2
Danehurst Cl SW19 ..... 11 E2
Danehurst Cres RH13 ..... 217 F2
Danehurst Ct KT17 ..... 76 F6
Danemore La RH9 ..... 142 E2
Danes Cl KT22 ..... 74 C5
Danes Hill Jun Sch KT22 ..... 74 D6
Danes Hill Sch KT22 ..... 74 D6
Danes Way KT22 ..... 74 D5
Danesbury Rd TW13 ..... 15 B7
Danescourt Cres SM1 ..... 59 C8
Danesfield GU23 ..... 90 F4
Danesfield Cl KT12 ..... 54 C8
Daneshill RH1 ..... 118 E2
Daneshill Cl RH1 ..... 118 E2
Danesmead KT11 ..... 74 A1

Danesrood GU1 ..... 130 F8
Daneswood Ave SE6 ..... 24 C5
Daneswood Cl KT13 ..... 53 C5
Danetree Cl KT19 ..... 57 C3
Danetree Rd KT19 ..... 57 D3
Danetree Sch KT19 ..... 57 C4
Daniel Cl SW17 ..... 20 E2
Daniel Ct ⬛ BR3 ..... 24 A1
Daniel Way SM7 ..... 78 B5
Daniell Way CR0, CR9 ..... 41 F1
Daniels La CR6 ..... 81 F4
Danley La GU27 ..... 207 A3
Danses Cl GU4 ..... 110 D3
Danvers Way CR3 ..... 100 C4
Dapdune Cl GU1 ..... 109 C1
Dapdune Rd GU1 ..... 109 D1
Daphne Ct KT4 ..... 57 E8
Daphne Dr GU16 ..... 85 D8
Darby Cl CR3 ..... 100 C5
Darby Cres TW16 ..... 35 C7
Darby Gdns TW16 ..... 35 C7
Darby Green La GU17 ..... 64 B6
Darby Green Rd GU17 ..... 64 B5
Darcy Ave SM6 ..... 60 C6
Darcy Cl CR5 ..... 100 B8
Darcy Pl KT21 ..... 75 F2
Darcy Rd Ashstead KT21 ..... 75 F2
Isleworth TW7 ..... 6 A6
Thornton Heath SW16 ..... 41 C7
Darell Prim Sch TW9 ..... 7 A4
Darell Rd TW9 ..... 7 A4
Darent House RH11 ..... 24 D3
Darenth Way RH6 ..... 160 F6
Darfield Rd GU1 ..... 110 A4
Dargate Cl SE19 ..... 22 F1
Dark La GU3 ..... 128 B4
Darlaston Rd SW19 ..... 19 E1
Darley Cl Addlestone KT15 ..... 52 C5
Croydon CR0 ..... 43 E3
Darley Dene Inf Sch KT15 ..... 52 C5
Darley Dr KT3 ..... 38 D7
Darley Gdns SM4 ..... 40 B3
Darleydale RH11 ..... 201 C3
Darleydale Cl GU47 ..... 45 D2
Darlington Ct SE6 ..... 24 F7
Darlington House ⬛ KT6 ..... 37 D2
Darlington Rd SE27 ..... 22 B3
Darmaine Cl CR2 ..... 61 C3
Darnley Pk KT13 ..... 53 B7
Darracott Cl GU15 ..... 66 B8
Darrell Ct BR2 ..... 44 E6
Dart Cl SL3 ..... 1 B8
Dart Ct RH19 ..... 186 A3
Dart Rd GU14 ..... 84 D6
Dartmouth Ave GU21 ..... 70 D5
Dartmouth Cl RG12 ..... 27 E6
Dartmouth Gn GU21 ..... 70 D5
Dartmouth House CR0 ..... 42 B2
Dartmouth Path GU21 ..... 70 D5
Dartmouth Pl Chiswick W4 ..... 7 E8
Forest Hill SE23 ..... 23 C6
Dartmouth Rd SE23, SE26 ..... 23 C5
Dartnell Ave KT14 ..... 71 C7
Dartnell Cl KT14 ..... 71 B7
Dartnell Cres KT14 ..... 71 B7
Dartnell Ct KT14 ..... 71 C7
Dartnell Park Rd KT14 ..... 71 C7
Dartnell Pl KT14 ..... 71 B7
Dartnell Rd CR0 ..... 42 F2
Darvel Cl GU21 ..... 69 A3
Darvills La GU9 ..... 125 C2
Darwall Dr SL5 ..... 28 D7
Darwin Cl RH12 ..... 217 F4
Darwin Gr GU11 ..... 105 C3
Daryngton Dr GU1 ..... 110 B1
Dashwood Cl
Bracknell RG12 ..... 27 D8
West Byfleet KT14 ..... 71 C7
Dashwood Ct TW3 ..... 5 C3
Dashwood House SE21 ..... 22 C5
Dassett Rd SE27 ..... 22 B3
Datchet Rd Forest Hill SE6 ..... 23 F6
Horton SL3 ..... 1 A4
Daux Hill RH12 ..... 217 B6
Davenant Rd CR0, CR9 ..... 61 B6
Davenport Cl TW11 ..... 17 A2
Davenport Lodge TW5 ..... 4 F7
Davenport Rd RG12 ..... 27 E8
Daventry Cl SL3 ..... 1 F6
Daventry Ct RG12 ..... 27 B8
David Cl UB3 ..... 3 E7
David House SE25 ..... 43 A6
David Livingstone Prim Sch
CR7 ..... 42 C8
David La ⬛ 42 E2
Davis's Rd GU27 ..... 23 C7
Davidson Inf Sch CR0 ..... 42 F2
Davidson Jun Sch CR0 ..... 42 E2
Davidson Lodge CR0 ..... 42 E2
Davidson Rd CR0 ..... 42 F3
Davies Cl Croydon CR0, SE25 ..... 43 A3
Farncombe GU7 ..... 150 D7
Davies Wlk TW7 ..... 5 D6
Davis Cl RH11 ..... 201 A1
Davis Gdns GU47 ..... 64 E7
Davis Rd Chessington KT9 ..... 57 A5
Weybridge KT13 ..... 52 F1
Davos Cl GU22 ..... 89 E8
Davy Cl RG40 ..... 25 C5
Dawell Dr TN16 ..... 83 C2
Dawes Ave TW7 ..... 6 A3
Dawes Ct KT10 ..... 55 B6
Dawes Green Cotts RH2 ..... 138 A3
Dawley Ride SL3 ..... 1 E6
Dawlish Ave SW18 ..... 20 B6
Dawn Cl TW4 ..... 4 E4
Dawn Redwood Cl SL3 ..... 1 A4

wn Wlk BR2 ....44 D7
wny Cl SL5 ....28 F8
wny Rd Camberley GU15 .65 B7
sbrook Rd SW20 ....20 D6
eat Bookham KT23 ....94 C1
andsworth SW17, SW18 ...20 D6
wny Hill GU24 ....87 F5
wneys Rd GU24 ....87 E5
wsmere Cl GU15 ....66 C5
wson Rd Byfleet KT14 ....71 E8
ngston u T KT1 ....37 F6
Feltham 35 C6
y Ct GU6 ....173 F2
y's Acre CR2 ....61 F1
ybrook Rd SW20 ....40 B6
wymerslea Ridge KT22 ....95 C6
ysbrook Rd SW2 ....21 F7
ysreys HRB RH1 ....162 A8
yspring GU7 ....109 B5
ytone House SW20 ....39 D8
Broome Rd TW13 ....15 C7
Burgh House 10 SW19 .....20 C1
Burgh Pk SM7 ....79 B4
Frene Rd SE23, SE26 .....23 F5
Havilland Dr KT13 ....93 B8
Havilland Rd Heston TW5 ..4 C7
Maldon 60 E3
Havilland Way TW19 ......2 E1
La Warr Rd RH19 ....185 F1
Lara Way GU21 ....69 D1
Montfort Par 1 SW16 .....27 F1
Montfort Rd SW16 ....21 E6
Ros Pl TW20 ....26 A1
Stafford Sch CR3 ....100 F6
arn Gdns CR4 ....40 E6
Vitre Gn RG40 ....25 F7
acon Cl Downside KT11 ...93 B8
allington CR8 ....60 E2
ackingham RG40 ....25 C8
acon Dr RH7 ....164 C4
acon Field GU2 ....109 A2
acon Rd KT2 ....37 F8
acons Wlk TW12 ....16 B4
adbrook La GU12 ....105 E3
al Rd SW17 ....21 A2
an Cl GU22 ....70 E3
an Ct Farncombe GU7 ...150 D6
Kingston u T KT1 ....18 A1
ar RG40 ....25 C7
an La CR3, CR5, RH1 .....99 D3
an Par GU15 ....65 F8
an Rd Croydon CR0 ....61 D6
rncombe GU7 ....150 D6
nham TW12 ....16 A3
sworth TW3 ....5 B2
an Wlk KT23 ....94 B1
anery Pl GU7 ....150 D4
anery Rd GU7 ....150 E6
anfield Gdns CR0 ....61 D6
anhill Ct SW14 ....7 B3
anhill Rd SW14 ....7 B3
anoak La Leigh RH2 ....159 D8
llow RH2 ....159 D8
ans Cl Chiswick W4 ....7 F1
uth Croydon CR0 ....61 F7
lton on t H KT20 ....97 B3
ans Ct GU20 ....48 D4
ans Gate Cl SE23 ....23 D5
ans La Nutfield RH1 .....120 A2
alton on t H KT20 ....97 B2
anngate KT22 ....95 C5
armer House 6 SW2 .....22 A8
oden Cl KT2 ....37 D3
oorah Cl TW7 ....5 E6
op Rd SW19 ....20 C1
con Pl CR3 ....100 C4
ham House SE6 ....24 C4
dsham Cl RH10 ....202 A5
dswell Dr GU4 ....111 A6
Rd TW9 ....6 F3
e Way KT19 ....57 E5
dman Cl GU2 ....106 A2
ep Dene GU27 ....207 E6
op Well Dr GU15 ....65 E5
epcut Bridge Rd GU16 ...86 C7
pdale Bracknell RG12 ....27 A5
mbledon SW19 ....19 D1
pdale Ave RH2 ....44 F5
pdene GU10 ....146 D7
pdene Ave
4 ....115 C1
pdene Ct SE22 ....44 E6
pdene Dr RH5 ....136 C7
pdene Gdns
eatham SW2 ....21 F8
pdene Lodge 8 SW2 .....21 F8
pdene Rd RH5 ....136 D8
pdene Point 10 SE26 ....23 D5
pdene Vale RH4 ....135 C1
pdene Wood RH5 ....136 D7
pfield Rd RG12 ....27 E7
pfield Way CR5 ....79 E3
pfields RH6 ....160 F5
prose Cl GU23 ....109 B5
pwell Cl TW7 ....6 A6
er Leap GU18 ....67 A8
r Park Cl KT2 ....18 B1
r Park Dr SW19 ....40 C7
r Park Rd SW19 ....40 C7
r Park Way BR4 ....63 F8

Deer Rock Hill RG12 ......27 C3
Deer Rock Rd GU15 ....65 F8
Deerbarn Rd GU2 ....109 B2
Deerbrook Rd SE24, SW2 ..22 B7
Deerhurst KT2 ....38 B8
Deerhurst Ct TW13 ....15 B4
Deerhurst Rd SW16 ....21 F3
Deerings Rd RH2 ....118 C1
Deerleap GU35 ....187 C4
Deerleap Rd RH4 ....135 B6
Deers Farm GU23, KT14 ...71 E3
Deerswood Cl
Caterham CR3 ....101 A3
Crawley RH11 ....201 B7
Deerswood Ct RH11 .....201 A7
Deerswood Lower Sch
RH11 ....201 A8
Deerswood Rd RH11 .....201 B7
Deerswood Upper Sch
RH11 ....201 A8
Deeside Rd SW17 ....20 D5
Defiant Way SM6 ....60 E3
Defoe Ave TW9 ....7 A7
Defoe Cl SW17, SW19 .....20 E2
Delabole Rd RH1 ....119 E6
Delamare Cres CR0 ....43 C3
Delamere Rd Reigate RH2 .139 C5
Wimbledon SW20 ....39 D8
Delaporte Cl KT17 ....76 E7
Delcombe Ave K4 ....39 C1
Delderfield KT21 ....95 D6
Delfont Cl RH10 ....202 D4
Delia St SW18 ....20 B8
Dell Cl Fetcham KT22 ....94 C4
Haslemere GU27 ....208 A7
Mickleham RH5 ....115 C8
Wallington SM6 ....60 D6
Dell Close Cotts RH5 ....115 C8
Dell Gr GU16 ....85 F2
Dell House CR2 ....61 C2
Dell La KT17 ....58 A5
Dell Rd KT17 ....58 A4
Dell The Brentford TW8 ...6 D7
Burgh Heath KT20 ....97 C6
East Grinstead RH19 ....186 B1
Englefield Green SL4 .....11 A5
Feltham TW14 ....15 B8
Heath End GU9 ....125 B6
Horley RH6 ....161 B4
Reigate RH2 ....118 A2
Sidlow RH6 ....160 C5
South Norwood SE19 .....42 F8
Woking GU21 ....69 C3
Dell Wlk KT3 ....38 E7
Dellbow Rd TW14 ....4 B2
Dellfield Cl BR3 ....44 C8
Delmey Cl CR0 ....61 F7
Delphian Ct 5 SW16 .....22 A3
Delta Bglws RH6 ....161 A1
Delta Cl Chobham GU24 ..49 F1
Worcester Park KT4 ....57 F7
Delta Dr RH6 ....161 A1
Delta House RH6 ....161 A1
Delta Rd Chobham GU24 ..49 F1
Woking GU21 ....70 A3
Worcester Park KT19, KT4 .57 F7
Delta Way TW20 ....32 C8
Delves KT20 ....97 D6
Delville Cl GU14 ....84 D3
Demesne Rd SM6 ....60 D6
Dempster Cl KT6 ....37 C2
Dempster House GU9 ....125 D8
Den Cl BR2, BR3 ....44 D6
Den Rd BR2 ....44 D6
Denbigh Cl SM1 ....58 F5
Denbigh Gdns TW10 ......6 F2
Denbigh Rd
Haslemere GU27 ....208 D5
Hounslow TW3 ....5 B5
Denby Dene GU12 ......106 B2
Denby Rd KT11 ....73 C7
Denchers Plat RH11 ....181 D1
Dencliffe TW15 ....14 A3
Dendy St SW12 ....21 A7
Dene Ave TW3 ....4 F4
Dene Cl 3 Bracknell RG12 .27 C8
Farnham GU10 ....146 E6
Haslemere GU27 ....208 C6
Hayes BR2 ....44 F1
Horley RH6 ....160 E5
Worcester Park KT4 ....57 F7
Dene Ct GU1 ....110 B3
Dene Gdns KT7 ....56 A8
Dene La GU10 ....146 E6
Dene La W GU10 ....146 E5
Dene Pl GU21 ....69 C1
Dene Rd Ashtead KT21 ....95 F8
Farnborough GU14 ....84 F3
Guildford GU1 ....130 E8
Dene St RH4 ....136 B7
Dene The
Abinger Hammer RH5 ...134 B3
Belmont SM2 ....77 F8
East Molesey KT12, KT8 ..35 F4
South Croydon CR2 ....62 D1
Dene Tye RH10 ....202 D7
Dene Wlk GU10 ....146 E6
Denefield Dr CR8 ....80 D4
Denehurst Gdns
Harmdale TW10 ....7 A3
Twickenham TW2 ....16 D7
Whitton TW2 ....16 D7
Denewood 6 KT17 ....76 E6
Denfield RH4 ....136 C5
Denham Cres CR4 ....40 F5
Denham Ct SE26 ....23 B5
Denham Gr RG12 ....27 C3

Denham Rd Egham TW20 ..12 A4
Ewell KT17 ....76 F7
Feltham TW14 ....3 F1
Denholm Gdns GU1, GU4 .110 A4
Denison Rd Feltham, Lower
Feltham TW13 ....3 F1
Mitcham SW19 ....20 D2
Denleigh Gdns KT18 .....36 E3
Denly Way GU18 ....48 C1
Denman Dr Ashford TW15 .14 B2
Claygate KT10 ....56 A5
Denmans RH10 ....202 D7
Denmark Ave SW19 ....19 F1
Denmark Ct Morden SM4 ..40 A4
2 Weybridge KT13 ....53 B7
Denmark Gdns SM5 ......59 F7
Denmark Rd
Carshalton SM5 ....59 F7
Croydon SM5 ....43 B4
Guildford GU1 ....130 E8
Kingston u T KT1 ....37 E6
Twickenham TW2 ....16 D5
Wimbledon SW19 ....19 D2
Denmark Sq GU12 ......105 C2
Denmark St
Aldershot GU11 ....105 D2
Twickenham TW2 ....16 D5
Denmead Rd GU12 ......27 E3
Denmead House 7 F1
Denmead Lower Sch
TW12 ....16 B1
Denmead Rd CR0 ....42 B1
Denmead Upper Sch
TW12 ....16 B1
Denmore Ct SM6 ....60 B5
Dennan Rd KT6 ....37 F1
Denne Par RH12, RH13 ...217 C1
Denne Rd Crawley RH11 ..201 D5
Horsham RH12 ....217 C1
Dennett Rd CR0 ....42 A2
Denning Ave CR0 ....61 A5
Denning Cl TW12 ....15 F3
Denningtons The KT4 ....57 E8
Dennis Cl Ashford TW15 ..14 D1
Redhill RH1 ....118 E3
Dennis House SM4 ....59 A6
Dennis Park Cres SW20 ..39 E8
Dennis Rd KT8 ....36 C5
Dennis Reeve Cl CR4 .....40 F8
Dennis Way GU1 ....109 E6
Dennistoun Cl GU15 .....65 D5
Densole Cl BR3 ....43 E8
Denton Cl RH1 ....140 A4
Denton Gr KT12 ....54 D7
Denton Rd Twickenham TW1 ..6 D1
Wokingham RG40 ....25 C6
Denton Way Frimley GU16 ..65 D2
Woking GU21 ....69 A2
Dents Gr KT20 ....117 F7
Denvale Wlk GU21 ....69 A2
Denwood SE23 ....23 D5
Denzil Rd GU2 ....130 B8
Departures Rd RH6 .....181 F8
Depot Rd Crawley RH11 ..201 A5
Epsom KT17 ....76 E6
Horsham RH13 ....217 E2
Hounslow TW3 ....5 D4
Derby Arms Rd KT18 .....76 F2
Derby Cl KT18 ....96 E8
Derby Hill SE23 ....23 C6
Derby Hill Cres SE23 ....23 C6
Derby Rd Cheam SM1, SM2 ..58 F3
Guildford GU2 ....108 F1
Haslemere GU27 ....208 B7
Hounslow TW3 ....5 B3
Merton SW19 ....20 A1
Mortlake SW14 ....7 B3
Surbiton KT5, KT6 ....38 A1
Thornton Heath CR0 ......42 B1
Derby Stables Rd KT18 ...76 F2
Derek Ave Hackbridge SM6 ..60 B6
Wallington CR0, SM6 .....60 B6
Derek Cl KT19 ....57 B5
Derek Horn Ct GU15 .....65 B6
Deri Dene Cl 8 TW19 .....2 E1
Dering Pl CR0 ....61 C6
Dering Rd CR0, CR9 ......61 C6
Derinton Rd SW17 ....21 A4
Deronda Rd SE24, SW2 ...22 B7
Deroy Cl SM5 ....59 F4
Derrick Ave CR2 ....61 C1
Derrick House 13 SW2 ...22 A7
Derrick Rd BR3 ....43 F5
Derry Cl GU12 ....105 F5
Derry Rd
Farnborough GU14 ....84 F8
Wallington CR0, SM6 .....60 E7
Derrydown GU22 ....89 C6
Derwent Ave
Ash Vale GU12 ....105 F4
Kingston u T KT1, SW15 ..18 E4
Derwent Cl
Addlestone KT15 ....52 D5
Claygate KT10 ....55 F5
Crawley RH11 ....200 F5
East Bedfont TW14 ....14 F7
Farnborough GU14 ....84 E4
Hale GU9 ....125 A6
Horsham RH13 ....218 B6
Oxshott KT22 ....74 D5
Derwent Dr CR8 ....80 E6
Derwent House
Penge SE20 ....43 B7
Reigate RH2 ....139 A7
Derwent Lodge KT4 ......58 B8
Derwent Rd
Lightwater GU18 ....67 B8
Penge SE20 ....43 B7

Derwent Rd *continued*
Thorpe Lea TW20 ....12 B1
Twickenham TW2 ....5 B1
West Barnes SM4 ....39 D3
Derwent Wlk SM6 ....60 B3
Desborough Cl TW17 .....34 A2
Desborough Ct SE25 .....43 A5
Desford Way TW15 ....13 F6
Desmond Anderson Cty
Fst Sch RH10 ....201 E2
Desmond Anderson Cty
Mid Sch RH10 ....201 E2
Despard House SW2 ......22 A6
Detherick Ct TW3 ....5 C3
Detillens La RH8 ....123 A6
Detling Rd RH11 ....201 C1
Dettingen Rd GU16 ......86 E8
Deutsche Schule TW10 ...17 D7
Devana End SM5 ....59 F7
Devas Rd SW20 ....39 C8
Devenish La GU20, SL5 ..29 D1
Devenish Rd
Ascot GU20, SL5 ....29 D2
Sunningdale GU20, SL5 ...29 D2
Deverill Ct SE20 ....43 C8
Devey Cl KT2 ....18 E1
Devil's La TW20 ....12 C2
Devitt Cl KT21 ....76 A3
Devoil Cl GU1 ....110 B5
Devoke Way KT12 ....54 D8
Devon Ave TW2 ....16 C7
Devon Bank GU2 ....130 C7
Devon Cl Kenley CR8 .....80 E3
Sandhurst GU47 ....64 D7
Devon Cres RH1, RH2 ...118 C1
Devon House
Caterham CR3 ....100 F3
Knaphill GU21 ....68 D2
Penge SE20 ....23 B1
Devon Rd Belmont SM2 ...58 E2
Hersham KT12 ....54 C6
Merstham RH1 ....119 C5
Devon Way Chessington KT9 .56 C6
West Ewell KT19 ....57 B5
Devon Waye TW5 ....4 F7
Devoncroft Gdns TW1 ....17 A8
Devonhurst Pl 5 W4 ......7 E8
Devonport Rd 8 GU21 ....69 E1
Devonshire Ave
Sheerwater GU21 ....70 D6
Sutton SM2 ....59 C3
Devonshire Cl Croydon CR0 ..44 A1
Feltham TW13 ....15 B6
6 Richmond TW9 ....6 F6
Devonshire Dr
Camberley GU15 ....65 F7
Long Ditton KT6 ....56 D8
Devonshire Gdns W4 .....7 C7
Devonshire House
14 Balham SW12 ....21 B8
Hounslow TW3 ....5 C4
Sutton SM2 ....59 C3
Devonshire Pl GU11 ....104 F1
Devonshire Prim Sch SM2 ..59 C3
Devonshire Rd Chiswick W4 ..7 E8
Feltham TW13 ....15 F5
Forest Hill SE23 ....23 C7
Hackbridge SM5, SM6 ....60 A6
Horsham RH13 ....217 D2
Mitcham SW17, SW19 ....20 D1
Sutton SM2 ....59 C3
Thornton Heath CR0 ......42 D2
Weybridge KT13 ....53 A6
Devonshire St W4 ....7 E8
Devonshire Way CR0, CR9 ..62 F8
Dewar Cl RH11 ....200 E5
Dewar House SW17 ......20 F7
Dewey St SW17 ....20 F7
Dewlands RH9 ....121 C4
Dewlands Cl GU6 ....174 E3
Dewlands La GU6 ....174 E3
Dewsbury Gdns KT4 ......58 A7
Dexter Dr RH19 ....205 E8
Diamedes Ave TW19 .....13 D7
Diamond Ct GU12 ......119 A2
Diamond Est SW17 ....20 E5
Diamond Hill GU15 ......65 E7
Diamond Ridge GU15 ....65 C5
Diana Gdns KT6 ....56 F8
Dianthus Cl KT16 ....32 E2
Dianthus Ct GU22 ....89 D8
Dianthus Pl RG42 ....8 B2
Dibdin Cl SM1 ....59 A7
Dibdin Rd SM1 ....59 A7
Diceland Rd SM7 ....77 F3
Dick Sheppard Sch SE24 ..22 A8
Dick Turpin Way TW14 ....3 F3
Dickens Cl
East Grinstead RH19 ....185 C1
Richmond TW10 ....17 E6
Dickens Dr KT15 ....51 F4
Dickens Rd RH10 ....201 E3
Dickenson's La SE25 .....43 A3
Dickenson's Pl SE25 .....43 A3
Dickerage Hill KT3 ....38 C6
Dickerage La KT3 ....38 C6
Dickerage Rd KT1, KT2, KT3 ..38 D7
Dickins Way RH13 ......217 F1
Dickinson Rd TW13 ......15 D3
Digby Pl CR0 ....61 F7
Digby Way KT14 ....71 F7
Diggers Rise KT18 ....76 C4
Dillenburg Cl SE26 ......23 E4
Dillon Gdns SW15 ....19 F8
Dilston Rd KT22 ....95 A8
Dingle Cl RH11 ....201 A3
Dingle Rd TW15 ....14 B3
Dingle The RH11 ....201 B6
Dingley La SW16 ....21 D6
Dingwall Ave CR0, CR9 ...61 C8

Dingwall Rd
Croydon CR0, CR9 ....61 D8
Wallington SM5 ....59 F2
Wandsworth SW18 ....20 C8
Dinsdale Cl GU22 ....70 A1
Dinton Rd Kingston u T KT2 ..17 F1
Merton SW19, SW20 ......20 B1
Dione Wlk RH11 ....200 E4
Dippenhall Rd GU10 ....124 C2
Dippenhall St GU10 ....124 A5
Dirdene Cl KT17 ....76 F7
Dirdene Gdns KT17 ......76 F7
Dirdene Gr KT17 ....76 F7
Dirtham La KT24 ....113 B6
Dirty La RH19 ....206 E2
Discovery Pk RH10 .....182 A2
Disraeli Ct 3 SL3 ....1 B8
Distillery Wlk 14 TW8 .....6 E8
Ditches La CR3, CR5 .....99 E6
Ditchling RG12 ....27 A2
Ditchling Hill RH11 .....201 C4
Ditton Cl KT7 ....37 A2
Ditton Grange Cl KT6 ....37 E1
Ditton Grange Dr KT6 ....37 D1
Ditton Hill KT6 ....56 D8
Ditton Hill Rd KT6 ......37 C1
Ditton Lawn KT7 ....37 A1
Ditton Pl 8 SE20 ....43 B8
Ditton Rd KT6 ....37 E1
Ditton Reach KT7 ....37 B3
Dittoncroft Cl CR0 ......61 E6
Dixon Ct KT13 ....53 D7
Dixon Pl BR4 ....44 B1
Dixon Rd SE25 ....42 F6
Dobbins Pl RH11 ....200 E5
Doble Ct CR2 ....81 A8
Dobson Rd RH11 ....181 D1
Dock Rd TW8 ....6 D7
Dockenfield St GU10 ...166 C6
Dockett Eddy La TW17 ...33 F1
Dockett Moorings KT16 ..33 F1
Dockwell Cl TW14 ....4 A3
Dockwell's Ind Est TW14 ..4 C2
Doctors Cl SE23 ....23 C3
Doctors La CR3 ....100 A3
Dodbrooke Rd SE27 .....22 B5
Dodd's La KT14 ....71 A5
Dodds Cres KT14 ....71 B5
Dodds Pk RH3 ....137 B7
Doel Cl SW19 ....20 C1
Dogflud Way GU9 ......125 C3
Doggett Rd Catford SE6 ..24 A8
Lewisham SE6 ....24 A8
Doghurst Ave UB7 ....3 B7
Doghurst Dr UB7 ....3 B7
Doghurst La CR5 ....98 F1
Doland Ct SW17 ....20 F3
Dolby Terr RH6 ....180 E6
Dollis Cl RH10 ....202 C5
Dollis Ct GU9 ....125 D3
Dollis Dr GU9 ....125 D3
Dolphin Cl
Haslemere GU27 ....207 E6
Kingston u T KT6 ....37 D4
Dolphin Ct Merton SW19 ..20 D1
Stanwell TW19 ....13 A5
2 Wallington SM6 ....60 B4
Dolphin Ct N TW19 ......13 A5
Dolphin Rd TW16 ....34 E8
Dolphin Rd N TW16 .....34 E8
Dolphin Rd S TW16 .....34 D8
Dolphin Rd W TW16 .....34 D8
Dolphin Sq W4 ....7 E8
Dolphin St KT1 ....37 E8
Doman Rd GU15 ....65 A4
Dome Hill CR3 ....120 E8
Dome Hill Peak CR3 ....100 E1
Dome Hill Pk SE26 ......22 E4
Dome Way RH1 ....119 A2
Dominion Cl TW3 ....5 D5
Dominion Rd CR0 ....42 F2
Donald Lynch House KT4 ..40 F7
Donald Rd CR0, CR9 .....42 F3
Donald Woods Gdns KT5 ..57 C8
Doncaster Wlk RH10 ....202 A4
Doncastle Rd RG12 ......26 F6
Donkey La
Abinger Common RH5 ...155 D8
Crawley RH10 ....182 D7
Donnafields GU24 ....68 A4
Donne Cl RH10 ....202 C8
Donne Gdns GU22 ....70 E4
Donne Pl CR4 ....41 B5
Donnington Cl GU15 .....65 B4
Donnington Ct 2 RH11 ..200 F3
Donnington Rd KT4 ......58 A8
Donnybrook RG12 ....27 A2
Donnybrook Rd SW16 ...21 D1
Donovan Cl KT19 ....57 D1
Donyngs Place Recn Ctr
RH1 ....118 E2
Doods Brow Sch RH1 ...119 F2
Doods Park Rd RH1 ....118 C1
Doods Rd RH2 ....118 C2
Doods Way RH2 ....118 D2
Doomsday Garden RH13 ..218 A1
Doone Cl TW11 ....17 A2
Dora Rd SW19 ....20 A4
Dora's Green La GU10 ..124 C5
Doradus Ct 32 SW19 ....19 D7
Doral Way SM5 ....59 F5
Doran Dr RH2 ....118 D1
Doran Gdns RH2 ....118 D1

Dorcas Ct GU15 . . . .**65** B3
Dorchester Ct
Reigate RH2 . . . .**118** C2
Staines TW18 . . . .**13** A4
🔢 **Streatham** SW16 . . . .**21** E6
Woking GU22 . . . .**70** A3
Dorchester Dr TW14 . . . .**3** E1
Dorchester Gr W4 . . . .**7** E8
Dorchester Mews
New Malden KT3 . . . .**38** D5
Twickenham TW1 . . . .**6** C1
Dorchester Prim Sch KT4 . . .**39** C1
Dorchester Rd Cheam SM4 . .**40** C2
Morden CR4 . . . .**40** C2
North Cheam KT4 . . . .**39** C1
Weybridge KT13 . . . .**53** B7
Dore Gdns SM4 . . . .**40** B2
Doreen Ct GU14 . . . .**84** E7
Dorian Dr SL5 . . . .**29** E8
Dorin Ct KT20 . . . .**97** F7
Dorien Rd SW20 . . . .**39** D7
Dorin Ct Pyrford GU22 . . . .**70** E4
Warlingham CR6 . . . .**101** B7
Doris Rd TW15 . . . .**14** D2
Dorking Bsns Pk RH4 . . . . .**136** A8
Dorking Cl KT4 . . . .**58** D8
Dorking (Deepdene) Sta
RH4 . . . .**115** C1
Dorking General Hospl
RH4 . . . .**136** B6
Dorking Mus RH4 . . . .**136** A7
Dorking Rd Chilworth GU4 . .**131** E3
Epsom KT18 . . . .**76** B4
Great Bookham KT23 . . . .**114** C8
Leatherhead KT22 . . . .**95** B3
Lower Kingswood KT20 . . . .**116** F7
Tadworth KT20 . . . .**97** C3
Walton on t H KT20 . . . .**97** C3
Warnham RH12, RH5 . . . .**198** B4
Dorking Sta RH4 . . . .**115** C1
Dorking West Sta RH4 . . . . .**136** A8
Dorlcote GU8 . . . .**170** E5
Dorlcote Rd SW18 . . . .**20** E8
Dorling Dr KT17 . . . .**76** F7
Dorly Cl TW17 . . . .**34** E4
Dorman's Cl RH7 . . . .**186** A8
Dormans RH1 . . . .**201** A5
Dormans Ave RH7 . . . .**165** A2
Dormans Gdns RH9 . . . .**185** E6
Dormans High St RH7 . . . . .**186** A8
Dormans Park Rd
Dormans Park RH19 . . . .**185** E6
East Grinstead RH19 . . . .**185** D3
Dormans Rd RH7 . . . .**165** A2
Dormans Sta RH7 . . . .**185** F8
Dormans Station Rd
Dormans Park RH7 . . . .**185** F7
Dormansland RH7 . . . .**185** F7
Dormansland Prim Sch
RH7 . . . .**186** A8
Dormer Cl RG45 . . . .**45** A5
Dormers Cl GU7 . . . .**150** D7
Dormy House The GU25 . . . .**30** F3
Dorney Gr KT13 . . . .**53** B8
Dorney Way TW4 . . . .**4** E2
Dornford Gdns CR5 . . . .**100** C8
Dornton Rd
South Croydon CR2 . . . .**61** D5
Upper Tooting SW12, SW17 . . .**21** C6
Dorrien Wlk SW16 . . . .**21** D6
Dorrington Ct SE25 . . . .**42** E7
Dorrit Cres GU3 . . . .**108** E3
Dorryn Ct SE26 . . . .**23** D3
Dorset Ave RH19 . . . .**185** C3
Dorset Ct Camberley GU15 . .**65** F8
Epsom KT17 . . . .**76** F7
Dorset Dr GU22 . . . .**70** B2
Dorset Gdns
East Grinstead RH19 . . . .**185** C3
Thornton Heath SW16 . . . .**41** F5
Dorset House 🔢 SE20 . . . .**43** B8
Dorset Rd Ash GU12 . . . .**106** B5
Ashford TW15 . . . .**13** D5
Belmont SM2 . . . .**59** A1
Merton SW19 . . . .**40** A7
Mitcham CR4 . . . .**40** E7
Penge BR3 . . . .**43** D6
Dorset Sq KT19 . . . .**57** D1
Dorset Way Byfleet KT14 . . .**52** D1
Twickenham TW2 . . . .**16** D7
Dorset Waye TW5 . . . .**4** F7
Dorsten Sq RH11 . . . .**200** F3
Dorton Way GU23 . . . .**91** B6
Douai Cl GU14 . . . .**85** C4
Douai Gr TW12 . . . .**36** C8
Douglas Ave KT3 . . . .**39** B5
Douglas Cl Guildford GU4 .**109** D6
Wallington SM6 . . . .**60** E4
Douglas Ct CR3 . . . .**100** D5
Douglas Dr Croydon CR0 . . .**63** A7
Godalming GU7 . . . .**150** F5
Douglas Gr GU10 . . . .**146** C5
Douglas Grace House
SW18 . . . .**19** E8
Douglas Houghton
House 🔢 RH1 . . . .**118** F2
Douglas House
Little Bookham KT23 . . . .**94** A3
Twickenham TW1 . . . .**6** B2
Douglas Mews SM7 . . . .**77** F3
Douglas Pl GU14 . . . .**85** A5
Douglas Rd
Addlestone KT15 . . . .**52** B7
Hounslow TW3 . . . .**5** B4
Kingston u T KT1 . . . .**38** B7

Douglas Rd continued
Reigate RH2 . . . .**118** B2
Stanwell TW19 . . . .**2** D1
Surbiton KT6 . . . .**37** F1
Thames Ditton KT10 . . . .**55** B8
Douglas Robinson Ct
SW16 . . . .**21** E1
Douglas Sq SM4 . . . .**40** A3
Doultons The TW18 . . . .**13** A2
Dounesforth Gdns SW18 . .**20** B7
Dove Cl Crawley RH11 . . . .**201** D8
Selsdon CR2 . . . .**81** D8
Dove Ct TW19 . . . .**13** E8
Dovecote Cl KT13 . . . .**53** B7
Dovecote Gdns 🔢 SW14 . . . . . .**7** D4
Dovedale Cl Guildford GU1 .**110** A4
Sandhurst GU47 . . . .**45** D2
Dovedale Cres RH11 . . . .**201** B4
Dovedale Rise CR4 . . . .**20** F1
Dovehouse Gn 🔢 KT13 . . . . . .**53** D6
Dover Ct GU6 . . . .**175** A3
Dover Gdns SM5 . . . .**59** F7
Dover House
🔢 Beckenham BR3 . . . .**24** A1
🔢 Penge SE20 . . . .**43** B8
Dover House Rd SW15 . . . . . .**19** B8
Dover Rd SE19 . . . .**22** D2
Dover Terr TW9 . . . .**7** A5
Dovercourt Ave CR7 . . . .**42** A5
Dovercourt La SM1 . . . .**59** C7
Dovercourt Rd SE21, SE22 . .**22** E8
Doverfield Rd
Guildford GU4 . . . .**110** A4
Streatham SW2 . . . .**21** E8
Dovers Green Inf Sch
RH2 . . . .**139** C5
Dovers Green Rd RH2 . . . . .**139** B4
Doversmead GU21 . . . .**68** E3
Doverton Rd CR2 . . . .**61** D5
Dowanhill Rd Se6 . . . .**24** D7
Dowdeswell Cl SW15 . . . .**7** E3
Dowding Cl RG45 . . . .**45** C6
Dowding Rd TN16 . . . .**83** D4
Dowell House SE22 . . . .**22** F5
Dower Ave SM6 . . . .**60** B2
Dower House GU8 . . . .**170** F8
Dower Wlk RH11 . . . .**201** A5
Dowes House 🔢 SW16 . . . .**21** E5
Dowlands La RH10, RH6 . . . .**183** D7
Dowlans Cl KT23 . . . .**114** A8
Dowlans Rd KT23 . . . .**114** B8
Dowler Ct 🔢 KT2 . . . .**37** F8
Dowman Cl 🔢 SW19 . . . .**20** B1
Down Hall Rd KT2 . . . .**37** D8
Down La GU3 . . . .**129** B4
Down Lodge Ct KT18 . . . .**76** E5
Down Rd Guildford GU1 . . . . .**110** B1
Teddington TW11 . . . .**17** B2
Down St KT8 . . . .**36** A4
Down Yhonda GU8 . . . .**148** C3
Downberry Prim Sch BR1 . .**24** E4
Downderry Rd BR1 . . . .**24** E4
Downe Cl RH6 . . . .**160** E5
Downe Golf Course BR6 . . .**83** E7
Downe Rd CR4 . . . .**40** F7
Downer Meadow GU7 . . . . . .**150** E8
Downes Cl TW1 . . . .**6** B1
Downfield 🔢 KT4 . . . .**39** A1
Downfield House KT3 . . . .**38** D1
Downham Enterprise Ctr
SE6 . . . .**24** F6
Downham La BR1 . . . .**24** D3
Downham Way BR1 . . . .**24** E4
Downhurst Rd GU6 . . . .**175** E6
Downing Ave GU2 . . . .**129** F8
Downing House 🔢 SW19 . . . . . .**20** A1
Downing St GU9 . . . .**125** B2
Downland
Burgh Heath KT18 . . . .**77** B1
Wallington CR5 . . . .**79** B5
Downland Ct RH11 . . . .**201** C4
Downland Dr RH11 . . . .**201** C3
Downland Gdns KT18 . . . .**77** B1
Downland Pl RH11 . . . .**201** C4
Downland Way KT18 . . . .**77** B1
Downlands Rd CR8 . . . .**79** F6
Downmill Rd RG12 . . . .**26** F7
Downs Ave KT18 . . . .**76** F4
Downs Bridge Rd
BR2, BR3 . . . .**44** D8
Downs Court Rd CR8 . . . .**80** B6
Downs Ct Purley CR8 . . . .**61** B1
🔢 Redhill RH1 . . . .**119** A4
🔢 Wimbledon SW19 . . . .**19** D1
Downs Est KT17 . . . .**77** D5
Downs Hill BR2, BR3 . . . .**44** D8
Downs Hill Rd KT18 . . . .**76** E5
Downs La KT22 . . . .**95** B3
Downs Rd
Ashstead KT18, KT21 . . . .**96** C7
Beckenham BR3 . . . .**44** B7
Coulsdon CR5 . . . .**79** D1
Epsom KT17, KT18 . . . .**76** E3
Mickleham RH5 . . . .**115** C7
Purley CR8 . . . .**80** B8
South Norwood CR7 . . . .**42** C8
Downs Side SM2 . . . .**78** C8
Downs The
Leatherhead KT22 . . . .**95** C2
Wimbledon SW19, SW20 . . . . . .**19** D1
Downs View Dorking RH4 .**115** D1
Hounslow TW7 . . . .**6** A6
Tadworth KT20 . . . .**97** B6
Downs View Lodge 🔢 KT6 .**37** E3
Downs View Rd KT23 . . . .**114** C8
Downs Way Epsom KT18 . . . . .**76** F3
Great Bookham KT23 . . . .**94** C1

Downs Way continued
Oxted RH8 . . . .**122** E8
Tadworth KT20 . . . .**97** B6
Downs Way City Inf Sch
RH8 . . . .**122** E8
Downs Wood KT18 . . . .**77** B2
Downsend Lodge Pre Prep
Sch KT22 . . . .**95** B6
Downsend Sch KT22 . . . .**95** D7
Downsend Sch (Epsom
Lodge) KT17 . . . .**76** F7
Downshire Way
Bracknell RG12, RG42 . . . .**27** A7
Bracknell RG12 . . . .**27** B6
Downside
Beacon Hill GU26 . . . .**188** D7
Epsom KT18 . . . .**76** E5
Twickenham TW1 . . . .**16** F5
Downside Bridge Rd KT11 .**73** B4
Downside Cl SW19 . . . .**20** C2
Downside Common Rd
KT11 . . . .**73** C1
Downside Ct RH1 . . . .**119** C6
Downside Orch GU22 . . . .**70** A2
Downside Rd
Cobham KT11 . . . .**73** B2
Guildford GU4 . . . .**131** B8
Sutton SM2 . . . .**59** E4
Downsman Ct RH10 . . . .**201** D3
Downsview Ave GU22 . . . .**89** F6
Downsview Ct GU1 . . . .**109** C5
Downsview Gdns
Dorking RH4 . . . .**136** B6
South Norwood SE19 . . . .**22** C1
Downsview Prim Sch
SE19 . . . .**22** C1
Downsview Rd
Headley Down GU35 . . . .**187** C5
Horsham RH12 . . . .**218** B6
South Norwood CR7, SE19 . . . . .**22** C1
Wimbledon SW2 Guildford GU1 .**110** E1
South Croydon CR2 . . . .**80** E8
Whyteleafe CR3 . . . .**80** F2
Downsway Cl KT20 . . . .**97** A6
Downsway The SM2 . . . .**59** C2
Downswood RH2 . . . .**118** D4
Downton Ave SW2 . . . .**21** F6
Downview Cl
Beacon Hill GU26 . . . .**188** D6
Dormansland RH7 . . . .**93** B8
Doyle Rd SE25 . . . .**43** A5
Dr Johnson Ave SW17 . . . .**21** B5
Dragon La KT13 . . . .**53** A1
Dragoon Ct GU11 . . . .**104** E2
Drake Ave Caterham CR3 . .**100** C5
Mytchett GU16 . . . .**86** A1
Staines TW18 . . . .**12** F3
Drake Cl Bracknell RG12 . . . .**27** B4
Horsham RH12 . . . .**217** E6
Drake Ct Dulwich SE19 . . . .**22** F3
Kingston u T KT5 . . . .**37** F5
Drake Rd Chessington KT9 . . .**57** A5
Crawley RH11 . . . .**201** E3
Horley RH6 . . . .**160** E3
Mitcham CR4 . . . .**41** A3
Thornton Heath CR0, CR9 . . . . . .**41** F2
Drake's Cl KT10 . . . .**55** A6
Drakefield Rd SW17 . . . .**21** A5
Drakes Ct SE23 . . . .**23** C7
Drakes Way GU22 . . . .**89** D5
Drakewood Rd SW16 . . . .**21** D1
Drax Ave SW20 . . . .**19** A1
Draxmont SW19 . . . .**19** E2
Dray Ct GU2 . . . .**130** B8
Draycot Rd KT6 . . . .**38** A1
Draycott RG12 . . . .**27** E4
Drayhorse Dr GU19 . . . .**47** E2
Draymans Way TW7 . . . .**5** F4
Drayton Cl Bracknell RG12 . .**27** D7
Fetcham KT22 . . . .**94** E3
Hounslow TW4 . . . .**4** F2
Drayton Ct Tolworth KT5 . . . . .**57** B8
West Byfleet KT14 . . . .**71** A6
Drayton Rd CR0, CR9 . . . .**61** B8
Dresden Way KT13 . . . .**53** C5
Drew House 🔢 SW16 . . . .**21** E5
Drew Pl CR3 . . . .**100** D4
Drewstead Rd SW16 . . . .**21** D6
Drift The
East Horsley KT11, KT24 . . . .**92** E3
Martyr's Green KT11 . . . .**73** D1
Drift Way SL3 . . . .**1** C7
Driftway The Banstead SM7 .**77** C4
Leatherhead KT22 . . . .**95** C4
Mitcham CR4 . . . .**41** A8
Driftway (Worple Road)
The KT27 . . . .**95** B4
Driftwood Dr CR8 . . . .**80** C2
Drill Hall Rd KT16 . . . .**33** A2
Drive Rd CR5 . . . .**99** F7
Drive Spur KT20 . . . .**98** B6
Drive The Artington GU3 . . . .**130** B5
Ashford TW15 . . . .**14** D1
Banstead SM7 . . . .**77** E3
Beckenham BR3 . . . .**44** A8
Belmont SM2 . . . .**77** E2
Cobham KT11 . . . .**73** F5
Copthorne RH10 . . . .**183** C3
Coulsdon CR5, CR8 . . . .**79** E5
Cranleigh GU6 . . . .**174** F2
Farnham GU9 . . . .**146** B7
Feltham TW14 . . . .**15** C8
Fetcham KT22 . . . .**94** E5
Godalming GU7 . . . .**150** F2
Guildford GU2 . . . .**108** F1
Guildford GU2 . . . .**130** A7
Headley KT18, KT22 . . . .**96** A3
Horley RH6 . . . .**161** A3

Drive The continued
Hounslow TW3, TW7 . . . .**5** D5
Ifold RH14 . . . .**212** D2
Kingston u T KT2 . . . .**18** C1
Leatherhead KT22, KT18 . . . .**95** F4
Morden SM4 . . . .**40** D4
Shackleford GU7, GU8 . . . .**149** E4
South Norwood CR7 . . . .**42** D5
Thames Ditton KT10 . . . .**36** C1
Thorpe GU25 . . . .**31** F4
Wallington CR8, SM6 . . . .**60** D1
West Ewell KT19 . . . .**57** F4
West Wickham BR4 . . . .**44** D2
Wimbledon SW19, SW20 . . . . . .**19** C1
Woking GU22 . . . .**89** B7
Wonersh GU5 . . . .**152** B6
Drivers Mead RH7 . . . .**164** D3
Drodges Cl GU5 . . . .**151** F8
Droitwich Cl Bracknell RG12 .**27** E6
Forest Hill SE26 . . . .**23** A5
Drove Rd GU4 . . . .**132** A7
Drovers Ct 🔢 KT1 . . . .**37** E7
Drovers Rd CR2 . . . .**61** D5
Drovers Way Ash GU12 . . . .**106** C1
Bracknell RG12 . . . .**27** F6
Hale GU9 . . . .**125** A6
Druid's Cl KT21 . . . .**95** F7
Druids Way BR2 . . . .**44** D5
Drumaline Ridge KT4 . . . .**57** E8
Drummond Cl RG12 . . . .**27** F8
Drummond Ct 🔢 GU1 . . . .**109** D1
Drummond Crr CR9 . . . .**61** C8
Drummond Gdns KT19 . . . . . .**76** B8
Drummond Rd
Crawley RH11 . . . .**200** E5
Croydon CR0, CR9 . . . .**61** C8
Guildford GU1 . . . .**109** D1
Drummonds Pl TW9 . . . .**6** E3
Drungewick La RH14 . . . .**213** D2
Drury Cl RH10 . . . .**202** D4
Drury Cres CR0, CR9 . . . .**61** A8
Dry Arch Rd SL5 . . . .**29** F3
Dryden RG12 . . . .**27** A2
Dryden Ct 🔢 TW10 . . . .**17** D4
Dryden Rd
Farnborough GU14 . . . .**84** F6
Wimbledon SW19 . . . .**20** C2
Drynham Pk KT13 . . . .**53** E7
Du Cane Ct SW12 . . . .**21** A7
Ducavel House SW2 . . . .**21** F7
Duck's Wlk TW1 . . . .**6** C2
Dudley Cl KT15 . . . .**52** C7
Dudley Dr SM4 . . . .**39** E2
Dudley Gr KT18 . . . .**76** C5
Dudley Rd Ashford TW15 . . . .**13** F4
East Bedfont TW14 . . . .**14** D7
Kingston u T KT1 . . . .**37** F6
Richmond TW9 . . . .**7** A5
Walton-on-T KT12 . . . .**35** A2
Wimbledon SW19 . . . .**20** A2
Dudset La TW5 . . . .**4** A6
Duffield Rd KT20 . . . .**97** B3
Duffins Orch KT16 . . . .**51** C3
Duke Cl RH10 . . . .**202** C2
Duke Of Cambridge Cl
TW2 . . . .**5** D1
Duke Of Cornwall Ave
GU15 . . . .**46** D1
Duke Of Edinburgh Rd
SM1 . . . .**59** D8
Duke of Kent Sch GU6 . . . .**154** D2
Duke St Richmond TW10, TW9 . .**6** D2
Sutton SM1 . . . .**59** D8
Woking GU21 . . . .**69** F2
Duke's Ave W4 . . . .**7** D8
Duke's Dr Farncombe GU7 .**150** B7
Newdigate RH5 . . . .**179** D6
Duke's Hill GU19 . . . .**47** E5
Duke's La
Old Windsor SL4, SL5 . . . .**10** B3
Windsor SL4, SL5 . . . .**9** F1
Duke's Ride RG45 . . . .**45** B5
Dukes Ave Hounslow TW4 . . . . .**4** E3
Kingston u T KT2, TW10 . . . .**17** D4
New Malden KT3 . . . .**38** F6
Richmond TW10 . . . .**17** C5
Dukes Cl Ashford TW15 . . . .**14** C4
Cranleigh GU6 . . . .**175** A2
Hale GU9 . . . .**125** A6
Hampton TW12 . . . .**15** F3
Dukes Covert GU19 . . . .**47** E6
Dukes Ct Addlestone KT15 . . .**52** C6
Beckenham BR3 . . . .**43** E6
Dukes Hill CR3, CR6 . . . .**101** E7
Dukes Pk GU11 . . . .**105** D6
Dukes Rd KT12 . . . .**54** D5
Dukes Ride RH5 . . . .**136** D4
Dukes Way BR4 . . . .**63** F7
Dukes Wlk GU9 . . . .**125** A6
Dukeshill Rd RG42 . . . .**45** B5
Dukeshill Rd RG42 . . . .**27** B8
Dukesthorpe Rd SE26 . . . .**23** D4
Dulverton Ct 🔢 KT6 . . . .**37** E4
Dulverton Rd CR2 . . . .**62** C1
Dulwich and Sydenham
Hill Golf Course SE21 . . . . . .**22** F6
Dulwich Bsns Ctr SE23 . . . . .**23** D7
Dulwich Coll (Endowed)
SE21 . . . .**22** E6
Dulwich Coll Picture Gal
SE21 . . . .**22** D8
Dulwich Coll Prep
Sch SE21 . . . .**22** E5
Dulwich Comm SE21 . . . .**22** E7
Dulwich Ct SE22 . . . .**23** D8
Dulwich Oaks The SE21 . . . . .**22** F5
Dulwich Village SE21 . . . .**22** E8

Dulwich Wood Ave SE19 . . . .**22**
Dulwich Wood Pk
SE21, SE19 . . . .**22**
Dumbarton Ct 🔢 SW2 . . . .**21**
Dumbleton Cl KT2 . . . .**38**
Dumphreys House 🔢
SW4 . . . .**21**
Dumville Dr RH9 . . . .**121**
Dunally Pk TW17 . . . .**34**
Dunbar Ave Beckenham BR3 .**43**
Thornton Heath CR7, SW16 . . . .**42**
Dunbar Ct Carshalton SM1 . . .**59**
Walton-on-T KT12 . . . .**35**
Dunbar Rd Frimley GU16 . . . . .**85**
Kingston u T KT3 . . . .**38**
Dunbar St SE27 . . . .**22**
Dunboe Pl TW17 . . . .**34**
Dunbridge House SW15 . . . . . .**7**
Duncan Dr Guildford GU1 . .**110**
Wokingham RG40 . . . .**25**
Duncan Gdns TW18 . . . .**13**
Duncan Rd
Burgh Heath KT20 . . . .**97**
Richmond TW9 . . . .**6**
Duncombe Ct TW18 . . . .**12**
Duncombe Hill SE23 . . . .**23**
Duncombe House 🔢
SW19 . . . .**19**
Duncombe Rd GU7 . . . .**150**
Duncroft Cl RH2 . . . .**117**
Dundaff Cl GU15 . . . .**66**
Dundas Cl RG12 . . . .**27**
Dundas Gdns KT8 . . . .**36**
Dundee Rd SE25 . . . .**43**
Dundela Gdns KT17, KT4 . . . . .**58**
Dundonald Prim Sch
SW19 . . . .**19**
Dundonald Rd SW19 . . . .**19**
Dundrey Cres RH1 . . . .**119**
Dundry House 🔢 SE26 . . . .**23**
Dunedin Dr CR3 . . . .**100**
Dunelm Gr SE27 . . . .**22**
Dunfee Way KT14 . . . .**71**
Dunfield Gdns SE6 . . . .**24**
Dunfield Rd SE6 . . . .**24**
Dungates La RH3 . . . .**117**
Dunheved Cl CR7 . . . .**42**
Dunheved Rd N CR7 . . . .**42**
Dunheved Rd S CR7 . . . .**42**
Dunheved Rd W CR7 . . . .**42**
Dunhill Point 🔢 SW15 . . . .**19**
Dunkeld Rd SE25 . . . .**42**
Dunkirk St 🔢 SE27 . . . .**22**
Dunleary Cl TW4 . . . .**15**
Dunley Dr CR0 . . . .**63**
Dunlin Cl RH1 . . . .**135**
Dunlin Ct 🔢 SE21 . . . .**22**
Dunlin Rise GU4 . . . .**110**
Dunmail Dr CR2, CR8 . . . .**80**
Dunmore GU2 . . . .**130**
Dunmore Rd SW20 . . . .**39**
Dunmow Cl TW13 . . . .**15**
Dunnets GU21 . . . .**68**
Dunnings Mill L Complex
RH19 . . . .**205**
Dunnock Ct 🔢 SE21 . . . .**22**
Dunnymans Rd SM7 . . . .**77**
Dunoon Gdns SE23 . . . .**23**
Dunoon Rd SE23 . . . .**23**
Dunottar Cl RH1 . . . .**139**
Dunraven Ave RH1 . . . .**140**
Dunraven House 🔢 TW9 . . . .**6**
Dunraven Lower Sch
SW16 . . . .**21**
Dunsborough Cotts GU23 .**91**
Dunsbury Cl SM2 . . . .**59**
Dunsdon Ave GU2 . . . .**130**
Dunsfold CE Prim Sch
GU8 . . . .**192**
Dunsfold Cl RH11 . . . .**200**
Dunsfold Common Rd
GU8 . . . .**192**
Dunsfold Rd
Alfold Crossways GU6 . . . .**193**
Bramley GU5, GU8 . . . .**173**
Dunsfold GU6, GU8 . . . .**193**
Plaistow GU8, RH14 . . . .**211**
Dunsfold Rise CR5 . . . .**79**
Dunsfold Way CR0 . . . .**63**
Dunsmore Rd KT12 . . . .**35**
Dunstable Rd
East Molesey KT8 . . . .**35**
Richmond TW10, TW9 . . . .**6**
Dunstall Pk GU14 . . . .**85**
Dunstall Rd SW19, SW20 . . . . . .**19**
Dunstall Way KT8 . . . .**36**
Dunstan Ct TW18 . . . .**13**
Dunstan Rd CR5 . . . .**79**
Dunstan's Rd SE22 . . . .**23**
Dunster Ave SM4 . . . .**39**
Dunster House SE6 . . . .**24**
Dunton Cl KT6 . . . .**37**
Dunton Ct 🔢 SE26 . . . .**23**
Dunton House 🔢 SW16 . . . .**21**
Dunvegan Cl KT8 . . . .**36**
Dupont Rd SW20 . . . .**39**
Duppas Ave CR0 . . . .**61**
Duppas Cl TW17 . . . .**34**
Duppas Ct CR0 . . . .**61**

ppas Hill La CR0 ....61 B6
ple Rd CR0 ....61 B6
ppas Hill Terr CR0, CR9 ...61 B7
ppas Jun Sch CR7 ...61 A6
ppas Rd CR0, CR9 ...24 B1
ra Den Cl BR3 ...40 F1
rand Cl SM5 ...
rban Rd Beckenham BR3 ...43 F1
lest Norwood SE27 ...22 D4
rfold Rd RH2 ...118 C1
rbla Rd RH2 ...217 D7
rfold Wood RH14 ...211 D5
rfold Wood
Woodlands Wlks GU8 ...211 C6
rford Cres SW15 ...19 B7
rham Ave BR4 ...44 F5
rham Cl Crawley RH10 ...201 C2
uildford GU2 ...108 F3
imbledon SW20 ...39 B7
rham Ct
atherhead KT22 ...95 A5
ddington TW11 ...16 E4
rham Hill BR1 ...24 F4
rham Rd Beckenham BR2 ...44 F6
ltham TW14 ...15 C2
andhurst GU47 ...45 E2
imbledon SW20 ...39 B8
rkins Rd RH19 ...185 D3
rleston Park Dr KT23 ...94 C2
rley Mead RG12 ...27 F4
riston Rd KT2 ...17 E2
rmford House SE6 ...24 B5
rning Rd SE19 ...22 D3
rmsford Ave
W18, SW19 ...20 A6
rmsford Rd SW18, SW19 ...20 A6
rrard Way TW7 ...34 D3
rrington Ave SW20 ...19 C1
rrington Park Rd SW20 ...39 C8
rch Barn Cl TW19 ...2 D1
rtch Gdns KT2 ...18 B2
tchells Copse RH12 ...217 F5
vton House SW2 ...22 B7
ytal Pl GU19 ...47 E3
xford TW14 ...38 A7
shurst La RH2 ...160 B7
velly La Haxted TN8 ...165 D8
rnstough TN8 ...144 D3
ehouse Rd GU8 ...169 C4
rning Rd TW12 ...36 B8
er's Field RH1 ...140 A5
ers Almshouses RH10 ...201 D7
kes Ct SW2 ...21 F7
kes Path GU2 ...70 C4
kes Way BR2 ...44 F6
kes Path SW19 ...19 D6
nevor Pl GU3 ...108 C5
nevor Rd TW10 ...6 E2
sart Ave KT2, TW10 ...17 C4
sart Ct KT2 ...17 C4
son Ct RH4 ...136 A7
son Wlk RH11 ...201 B1

dy Cl RH13 ...217 F2
gle Cl Crowthorne RG45 ...45 A7
allington SM6 ...60 E4
gle Ct 9 SE21 ...22 D6
gle Hill SE19 ...22 C2
gle House Sch GU47 ...45 B2
gle Rd Farnborough GU14 ...85 B2
uildford GU1 ...109 D1
gle Trad Est CR4 ...40 F3
gles Dr TN16 ...83 D1
gles Nest GU47 ...64 A8
ing Rd TW9 ...6 E8
dley Prim Sch SW16 ...21 C2
dley Rd SW16 ...21 C2
rl Rd SW14 ...7 C3
rle Gdns KT17 ...
rles Meadow RH12 ...218 B6
lest Norwood KT11 ...73 E7
leydene SL5 ...29 B1
ls Gr GU15 ...65 E6
borook Rd RH1 ...139 F7
lesfield Prim Sch SW18 ...20 C6
lesfield Sta SW18 ...20 C6
lsthorpe Rd SE26 ...23 D4
lswood Rd RG12 ...27 B2
lswood Ave CR7 ...42 A4
lswood Cl RH13 ...218 A4
lswood Ct RH1 ...139 F7
lswood Cty Inf & Nurs Sch RH1 ...140 A8
lswood House 2 SW2 ...21 F7
lswood Rd RH1 ...139 F7
lswood Sta RH1 ...139 F7
ly Commons RH10 ...201 F7
sby Cres SM4 ...40 B3
sedale House TW1 ...5 F2
shing La
odalming GU7, GU8 ...150 A3
ackleford GU7, GU8 ...149 F3
shing Point 5 SW15 ...19 B7
sington PF GU1 ...130 F7
st Ave Heath End GU9 ...125 D6
sby Cres SM4 ...40 B3
st Croydon Sta CR9 ...61 D8
st Dr Beckenham BR3 ...44 D8
allington SM5 ...59 F2
entworth GU25 ...31 B3
st Flexford La GU3 ...128 F6

East Gdns
Mitcham SW17, SW19 ...20 E2
Woking GU21 ...70 C2
East Gn GU17 ...64 D3
East Grinstead Rd RH7 ...164 D3
East Grinstead Sta RH19 ...185 D1
East Grinstead Town Mus
RH19 ...185 D1
East Hill Biggin Hill TN16 ...83 B1
Dormans Park RH19 ...185 E6
Oxted RH8 ...122 F6
South Croydon CR2 ...61 E1
Woking GU22 ...70 C2
East Hill Ct RH8 ...122 E5
East Hill Rd RH8 ...183 D5
East La Kingston u T KT1 ...37 D6
West Horsley KT24 ...92 D2
East Meads GU2 ...130 A8
East Park La RH7 ...163 C1
East Pk RH10, RH11 ...201 D5
East Pl SE27 ...22 C4
East Ramp TW6 ...3 B6
East Rd East Bedfont TW14 ...14 D8
Kingston u T KT2 ...37 E8
Merton SW19 ...20 C2
Reigate RH2 ...117 F2
Weybridge KT13 ...53 D3
Wimbledon SW19 ...20 C2
East Resr (Nature Reserve)
RH9 ...121 A3
East Ring GU10 ...127 A7
East Shalford La GU4 ...131 A3
East Sheen Ave SW14 ...7 D3
East Sheen Prim Sch SW14 ...7 E3
East St Brentford TW8 ...6 D7
Ewell KT17 ...76 E7
Farnham GU9 ...125 C3
Great Bookham KT23 ...94 B2
Horsham RH12 ...217 C1
Rusper RH12 ...199 F7
Turners Hill RH10, RH19 ...204 C4
East Station Rd GU22 ...105 B1
East Stratton Cl RG12 ...27 F4
East Surrey Coll RH1 ...119 A4
East Surrey Hospl RH1 ...118 E1
East Surrey Hospl The
RH1 ...140 A5
East Surrey Mus CR3 ...101 A3
East View La GU6 ...174 C3
East Way CR0 ...62 E7
East Whipley La
Rowly GU5 ...173 F7
Shamley Green GU5 ...173 F8
East Wlk RH2 ...118 B1
Eastbank Rd TW12 ...16 C3
Eastbourne Gdns SW14 ...7 C4
Eastbourne Rd
Blindley Heath RH9 ...142 E4
Chiswick W4 ...7 D7
Felbridge RH7 ...184 E8
Feltham TW13 ...15 D6
Godstone RH9 ...121 D2
Mitcham SW17 ...21 A2
Newchapel RH7, RH9 ...163 F5
South Godstone RH9 ...142 E4
Eastbrook Cl GU21 ...70 A3
Eastbury Gr W4 ...7 E8
Eastbury La GU3 ...129 A3
Eastbury Rd KT2 ...17 E1
Eastchurch Rd TW6 ...3 E4
Eastchurch Road Rdbt TW6 ...3 E5
Eastcote Ave KT8 ...36 A4
Eastcroft Ct GU1 ...131 A8
Eastcroft Mews RH11 ...216 F1
Eastcroft Rd KT19 ...57 E3
Eastdean Ave KT18 ...76 B5
Easter Way RH9 ...142 F5
Eastern Ave KT16 ...33 A6
Eastern Ind Area RG12 ...27 F7
Eastern La RG45 ...45 F4
Eastern Perimeter Rd TW14 ...3 F5
Eastern Rd
Aldershot GU12 ...105 E2
Bracknell RG12 ...27 D7
Eastern View TN16 ...83 C2
Eastfield Rd RH1 ...140 A8
Eastfields GU8 ...170 F5
Eastfields High Sch CR4 ...41 B7
Eastfields Rd CR4 ...41 A7
Eastgate SM7 ...77 F5
Eastgate Gdns GU1 ...130 E8
Easthampstead Park Sch
RG12 ...26 D3
Easthampstead Rd
Bracknell RG12 ...27 A7
Wokingham RG40 ...25 E4
Eastheath Ave RG41 ...25 B3
Eastheath Gdns RG41 ...25 B2
Eastlands Cl RH8 ...122 D8
Eastlands Cres SE21, SE22 ...23 B8
Eastlands Way RH8 ...122 D8
Eastleigh Cl SM2 ...59 B3
Eastleigh Way TW14 ...15 A7
Eastleigh Wlk 10 SW15 ...19 A8
Eastmead
Farnborough GU14 ...85 B3
Woking GU21 ...69 B2
Eastmearn Rd SE21, SE27 ...22 C6
Eastmont Rd KT10 ...55 F8
Eastney Rd CR0 ...42 B1
Eastnor Cl RH1 ...138 F6
Eastnor Rd RH1 ...138 F6
Eastry Ave BR2 ...44 F3
Eastry Rd SE19 ...22 D1
Eastway Crawley RH6 ...182 B7
Epsom KT19 ...

Eastway continued
Guildford GU2 ...108 F1
Merton SM4, SW20 ...39 E5
Wallington SM6 ...60 E6
Eastwell Cl BR3 ...23 E1
Eastwick Ct 8 SW19 ...19 D7
Eastwick Cty Inf Sch KT23 ...94 B3
Eastwick Cty Mid Sch
KT23 ...94 B3
Eastwick Dr KT23 ...94 B4
Eastwick Park Ave KT23 ...94 B3
Eastwick Rd
Great Bookham KT23 ...94 B2
Hersham KT12 ...54 B5
Eastwood Crawley RH10 ...201 F6
8 Weybridge KT13 ...53 D4
Eastwood Lodge GU5 ...151 F7
Eastwood Rd GU5 ...151 F7
Eastwood St SW16 ...21 C2
Eastworth Rd KT15, KT16 ...33 A1
Eaton Ct Guildford GU1 ...110 A3
Sutton SM2 ...59 D4
Eaton Dr KT2 ...18 A1
Eaton Ho GU1 ...130 F7
Eaton Park Rd KT11 ...73 D4
Eaton Pk KT11 ...73 E5
Eaton Rd Camberley GU15 ...65 B4
Isleworth TW3, TW7 ...6 A4
Sutton SM2 ...59 D4
Eatonville Rd SW17 ...20 F6
Eatonville Villas SW17 ...20 F6
Ebba's Way KT18 ...76 B4
Ebbage Ct 5 GU22 ...69 E1
Ebbisham Cl KT18 ...76 C4
Ebbisham La KT20 ...97 A4
Ebbisham Rd Epsom KT18 ...76 B5
North Cheam KT4 ...58 C8
Ebenezer Wlk CR4 ...41 C8
Ebisham Cl RH4 ...136 A7
Ebor Cotts SW15 ...18 E5
Ebsworth St SE23 ...23 D8
Ecclesbourne Inf Sch CR7 ...42 C4
Ecclesbourne Jun Sch
CR7 ...42 C4
Ecclesbourne Rd CR7 ...42 C4
Eccleshill Beckenham BR2 ...44 F5
Dorking RH5 ...136 C3
Echelford Cty Mid Sch
TW15 ...14 B3
Echelforde Dr TW15 ...14 A4
Echo Barn La GU10 ...145 E3
Echo Pit Rd GU1, GU4 ...130 E6
Ecob Cl GU3 ...108 F5
Ecton Rd KT15 ...52 B6
Ector Rd SE6 ...24 E6
Eddeys Cl GU35 ...187 B6
Eddeys La GU35 ...187 B6
Eddington Hill RH11 ...201 B1
Eddington Rd RG12 ...26 E3
Eddisbury House 7 SE26 ...23 A5
Eddy Rd GU12 ...105 C1
Eddystone Wlk TW19 ...13 E8
Ede Cl TW4 ...4 F4
Ede Ct KT17 ...76 F7
Ede's Cotts KT21 ...95 D8
Eden Cl KT15 ...52 B1
Eden Grove Rd KT14 ...71 E6
Eden Park Ave BR3 ...44 A4
Eden Park Sch BR3 ...43 F4
Eden Rd Crawley RH11 ...200 F4
Croydon CR0 ...61 D6
Penge BR3 ...43 E8
West Norwood SE27 ...22 B4
Eden St KT1, KT2 ...37 E7
Eden Vale
Dormans Park RH19 ...185 E5
East Grinstead RH19 ...185 E5
Eden Way Beckenham BR3 ...44 A3
Warlingham CR6 ...81 E1
Eden Wlk 5 KT1 ...37 E7
Edencourt Rd SW16 ...21 B2
Edencroft GU5 ...151 F7
Edenfield Gdns KT4 ...57 F7
Edenham High Sch CR0 ...43 F2
Edenhurst PF SM2 ...59 B4
Edenside Rd KT23 ...93 F3
Edensor Gdns W4 ...7 E7
Edensor Rd W4 ...7 E7
Edenvale Cl CR4 ...21 A1
Edenvale Rd CR4 ...21 A1
Ederline Ave SW16 ...42 A2
Edgar Cl RH10 ...202 E5
Edgar Ct KT3 ...38 E6
Edgar Rd
South Croydon CR2 ...61 D2
Tatsfield TN16 ...103 D6
Twickenham TW4 ...15 F8
Edgarley Terr SW6 ...7 D5
Edgbarrow Rise GU47 ...45 A2
Edgbarrow Sch RG45 ...45 C3
Edgbarrowhill Star RG45 ...45 A3
Edgcumbe Park Dr RG45 ...45 A5
Edge Cl KT13 ...53 A3
Edge Hill SW19 ...19 D1
Edge Hill Ct SW19 ...19 D1
Edge Point Cl SE27 ...22 B3
Edgeborough Ct 6 GU1 ...131 A7
Edgeborough Sch GU10 ...146 C3
Edgecombe Cl KT2 ...18 C1
Edgecombe House SW19 ...19 E8
Edgecoombe CR2 ...62 D2
Edgecumbe Ct 2 CR0 ...43 A1
Edgedale Cl RG45 ...45 B4
Edgefield Cl
Cranleigh GU6 ...174 C4
Redhill RH1 ...140 A4
Edgehill Ct KT12 ...35 C1

Edgehill House 2 RH1 ...118 F1
Edgehill Rd Mitcham CR4 ...41 B8
Purley CR2, CR8 ...61 B1
Edgeley KT23 ...93 E3
Edgell Cl GU25 ...31 F6
Edgell Rd TW18 ...12 F3
Edgemoor Rd GU16 ...66 C3
Edgewood Cl RG45 ...45 A7
Edgewood Gn CR0 ...43 D1
Edgeworth Cl CR3 ...81 A1
Edgington Rd SW16 ...21 D2
Edinburgh Cl GU12 ...106 A5
Edinburgh Ct Catford SE6 ...24 F7
3 Kingston u T KT1 ...37 E6
West Barnes SM4 ...39 C6
Edinburgh Dr TW15, TW18 ...13 D2
Edinburgh Rd SM1 ...59 D8
Edinburgh Way RH19 ...205 F7
Edith Gdns KT5 ...38 B2
Edith Rd
Thornton Heath SE25 ...42 D4
Wimbledon SW19 ...20 B2
Edmonds Ct 4 RG12 ...27 C8
Edmund Rd CR4 ...40 E6
Edna Rd SW20 ...39 D7
Edrich Rd RH11 ...201 A1
Edridge House 9 SE27 ...22 C3
Edridge Rd CR0, CR9 ...61 C7
Edward Alleyn House
SE21 ...22 E8
Edward Ave
Camberley GU15 ...65 A5
Morden CR4, SM4 ...40 D4
Edward Cl TW12 ...16 C3
Edward Ct TW18 ...13 C2
Edward II Ave KT14 ...71 F5
Edward Pauling House
TW14 ...14 E6
Edward Pauling Prim Sch
TW13 ...14 E6
Edward Pinner Ct 5 KT6 ...56 E8
Edward Rd Biggin Hill TN16 ...83 E1
Coulsdon CR5 ...79 D4
Croydon CR0 ...42 E2
Farnham GU9 ...146 C2
Hampton TW12 ...16 C3
Hatton TW14 ...3 E2
Penge SE20 ...23 D2
Windlesham GU20 ...48 D4
Edward St 2 KT6 ...37 D2
Edward Way TW15 ...13 E6
Edwards Cl KT4 ...58 D8
Edwin Cl KT24 ...92 D2
Edwin Rd
Twickenham TW1, TW2 ...16 E7
West Horsley KT24 ...92 D2
Edwin Stray House TW13 ...16 A5
Edwina Ct SM1 ...59 B6
Eelmoor Plain Rd GU11 ...104 D5
Eelmoor Rd
Aldershot GU11 ...104 D5
Farnborough GU14 ...84 F2
Eelmoor Road Trad Est
GU14 ...85 A2
Effingham Cl SM2 ...59 B3
Effingham Common Rd
KT24 ...93 C2
Effingham Ct
Mitcham SW19 ...20 E1
Woking GU22 ...89 E8
Effingham Lodge 9 KT1 ...18 B2
Effingham House
Golf Club GU4 ...113 D7
Effingham Junction Sta
KT24 ...93 A4
Effingham La RH10 ...183 E4
Effingham Lodge 1 KT6 ...37 F5
Effingham Rd
Burstow RH10, RH6 ...183 D6
Domewood RH10, RH6 ...183 D6
Reigate RH2 ...139 B8
Thames Ditton KT6, KT7 ...37 C2
Thornton Heath CR0 ...41 F2
Effort St SW17 ...20 E3
Effra Ct SE19 ...22 E1
Effra Rd SW19 ...20 B2
Egbury House SW15 ...7 F1
Egerton Ct
6 Guildford GU1 ...108 E1
6 Richmond TW10 ...6 E2
Egerton House W4 ...7 B8
Egerton PF KT13 ...53 C4
Egerton Rd Guildford GU2 ...129 F8
New Malden KT3 ...38 F5
Sandhurst GU15 ...64 F7
Sandhurst GU15 ...65 A7
South Norwood SE25 ...42 E6
Twickenham TW2 ...16 E8
Weybridge KT13 ...53 C4
Eggar's Ct GU12 ...105 B1
Eggar's Hill GU11 ...126 A8
Egham By-Pass TW20 ...11 F3
Egham Cl Cheam SM3 ...58 E8
Putney SW19 ...19 E6
Egham Cres SM3 ...58 D8
Egham Ct KT6 ...37 D4
Egham Hill Egham TW20 ...11 F1
Englefield Green TW20 ...11 D2
Egham Hill Rdbt TW20 ...11 E2
Egham Mus TW20 ...12 A3
Egham Sta TW20 ...12 A3
Egleston Rd SM4 ...40 B3
Egley Dr GU22 ...89 D5
Egley Rd GU22 ...89 D6
Eglinton Rd GU10 ...168 B7
Eglise Rd CR6 ...81 E2
Egmont Ave KT6 ...37 F1

Egmont Park Rd KT20 ...97 A2
Egmont Rd New Malden KT3 ...38 F5
Surbiton KT6 ...38 A1
Sutton SM2 ...59 C3
Walton-on-T KT12 ...35 B2
Egmont Way KT20 ...97 E8
Egremont Rd SE27 ...22 B3
Eight Acres GU26 ...188 C7
Eighteenth Rd CR4 ...41 E5
Eileen Rd SE25 ...42 E4
Eisenhower House KT8 ...37 C8
Eland Pl CR9 ...61 B7
Eland Rd Aldershot GU12 ...105 D1
Croydon CR0, CR9 ...61 B7
Elberon Ave CR0 ...41 E3
Elborough Rd SE25 ...43 A4
Elborough St SW18 ...20 A7
Elbow Meadow SL3 ...1 F6
Elcho Rd GU24 ...87 D8
Elder Cl GU4 ...110 A4
Elder Gdns 8 SE27 ...22 C3
Elder Oak Cl SE20 ...43 B8
Elder Rd Bisley GU24 ...68 A4
West Norwood SE27 ...22 C3
Elder Way RH5 ...136 C3
Elderberry Gr 10 SE27 ...22 C3
Eldergrove GU14 ...85 E2
Eldersley Cl RH1 ...118 F3
Eldersley Gdns RH1 ...118 F3
Elderslie Cl BR3 ...44 A3
Elderslie Rd SE26 ...24 A1
Eldertree Pl CR4 ...41 C8
Eldertree Way CR4 ...41 C8
Elderwood SE27 ...22 C3
Eldon Ave Croydon CR0 ...62 C8
Heston TW5 ...5 A7
Eldon Cl KT13 ...53 C5
Eldon Dr GU10 ...146 D5
Eldon Pk SE25 ...43 B5
Eldon Rd CR3 ...100 D6
Eldrick Ct TW14 ...14 D7
Eldridge Cl TW14 ...15 A7
Eleanor Ave KT19 ...57 D1
Eleanor Ct GU1 ...130 D7
Eleanor Gr SW13, SW14 ...7 E4
Eleanor House 3 SW19 ...40 B8
Elfin Gr TW11 ...16 F3
Elfrida Cres SE6 ...24 A4
Elfrida Inf & Jun Sch SE6 ...24 A4
Elgar Ave Crowthorne RG45 ...45 B7
Thornton Heath SW16 ...41 E6
Tolworth KT5, KT6 ...38 B2
Elgar House Kenley CR8 ...80 C5
Twickenham TW2 ...5 D1
Elgar Way RH13 ...218 B4
Elgal Cl 1 BR6 ...
Elgar Way RH13 ...183 A4
Elgin Ave TW15 ...13 E3
Elgin Cl RH13 ...217 F3
Elgin Cres Caterham CR3 ...101 A5
Harlington TW6 ...3 E5
Elgin Ct 6 CR0 ...61 C6
Elgin Gdns GU1 ...110 A2
Elgin Rd Croydon CR0 ...61 F8
Sutton SM1 ...59 C7
Wallington SM6 ...60 C4
Weybridge KT13 ...53 B5
Elgin Way GU16 ...85 F8
Eliot Bank SE23, SE26 ...23 B6
Eliot Bank Prim Sch SE23 ...23 B6
Eliot Cl GU15 ...66 B7
Eliot Dr GU27 ...207 E6
Eliot House 10 TW10 ...7 A2
Elizabeth Ave
Bagshot GU19 ...47 F2
Staines TW18 ...13 D2
Elizabeth Cl Bracknell RG12 ...27 C5
Cheam SM1 ...58 F8
Farncombe GU7 ...150 E7
Elizabeth Cotts 5 TW9 ...7 A6
Elizabeth Cres RH19 ...185 F3
Elizabeth Ct Horley RH6 ...161 A3
Sunbury TW16 ...35 C6
Teddington TW11 ...16 E3
West Barnes SM4 ...39 E2
Whyteleafe CR3 ...80 F8
Elizabeth Gdns Ascot SL5 ...29 B4
Sunbury TW16 ...35 C6
Elizabeth Hart Ct KT13 ...52 F5
Elizabeth House 3 RH1 ...101 A3
Elizabeth Rd
Farncombe GU7 ...150 E7
Wokingham RG40 ...25 D6
Elizabeth Way
Crawley RH10 ...202 C5
Feltham TW13 ...15 C4
Elizabethan Cl TW19 ...13 D8
Elizabethan Way
Crawley RH10 ...202 C5
Stanwell TW19 ...13 D8
Elkins Gdns GU4 ...110 A4
Ellacombe House 1 SW2 ...22 A8
Elland Rd KT12 ...54 D6
Ellenborough Cl RG12 ...27 D8
Ellenbridge Way CR2 ...61 E2
Elleray Ct GU12 ...106 A5
Elleray Rd TW11 ...16 F2
Ellerdine Rd TW3 ...5 C2
Ellerker Gdns TW10 ...6 E1
Ellerman Ave TW2, TW4 ...15 F7
Ellerslie Ct 3 SM6 ...60 B4
Ellerton Rd Surbiton KT6 ...37 F1
Wandsworth SW17, SW18 ...20 D7
Wimbledon SW20 ...19 A1
Ellery Cl GU6 ...174 E1
Ellery Rd SE19 ...22 D1

Elles Ave GU1 .... 110 C1
Elles Cl GU14 .... 85 B3
Elles Rd GU14 .... 84 F2
Ellesfield Ave RG12 .... 26 E5
Ellesmere Ave BR3 .... 44 B7
Ellesmere Ct Chiswick W4 ...... 7 D8
   Penge SE20 .... 43 B7
   Weybridge KT12 .... 53 E4
Ellesmere Dr CR2 .... 81 B5
Ellesmere Pl KT12 .... 53 E3
Ellesmere Rd
   Twickenham TW1 .... 6 C1
   Weybridge KT13 .... 53 E3
Ellice Rd RH8 .... 122 F6
Ellies Mews TW15 .... 13 E6
Ellingham GU22 .... 89 E8
Ellingham Prim Sch KT9 ..... 56 D3
Ellingham Rd KT9 .... 56 D4
Ellington Rd Feltham TW13 ... 14 F4
   Hounslow TW3 .... 5 B5
Ellington Way KT18 .... 77 B2
Elliot Cl RH10 .... 202 C4
Elliot Park GU12 .... 105 E2
Elliot Rise SL5 .... 28 D7
Elliott Ct GU21 .... 70 A3
Elliott Gdns TW17 .... 34 A5
Elliott Rd CR7 .... 42 B5
Ellis Ave GU2 .... 129 F7
Ellis Cl CR5 .... 99 F7
Ellis Farm Cl GU22 .... 89 D5
Ellis Rd Coulsdon CR5 .... 99 F7
   Crowthorne RG45 .... 45 B6
   Mitcham CR4 .... 40 F3
Ellisfield Dr SW15 .... 19 A8
Ellison Rd Barnes SW13 .... 7 F5
   Streatham SW16 .... 21 E1
Ellison Way
   Tongham GU10 .... 126 F7
   Wokingham RG40 .... 25 B6
Ellman Rd RH11 .... 200 F4
Ellora Rd SW16 .... 21 D3
Ellson Cl RH10 .... 202 C4
Ellswood Ct GU16 .... 37 D2
Elm Bank Gdns SW13 .... 7 E5
Elm Bank Mansions SW13 .... 7 E5
Elm Bridge La GU22 .... 90 A8
Elm Cl Box Hill KT20 .... 116 C5
   Carshalton SM5 .... 40 E2
   Leatherhead KT22 .... 95 B5
   Send Marsh GU23 .... 91 A3
   South Croydon CR2 .... 61 E4
   Stanwell TW19 .... 13 D7
   Tolworth KT5 .... 38 C2
   Twickenham TW13, TW2 .... 16 A6
   Warlingham CR6 .... 81 D2
   West Barnes SW20 .... 39 C5
   Woking GU21 .... 69 D4
Elm Cotts RH5 .... 115 C8
Elm Court Sch SE27 .... 22 C6
Elm Cres Heath End GU9 ...... 125 D7
   Kingston u T KT2 .... 37 E8
Elm Ct Catford SE6 .... 24 B7
   █ Charlton TW16 .... 14 F1
   Knaphill GU21 .... 68 D2
   Mitcham CR4 .... 40 F7
   Sandhurst GU47 .... 45 E2
Elm Dr Chobham GU24 .... 49 F1
   East Grinstead RH19 .... 186 A1
   Leatherhead KT22 .... 95 B4
   Sunbury TW16 .... 35 C7
   Winkfield SL4 .... 9 B7
Elm Gdns Burgh Heath KT18 .... 97 C8
   Claygate KT10 .... 55 F4
   Mitcham CR4 .... 41 D5
Elm Gr Bisley GU24 .... 68 A3
   Caterham CR3 .... 100 E5
   Cranleigh GU6 .... 174 A3
   Epsom KT18 .... 76 C5
   Heath End GU9 .... 125 C7
   Horsham RH13 .... 217 E1
   Kingston u T KT2 .... 37 E8
   Sutton SM1 .... 59 B6
   Wimbledon SW19 .... 19 E1
Elm Grove Par SM6 .... 60 A7
Elm Grove Rd
   Cobham KT11 .... 73 D3
   Farnborough GU14 .... 85 B4
Elm Hill Bglws GU3 .... 106 A3
Elm House █ KT2 .... 17 F1
Elm La GU10 .... 126 F8
   Forest Hill SE6 .... 23 F6
   Ockham GU23 .... 92 A8
Elm Park Rd SE25 .... 42 F6
Elm Pk Streatham SW2 .... 21 F8
   Sunningdale GU20, SL5 ...... 29 E1
Elm Pl GU11 .... 126 C8
Elm Rd Beckenham BR3 .... 43 F7
   Carshalton CR4, SM6 .... 41 A1
   Chessington KT9 .... 56 E6
   Claygate KT10 .... 55 F4
   East Bedfont TW14 .... 14 E7
   Farncombe GU7 .... 150 F8
   Heath End GU9 .... 125 D7
   Kingston u T KT3 .... 37 F8
   Kingston u T KT3 .... 38 D6
   Leatherhead KT22 .... 95 B5
   Mortlake SW14 .... 7 C3
   Purley CR8 .... 80 B6
   Redhill RH1 .... 118 E1
   South Norwood CR2 .... 42 D5
   Stoneleigh KT17 .... 57 F4
   Warlingham CR6 .... 81 D2
   Woking GU21 .... 69 D1
   Woking, Horsell GU21 .... 69 F4
Elm Rd W SM4 .... 39 F2
Elm Tree Ave KT10 .... 36 E2
Elm Tree Cl
   Addlestone KT16 .... 51 E8
   Ashford TW15 .... 14 B3
Elm View GU12 .... 106 B3
Elm Way North Cheam KT4 ..... 58 C7
   West Ewell KT19 .... 57 D5
Elm Wlk SW20 .... 39 D5
Elm Wood Prim Sch SE27 ..... 22 D5
Elmbank Ave
   Englefield Green TW20 ...... 11 B2
   Guildford GU2 .... 130 A8
Elmbourne Rd SW17 .... 21 B5
Elmbridge Ave KT5 .... 38 C3
Elmbridge Cotts GU6 .... 174 B3
Elmbridge La GU22 .... 89 F8
Elmbridge Rd GU6 .... 173 F2
Elmbrook Cl TW16 .... 35 B8
Elmbrook Rd SM1 .... 58 F6
Elmcott Rd SE21, SE27 .... 22 B6
Elmcroft
   Little Bookham KT23 .... 94 A3
   █ Woking GU22 .... 69 E1
Elmcroft Cl Chessington KT9 . 56 E7
   Feltham TW14 .... 3 F1
   Frimley GU16 .... 65 F2
Elmcroft Dr Ashford TW15 .... 14 A3
   Chessington KT9 .... 56 E7
Elmdene KT5 .... 38 C1
Elmdene Cl BR3 .... 43 F4
Elmdon Rd Hatton TW6 .... 3 F4
   Hounslow TW5 .... 4 C5
Elmer Cotts KT22 .... 95 A4
Elmer Gdns TW7 .... 5 D4
Elmer Mews KT22 .... 95 A5
Elmer Rd SE6 .... 24 C8
Elmer's Dr TW11 .... 17 B2
Elmers End Rd
   Beckenham BR3 .... 43 C6
   Penge BR3, SE20 .... 43 C6
Elmers End Sta BR3 .... 43 D5
Elmers Rd
   Croydon CR0, SE25 .... 43 A2
   Ockley RH5 .... 177 C4
Elmerside Rd BR3 .... 43 E5
Elmfield KT23 .... 94 A4
Elmfield Ave Mitcham CR4 .... 41 A8
   Teddington TW11 .... 16 F3
Elmfield House GU4 .... 110 C3
Elmfield Mansions █
   SW17 .... 21 A6
Elmfield Rd SW17 .... 21 A6
Elmfield Way CR2 .... 61 F2
Elmgate Ave TW13 .... 15 C5
Elmgrove Cl GU21 .... 88 D8
Elmgrove Rd Croydon CR0 ..... 43 B2
   Weybridge KT13 .... 53 A6
Elmhurst Ave CR4 .... 21 B1
Elmhurst Ballet Sch GU15 .... 65 D5
Elmhurst Ct Croydon CR0 ..... 61 D5
   Guildford GU1 .... 130 F8
Elmhurst Dr RH4 .... 136 B5
Elmhurst Lodge SM2 .... 59 C3
Elmhurst Sch for Boys
   CR2 .... 61 D5
Elmore Rd CR5 .... 99 A6
Elmpark Gdns CR2 .... 62 C1
Elms Cotts CR4 .... 40 F7
Elm Ct SW19 .... 20 B1
Elms Rd Aldershot GU11 ..... 105 A2
   Wokingham RG40 .... 25 B5
Elms The Ash GU10 .... 126 F8
   Ashford TW15 .... 14 A3
   Claygate KT10 .... 55 F3
   Croydon CR0 .... 42 C1
   Mortlake SW13 .... 7 F4
Elmscott Rd BR1 .... 24 F3
Elmshorn KT17 .... 77 C3
Elmside Guildford GU2 ...... 130 A8
   Milford GU8 .... 149 F1
   New Addington CR0 .... 63 B4
Elmsleigh Ct SM1 .... 59 B7
Elmsleigh Ctr The TW18 ...... 12 F4
Elmsleigh House █ TW2 ...... 16 D6
Elmsleigh Rd
   Farnborough GU14 .... 84 F4
   Staines TW18 .... 12 F3
   Twickenham TW2 .... 16 D6
Elmslie Cl KT18 .... 76 C5
Elmstead Rd
   Hinchley Wood KT10 .... 205 E8
Elmstead Cl KT19 .... 57 E5
Elmstead Gdns KT4 .... 58 A7
Elmstead Rd KT14 .... 71 A5
Elmsway TW15 .... 14 A3
Elmsworth Ave TW3 .... 5 B5
Elmsworth Ave TW3 .... 93 F3
Elmtree Cl KT14 .... 71 E6
Elmtree Rd TW11 .... 16 E3
Elmwood Ave TW13 .... 15 B5
Elmwood Cl Ashstead KT21 .... 75 D2
   Hackbridge SM6 .... 60 B8
   Stoneleigh KT17 .... 58 A3
Elmwood Ct KT21 .... 75 D2
Elmwood Ct SM1 .... 58 D3
Elmwood Inf Sch CR0 .... 42 B3
Elmwood Jun Sch CR0 .... 42 B2
Elmwood Rd Chiswick W4 .... 7 C8
   Knaphill GU21 .... 88 D8
   Mitcham CR4 .... 40 F6
   Redhill RH1 .... 119 B5
   Thornton Heath CR0 .... 42 B2
Elmworth Gr SE21 .... 22 D6
Elphinstone Ct SW16 .... 21 E2
Elsdon Rd GU21 .... 69 A1
Elsenham St SW18, SW19 TW ... 19 F6
Elsenwood Cres GU15 .... 66 A6
Elsenwood Dr GU15 .... 66 A7
Elsinore Ave TW19 .... 13 E8
Elsinore Rd SE23 .... 23 E7
Elsinore Way TW9 .... 7 B4
Elsley Cl GU16 .... 85 F6
Elsrick Ave SM4 .... 40 A4
Elstan Way CR0 .... 43 E2
Elstead Ct SM4 .... 39 E1
Elstead Gn GU8 .... 148 D4
Elstead House █ SW2 .... 21 F8
Elstead Rd Milford GU8 ..... 149 C3
   Shackleford GU7, GU8 ...... 149 E6
   The Sands GU10 .... 127 A2
Elsted Cl RH11 .... 201 B8
Elston Pl GU12 .... 126 C8
Elston Rd GU11, GU12 .... 126 C8
Elsworth Hill BR1 .... 24 E1
Elsworth Cl TW14 .... 14 E7
Elsworthy KT7 .... 36 E3
Elthorne Ct TW13 .... 15 C7
Elton Rd Kingston u T KT2 ... 38 A8
   Purley CR8 .... 79 C7
Elveden Cl GU22 .... 71 B2
Elveden Ct KT22 .... 95 C6
Elveden Rd KT11 .... 73 B3
Elvington Gn BR2 .... 44 F4
Elvino Rd SE26 .... 23 E3
Elwell Cl TW20 .... 12 A2
Elwill Way BR3 .... 44 D5
Ely Cl Crawley RH10 .... 201 F2
   Frimley GU16 .... 86 A7
   Kingston u T SW20 .... 39 B7
Ely Ct KT1 .... 38 A6
Ely House █ RH1 .... 118 F1
Ely Rd Hatton TW6 .... 3 F5
   Hounslow TW4 .... 4 C4
   Thornton Heath CR0 .... 42 D4
Elystan Ct SM6 .... 60 C2
Embankment The
   Twickenham TW1 .... 17 A7
   Wraysbury TW19 .... 11 C7
Embassy Ct
   Kingston u T KT6 .... 37 D4
   █ Wallington SM6 .... 60 B4
Embassy Gdns BR3 .... 43 F8
Ember Cl KT15 .... 52 D5
Ember Ctr KT12 .... 54 E8
Ember Farm Ave KT8 .... 36 D3
Ember Farm Way KT8 .... 36 D4
Ember Gdns KT10, KT8 .... 36 D2
Ember House BR1 .... 24 D3
Ember La KT10, KT8 .... 36 D2
Embercourt Rd
   KT10, KT7, KT8 .... 36 E3
Emberwood RH11 .... 201 D8
Embleton Rd GU35 .... 187 B6
Embleton Wlk TW12 .... 15 F3
Emerton Rd KT22 .... 94 D3
Emery Down Cl RG12 .... 28 A6
Emley Rd KT15 .... 52 B6
Emlyn La KT22 .... 95 A5
Emlyn Rd Horley RH6 .... 160 E4
   Redhill RH1 .... 140 A8
Emmanuel Cl GU2 .... 109 A4
Emmanuel House SE21 .... 22 C5
Emmanuel Rd SW12 .... 21 D7
Emmbrook Rd RG41 .... 25 A8
Emmbrook Sch The RG41 ...... 25 A8
Emmeline Ct KT12 .... 35 C1
Emmetts Cl GU21 .... 69 D2
Empire Villas RH1 .... 161 B7
Empress Ave GU14 .... 85 B5
Emsworth Cl RH10 .... 202 C3
Emsworth Ct █ SW16 .... 21 F5
Emsworth St SW2 .... 21 F6
Ena Rd SW16 .... 41 E6
Endale Cl SM5 .... 59 F8
Endeavour Way
   Wallington CR0 .... 41 E2
   Wimbledon SW19 .... 20 B4
Enderby House SE19 .... 42 F8
Endlesham Ct █ SW12 .... 21 A8
Endlesham Rd SW12 .... 21 A8
Endsleigh Cl CR2 .... 62 C1
Endsleigh Gdns
   Kingston u T KT6 .... 37 C3
Endsleigh Mansions █
   SW16 .... 54 C5
Endsleigh Rd RH1 .... 119 C6
Endway KT5 .... 38 B2
Enfield Rd Ash GU12 .... 106 B5
   Crawley RH11 .... 201 C2
   Frimley GU16 .... 3 E5
Enfield Road Rdbt TW6 .... 3 E5
Engadine Cl CR0 .... 61 F7
Engadine St SW18 .... 20 A7
Engalee RH19 .... 185 C2
Englefield Cl
   Englefield Green TW20 ...... 11 C2
   Thornton Heath CR0 .... 42 C3
Englefield Green Cty Inf Sch
   TW20 .... 11 C3
Englefield Rd GU21 .... 68 D2
Engleheart Dr TW14 .... 3 F1
Engleheart Rd SE6 .... 24 C8
Englehurst TW20 .... 11 C2
Englemere Pk SL5 .... 28 D5
Englemere Pond Nature
   Trail SL5 .... 28 C6
Englesfield GU15 .... 66 D5
Englewood Rd SW12 .... 21 C8
Enid Wood House RG12 .... 27 C7
Enmore Ave SE25 .... 43 A4
Enmore Gdns SW14 .... 7 D2
Enmore Rd SE25 .... 43 A4
Ennerdale RG12 .... 27 A5
Ennerdale Cl Cheam SM1 ..... 58 F6
   Crawley RH11 .... 201 B4
Ennerdale Cl continued
   East Bedfont TW14 .... 14 F7
Ennerdale Gr GU9 .... 125 A6
Ennerdale Rd TW9 .... 6 F5
Ennismore Ave GU1 .... 109 F1
Ennismore Gdns KT7 .... 36 E3
Ennor Ct KT4 .... 58 C6
Ensham Sch SW17 .... 20 F3
Ensham Sec Sch (Annexe)
   SW17 .... 20 E4
Ensign Cl Purley CR8 .... 61 A1
   Stanwell TW19 .... 13 D7
Ensign Way TW19 .... 13 D7
Enterdent Cotts RH9 .... 121 D2
Enterdent Rd RH9 .... 121 D2
Enterprise Cl CR0 .... 42 A1
Enterprise Est GU1 .... 109 E5
Enterprise House KT12 ...... 35 B2
Enterprise Way TW11 .... 16 F3
Envis Way GU3 .... 108 C4
Eothen Cl CR3 .... 101 A3
Epping Way RG12 .... 27 E5
Epping Wlk RH10 .... 201 F4
Epsom Bsns Pk KT17 .... 76 E8
Epsom Cl GU15 .... 65 C8
Epsom Coll KT17 .... 77 B5
Epsom Cty Prim Sch KT19 .... 76 D8
Epsom Downs Cty Inf Sch
   KT18 .... 96 D8
Epsom Downs Metro Ctr
   KT20 .... 97 B7
Epsom Downs Sta KT17 .... 77 B4
Epsom & Ewell High Sch
   KT19 .... 57 C5
Epsom General Hospl KT18 ... 76 C4
Epsom La N KT18, KT20 ...... 97 B7
Epsom La S KT20 .... 97 C5
Epsom Pl GU6 .... 174 F3
Epsom Rd
   Ashstead KT18, KT21 .... 76 A2
   Cheam SM4 .... 39 F2
   Crawley RH10 .... 202 A4
   Croydon CR0 .... 61 A6
   East Clandon GU4 .... 111 D3
   Ewell KT17 .... 76 F8
   Guildford GU4 .... 110 F2
   Guildford GU1 .... 130 F8
   Guildford, Merrow
      GU1, GU4 .... 110 C1
   Leatherhead KT22 .... 95 C6
   Morden SM4 .... 39 F2
   West Clandon GU4 .... 111 D3
   West Horsley GU4, KT24 .... 112 C6
Epsom Sq TW6 .... 3 F5
Epsom Sta KT18 .... 76 D6
Epworth Rd TW7, TW8 .... 6 A7
Eresby Dr BR3 .... 44 A1
Erica Cl GU24 .... 67 E6
Erica Ct GU22 .... 69 D1
Erica Dr RG40 .... 25 D5
Erica Gdns CR0 .... 63 A6
Erica Way Copthorne RH10 . 183 A2
   Horsham RH12 .... 217 D5
Eridge Ct RH10 .... 202 C6
Erin Cl BR1 .... 24 E1
Erindale Ct BR3 .... 44 A8
Eriswell Cres KT12 .... 53 F4
Eriswell Rd KT12 .... 53 F5
Erkenwald Cl KT16 .... 32 E3
Ermine Cl TW4 .... 4 C5
Ermyn Cl KT21 .... 95 D6
Ermyn Way KT21, KT22 .... 95 D6
Erncroft Way TW1 .... 5 F1
Ernest Ave SE27 .... 22 B4
Ernest Bevin Sch SW17 ...... 20 E6
Ernest Cl Beckenham BR3 .... 44 A4
   Farnham GU10, GU9 .... 146 B6
Ernest Cotts KT17 .... 57 F3
Ernest Gdns W4 .... 7 B8
Ernest Rd BR3 .... 43 F4
Ernest Sq KT1 .... 38 B7
Ernle Rd SW20 .... 19 C1
Erridge Rd SW19 .... 40 A7
Errol Gdns KT3 .... 39 A5
Erskine Cl Carshalton SM1 .. 59 E7
   Crawley RH11 .... 200 E2
Erskine Rd SM1, SM5 .... 59 E6
Esam Way SE27, SW16 .... 22 A3
Escombe Dr GU2 .... 109 B6
Escot Rd TW16 .... 14 E1
Escott Pl KT16 .... 51 D4
Esher Ave Cheam SM3 .... 58 D7
   Walton-on-T KT12 .... 35 A2
Esher Church Sch KT10 ...... 55 C5
Esher Cl KT10 .... 55 B5
Esher Cres TW6 .... 3 F5
Esher Ct KT17 .... 36 E2
Esher Cres TW6 .... 3 F5
Esher Gdns SW19 .... 19 D6
Esher Gn KT10 .... 55 B6
Esher Green Dr KT10 .... 55 B7
Esher Mews CR4 .... 40 F6
Esher Park Ave KT10 .... 55 B6
Esher Place Ave KT10 .... 55 B6
Esher Rd Camberley GU15 .... 47 A1
   East Molesey KT8 .... 36 D4
   Hersham KT10, KT12 .... 54 E6
Esher Sta KT10 .... 55 D8
Eskdale Gdns CR8 .... 80 D5
Eskdale Way GU15 .... 66 D4
Eskmont Ridge SE19 .... 22 E1
Esme House SW15 .... 7 F3
Esparto St SW18 .... 20 B8
Essame Cl RG40 .... 25 D6
Essenden Rd CR2 .... 61 E3
Essendene Cl CR3 .... 100 E4
Essendene Lodge Sch
   CR3 .... 100 E4
Essendene Rd CR3 .... 100 E4
Essex Ave TW7 5
Essex Cl Addlestone KT15 ... 52
   Frimley GU16 86
   South Norwood SE19 39
Essex Ct Barnes SW13 22
Essex Dr GU6 173
Essex Gr SE19 22
Essex Tower █ SE20 43
Estcots Cty Prim Sch
   RH19 186
Estcots Dr RH19 186
Estcourt Rd CR0, SE25 43
Estella Ave KT3, SW20 39
Estoria Cl SW2 22
Estreham Rd SW16 21
Estridge Cl TW3 5
Eswyn Rd SW17 20
Ethel Rd TW15 13
Ethelbert Rd SW20 39
Ethelbert St SW12 21
Ethelworth St █ SW2 22
Etherley Hill RH5 177
Etherow St SE22 23
Etherstone Gn SW16 22
Etherstone Rd SW16 22
Eton Ave Heston TW5 5
   New Malden KT3 38
Eton Cl SW18 20
Eton Ct TW18 12
Eton Pl GU9 125
Eton Rd U83 3
Eton St TW10 6
Ettrick Ct GU14 105
Etwell Pl KT5 37
Eureka Rd KT1 38
Europa Park Rd GU1 109
Eustace Cr RH19 205
Eustace Cres RG40 25
Eustace Rd GU4 110
Euston Rd CR0 42
Evans Cl RH10 202
Evans Gr TW13 16
Evans Rd SE6 24
Eve Rd Isleworth TW7 6
   Sheerwater GU21 70
Evedon RG12 27
Evelina Rd SE20 43
Eveline Rd CR4 40
Evelyn Ave GU11 126
Evelyn Cl Twickenham TW2 ... 16
   Woking GU22 89
Evelyn Cotts
   Abinger Common RH5 155
   South Godstone RH9 142
Evelyn Cres TW16 34
Evelyn Ct CR0 42
Evelyn Gdns Richmond TW9 6
   Tyler's Green RH9 121
Evelyn Rd Richmond TW9 6
   Richmond, Ham TW10 17
   Wimbledon SW19 20
Evelyn Terr █ TW9 6
Evelyn Way
   Stoke D'Abernon KT11 73
   Sunbury TW16 34
   Wallington SM6 60
Evelyn Woods Rd GU11 105
Evendon's Cl RG41 25
Evendon's La RG41 25
Evening Hill BR3 24
Evenlode Way GU47 64
Everard La CR3 101
Everest Ct
   South Norwood SE19 22
   Woking GU21 68
Everest Rd Camberley GU15 .. 65
   Crowthorne RG45 45
   Stanwell TW19 13
Everglade TN16 83
Everglades █ BR3 44
Evergreen Ct TW19 13
Evergreen Rd GU16 66
Evergreen Way TW19 13
Evergreens The GU8 171
Everlands Cl █ GU22 69
Eversfield Rd █ RH2 118
Eversfield Rd
   Horsham RH13 217
   Reigate RH2 118
   Richmond TW9 6
Eversley Cres TW7 5
Eversley Pk SW19 19
Eversley Rd
   South Norwood SE19 37
Eversley Way Croydon CR0 ... 62
   Thorpe TW20 32
Everton Rd CR0 43
Evesham Cl Belmont SM2 59
   Reigate RH2 117
Evesham Gn SM4 40
Evesham Rd Morden SM4 40
   Reigate RH2 118
Evesham Rd N RH3 117
Evesham Wlk GU47 45
Evesham Wlk GU47 45
Ewart Rd SE23 23
Ewelands RH6 161
Ewell By-Pass KT17 58
Ewell Court Ave KT19 57
Ewell Court Ave KT19 57
Ewell Downs Rd KT17 77
Ewell East Sta KT17 77
Ewell Grove Cty Inf Sch
   KT17 57
Ewell House KT17 57

ll House Gr KT17 .... 57 F1
ll Park Gdns KT17 .... 58 A3
ll Rd Cheam SM2, SM3 .. 58 D4
mes Ditton KT6, KT7 .... 37 F2
worth KT6 .... 38 B1
lme Rd SE23 .... 23 C2 ... 57 E2
urst Ave CR2 .... 61 F2
n Cres SW7 .... 22 A8
urst C of E Fst Sch ... 175 E5
urst Cl Crawley RH11 .. 201 C6
urst Cl SM2 .... 58 C2
urst Ct CR4 .... 40 D6
urst Rd Cranleigh GU6 174 E3
awley RH11 .... 201 C7
urst GU5, GU6 .... 154 E3
ns Cl GU12 .... 106 A2
ood La
grane RH5 .... 157 F6
esort GU5 .... 158 C6
hot Hill Cross GU10 .. 124 D7
erly Rd SE6 .... 24 A6
alibur Cl RH11 .... 200 E5
oright Cl RH11 .... 38 A7
range Rd Ascot SL5 ... 29 C4
awley RH10 .... 201 E6
forde Ave TW16 .... 14 A4
orge The 6 CR8 .... 80 A8
ter Ct Kingston u T KT6 . 37 E4
sham SW19 .... 20 E1
ter House TW10 .... 16 A6
ter Rd Ash GU12 ...... 106 A3
ydon CR0 .... 42 C1
ham TW13 .... 15 F5
ter Way TW19 .... 13 E4
oright Cl CR0 .... 43 D1
urst Cl KT20 .... 97 F3
urst Spur KT20 .... 97 F3
nrise Rd SE27 .... 217 B4
ewood Rd SE27 .... 22 C3
erly Rd SE21 .... 22 F8
ton Dr KT3 .... 53 A1

yc House TW10 .... 7 A7
tory Cotts TW10 ...... 124 D2
tory La CR0, CR9 ..... 61 B8
ng's Rd Feltham TW14 . 4 A2
n
Green Ct 1 CR4 ...... 40 D6
r La CR5, RH2 .... 98 D1
r Oak Cl KT22 .... 74 D7
St TW3 .... 5 C4
r View RH12 .... 217 A3
racre Hounslow TW7 ... 5 D5
an 38 E6
racres Bagsh Heath KT20 . 97 C6
bham KT11 .... 73 E7
ew Addington CR0 .... 62 F2
rbairn Ct CR8 .... 80 A6
rbourne KT11 .... 73 D6
rbourne Cl GU21 ..... 69 A1
rbourne La CR3 ...... 100 C4
rbourne Way GU22 ... 109 A4
rbriar Ct 13 KT8 .... 76 E6
rchildes Ave CR0 .... 82 D7
rchildes Cotts CR0 .. 82 F6
rchildes Prim Sch CR9 . 82 E6
rchildes Rd CR6 ..... 82 E4
rcroft SE26 .... 23 C4
rcross 87 B6
rdene CR5 .... 98 F6
rdene Rd CR0 .... 79 D2
rfax RG42 .... 27 A8
rfax Ave Ewell KT17 . 58 B2
rfax Ct KT12 .... 118 F2
rfax Cl KT12 .... 35 B1
rfax Mews GU14 ..... 85 D2
rfax Rd
cksham SM3 .... 44 A7
ast Grinstead RH19 .. 205 F8
ngston u T KT1 ...... 37 E7
eatherhead KT22 ..... 95 B6
uth Croydon CR0, CR9 . 61 E7
rfield Rise GU2 ..... 108 E2
rfield Cl 37 F7
rfield The GU9 ...... 125 C2
rfield W KT1 .... 37 E7

Fairfield Way Coulsdon CR5 . 79 D5
West Ewell KT19 .... 57 E5
Fairfield Wlk KT22 .... 95 B6
Fairfields Rd TW3 ..... 5 C4
Fairford SE6 .... 24 A7
Fairford Ave CR0 ..... 43 D4
Fairford Ct Croydon CR0 43 E4
Pyrford KT14 .... 70 F5
Reigate RH2 .... 118 B2
Fairford Ct SM2 .... 59 B3
Fairgreens KT4 .... 57 F7
Fairgreen Rd CR7 ..... 42 B4
Fairhaven TW20 ...... 11 F3
Fairhaven Ave CR0 .... 43 D3
Fairhaven Ct Croydon CR2 . 61 C5
6 Egham TW20 .... 11 F3
Fairhaven Rd RH1 .... 119 A5
Fairholme
East Bedfont TW14 .... 14 E8
2 New Malden KT3 ... 38 E5
Fairholme Cres KT21 .. 75 C2
Fairholme Gdns GU9 .. 125 C1
Fairholme Jun & Inf Schs
  TW14 .... 14 D7
Fairholme Rd
Ashford TW15 .... 13 F3
Cheam SM1 .... 58 F4
Thornton Heath CR0 .. 42 A2
Fairings The KT12 .... 54 B6
Fairlands Ave
Fairlands GU3 .... 108 C5
Sutton SM1 .... 59 A8
Thornton Heath CR7 .. 42 A4
Fairlands Ct GU3 ..... 108 C5
Fairlands Rd GU3 .... 108 D5
Fairlawn
Little Bookham KT23 .. 93 F3
Weybridge KT13 ...... 53 E5
Fairlawn Cl Claygate KT10 . 55 F4
Feltham TW13 .... 15 C4
Fairlawn Cres RH19 .. 185 B2
Fairlawn Dr
East Grinstead RH19 .. 185 B2
Redhill RH1 .... 139 E7
Reigate RH1 .... 139 E7
Fairlawn Gr SM7 ..... 78 A5
Fairlawn Pk Forest Hill SE26 . 23 E3
Woking GU21 .... 69 E4
Fairlawn Prim Sch SE23 . 23 E8
Fairlawn Rd Merton SW19 . 19 F1
Sutton SM2, SM5 ..... 78 C8
Fairlawnes SM6 ...... 60 B5
Fairlawns Addlestone KT15 . 110 C1
Guildford GU1 .... 110 C1
Horley RH6 .... 161 B2
Sunbury TW16 .... 35 A6
Twickenham TW1 ..... 6 B1
Woodham KT15 .... 70 F8
Fairlawns Cl TW18 ... 13 B2
Sandhurst GU47 ...... 64 E7
Fairmead Rd Heston TW5 . 4 B6
Kingston u T KT3 .... 38 D6
Sandhurst GU47 ...... 64 E7
Fairmead Rd CR0 .... 42 A2
Fairmeads KT11 ...... 73 F6
Fairmile Ave Cobham KT11 . 73 E5
Streatham SW16 ..... 21 D3
Fairmile Hts KT11 ... 74 A6
Fairmile La KT11 .... 73 E5
Fairmile Park Copse KT11 . 73 F6
Fairmile Park Rd KT11 73 F6
Fairoak Cl CR8 ...... 80 A4
Fairoak La
Chessington KT9, KT22, KT10 . 75 B8
Oxshott KT10, KT22, KT9 . 74 E8
Fairoaks Airport GU24 . 50 E1
Fairoaks Ct KT15 .... 52 B6
Fairs Rd KT22 .... 95 A8
Fairstone Ct RH6 .... 161 B4
Fairview KT17 .... 77 C8
Fairview Ave GU22 ... 69 E1
Fairview Cl Forest Hill SE26 . 23 E3
Woking GU22 .... 69 E1
Fairview Cotts GU25 . 31 D3
Fairview Ct Ashford TW15 . 13 E3
Kingston u T KT2 .... 38 B8
Fairview Dr TW17 .... 33 F4
Fairview Gdns GU9 .. 125 D6
Fairview House 17 SW2 . 21 F8
Fairview Pl SW2 ..... 21 F8
Fairview Rd Ash GU12 . 106 B3
Carshalton SM1, SM5 . 59 E8
Ewell KT17 .... 76 F8
Headley Down SL5 .. 187 C5
Thornton Heath SW16 41 F8
Wokingham RG40 .... 25 C6
Fairview Terr GU35 . 187 A6
Fairwater Dr KT15 ... 52 D2
Fairwater House TW11 . 17 A4
Fairway Chertsey KT16 . 33 A1
Copthorne RH10 ..... 183 B2
Crawley RH11 .... 200 D4
Guildford GU1 ...... 110 D1
Sutton SM5 .... 78 D8
West Barnes SW20 .. 39 C6

Fairway Cl
Copthorne RH10 ..... 183 A2
Croydon BR3, CR0 .... 43 E4
Hounslow TW4 .... 4 C2
West Ewell KT19 .... 57 C6
Woking GU23 .... 89 B3
Fairway Cty Inf Sch RH10 . 183 B3
Fairway East TW4 .... 4 C2
Fairway Gdns BR3 ... 44 D3
Fairway Hts GU15 ... 66 B6
Fairway The
East Molesley KT8 ... 36 B6
Frimley GU15 .... 66 A3
Godalming GU7 ...... 150 D7
Heath End GU9 ...... 125 D7
Kingston u T KT3 .... 38 D8
Leatherhead KT22 ... 75 A1
Pirbright GU22, GU24 . 88 C3
Weybridge KT13 .... 72 A8
Fairways Ashford TW15 . 14 B3
Beacon Hill GU26 ... 188 B6
2 Hounslow TW7 .... 5 E6
Kenley CR8 .... 80 C2
Teddington TW11 ... 17 D1
Fairways The KT10 .. 139 D6
Fairwell La KT24 .... 112 B7
Fairwyn Rd SE26 .... 23 E4
Fakenham Way GU47 . 45 D2
Falaise TW20 .... 11 F3
Falaise Cl GU11 .... 105 B3
Falcon Cl Chiswick W4 . 7 C8
Crawley RH11 ...... 201 D8
Lightwater GU18 .... 66 F8
Falcon Ct Frimley GU16 . 65 D1
Sheerwater GU21 ... 70 C6
5 West Norwood SE21 . 22 D6
Falcon Dr TW19 .... 2 E1
Falcon Rd Guildford GU1 . 109 D1
Hampton TW12 ...... 15 F1
Falcon Way Feltham TW14 . 4 A2
Sunbury TW16 ...... 34 E7
Falcon Wood KT22 .. 94 F8
Falconhurst
4 Kingston u T KT6 . 37 E4
Oxshott KT22 .... 74 A4
Falconry Ct KT1 .... 37 E6
Falcons Cl TN16 .... 83 D2
Falconwood
East Horsley KT24 .. 92 F3
Englefield Green TW20 . 11 A2
Falconwood Rd CR0 . 63 A3
Falcourt Cl SM1 .... 59 B5
Falkland Ct GU14 ... 105 E8
Falkland Gr RH4 ... 136 A6
Falkland House SE6 . 24 C4
Falkland Park Ave SE25 . 42 E6
Falkland Rd RH4 .... 136 A6
Fallow Deer Cl RH13 . 218 B4
Fallowfield Way RH6 . 161 B4
Fallsbrook Rd SW16 . 21 C2
Falmer Cl RH11 .... 201 D4
Falmouth Cl GU15 .. 66 A4
Falmouth Rd KT12 .. 54 C1
Falstone GU21 ...... 69 B1
Famet Ave CR8 ..... 80 C6
Famet Cl CR8 ...... 80 C6
Famet Wlk CR8 .... 80 C5
Fanchford Rd RH2 .. 117 E1
Fanes Cl RG42 ..... 26 E8
Fanfare The GU22 .. 70 C4
Fanshawe Rd TW10 . 17 C4
Faraday Ave RH19 .. 205 F6
Faraday Ct Wallington SM6 . 60 C5
Faraday Ctr The RH10 . 181 F2
Faraday House
2 Balham SW12 .... 21 B8
5 Hampton TW12 .. 15 F1
Faraday Rd Crawley RH10 . 181 F2
East Molesley KT8 .. 36 A5
Farnborough GU14 .. 85 C6
Wimbledon SW19 ... 20 B2
Faraday Way CR0, CR9 . 41 F2
Farcrosse Cl GU47 .. 64 C8
Fareham House 6 SW15 . 19 A7
Fareham Rd TW14 ... 4 A1
Farewell Pl CR4 .... 40 E8
Farhalls Cres RH12 . 217 F6
Faringdon Cl GU47 . 45 E2
Faringdon Dr RG12 . 27 D4
Farington Acres KT13 . 53 D7
Faris Barn Dr KT15 . 70 F8
Faris La KT15 ...... 70 F8
Farleigh Ave BR2 .. 44 F8
Farleigh Court Rd CR6 . 82 B5
Farleigh Ct Croydon CR2 . 61 C5
2 Guildford GU1 ... 109 D1
Farleigh Cty Prim Sch
  CR6 .... 81 E2
Farleigh Dean Cres CR0 . 82 B8
Farleigh House 7 KT2 . 18 B2
Farleigh Rd
Warlingham CR6 .... 81 E2
Woodham KT15 .... 71 A8
Farley Copse RG42 . 26 E8
Farley Croft BR2 ... 44 E7
Farley Ct GU14 .... 85 D2
Farley Heath Rd GU5 . 153 C6
Farley House SE26 . 23 C5
Farley Nursery KT24 . 92 D1
Farley Pk RH8 ..... 122 D5
Farley Pl SE25 .... 43 A5
Farley Rd Lewisham SE6 . 24 C8
South Croydon CR2 . 62 B2

Farleycroft 11 CR0 . 43 A1
Farleys Cl KT24 ... 92 C1
Farlington Pl SW15 . 19 B8
Farlington Sch RH12 . 216 B6
Farlton Rd SW18 ... 20 B8
Farm Ave
Horsham RH12 ..... 217 B3
Streatham SW16 ... 21 E4
Warlingham CR6 ... 81 B2
Farm Bsns Ctr SL5 .. 29 C4
Farm Cl Ascot SL5 . 29 C4
Bracknell RG42 .... 26 F8
Byfleet KT14 ...... 71 F7
Chertsey KT16 .... 32 A4
Coney Hall BR4 ... 63 F7
Crawley RH10 .... 202 A7
Crowthorne RG45 . 45 C7
East Grinstead RH19 . 206 B8
East Horsley KT24 . 112 F7
Farnham GU9 ..... 126 B1
Fetcham KT22 .... 94 E3
Guildford GU1 ... 109 D4
Lower Halliford TW17 . 34 A2
Loxwood RH14 ... 213 A3
Sutton SM2 ...... 59 D3
Wallington SM6 .. 60 C1
Warnham RH12 ... 216 F7
Farm Dr Croydon CR0 . 62 F8
Purley CR8 .... 79 F8
Farm Fields CR2 .. 80 F8
Farm La Addlestone KT15 . 52 A3
Ashtead KT21, KT18 . 76 B2
Croydon CR0 ..... 62 F8
East Horsley KT24 . 112 F7
Purley CR8 .... 60 C1
Send GU23 .... 90 C3
Wallington CR8 ... 60 C1
Farm Rd Aldershot GU12 . 105 E3
Frimley GU16 .... 65 D1
Morden SM4 ..... 40 B4
Old Woking GU22 . 90 B7
Staines TW18 .... 13 B2
Sutton SM2 ..... 59 D3
Thames Ditton KT7 . 37 A2
Warlingham CR6 . 101 E8
Farm View
North Cheam KT4 . 58 C7
Farm Way
Aldershot GU11 ... 105 D1
Farm Wlk GU2 ... 127 C8
Farmdale Rd SM2, SM5 . 59 E3
Farmer's Rd TW18 . 12 E3
Farmfield Dr RH6 .. 181 B8
Farmfield Hospl RH6 . 160 B2
Farmfield Rd BR1 .. 24 E3
Farmhouse Cl GU22 . 70 D4
Farmhouse Rd SW16 . 21 C1
Farmington Ave SM1 . 59 D7
Farmleigh Cl RH11 . 201 C4
Farmleigh Gr KT12 . 53 F5
Farmstead Rd SE6 . 24 B4
Farmview KT11 ... 73 D3
Farnaby Rd BR1, BR2 . 44 E8
Farnan Rd SW16 .. 21 E3
Farnborough Ave CR2 . 62 E3
Farnborough Bsns Ctr
  GU14 .... 84 F2
Farnborough Coll of Tech
  GU14 .... 85 B6
Farnborough Cres
Coney Hall BR2 ... 44 F1
South Croydon CR2 . 62 E2
Farnborough Gate Ret Pk
  GU14 .... 85 A7
Farnborough Grange Cty
  Jun Sch GU14 .... 85 A7
Farnborough Grange Inf
  Sch GU14 .... 85 A8
Farnborough Hill Sch
  GU14 .... 85 C5
Farnborough House 1
  SW15 .... 19 A7
Farnborough Ind Est
  GU14 .... 85 D6
Farnborough North Sta
  GU14 .... 85 D6
Farnborough Rd
Aldershot GU11 ... 104 E3
Farnborough GU14 . 85 C5
Heath End GU11, GU9 . 125 D7
Farnborough (Sixth Form)
  Coll GU14 .... 85 B6
Farnborough St GU14 . 85 D6
Farnborough Sta GU14 . 85 B5
Farncombe C of E Inf Sch
  GU7 .... 150 E7
Farncombe Hill GU7 . 150 D6
Farncombe St GU7 . 150 E6
Farncombe Sta GU7 . 150 F7
Farnell Mews SW5 . 53 B7

Farnham Rd
Elstead GU10, GU8 .. 148 C4
Guildford, Guildford Park
  GU1, GU2, GU3 .... 130 B7
Guildford, Onslow Village
  GU2, GU3 .... 129 E6
Farnham Rd Hospl GU2 . 130 B7
Farnham Sta GU9 .. 125 C2
Farnham Trad Est GU9 . 125 B8
Farnhurst La GU6, GU8 . 193 F4
Farningham GU12 .. 27 E3
Farningham Cres CR3 . 101 A4
Farningham Ct SW16 . 21 D1
Farningham Rd CR3 . 101 A4
Farnley GU21 ...... 68 F2
Farnley Rd UR7, SE25 . 42 D5
Farnsworth House 5
  SW27 .... 22 B3
Farquhar Rd Dulwich SE19 . 22 F3
Farquharson Rd CR0 . 42 C1
Farrell Cl GU15 .... 65 C3
Farren Rd SE23 .... 23 E6
Farrer's Pl CR0 .... 62 C6
Farriers Cl GU1 ... 110 A1
Farriers Ct KT17 ... 76 E7
Farriers Ct Belmont SM2 . 58 E3
Wimbledon SW19 .. 19 E1
Farriers Rd KT17 .. 76 E8
Farriers The GU5 .. 152 B5
Farthingfield House GU3 . 125 C3
Farthingham La GU6 . 175 E6
Farthings GU21 ... 68 E3
Farthings The 1 KT2 . 38 A8
Farwig La BR1 .... 44 F8
Fassett Rd KT1 .... 37 E5
Fauconberg Ct W4 . 7 C8
Fauconberg Rd W4 . 7 C8
Faulkner Pl GU19 . 47 F4
Faulkner's Rd KT12 . 54 C5
Faversham Rd
Beckenham BR3 ... 43 F7
Forest Hill SE6 ... 23 F7
Morden SM4 ..... 40 B3
Sandhurst GU47 .. 45 D1
Fawcett Cl SW16 .. 22 A4
Fawcett Rd CR0, CR9 . 61 C7
Fawcus Cl KT10 ... 55 E4
Fawler Mead RG12 . 27 F5
Fawley Cl GU6 .... 174 F2
Fawns Manor Cl TW14 . 14 C2
Fawns Manor Rd TW14 . 14 D2
Fawsley Cl SL3 .... 1 F7
Fay Rd RH12 ...... 217 C5
Faygate Bsns Ctr RH12 . 199 F1
Faygate La
Blindley Heath RH9 . 142 A3
Faygate RH12 ..... 199 F4
Rusper RH12 ..... 199 F4
Faygate Rd SW2 .. 21 F6
Faygate Sta RH12 . 199 C1
Fearn Cl KT24 .... 112 E6
Fearnley Cres TW12 . 15 F2
Fayland Ave SW16 . 21 C3
Featherbed La CR0 . 63 A1
Feathers La TW19 .. 2 A1
Featherstone KT24 . 92 D1
Featherstone Ave SE23 . 23 C6
Fee Farm Rd KT10 . 55 F3
Felbridge Ave RH10 . 202 D7
Felbridge Cl
East Grinstead RH19 . 185 C3
Frimley GU16 .... 65 F1
Streatham SW16 .. 22 A4
Sutton SM2 ..... 59 B2
Felbridge Ct
East Grinstead RH19 . 185 A4
Harlington UB3 .. 3 D8
Felbridge Ctr The RH19 . 185 A3
Felbridge Cty Prim Sch
  RH19 .... 184 F4
Felbridge Rd RH19 . 184 D3
Felcot Rd RH19 ... 184 C4
Felcote House RH2 . 138 F7
Felcott Cl KT12 ... 54 C7
Felcott Rd KT12 .. 54 C7
Felcourt Cotts RH19 . 185 C8
Felcourt La RH19 . 164 C1
Felcourt Rd
Dormans Park RH19, RH7 . 185 C7
Felcourt RH19, RH7 . 185 C2
Felday Glade RH5 . 155 C2
Felday Houses RH5 . 155 C7
Felday Rd RH5 .... 133 F3
Felix Dr GU4 ..... 111 A4
Felix La TW17 .... 34 F3
Felix Rd KT12 .... 35 A3
Fell Rd CR0, CR9 . 61 D7
Felland Way RH2 . 139 D5
Fellbrook TW10 ... 17 B5
Fellcott Way RH12 . 216 F1
Fellow Gn GU24 .. 67 F6
Fellow Green Rd GU24 . 67 F6
Fellowes Cl GU14 . 85 D1
Fellowes Rd SM1, SM5 . 59 E8
Fellows Rd GU14 .. 85 B1
Felmingham Rd SE20 . 43 C7
Felnex Trad Est SM6 . 60 A8
Felsberg Rd SW2 . 21 E8
Felside Ct KT13 ... 53 A6
Felstead Rd KT19 . 76 D8
Feltham Arena TW14 . 15 A5
Feltham Ave KT8 .. 36 E5
Feltham Corporate Ctr
  TW13 .... 15 B5

Feltham Hill Jun & Inf Schs TW13 ... 14 F5
Feltham Hill Rd
　Ashford TW15 ... 14 C2
　Feltham TW13 ... 15 B4
Feltham Rd Ashford TW15 ... 14 C4
　Mitcham CR4 ... 41 A2
　Redhill RH1 ... 139 F4
Feltham Sch The TW13 ... 15 C6
Feltham Sta TW13 ... 15 B7
Feltham Wlk RH1 ... 139 F4
Felthambrook Ind Ctr TW13 ... 15 B5
Felthambrook Ind Est TW13 ... 15 B5
Felthambrook Way TW13 ... 15 B3
Feltonfleet SchTrust Ltd KT11 ... 72 E6
Felwater Ct RH19 ... 185 A3
Fenby Cl RH13 ... 218 C4
Fenchurch Rd RH10 ... 202 B4
Fencote RG12 ... 27 D3
Fendall Rd KT19 ... 57 C5
Fender House RH12 ... 217 B2
Fengates Rd RH1 ... 118 E1
Fenhurst Ct RH12 ... 216 F1
Fenn's Way GU21 ... 69 E4
Fennel Cl Croydon CR0 ... 43 D1
　Farnborough GU14 ... 84 B4
　Guildford GU1 ... 110 B4
Fennel Cres RH11 ... 201 B2
Fennells Mead KT17 ... 57 F2
Fenner House KT12 ... 54 A6
Fenning Ct CR4 ... 40 E5
Fenns La GU24 ... 67 E5
Fenns Yd GU9 ... 125 B2
Fennscombe Ct GU24 ... 67 F6
Fenstanton Prim Sch SW2 ... 22 A7
Fenton Ave TW18 ... 13 C3
Fenton Cl RH1 ... 119 A1
Fenton House TW5 ... 5 A8
Fenton Rd RH1 ... 119 A1
Fentum Rd GU2 ... 109 A3
Fenwick Cl GU21 ... 69 B1
Fenwick Pl CR5 ... 37 F4
Ferguson Cl BR2, BR3 ... 44 D6
Fermandy La RH10 ... 184 A1
Fermor Rd SE23 ... 23 E7
Fern Ave CR4 ... 41 D5
Fern Cl Crowthorne RG45 ... 45 A7
　Frimley GU16 ... 66 C3
　Warlingham CR6 ... 81 E1
Fern Cotts RH5 ... 133 E4
Fern Gr TW14 ... 15 B8
Fern Lodge **15** SW16 ... 22 A3
Fern Rd GU7 ... 150 F6
Fern Towers CR3 ... 101 A2
Fern Wlk TW15 ... 13 D5
Fernbank Ave KT12 ... 35 E2
Fernbank Cres SL5 ... 28 D8
Fernbank Pl SL5 ... 28 D7
Fernbank Rd
　Addlestone KT15 ... 52 A5
　North Ascot SL5 ... 28 D8
Ferndale Cl GU10 ... 146 B3
Ferndale GU23 ... 108 E3
Ferndale Ave
　Addlestone KT16 ... 51 E7
　Hounslow TW4 ... 4 E4
Ferndale Rd Ashford TW15 ... 13 E3
　Banstead SM7 ... 77 F3
　Croydon SE25 ... 43 B4
　Woking GU21 ... 69 E2
Ferndell GU27 ... 208 C2
Ferndene Rise KT12 ... 150 E7
Ferndown Crawley RH10 ... 182 D2
　Horley RH6 ... 161 A1
　Kingston u T KT6 ... 37 E4
Ferndown Cl
　Guildford GU1 ... 131 A8
　Sutton SM2 ... 59 D4
Ferndown Gdns
　Cobham KT11 ... 73 C6
　Farnborough GU14 ... 84 E4
Ferney The TW18 ... 12 E3
Ferney Ct KT14 ... 71 D8
Ferney Meade Way TW7 ... 6 A5
Ferney Rd KT14 ... 71 D7
Fernhill Golf & Ctry Club GU6 ... 174 F6
Fernham Rd CR7 ... 42 C6
Fernhill KT22 ... 74 D5
Fernhill Cl
　Crawley Down RH10 ... 184 B1
　Farnborough GU17 ... 64 F1
　Hale GU9 ... 125 B6
　Woking GU22 ... 89 D7
Fernhill Ct GU17 ... 67 D3
Fernhill Cty Prim Sch GU14 ... 64 F1
Fernhill Dr GU9 ... 125 B6
Fernhill Gdns KT2 ... 17 E3
Fernhill La
　Farnborough GU17 ... 64 F1
　Hale GU9 ... 125 B6
　Woking GU22 ... 89 C7
Fernhill Pk GU22 ... 89 D7
Fernhill Rd
　Blackwater GU14, GU17 ... 64 E2
　Farnborough, Hawley GU14, GU17 ... 182 D7
　Farnborough, West Heath GU14, GU17 ... 84 E6

Fernhill Sch GU14 ... 64 F1
Fernhill Wlk GU17 ... 64 F1
Fernhurst Cl RH11 ... 201 B8
Fernhurst Rd Ashford TW15 ... 14 C4
　Croydon CR0 ... 43 B1
Fernihurst GU15 ... 65 F4
Fernihough Cl KT13 ... 72 A8
Fernlands Cl KT16 ... 51 E7
Fernlea KT23 ... 94 B3
Fernlea Rd Balham SW12 ... 21 B7
　Mitcham CR4 ... 41 A8
Fernleigh Cl Croydon CR0 ... 61 A6
　Walton-on-T KT12 ... 54 B7
Fernleigh Rise GU16 ... 86 C7
Fernley House GU7 ... 150 E8
Ferns Cl CR2 ... 62 B1
Ferns Mead GU9 ... 125 B1
Ferns The GU9 ... 125 C7
Fernside Ave TW13 ... 15 B4
Fernside Rd SW12 ... 21 A8
Fernthorpe Rd SW16 ... 21 C2
Fernwood
　New Addington CR0, CR2 ... 62 E2
　Putney SW19 ... 19 F7
Fernwood Ave SW16 ... 21 D4
Feroners Cl RH10 ... 202 A4
Ferrard Cl SL5 ... 28 D8
Ferraro Cl TW5 ... 5 A8
Ferrers Ave SM6 ... 60 D6
Ferrers Rd SW16 ... 21 D3
Ferring Cl RH11 ... 201 B8
Ferrings SE21 ... 22 E5
Ferris Ave CR0 ... 62 F7
Ferroners Ct RH10 ... 202 A4
Ferry Ave TW18 ... 12 E1
Ferry La Barnes SW13 ... 7 F8
　Brentford TW8 ... 6 E8
　Chertsey KT16 ... 33 A3
　Guildford GU2, GU3 ... 130 C5
　Laleham TW18 ... 33 C6
　Lower Halliford TW17 ... 34 A1
　Richmond TW9 ... 6 F8
　Wraysbury TW19 ... 12 B5
Ferry Rd East Molesey KT8 ... 36 A6
　Richmond TW11 ... 17 B3
　Thames Ditton KT7 ... 37 B3
　Twickenham TW1 ... 17 B7
Ferry Sq **1** TW8 ... 6 E8
Ferry Wks TW17 ... 34 A1
Ferrymoor TW10 ... 17 B5
Fetcham Common La KT22 ... 94 B6
Fetcham Park Dr KT22 ... 94 E4
Fetcham Village Cty Inf Sch KT22 ... 94 D5
Fettes Rd GU6 ... 174 F3
Fiddicroft Ave SM7 ... 78 C5
Field Cl Chessington KT9 ... 56 C5
　Cranford TW4 ... 4 B6
　East Molesey KT8 ... 36 B4
　Guildford GU4 ... 110 D3
　Hamsey Green CR2 ... 81 B5
　Harlington UB7 ... 3 C7
Field Ct Oxted RH8 ... 122 E8
　Wimbledon SW19 ... 20 A5
Field End Coulsdon CR5 ... 79 D5
　Farnham GU9 ... 125 F4
　West End GU24 ... 67 F6
Field La Brentford TW8 ... 6 C7
　Farncombe GU7 ... 150 F7
　Frimley GU16 ... 65 E1
　Teddington TW11 ... 17 A3
Field Pk RG12 ... 27 D8
Field Pl KT3 ... 38 F3
Field Rd Farnborough GU14 ... 64 F1
　Feltham TW14 ... 4 B1
Field Stores App GU11 ... 105 C3
Field View Egham TW20 ... 12 C3
　Feltham TW13 ... 14 D5
Field Way Aldershot GU12 ... 105 E3
　New Addington CR0 ... 63 B4
　Send Marsh GU23 ... 90 F2
　Tongham GU10 ... 126 F7
Field Wlk RH6 ... 162 C4
Fieldcommon La KT12 ... 35 F1
Fielden Pl RG12 ... 27 D7
Fieldend Horsham RH12 ... 218 B5
　Teddington TW11 ... 16 F4
Fieldend Rd SW16 ... 41 C8
Fielders Gn GU1 ... 110 A1
Fieldhouse Rd SW12 ... 21 C7
Fieldhouse Villas SM7 ... 78 E4
Fieldhurst Cl KT15 ... 52 B5
Fielding Ave TW2 ... 16 C5
Fielding Gdns RG45 ... 45 B4
Fielding House W4 ... 7 E8
Fielding Rd GU47 ... 64 E6
Fieldings The Forest Hill SE23 ... 23 C7
　Horley RH6 ... 161 C4
　Woking GU21 ... 68 F3
Fieldsend Rd SM3 ... 58 E5
Fieldside Rd BR1 ... 24 D3
Fieldview Horley RH6 ... 161 B4
　Wandsworth SW17, SW18 ... 20 D7
Fieldway GU27 ... 208 C2
Fife Rd Kingston u T KT2 ... 37 E7
　Mortlake SW14 ... 7 C2
Fife Way KT23 ... 94 A2
Fifehead Cl TW15 ... 13 E2
Fifield La GU10 ... 146 C2
Fifield Path **13** SE23 ... 23 D5
Fifth Cross Rd TW2 ... 16 D6
Figge's Rd CR4 ... 21 A1
Filby Rd KT9 ... 56 F4

Filey Cl Biggin Hill TN16 ... 103 B8
　Crawley RH11 ... 200 F4
　Sutton SM2 ... 59 C3
Filmer Ct GU7 ... 150 E5
Filmer Gr GU7 ... 150 E5
Finborough Rd SW17 ... 20 F2
Finch Ave SE27 ... 22 D4
Finch Cl GU21 ... 68 C2
Finch Dr TW14 ... 15 D8
Finch Rd **8** GU1 ... 109 D1
Finch's Cross RH8 ... 144 A8
Finchampstead Rd RG41, RG40 ... 25 B3
Finchdean House SW15 ... 18 F8
Finches Rise GU1 ... 110 C3
Findhorn Cl GU47 ... 64 D7
Findings The GU14 ... 84 E8
Findlay Dr GU3 ... 108 F5
Findon Ct KT15 ... 51 F5
Findon Rd RH11 ... 201 B8
Findon Way RH12 ... 216 D3
Finlay Gdns KT15 ... 52 C6
Finlays Cl KT9 ... 57 A5
Finmere RG12 ... 27 C2
Finnart Cl KT13 ... 53 C6
Finney Dr GU20 ... 48 D4
Finney La TW7 ... 6 A6
Finsbury Cl RH11 ... 201 C2
Finstock Gn RG12 ... 27 F5
Finton House Sch SW17 ... 20 F6
Fintry Pl GU14 ... 84 E7
Fintry Wlk GU14 ... 84 E7
Finucane Ct TW9 ... 6 F4
Fiona Cl KT23 ... 94 A3
Fir Acre Rd GU12 ... 106 A6
Fir Cl KT12 ... 35 A2
Fir Dr GU17 ... 64 B3
Fir Gr KT3 ... 38 F3
Fir Grange Ave KT13 ... 53 B5
Fir Rd Cheam SM3 ... 39 F1
　Feltham TW13 ... 15 D3
Fir Tree Alley **4** GU11 ... 105 A2
Fir Tree Ave GU27 ... 207 D6
Fir Tree Cl Ascot SL5 ... 29 A2
　Banstead KT17 ... 77 C4
　Crawley RH11 ... 181 B1
　Esher KT10 ... 55 C5
　Leatherhead KT22 ... 95 C4
　Streatham SW16 ... 21 C3
　Worcester Park KT19 ... 57 F8
Fir Tree Gdns CR0 ... 63 A6
Fir Tree Gr SM5 ... 59 F3
Fir Tree Rd
　Banstead KT17, SM7 ... 77 D5
　Guildford GU1 ... 109 D4
　Hounslow TW4 ... 4 E3
　Leatherhead KT22 ... 95 C4
Fir Tree Wlk RH2 ... 118 D1
Fir Wlk KT17, SM3 ... 58 D4
Firbank Cotts RH6 ... 183 C7
Firbank Dr GU21 ... 89 B8
Firbank La CR0 ... 89 B8
Firbank Pl TW20 ... 11 B2
Firbank Way RH19 ... 185 D1
Fircroft Cl GU22 ... 69 F1
Fircroft Ct **9** GU22 ... 69 F1
Fircroft Prim Sch SW17 ... 20 F5
Fircroft Rd Chessington KT9 ... 56 F6
　Upper Tooting SW17 ... 20 F6
Firdene KT5 ... 38 C1
Fire Bell Alley KT6 ... 37 E3
Fire Station Cotts SE8 ... 79 F6
Fire Station Flats **3** KT17 ... 76 E6
Fire Station Rd GU11 ... 105 B3
Fireball Hill SL5 ... 29 D2
Firefly Cl SM6 ... 60 E3
Firfield Rd Addlestone KT15 ... 52 A6
　Farnham GU9 ... 146 A2
Firfields KT13 ... 53 B4
Firglen Dr GU22 ... 89 B8
Firgrove Ct
　7 Farnborough GU14 ... 85 B4
　Farnham GU9 ... 125 C1
Firgrove Par **5** GU14 ... 85 B4
Firgrove Rd GU14 ... 85 B4
Firhill Rd SE6 ... 24 A5
Firlands Bracknell RG12 ... 27 C4
　Horley RH6 ... 161 B4
　Weybridge KT13 ... 53 E4
Firlands Ave GU15 ... 65 C5
Firle Cl RH10 ... 201 E8
Firmston House **8** SW14 ... 7 D4
Firs Ave Bramley GU5 ... 152 A6
　Mortlake SW14 ... 7 C3
Firsby Ave CR0 ... 43 D1
Firsdene Cl KT16 ... 51 D4
Firs La East Molesey KT8 ... 36 A6
　Mortlake SW14 ... 7 C3
　Sutton SM2 ... 59 B3
Firs The Artington GU3 ... 130 B5
　Bisley GU24 ... 68 A3
　6 Bracknell RG12 ... 27 F5
　Caterham CR3 ... 100 D6
　Claygate KT10 ... 55 E4
　2 Forest Hill SE26 ... 23 B3
　Hindhead GU26 ... 188 F4
　Mortlake SW14 ... 7 C3
　Sutton SM7 ... 59 B3
　Walton-on-T KT12 ... 35 B3
　West Ewell KT19 ... 57 E2

First Ave continued
　Woodham KT15 ... 52 B2
First Cl KT8 ... 36 C6
First Cross Rd TW2 ... 16 E6
First Quarter Bsns Pk KT19 ... 76 E8
Firstway SW20 ... 39 C7
Firsway GU2 ... 109 A2
Firswood Ave KT19 ... 57 F5
Firtree Ave CR4 ... 41 A7
Firtree Ct BR2 ... 44 F6
Firwood Cl GU21 ... 88 E8
Firwood Ct GU15 ... 65 C5
Firwood Dr GU15 ... 65 C5
Firwood Rd GU25 ... 30 E3
Fisher Cl Crawley RH10 ... 201 E4
　Croydon CR0 ... 42 F1
　Hersham KT12 ... 54 B6
Fisher La Chiddingfold GU8 ... 210 B7
　Dunsfold GU8 ... 211 B7
Fisher Rowe Cl GU5 ... 152 A6
Fisherdene KT10 ... 56 A3
Fisherman Cl TW10 ... 17 C4
Fishermen's Cl GU11 ... 105 E5
Fishers Ct Horsham RH12 ... 217 C4
　4 Teddington TW11 ... 16 F3
Fishers Wood SL5 ... 30 C1
Fishponds Cl RG41 ... 25 A4
Fishponds Est RG41 ... 25 A4
Fishponds Rd
　Upper Tooting SW17 ... 20 F4
　Wokingham RG41 ... 25 A4
Fitchet Cl RH11 ... 181 B1
Fitch Ct CR4 ... 41 A7
Fitchet Cl RH11 ... 201 B8
Fitzalan House **5** SE19 ... 22 E1
Fitzalan Rd Claygate KT10 ... 55 E3
　Horsham RH12, RH13 ... 218 A4
Fitzgeorge Ave KT2, KT3 ... 38 D8
Fitzgerald Ave SW14 ... 7 E4
Fitzgerald Rd Mortlake SW14 ... 7 D4
　Thames Ditton KT7 ... 37 A3
Fitzherbert House **11** TW10 ... 6 F1
Fitzjames Ave CR0 ... 62 A8
Fitzjohn Cl GU4 ... 110 C4
Fitzrobert Pl TW20 ... 12 A2
Fitzroy Cres W4 ... 7 D7
Fitzwarren Gdns SW19 ... 22 E1
Fitzwilliam Ave TW9 ... 6 F5
Fitzwilliam House TW9 ... 6 D3
Fitzwilliam Hts SE23 ... 23 C6
Five Acres RH10 ... 201 E8
Five Oaks Rd Broadbridge Heath RH12, RH13 ... 216 B2
　Slinfold RH12, RH13 ... 216 B2
Five Ways Bsns Ctr TW13 ... 15 B5
Flag Cl CR0 ... 43 D1
Flambard Way GU7 ... 150 D4
Flamborough Cl TN16 ... 103 B8
Flamsteed Hts RH11 ... 201 B1
Flanchford House **6** Leigh RH2 ... 138 D5
　Reigate RH2 ... 138 D5
Flanchford Rd RH2 ... 138 D3
Flanders Cotts GU5 ... 152 D4
Flanders Cres SW17, SW19 ... 20 F2
Flanders Ct TW20 ... 12 C3
Flatford House SE6 ... 24 C4
Flats The GU17 ... 64 C4
Flaxley Rd SM4 ... 40 B4
Flaxmore Ct CR7 ... 42 D7
Fleece Rd KT6 ... 37 C1
Fleet Rd Aldershot GU11 ... 104 D6
　Farnborough GU11 ... 84 A4
Fleet Terr SE6 ... 24 C8
Fleetside KT8 ... 36 A3
Fleetway TW20 ... 32 C6
Fleetwood Cl
　Chessington KT9 ... 56 C3
　South Croydon CR0 ... 61 F7
　Tadworth KT20 ... 97 D7
Fleetwood Ct
　1 Stanwell TW19 ... 2 E1
　West Byfleet KT14 ... 71 A6
Fleetwood Rd KT3 ... 38 B6
Fleetwood Sq KT3 ... 38 B6
Fleming Cl GU14 ... 85 D6
Fleming Ct CR0 ... 60 F5
Fleming Mead CR4, SW19 ... 20 F1
Fleming Way
　Crawley RH10, RH11 ... 181 F2
　Isleworth TW7 ... 5 F3
Flemish Fields KT16 ... 33 A2
Fletcher Cl Crawley RH10 ... 201 E4
　Ottershaw KT15, KT16 ... 51 E4
Fletcher Gdns RG42 ... 26 D8
Fletcher Rd KT16 ... 51 C4
Fletcher Cl RH13 ... 217 E1
Fleur Gates **7** SW19 ... 19 D8
Flexford Gn RG12 ... 26 E3
Flexford Rd GU3 ... 107 C1
Flexlands Sch GU24 ... 68 D5
Flint Cl Banstead SM7 ... 78 B5
　Crawley RH10 ... 202 B3
　Great Bookham KT23 ... 94 C1
　Redhill RH1 ... 118 F2
Flint Hill RH4, RH5 ... 136 B5
Flint Hill Cl RH4 ... 136 B4
Flintgrove RG12 ... 27 D8

Flintlock Cl TW19 ... 2 A2
Flitwick Grange GU8 ... 149 ..
Flock Mill Pl SW18 ... 20 B7
Flood La **4** TW1 ... 17 A7
Flora Gdns CR0 ... 82 ..
Floral Ct KT21 ... 75 ..
Floral House KT16 ... 51 ..
Florence Ave Addlestone KT15 ... 52 ..
　New Malden SM4 ... ..
　Woodham KT15 ... 70 ..
Florence Cl KT12 ... 35 ..
Florence Cotts
　Kingston u T SW15 ... 18 ..
　Winkfield SL4 ... ..
Florence Ct SW19 ... 19 ..
Florence Gdns Chiswick W4 ... 7 ..
　Staines TW18 ... 13 ..
Florence Rd Feltham **5** KT2 ... ..
　2 Kingston u T KT2 ... ..
　Penge BR3 ... ..
　Sanderstead GU47 ... 64 ..
　South Croydon CR2 ... 61 ..
　Walton-on-T KT12 ... 35 ..
　Wimbledon SW19 ... 20 ..
Florence Terr SW15 ... 18 ..
Florence Way SW12 ... 20 ..
Florian Ave SM1 ... 59 ..
Florida Cl Beckenham BR2 ... 44 ..
　Staines TW18 ... 13 ..
Florida Rd Shalford GU4 ... 130 ..
　South Norwood CR7 ... 42 ..
Florys Ct **7** SW19 ... 19 ..
Flower Cres KT16 ... 51 ..
Flower La
　Tyler's Green RH9 ... 121 ..
　Woldingham RH9 ... 121 ..
Flower Wlk GU2 ... 130 ..
Flowersmead SW17 ... 2 ..
Floyd's La GU22 ... 7 ..
Foden Rd GU11 ... 104 ..
Foley Mews KT10 ... 55 ..
Foley Rd Biggin Hill TN16 ... 83 ..
　Claygate KT10 ... 55 ..
Folly House SW12 ... ..
Folly Hill Cty Inf Sch GU9 ... 125 ..
Folly La RH5 ... 157 ..
Folly La N GU9 ... 125 ..
Folly La S GU9 ... 125 ..
Follyfield Rd SM7 ... 78 ..
Fontaine Ct BR3 ... 43 ..
Fontaine Rd SW16 ... 2 ..
Fontenoy Rd SW12, SW17 ... 21 ..
Fonthill Cl SE20 ... 43 ..
Fonthill Ct SE23 ... 23 ..
Fontley Way SW15 ... 19 ..
Fontmell Cl TW15 ... 14 ..
Fontmell Pk TW15 ... 14 ..
Fontwell Cl GU11 ... 202 ..
Forbes Chase GU47 ... 64 ..
Forbes Cl RH10 ... 202 ..
Forbes Ct SE19 ... 22 ..
Forburys GU1 ... ..
Ford Cl Ashford TW15 ... 14 ..
　Littleton TW17 ... 34 ..
　Thornton Heath CR7 ... 42 ..
Ford La GU10, GU9 ... 146 ..
Ford Manor Cotts RH7 ... 165 ..
Ford Manor Rd RH7 ... 165 ..
Ford Rd Ashford TW15 ... 13 ..
　Bisley GU24 ... 6 ..
　Chertsey KT16 ... 3 ..
　Chobham GU24 ... 4 ..
　Old Woking GU22 ... 9 ..
Fordbridge Ct TW15 ... 1 ..
Fordbridge Rd
　Ashford TW15 ... 13 ..
　Sunbury TW16 ... 35 ..
　Upper Halliford TW16, TW17 ... 34 ..
Fordel Rd SE6 ... ..
Fordingbridge Cl
　Chertsey KT16 ... 33 ..
　Horsham RH12 ... 217 ..
Fordington House SE26 ... 2 ..
Fordmill Rd SE6 ... ..
Fordwater Rd KT15, KT16 ... 33 ..
Fordwater Trad Est KT16 ... 33 ..
Fordwells Dr RG12 ... 2 ..
Fordyce House **8** SW16 ... 2 ..
Foreman Pk GU12 ... 106 ..
Foreman Rd GU12 ... 126 ..
Forest Cl Bracknell SL5 ... 28 ..
　Crawley Down RH10 ... 204 ..
　East Horsley KT24 ... 9 ..
　Horsham RH12 ... 21 ..
　Woking GU22 ... 7 ..
Forest Cres KT21 ... 7 ..
Forest Croft SE23 ... 2 ..
Forest Dene Ct SE27 ... 59 ..
Forest Dr Charlton TW16 ... 1 ..
　Kingswood KT20 ... 9 ..
Forest End Rd GU47 ... 4 ..
Forest Glade GU10 ... 14 ..
Forest Hill Bsns Ctr SE23 ... 23 ..
Forest Hill Ind Est SE23 ... 2 ..
Forest Hill Rd SE22, SE23 ... 2 ..
Forest Hill Sta SE23 ... 2 ..
Forest Hills GU15 ... 6 ..
Forest La KT24 ... 9 ..
Forest Lodge
　2 East Grinstead RH19 ... 205 ..
Forest Oaks RH13 ... 218 ..

For–Gai 247

orest Rd Cheam SM3, SM4 40 A2
Crawley RH12 218 D5
Crowthorne RG45 45 C5
East Horsley KT24 92 F2
Feltham TW13 15 C6
North Ascot RG42 8 D2
Richmond TW9 7 A7
Windsor SL4 9 E7
Winkfield RG42, SL5 8 D2
Woking GU22 70 D4
orest Ridge BR3 44 A6
orest Row Bsns Pk
RH18 206 F4
orest Row C of E Inf Sch
RH18 206 F2
orest Sch The RH13 217 F1
orest Side KT4 38 F1
orest View RH10 202 A3
orest View Rd RH19 205 E6
orest Way KT21 76 A3
orest Wlk GU6 173 F2
orestdale GU26 188 E3
orestdale Ctr The CR0 62 F3
orestdale Prim Sch CR0 62 F2
orester Rd RH10 201 E4
oresters Cl Knaphill GU21 68 F1
Wallington SM6 60 D3
oresters Dr CR8, SM6 60 D2
oresters Prim Sch SM6 60 D4
oresters Sq RG12 27 E6
oresters Way RG45 45 E8
orestfield Crawley RH10 202 B3
Horsham RH13 218 A3
orestholme Cl SE23 23 C6
orge Ave CR5 100 B7
orge Cl
Broadbridge Heath RH12 216 D4
Farnham GU9 125 D3
orge Dr KT10 56 A3
orge End GU21 69 E2
orge La
Broadbridge Heath RH12 216 D4
Cheam SM2, SM3 58 E3
Crawley RH10 202 A7
Farnborough GU11 105 A6
Feltham TW13 15 E3
Sunbury TW16 35 A6
orge Lane Inf Sch TW13 15 E3
orge Lane Jun Sch TW13 15 E3
orge Rd Crawley RH10 202 A7
Headley GU35 166 A1
orge Steading SM7 78 B4
orge The Harlington UB3 3 D8
Warnham RH12 216 E7
orge Wood RH10 182 D3
orge Wood Ind Est
RH10 182 B2
orgefield TN16 83 D3
orman Ct TW1 16 F7
orrest Gdns SW16 41 F6
orrester Path SE26 23 C4
orster House SE6 24 D5
orster Park Sch SE6 24 E5
orster Rd Beckenham BR3 43 E6
Streatham SW2 21 E8
Thornton Heath CR0 42 C2
orsyte Cres SE19 42 E8
orsyte Ct KT2 38 B8
orsyth Path GU21 70 D6
orsyth Rd GU21 70 C5
orsythe Shades BR3 44 C8
orsythia Pl GU1 109 C3
ort La RH2 118 B5
ort Narrien GU15 64 F7
ort Rd Box Hill KT20 116 B4
Guildford GU1 130 E6
ortescue Ave TW2 16 C5
ortescue Rd
Mitcham SW19 20 D1
Weybridge KT13 52 F6
orth Cl GU14 84 D6
ortrose Cl GU47 64 D7
ortrose Gdns SW12, SW2 21 E7
ortune Dr GU6 174 E1
ortyfoot Rd KT22 95 C6
orum The KT8 36 B5
orval Cl CR4 40 F4
oss Ave CR0, CR9 61 A5
oss Rd SW17 20 D4
osse Way KT14 70 F6
osseway RG45 45 A5
ossewood Dr GU15 65 D7
osterdown RH9 121 B6
osters Gr GU20 48 B6
osters La GU21 68 C2
oulser Rd SW17 21 A5
oulsham Rd CR7 42 D6
oundation Units GU1 109 F5
ounders Gdns SE19 22 C1
oundry Cl RH13 217 E4
oundry Ct KT16 33 A2
oundry La
Haslemere GU27 208 A6
Horsham RH12, RH13 217 E3
Horton SL3 1 B4
oundry Mews KT16 33 A2
ountain Ct
New Malden KT3 38 C5
Penge SE26 23 C2
ountain Dr Dulwich SE19 22 F4
Wallington SM5 59 F2
ountain Rd Redhill RH1 139 E7
South Norwood CR7 42 C7
Upper Tooting SW17 20 D4
ountains Ave TW13 15 F5
ountains Cl
Crawley RH11 201 A4
Feltham TW13 15 F5

Fountains Garth RG12 27 A6
Four Acres Cobham KT11 73 E6
Guildford GU1, GU4 110 C3
Four Seasons Cres SM3 58 F8
Four Square Ct TW4 5 A1
Four Wents KT11 73 C5
Fourth Cross Rd TW2 16 D6
Fourth Dr CR5 79 D3
Fowler Cl RH10 202 C4
Fowler Rd
Farnborough GU14 84 F3
Mitcham CR4 41 A7
Fowler's Rd GU11 105 D6
Fowlers La RG42 27 B8
Fowlers Mead GU24 49 E2
Fowlerscroft GU3 129 B2
Fox Cl Crawley RH11 181 B1
Weybridge KT13 53 D5
Woking GU22 70 D4
Fox Covert Fetcham KT22 94 D3
Lightwater GU18 67 A8
Fox Covert Cl SL5 29 C4
Fox Dene GU7 150 C2
Fox Gr KT12 35 B2
Fox Heath GU14 84 C3
Fox Hill SE19 22 F1
Fox Hill Gdns SE19 22 F1
Fox Hill Prim Sch RG12 27 B4
Fox Hills La GU12 106 C3
Fox Hills Rd KT16 51 B5
Fox La KT23 93 F3
Fox La N KT16 32 F1
Fox La S KT16 32 F1
Fox Rd Bracknell RG12 27 C5
Farnham GU10 146 C7
Haslemere GU27 207 E6
Fox Way GU10 124 D8
Fox Yd GU9 125 B2
Foxacre CR3 100 E5
Foxborough Hill GU5 151 D6
Foxborough Hill Rd GU5 151 D6
Foxbourne Rd SW17 21 A6
Foxbridge La RH14 212 C1
Foxburrows Ave GU2 108 F2
Foxcombe CR0 63 B4
Foxcombe Rd 6 SW15 19 A7
Foxdown Cl GU15 65 C5
Foxearth Cl TN16 83 E1
Foxearth Rd CR2 62 C2
Foxearth Spur CR2 62 C2
Foxenden Rd GU1 109 E1
Foxes Dale BR2 44 D6
Foxes Path GU4 89 F1
Foxglove Ave
Beckenham BR3 24 B1
Horsham RH12 217 E6
Foxglove Cl TW19 13 D7
Foxglove Gdns
Guildford GU4 110 C3
Purley CR8 79 F8
Foxglove La KT9 57 A6
Foxglove Way CR4 41 B1
Foxglove Wlk RH11 201 B3
Foxgrove Dr GU21 70 A4
Foxgrove Rd BR3 24 C1
Foxhanger Gdns GU22 70 A3
Foxheath RG12 27 E4
Foxhill Cres GU15 66 B8
Foxhills GU21 69 C2
Foxhills Cl KT16 51 C4
Foxholes Rudgwick RH12 214 D8
Weybridge KT13 53 D5
Foxhurst Rd GU12 106 A4
Foxlake Rd KT14 71 F7
Foxleigh Chase RH12 217 F5
Foxley Cl Blackwater GU17 64 C5
Redhill RH1 140 A4
Foxley Ct SM2 59 C3
Foxley Gdns CR8 80 B6
Foxley Hall CR8 80 A6
Foxley Hill Rd CR8 80 A7
Foxley La CR8 60 E1
Foxley Rd Purley CR8 80 B5
Thornton Heath CR7 42 B5
Foxoak Hill KT12, KT13 53 E1
Foxon Cl CR3 100 E6
Foxon La CR3 100 E6
Foxon Lane Gdns CR3 100 E6
Foxtail House TW3 5 C6
Foxton KT1 38 A6
Foxwarren KT10 55 F2
Foxwood Cl TW13 15 B5
Frailey Cl GU22 70 B3
Frailey Hill GU22 70 B3
Framfield Cl RH11 201 A8
Framfield Rd CR4 21 A1
Frampton Cl SM2 59 A3
Frampton Rd TW4 4 E2
France Hill Dr GU15 65 C5
France Hill Sch GU15 65 C2
Frances Ct SE25 42 F7
Franche Court Rd SW17 20 C5
Francis Ave TW13 15 A5
Francis Barber Cl SW16 21 F4
Francis Chichester Cl SL5 29 B4
Francis Cl Littleton TW17 34 A5
West Ewell KT19 57 D6
Francis Cnr KT24 133 B8
Francis Ct Guildford GU2 109 B3
Kingston u T KT5 37 E5
Francis Edwards Way
RH11 200 E2
Francis Gr SW19 19 F2
Francis Rd Caterham CR3 100 D5
Hounslow TW4 4 D5
Thornton Heath CR0 42 B2
Wallington SM6 60 C4
Francis Way GU15 66 C4

Franciscan Prim Sch
SW17 21 A3
Franciscan Rd SW17 21 A4
Frangate KT24 112 E8
Frank Dixon Cl SE21 22 E7
Frank Dixon Way SE21 22 E7
Frank Towell Ct TW14 15 A7
Frankland House 4 SW12 21 B8
Franklands Dr KT15 51 F3
Franklin Cl Kingston u T KT1 38 A6
West Norwood SE27 22 B5
Franklin Cres CR4 41 C5
Franklin Ct 2 GU2 108 F1
Franklin House BR2 44 E7
Franklin Ind Est SE20 43 C8
Franklin Rd Crawley RH10 202 C5
Penge SE20 43 C8
Walton-on-T KT12 35 A1
Franklin Way CR0, CR9 41 E2
Franklyn Rd
Godalming GU7 150 B3
Walton-on-T KT12 35 B3
Franks Ave KT3 38 C5
Franks House TW7 6 B3
Franks Rd GU2 109 A3
Franksfield GU5 154 E7
Fransfield Gr SE26 23 B5
Frant Cl SE20 23 C1
Frant Rd CR0, CR7 42 B4
Franthorne Way SE6 24 B5
Fraser Gdns RH4 136 A8
Fraser Mead GU47 64 E6
Fraser Rd RG42 27 B8
Frederick Cl SM1 58 F5
Frederick Gdns SM1 58 F5
Frederick Pl RG41 25 A6
Frederick Rd SM1 58 F5
Frederick Sanger Rd
GU2 129 D8
Frederick St GU11 105 A2
Free Prae Rd KT16 33 A1
Freeborn Way RG12 27 E7
Freedown La SM2 78 C6
Freehold Ind Ctr TW4 4 C2
Freelands Ave CR2 62 D2
Freelands Rd KT11 73 B5
Freeman Cl TW17 34 E5
Freeman Dr KT8 35 F5
Freeman House 13 SW2 21 E8
Freeman Rd
Morden CR4, SM4 40 D4
Warnham RH12 216 F8
Freemantle Rd GU19 47 F4
Freemantles Sch
(Specl Sch) KT16 32 E2
Freemason's Rd CR0 42 E1
Freesia Dr GU24 68 A3
Freethorpe Cl SE19 42 E8
French Gdns
Blackwater GU17 64 D4
Cobham KT11 73 C5
French La GU8 169 E3
French St TW16 35 C7
Frenchaye KT15 52 C5
Frenches Ct 4 RH1 119 A3
Frenches Rd RH1 119 B4
Frenches The RH1 119 A3
Frenchlands Hatch KT24 112 E8
Frensham RG12 27 D3
Frensham C of E Fst Sch
GU10 167 D7
Frensham Ct CR4 40 D6
Frensham Ctry Pk GU10 167 E5
Frensham Dr
New Addington CR0 63 C3
Roehampton SW15 19 A6
Frensham Heights Rd
GU10 146 A2
Frensham Heights Sch
GU10 146 A2
Frensham House 7 KT6 37 E4
Frensham La GU35, GU10 166 F2
Frensham Rd
Crowthorne RG45 45 B7
Farnham GU10, GU9 146 D6
Purley CR8 80 B5
Frensham Vale GU10 146 C4
Frensham Way KT17 77 C3
Fresham House BR2 44 F6
Freshborough Ct 1 GU1 130 F8
Freshfield KT20 117 E8
Freshfield Bank RH18 206 E2
Freshfield Cl RH10 202 A5
Freshfields CR0 43 F1
Freshford St SW17, SW18 20 C5
Freshmount Gdns KT19 76 B8
Freshwater Cl SW17 21 A2
Freshwater Rd SW17 21 A2
Freshwood Cl BR3 44 B8
Freshwood Way SM6 60 C2
Frewin Rd SW18 20 D7
Friar Mews SE27 22 B5
Friar's Gate GU2 130 A7
Friars Ave SW15 18 F5
Friars Croft GU4 110 C4
Friars Ct Farnham GU9 125 D7
5 Wallington SM6 60 B6
Friars Keep RG12 27 B5
Friars La TW9 6 D2
Friars Orch KT22 94 D6
Friars Rd GU25 31 D5
Friars Rise GU22 70 A1
Friars Rookery RH10 201 F6
Friars Stile Pl 9 TW10 6 E1
Friars Stile Rd TW10 6 E1
Friars Way KT16 33 A3
Friars Wood CR0 62 E2
Friary Bridge GU1 130 C7

Friary Ct GU21 68 F1
Friary Ho 4 GU1 130 C8
Friary Pas GU1 130 C7
Friary Rd Ascot SL5 29 B3
Wraysbury TW19 11 C8
Friary St GU1 130 C7
Friary The 5 GU1 130 C8
Friary Way RH10 201 E5
Friday Rd CR4 20 F1
Friday St Faygate RH12 198 E6
Ockley RH5 177 E4
Rusper RH12 198 E6
Warnham RH12 216 E7
Friday Street Rd RH5 155 E8
Friend Ave GU12 105 D1
Friends Cl RH11 181 D1
Friends' Rd CR0, CR9 61 D7
Friends Rd CR8 80 B7
Friendship Way RG12 27 B6
Friern Rd SE22 23 A8
Frimley Ave SM6 60 F5
Frimley Bsns Pk GU16 85 B8
Frimley CE Jun Sch GU16 85 E7
Frimley Cl
New Addington CR0 63 C3
Putney SW19 19 E6
Frimley Cres CR0 63 C3
Frimley Gdns CR4 40 E6
Frimley Green Rd GU16 85 E7
Frimley Grove Gdns GU16 65 E1
Frimley Hall Dr GU15 65 F6
Frimley High St GU16 85 D8
Frimley House CR4 40 E6
Frimley Park Hospl GU16 65 D2
Frimley Rd Ash Vale GU12 106 A8
Camberley GU15 65 B3
Chessington KT9 56 E5
Frimley GU15, GU16 65 C1
Frinton Rd SW17 21 A2
Friston Wlk RH11 201 A7
Frith End Rd GU34, GU35 166 A6
Frith Hill Rd
Farncombe GU7 150 D6
Frimley GU16 66 B1
Frith Knowle KT12 54 B5
Frith Pk RH19 185 E3
Frith Rd CR0, CR9 61 C8
Fritham Cl KT3 38 E3
Friths Dr RH2 118 B4
Frithwald Rd KT16 32 F2
Frobisher RG12 27 C2
Frobisher Cl CR8 80 C2
Frobisher Cres TW19 13 E8
Frobisher Ct Belmont SM2 58 F3
Forest Hill SE23 23 B6
Frobisher Gdns
Guildford GU1 110 A2
Stanwell TW19 13 E8
Frodsham Way GU47 45 E2
Frog Grove La GU3 107 F4
Frog Hall RG40 25 F5
Frog Hall Dr RG40 25 E5
Frog La Bracknell RG12 27 A6
Woking GU4 89 E2
Froggetts La RH5 176 C1
Frogmore Cl SM3 58 E7
Frogmore Comm
Coll GU46 64 A5
Frogmore Ct GU17 64 C4
Frogmore Cty Infs Sch
GU17 64 B5
Frogmore Cty Jun Sch
GU17 64 B5
Frogmore Gdns SM3 58 E6
Frogmore Gr GU17 64 C4
Frogmore Park Dr GU17 64 D4
Frogmore Rd GU17 64 C5
Frome Cl GU14 84 D6
Fromondes Rd SM3 58 E5
Fromow Gdns GU20 48 D4
Froxfield Down 6 RG12 27 F4
Fruen Rd TW14 14 F8
Fry Cl RH11 201 B1
Fry's Cross GU8 193 A2
Fryern Wood CR3 100 C3
Frylands Ct CR0 82 C8
Fryston Ave Croydon CR0 62 A8
Wallington CR5 79 B5
Fuchsia Way GU24 67 E6
Fuel Farm Rd RH6 181 E8
Fulbourn 4 KT1 38 A7
Fulbourne Cl RH1 118 E3
Fulford Rd Caterham CR3 100 D6
West Ewell KT19 57 D3
Fulham Cl RH11 201 B2
Fullbrook Ave KT15 71 A8
Fullbrook Cty Sec Sch
KT15 71 A8
Fullbrooks Ave KT4 38 F1
Fuller's Wood CR0 63 A6
Fullers Ave KT6 56 F8
Fullers Farm Rd KT24 112 B1
Fullers Rd Binstead GU10 145 D3
Rowledge GU10 145 D3
Fullers Vale GU35 187 A5
Fullers Way N KT6 56 F7
Fullers Way S KT9 56 E7
Fullers Wood La RH1 119 C1
Fullerton Cl KT14 71 F5
Fullerton Dr KT14 71 E5
Fullerton Rd Byfleet KT14 71 F5
Croydon CR0 42 F2
Sutton SM5 59 E2
Fullerton Way KT14 71 E5
Fullmer Way KT15 51 F1
Fulmar Cl 1 RH11 200 D5
Fulmar Ct 5 SE21 22 D6
Fulmar Dr RH19 186 B3

Fulmer Cl TW12 15 E3
Fulstone Cl TW4 4 F3
Fulvens GU5 133 E1
Fulwell Golf Course TW12 16 C4
Fulwell Park Ave TW2 16 C6
Fulwell Rd TW11, TW12 16 D4
Fulwell Sta TW11 16 D4
Fulwood Gdns TW1 6 A1
Fulwood Wlk SW19 19 E7
Furlong Cl CR4 41 B1
Furlong Rd RH4 135 C6
Furlong Way RH6 181 F8
Furlough The GU22 70 A2
Furmage St SW18 20 B8
Furnace Dr RH10 201 F4
Furnace Farm Rd RH10 202 A4
Furnace Par RH10 202 A4
Furnace Pl RH10 202 A4
Furnace Rd RH19 184 C3
Furneaux Ave SE27 22 B3
Furness Rd SM4 40 B3
Furniss Ct GU6 173 F2
Furnival Cl GU25 31 D3
Furrows Pl CR3 100 F4
Furrows The KT12 54 C8
Furse Cl GU15 66 C4
Further Green Rd SE6 24 E7
Furtherfield GU6 174 E4
Furtherfield Cl CR0 42 A3
Furze Cl Ash Vale GU12 106 A7
Redhill RH1 118 F2
Furze Ct CR0 62 A8
Furze Field KT22 74 E6
Furze Gr KT20 97 F6
Furze Hill Kingswood KT20 97 F6
Purley CR8 79 F8
Furze Hill Cres RG45 45 C4
Furze Hill Rd GU35 187 C4
Furze La
East Grinstead RH19 185 B4
Farncombe GU7, GU3 150 F8
Purley CR8 79 F8
Furze Rd Addlestone KT15 51 F4
Rudgwick RH12 214 D8
South Norwood CR7 42 C6
Furze Vale Rd GU35 187 B4
Furzebank SL5 29 D5
Furzedown Cl TW20 11 E2
Furzedown Dr SW17 21 B3
Furzedown Prim Sch
SW17 21 A2
Furzedown Rd
Streatham SW17 21 B3
Sutton SM2 78 C8
Furzefield RH11 201 C7
Furzefield Chase RH19 185 E6
Furzefield Cres RH2 139 C7
Furzefield Cty Prim Sch
RH1 119 D7
Furzefield Rd
East Grinstead RH19 185 D4
Horsham RH12 218 B5
Reigate RH2 139 C7
Furzehill RH1 118 E2
Furzeland House 2 KT3 38 E2
Furzemoors RG12 27 B4
Furzen La
Ellen's Green RH12, RH5 196 B4
Wallis Wood RH12, RH5 196 B4
Furzewood TW16 35 A8
Fyfield Cl
Beckenham BR2, BR3 44 D5
Blackwater GU17 64 D5

G

Gable Ct Forest Hill SE26 23 B4
9 Redhill RH1 119 A2
Gable End GU14 85 B4
Gable Lodge BR4 44 C1
Gables Ave TW15 13 F3
Gables Cl Ash Vale GU12 106 A5
Farnborough GU14 85 A4
Old Woking GU22 89 F7
Gables Ct GU22 89 F7
Gables The Banstead SM7 77 F2
Copthorne RH10 183 B3
Elstead GU8 148 C3
Horsham RH12 217 D4
Oxshott KT22 74 C7
Weybridge KT13 53 C5
Gabriel Cl TW13 15 D4
Gabriel Dr GU15 66 B4
Gabriel Rd RH10 202 C2
Gabriel St SE23 23 E8
Gadbridge La GU6 175 E4
Gadbrook Rd RH3 137 D4
Gadesden Rd KT19 57 C4
Gaffney Cl GU11 105 D7
Gage Cl RH10 184 C1
Gage Ridge RH18 206 E2
Gainsborough RG12 27 C3
Gainsborough Cl
Beckenham BR3 24 A1
Camberley GU15 65 F7
Farnborough GU14 85 D2
Thames Ditton KT10 36 E1
Gainsborough Ct
Dulwich SE21 22 E6
Walton-on-T KT12 54 A6
Gainsborough Dr
North Ascot SL5 28 D7
Sanderstead CR2 81 A6
Gainsborough Gdns TW7 5 D2

Gainsborough Mews SE26 . . **23** B5
Gainsborough Rd
  Crawley RH10 . . . . **201** F3
  Epsom KT19 . . . . **57** C1
  New Malden KT3 . . . . **38** D2
  Richmond TW9 . . . . **6** F4
Gaist Ave CR3 . . . . **101** B5
Galahad Ho RH1 . . . . **119** A2
Galahad Rd RH11 . . . . **200** E6
Galba Ct ⓵ TW8 . . . . **6** D7
Gale Cl Hampton TW12 . . . . **15** E2
  Mitcham CR4 . . . . **40** D6
Gale Cres SM7 . . . . **78** A2
Gale Dr GU18 . . . . **48** A1
Gales Cl GU4 . . . . **110** D3
Gales Dr RH10 . . . . **201** F6
Gales Pl RH10 . . . . **201** F6
Galgate Cl ⓵ SW19 . . . . . **19** E7
Gallery Rd Dulwich SE21 . . **22** D7
  Pirbright GU24 . . . . **87** D8
Galleymead Rd SL3 . . . . . . **1** F6
Gallop The
  South Croydon CR2 . . . . **62** B3
  Sutton SM2 . . . . **59** D2
Gallwey Rd GU11 . . . . **105** C3
Galpin's Rd CR4, CR7 . . . . . **41** F5
Galsworthy Rd
  Chertsey KT16 . . . . **33** A2
  Kingston u T KT2 . . . . **38** B8
Galton Rd SL5 . . . . **29** F3
Galvani Way CR0, CR9 . . . . **41** F1
Galvins Cl GU2 . . . . **109** A4
Gambles La GU23 . . . . **91** C2
Gambole Rd SW17 . . . . **20** E4
Gander Green Cres TW12 . . **36** A8
Gander Green La
  KT4, SM1, SM3 . . . . **58** F7
Gangers Hill CR3, RH9 . . . **121** F7
Ganghill GU1 . . . . **110** A3
Gannet Ct ⓵ SE21 . . . . . . **22** D6
Ganymede Ct RH11 . . . . . **200** E3
Gap Rd SW19 . . . . **20** B3
Gapemouth Rd GU16, GU24 . **86** E5
Garbetts Way GU10 . . . . . **126** F6
Garbrand Wlk KT17 . . . . . . **57** F2
Garden Ave CR4 . . . . **21** B1
Garden Cl Addlestone KT15 . **52** D6
  ⓵ Richmond TW9 . . . . **6** F8
  South Croydon CR0 . . . . **61** F7
Garden Flats SW16 . . . . . . **21** E5
Garden House La RH19 . . . **205** F7
Garden La SW2 . . . . **21** F7
Garden Pl RH12 . . . . **217** C4
Garden Rd Mortlake TW9 . . . **7** A4
  Penge SE20 . . . . **43** C8
  Walton-on-T KT12 . . . . **35** B2
Garden The KT24 . . . . **113** D7
Garden Wlk Beckenham BR3 . **43** F8
  Crawley RH11 . . . . **201** C6
  Hooley CR5 . . . . **99** B4
  Horsham RH12 . . . . **217** C4
Garden Wood Rd RH19 . . . **205** C8
Gardener's Hill Rd GU10 . . **146** B4
Gardener's Wlk KT23 . . . . . **94** B1
Gardeners Cl RH12 . . . . . . **216** E8
Gardeners Gn RH13 . . . . . **217** D1
Gardeners Gn RH12 . . . . . **199** C6
Gardeners Rd CR0 . . . . . . **199** F8
Gardenfields KT20 . . . . **97** E8
Gardenia Ct ⓵ BR3 . . . . . . **24** A1
Gardenia Dr GU24 . . . . **67** F6
Gardens The
  Beckenham BR3 . . . . **44** D7
  Esher KT10 . . . . **55** A6
  Hatton TW14 . . . . **3** D1
  Pirbright GU24 . . . . **87** F5
  Tongham GU10 . . . . **126** F7
Gardner House TW13 . . . . . **15** F6
Gardner Ind Est SE26 . . . . **23** F3
Gardner Rd GU1 . . . . **204** A8
Gardner Pl TW14 . . . . **4** B1
Gardner Rd GU1 . . . . **109** D1
Garendon Gdns SM4 . . . . . . **40** B2
Garendon Rd SM4 . . . . **40** B2
Gareth Cl KT4 . . . . **58** D8
Gareth Ct SW16 . . . . **21** D5
Garfield Prim Sch SW19 . . . **20** C2
Garfield Rd
  Addlestone KT15 . . . . **52** C6
  Camberley GU15 . . . . **65** C5
  ⓶ Twickenham TW1 . . . . **17** A7
  Wimbledon SW19 . . . . **20** C2
Garibaldi Rd RH1 . . . . **139** F8
Garland Rd RH19 . . . . **185** D2
Garland Way CR3 . . . . **100** D5
Garlands Rd
  Leatherhead KT22 . . . . **95** C6
  Redhill RH1 . . . . **118** F1
Garlichill Rd KT17, KT18 . . . **77** B2
Garlies Rd SE23 . . . . **23** E5
Garnet House KT4 . . . . **38** D1
Garnet Rd CR7 . . . . **42** D5
Garrad's Rd SW16 . . . . **21** D4
Garrard Rd SM7 . . . . **78** A3
Garrat La SW17, SW18 . . . . **20** C5

Garratt Cl CR0 . . . . **60** E6
Garratt La SW17, SW18 . . . **20** C5
Garratt Park Sec Sch
  SW18 . . . . **20** C5
Garratt Terr SW17 . . . . **20** E4
Garratts La SM7 . . . . **78** A3
Garraway House SE21 . . . . **22** F5
Garratt Cl RH10 . . . . **202** C4
Garrick Cl Hersham KT12 . . **54** B6
  ⓵ Richmond TW9 . . . . **6** D2
  Staines TW18 . . . . **13** A1
Garrick Cres CR0 . . . . **61** E8
Garrick Gdns KT8 . . . . **36** A6
Garrick House Chiswick W4 . . **7** E8
  ⓶ Kingston u T KT1 . . . . **37** E5
  ⓷ Streatham SW16 . . . . **21** C3
Garrick Rd TW9 . . . . **7** A5
Garrick Way GU16 . . . . **85** E7
Garrick Wlk RH10 . . . . **201** E3
Garrick's Ait KT8 . . . . **36** C7
Garrison Cl TW4 . . . . **4** F2
Garrison La KT9 . . . . **56** E3
Garrones The RH10 . . . . . . **202** E7
Garside Cl TW12 . . . . **16** B2
Garson La TW19 . . . . **11** D8
Garson Rd KT10 . . . . **54** F4
Garson's La SL4 . . . . **8** A7
Garston Gdns CR8 . . . . **80** D4
Garston La CR8 . . . . **80** D4
Garstons The KT23 . . . . **94** A2
Garswood RG12 . . . . **27** D3
Garth Cl ⓵ Farnham GU9 . . **146** A7
  Kingston u T KT2 . . . . **18** C3
  West Barnes SM4 . . . . **39** D2
Garth Ct W4 . . . . **7** D8
Garth High Sch SM4 . . . . . . **40** D3
Garth Hill Sch RG12 . . . . . . **27** C8
Garth Rd Chiswick W4 . . . . . . **7** D8
  Kingston u T KT2 . . . . **17** F3
  West Barnes SM4 . . . . **39** D2
Garth The Ash GU10, GU12 . **105** F1
  Cobham KT11 . . . . **73** E6
  Farnborough GU14 . . . . **85** D4
  Hampton TW12 . . . . **16** B2
Garthorne Rd SE23 . . . . . . **23** D8
Garthside TW10 . . . . **17** E3
Gartmoor Gdns SW19 . . . . . **19** F7
Garton Cl RH11 . . . . **200** E5
Garvens SE19 . . . . **22** E3
Gascoigne Rd
  New Addington CR0 . . . . **63** C2
  Weybridge KT13 . . . . **53** B7
Gasden Copse GU8 . . . . . . **170** D5
Gasden Dr GU8 . . . . **170** D5
Gasden La GU8 . . . . **170** D6
Gaskyns Cl RH12 . . . . **214** D7
Gassiot Rd SW17 . . . . **20** F4
Gassiot Way SM1 . . . . **59** D7
Gasson Wood Rd RH11 . . . **200** E4
Gaston Bell Cl TW9 . . . . **6** F4
Gaston Bridge Rd
  Shepperton TW17 . . . . **34** D3
  Upper Halliford TW17 . . . . . . **34** E4
Gaston Rd CR4 . . . . **41** A6
Gaston Way TW17 . . . . **34** D4
Gatcombe Ct BR3 . . . . **24** A1
Gate Ct ⓵ KT1 . . . . **53** B7
Gate House ⓶ KT6 . . . . **37** E1
Gate St GU5 . . . . **173** F8
Gateford Dr RH12 . . . . **217** F6
Gatehouse Cl KT2 . . . . **18** C1
Gates Cl RH10 . . . . **202** C2
Gates Green Rd BR4 . . . . . . **63** F7
Gatesden Rd KT22 . . . . **94** C4
Gateside Rd SW17 . . . . **20** F5
Gatestone Ct ⓵ SE19 . . . . . **22** E2
Gatestone Rd SE19 . . . . . . **22** E2
Gateway The GU21 . . . . **70** C5
Gateways Guildford GU1 . . . **131** B8
  ⓵ Kingston u T KT6 . . . . **37** E4
Gateways Ct SM6 . . . . **60** B5
Gateways The TW9 . . . . **6** D3
Gatfield Gr TW13 . . . . **16** A6
Gatfield House TW13 . . . . . **16** A6
Gatley Ave KT19 . . . . **57** B5
Gatley Dr GU1 . . . . **109** F4
Gatton Bottom
  Gatton RH2, RH1 . . . . **118** E7
  Lower Kingswood
  RH1, RH2 . . . . **119** B8
  Merstham RH1, RH2 . . . . . . **119** B8
Gatton Cl ⓵ Reigate RH2 . . **118** C3
  Sutton SM2 . . . . **59** B2
Gatton Park Ct RH1 . . . . . . **118** F4
Gatton Park Rd RH1, RH2 . . **118** E4
Gatton Point RH1 . . . . **119** A5
Gatton Rd Reigate RH2 . . . . **118** C4
  Upper Tooting SW17 . . . . **20** E4
Gatwick Airport Sta RH6 . . **182** B7
Gatwick Airport-London
  RH6 . . . . **181** F7
Gatwick Gate RH11 . . . . . . **181** E5
Gatwick Metro Ctr RH6 . . . **161** B4
Gatwick Park Hospl RH6 . . **160** E2
Gatwick Rd
  Crawley RH10 . . . . **182** A3
  Wandsworth SW18 . . . . **19** F8
Gatwick Way RH6 . . . . **181** F8
Gatwick Zoo RH6 . . . . **180** D6
Gauntlet Cres CR3, CR8 . . . **100** D7
Gauntlett Rd SM1 . . . . **59** D5
Gavell Rd KT11 . . . . **73** A6
Gaveston Cl KT14 . . . . **71** F6
Gaveston Rd KT22 . . . . **95** A7
Gavina Cl SM4 . . . . **40** E4
Gayfere Rd KT17 . . . . **58** A5
Gayhouse La RH1 . . . . **162** E8
Gayler Cl RH1 . . . . **120** F2

Gaynesford Rd
  Forest Hill SE23 . . . . **23** D6
  Wallington SM5 . . . . **59** F3
Gaysland Cotts RH7 . . . . . **143** A2
Gayton Cl KT21 . . . . **75** E1
Gayton Ct New Malden KT3 . **38** F4
  Reigate RH2 . . . . **118** A2
Gaywood Cl SW2 . . . . **22** A7
Gaywood Rd KT21 . . . . **75** F1
Geary Cl RH6 . . . . **162** B1
Gedge Ct CR4 . . . . **40** E5
Geffers Ride SL5 . . . . **28** E7
Gemini Cl RH11 . . . . **200** E4
Gemma Ct BR3 . . . . **43** F7
Genesis Bsns Pk GU21 . . . . **70** C4
Genesis Cl TW19 . . . . **13** F7
Geneva Cl TW17 . . . . **34** E7
Geneva Rd Kingston u T KT1 . **37** E5
  Thornton Heath CR7 . . . . **42** C4
Genoa Rd SE20 . . . . **43** C8
Gentles La GU30, GU35 . . . **187** A3
Genyn Rd GU2 . . . . **130** B8
George Abbot Sch GU1 . . . **110** A3
George Denyer Cl GU27 . . . **208** C7
George Eliot Cl GU8 . . . . . **170** F5
George Horley Pl RH5 . . . . **158** B1
George House ⓵ SE26 . . . . **23** B3
George Pinion Ct RH12 . . . **217** B3
George Rd Farncombe GU7 . . **150** F7
  Guildford GU1 . . . . **109** D1
  Kingston u T KT2 . . . . **18** C1
  Milford GU8 . . . . **149** F2
  New Malden KT3 . . . . **38** F4
George Sq SW19 . . . . **40** A6
George St
  Croydon CR0, CR9 . . . . **61** D8
  Hounslow TW3, TW5 . . . . **4** F5
  Pirbright GU24 . . . . **87** A6
  Richmond TW10 . . . . **6** D2
  Staines TW18 . . . . **12** F4
George Wyver Cl SW19 . . . . **19** E8
George's Rd TW16 . . . . **103** D7
Georgeham Rd GU47 . . . . . . **45** D2
Georgelands GU23 . . . . **91** B6
Georges Terr CR3 . . . . **100** D5
Georgetown Ct ⓵ SE19 . . . **22** E3
Georgia Rd
  Kingston u T KT3 . . . . **38** C5
  South Norwood CR7 . . . . **42** B8
Georgian Cl
  Camberley GU15 . . . . **65** E7
  Crawley RH10 . . . . **202** D5
  Staines TW18 . . . . **13** B4
Georgian Ct CR0, CR9 . . . . . **42** D1
Georgina Ct ⓵ TW1 . . . . **6** C1
Gerald Ct RH13 . . . . **217** E2
Gerald's Gr SM7 . . . . **77** D5
Geraldine Rd W4 . . . . **7** A8
Gerard Ave TW4 . . . . **16** A8
Gerard Rd SW13 . . . . **7** F6
Germander Dr GU24 . . . . . . **68** A4
Gerrards Mead SM7 . . . . . . **77** F3
Ghent St SE6 . . . . **24** A6
Ghyll Cres RH13 . . . . **217** F1
Gibb's Acre GU24 . . . . **87** F3
Gibbet La GU15 . . . . **66** A7
Gibbet Rd GU1 . . . . **131** A8
Gibbon Rd KT2 . . . . **17** F1
Gibbons Cl Crawley RH10 . . **202** C3
  Sandhurst GU47 . . . . **64** C8
Gibbs Ave SE19 . . . . **22** D3
Gibbs Brook La
  Crowhurst RH7, RH8 . . . . . . **143** D7
  Oxted RH7, RH8 . . . . **143** D7
Gibbs Cl SE19 . . . . **22** D3
Gibbs House
  ⓵ Balham SW12 . . . . **21** B8
  Bromley BR1 . . . . **24** F1
Gibbs Sq SE19 . . . . **22** D3
Giblets La RH12 . . . . **217** F7
Giblets Way RH12 . . . . **217** E7
Gibraltar Cres KT19 . . . . . . **57** E1
Gibson Cl Chessington KT9 . . **56** C5
  Isleworth TW7 . . . . **5** E4
Gibson Ct KT10 . . . . **55** F7
Gibson House SM1 . . . . **59** A6
Gibson Pl TW19 . . . . **2** C1
Gibson Rd SM1 . . . . **59** B5
Gibson's Hill
  South Norwood SW16 . . . . . . **22** A1
  South Norwood SW16 . . . . . . **22** A2
Gidd Hill CR5 . . . . **79** A3
Giffard Dr GU14 . . . . **84** F5
Giffard Way GU2 . . . . **109** A4
Giffards Cl RH19 . . . . **186** B1
Giffards Meadow GU9 . . . . **125** E1
Giggs Hill Rd KT7 . . . . **37** A2
Giggshill Gdns KT7 . . . . **37** A1
Gilbert Cl ⓵ SW19 . . . . **40** C8
Gilbert Rd Frimley GU15 . . . . **65** C2
  Merton SW19 . . . . **20** C1
Gilbert Scott Jun & Inf Sch
  CR2 . . . . **62** E3
Gilbert St TW7 . . . . **5** C4
Gilbey Rd SW17 . . . . **20** E4
Gilders Rd KT9 . . . . **56** F4
Giles Coppice SE19 . . . . **22** F4
Giles Travers Cl TW20 . . . . . **32** C6
Gilesmead KT18 . . . . **76** E5
Gilham La GU8 . . . . **206** E2
Gilham's Ave SM7 . . . . **77** E7
Gill Ave GU2 . . . . **129** E8
Gillett Ct RH13 . . . . **218** B4
Gillett House RH13 . . . . . . **218** B4
Gillett Rd CR7 . . . . **42** D5
Gillette Cnr TW7 . . . . **6** A7
Gillham's La GU27 . . . . **207** A5

Gilliam Gr CR8 . . . . **61** A1
Gillian Ave GU11, GU12 . . . **126** D8
Gillian Cl GU12 . . . . **126** D8
Gillian Park Rd SM3 . . . . . . **39** F1
Gilliat Dr GU4 . . . . **110** D3
Gilligan Cl RH12 . . . . **217** B2
Gilmais KT23 . . . . **94** C2
Gilmore Cres TW15 . . . . **14** A2
Gilpin Ave SW14 . . . . **7** D3
Gilpin Cl CR4 . . . . **40** E7
Gilpin Cres TW2 . . . . **16** B8
Gilpin Way UB3 . . . . **3** D7
Gilsland Rd CR7 . . . . **42** D5
Gilton Rd SE6 . . . . **24** E5
Gimcrack Hill KT22 . . . . **95** B5
Gingers Cl GU6 . . . . **174** F2
Ginhams Rd RH11 . . . . **201** B6
Gipsy Hill SE19, SE27 . . . . . **22** E3
Gipsy Hill Sta SE19 . . . . **22** E3
Gipsy La Bracknell RG12 . . . . **27** D7
  Wokingham RG40 . . . . **25** C4
Gipsy Rd SE21, SE27 . . . . . . **22** E4
Gipsy Road Gdns SE27 . . . . **22** C4
Girdwood Rd SW18, SW19 . . **19** E8
Girling Way TW14 . . . . **4** A4
Girton Cl GU47 . . . . **45** E1
Girton Gdns CR0 . . . . **63** A7
Girton Rd SE26 . . . . **23** D3
Gittens Cl BR1 . . . . **24** F4
Giunevere Ho RH1 . . . . **119** A2
Glade Cl KT6 . . . . **56** D8
Glade Gdns CR0 . . . . **43** E2
Glade House SL5 . . . . **29** D4
Glade Spur KT20 . . . . **98** B6
Glade The Ascot SL5 . . . . . . **29** C4
  Belmont SM2 . . . . **58** E2
  Binstead GU10 . . . . **145** B1
  Coulsdon CR5, CR8 . . . . **100** A8
  Crawley RH10 . . . . **202** A4
  Croydon CR0 . . . . **43** D3
  Fetcham KT22 . . . . **94** B5
  Heath End GU9 . . . . **125** D7
  Horsham RH13 . . . . **218** A3
  Kingswood KT20 . . . . **98** B6
  Mytchett GU16 . . . . **86** A2
  Sheerwater KT14 . . . . **70** E6
  Staines TW18 . . . . **13** B2
  Stoneleigh KT17 . . . . **58** A4
  West Wickham BR4 . . . . **63** B7
Glades The RH19 . . . . **186** B1
Gladeside CR0 . . . . **43** D3
Gladeside Cl CR6 . . . . **101** B7
Gladiator St SE23 . . . . **23** E8
Gladiator Way
  GU11, GU14 . . . . **105** A8
Gladioli Cl ⓵ TW12 . . . . . . **16** A2
Gladsmuir Cl KT12 . . . . **54** C8
Gladstone Ave Feltham TW14 . **4** B1
  Twickenham TW2 . . . . **16** D7
Gladstone Ct ⓵ SW19 . . . . **20** A1
Gladstone Gdns TW3 . . . . . . **5** C6
Gladstone Mews ⓷ SE20 . . **23** C1
Gladstone Pl KT8 . . . . **36** E4
Gladstone Rd
  Ashstead KT21 . . . . **75** D1
  Croydon CR0 . . . . **42** D2
  Horsham RH12 . . . . **217** D3
  Kingston u T KT1 . . . . **38** A6
  Merton SW19 . . . . **20** A1
  Surbiton KT6 . . . . **56** E8
Glamis Cl GU16 . . . . **85** F7
Glamis Ho ⓶ RH2 . . . . **118** F1
Glamorgan Cl CR4, SW16 . . . **41** E6
Glamorgan Rd KT1 . . . . **17** C1
Glanfield Rd BR3 . . . . **43** F6
Glanty The TW20 . . . . **12** B4
Glanville Dr RH13 . . . . **218** B4
Glanville Wlk ⓵ RH11 . . . . **201** A3
Glasbrook Ave TW2 . . . . **15** F7
Glasford St SW17 . . . . **20** F2
Glassmill La BR2 . . . . **44** F7
Glassonby Wlk GU15 . . . . . . **66** C5
Glastonbury Prim Sch SM4 . **40** B2
Glastonbury Rd Cheam CR4 . **40** A2
  Morden SM4 . . . . **40** A2
Glayshers Hill GU35 . . . . . . **187** B6
Glazebrook Cl SE21 . . . . **22** D6
Glazebrook Rd TW11 . . . . . . **16** F1
Glaziers La GU3 . . . . **107** C2
Gleave Cl RH19 . . . . **186** A2
Glebe Ave CR4 . . . . **40** E7
Glebe Cl Crawley RH10 . . . . **201** E7
  Great Bookham KT23 . . . . **94** A1
  Lightwater GU18 . . . . **48** C1
  Sanderstead CR2 . . . . **80** F8
Glebe Cotts Feltham TW13 . . **15** A5
  West Clandon GU4 . . . . **111** B3
Glebe Ct Guildford GU1 . . . **109** F1
  Mitcham CR4 . . . . **40** F6
Glebe Gdns Byfleet KT14 . . . **71** E5
  New Malden KT3 . . . . **38** E3
Glebe House TW13 . . . . **16** A5
Glebe Hyrst CR2 . . . . **80** F7
Glebe La
  Abinger Common RH5 . . . . . **155** D8
  Rushmoor GU10 . . . . **168** C5
Glebe Path CR4 . . . . **40** F6
Glebe Rd Ashstead KT21 . . . . **75** D1
  Belmont SM2 . . . . **58** E3
  Cranleigh GU6 . . . . **174** E4
  Dorking RH4 . . . . **135** F7
  Egham TW20 . . . . **12** C2
  Farnborough GU14 . . . . **85** A6
  Merstham CR5 . . . . **99** B3
  Staines TW18 . . . . **13** B3
  Wallington SM5 . . . . **59** F4
  Warlingham CR6 . . . . **81** D2
Glebe Sch BR4 . . . . **63** D8

Glebe Side TW1 . . . . **5** F1
Glebe Sq CR4 . . . . **40** F6
Glebe The Blackwater GU17 . . **64** E4
  Copthorne RH10 . . . . **183** B3
  Ewhurst GU6 . . . . **175** E6
  Felbridge RH19 . . . . **166** E1
  Horley RH6 . . . . **160** F3
  Leigh RH2 . . . . **138** A2
  New Malden KT3 . . . . **38** F1
  Streatham SW16 . . . . **21** D4
Glebe Way Coney Hall BR4 . . **63** E7
  Feltham TW13 . . . . **16** A5
  Sanderstead CR2 . . . . **80** F8
  West Wickham BR4 . . . . **63** D8
Glebeland Ctr RH4 . . . . **136** A7
Glebeland Gdns TW17 . . . . . **34** C3
Glebeland Rd GU15 . . . . **64** F4
Glebelands Claygate KT10 . . . **55** F2
  Crawley Down RH10 . . . . . . **204** A7
  East Molesey KT8 . . . . **36** B5
  Loxwood RH14 . . . . **212** F4
Glebelands Rd
  East Bedfont TW14 . . . . **15** A8
  Wokingham RG40 . . . . **25** C7
Glebelands Sch GU6 . . . . . **174** D3
Glebewood RG12 . . . . **27** C4
Gledhow Wood KT20 . . . . . . **98** B5
Gleeson Mews KT15 . . . . . . **52** C6
Glen Albyn Rd SW19 . . . . . . **19** D6
Glen Ave TW15 . . . . **14** A4
Glen Cl Beacon Hill GU26 . . **188** C6
  Kingswood KT20 . . . . **97** E4
  Littleton TW17 . . . . **34** A5
Glen Court Flats GU26 . . . . **188** C6
Glen Ct Addlestone KT15 . . . . **51** F5
  Bromley BR1 . . . . **24** F1
  ⓾ Penge SE20 . . . . **43** B8
  Staines TW18 . . . . **12** F3
Glen Dale Mews BR3 . . . . . . **44** B8
Glen Gdns CR0, CR9 . . . . . . **61** A6
Glen Innes GU47 . . . . **45** E3
Glen Rd Beacon Hill GU26 . . **188** C6
  Chessington KT9 . . . . **56** F7
  Grayshott GU26 . . . . **188** D3
Glen Road End SM6 . . . . **60** B2
Glen The The Addlestone KT15 . **51** F5
  Ascot SL5 . . . . **29** D5
  Beckenham BR2 . . . . **44** F6
  Croydon CR0 . . . . **62** D7
  Redhill RH1 . . . . **139** F6
Glen Vue RH19 . . . . **185** E3
Glen Wlk TW7 . . . . **5** D2
Glena Mount SM1 . . . . **59** C6
Glenalmond House TW15 . . **13** E6
Glenavon Cl KT10 . . . . **56** A4
Glenavon Ct KT4 . . . . **58** B8
Glenbow Rd BR1 . . . . **24** E2
Glenbuck Ct ⓺ KT6 . . . . . . **37** E3
Glenbuck Rd KT6 . . . . **37** E3
Glenburnie Rd SW17 . . . . . . **20** F5
Glencairn Rd SW16 . . . . **21** E3
Glencoe Cl GU16 . . . . **86** A1
Glencoe Rd KT13 . . . . **53** A7
Glendale Cl
  Horsham RH12 . . . . **218** A6
  Woking GU21 . . . . **69** C3
Glendale Dr GU4 . . . . **110** C5
Glendale Rise CR8 . . . . **80** B4
Glendene Ave KT24 . . . . **92** E1
Glendon House ⓵ RH10 . . . **201** D5
Glendower Gdns ⓶ SW14 . . . **7** D4
Glendower Rd SW14 . . . . **7** D4
Glendyne Cl RH19 . . . . **206** A8
Glendyne Way RH19 . . . . . . **206** A8
Gleneagle Lodge BR3 . . . . . **44** A8
Gleneagle Mews SW16 . . . . **21** D3
Gleneagle Rd SW16 . . . . **21** D3
Gleneagles Cl TW19 . . . . **2** D1
Gleneagles Ct
  ⓵ Crawley RH10, RH11 . . . **201** D5
  ⓷ Teddington TW11 . . . . **17** A2
Gleneagles Dr GU14 . . . . . . **84** C2
Gleneagles House RG12 . . . **26** E3
Gleneldon Mews SW16 . . . . **21** E4
Gleneldon Rd SW16 . . . . **21** E4
Glenfarg Rd SE6 . . . . **24** D7
Glenfield Cl RH3 . . . . **137** B5
Glenfield Cotts RH6 . . . . . . **180** D1
Glenfield House RG12 . . . . . **27** C5
Glenfield Rd Ashford TW15 . . **14** C2
  Banstead SM7 . . . . **78** B3
  Brockham RH3 . . . . **137** B5
  Streatham SW12 . . . . **21** C1
Glenhaven Dr TW19 . . . . **2** A2
Glenhurst Cl GU17 . . . . **64** E4
Glenhurst Ct SE19 . . . . **22** F3
Glenhurst Rise SE19 . . . . . . **22** C1
Glenhurst Rd TW8 . . . . **6** C8
Glenister Park Rd SW16 . . . **21** D1
Glenlea GU26 . . . . **188** E1
Glenlea Hollow
  GU26, GU27 . . . . **207** E6
Glenlyn Rd KT8 . . . . **36** B5
Glenmill TW12 . . . . **15** F3
Glenmore Cl KT15 . . . . **52** B1
Glenmore House ⓺ TW10 . . . **6** E2
Glenmount Rd GU16 . . . . . . **86** A3
Glenn Ave CR8 . . . . **80** B8
Glennie Ct SE21 . . . . **23** A8
Glennie Rd SE27, SW16 . . . . **22** B5
Glentanner Way SW17 . . . . . **20** D5
Glenthorne Ave CR0, CR9 . . **43** C1
Glenthorne Cl SM3 . . . . **40** A1
Glenthorne Gdns SM3 . . . . . **40** A1
Glenthorne High Sch SM3 . . **40** A1

thorne Rd KT1 . . . . .37 F5
thorpe Rd SM4 . . . . .39 D4
view CI RH10 . . . . .201 F8
ville Gdns GU26 . . . . . . .188 F4
ville Mews SW18 . . . . . . .20 A8
ville Rd KT2 . . . . .18 B2
nwood Bracknell RG12 . . .27 D5
rking RH5 . . . . .136 C5
gina Water GU25 . . . . . . .31 C8
nwood Rd
rest Hill SE6 . . . . .24 A7
unslow TW3 . . . . .5 D4
nwood Way CR0 . . . . .43 D3
be Farm La GU17 . . . . . .64 B5
rney Mead GU9 . . . . . . .126 A6
ry Mead RH5 . . . . .136 C4
ssop Rd CR2 . . . . .61 D2
ster CI GU21 . . . . .105 F5
ster CI GU21 . . . . .69 F3
ster Rd New Malden KT3 . .38 E5
d Woking GU22 . . . . .90 A7
nwood Rd
st Grinstead RH19 . . . . .206 A8
amley GU10 . . . . .85 E6
ames Ditton KT7 . . . . . . .37 A1
ucester Cres TW18 . . . . .13 D2
ucester CI Richmond TW9 . .7 A2
Surbiton KT6 . . . . .37 D2
ucester Dr TW18, TW19 . .12 D5
ucester Gdns
gshot GU19 . . . . .47 E3
tton SM1 . . . . .59 B8
ucester Lodge 5 CR0 . . .61 F8
ucester Rd
ershot GU11 . . . . .126 C2
nley GU22 . . . . .47 E3
awley RH10 . . . . .201 E2
oydon CR0 . . . . .42 F1
tham TW13 . . . . .15 C7
ildford GU2 . . . . .108 F3
mpton TW12 . . . . .16 B1
unslow TW4 . . . . .4 E2
ngston u T KT1, KT2 . . . . .38 B7
well RH1 . . . . .118 F2
chmond TW9 . . . . .7 A7
ddington TW11 . . . . .16 E3
ornton Heath CR0 . . . . . .42 E2
ickenham TW2 . . . . .16 C7
ver's Rd
arlwood RH6 . . . . .180 D7
gate RH7 . . . . .139 B8
vers Field GU27 . . . . . . .207 F6
xinia Wlk TW12 . . . . .16 A2
n ADT Tech Sch KT17 . . .76 F8
CI Ewell KT17 . . . . .58 A2
uth Norwood SE19, SE25 . .22 A5
n CI SE27 . . . . .22 A5
n Rd KT4, SM3 . . . . .58 B3
ndale Grange SM2 . . . . . .59 B4
nle PI RH12 . . . . .217 C2
nswood Frimley GU15 . . .65 F3
nwood GU10 . . . . .146 A4
st CI SE23 . . . . .23 C6
n Rd CR4 . . . . .40 F2
t Wharf TW8 . . . . .6 D7
aters Rd SL5 . . . . .28 C7
tsfield Rd TN16 . . . . . . .103 C7
dalming Ave SM6 . . . . . .60 F5
dalming Bsns Ctr GU7 . .150 F4
dalming Coll GU7 . . . . . .150 D2
dalming Cty Mid Sch
GU7 . . . . .150 F5
dalming Rd
nsfold GU8 . . . . .193 A8
ascombe GU8 . . . . .172 E3
dalming Sta GU7 . . . . . .150 D4
ddard CI Crawley RH10 . .202 B3
leton TW17 . . . . .33 F6
ddard House SW19 . . . . .19 D6
ddard Rd BR3 . . . . .43 E5
ddards La GU15 . . . . . . .65 B3
dfrey Ave TW2 . . . . .16 D8
dfrey Way TW4 . . . . .4 E1
dley Rd Byfleet KT14 . . . .71 F6
andsworth SW18 . . . . . . .20 D7
dolphin CI Sm2 . . . . . . .77 F8
dolphin CI SW15 . . . . .7 F4
dolphin House 7 SW2 . .22 A7
dric Cres CR0 . . . . .63 D1
dson Rd CR0, CR9 . . . . . .61 A7
dstone Farm RH1 . . . . .121 C3
dstone Tech Sch RH9 . .121 B3
dstone Green Rd RH9 . .121 B4
dstone Hill
ler's Green RH9 . . . . . . .121 C5
oldingham CR3, RH9 . . .121 B7
dstone House 1 KT2 . . . .18 B2
dstone Mount 3 CR3 . . .80 B7
dstone Rd
etchingley RH1 . . . . .120 F2
aterham CR3 . . . . .101 A3
enley CR3, CR8 . . . . .80 D4
eigate RH7 . . . . .144 E4
dhill, RH9 . . . . .121 C5
urley GR8 . . . . .80 D4
dton SM1 . . . . .59 C6
tteleafe CR3 . . . . .80 F9
dstone Sta RH9 . . . . . . .142 E5
dwin CI KT19 . . . . .57 C4
ffs CI RH11 . . . . .201 C5
ffs La RH11 . . . . .201 B6
ffs Park Rd RH11 . . . . . .14 D2
ffs Rd TW15 . . . . .14 D2
gmore Farm CI KT16 . . . .32 F2
gmore La KT16 . . . . .33 A2

Goidel CI SM6 . . . . .60 D6
Gold Cup La SL5 . . . . .28 D8
Goldcliff CI SM4 . . . . .40 A2
Goldcrest CI RH6 . . . . . . .160 E4
Goldcrest Way
New Addington CR0 . . . . . .63 D3
Wallington CR8 . . . . .60 D1
Golden CI 9 TW20 . . . . . . .6 D2
Golden Mews SE20 . . . . . .43 C8
Golden Orb Wood RG42 . . .26 D8
Goldfinch CI
Crawley RH11 . . . . .201 D8
Horsham RH12 . . . . .217 C7
Goldfinch Gdns GU4 . . . .110 D2
Goldfinch Rd CR0, CR2 . . .62 E1
Goldfort WIk GU21 . . . . . .68 E3
Goldhill GU10 . . . . .146 C6
Golding CI Chessington KT9 .56 C4
Crawley RH10 . . . . .202 C5
Goldings The GU1 . . . . . . .68 F3
Goldney Rd GU15 . . . . . . .66 C2
Goldrings Rd KT22 . . . . . .74 C6
Goldsmith Way RG45 . . . .45 B4
Goldsmiths CI GU21 . . . . .69 C1
Goldstone Farm View
KT23 . . . . .114 A8
Goldsworth Orch 6 GU21 . .69 A1
Goldsworth Park CI GU21 . .69 A2
Goldsworth Park Trad Est
GU21 . . . . .69 B3
Goldsworth Prim Sch
GU21 . . . . .69 C1
Goldsworth Road Ind Est
GU21 . . . . .69 D2
Goldwell Rd CR7 . . . . .41 F5
Gole Rd GU24 . . . . .87 D6
Golf CI Pyrford GU22 . . . . .70 E5
Goliath Rd North SW16 . . .41 E8
Golf CI KT2 . . . . .18 D1
Golf Club Rd
Weybridge KT13 . . . . .53 C1
Woking GU23 . . . . .89 B7
Golf Dr GU15 . . . . .65 F4
Golf Links Ave GU26 . . . .188 B6
Golf Rd CR8 . . . . .80 D1
Golf Side Belmont SM2 . . .77 E8
Twickenham TW2 . . . . . . .16 C8
Golf Side CI KT3 . . . . .38 E7
Goliath CI SM6 . . . . .60 E3
Gomer Gdns TW11 . . . . . .17 A2
Gomer PI TW11 . . . . .17 A2
Gomshall Ave SM6 . . . . . .60 E5
Gomshall La GU5 . . . . . .133 B4
Gomshall Rd KT17, SM2 . .58 D3
Gomshall Sta GU5 . . . . . .133 E4
Gong Hill Dr GU10 . . . . . .146 D4
Gong Hill Fresham Rd
GU10 . . . . .146 D4
Gonston CI SW19 . . . . . . .19 E6
Gonville Prim Sch CR7 . . .42 A4
Gonville Rd CR7 . . . . .41 F4
Good Shepherd RC Prim
Sch Catford BR1 . . . . .24 F4
New Addington CR0 . . . . . .63 B3
Goodbehere House 7
SE27 . . . . .22 C5
Gooden Cres GU14 . . . . . .84 F3
Goodenough Rd SW19 . . .19 F1
Goodenough Way CR5 . . . .99 F7
Goodhart Way BR4 . . . . . .44 E3
Gooding CI KT3 . . . . .38 C4
Goodings Gn RG40 . . . . . .25 F6
Goodland House 1 KT3 . . .38 E2
Goodman Cres SW2 . . . . .21 D6
Goodson House SM4 . . . . .40 C2
Goodways Dr RG12 . . . . . .27 D7
Goodwin CI Crawley RH11 .200 F3
Mitcham CR4 . . . . .40 D6
Goodwin Gdns CR0, CR2 . .61 B4
Goodwin Rd CR0 . . . . .61 B5
Goodwins CI RH19 . . . . . .185 D3
Goodwood CI
Camberley GU15 . . . . . . .65 C4
Crawley RH10 . . . . .202 A3
Morden SM4 . . . . .40 A5
Goodwood House SE26 . . .23 B2
Goodwood Parr BR3 . . . . .43 E5
Goodwood PI GU14 . . . . . .85 E3
Goodwood Rd RH1 . . . . . .118 F3
Goodwyns PI RH4 . . . . . .136 B5
Goodwyns Rd RH4 . . . . . .136 C4
Goose Gn GU5 . . . . .133 C4
Goose Green CI RH12 . . . .217 D5
Goose La GU22 . . . . .89 B5
Goose Rye Rd Woking GU3 .89 A7
Worplesdon GU3 . . . . .88 E1
Goossens CI 1 SM1 . . . . .59 C5
Gordon Ave
Camberley GU15 . . . . .65 C4
Isleworth TW1 . . . . .6 A3
Mortlake SW14 . . . . .7 E3
South Croydon CR2, CR8 . .61 C1
Gordon CI Addlestone KT16 .51 E7
Staines TW18 . . . . .13 B2
Gordon Cres
Camberley GU15 . . . . .65 C4
Croydon CR0 . . . . .42 F1
Gordon Dr Addlestone KT16 .51 E7
Shepperton TW17 . . . . . . .34 D2
Gordon Rd
Aldershot GU11 . . . . .105 A1
Ashford TW15 . . . . .13 E6
Beckenham BR3 . . . . .43 F6

Gordon Rd continued
Camberley GU15 . . . . .65 C5
Caterham CR3 . . . . .100 D6
Chiswick W4 . . . . .7 B8
Claygate KT10 . . . . .55 E3
Crowthorne RG45 . . . . . . .45 D3
Farnborough GU14 . . . . .105 D8
Horsham RH12 . . . . .217 D4
Hounslow TW3 . . . . .5 C3
Kingston u T KT2 . . . . . . .37 F8
Redhill RH1 . . . . .119 A4
Richmond TW9 . . . . .7 A5
Shepperton TW17 . . . . . . .34 D3
Surbiton KT5 . . . . .37 F2
Wallington SM5 . . . . .59 F4
Gordon's Sch GU24 . . . . . .67 E7
Gordondale Rd SW18, SW19 .20 A6
Gordons Way RH8 . . . . . .122 D7
Gore Rd SW20 . . . . .39 C7
Goring Rd TW18 . . . . .12 D3
Goring's Mead RH13 . . . .217 D1
Goring CI RH11 . . . . .200 E5
Gorrick Sq RG41 . . . . .25 A4
Gorringe Park Ave
CR4, SW17 . . . . .21 A1
Gorringe Park Mid Sch
CR4 . . . . .41 A8
Gorringes Bridd RH12 . . .217 D6
Gorse Bank GU10 . . . . . . .67 A8
Gorse CI Burgh Heath KT20 .97 B7
Copthorne RH10 . . . . . . .183 B2
Crawley RH11 . . . . .201 B1
Wrecclesham GU10 . . . . .146 B6
Gorse Cotts GU27 . . . . . .207 C8
Gorse Ct GU4 . . . . .110 C3
Gorse Dr RH6 . . . . .162 B3
Gorse End RH12 . . . . . . .217 D5
Gorse Hill La GU25 . . . . . .31 D5
Gorse Hill Rd GU25 . . . . . .31 D5
Gorse La Chobham GU24 . .49 E3
Wrecclesham GU10 . . . . .146 B6
Gorse Rd RG42 . . . . .8 B1
Gorse Rd Croydon CR0 . . .63 A7
Frimley GU16 . . . . .65 E2
Gorselands CI 125 C7
Gorselands CI Ash GU12 . .106 A5
Headley Down GU35 . . . .187 C4
West Byfleet KT14 . . . . . .71 C8
Gorsewood Rd GU21 . . . . .88 E7
Gort CI GU11 . . . . .105 E7
Gosberton Rd SW12 . . . . .21 A7
Gosbury Hill KT9 . . . . .56 E6
Gosden CI Crawley RH10 .202 A5
Shalford GU5 . . . . .151 F8
Gosden Comm GU5 . . . . .151 E8
Gosden Cotts GU5 . . . . . .152 A8
Gosden Hill Rd GU4 . . . .110 C5
Gosden House Sch GU5 . .151 E8
Gosden Rd GU24 . . . . .67 F6
Gosfield Rd KT19 . . . . .76 D7
Gosnell CI GU16 . . . . .66 E3
Gosport House 3 SW15 . . .19 A7
Gossops Dr RH11 . . . . .1 D3
Gossops Green Cty Fst
Sch RH11 . . . . .201 A5
Gossops Green Cty Mid
Sch RH11 . . . . .201 A5
Gossops Green La RH11 . .201 A5
Gossops Parr RH11 . . . . .200 F5
Gostling Rd TW2 . . . . .16 A7
Goston Gdns CR7 . . . . . . .42 A6
Gostrode La GU8 . . . . . . .210 A6
Gothic CI Harlington UB3 . . .3 A3
Sandhurst GU47 . . . . .45 E1
Gothic Rd TW2 . . . . .16 D6
Goudhurst CI RH10 . . . . .202 E6
Goudhurst House 10 SE20 .23 C1
Goudhurst Keep RH10 . . .202 E6
Goudhurst Rd BR1 . . . . . .24 F3
Gough House 4 KT1 . . . . .37 E7
Gough's La RG12 . . . . .27 D8
Gough's Meadow GU47 . . .64 B7
Gould CI Dulwich SE19 . . .121 E3
Guildford GU4 . . . . .110 B3
Gould Rd East Bedfont TW14 .14 E8
Twickenham TW2 . . . . . . .16 E7
Goulding Gdns CR7 . . . . . .42 C7
Government House Rd
GU11, GU14 . . . . .105 B7
Government Rd
Aldershot GU11 . . . . .105 E4
Farnborough GU11 . . . . .105 C6
Governor's Rd GU15 . . . . .64 F6
Govett Ave TW17 . . . . .34 C4
Govett Gr GU20 . . . . .48 D5
Gower Pk GU47 . . . . .64 B7
Gower Rd Horley RH6 . . . .160 E3
Hounslow TW7 . . . . .5 F8
Weybridge KT13 . . . . .53 D4
Gower The TW20 . . . . .32 C6
Gowland PI BR3 . . . . .43 F6
Graburn Way KT8 . . . . . . .36 D6
Grace Bennett CI GU14 . . .85 A7
Grace Bsns Ctr CR4 . . . . .40 E3
Grace House SE26 . . . . . . .23 B3
Grace Path SE26 . . . . .23 C4
Grace Rd Crawley RH11 . .201 A1
Thornton Heath CR0 . . . . .42 C3
Grace Reynolds Wlk 4
GU15 . . . . .65 C6
Gracedale Rd SW16, SW17 .21 B3
Gracefield Gdns SW16 . . .21 E5
Gracious Pond Rd GU24 . .50 A8
Gradient The SE26 . . . . . .23 A4
Graemesdyke Ave SW14 . . .7 B3
Graffham CI RH11 . . . . . .201 B8
Grafton CI Twickenham TW4 .15 F7

Grafton CI continued
West Byfleet KT14 . . . . . . .70 F6
Worcester Park KT4 . . . . . .57 E7
Grafton Ct TW14 . . . . .14 D7
Grafton Park Rd KT4 . . . . .57 E8
Grafton Rd Kingston u T KT3 .38 E6
Thornton Heath CR0 . . . . .42 A1
Worcester Park KT19, KT4 . .57 E7
Grafton Way KT8 . . . . .35 F5
Graham Ave CR4 . . . . .41 A8
Graham CI CR0 . . . . .63 A8
Graham Gdns KT6 . . . . . . .37 E1
Graham House
5 Balham SW12 . . . . .21 B8
Little Bookham KT23 . . . . .94 A3
Redhill RH1 . . . . .118 E3
Graham Rd Hampton TW12 .16 A4
Merton SW19 . . . . .19 F1
Mitcham CR4 . . . . .41 A8
Purley CR8 . . . . .80 A6
Windlesham GU20 . . . . . . .48 C4
Grainford Ct RG40 . . . . . . .25 D5
Grainger Rd TW7 . . . . .5 F5
Grampian Cl UB3 . . . . .3 D7
Grampian Rd GU47 . . . . . .45 A2
Granada St SW17 . . . . . . .20 F3
Granard House 8 SW11, SW12 .20 F8
Granary CI RH6 . . . . .161 A5
Granary Way RH12 . . . . . .217 A1
Grand Ave Camberley GU15 .65 A5
Tolworth KT5 . . . . .38 B3
Grand Avenue Prim Sch
KT5 . . . . .38 C3
Grand Avenue Prim Sch
(Upper Sch) KT5 . . . . . . .38 C3
Grand Dr KT3, SM4, SW20 .39 C5
Grand Par Crawley RH10 . .201 D6
Mortlake SW14 . . . . .7 C3
Tolworth KT6 . . . . .38 A1
Grand Stand Rd KT17, KT18 .77 A2
Grand View Ave TN16 . . . .83 C2
Granden Rd SW16 . . . . . . .41 E7
Grandfield Ct W4 . . . . .7 D8
Grandis Cotts GU23 . . . . . .91 B5
Grandison Rd KT4 . . . . . . .58 C7
Grange Ave
Crowthorne RG45 . . . . . . .45 B6
South Norwood SE25 . . . . .42 E7
Twickenham TW2 . . . . . . .16 E6
Grange CI Ashstead KT22 . .95 D7
Bletchingley RH1 . . . . . . .120 D7
Crawley RH10 . . . . .202 A8
East Molesey KT8 . . . . . . .36 B5
Godalming GU7 . . . . .151 A5
Guildford GU2 . . . . .109 B5
Heston TW5 . . . . .4 E7
Merstham RH1, RH2 . . . .119 B7
Wraysbury TW19 . . . . .11 F8
Grange Cres RH10 . . . . . .204 B7
Grange Ct Egham TW20 . . .11 F3
Hackbridge SM6 . . . . .60 B7
Littleton TW17 . . . . .34 A5
South Godstone RH9 . . . .142 E5
Staines TW18 . . . . .13 A3
Sutton SM2 . . . . .59 B3
Walton-on-T KT12 . . . . . . .54 A8
Grange Cty Inf Sch The
KT15 . . . . .52 D6
Grange Dr Merstham RH1 .119 B7
Woking GU21 . . . . .69 E4
Grange End RH6 . . . . . . .162 A3
Grange Farm Rd GU12 . . .106 A3
Grange Gdns Banstead SM7 .78 B6
South Norwood SE25 . . . . .42 E7
Grange Hill SE25 . . . . .42 E7
Grange La SE21 . . . . .22 F6
Grange Lodge SW19 . . . . .19 F3
Grange Mansions KT17 . . .57 F3
Grange Meadow SM7 . . . .78 B6
Grange Mills SW12 . . . . . .21 C7
Grange Park PI SW20 . . . .19 B1
Grange Park Rd CR7 . . . . .42 D5
Grange Pk Cranleigh GU6 .174 F3
Woking GU21 . . . . .69 E4
Grange PI TW18 . . . . .33 C7
Grange Rd Ash GU12 . . . .106 B1
Ashstead KT21, KT22 . . . .95 D7
Belmont SM2 . . . . .59 A3
Bracknell RG12 . . . . .27 C8
Camberley GU15 . . . . .65 D7
Caterham CR3 . . . . .101 A2
Chessington KT9 . . . . .56 E6
Crawley Down RH10 . . . . .204 B7
East Molesey KT8 . . . . . . .36 B5
Egham TW20 . . . . .11 F3
Farnborough GU14 . . . . . .85 B7
Guildford GU2, GU3 . . . .109 B5
Hersham KT12 . . . . .54 E6
Kingston u T KT1 . . . . .37 E6
Rushmoor GU10 . . . . . . .168 C7
South Croydon CR2 . . . . . .61 C2
South Norwood SE19, SE25 .42 E7
Sutton SM2 . . . . .59 B3
Tongham GU10 . . . . .126 E6
Woking GU21 . . . . .69 E4
Woodham KT15 . . . . .52 B1
Grange Specl Sch The
GU11 . . . . .126 B8
Grange The Chobham GU24 .49 E1
Croydon CR0 . . . . .62 F8
Frensham GU10 . . . . .167 D7
Horley RH6 . . . . .161 A6
New Malden KT3 . . . . .39 A4
Walton-on-T KT12 . . . . . . .34 F1
Wimbledon SW19 . . . . . . .19 D2
Worcester Park KT19 . . . . .57 D6
Grange Vale SM2 . . . . .59 B3
Grangecliffe Gdns SE25 . .42 E7

Grangefields Way GU4 . . .109 D6
Grangemill Rd SE6 . . . . . .24 A6
Grangemill Way SE6 . . . . .24 A6
Grangemount KT22 . . . . . .95 D7
Grangeway RH6 . . . . .162 A3
Grangewood La BR3 . . . . .23 F2
Granston CI GU35 . . . . . . .175 E5
Granston Way RH10 . . . . .204 C8
Grant CI TW17 . . . . .34 B3
Grant PI 2 CR0 . . . . .42 F1
Grant Rd Crowthorne RG45 .45 C4
Croydon CR0 . . . . .42 F1
Grant Way TW7, TW8 . . . . .6 A8
Grant Wlk SL5 . . . . .29 F1
Grantchester 3 KT1 . . . . .38 A7
Grantham CI GU47 . . . . . .45 E1
Grantham House TW16 . . .14 A6
Grantham Rd W4 . . . . .7 E7
Grantley Ave GU5 . . . . . .152 B6
Grantley CI GU4 . . . . .130 E2
Grantley House SW19 . . . .19 D7
Grantley Rd
Cranford TW4, TW5 . . . . . . .4 C5
Guildford GU2 . . . . .109 A2
Granton Rd SW16 . . . . . . .41 C8
Grants Cotts KT10 . . . . . . .55 D8
Grantham House TW16 . . .14 A6
Grantwood CI RH1 . . . . . .140 B4
Granville Ave
Feltham TW13 . . . . .15 A6
Hounslow TW3, TW4 . . . . . .5 A2
Granville CI Byfleet KT14 . .71 F6
South Croydon CR0 . . . . . .61 E8
Weybridge KT13 . . . . .53 C4
Granville Gdns SW16 . . . . .21 F1
Granville Rd
Limpsfield RH8 . . . . .123 A7
Merton SW19 . . . . .20 A1
Wandsworth SW18 . . . . . .19 F8
Weybridge KT13 . . . . .53 C4
Woking GU22 . . . . .89 F7
Granwood CI 5 TW7 . . . . . .5 F6
Grasmere Ave
Kingston u T SW15 . . . . . .18 E4
Merton SW19 . . . . .40 A6
Twickenham TW2 . . . . .5 B1
Grasmere CI
East Bedfont TW14 . . . . . .14 F7
Guildford GU1 . . . . .110 B2
Thorpe Lea TW20 . . . . . . .12 B1
Grasmere Ct SE26 . . . . . .23 A3
Grasmere Gdns RH12 . . .218 B6
Grasmere Rd Bromley BR1 .24 F1
Croydon SE25 . . . . .43 B4
Farnborough GU14 . . . . . .84 E4
Hale GU9 . . . . .125 A6
Lightwater GU18 . . . . .48 B1
Purley CR8 . . . . .80 B8
Streatham SW16 . . . . .21 F3
Grasmere Way KT14 . . . . .71 F7
Grassfield CI CR5 . . . . .99 C8
Grasslands RH6 . . . . .162 A3
Grassmere RH6 . . . . .161 C4
Grassmount
Forest Hill SE23 . . . . .23 B6
Wallington CR8 . . . . .60 C1
Grassway SW16 . . . . .60 C6
Grately House 10 SW15 . . .19 B7
Grattons Dr RH10 . . . . . . .182 C1
Grattons The RH13 . . . . . .215 E3
Gravel Hill
Leatherhead KT22 . . . . . . .95 B6
South Croydon CR0, CR2 . .62 E4
Gravel Hill CI GU10 . . . . .145 A3
Gravel Pits GU5 . . . . .133 C4
Gravel Pits La GU5 . . . . . .133 C4
Gravel Rd
Farnborough GU14 . . . . .105 D8
Hale GU9 . . . . .125 B7
Twickenham TW2 . . . . . . .16 E7
Graveley 7 KT1 . . . . .38 A7
Gravelly Hill CR3 . . . . . . .120 F7
Gravenel Gdns SW17 . . . .20 E3
Graveney GU27 . . . . .207 F4
Graveney Rd
Crawley RH10 . . . . .202 C5
Upper Tooting SW17 . . . . .20 E4
Graveney Sch SW17 . . . . .21 B3
Gravetts La GU3 . . . . .108 D4
Gravetye CI RH10 . . . . . . .202 A4
Gray Ct 8 KT2 . . . . .17 D4
Gray PI KT16 . . . . .51 D4
Gray's La KT21 . . . . .95 F8
Grayham Cres KT3 . . . . . .38 D5
Grayham Rd KT3 . . . . .38 D5
Graylands GU21 . . . . .69 E3
Graylands CI GU21 . . . . . .69 E3
Graylands CI 5 GU21 . . . .130 F8
Grays CI GU27 . . . . .208 E8
Grays Rd GU7 . . . . .150 F7
Grays Wood RH6 . . . . . . .161 C3
Grayscroft Rd SW16 . . . . .21 D1
Grayshot Dr GU17 . . . . . . .64 C5
Grayshott Prim Sch GU26 .188 D3
Grayshott Rd GU26, GU35 .188 D6
Grayswood Ave GU27 . . . .208 E8
Grayswood Point 14 SW15 .19 A7
Grayswood Rd
Grayswood GU27 . . . . . . .189 F1
Haslemere GU27 . . . . . . .189 F1

Grazely Ct SE19 ....22 E3
Great Austins GU9 ....146 D8
Great Bookham Cty Mid
  Sch KT23 ....94 A1
Great Brownings SE21 ......22 F4
Great Chertsey Rd
  Hounslow TW4, W4 ....7 D6
  Feltham TW13, TW7 ....16 A5
Great Elshams SM7 ....78 A3
Great George St GU7 ....150 E4
Great Goodwin Dr GU1 ....110 B3
Great Hollands Inf Sch
  RG12 ....26 F4
Great Hollands Jun Sch
  RG12 ....26 E4
Great Hollands Rd RG12 ...26 F3
Great Hollands Sq RG12 ...26 F3
Great House Ct ⁴ RH19 ...205 F8
Great Oaks Pk GU4 ....110 C5
Great Quarry GU1 ....130 D6
Great South-West Rd
  TW14, TW6, TW4, TW5 ....3 D2
  Feltham TW6, TW14 ....3 D2
  Hatton TW6, TW14 ....3 D2
  Hounslow TW5 ....4 B4
Great Tattenhams KT18 ....77 C1
Great West Rd
  Brentford TW8 ....6 B8
  Cranford TW5 ....4 F6
  Heston TW5 ....4 F6
  Hounslow TW5, TW7 ....5 C6
Great West Rd Cedars Rd
  W4 ....7 C8
Great West Road Chiswick
  W4 ....7 F8
Great West Road
  Ellesmere Rd W4 ....7 D8
Great West Road Hogarth La
  W4 ....7 D7
Great Woodcote Dr CR8 ....60 D1
Great Woodcote Pk
  CR8, SM6 ....60 D1
Greatfield Cl GU14 ....85 B8
Greatfield Rd GU14 ....85 B8
Greatford Dr GU1 ....110 D1
Greatham Rd RH10 ....202 C3
Greatham Wlk ⁶ SW15 .....19 A7
Greathed Manor RH7 ....165 C1
Greathurst End KT23 ....93 F3
Greatlake Ct RH6 ....161 B4
Greatstone House 18 SE20 23 C1
Greatwood Cl KT16 ....51 C2
Greaves Pl SW17 ....20 E4
Grebe Cres RH13 ....218 A1
Grebe Terr 4 KT1 ....37 E6
Grecian Cres SE19, SW16 ..22 B2
Green Acre GU11 ....104 F1
Green Acres CR0 ....61 F7
Green Bsns Ctr The TW20 ..12 C4
Green Cl Beckenham BR2 ....44 E6
  Carshalton SM5 ....59 F8
  Feltham TW13 ....15 E3
  Sutton SM1 ....59 F8
Green Court Ave CR0 ....62 B8
Green Court Gdns CR0 ......62 B8
Green Croft RG40 ....25 E8
Green Cross La GU10 ....168 A1
Green Ct TW16 ....14 F2
Green Curve SM7 ....77 F4
Green Dene
  East Horsley KT24 ....112 A3
  West Horsley KT24 ....112 E3
Green Dr Send Marsh GU23 ..90 F4
  Wokingham RG40 ....25 E4
Green Dragon Jun & Inf
  Sch TW8 ....6 E8
Green End KT9 ....56 E6
Green Farm Rd GU19 ....47 F3
Green Finch Cl RG45 ....45 A6
  Warlingham CR6 ....6 C1
Green Hedges Ave RH19 ..185 D2
Green Hedges Cl RH19 ....185 D2
Green Hill BR6 ....83 F7
Green Hill Cl GU15 ....66 C6
Green Hill Rd GU15 ....66 C6
Green House The ⑤ SW19 ..19 E7
Green La
  Addlestone KT15, KT16 .....51 E7
  Alfold Crossways GU6 ....193 F4
  Ascot SL5 ....29 E8
  Ashford TW16 ....14 F2
  Ashtead KT22 ....95 D6
  Ashtead, Lower
  Ashtead KT22 ....75 D1
  Bagshot GU19 ....47 F2
  Blackwater GU17 ....64 B4
  Blackwater, Hawley GU17 ..64 E4
  Burstow RH6 ....182 F6
  Byfleet KT14 ....71 F7
  Carshalton CR3 ....100 C5
  Cheam SM4 ....40 E3
  Chertsey KT15, KT16 ....51 E7
  Chessington KT9 ....56 E3
  Chobham GU24 ....49 F1
  Churt GU10 ....168 A1
  Cobham KT11 ....73 E7
  Copthorne RH10 ....183 F4
  Crawley, Northgate RH10 ..201 E8
  Crawley, Worth RH10 ....202 D6
  Cudworth RH5 ....179 D8
  Dockenfield GU10 ....166 A6
  East Molesey KT8 ....36 B4
  Egham TW20 ....12 B3
  Egham TW18 ....32 E8

Green La continued
  Farncombe GU7, GU3 ......150 E8
  Farnham GU9 ....146 A7
  Farnham, Weybourne GU9 125 F5
  Faygate RH12 ....198 F4
  Feltham TW13 ....15 E3
  Guildford GU1 ....110 B1
  Heath End GU9 ....125 F5
  Hersham KT12 ....54 B5
  Hounslow TW4 ....4 A2
  Kingsley Green GU27 ....208 B4
  Leatherhead KT22 ....95 D6
  Leigh RH2 ....158 E8
  Lingfield RH7 ....164 C4
  Lower Kingswood KT20 .....97 F1
  Milford GU8 ....170 E8
  Morden SM4 ....40 B3
  New Malden KT3 ....38 C4
  North Cheam KT4 ....39 A1
  Penge SE20 ....23 D1
  Purley CR8 ....60 D1
  Redhill RH1 ....118 E3
  Redhill, Whitebushes RH1 ..140 A4
  Reigate RH2 ....117 F1
  Sandhurst GU47 ....64 C7
  Shamley Green GU5 ....153 A7
  Shepperton TW17 ....34 C4
  South Norwood CR7, SW16 ..42 B8
  South Nutfield RH1 ....140 F1
  Streatham SW16 ....21 F1
  Tilford GU10 ....147 E6
  West Clandon GU4 ....111 B8
  West Horsley GU23, KT24 ...92 B3
  Wood St V GU3 ....108 A3
Green La E GU3 ....128 B8
Green La W GU12 ....127 E8
Green Lane Ave KT12 ....54 C5
Green Lane Cl
  Addlestone KT16 ....51 E8
  Byfleet KT14 ....71 F7
  Camberley GU15 ....65 C7
Green Lane Cotts GU10 ...167 F1
Green Lane Cty Inf Sch
  GU/ 129 C1
Green Lane Prim Sch KT4 ..39 B2
Green Lanes KT17 ....57 G7
Green Leaf Ave SM6 ....60 D6
Green Leas Ashford TW16 ..14 F2
  Kingston u T KT1 ....37 E6
Green Leas Cl TW16 ....14 F2
Green Man La TW14 ....4 A3
Green Mead KT12 ....54 F4
Green Pk TW18 ....12 E5
Green Sch for Girls The
  TW7 ....6 A6
Green St TW16 ....35 A7
Green La The Bracknell RG12 27 B5
  Broadbridge Heath RH12 ...216 D4
  Burgh Heath KT20 ....97 E8
  Carshalton SM6 ....60 A8
  Chiddingfold GU8 ....191 C5
  Claygate KT10 ....55 F4
  Copthorne RH10 ....183 B3
  Crawley RH11 ....201 C7
  Ewell KT17 ....77 A7
  Ewhurst GU6 ....124 B8
  Farnham GU9 ....126 A6
  Feltham TW13 ....15 B6
  Fetcham KT22 ....94 D3
  Frimley GU16 ....85 F6
  Hale GU9 ....125 C6
  Heston TW5 ....5 A8
  Kingston u T KT3 ....38 C7
  Merton SM4 ....39 E5
  New Addington CR0 ....62 F2
  R7 Richmond TW9 ....6 D2
  Staines TW18 ....126 E3
  Sutton SM1 ....59 B7
  The Sands GU10 ....126 E1
  Twickenham TW2 ....16 C6
  Tyler's Green RH9 ....121 C4
  Warlingham CR6 ....81 D1
  Whiteley Village KT12 ....53 E1
  Wimbledon SW19 ....19 D3
  Woldingham CR3 ....102 A4
Green View
  Chessington KT9 ....56 F3
  Godstone RH9 ....121 B4
Green Way
  Aldershot GU12 ....108 E3
  Redhill RH1 ....118 E3
  Sunbury TW16 ....35 A5
Green Wlk Crawley RH10 ..201 E8
  Hampton TW12 ....15 F2
Green Wood SL5 ....28 C8
Green Wrythe Cres SM5 ....40 E1
Green Wrythe La SM4, SM5 ..40 E2
Green Wrythe Prim Sch
  SM5 ....40 D3
Greena Ct TW16 ....35 A4
Greencroft Guildford GU1 ..110 B1
Greencroft Rd TW5 ....4 F6
Greene Fielde End TW18 ....13 D1
Greenfield Ave KT5 ....38 B3
Greenfield House 20
  SW19 ....19 D7
Greenfield Link CR5 ....79 E4
Greenfield Rd
  Farnham GU9, GU10 ....146 A7
  Slinfold RH13 ....216 D3
  Wrecclesham GU9 ....145 F7
Greenfield Sch GU22 ....89 E8
Greenfield Way RG45 ....45 A7
Greenfields Cl Horley RH6 ..160 E5
  Horsham RH12 ....218 A6
Greenfields Pl RH5 ....157 D7
Greenfields Rd
  Horley RH6 ....160 F5
  Horsham RH12 ....218 A5
Greenfields Sch
  East Grinstead RH19 ....205 D6
  Forest Row RH18 ....206 C1
Greenfields Way RH12 .....218 A6
Greenfinch Way RH12 ......217 D7
Greenford Rd SM1 ....59 B6
Greenham House TW7 ....5 D4
Greenham Wlk GU21 ....69 C1
Greenham Wood RG12 ......27 C3
Greenhanger GU10 ....188 A8
Greenhayes Ave SM7 ....78 A4
Greenhayes Cl RH2 ....118 C1
Greenhayes Gdns SM7 ......78 A4
Greenhayes Sch BR4 ....63 C8
Greenheys Pl GU22 ....69 F1
Greenhill SM1 ....59 C8
Greenhill Ave CR3 ....101 B6
Greenhill Cl
  Godalming GU7 ....150 D3
  Wrecclesham GU9 ....146 A7
Greenhill Gdns GU4 ....110 C4
Greenhill La CR6 ....81 F2
Greenhill Rd GU9 ....146 D8
Greenhill Way
  Farnham GU9 ....146 A7
  Wrecclesham GU9 ....146 A7
Greenhills GU16 ....69 E8
Greenholme GU15 ....66 D5
Greenhow RG12 ....27 A6
Greenhurst La RH8 ....123 A3
Greenhurst Rd SE27 ....22 A3
Greenlake Terr TW18 ....13 A3
Greenlands Rd
  Camberley GU15 ....65 B1
  Staines TW18 ....13 A4
  Weybridge KT13 ....53 C7
Greenlaw Gdns KT3 ....38 F2
Greenlea Pk SW19 ....40 E8
Greenleaf Cl 15 SW2 ....22 A8
Greenleas GU16 ....65 E2
Greenleaves Ct TW15 ....14 B2
Greenmead Cl SE25 ....43 A4
Greenmeads GU22 ....89 E5
Greenoak Rise TN16 ....83 C1
Greenoak Way SW19 ....19 D4
Greenock Rd SW16 ....41 D8
Greensand Cl RH1 ....119 D7
Greensand Rd GU1 ....130 E8
Greenside Cl Catford SE6 ...24 D6
  Guildford GU4 ....110 C3
Greenside Cotts GU23 ....91 C6
Greenside Rd CR0 ....42 A2
Greenside Wlk TN16 ....83 B1
Greensleeves Manor SM2 ..59 B4
Greenstede Ave RH19 .....185 F2
Greenvale Prim Sch CR7 ....81 D8
Greenvale Rd GU21 ....68 D1
Greenvale Spec Sch SE23 ..23 F5
Greenview Ave CR0 ....43 E3
Greenview Ct TW15 ....13 F4
Greenway
  Great Bookham KT23 ....94 B4
  Horsham RH12 ....217 B3
  Tatsfield TN16 ....103 C7
  Wallington SM6 ....60 C6
  West Barnes SW20 ....39 C5
Greenway Cl KT14 ....71 A6
Greenway Dr TW18 ....33 D8
Greenway Gdns CR0 ....62 F7
Greenway Jun Sch RH12 ..217 B3
Greenway The Epsom KT18 ..76 A5
  Hounslow TW4 ....4 F3
  Oxted RH8 ....122 E5
Greenways
  Beckenham BR3 ....44 A7
  Egham TW20 ....11 E3
  Forest Hill SE26 ....23 C4
  Hinchley Wood KT10 ....55 E6
  Sandhurst GU47 ....45 B1
  Walton on t H KT20 ....97 B2
Greenways Dr SL5 ....29 E1
Greenways The 2 TW1 ....6 A1
Greenways Wlk RH11 ......201 C2
Greenwich Cl RH11 ....201 C2
Greenwood
  ⁴ Bracknell RG12 ....27 F5
  5 Putney SW19 ....19 D8
Greenwood Cl
  Hinchley Wood KT7 ....37 A1
  Merton SM4 ....39 E5
  Woodham KT15 ....70 F8
Greenwood Ct 2 RH11 ....201 B1
Greenwood Dr RH1 ....140 A4
Greenwood Gdns CR3 ......101 A2
Greenwood La TW12 ....16 B3
Greenwood Pk KT2 ....18 E1
Greenwood Prim Sch CR4 ..41 D6

Greenwood Rd
  Crowthorne RG45 ....45 B6
  Hinchley Wood KT7 ....56 A8
  Isleworth TW7 ....5 F4
  Knaphill GU21 ....88 E7
  Mitcham CR4 ....41 D6
  Pirbright GU24 ....87 D2
  Thornton Heath CR0, CR9 ..42 C2
Greenwood The GU10 ......110 A1
Gregan Ct GU11 ....104 F1
Gregory Cl ⁷ Crawley RH10 202 C2
  Woking GU21 ....69 C2
Gregory Ct CR8 ....80 B6
Gregsons RH12 ....216 E8
Grena Gdns TW9 ....6 F3
Grena Rd TW10, TW9 ....6 F3
Grenaby Ave CR0 ....42 D2
Grenaby Rd CR0 ....42 D2
Grenadier Rd GU12 ....106 B4
Grenadiers Way GU14 ......84 C3
Grendon Cl RH6 ....160 F5
Grenehurst Pk RH5 ....178 B4
Grenfell Rd CR4, SW17 .....20 F2
Grennell Cl SM1 ....59 D8
Grennell Rd SM1 ....59 C8
Grenside Rd KT13 ....53 B7
Grenville Cl Cobham KT11 ..73 E6
  Tolworth KT5 ....38 C1
Grenville Gdns GU16 ....85 E6
Grenville Mews SW19 ......16 B3
Grenville Rd
  New Addington CR0 ....63 C2
  Shackleford GU8 ....149 D7
Gresham Ave CR6 ....81 F1
Gresham Ct RH8 ....122 F7
Gresham House
  2 Teddington TW11 ....16 E3
  7 Thames Ditton KT7 ....37 A2
Gresham Ind Est GU12 ....105 E2
Gresham Prim Sch CR2 ....81 A8
Gresham Rd Croydon SE25 ..43 A5
  Hampton TW12 ....16 A2
  Hounslow TW3, TW5 ....5 C6
  Lingfield RH7 ....164 C4
  Oxted RH8 ....122 F6
  Penge BR3 ....43 E7
  Staines TW18 ....13 A3
Gresham Way Frimley GU16 85 E6
  Wimbledon SW19 ....20 A5
Gresham Way East SW19 ..20 B5
Gresham Wlk RH10 ....201 E3
Gressenhall Rd SW18 ....19 F8
Greta Bank KT24 ....92 C1
Greville Ave CR2 ....62 D1
Greville Cl Ashstead KT21 ..95 E8
  Guildford GU2 ....108 E1
  Twickenham TW1 ....17 B8
Greville Ct Ashstead KT21 ..95 C2
  Fetcham KT23 ....94 C2
Greville Cty Prim Sch The
  KT21 ....75 F2
Greville Park Ave KT21 ......75 E1
Greville Park Rd KT21 ....75 E1
Greville Rd TW10 ....6 F1
Grey Alders KT17 ....77 C3
Grey Court Sch TW10 ....17 C5
Greycot Rd BR3 ....24 A3
Greyfields Cl CR8 ....80 B6
Greyfriars 11 SE26 ....23 A5
Greyfriars Dr Ascot SL5 ....29 B3
  Bisley GU24 ....68 A4
Greyfriars Rd GU23 ....91 A3
Greyhound Cl GU12 ....105 F1
Greyhound La SW16 ....21 D2
Greyhound Rd SM1 ....59 D5
Greyhound Slip RH10 ......202 D7
Greyhound Terr SW16 ....41 C8
Greylees Rd GU7 ....150 E5
Greys Ct GU11 ....104 E2
Greystead Pk GU10 ....145 E5
Greystead Rd SE23 ....23 C8
Greystoke Ct RG45 ....45 A4
Greystone Cl CR2 ....81 C8
Greystones Cl RH1 ....139 D7
Greystones Dr RH2 ....118 C3
Greyswood St SW16 ....21 B2
Greythorne Rd GU21 ....69 A1
Greywaters GU5 ....152 A6
Grice Ave TN16 ....83 C5
Grier Cl RH11 ....200 E5
Grierson House SW16 ....21 C4
Grieve Cl GU10 ....126 E7
Grieve Cl Ashstead KT21 ...95 D8
  Brentford TW8 ....6 E8
  Great Bookham KT23 ....94 B1
Griffin Ctr KT1 ....37 D7
Griffin Ctr The KT1 ....37 D7
Griffin Pk (Brentford FC)
  TW8 ....6 D8
Griffin Way
  Great Bookham KT23 ....94 A1
  Sunbury TW16 ....35 A7
Griffiths Cl KT4 ....58 B8
Griffiths Rd SW19 ....20 B1
Griffon Cl GU14 ....84 D3
Griggs Meadow GU8 ....170 F7
Grimwade Ave CR0 ....62 A7
Grimwood Rd TW1 ....16 F8
Grindall Cl CR0 ....61 B6
Grindley Gdns CR0 ....42 F3
Grindstone Cres GU21 ......68 B1
Grindstone Handle Cnr
  GU21 ....68 C1

Grinstead La RH19 ....20?
Grisedale Cl
  Crawley RH11 ....20..
  Sanderstead CR8 ....8?
Grisedale Gdns CR8 8
Grisedale Terr SE23 2
Grobars Ave GU21 6
Groom Cres SW18 ....2?
Groombridge Cl KT12 5
Groombridge House SE20 ..22
Groombridge Way RH12 ...216
Groomfield Cl SW17 ....2?
Grooms The RH10 ....20?
Grosslea SM4 40
Grosvenor Ave
  Mortlake SW14 ....7?
  Richmond TW10 6
  Wallington SM5, SM6 ....6¢
Grosvenor Ct
  Blackwater GU17 64
  Guildford GU4 11
  Morden SM4 40
  Penge SE19 ....2?
  5 Richmond TW10 6
  8 Sutton SM2 ....5?
Grosvenor Gdns
  Kingston u T KT2 17
  Mortlake SW14 ....7?
  Wallington SM6 60
Grosvenor Hill 8 SW19 1
Grosvenor Ho 8 GU1 ....13¬
Grosvenor Pl
  8 Oatlands Park KT13 53
  9 Woking GU21 ....6?
Grosvenor Rd
  Aldershot GU11 ....10¬
  Brentford TW8 ....
  Croydon SE25 ....4?
  East Grinstead RH19 ....18¬
  Godalming GU7 150
  Hounslow TW3, TW4 ....
  Langley Vale KT18, KT21 ....
  Richmond TW10 ....1?
  Staines TW18 ....1?
  Twickenham TW1 ....1?
  Wallington SM6 60
  West End GU24 48
  West Wickham BR4 ....6?
Groton Rd SW18 20
Grotto Rd Twickenham TW1 ..1¢
  Weybridge KT13 ....5?
Grove Ave Epsom KT17 ....7¬
  Sutton SM1, SM2 ....5¬
  Twickenham TW1 ....1?
Grove Cl Cranleigh GU6 174
  Forest Hill SE23 ....2?
  8 Kingston u T KT1 ....3?
  Old Windsor SL4 ....1?
Grove Cnr KT23 94
Grove Cres Feltham TW13 ...1?
  Kingston u T KT1 ....3?
  8 Kingston u T KT3 ....3¬
  Walton-on-T KT12 ....5?
Grove Cross Rd GU16 65
Grove Ct East Molesey KT8 ...3¬
  Egham TW20 ....1?
  Forest Hill SE23 ....2?
  Hounslow TW3 ....
  8 Kingston u T KT1 ....3?
  Kingston u T KT3 ....3?
Grove End GU19 ....4¬
Grove End La KT10 36
Grove End Rd GU9 ....14¢
Grove Farm Ctr CR4 ....4?
Grove Gdns TW11 ....1?
Grove Heath La GU23 ....9?
Grove Heath N GU23 ....9¬
Grove Heath Rd GU23 ....9¬
Grove House
  8 Epsom KT17 ....7¬
  Mitcham CR4 ....
  8 Redhill RH1 ....11¬
  Walton-on-T KT12 ....5?
Grove House Froebel Ed
  Inst SW15 ....
Grove House Prim Sch
  SE27 ....2?
Grove Jun & Inf Sch W4 7
Grove La Kingston u T KT1 ...3?
  Wallington CR5 ....7?
  Winkfield RG42 ....
Grove Park Bridge W4 7
Grove Park Gdns W4 7
Grove Park Rd W4 7
Grove Park Terr W4 7
Grove Pl KT13 53
Grove Prep Sch The
  GU26 ....18¬
Grove Rd Ash GU12 ....10¢
  Ashstead KT21 ....9¬
  Barnes SW13 ....
  Beacon Hill GU26 ....18¬
  Camberley GU15 ....6¬
  Cheam SM2 ....5¬
  Chertsey KT16 ....3?
  Cranleigh GU6 ....17¢
  East Molesey KT8 ....3¬
  Epsom KT17, KT18 ....7¬
  Godalming GU7 150
  Guildford GU1 ....11¬
  Horley RH6 ....16¬
  Hounslow TW3 ....
  Hounslow TW7 ....
  Kingston u T KT6 ....3?

ve Rd *continued*
field RH7 164 E5
ton SW19 20 C1
ham CR4 41 B7
mond TW10 6 F1
Richmond TW10 6 F2
epperton TW17 34 C3
ton SM2 59 A4
sfield TN16 103 C7
rnton Heath CR7 42 A5
ckenham TW2 16 D5
king GU21 69 F3
ve Rd Prim Sch TW3 5 A3
ve Shaw KT20 97 E3
ve Terr TW11 17 A4
ve The Addlestone KT15 52 B5
ershot GU11 105 A1
gin Hill TN16 83 E1
erham CR3 100 C6
lsdon CR5 79 D5
wley RH11 201 C6
am TW20 12 A3
om KT17 76 E6
nborough GU14 85 D1
nley GU16 65 D1
ley RH6 161 B2
nslow TW7 5 E6
rth Ascot SL5 28 C8
dington TW11 17 A4
Twickenham TW1 6 B1
ton-on-T KT12 35 B2
st Wickham BR4 63 C7
king GU21 69 F3
ve Way KT10 36 C1
ve Wood Hill CR5 79 D5
vebarns TW18 13 A2
vebell Ind Est GU9 145 F7
vefields Ave GU16 65 D1
vehill Ct BR1 24 F2
vehill Rd RH1 118 F1
veland Ave SW16 21 F1
veland Rd BR3 43 F6
veland Way KT3 38 D4
velands
st Molesey KT8 36 A5
nham GU10 146 E7
ley RH6 161 B2
gston u T KT1 37 D5
velands Rd CR8 79 F7
velands Sch KT12 35 B3
veley Rd TW13, TW16 14 F3
veside KT23 114 A8
veside Cl
shalton SM5 59 E8
eat Bookham KT23 114 A8
vestile Waye TW14 14 D8
vewood 9 TW9 7 A6
vewood Ct 6 TW7 5 E6
b St RH8 123 C6
ardian Ct GU8 148 C3
ards Ct SL5 30 B2
erdon Pl RG12 27 D2
ernsey Cl
wley RH11 201 A2
ildford GU4 110 A6
ston TW5 5 A7
ernsey Farm Dr GU21 69 D4
ernsey Gr SE24 22 C8
ldables La RH8, TN8 144 E7
ldcroft GU1 110 A1
ldersfield Rd SW16 21 E1
ldford Ave TW13 15 A6
ldford Business Park Rd
2 109 B2
ldford Castle GU1 130 D7
ldford Cath GU2 109 B1
ldford Coll
arkenfield House
1 109 D1
ldford Cty Sch GU2 130 B7
ldford & Godalming
-Pass Rd
mpton GU3 129 E6
ildford GU2 129 E6
ackleford GU7 149 F6
ildford Golf Club GU1 110 C1
ldford High Sch for
rls GU1 109 E1
ildford Ind Est GU2 109 A2
ildford Lodge Dr KT24 112 F6
ldford Mus GU1 130 D7
ldford Park Ave GU2 130 B8
ildford Park Rd GU2 130 C8
ildford Rd
inger Hammer RH5 134 C3
dlestone KT16 51 C5
dershot GU11, GU12 126 D7
h GU12, GU3 106 D3
gshot GU19 47 E3
sley GU24 67 F7
oadbridge Heath RH12 216 B6
ertsey KT16 32 F1
anleigh GU6 174 B6
rncombe GU7 151 B7
rnham GU10, GU9 125 F4
rnham, Runfold GU10 126 B4
tcham KT22 94 F3
imley GU16 85 F6
reat Bookham KT23 94 A1
orsham RH12 217 A2
ghtwater GU18, GU19 48 B1
ytchett GU16 86 B5
rmandy GU3 107 B4
tershaw KT16 51 C5
rbright GU3 88 C2
owhook RH12, RH13 215 C7
owly GU6 174 B6
udgwick RH12 214 C6

Guildford Rd *continued*
Shamley Green GU5 153 A1
Slinfold RH12, RH13 215 C7
Thornton Heath CR0 42 D3
West End GU24 67 F7
West End, Castle Green GU21, GU24 68 D6
Westcott RH4 135 C6
Windlesham GU19 47 F2
Woking GU22, GU4 89 E8
Woking, Westfield GU22, GU4 89 D4
Wotton RH5 134 C3
Guildford Rd E GU14 85 C1
Guildford Rd W GU14 85 C1
Guildford Road Trad Est GU9 125 D3
Guildford Sch of Acting GU2 130 D7
Guildford St Chertsey KT16 33 A2
Staines TW18 13 A2
Guildford Sta GU1 130 C8
Guildford Way SM6 60 E5
Guildown Ave GU2 130 B6
Guildown Rd GU2 130 C6
Guileshill La GU23 91 F5
Guilford Ave KT5 37 F4
Guillemont Fields GU14 84 D5
Guillemont Jun Sch GU14 84 D7
Guillemot Path 2 RH11 200 D5
Guinevere Rd RH11 200 E6
Guinness Ct Crawley RH11 201 C2
4 Knaphill GU21 68 F1
3 South Croydon CR0 61 F8
Gull Cl SM6 60 E3
Gulliver Ct CR0 61 B3
Gumbrells Cl GU3 108 C5
Gumley Gdns TW7 6 A4
Gumley House Convent Sch for girls TW7 6 A4
Gun Hill GU11 105 B3
Gun Pit Rd RH7 164 D4
Gunnell Cl SE25 43 A3
Gunnell Ct CR4 40 E8
Gunners Rd SW18 20 D6
Gunning Cl RH11 201 A3
Gunters Mead KT22 74 C8
Gunton Rd SW17 21 A2
Gurdon's La GU8 170 F2
Gurney Cres CR0 41 F1
Gurney Rd SM5 60 A6
Gurney's Cl 3 RH1 139 F8
Guy Rd CR0, SM6 60 D7
Guyatt Gdns CR4 41 A7
Gwydor Rd BR3 43 D6
Gwydyr Rd BR2 44 F6
Gwynne Ave CR0 43 D2
Gwynne Gdns RH19 185 C2
Gwynne House 6 SW2 21 F7
Gwynne Rd CR3 100 D4
Gwynne Vaughan Ave GU2 109 B5

H

H Jones Cres GU11 105 C3
Habershon Dr GU16 66 D2
Haccombe Rd SW19 20 C2
Hackbridge Inf Sch SM6 41 A1
Hackbridge Jun Sch SM5 41 A1
Hackbridge Park Gdns SM5 59 F8
Hackbridge Rd SM5, SM6 60 A8
Hackbridge Sta SM6 60 B8
Hackenden Cl RH19 185 E3
Hackenden La RH19 185 E3
Hacketts La GU22 70 F4
Hackhurst La RH5 133 F4
Hackington Cres BR3 24 A2
Haddenham Ct SW17 20 D4
Haddington Rd BR1 24 D4
Haddon Cl New Malden KT3 38 F4
Oatlands Park KT13 53 D6
Haddon Rd SM1 59 B6
Hadfield Rd TW19 2 D1
Hadleigh Cl SW20 39 F7
Hadleigh Dr SM2 59 B2
Hadleigh Gdns GU16 85 E6
Hadley Ct SL3 1 E6
Hadley Pl KT13 53 A3
Hadley Rd CR4 41 D5
Hadley Wood Rise CR8 80 B5
Hadleys GU10 145 E3
Hadlow Pl SE19 23 A1
Hadmans Cl RH12 217 C1
Hadrian Cl Stanwell TW19 13 E8
Wallington SM6 60 E3
Hadrian Ct 1 SM2 59 B3
Hadrian Way
Stanwell TW19 13 D8
Stanwell TW19 13 E8
Hadrians GU9 125 E4
Hafton Rd SE6 24 E6
Haggard Rd TW1 17 B8
Haig Pl SM4 40 A3
Haig Rd Aldershot GU12 105 C1
Biggin Hill TN16 83 E2
Sandhurst GU15 64 F6
Haigh Cres RH1 140 B7
Hailes Cl SW19 20 C2
Hailey Pl GU6 174 F4
Hailsham Ave SW2 21 F6
Hailsham Cl
Sandhurst GU47 45 D1
Surbiton KT6 37 D2
Hailsham Rd SW17 21 A2
Haines Ct KT13 53 D5

Haines Wlk SM4 40 B2
Haining Gdns GU16 86 A3
Hainthorpe Rd SE27 22 B4
Halcyon Ct TW18 33 B7
Haldane Pl SW18 20 B7
Hale Cty Prim Sch GU9 125 B7
Hale End RG12 27 F5
Hale Ends GU22 89 B6
Hale House Cl GU10 167 F1
Hale House La GU10 168 B2
Hale Pit Rd KT23 94 C1
Hale Pl GU9 125 E5
Hale Rd Farnham GU9 125 D4
Hale GU9 125 D5
Hale Rdbt GU9 125 E5
Hale Reeds GU9 125 E6
Hale St TW18 12 E4
Hale Way GU16 85 D8
Halebourne La GU24 49 A2
Hales Ct 5 TW11 17 A3
Hales Field GU27 208 C6
Hales House 3 SW12 21 B8
Hales Oak KT23 94 C1
Halesowen Rd SM4 40 B2
Haleswood KT11 73 C5
Halewood RG12 26 F3
Half Acre TW8 6 D8
Half Acre Mews TW8 6 D8
Half Moon Hill GU27 208 C6
Half Moon St GU19 47 E3
Half Way Cotts GU10 124 C3
Halford Rd TW10 6 E2
Halfpenny Cl GU4 131 D3
Halfpenny Cross KT11 73 A2
Halfpenny Ct SL5 30 B2
Halfpenny La
Guildford GU4 131 C5
Sunningdale SL5 30 A2
Halfway La GU7 150 B4
Haliburton Rd TW1, TW7 6 A3
Halifax Cl Crawley RH10 182 E1
Farnborough GU14 84 F3
Halifax St SE26 23 B5
Halimote Rd GU11 105 A1
Haling Down Pas CR8 61 C1
Haling Gr CR2 61 C3
Haling Manor High Sch CR2 61 B3
Haling Manor High Sch (Pampisford Wing) CR2 61 B2
Haling Park Gdns CR2 61 B4
Haling Park Rd CR2 61 C4
Haling Rd CR2 61 D4
Hall Cl Camberley GU15 65 E6
Farncombe GU7 150 E7
Hall Ct TW11 16 F3
Hall Dene Cl GU1 110 C2
Hall Dr SE26 23 C3
Hall Farm Dr TW2 16 D8
Hall Grove (Sch) GU19 48 A5
Hall Hill RH8 122 D4
Hall La UB3 3 D7
Hall Pl GU21 70 A3
Hall Place Dr KT13 53 E5
Hall Rd Bramley GU5 151 F6
Isleworth TW7 5 D2
Wallington SM6 60 B2
Hall Sch Wimbledon SW15 19 A5
Hall Way CR8 80 B6
Hallam Rd GU7 150 F5
Halland Ct RH10 202 A7
Hallane House SE27 22 C3
Halley Cl RH11 201 B1
Halley Dr SL5 28 D7
Halley's App GU21 69 A1
Halley's Ct 1 GU21 69 A1
Halley's Wlk KT15 52 C3
Hallgrove Bottom GU19 47 F5
Halliards The KT12 35 A3
Halliford Cl TW17 34 E6
Halliford Rd Sunbury TW16 35 A5
Upper Halliford TW16, TW17 34 F5
Halliford Sch TW17 34 C2
Hallington Cl GU21 69 B2
Hallmark Cl GU47 64 E8
Hallmead Rd SM1 59 B7
Hallowell Ave CR0 60 E6
Hallowell Cl CR4 41 A6
Hallowfield Way CR4 40 E6
Halls Farm Cl GU21 68 D2
Hallsland RH10 204 C8
Hallsland Way RH8 122 F3
Halnaker Wlk 9 RH11 200 F3
Halsford Croft RH19 185 B3
Halsford Gn RH19 185 B3
Halsford La RH19 185 C3
Halsford Park Cty Prim Sch RH19 185 C2
Halsford Park Rd RH19 185 C2
Halters End GU26 188 A3
Ham Cl TW10 17 C5
Ham Comm TW10 17 D5
Ham Farm Rd KT2, TW10 17 E4
Ham Gate Ave
Richmond TW10 17 E4
Richmond, Richmond Park TW10 18 A4
Ham House TW10 17 D3
Ham La Elstead GU8 148 E4
Englefield Green TW20 11 B4
Ham Ridings TW10 17 F3
Ham St TW10 17 C5
Ham The TW8 6 C7
Ham View CR0 43 E3
Hamble Ave GU17 64 D5
Hamble Cl GU21 69 A2
Hamble Ct KT1 17 D1

Hamble Wlk GU21 69 A2
Hambleden Ct RG12 27 E5
Hambledon Ct 9 SM6 60 B4
Hambledon Gdns SE25 42 F6
Hambledon Hill KT18 76 C3
Hambledon House 2 KT2 18 B2
Hambledon Inf Sch GU8 171 D2
Hambledon Pk GU8 171 B1
Hambledon Pl
Dulwich SE21 22 F7
Little Bookham KT23 94 A4
Hambledon Rd
Caterham CR3 100 D4
Godalming GU8, GU7 171 D5
Hambledon GU8, GU7 171 D5
Hydestile GU8, GU7 171 D5
Wandsworth SW18 19 F8
Hambledon Vale KT18 76 C3
Hambleton Cl Frimley GU16 66 B3
North Cheam KT4 58 C8
Hambleton Ct RH11 201 C4
Hambleton Hill RH11 201 C4
Hambridge Way SW2 22 A8
Hambro Rd SW16 21 D3
Hambrook Rd SE25 43 B6
Hamers House 10 SW2 22 A8
Hamesmoor Rd GU16 85 F4
Hamesmoor Way GU16 85 F4
Hamfield Cl RH8 122 C8
Hamilton Ave Cheam SM3 58 E8
Cobham KT11 73 A6
Pyrford GU22 70 E3
Tolworth KT6, SM3 57 A8
Hamilton Cl TW13 14 F3
Hamilton Cl GU19 47 E3
Hamilton Cl Chertsey KT16 32 F1
Epsom KT19 76 C7
Guildford GU2 109 A6
Purley CR8 80 B7
Hamilton Cres TW3 5 B2
Hamilton Ct Catford SE6 24 F7
Cobham KT11 73 A6
Croydon CR0 43 A1
Farnborough GU17 64 E1
Great Bookham KT23 94 B2
Hamilton Dr
Guildford GU2 109 A6
Sunningdale SL5 29 E2
Hamilton House
Chiswick W4 7 E8
10 Richmond TW9 7 A6
Hamilton Mews KT13 53 A6
Hamilton Par TW13 15 A4
Hamilton Pl Guildford GU2 109 A6
Kingswood KT20 97 F4
Sunbury TW16 15 B1
Hamilton Rd
Brentford TW8 6 D8
Feltham TW13 14 F4
Horsham RH12 217 B3
Merton SW19 20 B1
South Norwood CR7 42 D6
Twickenham TW2 16 E7
West Norwood SE27 22 D4
Hamilton Road Ind Est SE27 22 D4
Hamilton Road Mews 1 SW19 20 B1
Hamilton Way SM6 60 D2
Hamlash Cotts GU10 146 C2
Hamlash La GU10 146 C1
Hamlet Rd SE19 23 A1
Hamlet St RG42 27 E8
Hamlyn Gdns SE19 22 E1
Hamm Court Est KT13 52 F8
Hamm Moor La KT15 52 E6
Hammelton Ct BR1 44 F8
Hammelton Rd BR1 44 F8
Hammer Hill GU27 207 C4
Hammer La
Grayshott GU10, GU26 187 E6
Haslemere GU27, GU30 207 A6
Haslemere GU26 207 C8
Linchmere GU27 207 C5
Hammer Vale GU27 207 B6
Hammer Yd RH10 201 D5
Hammerfield Dr RH5 133 F3
Hammerpond Rd RH13 217 F1
Hammersley Rd GU11 105 C7
Hammerwood Copse GU27 207 D5
Hammerwood Rd RH19 206 E6
Hammond Ave CR4 41 B7
Hammond Cl
Hampton TW12 36 A8
Woking GU21 69 C4
Hammond Cty Jun Sch GU18 48 A1
Hammond Rd GU21 69 C4
Hammond Way GU18 48 B1
Hamond Cl CR2 61 B2
Hampden Ave BR3 43 E7
Hampden Cl RH10 182 E1
Hampden Rd
Beckenham BR3 43 E7
Kingston u T KT1 38 A6
Hamper's La RH13 218 A2
Hampers Ct RH13 217 D2
Hampshire Cl GU12 126 D7
Hampshire Ct
Addlestone KT15 52 C5
Barnes SW13 7 F5
Hampshire Rd GU15 65 F8
Hampstead La RH4 135 F6
Hampstead Rd RH4 136 A6
Hampton Cl SW20 19 C1
Hampton Court Ave KT8 36 E3
Hampton Court Cres KT8 36 D6

Hampton Court Palace KT8 36 F6
Hampton Court Par KT8 36 E5
Hampton Court Rd KT1, KT8 37 B6
Hampton Court Sta KT8 36 E5
Hampton Court Way KT10, KT7, KT8 36 E3
Hampton Farm Ind Est TW13 15 E5
Hampton Gr KT17 76 F8
Hampton Hill Bsns Pk TW12 16 C3
Hampton Hill Jun Mix Sch TW12 16 C3
Hampton Inf Sch TW12 16 A1
Hampton Jun Sch TW12 36 A8
Hampton La TW13 15 E4
Hampton Lodge RH6 161 A2
Hampton Rd Hale GU9 125 B6
North Cheam KT4 58 B8
Redhill RH1 139 F4
Teddington TW11, TW12 16 E3
Thornton Heath CR0 42 C3
Twickenham TW2 16 D5
Hampton Rd E TW13 15 F5
Hampton Rd W TW13 15 E5
Hampton Road Ind Pk CR0 42 C3
Hampton Sch TW12 16 A3
Hampton Sta TW12 36 A8
Hampton Way RH19 205 F7
Hampton Wick Inf Sch KT1 17 D1
Hampton Wick Sta KT1 37 C8
Hamsey Green Cty Inf Sch CR6 81 B3
Hamsey Green Cty Jun Sch CR6 81 B3
Hamsey Green Gdns CR6 81 C3
Hamsey Way CR2 81 B4
Hanbury Dr TN16 83 B6
Hanbury Path GU21 70 D5
Hanbury Rd RH11 200 E5
Hanbury Way GU15 65 C3
Hancock Rd SE19 22 D2
Hancocks Mount SL5 29 D3
Hancombe Rd GU47 45 A1
Handcroft Rd CR0 42 B1
Handel House TW2 5 D1
Handside Cl KT4 39 D1
Handsworth House 8 RH10 201 D5
Hanford Cl SW18 20 A7
Hanger Hill KT13 53 B5
Hanley Pl BR3 24 A1
Hannah Cl BR3 44 C6
Hannah Ct SW19 19 D1
Hannah Peschar Gall & Gdn RH5 177 A2
Hannay Wlk SW16 21 D6
Hannen Rd SE27 22 B5
Hannibal Rd TW19 13 E8
Hannibal Way CR0 60 F4
Hanning Lodge TW3 5 C3
Hanover Ave TW13 15 A6
Hanover Cl Cheam SM3 58 F6
Crawley RH10 201 F3
Englefield Green TW20 11 B2
Frimley GU16 65 E1
Merstham RH1 119 C7
Richmond TW9 7 A7
Hanover Ct Dorking RH4 135 F7
Horsham RH13 217 F3
1 Penge SE19 23 A1
Woking GU22 89 E8
Hanover Gdns
Bracknell RG12 26 F2
Farnborough GU14 84 E6
Hanover House KT6 38 A1
Hanover Rd SW19 20 C1
Hanover St CR0, CR9 61 B7
Hanover Terr TW7 6 A6
Hanover Wlk KT13 53 E7
Hansler Gr KT8 36 D5
Hanson Cl Balham SW12 21 B8
Beckenham BR3 24 B2
Camberley GU15 66 B7
Guildford GU1 109 F4
Mortlake SW14 7 C4
Hanworth Cl RG12 27 C3
Hanworth La KT16 32 F1
Hanworth Rd
Bracknell RG12 27 A2
Feltham TW13 15 B7
Hampton TW12 16 A3
Hounslow TW3, TW4 5 B2
Redhill RH1 139 F4
Sunbury TW16 15 A1
Twickenham TW4 15 F8
Hanworth Terr TW3 5 B3
Hanworth Trad Est
Chertsey KT16 32 F1
Feltham TW13 15 E5
Harberson Rd SW12 21 B7
Harbin House 5 SW2 22 A7
Harbledown Rd CR2 81 A8
Harborough Rd SW16 21 F4
Harbour Cl GU14 85 A8
Harbourfield Rd SM7 78 B4
Harbridge Ave SW15 19 A8
Harbury Rd SM5 59 E3
Harcourt Ave SM6 60 B6
Harcourt Cl Egham TW20 12 C2
Isleworth TW7 6 A4

Harcourt Field SM6 . . . . .60 B6
Harcourt Lodge **2** SM6 . . . . . .60 B6
Harcourt Rd Bracknell RG12 . .27 B4
  Camberley GU15 . . . . .65 B5
  Merton SW19 . . . . .20 A1
  Thornton Heath CR7 . . . . .42 A3
  Wallington SM6 . . . . .60 B6
Harcourt Way RH9 . . . . .142 E6
Hardcastle Cl SE25 . . . . .43 A3
Hardcourts Cl BR4 . . . . .63 B7
Hardel Rise SW2 . . . . .22 B7
Hardel Wlk SE24, SW2 . . . . .22 A8
Hardell Cl TW20 . . . . .12 A3
Hardham Cl RH11 . . . . .201 A8
Harding Cl Kingston u T KT2 . .37 F8
  South Croydon CR0 . . . . .61 F7
Harding Ct SE25 . . . . .42 F7
Harding House SM6 . . . . .60 E2
Harding Pl SE23 . . . . .23 E8
Harding Rd KT18 . . . . .96 E8
Hardings La SE20 . . . . .23 D2
Hardman Rd KT2 . . . . .37 E7
Hardwell Way RG12 . . . . .27 E5
Hardwick Cl KT22 . . . . .74 C4
Hardwick La KT16 . . . . .32 D1
Hardwick Rd RH1 . . . . .139 D7
Hardwicke Ave TW5 . . . . .5 A6
Hardwicke Rd
  Reigate RH2 . . . . .118 A2
  Richmond TW10 . . . . .17 C4
Hardy Cl Crawley RH10 . . . . . .202 C7
  Dorking RH5 . . . . .136 B3
  Horley RH6 . . . . .160 E3
  Horsham RH12 . . . . .217 B4
Hardy Gn RG45 . . . . .45 B4
Hardy Rd SW19 . . . . .20 B1
Hardys Cl KT8 . . . . .36 E5
Hare Hill KT15 . . . . .51 F4
Hare Hill Cl GU22 . . . . .71 A4
Hare La Claygate KT10 . . . . . . .55 E4
  Crawley RH11 . . . . .201 B8
  Farncombe GU7 . . . . .150 F6
  Horne RH7 . . . . .163 D5
Harebell Hill KT11 . . . . .73 E5
Harecroft
  Dorking RH4, RH5 . . . . .136 C4
  Fetcham KT23 . . . . .94 C3
Haredon Cl SE23 . . . . .23 D8
Harefield KT10 . . . . .55 E7
Harefield Ave SM2 . . . . .58 E3
Harefield Rd SW16 . . . . .21 F1
Harelands Cl GU21 . . . . .69 C2
Harelands La GU21 . . . . .69 C2
Harendon KT20 . . . . .97 D6
Hares Bank CR0 . . . . .63 D1
Harestone Dr CR3 . . . . .100 F2
Harestone Hill CR3 . . . . .100 F2
Harestone La CR3 . . . . .100 E2
Harestone Valley Rd CR3 . .100 F2
Harewood Cl
  Crawley RH10 . . . . .182 A1
  Reigate RH2 . . . . .118 C4
Harewood Gdns CR2 . . . . .81 C4
Harewood Rd
  Guildford GU4 . . . . .110 C4
  Hounslow TW7 . . . . .5 F6
  Mitcham SW17 . . . . .20 E2
  South Croydon CR2 . . . . .61 E4
Harfield Rd TW16 . . . . .35 D7
Harkness Cl KT17 . . . . .77 C3
Harland Ave CR0 . . . . .62 A7
Harland Fst Sch CR4 . . . . .40 D7
Harlech Cl **1** SE23 . . . . .23 C7
Harlech Gdns TW5 . . . . .4 C7
Harlech Rd GU17 . . . . .64 D4
Harlequin Ave TW8 . . . . .6 A8
Harlequin Cl TW7 . . . . .5 E2
Harlequin Rd IW11 . . . . .17 B1
Harlington Cl UB7 . . . . .3 C7
Harlington Cnr UB3 . . . . .3 D6
Harlington Rd
  E TW13, TW14 . . . . .15 C7
Harlington Rd W TW14 . . . . . . .4 B1
Harlow Ct **4** RH2 . . . . .118 D1
Harman Pl CR8 . . . . .80 B8
Harman Rd RH19 . . . . .186 B1
Harmans Mead RH19 . . . . . . .186 B1
Harmans Water Cty Inf Sch
  RG12 . . . . .27 E4
Harmans Water Cty Jun Sch
  RG12 . . . . .27 E4
Harmans Water Rd RG12 . . . .27 D4
Harmar Cl RG40 . . . . .25 E6
Harmes Way GU4 . . . . .105 D7
Harmondsworth La UB7 . . . . . .2 E8
Harmondsworth Prim Sch
  UB7 . . . . .2 D8
Harmony Cl Crawley RH11 . . .200 E4
  Wallington SM6 . . . . .60 E2
Harms Gr GU4 . . . . .110 C4
Harold Rd Carshalton SM1 . . . .59 D6
  Crawley RH10 . . . . .202 D5
  South Norwood SE19 . . . . .22 D1
Haroldslea RH6 . . . . .161 D1
Haroldslea Cl RH6 . . . . .161 C1
Haroldslea Dr RH6 . . . . .161 D1
Harpenden Rd SE27, SW16 . . .22 B6
Harper Dr RH10 . . . . .202 C2
Harper's Rd GU12 . . . . .106 C2
Harpesford Ave GU25 . . . . . . .31 C4
Harps Oak La RH1, RH2 . . . . .99 A2
Harpurs KT20 . . . . .97 D5
Harrier Cl GU6 . . . . .174 E4
Harrier Ct RH10 . . . . .182 D1
Harriet Gdns CR0 . . . . .62 A8

Harriet Tubman Cl SW2 . . . . . .22 A8
Harrington Cl Leigh RH2 . . . .138 A2
  Wallington CR0 . . . . .60 E8
Harrington Ct **7** CR0 . . . . . . .61 DB
Harrington Rd SE25 . . . . .43 B5
Harriotts Cl KT22 . . . . .95 C7
Harriotts La KT21, KT22 . . . . . .95 C8
Harris City Tech Coll SE19 . .42 F8
Harris Lodge SE6 . . . . .24 C7
Harris Way TW16 . . . . .34 E8
Harrison Cl RH2 . . . . .139 B8
Harrison Ct TW17 . . . . .34 B4
Harrison's Rise CR0, CR9 . . . . .61 B7
Harrodian Sch SW13 . . . . .7 F7
Harrogate Ct **8** SE26 . . . . .23 A5
Harrow Bottom Rd GU25 . . . .31 F3
Harrow La GU7 . . . . .150 E7
Harrow Lodge SM2 . . . . .59 D4
Harrow Rd Ashford TW15 . . . .14 A6
  Carshalton SM1, SM2, SM5 . . .59 F4
  Warlingham CR6 . . . . .81 F3
Harrow Rd E RH4 . . . . .136 B6
Harrow Rd W RH4 . . . . .136 A6
Harrow Way TW17 . . . . .34 C7
Harrowdene GU6 . . . . .174 E4
Harrowdene Ct SW19 . . . . . . .19 E3
Harrowdene Gdns TW11 . . . . .17 A1
Harrowlands Pk RH4 . . . . . . .136 B6
Harrowsley Ct RH6 . . . . .161 B4
Harrow La T Bletchingley RH1 .120 E2
  1 Bracknell RG42 . . . . .27 B8
  Farnborough GU14 . . . . .84 E8
Hart Dene Cl GU19 . . . . .47 E3
Hart Dyke Cl RG41 . . . . .25 B2
Hart Gdns RH4 . . . . .136 B8
Hart House SW2 . . . . .22 A7
Hart Rd Byfleet KT14 . . . . .71 E6
  Dorking RH4 . . . . .136 B8
Hart The GU9 . . . . .125 B2
Hart's La RH9 . . . . .142 D7
Harte Rd TW3 . . . . .4 F5
Hartfield Cres SW19 . . . . .19 F1
Hartfield Gr SE20 . . . . .43 C8
Hartfield Rd
  Chessington KT9 . . . . .56 D5
  Forest Row RH18 . . . . .206 F2
  Merton SW19 . . . . .20 A1
Hartford Rd KT19 . . . . .57 B4
Hartford Rise GU15 . . . . .65 D6
Hartham Cl TW7 . . . . .6 A6
Hartham Rd TW7 . . . . .6 A6
Harting Ct RH11 . . . . .200 F3
Hartington Cl W4 . . . . .7 B7
Hartington Pl RH2 . . . . .118 A3
Hartington Rd Chiswick W4 . . .7 C6
  Twickenham TW1 . . . . .6 B1
Hartland Cl KT15 . . . . .52 C2
Hartland Pl GU14 . . . . .85 A7
Hartland Rd
  Addlestone KT15 . . . . .52 A3
  Cheam SM4 . . . . .40 D2
  Hampton TW12 . . . . .16 B4
  Isleworth TW7 . . . . .6 A4
Hartland Way Croydon CR0 . .62 E8
  Morden SM4 . . . . .39 F2
Hartlands The TW5 . . . . .4 B8
Hartley Cl GU17 . . . . .64 B5
Hartley Down CR5, CR8 . . . . .79 F5
Hartley Farm CR8 . . . . .79 F4
Hartley Hill CR8 . . . . .79 F4
Hartley Old Rd CR8 . . . . .79 F5
Hartley Rd CR0 . . . . .42 C2
Hartley Way CR5, CR8 . . . . . . .79 F4
Harts Gdns GU2 . . . . .109 B4
Harts Leap Cl GU47 . . . . .45 B1
Harts Leap Rd GU47 . . . . .64 A8
Harts Yd **14** GU9 . . . . .125 B2
Hartscroft CR0 . . . . .62 E2
Hartsgrove GU8 . . . . .191 B5
Hartshill Wlk GU21 . . . . .69 B3
Hartspiece Rd RH1 . . . . .140 B7
Hartswood RH5 . . . . .136 D4
Hartswood Ave RH2 . . . . .139 A5
Hartswood House TW10 **2** .21 E7
Harvard Hill W4 . . . . .7 B8
Harvard Rd Hounslow TW7 . . . .5 E6
  Sandhurst GU47 . . . . .45 E1
Harvest Bank Rd BR4 . . . . .63 F7
Harvest Ct Beckenham BR3 . .24 A1
  Littleton TW17 . . . . .34 A5
Harvest Hill
  East Grinstead RH19 . . . . .205 E8
  Godalming GU7 . . . . .150 D4
Harvest La KT7 . . . . .37 A3
Harvest Rd Crawley RH10 . .202 C4
  Englefield Green TW20 . . . . . . .11 D2
  Feltham TW13 . . . . .15 A5
Harvest Ride
  RG12, RG42, SL5 . . . . .28 A8
Harvester Rd KT19 . . . . .57 D1
Harvesters RH12 . . . . .217 D5
Harvesters Cl TW7 . . . . .5 D2
Harvestside RH6 . . . . .161 C4
Harvey Cl RH11 . . . . .201 A1
Harvey Dr TW12 . . . . .36 A8
Harvey Rd
  Farnborough GU14 . . . . .84 C5
  Guildford GU1 . . . . .130 E8
  Twickenham TW4 . . . . .15 F8

Harvey Rd *continued*
  Walton-on-T KT12 . . . . .35 A2
Harwarden Cl RH10 . . . . .204 C8
Harwood Ave CR4 . . . . .40 E6
Harwood Gdns SL4 . . . . .11 B8
Harwood Pk RH1 . . . . .161 A8
Harwood Rd RH12, RH13 . . .218 A3
Harwoods Cl **3** RH19 . . . . . .205 F7
Harwoods La RH19 . . . . .205 F7
Hascombe Dr RH1 . . . . .201 A5
Hascombe House **11** SW15 .19 B7
Haseley End SE23 . . . . .23 C8
Haseltine Prim Sch SE6 . . . .23 F4
Haseltine Rd SE26 . . . . .23 F4
Haslam Ave SM3, SM4 . . . . . . .39 E1
Hasle Dr GU27 . . . . .208 B6
Haslemere Ave
  Cranford TW5 . . . . .4 C5
  Mitcham CR4, SW19 . . . . .40 D7
  Wimbledon SW18 . . . . .20 B6
Haslemere Cl Frimley GU16 . .66 C3
  Hampton TW12 . . . . .15 F3
  Wallington SM6 . . . . .60 E5
Haslemere & District
  Hospl GU27 . . . . .208 D7
Haslemere Educational
  Mus GU27 . . . . .208 D7
Haslemere Fst Sch GU4 . . . . .40 D7
Haslemere & Heathrow Est
  The TW4 . . . . .4 B4
Haslemere Ind Est
  Feltham TW14 . . . . .4 A2
  Wimbledon SW18 . . . . .20 B6
Haslemere Prep Sch
  GU27 .208 D5
Haslemere Rd Brook GU8 . . .170 C5
  Kingsley Green GU27 . . . . .208 B1
  Thornton Heath CR7 . . . . .42 B4
  Witley GU8 . . . . .170 C5
Haslemere Sta GU27 . . . . . . .208 B6
Haslett Ave E RH10 . . . . .202 A6
Haslett Ave W
  RH10, RH11 . . . . .201 D5
Haslett Rd TW17 . . . . .34 E7
Hassall Ct GU22 . . . . .90 A6
Hassocks Cl SE23, SE26 . . . . .23 B5
Hassocks Ct **3** RH11 . . . . . .200 F3
Hassocks Rd SW16 . . . . .41 D8
Haste Hill GU27 . . . . .208 D5
Hastings Dr KT6 . . . . .37 C3
Hastings Pl **1** CR0 . . . . .42 F1
Hastings Rd Crawley RH10 . .202 C6
  Croydon CR0 . . . . .42 F1
Hatch Cl Addlestone KT15 . . . .52 B7
  Alfold Crossways GU6 . . . . .194 A3
Hatch End
  Forest Row RH18 . . . . .206 F2
  Windlesham GU20 . . . . .48 C4
Hatch Gdns KT20 . . . . .97 D7
Hatch Hill GU27 . . . . .208 B1
Hatch La
  Harmondsworth TW6, UB7 . . . .2 D7
  Kingsley Green GU27 . . . . .208 B2
  Ockham GU23 . . . . .72 B1
  Ockham GU23 . . . . .92 B7
  South Nutfield RH1 . . . . .140 F3
  Wormley GU8 . . . . .190 D8
Hatch Pl TW10 . . . . .17 F3
Hatch Rd SW16 . . . . .41 E7
Hatch Ride RG45 . . . . .45 A5
Hatch Ride Cty Prim Sch
  RG45 . . . . .45 B7
Hatches The
  Farnham GU9 . . . . .145 F8
  Frimley GU16 . . . . .85 F6
Hatchet La SL4, SL5 . . . . .9 B5
Hatchett Rd TW14 . . . . .14 C7
Hatchetts Dr GU27 . . . . .207 E7
Hatchford Park Sch KT11 . .72 E1
Hatchgate RH6 . . . . .160 F2
Hatchgate Copse RG12 . . . . .26 E3
Hatchlands RH11 . . . . .218 A7
Hatchlands Rd RH1 . . . . .118 E2
Hatfield Cl Belmont SM2 . . . . .59 B2
  West Byfleet KT14 . . . . .71 A7
Hatfield Gdns GU14 . . . . .85 E3
Hatfield House **8** KT6 . . . . .37 E4
Hatfield Mead SM4 . . . . .40 A4
Hatfield Prim Sch SM4 . . . . . .39 E3
Hatfield Rd KT21 . . . . .95 F8
Hatfield Wlk RH11 . . . . .200 E2
Hathaway Cl **1** RH1 . . . . . . .119 A2
Hathaway Rd CR0 . . . . .42 A2
Hatherleigh Cl
  Chessington KT9 . . . . .56 D5
  Morden SM4 . . . . .40 A5
Hatherleigh House SM4 . . . . .40 A5
Hatherley Rd TW9 . . . . .6 F4
Hatherop Rd TW12 . . . . .15 F1
Hathersham Cl RH6 . . . . .162 A4
Hathersham La RH1, RH6 . . . .161 F6
Hathersley House **3** SW2 . .22 A8
Hatherwood GU7 . . . . .65 E6
Hatton Cross Rdbt TW6 . . . . . .3 F4
Hatton Cross Sta TW6 . . . . . . .3 F3
Hatton Gdns CR4 . . . . .40 F4
Hatton Gn TW14 . . . . .4 A3
Hatton Hill GU20 . . . . .48 C4
Hatton Rd
  East Bedfont TW14 . . . . .14 D8
  Hatton TW14, TW6 . . . . .3 F2
  Thornton Heath CR0 . . . . .42 A1
Havana Rd SW18, SW19 . . . . .20 A6
Havelock Cotts GU22 . . . . . . .89 D5
Havelock Hall **8** CR0 . . . . . .42 F1

Havelock House
  4 Croydon CR0 . . . . .42 F1
  Farnborough GU14 . . . . .105 C8
  Forest Hill SE23 . . . . .23 C7
Havelock Rd Croydon CR0 . . .61 F8
  Wimbledon SW19 . . . . .20 C3
  Wokingham RG41 . . . . .25 A4
Havelock St RG41 . . . . .25 A6
Havelock Wlk SE23 . . . . .23 C6
Haven Cl SW19 . . . . .19 D5
Haven Ct BR3 . . . . .44 C7
Haven Gdns RH10 . . . . .184 B1
Haven Rd Ashford TW15 . . . . .14 B5
  Rudgwick RH12, RH14 . . . . . . .214 D3
Haven The Ashford TW16 . . . . .15 A1
  Richmond TW9 . . . . .7 A4
Haven Way GU9 . . . . .125 E6
Havenbury Est RH4 . . . . .136 A8
Havenbury Ind Est RH4 . . . . .135 F8
Havengate RH12 . . . . .217 F5
Haverfield Gdns TW9 . . . . .7 A7
Haverfield Rd SW12 . . . . .21 C7
Havers Ave KT12 . . . . .54 D5
Haversham Cl
  Crawley RH10 . . . . .201 F6
  Twickenham TW1 . . . . .6 D1
Haversham Dr RG12 . . . . .27 B3
Haversham House RH6 . . . . .161 B5
Havisham Pl SW16 . . . . .22 B1
Hawarden Gr SE24 . . . . .22 C8
Hawarden Rd CR3 . . . . .100 C6
Hawes Down Schs BR4 . . . . .44 D1
Hawes La BR4 . . . . .63 E8
Hawes Rd KT20 . . . . .97 D7
Haweswater Ho TW1 . . . . .5 F2
Hawk La RG12 . . . . .27 D5
Hawk's Hill KT22 . . . . .94 F4
Hawke Rd SE19 . . . . .22 E2
Hawkedale Fst Sch TW16 . . .34 F6
Hawker Cl SM6 . . . . .60 E3
Hawker Ct **14** KT2 . . . . .18 A1
Hawkesbourne Rd RH12 . . .217 F5
Hawkes Leap GU20 . . . . .48 B6
Hawkes Rd CR4 . . . . .40 F8
Hawkesbourne Rd RH12 . . .217 F5
Hawkesfield Rd SE23 . . . . .23 F6
Hawkesley Cl TW1 . . . . .17 A4
Hawkesmoor Rd RH11 . . . . .200 E4
Hawkesmoor Dr RH5 . . . . . . .157 C4
Hawksworth Dr GU19 . . . . . . .47 E1
Hawkewood Rd TW16 . . . . . . .35 A6
Hawkfield Cl TW7 . . . . .5 D5
Hawkhirst Rd CR8 . . . . .80 E3
Hawkhurst KT11 . . . . .74 A5
Hawkhurst Gdns KT9 . . . . . . .56 E6
Hawkhurst Rd SW16 . . . . .41 D8
Hawkhurst Way
  New Malden KT3 . . . . .38 D4
  West Wickham BR4 . . . . .63 B8
Hawkhurst Wlk RH10 . . . . . .202 B4
  Teddington TW11 . . . . .17 B2
Hawkins Way Catford SE6 . . .24 A3
  Wokingham RG40 . . . . .25 E6
Hawkley Gdns SE27 . . . . .22 B6
Hawkridge RH12 . . . . .195 E1
Hawkridge Ct RG12 . . . . .27 E5
Hawksbrook La BR3 . . . . .44 B4
Hawkshead Cl BR1 . . . . .24 C1
Hawkshill Cl KT10 . . . . .55 A4
Hawkshill Way KT10 . . . . .55 A4
Hawkswell Cl GU21 . . . . .68 F2
Hawkswell Wlk GU21 . . . . .68 F3
Hawkswood Ave GU16 . . . . . .65 F2
Hawkswood House RG42 . . . .26 E8
Hawkwood Dell KT23 . . . . . . .94 A1
Hawkwood Rise KT23 . . . . . . .94 A1
Hawley Cl TW12 . . . . .15 F2
Hawley Ct GU14 . . . . .84 E8
Hawley Garden Cotts
  GU17 . . . . .64 E3
Hawley Gn GU17 . . . . .64 E3
Hawley La GU14 . . . . .85 B8
Hawley Lodge GU14 . . . . .64 F2
Hawley Place Sch GU17 . . . . .64 E1
Hawley Rd GU14, GU17 . . . . . .64 F3
Hawley Way TW15 . . . . .14 B3
Hawmead RH10 . . . . .204 C8
Haworth Rd RH10 . . . . .202 C5
Hawth (Arts Ctr) The
  RH10 .201 F5
Hawth Ave RH10 . . . . .201 F4
Hawth Cl RH10 . . . . .201 E4
Hawthorn Cl Banstead SM7 . .77 E5
  Bracknell RG42 . . . . .27 A8
  Cranford TW5 . . . . .4 B7
  Crawley RH11 . . . . .181 C1
  Horsham RH12 . . . . .217 C4
  Redhill RH1 . . . . .140 A4
  Woking GU22 . . . . .89 E7
Hawthorn Cres
  Selsdon CR2 . . . . .81 C8
  Upper Tooting SW17 . . . . .21 A3
Hawthorn Ct Richmond TW9 . .7 B7
  8 West Norwood SW16 . . . . .22 A3
Hawthorn Dr BR4 . . . . .63 E6
Hawthorn Gr SE20 . . . . .43 B8
Hawthorn Hatch TW8 . . . . .6 B7

Hawthorn La
  Newell Green SL4 . . . .
  Rowledge GU10 . . . . .14█
Hawthorn Rd Brentford TW8 . . . .
  Carshalton SM1, SM2, SM5 . . . .5█
  Frimley GU16 6
  Godalming GU7 15
  Send Marsh GU23 9
  Wallington SM5, SM6 6
  Woking GU22 8
Hawthorn Way Bisley GU24 . .68█
  Redhill RH1 . . . . .14█
  Upper Halliford TW17 . . . . .3█
  Woodham KT15 . . . . .5█
Hawthorndene Cl BR2 6
Hawthorndene Rd BR2 6
Hawthorne Ave
  Biggin Hill TN16 . . . . .8█
  Carshalton SM5 6
  Winkfield SL4 . . . .
Hawthorne Cl
  Aldershot GU12 12
  Sutton SM1 5
Hawthorne Cotts RH6 . . . . . .6█
Hawthorne Cres GU17 . . . . . . .6█
Hawthorne Ct TW19 . . . . .1█
Hawthorne Dr SL4 . . . .
Hawthorne Pl KT17 7
Hawthorne Rd TW20 1
Hawthorne Way
  Guildford GU4 11
  Stanwell TW19 . . . . .1█
  Winkfield SL4 . . . .
Hawthorns The
  Belmont SM2 5
  Ewell KT17 . . . . .5█
  Oxted RH8 . . . . .12█
  Poyle SL3 . . . .
Haxted Mill Mus TN8 . . . . . .16█
Haxted Rd
  Haxted RH7, TN8 . . . . .16█
  Lingfield RH7, TN8 . . . . .16█
Haybarn Dr RH12 . . . . .21█
Haycroft Cl CR8 . . . . .8█
Haycroft Rd KT6 . . . . .5█
Hayden Ct KT15 5
Haydn Ave CR8 . . . . .8█
Haydon House **2** TW11 . . . .1█
Haydon Park Rd SW19 . . . . . .2█
Haydon Pl GU1 . . . . .13█
Haydon's Rd SW19 . . . . .2█
  Wimbledon SW19 . . . . .2█
Haydons Road Sta SW19 . . . .2█
Hayes Barton GU22 . . . . .7█
Hayes Chase BR4 . . . . .4█
Hayes Cres SM3 . . . . .5█
Hayes Ct Streatham SW12 . . .2█
  Wimbledon SW19 . . . . .2█
Hayes Hill BR2 . . . . .4█
Hayes Hill Rd BR2 . . . . .4█
Hayes La
  Beckenham BR2, BR3 . . . . .4█
  Kenley CR8, CR3 . . . . .8█
  Purley CR8 . . . . .8█
  Slinfold RH13 215
Hayes Mead Rd BR2 4
Hayes Prim Sch The BR2 . . . .8█
Hayes Sta BR2 4
Hayes The KT18 . . . . .9█
Hayes Way BR3 . . . . .4█
Hayes Wlk RH6 162
Hayesend House SW17 . . . . . .2█
Hayeswood House **2** BR2 . .4█
Hayfields RH6 161
Haygarth Pl SW19 . . . . .19█
Haygreen Cl KT2 . . . . .1█
Haylett Gdns KT1 . . . . .3█
Hayling Ave TW13 15
Hayling Ct Cheam SM3 . . . . . .5█
  Crawley RH11 . . . . .20█
Haymeads Dr KT10 . . . . .5█
Haymer Gdns KT4 . . . . .5█
Hayne Rd BR3 . . . . .4█
Haynes La SE19 . . . . .2█
Haynt Wlk SW20 . . . . .3█
Hays Bridge Bsns Ctr
  RH9 163
Hays Bridge House RH9 163
Hays Wlk SM2 . . . . .5█
Haysleigh Gdns SE20 43
Haysleigh House SE20 43
Haywain The RH8 122
Hayward Cl SW19 . . . . .4█
Hayward Rd KT7 . . . . .5█
Haywardens RH7 164
Haywards RH10 182
Haywood RG12 27
Hazel Ave
  Farnborough GU14 . . . . .8█
  Guildford GU1 109
Hazel Bank Ewhurst GU6 175
  South Norwood SE25 . . . . .42█
  Tolworth KT5 . . . . .3█
Hazel Cl Brentford TW8 6
  Crawley RH11 181
  Crawley Down RH10 204
  Croydon CR0 43
  Englefield Green TW20 11
  Mitcham CR4 41
  Reigate RH2 139
  Twickenham TW2 . . . . .1█
Hazel Ct Guildford GU1 109
  Warlingham CR6 . . . . .8█
  8 West Norwood SW16 22
Hazel Dr GU23 90

azel Gr Forest Hill SE26 ......23 D4
Haslemere GU26 ....188 E2
Staines TW18 ....13 C2
azel Mead KT17 ....58 A1
azel Par KT22 ....94 C5
azel Rd Ash GU22 ....127 C8
Mytchett GU16 ....86 A2
Reigate RH2 ....139 C7
azel Way Chipstead CR5 ......78 F1
Crawley Down RH10 ....204 C8
Fetcham KT22 ....94 C4
azel Wlk RH5 ....136 C4
azelbank Cl TN16 ....33 C1
azelbank Rd Catford SE6 .....24 E6
Chertsey KT16 ....33 C2
azelbury Cl SW19 ....40 A7
azeldene KT15 ....52 C5
azeldene Ct CR8 ....80 D4
azelhurst Beckenham BR3 .....44 D8
Horley RH6 ....161 C4
azelhurst Cl GU4 ....110 B6
azelhurst Ct Crawley RH22 ...212 F1
azelhurst Ct St6 ....24 C3
azelhurst Dr RH10 ....202 E6
azel Hill RG12 ....27 C6
azell Rd GU9 ....124 F1
azelmere Cl Hatton TW14 ....3 E1
Leatherhead KT22 ....95 B8
azelmere Ct 12 SW2 ....21 F7
azelwick Ave RH10 ....202 B8
azelwick Mill La RH10 .....202 A8
azelwick Rd RH10 ....202 A7
azelwick Sch RH10 ....202 A8
azelwood RH11 ....201 A5
azelwood Ave SM4 ....40 B5
azelwood Ct RH10 ....203 F8
azelwood Cotts
Cranleigh GU6 ....194 D4
Godalming GU7 ....150 D4
azelwood Rd 16 ....37 E3
azelwood Ce CR7 ....81 B6
azelwood House BR2 ....44 E6
azelwood La CR5 ....98 F8
azelwood Lodge BR4 ......44 C2
azelwood Rd
Knaphill GU21 ....68 E1
Oxted RH8 ....123 B3
azelwood Sch RH8 ....123 A4
azeldean Rd CR0, CR9 ....61 D8
azeldon Cross RH19 ......205 B6
azeldene Rd W4 ....7 C8
azelmere Gdns KT4 ......39 A1
azlitt Cl TW13 ....15 E4
azon Way KT19 ....76 C7
adcorn PK CR7 ....41 F5
adcorn Rd Bromley BR1 ..24 F3
Thornton Heath CR7 .....41 F5
adington Cl RG40 ......25 D8
adington Dr RG40 ......25 C8
adington Rd SW18 .....20 C6
adlam Rd SW4 ....21 D8
adley Ave SM6 ....164 D4
adley Cl
Chessington KT19 .....57 A4
Crawley RH10 ....182 D1
adley Common Rd
KT18, KT20 ....116 D7
adley Ct SE26 ....23 C3
adley Dr
Burgh Heath KT18 ....97 B8
New Addington CR0 ...63 C3
adley Gr
Burgh Heath KT18 ....97 C7
Headley KT20 ....116 D7
adley Heath App KT20 .116 B4
adley Rd Ashstead KT18 .96 C6
Grayshott GU26 .....188 C3
Headley KT18 ....96 A4
Headley KT20 ......188 C3
Langley Vale KT21 ..96 C8
Leatherhead KT18, KT22 .95 E4
Mickleham RH5 ......115 E7
adon Ct GU9 ....125 D1
adway Cl TW10 .....17 C4
adway The KT17 ....57 F2
Hearn Vale GU35 ...187 A7
Hearn Wlk RG12 ....27 E8
Hearne Dr W4 ......7 A8
Hearnville Prim Sch SW17 .21 A7
Hearnville Rd SW17 .21 A7
Hearsey Gdns GU17 .64 C6
Heath Bsns Ctr The SW17 .5 C3
Heath Cl Banstead SM7 .78 B5
Heath Cl
Brookwood GU23 ....88 A7
Send GU23 ....90 B5
Sutton SM2 ....59 C2
Walton on t H KT18 .97 A2
West Barnes SW20 ..39 C5
Heath Cts Sch GU9 .125 E6
Heath Ends TW1 ...16 F6
Heath Gr Ashford TW16 .14 F1
Heath SE20 ......23 C1

Heath Hill
Dockenfield GU10 ....166 E3
Dorking RH4 ....136 B7
Heath Hill Rd N RG45 .....45 B5
Heath Hill Rd S RG45 .....45 B4
Heath House
Thornton Heath CR7 ....42 A4
Weybridge KT13 ....53 A6
Heath La Albury GU5 ......132 E2
Crondall GU10 ....141 B1
Godalming GU7, GU8 ....151 A2
Heath End GU9 ....125 C7
Heath Mead SW19 ....19 D5
Heath Mill La SW3 ....88 C2
Heath Rd Bagshot GU19 ...47 E3
Caterham CR3 ....100 D3
Isleworth TW3, TW7 ......5 C3
Oxshott KT22 ....207 D5
Twickenham TW1 ....16 F7
Weybridge KT13 ....53 A5
Woking GU21 ....69 F4
Heath Ridge Gn KT11 .....74 A6
Heath Rise Camberley GU15 .65 D5
Hayes BR2 ....44 F3
Virginia Water GU25 .....31 D5
Westcott RH4 ....135 C5
Heath The CR3 ....100 C3
Heath View KT24 ....92 F2
Heath Way KT21 ....217 D5
Heathacre SL3 ....1 E6
Heatham Pk TW2 ....16 E7
Heathbridge KT13 ....53 A4
Heathcote KT22 ....97 D5
Heathcote Cl GU22 ....106 A3
Heathcote Dr RH19 ....185 C2
Heathcote Rd Ash GU12 ..106 B3
Camberley GU15 ....65 D5
Epsom KT18 ....76 E6
Twickenham TW1 ....6 B2
Heathcroft Ave TW16 ...14 F1
Heathdale Ave TW4 .....4 E4
Heathden KT20 ....77 E1
Heathdene Rd
Streatham SW16 ....21 F1
Wallington SM5, SM6 ..60 B3
Heathdown Rd GU22 ....70 D4
Heathedge SE23, SE26 .23 B6
Heathend Rd Aldershot GU11 .104 E1
Ash GU12 ....106 B5
Copthorne RH10 ......183 B2
Guildford GU23 ......109 B3
Hampton TW12 ....217 D5
Horsham RH12 ....217 D5
Isleworth TW7 ....5 D2
Heatheridge GU22 ...97 E5
Lewisham SE13 ......24 D7
Woking GU21 ....69 C4
Woodham KT15 ....52 B1
Wrecclesham GU9 ....145 F6
Heather Cotts GU12 .106 A8
Heather Cl
Chobham GU24 ....49 E3
South Croydon CR2 ..62 D2
Heather Way
Chobham GU24 ....49 E3
South Croydon CR2 ..62 D2
Heather Wlk
Crawley RH11 ......201 B3
Pirbright GU24 ....87 D7
Smallfield RH6 ....162 C3
Twickenham TW4 ...4 D2
Whiteleys Village KT12 .53 F1
Heatherdale Cl KT2 ..18 B1
Heatherdale Rd GU15 .65 D4
Heatherdeane KT24 ...92 D2
Heatherden Cl CR4 ...40 E5
Heatherdene Mansions 2
TW1 ....6 D1
Heatherlands
Ashford TW15 ......15 A2
Horley RH6 ....161 B4
Heatherley Cl GU15 .65 B5
Heatherley Rd GU15 .65 B5
Heathermount Dr RG45 .45 A6
Heathermount Sch SL5 .29 D3
Heathers Land RH4 ..136 C4
Heathers The TW19 ..13 F8
Heatherset Cl KT13 .55 C5
Heatherset Gdns SW16 .21 F1
Heatherside Dr GU25 .31 A3
Heatherside Rd KT19 .57 D3
Heathervale Rd KT15 .52 E8
Heathervale Rd KT15 .52 E8
Heatherway
Crowthorne RG45 ...45 A5
Felbridge RH19 ....184 F7
Heatherwood Hospl SL5 .28 E6
Heathervale Cobham KT11 .74 A5
Crawley RH10 ......202 D8
Reigate RH2 ......138 D8
Heathfield Ave Ascot SL5 .29 E4
Wandsworth SW18 ..20 D8
Heathfield Cl
Godalming GU7 ....150 E2
Woking GU22 ......70 A1
Heathfield Ct Ashford TW15 .13 E5

Heathfield Ct continued
Penge SE20 ....23 C1
Wandsworth SW18 ....20 D8
Heathfield Dr
Mitcham SW19 ....20 E1
Redhill RH1 ....139 E4
Heathfield Gdns CR0 ......61 D6
Heathfield Inf Sch TW2 ...16 A7
Heathfield Jun Sch TW2 ...16 A7
Croydon CR0 ....61 D6
Heathfield N TW1, TW2 ....16 B8
Heathfield Rd Bromley BR1 .24 F1
Croydon CR0 ....61 D6
Hersham KT12 ....54 E6
Keston BR2 ....44 C5
Wandsworth SW18 ....20 D8
Woking GU22 ....70 A1
Heathfield S TW1, TW2 ..16 F8
Heathfield Sch SL5 ....28 F7
Heathfield Sq SW18 ...20 D8
Heathfield Vale CR2 ..62 E2
Heathhurst Rd CR2 ...61 F2
Heathland Sch The TW4 .4 F1
Heathland St GU11 ...105 A2
Heathlands Tadworth KT20 .97 D5
Upper Tooting SW17 ..21 B6
Weybridge KT13 .....53 C5
Heathlands Cl
Sunbury TW16 ......35 A7
Twickenham TW1 ....16 F7
Woking GU21 ......69 E5
Heathlands Country Mkt
RG40 ....25 E1
Heathlands Ct
Hounslow TW4 ....4 E1
Mitcham CR4 .....41 A6
Heathlands Rd RG40 .25 E2
Heathlands Sch SW19 .19 C5
Heathlands Way TW4 .4 D2
Heathmere Prim Sch
SW15 ....19 A7
Heathmoors RG12 ...27 C4
Heathpark Dr GU22 .89 E3
Heathrise GU23 ...91 B4
Heathrow GU5 ....133 C4
Heathrow Airport London
TW6 ....3 A5
Heathrow Bvd UB7 ..2 A2
Heathrow Causeway Est
TW4 ....4 B4
Heathrow Central Sta TW6 .2 B6
Heathrow Cl TW6 ...2 B6
Heathrow International
Trad Est TW4 ...4 D4
Heathrow Sch UB7 .2 D7
Heathrow Terminal 4 Sta
TW6 ....3 C1
Heathshot 8 TW10 .6 E1
Heathside
Hinchley Wood KT10 .55 E7
Twickenham TW4 ...4 F1
Weybridge KT13 ..53 B5
Heathside Cl KT10 .55 E7
Heathside Cres GU22 .69 F2
Heathside Ct GU22 .97 C4
Heathside Gdns GU22 .70 A2
Heathside La GU22 .188 D6
Heathside Park Rd GU22 .70 A2
Heathside Pk GU15 .66 C7
Heathside Rd GU22 .69 F1
Heathside Sch KT13 .52 F4
Heathvale Bridge
Rd GU12 ....106 A6
Heathview Ct SW19 .19 D6
Heathview Gdns SW15 .19 C8
Heathview Rd
Thornton Heath CR7 .42 A5
Witley GU8 ......170 E7
Heathway Camberley GU15 .65 D5
Caterham CR3 ....100 D2
Croydon CR0 .....62 F7
East Horsley KT24 .93 A3
North Ascot SL5 .28 E8
Heathway Cl GU15 .65 D5
Heathwood Ct
Hinchley Wood KT10 .97 C4
Heathwood Cl
Hounslow TW3 ...5 B3
Heathwood Point SE26 .23 D5
Heathyfields Rd GU9 .125 A6
Heaton Rd CR4 ..21 A1
Heavers Farm Prim Sch
SE25 ....42 F4
Hebdon Rd SW17 .20 F5
Heddon Cl TW7 ..6 A3
Hebdon Wlk 1 GU21 .69 B1
Hedge Cnr KT20 .97 C4
Hedge Croft Cotts GU23 .91 B6
Hedgecourt Pl RH19 .184 E4
Hedgegate Ct 2 W11 .208 B5
Hedgeley Ca GU21 .69 C3
Hedgeside RH11 ...201 C1
Hedgeway GU2 ...130 A7
Hedingham Cl RH6 .161 C4
Hedley Rd TW4 ..4 B5
Heelas Rd RG41 .25 A5
Heenan Cl GU16 .85 E7
Heighton Gdns CR0 .61 B5
Heights Cl Banstead SM7 .77 E3
Wimbledon SW20 ..19 B1
Heights The BR3 .24 C1
Helder Gr SE12 .24 F8
Helder St CR2 ..61 D4
Heldmann Cl CR4 .21 A1
Helen Ave TW14 .15 B8
Helen Cl KT8 ..36 B5
Helen Cl GU3 ..108 D8
Helena Cl SM6 .60 E3
Helford Wlk 3 GU21 .69 A1

Helgiford Gdns TW16 .....14 E1
Helicon House RH11 .....201 C5
Helix Ho TW7 ....6 B5
Helksham Cl GU47 ......45 D1
Helme Cl SW19 ....19 F3
Helmsdale Bracknell RG12 .27 E4
8 Woking GU21 ....69 B1
Helmsdale Rd SW16 ....21 D1
Helston Cl GU16 ......86 A7
Helvellyn Cl TW20 ....12 C1
Helvetia St SE6 .....23 F6
Hemingford Rd SM3 ...58 B6
Hemlock Cl KT20 ....97 D8
Hemming Cl 7 TW12 .36 A8
Hempshaw Ave SM7 ..78 F3
Hemsby Rd KT9 .....56 F4
Hemsby Wlk RH10 ..202 B4
Henage Cnr GU24 ..49 F1
Henbane Ct 2 RH11 .201 B2
Henbit Cl KT20 ..97 B8
Henchley Dene GU4 .110 D4
Henderson Ave GU2 .109 B5
Henderson Hospl SM2 .59 B2
Henderson Rd
Biggin Hill TN16 ..83 C7
Crawley RH11 .....201 B1
Thornton Heath CR7 .42 D3
Wandsworth SW18 ..20 E8
Henderson Way RH12 .216 F1
Hendfield Ct 5 SM6 .60 B4
Hendham Rd SW17 ..20 F6
Hendon Terr TW15 ..14 D2
Hendon Way TW19 ..2 D1
Hendrick Ave SW12 .20 F8
Heneage Cres CR0 .63 C1
Henfield Cotts RH5 .39 F8
Henfold Cotts RH5 .158 A2
Henfold Dr RH5 ...157 E3
Henfold La RH5 ...157 F5
Hengelo Gdns CR4 .40 D5
Hengist Cl RH12 ..217 A1
Hengist Way BR2, BR3 .44 F5
Hengrave Rd SE23 ..23 C8
Hengrove Cres TW15 .13 D5
Henhurst Cross La RH5 .157 A2
Henley Ave SM3 ..58 E7
Henley Bank GU2 .130 A7
Henley Cl Crawley RH10 .202 D3
Farnborough GU14 .84 E8
Hounslow TW7 ....5 F6
Henley Ct Mitcham CR4 .41 A6
Old Woking GU22 .90 A7
Henley Dr Frimley GU16 .85 E7
Kingston u T KT2 .19 A1
Henley Gate GU3 .107 D8
Henley Lodge SE25 .42 F5
Henley Way TW13 .15 D3
Henlow Cl SE6 ..82 A2
Hennel Cl SE23 .23 C5
Hennessy Cl GU22 .89 A5
Henry Cavendish Prim Sch
SW12 ....21 C7
Henry Doulton Dr SW17 .21 B4
Henry Hatch Ct SM2 .59 C3
Henry Peters Dr TW11 .16 E3
Henry Tyndale Sch GU14 .85 B7
Hensford Gdns SE26 .23 B4
Henshaw Cl RH11 .200 F4
Henslow Way GU21 .70 D5
Henson Rd RH10 .202 B7
Hensworth Rd TW15 .13 D3
Henty Cl RH11 ..200 E3
Hepburn Gdns BR2 .44 F1
Hepple Cl TW7 ..6 B5
Hepplewhite Cl RH11 .201 B1
Hepworth Croft GU47 .64 E6
Hepworth Ct SM3 .40 A1
Hepworth Rd SW16 .21 E1
Hepworth Way KT12 .34 F1
Heracles Cl SM6 .60 E3
Herald Ct 5 GU12 .105 B1
Herald Gdns SM6 .60 B7
Herbert Ct RG12 .27 E4
Herbert Cres GU21 .68 E1
Herbert Gdns W4 .7 B8
Herbert Rd Kingston u T KT1 .37 F6
Merton SW19 ....19 F1
Hereford Cl Crawley RH10 .202 D6
Epsom KT18 .....76 D6
Guildford GU2 ..108 F3
Staines TW18 ...33 B8
Hereford Copse GU22 .89 B8
Hereford Ct CR0 .42 F1
Hereford Ho 2 TW10 .6 D2
Hereford La GU9 .125 B7
Hereford Rd TW13 .15 D3
Hereford Way KT9 .56 D5
Hereward Ave CR8 .61 A1
Hereward Rd SW17 .20 F4
Heriot Rd KT16 .33 A2
Heritage 5 KT20 .97 D1
Heritage Cl GU12 .27 E8
Heritage House GU22 .89 E8
Heritage Lawn RH6 .161 C4
Herlwyn Gdns SW17 .20 F4
Hermes House BR3 .43 E8
Hermes Way SM6 .60 D3
Hermitage 5
Claygate KT10 .55 F4
Farnborough GU14 .85 D1
Frimley GU16 ..85 E7
Littleton TW17 .34 B5
Hermitage Ct TW18 .12 F3
Hermitage Cty Jun Sch The
GU21 ....88 E8

Hermitage Dr SL5 ....28 E7
Hermitage Gdns SE19 ....22 C1
Hermitage La Croydon CR0 .43 A3
East Grinstead RH19 ....205 F8
Streatham SW16 ....21 F1
Hermitage Par SL5 .....29 A6
Hermitage Rd
East Grinstead RH19 ...185 D3
Kenley CR8 ....80 C3
Knaphill GU21 ....88 D8
South Norwood SE19 ..22 D2
Hermitage The Barnes SW13 .7 F6
Feltham TW13 ....14 F5
Forest Hill SE23 .....22 F6
Kingston u T KT1 ....37 D5
Richmond TW10 ......6 E2
Hermitage Woods Cres
GU21 ....88 E7
Hermits Rd RH10 ....201 F7
Hermonger La RH12 ..195 F2
Herndon Cl TW20 ...12 A4
Herne Rd KT6 ......56 E8
Heron Cl Cheam SM1 .58 F5
Crawley RH11 .....201 C8
Guildford GU2 ....109 B4
Mytchett GU16 ...85 F4
North Ascot SL5 .28 D8
Heron Ct Dorking RH4 .136 A8
6 Kingston u T KT1 .37 E6
Stanwell TW19 ...13 E7
6 West Norwood SE21 .22 D6
Heron Dale RH15 .52 D5
Heron House KT1 .37 C8
Heron Pl RH1 ....205 F8
Heron Rd Croydon CR0 .61 E8
Isleworth TW1 ...6 B3
Heron Sq 6 TW10 .174 E1
Heron Shaw GU6 .6 D2
Heron Way RH13 .218 A1
Heron Way Cty Prim Sch
RH13 ....218 A1
Heron Wlk GU21 .70 C5
Heron Wood Rd GU12 .126 D7
Herondale Bracknell RG12 .27 C3
Haslemere GU27 ..207 E6
Selsdon CR2 .....62 E7
Herondale Ave SW18 .20 E7
Heronfield TW20 .11 C2
Herons The KT22 .54 A4
Herons Croft KT13 .53 D4
Herons L Ctr The GU27 .207 F6
Herons Lea RH10 .184 A4
Herons Pl TW7 ..6 B4
Herons Way RH1 .87 D6
Herons Wood Ct RH6 .161 B4
Heronscourt GU18 .67 C8
Heronsgate Cty Prim Sch
RH19 ....206 A8
Herrett St GU12 .126 D8
Herretts Gdns GU12 .105 D1
Herrick Cl Crawley RH10 .202 D6
Frimley GU16 ...66 C3
Herrings La GU24 .17 D4
Herschel Wlk 9 RH11 .201 B1
Herschell Rd SE23 .23 E8
Hersham Cl SW15 .19 B8
Hersham Ct 2 KT12 .54 C6
Hersham Gdns KT12 .54 C6
Hersham Rd Hersham KT12 .54 B6
Walton-on-T KT12 .54 B7
Hersham St KT12 .54 E8
Hersham Trad Est KT12 .54 E8
Hertford Ave SW14 .7 E3
Hertford Lodge 10 SW19 .19 E7
Hertford Rd CR4 .41 E5
Hertford Way CR4 .41 E5
Hesiers Hill CR6 .82 E2
Hesiers Rd CR6 .82 F3
Hesketh Cl GU6 .174 E3
Heslop Ct 2 SW12 .21 A7
Heslop Rd SW12 .20 F7
Hessle Gr KT17 .76 F8
Hester Terr TW9 .7 A4
Hestermann Way CR0, CR9 .41 F1
Heston Ave TW5 .4 E7
Heston Comm Sch TW5 .5 A7
Heston Grange TW5 .4 F8
Heston Grange La TW5 .4 F8
Heston Ind Mall TW5 .5 A7
Heston Inf Sch TW5 .5 A7
Heston Jun Sch TW5 .5 A7
Heston Phoenix
Distribution Pk TW5 .4 C8
Heston Rd Heston TW5 .5 A7
Redhill RH1 ......140 A4
Heston Wlk RH1 ..139 F4
Hetherington Rd TW17 .34 C7
Hethersett Cl RH2 .118 C4
Hetley Gdns 5 SE19 .22 F1
Heverfield Ct CR4 .20 F1
Hevers Ave RH6 .161 A4
Hewitt Cl CR0 ..63 A7
Hewitts Ind Est GU6 .173 F2
Hewlett House 8 SW8 .21 C8
Hexham Cl Crawley RH10 .202 E6
Hexham Gdns 7 TW7 .6 A7
Hexham Rd Cheam SM4 .40 B1
West Norwood SE27 ..22 C6
Hextalls La RH1 .120 E6

Heybridge Ave SW16 ....21 F2
Heydon Ct BR4 ....63 E8
Heyford Ave SW20 ....39 F6
Heyford Rd CR4 ....40 C7
Heymede KT22 ....95 C4
Heythorp St SW18 ....19 F6
Heythorpe Cl GU21 ....68 F2
Heyward Ct SM2 ....59 A4
Heywod Dr GU19 ....47 D3
Hibernia Gdns TW3 ....5 A3
Hibernia Rd TW3 ....5 A3
Hickey's Almshouses **7**
    TW9 ....6 F3
Hickling Wlk RH10 ....202 B4
Hickmans Cl RH9 ....121 C3
Hicks La GU17 ....64 B5
Hidaburn Ct **7** SW16 .....21 C4
Hidcote Gdns SW20 ....39 B6
Hidcote House SM2 ....59 C3
Hidecote Cl GU22 ....70 B3
Higgins Wlk TW12 ....15 E2
Higgs La GU19 ....47 D3
High Ashton **11** KT2 ....18 B1
High Ashurst (Outdoor Ctr)
    RH5 ....116 A7
High Barn Rd KT24, RH5 ...113 E3
High Beech Bracknell RG12 ..27 F5
    South Croydon CR2 ....61 E3
High Beeches
    Banstead KT17, SM7 ....77 D5
    Frimley GU16 ....65 D2
High Beeches Cl CR8 ....60 D1
High Broom Cres BR4 ....44 B2
High Cedar Dr SW20 ....19 B1
High Close Sch RG40 ....25 C7
High Coombe Pl KT2 ....18 D1
High Down Rd SM2 ....78 B8
High Dr
    Kingston u T KT2, KT3 ....38 C7
    Oxshott KT22 ....74 D5
    Woldingham CR3 ....102 A5
High Fields SL5 ....29 F4
High Foleys KT10 ....56 B3
High Gables BR2 ....44 E7
High Garth KT10 ....55 C4
High Hill Rd Chelsham CR6 ..82 C5
    Fickleshole CR6 ....82 C5
High La Haslemere GU27 ...208 C8
    Warlingham CR3, CR6 ....101 F8
High Level Dr SE26 ....23 A4
High Limes **2** SE19 ....22 E2
High Loxley Rd GU8 ....193 B7
High Mead BR4 ....63 E8
High Meadow CI RH4 ......136 B6
High Meadow Pl KT16 ......32 F7
High Oaks RH11 ....201 B4
High Par The SW16 ....21 E5
High Park Ave
    East Horsley KT24 ....92 F1
    Richmond TW9 ....7 A6
High Park Rd
    Farnham GU9 ....125 C3
    Richmond TW9 ....7 A6
High Path SW19 ....40 C8
High Path Rd GU1 ....110 C1
High Pewley GU1 ....130 E7
High Pine Cl KT13 ....53 C5
High Pines CR6 ....101 C8
High Pitfold GU26 ....188 D1
High Ridge Byfleet KT14 ....71 E6
    Chipstead CR5, RH2 ....98 F4
    Knaphill GU21 ....68 E1
    Lower Kingswood CR5, RH2 .98 F4
High Ridge GU7 ....150 D2
High St Addlestone KT15 ....52 B6
    Aldershot GU11 ....105 A2
    Aldershot GU11, GU12 ....105 B1
    Ascot SL5 ....29 A6
    Ascot, Sunninghill SL5 .....29 D4
    Bagshot GU19 ....47 E3
    Banstead SM7 ....78 B4
    Beckenham BR3 ....20 E2
    Bletchingley RH1 ....120 D2
    Bracknell RG12 ....27 B7
    Bracknell RG12 ....27 C7
    Bramley GU5 ....151 F6
    Brentford TW8 ....6 D7
    Brentford, Brentford End TW8 .6 D7
    Camberley GU15 ....65 D6
    Carshalton SM5 ....60 A6
    Caterham CR3 ....100 E4
    Cheam SM1, KT17 ....58 D4
    Chobham GU24 ....68 E8
    Claygate KT10 ....55 F4
    Cobham KT11 ....73 B4
    Colnbrook SL3 ....1 C7
    Cranford TW5 ....4 C2
    Cranleigh GU6 ....174 D3
    Crawley RH10 ....201 D6
    Crowthorne RG45 ....45 C4
    Croydon CR0, CR9 ....61 C7
    Croydon, Woodside SE25 ...43 A5
    Dorking RH4 ....136 B8
    East Grinstead RH19 ......205 F8
    East Molesey KT8 ....36 A5
    4 Egham TW20 ....11 F3
    Epsom KT17, KT18 ....76 D6
    Esher KT10 ....55 B6
    Ewell KT17 ....58 A2
    Farnborough GU14 ....105 D8
    Feltham TW13 ....15 A6
    Godalming GU7 ....150 D4
    Godstone RH9 ....121 C4
    Great Bookham KT23 ......94 B2
    Guildford GU1, GU2 ......130 D7

High St *continued*
    Hampton TW12 ....16 C2
    Harlington UB3 ....3 D8
    Harmondsworth UB7 ....2 D8
    Haslemere GU27 ....208 D7
    Heston TW5 ....4 B7
    Horley RH6 ....161 B3
    Houslow TW3 ....5 B4
    Kingston u T KT1 ....37 D6
    Knaphill GU21 ....68 C2
    Leatherhead KT22 ....95 B6
    Limpsfield RH8 ....123 B7
    Lingfield RH7 ....164 D4
    Merstham RH1 ....119 B7
    New Malden KT3 ....38 E5
    Nutfield RH1 ....119 F2
    Old Woking GU22 ....90 B6
    Oxshott KT22 ....74 D5
    Oxted RH8 ....122 D5
    Penge SE19, SE20, BR3 .....23 C1
    Purley CR8 ....80 A8
    Redhill RH1 ....118 F2
    Reigate RH2 ....118 A1
    Ripley GU23 ....91 C6
    Rowledge GU10 ....145 E4
    Rusper RH12 ....199 D7
    Sandhurst GU47 ....64 A8
    Sandhurst, Little
    Sandhurst GU47 ....45 A1
    Shepperton TW17 ....34 C3
    South Norwood CR7, SE25 ..42 D5
    South
    Norwood,Woodside SE25 ...43 A6
    Staines TW18 ....12 F4
    Stanwell TW19 ....2 D1
    Sunningdale SL5 ....30 A4
    Sutton SM1, SM2 ....59 B4
    Sutton SM1 ....59 B6
    Tadworth KT20 ....97 C4
    Teddington TW11 ....17 A3
    Teddington, Hampton
    Hill TW12 ....16 C2
    Teddington, Hampton
    Wick KT1 ....37 D8
    Thames Ditton KT7 ....37 A3
    Twickenham TW2 ....16 C8
    Tyler's Green RH9 ....121 C4
    Walton-on-T KT12 ....35 C1
    West End GU24 ....67 F7
    West Wickham BR4 ....44 B1
    Weybridge KT13 ....53 A6
    Wimbledon SW19 ....19 D3
    Woking GU21 ....69 F2
    Woking, Horsell GU21 ......69 F3
    Wokingham RG40 ....25 D7
High St Mews SW19 ....19 E3
High Standing CR3 ....100 C2
High Street Collier's Wood
    SW17, SW19 ....20 D2
High Street Gn GU8 ....191 F2
High Street Harlington TW6 ..3 D7
High The SW16 ....21 E5
High Thicket Rd GU10 ....166 D5
High Tree CI KT15 ....52 A5
High Trees Croydon CR0 ....43 E1
    Streatham SW2 ....22 A7
High Trees CI CR3 ....100 F5
High Trees Ct
    Caterham CR3 ....100 F4
    Sidlow RH6 ....160 A4
High Trees Rd RH2 ....139 D8
High View Belmont SM2 ....77 F8
    Gomshall GU5 ....133 C4
    5 Penge SE19 ....22 F1
High View Ave CR0, SM6 ...60 F5
High View Cl
    Farnborough GU14 ....85 A4
    South Norwood SE19, SE25 .42 F7
High View Lodge **18** GU11 105 A2
High View Prim Sch SM6 ...60 F5
High View Rd
    Farnborough GU14 ....85 A4
    Guildford GU2 ....129 C6
    Lightwater GU18 ....66 F8
    South Norwood SE19 ......42 F7
Higham Ct RH11 ....136 B4
Highams Hill RH11 ....200 F5
Highams La GU20, GU24 ...49 A5
Highbarrow Rd CR0 ....43 A1
Highbirch Cl RH12 ....218 B5
Highbury Ave CR7 ....42 B7
Highbury Cl
    New Malden KT3 ....38 C4
    West Wickham BR4 ....63 B8
Highbury Cres GU15 ....66 A8
Highbury Gr GU27 ....208 C8
Highbury Rd SW19 ....19 E4
Highclere Ascot SL5 ....29 C4
    Guildford GU1 ....110 A4
Highclere Cl Bracknell RG12 .27 E7
    Kenley CR8 ....80 C4
Highclere Ct GU21 ....68 D2
Highclere Dr GU15 ....66 A7
Highclere Gdns GU21 ......68 D2
Highclere Rd
    Aldershot GU12 ....126 D8
    Kingston u T KT3 ....38 D6
    Knaphill GU21 ....68 D2
Highclere St SE26 ....23 E4
Highcliffe BR3 ....44 B8
Highcliffe Dr SW15 ....7 F1
Highcotts La GU4, GU23 ...91 A1
Highcroft
    Beacon Hill GU26 ....188 D6
    Milford GU8 ....170 F8
    Purley CR8 ....79 F5
    Shamley Green GU5 ....152 E4
    2 Surbiton KT5 ....37 F4
Highcroft Ct KT23 ....94 A4

Highcroft Dr RH12 ....195 E1
Highcross Way **4** SW15 ..19 A7
Highdaun Dr SW16 ....41 F5
Highdene **6** GU22 ....69 F1
Highdown KT4 ....57 F6
Highdown Ct RH10 ....202 B3
Highdown Way RH12 ......217 F6
Higher Alham RG12 ....27 F2
Higher Dr
    Belmont KT17, SM7 ....77 D6
    East Horsley KT24 ....112 E8
    Purley CR8 ....80 A6
Higher Gn KT17 ....77 A6
Highercombe Rd GU27 ....208 E8
Highfield Bracknell RG12 ...26 F3
    Feltham TW15 ....15 A2
    Guildford GU4 ....130 F1
    Oxshott KT22 ....74 B5
    Woodmansterne SM7 ......78 E2
Highfield Ave GU11 ....126 A8
Highfield Cl
    Aldershot GU11 ....126 B8
    Englefield Green TW20 ....11 C2
    Farnborough GU14 ....84 F4
    Farnham GU9 ....146 B7
    Long Ditton KT6 ....37 C1
    Oxshott KT22 ....74 B5
    Rowledge GU10 ....145 E4
Highfield Cres GU26 ....188 F4
Highfield Ct
    Englefield Green TW20 ....11 D2
    Mitcham CR4 ....40 E5
Highfield Dr
    Beckenham BR2 ....44 F5
    West Ewell KT19 ....57 F4
    West Wickham BR4 ....63 C7
Highfield Gdns GU11 ......126 B8
Highfield La GU27 ....22 E3
Highfield Inf Sch BR2 ......44 E5
Highfield Jun Sch BR2 .....44 E5
Highfield La
    Puttenham GU3 ....128 A3
    Thursley GU8 ....169 B2
Highfield Path GU14 ....84 F4
Highfield Rd
    Biggin Hill TN16 ....83 C3
    Carshalton SM1 ....59 E5
    Caterham CR3 ....101 A6
    Chertsey KT16 ....33 A1
    East Grinstead RH19 ......185 D3
    Farnborough GU14 ....84 F4
    Feltham TW13 ....15 A7
    Hounslow TW7 ....5 F7
    Purley CR8 ....61 A1
    Tolworth KT5 ....38 C2
    Upper Halliford TW16 ......34 F4
    Walton-on-T KT12 ....35 A1
    West Byfleet KT14 ....71 A6
Highfield Sch SW18 ....20 B8
Highfields Ashtead KT21 ...95 D8
    East Horsley KT24 ....112 F7
    Fetcham KT22 ....94 D3
    Forest Row RH18 ....206 F2
    Richmond TW10 ....6 D2
Highgate Ct Crawley RH11 201 C2
    Farnborough GU14 ....85 A4
Highgate House **11** SE26 .23 A5
Highgate La GU14 ....85 C5
Highgate Rd RH18 ....206 F1
Highgate Wlk SE23 ....23 C6
Highgrove **2** GU14 ....85 B7
Highgrove Ct BR3 ....24 A1
Highgrove House GU4 ....110 C3
Highland Cotts SM6 ....60 C6
Highland Croft BR3 ....24 B2
Highland Lodge **8** SE19 ..22 F1
Highland Pk TW13 ....14 F4
Highland Rd
    Aldershot GU12 ....105 D2
    Beare Green RH5 ....157 D3
    Bromley BR1, BR2 ....44 F8
    Camberley GU15 ....65 E8
    Purley CR8 ....80 A5
    West Norwood SE19 ....22 E2
Highlands Ave
    Horsham RH13 ....217 E2
    Leatherhead KT22 ....95 C5
Highlands Cl
    Farnham GU9 ....146 B7
    Hounslow TW3 ....5 B6
    Leatherhead KT22 ....95 B5
Highlands Cres RH13 ......217 E2
Highlands Ct SE19 ....22 E2
Highlands Heath SW15 ....19 C8
Highlands La GU22 ....89 B6
Highlands Pk KT22 ....95 D4
Highlands Rd
    Heath End GU9 ....125 C7
    Horsham RH13 ....217 F2
    Leatherhead KT22 ....95 C5
    Reigate RH2 ....118 D2
Highlands The KT24 ....92 E2
Highmead Gu7 ....150 F6
Highpoint KT13 ....53 A5
Highridge Cl KT18 ....76 E5
Highridge Ct KT17 ....58 A1
Highview CR3 ....100 E2
Highview Cres GU15 ....46 F1
Highview Ct
    2 Pulney SW19 ....19 E7
    2 Reigate RH2 ....118 D1
Highview High Sch SM6 ....60 C3
Highway RG45 ....45 A5
Highway The SM2 ....59 C2
Highwayman's Ridge
    GU20 ....48 B6
Highwold CR5 ....79 A1
Highwood Cl CR8 ....80 C2

Highwoods Caterham CR3 .100 E2
    Leatherhead KT22 ....95 C6
Hilary Ave CR4 ....41 A6
Hilary Dr RG45 ....45 B6
Hilbert Rd SM3 ....58 D7
Hilborough Cl SW19 ....20 C1
Hildenborough Gdns BR1 ..24 F2
Hildenbrough House BR3 ...23 F1
Hildenlea Pl BR2 ....44 E7
Hildenley Cl RH1 ....119 D7
Hildens The RH4 ....135 C5
Hilder Gdns GU14 ....85 D3
Hilders La TN8 ....144 F4
Hilders The KT21 ....76 B2
Hiddicth House **7** TW10 ....6 E1
Hildreth St SW12 ....21 B7
Hildreth Street Mews
    SW12 ....21 B7
Hilgay GU1 ....109 F1
Hilgay Cl GU1 ....109 F1
Hilgay Ct GU1 ....109 F1
Hill Cl Purley CR8 ....80 C6
    Woking GU21 ....69 D3
    Wonersh GU5 ....152 B6
Hill Copse View RG12 ......27 E8
Hill Cres Kingston u T KT5 .37 F4
    North Cheam KT4 ....58 C8
Hill Crest
    Dormans Park RH19 ....185 E6
    Elstead GU8 ....148 D4
Hill Crest Dr GU10 ....146 F6
Hill Ct La Farncombe GU7 .150 E6
    Haslemere GU27 ....208 B6
    8 Kingston u T KT2 .....18 B1
    14 Kingston u T KT6 ....37 E4
Hill Dr SW16 ....41 F6
Hill Field Rd TW12 ....15 F8
Hill Gr TW13 ....15 F6
Hill House Cl RH10 ....204 A5
Hill House Dr
    Hampton TW12 ....36 A8
    Reigate RH2 ....139 B7
    Weybridge KT13 ....72 A8
Hill House Rd SW16 ....21 F3
Hill La KT20 ....97 E6
Hill Manor RH12 ....217 B2
Hill Mead RH12 ....217 B3
Hill Park Dr KT22 ....94 F8
Hill Rd Beacon Hill GU26 ..188 C6
    Carshalton SM5 ....59 E4
    Fetcham KT22 ....94 B5
    Grayshott GU26 ....188 C2
    Haslemere GU27 ....208 C6
    Heath End GU9 ....125 D7
    Mitcham CR4 ....21 B1
    Purley CR8 ....79 F7
    Sutton SM1 ....59 B5
Hill Rise Dorking RH4 ......115 A1
    Forest Hill SE23 ....23 B7
    Hinchley Wood KT10 ....56 B8
    Richmond TW10 ....6 D2
Hill The CR3 ....100 F3
Hill Top SM3, SM4 ....39 F2
Hill View CR4 ....41 E5
Hill View Cl Purley CR8 ....80 B8
    Tadworth KT20 ....97 C6
Hill View Cres GU2 ....109 B3
Hill View Ct **16** GU22 .....69 E1
Hill View Rd Claygate KT10 .56 A3
    Farnham GU9 ....124 F2
    Twickenham TW1 ....6 A1
    Woking GU22 ....69 E1
Hillacre GU3 ....100 E2
Hillard Ct SM6 ....60 D4
Hillars Heath Rd CR5 ......79 E4
Hillary Cl
    East Grinstead RH19 .....186 A3
    3 Farnham GU9 ....146 B7
Hillary Cres KT12 ....35 C1
Hillary Ct TW19 ....13 E2
Hillary House **11** RH1 ...118 F2
Hillary Rd GU9 ....146 A7
Hillbarn CR2 ....80 E8
Hillberry RG12 ....27 C2
Hillbrook Gdns KT13 ....53 A3
Hillbrook Prim Sch
    & Hillcroft Sch Annexe
    SW17 ....21 A4
Hillbrook Rd SW17 ....21 A4
Hillbrook Rise GU9 ....125 B6
    New Malden KT3 ....38 E4
    3 Reigate RH2 ....118 C1
Hillbrow Cl GU3 ....108 B2
Hillbrow Cotts RH9 ....121 C3
Hillbrow Ct RH9 ....121 C3
Hillbrow Rd Catford BR1 ...24 E2
    Esher KT10 ....55 C5
Hillbury Cl CR6 ....81 C1
Hillbury Gdns CR6 ....81 C1
Hillbury Rd
    Upper Tooting SW17 ......21 B5
    Warlingham CR3, CR6 ....81 B1
Hillcote Ave SW16 ....22 B1
Hillcrest Heath End GU9 ..125 D8
    Weybridge KT13 ....53 B7
Hillcrest Ave KT16 ....51 E6
Hillcrest Cl
    Beckenham BR3 ....43 F3
    Crawley RH10 ....202 D6
    Epsom KT18 ....76 F4
    Forest Hill SE26 ....23 A4
Hillcrest Ct Sutton SM2 ....59 D4
    Weybridge KT13 ....53 B7
Hillcrest Gdns KT10 ....55 F7
Hillcrest House GU4 ....110 C3
Hillcrest Par CR5 ....79 B5

Hillcrest Rd
    Biggin Hill TN16 ....83 D3
    Camberley GU15 ....66 B7
    Guildford GU2 ....108 F2
    Kenley CR3 ....80 D3
    Purley CR8 ....60 F1
Hillcrest View BR3 ....43 F3
Hillcroft Ave CR5, CR8 .....79 D6
Hillcroft Coll KT6 ....37 E3
Hillcroft Cty Prim Sch
    Caterham CR3 ....100 E4
    Whyteleafe CR3 ....100 F6
Hillcroome Rd SM2 ....59 D4
Hillcross Ave Merton SM4 ..39 E4
    West Barnes SM4 ....39 E4
Hillcross Mid Sch SM4 .....39 F5
Hilldale Rd SM1 ....58 F6
Hilldeane Rd CR8 ....61 A1
Hilldown Ct SW16 ....21 E1
Hilldown Rd
    Streatham SW16 ....21 E1
    Wickham BR2 ....44 F1
Hilley Field La KT22 ....94 C6
Hillfield Ave SM4 ....40 E4
Hillfield Cl Guildford GU1 .110 C3
    Redhill RH1 ....119 A1
Hillfield Rd RH1 ....119 A1
Hilford Pl RH1 ....140 A3
Hillgate GU26 ....188 D5
Hillgate PI SW12 ....21 B8
Hillhouse La RH12 ....194 F1
Hillhurst Gdns CR3 ....100 E7
Hillier Gdns CR0 ....61 A5
Hillier House GU1 ....130 B7
Hillier Lodge TW12 ....16 D3
Hillier Mews GU1 ....110 A1
Hillier PI KT9 ....56 C6
Hillier Rd GU1 ....110 A1
Hillier's La CR0, SM6 ....60 E7
Hillingdale Biggin Hill TN16 .203 D1
    Crawley RH11 ....201 D1
Hillingdon Ave TW19 ......13 E7
Hillmead RH11 ....200 F6
Hillmont Rd KT10 ....55 E7
Hillmore Gr SE26 ....23 E3
Hillmount **18** GU22 ....69 E1
Hillrise Brands Hill SL3 ......1 A8
    Walton-on-T KT12 ....34 F2
Hills Farm La RH12 ....216 F1
Hills Pl RH12 ....217 A2
Hillsborough Ct GU14 .....84 E8
Hillsborough Pk GU15 .....66 C5
Hillside Ascot SL5 ....29 C4
    Banstead SM7 ....77 E4
    Crawley Down RH10 ......204 B8
    Forest Row RH18 ....206 E3
    Horsham RH13 ....217 E2
    Sandhurst GU15 ....64 F7
    Wentworth GU25 ....31 C3
    Wimbledon SW19 ....19 D2
    Woking GU22 ....89 D7
Hillside Ave CR8 ....80 B8
Hillside Cl Banstead SM7 ...77 E3
    Brockham RH3 ....137 A8
    Crawley RH11 ....201 B4
    East Grinstead RH19 .....185 E3
    Headley Down GU35 ......187 A8
    Knaphill GU21 ....68 D2
    Merstham RH1 ....119 E7
    7 Kingston u T KT2 .....18 B1
Hillside Gdns
    Addlestone KT15 ....51 F1
    Brockham RH3, RH1 ....116 A3
    Streatham SW2 ....22 A6
    Wallington SM6 ....60 D3
Hillside La Coney Hall BR2 ..63 F8
    Heath End GU9 ....125 D8
Hillside Pk SL5 ....29 F1
Hillside Rd
    Aldershot GU11 ....126 A8
    Ash GU12 ....106 B1
    Ashtead KT21 ....75 F2
    Beckenham BR2 ....44 F6
    Belmont SM2 ....59 B1
    Coulsdon CR5 ....79 B4
    Croydon CR0 ....61 B8
    East Ewell KT17 ....58 C1
    Farnham GU10 ....146 C1
    Heath End GU9 ....125 E6
    Kingston u T KT5 ....38 A4
    Linchmere GU27 ....207 A1
    Streatham SW2 ....22 A6
    Tatsfield TN16 ....103 E6
    Warlingham CR3, CR6 ....101 A8
    Whyteleafe CR3, CR6 ......81 A1
Hillside Way GU7 ....150 D4
Hillsmead Way CR2 ....81 B6
Hillspur Cl GU2 ....108 F2
Hillspur Rd GU2 ....108 F2
Hilltop Cl Ascot SL5 ....29 E1
    Guildford GU3 ....108 F5
Hilltop Ct SE19 ....22 C4
Hilltop Cl SL9 ....42 D8
Hilltop La CR3, RH1 ....100 A4
Hilltop Rd Kenley CR3 ......80 D3
    Reigate RH2 ....139 C6
Hilltop Rise KT23 ....94 C2
Hilltop Wlk CR3 ....101 E6
Hillview CR3 ....100 E2
Hillview Whyteleafe CR3 ...80 F7
    Wimbledon SW20 ....19 B1
Hillview Ct SE19 ....19 E8
Hillview Dr SE20 ....43 B8
Hillview Mid Sch 51 B7
Hillview Rd SM1 ....59 D7
Hillworth BR3 ....44 B8
Hillworth Rd SW2 ....22 A8
Hilly Mead SW19 ....19 E1

ybarn Rd RH11 . . . . .180 C1
ea Point ⁊ SW15 . . . . .19 B7
on Ct RH6 . . . . .161 C4
on Way CR2 . . . . .81 B4
ley Rd SW17 . . . . .20 F2
chcliffe Cl SM6 . . . . .60 F3
chley Cl KT10 . . . . .55 F7
chley Dr KT10 . . . . .55 F7
chley Way KT10 . . . . .56 A7
chley Wood Prim Sch
  KT10 . . . . .56 A8
chley Wood Sta KT10 . . . .56 B7
dell Cl GU14 . . . . .85 A8
dhead Cl RH11 . . . . .201 C4
dhead Point ⁊ SW15 . . . .19 B7
dhead Rd GU26, GU27 . . . .188 F2
dhead Way SM6 . . . . .60 E5
dsley's Pl SE23 . . . . .23 C6
kler Cl SM6 . . . . .60 E3
stock Cl GU14 . . . . .85 A5
kler Cl SM6 . . . . .60 E3
ton Ave TW4 . . . . .4 D3
ton Cl RG45 . . . . .45 B7
ton Dr RG45 . . . . .45 B7
ton Rd SM6 . . . . .60 C4
ley Ct GU1 . . . . .130 B7
ley Ct GU1 . . . . .130 B7
hcock Cl ⁊ TW17 . . . . .33 F6
chings Way RH2 . . . . .139 A5
ner Green Hospl SE13 . . .24 D8
ner Green La SE13 . . . . . . .24 E8
nver Cl GU2 . . . . .130 C6
nerfield Prim Sch SW2 . . .22 A6
nerfield Rd SW16, SW27 . .22 A5
nerhooks Hill RG42 . . . . . . .26 E8
nermoor Rd TW19 . . . . .2 A2
nerwood Gu6 . . . . .174 E2
nerwood Cl RH7 . . . . .118 E3
nerwood Ct SE21 . . . . .22 E7
nerwood Dr SE19, SE21 . .22 E7
adly Rd SM6 . . . . .21 D6
art Cl SE7 . . . . .42 D6
art Pl ⁊ TW10 . . . . .6 F1
art Rd L14 . . . . .58 B7
obs Ind Est RH7 . . . . .184 D7
obs Rd Crawley RH11 . . . .201 A2
  West Norwood SE27 . . . . . .22 A5
olli Wlk KT5 . . . . .37 F3
cken Mead RH10 . . . . .202 D8
ckering Gdns GU22 . . . . . .70 B1
ckering Rd GU22 . . . . .70 B1
ckerfield Cl GU23 . . . . .88 B1
dge La SL5 . . . . .9 A2
dges Cl GU19 . . . . .47 E1
dgkin Cl RH10 . . . . .202 C5
dgson Gdns GU1, GU4 . . .109 C3
e Bridge Sch GU22 . . . . . . .90 C8
e Cotts GU5 . . . . .154 B4
e La Hascombe GU8 . . . . .172 D4
aslake GU5, RH5 . . . . .154 F8
ebridge Golf Ctr GU22 . . .90 C8
ebrook Glade GU2 . . . . . . .130 B8
garth Ave TW15 . . . . .14 C2
garth Bsns Pk W4 . . . . .7 E8
garth Cl GU47 . . . . .64 E6
garth Cres
  tcham CR4, SW19 . . . . .40 D8
  orough Heath CR0 . . . . .42 C2
garth Ct Dulwich SE19 . . . .22 F4
  ston TW5 . . . . .4 E7
garth Gdns TW5 . . . . .4 E7
garth House ⁊ SE27 . . . . .22 C4
garth La W4 . . . . .7 D8
garth Rd RH10 . . . . .201 F3
garth Roundabout W4 . . . . .7 E8
garth Way KT12 . . . . .36 C8
ghatch La GU9 . . . . .125 A6
goak La SL4 . . . . .8 A1
jscross La CR5 . . . . .98 F5
gsmill Way KT11 . . . . .73 C5
gspudding La RH5 . . . . . .158 C1
ogbrook Cl Gu9 . . . . .69 F1
obrook Cl TW20 . . . . .125 F8
obrook Cty Prim Sch
  RH12 . . . . .217 E2
obrook Sch SW2 . . . . .21 F7
obrook Meadow TW20 . . .12 D2
obrook School La RH12 . .217 E2
obrook Way GU11 . . . . . .126 B7
con Ct RH1 . . . . .119 A4
der Rd Aldershot GU12 . .105 C1
kfield RH1 . . . . .202 B3
dderness Way SE27 . . . . . .22 B4
ddernesse Rd
  eworth TW7 . . . . .6 A6
  Upper Tooting SW17 . . . . . .21 A6
ddlast La GU27 . . . . .208 F7
dsworth House ⁊ SW2 . . .22 A8
le Hill RH4 . . . . .135 B7
mbledon SW20 . . . . .39 B8
land Cl Coney Hall BR2 . . .63 F8
rnham GU9 . . . . .146 E8
edhill RH1 . . . . .118 F1

Holland Cres RH8 . . . . .123 A2
Holland Cty Jun Sch
  RH8 .123 A1
Holland Dr SE23 . . . . .23 E5
Holland Gdns TW20 . . . . . . .32 F7
Holland Rd RH8 . . . . .123 A2
Holland Pines RG12 . . . . . . .26 F2
Holland Rd Croydon SE25 . . .43 A4
  Oxted RH8 . . . . .123 A1
Holland Way BR2 . . . . .63 F8
Hollands Field RH13 . . . . . .216 E4
Hollands The
  Feltham TW13 . . . . .15 D4
  New Malden KT4 . . . . .38 F1
Hollands Way
  East Grinstead RH19 . . . . .186 A4
  Warnham RH12 . . . . .216 F8
Holles Cl TW12 . . . . .16 A3
Hollies Ave KT14 . . . . .70 F6
Hollies Cl
  South Norwood SW16 . . . . .22 A2
  Twickenham TW1 . . . . .16 F6
Hollies Ct KT15 . . . . .52 C5
Hollies Way ⁊ SW12 . . . . . .21 A8
Hollin Ct RH10, RH11 . . . . .181 E1
Hollingbourne Cres
  RH11 . . . . .201 C1
Hollingsworth Rd CR0, CR2 .62 B4
Hollington Cres KT3 . . . . . . .39 A3
Hollingworth Cl KT8 . . . . . . .35 F5
Hollingworth Ct ⁊ KT6 . . . .37 D2
Hollis Wood Dr GU10 . . . . .145 E5
Hollman Gdns SW16 . . . . . .22 B2
Hollow Cl GU2 . . . . .130 B8
Hollow La
  Dormansland RH19, RH7 . .186 D6
  Virginia Water GU25 . . . . . . .31 C6
  Wotton RH5 . . . . .134 D2
Hollow The Crawley RH11 . .200 F5
  Shackleford GU7 . . . . .149 F4
Holloway Dr GU25 . . . . .31 E5
Holloway Hill
  Godalming GU7 . . . . .150 D4
  Lyne KT16 . . . . .51 D8
Holloway La TW19 . . . . .2 E8
Holloway St TW3 . . . . .5 B4
Holly Acre Frimley GU16 . . . .66 B2
  Walton-on-T KT12 . . . . .35 D1
Holly Ave KT15 . . . . .52 A1
Holly Bank Rd GU22 . . . . . . .89 B7
Holly Bush Ind Pk GU12 . .105 E5
Holly Bush La
  Farnborough GU14 . . . . . . .105 E6
  Hampton TW12 . . . . .15 F1
Holly Cl Aldershot GU12 . . .105 C2
  Crawley RH10 . . . . .202 A8
  Englefield Green TW20 . . . . .11 B2
  Farnborough GU14 . . . . . . .105 E6
  Feltham TW13 . . . . .15 E3
  Headley Down GU35 . . . . . .187 C5
  Longcross KT16 . . . . .50 B7
  Woking GU21 . . . . .89 B7
Holly Cott KT7 . . . . .37 A1
Holly Cres BR3 . . . . .43 F4
Holly Ct ⁊ Belmont SM2 . . . .59 A3
  Leatherhead KT22 . . . . .95 C6
Holly Gn KT13 . . . . .53 D6
Holly Grove Cl TW3 . . . . .4 F3
Holly Hedge Cl GU16 . . . . . .65 E2
Holly Hedge Rd
  Cobham KT11 . . . . .73 B5
  Frimley GU16 . . . . .65 E2
Holly Hill Dr SM7 . . . . .78 A3
Holly Hock Cl GU8 . . . . .68 A4
Holly Hough KT20 . . . . .116 B5
Holly Lea Banstead SM7 . . . .78 C2
  Godalming GU7 . . . . .150 C4
  Woodmansterne SM7 . . . . . .78 C2
  Worplesdon GU3 . . . . .108 D7
Holly La E SM7 . . . . .78 B3
Holly La W SM7 . . . . .78 B2
Holly Lea GU4 . . . . .109 D7
Holly Lodge Mid
  Sch GU22 . . . . .105 F8
Holly Rd Aldershot GU12 . .105 D1
  Farnborough GU14 . . . . .16 C2
  Hampton TW12 . . . . .16 C2
  Hounslow TW3 . . . . .5 B3
  Reigate RH2 . . . . .139 B7
  Twickenham TW1 . . . . .17 A7
Holly Ridge GU8 . . . . .67 E6
Holly Spring Cty Inf Sch
  RG12 .27 E7
Holly Spring Cty Jun Sch
  RG12 .27 E7
Holly Spring La RG12 . . . . . .27 D8
Holly Tree Rd SE3 . . . . .100 E5
Holly Way Blackwater GU17 .64 E5
  Mitcham CR4 . . . . .41 D6
Holly Wlk SL4 . . . . .9 E4
Hollybank GU21 . . . . .67 F6
Hollybank Cl TW12 . . . . .16 A3
Hollybank Rd KT14 . . . . .71 A5
Hollybush Rd
  Crawley RH10 . . . . .201 E8
  Kingston u T KT2 . . . . .17 E3
Hollybush Ride GU19, GU20 .47 F6
Hollycombe TW20 . . . . .11 D4
Hollycroft Cl
  Harmondsworth UB7 . . . . . . .3 A8
  South Croydon CR2 . . . . .61 E5
Hollycroft Gdns UB7 . . . . . . .3 A8
Hollydene BR1 . . . . .44 F8
Hollyfield Rd KT5 . . . . .37 F2

Hollyfields Sch KT6 . . . . . . .37 E4
Hollyfields Cl GU15 . . . . . . .65 B5
Hollymead SM5 . . . . .59 F7
Hollymead Rd CR5 . . . . .79 A1
Hollymeoak Rd CR5 . . . . . . .79 B1
Hollymoor La KT19 . . . . .57 D1
Hollymount Prim Sch
  SW20 . . . . .39 C8
Hollyridge GU27 . . . . .208 B6
Hollytree Cl SW19 . . . . .19 D7
Hollytree Gdns GU16 . . . . . .85 D8
Hollywoods CR0 . . . . .62 F2
Holm Cl KT15 . . . . .70 E7
Holm Ct Dorking RH4 . . . . .136 B4
  Farncombe GU7 . . . . .150 D7
Holman Ct KT17 . . . . .58 A5
Holman Rd KT19 . . . . .57 C5
Holmbank Dr TW17 . . . . . . .34 E5
Holmbrook Cl GU14 . . . . . . .84 C4
Holmbury Ave RG45 . . . . . . .45 A7
Holmbury Cl RH11 . . . . .201 C4
Holmbury Ct
  Mitcham SW19 . . . . .20 E1
  Upper Tooting SW17 . . . . . .20 F5
Holmbury Dr RH5 . . . . .136 C4
Holmbury Gr CR0 . . . . .62 F3
Holmbury Hill Rd RH5 . . . .155 B3
Holmbury Rd RH5 . . . . .155 D1
Holmbush Cl RH12 . . . . . . .217 D6
Holmcroft Crawley RH10 . .201 E5
  Walton on t H KT20 . . . . .97 B2
Holmdene Cl BR3 . . . . .44 C7
Holme Chase KT13 . . . . .53 C4
Holme Cl RG45 . . . . .45 A7
Holmes Cl Ascot SL5 . . . . . .29 C3
  Woking GU23 . . . . .89 F6
  Wokingham RG41 . . . . .25 A4
Holmes Cres RG41 . . . . .25 A4
Holmes Rd Merton SW19 . .20 C1
  Twickenham TW1 . . . . .16 F6
Holmesdale Cl SE25 . . . . . . .43 A6
Holmesdale Ave SW14 . . . . . .7 B3
Holmesdale Cl
  Guildford GU1 . . . . .110 B2
  South Norwood SE25 . . . . . .42 F6
Holmesdale Rd
  Dorking RH5 . . . . .136 C3
  Reigate RH2 . . . . .118 B2
  Richmond TW9 . . . . .7 A6
  South Norwood SE25 . . . . . .42 E5
  South Nutfield RH1 . . . . . . .140 F7
  Teddington TW11 . . . . .17 C2
  Thornton Heath CR0 . . . . . . .42 D4
Holmethorpe Ave RH1 . . . .119 B4
Holmethorpe Ind
  Est RH1 . . . . .119 B4
Holmewood Cl RG41 . . . . . .25 A2
Holmewood Gdns SW2 . . . .21 F8
Holmewood Rd
  South Norwood SE25 . . . . . .42 E6
  Streatham SW2 . . . . .21 F8
Holmgrove House CR8 . . . . .80 A7
Holming End KT22 . . . . .218 B5
Holmlea Ct ⁊ CR0 . . . . .61 E7
Holmlea Rd SM6 . . . . .60 D4
Holmlea Wlk SL3 . . . . .1 B7
Holmoaks House BR3 . . . . . .44 C7
Holmsdale Cl Inf Sch
  RH2 .118 B3
Holmsley Cl SE26, SE6 . . . .23 C4
Holmsley Ct ⁊ SW16 . . . . . .21 D6
Holmwood ⁊ KT5 . . . . .37 F3
Holmwood Cl CR2 . . . . .80 F6
Holmwood
  Cl Addlestone KT15 . . . . . . .52 A5
  Cheam SM2 . . . . .58 D3
  East Horsley KT24 . . . . .112 E6
Holmwood Gdns SM6 . . . . . .60 B4
Holmwood Rd
  Belmont SM2, SM1, SM2 . .58 B4
  Chessington KT9 . . . . .56 D5
Holmwood Sta RH5 . . . . . . .157 C4
Holmwood View Rd RH5 . .136 B1
Holne Chase SM4 . . . . .40 A3
Holstein Ave KT13 . . . . .53 A6
Holsworthy Way KT9 . . . . . .56 C5
Holt Cl GU14 . . . . .85 C7
Holt La RG41 . . . . .25 B7
Holt Pound La GU10 . . . . . .145 C5
Holt Sch The RG41 . . . . .25 B7
Holt The Morden SM4 . . . . . .40 A5
  Wallington SM6 . . . . .60 D6
Holt Wood CR6 . . . . .82 A3
Holton Heath ⁊ RG12 . . . . .27 F5
Holtwood Rd KT22 . . . . .74 C6
Holtye Ave RH19 . . . . .186 A3
Holtye Rd RH19 . . . . .186 B3
Holtye Wlk RH10 . . . . .202 A4
Holy Cross Catholic Prim
  Sch 24 C7
Holy Cross Hospl SE7 . . . .207 F7
Holy Cross RC Convent
  Sch KT3 . . . . .38 E4
Holy Cross RC Prep Sch
  KT2 . . . . .18 C1
Holy Family RC Prim Sch
  The KT15 . . . . .52 B6
Holy Ghost RC Prim Sch
  SW12 .21 A8
Holy Trinity C of E Inf Sch
  SW17 .20 F6
Holy Trinity C of E Prim Sch
  Forest Hill SE23 . . . . .23 C6
  Streatham SW2 . . . . .21 F8
  West End GU24 . . . . .68 A7
  Wimbledon SW19 . . . . .20 B2
Holy Trinity CE Aided Sch
  SL5 . . . . .30 A3

Holy Trinity CE Jun Sch
  TW10 . . . . .7 A3
Holy Trinity CE Sch The
  RH11 .201 A4
Holy Trinity Church of
  England Jun Sch SM6 . . . . .60 C6
Holy Trinity Sch GU1 . . . . .130 F7
Holybourne Ave SW15 . . . . .19 A8
Holyhead Ct KT1 . . . . .37 D5
Holyhook Cl RG45 . . . . .45 A6
Holyoake Ave GU21 . . . . . . .69 C2
Holyoake Cres GU21 . . . . . . .69 C2
Holyrood RH19 . . . . .206 A8
Holyrood Pl RH11 . . . . .201 B2
Holywell Cl
  Farnborough GU14 . . . . .85 A7
  Stanwell TW19 . . . . .13 E7
Holywell Way TW19 . . . . . . .13 E7
Homan House ⁊ SW4 . . . . . .21 D8
Hombrook Dr RG42 . . . . .26 E8
Hombrook House RG42 . . . .26 E8
Home Cl Carshalton SM5 . . .59 F8
  Crawley RH10 . . . . .202 C8
  Fetcham KT22 . . . . .94 D6
Home Ct KT6 . . . . .37 D4
Home Farm Cl
  Betchworth RH3 . . . . .137 E8
  Burgh Heath KT18 . . . . .77 D2
  Esher KT10 . . . . .55 B4
  Farnborough GU14 . . . . .85 D6
  Ottershaw KT16 . . . . .51 A3
  Thames Ditton KT7 . . . . .36 F2
  Upper Halliford TW17 . . . . .34 E5
  Surbiton KT6, KT19 . . . . . . .56 E7
Home Farm Cotts GU4 . . . .149 C5
Home Farm Gdns KT12 . . . .54 C8
Home Farm Rd GU7 . . . . . .150 F2
Home Meadow SM7 . . . . . . .78 B5
Home Park Cl GU5 . . . . .151 F6
Home Park Rd SW19 . . . . . .19 F4
Home Park Wlk KT1 . . . . . . .37 D5
Home Pk RH8 . . . . .123 A4
Homebeech House ⁊
  GU22 .69 E1
Homecoppice House ⁊
  BR1 . . . . .24 F1
Homecourt TW14 . . . . .15 A7
Homecroft Rd SE26 . . . . . . .23 C3
Homefield Morden SM4 . . . .40 A5
  Thursley GU8 . . . . .169 C3
Homefield Cl Horley RH6 . .161 B4
  Leatherhead KT22 . . . . .95 C6
  Woodham KT15 . . . . .70 E7
Homefield Gdns
  Burgh Heath KT20 . . . . .97 C7
  Mitcham CR4, SW19 . . . . . . .40 D7
Homefield House ⁊ 23 D5
  SE26 .23 D5
Homefield Pk SM1, SM2 . . .59 B4
Homefield Prep Sch SM1 . .59 A5
Homefield Rd
  Coulsdon CR3, CR5 . . . . . .100 B7
  Walton-on-T KT12 . . . . .35 E2
  Warlingham CR6 . . . . .101 C8
  Wimbledon SW19 . . . . .19 E3
Homegreen House ⁊ SM6 .60 C6
Homeland Dr SM2 . . . . .59 B2
Homelands GU1 . . . . .95 C6
Homelands Dr SE19 . . . . . . .22 E1
Homelea Cl GU14 . . . . .85 B8
Homeleigh Cres GU12 . . . .106 A8
Homeleigh Ct ⁊ SW16 . . . . .21 E5
Homemead SW12 . . . . .21 B6
Homemead Rd CR0 . . . . .41 C3
Homepark House GU9 . . . . .125 C3
Homer Rd CR0 . . . . .43 D3
Homersham Rd KT1 . . . . . . .38 B7
Homesdale Rd CR3 . . . . . . .100 D4
Homestall GU2 . . . . .108 D2
Homestall Rd RH19 . . . . . . .206 E8
Homestead GU6 . . . . .174 F4
Homestead Gdns KT10 . . . .55 E5
Homestead Rd
  Caterham CR3 . . . . .100 D4
  Staines TW18 . . . . .13 B2
Homestead Way CR0 . . . . . .82 D7
Homestead The BR3 . . . . . . .24 A1
Homewalk House SE26 . . . .23 C4
Homewater House ⁊
  KT17 .76 E6
Homewaters Ave TW16 . . . .34 F8
Homewood GU6 . . . . .175 A3
Homewood Cl TW12 . . . . . . .15 F2
Homewood Gdns SE25 . . . . .42 E4
Homewoods ⁊ SW12 . . . . . .21 C8
Homildon House ⁊ SE26 . . .23 A5
Homington Ct KT2 . . . . .17 E1
Homstead The RH6 . . . . . . .162 B1
Honey End La RG30 . . . . . . .41 C1
Honey Hill RG40 . . . . .26 A1
Honey Yard Bsns Pk
  GU9 .125 D2
Honey Hill RG40 . . . . .26 A1
Honeybrook Rd
  SW12, SW4 . . . . .21 C8
Honeycrock La RH1 . . . . . . .140 B2
Honeyhill Rd RG42 . . . . .27 A8
Honeypot La TN8 . . . . .144 D4
Honeypots Rd GU22 . . . . . . .89 D5
Honeysuckle Bottom
  KT24 .112 E2
Honeysuckle Cl
  Crowthorne RG45 . . . . .45 A7
  Horley RH6 . . . . .161 C4
Honeysuckle Gdns CR0 . . . .43 D1
Honeysuckle La
  Crawley RH11 . . . . .181 C1
  Dorking RH5 . . . . .136 C4
  Headley Down GU35 . . . . . .187 B5

Honeysuckle Wlk RH12 . . .218 A5
Honeywood La
  Ockley RH5 . . . . .196 F5
  Rowhook RH5 . . . . .196 F5
Honeywood Rd
  Horsham RH13 . . . . .218 A4
  Isleworth TW7 . . . . .6 A3
Honeywood Wlk SM5 . . . . . .59 F6
Honister Hts CR8 . . . . .80 E5
Honister Wlk GU15 . . . . .66 D4
Honley Rd SE6 . . . . .24 B8
Honnor Rd TW18 . . . . .13 D1
Honor Oak Rd SE23 . . . . . . .23 C8
Hood Ave SW14 . . . . .7 C2
Hood Cl CR0, CR9 . . . . .42 B1
Hood Rd SW20 . . . . .18 F1
Hook Heath Ave GU22 . . . . .89 C8
Hook Heath Gdns GU22 . . .88 F6
Hook Heath Rd GU22 . . . . . .89 B6
Hook Hill CR2 . . . . .61 E1
Hook Hill La GU22 . . . . .89 C6
Hook Hill Pk GU22 . . . . .89 B6
Hook House SW27 . . . . .22 B3
Hook La Gomshall GU5 . . . .133 C2
  Puttenham GU3 . . . . .128 D3
  West End GU24 . . . . .67 C6
Hook Mill La GU18 . . . . .48 D2
Hook Rd Chessington KT6 . .56 F7
  Epsom KT19, KT17 . . . . .57 C2
  Ewell KT19 . . . . .76 D8
  Surbiton KT6, KT19 . . . . . . .56 E7
Hook Rise N Surbiton KT6 . .56 F7
  Tolworth KT6, KT9 . . . . .57 B8
Hook Rise S KT6, KT9 . . . . .57 B8
Hook Rise South Ind Est . .57 A7
Hook Underpass KT6 . . . . . .56 F7
Hooke Rd KT24 . . . . .92 F2
Hookfield KT18, KT19 . . . . . .76 C6
Hookhouse Rd GU8 . . . . . . .192 D6
Hookley Cl GU8 . . . . .148 E3
Hookley La GU8 . . . . .148 E3
Hookstile La GU9 . . . . .125 C1
Hookstone La GU24 . . . . . . .67 F8
Hookwood Bglws RH6 . . . .123 B6
Hookwood Cnr RH8 . . . . . .123 B7
Hooley La RH1 . . . . .139 F8
Hoover House SE6 . . . . .24 C4
Hope Ave RG12 . . . . .27 E2
Hope Cl SM1 . . . . .59 C5
Hope Ct RH11 . . . . .201 B1
Hope Fountain GU15 . . . . . .65 F4
Hope Grant's Rd GU11 . . . .105 A4
Hope La GU9 . . . . .125 B6
Hope Pk BR1 . . . . .24 F1
Hope St GU8 . . . . .148 D4
Hopeman Cl GU47 . . . . .64 D7
Hopes Cl TW5 . . . . .5 A8
Hopfield RH6 . . . . .71 E6
Hophurst Cl RH10 . . . . .204 B8
Hophurst Dr RH10 . . . . .204 B8
Hophurst Hill RH10, RH19 .184 D2
Hophurst La RH10 . . . . .184 B1
Hopkins Ct RH11 . . . . .201 B1
Hoppety The KT20 . . . . .97 D5
Hoppingwood Ave KT3 . . . .38 E6
Hopton Gdns KT3 . . . . .39 A3
Hopton Rd SW16 . . . . .21 E3
Hopwood Cl SW17 . . . . .20 C5
Horace Rd KT1 . . . . .37 F6
Horatio Ave RG42 . . . . .27 E8
Horatius Way CR0 . . . . .60 F4
Hordern House RH12 . . . . .217 A1
Horewood Rd RG12 . . . . . . .27 B3
Horley City Int Sch RH6 . .161 A3
Horley Lodge La RH1 . . . . .161 A8
Horley Rd Crawley RH6 . . .181 B7
  Hookwood RH6 . . . . .181 B7
  Redhill RH1 . . . . .139 F5
Horley Row RH6 . . . . .161 A4
Horley Sta RH6 . . . . .161 B2
Hormer Cl GU47 . . . . .45 D1
Horn Rd GU14 . . . . .84 E5
Hornbeam Cl
  Farnborough GU14 . . . . .84 C5
  Horsham RH13 . . . . .217 F1
  Sandhurst GU47 . . . . .45 D1
Hornbeam Cres TW8 . . . . . . .6 B7
Hornbeam Rd
  Guildford GU1 . . . . .109 C3
  Reigate RH2 . . . . .139 C6
Hornbeam Terr SM5 . . . . . . .40 E1
Hornbeam Wlk KT12 . . . . . .54 F6
Hornbrook Cl RH12 . . . . . . .217 F3
Hornbrook Ho ⁊ RH12 . . . .217 F3
Hornchurch Cl KT2 . . . . .17 D3
Hornchurch Hill CR3 . . . . . .80 F1
Horndean Cl
  Crawley RH10 . . . . .182 D2
  Roehampton SW15 . . . . .19 A7
Horndean Rd RG12 . . . . .27 F3
Horne Rd TW17 . . . . .34 A5
Hornecourt Hill RH6 . . . . . .162 F7
Horner La CR4 . . . . .40 D7
Hornhatch GU4 . . . . .131 B3
Hornhatch Cl GU4 . . . . .131 B3
Hornhatch La GU4 . . . . .131 B2
Horniman Dr SE23 . . . . .23 B7
Horniman Grange ⁊ SE23 .23 C7
Horniman Mus & Gdns
  SE23 .23 B7
Horniman Prim Sch SE23 . .23 B7
Hornshill La RH12 . . . . .213 F7
Horsa Cl SM6 . . . . .60 E3

Horse Fair KT1 ....37 D7
Horse Gate Ride SL5 ....29 A3
Horse Hill RH6 ....160 B4
Horsebrass Dr GU19 ....47 E2
Horsecroft SM7 ....77 F2
Horsell Birch Woking GU21 .69 A4
  Woking GU21 ....69 B4
Horsell C of E Sch GU21 .69 C3
Horsell Common Rd GU21 .69 C5
Horsell Ct KT16 ....33 B2
Horsell Moor GU21 ......69 D2
Horsell Park Cl GU21 ...69 D3
Horsell Pk GU21 ....69 E3
Horsell Rise GU21 ......69 E4
Horsell Rise Cl GU21 ...69 D4
Horsell Vale GU21 ......69 E3
Horsell Village Cty Inf Sch
  GU21 ....69 D4
Horsell Way GU21 ....69 C3
Horseshoe Bend GU26 ...188 B3
Horseshoe Cl
  Camberley GU15 ......65 F8
  Crawley RH10 ....202 D7
Horseshoe Cres GU15 ...65 F8
Horseshoe La
  Ash Vale GU12 ....106 A7
  Cranleigh GU6 ....174 D4
Horseshoe La E GU1 ....110 C2
Horseshoe La W GU1 ...110 B1
Horseshoe Ridge KT13 ..72 C8
Horseshoe The
  Banstead SM7 ....77 F4
  Coulsdon CR5, CR8 ....79 D6
  Godalming GU7 ....150 C3
Horsham Bsns Pk RH12 .198 C4
Horsham Hospl RH12 ...217 C3
Horsham Mus RH12 .....217 C1
Horsham Rd Alfold GU6 .193 F8
  Beare Green RH5 .....157 C4
  Beare Green, Holmwood
  Cnr RH5 ....157 C6
  Bramley GU5, GU4 ....151 E7
  Bramley, Palmers Cross
  GU5, GU6 ....173 D5
  Capel RH5 ....178 C2
  Capel RH5 ....178 D8
  Cranleigh GU6 ....174 E1
  Cranleigh GU6, RH12 ..194 C1
  Crawley RH11 ....201 B4
  Crawley, Palmers Cross
  GU5, GU6 ....173 D5
  Dorking RH4 ....136 A6
  Dorking, Mid
  Holmwood RH5 ....136 B2
  East Bedfont TW14 .....3 C1
  Ellen's Green GU6 ....176 B1
  Ewhurst GU6 ....175 F3
  Holmbury St M GU5,
  RH5, GU6 ....155 C5
  Rowhook RH5, RH12 ..196 D5
  Rusper RH12 ....199 B5
  Sandhurst GU47 ......45 D1
  Shalford GU4 ....130 E3
  South Holmwood RH5 .157 C6
  Wallis Wood RH12, RH5 .196 D5
  Wallis Wood, Mayes Green
  RH5, GU6 ....196 E4
Horsham Sta RH12 .....217 D2
Horsley Cl KT19 ....76 D6
Horsley Dr Kingston u T KT2 .17 D3
  New Addington CR0 ...63 C3
Horsley Rd KT11, KT24 .93 B7
Horsley Sta KT24 ....91 C6
Horsneile La RG42 ......27 B8
Horton Country Park
  KT19 ....57 A3
Horton Hill KT19 ....76 C8
Horton Hospl KT19 .....76 B8
Horton La KT19, KT18 ..57 B2
Horton Park Children's
  Farm KT19 ....57 A1
Horton Rd Colnbrook SL3 .1 A6
  Horton SL3 ....1 A6
  Poyle SL3, TW19 ....1 E4
  Stanwell TW19 ....2 A2
Horton Trad Est SL3 ...1 C4
Horton Way CR0 ....43 D4
Horvath Cl KT13 ....53 D6
Hosack Rd SW12, SW17 .21 A6
Hoskins Pl RH19 ....186 A4
Hoskins Place Ind Est
  GU15 ....65 B3
Hoskins Rd RH8 ....122 E6
Hospital Bridge Rd TW2 .16 B7
Hospital Hill GU11 .....105 A3
Hospital of the Holy Trinity
  (Almshouses) CR9 ....61 C8
Hospital Rd
  Aldershot GU11 ......105 B3
  Hounslow TW3 ....5 A4
Hospital Way SE13 .....24 D7
Hotham Cl KT8 ....36 A6
Hotham Rd SW19 ....20 C1
Houlton Rd TW10 ....6 E2
Houghton Cl TW12 .....15 E2
Houghton Rd RH10 ....202 C3
Houlder Cres CR0 ......61 B4
Houlton Cl GU19 ....47 F4
Hound House Rd GU5 .154 A5
Hounslow Ave TW3 .....5 B2
Hounslow Bsns Pk TW3 .5 B3
Hounslow Central Sta TW3 .5 B4
Hounslow East Sta TW3 .5 C5
Hounslow Ed Ctr (Specl Sch)
  The TW4 ....4 E4

Hounslow Gdns TW3 ....5 B2
Hounslow Heath Jun & Inf
  Schs TW4 ....4 E4
Hounslow Manor Sch TW3 .5 C4
Hounslow Rd
  Feltham, Hanworth TW13 .15 D4
  Feltham, North Feltham TW14 .4 B1
  Twickenham TW2, TW3 .5 C1
Hounslow Sta TW3 ......5 B2
Hounslow Town Prim Sch
  TW3 ....5 D4
Hounslow West Sta TW3 .4 E5
Houseman Rd GU14 ....84 F6
Houston Ct KT19 ....76 E6
Houston Rd SE23, SE6 ..23 E5
Houstoun Ct TW5 ....4 D5
Hove Gdns SM1 ....40 B1
Hovenden House GU15 ..22 E4
How La CR5 ....79 A1
Howard Ave KT17 ......58 A1
Howard Cl Ashford TW16 .14 F2
  Ashtead KT21 ....75 F1
  Hampton TW12 ....16 C2
  Leatherhead KT22 .....95 C4
  Walton on t H KT20 ...97 A2
  West Horsley KT24 ....92 D2
Howard Cole Way GU11 .104 E2
Howard Ct Beckenham BR3 .44 C7
  Effingham KT24 ......113 D8
  Reigate RH2 ....118 B2
Howard Dr GU14 ....84 B4
Howard Gdns GU1 .....110 B2
Howard House Penge SE20? .43 C8
  Reigate RH2 ....118 B2
Howard of Effingham Sch
  KT24 ....113 E8
Howard Prim Sch CR0 ..61 E8
Howard Rd Coulsdon CR5 .79 D5
  Crawley RH11 ....200 D2
  Croydon SE25 ....43 A3
  Dorking RH4 ....136 A7
  Dorking, North
  Holmwood RH5 ....136 C3
  East Horsley KT24 ....93 A4
  Great Bookham KT23 ..114 C8
  Horsham RH13 ....218 A4
  Isleworth TW7 ....5 F4
  New Malden KT3 ......38 E5
  Reigate RH2 ....139 B8
  Surbiton KT5 ....37 F3
  Wokingham RG40 .....25 C5
Howard Ridge GU4 ....109 A6
Howard St KT7 ....37 B3
Howards Cl GU22 ....90 A7
Howards Crest Cl BR3 ..44 C7
Howards La KT15 ....51 F3
Howards Rd GU22 ......89 F7
Howberry Rd CR7 ....42 D7
Howden Ct SE25 ....42 F7
Howden Rd SE25 ....42 F7
Howe Dr CR3 ....100 D5
Howell Hill Cl KT17 ....77 C8
Howell Hill Gr KT17 ....58 C1
Howgate Rd SW14 ......7 D4
Howitts Cl KT10 ....55 A5
Howland House **9** SW16 .21 E5
Howley Rd CR0, CR9 ...61 C7
Howmic Ct **1** TW1 .....6 C1
Howorth Ct RH12 ....27 E5
Howson Terr TW10 ....6 E1
Hoylake Cl RH11 ......200 D5
Hoylake Gdns CR4 .....41 C6
Hoyle Hill RH5 ....157 D1
Hoyle Rd SW17 ....20 E3
Hrmondsworth Moor
  Ctry Pk UB7 ....3 B2
Hubbard Dr KT19 ......56 C4
Hubbard Rd SE27 ......22 C4
Hubberholme RG12 ....27 A6
Huddleston Cres RH4 .119 D7
Hudson Cl Guildford GU2 .108 F1
  4 Merton SW19 ......40 B8
Hudson Rd Crawley RH10 .201 E4
  Harlington UB7 ....3 D8
Hugdens Rd KT20 ......97 C6
Huggins Pl SW2 ....21 F7
Hugh Herland KT1 .....37 E6
Hughenden Rd KT4 .....39 A2
Hughes Cl CR0 ....42 A1
Hughes Rd Ashford TW15 .14 C2
  Wokingham RG40 .....25 E7
Hughes Wlk CR0 ....42 C2
Huhtholth La GU5 .....152 D4
Hullmead GU5 ....152 E4
Hulton Cl KT22 ....95 C4
Hulverston Cl SM2 .....59 B2
Humber Way GU47 .....64 D8
Humbolt Cl GU2 ......108 F1
Humber Rd TW20 ....12 A4
Humphrey Cl KT22 .....94 C5
Humphries Yd RG12 ....27 C5
Hungerford Cl GU47 ...64 E4
Hungerford Sq **3** KT13 .53 D6
Hungry Hill La GU23 ...91 D3
Hunston Cl
  Colnbrook SW3 ....1 C3
  Crawley RH11 ....200 D5
Hunston Rd SM4 ....40 B1
Hunter Cl SW12 ....21 A7
Hunter House RH10 ...201 D3
Hunter Rd
  Crawley RH10, RH11 ..201 D4
  Guildford GU1 ....130 E8
  South Norwood CR7 ...42 D6
  Wimbledon SW20 ......39 C8
Hunters Chase RH9 ....142 F6

Hunters Cl KT19 ....76 C6
Hunters Ct **5** TW9 ......6 D2
Hunters Meadow SE19 .22 E4
Hunters Rd KT9 ....56 E6
Hunters The BR3 ....44 C8
Hunters Way CR0 ......61 E6
Huntersfield Cl RH2 ...118 B4
Hunting Cl KT10 ....55 A6
Hunting Gate Dr KT9 ..56 E3
Hunting Gate Mews
  Sutton SM1 ....59 B7
  Twickenham TW2 ......16 E7
Huntingdon Cl SW16 ...41 E5
Huntingdon Ct SW14 ....7 C3
Huntingdon Gdns
  Chiswick W4 ....7 C7
  Worcester Park KT4 ...58 C7
Huntingdon Rd
  Redhill RH1 ....118 F1
  Woking GU21 ....68 F2
Huntingfield CR0 ....62 F3
Huntingfield Way TW20 .12 D2
Huntingford Cl GU26 ..188 C7
Huntley House **7** SE21 .22 E4
Huntley Way SW20 .....39 A7
Huntly Rd SE25 ....42 E5
Hunts Cl GU2 ....108 D2
Hunts Hill Rd GU3 ....107 A4
Hunts Slip Rd SE21 ...22 E4
Huntsman Cl TW13 .....15 B4
Huntsman's Mews GU16 .85 F3
Huntsmans Cl
  Fetcham KT22 ....94 D3
  Warlingham CR6, CR3 .100 C6
Huntsmans Meadow SL5 .28 F8
Huntsmoor Rd KT19 ...57 D5
Hunwicke Rd SE6 ......24 A7
Huntsworth Ct SE6 ....24 A7
Hurland La GU30, GU35 .187 A3
Hurlands Bsns Ctr GU9 .125 F4
Hurlands Cl GU10, GU9 .125 F4
Hurlands La GU8 ......192 F2
Hurlands Pl GU9 ......125 F4
Hurley Cl KT12 ....54 B8
Hurley Ct RG12 ....27 E5
Hurley Gdns GU4 .....110 A4
Hurlford GU21 ....69 A2
Hurlstone Rd SE25 ....42 E4
Hurn Court Rd TW5 .....4 D5
Hurn Ct TW5 ....4 D5
Hurnford Cl CR2 ....61 E1
Huron Dr SW17 ....21 A5
Hurricane Rd SM6 ......60 E3
Hursley Ct **1** KT16 ....37 D2
Hurst Ave RH12 ......217 D3
Hurst Cl Chessington KT9 .57 A5
  Crawley RH11 ....201 A1
  Hayes BR2 ....44 F5
  Woking GU22 ....89 C7
Hurst Croft GU1 ....130 E6
Hurst Ct Beckenham BR3 .24 A1
  Horsham RH12 ....217 D3
  South Norwood SE25 .42 F5
Hurst Dr KT20 ....97 A1
Hurst Farm Cl GU8 ...149 F7
Hurst Farm Rd RH19 ..205 D2
Hurst Gr KT12 ....34 F1
Hurst Green Cl RH8 ..123 A3
Hurst Green Cty Prim Sch
  RH8 ....123 A3
Hurst Green Rd RH8 ..122 F3
Hurst Green Sta RH8 .122 F3
Hurst Hill Cotts SL5 ..152 B4
Hurst House **7** SE26 ..23 B3
Hurst La East Molesey KT8 .36 C6
  Headley KT18 ....96 D4
  Thorpe TW20 ....32 B6
Hurst Lodge Cl SL3 ....53 D4
Hurst Lodge Sch SL5 ..29 A3
Hurst Park Cty Prim Sch
  KT8 ....36 A6
Hurst Rd Aldershot GU11 .105 C4
  Croydon CR0 ....61 D5
  East Molesey KT8, KT12 .36 C4
  Epsom KT19 ....76 D8
  Farnborough GU14 ...85 B5
  Horley RH6 ....160 E4
  Headley Down GU35 ..187 B6
  Horsham RH12 ....217 D3
  Walton-on-T KT8&KT12 .35 D5
Hurst View Rd CR2 .....61 E3
Hurst Way Pyrford GU22 .70 F7
  South Croydon CR2 ...61 E4
Hurstbourne KT10 .....55 F4
Hurstbourne House SW15 .7 F1
Hurstbourne Priors CR2 .61 E4
Hurstbourne Rd SE23 ..23 E7
Hurstcourt Rd SM1 ....59 B8
Hurstdene Ave Hayes BR2 .44 F5
  Staines TW18 ....13 B2
Hurstfield Rd KT8 ......36 A6
Hurstlands RH8 ....123 A3
Hurstleigh Cl RH1 ....118 F3
Hurstleigh Dr RH1 ....118 F3
Hurstmere Ct GU26 ...188 D2
Hurstmere Grange CR0 .61 A2
Hurstwood SL5 ....29 A3
Hurtmore Chase GU7 ..150 B7
Hurtmore Rd
  Farncombe GU7 ......150 B7
  Shackleford GU7 .....150 B7
Hurtwood House Sch
  (International Sixth
  Form Coll) RH5 ......155 A2
Hurtwood Rd KT12 .....35 F2
Hussar Ct GU11 ....104 E2
Hussars Cl TW4 ....4 E4

Hutchingson's Rd CR0 .82 C8
Hutchins House **3** SW4 .21 D8
Hutchins Way RH6 ....160 F5
Hutsons Cl RG40 ....25 D8
Hutton Cl GU20 ....48 D3
Hutton Rd GU12 ......106 A6
Huxley Cl GU7 ....150 D7
Huxley Rd GU7 ....129 D8
Hyacinth Cl **3** TW12 ..16 A2
Hyacinth Rd SW15 .....19 A7
Hyde Cl TW16 ....14 E2
Hyde Dr RH11 ....200 E5
Hyde Farm Sch SW12 .21 D7
Hyde Heath Ct RH10 ..202 E8
Hyde La
  Beacon Hill GU10, GU8 .168 E1
  Thursley GU8 ....169 A2
Hyde Rd Richmond TW10 .6 F2
  Sanderstead CR2, CR8 .80 E6
Hyde Terr TW15, TW16 .14 E2
Hyde Wlk SM4 ....40 A2
Hydestile Cotts GU8 ..171 D5
Hydethorpe Rd SW12 ..21 C7
Hydons The GU8 ......171 E5
Hylands Cl Crawley RH10 .202 A5
  Epsom KT18 ....76 C4
Hylands Mews KT18 ...76 C4
Hylands Rd KT18 ......76 C4
Hylton Lodge KT12 ....54 C5
Hyndewood **14** SE23 ..23 D5
Hyperion Ct RH11 ....200 E4
Hyperion House **1** SW2 .21 F8
Hyperion Pl KT19 ......57 D2
Hyperion Wlk RH6 ....161 B1
Hyrstdene CR0 ....61 B6
Hythe Cl RG12 ....27 E4
Hythe End Rd TW19 ...12 D2
Hythe Field Ave TW20 .12 D2
Hythe Park Rd TW20 ..12 D2
Hythe Rd Egham TW18 .12 D3
  South Norwood CR7, SE25 .42 D7
Hythe Sch The TW18 ..12 D3
Hythe The TW18 ....12 D3

I

Ian Ct SE23 ....23 C6
Iberian Ave CR0, SM6 .60 E6
Iberian Way GU15 .....66 B6
Ibis La W4 ....7 C6
Ibsley Gdns SW15 .....19 A7
Ibstock Place Sch SW15 .7 E2
Icehouse Wood RH8 ...122 F4
Icklesham House **9**
  RH11 ....200 F3
Icklingham Gate KT11 .73 C7
Icklingham Rd KT11 ...73 D6
Iden Cl BR2 ....44 E6
Idlecombe Rd SW17 ...21 A2
Idmiston Rd
  New Malden KT4 ......38 F2
  West Norwood SE21, SE27 .22 C6
Idmiston Sq KT4 ......38 F2
Ifield Ave RH11 ....201 A4
Ifield Cl RH1 ....139 E7
Ifield Com Sch RH11 ..201 A7
Ifield Cty Mid Sch RH11 .201 A6
Ifield Fst Sch RH11 ...201 A8
Ifield Gn RH11 ....201 A8
Ifield Rd Charlwood RH6 .180 E5
  Crawley RH11 ....200 E6
  Crawley, West Green RH11 .201 C6
Ifield St RH11 ....200 F8
Ifield Sta RH11 ....201 A6
Ifield Wood RH11 .....180 E1
Ifold Bridge La RH14 .212 D3
Ifold Rd RH1 ....140 A4
Ifoldhurst RH14 ......212 C2
Ightham House BR3 ...23 F1
Ikona Ct KT13 ....53 C5
Ildersly Gr SE21 ....22 D6
Ilex Cl
  Englefield Green TW20 .11 B1
  Sunbury TW16 ....35 B8
Ilex House KT15 ....52 A1
Ilex Way SW16 ....22 A3
Ilford Ct GU6 ....173 F2
Ilfracombe Rd BR1 ....24 F5
Ilkley Cl SE19 ....22 D2
Illingworth Cl CR4 ....40 D6
Illingworth Gr RG12 ..27 F8
Imber Cl KT7 ....36 D1
Imber Court Trad Est KT8 .36 E2
Imber Cross KT7 ....36 F3
Imber Gr KT10 ....36 D3
Imber Rd KT10 ....36 D3
Imberhorne La RH19 ..185 B2
Imberhorne Lower Sch
  RH19 ....185 D3
Imberhorne Sch RH19 .185 B3
Imberhorne Way RH19 .185 B3
Imjin Cl GU11 ....105 B3
Immanuel & St Andrew
  C of E Prim Sch SW16 .21 D2
Impact Ct SE20 ....43 B7
Imperial Gdns CR4 ....41 B6
Imperial House GU25 .31 A1
Imperial Rd TW14 ......3 D1
Impington **6** KT1 ....38 A7
Imran Ct GU12 ....106 A8
Ince Rd KT12 ....53 E4
Inchmery Rd SE6 ......24 C6
Inchwood Bracknell RG12 .27 C1
  Croydon BR4, CR0 .....63 B6

Independent Bsns Pk The
  RH19 ....18?
Ingatestone Rd SE25 ..4?
Ingham Cl CR2 ....6?
Ingham Dr CR2 ....6?
Ingle Dell GU15 ....6?
Ingle House SW12 .....2?
Inglebom Dr CR8 ......8?
Ingleby Way SM6 ....6?
Inglehurst KT15 ....5?
Inglemere Ct CR4, SW17 .2?
Inglemere Rd
  Forest Hill SE23 ......2?
  Mitcham CR4, SW17 ...2?
Ingleside SL3 ....?
Ingleside Cl BR3 ....2?
Inglewood CR0 ....4?
Inglewood **2** BR1 ......2?
Inglis Rd CR0 ....4?
Ingram Ct RH12 ....21?
Ingram High Sch for Boys
  CR7 ....4?
Ingram House SW13 ...3?
Ingram Rd CR7 ....4?
Ingrams Almshouses TW7 .6?
Ingrams Cl KT12 ....5?
Ingress St **4** W4 ......7?
Ingrebourne House BR1 .2?
Inholmes La RH5 ......13?
Inkerman Rd GU21 .....6?
Inkerman Way GU21 ...6?
Inman Rd SW18 ....2?
Inner Park Rd SW19 ..1?
Inner Ring E TW6 ......?
Inner Ring W TW6 .....?
Innes Cl SW20 ....3?
Innes Gdns SW15 .....?
Innes Rd RH12 ....21?
Innes Yd CR0, CR9 .....6?
Innings La RG12 ....2?
Innisfail Gdns GU11 ...10?
Inst of Oceanographic
  Sciences GU8 ....17?
Institute Rd
  Aldershot GU12 ......10?
  Westcott RH4 ....13?
Instone Cl SM6 ....6?
Instow Gdns GU14 ......8?
Inval Hill GU27 ....20?
Inveresk Gdns KT4 .....5?
Inverness Ct SE6 ....2?
Inverness Rd Hounslow TW3 .5?
  Cheam KT4 ....3?
Inverness Way GU47 ...6?
Invicta Cl TW14 ....?
Invicta Ct KT9 ....5?
Invincible Rd GU14 ....8?
Inwood Ave Coulsdon CR5 .10?
  Hounslow TW3 ....?
Inwood Bsns Pk TW3 ..?
Inwood Cl CR0 ....?
Inwood Ct **1** KT12 ....5?
Inwood Rd TW3 ....?
Iona Cl Crawley RH11 ..20?
  Forest Hill SE17, SE23 .2?
Ipsley Lodge GU10 ....12?
Ipswich Rd SW17 ......2?
Irene Rd KT11 ....7?
Ireton Ave KT13 ....7?
Iris Cl Croydon CR0 .....4?
  Surbiton KT6 ....3?
Iris Rd Bisley GU24 ....6?
Iron La GU5 ....15?
Irons Bottom Rd RH2 .15?
Irvine Ct CR7 ....4?
Irvine Dr GU14 ....8?
Irvine Pl GU25 ....3?
Irving Wlk RH10 ......20?
Irwin Dr RH12 ....21?
Irwin Rd GU2 ....13?
Isabel Cotts KT18 ......7?
Isabella Ct **8** TW10 ...?
Isbells Dr RH2 ....13?
Isham Rd SW16 ....4?
Isis Ct W4 ....?
Isis St SW18 ....2?
Isis Way GU47 ....6?
Island Cl TW18 ....1?
Island Cotts The KT11 .7?
Island Farm Ave KT8 ..3?
Island Farm Rd KT8 ...3?
Island House SW19 ....2?
Island Rd CR4, SW19 ..2?
Islay Gdns TW4 ....?
Isleworth Bsns Complex
  TW7 ....?
Isleworth Sta TW7 .....?
Isleworth & Syon Sch
  for Boys TW7 ....?
Isleworth Town Sch TW7 .?
Itchingwood Common Rd
  RH8 ....12?
Ivanhoe Cl RH11 ......18?
Ivanhoe House **11** SW12 .2?
Ivanhoe Rd TW4 ....?
Iveagh Cl RH11 ....20?
Iveagh Ct Beckenham BR3 .4?
  Bracknell RG12 ....2?
Iveagh Rd GU2 ....13?
Ively Rd GU14 ....8?
Ively Rdbt GU11 ....8?
Iverna Gdns TW14 .....?
Ivers Way CR0 ....6?

Ivestor Terr SE23 . . . . .23 C8
Ivor Cl GU1 . . . . .131 A8
Ivory Vlk RH11 . . . . .200 C3
Ivy Cl TW16 . . . . .35 C7
Ivy Dene La RH19 . . . . .206 D6
Ivy Dr GU18 . . . . .67 A7
Ivy Gdns CR4 . . . . .41 D6
Ivy House CR0 . . . . .43 D1
Ivy Lea Farnham GU9 . . . . . .125 B2
 Hounslow TW4 . . . . .4 F3
 Woking GU22 . . . . .70 B1
Ivy Mill La RH1 . . . . .121 B3
Ivy Mill La
 Bletchingley RH1, RH9 . . .121 B3
 Godstone RH1, RH9 . . . . .121 B3
Ivy Rd Aldershot GU12 . . . . .105 E2
 Hounslow TW3 . . . . .5 B3
 Tolworth KT6 . . . . .38 A1
 Upper Tooting SW17 . . . . .20 E3
Ivybank GU7 . . . . .150 E6
Ivybridge Cl 3 TW1 . . . . .17 A8
Ivybridge Jun & Inf Sch
 TW1 . . . . .17 A8
Ivychurch Cl SE20 . . . . .23 C1
Ivydale Rd SM5 . . . . .59 F8
Ivyday Gr SW16 . . . . .21 F5
Ivydene
 East Molesey KT12, KT8 . . .35 F5
 Knaphill GU21 . . . . .68 B1
Ivydene Cl Redhill RH1 . . . . .140 B4
 Sutton SM1 . . . . .59 C6
Ivymount Rd SE27 . . . . .22 A5

J

Jackass La RH9 . . . . .121 F4
Jackdaw Cl RH11 . . . . .201 C8
Jackdaw La RH12 . . . . .217 E6
Jackman's La GU21 . . . . .89 B8
Jackson Cl Bracknell RG12 . .27 A4
 Crawley GU6 . . . . .173 F2
 Epsom KT18 . . . . .76 D5
Jackson's Pl CR0 . . . . .42 E1
Jackson's Way CR0 . . . . .63 B7
Jacob Cl RG42 . . . . .26 C7
Jacob Rd GU15 . . . . .65 A7
Jacobean Cl RH10 . . . . .202 C5
Jacobs Well Rd GU4 . . . . . . .109 D6
Jaggard Way SW12 . . . . .20 F8
Jail La TN16 . . . . .83 E3
Jamaica Rd SE27 . . . . .22 B3
James Boswell 1 SW16 . . . . .22 A4
James Dixon Prim Sch
 SE20 . . . . .23 B1
James Est CR4 . . . . .40 F7
James Rd Camberley GU15 . .65 A5
 Shalford GU3 . . . . .130 C1
James St TW3 . . . . .5 C4
James Watt Way RH10 . . . . .182 A4
James Way GU15 . . . . .65 B2
Jameston RG12 . . . . .27 C1
Jamieson House TW4 . . . . . . .15 F8
Jamnagar Cl TW18 . . . . .12 F2
Janoway Hill GU21 . . . . .89 C8
Japonica Cl GU21 . . . . .69 C1
Japonica Ct GU12 . . . . .105 F1
Jarrett Cl SW2 . . . . .22 B7
Jarvis Rd CR2 . . . . .61 D4
Jasmin Rd KT19 . . . . .57 B5
Jasmine Cl Redhill RH1 . . . . .140 A4
 Woking GU21 . . . . .68 F3
Jasmine Ct Horsham RH12 . .217 C2
 1 Wallington SM6 . . . . . . .60 B6
Jasmine Gdns CR0 . . . . .63 B7
Jasmine Way KT7 . . . . .36 E5
Jason Cl Redhill RH1 . . . . . .139 E4
Jasons Dr GU4 . . . . .110 C4
Jasper Rd KT4 . . . . .38 D1
Jasper Rd Dulwich SE19 . . . .22 F2
 West Norwood SE19 . . . . .22 F2
Javelin Ct RH10 . . . . .182 D1
Jawahar Bagh SE13 . . . . .22 C4
Jay Ave KT15 . . . . .52 D7
Jay's La Fisherstreet GU27 . .209 C3
Jays Nest Cl GU17 . . . . .64 D4
Jayson Ct 2 CR0 . . . . .43 A1
Jeal Oakwood Ct KT18 . . . . .76 E5
an Humbert House 2
 E27 . . . . .22 D4
Jean's Ct 10 RH11 . . . . .201 B1
Jeddere Cotts RH7 . . . . .165 A2
Jeffries Pas GU1 . . . . .130 D8
Jeffries Rd KT24 . . . . .112 C5
Jeffs Cl TW12 . . . . .16 B2
Jeffs Rd SM1 . . . . .58 F6
Jefton Ct SW6 . . . . .60 C4
Jemmett Ct KT2 . . . . .38 B8
Jengar Cl SM1 . . . . .59 B6
Jenkins' Hill London Rd
 GU19 . . . . .47 D2
 nkins Pl GU11 . . . . .105 D8
Jenner Dr GU24 . . . . .68 A6
Jenner Rd Crawley RH10 . . . .181 F3
 Guildford GU1 . . . . .130 E8
Jennett Rd CR0, CR9 . . . . . . .61 A7
Jennifer Rd BR1 . . . . .24 F5
Jenny La RH7 . . . . .185 F1
Jennys Wlk GU15 . . . . .52 C2
nson Way SE19 . . . . .22 F1
ppo's La CR4 . . . . .40 F5
rome Cnr GU47 . . . . .45 E2

Jersey Cl Addlestone KT16 . . .51 F7
 Guildford GU4 . . . . .110 B6
Jersey Rd Crawley RH11 . . . .201 A2
 Hounslow TW5, TW7 . . . . . .5 D7
 Mitcham SW17 . . . . .21 A2
Jerviston Gdns SW16 . . . . . . .22 A2
Jesmond Cl CR4 . . . . .41 B6
Jesmond Rd CR0 . . . . .42 F2
Jessamy Rd KT13 . . . . .53 B8
Jesses La GU5 . . . . .154 C8
Jessie's Hollow GU5 . . . . . . .133 C1
Jessiman Terr TW17 . . . . .34 A4
Jessops Way CR0, CR4 . . . . .41 C3
Jeston House 10 SE27 . . . . . .22 B5
Jevington RG12 . . . . .27 C1
Jewell House 3 SE21 . . . . . . .22 E4
Jewels Hill Biggin Hill TN16 . .83 A6
Jeypore Rd SW18 . . . . .20 C8
Jig's La S RG42 . . . . .27 E8
Jillian Cl TW12 . . . . .16 A1
Jobson's La
 Fisherstreet GU27 . . . . . . .209 D3
 Lurgashall GU27 . . . . .209 D1
Jocelyn Rd TW9 . . . . .6 E4
Jock's La RG42 . . . . .26 E8
Jockey Mead RH12 . . . . .217 A1
Jodrell Cl TW7 . . . . .6 A6
Joe Hunte Ct 2 SW27 . . . . . .22 B3
John Austin Cl KT2 . . . . .37 F8
John Baird Ct SE26 . . . . .23 D4
John Barker House 14 SE20 . .23 C1
John Barter House TW3 . . . . .4 F5
John Busch Sch TW7 . . . . . . .6 B6
John Cl GU11, GU9 . . . . . . .125 E8
John Cobb Rd KT13 . . . . .53 A3
John Dee House 6 SW14 . . . .7 D4
John Fisher Sch The CR8 . . .60 E1
John Gale Ct KT17 . . . . .57 F7
John Kaye Ct TW17 . . . . .34 A4
John Kirk House 6 SW16 . . . .21 E5
John Nightingale Sch KT8 . . .35 F6
John Nike Way RG12 . . . . . . .26 C7
John Paul II RC Sec Sch
 SW19 . . . . .19 D8
John Pounds House
 RH11 . . . . .201 D4
John Ruskin Sixth Form
 Coll CR2 . . . . .62 E3
John Russell Cl GU4 . . . . . .109 A4
John St South SE25 . . . . .43 A5
 Hounslow TW3, TW5 . . . . . .5 A3
John Wesley Ct 5 TW1 . . . . .17 A7
John Wiskar Dr GU6 . . . . . .174 D2
John's Rd TN16 . . . . .103 D7
John's Terr CR0 . . . . .42 E1
Johns La SM4 . . . . .40 C4
Johns Wlk CR3 . . . . .101 A8
Johnsdale RH8 . . . . .122 F6
Johnson Rd Heston TW5 . . . . .4 C7
 Thornton Heath CR0 . . . . . .42 D2
Johnson's Cl SM5 . . . . .59 F7
Johnson's Cl CR5 . . . . .59 F7
Johnsons Dr TW12 . . . . .36 C8
Johnston Gr GU4 . . . . .109 A5
Johnston Wlk GU2 . . . . .109 A5
Joinville Pl KT15 . . . . .52 D6
Jolesfield RH11 . . . . .200 F3
Jolliffe Rd RH1 . . . . .99 C1
Jones Cnr SL5 . . . . .28 E8
Jones Wlk 6 TW10 . . . . .6 F1
Jonquil Gdns 5 TW12 . . . . . .16 A2
Jonson Cl CR4 . . . . .41 B6
Jordan Cl CR2 . . . . .80 E6
Jordans Cl Crawley RH11 . . . .201 D8
 Guildford GU1 . . . . .110 A2
 Redhill RH1 . . . . .140 B4
 Stanwell TW19 . . . . .13 C8
Jordans Cres RH11 . . . . .181 D1
Jordans The RH19 . . . . .205 E8
Josef Perrin House 1
 SE27 . . . . .22 D4

Jubilee Way continued
 Merton SW19 . . . . .40 B8
 Tolworth KT4, KT9 . . . . . . .57 B7
Jubilee Wks SW19 . . . . .40 C7
Jubilee Wlk RH10 . . . . .202 A6
Judge Wlk KT10 . . . . .55 E4
Judge's Terr RH19 . . . . .205 E8
Julian Cl GU21 . . . . .69 C1
Julian Hill KT13 . . . . .53 B3
Julian Hill Sch KT13 . . . . . . .53 B3
Julian Tayler Path SE23 . . . . .22 E4
Julians Prim Sch SW16 . . . . .22 A4
Julians Cl SW16 . . . . .22 A4
Juliet Gdns RG42 . . . . .27 F8
Julius Cl TW8 . . . . .6 E7
Julius Hill RG42 . . . . .27 F8
Jumps Rd GU10 . . . . .168 B3
Junction Pl GU27 . . . . .207 F6
Junction Rd Ashford TW15 . .14 C3
 Croydon CR2 . . . . .61 D5
 Dorking RH4 . . . . .136 A7
 Lightwater GU18 . . . . .48 B1
June Cl CR5 . . . . .79 B5
June La RH1 . . . . .140 B2
Junewood Cl KT15 . . . . .70 F8
Juniper RG12 . . . . .27 C1
Juniper Cl Biggin Hill TN16 . .83 E2
 Chessington KT9 . . . . .56 E5
 Guildford GU1 . . . . .109 C6
 Reigate RH2 . . . . .139 C7
Juniper Ct Belmont SM2 . . . .59 A4
 Hounslow TW3 . . . . .5 B3
 4 Kingston u T GU24 . . . . .68 A4
Juniper Gdns Ashford TW16 . .14 F2
 Mitcham CR4 . . . . .41 A8
Juniper Hall (Field Study
 Ctr) RH5 . . . . .115 C6
Juniper Pl GU4 . . . . .130 D2
Juniper Rd Crawley RH11 . . .181 C1
 Farnborough GU14 . . . . . . .84 C5
 Reigate RH2 . . . . .139 C7
Juniper Terr GU4 . . . . .130 D2
Juniper Way GU12 . . . . .105 F1
Jura Cl RH11 . . . . .201 B3
Justin Cl TW8 . . . . .6 D7
Jutland Gdns CR5 . . . . .99 F7
Jutland Pl TW20 . . . . .12 C3
Jutland Rd SE6 . . . . .24 C8
Juxon Cl RH11 . . . . .200 F4

K

Kaithwood House RH12 . . . . .218 B5
Kangley Bridge Rd SE26 . . .23 F3
Kangley Bridge Rd
 Forest Hill SE26 . . . . .23 F3
 Penge SE26 . . . . .23 F3
Karen Ct BR1 . . . . .44 F8
Kashmir Cl KT15 . . . . .52 D2
Katharine Rd 1 TW1 . . . . . . .17 A7
Katharine St CR0, CR9 . . . . .61 C7
Katherine Cl KT15 . . . . .52 A4
Katherine Ct SE23 . . . . .23 C7
Kathleen Moore Ct BR4 . . . .63 C8
Kay Ave KT15 . . . . .52 E7
Kay Cres GU35 . . . . .187 B6
Kaye Ct GU1 . . . . .109 C5
Kaye Don Way KT13 . . . . .53 A1
Kayemoor Rd SM2 . . . . .59 E4
Kaynes Pk SL5 . . . . .28 E8
Keable Rd GU10 . . . . .145 E7
Kearton Cl CR8 . . . . .80 C2
Keates Grn RG42 . . . . .27 B8
Keats Ave RH1 . . . . .119 B3
Keats Cl Horsham RH12 . . . . .217 F7
 Mitcham SW17, SW19 . . . . .20 D2
Keats House BR3 . . . . .24 B2
Keats Pl RH19 . . . . .185 D1
Keats Way Crowthorne RG45 . .45 B6
 Croydon CR0 . . . . .43 C3
Keble Cl Crawley RH10 . . . . .182 D1
 New Malden KT4 . . . . .38 F1
Keble St SW17 . . . . .20 C4
Keble Way GU47 . . . . .45 F2
Kedeston Ct SM3 . . . . .40 B1
Keedonwood Rd
 Bromley BR1 . . . . .24 F3
 Catford BR1 . . . . .24 F3
Keeley Rd CR0, CR9 . . . . . . .61 C8
Keeling House 2 TW11 . . . . . .16 E3
Keen's Rd CR0 . . . . .61 C6
Keens Cl SW16 . . . . .21 D3
Keens La GU2, GU3 . . . . . . .108 F5
Keens Park Rd GU3 . . . . .108 F5
Keep Hatch Cty Inf Sch
 RG40 . . . . .25 D7
Keep Hatch Cty Jun Sch
 RG40 . . . . .25 D7
Keep The Catford SE6 . . . . . .24 B7
 Kingston u T KT2 . . . . .17 F1
Keepers Cl GU4 . . . . .110 D4
Keepers Combe RG12 . . . . . .27 D3
Keepers Mews TW11 . . . . . . .17 C2
Keepers Terr GU25 . . . . .31 B4
Keepers Wlk GU25 . . . . .31 D4
Keephatch Rd RG40 . . . . .25 F7
Keevil Dr SW19 . . . . .19 E8
Keir Hardie House 7
 RH11 . . . . .201 B1
Keith Lucas Rd GU14 . . . . . . .84 F2
Keith Park Cres TN16 . . . . . .83 C7
Keldholme RG12 . . . . .27 A6
Kelling Gdns CR0 . . . . .42 B2
Kellino St SW17 . . . . .20 F4
Kelmscott Cl KT17 . . . . .54 E7
Kelmscott 5 SE23 . . . . .23 D5
Kelsey Cl RH6 . . . . .160 F3

Kelsey Gate BR3 . . . . .44 B7
Kelsey La BR3 . . . . .44 A6
Kelsey Park Ave BR3 . . . . . . .44 B7
Kelsey Park Rd BR3 . . . . .44 A7
Kelsey Park Sch BR3 . . . . . . .44 A6
Kelsey Sq BR3 . . . . .44 A7
Kelsey Way BR3 . . . . .44 A6
Kelso Cl RH10 . . . . .202 E7
Kelso Ct SE20 . . . . .23 B1
Kelvedon Cl KT2 . . . . .18 A2
Kelvedon Cl KT12 . . . . .53 F3
Kelvedon Ct KT2 . . . . .18 A2
Kelvin Ave KT22 . . . . .94 F8
Kelvin Bsns Ctr RH10 . . . . . .181 F2
Kelvin Cl KT19 . . . . .57 A4
Kelvin Ct Chiswick W4 . . . . . .7 C7
 Isleworth TW7 . . . . .5 F5
 6 Penge SE20 . . . . .43 B8
 8 Twickenham TW1 . . . . . . .6 B1
Kelvin Dr TW1 . . . . .6 B1
Kelvin Gdns CR0 . . . . .41 E2
Kelvin Grove Chessington KT9 . .56 E7
Kelvin Grove Prim Sch
 Forest Hill SE26 . . . . .23 B5
 Forest Hill SE23 . . . . .23 B5
Kelvin La RH10 . . . . .181 F2
Kelvin Way RH10 . . . . .181 F2
Kelvinbrook KT8 . . . . .36 B6
Kelvington Cl CR0 . . . . .43 E2
Kelyway House 10 SW2 . . . . .22 A8
Kemble Cl Weybridge KT13 . .53 D6
 Kemble Cotts KT15 . . . . . . .52 A6
Kemble Rd
 Croydon CR0, CR9 . . . . .61 B7
 Forest Hill SE23 . . . . .23 D7
Kembleside Rd TN16 . . . . . .103 C1
Kemerton Rd
 Beckenham BR3 . . . . .44 B7
 Croydon CR0 . . . . .43 B2
Kemishford GU22 . . . . .89 A4
Kemnal Pk GU27 . . . . .208 D7
Kemp Ct GU19 . . . . .47 F2
Kemp Gdns CR0 . . . . .42 C3
Kempshott Rd
 Horsham RH11 . . . . .217 B4
 Streatham SW16 . . . . .21 E1
Kempson House SE1 . . . . .59 B2
Kempton Ave TW16 . . . . .35 B8
Kempton Ct
 Farnborough GU14 . . . . . . .84 F2
 Sunbury TW16 . . . . .35 B8
Kempton Park Race Course
 TW16 . . . . .15 C1
Kempton Park Sta TW16 . . .15 B1
Kempton Wlk CR0 . . . . .43 E3
Kemsing Cl Coney Hall BR2 . .63 F8
 Thornton Heath CR7 . . . . . .42 C5
Kemsley Rd TN16 . . . . .103 D8
Kendal Cl
 East Bedfont TW14 . . . . . . .14 F7
 Farnborough GU14 . . . . . . .84 E4
 Redhill RH2 . . . . .118 D2
Kendal Ct 7 CR0 . . . . .42 E1
Kendal Gdns SM1 . . . . .59 C8
Kendal Gr GU15 . . . . .66 D4
Kendal House
 5 Croydon CR0 . . . . .42 E1
 3 Penge SE26 . . . . .23 B2
Kendale Cl RH10 . . . . .202 C2
Kendale Rd BR1 . . . . .24 E3
Kendall Ave Penge BR3 . . . . .43 E7
 South Croydon CR2 . . . . . .61 D2
Kendall Ave S CR2 . . . . .61 D1
Kendall Cl 4 SE19 . . . . .22 F1
Kendall House SE12 . . . . .24 F8
 Penge BR3 . . . . .43 E7
Kendall Rd Isleworth TW7 . . .6 A6
 Penge BR3 . . . . .43 E7
Kendor Ave KT19 . . . . .76 C6
Kendra Hall Rd CR2 . . . . .61 B3
Kendrey Gdns TW2 . . . . .16 E8
Kendrick Cl RG40 . . . . .25 C5
Kenilford Rd SW12 . . . . .21 B8
Kenilworth Ave
 Bracknell RG12 . . . . .27 D8
 Oxshott KT11 . . . . .74 B5
 Wimbledon SW19 . . . . .20 A4
Kenilworth Cl
 Banstead SM7 . . . . .78 B3
 Crawley RH11 . . . . .201 B2
Kenilworth Ct TW2 . . . . .16 E6
Kenilworth Dr KT12 . . . . .54 D7
Kenilworth Gdns TW18 . . . . .13 C3
Kenilworth Rd
 Ashford TW15, TW19 . . . . . .13 D5
 Farnborough GU14 . . . . . . .84 C5
 Penge SE20 . . . . .43 D8
 Stoneleigh KT17 . . . . .58 A5
Kenilworth Terr 3 SM2 . . . . .59 A3
Kenley Cl CR3 . . . . .100 F7
Kenley Gdns CR7 . . . . .42 B5
Kenley House 5 CR3 . . . . . . .43 A1
Kenley La CR8 . . . . .80 D3
Kenley Prim Sch CR3 . . . . . .80 E3
Kenley Rd
 Headley Down GU35 . . . . . .187 C5
 Kingston u T KT1, KT3 . . . . .38 B7
 Merton SW19 . . . . .40 A6
 Twickenham TW1 . . . . .6 B1
Kenley Sta CR8 . . . . .80 C5
Kenley Wlk SM3 . . . . .58 B6
Kenlor Rd SW17 . . . . .20 D3
Kenmara Cl RH10 . . . . .182 A1
Kenmara Ct RH10 . . . . .182 A2
Kenmare Dr CR4 . . . . .20 F1
Kenmare Rd CR7 . . . . .42 A3
Kenmore Cl Frimley GU16 . . .85 D8
 Richmond TW9 . . . . .7 A7

Kenmore Rd CR8 . . . . .80 B5
Kennard Ct RH18 . . . . .206 E3
Kennedy Ave RH19 . . . . .185 D3
Kennedy Cl CR4 . . . . .41 A7
Kennedy Ct TW15 . . . . .14 C3
Kennedy Rd RH13 . . . . .217 D1
Kennel Ave SL5 . . . . .28 F8
Kennel Cl
 Fetcham KT22, KT23 . . . . . .94 C3
 North Ascot SL5 . . . . .8 F2
Kennel Gn SL5 . . . . .28 E8
Kennel La Fetcham KT22 . . . .94 C4
 Frensham GU10 . . . . .146 C2
 Hookwood RH6 . . . . .160 D2
 Windlesham GU20 . . . . .28 D3
Kennel Ride SL5 . . . . .8 F1
Kennel Wood SL5 . . . . .28 F8
Kennel Wood Cres CR0 . . . . .82 D8
Kennels La GU14 . . . . .84 C2
Kennet Cl Ash GU12 . . . . . .106 A5
 Crawley RH11 . . . . .200 F5
 Farnborough GU14 . . . . . . .84 E6
Kennet House 6 RH1 . . . . . .118 F2
Kennet Rd TW7 . . . . .5 F4
Kennet Sq CR4 . . . . .40 E8
Kenneth Rd SM7 . . . . .78 D4
Kennodies SE21 . . . . .22 D6
Kenrick Sq RH1 . . . . .120 E1
Kensington Ave CR7 . . . . . . .42 A8
Kensington Avenue Inf Sch
 CR7 . . . . .42 A8
Kensington Avenue Jun Sch
 CR7 . . . . .42 A8
Kensington Rd RH11 . . . . . .201 C2
Kensington Terr CR2 . . . . . . .61 D3
Kent Cl Mitcham CR4, SW16 .41 E5
 Staines TW18 . . . . .13 D2
Kent Dr TW11 . . . . .16 D3
Kent Gate Way
 Addington SL5 . . . . .63 B5
 New Addington CR0, CR2 . . .63 B5
Kent Hatch Rd
 Limpsfield RH8, TN8 . . . . . .123 D4
 The Chart RH8, TN8 . . . . . .123 D4
Kent House La BR3 . . . . .23 E3
Kent House Rd
 Forest Hill SE26, BR3 . . . . . .23 E2
 Penge SE26, BR3 . . . . .23 E2
Kent House Sta BR3 . . . . . . .43 E8
Kent House Station App
 BR3 . . . . .43 D8
Kent Lodge 3 SW19 . . . . . . .19 D7
Kent Rd East Molesey KT8 . . .36 C5
 Kingston u T KT1 . . . . .37 D6
 Richmond TW9 . . . . .7 A7
 West Wickham BR4 . . . . . . .44 B1
 Windlesham GU20 . . . . .48 B5
 Woking GU22 . . . . .70 C3
Kent Tower SE20 . . . . .23 B1
Kent Way KT6 . . . . .56 F8
Kentigern Dr RG45 . . . . .45 E5
Kenton Ave TW16 . . . . .35 C7
Kenton Cl Bracknell RG12 . . .27 D7
 Frimley GU16 . . . . .65 F1
Kenton Ct SE26 . . . . .23 E5
Kenton Rd KT17 . . . . .68 F2
Kentwyns Rise RH1 . . . . .140 F8
Kenwood Cl UB7 . . . . .3 A8
Kenwood Dr
 Beckenham BR3 . . . . .44 C6
 Hersham KT12 . . . . .54 B5
Kenwood Pk KT13 . . . . .53 D4
Kenwood Ridge CR8 . . . . . . .80 B2
Kenworth Gr GU18 . . . . .48 A1
Kenwyn Rd SW20 . . . . .39 C8
Kenya Ct RH6 . . . . .160 F4
Kenyngton Dr TW16 . . . . .15 A3
Kenyngton Manor Prim Sch
 TW16 . . . . .15 A2
Kenyons KT24 . . . . .112 B7
Keogh Barracks GU16 . . . . . .86 B1
Keogh Cl GU12 . . . . .86 B2
Keppel Rd RH4 . . . . .115 B1
Keppel Spur SL4 . . . . .11 B8
Kepple Pl GU19 . . . . .47 F3
Kerria Way GU24 . . . . .67 F6
Kerrill Ave CR5 . . . . .100 A8
Kerrisdale Cotts GU27 . . . . .149 E7
Kerry Terr GU21 . . . . .70 B3
Kersey Dr CR2 . . . . .81 D7
Kershaw House 7 SE27 . . . . .22 B3
Keston Ave
 Coulsdon CR5, CR8 . . . . . .100 B8
 Woodham KT15 . . . . .71 A8
Keston Rd CR7 . . . . .42 A3
Keston Rd SM1 . . . . .58 F7
Kestrel Cl
 Crawley RH11 . . . . .201 C8
 Frimley GU15 . . . . .66 D4
 Sutton SM1 . . . . .59 C6
Kestrel Rd GU18 . . . . .67 B8
Kestrel Way GU9 . . . . .146 A8
Keswick Ave
 Kingston u T KT2, SW15 . . . .18 E3
 Merton SW19 . . . . .40 A6
 Upper Halliford TW17 . . . . .34 E6
Keswick Cl Crawley RH11 . . . .200 D4
 Frimley GU15 . . . . .66 D4
 Sutton SM1 . . . . .59 C6
Keswick Dr GU18 . . . . .67 B8
Keswick Rd
 Fetcham KT22, KT23 . . . . . .94 C2

Keswick Rd continued
Thorpe Lea TW20 . . . . **12** B1
Twickenham TW2 . . . . **5** C1
West Wickham BR4 . . . . **63** E8
Witley GU8 . . . . **170** D6
Kettering Ct CR7 . . . . **42** C5
Kettering St SW16 . . . . **21** C2
Kettlewell Cl GU21 . . . . **69** E4
Kettlewell Dr GU21 . . . . **69** E5
Kettlewell Hill GU21 . . . . **69** E4
Ketton Grn RH1 . . . . **119** D7
Kevan Dr GU23 . . . . **90** E2
Kevin Cl TW4 . . . . **4** D5
Kew Bridge Rd TW8 . . . . **6** F8
Kew Cres SM3 . . . . **58** F7
Kew Foot Rd TW9 . . . . **6** E4
Kew Gardens Rd TW9 . . . . **7** A6
Kew Gardens Sta TW9 . . . . . . **7** A6
Kew Gn TW9 . . . . **6** F6
Kew Lodge **10** TW9 . . . . **6** F6
Kew Observatory TW9 . . . . **6** C4
Kew Palace TW9 . . . . **6** E7
Kew Rd TW9 . . . . **6** F4
Kew Ret Pk TW9 . . . . **7** B6
Key Cross GU10 . . . . **147** D5
Keymer Cl TW16 . . . . **83** D3
Keymer Rd Crawley RH11 . . **201** D4
 Streatham SW2 . . . . **21** F6
Keynsham Rd SM4 . . . . **40** B1
Keynsham Way GU47 . . . . . . **45** D2
Keynsham Wlk SM4 . . . . **40** B1
Keysham Ave TW5 . . . . **4** A6
Keywood Dr TW16 . . . . **15** A2
Khama Rd SW17 . . . . **20** E4
Khartoum Rd
 Upper Tooting SW17 . . . . . . **20** D4
 Witley GU8 . . . . **170** E6
Kibble Gn RH12 . . . . **27** C3
Kidborough Down KT23 . . . **114** A8
Kidborough Rd RH11 . . . . . . **200** F4
Kidbrooke Park
 (Michael Hall Sch)
 RH18 . . . . **206** D1
Kidbrooke Rise RH18 . . . . . . **206** E2
Kidderminster Rd CR0 . . . . . **42** C2
Kidmans Cl RH12 . . . . **217** F5
Kidworth Cl RH6 . . . . **160** F5
Kielder Wlk GU15 . . . . **66** C4
Kier Pk SL5 . . . . **29** C6
Kilberry Cl TW7 . . . . **5** D6
Kilcorral Cl KT17 . . . . **77** A5
Kilasser Ct KT20 . . . . **97** C4
Kilkearn Rd SE6 . . . . **24** D7
Killester Gdns KT17, KT4 . . **58** B6
Killick House SM1 . . . . **59** B6
Killicks **174** F4
Killieser Ave SW2 . . . . **21** E6
Kilingbeck House TW16 . . . . . **14** E1
Killinghurst La GU27,GU8 . . **209** D6
Killross Rd TW14 . . . . **14** D7
Kilmarnock Pk RH2 . . . . **118** B2
Kilmartin Ave SW16 . . . . **42** A6
Kilmartin Gdns GU16 . . . . . . **65** F1
Kilmington Cl RG12 . . . . **27** D2
Kilmiston Ave TW17 . . . . **34** C3
Kilmiston House TW17 . . . . . . **34** C3
Kilmore Dr GU15 . . . . **66** B4
Kilmorey Gdns TW1 . . . . **6** B3
Kilmorey Rd TW1 . . . . **6** B4
Kilmorie Prim Sch SE23 . . . **23** E6
Kilmorie Rd SE23 . . . . **23** E6
Kilmuir Cl GU47 . . . . **64** D7
Kiln Cl UB3 . . . . **3** D8
Kiln Copse GU4 . . . . **174** E4
Kiln Fields GU27 . . . . **208** C8
Kiln La Bracknell RG12 . . . . . **27** A7
 Brockham RH3 . . . . **116** C1
 Ewell KT17 . . . . **76** E8
 Farnham GU10, GU9 . . . . **146** C6
 Horley RH6 . . . . **161** A5
 Ripley GU23 . . . . **91** B3
 Sunningdale SL5 . . . . **30** A4
Kiln Meadows GU3 . . . . **108** C5
Kiln Mews SW17 . . . . **20** D3
Kiln Rd RH10 . . . . **204** B7
Kiln Way Aldershot GU11 . . **126** B7
 Grayshott GU26 . . . . **187** E5
Kiln Wlk RH1 . . . . **140** A4
Kilnfield Rd RH12 . . . . **213** F4
Kilnmead RH10, RH11 . . . . **201** E7
Kilnmead Cl RH10 . . . . **201** E7
Kilnside KT10 . . . . **56** A3
Kilnwood La
 Crawley RH12 . . . . **200** B3
 Faygate RH12 . . . . **199** F3
Kilross Rd TW14 . . . . **14** D7
Kilrue La KT12 . . . . **53** F6
Kilrush Terr GU21 . . . . **69** F3
Kilsha Rd KT12 . . . . **35** C3
Kimber Ct GU4 . . . . **110** D3
Kimber Ctr The SW18 . . . . . . **20** A8
Kimber Rd SW18 . . . . **20** B8
Kimberley RG12 . . . . **27** C1
Kimberley Ct RH6 . . . . **160** E3
Kimberley Pl **5** CR8 . . . . **80** A8
Kimberley Rd
 Crawley RH10 . . . . **202** B7
 Penge BR3 . . . . **43** D7
 Thornton Heath CR0, CR7 . . **42** B3
Kimberley Ride KT11 . . . . **74** B6
Kimberley Wlk KT12 . . . . **35** B2
Kimbers La GU9 . . . . **125** D3
Kimble Rd Mitcham SW17 . . **20** D2
 Mitcham SW17 . . . . **20** D2
Kimbolton Cl SE12 . . . . **24** F8

Kimmeridge RG12 . . . . **27** E3
Kimpton Bsns Ctr SM3 . . . . . **58** F8
Kimpton House SW15 . . . . . . **19** A8
Kimpton Ind Est SM3 . . . . . . **58** F8
Kimpton Rd SM3 . . . . **58** F8
Kinburn Dr TW20 . . . . **11** E3
Kindell House **4** SW14 . . . . **7** D4
Kindersley Ct RH19 . . . . **186** B3
Kindauns Rd SW7 . . . . **22** A6
King Acre Ct TW18 . . . . **12** E5
King Alfred Ave SE6 . . . . **24** A4
King Athelstan Prim Sch
 KT1 . . . . **37** F6
King Charles Cres KT5 . . . . . . **37** F2
King Charles' Rd KT5, KT6 . . **37** F3
King Charles Wlk **6** SW19 . . **19** E7
King Edward Dr KT6 . . . . **56** E7
King Edward's Gr TW11 . . . . . **17** C2
King Edward's Sch GU8 . . . **170** F1
King Edwards Rd SL5 . . . . . . **28** E8
King Edwards Rise SL5 . . . . . **28** E8
King Gdns Mews SE23 . . . . . . **23** C6
King George Ave
 East Grinstead RH19 . . . . . **185** C3
 Walton-on-T KT12 . . . . **35** D1
King George Cl TW16 . . . . . . **14** E3
King George Sq TW10 . . . . . . **6** E1
King George VI Ave TW16 . . **83** D3
King George VI Ave CR4 . . . . **41** D8
King George's Cotts GU8 . . **192** F6
King George's Dr KT15 . . . . . **52** A1
King George's Lodge
 GU2 . . . . **109** A4
King George's Trad Est
 KT9 . . . . **57** A6
King Henry's Dr
 New Addington CR0 . . . . **63** B3
 West Wickham CR0 . . . . **82** E8
King Henry's Rd KT1, KT3 . . **38** B6
King St Chertsey KT16 . . . . . . **33** A1
 East Grinstead RH19 . . . . . **185** E1
 Richmond TW10, TW9 . . . . . . **6** D2
 Twickenham TW1 . . . . **17** A7
King Street Par **8** TW1 . . . . . **17** A7
King William IV Gdns
 SE20 . . . . **23** C2
King's Ave Ashford TW16 . . . . **14** F2
 Hounslow TW3, TW5 . . . . **5** B6
King's Cl Staines TW18 . . . . . **13** D1
 Thames Ditton KT7 . . . . **37** A2
King's Coll Sch SW19 . . . . . . **19** D2
King's Court Prim Sch
 SL4 . . . . **9** A7
King's Ct
 Aldershot GU10, GU12 . . . . **126** E8
 Beckenham BR3 . . . . **44** B6
 Wimbledon SW19 . . . . **20** A2
King's Dr KT7 . . . . **37** B2
King's Head La KT14 . . . . **71** D8
King's House Jun Sch
 TW10 . . . . **6** F2
King's House Sch TW10 . . . . . . **6** F2
King's Keep GU47 . . . . **45** B1
King's La SM1, SM2 . . . . **59** D5
King's Paddock TW12 . . . . . . **36** C8
King's Pas KT2 . . . . **37** D8
King's Rd Aldershot GU11 . . **104** F1
 Ascot SL5 . . . . **29** D4
 Cranleigh GU6 . . . . **174** F5
 Crowthorne RG45 . . . . **45** C5
 Croydon SE25 . . . . **43** A6
 Egham TW20 . . . . **12** A4
 Farncombe GU7 . . . . **150** F6
 Haslemere GU27 . . . . **208** A7
 Horsham RH12, RH13 . . . . **217** E3
 Long Ditton KT6 . . . . **37** C1
 Mortlake SW14 . . . . **7** D4
 Teddington TW11, TW12 . . . . **16** D3
 Twickenham TW1 . . . . **6** B1
 Wimbledon SW19 . . . . **20** A2
King's Shade Wlk **1** KT18 . . . . **76** D6
King's Terr **3** TW7 . . . . **6** A4
King's Way GU24 . . . . **87** D8
King's Wlk GU15 . . . . **64** F6
Kingcup Cl CR0 . . . . **43** D1
Kingcup Dr GU24 . . . . **68** A4
Kingfield Cl GU22 . . . . **89** F7
Kingfield Dr GU22 . . . . **89** F7
Kingfield Gdns GU22 . . . . **89** F7
Kingfield Rd GU22 . . . . **89** F7
Kingfield Sch GU22 . . . . **90** A7
Kingfisher Cl
 Crawley RH11 . . . . **182** A1
 Farnborough GU14 . . . . **84** D6
 Hersham KT12 . . . . **54** D5
 Putney SW19 . . . . **19** E6
Kingfisher Ct Cheam SM1 . . **58** F5
 Dorking RH4 . . . . **136** A8
 East Molesey KT8 . . . . **36** B5
 Isleworth TW3 . . . . **5** B3
 Sheerwater GU21 . . . . **70** C5
Kingfisher Dr
 Guildford GU4 . . . . **110** C3
 Redhill RH1 . . . . **119** A3
 Staines TW18 . . . . **12** F4
 Teddington TW10 . . . . **17** B4
Kingfisher Gdns CR2 . . . . **62** D1
Kingfisher Lodge **3** TW11 . . . **17** A4
Kingfisher Rise RH19 . . . . . . **205** F8
Kingfisher Sports Ctr The
 KT1 . . . . **37** E7
Kingfisher Way
 Beckenham CR0 . . . . **43** D4
 Horsham RH12 . . . . **217** C5

Kingfisher Wlk GU12 . . . . . . **105** F2
Kingham Cl SW18 . . . . **20** C8
Kings Ave Ash GU10, GU12 . **126** F8
 Bromley BR1 . . . . **24** F2
 Byfleet KT14 . . . . **71** D7
 New Malden KT3 . . . . **38** F5
 Redhill RH1 . . . . **139** E7
 Streatham SW12, SW4 . . . . . **21** D8
 Wallington SM5 . . . . **59** F3
Kings Chase KT8 . . . . **36** C6
Kings Cl KT12 . . . . **35** B1
Kings Copse **2** RH19 . . . . . . **205** F8
Kings Cres GU15 . . . . **65** C8
Kings Cross La RH1 . . . . **140** E6
Kings Ct Horsham RH13 . . . **217** E3
 10 Kingston u T KT2 . . . . . . **18** A1
 11 Roehampton SW15 . . . . **19** A8
 Tadworth KT20 . . . . **97** C5
 8 Wallington SM6 . . . . **60** B4
Kings Dr KT5 . . . . **38** A3
Kings Dr The KT12 . . . . **53** F2
Kings Farm Ave TW10 . . . . **7** A3
Kings Gate GU7 . . . . **150** F6
Kings Hall Rd BR3 . . . . **43** E8
Kings Keep KT6 . . . . **37** E5
Kings La
 Englefield Green TW20 . . . . . **11** A2
 Windlesham GU20 . . . . **48** E5
 Wrecclesham GU10 . . . . . . **145** F6
Kings' Manor Sch GU2 . . . . **108** E1
Kings Mead
 Smallfield RH6 . . . . **162** B3
 South Nutfield RH1 . . . . . . **140** E7
Kings Mead Pk KT10 . . . . **55** E3
Kings Mill La
 Salfords RH1 . . . . **140** D5
 South Nutfield RH1 . . . . . . **140** D5
Kings Rd Belmont SM2 . . . . . **59** A3
 Biggin Hill TN16 . . . . **83** C2
 Feltham TW13 . . . . **15** C7
 Horley RH6 . . . . **161** A3
 Mitcham CR4 . . . . **41** A6
 Richmond TW10, TW9 . . . . . . **6** F2
 Shalford GU4 . . . . **130** E2
 Walton-on-T KT12 . . . . **35** B1
 West End GU24 . . . . **68** A6
 Woking GU21 . . . . **70** A3
 Wonersh GU5 . . . . **71** B8
Kings Ride Gate TW10 . . . . **7** A3
Kings Way CR0 . . . . **60** F5
Kings Wlk GU21 . . . . **81** B5
Kings's Rd **2** GU1 . . . . **109** D1
Kingsbridge House 11
 SE20 . . . . **43** B8
Kingsbridge Rd
 Walton-on-T KT12 . . . . **35** B2
 West Barnes SM4 . . . . **39** D2
Kingsbrook KT22 . . . . **95** A5
Kingsbury Cres TW18 . . . . . . **12** D4
Kingsbury Dr SL4 . . . . **11** B8
Kingsclear Pk GU15 . . . . **65** D4
Kingsclere Cl SW15 . . . . **19** A8
Kingscliffe Gdns SW19 . . . . . **19** F7
Kingscote Hill RH11 . . . . . . **201** B4
Kingscote Rd
 Croydon CR0, CR9 . . . . **43** B2
 Kingston u T KT3 . . . . **38** D6
Kingscote Sta RH19 . . . . **204** F4
Kingscourt Rd SW16 . . . . **21** E5
Kingscourt Cty Inf Sch
 TW18 . . . . **13** A2
Kingscroft Cty Jun Sch
 TW18 . . . . **13** A2
Kingscroft La RG42 . . . . **8** A6
Kingscroft Rd
 Leatherhead KT22 . . . . **95** B7
 Woodmansterne SM7 . . . . . . **78** E4
Kingsdale Rd SE20 . . . . **23** D1
Kingsdale Sch SE21 . . . . **22** F5
Kingsdene KT20 . . . . **97** B5
Kingsdown **11** SW19 . . . . **19** D7
Kingsdown Ave CR2, CR8 . . . **61** C2
Kingsdown Rd Cheam SM3 . . **58** E5
 Ewell KT17 . . . . **77** A6
Kingsdowne Rd KT6 . . . . **37** F2
Kingsfield GU5 . . . . **152** E6
Kingsfold Bsns Pk RH1 . . . . **140** A8
Kingsfold Ct RH12 . . . . **198** B5
Kingsford Ave SM6 . . . . **60** E3
Kingsgate Bsns Ctr KT2 . . . . **37** E8
Kingsgate Rd KT2 . . . . **37** E8
Kingslake Ct **2** GU21 . . . . **68** F1
Kingsland RH5 . . . . **158** B1
Kingsland Ct RH10 . . . . **202** A6
Kingslea KT22 . . . . **95** A7
Kingslea Horsham RH13 . . . **217** E3
 Leatherhead KT22 . . . . **95** A7
Kingslee Ct **5** SM2 . . . . **59** B3
Kingsleigh Pl CR4 . . . . **40** F6
Kingsley Ave Banstead SM7 . . **78** A4
 Camberley GU15 . . . . **65** C5
 Carshalton SM1 . . . . **59** E8
 Englefield Green TW20 . . . . . **11** B2
 Hounslow TW3 . . . . **5** C5
Kingsley Cl
 Crowthorne RG45 . . . . **45** B3
 Horley RH6 . . . . **160** F3
Kingsley Ct
 Worcester Park KT4 . . . . **57** F8
 8 Kingston u T KT2 . . . . . . **18** A1
Kingsley Dr KT4 . . . . **57** F8
Kingsley Gr RH2 . . . . **139** B5
Kingsley House **3** KT6 . . . . . . **37** E4
Kingsley Inf Sch CR9 . . . . . . **42** A1
Kingsley Jun Sch CR9 . . . . . . **42** A1
Kingsley Rd Crawley RH11 . **201** A3

Kingsley Rd continued
 Farnborough GU14 . . . . **84** F6
 Horley RH6 . . . . **160** F5
 Hounslow TW3 . . . . **5** C5
 Thornton Heath CR0 . . . . . . **42** A1
 Wimbledon SW19 . . . . **20** B3
Kingslyn Cres SE19 . . . . **42** E8
Kingslyn Cres SE19 . . . . **42** E8
Kingsmead **Bigin Hill TN16** . . **83** D3
 Cranleigh GU6 . . . . **174** E3
 Farnborough GU14 . . . . **85** B4
 Frimley GU16 . . . . **85** E7
 Richmond TW10 . . . . **6** F1
 Weybridge KT13 . . . . **53** D4
 Woking GU21 . . . . **70** A3
Kingsmead Ave
 Mitcham CR4 . . . . **41** C6
 North Cheam KT4 . . . . **58** B7
 Sunbury TW16 . . . . **35** C7
 Tolworth KT6 . . . . **57** A8
Kingsmead Cl
 Horsham RH12 . . . . **218** B6
 Teddington TW11 . . . . **17** B2
 West Ewell KT19 . . . . **57** D3
Kingsmead Ct BR1 . . . . **24** F1
Kingsmead Lodge SM2 . . . . . **59** D4
Kingsmead Pl RH12 . . . . **216** C3
Kingsmead Rd
 Broadbridge Heath RH12 . . **216** D3
 Streatham SW2 . . . . **22** A6
Kingsmead Sh Ctr GU14 . . . **85** B3
Kingsmere Rd **84** B7
Kingsmere Rd
 Bracknell RG42 . . . . **26** F8
 Putney SW19 . . . . **19** D6
Kingsnympton Pk KT2 . . . . . . **18** B2
Kingsridge SW19 . . . . **19** E6
Kingsthorpe Rd SE26 . . . . . . **23** D4
Kingston Ave New Cheam SM3 . . **58** E7
 East Horsley KT24 . . . . **92** E1
 Feltham TW14 . . . . **3** F1
 Leatherhead KT22 . . . . **95** B6
Kingston Bsns Ctr KT9 . . . . . **56** F7
Kingston By - Pass KT6 . . . . . **37** B8
Kingston By-Pass
 KT6, KT7, KT9 . . . . **56** E7
Kingston Cl TW11 . . . . **17** B2
Kingston Coll of F Ed KT1 . . **37** D6
Kingston Coll of F Ed
 (M V Annex) KT2 . . . . **37** D6
Kingston Cres BR3 . . . . **43** F8
Kingston Gdns CR0 . . . . **60** E7
Kingston Gram Sch KT2 . . . . **37** E6
Kingston Hall Rd KT1 . . . . **37** D6
Kingston Hill KT2 . . . . **18** C2
Kingston Hill Pl KT2, TW10 . . **18** C4
Kingston Hospl KT2 . . . . **38** B8
Kingston House Gdns
 KT22 . . . . **95** B6
Kingston La
 Teddington TW11 . . . . **17** B2
 West Horsley KT24 . . . . **112** A8
Kingston Lodge **1** KT3 . . . . . . **38** E5
Kingston Mus KT1 . . . . **37** E7
Kingston Poly (Gipsy Hill
 Ctr) KT2 . . . . **18** C2
Kingston Rd
 Ashford TW15, TW17 . . . . . . **13** F2
 Ashstead KT22, KT9 . . . . **75** A3
 Camberley GU15 . . . . **47** A1
 Ewell KT17, KT19, KT4,
 KT5, KT6 . . . . **57** D6
 Kingston u T KT1, KT3 . . . . . **38** C5
 Leatherhead KT22 . . . . **75** A1
 Merton SW19, SW20 . . . . . . **39** E7
 New Malden KT3 . . . . **38** E5
 Putney SW15, SW19 . . . . . . **19** B7
 Roehampton SW15, SW19 . . **19** B7
 Staines TW15, TW18 . . . . . . **13** B1
 Teddington TW11 . . . . **17** B2
 Tolworth KT17, KT19, KT4,
 KT5, KT6 . . . . **57** D6
 Worcester Park KT17, KT19,
 KT4 . . . . **57** D6
Kingston Rise KT15 . . . . **52** A1
Kingston Sq SE19 . . . . **22** D3
Kingston Sta KT2 . . . . **37** E8
Kingston Univ
 Kingston u T KT2 . . . . **37** E6
 Kingston u T KT1, KT3 . . . . . **38** E6
Kingston Univ Annex KT1 . . . **37** E7
Kingston Univ
 Roehampton Vale Ctr
 SW15 . . . . **18** E5
Kingston Vale SW15 . . . . **18** E5
Kingstons Ind Est GU12 . . . **105** E2
Kingsway Aldershot GU11 . . **104** E1
 Blackwater GU17 . . . . **64** E5
 Coney Hall BR4 . . . . **63** F7
 Mortlake SW14 . . . . **7** C4
 Stanwell TW19 . . . . **2** A2
 West Barnes KT3 . . . . **39** C4
 Woking GU21 . . . . **69** D3
Kingsway Ave Selsdon CR2 . . **62** D2
 Woking GU21 . . . . **69** D3
Kingsway Bsns Pk GU21 . . . . **70** C5
Kingsway Bsns Pk The
 TW12 . . . . **35** F8
Kingsway Rd SM3 . . . . **58** E3
Kingsway Terr KT13 . . . . **53** A2
Kingsway The KT17 . . . . **77** F1
Kingswear House SE23 . . . . . **23** F1
Kingswick Cl SL5 . . . . **29** D5
Kingswick Dr SL5 . . . . **29** D5
Kingswood Ave
 Beckenham BR2, BR3 . . . . . **44** E5
 Hampton TW12 . . . . **16** B2

Kingswood Ave continued
 Hamsey Green CR2 . . . . **81** C4
 Hounslow TW3, TW5 . . . . **4** F5
 Thornton Heath CR7 . . . . . . **42** A4
Kingswood Cl
 Englefield Green TW20 . . . . . **11** D4
 Guildford GU1 . . . . **110** C2
 New Malden KT3 . . . . **38** F3
 Surbiton KT6 . . . . **37** E2
 Weybridge KT13 . . . . **53** B3
Kingswood Ct
 8 Richmond TW10 . . . . **6** F2
 Woking GU21 . . . . **69** F3
Kingswood Cty Prim Sch
 KT20 . . . . **117** F7
Kingswood Dr
 Belmont SM2 . . . . **59** B2
 Carshalton SM5 . . . . **40** F3
 Dulwich SE19, SE21 . . . . . . **22** F4
Kingswood Firs GU26 . . . . . **188** C2
Kingswood Golf Course
 . . . . **98** A.
Kingswood Hall of
 Residence TW20 . . . . **11** D4
Kingswood House **3** KT3 . . . **18** B2
Kingswood House Sch
 KT18 . . . . **76** C6
Kingswood La CR6 . . . . **81** C4
Kingswood Pk KT20 . . . . **97** E5
Kingswood Prim Sch
 SE27 . . . . **22** D:
Kingswood Rd
 Beckenham BR2 . . . . **44** E3
 Merton SW19 . . . . **39** F7
 Penge SE20 . . . . **23** C:
 Streatham SW2 . . . . **21** F8
 Tadworth KT20 . . . . **97** B:
Kingswood Rise TW20 . . . . . . **11** D:
Kingswood Sta KT20 . . . . **97** F7
Kingswood Way
 Hamsey Green CR2 . . . . **81** C:
 Selsdon CR2 . . . . **81** D:
 Wallington SM6 . . . . **60** E:
Kingsworth Cl BR3 . . . . **43** E:
Kingsworthy Cl KT1 . . . . **37** F:
Kinloss Rd SM5 . . . . **40** C:
Kinnaird Ave Bromley BR1 . . **24** F:
 Chiswick W4 . . . . **7** C:
Kinnaird Cl BR1 . . . . **24** F:
Kinnear Ct SW20 . . . . **39** D:
Kinnersley Wlk RH2 . . . . **139** B:
Kinnibrugh Dr RH7 . . . . **165** A:
Kinross Ave Ascot SL5 . . . . . . **28** F:
 Worcester Park KT4 . . . . **58** A:
Kinross Cl TW16 . . . . **14** F:
Kinross Ct SL5 . . . . **28** F:
Kinross Dr TW16 . . . . **14** F:
Kinsey House SE21 . . . . **22** E:
Kintyre Cl SW16 . . . . **41** F:
Kintyre Ct **17** SW2 . . . . **21** E:
Kinver Rd SE26 . . . . **23** C:
Kipings KT20 . . . . **97** D:
Kipling Cl RH10 . . . . **202** C:
Kipling Ct RH13 . . . . **218** A:
Kipling Dr SW17 . . . . **20** E:
Kipling Way RH19 . . . . **185** C:
Kirby Cl KT19 . . . . **57** F:
Kirby Rd GU21 . . . . **69** C:
Kirby Way KT12 . . . . **35** C:
Kirdford Dr RH11 . . . . **201** A:
Kirk Rise SM1 . . . . **59** B:
Kirkby Ct GU16 . . . . **65** F:
Kirkdale SE26 . . . . **23** C:
Kirkdale Cty . . . . **109** A:
Kirkgate The **2** KT17 . . . . **76** E:
Kirkham Cl GU47 . . . . **45** A:
Kirkland Ave GU21 . . . . **68** F:
Kirkleas Rd KT6 . . . . **37** E:
Kirklees Rd CR7 . . . . **42** A:
Kirkley Rd SW19 . . . . **40** A:
Kirkly Cl CR2 . . . . **61** E:
Kirkstall Gdns SW2 . . . . **21** E:
Kirkstall Rd SW2 . . . . **21** E:
Kirkstone Cl GU15 . . . . **66** D:
Kirkstone Way BR1 . . . . **24** E:
Kirrane Cl KT3 . . . . **38** F:
Kirriemuir Gdns GU12 . . . . . **106** B:
Kirtley Rd SE26 . . . . **23** E:
Kitchener Rd
 Farnborough GU11 . . . . **105** C:
 South Norwood CR7 . . . . . . **42** D:
Kitchenride Cnr KT16 . . . . **51** A:
Kites Cl RH11 . . . . **201** A:
Kithurst Cl RH11 . . . . **201** C:
Kitley Gdns SE19 . . . . **42** F:
Kitsmead RH10 . . . . **183** A:
Kitsmead La KT16 . . . . **50** D:
Kittiwake Cl
 Crawley RH11 . . . . **201** C:
 Selsdon CR0, CR2 . . . . **62** E:
Kittiwake Pl SM1 . . . . **58** F:
Klondyke Villas GU27 . . . . . **190** F:
Knaggs House **1** TW11 . . . . . **16** E:
Knapdale Cl SE23 . . . . **23** B:
Knaphill Cty Inf Sch GU21 . . **68** D:
Knaphill Cty Jun Sch
 GU21 . . . . **68** E:
Knaphill Rd SE6 . . . . **24** A:
Knaphill War SL5 . . . . **13** E:
Knapton Mews SW17 . . . . **21** A:
Knaresborough Dr SW18 . . . . **20** B:
Kneller Gdns TW7 . . . . **5** D:
Kneller Rd New Malden KT3 . . **39** A:
 Twickenham TW2 . . . . **5** C:
Knepp Cl RH10 . . . . **202** D:
Knight's Hill SE19, SE27 . . . . **22** C:

iph't Hill Sq SE27 . . . . 22 B4
ight's Pk KT1 . . . . 37 E6
roydon CR2 . . . . 61 B2
ighton Park Rd SE26 . . . 23 D3
ighton Rd RH1 . . . . 140 A7
ights Gdns La GU8 . . . . . 193 A2
ights Cl TW20 . . . . 12 D2
ights Ct Kingston u T KT1 . 37 E6
enge BR3 . . . . 43 E8
ights Pl RH1 . . . . 119 A2
ights Rd GU19 . . . . 125 E7
ights Way GU15 . . . . 66 C4
ightsbridge Cres TW18 . 13 B2
ightsbridge Ho 16 GU1 . 130 F8
ightsbridge Rd GU15 . . . 65 E7
Aldershot . . . .
acknel RG12 . . . . 27 B1
cking GU21 . . . . 68 F1
ightwood Cl RH12 . . . . . . 217 E3
ightwood Cres KT3 . . . . 38 E3
igh Hill KT11 . . . . 73 F6
ob Hill RH12 . . . . 198 A1
obfield RH5 . . . . 154 F8
ockhundred La GU26 . . 207 C8
ole Cl Crawley RH10 . . . 202 D7
oydon CR0 . . . . 43 C3
ole Gr RH10 . . . . 185 C3
ole Wood SL5 . . . . 29 C1
oll Ct SE19 . . . . 22 F3
oll Park Rd KT16 . . . . 32 F1
oll Quarry GU7 . . . . 150 E6
oll Rd Camberley GU15 . 65 D6
orking RH4 . . . . 136 A5
oll The Beckenham BR3 . 44 B8
Hersham KT11 . . . . 74 A6
atherhead KT22 . . . . 95 C6
oll Wood GU7 . . . . 150 D6
ollmead KT24 . . . . 92 F1
ollmead Prim Sch KT4 . 57 C8
oll's The KT17 . . . . 77 C3
olly's Cl GU21 . . . . 69 B1
olly's Rd SE27, SW16 . . 22 A5
ollys Rd GU11 . . . . 104 F3
oll Park House KT22 . . 74 C4
olt GU21 . . . . 70 B1
owl Hill Sch The GU8 . 87 E5
owle Ct RH10 . . . . 183 C3
owle Dr RH10 . . . . 183 B3
owle Gdns KT14 . . . . 70 F6
owle Gn TW18 . . . . 13 A3
owle Gr GU25 . . . . 31 C2
owle Grove Cl GU25 . . . 31 C2
owle Hill GU25 . . . . 31 C2
owle La GU6, RH12 . . . . 194 D4
owle Lodge CR3 . . . . 101 A4
owle Park Ave TW18 . 13 B3
owle Pk KT11 . . . . 73 E4
owle Rd TW2 . . . . 16 E7
wlton Gn BR2 . . . . 44 F4
x Rd GU2 . . . . 109 B6
aat Ct GU11 . . . . 104 F2
ima Cl GU1 . . . . 105 B3
nowla Cl TN16 . . . . 83 D4
ringa CR6 . . . . 101 B8
da Cl TW17 . . . . 33 F6
sel Wlk TW9 . . . . 7 A6
tina Ct SM2 . . . . 59 A4
oner Rd GU15 . . . . 65 B3
ia Gdns SW16 . . . . 41 F8
esi Cl RG12 . . . . 27 B6
aston Ave CR7 . . . . 42 C4
aston Cres CR0, CR7 . 42 C4
aston House 7 SW2 . . 21 F7
aston Rd CR0, CR7 . . . 42 C4
ersley CI SW17 . . . . 59 F7

traite RC Girls Sch
12 . . . . 21 C8
urnam Ct SW16 . . . . . . 22 A3
urnam Ave SM1 . . . . . . 59 E7
12 . . . .
Aldershot GU11 . . . . 105 A1
ndford GU1 . . . . 109 C4
urnam Cres TW16 . . . . 35 B8
urnam Ct CR4 . . . . 41 A7
urnam Gdns CR0 . . . . 43 D1
urnam Gr Brands Hill SL3 . 1 B8
nslow TW3 . . . . 4 F3
gston u T KT3 . . . . 38 D7
urnam Pas 1 GU11 . 105 A1
urnam Pl TW20 . . . . 11 B2
12 . . . .
urnam Rd
ershot GU11 . . . . 105 A2
rtsey KT16 . . . . 33 A1
om KT18 . . . . 76 E6
th End GU9 . . . . 125 E7
ton SW19 . . . . 20 C1
urnam Way CR4 . . . . . . 41 A7
 king GU22 . . . . 89 D7
urnam Way TW19 . . . . 13 F7
urnums The GU17 . . . . 64 B5
wley Ave CR5 . . . . 100 A7
wley Ct SM2 . . . . 59 A3
y Dr Coulsdon CR5 . . . 100 B7
nm Rd CR4 . . . . 35 F8
ford Rd CR5 . . . . 78 F1
urnford Cl SW19 . . . . . . 20 C2
am Cl CR5 . . . . 100 A7
od St SE27 . . . . 22 C3
roke Cotts 2 RH11 . . 119 A2

Ladbroke Ct 7 RH1 . . . . 119 A3
Ladbroke Gr RH1 . . . . 119 A2
Ladbroke Hurst RH7 . . . 165 A1
Ladbroke Rd Epsom KT18 . 76 D5
Horley RH6 . . . . 161 B5
Redhill RH1 . . . . 119 A3
Ladbrook Rd SE25 . . . . . . 42 D5
Ladderstile Ride
Kingston u T KT2 . . . . 18 C3
Richmond KT2, TW10 . . . 18 B3
Ladlands SE22 . . . . 23 A8
Lady Booth Rd 2 KT1 . . 37 E7
Lady Eleanor Holles Sch
The (Jeun Girls) TW12 . 16 B3
Lady Eleanor Holles Sch
The (Senior Gs) TW12 . 16 B3
Lady Hay KT4 . . . . 57 F8
Lady Margaret Rd
Crawley RH11 . . . . 201 A2
Sunningdale SL5 . . . . 29 F2
Lady Margaret Wlk RH1 . 201 A2
Ladybank RG12 . . . . 27 B1
Ladycross GU8 . . . . 170 E8
Ladycross Mews GU8 . . 170 F7
Ladygate CI RH5 . . . . . . 136 D8
Ladygate Dr GU26 . . . . . 188 A3
Ladygrove CR2 . . . . 62 D1
Ladygrove Dr GU4 . . . . . 110 B6
Ladymead GU1 . . . . 109 C2
Ladymead Cl RH10 . . . . 202 C3
Ladymead Retail Ctr GU1 . 109 E2
Ladythorpe Cl KT15 . . . . 52 B6
Ladywood Ave GU14 . . 84 E8
Ladywood Rd KT6 . . . . . . 57 A8
Laffan's Rd GU11 . . . . . . 104 E6
Lafone Ave TW13 . . . . 15 C6
Lafone House 11 SW2 . 21 F8
Lagham Pk RH9 . . . . 142 E6
Lagham Rd RH9 . . . . 142 F5
Laglands Cl RH2 . . . . 118 C3
Laings Ave CR4 . . . . 40 F7
Laings Cnr CR4 . . . . 40 F8
Lainlock Pl TW3 . . . . 5 B6
Lainson St SW18 . . . . 20 A8
Laird Ct GU19 . . . . 47 E1
Lairdale Cl SE21 . . . . 22 C8
Laitwood Rd SW12 . . . . . 21 B7
Lake Cl Byfleet KT14 . . . . 71 D7
8 Wimbledon SW19 . . . . 19 F3
Lake Cotts GU18 . . . . 169 F4
Lake End Way RG45 . . . . 45 A4
Lake Gdns Hackbridge SM6 . 60 B7
Richmond TW10 . . . . 17 B6
Lake House 4 SW27 . . . 22 B3
Lake La Dockenfield GU10 . 166 E6
Horley RH1, RH6 . . . . 161 C6
Lake Rd Croydon CR0 . . 62 F8
Frimley GU16 . . . . 85 F6
Ockley RH5 . . . . 177 D6
Virginia Water GU25 . . . . 31 B5
8 Wimbledon SW19 . . . . 19 F3
Lake Side The GU17 . . . . 64 D4
Lake View RH5 . . . . 136 C4
Lake View
Copthorne RH10 . . . . 184 C4
Domewood RH10 . . . . . . 184 C4
Dormans Park RH19 . . . 185 F5
Dormansland RH19 . . . . 185 F5
Lakehall Gdns CR7 . . . . . 42 B4
Lakehall Rd CR7 . . . . 42 B4
Lakehurst Rd KT19 . . . . . 57 E5
Lakeland Dr GU16 . . . . . . 65 E1
Lakeman Ct CR7 . . . . 42 C7
Lakers La KT24 . . . . 212 F1
Lakers Rise SM7 . . . . 78 E3
Lakes Cl GU4 . . . . 131 C3
Lakeside Beckenham BR3 . 44 B6
3 Bracknell RG42 . . . . . . 27 C8
Horsham RH12 . . . . 217 C5
10 Kingston u T KT2 . . . . 18 B1
Knaphill GU21 . . . . 88 E8
Oatlands Park KT13 . . . . 53 E8
Redhill RH1 . . . . 119 A1
West Ewell KT19 . . . . 57 E4
Lakeside Cl Ash Vale GU12 . 105 F4
Knaphill GU21 . . . . 88 E8
South Norwood SE25 . . . 43 A7
Lakeside Cty Prim Sch
GU16 . . . . 65 F1
Lakeside Dr KT10 . . . . 55 C4
Lakeside Est SL3 . . . . 2 A8
Lakeside Gdns GU14 . . 84 D7
Lakeside Grange KT13 . 53 C7
Lakeside Rd
Ash Vale GU1, GU12 . . . 105 F4
Colnbrook SL3 . . . . 1 F7
Farnborough GU14 . . . . . 105 A7
Lakeview Rd SE27 . . . . . . 22 B3
Lakeham Ct E Prim Sch
TW16 . . . . 14 E7
Laleham Ct GU21 . . . . 69 E3
Laleham Lea Prep Sch
CR8 . . . . 60 E1
Laleham Rd Catford SE6 . 24 B8
Lewisham SE6 . . . . 24 C8
Littleton TW17 . . . . 34 A4
Shepperton TW17 . . . . . . 34 B3
Staines TW18 . . . . 12 F2
Lamb's Bsns Pk RH5 . . 142 C5
Lamberhurst Rd SE27 . 22 A3
Lamberhurst Wlk RH10 . 202 A5
Lambert Ave TW9 . . . . 7 B4
Lambert Cl TN16 . . . . 83 D3
Lambert Cotts RH1 . . . . 120 E2
Lambert Cres GU17 . . . . . 64 C4
Lambert Rd SM7 . . . . 78 B5

Lambert's Pl CR0 . . . . 42 D1
Lambert's Rd KT6 . . . . 37 F4
Lambeth Cl RH11 . . . . . . 201 B2
Lambeth Inst Strand Ctr
SW2 . . . . 21 F8
Lambeth Prospect SE19 . 22 D2
Lambeth Rd CR0 . . . . 42 B1
Lambly Hill GU25 . . . . 32 A5
Lamborne Cl GU47 . . . . . 45 A1
Lambourn Cl RH19 . . . . 185 E3
Lambourne Ave SW19 . . 19 F4
Lambourne Cl RH10 . . . 201 F4
Lambourne Cres GU21 . 70 D6
Lambourne Dr
Bagshot GU19 . . . . 47 D2
Cobham KT11 . . . . 73 D4
Lambourne Gr
Bracknell RG12 . . . . 27 E7
Kingston u T KT1 . . . . 38 B7
Lambourne Way GU10 . 126 F7
Lambs Cres RH12 . . . . . 217 F5
Lambs Farm Cl RH12 . . 218 A5
Lambs Farm Rd RH12 . 218 A5
Lambs Green Rd RH12 . 199 B7
Lambton Rd SW20 . . . . . . 39 C8
Lambyn Croft RH6 . . . . . 161 C4
Lamerock Rd BR1 . . . . 24 F4
Lammas Ave CR4 . . . . 41 A7
Lammas Cl GU7 . . . . 151 A6
Lammas Ct
Farncombe GU7 . . . . 150 E6
Stanwell TW19 . . . . 12 D5
Lammas Dr TW18 . . . . 12 D4
Lammas Gate GU7 . . . . . 150 F6
Lammas Gn SE26 . . . . 23 B5
Lammas Hill KT10 . . . . . . 55 A5
Lammas Rd
Godalming GU7 . . . . 151 A5
Richmond TW10 . . . . 17 C4
Lammermoor Rd SW12 . 21 B8
Lampard La GU10 . . . . . . 167 E2
Lampeter Cl 4 GU22 . . . 69 E1
Lampton Ave TW5 . . . . 5 B6
Lampton Ct TW5 . . . . 5 B6
Lampton House Cl SW19 . 19 D4
Lampton Park Rd TW3 . . 5 B5
Lampton Rd TW3, TW5 . . 5 B5
Lampton Sch TW5 . . . . 5 A6
Lanain Ct SE12 . . . . 24 F8
Lanark Cl RH12 . . . . 217 B2
Lancaster Ave
Farnham GU9 . . . . 146 D8
Mitcham CR4 . . . . 41 E4
West Norwood SE21, SE27 . 22 C6
Wimbledon SW19 . . . . 19 D3
Lancaster Cl
Ash Vale GU12 . . . . 105 F5
Beckenham BR2 . . . . 44 F5
Crawley RH10 . . . . 182 D1
Englefield Green TW20 . . 11 D3
Kingston u T KT2 . . . . 17 D3
Stanwell TW19 . . . . 2 E1
Woking GU21 . . . . 70 A3
Lancaster Cotts 1 TW10 . 6 E2
Lancaster Ct
1 Banstead SM7 . . . . 77 F5
2 Belmont SM2 . . . . 59 A3
Epsom KT19 . . . . 57 D1
Stanwell TW19 . . . . 13 E7
Walton-on-T KT12 . . . . 35 B2
Lancaster Dr
Camberley GU15 . . . . 65 D6
East Grinstead RH19 . . 186 A3
Lancaster Gdns
Kingston u T KT2 . . . . 17 D3
Wimbledon SW19 . . . . 19 E3
Lancaster House
Bracknell RG12 . . . . 27 B4
Wandsworth SW18 . . . . . 20 B8
Lancaster Mews 3 TW10 . 6 E1
Lancaster Pk Houston TW5 . 6 E2
Lancaster Pl Houslow TW5 . 4 C5
Twickenham TW1 . . . . 17 A8
Wimbledon SW19 . . . . 19 D3
Lancaster Rd
South Norwood SE25 . . . 43 A6
Wimbledon SW19 . . . . 19 E3
Lancaster Way GU14 . . . 85 C7
Lancelot Cl RH11 . . . . . . 200 E6
Lancelot Ho RH1 . . . . . . 119 A2
Lancer Ct GU11 . . . . 104 E2
Lanchester Dr RG45 . . . . 45 C7
Lancing Cl RH11 . . . . 201 A8
Lancing Ct RH12 . . . . . . 218 A6
Lancing Rd Feltham TW13 . 14 F6
Thornton Heath CR0 . . . . 41 F2
Landen Ct RG40 . . . . 25 B4
Landen Pk RH6 . . . . 160 E5
Landgrove Rd SW19 . . . . 20 A3
Landon Way TW15 . . . . . . 14 B2
Landscape Rd CR6 . . . . . 101 B8
Landsdowne Cl KT5 . . . . 57 B8
Landseer Cl Mitcham SW19 . 40 D8
Sandhurst GU47 . . . . 64 E6
Landseer Rd
Cheam SM1, SM2 . . . . . . 59 A4
New Malden KT3 . . . . 38 D2
Lane Cl KT15 . . . . 52 B5
Lane End Epsom KT18 . . 76 B5
Hambledon GU8 . . . . 191 B8
Lane End Dr GU21 . . . . . . 68 C2
Lane House RH13 . . . . . . 217 D2
Lane The Chertsey KT16 . 33 A6
Ifold RH14 . . . . 212 C4
Thorpe GU25 . . . . 31 E6

Lane The continued
Thursley GU8 . . . . 169 C4
Lanercost Cl SW2 . . . . 22 A6
Lanercost Rd
Crawley RH11 . . . . 201 C5
Streatham SW2 . . . . 22 A6
Lanesborough Prep Sch
GU1 . . . . 109 D1
Lang Cl KT23 . . . . 94 B4
Langaller La KT22 . . . . . . 94 A6
Langborough Rd RG40 . 25 C5
Langbourne Prim Sch
SE21 . . . . 22 E5
Langbourne Way KT10 . 56 A4
Langcroft Cl SM5 . . . . 59 F7
Langdale Ave CR4 . . . . . . 40 F6
Langdale Cl
Farnborough GU14 . . . . . 84 E4
Mortlake SW14 . . . . 7 B3
Woking GU21 . . . . 69 C3
Langdale Dr SL5 . . . . 28 E2
Langdale Rd
Thornton Heath CR7 . . . . 42 A5
Langdon Cl GU15 . . . . 66 C4
Langdon Pl SW14 . . . . 7 C4
Langdon Rd SM4 . . . . 40 C4
Langdon Wlk SM4 . . . . . . 40 C4
Langham Cl GU7 . . . . 150 F4
16 Twickenham TW1 . . . . . 6 C1
Wimbledon SW20 . . . . 39 C7
Langham Dene CR8 . . . . 80 B4
Langham Gdns TW10 . . . 17 C4
Langham House Cl TW10 . 17 C4
Langham Pk GU7 . . . . . . 150 F4
Langham Pl Chiswick W4 . 7 E8
Egham TW20 . . . . 11 F3
Langham Rd
Teddington TW11 . . . . 17 B2
Wimbledon SW20 . . . . 39 C8
Langholm Cl SW12 . . . . . 21 D8
Langhorn Dr TW2 . . . . 16 E8
Langhurst Cl RH12 . . . . 198 D3
Langhurst La RH12 . . . . 198 D3
Langhurstwood Rd RH12 . 198 D3
Langland Gdns CR0 . . . . 62 F8
Langlands Rise KT19 . . . 76 C6
Langley Ave
North Cheam KT4, SM3 . 58 D8
Surbiton KT6 . . . . 37 E1
Langley Cl Guildford GU1 . 109 D2
Langley Vale RH6 . . . . . . 196 D8
Langley Cres UB3 . . . . 3 F7
Langley Ct RH2 . . . . 118 B2
Langley Dr
Aldershot GU11 . . . . 126 A8
Camberley GU15 . . . . 65 D6
Crawley RH11 . . . . 201 D8
Langley Gr KT3 . . . . 38 E7
Langley Green Cty Fst Sch
RH11 . . . . 181 D1
Langley Green Cty Mid Sch
RH11 . . . . 201 C8
Langley La RH11 . . . . . . 201 D8
Langley Oaks Ave CR2 . 62 A1
Langley Par RH11 . . . . . 181 C1
Langley Park Golf Course
BR3 . . . . 44 B7
Langley Park Rd SM1, SM2 . 59 C3
Langley Park Sch for Boys
BR3 . . . . 44 B3
Langley Park Sch for Girls
BR3 . . . . 44 A3
Langley Pl RH11 . . . . 181 C1
Langley Rd Beckenham BR3 . 43 E5
Isleworth TW7 . . . . 5 F5
Merton SW19 . . . . 40 A8
Selsdon CR2 . . . . 62 D2
Surbiton KT6 . . . . 37 E2
Langley Vale Rd KT18, KT21 . 76 E1
Langley Way BR4 . . . . 44 E2
Langley Wlk
Crawley RH11 . . . . 181 B1
Woking GU22 . . . . 89 E8
Langmans Way GU21 . . 68 E3
Langmead St SE27 . . . . . 22 C4
Langport Ct KT12 . . . . 35 C1
Langridge Dr RH19 . . . . 205 E8
Langridge House RH12 . 217 B2
Langridge Mews TW12 . 15 F2
Langroyd Rd SW17 . . . . . 20 F6
Langshott RH6 . . . . 161 D4
Langshott Cl KT15 . . . . . . 70 F8
Langshott Cty Inf Sch
RH6 . . . . 161 C3
Langshott La RH6 . . . . . 161 C3
Langsmead RH7 . . . . 163 E8
Langthorne Ct BR1 . . . . . 24 F5
Langthorne St SW6 . . . . . 6 B1
Langton Ave KT17 . . . . . . 77 A5
Langton Cl Addlestone KT15 . 52 B7
Woking GU21 . . . . 68 F2
Langton Dr GU35 . . . . . . 187 A7
Langton House 5 SW16 . 21 C4
Langton Pl SW18 . . . . 20 A7
Langton Rd KT8 . . . . 36 C5
Langton Rise SE22, SE23 . 23 B8
Langton Way Egham TW20 . 12 C2
South Croydon CR0 . . . . 61 E6
Langwood Chase TW11 . 17 C2
Lanigan Dr TW3 . . . . 5 B2
Lankton Cl BR3 . . . . 44 C8
Lansbury Ave TW14 . . . . . 4 B1
Lansbury Rd RH11 . . . . 201 B1
Lansdell Rd CR4 . . . . 41 A7

Lansdown GU1 . . . . 110 A1
Lansdown Cl
Horsham RH12 . . . . 218 B6
Knaphill GU21 . . . . 88 F8
Walton-on-T KT12 . . . . 35 C1
Lansdown Cl
Twickenham TW1 . . . . 16 F7
Wimbledon SW20 . . . . 19 D1
Lansdowne Copse 1 KT4 . 58 A8
Lansdowne Ct Purley CR8 . 61 B1
2 Worcester Park KT4 . . 58 A8
Lansdowne Hill SE27 . . 22 B5
Lansdowne Pl SE19 . . . . 22 F1
Lansdowne Rd
Aldershot GU11 . . . . 105 A1
Croydon CR0 . . . . 42 D1
Frimley GU16 . . . . 86 A8
Hounslow TW3 . . . . 5 B4
Purley CR8 . . . . 80 A7
Staines TW18 . . . . 13 B1
West Ewell KT19 . . . . 57 D2
Wimbledon SW20 . . . . 19 C1
Lansdowne Wood Cl 11
SE27 . . . . 22 B5
Lanswood Ct KT4 . . . . 58 A8
Lantern Ct SW20 . . . . 39 C8
Lanyon Cl RH12 . . . . 218 A6
Lanyon Mews RH12 . . . 218 A6
Lapse Wood Wlk SE22 . 23 B7
Lapwing Cl Horsham RH13 . 217 F3
Selsdon CR0, CR2 . . . . . . 62 E1
Lapwing Ct KT6 . . . . 57 A7
Lapwing Gr GU4 . . . . 110 D3
Lara Cl KT9 . . . . 56 E3
Larbert Rd SW16 . . . . 21 C1
Larby Pl KT17 . . . . 57 E1
Larch Ave Ascot SL5 . . . . 29 E4
Guildford GU1 . . . . 109 C4
Wokingham RG41 . . . . 25 A8
Larch Cl Camberley GU15 . 65 E8
Kingswood KT20 . . . . 97 F8
Reigate RH1 . . . . 139 C7
Upper Tooting SW12 . . . . 21 B6
Warlingham CR6 . . . . 101 E8
Larch Cres KT19 . . . . 57 B4
Larch End RH1 . . . . 217 B4
Larch Rd GU35 . . . . 187 B6
Larch Tree Way CR0 . . . . 62 F7
Larch Way GU14 . . . . 84 C3
Larches Ave SW14 . . . . 7 D3
Larches The
Horsham RH12 . . . . 218 C6
Woking GU21 . . . . 69 E3
Larches Way
Blackwater GU17 . . . . 64 B5
Crawley Down RH10 . . . 204 C8
Larchvale Ct 2 SM2 . . . . 59 B3
Larchwood 8 RG12 . . . . 27 F5
Larchwood Cl SM7 . . . . . 77 E4
Larchwood Dr TW20 . . . . 11 B2
Larchwood Glade GU15 . 66 A7
Larchwood Rd GU21 . . . 88 D8
Larcombe Cl CR0 . . . . 61 F6
Larges Bridge Dr RG12 . 27 D6
Larges La RG12 . . . . 27 C7
Largewood Ave KT6 . . . . 57 A8
Lark Ave TW18 . . . . 12 F5
Lark Rise Crawley RH11 . 201 C8
East Horsley KT24 . . . . . 112 E4
Larkbere Rd SE26 . . . . . . 23 E4
Larkfield Cobham KT11 . 73 A6
Ewhurst GU6 . . . . 175 E4
Larkfield Cl 2 Coney Hall BR2 . 63 F8
Farnham GU9 . . . . 124 F2
Larkfield Ct RH6 . . . . 162 A3
Larkfield Rd Farnham GU9 . 124 F2
Richmond TW9 . . . . 6 E3
Larkhall Cl KT12 . . . . 54 C5
Larkham Cl TW13 . . . . 14 E5
Larkin Cl CR5 . . . . 79 F2
Larkins Rd RH6 . . . . 181 D7
Larks Way GU21 . . . . 68 C3
Larksfield
Englefield Green TW20 . . 11 C1
Horley RH6 . . . . 161 B4
Larkspur Cl GU11 . . . . . . 126 A7
Larkspur Way
Dorking RH5 . . . . 136 D4
West Ewell KT19 . . . . 57 C5
Larkswood Cl GU47 . . . . 45 A1
Larkswood Dr RG45 . . . . 45 B5
Lascombe La GU3 . . . . . 128 B4
Lashmere Copthorne RH10 . 183 D2
Cranleigh GU6 . . . . 174 B3
Laski Cl RH11 . . . . 201 B1
Lasswade Ct KT16 . . . . . . 32 F2
Lasswade Rd KT16 . . . . . . 32 F2
Lastingham Ct TW18 . . . 13 A2
Latchmere Cl KT2, TW10 . 17 E2
Latchmere Jun & Inf Schs
KT2 . . . . 17 F2
Latchmere La
Kingston u T KT2, TW10 . 17 F3
Richmond KT2, TW10 . . . 17 F3
Latchmere Rd KT2 . . . . . . 17 F2
Latchwood La GU10 . . . 146 D5
Lateward Rd TW8 . . . . 6 D8
Latham Ave GU16 . . . . . . 65 E2
Latham Cl 1 Biggin Hill TN16 . 83 C3
5 Twickenham TW1 . . . . 17 A8
Latham's Way CR0 . . . . . . 60 F8
Lathwood House 6 SE26 . 23 B3
Latimer RG12 . . . . 27 B1

Latimer Cl Crawley RH11 ....181 D1
North Cheam KT4 ....58 B6
Woking GU22 ....70 B3
Latimer Cres GU7 ....150 E3
Latimer Rd
Croydon CR0, CR9 ....61 B7
Godalming GU7 ....150 E4
Teddington TW11 ....16 F3
Wimbledon SW19 ....20 B2
Wokingham RG41 ....25 B5
Latton Cl Esher KT10 ....55 B6
Walton-on-T KT12 ....35 E2
Latymer Cl KT13 ....53 C6
Laud Dr RH10 ....202 D5
Laud St CR0, CR9 ....61 C7
Laud Way RG40 ....25 E6
Lauder Cl GU16 ....65 E2
Lauderdale GU14 ....84 D3
Lauderdale Dr TW10 ....17 D5
Lauderdale House TW18 ..12 F3
Laughton Rd RH12 ....217 F5
Launceston Ct CR7 ....42 A3
Laundry La GU47 ....64 E5
Laundry Rd GU1 ....130 C8
Laundry Way RH5 ....178 C5
Lauradale RG12 ....27 A5
Laurel Ave
Englefield Green TW20 .....11 B3
Twickenham TW1 ....16 F7
Laurel Cl Camberley GU15 ..65 D4
Crawley RH10 ....202 A3
Farnborough GU14 ....84 C3
Poyle SL3 ....1 E7
Upper Tooting SW17 ....20 E3
Laurel Cres Croydon GU1 ...70 D6
Sheerwater GU21 ....70 C6
Laurel Ct SL25 ....42 E4
Laurel Dene RH19 ....185 F1
Laurel Dr RH8 ....122 F4
Laurel Gdns
Aldershot GU11 ....126 A7
Hounslow TW4 ....4 E3
Woodham KT15 ....52 B1
Laurel Gr Forest Hill SE26 ..23 E4
Penge SE20 ....23 C1
Rowledge GU10 ....145 F5
Wrecclesham GU10 ....146 A5
Laurel House SM4 ....40 B4
Laurel Manor SM2 ....59 C3
Laurel Rd Teddington TW12 ..16 D3
Wimbledon SW20 ....39 B8
Laurel Wlk RH13 ....217 F1
Laureldene GU3 ....107 B1
Laurels The Banstead SM7 ..77 F1
Cobham KT11 ....73 E4
Crawley RH10 ....182 A1
Heath End GU9 ....125 F7
4 Oatlands Park KT13 ......53 D7
Laurier Rd CR0 ....42 E2
Lauriston Cl GU21 ....68 D2
Lauriston Rd SW19 ....19 D2
Lausor Rd TW19 ....13 C8
Laustan Cl GU1 ....110 C2
Lavant Cl RH11 ....200 F5
Lavender Ave Mitcham CR4 ..40 F8
North Cheam KT4, SM3 ....58 C7
Lavender Cl
Caterham CR3 ....100 C2
Coulsdon CR5 ....99 C8
Redhill RH1 ....140 B4
Wallington SM5 ....60 B6
Lavender Ct KT8 ....36 B6
Lavender Gr GU14 ....46 E8
Lavender La GU10 ....145 F4
Lavender Park Rd KT14 ....71 A6
Lavender Pk SL5 ....28 C6
Lavender Rd
Carshalton SM1 ....59 D6
Thornton Heath CR0 ....41 F3
Wallington SM5 ....60 A6
West Ewell KT19 ....57 B4
Woking GU22 ....70 B4
Lavender Vale SM6 ....60 D4
Lavender Way CR0 ....43 D3
Lavengro Rd SE27 ....22 C6
Laverock Sch RH8 ....122 E7
Laverstoke Gdns SW15 ....19 A8
Lavington Cl RH11 ....201 A7
Lavington Rd CR0 ....60 F6
Lavinia Ct BR1 ....24 E1
Lawbrook La
Gomshall GU5 ....154 C7
Peaslake GU5 ....154 C7
Lawday Link GU9 ....125 A7
Lawday Pl GU9 ....125 A7
Lawday Place La GU9 .....125 A7
Lawdon Gdns CR0 ....61 B6
Lawford Cl SM6 ....60 E2
Lawford Gdns CR8 ....80 C3
Lawford Rd W4 ....7 C7
Lawford's Hill Cl GU3 .....88 C3
Lawford's Hill Rd GU3 ....88 C3
Lawman Ct KT7 ....37 A3
Lawn Cl KT3 ....38 E7
Lawn Cres TW9 ....7 A5
Lawn Rd Beckenham BR3 ..23 F1
Guildford GU1 ....130 C6
Lawns Rd RH12 ....195 A3
Lawns The Belmont SM2 ...58 E3
Farnborough GU14 ....84 E3
Milford GU8 ....149 F1
North Ascot SL5 ....28 D6
Purley CR8 ....61 B1
South Norwood SE19 ......42 D8
1 Wimbledon SW19 ....19 F3

Lawnsmead Cotts GU5 ...152 B7
Lawnwood Ct GU7 ....151 A5
Lawrence Ave KT3 ....38 E2
Lawrence Cl
Guildford GU4 ....110 B6
Wokingham RG40 ....25 D6
Lawrence Cres GU21 ......48 D4
Lawrence Est TW4 ....4 C3
Lawrence Gr RG42 ....26 D8
Lawrence La RH3 ....117 B3
Lawrence Lodge GU15 .....65 C7
Lawrence Rd
Hampton TW12 ....15 F1
Hounslow TW4 ....4 C3
Richmond TW10 ....17 C4
South Norwood SE25 ......42 F5
Lawrence Way GU11 ....64 F4
Lawrence Weaver Cl SM4 ..40 A3
Lawrie Park Ave SE26 .....23 B3
Lawrie Park Cres SE26 ....23 B3
Lawrie Park Gdns SE26 ...23 B3
Lawrie Park Rd
Forest Hill SE19, SE26 ....23 C3
Penge SE19, SE26 ....23 C3
Laws Cl RH11 ....200 E5
Law Terr GU11 ....105 C3
Lawson Cl SW19 ....19 D5
Lawson Ct KT6 ....37 D2
Lawson Way SL5 ....30 A6
Lawson-Hunt Ind Pk
RH12 ....216 C4
Laxton Ct CR7 ....42 C5
Laxton Gdns RH1 ....119 D7
Layard Rd CR7 ....42 D7
Layburn Cres SL3 ....1 A8
Layhams Rd
Coney Hall BR2, BR4, CR6 ..63 F5
West Wickham BR2 ....63 F1
Layton Cres CR0 ....61 B5
Layton Ct KT13 ....53 B6
Layton Pl TW9 ....7 A6
Layton Rd TW3 ....5 B3
Layton's La TW16 ....34 F7
Le Chateau CR0 ....61 D7
Le Marchant Rd
GU15, GU16 ....65 F3
Le May Cl RH6 ....161 A4
Le Personne Rd CR3 ......100 D5
Lea Cl Ash GU12 ....106 A1
Crawley RH11 ....200 F5
Farnham GU9 ....126 A6
Lea Croft RG45 ....45 B6
Lea Ct GU9 ....125 F7
Lea Rd Beckenham BR3 ....44 A7
Camberley GU15 ....65 B2
Lea The TW20 ....12 C1
Lea Way GU12 ....105 F3
Leach Gr KT22 ....95 C5
Leacroft Staines TW18 ....13 B4
Sunningdale SL5 ....30 A4
Leacroft Ave SW12 ....20 F8
Leacroft Cl Kenley CR8 ...80 C3
Staines TW18 ....13 B4
Leaf Cl KT7, KT8 ....36 E4
Leaf Gr SE27, SW16 ......22 A3
Leafield Cl
South Norwood SW16 .....22 B2
Woking GU21 ....69 B1
Leafield Copse RG12 .....27 F5
Leafield Rd
Merton SW19, SW20 ......39 F6
Sutton SM1 ....59 A8
Leafy Way CR0 ....62 A8
Leamington Ave SM4 .....39 E3
Leamington Cl TW3 ....5 C2
Leamington Ct 4 SE26 ...23 A5
Leander Ct 5 KT6 ....37 D2
Leander Rd
4 Streatham SW2 ....21 F8
Thornton Heath CR7 ......41 F5
Leapale La GU1 ....130 D8
Leapale Rd GU1 ....130 D8
Leas Cl KT9 ....56 F3
Leas La CR6 ....81 D1
Leas Rd Guildford GU1 ..130 C8
Warlingham CR6 ....81 D1
Leaside KT23 ....94 A4
Leather Cl CR4 ....41 A7
Leatherhead By-Pass Rd
KT22 ....95 D5
Leatherhead General Hospl
KT22 ....95 C5
Leatherhead Golf Club
KT22 ....75 A3
Leatherhead Mus of
Local History KT22 ....95 B5
Leatherhead Rd
Ashtead KT21, KT22 ....95 E7
Chessington KT9 ....75 C6
Leatherhead KT22, KT23 ..94 C2
Great Bookham KT22, KT23 ..94 C2
Oxshott KT22 ....74 D4
Leatherhead Sta KT22 ....95 A6
Leaveland Cl BR3 ....44 A5
Leaves Gn RG12 ....27 D3
Leaves Green Cres BR2 ...83 C8
Leaves Green Rd BR2 .....83 D8
Leaview Cl GU12 ....105 F3
Leazes Ave CR3 ....100 A4

Leckhampton Pl SW2 ......22 A8
Leconfield Ave SW13, SW15 ..7 F4
Ledbury Pl CR0 ....61 C6
Ledbury Rd
Croydon CR0, CR9 ....61 D6
Reigate RH2 ....118 A2
Ledger Cl GU1 ....110 B3
Ledger Dr KT15 ....51 F4
Ledgers Rd CR6 ....82 B1
Ledrington Rd SE19 ....23 A2
Lee Ct GU11 ....126 C8
Lee Hollow GU5 ....133 C1
Lee Rd Aldershot GU11 ..104 C2
Merton SW19 ....40 B8
Lee St RH6 ....160 E4
Leech La KT18, KT22 ......96 C1
Leechcroft Rd SM6 ....60 A7
Leechpool La RH12, RH13 ..218 A4
Leechpool Lane Cty Prim
Sch RH13 ....218 A4
Leechpool & Owlbeech
Nature Reserve RH13 ....218 C4
Leeds Cl Carshalton SM5 ..59 F7
Catford SE6 ....24 B5
Leegate Cl GU21 ....69 B3
Leehurst GU8 ....149 F4
Lees The CR0 ....62 F8
Leeson House 8 TW1 ....17 B8
Leeward Gdns SW19 ....19 F2
Leewood Way KT24 ......113 D8
Legge Cres GU11 ....104 E1
Legion Ct SM4 ....40 A3
Legrace Ave TW4, TW5 .....4 F5
Legsheath La RH19 ......205 D1
Leicester RG12 ....27 E2
Leicester Ave CR4 ....41 E5
Leicester Cl KT4 ....58 C6
Leicester House 2 KT7 ...37 A2
Leicester Rd CR0 ....42 E2
Leigh Cl Addlestone KT15 ..51 F3
New Malden KT3 ....38 D5
Leigh Court Cl KT11 ......73 D5
Leigh Cres CR0 ....63 C3
Leigh Ct CR0 ....62 A8
Leigh Hill Rd KT11 ....73 D5
Leigh House 4 KT2 ....18 B2
Leigh La GU9 ....146 E8
Leigh Orchard Cl SW16 ...21 F5
Leigh Pl KT11 ....73 C5
Leigh Place La RH9 ......121 E3
Leigh Place Rd RH2 ......138 A3
Leigh Rd Betchworth RH3 ..137 C2
Cobham KT11 ....73 D5
Isleworth TW3 ....5 F3
Leigham Ave SW16 ....21 E5
Leigham Court Rd
SE27, SW16, SW21 ....22 A4
Leigham Dr TW7 ....5 E7
Leigham Hall 3 SW16 ....21 E5
Leigham Hall Par 2 SW16 ..21 E5
Leigham Vale
SE27, SW16, SW2 ....22 A4
Leighlands RH10 ....202 C8
Leighton Gdns
Sanderstead CR2 ....81 B6
Thornton Heath CR0 ......42 B1
Leighton House 7 KT6 ....37 E3
Leighton St CR0 ....42 B1
Leighton Way KT18 ....76 D5
Leinster Ave SW14 ....7 C3
Leisure La KT14 ....71 B7
Leith Cl RG45 ....45 A7
Leith Gr RH5 ....157 D4
Leith Hill Ave
Abinger Common RH5 ....155 F5
Wotton RH5 ....156 A3
Leith Hill Tower RH5 ....156 B3
Leith House Reigate RH2 ..139 A6
4 Streatham SW2 ....21 F8
Leith Lea RH5 ....157 D4
Leith Rd Beare Green RH5 ..157 D4
Ewell KT17 ....76 E7
Leith Towers 11 SM2 .....59 B3
Leith Vale Cotts RH5 ....177 A2
Leith View RH5 ....136 C3
Leith View Rd RH12 .....218 A5
Leithcote Gdns SW16 .....21 F4
Leithcote Path SW16 .....21 F5
Lela Ave TW4, TW5 ....4 C5
Lemington Gr RG12 ....27 B3
Lemmington Way RH12 ..218 A7
Lemon's Farm Rd RH5 ...155 F6
Lendore Rd GU16 ....85 D8
Lenelby Rd KT6 ....38 A1
Leney Cl RG40 ....25 D8
Lenham Rd
South Norwood CR7 ....42 D7
Sutton SM1 ....59 C5
Lennard Ave BR4 ....63 E8
Lennard Ct BR4 ....63 E8
Lennard Rd
Penge BR3, SE20, SE26 ...23 E2
Thornton Heath CR0 ......42 C1
Lennox Ct 10 RH1 ....119 A2
Lennox Gdns CR0 ....61 B6
Lennox Gdns Cl 133 D1
Lenton Rise TW9 ....6 E4
Leo Ct 4 TW8 ....6 D8
Leof Cres SE6 ....24 B3
Leominster Rd SM4 ....40 C3
Leominster Wlk SM4 .....40 C4
Leonard Ave SM4 ....40 C4
Leonard Cl GU16 ....85 D8
Leonard Rd CR4, SW16 ...41 C8
Leonardslee Ct RH10 ....202 B3
Leopold Ave
Farnborough GU14 ....85 B5

Leopold Ave continued
Wimbledon SW19 ....19 F3
Leopold Rd Crawley RH11 ..201 C6
Wimbledon SW19 ....19 F4
Leopold Terr SW19 ....20 A3
Leppington RG12 ....27 B2
Leret Way KT22 ....95 B6
Lesbourne Rd RH2 ....139 B8
Lescombe Cl SE23 ....23 E5
Lescombe Rd SE23, SE6 ..23 E5
Lesley Cl 3 SM6 ....60 B6
Leslie Gdns SM2 ....59 A3
Leslie Gr CR0 ....42 E1
Leslie Park Rd CR0 ....42 E1
Leslie Rd Chobham GU24 ..49 E1
Dorking RH4 ....115 D1
Lessing St SE23 ....23 E8
Lessingham Ave SW17 ....21 A4
Lessness Rd SM4 ....40 C4
Lestor Ct SW7 ....40 F7
Letchworth Ave TW14 .....14 F8
Letchworth Cl RH11 .....200 E3
Letchworth St SW17 ......20 F4
Letcombe Sq RG12 ....27 F5
Levana Cl SW19 ....19 E7
Levehurst House SE27 ....22 C3
Levendale Rd SE23, SE6 ..23 F6
Leveret Cl CR0 ....82 D8
Leveret La RH11 ....201 B8
Leverkusen Rd RG12 ......27 B6
Levern Dr GU9 ....125 E7
Leverson St SW16 ....21 C2
Leveson Rd 8 SW16 ......21 C3
Levett Rd KT22 ....95 B7
Levylsdene GU1 ....110 D1
Lewes Cl RH10 ....202 C6
Lewes Ct 5 CR4 ....40 F6
Lewes House GU27 ......208 C3
Lewes Rd
Ashurst Wood RH19 ......206 C6
East Grinstead RH19 ....206 C6
Forest Row RH18 ....206 E2
Lewesdon Cl 16 SW19 ...19 E7
Lewin Ct SW16 ....21 E2
Lewin Rd Mortlake SW14 ...7 D4
Streatham SW16 ....21 D2
Lewins Rd KT18 ....76 B5
Lewis Cl KT15 ....52 C6
Lewis Rd Mitcham CR4 ....40 E7
18 Richmond TW10 ....6 D2
Sutton SM1 ....59 B6
Lewis Sports & L Ctr SE19 ..42 F8
Lewisham Cl RH11 ....201 C2
Lewisham Way GU47 ......45 D2
Lexden Rd CR4 ....41 C6
Lexington Ct CR8 ....80 C8
Lexton Gdns SW12 ....21 D7
Ley Rd GU14 ....85 A8
Leyborne Pk TW9 ....7 A6
Leybourne Ave KT14 ......71 F6
Leybourne Cl Byfleet KT14 ..71 F6
Crawley RH11 ....201 C1
Leyburn Gdns CR0 ....61 E8
Leycester Cl GU20 ....48 B6
Leyfield KT4 ....38 F1
Leylands La TW19 ....2 A2
Leylands Rd
Abinger Common RH5 ....155 F5
Wotton RH5 ....156 A6
Leys Ave RG12 ....27 F4
Leys Rd KT22 ....74 E6
Leys The KT12 ....54 E6
Leyside RG45 ....45 A5
Leyton Rd SW19 ....20 C1
Liberty Ave SW19 ....40 D8
Liberty Hall Rd KT15 ......52 A5
Liberty La KT15 ....52 B5
Liberty Mid Sch CR4 .....40 E7
Liberty Rise KT15 ....52 A4
Licensed Victuallers Sch
SL5 ....28 C6
Lichfield Ct
Kingston u T KT6 ....37 E4
Richmond TW9 ....6 E3
Lichfield Gdns TW10, TW9 ..6 E2
Lichfield Rd Hounslow TW4 ..4 C4
Richmond TW9 ....6 F6
Lichfield Terr 1 TW9 ....6 E2
Lichfield Way CR2 ....62 D2
Lickfolds Rd GU10 ....145 E3
Liddell Cl RG40 ....25 F8
Liddell Way SL5 ....28 F5
Liddell Ct 3 CR8 ....80 A7
Liddington Hall Dr GU3 ..108 E4
Liddington Hall Est GU3 ..108 E4
Liddington New Rd GU3 ..108 E4
Lidiard Rd SW18 ....20 C6
Lido Rd GU1 ....130 D2
Lidsey Cl RH10 ....202 C4
Lidstone Cl GU21 ....69 B2
Lightwater Cty Prk GU18 ..47 F1
Lightwater Meadow GU18 ..67 B8
Lightwater Rd GU18 ......48 C1
Lightwater Village Cty Inf
Sch GU18 ....48 C1
Lightwood RG12 ....27 D3
Lilac Ave GU22 ....89 D7
Lilac Cl GU1 ....109 C5
Lilac Gdns CR0 ....63 A7
Lilian Rolfe House 5
SE27 ....22 D4
Lilleshall Rd SM4 ....40 D3
Lilley Dr KT20 ....98 B5
Lillie Rd TN16 ....103 D7
Lilliput Childrens Ctr KT12 ..54 C5
Lily Hill Dr RG12 ....27 E6
Lily Hill Rd RG12 ....27 F7
Lilyfields Chase GU6 ....175 E4

Lime Ave Camberley GU15 ..66 A1
Horsham RH12 ....218 A4
Winkfield SL4 ....9 F1
Lime Cl Carshalton SM5 ...59 F8
Copthorne RH10 ....183 E8
Crawley RH11 ....181 C5
Reigate RH2 ....139 E8
West Clandon GU4 ....111 E8
Lime Cres TW16 ....35 C8
Lime Ct CR4 ....40 E7
Lime Gr Addlestone KT15 ..52 A2
Guildford GU1 ....109 F3
Kingston u T KT3 ....38 E8
Twickenham TW1 ....6 A1
Warlingham CR6 ....81 D7
West Clandon GU4 ....111 F8
Woking GU22 ....89 F8
Lime Lodge 3 TW16 ....14 F1
Lime Meadow Ave CR2 ....81 B5
Lime Rd TW9 ....7 A4
Lime Tree Ave KT10, KT7 ..36 E4
Lime Tree Cl KT23 ....94 B4
Lime Tree Ct KT21 ....75 F1
Lime Tree Gr CR0 ....63 A7
Lime Tree Rd TW5 ....5 C6
Lime Tree Wlk
Coney Hall BR4 ....63 F7
Thorpe GU25 ....31 A5
Lime Wlk RG12 ....27 D4
Limebush Cl KT15 ....52 C6
Limecroft Cl KT19 ....57 D3
Limecroft Rd GU21 ....68 C1
Limekiln Pl SE19 ....22 F1
Limerick Cl Bracknell RG42 ..27 A1
Streatham SW12 ....21 C8
Limes Ave 6 SW12 ....21 A8
Limerick House GU22 .....70 A1
Limes Ave Barnes SW13 ....7 F5
Carshalton SM5 ....40 E1
Croydon CR0, CR9 ....61 A6
Horley RH6 ....161 A1
Penge SE20 ....23 B1
Limes Cl TW15 ....14 A3
Limes Ct BR3 ....44 A8
Limes Field Rd 1 SW14 ....7 E4
Limes Rd Beckenham BR3 ..44 B7
Egham TW20 ....11 F1
Farnborough GU14 ....84 F1
Thornton Heath CR0 ......42 B3
Weybridge KT13 ....53 A6
Limes The Belmont SM2 ...59 B4
Dormans Park RH19 .....185 C6
East Molesey KT8 ....36 A6
Woking GU21 ....70 A2
Woking, Horsell GU21 .....69 C4
Limetree Ct SW17 ....20 E6
Limetree Pl CR4 ....41 A8
Limetree Wlk 2 SW17 ....21 A3
Limeway Terr RH4 ....115 B2
Limewood Cl GU21 ....88 E7
Limpsfield Ave
Putney SW19 ....19 E6
Thornton Heath CR7 ......41 F4
Limpsfield CE Inf Sch
RH8 ....123 B7
Limpsfield Chart
Golf Club RH8 ....123 D6
Limpsfield Grange Sch
RH8 ....123 B8
Limpsfield Rd
Chelsham CR6 ....102 B6
Sanderstead, Green CR2, CR6 ..81 D3
Sanderstead CR2, CR6 ....81 B2
Warlingham CR2, CR6 ....81 D4
Linacre Dr
Cranleigh GU6, RH12 ....195 F4
Ewhurst GU6, RH12 .....194 E4
Linchmere Pl RH11 ......201 A7
Linchmere Rd
Lewisham SE12 ....24 F8
Linchmere, Hammer GU27 ..207 F3
Lincoln Ave
Twickenham TW2 ....16 C6
Wimbledon SW19 ....19 E5
Lincoln Cl Ash Vale GU12 ..106 A7
Croydon SE25 ....43 A3
Frimley GU15 ....65 E1
Horley RH6 ....161 B2
Lincoln Ct CR0 ....42 E2
Lincoln Dr GU22 ....70 E3
Lincoln Lodge 3 KT13 ....53 A6
Lincoln Rd Croydon SE25 ..43 A5
Dorking RH4 ....136 B5
Feltham TW13 ....16 A5
Guildford GU2 ....108 F3
Kingston u T KT3 ....38 D5
Mitcham CR4 ....41 E4
Worcester Park KT4 ....58 B8
Lincoln Terr 4 SM2 ....59 A3
Lincoln Way TW16 ....34 E8
Lincolns Mead RH7 ......163 E8
Lincombe Rd BR1 ....24 F1
Lind Rd SM1 ....59 C5
Linda Ave KT9 ....56 F5
Lindale Cl GU25 ....30 F5
Lindale SW19 ....19 E6
Linden 3 RG12 ....27 C5
Linden Ave Coulsdon CR5 ..79 C2
Thornton Heath CR7 ......42 A5
Houslow TW3 ....5 B2
Thornton Heath CR7 ......42 A5
Linden Bridge Sch KT4 ....57 E7

Linden Cl Crawley RH10 ....202 A3
Horsham RH12 ....217 E4
Tadworth KT20 ....97 D7
Thames Ditton KT7 ......37 A2
Woodham KT15 ....71 A8
Linden Ct KT22 ....37 F7
Linden Ct Beckenham BR3 ..44 B6
Camberley GU15 ....65 F7
Englefield Green TW20 ...11 B2
Leatherhead KT22 ......95 B6
Penge SE20 ....23 B1
Linden Dr CR3 ....100 C3
Linden Gdns KT22 ......95 C6
Linden Gr Kingston u T KT3 ..38 E6
Penge SE20 ....23 C2
Teddington TW11 ....16 F3
Walton-on-T KT12 ......53 F8
Warlingham CR6 ....81 E1
Linden Lea RH4 ....136 C5
Linden Leas RH4 ....63 D8
Linden Lodge Sch TW19 ..19 E7
Linden Pit Path KT22 ....95 B6
Linden Pl Ewell KT17 ....76 E7
Mitcham CR4 ....40 E5
Staines TW18 ....13 A4
Linden Rd Guildford GU1 ..109 D1
Hampton TW12 ....16 A3
Headley Down GU35 ....187 C5
Leatherhead KT22 ......95 B6
Weybridge KT13 ....53 C2
Linden Way
Send Marsh GU23 ......90 F3
Shepperton TW17 ......34 C4
Wallington CR8 ....60 C1
Woking GU22 ....89 F6
Lindenhill Rd RG42 ......26 F8
Lindens Cl KT24 ....113 E7
Lindens The Chiswick W4 ..7 D6
Copthorne RH10 ......183 B3
Farnham GU9 ....125 D1
New Addington CR0 ....63 C4
Lindfield Gdns GU1 ....109 F2
Lindfield Rd CR0 ....42 F3
Lindgren Wlk RH11 ....201 B1
Lindisfarne Rd SW20 ....19 A1
Lindley Ct Teddington KT1 ..37 C8
West Byfleet KT14 ......71 B7
Lindley Rd
Tyler's Green RH9 ....121 C5
Walton-on-T KT12 ......54 D7
Lindon Bennett Sch TW13 ..15 D3
Lindores Rd SM5 ....40 C1
Lindsay Cl Chessington KT9 ..56 E3
Epsom KT18 ....76 C6
Stanwell TW19 ....2 D2
Lindsay Dr TW17 ....34 D3
Lindsay Rd Hampton TW12 ..16 B4
Cheam KT4 ....58 B8
Woodham KT15 ....71 B8
Lindsey Cl CR4, SW16 ..41 E5
Lindum Dene GU11 ....105 A1
Lindum Rd TW11 ....17 C1
Lindums The BR3 ....23 F2
Lindway SE27 ....22 B3
Linersh Dr GU5 ....152 A6
Linersh Wood GU5 ....152 A6
Linersh Wood Cl GU5 ..152 B5
Lines Rd GU11 ....105 D7
Linfield Cl KT12 ....54 B5
Linford Ct CR4 ....40 E8
Ling Cres GU35 ....187 B6
Ling Ct GU18 ....66 F7
Ling's Coppice SE21 ....22 D6
Lingfield Ave KT1, KT5 ..37 E5
Lingfield Common Rd
RH7 ....164 C6
Lingfield Ct SW19 ......19 D2
Lingfield Dr RH10 ......202 E7
Lingfield Gdns CR5 ....100 B8
Lingfield Hospital Sch
RH7 ....165 A4
Lingfield House SE26 ...23 B2
Lingfield Park Race Course
RH7 ....164 E2
Lingfield Prim Sch RH7 ..164 D4
Dormans Park RH19 ....185 D3
East Grinstead RH19 ...185 F4
Edenbridge TN8 ....165 F8
Haxted TN8 ....185 A5
North Cheam KT4 ......58 C7
Wimbledon SW19 ......19 D2
Lingfield Sta RH7 ......164 E4
Lingfield Rd SW17 ......20 B5
Lingwood RG12 ....27 C3
Lingwood Gdns TW7 ....5 E7
Link La SM6 ....60 E6
Link Prim Day Sch The
CR0 ....60 E6
Link Rd Addlestone KT15 ..52 E6
Carshalton CR4, SM6 ...41 A1
East Bedfont TW14 ....14 D8
Link Sec Day Sch The CR0 ..60 F6
Link The Crawley RH11 ..201 D6
Teddington TW11 ......16 F2
Link Way Richmond TW10 ..17 B6
Staines TW18 ....13 B2
Link's Rd KT17 ....77 A5
Linkfield E Molesey KT8 ..36 A6
Linkfield Cnr RH1 ......118 E1
Linkfield Gdns RH1 ....118 E1
Linkfield La RH1 ....118 E2
Linkfield Rd TW7 ....5 F5
Linkfield St RH1 ....118 E1
Linklater's Cotts GU14 ...84 B6
Links Ave SM4 ....40 A5

Links Brow KT22 ....94 E4
Links Cl Ashstead KT21 ..75 C2
Ewhurst GU6 ....175 E6
Links Gdns SW16 ......22 A1
Links Green Way KT11 ..74 A5
Links Pl KT21 ....75 D2
Links Prim Sch SW17 ...21 A2
Links Rd Ashford TW15 ..13 E3
Ashtead KT21 ....75 C2
Bramley GU5 ....151 E7
Mitcham SW16, SW17 ...21 A2
West Wickham BR4 ....44 B1
Links The North Ascot SL5 ..28 E7
Walton-on-T 54 A8
Links View RH3, RH5 ...116 A1
Links View Rd Croydon CR0 ..63 A7
Hampton TW12 ....16 C3
Links Way Beckenham BR3 ..44 A3
Effingham KT24 ....113 E7
Farnborough GU14 ....84 C3
Mitcham SW17 ....21 A2
Linkscroft Ave TW15 ...14 B2
Linkside KT3 ....38 E7
Linkside E GU26 ......188 C7
Linkside N GU26 ......188 B7
Linkside S GU26 ......188 B7
Linkside W GU26 ......188 C6
Linkway Camberley GU15 ..65 C4
Crawley RH6 ....182 C7
Crowthorne RG45 ......45 A3
Guildford GU2 ....108 F2
West Barnes SW20 ....39 B5
West Barnes SW20 ....39 B6
Woking GU22 ....70 C2
Linkway The SM2 ......59 C2
Linley Ct 1 Dulwich SE22 ..22 E4
Sutton SM1 ....59 C6
Linnell Rd RH1 ....140 B8
Linnet Cl CR2 ....62 D1
Linnet Gr GU4 ....110 D3
Linnet Mews SW12 ....21 A8
Linsford Bsns Pk GU16 ..85 F3
Linsford La GU16 ......85 F3
Linstead Rd GU14 ......84 E8
Linstead Way SW18, SW19 ..19 E8
Linton Cl CR4, SM5 ....40 F2
Linton Gr SE27 ....22 C3
Linton's La KT17 ......76 E7
Lintott Ct TW19 ....2 D1
Lintott Gdns RH13 ....217 E3
Lion and Lamb Way 7
GU9 ....125 B2
Lion and Lamb Yd 7
GU9 ....125 B2
Lion Ave TW1 ....16 F7
Lion Cl Haslemere GU27 ..207 F7
Walton on T 33 E6
Lion Ctr The TW13 ....15 E5
Lion Gate Gdns TW9 ...6 F4
Lion Gn GU27 ....207 F6
Lion Green Rd CR5 ....79 D3
Lion La Haslemere GU27 ..207 F7
Turners Hill RH10 ....204 A4
Lion Mead GU27 ......207 E6
Lion Park Ave KT9 ....57 A6
Lion Rd Thornton Heath CR0 ..42 C4
Twickenham TW1, TW2 ..16 F7
Lion Ret Pk GU22 ......70 B3
Lion Way TW8 ....6 D7
Lion Wharf Rd TW7 ....6 A4
Liphook Cres SE23 ....23 C8
Liphook Rd
Haslemere GU27 ......208 B4
Linchmere GU27 ......207 B4
Lipsham Cl SM7 ....78 D6
Lisbon Ave TW2 ......16 C6
Liscombe RG12 ....27 B2
Liscombe House RG12 ..27 B2
Liskeard Dr 3 GU14 ...85 A6
Lisle Cl SW17 ....21 B4
Lismore 3 SW19 ......19 F3
Lismore Cl TW7 ....6 A5
Lismore Cres RH11 ....201 B3
Lismore Rd CR2 ....61 E4
Lissoms Rd CR5 ....79 A1
Lister Ave RH19 ......205 F6
Lister Cl SW19 ....40 E8
Lister Ct 8 CR4 ....80 B7
Litchfield Ave SM4 ....39 F2
Litchfield Rd SM1 ......59 C6
Litchfield Way GU2 ...129 F7
Lithgow's Rd TW14, TW6 ..3 F3
Little Acre BR3 ....44 A6
Little Austins Rd GU9 ..146 D8
Little Birch Cl KT15 ...52 D2
Little Bookham St KT23 ..93 F2
Little Bornes SE21 ....22 E4
Little Borough RH3 ....137 A7
Little Brownings SE23 ..23 B6
Little Browns La TN8 ..144 F4
Little Collins RH1 ....162 B7
Little Common La RH1 ..120 C3
Little Comptons RH13 ..217 F2
Little Crabtree RH11 ...201 C7
Little Cranmore La KT24 ..112 C6
Little Ct BR4 ....44 E1
Little Dimocks SW12 ...21 B6
Little Elms UB3 ....3 D8
Little Ferry Rd TW1 ...17 B7
Little Gn GU8 ....148 C4
Little Grebe RH12 ....217 C5
Little Green La
Addlestone KT16 ......51 E7
Wrecclesham GU9 ....146 B6
Little Halliards KT12 ...35 A3
Little Hatch RH12 ....217 F5

Little Haven La RH12 ..217 F5
Little Heath La KT11 ...74 A5
Little Heath Rd GU24 ..49 E2
Little Hide GU1 ....110 B3
Little King St SE19 ....22 E2
Little King St RH19 ...185 E1
Little London Shere GU5 ..132 F2
Little London GU6 ....170 E5
Little Lullenden KT22 ..164 E5
Little Manor Gdns GU6 ..174 E2
Little Mead GU21 ......68 F3
Little Mead Ind Est SW19 ..40 C8
Little Moor GU47 ......45 C1
Little Moreton Cl KT14 ..71 B7
Little Orch Woking GU21 ..70 A5
Woodham KT15 ....71 A8
Little Orchard Way GU4 ..130 E1
Little Orchards KT18 ...76 E5
Little Paddock GU15 ...66 A8
Little Park Dr TW13 ...15 E6
Little Park Enterprises
RH4 ....180 D3
Little Platt GU2 ....108 D2
Little Queens Rd TW11 ..16 F2
Little Ringdale RG12 ...27 E5
Little Roke Ave CR8 ...80 B5
Little Roke Rd CR8 ....80 C5
Little St St Leonards SW14 ..7 C4
Little Sutton La SL3 .....1 B8
Little Tangley Flats GU5 ..131 C1
Little Thatch GU7 ....150 F6
Little Thurbans Cl GU9 ..146 A6
Little Tumners Ct GU7 ..150 E6
Little Warren Cl GU4 ...131 B7
Little Wellington St 9
GU11 ....105 A2
Little Wildwood GU6 ..174 F1
Little Woodcote
La CR8, SM5, SM6 ....79 B8
Littlebourne 2 SE13 ...24 E8
Littlebrook Cl CR0 ....43 D3
Littlecote Cl SW19 ....19 E8
Littlecroft Rd 1 TW20 ..11 E3
Littledale Cl RG12 ....27 E6
Littledown Cl GU15 ...66 A4
Fairlands GU3 ....108 D5
8 Kingston u T KT1 ...37 E7
Littlefield Cotts GU3 ..108 B6
Littlefield Cl GU7 ....2 D7
Littlefield Ct UB7 ....2 D7
Littlefield Way GU3 ...108 D5
Littleford La GU4, GU5 ..152 F7
Littlehaven Cty Inf Sch
RH12 ....217 F5
Littleheath Rd CR2 ....62 B2
Littlemead KT10 ......55 D6
Littlers Cl SW19 ......40 D8
Littlestone Cl BR3 ....24 A2
Littleton C of E Fst Sch
TW17 ....34 A4
Littleton Cross GU3 ...130 A4
Littleton House 4 RH2 ..118 A2
Littleton La Artington GU3 ..130 A3
Littleton TW17, TW18 ...33 E4
Reigate RH2 ....138 E7
Littleton Rd TW15, TW17 ..14 C1
Littleton St SW18 ......20 C6
Littlewick Cotts GU21 ..68 F4
Littlewood GU6 ....174 F3
Littlewood House CR2 ..81 B5
Littleworth Ave KT10 ..55 D5
Littleworth Common Rd
KT10 ....55 D7
Littleworth La KT10 ...55 D6
Littleworth Pl KT10 ...55 D6
Littleworth Rd
Hinchley Wood KT10 ..55 E6
Tilehurst GU10, GU8 ...148 C8
The Sands GU10 ......126 D3
Liverpool Rd
Kingston u T KT2 ......18 A1
South Norwood CR7 ...42 C6
Livesey Cl KT1 ....37 F6
Livingstone Ct TW19 ..13 D5
Livingstone Rd
Caterham CR3 ....100 D5
Crawley RH10 ....201 E4
Horsham RH13 ......217 D1
Hounslow TW3 ....5 C3
South Norwood CR7 ...42 D7
Llanaway Cl GU7 ......150 F6
Llanaway House GU7 ..150 F6
Llanaway Rd GU7 ....150 F6
Llangar Gr RG45 ......45 A5
Llanthony Rd SM4 ....40 D4
Llanvair Cl SL5 ....29 A3
Llanvair Dr SL5 ....28 F3
Llewellyn Ct SE20 ....43 C8
Lloyd Ave
Thornton Heath SW16 ..41 E8
Wallington CR5 ....79 B5
Lloyd Ct 6 SE27 ......22 B5
Lloyd House RH13 ....24 B2
Lloyd Park Ave CR0 ...61 F6
Lloyd Rd KT4, SM5 ....58 D7
Lloyds Ct RH10 ......181 E1
Lloyds Way BR3 ....43 E4
Lobelia Rd GU24 ......68 A4
Lochaline St W6 ....7 E3
Lochinvar St SW12 ....21 B8
Lochner Rd GU11 ....105 C1
Lock Cl GU21, KT15 ...70 E7
Lock La GU22, GU23, KT14 ..71 C3
Lock Rd Farnborough GU11 ..105 C3
Guildford GU1 ....109 D4
Richmond TW10 ......17 C4
Lock's La CR4 ....41 A7

Locke King Rd KT13 ...53 A3
Locke King Ct KT13 ...53 A3
Locke-King GU11 ......53 A3
Lockesley Sq KT6 ....37 D3
Lockfield Cotts GU21 ..69 A1
Lockfield Dr GU21 ....68 F2
Lockhart Rd KT11 ....73 C6
Lockhursthatch La GU5 ..153 E6
Locks Meadow RH7 ...165 A1
Locks Ride SL5 ....8 C2
Locksley Dr GU21 ....68 F2
Locksmeade Rd TW10 ..17 C4
Lockswood GU24 ......88 B7
Lockton Chase SL5 ....28 D6
Lockton House RG40 ..25 C6
Lockwood Cl
Farnborough GU14 ....84 E8
Forest Hill SE26 ......23 D4
Horsham RH12 ......218 A5
Lockwood Ct RH10 ...201 F8
Lockwood Path TW20 ..70 E6
Lockwood Way KT9 ...57 A5
Lodden Lodge SM2 ...59 C3
Loddon Cl GU15 ......66 A6
Loddon Rd GU14 ......84 E8
Loddon Way GU14 ....106 A1
Loder Cl GU21 ....70 D6
Lodge Ave CR0, CR9 ..61 A7
Lodge Cl Crawley RH11 ..201 C6
Dorking RH5 ....136 C3
E Ewell KT17 ....58 C1
East Grinstead RH19 ..185 D1
Englefield Green TW20 ..11 D3
Fetcham KT22 ....94 D5
Stoke D'Abernon KT11 ..73 F3
Lodge Gdns BR3 ......43 F4
Lodge Hill CR8 ....80 A4
Lodge Hill Cl GU10 ...146 D6
Lodge Hill Rd GU10 ..146 E7
Lodge La Beckenham BR3 ..44 B5
New Addington CR0, R9 ..63 B3
Salfords RH1 ....139 F1
South Croydon CR0 ...63 A4
South Holmwood RH5 ..157 F8
Lodge Pl SM1 ....59 B5
Lodge Rd Fetcham KT22 ..94 D5
Sutton SM1 ....59 B5
Thornton Heath CR0 ..42 B2
Wallington SM6 ....60 B5
Lodge Way Ashford TW15 ..13 E6
Thornton Heath CR0 ..34 C7
Lodgebottom Rd
KT22, RH5 ....116 A8
Lodsworth GU11 ......105 A1
Lofthouse Pl KT9 ......56 C4
Logan Cl TW4 ....4 F4
Logmore La RH4 ......135 D3
Lois Dr TW17 ....34 B4
Lollesworth La KT24 ..112 C8
Loman Rd GU16 ....86 A6
Lomas Cl CR0 ....63 C3
Lombard Bsns Pk
Merton SW19 ....40 B7
Thornton Heath CR0 ..41 F2
Lombard Rd SW19 ....40 B7
Lombard St GU3 ......107 A2
Lombardy Cl GU21 ....69 A1
Lomond Gdns CR2 ....62 E3
Loncin Mead Ave KT15 ..52 C2
London Butterfly House
4 ....8 B6
London Cotes KT24 ...112 F4
London Fields
House RH11 ....201 C2
London Inst The SW17 ..21 A3
London La Bromley BR1 ..24 F1
Shere GU5 ....133 A5
London Rd Ascot SL5 ..29 D5
Ashford TW15, TW18,
TW19, TW14 ....13 D5
Bagshot GU15, GU19 ...47 F3
Blackwater GU15, GU17 ..64 E4
Bracknell RG42 ....26 B6
Bracknell RG12, SL5 ...28 C6
Brands Hill SL3 ....2 E7
Brentford TW7,TW8 ....6 B6
Bromley BR1 ....24 F1
Camberley GU15 ......65 D3
Caterham CR3 ....100 D4
Cheam KT17 ....58 C6
Crawley RH10 ....181 E3
Dorking RH4 ....115 C8
East Grinstead RH19 ..185 C3
Ewell KT17 ....58 C6
Fetcham GU24 ....49 E1
Forest Hill SE23 ......23 D5
Forest Row RH18 ....206 E4
Guildford GU1 ....109 D4
Guildford, Burpham
GU1, GU4 ....110 B4
Hackbridge SM6, CR4 ..60 B7
Hindhead GU26 ......188 F4
Horsham RH12 ......217 C2
Hounslow TW3, TW7, TW1,
TW8 ....5 B4
Isleworth TW7, TW8 ...6 B6
Kingston u T KT1, KT2 ..37 E7
Mitcham CR4, SW17 ...40 F6
Morden SM4 ....40 A6
North Cheam KT4, SM3, SM4 ..58 C6
Redhill RH1 ....118 E3
Reigate RH2 ....118 A2
Send Marsh GU23 ....90 A1

London Rd continued
Stoneleigh KT17, KT4, SM3 ..58 C6
Sunningdale, Blacknest SL5 ..30 B6
Sunningdale, Shrubs Hill SL5 ..30 C4
Thornton Heath CR0,
CR7, SW16 ....42 A3
Twickenham TW1 ......17 A7
Virginia Water GU25 ...31 B7
Wentworth SL5, GU25 ..30 C4
Westhumble RH4 ......115 C3
Windlesham GU19, GU20 ..47 D1
Wokingham RG42, RG12 ..26 C7
London Rd N RH1 ......99 B2
London Rd S
Merstham RH1 ....119 B6
Redhill RH1 ....119 B6
London Road Sta GU1 ..109 E1
London St KT16 ....33 A3
Lone Oak RH6 ....162 B1
Lonesome La
Reigate RH1, RH2 ....139 C3
Salfords RH1, RH2 ....139 D3
Lonesome Prim Sch CR4 ..41 B7
Lonesome Way CR4 ....41 C8
Long Acre RH10 ......204 A8
Long Beech Dr GU14 ..84 C3
Long Bridge GU9 ......125 C2
Long Cl RH10 ....202 D6
Long Copse Cl KT23 ...94 B4
Long Ditton Cty Inf Sch
KT6 ....37 C1
Long Dyke GU1 ......110 B3
Long Garden Mews 3
GU9 ....125 B2
Long Garden Way GU9 ..125 B2
Long Garden Wlk GU9 ..125 B2
Long Garden Wlk E 2
GU9 ....125 B2
Long Garden Wlk W 1
GU9 ....125 B2
Long Gore GU7 ......150 E8
Long Grove Rd KT19 ...57 B1
Long Hill The Sands GU10 ..126 E1
Woldingham CR3 ....101 F6
Long Hill Rd RG12, SL5 ..28 A7
Long Houses GU24 ....63 D3
Long La Croydon CR0 ..43 C3
Stanwell TW15, TW19 ..13 F7
Long Lodge Dr KT12 ...54 C7
Long Meadow BR3, BR4 ..44 C2
Long Mickle GU47 ....45 B1
Long Rd The GU14 ....146 A2
West Horsley KT24 ....92 B3
Long Shaw Ockham GU23 ..92 B3
Long Wlk Burgh Heath KT18 ..78 D5
Kingston u T KT3 ......38 C6
Long Wlk The SL4 ....10 C7
Long's Way RG40 ......25 E7
Longacre GU12 ......106 A2
Longacre Pl SM5 ......60 A4
Longbourne Gr SL5 ...152 D4
Longbourne Go GU7 ..150 E8
Longboyds KT11 ......73 B4
Longbridge Gate RH6 ..181 E8
Longbridge Rd
Crawley RH6 ....181 F8
Horley RH6 ....160 F1
Longbridge Rdbt RH6 ..160 E2
Longbridge Wlk RH6 ..160 F1
Longchamp Cl RH6 ...161 C3
Longcroft Ave SM7 ....78 C5
Longcross Rd
Longcross KT16, GU24 ..50 C3
Longcross Sta GU25 ...30 F1
Longdene Rd GU27 ...208 B6
Longdown GU27 ......16 A4
Longdown La N KT17 ..77 A6
Longdown La S KT17, KT18 ..76 A4
Longdown Lodge GU47 ..64 B8
Longdown Rd Catford SE6 ..24 B4
Ewell KT17 ....77 A6
Farnham GU10 ......146 C5
Guildford GU4 ....131 B6
Sandhurst GU47 ......45 B1
Longfellow Cl RH12 ..217 E2
Longfellow Rd KT4 ....39 B1
Longfield BR1 ....44 F8
Longfield Ave
Mitcham SW19 ....40 A8
Mortlake SW14 ....7 B2
Longfield Cl GU14 ....84 F8
Longfield Cres
Burgh Heath KT20 ....97 C7
Forest Hill SE23, SE26 ..23 C5
Longfield Dr Mitcham SW19 ..40 E8
Mortlake SW14 ....7 B2
Longfield Rd Ash GU12 ..106 A2
Dorking RH4 ....136 A8
Horsham RH12 ......217 A1
Longfield St SW18 ....20 A8
Longford Ave Feltham TW14 ..3 F1
Stanwell TW19 ....13 E7
Longford Cl
Camberley GU15 ......65 D7
Hampton TW12 ......16 A4
Longford Ct KT19 ....57 C6
Longford Gdns SM1 ..59 C8
Longford House
Catford BR1 ....24 D3
5 Hampton TW12 ....16 A4
Longford Ind Est TW12 ..16 B7
Longford Rdbt TW6, UB7 ..2 B6
Longford Sch TW14 ...14 F8
Longford Way TW19 ..13 E7

Longford Wlk **9** SW2 ..... 22 A8
Longheath Dr KT23 ..... 93 E3
Longheath Gdns CR0 ..... 43 C4
Longhedge House SE26 ..... 23 A4
Longhill Rd SE6 ..... 24 D5
Longhope Dr GU10 ..... 146 A6
Longhurst Rd
  Crawley RH11 ..... 201 A1
  Croydon CR0 ..... 43 B3
  East Horsley KT24 ..... 112 E6
Longlands Ave CR5 ..... 79 A5
Longlands Ct CR4 ..... 41 A8
Longlands Way GU15 ..... 66 D5
Longleat Sq GU14 ..... 85 E3
Longleat Way TW14 ..... 14 D8
Longmead Rd Farnham GU9 125 D1
  Thornton Heath CR0 ..... 42 B2
  Upper Tooting SW17 ..... 20 F2
Longmead GU1 ..... 110 C1
Longmead Bsns Ctr KT19 ..... 76 D8
Longmead Cl CR3 ..... 100 E5
Longmead House SE27 ..... 22 C3
Longmead Rd Epsom KT19 ..... 57 E1
  Thames Ditton KT7 ..... 36 F2
  Upper Tooting SW17 ..... 20 F3
Longmeadow
  Frimley GU15,GU16 ..... 65 F3
  Little Bookham KT23 ..... 93 F2
Longmere Gdns KT20 ..... 97 C8
Longmere Rd RH10 ..... 201 D8
Longmoors RG42 ..... 26 D8
Longmore Rd KT12 ..... 54 E6
Longpoles Rd GU6 ..... 174 F2
Longridge Gr GU22 ..... 70 E5
Longs Cl GU22 ..... 71 A3
Longs Ct **7** TW9 ..... 6 F3
Longshaw Way CR3 ..... 101 A3
Longshot Ind Est RG12 ..... 26 F7
Longshot La RG12 ..... 26 E7
Longside Cl TW20 ..... 32 C8
Longstaff Cres SW18 ..... 20 A8
Longstaff Rd SW18 ..... 20 B8
Longstone Rd SW17 ..... 21 B3
Longthornton Rd SW16 ..... 41 D7
Longton Ave SE26 ..... 23 A4
Longton Gr SE26 ..... 23 B4
Longwater Rd RG12 ..... 27 C3
Longwood Dr SW15 ..... 19 B8
Longwood Rd CR8 ..... 80 D3
Longwood View 202 A3
Longyard House RH6 ..... 161 B5
Lonsdale Gdns CR7,SW16 ..... 41 F5
Lonsdale Mews **1** TW9 ..... 7 A6
Lonsdale Rd Barnes SW13 ..... 7 F7
  Croydon SE25 ..... 43 B5
  Dorking RH4 ..... 136 B8
  Weybridge KT13 ..... 53 A3
Look Out Discovery Ctr
  The RG12 ..... 27 C4
Loop Rd Epsom KT18 ..... 76 C3
  Old Woking GU22 ..... 89 F7
Loppets Rd RH10 ..... 201 F3
Loraine Gdns KT21 ..... 75 E2
Loraine House **4** SM5 ..... 60 B6
Loraine Rd W4 ..... 7 B8
Lord Chancellor Wlk KT12 ..... 38 C8
Lord Knyvett Cl TW19 ..... 2 D1
Lordell Pl SW19 ..... 19 C2
Lords Cl Feltham TW13 ..... 15 C6
  West Norwood SE21 ..... 22 C6
Lordsbury Field SM6 ..... 60 C1
Lordsgrove Cl KT20 ..... 97 B7
Lordshill Rd GU5 ..... 152 C5
Lordship La SE21,SE22 ..... 23 A8
Loretto Cl GU6 ..... 175 A3
Lorian Dr RH2 ..... 118 C2
Loriners RH10 ..... 201 D3
Lorne Ave CR0 ..... 43 D2
Lorne Gdns Croydon CR0 ..... 43 D2
  Knaphill GU21 ..... 88 D8
Lorne Rd **2** TW10 ..... 6 F2
Lorne The KT23 ..... 94 A1
Lorraine Ct BR3 ..... 44 C8
Lorraine Cty Ind Sch GU15 65 E8
Lorraine Rd GU15 ..... 65 E8
Lory Ridge GU19 ..... 47 E4
Loseberry Rd KT10 ..... 55 D5
Loseley Ho GU3 ..... 129 E5
Loseley Rd GU7 ..... 150 E8
Lothian Rd GU24 ..... 87 A6
Lothian Wood KT20 ..... 97 B5
Lotus Rd TN16 ..... 83 F1
Loubet St SW17 ..... 20 F2
Loudwater Cl TW16 ..... 35 A5
Loudwater Rd TW16 ..... 35 A5
Loughborough RG12 ..... 27 E3
Louis Fields GU3 ..... 108 C5
Louisa Ct TW2 ..... 16 E6
Louisa House SW15 ..... 7 F3
Louise Margaret
  Maternity Hospl GU11 ..... 105 B3
Louise Margaret Rd GU11 105 C3
Louisville Rd SW17 ..... 21 A5
Louvain Rd SW15 ..... 4 E7
Lovatt Ct SW12 ..... 21 B7
Love La Cheam SM3 ..... 58 E4
  Croydon SE25 ..... 43 B6
  Godstone RH9 ..... 121 C3
  Long Ditton KT6 ..... 56 D8
  Mitcham CR4 ..... 40 E6
  Morden SM4 ..... 40 B2
  Sutton SM1 ..... 59 A4
  Walton on t H KT20 ..... 97 A1
Loveday House **2** SW2 ..... 22 A7

Lovedean Ct RG12 ..... 27 E3
Lovekyn Cl KT1 ..... 37 F7
Lovel La SL5 ..... 9 A3
Lovel Rd SL5 ..... 9 A4
Lovelace Cl KT24 ..... 93 A4
Lovelace Dr GU22 ..... 70 F3
Lovelace Gdns
  Hersham KT12 ..... 54 C5
  Surbiton KT6 ..... 37 D2
Lovelace Prim Sch KT9 ..... 56 C5
Lovelace Rd Bracknell RG12 26 E5
  Surbiton KT6 ..... 37 D2
  West Norwood SE21 ..... 22 C7
Lovelands La
  Lower Kingswood KT20 ..... 118 B8
  West End GU24 ..... 68 C6
Loveletts RH11 ..... 201 A5
Lovell House **4** SW19 ..... 40 B8
Lovell Rd TW10 ..... 17 C5
Lovells Cl GU18 ..... 48 B1
Lovelock Cl CR8 ..... 80 C2
Lovers La GU10 ..... 167 C7
Lovett Dr SM5 ..... 40 D2
Lovett House **9** GU25 ..... 125 B2
Lovett Rd TW20 ..... 12 C4
Low Cross Wood La SE21 ..... 22 F5
Low La GU9 ..... 126 B6
Lowbury RG12 ..... 27 E5
Lowburys RH4 ..... 136 B4
Lowdells Cl RH19 ..... 185 C4
Lowdells Dr RH19 ..... 185 D4
Lowdells La RH19 ..... 185 C3
Lower Addiscombe Rd
  CR0 ..... 42 E1
Lower Barn Cl RH1 ..... 217 F5
Lower Barn Rd CR8 ..... 80 D6
Lower Breache Rd GU6 ..... 176 B4
Lower Bridge Rd RH1 ..... 118 F1
Lower Broadmoor Rd
  RG45 ..... 45 D4
Lower Charles St GU15 ..... 65 D6
Lower Church La **15** GU9 125 B2
Lower Church St CR0,CR9 ..... 61 B8
Lower Coombe St
  CR0,CR9 ..... 61 C6
Lower Court Rd KT19 ..... 76 C8
Lower Ct KT19 ..... 76 D8
Lower Dene RH19 ..... 186 A1
Lower Downs Rd SW20 ..... 39 D8
Lower Dunnymans **4** SM7 77 F5
Lower Eashing GU7 ..... 149 F4
Lower Edgeborough Rd
  GU1 ..... 130 F8
Lower Farm Rd KT23,KT24 93 C3
Lower Farnham Rd
  GU11,GU12 ..... 126 C7
Lower Forecourt RH6 ..... 182 B7
Lower George St **3** TW10 6 D2
Lower Gn KT12 ..... 54 D5
Lower Gn W CR4 ..... 40 E6
Lower Grn Rd
  Esher KT10 ..... 55 C8
  Thames Ditton KT10 ..... 55 C8
Lower Grove Rd TW10 ..... 6 F2
Lower Guildford Rd GU21 68 D1
Lower Ham La GU8 ..... 148 E4
Lower Ham Rd KT2 ..... 17 D2
Lower Hampton Rd
  TW12,TW16 ..... 35 D7
Lower Hanger GU27 ..... 207 D6
Lower Hill Rd KT19 ..... 76 B7
Lower House Rd GU8 ..... 169 F2
Lower Manor Rd
  Farncombe GU7 ..... 150 F6
  Milford GU8 ..... 149 E1
Lower Marsh La KT1,KT5 ..... 38 A5
Lower Mere RH19 ..... 205 F8
Lower Mill Field GU19 ..... 47 D2
Lower Morden La SM4 ..... 39 E3
Lower Mortlake Rd TW9 ..... 6 F4
Lower Moushill La GU8 ..... 149 E1
Lower Nelson St **4** GU11 105 A2
Lower Northfield **5** SM7 ..... 77 F5
Lower Park Rd CR5 ..... 78 F1
Lower Peryers KT24 ..... 112 E7
Lower Pillory Down SM5 ..... 79 B7
Lower Rd Effingham KT24 113 D8
  Fetcham KT22,KT23,KT24 94 A3
  Forest Row RH18 ..... 206 F3
  Grayswood GU27 ..... 189 F2
  Great Bookham KT22,
   KT23,KT24 ..... 94 C3
  Purley CR8 ..... 80 B6
  Reigate RH1 ..... 139 D7
  Sutton SM1 ..... 59 C6
Lower Richmond Rd
  SW14,TW9 ..... 7 A4
Lower Sandfields GU23 ..... 90 D3
Lower Sawleywood **2** SM7 77 F5
Lower Shott 94 B1
Lower South St GU7 ..... 150 D4
Lower South View GU9 ..... 125 C3
Lower Sq RH18 ..... 206 E3
Lower St Haslemere GU27 208 C6
  Shere GU5 ..... 133 A4
Lower Sunbury Rd TW12 ..... 36 A7
Lower Sydenham Sta SE26 23 F3
Lower Tanbridge Way
  RH12 ..... 217 B2
Lower Teddington Rd
  KT1 ..... 37 C8
Lower Village Rd SL5 ..... 29 C4
Lower Weybourne La
  Farnham GU9 ..... 125 F6
  Heath End GU9 ..... 125 F6
Lower Wood Rd KT10 ..... 56 B4
Lowestoft Wlk RH10 ..... 202 B4
Loweswater Wlk GU15 ..... 66 D4

Lowfield Cl GU18 ..... 67 A8
Lowfield Heath Rd
  Charlwood RH6 ..... 180 F5
  Crawley RH6 ..... 180 F5
Lowfield Rd RH13 ..... 215 D3
Lowfield Way RH11 ..... 181 E5
Lowicks Rd GU10 ..... 168 C6
Lowlands Rd
  Blackwater GU17 ..... 64 C4
  Stanwell TW19 ..... 2 D2
Lowndes Bldgs GU9 ..... 125 B3
Lowood Ct SE19 ..... 22 F3
Lowry Cl GU47 ..... 64 D6
Lowry Cres CR4 ..... 40 E7
Lowther Hill SE23 ..... 23 E8
Lowther Rd Barnes SW13 ..... 7 F6
  Kingston u T KT2 ..... 37 F8
Lowthorpe **9** GU21 ..... 69 A1
Loxford Ct GU6 ..... 173 F2
Loxford Rd CR3 ..... 100 F2
Loxford Way CR3 ..... 100 F2
Loxley Cl SE26 ..... 23 D3
Loxley Rd Hampton TW12 ..... 15 E4
  Wandsworth SW18 ..... 20 D7
Loxton Rd SE23 ..... 23 E7
Loxwood Cl TW14 ..... 14 E7
Loxwood Cty Prim Sch
  RH14 ..... 213 A4
Loxwood Rd Alfold GU6 ..... 193 F2
  Alfold Crossways GU6 ..... 193 F2
  Ifold RH14 ..... 212 A2
  Loxwood RH12,RH14 ..... 213 D4
  Loxwood, Alfold Bars
   GU6,RH14 ..... 212 F8
  Plaistow RH14 ..... 212 A2
  Rudgwick RH12 ..... 214 A6
Loxwood Wlk RH11 ..... 201 A8
Lucan Dr TW18 ..... 13 D1
Lucas Cl RH19 ..... 186 A1
Lucas Ct SE26 ..... 23 E3
Lucas Field GU27 ..... 207 E6
Lucas Green GU24 ..... 67 D4
Lucas Green Rd GU24 ..... 67 E5
Lucas Rd Penge SE20 ..... 23 C2
  Warnham RH12 ..... 216 F8
Lucerne Cl GU22 ..... 89 E8
Lucerne Ct **8** BR3 ..... 24 A1
Lucerne Dr RH10 ..... 202 D4
Lucerne Rd CR7 ..... 42 C5
Lucie Ave TW15 ..... 14 B2
Lucien Rd
  Upper Tooting SW17 ..... 21 A4
  Wimbledon SW19 ..... 20 B6
Lucille Ho SE26 ..... 23 D3
Luckley Oakfield Sch
  RG40 ..... 25 B3
Luckley Path RG40 ..... 25 B3
Luckley Rd RG41 ..... 25 B3
Luckley Wood RG41 ..... 25 B3
Lucraft House **12** SW2 ..... 21 E8
Luddington Ave
  GU25,TW20 ..... 31 F7
Ludford Cl CR0 ..... 61 B6
Ludgrove Sch RG40 ..... 25 D3
Ludlow RG12 ..... 27 A2
Ludlow Cl GU16 ..... 86 A7
Ludlow Rd Feltham TW13 ..... 15 A4
  Guildford GU2 ..... 130 B8
Ludovick Wlk SW15 ..... 7 E3
Ludshott Gr GU35 ..... 187 A4
Ludwell La KT11 ..... 125 E8
Luke Rd E GU11 ..... 125 F8
Lullarook Cl TN16 ..... 83 C3
Lullington Rd SE20 ..... 23 A1
Lulworth Ave TW5,TW7 ..... 5 C7
Lulworth Cl Crawley RH11 201 B3
  Farnborough GU14 ..... 85 A7
Lulworth Cres CR4 ..... 40 E7
Lumley Ct RH6 ..... 161 A4
Lumley Gdns SM3 ..... 58 E5
Lumley House **4** GU11 ..... 105 A2
Lumley Rd Cheam SM1,SM3 58 E5
  Horley RH6 ..... 161 A3
Luna Rd CR7 ..... 42 C6
Lunar Cl TN16 ..... 83 D3
Lundy Cl RH11 ..... 201 C3
Lunghurst Rd CR3 ..... 102 A5
Lunham Rd SE19 ..... 22 E2
Lupin Cl Bagshot GU19 ..... 47 C1
  Croydon CR0 ..... 43 D1
  Streatham SW2 ..... 22 A6
Lupin Ride RG45 ..... 45 B8
Lupus Ct SE19 ..... 42 D8
Luscombe Ct BR2 ..... 44 E7
Lushington Dr KT11 ..... 73 B5
Lushington House KT12 ..... 35 C3
Lushington Rd SE6 ..... 24 C3
Lusted Hall La
  Biggin Hill TN16 ..... 103 C7
  Tatsfield TN16 ..... 103 C7
Lusteds Cl RH4 ..... 136 C4
Lutea House SM2 ..... 59 C3
Luther Rd TW11 ..... 16 F3
Lutwyche Rd SE23,SE6 ..... 23 F6
Lutyens Cl RH11 ..... 200 E4
Luxford Cl RH12 ..... 217 F5
Luxford's La
  Ashurst Wood RH19 ..... 206 B6
  Forest Row RH19 ..... 206 B6
Lyall Ave SE21 ..... 22 F4
Lyall Pl GU9 ..... 125 B7
Lycett House **10** SW2 ..... 21 E8
Lych Way GU21 ..... 69 D3
Lyconby Gdns CR0 ..... 43 E2
Lydbury RG12 ..... 27 F6
Lydden Gr SW18 ..... 20 B8
Lydden Rd SW18 ..... 20 B8
Lydele Cl GU21 ..... 69 F4

Lydford Cl
  2 Farnborough GU14 ..... 85 A7
  Frimley GU16 ..... 86 A7
Lydhurst Ave SW2 ..... 21 F6
Lydney RG12 ..... 27 B2
Lydney Cl SW19 ..... 19 E6
Lydon House RH11 ..... 181 D1
Lye Copse Ave GU14 ..... 85 B8
Lye The KT20 ..... 97 C5
Lye View Cotts GU21 ..... 89 A8
Lyefield La GU6,RH5 ..... 176 C5
Lyfield KT11,KT22 ..... 74 B5
Lyford Rd SW18 ..... 20 E7
Lyham Rd SW2 ..... 21 E8
Lyle Cl CR4 ..... 41 A2
Lymbourne Cl SM2 ..... 59 A1
Lymden Gdns RH2 ..... 139 B7
Lyme Regis Rd SM7 ..... 77 F2
Lymer Ave SE19 ..... 22 F3
Lymescote Gdns SM1 ..... 59 A8
Lyminge Gdns SW17,SW18 20 E7
Lymington Cl SW16 ..... 41 D7
Lymington Ct SM1 ..... 59 C7
Lymington Gdns KT19 ..... 57 F5
Lyn Ct GU1 ..... 131 A8
Lynch Rd GU9 ..... 125 E2
Lynchen Cl TW5 ..... 4 B6
Lynchford La GU11,GU13 105 E8
Lynchford Rd GU14 ..... 105 D8
Lyncroft Gdns Ewell KT17 57 F2
  Isleworth TW3 ..... 5 C2
Lyndale Ct **3** RH1 ..... 119 A4
Lyndale Rd RH1 ..... 119 A4
Lyndhurst Ave
  Aldershot GU11 ..... 126 C6
  Blackwater GU17 ..... 64 C6
  Mitcham SW16 ..... 41 D7
  Sunbury TW16 ..... 35 A6
  Tolworth KT5 ..... 38 B1
  Twickenham TW2,TW4 ..... 16 A7
Lyndhurst Cl
  Bracknell RG12 ..... 28 A6
  Crawley RH11 ..... 201 D5
  South Croydon CR0 ..... 61 F7
  Woking GU21 ..... 69 D4
Lyndhurst Ct **7** SM2 ..... 59 A3
Lyndhurst Dr KT3 ..... 38 F2
Lyndhurst Farm Cl RH19 184 D4
Lyndhurst House **3** SW15 19 A8
Lyndhurst Rd Ascot SL5 ..... 29 A1
  Coulsdon CR5 ..... 79 A3
  Reigate RH2 ..... 139 A6
  Thornton Heath CR7 ..... 42 A5
Lyndhurst Sch GU15 ..... 65 B5
Lyndhurst Way
  Addlestone KT16 ..... 59 A2
  Belmont SM2 ..... 59 A2
Lyndon Ave SM6 ..... 60 A7
Lyndon Yd SW17 ..... 20 B4
Lyndsey Cl GU14 ..... 84 B4
Lyne Cl GU25 ..... 31 F3
Lyne Crossing Rd
  KT16,TW20 ..... 32 B3
Lyne Ct GU25 ..... 31 F2
Lyne La
  Chertsey KT16,TW20 ..... 32 A3
  Lyne KT16 ..... 32 A2
Lyne & Longcross Inf Sch
  KT16 ..... 51 B8
Lyne Place Manor GU25 ..... 31 F2
Lyne Rd GU25 ..... 31 E3
Lynegrove Ave TW15 ..... 14 C3
Lyneham Rd RG45 ..... 45 B5
Lynfield Ct SE23 ..... 23 D8
Lynmouth Ave SM4 ..... 39 D2
Lynmouth Gdns TW5 ..... 4 D3
Lynn Cl TW15 ..... 14 D3
Lynn Ct Streatham SW16 ..... 21 D3
  Whyteleafe CR3 ..... 80 F1
Lynn Rd SW12 ..... 21 B8
Lynn Way GU14 ..... 84 F7
Lynn Wlk RH2 ..... 139 B6
Lynn Wood Rd GU14 ..... 84 F3
Lynne Cl
  South Croydon CR2 ..... 62 D1
  Shalford GU4 ..... 130 E3
Lynne Ct Forest Hill SE23 ..... 23 E8
  Farnham GU9 ..... 146 A7
  Isleworth TW7 ..... 5 F5
Lynscott Way CR2 ..... 61 B2
Lynsted Ct BR3 ..... 43 E7
Lynton Cl Chessington KT9 56 E6
  East Grinstead RH19 ..... 186 A2
  Farnham GU9 ..... 146 A7
  Isleworth TW7 ..... 5 F3
Lynton Ct SM7 ..... 59 C4
Lynton Park Ave RH19 ..... 186 A2
Lynton Prep Sch KT17 ..... 76 F8
Lynton Rd New Malden KT3 38 D4
  Thornton Heath CR0,CR7 42 A3
Lynwick St Rudgwick RH12 214 D8
  Rudgwick RH12 ..... 214 C8
  Rudgwick, Cox Green RH12 195 D1
Lynwood GU2 ..... 130 B8
Lynwood Ave Egham TW20 11 F2
  Epsom KT17 ..... 76 F5
  Wallington CR5 ..... 79 B4
Lynwood Chase **1** RG12 ..... 27 C8
Lynwood Cl GU21 ..... 70 D5
Lynwood Cres SL5 ..... 29 E3
Lynwood Ct RH12 ..... 217 D2
Lynwood Dr Mytchett GU16 86 A3
  North Cheam KT4 ..... 58 A8
Lynwood Flats SL5 ..... 29 E4
Lynwood Gdns CR0 ..... 60 F6

Lynwood Rd Epsom KT17 ..... 76 F5
  Redhill RH1 ..... 119 A4
  Thames Ditton KT7 ..... 36 F1
  Upper Tooting SW17 ..... 20 F5
Lynx Hill KT24 ..... 112 F7
Lyon Cl RH10 ..... 202 C3
Lyon Ct RH13 ..... 217 E1
Lyon Rd Crowthorne RG45 ..... 45 C4
  Merton SW19 ..... 40 C8
  Walton-on-T KT12 ..... 54 E8
Lyon Way GU16 ..... 65 C1
Lyon Way Ind Est GU16 ..... 65 C2
Lyons Cl RH13 ..... 215 D3
Lyons Ct RH4 ..... 136 B8
Lyons Dr GU2 ..... 109 A4
Lyons Rd RH13 ..... 215 E3
Lyonsdene KT20 ..... 117 F3
Lyric Cl RH10 ..... 202 C5
Lyric Mews SE26 ..... 23 C4
Lyric Rd SW13 ..... 7 F6
Lysander Rd CR0 ..... 60 F5
Lysias Rd SW12 ..... 21 B8
Lysons Ave GU12 ..... 105 F3
Lysons Rd GU11 ..... 105 A1
Lyster Mews KT11 ..... 73 C4
Lytchet Minster Cl **4** RG12 27 F2
Lytchgate Cl CR2 ..... 61 E3
Lytcott Dr KT8 ..... 35 F2
Lytham RG12 ..... 26 E2
Lytham Ct SL5 ..... 29 C4
Lytton Dr RH10 ..... 202 C2
Lytton Gdns SM6 ..... 60 E6
Lytton House **3** TW12 ..... 16 B2
Lytton Rd GU22 ..... 70 B2
Lyveden Rd SW17,SW19 ..... 20 E2
Lywood Cl KT20 ..... 97 C5

M

Mabbotts KT20 ..... 97 C1
Mabel St GU21 ..... 69 C2
Maberley Cres SE19 ..... 23 A1
Maberley Ct SE19 ..... 23 A1
Maberley Rd Penge SE19 ..... 23 A1
  Penge, Elmers End BR3 ..... 43 C1
Macadam Ave RG45 ..... 45 C1
MacArthur House **4** SW2 21 E8
Macaulay Ave KT10 ..... 55 F8
Macaulay Ct CR3 ..... 100 C5
Macaulay Rd CR3 ..... 100 C5
Macbeth Ct RG42 ..... 27 E8
Macclesfield Rd CR0,SE25 43 C4
Macdonald Ct TW3 ..... 5 C6
Macdonald Rd
  Heath End GU9 ..... 125 A8
  Lightwater GU18 ..... 67 A8
Macfarlane La TW7 ..... 6 A8
MacGregor House SW12 ..... 21 C7
Mackenzie Rd BR3 ..... 43 D7
Mackie House SW2 ..... 22 A8
Mackie Rd **1** SW2 ..... 22 A8
Mackies Hill GU5 ..... 154 E1
Macklin House SE23 ..... 23 B8
Mackrells RH1 ..... 139 C1
Macleod Rd RH13 ..... 217 E1
Macmillan House SM7 ..... 77 F7
Macphail Cl RG40 ..... 25 E8
Maddison Cl TW11 ..... 16 F2
Maddox La KT23 ..... 93 F3
Maddox Pk KT23 ..... 93 E3
Madehurst Cl RH11 ..... 200 F7
Madeira Ave Bromley BR1 ..... 24 F3
  Horsham RH12 ..... 217 C3
Madeira Cl KT14 ..... 71 A6
Madeira Cres KT14 ..... 70 F6
Madeira Rd Mitcham CR4 ..... 40 F5
  Streatham SW16 ..... 21 E4
  West Byfleet KT14 ..... 71 A6
Madeira Wlk KH1,RH2 ..... 118 C1
Madeline Rd SE20 ..... 23 A1
Madgehole La GU5 ..... 153 B9
Madingley RG12 ..... 27 A1
Madingley Ct TW1 ..... 6 D1
Madison Gdns BR2 ..... 44 F6
Madox Brown End GU47 ..... 64 D6
Madrid Rd GU2 ..... 130 B7
Maesmaur Rd TN16 ..... 103 D2
Mafeking Ave TW8 ..... 6 E8
Mafeking Rd TW19 ..... 12 A6
Magazine Cotts GU4 ..... 131 C1
Magazine Pl KT22 ..... 95 B5
Magazine Rd GU3 ..... 108 B8
Magdala Rd Isleworth TW7 6 A4
  South Croydon CR2 ..... 61 D3
Magdalen Cl KT14 ..... 71 A5
Magdalen Cres KT14 ..... 71 A5
Magdalen Ct SE25 ..... 43 A4
Magdalen Rd SW17,SW18 20 D2
Magdalene Cl RH10 ..... 182 C1
Magdalene Rd
  Littleton TW17 ..... 33 F5
  Sandhurst GU47 ..... 45 A1
Magellan Terr RH10 ..... 182 A1
Magna Carta La TW19 ..... 11 D7
Magna Carta Sec Sch
  TW20 ..... 12 D1
Magna Rd TW20 ..... 11 C2
Magnolia Cl
  Kingston u T KT2 ..... 18 B2
  Sandhurst GU47 ..... 45 C1
Magnolia Ct
  3 Belmont SM2 ..... 59 B3
  Horley RH6 ..... 161 A3
  Penge SE26 ..... 23 C4
  Richmond TW9 ..... 7 A7
  Wallington SM6 ..... 60 B5
Magnolia Dr TN16 ..... 83 D3

Magnolia Rd W4 . . . . 7 B8
Magnolia Way
  Dorking RH5 . . . . 136 C5
  West Ewell KT19 . . . . 57 C5
Magnolia Wharf W4 . . . . 7 B8
Magpie Cl Coulsdon CR5 . . . . 79 C1
  Crondall GU10 . . . . 124 D8
Magpie Wlk RH10 . . . . 201 F8
Maguire Dr Frimley GU16 . . . 66 C3
  Richmond TW10 . . . . 17 C4
Mahonia Cl GU24 . . . . 67 F6
Maida Rd GU11 . . . . 105 B4
Maiden La RH11 . . . . 201 C8
Maiden's Gn SL4 . . . . 8 B6
Maidenbower Cty Fst Sch
  RH10 . . . . 202 C4
Maidenbower Dr RH10 . . . . 202 D4
Maidenbower La RH10 . . . . . 202 C4
Maidenbower Pl RH10 . . . . . 202 C4
Maidenbower Sq RH10 . . . . . 202 C4
Maidenshaw Rd KT19 . . . . . . 76 D7
Maids of Honour Row **4**
  TW9 . . . . 6 D2
Maidstone Cres GU24 . . . . . . 87 D6
Main Dr RG12, SL5 . . . . 28 B8
Main Rd TN16 . . . . 83 C5
Main St Chertsey KT15 . . . . . 52 E7
  Feltham TW13 . . . . 15 D3
Mainprize Rd RG12 . . . . 27 E7
Mainstone Cl GU16 . . . . 86 C7
Mainstone Rd GU24 . . . . 67 F3
Mainwaring Ct GU4 . . . . 41 A7
Mais House SE26 . . . . 23 B6
Maise Webster Cl TW19 . . . 13 D8
Maisonettes The SM1 . . . . . . 58 F5
Maitland Cl Hounslow TW4 . . . 4 F4
  Walton-on-T KT12 . . . . 54 E8
  West Byfleet KT14 . . . . 71 A6
Maitland Rd
  Farnborough GU14 . . . . 105 B8
  Penge SE26 . . . . 23 D2
Maitlands Cl GU10 . . . . 126 F6
Maizecroft RH6 . . . . 161 C4
Majestic Way CR4 . . . . 40 F7
Major's Farm Rd SL3 . . . . 1 A8
Major's Hill RG12 . . . . 28 D5
Malacca Farm GU4 . . . . 111 B7
Malan Cl TN16 . . . . 83 E2
Malcolm Cl SE20 . . . . 23 C1
Malcolm Dr KT6 . . . . 37 E1
Malcolm Gdns RH6 . . . . 160 D1
Malcolm Prim Sch SE20 . . . . 23 C1
Malcolm Rd Coulsdon CR5 . . 79 D4
  Croydon CR0, SE25 . . . . 43 A3
  Penge SE20 . . . . 23 C1
  Wimbledon SW19 . . . . 19 F2
Malden Ave SE25 . . . . 43 B6
Malden Ct KT3 . . . . 39 B6
Malden Golf Course KT4 . . . 38 F7
Malden Green Ave KT4 . . . . 39 A1
Malden Hill KT3 . . . . 38 F6
Malden Hill Gdns KT3 . . . . . 38 F6
Malden Manor Prim Sch
  KT3 . . . . 38 E2
Malden Manor Sta KT3 . . . . 38 E2
Malden Parochial CE
  Prim Sch KT4 . . . . 38 E1
Malden Pk KT3 . . . . 38 F3
Malden Rd Cheam KT4, SM3 . 58 D5
  New Malden KT3, KT4 . . . . . . 38 F2
  Walton-on-T KT12 . . . . 39 A5
Malden Way (Kingston
  By Pass) KT3, KT5 . . . . 38 E4
Maldon Ct SM6 . . . . 60 C5
Maldon Rd SM6 . . . . 60 B5
Malet Cl TW20 . . . . 12 D2
Maley Ave SE27 . . . . 22 B6
Malham Cl RH10 . . . . 202 C3
Malham Fell RG12 . . . . 27 A5
Malham Rd Ind Est SE23 . . . 23 D7
Mall The Brentford TW8 . . . . . 6 D8
  Croydon CR9 . . . . 61 C8
 6 Guildford GU1 . . . . 130 C8
  Hersham KT12 . . . . 54 D5
  Kingston u T KT6 . . . . 37 D4
  Mortlake SW14 . . . . 7 C2
Mall The (Prep Sch) TW2 . . 16 D5
Mallard Cl Ash GU12 . . . . . . 105 F2
  Haslemere GU27 . . . . 207 E6
  Horley RH6 . . . . 161 A5
  Horsham RH12 . . . . 217 C5
  Redhill RH1 . . . . 119 A4
  Twickenham TW4 . . . . 16 A8
Mallard Ct Dorking RH4 . . . 136 A8
 6 Richmond TW9 . . . . 6 D1
Mallard Pl
  East Grinstead RH19 . . . . . 205 F8
  Twickenham TW1 . . . . 17 A5
Mallard Rd CR2 . . . . 62 D1
Mallard Way SM6 . . . . 60 C2
Mallard Wlk BR3, CR0 . . . . . 43 D4
Mallard's Reach KT13 . . . . . . 53 D6
Mallards The Frimley GU16 . . 65 F2
  Laleham TW18 . . . . 33 B7
Mallards Way GU18 . . . . 67 A8
Malling Cl CR0 . . . . 43 C3
Malling Gdns SM4 . . . . 40 C4
Malling House **6** BR3 . . . . . 24 A1
Malling Way BR2 . . . . 44 F2
Mallinson Rd SM6 . . . . 60 D7
Mallow Cl
  Burgh Heath KT20 . . . . 97 B8
  Croydon CR0 . . . . 43 D1
  Horsham RH12 . . . . 217 E6
Mallow Cres GU4 . . . . 110 C4
Mallowdale Rd RG12 . . . . . . 27 E2
Malloy Ct GU21 . . . . 70 A3

Malmains Cl BR3 . . . . 44 D5
Malmains Way BR3 . . . . 44 D5
Malmesbury Fst Sch SM4 . . 40 C4
Malmesbury Mid Sch SM4 . 40 C3
Malmesbury Rd SM4 . . . . . . 40 C3
Malmstone Ave RH1 . . . . . . 119 D6
Malt Hill TW20 . . . . 11 E3
Malt House SL4 . . . . 11 B8
Malt House Ct SL4 . . . . 11 B8
Malt House Rd SL4 . . . . 1 B8
Maltby Rd KT9 . . . . 57 A4
Malthouse Ct GU4 . . . . 130 E4
Malthouse Dr TW13 . . . . 15 D3
Malthouse La
  Pirbright GU24, GU3 . . . . . . 88 C2
  West Green GU27 . . . . 67 F7
Malthouse Mead GU8 . . . . . 170 F5
Malthouse Rd RH10, RH11 . 201 D4
Malthouses The GU6 . . . . . . 174 E3
Maltings The Byfleet KT14 . . 71 F6
  Oxted RH8 . . . . 122 F4
  Staines TW18 . . . . 12 E4
Maltings La GU8 . . . . 171 C1
Malton House SE25 . . . . 42 E5
Malus Cl KT15 . . . . 51 F3
Malus Dr KT15 . . . . 51 F3
Malvern Cl Mitcham CR4 . . . 41 C6
  Ottershaw KT16 . . . . 51 C4
  Penge SE20 . . . . 43 A2
  Surbiton KT6 . . . . 37 E1
Malvern Ct Belmont SM2 . . . 59 A3
  Brands Hill SL3 . . . . 1 A8
  Guildford GU1 . . . . 118 F8
 3 Surbiton KT6 . . . . 37 E1
Malvern Dr TW13 . . . . 15 D3
Malvern Rd Crawley RH11 . . 201 C5
  Farnborough GU14 . . . . 84 D7
  Hampton TW12 . . . . 16 A1
  Harlington UB3 . . . . 3 E7
  Surbiton KT6 . . . . 37 E1
  Thornton Heath CR7 . . . . . . 42 A5
Malyons The TW17 . . . . 34 D3
Manatee Pl SM6 . . . . 60 D7
Manby Lodge Cty Inf Sch
  KT13 . . . . 53 C5
Manchester Rd CR7 . . . . 42 C6
Mandeville Cl
  Guildford GU2 . . . . 109 A4
  Merton SW19 . . . . 39 E8
Mandeville Ct TW20 . . . . 12 A4
Mandeville Dr KT6 . . . . 37 D1
Mandeville Rd
  Isleworth TW7 . . . . 6 A5
  Littleton TW17 . . . . 34 A4
Mandora Rd GU11 . . . . 105 B4
Mandrake Rd SW17 . . . . 20 F5
Manfield Cty Fst Sch
  GU12 . . . . 106 B2
Manfield Pk GU6 . . . . 174 B5
Manfield Rd GU12 . . . . 106 A2
Mangles Ct **1** GU1 . . . . 130 C8
Mangles Rd GU1 . . . . 109 D3
Manley Bridge Rd
  Rowledge GU10 . . . . 145 E4
  Wrecclesham GU10 . . . . 145 E4
Mann's Cl TW7 . . . . 5 F2
Mannamead Cl KT18 . . . . . . 96 E8
Mannamead Rd KT18 . . . . . . 96 E8
Manning Cl RH19 . . . . 185 D2
Manning Ct RH19 . . . . 185 D2
Mannings Cl RH10 . . . . 182 D1
Manningtree Cl SW19 . . . . . . 19 E7
Manoel Rd TW2 . . . . 16 C6
Manor Ave Caterham CR3 . . 100 E3
  Hounslow TW4 . . . . 4 D5
Manor Chase KT13 . . . . 53 B5
Manor Cl
  East Horsley KT24 . . . . 112 E7
  Haslemere GU27 . . . . 207 E6
  Horley RH6 . . . . 160 F4
  New Malden KT4 . . . . 38 E1
  Pyrford GU27 . . . . 70 F3
  South Godstone RH9 . . . . . 142 F5
  Tongham GU10 . . . . 126 F7
  Warlingham CR6 . . . . 81 E2
Manor Cotts GU21 . . . . 68 E5
Manor Cres Byfleet KT14 . . . 71 F6
  Guildford GU2 . . . . 109 B3
  Haslemere GU27 . . . . 207 E6
  Pirbright GU24 . . . . 87 D7
  Surbiton KT5 . . . . 38 A3
Manor Ct Horsham RH12 . . 218 A5
  Kingston u T KT2 . . . . 38 A8
  Streatham SW16 . . . . 21 E5
  Twickenham TW2 . . . . 16 C6
  Weybridge KT13 . . . . 53 B6
Manor Dr Feltham TW13 . . . 15 D3
  Hinchley Wood KT10 . . . . . . 56 A7
  Horley RH6 . . . . 160 F3
  Sunbury TW16 . . . . 35 A7
  Surbiton KT5 . . . . 38 A4
  West Ewell KT19 . . . . 57 A4
  Woodham KT15 . . . . 52 A1
Manor Dr N KT3, KT4 . . . . . . 38 D2
Manor Dr The KT4 . . . . 38 E1
Manor Farm Ave TW17 . . . . 34 B3
Manor Farm Bsns Ctr
  GU10 . . . . 126 F5
Manor Farm Cl GU12 . . . . . 105 F1
Manor Farm Ct TW20 . . . . . . 12 A3
Manor Farm La TW20 . . . . . . 12 A3
Manor Farm Rd CR7, SW16 . 42 A7
Manor Fields
  Horsham RH12, RH1 . . . . . . 218 A4
  Milford GU8 . . . . 149 E2
  Seale GU10 . . . . 127 B4

Manor Fst Sch The KT14 . . . 71 E5
Manor Gdns
  Effingham KT24 . . . . 113 D7
  Farncombe GU7 . . . . 150 F5
  Farnham GU10 . . . . 146 D5
  Guildford GU2 . . . . 109 B3
  Hampton TW12 . . . . 16 C1
  Merton SW19, SW20 . . . . 39 F7
  Richmond TW10, TW9 . . . . . . 6 F3
  South Croydon CR2 . . . . 61 F4
  Sunbury TW16 . . . . 35 A7
Manor Gn GU8 . . . . 149 E1
Manor Gr Beckenham BR3 . . 44 B7
  Richmond TW9 . . . . 7 A4
Manor Green Rd KT19 . . . . . 76 C6
Manor Hill SM7 . . . . 78 F4
Manor House SM6 . . . . 60 B5
Manor House Ct KT18 . . . . . 76 C6
Manor House Dr SL5 . . . . 9 A1
Manor House Flats GU10 . . 146 D6
Manor House Sch KT23 . . . 113 E8
Manor House The GU15 . . . . 65 D6
Manor House Way TW7 . . . . . 6 B4
Manor La Feltham TW13 . . . . 15 A6
  Harlington UB3 . . . . 3 D8
  Lewisham SE12 . . . . 24 F8
  Lower Kingswood KT20 . . . 118 A6
  Shamley Green GU5 . . . . . . 152 E3
  Sunbury TW16 . . . . 35 B7
  Sutton SM1 . . . . 59 C5
Manor Lea GU27 . . . . 207 D6
Manor Lea Cl GU8 . . . . 149 E2
Manor Lea Rd GU8 . . . . 149 E2
Manor Leaze TW20 . . . . 12 B3
Manor Lodge GU2 . . . . 109 B3
Manor Mount SE23 . . . . 23 C7
Manor Park Cl BR4 . . . . 44 B1
Manor Park Ctr (Coll
  of Tech) GU15 . . . . 105 B1
Manor Park Ind Est GU12 . 105 C1
Manor Park Prim Sch SM1 . 59 C5
Manor Park Rd Sutton SM1 . 59 C5
  West Wickham BR4 . . . . 44 B1
Manor Pk Richmond TW9 . . . . 6 F3
Manor Pl
  Staines TW18 . . . . 12 D5
  East Bedfont TW14 . . . . 15 A7
  Great Bookham KT23 . . . . . . 94 A1
  Mitcham CR4 . . . . 41 C6
  Staines TW18 . . . . 13 B3
  Sutton SM1 . . . . 59 B6
Manor Rd
  Aldershot GU11, GU12 . . . . 126 A8
  Ash GU10, GU12 . . . . 126 F8
  Ashford TW15 . . . . 14 A3
  Beckenham BR3 . . . . 44 B7
  East Grinstead RH19 . . . . . 185 C2
  East Molesey KT8 . . . . 36 D5
  Farnborough GU14 . . . . 85 D5
  Guildford GU2 . . . . 109 B3
  Horsham RH12 . . . . 218 A5
  Merstham RH1 . . . . 119 C6
  Merton SW20 . . . . 39 F7
  Mitcham CR4 . . . . 41 C6
  Reigate RH2 . . . . 117 F3
  Richmond TW10, TW9 . . . . . . 6 F3
  Teddington TW11 . . . . 17 B3
  Tatsfield TN16 . . . . 83 D2
  Send Marsh GU23 . . . . 90 F4
  Teddington TW11 . . . . 17 A3
  Wallington SM5, SM6 . . . . . . 60 B5
  Walton-on-T KT12 . . . . 34 F2
  West Wickham BR4 . . . . 63 B8
  Woking GU21 . . . . 69 C3
  Wokingham RG41 . . . . 25 C2
Manor Rd N
  Hackbridge SM5, SM6 . . . . . 60 B6
  Hinchley Wood KT10 . . . . . . 56 A8
Manor Rd S KT10 . . . . 55 E6
Manor Royal RH10, RH11 . . 181 E1
Manor Royal Ind Est
  RH10 . . . . 181 E2
Manor Way Bagshot GU19 . . 47 F3
  Beckenham BR3 . . . . 44 A6
  Egham TW20 . . . . 11 D2
  Guildford GU2 . . . . 129 F6
  Mitcham CR4, SW16 . . . . 41 C6
  New Malden KT4 . . . . 38 F1
  Old Woking GU22 . . . . 90 B6
  Oxshott KT22 . . . . 74 E4
  Purley CR8 . . . . 79 E7
  South Croydon CR2 . . . . 61 F4
  Woodmansterne SM7 . . . . . . 78 F3
Manor Way The SM6 . . . . 60 B6
Manor Wlk
 3 Aldershot GU12 . . . . 105 B1
  Weybridge KT13 . . . . 53 B5
Manor Wood Rd CR8 . . . . . . 79 E6
Manorcroft Sch TW20 . . . . . 12 A2
Manorcrofts Rd TW20 . . . . . 12 A2
Manorfield Cl RH7 . . . . 143 E6
Manorfields RH11 . . . . 200 D2
Manorgate Rd KT2 . . . . 38 A8
Manorhouse La KT23 . . . . . 112 B7
Mansard Beeches SW17 . . . 21 A3
Manse Cl UB3 . . . . 3 D8
Mansel Cl GU2 . . . . 109 B6
Mansel Rd SW19 . . . . 19 F2
Mansell Cl SL4 . . . . 9 C6
Mansfield Cl SL5 . . . . 28 D7
Mansfield Cres RG12 . . . . . . 27 B3
Mansfield Dr RH1 . . . . 119 D6
Mansfield Pl SL5 . . . . 28 D8

Mansfield Rd
  Chessington KT9 . . . . 56 D5
  South Croydon CR2 . . . . 61 D4
  Wokingham RG41 . . . . 25 A5
Manship Rd CR4 . . . . 21 A1
Manston Cl SE20 . . . . 43 C8
Manston Dr RG12 . . . . 27 C3
Manston Gr KT2 . . . . 17 D3
Manston Rd GU4 . . . . 110 A5
Mantilla Rd SW17 . . . . 21 A4
Mantlet Cl SW16 . . . . 21 C1
Manville Ct GU4 . . . . 130 E1
Manville Gdns SW17 . . . . . . 21 B5
Manville Rd SW17 . . . . 21 B5
Many Gates SW12 . . . . 21 B6
Manygate La TW17 . . . . 34 C3
Maori Rd GU1 . . . . 130 F8
Mapel Ct **3** RG12 . . . . 27 F5
Maple Cl Ash Vale GU12 . . . 106 A7
  Blackwater GU17 . . . . 64 C5
  Crawley RH11 . . . . 181 C1
  Hampton TW12 . . . . 15 F2
  Horsham RH12 . . . . 218 A5
  Mitcham CR4 . . . . 41 B8
  Whyteleafe CR3 . . . . 80 F2
Maple Ct Catford SE6 . . . . . . 24 B7
 2 Croydon CR0 . . . . 61 C6
  Englefield Green TW20 . . . . . 11 B2
  Kingston u T KT3 . . . . 38 D6
 11 West Norwood SW16 . . . 22 A3
Maple Dr Crowthorne RG45 . 45 C7
  East Grinstead RH19 . . . . . 186 A1
  Lightwater GU18 . . . . 66 F8
Maple Gdns TW5, TW19 . . . 13 E6
Maple Gr Brentford TW8 . . . . 6 B7
  Guildford GU1 . . . . 109 D3
  Woking GU22 . . . . 89 E6
Maple Gr Bsns Ctr TW4 . . . . 4 C3
Maple Ho **6** RH2 . . . . 118 F1
Maple House **2** KT6 . . . . . . 37 E4
Maple Ind Est TW13 . . . . 15 A5
Maple Inf Sch KT6 . . . . 37 D4
Maple Leaf Cl
  Biggin Hill TN16 . . . . 83 D3
  Farnborough GU14 . . . . 84 F3
Maple Leaf Dr GU16 . . . . 65 F1
Maple Pl KT17 . . . . 77 D5
Maple Rd Ashstead KT21 . . . 95 D8
  Kingston u T KT6 . . . . 37 D4
  Penge SE20 . . . . 43 C8
  Redhill RH1 . . . . 139 F5
  Send Marsh GU23 . . . . 91 A3
  Whyteleafe CR3 . . . . 80 F2
Maple Way Feltham TW13 . . 15 B5
  Headley Down GU35 . . . . . . 187 B6
  Hooley CR5 . . . . 99 B5
Maple Wlk Aldershot GU12 . 126 D8
  Sutton SM2 . . . . 59 B1
Mapledale Ave CR0 . . . . 62 B7
Mapledrakes Cl GU6 . . . . . . 175 E5
Mapledrakes Rd GU6 . . . . . 175 E5
Maplehatch Cl GU7 . . . . 150 E2
Maplehurst Beckenham BR2 . 44 E7
  Fetcham KT22 . . . . 94 D4
Maplehurst Cl KT1 . . . . 37 E5
Maplehurst Ct GU2 . . . . 109 A3
Mapleleaf Cl CR2 . . . . 81 D8
Maples The Banstead SM7 . . 78 B5
  Ottershaw KT16 . . . . 51 C4
  Wallington SM6 . . . . 17 C1
Maplestead Rd SW2 . . . . 21 F8
Maplethorpe Rd CR7 . . . . . . 42 B5
Maple Hill TW1 . . . . 17 C8
Maple Hill Gdns TW1 . . . . . . 17 B8
Marble Hill Gdns TW1 . . . . . 17 B8
Marbles Way KT20 . . . . 97 D8
March Rd **6**
  Twickenham TW1 . . . . 17 A8
  Weybridge KT13 . . . . 53 A5
Marcheria Cl RG12 . . . . 27 B3
Marches Rd RH12 . . . . 197 E4
Marchmont House **10**
  SW16 . . . . 21 C3
Marchmont Rd
  Richmond TW10 . . . . 6 F2
  Wallington SM6 . . . . 60 C3
Marchside Cl TW5 . . . . 4 D6
Marcus Ct Brentford TW8 . . . . 6 E7
Marcus Rd TW14 . . . . 14 D7
Marcuse Rd CR3 . . . . 100 D4
Mardale GU15 . . . . 66 C4
Mardell Rd CR0 . . . . 43 D4
Marden Ave BR2 . . . . 44 F3
Marden Cres CR0 . . . . 41 F3
Marden Lodge Cty Prim
  Sch CR3 . . . . 101 B6
Marden Rd CR0 . . . . 41 F3
Mardens The RH11 . . . . 201 B7
Mare Hill GU8 . . . . 170 E5
Mare Hill Cotts GU8 . . . . . . 170 D4
Mare La GU8 . . . . 170 E5
Mares Field House GU4 . . . 110 D2
Mareschal Rd GU2 . . . . 130 C7
Marfield Cl KT4 . . . . 39 B1
Marfleet Cl SM5 . . . . 59 E8
Margaret Ct **11** TW18 . . . . 13 D2
Margaret Lockwood Cl
  KT1 . . . . 37 F5
Margaret Rd GU1 . . . . 130 D8
Margaret Roper RC Prim
  Sch CR8 . . . . 61 A1
Margaret Way CR8 . . . . 100 B8
Margery Gr KT20 . . . . 117 E6
Margery La KT20, RH2 . . . . 118 A6
Margin Dr SW19 . . . . 19 D4
Marham Gdns Morden SM4 . 40 C3
  Wandsworth SW17, SW18 . . 20 E7

Maria Theresa Cl KT3 . . . . . 38 D4
Marian Cl SM1 . . . . 59 B5
Marian Rd CR4, SW16 . . . . . 41 C8
Marian Vian Prim Sch BR3 . 43 E4
Mariette Way SM6 . . . . 60 E2
Marigold Cl RG45 . . . . 45 A6
Marigold Ct GU1 . . . . 109 E4
Marigold Dr GU24 . . . . 68 A4
Marigold Way CR0 . . . . 43 D1
Marina Ave KT3 . . . . 39 B4
Marina Cl KT16 . . . . 33 C1
Marina Way TW11 . . . . 17 D1
Mariner Gdns TW10 . . . . 17 C5
Mariners Dr
  Farnborough GU14 . . . . 85 C6
  Normandy GU3 . . . . 107 B4
Marion Ave TW17 . . . . 34 B4
Marion Ct SW17 . . . . 20 D3
Marion Rd Crawley RH10 . . . 202 B3
  Thornton Heath CR7 . . . . . . 42 B5
Marist RC Prim Sch KT14 . . 70 F6
Marius Mansions **3** SW17 . 21 A6
Marius Rd SW17 . . . . 21 A6
Marjoram Cl
  Farnborough GU14 . . . . 84 B4
  Guildford GU2 . . . . 109 A5
Marjorie Fosters Way
  GU24 . . . . 87 D8
Marjory Kinnon Sch TW14 . . 3 E2
Mark Oak La KT22 . . . . 94 A6
Mark St RH2 . . . . 118 B2
Mark Way GU7 . . . . 150 B8
Markedge La CR5, RH2 . . . . 98 F2
Markenfield Rd GU1 . . . . . . 109 D1
Markenhorn GU7 . . . . 150 D7
Market Par Croydon SE25 . . . 43 A5
  Feltham TW13 . . . . 15 E6
Market Pl Brentford TW8 . . . . 6 C7
  Kingston u T KT1 . . . . 37 D7
  Wokingham RG40 . . . . 25 C5
Market Rd TW9 . . . . 7 A4
Market St Horsham RH12 . . 217 C1
  Reigate RH2 . . . . 118 A1
  Staines TW18 . . . . 12 E4
Market St Bracknell RG12 . . 27 B7
  Guildford GU1 . . . . 130 D8
Market The SM1, SM4, SM5 . 40 C1
Marketfield Way **14** RH2 . . 118 F1
Marketfield Way RH1 . . . . . 119 A1
Markfield CR0 . . . . 63 A6
Markfield Rd CR3 . . . . 101 B2
Markham Ct GU15 . . . . 65 D6
Markham House **9** SE21 . . 22 E4
Markham Mews RG40 . . . . . 25 C6
Markham Rd RH5 . . . . 178 C5
Markhole Cl TW12 . . . . 15 F1
Marks Rd Warlingham CR6 . . 81 E1
  Wokingham RG41 . . . . 25 A8
Marksbury Ave TW9 . . . . 7 A4
Markville Gdns CR3 . . . . 101 A2
Markway The TW16 . . . . 35 C7
Markwell Cl SE26 . . . . 23 B4
Markwick La GU8 . . . . 172 C2
Marlang Ct BR3 . . . . 44 D8
Marlborough Rd TW7, TW8 . . 6 B7
Marlborough **11** SW19 . . . . 19 F2
Marlborough Cl
  Crawley RH11 . . . . 201 C2
  Hersham KT12 . . . . 54 D7
  Horsham RH12 . . . . 217 D5
  Mitcham SW19 . . . . 20 D2
Marlborough Ct
  Dorking RH4 . . . . 136 B7
  Wallington SM6 . . . . 60 C3
  Wokingham RG40 . . . . 25 D7
Marlborough Cty Inf Sch
  GU11 . . . . 105 C2
Marlborough Dr KT13 . . . . . . 53 C7
Marlborough Gdns KT6 . . . . 37 D2
Marlborough House SW19 . . 19 F1
Marlborough Jun & Inf Sch
  GU11 . . . . 6 A6
Marlborough Rd
  Ashford TW15 . . . . 13 E3
  Dorking RH4 . . . . 136 B7
  Feltham TW13 . . . . 15 D6
  Hampton TW12 . . . . 16 A2
  Mitcham SW19 . . . . 20 E2
  Richmond TW10 . . . . 6 F1
  South Croydon CR2 . . . . 61 C3
  Sutton SM1 . . . . 59 A8
  Woking GU21 . . . . 70 A3
Marlborough Rise GU15 . . . . 65 E6
Marlborough Trad Est TW9 . . 7 B5
Marlborough View GU14 . . . 84 C5
Marld The KT21 . . . . 75 F1
Marler Rd SE23 . . . . 23 F7
Marles La RH14 . . . . 214 C1
Marley Cl KT15 . . . . 51 F4
Marley Combe Rd GU27 . . . 207 F4
Marley Croft TW18 . . . . 12 E5
Marley Hanger GU27 . . . . . . 208 A3
Marley Rise RH4 . . . . 136 A4
Marlfield Ct KT3 . . . . 38 F2
Marlin Cl TW16 . . . . 14 E2
Marling Ct TW12 . . . . 15 E2
Marlings Cl CR3 . . . . 80 E2
Marlins Cl **3** SM1 . . . . 59 C5
Marlow Ct **3** SW19 . . . . 5 F1
Marlow Cres TW1 . . . . 16 F8
Marlow Ct RH10 . . . . 201 D7
Marlow Dr SM3 . . . . 58 D7

Marlow House TW11 ....17 A4
Marlow Rd SE20, SE25 .....43 B7
Marlowe Ct Dulwich SE19 ...22 F3
  6 Kingston u T KT2 ....37 D1
Marlowe House KT1 ....37 D5
Marlowe Lodge CR0 ....62 E8
Marlowe Sq CR4 ....41 C5
Marlowe Way CR0 ....60 E8
Marlpit Ave CR5 ....79 E2
Marlpit CI RH19 ....185 E4
Marlpit La CR5 ....79 E2
Marlyns CI GU4 ....110 A4
Marlyns Dr GU1, GU4 ......110 A4
Marmion House **15** SW12 ...21 B8
Marmot Rd TW4 ....4 D4
Marncrest Ct KT12 ....54 B5
Marnell Way TW4 ....4 D4
Marneys CI KT18 ....76 A4
Marnfield Cres SW2 ....21 F7
Maroons Way SE6 ....24 A3
Marquee Towers SW16 ......21 F1
Marquis Ct **1** KT1 ....37 E5
Married Quarters CR3 .....100 C5
Marriott CI TW14 ....3 D1
Marriott House SE6 ....24 C4
Marriott Lodge CI KT15 ...52 C6
Marrowbrook CI GU14 ......85 A4
Marrowbrook La GU14 ......85 A3
Marrowells KT13 ....53 F7
Marryat PI SW19 ....19 E3
Marryat Rd SW19 ....19 E3
Marsh Ave Epsom KT19 .....57 E1
  Mitcham CR4 ....41 A7
Marsh Ct Crawley RH11 ....201 B1
  3 Merton SW19 ....40 C8
Marsh Farm Rd TW2 ....16 F7
Marsh La KT15 ....52 B6
Marshall CI
  Farnborough GU14 ....84 F7
  Frimley GU16 ....66 D2
  Hounslow TW4 ....4 F2
  Sanderstead CR2 ....81 A6
Marshall House **3** KT3 ..38 E5
Marshall Par GU22 ....70 F4
Marshall PI KT15 ....52 C2
Marshall Rd Crawley RH10 .202 C4
  Farncombe GU7 ....150 E6
  Sandhurst GU47 ....64 D6
Marshall's Rd SM1 ....59 B6
Marshalls GU9 ....146 B8
Marsham CI **15** SW19 .....19 C7
Marsham Ct **15** SW19 ....19 C7
Marsfields C of E Fst Sch
  KT16 ....51 E4
Marshwood Rd GU18 ....67 D8
Marston KT19 ....76 F1
Marston Ave KT9 ....56 E4
Marston Ct KT12 ....35 C1
Marston Dr
  Farnborough GU14 ....85 B7
  Warlingham CR6 ....81 E2
Marston House RH1 ....118 F2
Marston Rd Farnham GU9 ..124 F2
  Richmond TW11 ....17 B3
  Woking GU21 ....69 B2
Marston Way
  North Ascot SL5 ....28 E7
  South Norwood SE19 ......22 C1
Martel CI GU15 ....66 C7
Martell Rd SE21 ....22 D5
Martens PI GU7 ....150 E6
Martin CI Crawley RH11 ...201 D8
  Selsdon CR2 ....62 D1
  Warlingham CR6 ....81 B3
Martin Cres CR0 ....42 A1
Martin Ct SW19 ....20 A1
Martin Dr SM4, SW19 ....40 A6
Martin House **3** KT3 ....38 E5
Martin Rd GU2 ....109 A3
Martin Way Frimley GU16 ..65 E2
  Merton SW19 , SW20, SM4 .39 E6
  Woking GU21 ....69 A1
Martin's Heron Sta RG12 ..27 F5
Martin's Rd BR2 ....44 F7
Martindale SW14 ....7 C2
Martindale Ave GU15, GU16 .66 C4
Martindale CI GU4 ....110 D3
Martindale Rd
  Balham SW12 ....21 B8
  Hounslow TW4 ....4 E4
  Woking GU21 ....69 A1
Martineau CI KT10 ....55 F6
Martineau Dr RH4 ....136 B5
Martingale CI TW16 ....35 A5
Martingale Ct GU11 ......104 E2
Martingales CI TW10 ......17 D5
Martins CI Blackwater GU17 .64 D4
  Guildford GU1 ....110 C2
  West Wickham BR4 ....63 D8
Martins Dr RG41 ....25 B7
Martins La RG12 ....27 E6
Martins The
  Crawdown RH10 ....204 C8
  Forest Hill SE26 ....23 B3
Martins Wood GU8 ....170 E7
Martinsyde GU22 ....70 C2
Martlet Cnr RH12 ....214 D7
Martletts CI RH12 ....217 C5
Martletts The RH10 ....201 E6
Marton Ct SE16 ....24 A5
Marts The RH12 ....214 D7
Martyns PI RH19 ....206 A8
Martyr Rd GU1 ....130 D8
Martyrs Ave RH11 ....181 D1
Martyrs La GU21 ....70 B7

Marvell CI RH10 ....202 C8
Marwell CI BR4 ....63 F8
Mary Adelaide CI SW15 ....18 E5
Mary Rd GU1 ....130 C8
Mary Rose CI TW12 ....36 A8
Mary Vale GU7 ....150 D2
Mary's Terr TW1 ....17 A8
Marygold House TW3 ....5 C6
Maryhill CI CR8 ....80 C2
Maryland Ct KT1 ....38 B7
Maryland Rd CR7 ....42 B8
Maryland Way TW16 ....35 A1
Marymount International Sch
  KT2 ....18 C1
Masefield CI **15** KT16 ..37 D2
Masefield Gdns RG45 ......45 B3
Masefield Rd
  Crawley RH11 ....200 E3
  Hampton TW13 ....15 F4
Masefield Way TW19 ....13 F7
Maskall Ct SW12 ....22 A7
Maskani Wlk SW16 ....21 C1
Maskell Rd SW17 ....20 C5
Maskell Way GU14 ....84 D3
Mason CI
  East Grinstead RH19 .....185 E2
  Hampton TW12 ....35 F8
  Wimbledon SW20 ....39 D8
Mason Ct **15** SE19 ......22 F1
Mason Rd Crawley RH10 ...201 E4
  Farnborough GU14 ....84 E6
Mason Way GU11 ....126 B7
Mason's Ave CR0, CR9 .....61 C7
Mason's Bridge Rd
  Redhill RH1 ....140 C3
  Salfords RH1 ....140 C3
Mason's PI CR4 ....40 F8
Masonic Hall Rd KT16 .....32 F3
Masons Paddock RH4 .....115 A1
Massetts Rd RH6 ....161 A2
Massingberd Way SW17 ....21 B4
Master CI RH8 ....122 E6
Mastin House SW18 ....20 A7
Maswell Park Cres TW3 ....5 C2
Maswell Park Rd TW3 ......5 C3
Matham Rd KT8 ....36 D4
Mathew Terr GU11 ....105 C2
Mathews CI GU14 ....105 C8
Mathews CI KT18 ....76 C6
Mathisen Way SL3 ....1 E6
Mathon Ct GU1 ....109 F1
Matilda CI SE19 ....22 D1
Matlock Cres SM3 ....58 B6
Matlock Gdns SM1, SM3 ...58 B6
Matlock PI SM1, SM3 ......58 B6
Matlock Rd CR3 ....100 E6
Matlock Way KT3 ....38 D8
Matthew Arnold CI
  Chertsey KT16 ....73 A5
  Staines TW18 ....13 C2
Matthew Arnold Sch The
  TW18 ....13 C2
Matthew Ct CR4 ....41 E8
Matthew Rd GU9 ....125 E8
Matthew's Gdns CR0 ......82 D8
Matthew's Dr RH2 ....139 A5
Matthews Ct SL5 ....29 D5
Matthews Dr RH10 ....202 C3
Matthews La TW18 ....12 H2
Matthews Rd GU15 ....66 A8
Matthewsgreen Rd RG41 ...25 A8
Matthey PI RH10 ....182 D1
Matthias Ct **15** TW10 ....6 E1
Maultway CI GU15 ....66 B8
Maultway Cres GU15 ......66 B8
Maultway N GU15 ....47 B1
Maultway The
  Camberley GU15, GU16 ....66 D6
  Frimley GU15, GU16 ......66 D6
Maunsell Pk RH10 ....202 B6
Maurice Ave CR3 ....100 D5
Maurice Ct **3** TW8 ....6 D7
Mavery Ct BR1 ....24 F1
Mavins Rd GU9 ....146 D8
Mavis Ave KT19 ....57 E5
Mavis CI KT19 ....57 E5
Mawbey Rd KT16 ....51 D4
Mawson CI SW20 ....39 E7
Mawson La W4 ....7 F8
Maxine Ct GU47 ....45 B1
Maxton Wlk RH11 ....201 B2
Maxwell CI CR0 ....41 E1
Maxwell Ct SE21 ....23 A7
Maxwell Dr KT14 ....71 C8
Maxwell Rd TW15 ....14 C2
Maxwell Way RH10 ....182 A1
May CI Chessington KT9 ....56 F4
  Godalming GU7 ....150 B2
  2 Sandhurst GU47 .....64 D8
May Cotts CR5 ....98 B2
May Cres GU12 ....105 E1
May Ct **2** SW19 ....40 C8
May Rd TW2 ....16 E7
May's Hill Rd BR2 ....44 E6
Maybelle CI RH5 ....157 D3
Mayberry PI RH15 ....37 F2
Maybourne CI SE26 ....23 B3
Maybourne Grange CR0 ....61 E8
Maybourne Rise GU22 .....89 D3
Maybury CI
  Burgh Heath KT20 ....97 E8
  Frimley GU16 ....85 D8
  Tadworth KT20 ....70 B2
Maybury Ct Inf Sch GU21 .70 A3
Maybury Hill GU21, GU22 ..70 A3
Maybury Rd GU21 ....70 A3

Maybury Rough GU22 ......70 B2
Maybury St SW17 ....20 E3
Maycroft BR2 ....44 F1
Maycross Ave SM4 ....40 A5
Mayday Hospl CR7 ....42 B3
Mayday Rd CR7 ....42 B3
Maydwell Ave RH13 ....215 C2
Mayfield Rd CR7 ....41 F4
Mayell CI KT22 ....95 C4
Mayes CI RH11 ....81 D1
Mayes La RH12 ....197 F3
Mayfair Ave
  New Malden KT4 ....39 A1
  Twickenham TW2 ....16 C8
Mayfair CI Beckenham BR3 .44 B8
  Surbiton KT6 ....37 E1
Mayfair Ct Beckenham BR3 .44 B8
  5 South Croydon CR0 ..61 F8
Mayfield Crawley RH10 ....202 D6
  Dormansland RH7 ....165 A1
  Hersham KT12 ....54 A6
  Rowledge GU10 ....145 F3
Mayfield Ave KT15 ....52 C1
Mayfield CI Ashford TW15 .14 B2
  Farnham GU9 ....126 B6
  Hersham KT12 ....54 A6
  Hinchley Wood KT7 ....37 B1
  Penge SE20 ....43 B8
  Redhill RH1 ....140 A3
  Weybridge KT15 ....52 C1
Mayfield Cres CR7 ....41 F5
Mayfield Gdns Staines TW18 .13 A2
  Walton-on-T KT12 ....54 A6
Mayfield Gr KT23 ....114 A8
Mayfield Rd
  Camberley GU15 ....65 B1
  Farnborough GU14 ....84 F7
  Hersham KT12 ....54 A6
  Merton SW19 ....39 F8
  South Croydon CR2 ....61 D2
  Sutton SM2 ....59 D2
  Weybridge KT13 ....52 F5
Mayflower CI RH10 ....202 D5
Mayford CI Balham SW12 ..20 F8
  Penge BR3 ....43 D6
  Woking GU22 ....89 D5
Mayford Rd SW12 ....21 A7
Mayhurst Ave GU22 ....70 C3
Mayhurst CI GU22 ....70 C3
Mayhurst Cres GU22 ......70 C3
Maynard Ct TW18 ....13 A4
Maynooth Gdns CR4 ......40 F2
Mayo Rd
  Thornton Heath CR0 ......42 D4
  Walton-on-T KT12 ....35 A2
Mayow Rd SE23, SE26 .....23 D4
Maypole Rd
  Ashurst Wood RH19 ......206 E6
  East Grinstead RH19 ....185 D2
Mayroyd Ave KT6 ....57 A8
Mays CI KT13 ....52 F1
Mays Cnr GU23 ....90 D3
Mays Gr GU23 ....90 D4
Mays Rd
  Teddington TW11, TW12 ...16 D3
  Wokingham RG40 ....25 E6
Maysfield Rd GU23 ....90 D4
Maytree CI GU1 ....109 C5
Maytree Ct CR4 ....41 A6
Maytree Wlk SW2 ....22 A6
Maytrees GU21 ....68 C2
Maywater CI CR2 ....80 D8
Maywood CI BR3 ....24 B1
Maywood Dr GU15 ....66 A7
Maze Rd TW9 ....7 A7
McAlmont Ridge GU7 .....150 D7
McCarthy Rd TW13 ....15 D3
McCormick House **9** SW2 .22 A7
McDonald House **1** KT2 ..17 F1
Mcdonald's Almshouses
  GU9 ....125 A1
McDonough CI KT9 ....56 E6
McDougall Ct TW9 ....7 A5
McGechie Ho RH19 ....185 D3
Mcindoe Rd RH19 ....185 D3
McIntosh CI SM6 ....60 E3
McIver CI RH19 ....184 F4
McKay CI GU11 ....105 C3
McKay Rd SW20 ....19 C2
Mckay Trad Est SL3 ....1 E5
McKinlay Ct BR3 ....43 F7
Mcleod Ct SE21 ....23 A7
McLeod House SE23 ....23 C6
McMillan Ct SE6 ....24 F7
McNaughton CI GU14 .....84 D3
McRae La CR4 ....40 F2
Meachen Ct RG40 ....25 C6
Mead Ave RH1 ....140 A1
Mead Cl Cranleigh GU6 ...174 F2
  Egham TW20 ....12 B2
  Redhill RH1 ....119 A4
Mead Cres Carshalton SM1 .59 E6
  Little Bookham KT23 .....94 A2
  Walton-on-T KT12 ....54 D8
  Woking GU21 ....68 E3
Mead Cty Inf Sch The KT19 .57 F6
Mead Dr CR5 ....79 E5
Mead End KT21 ....75 F3
Mead La Chertsey KT16 ....33 C2
  Farnham GU9 ....125 B2
Mead Path SW17 ....20 D2
Mead PI CR0 ....42 C1

Mead Rd Caterham CR3 ...100 F4
  Cranleigh GU6 ....174 E3
  Crawley RH10 ....201 F7
  Hersham KT12 ....54 E6
  Hindhead GU26 ....188 F4
  Richmond TW10 ....17 C5
Mead The Ashstead KT21 ..95 E8
  Beckenham BR3 ....44 C8
  Dorking RH4 ....136 C4
  Farnborough GU14 ....85 B3
  Wallington SM6 ....60 D4
  West Wickham BR4 ....44 D1
Mead Way Coulsdon CR5 ...79 F1
  Croydon CR0 ....62 E8
  Guildford GU1, GU4 .....110 C6
  Hayes BR2 ....44 F3
Meadcroft House 4 KT3 ..38 E2
Meade CI W4 ....7 A8
Meade CI W4 ....47 F3
  Walton on t H KT20 ....97 A3
Meadhurst Pk TW16 ....34 F6
Meades The RH7 ....165 A1
Meadfoot Rd SW16 ....41 C8
Meadhurst Pk TW16 ....14 E2
Meadhurst Rd KT16 ....33 B1
Meadhurst Sports Club
  TW16 ....14 F3
Meadlands Dr TW10 ....17 D6
Meadlands Prim Sch
  TW10 ....17 C4
Meadow App RH10 ....183 A3
Meadow Ave CR0 ....43 D3
Meadow Bank
  East Horsley KT24 ....112 E8
  Farnham GU9 ....125 B1
Meadow Bglws GU4 ....131 B3
Meadow Brook Ind Ctr
  RH10 ....182 A1
Meadow CI Ash Vale GU12 ..85 F1
  Blackwater GU17 ....64 D4
  Catford SE6 ....24 A3
  Copthorne RH10 ....183 A3
  Farncombe GU7 ....150 E7
  Horsham RH12 ....218 A5
  Hinchley Wood KT10 ......55 F7
  Milford GU8 ....149 A1
  Purley CR8 ....79 D6
  Richmond TW10 ....17 E7
  Sutton SM1 ....59 C8
  Twickenham TW4 ....16 A8
  West Barnes SW20 ....39 C5
Meadow Cotts GU24 ....67 F7
Meadow Croft CI RH6 .....182 C8
Meadow Ct Epsom KT18 ...76 C6
  Farnborough GU14 ....84 F4
  Staines TW18 ....12 B3
Meadow Dr GU23 ....90 F4
Meadow Farm La RH12 ...217 F7
Meadow Gdns TW18 ....12 D3
Meadow Hill
  Coulsdon CR5, CR8 ....79 C6
  New Malden KT3 ....38 E3
  Purley CR5, CR8 ....79 C6
Meadow House GU4 ....110 D2
Meadow La KT22 ....94 C5
Meadow PI W4 ....7 E7
Meadow Rd Ashford TW15 ..14 C3
  Ashstead KT21 ....75 E2
  Bromley BR2 ....44 E7
  Carshalton SM1 ....59 E5
  Claygate KT10 ....55 E4
  Farnborough GU14 ....85 B7
  Feltham TW13 ....15 E6
  Guildford GU4 ....110 A5
  Merton SW19 ....20 C1
  Wentworth GU25 ....30 E4
  Wokingham RG41 ....25 A5
Meadow Rise Coulsdon CR5 .79 D6
  Knaphill GU21 ....68 C2
Meadow Stile CR0, CR9 ...61 C7
Meadow The RH10 ....183 A3
Meadow Vale GU27 ....208 A6
Meadow Vale Prim Sch
  RG42 ....26 F8
Meadow View RH6 ....162 C3
Meadow View Rd CR7 .....42 B4
Meadow Way
  Addlestone KT15 ....52 B6
  Aldershot GU12 ....105 F3
  Blackwater GU17 ....64 C5
  Bracknell RG42 ....27 A8
  Burgh Heath KT20 ....77 E2
  Chessington KT9 ....56 E5
  Great Bookham KT23 ......94 B4
  Reigate RH2 ....139 B5
  Rowledge GU10 ....145 F3
  West End GU24 ....67 F6
  West Horsley KT24 ....92 D1
Meadow Waye TW5 ....4 E4
Meadow Wlk
  Hackbridge SM6 ....60 B7
  Walton on t H KT20 ....97 B3
  West Ewell KT17, KT19 ...57 F3
  Wokingham RG41 ....25 A6
Meadowbank KT5 ....37 F3
Meadowbank
  Gdns TW4, TW5 ....4 B6
Meadowbank Rd GU18 .....48 C1
Meadowbrook RH8 ....122 D5
Meadowbrook CI SL3 ....1 F6
Meadowbrook Rd RH4 ....136 A7
Meadowcroft CI
  Crawley RH11 ....200 F5
  East Grinstead RH19 ....185 C2
Meadowcroft Cty Fst Sch
  KT16 ....51 F7

Meadowfield CI KT3 ....39 C5
Meadowlands
  Cobham KT11 ....73 A6
  Crawley RH11 ....201 C6
  Oxted RH8 ....123 A4
  West Clandon GU4 ....111 B5
Meadowlea CI UB7 ....2 D8
Meadows End TW16 ....35 A8
Meadows Leigh CI KT13 ...53 C7
Meadows The Ash GU12 ..106 B2
  Churt GU10 ....167 F1
  Guildford GU2 ....130 C6
  Sandhurst GU47 ....64 E5
  Warlingham CR6 ....81 A2
Meadowside
  Great Bookham KT23 ......94 A4
  Horley RH6 ....161 B4
  Twickenham TW1 ....17 D8
  Walton-on-T KT12 ....54 E8
Meadowside Rd SM2 ....58 E2
Meadowview TW19 ....1 F2
Meadowview Rd
  Catford SE6 ....24 A3
  Reigate RH2 ....118 F4
  West Ewell KT19 ....57 E5
Meadow CI GU7 ....150 F1
Meadow Lock GU7 ....151 A6
Meads Cty Prim Sch The
  RH19 ....205 E3
Meads Rd GU1 ....110 B1
Meads The Cheam SM3 ...58 E7
  East Grinstead RH19 ....205 E7
  Haslemere GU27 ....207 F6
  Weybridge KT13 ....53 D4
Meadside 4 Epsom KT18 ..76 D6
  7 Woking GU22 ....69 F1
Meadside CI BR3 ....43 E8
Meadsview CI **3** GU14 ...85 B4
Meadvale RH1 ....216 F2
Meadvale Rd CR0 ....43 A3
Meadway Ashford TW15 ...14 C8
  Beckenham BR3 ....44 C8
  Effingham KT24 ....113 E7
  Epsom KT19 ....76 C7
  Esher KT10 ....55 B2
  Frimley GU16 ....66 F2
  Haslemere GU27 ....207 F6
  Oxshott KT22 ....74 E5
  Staines TW18 ....13 A1
  Tolworth KT5 ....38 C1
  Twickenham TW2 ....16 D7
  Warlingham CR6 ....81 C3
  West Barnes SW20 ....39 C5
Meadway CI TW18 ....13 A1
Meadway Dr
  New Haw KT15 ....52 C3
  Woking GU21 ....69 D4
Meadway The RH6 ....161 C3
Meaford Way SE20 ....23 B1
Meare CI KT20 ....97 D4
Meath Green Ave RH6 ....160 F5
Meath Green Cty Jun Sch
  RH6 ....160 F5
Meath Green La
  Horley RH1, RH6 ....160 E6
  Salfords RH1, RH6 ......160 E6
Meath Sch KT16 ....51 D3
Medawar Rd GU2 ....129 D8
Medcroft Gdns SW14 ......7 C3
Mede CI TW19 ....11 D7
Mede Ct TW18 ....12 E5
Mede Field KT22 ....94 D3
Medfield St SW15 ....19 B8
Medhurst CI GU24 ....49 E2
Medina Ave KT10 ....55 E7
Medlake Rd TW20 ....12 C2
Medland CI CR4 ....41 A1
Medlar CI Crawley RH11 ..181 C1
  Guildford GU1 ....109 C3
Medlar Dr GU17 ....64 F3
Medora Rd SW2 ....21 F8
Medway RH10 ....204 A5
Medway CI CR0 ....43 C3
Medway Dr Farnborough GU14 .84 F8
  South Norwood SE25 ......42 E4
Medway Dr
  East Grinstead RH19 ....205 D6
  Farnborough GU14 ....84 F8
Medwin Wlk RH12 ....217 C2
Medwyn Wlk RH12 ....217 C2
Melbourne CI SM6 ....60 C5
Melbourne Ct Penge SE20 .23 A1
  Twickenham TW2 ....16 D7
Melbourne Mews SE6 ....24 C8
Melbourne Rd
  Merton SW19 ....40 A8
  Teddington TW11 ....17 C2
  Wallington SM6 ....60 C5
Melbury CI Byfleet KT14 ...71 A1
  Chertsey KT16 ....32 A2
  Claygate KT10 ....56 B4
  West Byfleet KT14 ....71 A5
Melbury Gdns SW20 ....39 B8
Melbury House TW2 ....16 D6
Meldone CI KT5 ....38 B3
Meldone CI KT5 ....38 B3
Meldrum CI RH8 ....123 A3
Melfield Gdns SE6 ....24 C3
Melfont Ave CR7 ....42 A5
Melford CI KT9 ....56 F5
Melford Ct Dulwich SE22 ..23 A8
  Sutton SM2 ....59 C3
Melford Rd SE21, SE22 ....23 A7
Melfort Rd CR7, SW16 ....42 B6
Melinda CI BR6 ....84 D6
Melksham Rd RH13 ....217 E1
Meller CI SM6 ....60 A4
Mellersh Hill Rd GU5 ....152 C6

...sh Ct KT6 .... 37 E3
.son Rd SW17 .... 20 E3
.or Cl KT12 .... 35 F2
.or Ct 2 SW19 .... 20 C1
.or House 2 SE21 .... 22 E4
.wer St 78 C5
.ows Rd SM6 .... 60 D5
.ody Rd TN16 .... 83 C1
.ose Ave
  ..borough GU14 .... 84 C5
  ..ham CR4 .... 21 B1
  ..nton Heath SW16 .... 42 A6
  ..kenham TW2 .... 16 B8
  ..abledon SW19 .... 20 A5
.ose Gdns
  ..sham KT12 .... 54 C5
  ..ston u t KT3 .... 38 D6
.ose Rd Barnes SW13 .... 7 F5
  ..gh Hill TN16 .... 83 C3
  ..lsdon CR5 .... 79 B8
  ..leworth SW19 .... 40 A8
  ..bridge KT13 .... 53 A5
.ose Sch CR4 .... 40 E6
.ose Tudor SM6 .... 60 E5
.sa Rd SM4 .... 40 C3
.on Ct 8 Croydon CR0 .... 61 C6
  ..Twickenham TW1 .... 17 B8
.on Fields KT19 .... 57 D2
.on Pl KT19 .... 57 D2
.on Rd RH1 .... 119 C5
.ville Ave Frimley GU16 .... 65 F1
  ..th Croydon CR0, CR2 .... 61 F5
  ..bledon SW20 .... 19 A1
.in Ct 11 TW9 .... 7 A6
.in Rd SE20 .... 43 C8
  ..inshaw KT22 .... 95 C6
  ..nbury Cl GU16 .... 86 A7
  ..bury Wlk RG12 .... 27 F5
.norial Cl TW5 .... 4 F8
  ..ory Cotts 97 E8
  ..dip Cl Forest Hill SE26 .... 23 C4
  ..dip House 13 F1
  ..dip 8 Cheam KT4 .... 58 C8
  ..dip Wlk RH1 .... 201 B6
  ..borough GU14 .... 84 E7
.dip Way GU1 .... 125 D1
  ..o Gdns SE19 .... 22 D1
.worth KT20 .... 97 B5
  ..an Ct TW7 .... 5 E5
  ..apham Rd CR4, SW6 .... 41 C8
.antum Way
  ..ston SW19 .... 40 C8
  ..eam SW19 .... 40 C8
.cer Cl Crawley RH12 .... 202 C3
  ..ames Ditton KT7 .... 36 F2
  ..cer Rd RH12 .... 217 C8
  ..chiston Rd SE6 .... 24 D6
.cia Wlk 8 GU21 .... 69 F2
  ..cury Cl RH11 .... 200 E3
  ..cury Ctr TW14 .... 4 B2
  ..ce Cl SW15 .... 19 D8
  ..e End CR0 .... 43 D2
  ..e Rd Oatlands Park KT13 .... 53 D7
  ..epperton TW17 .... 34 B3
  ..worth KT20 .... 78 C4
  ..lton on t KT20 .... 97 B4
.ebank RH5 .... 157 D4
  ..ebank La CR0, SM6 .... 60 F5
  ..efield Gdns KT20 .... 97 D8
  ..etune Ct SM4 .... 39 F6
  ..evale Cres SM4 .... 40 C3
  ..eway Industry TW2 .... 16 E7
  ..eway Rd TW2 .... 16 E7
  ..eworth Ct BR2 .... 44 F4
  ..eworth Dr RH10 .... 202 D8
  ..ridian Ct Catford SE6 .... 24 F7
  ..oft Gdns KT20 .... 97 C6
  ..ningscale SL5 .... 29 B1
  ..ridian Gr RH6 .... 161 C4
  ..ridian Way RH11 .... 185 F3
  ..rland Cl KT12 .... 97 C7
  ..rland Gn KT20 .... 97 C7
  ..rland Rise KT18, KT20 .... 97 C8
.rland Rise Cty Prim Sch
  ..KT20 .... 97 C8
.he Common Rd RH8 .... 144 B7
  ..lewood RG12 .... 27 D4
  ..lewood Cl SL3 .... 100 D7
  ..lewood Ct CR4 .... 40 E6
  ..th Croydon CR0 .... 61 C6
.lin Cl Crawley RH11 .... 200 E6
  ..lin Cl 8 SW19 .... 19 D8
  ..rrick House RH2 .... 118 C1
.ricks St SW14 .... 7 B3
  ..rrilands Rd KT4 .... 39 C1
  ..rrilyn Cl KT10 .... 56 A4
.rict Wood Coll
  ..(agricultural) GU3 .... 108 C7
  ..ritt Gdns KT9 .... 56 C4
.rrivale Gdns GU21 .... 69 C2
.rrow Bsns Ctr GU4 .... 110 D4
  ..rrow CE Fst Sch GU4 .... 110 C4
  ..rrow Chase GU1 .... 110 D1
.rrow Common Rd GU4 .... 110 D4

Merrow Copse GU1 .... 110 B2
Merrow Croft GU1 .... 110 C2
Merrow Ct Guildford GU1 .... 110 D1
  ..Mitcham CR4 .... 40 D7
Merrow La GU4 .... 110 C5
Merrow Rd SM2 .... 58 D2
Merrow St GU1, GU4 .... 110 D2
Merrow Way CR0 .... 63 C4
Merrow Woods GU1 .... 110 B3
Merryacres GU8 .... 170 E6
Merryfield Dr RH12 .... 217 A3
Merryhill Rd RG42 .... 27 B8
Merryhills Cl TN16 .... 83 D3
Merryhills La RH14 .... 213 A5
Merrylands KT16 .... 51 E7
Merrylands Ct KT23 .... 93 F4
Merrylands Farm KT23 .... 93 F3
Merrylands Rd KT23 .... 93 F3
Merryman Dr RG45 .... 45 A7
Merrymeet KT20 .... 77 E5
Merryweather Ct 11 KT3 .... 38 E4
Merrywald KT22 .... 95 C6
Merrywood Gr KT20 .... 117 E5
Merrywood Pk Frimley GU15 .... 65 F4
  ..Reigate RH2 .... 118 B3
Merryworth Cl GU12 .... 105 F1
Mersham Pl Penge SE20 .... 43 B8
  ..South Norwood CR7 .... 42 D7
Mersham Rd CR7 .... 42 D7
Merstham Cty Prim Sch
  ..RH1 .... 119 C6
Merstham Rd RH1 .... 120 A5
Merstham Sta RH1 .... 119 C7
Merton Abbey Prim Sch
  ..SW19 .... 40 B8
Merton Cl GU47 .... 45 F2
Merton Gdns KT20 .... 97 D8
Merton Hall Gdns SW20 .... 39 E8
Merton Hall Rd
  ..SW19, SW20 .... 39 E8
Merton High St SW19 .... 20 C1
Merton Ind Pk CR4 .... 40 D4
Merton Ind Pk New CR4 .... 40 C8
Merton Mansions SW20 .... 39 D7
Merton Park Fst
  ..Sch SW19 .... 40 A7
Merton Park Sta SW19 .... 40 A7
Merton Park Sta SW19 .... 40 A8
Merton Pl 8 SW19 .... 20 C1
Merton Rd Croydon SE25 .... 43 A4
  ..Merton SW19 .... 20 B1
  ..Wandsworth SW18 .... 20 A7
Merton Road Ind Est
  ..SW18 .... 20 A8
Merton Tech Coll SM4 .... 39 F4
Merton Tech Coll (Annexe)
  ..SW19 .... 20 A8
Merton Way
  ..East Molesey KT8 .... 36 C6
  ..Leatherhead KT22 .... 95 A8
Mervyn Rd TW17 .... 34 C2
Metana Ho RH10 .... 182 A3
Metcalf Rd TW15 .... 14 B3
Metcalf Way RH11 .... 181 D2
Metcalfe Wlk TW13 .... 15 E4
Meteor Way SM6 .... 60 E3
Meteorological Off (HQ)
  ..RG12 .... 27 D7
Metro Bsns Ctr The SE26 .... 23 F3
Metro Ctr SM4 .... 39 D2
Metro Ind Ctr TW7 .... 5 E5
Meudon Ave GU14 .... 85 A4
Meudon Ct KT6 .... 37 D4
Meville Ct GU2 .... 130 C6
Mews Ct RH19 .... 205 F6
Mews The Banstead SM7 .... 78 B4
  ..Broadbridge Heath RH12 .... 216 D4
  ..Dunsfold GU8 .... 192 F6
  ..11 Farnham GU9 .... 125 B2
  ..Guildford GU1 .... 130 C8
Mewsend TN16 .... 83 D1
Meyer House 1 SW12 .... 21 B8
Meyrick Cl GU21 .... 68 E3
Mezel Hill Cotts SL4 .... 10 C3
Miall Wlk SE26 .... 23 E4
Michael Cres RH6 .... 161 A1
Michael Fields RH18 .... 206 E2
Michaelmas Cl SW20 .... 39 C6
Michaelson House 4
  ..SE21 .... 22 E4
Michel's Row 2 TW9 .... 6 E3
Micheldever Way RG12 .... 27 F4
Michelet Cl GU18 .... 48 B1
Michelham Gdns
  ..Burgh Heath KT20 .... 97 C7
  ..Twickenham TW1 .... 16 F5
Michell Cl RH12 .... 217 A2
Michels Almshouses 1
  ..TW10 .... 6 E2
Michelsdale Dr 3 TW9 .... 6 E3
Mickle Hill GU47 .... 45 A1
Micklefield Prep Sch
  ..RH2 .... 118 A2
Mickleham Dr KT22, RH5 .... 95 C1
Mickleham Gdns SM3 .... 58 E4
Mickleham Hall RH5 .... 115 C7
Mickleham Way CR0 .... 63 D3
Mid Holmwood La RH5 .... 136 B1
Mid St RH1 .... 119 F1
  ..South Nutfield RH1 .... 140 F7
Middle Ave GU9 .... 146 D8
Middle Bourne La GU10 .... 146 B6
Middle Church La 12 GU9 .... 125 B2
Middle Cl Coulsdon CR5 .... 100 A7
  ..Ewell KT17 .... 76 E7
  ..Frimley GU15 .... 66 C6

Middle Farm Cl KT24 .... 113 D8
Middle Farm Pl KT24 .... 113 D8
Middle Gn TW18 .... 13 D1
Middle Gordon Cl GU15 .... 65 D5
Middle Green Cl 8 KT5 .... 37 F3
Middle Hill
  ..Aldershot GU11 .... 105 A3
  ..Englefield Green TW20 .... 11 D3
  ..Frensham GU10 .... 146 C1
Middle Farm Cl KT17 .... 76 F2
  ..Teddington TW11 .... 16 F2
Middle Mill KT1 .... 37 F6
Middle Old Pk GU9 .... 124 F4
Middle Rd
  ..Leatherhead KT22 .... 95 B6
  ..Merton SW16 .... 41 D7
Middle Row 11 RH19 .... 205 F8
Middle St Brockham RH3 .... 137 C5
  ..Croydon CR0, CR9 .... 61 C7
  ..Horsham RH12 .... 217 C2
  ..Shere GU5 .... 133 A4
Middle Way SW16 .... 41 D7
Middlefield
  ..Farnham GU9 .... 146 A7
  ..Horley RH6 .... 161 C4
Middlefields CR0 .... 62 E2
Middlemarch GU8 .... 170 E5
Middlemead Cl KT23 .... 94 A2
Middlemead Rd KT23 .... 93 F2
Middlemoor Rd GU16 .... 85 E8
Middlesex Cl TN13 .... 23 C1
Middlesex House 8 SE20 .... 23 C1
Middlesex Rd CR4 .... 41 E4
Middleton Gdns GU14 .... 84 E6
Middleton Rd
  ..Camberley GU15 .... 65 F7
  ..Carshalton CR4, SM5 .... 40 D2
  ..Downside KT11 .... 93 C8
  ..Epsom KT19 .... 57 D1
  ..Horsham RH12 .... 217 A2
  ..Morden SM4 .... 40 D2
Middleton Way RH11 .... 200 E5
Midgarth Cl KT22 .... 74 D6
Midgley Rd RH10 .... 201 F8
Midholm Rd CR0 .... 62 E8
Midhope Cl GU22 .... 89 E8
Midhope Gdns GU22 .... 89 E8
Midhope Rd GU22 .... 89 E8
Midhurst SE26 .... 23 C2
Midhurst Ave CR0 .... 42 A2
Midhurst Cl RH11 .... 201 A7
Midhurst Rd GU27 .... 208 B5
Midleton Cl GU8 .... 149 F2
Midleton Industrial
  ..Estate Rd GU2 .... 109 B2
Midleton Rd
  ..Guildford GU2 .... 109 B2
  ..Kingston u t KT3 .... 38 C7
Midmoor Rd
  ..Streatham SW12 .... 21 C7
  ..Wimbledon SW19 .... 39 E8
Midsummer Ave TW4 .... 4 F3
Midsummer Wlk GU21 .... 69 D3
Midway Cheam SM3, SM4 .... 39 F2
  ..Walton-on-T KT12 .... 54 B8
Midway Ave Chertsey KT16 .... 33 A6
  ..Chertsey KT16 .... 33 A6
  ..Thorpe TW20 .... 32 B6
Midway Cl TW19 .... 13 B5
Miena Way KT21 .... 75 D2
Mike Hawthorn Dr GU9 .... 125 C3
Milbanke Ct RG12 .... 26 F7
Milbanke Way RG12 .... 26 F7
Milborne Rd RH10 .... 202 C2
Milborough Cres SE12 .... 24 E8
Milbourne La KT10 .... 55 C6
Milbourne Lodge Jun Sch
  ..KT10 .... 55 C5
Milbourne Lodge Sch
  ..KT10 .... 55 C4
Milbrook SW19 .... 55 C4
Milburn House 10 SW20 .... 39 B7
Milburn Wlk KT18 .... 76 D4
Milden Cl GU16 .... 86 A6
Milden Gdns GU16 .... 85 F6
Mile Path GU22 .... 89 B7
Mile Rd
  ..Carshalton CR4, SM6 .... 41 A1
  ..Wallington CR0, CR4,
  ..CR9, SM6 .... 41 C1
Miles Cl CR9 .... 61 B8
Miles La Cobham KT11 .... 73 E6
  ..South Godstone RH9 .... 142 F7
  ..Tandridge RH8, RH9 .... 143 A7
Miles Pl GU18 .... 66 F7
Miles Rd Ash GU12 .... 106 B3
  ..Epsom KT19 .... 76 D7
  ..Mitcham CR4 .... 40 E6
Miles's Hill
  ..Holmbury St M RH5 .... 155 C3
  ..Peaslake RH5 .... 155 C3
Milestone Cl Ripley GU23 .... 91 B5
  ..Sutton SM2 .... 59 D3
Milestone Rd SE19 .... 22 F2
Milford By Pass Rd GU8 .... 149 D2
Milford Gdns CR0 .... 43 D1
Milford Gr SM1 .... 59 C6
Milford Heath Rd GU8 .... 170 E6
Milford Hosp GU7 .... 171 C8
Milford Lodge GU8 .... 170 F8
Milford Mews SW16 .... 21 F5
Milford Rd GU8 .... 148 E4
Milford Sta GU8 .... 171 A7
Milking La
  ..Biggin Hill, Downe BR6 .... 83 E7
  ..Biggin Hill, Leaves Green BR2 .... 83 D8
Mill Bay La RH12 .... 217 B1

Mill Cl Bagshot GU19 .... 47 D3
  ..Carshalton SM5 .... 60 A8
  ..East Grinstead RH19 .... 205 F7
  ..Great Bookham KT23 .... 94 A3
  ..Haslemere GU27 .... 207 E6
  ..Horley RH6 .... 160 E4
  ..Wokingham RG41 .... 25 A7
Mill Copse Rd GU27 .... 208 B4
Mill Cotts
  ..East Grinstead RH19 .... 205 E7
  ..Rudgwick RH12 .... 214 D5
Mill Farm Ave TW16 .... 14 E1
Mill Farm Cres TW4 .... 15 E7
Mill Farm Rd RH13 .... 218 A4
Mill Field GU19 .... 47 D3
Mill Gdns SE26 .... 23 B5
Mill Gn CR4 .... 41 A2
Mill Green Bsns Pk CR4 .... 41 A2
Mill Green Rd CR4 .... 41 A2
Mill Hill RH3 .... 137 B8
Mill Hill La RH3 .... 116 B1
Mill House La KT16 .... 32 B5
Mill La Ascot SL5 .... 30 A7
  ..Bracknell RG42 .... 26 F5
  ..Bramley GU5 .... 151 F6
  ..Byfleet KT14 .... 71 F6
  ..Carshalton SM5 .... 60 A7
  ..Chiddingfold GU8 .... 191 B3
  ..Chilworth GU4, GU5 .... 131 F4
  ..Copthorne RH10 .... 183 C3
  ..Crawley RH11 .... 201 A8
  ..Croydon CR0 .... 61 A7
  ..Dorking RH4 .... 136 B8
  ..Dunsfold GU8 .... 192 F4
  ..Ewell KT17 .... 57 F2
  ..Felbridge RH19 .... 184 F4
  ..Felcourt RH7 .... 164 F2
  ..Fetcham KT22 .... 95 A5
  ..Forest Green RH5 .... 176 D7
  ..Frensham GU10 .... 167 B7
  ..Godalming GU7 .... 150 D4
  ..Guildford GU1 .... 130 D7
  ..Hookwood RH6 .... 160 D3
  ..Horton SL3 .... 1 C4
  ..Kingsley Green GU27 .... 208 C3
  ..Merstham RH1 .... 119 C6
  ..Ockham GU23 .... 91 D8
  ..Oxted RH8 .... 122 F2
  ..Parkgate RH5 .... 158 D5
  ..Pirbright GU24 .... 87 C3
  ..Shalford GU3 .... 130 C1
  ..The Chart RH8 .... 123 F4
  ..Thorpe KT16, TW20 .... 32 C5
  ..Witley GU8 .... 170 F5
Mill Lane Trad Est CR0 .... 60 F7
Mill Mead TW18 .... 12 F4
Mill Pl KT1 .... 37 F6
Mill Plat Isleworth TW7 .... 6 A5
  ..Isleworth TW7 .... 6 B4
Mill Plat Ave TW7 .... 6 A5
Mill Pond Rd GU20 .... 48 B6
Mill Rd Cobham KT11 .... 73 C4
  ..Crawley RH10 .... 202 B7
  ..Epsom KT17 .... 76 F7
  ..Ewell KT17 .... 76 F7
  ..Kingswood KT20 .... 97 D4
  ..Merton SW19 .... 20 C1
  ..South Norwood RH5 .... 157 D7
  ..Thames Ditton KT7 .... 53 A8
  ..Twickenham TW2 .... 16 C6
Mill Ride SL5 .... 28 D8
Mill Shaw RH8 .... 122 F3
Mill St Outwood SL3 .... 1 C7
  ..Kingston u t KT1 .... 37 E6
  ..Redhill RH1 .... 139 F8
Mill Stream GU9 .... 125 E6
Mill Vale BR2 .... 44 F7
Mill View Cl KT17 .... 57 F3
Mill View Gdns CR0 .... 62 D7
Mill Way
  ..East Grinstead RH19 .... 205 E7
  ..Feltham TW14 .... 4 B2
  ..Headley KT22 .... 96 A3
Millais RH13 .... 218 A3
Millais Cl RH11 .... 200 F2
Millais Ct RH13 .... 218 A4
Millais Rd KT3 .... 38 E2
Millais Sch RH13 .... 217 F2
Millais Way KT19 .... 57 C6
Millan Cl KT15 .... 52 B1
Milland House 11 SW15 .... 19 A7
Milland La GU8, GU30 .... 207 B2
Millbank The RH10 .... 201 E2
Millbourne Rd TW13 .... 15 E4
Millbrook Guildford GU1 .... 130 D7
  ..Oatlands Park KT13 .... 53 E6
Millcombe Cl 8 GU21 .... 69 B1
Millcroft House SE6 .... 24 B4
Miller House 9 SW2 .... 21 E8
Miller Rd Croydon CR0 .... 41 F1
  ..Wimbledon SW19 .... 20 D2
Millers Cl TW18 .... 13 B3
Miller's Ct TW20 .... 12 D2
Miller's La RH1 .... 162 C7
Millers Copse
  ..Langley Vale KT18 .... 96 D8
  ..Outwood RH1 .... 162 B7
Millers Gate RH12 .... 217 D6
Millers Mead Ct SW19 .... 20 D1
Millfarm Bsns Pk TW4 .... 15 E8
Millfield Charlton TW16 .... 34 D8
  ..Kingston u t KT1 .... 37 F6
Millfield La KT20 .... 98 A2
Millfield Rd TW4 .... 15 F7

Millford 69 B2
Millford Cty Inf Sch GU8 .... 149 F1
Millgate Ct GU9 .... 125 D3
Millhedge Cl KT11 .... 73 E3
Millholme Wlk GU15 .... 66 C4
Millhouse Pl SE27 .... 22 B4
Millins Cl GU47 .... 45 E1
Millmead Byfleet KT14 .... 71 F7
  ..Guildford GU2 .... 130 C7
  ..Wokingham RG41 .... 25 A7
Millmead Terr GU2 .... 130 C7
Millpond Cotts GU8 .... 172 E4
Millpond Ct KT15 .... 52 E5
Mills Ho SW8 .... 105 D3
Mills Spur SL4 .... 11 B8
Mills Rd KT12 .... 54 C5
Millside SM5 .... 59 F8
Millside Ct KT23 .... 94 A2
Millside Pl TW7 .... 6 B5
Millstream The GU27 .... 207 E5
Millthorpe Rd RH12 .... 217 F4
Millview Cl RH1 .... 118 D3
Millway RH2 .... 118 D1
Millwood RH10 .... 204 E5
Millwood Rd TW3, TW7 .... 5 C2
Milman Cl RG12 .... 28 A7
Milne Cl RH11 .... 200 E3
Milne Pk E CR0 .... 82 D8
Milne Pk W CR0 .... 82 D8
Milner App CR3 .... 101 A6
Milner Cl CR3 .... 101 A5
Milner Dr Cobham KT11 .... 73 F7
  ..Twickenham TW2 .... 16 D8
Milner Rd Caterham CR3 .... 101 A6
  ..Kingston u t KT1 .... 37 D6
  ..Merton SW19 .... 40 B8
  ..Morden CR4, SM4 .... 40 D4
  ..South Norwood CR7 .... 42 D5
Milnthorpe Rd W4 .... 7 D8
Milnwood Rd RH12 .... 217 C3
Milstead Cl KT20 .... 97 B5
Milton Ave Carshalton SM1 .... 59 C6
  ..Croydon CR0 .... 42 D2
  ..Westcott RH4 .... 135 D6
Milton Cl Bracknell RG12 .... 27 B3
  ..Carshalton SM1 .... 59 D7
  ..Horton SL3 .... 1 A4
Milton Cres RH19 .... 205 C8
Milton Ct Kingston u t KT12 .... 16 E5
  ..Twickenham TW2 .... 16 E5
  ..Wokingham RG40 .... 25 B7
Milton Dr Littleton TW17 .... 33 E5
  ..Wokingham RG40 .... 25 B6
Milton Gdns Epsom KT18 .... 76 E5
  ..Stanwell TW19 .... 13 F7
  ..Wokingham RG40 .... 25 B6
Milton Grange GU12 .... 106 A5
Milton House
  ..12 Beckenham BR3 .... 24 A1
  ..8 Kingston u t KT2 .... 18 B2
  ..Sutton SM1 .... 59 A7
Milton Lodge TW1 .... 16 F8
Milton Mount RH10 .... 182 D1
Milton Mount La RH10 .... 202 D8
Milton Mount Cty Fst &
  ..Mid Sch RH10 .... 202 C8
Milton Rd Addlestone KT15 .... 52 A4
  ..Caterham CR3 .... 100 D6
  ..Crawley RH10 .... 202 C2
  ..Croydon CR0 .... 42 D2
  ..Egham TW20 .... 11 F3
  ..Hampton TW12 .... 36 B8
  ..Horsham RH12 .... 217 C3
  ..Mitcham CR4 .... 21 A1
  ..Sutton SM1 .... 59 A6
  ..Wallington SM6 .... 60 C4
  ..Walton-on-T KT12 .... 54 D7
  ..Wimbledon SW19 .... 20 C2
  ..Wokingham RG40, RG41 .... 25 B6
Milton St RH4 .... 135 D6
Milton Way RH13 .... 94 C2
Miltoncourt La RH4 .... 135 E4
Miltons Cres GU7 .... 150 B2
Milverton House SE23 .... 23 E5
Milward Gdns RG12 .... 26 C7
Mina Rd SW19 .... 40 A8
Minard Rd SE6 .... 24 E7
Minchin Cl KT22 .... 95 A5
Mincing La GU24 .... 49 F2
Minden Rd Cheam SM3 .... 58 F8
  ..Penge SE20 .... 43 B8
Mindelheim Ave RH19 .... 186 B2
Minehead Rd SW16 .... 21 F3
Minehurst Rd GU16 .... 85 F4
Minerva Cl TW19 .... 2 E1
Minerva Rd KT1 .... 37 F7
Minimax Cl TW14 .... 4 A1
Mink Ct TW4 .... 4 C5
Minley Cl GU14 .... 84 E4
Minley Rd Blackwater GU17 .... 64 B4
  ..Farnborough GU14 .... 84 D5
Minniedale KT5 .... 37 F4
Minorca Ave GU16 .... 66 E1
Minorca Rd Frimley GU16 .... 66 E1
  ..Weybridge KT13 .... 53 A6
Minshull Pl 8 BR3 .... 24 A1
Minstead Cl RG12 .... 27 F6
Minstead Gdns SW15 .... 18 F8
Minstead Way KT3 .... 38 E3
Minster Ave SM1 .... 59 A8
Minster Ct Camberley GU15 .... 65 F5
  ..Camberley, York Town GU15 .... 64 F4
Minster Dr CR0 .... 61 E6
Minster Gdns KT8 .... 35 F5

Minster Rd GU7 ....150 E1
Minsterley Ave
 TW16, TW17 ....34 E5
Minstrel Gdns KT5 ....37 F5
Mint Gdns RH4 ....136 A8
Mint La KT20 ....118 A6
Mint Rd
 Wallington SM5, SM6 ....60 B6
 Woodmansterne SM7 .....78 C3
Mint St GU7 ....150 D4
Mint The GU7 ....150 D4
Mint Wlk Croydon CR0, CR9 ..61 C7
 Knaphill GU21 ....68 E2
 Warlingham CR6 ....81 D2
Miranda Wlk RH11 ......200 E4
Mirfield Ct SE20 ....43 A7
Misbrooks Green Rd
 RH5 ....178 E8
Missenden Cl TW14 ......14 F7
Missenden Gdns SM4 ....40 C3
Mission Sq **18** TW8 .....6 E8
Mistletoe Cl CR0 ....43 D1
Mistley Ct **4** KT18 .....76 D6
Misty's Field KT12 ......35 C1
Mitcham Garden Village
 CR4 ....41 A4
Mitcham Ind Est CR4 ....41 A8
Mitcham Junc CR4 ......41 A4
Mitcham La SW16 ....21 C3
Mitcham Pk CR4 ....40 F5
Mitcham Rd
 Camberley GU15 ....47 A1
 Thornton Heath CR0, CR9 ..41 F3
 Upper Tooting SW17 ....20 F2
Mitcham Sta CR4 ....40 E5
Mitchell Gdns RH13 ....215 E3
Mitchell's Row GU4 ....130 C1
Mitchells Cl GU4 ......130 E3
Mitchells Cotts GU4 ...131 E1
Mitchells Rd RH10 .....201 F6
Mitchley Ave CR2, CR8 ..80 D6
Mitchley Gr CR2 ....81 A6
Mitchley Hill CR2 ......80 F6
Mitchley View CR2 ......81 A6
Mitford Cl KT9 ....56 C4
Mitford Wlk **11** RH11 ...201 A3
Mitre Cl Shepperton TW17 ..34 D3
 Sutton SM2 ....59 D3
Mixbury Gr KT13 ....53 D4
Mixnams La KT16 ....33 A6
Mizen Cl KT11 ....73 D5
Mizen Way KT11 ....73 D4
Moat Ct Ashstead KT21 ..75 E2
 Ottershaw KT16 ....51 C4
Moat Rd RH19 ....185 E2
Moat Side TW13 ....15 C4
Moat The KT3 ....38 E8
Moat Wlk RH10 ....202 C7
Moatside La RH1 ......140 F3
Moberly Rd SW4 ....21 D8
Model Cotts SW14 ....7 C4
Moffat Ct
 Upper Tooting SW17 ....20 E4
 Wimbledon SW19 ....20 A2
Moffat Rd
 South Norwood CR7 ....42 D7
 Upper Tooting SW17 ...20 D7
Moffats Cl GU47 ....64 A8
Mogador Cotts KT20 ...117 D7
Mogador Rd KT20 ......117 E7
Mogden La TW7 ....5 F2
Moir Cl CR2 ....62 A2
Moira Ct SW17 ....21 A6
Mole Abbey Gdns KT8 ..36 B6
Mole Bsns Pk KT22 .....95 A6
Mole Cl Crawley RH11 ...201 B8
 Farnborough GU14 ......84 D6
Mole Ct KT19 ....57 C6
Mole House KT12 ....54 E5
Mole Rd Fetcham KT22 ..94 D6
 Hersham KT12 ....54 D5
Mole St RH5 ....177 B5
Mole Valley Pl KT21 ....95 D8
Molember Ct KT7 ....36 E5
Molember Rd KT8 ....36 E4
Moles Cl RG40 ....25 D5
Moles Hill KT22 ....74 D8
Molesey Ave KT12, KT8 ..36 A4
Molesey Cl KT12 ....54 E6
Molesey Dr SM2 ....58 E7
Molesey Hospl KT8 .....36 A4
Molesey Park Ave KT8 ..36 B4
Molesey Park Rd KT8 ...36 C4
Molesey Rd
 East Molesey KT12 .....35 E2
 Hersham KT12 ....54 D5
Molesham Cl KT8 ....36 B6
Molesham Way KT8 .....36 B6
Molesley Rd Hersham KT12 ..54 E8
 Walton-on-T KT12 ......54 E8
Molesworth Rd KT11 ...73 A6
Moliner Ct **4** BR3 .....24 A1
Molins Ct **5** RH11 .....201 A3
Mollie Davis Ct SE19 ...22 F2
Mollison Dr SM6 ....60 E3
Molly Huggins Cl SW12 ..21 C8
Molly Millar Bridge RG41 ..25 B4
Molly Millar's La RG41 ..25 A4
Molyneux Dr SW17 .....21 B4
Molyneux Rd
 Farncombe GU7 ....150 F7
 Weybridge KT13 ....53 A5
 Windlesham GU20 ......48 D4
Monahan Ave CR8 ....79 F8

Monarch Cl Coney Hall BR4 ..63 F6
 Crawley RH11 ....201 A3
 East Bedfont TW14 .....14 E8
Monarch Mews
 SE27, SW16 ....22 A3
Monarch Par CR4 ....40 F7
Monaveen Gdns KT8 ....36 B6
Monby Lodge Inf Sch
 KT13 ....53 C5
Mondial Way UB7 ....3 C7
Money Ave CR3 ....100 E5
Money Rd CR3 ....100 D5
Monivea Rd BR3 ....23 F1
Monk's Wlk
 Farnham GU10, GU9 ....146 F8
 Reigate RH2 ....118 B1
Monkleigh Rd SM4, SW20 ..39 E5
Monks Ave KT8 ....35 F4
Monks Cl Ascot SL5 ....29 B3
 Farnborough GU14 ......85 C4
Monks Cres
 Addlestone KT15 ....52 B5
 Walton-on-T KT12 ......35 B8
Monks Ct RH2 ....118 B1
Monks Dr SL5 ....29 B3
Monks Gn KT22 ....94 D6
Monks La
 Limpsfield RH8, TN8 ...144 E6
 Rowhook RH5 ....196 F5
Monks Orchard Rd
 Beckenham BR3, CR0 ....44 A1
 Croydon BR3, CR0 ......44 A1
Monks Orchard Sch CR0 ..43 D4
Monks Rd Banstead SM7 ..78 A3
 Virginia Water GU25 ...31 D5
Monks Way Beckenham BR3 ..44 A3
 Harmondsworth UB7 .....2 E8
 Staines TW18 ....13 D1
Monks' Well GU10 .....147 C8
Monks Wlk SL5 ....29 B3
Monksdene Gdns SM1 ..59 B7
Monksfield RH10 ......201 F7
Monkshanger GU9 .....125 E2
Monkshood Cl RG40 ....25 E7
Monkswell La CR5 ......98 B2
Monkton La GU9 ....125 E5
Monkton Pk GU9 ....125 F4
Monmouth Ave KT1 ....17 C1
Monmouth Cl CR4, SW16 ..41 E5
Mono La TW13 ....15 B6
Monro Dr GU2 ....109 B4
Monroe Dr SW14 ....7 B2
Mons Cl GU11 ....105 E7
Mons Wlk TW20 ....12 C3
Monsell Gdns TW18 ....12 E3
Monson Rd RH1 ....118 F4
Montacute Cl GU14 ....85 D4
Montacute Rd
 Forest Hill SE23, SE6 ..23 F8
 Morden SM4 ....40 D3
 New Addington CR0 .....63 C2
Montagu Gdns SM6 ....60 D6
Montague Ave CR2 .....80 E7
Montague Cl
 Camberley GU15 ....65 B5
 Lightwater GU18 ....48 A1
 Walton-on-T KT12 .....35 A2
Montague Dr CR3 ......100 C5
Montague Rd
 Hounslow TW3 ....5 B4
 Merton SW19 ....20 B1
 Richmond TW10 ....6 E1
 Thornton Heath CR0 ....42 B1
Montana Cl CR2 ....61 D1
Montana Gdns
 Beckenham SE6 ....23 F3
 Sutton SM1 ....59 C5
Montana Rd
 Upper Tooting SW17 ...21 A5
 Wimbledon SW20 ....39 C8
Montem Rd Forest Hill SE23 ..23 F8
 New Malden KT3 ....38 E5
Montford Rd TW16 .....35 A5
Montfort Pl SW19 ......19 D7
Montfort Rise RH1 ....139 F1
Montgomerie Dr GU2 ..109 A6
Montgomery Ave KT10 ..55 E8
Montgomery Cl
 Mitcham CR4 ....41 E5
 Sandhurst GU47 ....64 B8
Montgomery Ct Chiswick W4 ..7 C8
 Leatherhead KT22 ......95 C7
Montgomery House **5**
 SW14 ....7 D4
Montgomery Rd
 Farnborough GU14 .....84 F3
 Woking GU22 ....69 E1
Montpelier Ct BR2 ....44 F5
Montpelier Rd
 Purley CR2, CR8 ....61 B1
 South Croydon CR2, CR8 ..61 B1
 Sutton SM1 ....59 C6
Montpelier Row TW1 ...17 C8
Montrave Rd SE20 .....23 C1
Montreil Rd SW2 ....21 E6
Montreux Ct RH11 .....201 B6
Montrose Ave TW2 .....16 B8
Montrose Cl Ashford TW15 ..14 C3
 Frimley GU16 ....85 F7
Montrose Gdns
 Mitcham CR4 ....40 F7
 Oxshott KT22 ....74 D7
 Sutton SM1 ....59 B8
Montrose Rd TW14 ......3 D1
Montrose Way SE23 ....23 D7
Montrose Wlk KT13 ....53 B7

Montrouge Cres KT17 ..77 C3
Montserrat Cl SE19 ....22 D3
Monument Bridge
 Ind Est E GU21 ....70 B4
Monument Bridge
 Ind Est W GU21 ....70 A4
Monument Hill KT13 ...53 B6
Monument Hill Cty Prim
 Sch GU22 ....56 E5
Monument Rd
 Weybridge KT13 ....53 B7
 Woking GU21 ....70 B4
Monument Way E GU21 ..70 B4
Monument Way W GU21 ..70 A4
Moon Ct KT22 ....94 D6
Moon's La RH19, RH7, TN8 ..186 E8
Moons Hill GU10 ......146 C2
Moons La RH11 ....217 E1
Moor Cl GU47 ....45 E1
Moor House Sch RH8 ..122 F3
Moor La Chessington KT9 ..56 E5
 Harmondsworth UB7 ....2 C8
 Lingfield RH7, TN8 ....165 D3
 Staines TW18 ....12 D6
 Stanwell TW19 ....12 D6
 Woking GU22 ....89 F5
Moor Lane Jun Sch KT9 ..56 F5
Moor Mead Rd TW1 ......6 A1
Moor Park Cres RH11 ..200 D5
Moor Park Gdns KT2 ...18 E1
Moor Park House RG12 ..26 E3
Moor Park La GU10, GU9 ..126 A2
Moor Park Way GU9 ...125 F2
Moor Pl
 East Grinstead RH19 ..185 D2
 Windlesham GU20 ......48 B5
Moor Rd Farnborough GU14 ..85 A8
 Frimley GU16 ....85 F8
 Linchmere GU27 ....207 C5
Moorcroft RH9 ....121 C3
Moorcroft Cl RH11 ....201 B7
Moorcroft Rd SW16 ....21 E5
Moordale Ave RG42 ....26 E8
Moore Cl Addlestone KT15 ..52 B5
 Ash GU10 ....126 F8
 Mitcham CR4 ....41 B7
 Mortlake SW14 ....7 C4
 Wallington SM6 ....60 E3
Moore Ct RH12 ....217 A1
Moore Grove Cres TW20 ..11 F1
Moore House **1** SE27 ..22 C4
Moore Rd Pirbright GU24 ..87 B6
 South Norwood SE19 ...22 C2
Moore Way SM2 ....59 A2
Moore's Rd RH4, RH5 ..136 B8
Mooreland Rd BR1 .....24 F1
Moores Gn RG40 ....25 E8
Moorfield GU27 ....207 F5
Moorfield Ctr The GU1 ..109 D5
Moorfield Rd
 Chessington KT9 ....56 E5
 Guildford GU1 ....109 E5
Moorfields Cl TW18 ....32 E8
Moorfields Ct **4** SW16 ..21 C4
Moorhayes Dr TW18 ....33 C6
Moorhead Rd RH12 ....218 B5
Moorholme GU22 ......89 E8
Moorhouse Rd RH8 ...123 F5
Moorhurst La RH5 .....157 B4
Moorings The
 East Grinstead RH19 ..185 A3
 Hindhead GU26 ....188 E3
Moorland Cl
 Twickenham TW4 ......16 A8
Moorland Rd UB7 ......2 C8
Moorlands KT12 ....54 A7
Moorlands Cl GU26 ...188 E4
Moorlands Pl GU15 ....65 A4
Moorlands Rd GU15 ....65 B4
Moorlands The GU22 ..89 F6
Moormead Dr KT19 ....57 E5
Moormede Cres TW18 ..12 F4
Moors La GU8 ....148 C3
Moors The GU10 ......126 F7
Moorside Cl GU14 .....65 A1
Moorside Rd BR1 ......24 F4
Moorsom Way CR5 .....79 D2
Moray Ave GU47 ....64 D7
Moray House **1** KT6 ..37 E4
Mordaunt Dr RG45 ....45 B3
Mordaunt Gdns SW17 ..20 F3
Morden Cl Bracknell RG12 ..27 F5
 Burgh Heath KT20 .....97 D7
Morden Court Par SM4 ..40 A5
Morden Farm Mid Sch
 SM4 ....39 E2
Morden Gdns CR4 .....40 D5
Morden Hall Park SW19 ..40 C6
Morden Hall Rd
 SM4, SW19 ....40 C5
Morden House SM4 ....40 C5
Morden Park Sch Sports Ctr
 SM4 ....39 F2
Morden Rd Merton SW19 ..40 B7
 Mitcham CR4, SM4, SW19 ..40 D5
Morden Road Sta SW19 ..40 D5
Morden South Sta SM4 ..40 A4
Morden Sta SW19 ......40 A4
Morden Way SM3 ......40 A2
More Circ GU7 ....150 E7
More Cl CR8 ....80 A8
More House Sch GU10 ..146 C2
More La KT10 ....55 B7
More Rd GU7 ....150 E7
Morecambe Cl RH11 ...200 F4

Morecoombe Cl KT2 ....18 B1
Morecote Cl GU4 ......130 E2
Moreland Ave SL3 ......1 C7
Moreland Cl SL3 ....1 C7
Morella Cl GU25 ....31 D5
Morella Rd SW11, SW12 ..20 F8
Moremead Rd SE6 .....24 A4
Morena St SE6 ....24 B8
Moresby Ave KT5 ......38 B2
Moreton Ave TW7 ....5 E6
Moreton Cl GU10 .....167 E1
Moreton Green Est Sch
 SM4 ....40 D4
Moreton House SW17 ..20 D4
Moreton Rd
 North Cheam KT4 ......58 B8
 South Croydon CR2 ....61 D5
Morgan Ct TW15 ....14 B3
Moring Rd SW17 ....21 A4
Morkyns Wlk SE21 .....22 E5
Morland Ave CR0 ......42 E1
Morland Cl **7** Hampton TW12 ..15 F3
 Mitcham CR4 ....40 E6
Morland Rd
 Aldershot GU11 ....126 C6
 Croydon CR0 ....42 F2
 Penge SE20 ....23 D2
 Sutton SM1 ....59 C5
Morland's Rd GU11 ....105 D5
Morley Ct Beckenham BR3 ..44 D8
 Beckenham BR2 ....44 F5
 Sunningdale SL5 ......29 F3
Morley House TW2 .....21 B8
Morley Rd Cheam SM3 ..39 F1
 Farnham GU9 ....125 D1
 South Croydon CR2 ....61 F1
 Twickenham TW1 ....6 D1
Morningside Rd KT4 ...58 C8
Mornington Cl TN16 ...83 D2
Mornington Cres TW5 ..4 B6
Mornington Rd TW15 ..14 C3
Mornington Wlk TW10 ..17 C4
Morrell Ave
 Horsham RH12 ....217 F6
 Horsham RH12 ....218 A6
Morris Cl BR3, CR0 ....43 E4
Morris Gdns SW18 ....20 A8
Morris Rd
 Farnborough GU14 ....105 D8
 Isleworth TW7 ....5 F4
 South Nutfield RH1 ...140 E7
Morrish Rd SW2 ....21 E8
Morrison Ave KT21 ....75 D1
Morrison House SW2 ..22 A7
Morriss Ct **3** RH12 ..218 F1
Morston Cl KT20 ......97 B7
Mortaine Rd TW15 .....13 D5
Mortimer Cl SW16 .....21 D6
Mortimer Cres KT4 ....57 D7
Mortimer Lodge **11** SW19 ..19 E7
Mortimer Rd
 Biggin Hill TN16 ......83 C7
 Capel RH5 ....178 D6
 Mitcham CR4 ....40 F8
Mortimer Sch SW16 ...21 D6
Mortlake Cl CR0 ....60 E7
Mortlake Dr CR4 ....40 E8
Mortlake High St SW14 ..7 D4
Mortlake Rd SW14, TW9 ..7 A6
Mortlake Sta SW14 .....7 C4
Morton KT20 ....97 E6
Morton Cl Frimley GU16 ..85 F7
 Woking GU21 ....69 D4
Morton Gdns SM6 ......60 C5
Morton Rd
 East Grinstead RH19 ..205 E7
 Morden CR4, SM4 ......40 D4
 Woking GU21 ....69 D4
Morval Cl GU14 ....84 E4
Morven Rd SW17 ......20 F5
Moselle Cl GU14 ......84 D5
Moselle Rd TN16 ......83 F1
Mospey Cres KT17 .....76 F4
Moss Gdns CR2 ....62 D3
Moss La GU7 ....150 D4
Moss Lane Cty Inf Sch
 GU7 ....150 D4
Mossfield KT11 ....73 A6
Mosslea Rd Kenley CR3 ..80 F2
 Penge SE20 ....23 C2
Mossville Gdns SM4, SW20 ..39 F5
Mostyn Rd SW19 ......39 F2
Mostyn Terr RH1 .....140 A8
Motspur Park Sta SW20 ..39 B4
Motspur Pk SW20 ......39 A4
Motts Hill La
 Tadworth KT20 ....97 A4
 Walton on t H KT20 ...97 A4
Mouchotte Cl TN16 ....83 C7
Moulton Ave TW3, TW5 ..4 F5
Mount Adon Pk SE21, SE22 ..22 E8
Mount Angelus Rd SW15 ..18 F8
Mount Ararat Rd TW10 ..6 E2
Mount Arlington BR2 ..44 E7
Mount Ash Rd SE26 ...23 B5
Mount Ave CR3 ....100 C3
Mount Cl Crawley RH10 ..202 D7
 Ewhurst GU6 ....175 E5
 Fetcham KT22 ....94 F4
 Kenley CR8 ....80 D3
 Wallington SM5 ....60 A2
 Woking GU22 ....89 D8
Mount Cl The GU15 ....30 C1
Mount Ct **1** Guildford GU2 ..130 C7
 2 Kingston u T KT2 ..18 B1
 West Wickham BR4 .....63 E8

Mount Dr The RH2 1
Mount Ephraim La SW16 ..
Mount Ephraim Rd SW16 ..
Mount Felix KT12 ......
Mount Gdns SE26 ......
Mount Hermon Cl GU22 ..
Mount Hermon Rd GU22 ..
Mount La Bracknell RG12 ..
 Turners Hill RH10 20
Mount Lee TW20 ....
Mount Nod Rd SW16, SW2 ..
Mount Park Ave CR2 ..
Mount Pk SM5 ....
Mount Pl GU1 1
Mount Pleasant
 Biggin Hill TN16 .....
 Bracknell RG12 ....
 Farnham GU9 1
 Ewell KT17 ....
 Farnham GU9 1
 Guildford GU2 ....
 Sandhurst GU47 ......
 West Horsley KT24 ....
 West Norwood SE27 ...
 Weybridge KT13 ....
 Wokingham RG41 ......
Mount Pleasant Cl GU18 ..
Mount Pleasant Rd
 Aldershot GU12 1
 Caterham CR3 ....
 Kingston u T KT3 .....
 Lingfield RH7 ....
Mount Prim Sch The KT3 ..
Mount Rd Chessington KT9 ..
 Chobham GU24 ....
 Cranleigh GU6 ....
 Feltham TW13 ....
 Kingston u T KT3 .....
 Mitcham CR4 ....
 South Norwood SE19 ..
 Wimbledon SW18, SW19 ..
 Woking GU22 ....
Mount Rise Forest Hill SE23 ..
 Reigate RH1 ....
Mount St RH4 1
Mount The Cranleigh GU6 ..1
 Esher KT10 ....
 Ewell KT17 ....
 Ewhurst GU6 1
 Fetcham KT22 ....
 Grayswood GU27 ......
 Guildford GU2 ....
 Headley Down GU35 ...
 Lower Kingswood KT20 ..
 New Malden KT3 ......
 North Cheam KT4 .....
 Oatlands Park KT13 ...
 Rusper RH11, RH12 ...20
 Rusper RH12 ....
 Warlingham CR6 ......
 Wentworth GU25 .....
 Woking GU21, GU22 ...
Mount View RH1 ......
Mount View Rd KT10 ..
Mount Villas SE27 ....
Mount Way SM5 ......
Mountacre Cl SE26 ...
Mountbatten Cl
 Crawley RH11 2
 6 West Norwood SE19 ..
Mountbatten Ct **13**
 GU11 1
Mountbatten Gdns BR3 ..
Mountbatten Rise GU47 ..
Mountcombe Cl KT6 ...
Mountearl Gdns
 SW16, SW2 ....
Mountfield Cl SE6 ....
Mountfield Rd BR2 ...
Mounts Hill SL4, SL5 ..
Mountsfield Ct TW19 ..
Mountside Caterham CR3 ..10
 Guildford GU3 13
Mountview **5** RH8 ...
Mountview Cl RH1 13
Mountview Dr RH1 13
Mountwood KT8 ......
Mountwood Cl CR2 ...
Mousehill La GU8 17
Moushill La GU8 17
Mowat Ct KT4 ....
Mowbray Ave KT14 ...
Mowbray Cres TW20 ..
Mowbray Dr RH11 20
Mowbray Gdns RH4 ...1
Mowbray Rd
 Richmond TW10 ......
 South Norwood SE19 ..
Mower Cl RG40 ......
Mower Pl GU6 17
Moyne Ct **3** GU21 ...
Moyne Rd RH11 20
Moyser Rd SW16, SW17 ..
Muchelney Rd SM4 ...
Muckhatch La TW20 ..
Mudie House **3** SW2 ..
Muggeridge's Hill
 Capel RH2, RH5 19
 Rusper RH12, RH5 19
Muirdown Ave SW14 ..
Muirfield Cl RH11 20
Muirfield House RG12 ..
Muirfield Rd GU21 ....
Muirkirk Rd SE6 .....
Mulberries The KT22 ..
Mulberry Ave TW19 ...
Mulberry Bsns Pk RG41 ..

berry Cl Ash GU12 . . . . 106 A4
vthorne RG45 . . . . 45 C4
sham RH12 . . . . 217 C5
Sandhurst GU47 . . . . 64 D8
eatham SW16 . . . . 21 E4
ybridge KT13 . . . . 53 B7
berry GU21 . . . . 69 E5
berry Cres TW8 . . . . 6 C7
berry Ct
Bracknell RG12 . . . . 27 F4
urbiton KT6 . . . . 37 D2
ckenham TW1 . . . . 16 F5
kingham RG40 . . . . 25 C6
berry Gdns 42 F1
berry Mews **El** SM6 . . . . 60 C4
berry Rd RH11 . . . . 181 B1
berry Trees TW17 . . . . 34 D2
grave Chambers SM2 . . . . 59 B4
grave Manor SM2 . . . . 59 B4
grave Rd
mont SM2 . . . . 59 A4
ydon CR0, CR9 . . . . 61 D7
mley GU16 . . . . 65 F2
grave Way GU21 . . . . 68 E1
holland Cl CR4 . . . . 41 B7
lards Cl CR4 . . . . 40 F1
lein Wlk RH11 . . . . 201 A2
lens Rd RW20 . . . . 12 C3
lins Path TW14 . . . . 7 D4
roy Dr GU15 . . . . 66 A6
ton Rd SW18 . . . . 20 D8
caster Rd TW15 . . . . 14 A4
caster Rd TW15 . . . . 14 B3
ncies Mews SE6 . . . . 24 C6
nday's Boro Rd GU3 . . . . 128 A4
nday's Boro Rd GU3 . . . . 128 B4
nnings Dr GU47 . . . . 64 E6
nnings Gdns TW1 . . . . 5 D2
no Way GU14 . . . . 105 D8
nroe House RH2 . . . . 139 A6
nslow Gdns SM1 . . . . 59 D6
nstead Ct TW2 . . . . 16 E6
nstead Heath Rd
dals, GU5, GU7, GU8 . . . . 151 C3
dalming GU5, GU7, GU8 . . . . . 151 C3
nstead Pk GU8 . . . . 151 C2
nstead View GU3 . . . . 130 C4
nstead View Rd GU5 . . . . 151 D5
ster Ave TW4 . . . . 4 E2
ster Ct TW11 . . . . 17 C2
ster Rd TW11 . . . . 17 C2
doch Cl TW18 . . . . 13 A3
doch Rd RG40 . . . . 25 D5
rraye Ave TW3 . . . . 5 B2
rray Ct
cot SL5 . . . . 29 C3
 whitley RH11 . . . . 201 A1
rham RH13 . . . . 218 B4
rray Gn GU21 . . . . 70 C5
rray House RG16 . . . . 51 D4
rray Rd
rnborough GU14 . . . . 84 F3
chmond TW15, KT16 . . . . 51 D5
chmond TW10 . . . . 17 C6
mbledon SW19 . . . . 19 D2
kingham RG41 . . . . 25 A6
rray's La KT14 . . . . 71 E5
rray's Rd GU11 . . . . 105 D5
rrell Rd GU12 . . . . 106 A3
rrellhill La RG42 . . . . 26 C8
rrells Cl GU15 . . . . 65 B3
rrells Wlk KT23 . . . . 94 A3
rreys The KT21 . . . . 75 D1
schamp Inf Sch SM5 . . . . 59 E8
schamp Jun Sch SM5 . . . . . . 59 E8
schamp Rd SM1, SM5 . . . . . . 59 E8
seum Hill GU27 . . . . 208 D6
seum of Richmond

N

Naafi Rdbt GU11 . . . . 105 B2
Nadine Ct SM6 . . . . 60 C2
Nailsworth Cres RH1 . . . . 119 D6
Nairn Cl GU16 . . . . 65 E2
Nairn Ct **El** Wallington SM6 . . . 60 C4
Wimbledon SW19 . . . . 20 B2
Naldrett Cl RH12 . . . . 217 F4
Naldretts La RH12 . . . . 214 D5
Nailhead Rd TW13 . . . . 15 C3
Namba Roy Cl SW16 . . . . 21 F4
Namton Dr CR7, SW16 . . . . . . 41 F5
Napier Cl Crowthorne RG45 . . . . 45 C4
Napier Ct GU22 . . . . 42 F1
Napier Ct Caterham CR3 . . . . . 100 E5
10 Croydon CR0 . . . . 61 F8
El Surbiton KT6 . . . . 37 D2
Woking GU21 . . . . 69 E3
Napier Dr GU15 . . . . 66 A8
Napier Gdns GU1 . . . . 110 B2
Napier Lodge TW15 . . . . 14 D2
Napier Rd Ashford TW15 . . . . . 14 D1
Crowthorne RG45 . . . . 45 C4
Croydon SE25 . . . . 43 B5
Harmondsworth TW6 . . . . 2 F5
Isleworth TW7 . . . . 6 A3
South Croydon CR2 . . . . 61 D3
Napier Way RH10 . . . . 182 A1
Napier Wlk TW15 . . . . 14 D1
Napoleon Ave GU14 . . . . 85 B6
Napoleon Rd TW1 . . . . 17 B8
Napper Cl SL5 . . . . 28 D7
Napper Pl GU6 . . . . 174 E1
Narrow La CR6 . . . . 101 B8
Naseby Cl GU21 . . . . 27 B1
Naseby Ct TW7 . . . . 5 E6
Naseby Rd SE19 . . . . 22 D2
Nash Dr **El** RH1 . . . . 119 A3
Nash Gdns North Ascot SL5 . . . . 28 E7
Redhill RH1 . . . . 118 F3
Nash Rd RH10 . . . . 201 E3
Nassau Rd SW13 . . . . 7 F6
Nasturtium Dr GU24 . . . . 68 A4
Natal Rd
South Norwood CR7 . . . . 42 D6
Streatham SW16 . . . . 21 D2
Natalie Cl TW14 . . . . 14 D8
Natalie Mews TW2 . . . . 16 D5
National Physical
Laboratory TW1 . . . . 16 E2
National Wks TW4 . . . . 4 F4
Nayland House SE6 . . . . 24 C4
Neale Cl RH19 . . . . 185 C3
Neath Gdns SM4 . . . . 40 C3
Neb La KRB 122 D4
Needles Bank RH9 . . . . 121 B4
Needles Cl RH12 . . . . 217 B1
Neelem Ct GU14 . . . . 85 C1
Neil Cl TW15 . . . . 14 C3
Neil Wates Cres **El** SW2 . . . . . 22 A7
Nelgarde Rd Catford SE6 . . . . . 24 A8
Lewisham SE6 . . . . 24 A8
Nell Ball RH14 . . . . 211 E2
Nell Gwynn Ave TW17 . . . . . . 34 D3
Nell Gwynne Ave SL5 . . . . 29 D5
Nell Gwynne Cl SL5 . . . . 29 D5
Nello James Gdns SE27 . . . . . . 22 D4
Nelson Cl
Biggin Hill TN16 . . . . 83 E2
Bracknell RG12 . . . . 27 E7
Crawley RH10 . . . . 202 C5
East Bedfont TW14 . . . . 14 F7
Heath End GU9 . . . . 125 D8
Thornton Heath CR0 . . . . 42 B1
Walton-on-T KT12 . . . . 35 B1
Nelson Ct Carshalton SM5 . . . . . 59 F5
Chertsey KT16 . . . . 33 A1
Nelson Gdns
Guildford GU1 . . . . 110 A3
Twickenham TW3, TW4 . . . . 5 A1
Nelson Grove Rd SW19 . . . . . . 40 C8
Nelson Ho **El** GU11 . . . . 105 A2
Nelson Hospl SM4 . . . . 39 F7
Nelson Prim Sch TW2 . . . . 5 B1
Nelson Rd Ashford TW15 . . . . . 13 E3
Caterham CR3 . . . . 100 D4
Harmondsworth TW6 . . . . 2 E5
Heath End GU9 . . . . 125 D8
Horsham RH12 . . . . 217 C3
Merton SW19 . . . . 20 C1
New Malden KT3 . . . . 38 D4
Twickenham TW2, TW4 . . . . 16 A8
Nelson St **El** GU11 . . . . 105 A2
Nelson Trad Est SW19 . . . . . . 40 B8
Nelson Way GU15 . . . . 64 F4
Nelson Wlk KT19 . . . . 57 B6
Nene Rd TW6, UB7 . . . . 3 B6
Nepean St **El** SW15 . . . . 19 A8
Neptune Cl RH11 . . . . 200 E4
Nesbit Ct RH11 . . . . 200 E3
Nesbitt Sq SE19 . . . . 22 E1
NESCOT Epsom's Coll of
FE & HE KT17 . . . . 77 A8
Nether Mount GU2 . . . . 130 B7
Netheravon Rd S W4 . . . . 7 F8
Netheravon Rd S W4 . . . . 7 E8
Netherby Rd SE23 . . . . 23 C8
Netherby Rd GU21 . . . . 68 F2
Nethercote Ave GU21 . . . . 68 F2
Netherfield Rd SW17 . . . . 21 A5
Netherlands The SM5 . . . . 59 C8
Netherleigh Pk RH1 . . . . 140 D6
Nethern Court Rd CR3 . . . . . . 102 A4
Netherne La CR5 . . . . 99 C5

Netherton RG12 . . . . 27 A5
Netherton Rd TW1 . . . . 6 B2
Netherwood RH11 . . . . 201 B4
Netherwood Ct GU7 . . . . 150 E5
Netley Cl Cheam SM3 . . . . 58 D5
New Addington CR0 . . . . 63 C3
Netley Dr KT12 . . . . 35 F2
Netley Gdns SM4 . . . . 40 C2
Netley Rd Brentford TW8 . . . . . . 6 E8
Morden SM4 . . . . 40 C2
Netley Rd **[V]** TW6 . . . . 3 D6
Netley St GU14 . . . . 105 C8
Nettlecombe RG12 . . . . 27 D3
Nettlecombe Cl SM2 . . . . 59 B2
Nettlefold Pl SE27 . . . . 22 B5
Nettles Terr **El** GU1 . . . . 109 D1
Nettlestead Cl BR3 . . . . 23 F1
Nettleton Rd TW6 . . . . 3 B6
Nettlewood Rd SW16 . . . . 21 D1
Neuchatel Rd SE6 . . . . 23 F6
Nevada Cl
Farnborough GU14 . . . . 84 D3
Kingston u T KT3 . . . . 38 C5
Nevelle Cl RG42 . . . . 26 D8
Nevile Cl RH11 . . . . 201 A3
Neville Ave KT3 . . . . 38 D8
Neville Cl Banstead SM7 . . . . . . 78 B5
Esher KT10 . . . . 54 F4
Hounslow TW3 . . . . 5 B5
Neville Ct **[10]** SW2 . . . . 21 C8
Neville Duke Rd GU14 . . . . . . 84 F8
Neville Rd Croydon CR0 . . . . . . 42 D2
Kingston u T KT1 . . . . 38 A7
Richmond TW10 . . . . 17 C6
Neville Wlk SM5 . . . . 40 E2
Nevis Rd SW17 . . . . 21 A6
New Barn La Kenley CR3 . . . . . . 80 E3
Kenley CR3 . . . . 177 A3
New Barns Ave CR4 . . . . 41 D5
New Beckenham Sta BR3 . . . . 23 F1
New Belmont House **El**
SE23 . . . . 23 C7
New Berry La KT12 . . . . 54 D5
New Chapel La TW13 . . . . 15 B7
New Church Ct **El** SE19 . . . . . 23 A1
New Cl Feltham TW13 . . . . 15 E3
Merton SW19 . . . . 40 C6
New Colebrooke Ct SM5 . . . . . 60 A3
New Cotts
Betchworth RH3 . . . . 116 D4
Sidlow RH2 . . . . 138 F1
Turners Hill RH10 . . . . 204 A4
New Cross Rd GU2 . . . . 109 B3
New Cswy RH2 . . . . 139 C6
New Ct KT15 . . . . 52 C7
New Dawn Cl GU14 . . . . 84 D3
New Epsom & Ewell
Cottage Hospl TW4 . . . . 56 E6
New Farthingdale RH7 . . . . . . 186 B8
New Forest Cotts GU22 . . . . . . 89 F7
New Forest Ride RG12 . . . . . . 27 F4
New Green Pl SE19 . . . . 22 E2
New Haw La KT15 . . . . 52 A1
New Haw Rd KT15 . . . . 52 C4
New Heston Rd TW5 . . . . 4 F7
New House Farm La GU3 . . . . 108 C2
New Inn La GU4 . . . . 110 B4
New Inn La GU4 . . . . 110 B4
New Kelvin Ave TW11 . . . . . . 16 E2
New La GU22, GU4 . . . . 89 F3
New Lodge Dr RH8 . . . . 122 F7
New Malden Sta KT3 . . . . 38 E6
New Meadow SL5 . . . . 28 D8
New Mile Rd SL5 . . . . 29 C8
New Moorhead Dr RH12 . . . . 218 C6
New North Rd RH2 . . . . 138 F6
New Par TW15 . . . . 13 E4
New Park Ct **El** SW2 . . . . 21 E8
New Park Par **El** SW2 . . . . . . 21 E8
New Park Rd Ashford TW15 . . . 14 C3
Cranleigh GU6 . . . . 174 F2
Streatham SW2 . . . . 21 E8
New Pl CR0 . . . . 63 A4
New Place Gdns RH7 . . . . 164 E4
New Pond Rd
Artington GU3 . . . . 129 E1
Compton GU3 . . . . 129 E1
New Poplars The GU2 . . . . . . 106 A1
New Rd Albury GU5 . . . . 132 D3
Bagshot GU19 . . . . 47 F3
Blackwater GU17 . . . . 64 E4
Bracknell RG12 . . . . 27 D7
Brentford TW8 . . . . 6 D8
Carshalton SM5 . . . . 41 A1
Chilworth GU4 . . . . 131 B3
Crowthorne RG45 . . . . 45 B5
East Bedfont TW14 . . . . 3 D1
East Clandon GU4 . . . . 111 E4
East Molesey KT8 . . . . 36 A6
Egham TW18 . . . . 12 C4
Esher KT10 . . . . 55 B6
Feltham TW13 . . . . 14 E6
Feltham TW13 . . . . 15 E3
Forest Green RH5 . . . . 176 E6
Gomshall GU5 . . . . 133 C4
Hamptn TW4, UB7 . . . . 3 C7
Harlington TW6 . . . . 3 C6
Hydestile GU8 . . . . 171 F5
Kingston u T KT2 . . . . 18 A1
Limpsfield RH8 . . . . 123 B5
Linchmere GU27 . . . . 207 F5
Littleton TW17 . . . . 34 A5
Milford GU8 . . . . 170 E8
North Ascot SL5 . . . . 8 F1
Oxshott KT10, KT22 . . . . 74 F8

New Rd continued
Richmond TW10 . . . . 17 C4
Sandhurst GU47 . . . . 64 A8
Smallfield RH6 . . . . 162 B3
Tadworth KT20 . . . . 97 C4
Tandridge RH8, RH9 . . . . 143 A7
Tongham GU10 . . . . 126 F6
Weybridge KT13 . . . . 53 C5
Windlesham GU19, GU20 . . . . . 48 A4
Wormley GU8 . . . . 170 E1
Wormley GU8 . . . . 191 A8
New Rd Units TW3 . . . . 5 B8
New Residences KT16 . . . . 51 C7
New Scotland Hill City Prim
Sch GU47 . . . . 45 A2
New Sq TW14 . . . . 14 C7
New St Crawley RH10 . . . . 202 A7
Horsham RH13 . . . . 217 D2
Staines TW18 . . . . 13 A4
New Town Rd RH10 . . . . 183 B3
New Victoria Hospl The
KT3 . . . . 38 E8
New Way GU7 . . . . 150 C4
New Wickham La TW20 . . . . . . 12 B1
New Wokingham Rd RG45 . . . 45 A6
New Woodlands Sch BR1 . . . . 24 E4
New Zealand Ave KT12 . . . . . . 34 F1
Newall Rd TW6 . . . . 3 C6
Newark Cl Guildford GU4 . . . . 110 B6
Ripley GU23 . . . . 91 A6
Newark Ct KT12 . . . . 35 C1
Newark La
Ripley GU22, GU23 . . . . 91 A6
Woking GU22 . . . . 90 F8
Newark Rd Crawley RH10 . . . . 201 F8
South Croydon CR2 . . . . 61 D4
Windlesham GU20 . . . . 48 B6
Newbolt Ave SM3 . . . . 58 D5
Newborough Gn KT3 . . . . 38 D5
Newborough House SW19 . . . 20 D1
Newbridge Cl RH12 . . . . 216 C3
Newbridge Ct
Cranleigh GU6 . . . . 174 B3
Upper Tooting SW17 . . . . 20 C4
Newbridge Point **El** SE23 . . . 23 D5
Newbury Gdns KT19 . . . . 57 F6
Newbury Rd TW6 . . . . 3 C6
Newchapel Rd
Lingfield RH7 . . . . 164 B3
Newchapel RH7 . . . . 163 F2
Newcome Gdns SW16 . . . . 21 E4
Newcome Pl GU12 . . . . 126 E7
Newcome Rd GU9 . . . . 125 E6
Newdigate Endowed CE
Inf Sch RH5 . . . . 158 B1
Newdigate Rd
Beare Green RH5 . . . . 157 E2
Rusper RH12 . . . . 199 C8
Newenham Rd KT23 . . . . 94 A1
Newent Cl SM5 . . . . 40 F1
Newfield Ave GU14 . . . . 84 E7
Newfield Cl TW12 . . . . 36 A8
Newfield Rd GU12 . . . . 106 A6
Newfoundland Rd GU16 . . . . . 86 B8
Newgate CR0 . . . . 42 C1
Newgate Cl TW13 . . . . 15 E5
Newhache RH7 . . . . 165 A1
Newhall Gdns KT12 . . . . 54 C8
Newhaven Cres TW15 . . . . . . 14 D3
Newhaven Rd SE25 . . . . 42 D4
Newhouse Cl KT3 . . . . 38 E2
Newhouse Wlk SM4 . . . . 40 C2
Newland House Sch TW1 . . . . 16 F4
Newland House Sch Annex
TW1 . . . . 16 F4
Newlands
Thames Ditton KT7 . . . . 36 E1
Woking GU22 . . . . 89 F6
Newlands Cl Hersham KT12 . . . 54 E6
Horley RH6 . . . . 160 F5
Newlands Cnr GU4 . . . . 132 A2
Newlands Cres RH19 . . . . 185 E1
Newlands Croft SE20 . . . . 23 D8
Newlands Ct
Addlestone KT15 . . . . 52 B5
Caterham CR3 . . . . 100 C6
Streatham SW16 . . . . 21 E3
Newlands Dr Ash GU12 . . . . . 106 B4
Poyle SL3 . . . . 1 E4
Newlands Estate GU8 . . . . . . 170 F5
Newlands Flats GU1 . . . . 109 F2
Newlands Pk
Copthorne RH10 . . . . 183 E3
Forest Hill SE20, SE26 . . . . 23 D3
Penge SE26 . . . . 23 D3
Newlands Pl RH18 . . . . 206 F3
Newlands Rd
Camberley GU15 . . . . 65 B1
Crawley RH11 . . . . 201 C5
Horsham RH12 . . . . 217 C4
Thornton Heath SW16 . . . . 41 D7
Newlands The SM6 . . . . 60 D3
Newlands Way KT9 . . . . 55 F5
Newlands Wood CR0 . . . . 62 F2
Newman Cl RH10 . . . . 202 C4
Newman Rd Croydon CR0 . . . . 41 F1
Harlington TW6 . . . . 3 B6
Newmarket Rd RH10 . . . . 202 A4
Newminster Rd SM4 . . . . 40 C3
Newnham Cl CR7 . . . . 42 C7
Newnham House SE6 . . . . 24 C5
Newport Jun Sch GU12 . . . . . 105 D1
Newport Rd
Aldershot GU12 . . . . 105 D1
Harmondsworth TW6 . . . . 2 E6
Newquay Rd SE6 . . . . 24 C6

Newry Rd TW1 . . . . 6 A2
Newsham Rd **El** GU21 . . . . . . 68 F2
Newstead Cl GU7 . . . . 150 D6
Newstead Hall RH6 . . . . 161 D1
Newstead House SE12 . . . . . . 24 F8
Newstead Rise CR3 . . . . 101 B1
Newstead Way SW19 . . . . 19 D5
Newton Ave RH19 . . . . 205 F6
Newton Rd Crawley RH10 . . . . 181 F2
Farnborough GU14 . . . . 85 D6
Isleworth TW7 . . . . 5 F5
Merton SW19 . . . . 19 E1
Purley CR8 . . . . 79 C7
Newton Way GU10 . . . . 126 F7
Newton Wood Rd KT21 . . . . . . 75 F3
Newtown Ct RH13 . . . . 217 E1
Newtown Rd GU47 . . . . 64 B8
Nicholas Gdns GU22 . . . . 70 F3
Nicholas House SE26 . . . . 23 B2
Nicholas Lodge GU10 . . . . 55 A8
Nicholas Rd CR0 . . . . 60 E6
Nicholass Ct **El** CR8 . . . . 80 B7
Nicholes Rd TW3 . . . . 5 A3
Nicholes Rd **[V]** 56 C4
Nicholsfield RH14 . . . . 212 F4
Nicholson Rd CR0 . . . . 42 F1
Nicholson Wlk **El** TW20 . . . . . 12 A3
Nicol Cl **[6]** TW1 . . . . 6 B1
Nicola Cl CR2 . . . . 61 C4
Nicosia Rd SW18 . . . . 20 E8
Niederrald Rd SE26 . . . . 23 E4
Nightingale Ave KT24 . . . . 92 D2
Nightingale Cl
Carshalton SM5 . . . . 60 A8
Chiswick W4 . . . . 7 C8
Crawley RH11 . . . . 201 C8
East Grinstead RH19 . . . . 205 D7
Farnborough GU14 . . . . 84 C6
Nightingale Cres
Bracknell RG12 . . . . 27 D4
West Horsley KT24 . . . . 92 C2
Nightingale Ct
[2] Knaphill GU21 . . . . 68 F1
Penge SE26 . . . . 22 F2
El Redhill RH1 . . . . 119 A2
Nightingale Dr
Mytchett GU16 . . . . 86 A3
West Ewell KT19 . . . . 57 B4
Nightingale Gdns
Balham SW11, SW12 . . . . 20 F8
Hamgill RH11 . . . . 17 E8
Nightingale Rd Ash GU12 . . . 106 C3
Carshalton SM5 . . . . 60 A8
East Horsley KT24 . . . . 92 F2
East Molesey KT8 . . . . 36 B4
Esher KT10 . . . . 54 F4
Farncombe GU7 . . . . 150 E6
Guildford GU1 . . . . 109 E1
Hampton TW12 . . . . 16 A2
Horley RH6 . . . . 160 F4
Selsdon CR2 . . . . 62 D1
Walton-on-T KT12 . . . . 35 B2
Nightingale Sq SW12 . . . . 21 A8
Nightingale Way KT22 . . . . . . 120 E2
Nightingales The KT16 . . . . . . 13 F7
Nighjar Cl GU10 . . . . 124 D8
Nimbus Rd KT19 . . . . 57 D1
Nimrod Ct RH10 . . . . 182 D1
Nimrod Rd SW16, SW17 . . . . . 21 B3
Nine Elms Cl TW14 . . . . 14 F7
Nine Mile Ride
Bracknell RG12, RG40 . . . . 26 F1
Crowthorne RG12, RG40 . . . . . 26 F1
Nineacres Way CR5 . . . . 79 E3
Ninehams Cl CR3 . . . . 100 D7
Ninehams Gdns CR3 . . . . 100 D7
Ninehams Rd
Caterham CR3 . . . . 100 D6
Tatsfield TN16 . . . . 103 D6
Nineteenth Rd CR4 . . . . 41 D5
Ninfield Ct RH11 . . . . 200 F2
Niton Rd TW9 . . . . 7 A4
Niven Cl RH10 . . . . 202 D5
Nobel Dr TW6 . . . . 3 E7
Noble Cnr TW5 . . . . 5 B6
Noble Ct CR4 . . . . 40 D7
Noble St KT12 . . . . 54 C6
Nobles Way TW20 . . . . 11 E2
Noel Ct TW4 . . . . 4 F4
Noel St SE23 . . . . 23 E8
Noke Dr RH1 . . . . 119 A2
Nonsuch Court Ave KT17 . . . . 58 B1
Nonsuch Ct SM3 . . . . 58 E4
Nonsuch High Sch for Girls
SM3 . . . . 58 D3
Nonsuch Ind Est KT17 . . . . . . 76 E8
Nonsuch Prim Sch KT17 . . . . . 58 B1
Nonsuch Wlk SM2 . . . . 58 D1
Noons Corner Rd RH5 . . . . . . 156 A8
Norbiton Ave KT1, KT2 . . . . . . 38 A7
Norbiton Common Rd
KT1, KT3 . . . . 38 B6
Norbiton Hall KT2 . . . . 37 F7
Norbiton Sta KT1 . . . . 38 A8
Norbury Ave Isleworth TW3 . . . . 5 D3
Thornton Heath SW16 . . . . 41 F7
Norbury Cl SW16 . . . . 42 A7
Norbury Court Rd SW16 . . . . . 41 F7
Norbury Cres SW16 . . . . 42 A7
Norbury Cross SW16 . . . . 41 E6

Norbury Hill SW16 ....22 B1
Norbury Manor Girls
  High Sch CR7 ....42 A8
Norbury Rd Reigate RH2 ...117 F1
  South Norwood CR7 ....42 C6
Norbury Rise SW16 ....41 E6
Norbury Sta SW16 ....41 E6
Norbury Trad Est SW16 ......41 F7
Norbury Way KT23 ....94 C2
Norcroft Gdns SE22 ....23 A8
Norcutt Rd TW2 ....16 E7
Norfolk Ave CR2 ....62 A1
Norfolk Cl Crawley RH11 ...200 E2
  Horley RH6 ....161 A2
  ☑ Twickenham TW1 ....6 B1
Norfolk Cotts RH1 ....140 E7
Norfolk Ct Dorking RH5 ....136 D3
  Horsham RH12 ....218 B5
  Surbiton KT5 ....37 F3
Norfolk Farm Cl GU22 ....70 D3
Norfolk Farm Rd GU22 ......70 D3
Norfolk House
  ☑ Croydon CR0 ....61 D8
  ☑ Merton SW19 ....20 C1
  Penge SE20 ....43 C8
Norfolk House Rd SW16 ....21 E5
Norfolk La RH5 ....136 B1
Norfolk Rd Claygate KT10 ..55 E5
  Dorking RH4 ....136 A7
  Feltham TW13 ....15 C7
  Horsham RH12, RH11 ......217 D2
  Mitcham SW19 ....20 E1
  South Holmwood RH5 ....157 C6
  South Norwood CR7 ....42 C6
Norfolk Terr RH12, RH13 ..217 D2
Norgrove St SW12 ....21 A8
Norheads La
  Biggin Hill TN16 ....83 B2
  Chelsham TN16 ....83 B2
Norhyrst Ave SE25 ....42 F6
Nork Gdns SM7 ....77 E5
Nork Rise SM7 ....77 D3
Nork Way KT17, SM7 ....77 D4
Norlands La
  Egham TW18, TW20 ....32 E7
  Thorpe TW18, TW20 ....32 E7
Norley Vale SW15 ....19 A7
Norman Ave Ewell KT17 .....76 F7
  Feltham TW13 ....15 E6
  South Croydon CR2, CR8 ...61 C1
  Twickenham TW1 ....17 C8
Norman Colyer Ct KT19 .....57 D1
Norman Cres TW5 ....4 D7
Norman Ct Farnham GU9 ..125 C1
  ☑ Hampton TW12 ....36 A8
  Streatham SW16 ....21 E5
Norman House
  Feltham TW13 ....15 F6
  Lower Halliford TW17 ....34 A2
Norman Keep RG42 ....27 F8
Norman Rd Ashford TW15 ..14 A3
  Merton SW19 ....20 C1
  Sutton SM1 ....59 A5
  Thornton Heath CR7 ....42 B4
Norman's Rd RH1, RH6 ....162 C5
Normandy RH12 ....217 C1
Normandy Cl
  Crawley RH10 ....202 C4
  ☑ East Grinstead RH19 ....205 F8
  Forest Hill SE26 ....23 E5
  Frimley GU16 ....86 E8
Normandy Gdns RH12 ......217 C1
Normandy Wlk TW20 ....12 C3
Normanhurst TW15 ....14 A3
Normanhurst Cl RH10 ......201 F6
Normanhurst Dr TW1 ....6 B2
Normanhurst Rd
  Streatham SW2 ....21 F6
  Walton-on-T KT12 ....54 D8
Normansfield Ave TL18, KT8 17 C1
Normansfield Hospl KT8 ...17 C1
Normanton RH2 ....117 D2
Normanton Ave
  SW18, SW19 ....20 A6
Normanton Rd CR2 ....61 E4
Normanton St SE23 ....23 D6
Normington Cl SW16 ....22 A3
Norrels Dr KT24 ....92 F1
Norrels Ride KT24 ....92 F2
Norreys Ave RG40 ....25 D7
Norris Hill Rd GU13, GU14 104 A8
Norris Rd TW18 ....12 F4
Norstead Pl SW15 ....19 A6
North Acre SM7 ....77 F3
North Ash RH12 ....217 A4
North Ave Heath End GU9 .125 D7
  ☑ Richmond TW9 ....7 A6
  Wallington SM5 ....60 A3
  Whiteley Village KT12 ....73 B3
North Camp Sta GU12 ....105 F8
North Cl Ash GU12 ....105 E1
  Crawley RH10 ....201 F7
  Dorking RH5 ....136 C3
  East Bedfont TW14 ....3 D1
  Farnborough GU14 ....85 A8
  Merton SM4 ....39 E5
North Comm KT13 ....53 C6
North Crofts SE21 ....23 B7
North Dene TW5 ....5 B6
North Down CR2 ....80 E7
North Downs Cres CR0 ......63 B7
North Downs Golf Course
  CR3 ....102 A2

North Downs Rd CR0 ....63 C1
North Dr Beckenham BR3 ....44 B5
  Hounslow TW3, TW7 ....5 C5
  Pirbright GU24 ....87 C6
  Streatham SW16 ....21 C4
  Wentworth GU25 ....30 E4
North End CR0, CR9 ....61 C8
North End La SL5 ....30 B2
North Farm Rd GU14 ....84 F8
North Farnborough Cty Inf
  Sch GU14 ....85 D5
North Feltham Trad Est
  TW14 ....15 E8
North Gate Rd GU14 ....85 C2
North Gdns SW19 ....20 D1
North Gn RG12 ....27 D8
North Gr KT16 ....32 F3
North Hatton Rd TW6 ....3 D6
North Heath Cl RH12 ....217 D5
North Heath Cty Prim Sch
  RH12 ....217 D6
North Heath Est RH12 ......217 D6
North Heath La RH12 ....217 E6
North Holmes Cl RH12 .....218 B5
North Hyde La TW5 ....4 F8
North La
  Aldershot GU11, GU12 .....105 D2
  Teddington TW11 ....16 F2
North Lodge Dr SL5 ....28 C7
North Mead Crawley RH10 .201 E8
  Redhill RH1 ....118 F4
North Minden House
  GU16 ....86 D7
North Moors GU1 ....109 E6
North Munstead La GU8 ...151 A1
North Par Chessington KT9 ..56 F5
  Faygate RH12 ....217 C3
North Park La GU9 ....121 A5
North Pl Mitcham SW19 .....20 F1
  Teddington TW11 ....16 F2
North Pole La BR2 ....63 F4
North Rd Ash Vale GU12 ...105 F4
  Brentford TW8 ....6 E8
  Crawley RH10 ....202 A7
  East Bedfont TW14 ....3 D1
  Guildford GU2 ....109 B4
  Hersham KT12 ....54 C5
  Heston TW5 ....4 C8
  Kingston u T KT6 ....37 D3
  Mitcham SW17, SW19 ....20 D2
  Reigate RH2 ....138 F6
  Richmond TW9 ....7 A5
  West Wickham BR4 ....44 B1
  Wimbledon SW17, SW19 ....20 C2
  Winkfield SL5 ....28 A8
  Woking GU21 ....70 A3
North Sheen Sta TW10 ....7 A3
North Side GU10 ....126 F7
North St Carshalton SM5 ....59 F6
  Dorking RH4 ....136 A7
  Egham TW20 ....11 F2
  Farncombe GU7 ....150 E7
  Guildford GU1 ....130 D8
  Horsham RH12, RH13 ......217 D3
  Isleworth TW7 ....6 A4
  Leatherhead KT22 ....95 A6
  Redhill RH1 ....118 F2
  Turners Hill RH10 ....204 A4
  Winkfield SL4 ....9 A6
North Station App RH1 ....140 F7
North Terminal App RH6 ..181 F8
North View SW19 ....19 D3
North View Cres KT18 ....77 C2
North Weald La KT2 ....17 D1
North Weylands Ind Est
  KT12 ....54 E8
North Wlk CR0 ....63 C5
North Worple Way SW14 .....7 D4
Northampton Cl RG12 ....27 E6
Northampton Rd CR0, CR9 ..62 A8
Northanger Rd SW16 ....21 E2
Northborough Rd SW16 ....41 E7
Northbourne GU7 ....150 F8
Northbrook Coll of Design
  & Tech RH12 ....217 C4
Northbrook Copse RG12 ....27 F3
Northbrook Rd
  Aldershot GU11 ....126 B8
  Thornton Heath CR0 ....42 D4
Northcliffe Cl KT4 ....57 E7
Northcote KT15 ....52 D6
Northcote Ave
  Isleworth TW7 ....6 A2
  Tolworth KT5 ....38 B2
Northcote Cl KT24 ....92 C2
Northcote Cres KT24 ....92 C2
Northcote La GU5 ....152 B6
Northcote Pk KT22 ....74 C4
Northcote Rd
  Ash Vale GU12 ....106 A7
  Farnborough GU14 ....85 A5
  Isleworth TW1, TW7 ....6 A2
  Kingston u T KT3 ....38 D6
  Thornton Heath CR0 ....42 D3
  West Horsley KT24 ....92 C2
Northcott RG12 ....27 A1
Northcroft Cl TW20 ....11 B3
Northcroft Gdns TW20 ....11 B3
Northcroft Rd
  Englefield Green TW20 ......11 B3
  West Ewell KT19 ....57 E3
Northcroft Villas TW20 ......11 B3
Northdown Cl RH12 ....217 F4
Northdown Ct RH9 ....121 C5
Northdown La GU1 ....130 E6
Northdown Rd
  Croydon CR0 ....61 C5
  Isleworth TW7 ....5 F5
  Upper Tooting SW17 ....20 F7

Northdown Terr RH19 ....185 D3
Northdowns GU6 ....174 E1
Northend Ct KT23 ....94 C1
Northern Perimeter Rd
  Harlington TW6 ....3 B6
  Hatton TW6 ....3 E6
Northern Perimeter Road
  (W) TW6 ....3 A5
Northernhay Wlk SM4 ....39 E5
Northey Ave Belmont SM2 ..58 E1
  East Ewell SM2 ....58 E1
Northfield Lightwater GU18 ..67 B8
  Shalford GU4 ....130 E1
  Witley GU8 ....170 F4
Northfield Cl GU12 ....105 D1
Northfield Cres SM3 ....58 E6
Northfield Ct TW18 ....33 B8
Northfield Pl KT13 ....53 B3
Northfield Rd Cobham KT11 ..73 B6
  Heston TW5 ....4 D7
  Staines TW18 ....33 B8
Northfields KT21 ....95 E8
Northgate Ave RH10 ....201 F7
Northgate Cty Fst Sch
  RH10 ....201 E7
Northgate Cty Mid Sch
  RH10 ....201 E7
Northgate Dr GU15 ....66 A7
Northgate Pl RH10 ....201 E7
Northgate Rd
  Crawley RH10, RH11 ....201 D6
  Crawley, North
    Terminal RH6 ....181 F8
Northington Cl RG12 ....27 F3
Northlands Bglws RH5 ......158 B1
Northlands Rd
  Faygate RH12 ....198 F2
  Horsham RH12 ....217 E2
  Warnham RH12 ....197 D2
Northmead GM Jun Sch
  GU2 ....109 B4
Northmead [4] SE23 ....23 D5
Northolt Rd TW6 ....2 E6
Northover BR1 ....24 F5
Northrop Rd TW6 ....3 E6
Northspur Rd SM1 ....59 A7
Northstead Rd SW2 ....22 A6
Northumberland Ave TW7 ...6 A7
Northumberland Cl TW19 ...2 E1
Northumberland Cres
  TW14 ....3 E1
Northumberland Gdns
  Hounslow TW7 ....6 A7
  Mitcham CR4 ....41 D4
Northumberland Pl [26]
  TW10 ....6 E2
Northway Crawley RH6 .....181 F8
  Farncombe GU7 ....150 B7
  Guildford GU2 ....109 A3
  Merton SM4, SW20 ....39 E5
  Wallington SM6 ....60 C6
Northway Rd CR0 ....42 F2
Northwood Ave
  Knaphill GU21 ....68 D1
  Purley CR8 ....80 B6
Northwood Pk RH10 ....182 A2
Northwood Rd
  Forest Hill SE23 ....23 F7
  Harmondsworth TW6 ....2 D6
  South Norwood CR7 ....42 C7
  Wallington SM6 ....60 D4
Northwood Way [4] SE19 ..22 E2
Norton Ave KT5 ....38 B2
Norton Ct BR3 ....43 F8
Norton Gdns SW16 ....41 E7
Norton House [4] KT3 ....38 B5
Norton Pk SL5 ....29 C4
Norton Rd Frimley GU15 ....66 D4
  Wokingham RG40 ....25 C5
Norwegian Sch SW19 ....19 C1
Norwich Ave GU15 ....65 E3
Norwich Rd Crawley RH10 .202 B5
  South Norwood CR7 ....42 C6
Norwood Cl
  Effingham KT24 ....113 C7
  Twickenham TW2 ....16 D6
Norwood Cres TW6 ....3 C6
Norwood Farm La KT11 .....73 B8
Norwood Heights Sh Ctr
  SE19 ....22 E2
Norwood High St SE27 ......22 C4
Norwood Hill RH6 ....159 C3
Norwood Hospl SE19 ....22 D2
Norwood Junction Sta
  SE25 ....43 A5
Norwood Park Rd SE27 .....22 C3
Norwood Rd
  Effingham KT24 ....113 C7
  Streatham SE24, SE27 ....22 B7
  West Norwood SE24, SE27 .22 B7
Norwood Sch
  West Norwood SE27 ....22 C3
  West Norwood SE27 ....22 C4
Norwoodhill Rd RH6 ....159 F2
Noseby Ct KT12 ....54 D8
Notley End GU20 ....11 C1
Notre Dame Jun Sch
  RH7 ....164 F3
Notre Dame RH7 ....164 F3
Notson Rd SE25 ....43 B5
Nottingham Cl GU21 ....68 F1
Nottingham Ct [5] GU21 ....68 F1
Nottingham Rd
  Croydon CR2 ....61 C5
  Isleworth TW7 ....5 F5
  Upper Tooting SW17 ....20 F7

Nova Mews SM4 ....39 E2
Nova Rd CR0 ....42 C2
Nower Lodge Sch RH4 .....136 A6
Nower Rd RH4 ....136 A6
Nowhurst La RH12 ....216 A5
Noyna Rd SW17 ....20 F5
Nuffield Ct TW5 ....4 F7
Nuffield Dr GU47 ....45 E1
Nuffield Hospl GU2 ....108 E1
Nugee Ct RG45 ....45 B5
Nugent Ct Guildford GU2 ..109 B4
  Streatham SW16 ....21 C4
Nugent Rd Guildford GU2 ..109 B8
  South Norwood SE25 ....42 F6
Numa Ct TW8 ....6 D7
Nunappleton Way RH8 .....123 A3
Nuneaton RG12 ....27 E3
Nuneham SW16 ....21 D3
Nuns Wlk GU25 ....31 D4
Nuptown La SL4 ....8 A8
Nursery Ave CR0 ....43 D1
Nursery Cl Capel RH5 ......178 C5
  Croydon CR0 ....62 D8
  Ewell KT17 ....57 E1
  Feltham TW14 ....15 B8
  Frimley GU16 ....85 F7
  Walton-on-T KT12 ....33 B2
  Woking GU21 ....69 C3
  Woodham KT15 ....51 F1
Nursery Cotts GU21 ....88 F8
Nursery Gdns
  Chilworth GU4 ....131 B3
  Hounslow TW4 ....4 F2
  Staines TW18 ....13 B1
  Sunbury TW16 ....34 F7
Nursery Hill GU5 ....152 D5
Nursery La Hookwood RH6 .160 D2
  North Ascot SL5 ....28 C8
Nursery Rd
  Farncombe GU7 ....150 F7
  Knaphill GU21 ....68 D2
  Merton SW19 ....40 B7
  Mitcham CR4 ....40 E6
  South Norwood CR7, SE25 ..42 D5
  Sunbury TW16 ....34 F7
  Sutton SM1 ....59 C6
  Walton-on-T KT20 ....97 B2
  Wimbledon SW19 ....19 E1
Nurserylands RH11 ....201 A6
Nurston House SW19 ....19 D2
Nutbourne GU9 ....125 E2
Nutbourne Cotts GU8 ....72 F1
Nutbourne Ct TW18 ....12 F1
Nutcombe La Dorking RH4 .135 F7
  Haslemere GU26, GU27 ....188 E1
Nutcroft Gr KT22 ....94 E6
Nutfield CR8 ....80 C8
Nutfield Church Prim Sch
  RH1 ....140 F8
Nutfield Ct SM5 ....59 E7
Nutfield Ct Camberley GU15 ..65 D7
Nutfield Rd RH1 ....119 F2
Nutfield Marsh Rd RH1 ....119 E4
Nutfield Rd Coulsdon CR5 ...79 A3
  Merton SW19 ....19 C5
  Nutfield RH1 ....119 C1
  Redhill RH1 ....119 C1
  Thornton Heath CR7 ....42 B5
Nutfield Sta RH1 ....140 E7
Nutfield Way KT19 ....57 C4
Nuthatch Gdns RH2 ....139 C5
Nuthatch Way RH12 ....217 D7
Nuthurst RG12 ....27 E4
Nuthurst Ave
  Cranleigh GU6 ....174 E3
  Streatham SW2 ....21 A6
Nuthurst Cl RH11 ....201 A7
Nutley RG12 ....27 A1
Nutley Ct RH1 ....118 A1
Nutley La RH2 ....117 F2
Nutmeg Ct GU14 ....84 C5
Nutshell La GU9 ....125 C6
Nutty La TW17 ....34 C6
Nutwell St SW17 ....20 E3
Nutwood GU7 ....150 D6
Nutwood Ave RH3 ....137 C8
Nutwood Cl RH3 ....137 C8
Nyefield Pk KT20 ....97 A1
Nylands Ave TW9 ....7 A5
Nymans Cl RH12 ....217 F6
Nymans Ct RH10 ....202 B3
Nymans Gdns SW20 ....39 B6
Nyon Gr SE23, SE6 ....23 F6

O

O'Connor Rd GU11 ....105 E7
Oak Ave Croydon CR0 ....63 B8
  Egham TW20 ....12 D1
  Hampton TW12, TW13 ......15 E2
  Heston TW5 ....4 E7
  Sandhurst GU47 ....45 D1
Oak Bank CR0 ....63 C4
Oak Cl Box Hill KT20 ....116 B5
  Chiddingfold GU8 ....191 A4
  Copthorne RH10 ....183 A3
  Farncombe GU7 ....150 D6
  Oak Cnr RH5 ....157 C4
Oak Cottage Cl Catford SE6 24 F7
  Wood St V GU3 ....108 C2
Oak Cotts GU27 ....207 E6
Oak Croft RH19 ....206 A8
Oak Ct Crawley RH10 ....181 D2
Oak Dr KT20 ....116 B5
Oak Dell RH10 ....202 E2
Oak End KT15 ....52 D6
Oak End Way KT15 ....70 F7

Oak Farm Cl GU17 ....64 C5
Oak Farm Com Sch GU17 ..64 C5
Oak Gdns CR0 ....63 B8
Oak Glade KT19 ....76 B8
Oak Gr Cranleigh GU6 ....174 F1
  Loxwood RH14 ....213 E4
  Sunbury TW16 ....15 A1
  West Wickham BR4 ....44 A1
Oak Grange Rd GU4 ....111 C5
Oak Grove Cres GU15 ....64 F4
Oak Grove Rd SE20 ....43 C8
Oak Hill Epsom KT18 ....76 E5
  Guildford GU4 ....110 C3
  Surbiton KT6 ....37 F2
  Wood St V GU3 ....108 B3
Oak Hill Cres KT6 ....37 F2
Oak Hill Gr KT6 ....37 F3
Oak Hill Rd KT6 ....37 F2
Oak House SE20 ....43 B8
Oak La
  Broadbridge Heath RH12 ..216 D3
  Englefield Green TW20 ......11 C3
  Isleworth TW7 ....5 E3
  Twickenham TW1 ....17 A7
  Woking GU22 ....70 A1
Oak Leaf Cl KT19 ....76 B8
Oak Lodge
  ☑ Charlton TW16 ....14 F1
  Crowthorne RG45 ....45 C5
Oak Lodge Cl KT12 ....54 C5
Oak Lodge Dr
  Salfords RH1 ....140 A1
  West Wickham BR4 ....44 A1
Oak Lodge Prim Sch BR4 ..44 A1
Oak Lodge Sch SW12 ....21 C7
Oak Mead GU7 ....150 D7
Oak Park Gdns SW19 ....19 D7
Oak Pk KT14 ....70 D6
Oak Rd Caterham CR3 ......100 D4
  Cobham KT11 ....73 C6
  Crawley RH11 ....201 D6
  Farnborough GU14 ....85 B5
  Kingston u T KT3 ....38 D6
  Leatherhead KT22 ....95 B5
  Reigate RH2 ....118 A3
Oak Ridge RH4 ....136 A5
Oak Row CR4 ....41 D8
Oak Tree Cl
  Aldershot GU12 ....126 D8
  Ash Vale GU12 ....85 F3
  Guildford, Burpham GU4 ..110 C4
  Guildford, Jacobswell GU4 ..109 D6
  Knaphill GU21 ....68 D1
  Wentworth GU25 ....30 E4
Oak Tree Dr
  Englefield Green TW20 ......11 C3
  Guildford GU1 ....109 D5
Oak Tree La GU27 ....207 E8
Oak Tree Rd Knaphill GU21 ..68 D1
  Milford GU8 ....149 E2
Oak Tree View GU9 ....125 E4
Oak Tree Way RH13 ....217 F6
Oak Way Ashstead KT21 ....75 D1
  Crawley RH10 ....201 F3
  Croydon CR0 ....43 D3
  East Bedfont TW14 ....14 E7
  Reigate RH2 ....139 C7
Oak Wlk RH12 ....195 E3
Oak's Rd GU21 ....69 E3
Oakapple Cl Crawley RH11 .201 A1
  Hamsey Green CR2 ....81 A5
Oakbank Fetcham KT22 .....94 A4
  Woking GU22 ....89 E5
Oakbank Ave KT12 ....35 F2
Oakbrook BR3 ....44 B8
Oakcombe Cl KT3 ....38 E8
Oakcroft Bsns Ctr KT9 ......56 F6
Oakcroft Cl KT14 ....70 E6
Oakcroft House [3] KT3 ......38 E8
Oakcroft Rd
  Chessington KT9 ....56 F6
  Pyrford KT14 ....70 E6
Oakcroft Villas KT9 ....56 F6
Oakdale RG12 ....27 E4
Oakdale Rd Epsom KT19 ....57 E1
  Streatham SW16 ....21 E3
  Weybridge KT13 ....53 A7
Oakdale Way CR4 ....40 F2
Oakdene Chobham GU24 ....49 B8
  Kingswood KT20 ....97 F4
  Sunningdale SL5 ....29 F2
  ☑ West Norwood SE19 ....22 E2
Oakdene Ave KT7 ....37 A1
  Great Bookham KT23 ....114 A8
Oakdene Cl KT23 ....114 A8
Oakdene Ct KT5 ....38 B2
Oakdene Lodge SE20 ....23 A1
Oakdene Mews SM3 ....39 F1
Oakdene Par KT11 ....73 A5
Oakdene Rd
  Brockham RH3 ....137 B5
  Cobham KT11 ....73 C6
  Great Bookham KT23 ....114 A8
  Little Bookham KT23 ....94 A3
  Redhill RH1 ....119 A3
  Shalford GU3 ....130 C1
Oaken Coppice KT21 ....96 A8
Oaken Copse GU15 ....66 C7
Oaken Copse Cres GU14 ....85 A7
Oaken Dr KT10 ....55 F3
Oaken La KT10 ....55 E5
Oakengates RG12 ....27 A1
Oakenshaw Cl KT6 ....37 E2
Oakfield Plaistow RH14 ....211 D1
  Woking GU21 ....68 F3
Oakfield Cl New Malden KT3 ..38 F4

akfield Cl continued
Weybridge KT13 .....53 C6
akfield Cl Crawley RH11 .....
akfield Ct RG4 .....61 C4
Wokingham RG41 .....25 A5
akfield City Jun Sch
T22 .....94 D4
akfield Dr RH2 .....118 B3
akfield Gdns
Beckenham BR3 .....44 A4
Carshalton SM5 .....40 F1
8 Dulwich SE19 .....22 D3
akfield Glade KT13 .....53 C6
akfield Rd Ashford TW15 .....14 B3
snstead KT21 .....75 E1
Blackwater GU17 .....64 F3
Cobham KT11 .....73 B5
...enge SE20 .....23 B1
hornton Heath CR0 .....42 A1
...imble SW19 .....19 D5
akfield Sch Dulwich SE21 .....22 D7
ayrford GU22 .....70 F4
akfield Way RH19 .....185 F3
akfields Camberley GU15 .....65 B5
...rawley RH10 .....202 D7
uildford GU3 .....108 F3
Vallis Wood RH5 .....196 D8
Valton-on-T KT12 .....35 A1
/est Byfleet KT14 .....71 B5
khall Cl TW16 .....14 F3
khall Dr TW16 .....14 F3
kham Cl SE6 .....23 F6
kham Dr BR2 .....44 F5
khaven RH10, RH11 .....201 D4
khill Cl KT21 .....75 C1
khill Ct 8 Surbiton KT6 .....37 D3
...imbledon SW19 .....19 D1
khill Gdns KT13 .....53 E8
khill Lodge CR8 .....80 A6
khill Rd Addlestone KT15 .....51 F4
snstead KT21 .....75 C1
eckenham BR3 .....44 C7
eadley Down GU35 .....187 B5
orsham RH13 .....217 E2
enge RH12 .....139 B8
shan SM1 .....59 C7
hornton Heath SW16 .....41 F8
khurst Cobham GU24 .....49 E2
ayshott GU26 .....188 D3
khurst Cl 8 TW11 .....16 E3
khurst Gdns RH19 .....185 C2
khurst Grange Sch
.....100 D1
khurst La RH14 .....212 E7
khurst Rd RH17 .....57 D4
khurst Rise SM5 .....59 E1
khurst Way 8 KT1 .....38 A7
kington Dr TW16 .....35 C7
kland Ave GU19 .....125 E7
kland Way KT19 .....57 E4
klands Croydon CR0 .....61 B5
tcham KT22 .....94 D3
...eslemere GU27 .....208 C7
asley RH6 .....161 C3
...rsham RH13 .....217 E2
klands Cl Ewell KT19 .....57 E3
klands Gdns 80 C5
...ith Godstone RH9 .....142 E5
ames Ditton KT10 .....36 D1
ornton Heath CR7 .....42 A5
est Wickham BR4 .....63 B7
klands Cl
...essington KT9 .....56 C6
klands Rd Ascot SL5 .....8 F1
uilford GU4 .....130 E1
klands Ct KT15 .....52 B7
klands Cty Jun Sch
45 .....45 A6
klands Dr North Ascot SL5 .....8 F1
dhill RH1 .....140 B7
...ingham RG41 .....25 A5
klands Gdns CR8 .....80 C5
klands Inf Sch
...gin Hill TN16 .....83 C3
...imble RG45 .....45 A6
klands La
...gin Hill TN16 .....83 C5
...imble RG45 .....45 B7
klands Pk RG41 .....24 E1
klands Rd Bromley BR1 .....24 E1
...imble SW14 .....7 D4
klands Sch TW3 .....5 D4
klands Way
...allington SM6 .....97 C5
...ilington SM6 .....60 D3
...lands Rd Ashstead KT22 .....74 E2
...berhead KT22 .....74 E2
...ea GU12 .....106 A5
...ea Ct CR2 .....61 D2
eigh Epsom KT18 .....76 E5
atwater GU18 .....67 C8
eigh Ave KT6 .....57 B8
teigh Ct Oxted RH8 .....122 E6
...ge SE20 .....23 B1
eigh Rd RH12 .....217 F4
eigh Way Mitcham CR4 .....41 B8
Tolworth KT6 .....38 B1
...ey Ave CR0 .....60 E6
...ey Cl Addlestone KT15 .....52 B6
st Grinstead RH19 .....206 B7
...nslow TW7 .....5 D6
...ey Cotts RH19 .....206 C7
...ey Ct
shalton CR4 .....41 A2
Redhill RH1 .....119 A2
...ey Dell GU4 .....110 C3
...ey Gdns SM7 .....78 B4

Oakley House GU7 .....150 E8
Oakley Rd Camberley GU15 .....65 B4
Croydon SE25 .....43 B6
Whytleafe CR6 .....81 B5
Oakman House 20 SW19 .....19 D7
Oakmead Gn KT18 .....76 C4
Oakmead Pl CR4 .....40 E8
Oakmead Rd
Upper Tooting SW12 .....21 B7
Wallington CR0 .....41 D3
Oakridge GU4 .....67 F6
Oakridge La BR1 .....24 D3
Oakridge Rd BR1 .....24 D3
Oaks Ave Feltham TW13 .....15 E6
North Cheam KT4 .....58 B6
West Norwood SE19, SE27 .....22 E3
Oaks Cl Horsham RH13 .....218 B6
Leatherhead KT22 .....95 A6
Oaks Ct KT22 .....95 A6
Oaks La South Croydon CR0 .....62 C7
South Holmwood RH5 .....157 B8
Oaks Pk Purley CR8 .....80 B5
Reigate RH2 .....118 D2
South Croydon CR0 .....62 C6
Oaks Sports Ctr SM5 .....78 F8
Oaks The Bracknell RG12 .....27 D7
Dorking RH4 .....136 B4
East Grinstead RH19 .....206 B8
Epsom KT18 .....76 F5
Farnborough GU14 .....84 D3
Staines TW18 .....12 F4
West Byfleet KT14 .....71 A5
Wimbledon SW19 .....19 E2
Oaks Track SM5, SM6 .....60 B1
Oaks Way Burgh Heath KT18 .....97 B8
Long Ditton KT6 .....37 D1
Purley CR8 .....80 C5
Wallington SM5 .....59 F3
Oaksford Ave SE26 .....23 B5
Oakshade Rd Catford BR1 .....24 D4
Oxshott KT22 .....74 C5
Oakshaw RH8 .....122 D8
Oakshaw Rd SW18 .....20 B8
Oakside Ct RH6 .....161 C4
Oakside La RH6 .....161 C4
Oaktree Way GU47 .....45 A1
Oaktrees Ash GU12 .....105 F1
Hale GU9 .....125 B6
Oakview RH8 .....122 D8
Oakview Gr CR0 .....43 E1
Oakview Rd SE6 .....24 B8
Oakway Aldershot GU12 .....126 E8
Beckenham BR2 .....44 D7
Knaphill GU21 .....88 E8
West Barnes SW20 .....39 C5
Oakway Dr GU16 .....85 D1
Oakwood Guildford GU2 .....109 A6
Wallington SM6 .....60 B2
Oakwood Ave
Beckenham BR2, BR3 .....44 C7
Mitcham CR4 .....40 D7
Purley CR8 .....80 C7
Oakwood Cl
East Horsley KT24 .....112 E8
Redhill RH1 .....119 A1
South Nutfield RH1 .....140 F7
Oakwood Ct
Beckenham BR3 .....44 C7
Bisley GU24 .....68 A3
Oakwood Dr
East Horsley KT24 .....112 E8
West Norwood SE19 .....22 E2
Oakwood Gdns
Knaphill GU21 .....68 B1
Sutton SM1 .....59 A8
Oakwood Ind Pk RH1 .....182 A2
Oakwood Independent Sch
CR8 .....80 C7
Oakwood Pk RH18 .....206 F2
Oakwood Pl CR0 .....42 A3
Oakwood Rd
Bletchingley RH1 .....120 A6
Bracknell RG12 .....27 E7
Horley RH6 .....161 B4
Knaphill GU21 .....88 E8
Thornton Heath CR0, CR7 .....42 A3
Thorpe GU25 .....31 C4
Wimbledon SW20 .....39 A8
Windlesham GU20 .....48 E4
Oakwood Rise CR3 .....100 E2
Oakwood Sch CR3 .....100 E3
Oareborough RG12 .....27 E5
Oast House Cl TW19 .....11 E8
Oast House Cres GU9 .....125 D6
Oast House La GU9 .....125 D6
Oast La GU11 .....126 B7
Oast Rd RH8 .....122 E5
Oates Cl BR2 .....44 D6
Oates Wlk RH10 .....201 F3
Oatfield Rd KT20 .....97 B6
Oatlands Crawley RH11 .....201 A5
Horley RH6 .....161 C4
Oatlands Ave
Oatlands Park KT13 .....53 E6
Weybridge KT13 .....53 E6
Oatlands Chase KT12, KT13 .....53 E7
Oatlands Cl KT13 .....53 D6
Oatlands Ct 8 SW19 .....19 D7
Oatlands Cty Inf Sch KT13 .....53 D6
Oatlands Dr
Oatlands Park KT13, KT12 .....53 D7
Weybridge KT13 .....53 D7
Oatlands Gn KT13 .....53 D7
Oatlands Mere KT13 .....53 D7
Oatlands Rd KT20 .....97 E8
Oban Rd SE25 .....42 D5
Obelisk Way GU15 .....65 C6

Oberon Way
Crawley RH11 .....200 E3
Littleton TW17 .....33 E6
Obersvel Way GU11 .....126 F2
Observatory Rd SW14 .....7 C3
Observatory Wlk 4 RH1 .....118 F1
Occam Rd GU2 .....129 D8
Ockenden Cl GU22 .....69 F1
Ockenden Gdns GU22 .....69 F1
Ockenden Rd GU22 .....69 F1
Ockfields GU8 .....149 F1
Ockford Ct GU7 .....150 D4
Ockford Dr GU7 .....150 C3
Ockford Rdg GU7 .....150 C3
Ockford Rd GU7 .....150 D4
Ockford Ridge GU7 .....150 B2
Ockham Dr KT24 .....92 D3
Ockham La Downside KT11 .....92 D7
Martyr's Green GU23 .....92 D7
Ockham Rd N GU23 .....92 D7
Ockham Rd N
Ockham GU23 .....92 C3
West Horsley KT24 .....92 C3
Ockham Rd S KT24 .....112 E7
Ockley Ct GU4 .....110 B6
Ockley House 8 KT2 .....18 B2
Ockley Rd Ewhurst GU6 .....175 F6
Forest Green GU6, RH5 .....176 C7
Ockley RH5 .....177 B7
Streatham SW16 .....21 E5
Thornton Heath CR0, CR9 .....41 F2
Wotton GU6, RH5 .....177 C7
Ockley Sta RH5 .....178 A5
Ockleys Mead GU7 .....121 C5
Octagon Rd KT12 .....53 E1
Octavia RG12 .....27 A1
Octavia Cl CR4 .....40 E4
Octavia Rd TW7 .....5 F4
Octavia Way SW16 .....13 A2
October Cl BR2 .....44 F6
Odard Rd KT8 .....36 A5
Odette House 8 SE27 .....22 D4
Odiham Rd
Crondall GU9, GU10 .....124 D7
Heath End GU10, GU9 .....124 D7
Ogden House TW13 .....15 E4
Okeburn Rd SW17 .....21 A3
Okehurst Rd RH14 .....214 C1
Okingham Cl GU47 .....45 D1
Olaf Palme House TW13 .....15 B5
Old Acre KT14 .....71 A5
Old Ave
Sheerwater GU21, KT14 .....70 E6
Weybridge KT13 .....53 C3
Old Avenue Cl KT14 .....70 E6
Old Barn Cl SM2 .....58 E3
Old Barn Dr RH5 .....178 D6
Old Barn La Churt GU10 .....168 A5
Kenley CR3 .....80 F3
Old Barn Rd KT18 .....76 C2
Old Barn View GU7 .....150 C2
Old Bisley Rd GU16 .....66 C3
Old Bracknell Cl RG12 .....27 B6
Old Bracknell La E RG12 .....27 B6
Old Bracknell La W RG12 .....27 B6
Old Bridge St KT1 .....37 D7
Old Brighton Rd RH11 .....181 E5
Old Bromley Rd BR1 .....24 D3
Old Charlton Rd TW17 .....34 C4
Old Chertsey Rd GU24 .....50 C1
Old Chestnut Ave KT10 .....55 B4
Old Church La GU9 .....146 D7
Old Church Path KT10 .....55 B6
Old Claygate La KT10 .....56 A6
Old Common Rd KT11 .....73 B7
Old Compton La GU9 .....125 F2
Old Control Rd RH6 .....181 D6
Old Convent The RH19 .....185 E2
Old Cote Dr TW5 .....5 A8
Old Cotts GU9 .....130 C2
Old Court Rd GU2 .....130 A8
Old Crawley Rd RH12 .....218 C7
Old Cross Tree Way GU12 .....127 B8
Old Ct KT11 .....95 E8
Old Dean Rd GU15 .....65 D7
Old Deer Park Gdns TW9 .....6 E4
Old Denne Rd RH12 .....217 C1
Old Dock Cl TW9 .....7 A8
Old Elstead Rd GU8 .....149 E2
Old Esher Cl KT12 .....54 D5
Old Esher Rd KT12 .....54 D5
Old Farleigh Rd
Chelsham CR0, CR2, CR6 .....81 E6
Selsdon CR0, CR6, CR2 .....81 E6
Old Farm Cl TW4 .....4 F3
Old Farm Pl GU12 .....105 F5
Old Farm Rd
Guildford GU1 .....109 D4
Hampton TW12 .....15 F2
Old Farmhouse Dr KT22 .....74 D4
Old Farnham La
Bentley GU10 .....124 A1
Farnham GU9 .....146 C8
Old Ford House GU10 .....67 F7
Old Forge Cres TW17 .....34 B3
Old Fox Cl CR3 .....100 B6
Old Frensham Rd
Frensham GU10 .....146 E4
Frensham GU10 .....146 E4
Old Green La GU15 .....65 C7
Old Guildford Rd
Mytchett GU12, GU16 .....86 C4
Markham RH12 .....216 E4
Old Haslemere Rd GU27 .....208 C5
Old Heath Way GU9 .....125 C7
Old Hill GU22 .....89 D7
Old Horsham Rd RH11 .....201 B4

Old Hospital Cl
SW12, SW17 .....20 F7
Old House Cl Ewell KT17 .....57 F1
Wimbledon SW19 .....19 E3
Old House Gdns 8 TW1 .....6 C1
Old Kiln GU9 .....125 B2
Old Kiln La GU10 .....167 F2
Old Kiln Court Yd 18 GU9 .....125 B2
Old Kiln La Brockham RH4 .....137 C8
Churt GU10 .....167 F2
Old Kingston Rd KT4 .....57 C7
Old La Aldershot GU11 .....126 A7
Aldershot, North Town GU12 .....105 E3
Dockenfield GU10 .....166 F4
East Horsley KT11 .....93 A5
Martyr's Green KT11 .....92 E2
Ockham GU23, KT11 .....92 B1
Oxted RH8 .....122 F5
Tatsfield TN16 .....103 D6
Old La Trad Est SM1 .....59 A4
Old Lands Hill RG12 .....27 D8
Old Lane Gdns KT11 .....92 B1
Old Lodge Cl GU7 .....150 B3
Old Lodge La CR8 .....80 A3
Old Lodge Pl 7 TW1 .....6 B1
Old London Rd
Epsom KT17, KT18 .....77 A2
Mickleham RH5 .....115 C8
Old Malden La KT4 .....57 E8
Old Malt Way GU21 .....69 D2
Old Manor Cl RH11 .....201 A8
Old Manor Dr TW7 .....5 C1
Old Manor Gdns GU4 .....131 C3
Old Martyrs RH11 .....181 D1
Old Merrow St GU4 .....110 D3
Old Mill La KT17 .....119 B7
Old Mill Pl GU27 .....207 F7
Old Millmeads RH12 .....217 C5
Old Museum Ct GU27 .....208 D6
Old Nursery Rd TW15 .....14 B3
Old Oak Ave CR5 .....98 E8
Old Orch Byfleet KT14 .....71 F7
Sunbury TW16 .....35 B8
Old Orchard The GU9 .....146 A8
Old Palace La TW9 .....6 C2
Old Palace Rd
Croydon CR0 .....61 C7
Guildford GU2 .....130 A8
Weybridge KT13 .....53 B7
Old Palace Sch CR9 .....61 B7
Old Palace Terr 8 TW9 .....6 D2
Old Palace Yd 7 TW9 .....6 D2
Old Park Cl GU9 .....125 A4
Old Park La Farnham GU9 .....125 A4
Hale GU9 .....125 A4
Old Park Mews TW5 .....4 F7
Old Parvis Rd KT14 .....71 C7
Old Pasture Rd GU16 .....65 F3
Old Pharmacy Ct RG45 .....45 C4
Old Pond Ct GU15 .....65 C1
Old Portsmouth Rd
Artington GU2, GU3, GU7 .....130 C3
Frimley GU15 .....66 A5
Shalford GU2, GU3, GU7 .....130 C3
Thursley GU8 .....169 D4
Old Pottery Cl RH2 .....139 B7
Old Quarry The GU27 .....207 F4
Old Rd Addlestone KT15 .....51 F3
Buckland RH3 .....116 F1
East Grinstead RH19 .....185 F1
Old Rectory Cl
Bramley GU5 .....151 F6
Walton on t H KT20 .....97 A3
Old Rectory Dr GU12 .....106 B2
Old Rectory Gdns
Farnborough GU14 .....85 D4
Godalming GU7 .....150 F2
Old Rectory La KT24 .....92 E1
Old Redstone Dr RH1 .....140 A8
Old Reigate Rd
Brockham RH3 .....116 C1
Dorking RH4 .....115 F2
Old Sawmill La RH4 .....45 C6
Old School Cl Ash GU12 .....106 A3
Merton SW19 .....40 A7
Penge BR3 .....43 E7
Old School Ct
Leatherhead KT22 .....95 B5
Wraysbury TW19 .....11 E8
Old School La
Brockham RH3 .....137 A7
Newdigate RH5 .....158 B1
Old School Mews KT13 .....53 D6
Old School Pl
Lingfield RH7 .....164 D4
Woking GU22 .....89 F6
Old School Sq KT7 .....36 F3
Old Schools La KT17 .....57 F2
Old St Mary's KT24 .....112 B6
Old Station App KT22 .....95 A6
Old Station Cl RH10 .....204 B7
Old Station Rd GU7 .....150 E6
Old Surrey Mews The
RH9 .....121 C5
Old Swan Yd SM5 .....59 F6
Old Town CR0 .....61 B7
Old Town Mews GU22 .....125 A2
Old Tye Ave TN16 .....83 E3
Old Westhall Cl CR6 .....101 C8
Old Wickhurst La RH12 .....216 D2
Old Woking Rd
Old Woking GU22 .....90 C8
Pyrford GU22, KT14 .....70 D3
West Byfleet KT14 .....71 A6
Woking GU22 .....90 C8
Old Wokingham Rd
Bracknell RG45 .....45 C7
Crowthorne RG45 .....45 C7

Oldacre GU24 .....67 F7
Oldbury RG12 .....26 F6
Oldbury Cl Frimley GU16 .....85 F8
Horsham RH12 .....218 A7
Oldbury Rd KT16 .....32 E2
Olde Farm Dr GU17 .....64 B5
Olden La CR8 .....80 A7
Oldfield Gdns KT21 .....95 D8
Oldfield House SW16 .....21 E4
Oldfield House SW12 .....35 F8
Oldfield Rd Hampton TW12 .....35 F8
Horley RH6 .....160 F1
Wimbledon SW19 .....19 E2
Oldfields Rd SM1, SM3 .....59 B8
Oldfields Trad Est SM1 .....59 A7
Oldfieldwood GU22 .....70 B2
Oldham House SE21 .....22 E4
Oldhouse La Bisley GU24 .....68 A5
West End GU24 .....48 C1
Windlesham GU18 .....48 C8
Olding House 6 SW12 .....21 C8
Oldridge Rd SW12 .....21 B8
Oldstead RG12 .....27 A1
Oldstead Rd BR1 .....24 D4
Oldwood Chase GU14 .....84 C3
Oleander Cl RG45 .....45 A7
Olive Rd 8 SW19 .....20 C1
Oliver Ave SE25 .....42 E5
Oliver Cl Addlestone KT15 .....52 B6
Brentford W4 .....7 B8
Oliver Gr SE25 .....42 F5
Oliver Rd Ascot SL5 .....29 B5
Horsham RH12 .....217 A1
Kingston u T KT3 .....38 F5
Sutton SM1 .....59 D6
Olivier Rd RH10 .....202 D5
Ollerton RG12 .....27 A1
Olley Cl SM6 .....60 E4
Olveston Wlk SM4, SM5 .....40 D3
Olyffe Dr BR3 .....44 C8
Omega Rd GU21 .....70 A3
Omega Way TW20 .....32 C8
One Tree Cnr GU1 .....131 B8
One Tree Hill Rd GU4 .....131 B7
Ongar Cl KT15 .....52 A4
Ongar Hill KT15 .....52 A4
Ongar Pl KT15 .....52 A4
Ongar Place Inf Sch KT15 .....52 A4
Ongar Rd KT15 .....52 A4
Onslow Ave Belmont SM2 .....77 F8
Richmond TW10 .....6 E2
Onslow Avenue Mansions
TW10 .....6 E2
Onslow Cl
Thames Ditton KT7 .....36 E1
Woking GU22 .....70 A2
Onslow Cres GU22 .....70 A2
Onslow Cty Inf Sch GU2 .....129 F7
Onslow Dr SL5 .....9 A1
Onslow Gdns
Sanderstead CR2 .....81 A7
Thames Ditton KT7 .....36 E1
Wallington SM6 .....60 C3
Onslow House TW18 .....37 F8
Onslow Lodge 8 SW2 .....22 A8
Onslow Mews KT16 .....33 A3
Onslow Rd Guildford GU1 .....109 D1
Hersham KT12 .....54 A5
New Malden KT3 .....39 A5
Richmond TW10 .....6 E2
Sunningdale SL5 .....30 B2
Thornton Heath CR0 .....42 A1
Onslow St GU1 .....130 C8
Onslow Way Pyrford GU22 .....70 F4
Thames Ditton KT7 .....36 E1
Ontario Cl RH6 .....162 A2
Onyx House KT4 .....38 D1
Opal House KT4 .....38 D1
Openview SW17, SW18 .....20 D6
Opladen Way RG12 .....27 E4
Opossum Dr TW4 .....4 C4
Opus Park GU4 .....109 D6
Oracle Ctr RG12 .....27 C7
Orangery The TW10 .....17 C6
Orchard Ave Ashford TW15 .....14 C2
Carshalton CR4 .....41 A1
Croydon CR0 .....43 E1
Hatton TW14 .....3 D2
Heston TW5 .....4 E7
Hinchley Wood KT7 .....56 A8
Kingston u T KT3 .....38 E6
Woodham KT15 .....70 F8
Orchard Bsns Ctr SE26 .....23 F3
Orchard Bsns Ctr The
RH1 .....161 A8
Orchard Cl
Ash Vale GU12 .....106 A5
Ashford TW15 .....14 C2
Ashstead KT21 .....95 D7
Banstead SM7 .....78 B5
East Horsley KT24 .....92 F2
Farnborough GU17 .....64 F1
Farnham GU9 .....126 A6
Fetcham KT22 .....94 D5
Flexford GU3 .....107 B1
Guildford GU1 .....110 B1
Horley RH6 .....160 F1
Leatherhead KT22 .....94 F8
Walton-on-T KT12 .....35 B2
West Barnes SW20 .....39 C5
West End GU24 .....67 B4
West Ewell KT19 .....57 B4
Woking RG40 .....70 B3
Wokingham RG40 .....25 D6

Orchard Cotts
Charlwood RH6 180 F7
Lingfield RH7 165 B3
Orchard Ct Barnes SW13 7 F4
Bracknell RG12 27 C7
Croydon BR3 44 A1
Harmondsworth UB7 2 C7
Hounslow TW7 5 D7
Wallington SM6 60 B5
Walton-on-T KT12 34 F1
Orchard Cty Fst Sch The
KT8 36 D5
Orchard Dene KT14 71 A6
Orchard Dr Sunbury TW17 34 E6
Woking GU21 69 F4
Orchard End
Caterham CR3 100 E5
Fetcham KT22 94 C3
Oatlands Park KT13 53 E8
Rowledge GU10 145 F3
Orchard Gate
Sandhurst GU47 64 B8
Thames Ditton KT10 36 D1
Orchard Gdns
Aldershot GU11 126 C8
Chessington KT9 56 E6
Cranleigh GU6 174 F2
Effingham KT24 113 E7
Epsom KT18 76 C4
Sutton SM1 59 A5
Orchard Gr Croydon CR0 43 E2
Penge SE20 23 A1
Orchard Hill
Rudgwick RH12 214 C7
Windlesham GU20 48 D3
Orchard House
Guildford GU4 110 D2
Tongham GU10 126 F7
Orchard House Cheyne Ctr (Hospl) BR4 63 C7
Orchard Jun & Inf Sch The
TW3 5 A3
Orchard La
Thames Ditton KT8 36 D3
Wimbledon SW20 39 B8
Orchard Lea Cl GU22 70 E4
Orchard Mains GU22 89 C8
Orchard Pl RG40 25 C6
Orchard Rd Brentford TW8 6 C8
Chessington KT9 56 E6
Dorking RH4 136 B6
Farnborough GU14 85 A4
Farnham GU9 126 A6
Guildford, Burpham GU4 110 B5
Guildford, Onslow Village GU2 129 F7
Hampton TW12 15 F1
Hamsey Green CR2 81 B5
Horsham RH13 217 E2
Hounslow TW4 5 A2
Kingston u T KT1 37 E7
Mortlake TW9 7 A4
Reigate RH2 118 B1
Shalford GU4 130 E3
Shere GU5 133 A4
Smallfield RH6 162 C3
Sunbury TW16 15 B1
Sutton SM1 59 A6
Twickenham TW1 6 B2
Orchard Rise Croydon CR0 43 F1
Kingston u T KT2 38 C8
Mortlake TW10 7 B3
Orchard School Sports Ctr
SE20 43 A8
Orchard St
Crawley RH10, RH11 201 D6
Thames Ditton KT7 37 B2
Orchard The Banstead SM7 78 A4
Dorking RH5 136 C3
Ewell KT17 57 F1
Ewell KT17, KT19 57 F3
Haslemere GU27 207 F5
Hounslow TW3 5 C5
Lightwater GU18 67 B8
Thorpe GU25 31 E4
Weybridge KT13 53 B6
Woking GU22 89 E5
Orchard Way
Addlestone KT15 52 B4
Aldershot GU11, GU12 126 C8
Ashford TW15 13 F6
Beckenham BR3, CR0 43 E3
Camberley GU15 65 B2
Carshalton SM1 59 D6
Croydon BR3, CR0 43 E3
Dorking RH4 136 B6
East Grinstead RH19 185 E1
Esher KT10 55 C4
Flexford GU3 107 B1
Lower Kingswood KT20 97 F1
Oxted RH8 123 A2
Reigate RH2 139 B6
Send GU23 90 C2
Orchard Way Prim Sch
CR0 43 E2
Orchardfield Rd GU7 150 F7
Orchardleigh KT22 95 B5
Orchards Cl KT14 71 A5
Orchards The
Ashford TW15 14 D3
[4] Crawley RH11 200 D5
Horsham RH12 217 F5
Orchid Dr GU24 68 A4
Orchid Mead SM7 78 B5
Orde Cl RH10 182 D1
Ordnance Cl TW13 15 A6
Ordnance Rd GU11 105 C3
Ordnance Rdbt GU11 105 B2
Oregano Way GU2 109 A6
Oregon Cl KT3 38 C5
Orestan La KT24 113 C8
Orford Ct Wallington SM6 60 C5
West Norwood SE27 22 B6
Orford Gdns TW1 16 F6
Orford Rd SE6 24 B5
Oriel Cl Crawley RH10 182 C1
Mitcham CR4 41 D6
Oriel Ct [6] CR0 42 D1
Oriel Hill GU15 65 D4
Oriel Jun & Inf Sch TW13 15 E5
Oriental Cl GU22 70 A2
Oriental Rd Ascot SL5 29 D5
Woking GU22 70 A3
Orion RG12 27 A1
Orion Ct RH11 200 D4
Orion Ctr The CR0 60 E8
Orlando Gdns KT19 57 D1
Orlean Ct KT12 54 C8
Orleans Cl KT10 55 D8
Orleans Ct [10] TW1 17 B8
Orleans Inf Sch TW1 17 B8
Orleans Park Sec Sch
TW1 17 B8
Orleans Rd
South Norwood SE19 22 D2
[10] Twickenham TW1 17 C8
Orltons La RH12 179 F2
Ormanton Rd SE26 23 A4
Orme Rd KT1, KT3 38 B7
Ormeley Rd SW12 21 B7
Ormerod Gdns CR4 41 A8
Ormesby Wlk RH10 202 B4
Ormond Ave
Hampton TW12 36 B8
[22] Richmond TW10 6 D2
Ormond Cres TW12 36 B8
Ormond Dr TW12 16 B1
Ormond Rd TW10 6 D2
Ormonde Ave KT19 57 D1
Ormonde Lodge (West London Ins of Higher Education) TW1 6 B2
Ormonde Rd
Farncombe GU7 150 E6
Mortlake SW14 7 C4
Woking GU21 69 C3
Wokingham RG41 25 A5
Ormsby SM2 59 B3
Ormside Way RH1 119 B4
Ormuz Cotts RH7 164 C4
Orpin Rd RH1 119 C5
Orpwood Cl TW12 15 F2
Orwell Cl GU14 84 E6
Orwell Gdns RH2 139 B7
Orwell House [7] RH1 118 F2
Osborn La SE23 23 E8
Osborn Rd GU9 125 D4
Osborne Ave TW19 13 F7
Osborne Cl Beckenham BR3 43 E5
Feltham TW13 15 D3
Frimley GU16 85 F8
Osborne Ct Crawley RH11 201 B2
Farnborough GU14 105 C8
[10] Surbiton KT6 37 E3
Osborne Dr GU18 67 A8
Osborne Gdns CR7 42 C7
Osborne Pl SM1 59 D5
Osborne Rd Egham TW20 11 F2
Farnborough GU14 105 C8
Hounslow TW3, TW4 4 F4
Kingston u T KT2 17 E1
Redhill RH1 119 A4
South Norwood CR7 42 C7
Walton-on-T KT12 35 A1
Wokingham RG40 25 C6
Osbourne Terr [1] SW17 21 A3
Osier Pl TW20 12 C2
Osier Way
Banstead KT17, SM7 77 E5
Mitcham CR4 40 F4
Oslac Rd SE6 24 B3
Oslo Ct SW19 20 D1
Osman's Cl RG42 8 B1
Osmond Gdns SM6 60 C5
Osmund Cl RH10 202 E6
Osnaburgh Bank RH19 185 E6
Osnaburgh Hill GU15 65 B5
Osney Cl RH11 201 C5
Osney Wlk SM4, SM5 40 D3
Osprey Cl Cheam SM1 58 F5
Fetcham KT22 94 C5
Osprey Gdns CR0, CR2 62 E1
Ospringe Cl [9] SE20 23 C1
Ostade Rd SW2 21 F8
Osterley Ave TW7 5 D7
Osterley Cl RG40 25 F5
Osterley Cres TW7 5 F6
Osterley Ct TW7 5 D6
Osterley Lodge [1] TW7 5 E6
Osterley Rd TW7 5 E6
Osterley Sta TW7 5 D7
Osterly Gdns CR7 42 C7
Oswald Cl KT22 94 C5
Oswald Rd KT22 94 C5
Osward CR0 62 F1
Osward Rd SW12, SW17 20 F6
Otford Cl SE20 43 C8
Othello Gr RG42 27 E8
Otho Ct [5] TW8 6 D7
Otter Cl Crowthorne RG45 45 A7
Ottershaw KT16 51 B4
Otter Mdw KT22 94 F8
Otterbourne Pl RH19 185 B1
Otterbourne Rd [1]
CR0, CR9 61 C8
Otterburn Gdns TW7 6 A7
Otterburn St SW17 20 F2
Otterden St SE6 24 A4
Ottermead La KT16 51 C4
Ottershaw House CR4 40 D7
Ottershaw Pk KT16 51 A3
Ottways Ave KT21 95 D8
Ottways La KT21, KT22 95 D8
Otway Cl RH11 200 F4
Oulton Wlk RH10 202 B4
Our Lady of the Rosary RC Sch TW18 13 A2
Our Lady Queen of Heaven RC Prim Sch SW19 19 D8
Our Lady Queen Of Heaven RC Sch RH11 201 B8
Our Lady & St Philip Neri Prim Sch SE26 23 E4
Our Lady & St Philip Neri RC Sch Forest Hill SE23 23 D5
Forest Hill SE26 23 E4
Our Lady's Prep Sch RG45 45 B5
Our Ladys RC First Sch
KT16 33 A1
Ouseley Rd
Upper Tooting SW12 20 F7
Wraysbury TW19 11 D8
Outdowns KT24 113 B5
Outram Pl KT13 53 C5
Outram Rd CR0 61 F8
Outwood House [6] SW2 21 F8
Outwood La
Bletchingley RH1 141 D7
Chipstead CR5, KT20 98 C6
Kingswood CR5, KT20 98 C6
Outwood RH1 141 D1
Oval Prim Sch CR0 42 E1
Oval Rd CR0 42 E1
Oval The Banstead SM7 78 A5
Farncombe GU7 150 F7
Guildford GU2 130 A8
Wood St V GU3 108 B2
Overbrae BR3 24 A3
Overbrook Godalming GU7 151 A5
West Horsley KT24 112 B6
Overbury Ave BR3 44 C6
Overbury Cres CR0 63 C1
Overbury Ct BR3 44 C6
Overdale Ashstead KT21 75 E3
Bletchingley RH1 120 C2
Dorking RH5 136 D8
Overdale Ave KT3 38 D7
Overdale Rise GU16 65 E3
Overdene Dr RH11 201 A6
Overdown Rd SE6 24 B4
Overford Cl GU6 174 E2
Overford Dr GU6 174 E2
Overhill CR6 101 C8
Overhill Rd
Dulwich SE21, SE22 23 A8
Wallington CR8 61 A1
Overhill Way BR3 44 D4
Overlord Cl GU15 65 C8
Overstand Cl BR3 44 A4
Overstone Gdns CR0 43 F2
Overthorpe Cl GU21 68 E2
Overton Cl Aldershot GU11 126 C6
Hounslow TW7 5 F6
Overton House SW15 18 F8
Overton Rd SM2 59 A3
Overton Shaw RH19 185 E4
Overton's Yd CR0, CR9 61 C7
Oveton Way KT23 94 B1
Ovett Cl SE19 22 E2
Ovington Ct GU21 68 F3
Owen Cl CR0 42 D3
Owen House Feltham TW14 15 A8
[6] Twickenham TW1 17 B8
Owen Pl KT22 95 B5
Owen Rd Farncombe GU7 150 F6
Windlesham GU20 48 D5
Owen Wlk [7] SE20 23 A1
Owens Way SE23 23 E8
Owl Cl CR2 62 D1
Owlbeech Ct RH13 218 B4
Owlbeech Pl RH13 218 B4
Owlbeech Way RH13 218 B4
Owletts RH10 202 D7
Owlscastle Cl RH12 217 D5
Owlsmoor Cty Prim Sch
GU47 45 E1
Owlsmoor Rd GU47 45 D1
Ownstead Gdns CR2 80 F8
Ownsted Hill CR0 63 D1
Oxdowne Cl KT11 74 B5
Oxenden Ct GU10 126 E8
Oxenden Rd GU10, GU12 126 F8
Oxenhope RG12 27 A5
Oxford Ave Harlington TW6 3 F7
Merton SW20 39 E7
Oxford Cl
Littleton TW15, TW17 14 C1
Mitcham CR4 41 C6
Oxford Cres KT3 38 D3
Oxford Ct Epsom KT18 76 E5
[17] Kingston u T KT6 37 E4
Oxford Gdns W4 7 A8
Oxford Rd
Carshalton SM2, SM5 59 E5
Crawley RH10 201 F2
Farnborough GU14 85 C1
Guildford GU1 130 D7
Horsham RH13 217 E2
Redhill RH1 118 E2
Sandhurst GU47 45 E2
South Norwood SE19 22 D2
Oxford Rd continued
Teddington TW11, TW12 16 D3
Wallington SM6 60 C5
Wokingham RG41 25 A6
Oxford Terr GU1 130 D7
Oxford Way TW13 15 D4
Oxleigh Cl KT3 38 E4
Oxlip Cl CR0 43 D1
Oxshott Rd Ashstead KT22 74 F3
Leatherhead KT22 75 A2
Oxshott Rise KT11 73 E5
Oxshott Sta KT22 74 C6
Oxshott Way KT11 73 E4
Oxted Cl CR4 40 D6
Oxted Cty Sch RH8 122 F7
Oxted Gn GU8 170 E7
Oxted Hospl RH8 122 D7
Oxted Rd Tandridge RH9 121 D4
Tyler's Green RH9 121 D4
Oxted Sta RH8 122 E6
Oxtoby Way SW16 41 D8
Oyster La KT14 71 E7

P

Pacific Cl TW14 14 F7
Packer Cl RH19 186 A3
Packham Ct KT4 58 C7
Packway GU9 146 E7
Padbrook RH8 123 A6
Padbury Cl TW14 14 D7
Padbury Oaks UB7 2 B6
Paddock Cl
Beare Green RH5 157 D4
Camberley GU15 66 A6
Cobham KT11 73 C5
Forest Hill SE26 23 D4
Hambledon GU8 171 C1
Lingfield RH7 164 C4
New Malden KT4 38 E1
Oxted RH8 122 F4
Paddock Ct SW20 39 C5
Paddock Gdns
East Grinstead RH19 205 E7
South Norwood SE19 22 E2
Paddock Gr RH5 157 D4
Paddock House GU4 110 D2
Paddock Sch SW15 7 F3
Paddock The
Addington CR0 63 A4
Bracknell RG12 27 C6
Cranleigh GU6 174 D3
Crawley RH10 202 D7
Crowthorne RG45 45 A6
Ewhurst GU6 175 E4
Godalming GU7 150 F3
Grayshott GU26 188 A4
Guildford GU1 110 D2
Haslemere GU27 208 A8
Westcott RH4 135 C6
Paddock Way
Grayswood GU27 190 A2
Oxted RH8 122 F4
Sheerwater GU21 70 B5
Paddock Wlk CR6 101 B8
Paddockhurst Rd
Crawley RH11 201 A5
Crawley RH10 203 C2
Paddocks Cl KT21 75 E1
Paddocks Mead GU21 68 F3
Paddocks Rd GU4 110 A5
Paddocks The
Flexford GU3 107 C1
Great Bookham KT23 94 B1
Oatlands Park KT13 53 E7
Woodham KT15 52 B1
Paddocks Way
Ashstead KT21 75 E1
Chertsey KT16 33 B1
Padstow Wlk
Crawley RH11 200 F4
East Bedfont TW14 14 F7
Padua Rd SE20 43 C8
Padwick Rd RH13 218 A2
Page Cl TW12 15 E2
Page Cres CR0 61 B5
Page Croft KT15 52 B8
Page Ct RH13 217 D1
Page Rd TW14 3 D1
Page's Croft RG40 25 D5
Page's Yd W4 7 E8
Pageant Wlk CR0 61 E7
Pagehurst Rd CR0 43 B2
Paget Ave SM1 59 D7
Paget Cl Camberley GU15 66 B7
Hampton TW12 16 D4
Paget La TW7 5 E4
Paget Pl Kingston u T KT2 18 C2
Thames Ditton KT7 36 F1
Pagewood Cl RH10 202 D4
Pagoda Ave TW9 6 F4
Paice Gn RG40 25 D7
Pain's Cl CR4 41 B7
Paines Hill RH8 123 C4
Paisley Rd SM5 40 D1
Pakenham Cl SW12 21 A7
Pakenham Rd RG12 27 D2
Palace Ct
South Norwood CR7 42 D5
Streatham SW2 22 A6
Woking GU21 70 A3
Palace Dr KT13 53 B7
Palace Gn CR0 62 F3
Palace Gr SE19 22 F1
Palace Rd East Molesey KT8 36 D6
Kingston u T KT1 37 D5
Penge SE19 22 F1
Palace Rd continued
Streatham SE27, SW16, SW2 2…
Woodham KT15 5…
Palace Sq SE19 2…
Palace View CR0 6…
Palestine Gr SW19 4…
Palewell Common Dr SW14 …
Palewell Pk SW14 …
Palgrave House [4] TW2 1…
Pallingham Dr RH10 20…
Palm Ct BR3 4…
Palm Gr GU1 10…
Palmer Ave KT4, SM3 5…
Palmer C of E Jun Sch The
RG40 2…
Palmer Cl Crowthorne RG45 4…
Heston TW5 …
Horley RH6 16…
Redhill RH1 14…
West Wickham BR4 6…
Palmer Cres
Kingston u T KT1 3…
Ottershaw KT16 5…
Palmer Rd RH10 20…
Palmer School Rd RG40 2…
Palmer's Lodge GU2 13…
Palmers Gr KT8 3…
Palmers Rd Mortlake SW14 …
Thornton Heath SW16 4…
Palmersfield Rd SM7 7…
Palmerston Cl
Farnborough GU14 8…
Woking GU21 7…
Palmerston Ct [9] KT6 3…
Palmerston Gr [4] SW19 2…
Palmerston House SM7 7…
Palmerston Rd
Carshalton SM5 6…
Hounslow TW3 …
Merton SW19 2…
Mortlake SW14 …
Sutton SM1 5…
Thornton Heath CR0 4…
Twickenham TW2 …
Pampisford Rd
Croydon CR2, CR8 6…
Purley CR2, CR8 6…
Pams Way KT19 5…
Pan's Gdns GU15 6…
Pandora Ct [4] KT6 3…
Pangbourne Ct SW17 2…
Pankhurst Cl TW7 …
Pankhurst Ct [11] RH11 20…
Pankhurst Dr RG12 2…
Pankhurst Rd KT12 3…
Panmuir Rd SW20 3…
Panmure Rd SE26 2…
Pannell Cl RH19 18…
Pannells GU10 14…
Pannells Cl KT16 3…
Pannells Ct GU1 13…
Pantile Rd KT13 5…
Pantiles Cl GU21 6…
Paper Mews RH4 13…
Papercourt La GU23 9…
Papplewick Sch SL5 2…
Papworth Way SW2 2…
Parade Cl GU23 9…
Parade Mews SE27, SW2 2…
Parade The Ash GU12 10…
Ashford TW16 1…
Burgh Heath KT20 9…
Claygate KT10 5…
Coulsdon CR5 8…
Epsom KT18 7…
[2] Kingston u T KT2 3…
Wallington CR0 6…
Wentworth GU25 3…
Paradise Rd TW10 …
Paragon Gr KT5 3…
Parbury Rise KT9 5…
Parchmore Rd CR7 4…
Parchmore Way CR7 4…
Pares Cl GU21 6…
Parfew Ct SE22 2…
Parfitts Cl GU9 12…
Parfour Dr CR8 8…
Parham Rd RH11 20…
Parish Church C of E Inf & Jun Schs CR9 6…
Parish Cl Ash GU12 10…
Hale GU9 12…
Parish Ct KT6 3…
Parish House [6] RH11 20…
Parish La SE20, SE26 2…
Parish Rd GU14 10…
Park Ave Bromley BR1 2…
Camberley GU15 6…
Caterham CR3 10…
Egham TW20 1…
Isleworth TW3 …
Mitcham CR4 2…
Mortlake SW14 …
Peper Harow GU8 14…
Salfords RH1 13…
Staines TW18 1…
Upper Halliford TW17 3…
Wallington SM5 6…
West Wickham BR4 6…
Wokingham RG40 2…
Park Ave E KT17 5…
Park Ave W KT17 5…
Park Avenue Mews CR4 2…
Park Barn Dr GU2, GU3 10…
Park Barn E GU2 10…
Park Chase
Godalming GU7 15…
Guildford GU1 10…

rk Cl Binstead GU10 145 A2
rockham RH3 137 B4
sher KT10 55 A4
etcham KT22 94 D3
rayswood GU27 190 A1
ampton TW12 36 C8
sleworth TW3, TW7 5 C2
ingston u T KT2 38 A8
atlands Park KT13 53 F8
Vallington SM5 59 F4
Voodham KT15 52 C1
rk Close Cotts TW20 10 F3
rk Copse RH5 136 D7
rk Corner Dr KT24 112 E7
rk Cotts 10 TW1 6 B1
rk Cres Sunningdale SL5 29 F3
wickenham TW2 16 D7
rk Ct Beckenham BR3 44 B6
arnham GU9 125 D3
lew Malden KT3 38 D5
eddington KT1 37 C8
pper Tooting SW12 21 A7
Vallington SM6 60 E5
Vest Norwood SE21 22 D5
Voking GU22 69 F1
rk Dr Bramley GU5 151 F6
ranleigh GU6 174 F3
Aortlake SW14 7 D3
unningdale SL5 29 F3
Veybridge KT13 53 B5
Voking GU22 69 F1
rk End BR1 44 F8
rk Farm Cl RH12 217 D7
rk Farm Ind Est GU15 65 C1
rk Farm Rd
lorsham RH12 217 D7
ingston u T KT2 17 E1
rk Gate Cotts GU6 174 C3
rk Gate Ct
eddington TW12 16 C3
1 Woking GU22 69 E1
rk Gdns KT2 17 F3
rk Gn KT23 94 A3
rk Hall Rd Dulwich SE21 22 D5
eigate RH2 118 A3
Vest Norwood SE21 22 D5
rk Hall Road Trad Est
E21 22 D5
rk Hill Forest Hill SE23 23 C7
ichmond TW10 6 F1
Vallington SM5 59 F4
rk Hill Cl SM5 59 E5
rk Hill Ct
outh Croydon CR0 61 E8
pper Tooting SW17 20 F5
rk Hill Inf Sch CR0 61 E7
rk Hill Jun Sch CR0 61 E7
rk Hill Rd
eckenham BR2 44 E7
well KT17 76 F8
outh Croydon CR0, CR2 61 E7
Vallington SM6 60 B3
rk Hill Rise CR0 61 F7
rk Hill Sch KT2 18 A1
rk Ho 8 GU11 105 A1
rk Horsley KT24 113 A6
rk House Penge SE26 23 A3
eigate RH2 138 F7
rk House Cotts GU6 174 F3
rk House Dr RH2 138 F7
rk House Gdns TW1 6 C2
rk House Mid Sch
W19 19 F4
rk La Ashstead KT21 96 A8
shurst Wood RH19 206 D6
rook GU8 190 A8
amberley GU15 65 C5
heam SM3 58 E4
ranford TW5 4 A7
roydon CR0, CR9 61 D7
uildford GU4 110 D3
ooley CR5 99 D6
orton SL3 1 A4
ingfield RH7 164 F5
ckley RH5 177 F7
eigate RH2 138 E8
ichmond TW9 6 D3
eddington TW11 16 F2
Vallington SM5, SM6 60 A5
Vinkfield SL4 9 B7
rk La E RH2 139 A7
rk Lawn CR7 42 C7
rk Lawn Rd KT13 53 C6
rk Ley Rd CR3 101 D6
rk Mansions SE26 23 C5
rk Mead Cty Inf Sch
U6 175 A3
rk Mead Jun Sch GU6 175 A3
rk Mews TW19 13 F8
rk Pl Hampton TW12 16 C2
lorsham RH12 217 C1
3 Woking GU22 69 F1
rk Prim Sch GU11 126 C7
rk Rd Albury GU5 132 E2
ldershot GU11 126 B8
shford TW15 14 B3
shstead KT21 75 E1
anstead SM7 78 C3
eckenham BR3 23 F1
racknell RG12 27 D8
urstow RH6 162 C1
amberley GU15 65 C4
aterham CR3 100 E4
heam SM3 58 E4
hiswick W4 7 D8
rowhurst RH7 143 E2
ormans Park RH19 185 F6
ast Grinstead RH19 185 D1

Park Rd *continued*
East Molesey KT8 36 C5
Egham TW20 12 A4
Esher KT10 55 B6
Farnborough GU11, GU14 105 E8
Farnham GU9 125 D4
Faygate RH12 199 F1
Feltham TW13 15 D4
Fickleshole CR6 82 E5
Forest Row RH18 206 F2
Godalming GU7 150 E2
Guildford GU1 109 D1
Hackbridge SM6 60 B8
Hampton TW12 16 C3
Haslemere GU27 208 C5
Isleworth TW3, TW7 5 C2
Isleworth TW7 6 B5
Kenley CR8 80 C4
Kingston u T KT2, TW10 18 A1
Limpsfield RH8 122 F7
Lower Halliford TW17 34 A1
Mitcham SW19 20 E2
New Malden KT3 38 D5
Redhill RH1 118 F3
Richmond TW10 6 F1
Sandhurst GU47 64 C8
Slinfold RH13 215 D3
South Norwood SE25 42 E5
Stanwell TW19 2 C1
Sunbury TW16 15 B1
Surbiton KT5 37 C8
Teddington TW11 16 F2
Teddington, Hampton
Wick KT1 37 C8
Twickenham TW1 6 C1
Wallington SM6 60 B5
Woking GU22 70 A2
Wokingham RG40 25 B6
Woodmansterne CR5,
KT20, SM7 78 C3
Park Rise Forest Hill SE23 23 E7
Horsham RH12 217 B4
Leatherhead KT22 95 B6
Park Rise Cl KT22 95 B6
Park Rise Rd SE23 23 E7
Park Road House 3 KT2 18 A1
Park Row GU9 125 B3
Park Sch The GU22 70 A2
Park Sheen SW14 7 B3
Park Side KT15 52 C1
Park Sq 1 KT10 55 B6
Park St Bagshot GU19 47 E3
Camberley GU15 65 C5
Croydon CR0, CR9 61 C8
Guildford GU1, GU2 130 C7
Horsham RH12 217 D2
Poyle SL3 1 D6
Slinfold RH13 215 C3
Teddington TW11 16 E2
Park Terr Carshalton SM5 59 E7
New Malden KT4 39 A1
Park Terr E RH13 217 D1
Park Terr W RH13 217 D1
Park The Forest Hill SE23 23 C7
Great Bookham KT23 94 A3
Wallington SM5 59 F5
Park View Addlestone KT15 52 C5
Bagshot GU19 47 D3
Crawley RH11 201 C5
Great Bookham KT23 94 A2
Horley RH6 161 A3
Morden CR4 40 D4
New Malden KT3 38 F6
Purley CR8 80 B8
Tandridge RH8 143 B5
Park View Ct GU22 89 F8
Park View Rd
Salfords RH1 140 A1
Woldingham CR3 101 F5
Park Way Crawley RH10 202 C7
East Molesey KT8 36 B6
Feltham TW14 15 B8
Great Bookham KT23 94 A4
Horsham RH12 217 C2
Park Wood Cl SM7 77 D4
Park Wood Rd SM7 77 D4
Park Wood View SM7 77 D4
Park Works Rd RH1 119 E2
Parkcroft Rd SE12 24 F8
Parkdale Cres KT4 57 D7
Parke Rd TW16 35 A5
Parker Cl RH10 202 D5
Parker Ct SW19 19 E1
Parker Rd CR0, CR9 61 C6
Parker's Cl KT21 95 E8
Parker's Hill KT21 95 E8
Parker's La Ashstead KT21 95 F8
Winkfield RG42 8 B5
Parkers Ct GU19 47 E3
Parkfield Godalming GU7 150 F2
Horsham RH12 217 C3
3 Hounslow TW7 5 E6
Parkfield Ave
Feltham TW13 15 A5
Mortlake SW14 7 E3
Parkfield Cl RH11 200 F6
Parkfield Cres TW13 15 A5
Parkfield Par TW13 15 A5
Parkfield Rd TW13 15 A5
Parkfields Croydon CR0 43 F1
Oxshott KT22 74 D8
Parkfields Ave SW20 39 B7
Parkfields Cl SM5 60 A6
Parkfields Rd TW10 17 F3
Parkgate Cl KT2 18 B2
Parkgate Gdns SW14 7 D2
Parkgate Rd
Newdigate RH5 158 C3

Parkgate Rd *continued*
Parkgate RH5 158 C3
Reigate RH2 139 B8
Wallington SM5, SM6 60 B5
Parkham Ct BR2 44 E7
Parkhill Cl GU17 64 D4
Parkhill Rd GU17 64 D4
Parkhurst KT19 57 C1
Parkhurst Cotts GU10 187 F8
Parkhurst Fields GU10 167 F1
Parkhurst Gr RH6 160 F4
Parkhurst Rd
Carshalton SM1 59 D6
Guildford GU2 109 B2
Horley RH6 160 E4
Parkin House SE20 23 D1
Parkland Dr RG12 27 E8
Parkland Gdns 12 SW19 19 D7
Parkland Gr Ashford TW15 14 A4
Heath End GU9 125 F8
Hounslow TW7 5 F6
Parkland Rd TW15 14 A4
Parklands Addlestone KT15 52 C5
Dorking RH5 136 B3
Great Bookham KT23 94 A4
Kingston u T KT5 37 F4
Oxted RH8 122 E4
Redhill RH1 119 A3
Parklands Cl SW14 7 C2
Parklands Ct TW5 4 D5
Parklands Pl GU1 110 B1
Parklands Rd SW16, SW17 21 B3
Parklands Way KT4 57 E8
Parklawn Ave Epsom KT18 76 B6
Horley RH6 160 F5
Parkleigh Ct SW19 40 B7
Parkleigh Rd SW19 40 B7
Parkleys
Kingston u T KT2, TW10 17 D4
Richmond KT2, TW10 17 D4
Parkpale La RH3 137 A4
Parkshot TW9 6 E3
Parkside Beckenham BR3 44 B7
Cheam SM3 58 E4
Crawley RH10 201 E6
East Grinstead RH19 185 C1
Hale GU9 125 C6
Teddington TW12 16 C3
Wimbledon SW19 19 D4
Parkside Ave SW19 19 D3
Parkside Cl
East Horsley KT24 92 F2
Penge SE20 23 C1
Parkside Cres KT5 38 C3
Parkside Ct KT13 53 A6
Parkside Gdns
Coulsdon CR5 79 B2
Wimbledon SW19 19 D4
Parkside Hospl SW19 19 D5
Parkside Mews RH12 217 D2
Parkside Pl KT24 92 F2
Parkside Prep Sch KT11 74 A1
Parkside Rd Hounslow TW3 5 B2
Sunningdale SL5 30 A4
Parkstone Dr GU15 65 C4
Parkthorne Rd SW12 21 D8
Parkview Lodge BR3 44 B6
Parkview Rd CR0, CR9 43 A1
Parkview Vale GU4 110 C3
Parkway Camberley GU15 65 C3
Crowthorne RG45 45 A5
Dorking RH4 136 A8
Guildford GU1 109 E2
Horley RH6 161 A3
New Addington CR0, CR9 63 C1
Oatlands Park KT13 53 D6
West Barnes SM4, SW20 39 D5
Parkway Sch The TW5 4 A7
Parkway The TW5 4 B7
Parkway Trad Est TW5 4 C8
Parkwood BR3 24 A1
Parkwood Ave KT10 36 C1
Parkwood Gr TW16 35 A6
Parkwood Rd
Biggin Hill TN16 103 F6
Hounslow TW7 5 F6
Nutfield RH1 119 E2
Wimbledon SW19 19 F3
Parley Dr GU21 69 C1
Parliament Mews SW14 7 C5
Parliamentary Rd GU24 87 A6
Parnall House 11 SE19 22 E4
Parnell Cl RH10 202 D4
Parnham Ave GU18 67 D8
Parr Ave KT17 58 B2
Parr Cl KT22 94 F7
Parr Ct TW13 15 C4
Parr's Pl TW12 16 A1
Parris Croft RH4 136 C4
Parrs Cl CR2 61 D2
Parry Cl Horsham RH13 218 C4
Stoneleigh KT17 58 A3
Parry Dr KT13 53 A1
Parry Rd SE25 42 E6
Parsley Gdns CR0 43 D1
Parson's Mead CR0 42 B1
Parson's Mead Sch KT21 95 E8
Parson's Pightle CR5 100 A7
Parsonage Bsns Pk RH12 217 E4
Parsonage Cl
Warlingham CR6 81 F3
Westcott RH4 135 C5
Parsonage Farm Cty Inf
Sch GU14 84 C5
Parsonage La RH4 135 C6
Parsonage Rd
Cranleigh GU6 174 D3
Englefield Green TW20 11 D3

Parsonage Rd *continued*
Horsham RH12, RH13 217 E4
Parsonage Sq RH4 136 A7
Parsonage Way
Frimley GU16 65 E1
Horsham RH12 217 E4
Parsons Cl
Haslemere GU27 208 C8
Horley RH6 160 E4
Parsons Field GU47 64 B8
Parsons Gn GU27 208 C8
Parsons Green Ct GU1 109 D3
Parsons House 21 SW12 21 E8
Parsons La GU26 188 D6
Parsons Mead KT8 36 C6
Parsonsfield Cl SM7 77 D4
Parsonsfield Rd SM7 77 D4
Parthia Cl KT20 97 B8
Partridge Cl
Crondall GU10 124 D8
Frimley GU16 65 E1
Partridge Knoll CR8 80 B6
Partridge La
Newdigate RH5 179 F3
Parkgate RH5 158 E2
Partridge Mead SM7 77 C4
Partridge Rd 8 TW12 16 A2
Partridge Way GU4 110 D3
Parvis Rd Byfleet KT14 71 D7
West Byfleet KT14 71 D7
Paschal Rd GU15 65 F8
Passfields SE6 24 C5
Passingham House TW5 5 A8
Pastens Rd RH8 123 C4
Pasture Rd SE6 24 F7
Pasture The RH10 202 C6
Pasture Wood Rd RH5 155 D6
Patching Cl RH11 200 F7
Patchings RH13 217 F3
Paterson Cl GU16 66 C3
Pates Manor Dr TW14 14 D8
Path Link RH10 201 F7
Path The SW19 40 B8
Pathfield GU8 191 B4
Pathfield Cl
Chiddingfold GU8 191 B4
Rudgwick RH12 214 D7
Pathfield Rd
Rudgwick RH12 214 D7
Streatham SW16 21 D2
Pathfields GU5 133 A4
Pathfields Cl GU27 208 D7
Pathfinders The GU14 84 C3
Pathway The GU23 90 F2
Patmore La KT12 53 F4
Patricia Gdns SM2 78 A8
Patrington Cl RH11 201 A3
Patten Ash Dr RG40 25 E7
Patten Rd SW18 20 E8
Pattenden Rd SE23, SE6 23 F7
Patterdale Cl Catford BR1 24 E2
Crawley RH11 201 C4
Patterson Ct SE19 22 F2
Patterson Rd SE19 22 F2
Paul Cl GU11 125 E8
Paul Gdns CR0 61 F8
Paul Vanson Ct KT12 54 D4
Paul's Pl KT21 96 B8
Pauline Cres TW2 16 C7
Pauls Mead RH7 164 E5
Paved Ct 9 TW9 6 D2
Pavement The 11 SE27 22 C4
Pavilion Gdns TW18 13 B1
Pavilion Rd GU11 104 E1
Pavilion Way RH19 205 E8
Pavilions End The GU15 65 D3
Paviors GU9 125 C3
Pawley Cl GU10 126 F7
Pawleyne Cl SE20 23 C1
Pawson's Rd CR0 42 C4
Pax Cl RH11 200 E4
Paxton Cl Richmond TW9 6 F5
Walton-on-T KT12 35 C2
Paxton Ct Forest Hill SE26 23 E4
Mitcham CR4 40 F7
Paxton Gdns GU21 70 E7
Paxton Pl SE27 22 E4
Paxton Prim Sch SE19 22 E2
Paxton Rd SE23 23 E5
Payley Dr RG40 25 E8
Payne Cl RH10 202 D8
Paynesfield Ave SW14 7 D4
Paynesfield Rd
Tatsfield TN16 103 D7
Tatsfield TN16 103 D8
Peabody Est SE24 22 C8
Peabody Hill SE21 22 C7
Peabody Rd GU11, GU14 105 D8
Peacemaker Cl RH11 200 E4
Peach St RG40 25 C6
Peach Tree Cl GU14 85 A7
Peaches Cl SM2 58 E3
Peacock Ave TW14 14 D7
Peacock Cotts RG12 26 C5
Peacock Gdns CR0, CR2 62 E1
Peacock La RG12 26 D6
Peacock Wlk 9 RH11 201 A3
Peacocks Sh Ctr The
GU21 69 E2
Peak Hill SE26 23 C4
Peak Hill Ave SE26 23 C4
Peak Hill Gdns SE26 23 C4
Peak Rd GU2 109 A4
Peak The SE26 23 C5
Peakfield GU10 167 C7
Peaks Hill CR8 60 E1
Peaks Hill Rise CR8 60 E1
Peall Rd CR0 41 F3

Pear Ave TW17 34 E6
Pear Tree Cl
Addlestone KT15 52 A5
Mitcham CR4 40 E7
Pear Tree Ct GU15 66 B8
Pear Tree Hill RH1 161 A8
Pear Tree La GU10 145 F3
Pear Tree Rd
Addlestone KT15 52 A5
Ashford TW15 14 C3
Pearce Cl CR4 41 A7
Pearce House 7 SW2 21 E8
Pearcefield Ave 5 SE23 23 C7
Pearfield Rd SE23 23 E5
Pearl Ct GU21 68 E3
Pearmain Cl TW17 34 B4
Pears Rd TW3 5 C4
Pearson Ct SM4 40 B4
Pearson Rd RH10 202 C6
Peartree Ave SW17 20 C5
Peartree Cl CR2 81 B5
Peary Cl RH12 217 D6
Peaslake La GU5 154 D6
Peaslake Sch GU5 154 E7
Peat Comm GU8 148 C2
Peatmore Ave GU22 71 A3
Peatmore Cl GU22 71 A3
Peatmore Dr GU24 87 C6
Pebble Cl KT20 116 E6
Pebble Hill KT24 112 C2
Pebble Hill Cotts RH8 123 B6
Pebble La KT18, KT21 96 A5
Pebblehill Rd
Betchworth KT20, RH3 116 E5
Box Hill KT20, RH3 116 E5
Pebworth Ct 8 RH1 119 A3
Pebworth Lodge SE25 42 F5
Peckarmans Wood
SE21, SE26 23 A5
Peek Cres SW19 19 D3
Peeks Brook La
Crawley RH6 182 E7
Horley RH6 161 F2
Peel Ave GU16 86 A7
Peel Ct GU14 105 C8
Peel Ctr The RG12 27 B7
Pegasus Ave GU12 105 E2
Pegasus Cl GU27 207 D5
Pegasus Ct Crawley RH11 200 E4
Farnborough GU14 85 E1
Kingston u T KT1 37 D6
Pegasus Rd
Croydon CR0, CR9 61 A4
Farnborough GU14 84 F7
Pegasus Way RH19 186 B3
Pegg Rd TW5 4 D7
Peggotty Pl GU47 45 E2
Pegler Way RH11 201 D6
Pegwell Cl RH11 200 F4
Peket Cl TW18 32 E8
Peldon Ct TW10 6 F2
Pelham Ct Crawley RH11 201 B2
Great Bookham KT23 94 C1
Horsham RH12 217 B2
Staines TW18 13 B3
Pelham Ct Bsns Ctr RH11 201 B2
Pelham Dr RH11 201 A2
Pelham House CR3 100 F3
Pelham Pl RH11 201 B2
Pelham Prim Sch SW19 20 A1
Pelham Rd Merton SW19 20 A1
Penge BR3, SE20 43 C7
Pelham Way KT23 94 C1
Pelhams Cl KT10 55 A6
Pelhams Wlk KT10 55 A6
Pelinore Rd SE6 24 E6
Pelling Hill SL4 11 B7
Pelton Ave SM2 59 B1
Pelton Ct CR2 61 C4
Pemberley Chase KT19 57 B5
Pemberley Cl KT19 57 B5
Pemberton House SE26 23 A4
Pemberton Pl KT10 55 C7
Pemberton Rd KT8 36 C5
Pembley Gn RH10 183 E3
Pembridge Ave TW4 15 F7
Pembroke RG12 27 A1
Pembroke Ave
Hersham KT12 54 D6
Surbiton KT5 38 B4
Pembroke Broadway
GU15 65 C5
Pembroke Cl Ascot SL5 29 D4
Banstead SM7 78 B2
Pembroke Ct GU22 70 B3
Pembroke Gdns GU22 70 A1
Pembroke Mews SL5 29 D4
Pembroke Pl TW7 5 E5
Pembroke Rd
Crawley RH10 182 C1
Mitcham CR4 41 A7
South Norwood SE25 42 E5
Woking GU22 70 A2
Pembroke Villas TW9 6 D3
Pembroke Lodge 2 SW16 21 F5
Pembury Ave
New Malden KT4 39 A2
North Cheam KT4 39 A2
Pembury Cl Hayes BR2 44 F2
Wallington CR5 79 A5
Pembury Ct UB3 3 D8
Pembury Pl GU12 105 C1
Pembury Rd SE25 43 A5
Pemdevon Rd CR0 42 A2
Penarth Ct SM2 59 C3

Penates KT10 . . . . 55 D6
Penberth Rd SE6 . . . . 24 C7
Penceat Ct SE20 . . . . 43 C7
Pendarves Rd SW20 . . . . . . 39 C8
Pendell Ave U83 . . . . 3 F7
Pendell Rd RH1 . . . . 120 B4
Pendennis Cl KT14 . . . . 71 A5
Pendennis Rd SW16 . . . . . . 21 E4
Penderel Rd TW3 . . . . 5 A2
Penderry Rise SE6 . . . . 24 D6
Pendine Pl RG12 . . . . 27 B4
Pendle House **16** SE26 . . . 23 A5
Pendle Rd SW16 . . . . 21 B3
Pendlebury RG12 . . . . 27 A2
Pendleton Cl RH1 . . . . 139 F7
Pendleton Rd RH1 . . . . . . 139 E6
Pendragon Rd BR1 . . . . 24 F5
Pendragon Way GU15 . . . . 66 D3
Penerley Rd SE6 . . . . 24 B7
Penfold Cl CR0, CR9 . . . . . . 61 A7
Penfold Croft GU9 . . . . 125 F4
Penfold Ct CR4 . . . . 41 A7
Penfold Rd RH10 . . . . 202 B2
Penge East Sta SE20 . . . . . 23 C2
Penge La SE20 . . . . 23 D1
Penge Rd SE20, SE25 . . . . . 43 A6
Penge West Sta SE20 . . . . . 23 B2
Pengilly Rd GU9 . . . . 125 B1
Penhurst GU21 . . . . 69 F5
Peninsula Cl GU15 . . . . 66 B7
Peninsular Cl TW14 . . . . 3 E1
Penistone Rd SW16 . . . . . . 21 E1
Penn Cl RH11 . . . . 181 D1
Pennards The TW16 . . . . . . 35 C6
Pennefather's Rd GU11 . . 104 F3
Penner Cl SW19 . . . . 19 E6
Penners Gdns KT6 . . . . 37 E2
Pennine Cl RH11 . . . . 201 B6

Pennine Way
Farnborough GU14 . . . . 84 E7
Harlington U87 . . . . 3 D7
Pennings Ave GU2, GU3 . . 108 F3
Pennington Cl **10** SE27 . . 22 D4
Pennington Dr KT13 . . . . . . 53 F7
Pennington Lodge **18** KT5 . 37 E4
Penns Wood GU14 . . . . 85 D1
Penny Dr GU3 . . . . 108 B2
Penny La TW17 . . . . 34 E2
Penny Mews TW12 . . . . 21 B8
Penny Royal SM6 . . . . 60 D4
Pennycroft CR0 . . . . 62 F2
Pennyfield KT11 . . . . 73 A6
Pennymead Dr KT24 . . . . . 112 F8
Pennymead Rise KT24 . . . 112 F8
Pennypot La GU24 . . . . 68 C7
Penrhyn Cl GU11 . . . . 105 B1
Penrhyn Cres SW14 . . . . 7 C3
Penrhyn Gdns KT1 . . . . 37 D5
Penrhyn Rd KT1 . . . . 37 E6
Penrith Cl Beckenham BR3 . 44 B8
Redhill RH2 . . . . 118 C2
Penrith Pl SE27 . . . . 22 B6
Penrith Rd New Malden KT3 . 38 D5
South Norwood CR7 . . . . 42 C7
Penrith St SW16 . . . . 21 C2
Penrose Ct TW20 . . . . 11 C2
Penrose Rd KT22 . . . . 94 C5
Penryn Dr GU35 . . . . 187 C5
Penryn House **3** RH1 . . . 119 A3
Pensfold La RH12, RH13 . . 214 E5
Pensford Ave TW9 . . . . 7 A5
Pensford Ct RH45 . . . . 45 B7
Penshurst Cl RH10 . . . . . . 202 D7
Penshurst Gn BR2 . . . . 44 F4
Penshurst Rd CR7 . . . . 42 B4
Penshurst Rise GU16 . . . . . 85 F8
Penshurst Way SM2 . . . . . . 59 A3
Penshurst Wlk BR2 . . . . 44 F4
Pentelow Gdns TW14 . . . . . . 4 A1
Penthorpe SM RH12 . . . . . 214 C7
Pentland Ave TW17 . . . . . . 34 A4
Pentland Pl GU14 . . . . 84 E7
Pentlands BR3 . . . . 44 C8
Pentlands Cl CR4 . . . . 41 B6

Pentney Rd
Streatham SW12 . . . . 21 C7
Wimbledon SW19, SW20 . . . 39 E8
Penton Ave TW18 . . . . 32 F8
Penton Ct TW18 . . . . 12 F2
Penton Hall TW18 . . . . 33 A8
Penton Hall Dr TW18 . . . . . 33 A8

Penton Hook Marina
TW18 . . . . 33 A6
Egham TW18 . . . . 32 F7
Penton Hook Rd TW18 . . . 33 A8
Penton House SM2 . . . . 59 C3
Penton Rd TW18 . . . . 12 F1
Pentreath Ave GU2 . . . . . . 129 F8
Penwerris Ave TW5, TW7 . . . 5 C7
Penwerris Ct TW7 . . . . 5 C7
Penwith Dr GU27 . . . . 207 E5
Penwith Rd SW18 . . . . 20 B6
Penwith Wlk GU22 . . . . 89 D8
Penwood End GU22 . . . . . . 89 B6
Penwood Gdns RG12 . . . . . 26 D3
Penwood House SW15 . . . . . 7 F1

Penwortham Prim Sch
SW17 . . . . 21 B1

Penwortham Rd
South Croydon CR2 . . . . 61 D1
Streatham SW16 . . . . 21 C2
Peper Harow La GU8 . . . . . 149 C6
Peperham House GU27 . . . 208 C7
Peperham Rd GU27 . . . . . . 208 C8
Peperharow Rd GU7 . . . . . 150 C6

Peppard Rd RH10 . . . . 202 D3
Pepper Cl CR3 . . . . 100 E2
Pepperbox La GU6 . . . . 173 E4
Peppermint Cl CR0 . . . . 41 E2
Pepys Cl Ashstead KT21 . . . 76 A2
Brands Hill SL3 . . . . 1 B8
Pepys Rd SW20 . . . . 39 C8
Perak Ct KT6 . . . . 38 C2
Percheron Cl TW7 . . . . 5 F4
Percheron Dr GU21 . . . . 88 C8
Percival Rd Feltham TW13 . . 14 F6
Mortlake SW14 . . . . 7 C3
Percival Way KT19 . . . . 57 D6
Percy Ave TW15 . . . . 14 A3
Percy Bilton Ct TW5 . . . . 5 B6
Percy Bryant Rd TW16 . . . . 14 E1
Percy Ct **1** KT5 . . . . 37 F3

Percy Gdns
Isleworth TW7 . . . . 6 A4
New Malden KT3 . . . . 38 E5
Percy House **4** SW16 . . . . 21 C4
Percy Rd Carshalton CR4 . . . 41 A2
Croydon SE25 . . . . 43 A4
Guildford GU2 . . . . 109 B3
Hampton TW12 . . . . 16 A1
Horsham RH12 . . . . 217 B3
Isleworth TW7 . . . . 6 A4
Penge SE20 . . . . 43 D8
Twickenham TW2 . . . . 16 C7
Percy Way TW2 . . . . 16 C7

Peregrine Cl
Bracknell RG12 . . . . 27 B4
Cranleigh GU6 . . . . 174 E4
Peregrine Gdns CR0 . . . . . . 62 E8
Peregrine Rd TW16 . . . . 34 F7

Peregrine Way
SW19, SW20 . . . . 19 C1

Performing Arts & Tech Sch
SE25 . . . . 42 D3
Perifield SE21 . . . . 22 C7
Perimeter Rd E RH6 . . . . . 182 B6
Perimeter Rd N RH6 . . . . . 181 D7
Perimeter Rd S RH6 . . . . . 181 C5
Perkins Cl TW15 . . . . 13 F3
Perkins Way RG41 . . . . 25 A5
Perkstead Ct **7** RH11 . . . 201 A3
Perleybrooke La GU21 . . . . 69 A2
Perowne St GU11 . . . . 104 F2
Perram Wks GU4 . . . . 110 C4
Perran Rd SE24, SW2 . . . . . 22 B6
Perran Wlk **16** TW8 . . . . . . 6 E8
Perrin Cl TW15 . . . . 13 F3
Perrin Ct GU21 . . . . 70 B4
Perring Ave GU14 . . . . 84 F8
Perrior Rd GU7 . . . . 150 E7
Perry Ave RH19 . . . . 185 E3
Perry Cl GU7 . . . . 151 B5
Perry Hill SE23, SE6 . . . . . . 23 F5
Perry House **24** SW2 . . . . 21 F8
Perry How KT4 . . . . 38 F1
Perry Oaks RG12 . . . . 27 F2
Perry Oaks Dr TW6, UB7 . . . 2 C5
Perry Rise SE23, SE6 . . . . . . 23 E5
Perry Vale SE23 . . . . 23 D6
Perry Way Bracknell RG12 . 27 E7
Farnham GU9 . . . . 125 B7
Lightwater GU18 . . . . 48 B1

Perryfield House 7
RH11 . . . . 201 D5
Perryfield Rd RH11 . . . . . . 201 D5
Perryfield Way TW10 . . . . . 17 B6
Perrylands RH6 . . . . 180 F7
Perrylands La RH6 . . . . 162 A2

Perrymount Prim Sch
SE23 . . . . 23 D6
Perryn Ct **2** TW1 . . . . 17 A8
Perrywood Bsns Pk RH1 . 140 B1
Persant Rd SE6 . . . . 24 E6
Perseverance Cotts GU23 . 91 C6
Persfield Mews KT17 . . . . . 58 A1
Pershore Gr SM5 . . . . 40 D3
Perth Cl Crawley RH11 . . . 181 D1
Wimbledon SW20 . . . . 39 A7
Perth Rd BR3 . . . . 44 C7
Perth Way RH12 . . . . 217 F4
Perystreete SE23 . . . . 23 C6
Petauel Rd TW11 . . . . 16 E3
Petavel Rd TW11 . . . . 16 E2
Peter Ave RH8 . . . . 122 D6
Peter Kennedy Ct CR0 . . . . 43 F3
Peter's Path SE26 . . . . 23 B4

Peterborough Rd
Carshalton CR4, SM4, SM5 . 40 E3
Crawley RH10 . . . . 201 E2
Guildford GU2 . . . . 108 F3
Peterhouse Cl GU47 . . . . . . 45 F2
Peterhouse Par RH10 . . . . 182 C1
Peterlee Wlk RH11 . . . . . . 200 E2

Petersfield Ave
TW18 . . . . 13 C2
Petersfield Cres CR5 . . . . . . 79 E4
Petersfield Rd TW18 . . . . . . 13 C2
Petersfield Rise SW15 . . . . 19 B7
Petersham Ave KT14 . . . . . . 71 E7
Petersham Cl Byfleet KT14 . 71 E7
Cheam SM1 . . . . 59 A5
Richmond TW10 . . . . 17 D6
Petersham Rd TW10 . . . . . . 17 E7
Peterstow Cl SW19 . . . . 19 E6
Peterwood Pk CR0 . . . . 60 F8
Peterwood Way CR0 . . . . . . 60 F8
Petrel Ct **2** SE21 . . . . 22 D6
Petridge Rd RH1 . . . . 139 F4
Petters Rd KT21 . . . . 75 F3
Petts La TW17 . . . . 34 A5
Petworth Cl Coulsdon CR5 . 99 C8
Frimley GU16 . . . . 85 F8

Petworth Ct Crawley RH11 . 200 F3
Haslemere GU27 . . . . 208 D6
Petworth Dr RH12 . . . . 217 F7
Petworth Gdns 39 B6

Petworth Rd
Chiddingfold GU8 . . . . 191 C4
Chiddingfold,
Ansteadbrook GU27 . . . . . 209 B6
Witley GU8 . . . . 170 F5
Wormley GU8 . . . . 171 A1

Pevensey Cl
Crawley RH10 . . . . 202 C5
Hounslow TW7 . . . . 5 C6
Pevensey Ct SW16 . . . . 22 A5
Pevensey House RH12 . . . 217 F5
Pevensey Rd Feltham TW13 . 15 E7
Upper Tooting SW17 . . . . . . 20 D4
Pevensey Way GU16 . . . . . . 86 A8
Peverel Rd RH11 . . . . 200 E5
Peveril Dr TW11 . . . . 16 D3
Pewley Bank GU1 . . . . 130 E7
Pewley Hill GU1 . . . . 130 E7
Pewley Point GU1 . . . . 130 E7
Pewley Way GU1 . . . . 130 F7
Pewsey Vale RG12 . . . . 27 F4
Peyton's Cotts RH1 . . . . . . 119 F3
Pharaoh Cl CR4 . . . . 40 F2
Pheasant Cl CR8 . . . . 80 B6
Philanthropic Rd RH1 . . . 140 B8
Philip Gdns CR0 . . . . 62 F8
Philip Rd TW18 . . . . 13 D2

Philip Southcote Sch
KT15 . . . . 52 C8
Philips House GU26 . . . . . . 188 B3
Phillips Cl Ash GU10 . . . . . 126 E8
Crawley RH10 . . . . 202 C2
Godalming GU7 . . . . 150 D2
Phillips Cotts GU7 . . . . 150 B4
Phillips Hatch GU5 . . . . . . 152 C8
Philpot La GU24 . . . . 68 A3

Phipp's Bridge Rd
CR4, SW19 . . . . 40 D6
Phoenix Bsns Pk RG12 . . . 26 C7
Phoenix Cl BR4 . . . . 63 E8
Phoenix Coll SM4 . . . . 40 C4

Phoenix Ct
18 Aldershot GU11 . . . . . 105 A2
Croydon SE25 . . . . 43 A4
Guildford GU1 . . . . 130 D7
Phoenix La RH19 . . . . 206 E6
Phoenix Pl TW18 . . . . 13 A3
Phoenix Rd SE20 . . . . 23 C2
Phoenix Way TW5 . . . . 4 D8
Phyllis Ave KT3 . . . . 39 B4
Phyllis House CR0 . . . . 61 B6
Piccards The GU2 . . . . 130 C5
Pickering RG12 . . . . 27 A5
Pickering Gdns SE25 . . . . . 42 F3
Picket Post Cl RG12 . . . . . . 27 F6
Pickets St SW12 . . . . 21 B8
Picketts Hill GU35 . . . . 166 C1
Picketts La RH1 . . . . 161 C8
Pickford St GU11 . . . . 105 B2
Pickhurst Gn BR2 . . . . 44 F2
Pickhurst Inf Sch BR2 . . . . 44 F3
Pickhurst Jun Sch BR2 . . . 44 F3
Pickhurst La BR2, BR3, BR4 . 44 F2
Pickhurst Mead BR2 . . . . . 44 F2
Pickhurst Pk BR2 . . . . 44 F4
Pickhurst Rd GU8 . . . . 191 D2
Pickins Piece SL3 . . . . 1 A5
Pickwick Cl TW4 . . . . 4 E2
Pickwick Rd SE21 . . . . 22 E8
Picquets Way KT20, SM7 . . 77 F2
Picton Cl GU15 . . . . 66 B7
Picton House **1** SW4 . . . . 21 E8
Pier Rd TW14 . . . . 4 B2
Pierrefondes Ave GU14 . . . 85 B5
Pierrepoint SE25 . . . . 43 A5
Pierson House **12** SE19 . . 22 E4
Pigbush La RH14 . . . . 213 A7
Pigeon La TW12 . . . . 16 A4

Pigeonhouse La
Lower Kingswood CR5 . . . . . 98 C3
Winkfield SL4, SL5 . . . . 8 E4
Piggott Ct RH13 . . . . 217 E1
Pigott Ct RG40 . . . . 25 D8
Pigott Rd RG40 . . . . 25 D8
Pike Cl GU11 . . . . 105 C2
Pikes Hill KT17 . . . . 76 E6
Pikes La RH7 . . . . 143 E2
Pikethorne SE23 . . . . 23 D6
Pilgrim Cl SM4 . . . . 40 B2
Pilgrim Hill SE27 . . . . 22 C4
Pilgrim House GU1 . . . . . . 130 D7
Pilgrim's Way GU22 . . . . . . 89 E8

Pilgrims' Way
Guildford GU4 . . . . 130 E5
Reigate RH2 . . . . 118 B3
Pilgrims Way Shere GU5 . . 133 A4
Westhumble RH5 . . . . 115 B4
Pilgrims La Caterham CR3 . 100 B1
Tatsfield RH8 . . . . 103 D3
Titsey RH8 . . . . 103 D3
Pilgrims Pl RH2 . . . . 118 A3
Pilgrims View GU12 . . . . . 127 C8
Pilgrims Way GU4 . . . . 68 A3

**Pilgrims Way Prim
Sch The** GU9 . . . . 146 B8
Pilsden Cl SW19 . . . . 19 D7
Pilton Est The CR9 . . . . 61 B8

Pimms Cl GU4 . . . . 110 A5
Pinckards GU8 . . . . 191 B5
Pincott La KT24 . . . . 112 B6
Pincott Rd SW19 . . . . 40 C8
Pine Ave Camberley GU15 . 65 D3
West Wickham BR4 . . . . 44 B1
Pine Bank GU26 . . . . 188 E4
Pine Cl Ash Vale GU12 . . . 106 A6
Crawley RH11 . . . . 181 C1
Kenley CR8 . . . . 80 D2
Penge SE20 . . . . 43 C8
Sandhurst GU15 . . . . 64 E7
Woking GU21 . . . . 69 C3
Woodham KT15 . . . . 71 B8
Pine Coombe CR0 . . . . 62 D6
Pine Cres SM5 . . . . 78 D8
Pine Croft Rd RG41 . . . . . . 25 A2
Pine Ct Bracknell RG12 . . . 27 E5
2 Weybridge KT13 . . . . . . 53 C5
Pine Dean KT23 . . . . 94 B2
Pine Dr GU17 . . . . 64 E3
Pine Gdns Horley RH6 . . . 161 A2
Surbiton KT5 . . . . 38 A3

Pine Gr
East Grinstead RH19 . . . . . 185 B3
Farnham GU10 . . . . 146 E6
Weybridge KT13 . . . . 53 C5
Windlesham SW19 . . . . 19 F3
Wimbledon GU20 . . . . 48 D4
Pine Grove Mews **3** KT13 . 53 C5
Pine Hill KT18 . . . . 76 D4
Pine Mount Rd GU15 . . . . . 65 D4
Pine Pl KT17 . . . . 77 D5
Pine Rd GU22 . . . . 89 C7
Pine Ridge SM5 . . . . 60 A2

Pine Ridge Cty Inf Sch
GU15 . . . . 47 A1
Pine Ridge Dr GU10 . . . . . 146 B6
Pine Ridge Golf Ctr GU16 . 66 D2
Pine Shaw RH10 . . . . 202 D7
Pine Tree Cl TW5 . . . . 4 B6
Pine Tree Hill GU22 . . . . . . 70 D3
Pine Trees Bsns Pk TW18 . 12 E3
Pine View GU35 . . . . 187 C6

Pine View Cl
Chilworth GU4 . . . . 131 F3
Farnham GU9 . . . . 126 A5
Haslemere GU27 . . . . 208 D8
Pine Way TW20 . . . . 11 B2
Pine Way Cl RH19 . . . . 205 E7
Pine Wlk Caterham CR3 . . 100 F5
Cobham KT11 . . . . 73 D5
East Horsley KT24 . . . . 112 F7
Great Bookham KT23 . . . . . . 94 B2
Sanderstead KT5 . . . . 38 A3
Sutton SM5 . . . . 59 D1
Woodmansterne CR5, SM7 . 78 F2
Pine Wood TW16 . . . . 35 A8
Pineacre Cl GU22 . . . . 72 B2
Pinecote Dr SL5 . . . . 29 F2
Pinefields Cl TW15 . . . . 52 B6
Pinefields Cl RG45 . . . . 45 C3
Pinehill Rd RG45 . . . . 45 C3
Pinehurst Rise GU47 . . . . . 64 C8
Pinehurst Ascot SL5 . . . . . . 29 D4
Horsham RH12 . . . . 217 C4
8 Woking GU22 . . . . 69 E1
Pinehurst Ave GU14 . . . . . . 85 B2
Pinehurst Cl KT20 . . . . 98 A5
Pinehurst Cotts GU14 . . . . 85 B2
Pinel Cl GU25 . . . . 31 E5
Pines Ct **1** SW19 . . . . 19 D7
Pines Cty Inf Sch RG12 . . . 27 A2
Pines Cty Jun Sch RG12 . . 27 A2
Pines The Camberley GU15 . 65 F7
Dorking RH4 . . . . 136 B6
Guildford GU3 . . . . 108 E3
Horsham RH12 . . . . 218 C5
Purley CR8 . . . . 80 C6
South Norwood SE19, SW16 . 22 B2
Sunbury TW16 . . . . 35 A6
Pinetrees Cl RH10 . . . . 183 B3
Pinewood Ave
Crowthorne RG45 . . . . 45 C6
Woodham KT15 . . . . 52 C1

Pinewood Cl
Broadbridge Heath RH12 . 216 D3
South Croydon CR0 . . . . 62 E7
Woking GU21 . . . . 70 A4
Pinewood Cres GU14 . . . . . 84 C5

Pinewood Ct
Addlestone KT15 . . . . 52 B6
Woking GU21 . . . . 70 A3
Pinewood Dr TW18 . . . . 13 A3
Pinewood Gdns GU19 . . . . 47 C3
Pinewood Gr KT15 . . . . 52 B1
Pinewood Inf Sch GU14 . . 84 D7
Pinewood Mews TW19 . . . . 2 D1

Pinewood Pk
Farnborough GU14 . . . . 84 C7
Woodham KT15 . . . . 71 B8
Pinewood Pl KT19 . . . . 57 D6

Pinewood Rd
Feltham TW13 . . . . 15 B5
Normandy GU12 . . . . 106 D3
Wentworth GU25 . . . . 31 A5
Pinfold Rd SW16 . . . . 21 E4
Pinglestone Cl TW6, UB7 . . 2 E7
Pinkcoat Cl TW13 . . . . 15 B5
Pinkerton Pl SW16 . . . . 21 D4
Pinkham La RH13 . . . . 216 A2
Pioneers Ind Pk CR9 . . . . . 41 E1
Piper Rd KT1 . . . . 38 A6
Piper's End GU25 . . . . 31 D5
Pipers Cl KT11 . . . . 73 D3
Pipers Croft GU14 . . . . 85 A3
Pipers Gdns CR0 . . . . 43 E2
Pipers Patch **11** GU14 . . . 85 B4

Pipewell Rd SM5 . . . . 40 E3
Pippbrook Gdns RH4 . . . . 136 B8
Pippin Cl CR0 . . . . 43 F3
Pippins Ct TW15 . . . . 14 B3
Piquet Rd BR3 . . . . 43 E8
Pirbright Cres CR0 . . . . 63 C7

Pirbright Cty Prim Sch
GU24 . . . . 87 E3
Pirbright House **11** KT2 . . 18 A1

Pirbright Rd
Farnborough GU14 . . . . 85 A5
Normandy GU3 . . . . 107 A1
Wandsworth SW18 . . . . 20 A7
Pirbright Terr GU24 . . . . 87 F4
Pirles Pl RH12 . . . . 217 C1
Pisley La RH5 . . . . 177 E5
Pit Farm Rd GU1 . . . . 110 C1
Pit Wood Gn KT20 . . . . 97 C6
Pitcairn Rd CR4 . . . . 20 F1
Pitchfont La CR6, RH8 . . . 102 F2
Pitfold Ave GU27 . . . . 207 E6
Pitfold Cl GU27 . . . . 207 F6
Pitlake CR0, CR9 . . . . 61 B8
Pitland St RH5 . . . . 155 E8
Pitson Cl KT15 . . . . 52 E6
Pitt Cres SW19 . . . . 20 B4
Pitt Pl KT17 . . . . 76 E5
Pitt Rd Epsom KT17 76
Thornton Heath CR0, CR7 . . 42 B4
Pitt Way GU14 . . . . 84 F4
Pitts Rd GU11 . . . . 105 E5
Pittville Gdns SE25 . . . . 43 A6
Pixfield Ct BR2 . . . . 44 F7
Pixham Firs RH4 . . . . 115 C4
Pixham La RH4 . . . . 115 C4
Pixholme Ct RH4 . . . . 115 C4
Pixholme Gr RH4 . . . . 115 C4
Pixton Way CR0, CR2 . . . . . 62 F2
Place Ct GU11 126
Place Farm Rd RH1 120
Placehouse La CR5 80

Plaistow Cty Inf Sch
RH14 211

Plaistow Rd
Chiddingfold GU8 . . . . 210 B8
Dunsfold GU8 . . . . 192 E7
Ifold RH14 212
Loxwood RH14 212
Plaistow St RH7 . . . . 164 D4
Plane St SE26 23
Plane Tree Cres TW13 15
Plane Tree Wlk **4** SE19 . . 22
Planes The KT16 33
Plantagenet Cl KT19 57
Plantagenet Pk RG42 27
Plantain Cres RH11 201
Plantation La CR6 101
Plantation Row GU15 65
Plassy Rd SE6 24
Plat The RH12 217
Platt Meadow GU24 110
Platt The RH7 186
Platt's Eyot TW12 36
Plaws Hill GU5 154
Playden Ct **8** RH11 201
Playgreen Way SE6 24
Playground Cl BR3 43
Pleasant Gr CR0 62
Pleasant Pl KT12 54
Pleasure Pit Rd KT21 76
Plesman Way SM6 60
Plevna Rd TW12 36
Pleydell Ave SE19 22
Plough Cl RH11 200
Plough Ind Est KT22 95
Plough La Downside KT11 . 73
Ewhurst GU6 175
Horsham RH12 217
Purley CR0, CR8, SM6 60
Wallington, Bandonhill
CR0, SM6 60
Wallington, Russell Hill SM6 . 60
Wimbledon SW17, SW19 . . . 20
Wokingham RG40 25
Plough Lane CR0, SM6 60

Plough Rd
Dormansland RH7 165
Smallfield RH6 162
West Ewell KT19 57
Ploughlands RG42 26
Ploughmans End TW7 5
Plover Cl Crawley RH11 . . 201
Staines TW18 12
Plovers Rd RH13 217
Plovers Rise GU24 87
Plowman House SW19 19
Plummer La CR4 40
Plummer Rd SW4 21
Plumpton Way SM5 59
Plumtree Cl SM6 60
Pocket Cl RG12 26
Pockford Rd GU8 191
Pocklington Ct SW15 19
Point (L Ctr) The RG12 . . . 27
Point Royal RG12 27
Pointers Hill RH4 135
Pointers Rd KT11 72
Pointers The KT21 95
Polden Cl GU14 84
Polecroft La SE6 23
Poles La RH11, RH6 181
Polesden Gdns SW20 39
Polesden La Ripley GU23 . . 91
Send Marsh GU23 91
Polesden Lacey KT23 114
Polesden Rd KT23 114
Polesden View KT23 114
Polesteeple Hill TN16 83

Police Station Rd KT12 . . . . 54 C4
Pollard Gr GU15 . . . . 66 C4
Pollard House T14 . . . . 58 C6
Pollard Rd Morden SM4 . . . . 40 D4
Woking GU22 . . . . 70 B3
Pollardrow Ave RG42 . . . . . . 26 F8
Pollards RH11 . . . . 201 A5
Pollards Cres SW16 . . . . 41 E6
Pollard's Dr RH13 . . . . 217 F2
Pollards Hill N SW16 . . . . . . 41 F6
Pollards Hill S SW16 . . . . . . 41 F6
Pollards Hill S SW16 . . . . . . 41 F6
Pollards Hill W SW16 . . . . . . 41 F6
Pollards Oak Cres RH8 . . . . 123 A3
Pollards Oak Rd RH8 . . . . . . 123 A3
Pollards Wood Hill RH8 . . 123 B5
Pollards Wood Rd
Hampsfield RH8 . . . . 123 B4
Thornton Heath SW16 . . . . . 41 E6
Polsted La GU3 . . . . 129 C3
Polsted Rd SE6 . . . . 23 F8
Poltimore Rd GU2 . . . . 130 B7
Polworth Rd SW16 . . . . 21 E3
Polyanthus Way RG45 . . . . . 45 B8
Pond CI Hersham KT12 . . . . . 54 A4
Oxwood RH14 . . . . 212 F5
Pond Copse La RH14 . . . . . 212 F5
Pond Cottage La BR3, BR4 . 44 A1
Pondcroft RH19 . . . . 22 E7
Pond Farm CI RH10 . . . . 97 B3
Pond Head La
Forest Green RH5 . . . . 176 E5
Wallis Wood RH5 . . . . 176 C3
Pond Hill Gdns SM3 . . . . 58 E4
Pond House GU10 . . . . 110 D2
Pond La Frensham GU10 . . 167 C5
Puttenham GU3 . . . . 128 A4
Pond Meadow GU2 . . . . . . 108 E2
Pond Meadow Sch GU2 . . 108 E2
Pond Moor Rd RG12 . . . . 27 B4
Pond Piece KT22 . . . . 74 B6
Pond Rd Egham TW20 . . . . . . 12 C2
Headley Down GU35 . . . . . . 187 B4
Woking GU22 . . . . 89 B7
Pond Way
East Grinstead RH19 . . . . . 186 B1
Teddington TW11 . . . . 17 C2
Pond Wood Rd RH10 . . . . 202 A8
Pondfield House SE27 . . . . . 22 C3
Pondfield Rd
Rudgwick GU6 . . . . 150 F7
Kenley CR8 . . . . 80 B3
Wrecclesham GU10 . . . . . . 145 F6
Godalming, Charterhouse
GU7 . . . . 150 E6
Godalming GU7 . . . . 150 E5
Ponds La GU5 . . . . 153 D2
Ponsonby Rd SW15 . . . . 19 B8
Pontefract Rd BR1 . . . . 24 F3
Pook House SW2 . . . . 22 A7
Pony Chase KT11 . . . . 73 F6
Pook Hill GU8 . . . . 190 F3
Pool CI BR3 . . . . 24 A3
Pool CI SE6 . . . . 24 A6
Pool End CI TW17 . . . . 34 A4
Pool Rd Aldershot GU11 . . 126 C7
West Molesey KT12, KT8 . . . 35 F4
Poole Court Rd TW5 . . . . 4 E5
Poole Ct TW5 . . . . 4 E5
Poole Rd West Ewell KT19 . . 57 D4
Woking GU21 . . . . 69 E1
Pooley Ave TW20 . . . . 12 B3
Pooley Green CI TW20 . . . . . 12 C3
Pooley Green Rd TW20 . . . . 12 C3
Poole Ct Bedfont TW14 . . . . 14 F7
Penge, Clock House
SE20 . . . . 22 D7
Poole Court Rd TW5 . . . . 4 E5
Pope CI TW14 . . . . 14 F7
Pope's Ave TW2 . . . . 16 E6
Pope's Gr TW1, TW2 . . . . 16 F6
Pope's CI SL3 . . . . 1 C7
Popes Gr CR0 . . . . 62 F7
Popes La Brentford 6 B8
Popes Mead GU27 . . . . 208 C2
Popeswood Rd
Binfield RG42 . . . . 26 D8
Bracknell RG12 . . . . 27 F4
Popham CI RG12 . . . . 27 F4
Popham Gdns TW9 . . . . 7 B4
Popham Ave
Hatherwood KT22 . . . . 95 C5
Ockham CR4 . . . . 40 F8
Poplar CI Crawley RH11 . . 181 C1
Colnbrook SL3 . . . . 86 A3
Poplar Cotts GU3 . . . . 108 E4
Poplar Cres KT19 . . . . 57 C4
Poplar Ct
Streatham SW16 . . . . 21 F5
Twickenham TW1 . . . . 6 C1
Wimbledon SW19 . . . . 20 A3
Poplar Dr KT17, SM7 . . . . . . 77 D5
Poplar Farm CI KT19 . . . . . . 57 C4
Poplar Fst Sch SW19 . . . . . . 40 A6
Poplar Gdns KT3 . . . . 38 D7
Poplar Gr Kingston u t KT3 . 38 D6
Woking GU22 . . . . 89 E8
Poplar La BR3 . . . . 44 C3
Poplar Rd Ashford TW15 . . . 14 C3
Cheam SM3 . . . . 39 F1
Leatherhead KT22 . . . . 95 C5
Merton SW19 . . . . 40 A7
Shalford GU4 . . . . 130 E2
Poplar Rd S SM4, SW19 . . . 40 A6
Poplar Way TW13 . . . . 7 B4
Poplar Wlk Caterham CR3 . 100 E4

Croydon CR0 . . . . 42 C1
Heath End GU9 . . . . 125 D7
Poplars CI GU14 . . . . 84 D6
Poplars The Ascot SL5 . . . . . 29 A4
Horsham RH13 . . . . 217 E3
Poppy La CR0, CR9 . . . . 43 C2
Poppy PI RG40 . . . . 25 B6
Poppyhills Rd GU15 . . . . 65 F8
Porchester SL5 . . . . 29 A5
Porchester Mead BR3 . . . . . 24 B2
Porchester Rd KT1 . . . . 38 B7
Porchfield CI SM2 . . . . 59 B1
Porlock House T SE26 . . . . . 23 A5
Porridge Pot Alley GU2 . . 130 C7
Port Way GU24 . . . . 68 A3
Portal CI SE27 . . . . 22 A5
Porteridges RH4 . . . . 136 C4
Portesbery Hill Dr GU15 . . . 65 E6
Portesbery Rd GU15 . . . . 65 E6
Portesbery Sch GU15 . . . . . . 65 D6
Porthcawe Rd SE26 . . . . 23 F4
Portia Gr RG42 . . . . 27 E8
Portland Ave KT3 . . . . 38 F2
Portland Cotts CR0 . . . . 41 D2
Portland Cres TW13, TW15 . 14 D4
Portland Dr RH1 . . . . 119 D6
Portland House
B East Grinstead RH19 . . . 205 F8
Merstham RH1 . . . . 119 D6
20 Streatham SW2 . . . . 21 F7
Portland House Mews
KT18 . . . . 76 D5
Portland PI El Croydon SE25 . 43 A5
Ewell KT17 . . . . 76 E7
Portland Rd Ashford TW15 . 13 E5
Croydon SE25 . . . . 43 A5
Dorking RH4 . . . . 136 A8
East Grinstead RH19 . . . . . 205 F8
Kingston u t KT1 . . . . 37 F6
Mitcham CR4 . . . . 40 E7
Portland Terr TW9 . . . . 6 D3
Portley La CR3 . . . . 100 E6
Portley Wood Rd CR3 . . . . 101 A7
Portman Ave SW14 . . . . 7 D4
Portman CI El RG42 . . . . 27 A8
Portman Rd KT1 . . . . 37 F7
Portmore Park Rd KT13 . . . . 53 A6
Portmore Quays KT13 . . . . . 52 F6
Portmore Way KT13 . . . . 53 A7
Portnall Dr GU25 . . . . 30 F4
Portnall Rd GU25 . . . . 30 F4
Portnall Rise GU25 . . . . 30 F3
Portnalls CI CR5 . . . . 79 B3
Portnalls Rd CR5 . . . . 79 B2
Portnalls Rise CR5 . . . . 79 C3
Portobello House El
SW27 . . . . 22 B3
Porton Ct KT6 . . . . 37 C3
Portsea House El SW15 . . . . 19 B7
Portsmouth Ave KT7 . . . . . . 37 A2
Portsmouth Rd
Camberley GU15 . . . . 66 A7
Cobham KT10, KT11 . . . . 73 D3
Downside KT11 . . . . 72 F6
Esher KT10 . . . . 55 A4
Esher KT10 . . . . 55 D7
Godalming GU2, GU8 . . . . . 150 B2
Guildford GU2 . . . . 108 E2
Haslemere GU26 . . . . 188 E2
Hinchley Wood KT10, KT7 . . 55 E8
Hindhead GU26 . . . . 188 E2
Kingston u T KT1, KT6 . . . . . 37 C3
Milford GU8 . . . . 149 E1
Ockham GU23 . . . . 91 F7
Putney SW15 . . . . 19 C8
Ripley GU23 . . . . 91 B4
Send Marsh GU23 . . . . 91 B4
Thames Ditton KT6, KT7 . . . 37 C3
Thursley GU8 . . . . 169 D3
Wisley GU23, KT11 . . . . 72 D3
Witley GU8 . . . . 170 B6
Portswood PI SW15 . . . . 7 F1
Portugal Gdns TW2 . . . . 16 C6
Portugal Rd GU21 . . . . 69 F3
Portway KT17 . . . . 58 A2
Portway Cres KT17 . . . . 58 A2
Post House La KT23 . . . . 94 A2
Pot La GU22 . . . . 90 D7
Postford Mill Cotts GU4 . . 131 F5
Postmill CI CR0, CR9 . . . . . . 62 D7
Potley Hill Cty Prim Sch
GU46 . . . . 64 A5
Potley Hill Rd GU46 . . . . 64 A5
Potter CI CR4 . . . . 41 B7
Potter's La SW16 . . . . 21 D2
Potterhill Ct TW11 . . . . 17 B1
Potteries La GU16 . . . . 85 F4
Potteries The
Farnborough GU14 . . . . 84 D6
Ottershaw KT16 . . . . 51 E4
Potterne CI B SW15, SW19 . 19 D7
Potters CI Croydon CR0 . . . . 43 E1
Milford GU8 . . . . 149 F2
Potters Cres GU12 . . . . 106 B2
Potters Croft RH13 . . . . 217 E2
Potters Gate CE Prim Sch
GU9 . . . . 125 A2
Potters Gr KT3 . . . . 38 B5
Potters La GU23 . . . . 90 B2
Potters Way RH2 . . . . 139 C5
Pottersfield RH10 . . . . 201 D7
Pottery Ct GU10 . . . . 145 F6
Pottery La GU10 . . . . 145 F6
Pottery Rd TW8 . . . . 6 E8
Poulett Gdns TW1 . . . . 17 A7
Poullett House SW2 . . . . 22 B7
Poulton Ave SM1, SM5 . . . . . 59 D7

Pound CI Godalming GU7 . . 150 E4
Long Ditton KT6 . . . . 37 C1
Loxwood RH14 . . . . 212 F5
Pound Cres KT22 . . . . 94 D6
Pound Ct Ashstead KT21 . . . 75 F1
Wood St V GU3 . . . . 108 B2
Pound Farm La GU12 . . . . . 106 D1
Pound Field GU1 . . . . 109 D1
Pound Hill GU3 . . . . 108 B2
Pound Hill Cty Fst & Mid
Schs RH10 . . . . 202 C7
Pound Hill Par RH10 . . . . . 202 C7
Pound Hill PI RH10 . . . . 202 C6
Pound La Epsom KT19 . . . . . 76 D8
Godalming GU7 . . . . 150 E4
Windlesham GU20 . . . . 48 C4
Wood St V GU3 . . . . 108 B2
Pound PI GU4 . . . . 130 E3
Pound Place CI GU4 . . . . . . 130 F3
Pound Rd Aldershot GU12 . 105 C1
Banstead SM7 . . . . 78 A2
Chertsey KT16 . . . . 33 B2
Pound St SM5 . . . . 59 F5
Poundfield Gdns GU22 . . . . 90 C7
Poundfield La RH14 . . . . . . 212 E8
Povey Cross Rd RH6 . . . . . . 160 E1
Powder Mill La TW2, TW4 . . 16 A7
Powderham Ct GU21 . . . . . . 68 D1
Powell CI Chessington KT9 . 56 D5
Guildford GU2 . . . . 129 F7
Horley RH6 . . . . 160 E4
Wallington SM6 . . . . 60 E3
Powell Corderoy Prim Sch
RH4 . . . . 135 F6
Powell Ct CR0 . . . . 61 C6
Powell's Wlk W4 . . . . 7 F8
Powers Ct Mortlake CR4 . . . 14 C4
Powers Ct TW1 . . . . 17 D8
Pownall Gdns TW3 . . . . 5 B3
Pownall Rd TW3 . . . . 5 B3
Poyle 14 Trad Est SL3 . . . . . . 1 E4
Poyle Fst Sch SL3 . . . . 1 F6
Poyle Gdns RG12 . . . . 27 D8
Poyle House GU4 . . . . 110 D2
Poyle New Cotts SL3 . . . . 1 F5
Poyle Rd Guildford GU1 . . . 130 E7
Poyle SL3 . . . . 1 E5
Tongham GU10 . . . . 127 B7
Poyle Tech Ctr The SL3 . . . . . 1 E5
Poynders Gdns SW12, SW4 . 21 C8
Poynders Rd SW12, SW4 . . . 21 C8
Poynes Rd RH6 . . . . 160 E5
Poynings Rd RH11 . . . . 200 E5
Prairie CI KT15 . . . . 52 B7
Prairie Rd KT15 . . . . 52 B7
Pratts Cnr GU6 . . . . 193 A8
Pratts La KT12 . . . . 54 D6
Precinct The
Cranleigh GU6 . . . . 174 E4
East Molesey KT8 . . . . 36 B6
Egham TW20 . . . . 12 A3
Precincts The SM4 . . . . 40 A3
Prendergast House El
SW4 . . . . 21 D8
Prentice CI GU14 . . . . 85 B8
Prentice Ct El SW19 . . . . 19 F3
Prentis Rd SW16 . . . . 21 D4
Presburg Rd KT3 . . . . 38 E4
Presbury Ct GU21 . . . . 68 F2
Prescott KT1 . . . . 26 F2
Prescott Rd SL3 . . . . 1 E5
Presentation Mews SW2 . . . 21 F7
Prestbury Cres SM7 . . . . 78 F3
Preston CI TW2 . . . . 16 E5
Preston Ct KT12 . . . . 35 C1
Preston Dr KT19 . . . . 57 F4
Preston Gr KT21 . . . . 75 C2
Preston La KT20 . . . . 97 C7
Preston PI TW10 . . . . 6 E2
Preston Rd Littleton TW17 . . 34 A4
South Norwood SE19 . . . . . . 22 B2
Wimbledon SW20 . . . . 18 F1
Prestwick CI RH11 . . . . 200 D5
Prestwick La
Chiddingfold GU8 . . . . 190 C3
Grayswood GU8 . . . . 190 C3
Prestwood CI RH11 . . . . . . 181 B1
Prestwood Gdns CR0 . . . . . . 42 C2
Prestwood La
RH11, RH12, RH6 . . . . 180 E2
Pretoria Rd Chertsey KT16 . . 32 F1
Streatham SW16 . . . . 21 C3
Pretty La CR5 . . . . 99 C6
Prey Heath CI GU22 . . . . 89 C3
Prey Heath Rd GU22 . . . . . . 89 B3
Preymead Ind Est GU9 . . . 126 B7
Price CI SW17 . . . . 20 F5
Price Rd CR0 . . . . 61 B5
Priddy's Way TW12 . . . . 15 E2
Prices La RH2 . . . . 139 B6
Prickley Wood BR2 . . . . 44 F3
Priddy's Yd 4 CR9 . . . . 61 C8
Prides Crossing SL5 . . . . 9 A1
Pridham Rd CR7 . . . . 42 D5
Priest Ave RG40 . . . . 25 F5
Priest Croft CI RH11 . . . . . . 201 A6
Priest Hill Englefield Green
TW19, TW20 . . . . 11 C6
Nutfield RH8 . . . . 123 B6
Priest Hill Sch Sports Ctr
KT17 . . . . 77 B8
Priest La GU24 . . . . 67 C5
Priestfield Rd SE23 . . . . 23 E5
Priestley Gdns GU22 . . . . . . 90 A7
Priestley Rd
Guildford GU2 . . . . 129 D8
Mitcham CR4 . . . . 41 A7
Priestley Way RH10 . . . . . . 182 A3

Priests Bridge SW14, SW15 . . 7 E4
Priestwood Ave RG42 . . . . . 26 F8
Priestwood Court Rd
RG42 . . . . 27 A8
Priestwood Sq El RG42 . . . . 27 A8
Prim Sch of Our Lady
Immaculate KT6 . . . . 38 B1
Primrose Ave RH6 . . . . 161 B1
Primrose Ct Carshalton CR4 . 41 B1
Catford SE6 . . . . 24 C3
Crawley RH11 . . . . 201 B3
Primrose Copse RH12 . . . . 217 E7
Primrose Ct
New Malden KT4 . . . . 39 A2
El Streatham SW12 . . . . 21 D8
Primrose Dr GU24 . . . . 68 A4
Primrose Gdns GU14 . . . . . . 84 E3
Primrose House El TW9 . . . . . 6 F6
Primrose La CR0 . . . . 43 D1
Primrose Rd KT12 . . . . 54 C5
Primrose Ridge GU7 . . . . . 150 B2
Primrose Way
Bramley GU5 . . . . 151 D5
Sandhurst GU47 . . . . 45 B1
Primrose Wlk
Bracknell RG12 . . . . 27 C4
Ewell KT17 . . . . 57 F3
Prince Albert Dr SL5 . . . . 28 D4
Prince Albert Sq RH1 . . . . . 140 A4
Prince Andrew Way SL5 . . . . 28 D7
Prince Charles Cres GU14 . . 85 C8
Prince Charles Way SM6 . . . 60 B7
Prince Consort Dr SL5 . . . . . 28 D4
Prince Consort's Dr
Old Windsor SL4 . . . . 10 A6
Winkfield SL4 . . . . 9 F4
Prince Dr GU47 . . . . 45 A1
Prince George's Ave
SW20 . . . . 39 C7
Prince Georges Rd SW19 . . 40 D8
Prince of Wales' Rd SM1 . . . 59 D8
Prince of Wales Rd RH1 . . . 141 A2
Prince of Wales Wlk El
GU15 . . . . 65 C6
Prince Rd SE25 . . . . 42 E4
Prince Regent Rd TW3 . . . . . . 5 C4
Prince William Ct TW15 . . . 13 F3
Prince's Ave
Farnborough GU11 . . . . 105 C5
Farncombe GU7 . . . . 150 C7
Prince's CI TW11, TW12 . . . . 16 D3
Prince's Dr KT22 . . . . 74 E7
Prince's Rd Mortlake SW14 . . 7 E4
Redhill RH1 . . . . 139 F7
Teddington TW11, TW12 . . . 16 C3
Weybridge KT13 . . . . 53 C5
Wimbledon SW19 . . . . 20 A2
Prince's St TW10, TW9 . . . . . . 6 E2
Princes Ave
Hamsey Green CR2 . . . . 81 B4
Tolworth KT6 . . . . 57 A8
Wallington SM5 . . . . 59 F7
Princes CI Bagshot GU19 . . . 47 E1
Hamsey Green CR2 . . . . 81 B4
Princes Ct New Malden KT3 . 38 F6
Weybridge KT13 . . . . 53 B5
Princes Gdns GU3 . . . . 108 E3
Princes Mead GU14 . . . . 85 B4
Princes Mews TW3 . . . . 5 A3
Princes Rd Ashford TW15 . . 13 F3
Egham TW20 . . . . 12 A3
Feltham TW13 . . . . 14 F5
Kingston u T KT2 . . . . 18 A1
Penge SE20 . . . . 23 D2
Richmond TW10 . . . . 6 F2
Richmond, Kew TW9 . . . . 6 F6
Princes St SM1 . . . . 59 D6
Princes Way
Aldershot GU11 . . . . 105 A2
Coney Hall BR4 . . . . 63 F7
Croydon CR0 . . . . 60 F5
Putney SW15, SW19 . . . . . . 19 E7
Princess Anne Rd RH12 . . 214 D6
Princess Ct
Aldershot GU14 . . . . 105 C8
El Wimbledon SW19 . . . . . . 19 D1
Princess Gdns GU22 . . . . . . 70 B3
Princess House El RH1 . . . . 119 A2
Princess Margaret Rd
RH12 . . . . 214 D7
Princess Mary's Rd KT15 . . 52 C6
Princess Rd Crawley RH11 . 201 C6
Thornton Heath CR0 . . . . . . 42 C3
Woking GU22 . . . . 70 C3
Princess Sq RG12 . . . . 27 B7
Princess Way
Camberley GU15 . . . . 65 C5
Redhill RH1 . . . . 119 A2
Princethorpe Rd SE26 . . . . . 23 D4
Princeton Mews El KT2 . . . . 38 A8
Pringle Gdns Purley CR8 . . . 60 F1
Streatham SW16 . . . . 21 C4
Prins Willem-Alexander
Sch GU22 . . . . 70 C2
Prior Ave SM2, SM5 . . . . 59 E3
Prior Croft CI GU15 . . . . 66 A4
Prior End GU15 . . . . 66 A4
Prior Heath Cty Inf Sch
GU15 . . . . 66 A5
Prior Rd GU15 . . . . 66 A5
Prioress Rd SE27 . . . . 22 B5
Priors CI GU14 . . . . 85 B8
Priors Croft GU22 . . . . 90 A7
Priors Ct Ash GU12 . . . . 105 E1
Woking GU21 . . . . 69 A1
Priors Field Sch GU7 . . . . . 129 A1
Priors Hatch La GU7 . . . . . 128 F1

Pol–Pun 273

Priors Lodge El TW10 . . . . 6 E1
Priors Mead KT23 . . . . 94 C2
Priors The KT21 . . . . 95 D8
Priors Wlk RH10 . . . . 201 F6
Priors Wood GU27 . . . . 207 F6
Priorsfield Rd GU27 . . . . . . 129 A1
Priorswood GU3 . . . . 128 F2
Priory Ave SM3 . . . . 58 D6
Priory C of E Mid Sch
SW19 . . . . 20 B3
Priory CI Beckenham BR3 . . . 43 E6
Dorking RH4 . . . . 136 A5
Hampton TW12 . . . . 35 F8
Horley RH6 . . . . 160 F4
El Merton SW19 . . . . 40 A8
Sheerwater GU21 . . . . 70 D6
Sunbury TW16 . . . . 15 A1
Sunningdale SL5 . . . . 30 A2
Walton-on-T KT12 . . . . 54 A7
Priory Cres Cheam SM3 . . . . 58 D6
South Norwood SE19 . . . . . . 22 C1
Priory Ct Camberley GU15 . . 64 F5
Cheam SM3 . . . . 58 D6
Cheam SM1 . . . . 58 F5
Egham TW20 . . . . 12 C2
Hounslow TW3 . . . . 5 B3
Roehampton SW15 . . . . 7 F3
Priory Dr RH2 . . . . 139 A7
Priory Gdns Hampton TW12 . 35 F8
Mortlake SW13 . . . . 7 F4
South Norwood SE25 . . . . . . 42 F5
Priory Gn TW18 . . . . 13 B3
Priory Hospl The SW15 . . . . . 7 E3
Priory House SE6 . . . . 24 B7
Priory La East Molesey KT8 . 36 B5
Frensham GU10 . . . . 167 E8
Roehampton SW15 . . . . 7 F3
Priory Lodge BR4 . . . . 63 E7
Priory Mews TW18 . . . . 13 B3
Priory PI KT12 . . . . 54 A7
Priory Rd Cheam SM3 . . . . . 58 D6
Chessington KT9 . . . . 56 E7
Forest Row RH18 . . . . 206 D2
Hampton TW12 . . . . 16 A1
Isleworth TW3 . . . . 5 C2
Mitcham SW19 . . . . 20 D1
Reigate RH2 . . . . 139 A6
Richmond TW9 . . . . 7 A7
Sunningdale SL5 . . . . 30 A2
Thornton Heath CR0 . . . . . . 42 A2
Winkfield SL5 . . . . 28 D8
Priory Sch SE25 . . . . 42 F5
Priory Sch The SM7 . . . . 78 A4
Priory' St GU14 . . . . 85 D4
Priory The Croydon CR0 . . . . 61 A7
Godstone RH9 . . . . 121 B3
El Kingston u T KT6 . . . . 37 E4
Priory Way UB7 . . . . 2 E8
Priory Wlk RG12 . . . . 27 E8
Priscilla House El TW16 . . . . 14 F1
Probyn Rd SW2 . . . . 22 B6
Proctor CI Crawley RH10 . . 202 C4
Mitcham CR4 . . . . 41 B8
Proctor Gdns KT23 . . . . 94 B2
Proctors CI TW14 . . . . 15 A7
Proctors Rd RG40 . . . . 25 F6
Profumo Rd KT12 . . . . 54 D5
Progress Bsns Pk CR9 . . . . . 60 F8
Progress Way CR0 . . . . 60 F8
Promenade Approach Rd
W4 . . . . 7 E2
Promenade De Verdun
CR8 . . . . 79 D8
Promenade The W4 . . . . 7 E6
Prospect Ave GU14 . . . . 85 B6
Prospect CI Forest Hill SE26 . 23 B4
Hounslow TW5 . . . . 4 F6
Prospect Cotts RG42 . . . . . . 26 D8
Prospect Cres TW2 . . . . 5 C1
Prospect La TW20 . . . . 11 A3
Prospect PI Crawley RH11 . 201 C6
Ewell KT17 . . . . 76 E6
Staines TW18 . . . . 13 B3
Wimbledon SW20 . . . . 19 B1
Prospect Rd Ash GU12 . . . 106 A3
Farnborough GU14 . . . . 85 A5
Rowledge GU10 . . . . 145 E3
Thames Ditton KT6 . . . . 37 C2
Prossers KT20 . . . . 97 D6
Providence House GU19 . . . 47 E3
Providence La UB3 . . . . 3 D7
Providence PI Ewell KT17 . . 76 E7
Farnham GU9 . . . . 125 C2
Provincial Terr SE20 . . . . 23 D1
Prune Hill TW20 . . . . 11 E1
Prunus CI GU24 . . . . 67 E6
Public Record Office TW9 . . . 7 A7
Puckridge Hill Rd GU11 . . 104 E5
Puckshill GU21 . . . . 68 D2
Puckshott Way GU27 . . . . . 208 D8
Puddenhole Cotts RH4 . . . 116 A2
Pudding La RH6 . . . . 180 E7
Puffin CI Beckenham BR3 . . . 43 D4
Puffin Rd RH11 . . . . 200 D5
Pulborough Rd SW18 . . . . . . 19 F8
Pulborough Way TW4 . . . . 4 C3
Pullman Ct SW2 . . . . 21 F7
Pullman La GU7 . . . . 150 C2
Pullmans PI TW18 . . . . 13 A3
Pump Alley El TW8 . . . . 6 D7
Pump La SL5 . . . . 29 E8
Pump Pail N CR0, CR9 . . . . . 61 C7
Pump Pail S CR0, CR9 . . . . . 61 C7
Pumping Station Rd W4 . . . . . 7 E8
Punch Copse Rd RH10 . . . . 201 F7

Punchbowl La RH4, RH5 . . .136 D6
Punnetts Ct RH11 . . . . .200 F2
Purbeck Ave KT3 . . . . .38 F3
Purbeck Cl RH1 . . . . .119 D7
Purbeck Ct 4 GU2 . . . . .108 E1
Purbeck Dr GU21 . . . . .69 F5
Purberry Gr KT17 . . . . .57 F1
Purberry Shot KT17 . . . . .57 F1
Purbrook Ct RG12 . . . . .27 E3
Purbrook House 2 SW15 . .19 B7
Purcell House TW2 . . . . .5 D1
Purcell Rd Crowthorne RG45 . . . .200 F3
Crowthorne RG45 . . . . .45 B7
Purcell's Cl KT21 . . . . .75 F1
Purdey Ct 8 KT4 . . . . .39 A1
Purley Bury Ave CR8 . . . . .80 C8
Purley Bury Cl CR8 . . . . .80 C8
Purley Cl RH10 . . . . .202 D3
Purley Ct CR8 . . . . .61 B1
Purley & District War
Memorial Hospl CR8 . . . . . . .80 A8
Purley Downs Rd CR2 . . . . . . .80 E8
Purley Hill CR8 . . . . .80 B7
Purley Knoll CR8 . . . . .80 A8
Purley Oaks Prim Sch
CR2 .61 D3
Purley Oaks Rd CR2 . . . . .61 D1
Purley Oaks Sta CR2 . . . . .61 D2
Purley Par 2 CR8 . . . . .80 A8
Purley Park Rd CR8 . . . . .61 B1
Purley Rd Purley CR8 . . . . .80 A8
South Croydon CR2 . . . . .61 D3
Purley Rise CR8 . . . . .79 F7
Purley Sta CR8 . . . . .80 A7
Purley Vale CR8 . . . . .80 B6
Purley View Terr CR7 . . . . .61 A4
Purley Way
Croydon CR0, CR9 . . . . .61 A4
Frimley GU16 . . . . .85 E8
Purley CR8 . . . . .80 A8
Thornton Heath CR0, CR9 . . . . . .41 F1
Purmerend Cl GU14 . . . . .84 C5
Pursers Hollow GU5 . . . . .154 D8
Pursers La GU5 . . . . .154 D8
Purslane RG40 . . . . .25 D5
Purton Rd RH12 . . . . .217 B4
Putney Heath SW15 . . . . .19 B8
Putney Hill SW15 . . . . .19 D8
Puttenham Common
Nature Trails GU3 . . . . .148 E8
Puttenham Heath Rd
Puttenham GU3 . . . . .128 E3
Wanborough GU3 . . . . .128 E3
Puttenham Hill GU3 . . . . .128 C5
Puttenham La GU3, GU8 . . . . .128 C1
Puttenham Rd GU10 . . . . .127 C4
Puttenham Sch CE (VA)
GU3 .128 C4
Puttock Cl GU27 . . . . .207 D5
Pye Cl CR3 . . . . .100 D4
Pyecombe Ct 4 RH11 . . . . . . .200 F3
Pyegrove Chase RG12 . . . . . . .27 E2
Pyestock Cres GU14 . . . . .84 C4
Pylbrook Rd SM1 . . . . .59 B7
Pyle Hill GU22, GU4 . . . . .89 D3
Pymers Mead Dulwich SE21 . . .22 C7
West Norwood SE21 . . . . .22 C7
Pyne Rd KT6 . . . . .38 A1
Pyrcroft Grange Prim Sch
KT16 .32 E3
Pyrcroft La KT13 . . . . .53 B5
Pyrcroft Rd KT16 . . . . .32 E2
Pyrford Common Rd GU22 . . .70 E2
Pyrford Cty Prim Sch
GU22 . . . . .71 A3
Pyrford Heath GU22 . . . . .70 F3
Pyrford Rd
Pyrford GU22, KT14 . . . . .71 A4
West Byfleet GU22, KT14 . . . . . .71 A4
Woking GU22, KT14 . . . . .71 A4
Pyrford Woods Cl GU22 . . . . . .70 F4
Pyrford Woods Rd GU22 . . . . .70 F4
Pyrland Rd TW10 . . . . .6 F1
Pyrmont Gr SE27 . . . . .22 B5
Pyrmont Rd W4 . . . . .7 A8
Pytchley Cres SE19 . . . . .22 C2

Q

Quadrangle Lodge SW19 . . . .20 A2
Quadrangle The GU2 . . . . . . .130 A8
Quadrant Ct RG12 . . . . .27 E6
Quadrant Rd Richmond TW9 . . . .6 D3
Thornton Heath CR7 . . . . .42 B5
Quadrant The
Ash Vale GU12 . . . . .106 A4
Merton SW20 . . . . .39 E8
Richmond TW9 . . . . .6 D3
Sutton SM2 . . . . .59 C4
Quail Cl RH12 . . . . .217 D7
Quail Gdns CR0 . . . . .62 E1
Quakers Way GU3 . . . . .108 C5
Qualitas RG12 . . . . .26 F1
Quality St RH1 . . . . .119 A4
Quantock Cl
Crawley RH11 . . . . .201 B6
Harlington UB3 . . . . .3 D7
Quantock Dr KT4 . . . . .58 C8
Quarr Rd SM5 . . . . .40 E3
Quarry Bank GU18 . . . . .67 A8
Quarry Cl Horsham RH12 . .217 F6
Oxted RH8 . . . . .122 C6
Quarry Hill GU7 . . . . .150 B3
Quarry Hill Pk RH2 . . . . .118 C4

Quarry Park Rd SM1 . . . . .58 F4
Quarry Rd Oxted RH8 . . . . . . .122 E5
Shackleford GU7 . . . . .150 A7
Woldingham RH9 . . . . .121 C7
Quarry Rise Cheam SM1 . . . . . .58 F4
East Grinstead RH19 . . . . .186 A3
Quarry St GU1 . . . . .130 D7
Quarry The RH3 . . . . .116 D3
Quarter Mile Rd GU7 . . . . . . .150 E2
Quarterbrass Farm Rd
RH12 . . . . .217 D7
Quartermaine Ave GU22 . . . . .89 F5
Quarters Rd GU14 . . . . .85 C2
Quay West TW11 . . . . .17 B3
Quebec Cl RH6 . . . . .162 A3
Quebec Gdns GU17 . . . . .64 D4
Queen Adelaide Ct SE20 . . . .23 C2
Queen Adelaide Rd SE20 . . . .23 C1
Queen Alexandra's Ct 5
SW19 . . . . .19 F3
Queen Anne Ave BR2 . . . . .44 F6
Queen Anne Dr KT10 . . . . .55 E3
Queen Anne's Cl SL4 . . . . .10 B5
Queen Anne's Gdns
Leatherhead KT22 . . . . .95 B6
Mitcham CR4 . . . . .40 F6
Queen Annes Cl TW2 . . . . .16 D5
Queen Annes Ct KT22 . . . . . . .95 B6
Queen Annes Gate GU9 . . . . .125 D7
Queen Eleanor's C of E
Jun Sch GU2 . . . . .130 A8
Queen Eleanor's Rd GU2 . . .129 H8
Queen Elizabeth Dr GU11 . .104 F2
Queen Elizabeth Gdns
SM4 . . . . .40 A5
Queen Elizabeth Hospl
SM7 . . . . .78 C1
Queen Elizabeth II
Jubilee Sch The RH13 . . .217 F1
Queen Elizabeth Rd
Camberley GU15 . . . . .46 D1
Kingston u T KT2 . . . . .37 F7
Rudgwick RH12 . . . . .214 D7
Queen Elizabeth Way
Guildford GU1 . . . . .90 A8
Queen Elizabeth's Dr CR0 . . .63 D1
Queen Elizabeth's Gdns
CR0 . . . . .63 D1
Queen Elizabeth's Wlk
SM6 . . . . .60 D6
Queen Mary Ave
Camberley GU15 . . . . .65 A5
West Barnes SM4, SW20 . . . . . .39 D4
Queen Mary Cl
Tolworth KT9 . . . . .57 A8
Woking GU22 . . . . .70 C3
Queen Mary Rd
Charlton TW17 . . . . .34 C7
South Norwood SE19 . . . . .22 B2
Queen Mary's Ave SM5 . . . . . .59 F3
Queen Mary's Dr KT15 . . . . . .52 A1
Queen St Aldershot GU12 . . .105 B2
Chertsey KT16 . . . . .33 A1
Croydon CR0, CR9 . . . . .61 C6
Godalming GU7 . . . . .150 E4
Gomshall GU5 . . . . .133 C4
Horsham RH13 . . . . .217 D1
Queen Victoria Cross
Roads GU15 . . . . .65 A6
Queen Victoria Ct GU14 . . . . .85 B5
Queen Victoria Hospl
The RH19 . . . . .185 F3
Queen Victoria Way GU24 . . .87 D8
Queen's Ave
Aldershot GU11 . . . . .105 B5
Farnborough GU11 . . . . .105 B5
Queen's C of E Jun Mix
Sch The TW9 . . . . .7 A7
Queen's C of E Jun Sch The
TW9 . . . . .7 A7
Queen's Cl
Farnborough GU14 . . . . .105 B8
North Ascot SL5 . . . . .28 E8
Wallington SM6 . . . . .60 B5
Queen's Ct Beckenham BR3 . .44 A8
Croydon CR2 . . . . .61 C5
Farnborough GU14 . . . . .105 C8
1 Kingston u T KT2 . . . . .18 A1
5 Richmond TW10 . . . . .6 E1
Staines TW18 . . . . .13 D2
Thornton Heath CR7 . . . . .42 A4
Queen's Dr
Farncombe GU7 . . . . .150 C7
Guildford GU2 . . . . .109 A4
Thames Ditton KT7 . . . . .37 A3
Queen's Gate Rd GU14 . . . . .105 B8
Queen's Gdns TW5 . . . . .4 E6
Queen's Hospl CR0 . . . . .42 C3
Queen's House TW11 . . . . . . .16 F2
Queen's Mead GU8 . . . . .191 B4
Queen's Mead Rd BR2 . . . . . . .44 F7
Queen's Park Rd CR3 . . . . . . .100 E4
Queen's Pl Ascot SL5 . . . . .29 A6
Morden SM4 . . . . .40 A5
Queen's Rd Ascot SL5 . . . . . . .29 D4
Beckenham BR3 . . . . .43 E7
East Grinstead RH19 . . . . .185 E1
Egham TW20 . . . . .11 F2
Feltham TW13, TW14 . . . . .15 B7
Guildford GU1 . . . . .109 D1
Hampton TW12 . . . . .16 B4
Horley RH6 . . . . .161 A3
Hounslow TW3 . . . . .5 B3
Kingston u T KT2 . . . . .18 A1
Knaphill GU21 . . . . .68 D1

Queens Rd continued
Mitcham CR4 . . . . .40 D6
Mortlake SW14 . . . . .7 D4
New Malden KT3 . . . . .38 F4
Richmond TW10 . . . . .6 F1
Richmond, Richmond Park
KT2, TW10 . . . . .18 A3
Teddington TW11 . . . . .16 F2
Thames Ditton KT7 . . . . .36 F4
Thornton Heath CR0 . . . . .42 C3
Wallington SM6 . . . . .60 B5
Wimbledon SW19 . . . . .20 A2
Queen's Rdbt GU11 . . . . .105 B7
Queen's Rise TW10 . . . . .6 F1
Queen's Terr TW7 . . . . .6 A3
Queen's Way GU24 . . . . .87 D8
Queendale Ct GU21 . . . . .68 F3
Queenhill Rd CR2 . . . . .62 B1
Queenhythe Rd GU4 . . . . . . .109 D7
Queens Acre SM2, SM3 . . . . . .58 E3
Queens Ave Byfleet KT14 . . . .71 D7
Feltham TW13 . . . . .15 C4
Queens Cl Bisley GU24 . . . . . .68 A3
Walton on t H KT20 . . . . .97 A3
Queens Court Ride KT11 . . . . .73 A6
Queens Cres TW10 . . . . .6 F2
Queens Ct 3 Redhill RH1 . .119 A2
Weybridge KT13 . . . . .53 E4
Queens Dr Oxshott KT22 . . . . .74 C8
Surbiton KT5 . . . . .38 A3
Queens Gate RH4 . . . . .182 A8
Queens Hill Rise SL5 . . . . .29 C6
Queens Keep
Camberley GU15 . . . . .65 D5
10 Twickenham TW1 . . . . .6 C1
Queens La GU9 . . . . .125 B7
Queens Park Gdns TW13 . . . .14 F5
Queens Pine RG12 . . . . .27 E3
Queens Pl KT12, KT13 . . . . . . .53 E5
Queens Rd Aldershot GU11 . .104 F2
Belmont SM2 . . . . .78 A8
Bisley GU24 . . . . .67 F1
Camberley GU15 . . . . .65 B4
Farnborough GU14 . . . . .105 D8
Hale GU9 . . . . .125 C6
Hersham KT12 . . . . .54 A6
Morden SM4 . . . . .40 A5
Twickenham TW1 . . . . .17 A7
Weybridge KT13 . . . . .53 E5
Queens Reach KT8 . . . . .36 E5
Queens Sq RH10 . . . . .201 D6
Queens Way Croydon CR0 . . . .60 F5
Feltham TW13 . . . . .15 C4
Queens Wlk TW15 . . . . .13 D4
Queensberry House 6
TW9 . . . . .6 D2
Queensbridge Pk TW7 . . . . . . .5 E2
Queensbury Ct CR7 . . . . .42 C7
Queensbury Pl GU17 . . . . .64 C3
Queenscroft Rd SM3 . . . . .58 C6
Queensgate KT11 . . . . .73 D7
Queenshill Lodge SL5 . . . . . . .29 B6
Queensland Ave SW19 . . . . . .40 B8
Queensmead GU14 . . . . .85 B3
Queensmead Ave KT17 . . . . . .58 B1
Queensmere Cl SW19 . . . . . . .19 D6
Queensmere Rd SW19 . . . . . .19 D6
Queensmere
(Southlands Coll) SW19 . .19 D6
Queensthorpe Rd SE26 . . . . .23 D4
Queensway Hl SW12, SW4 . . .21 D8
Queensway Coney Hall BR4 . .63 F6
Cranleigh GU6 . . . . .174 F2
Crawley RH10 . . . . .201 E6
East Grinstead RH19 . . . . .185 E1
Frimley GU16 . . . . .86 A7
Hersham KT12 . . . . .54 B5
Horsham RH13 . . . . .217 C1
Redhill RH1 . . . . .118 F2
Sunbury TW16 . . . . .35 B7
Queensway N KT12 . . . . .54 C6
Queensway S KT12 . . . . .54 C5
Queenswood Ave
Hampton TW12 . . . . .16 B2
Hounslow TW3, TW5 . . . . .4 F5
Thornton Heath CR7 . . . . .42 A4
Wallington SM6 . . . . .60 D6
Queenswood Ct 11 SE27 . . . .22 D4
Queenswood Rd
Forest Hill SE23 . . . . .23 E5
Knaphill GU21 . . . . .88 D3
Quennel House 7 SW12 . . . .21 C8
Quennell Ct KT11 . . . . .95 F8
Quennells Hill GU10 . . . . . . .145 E6
Quentin Way GU25 . . . . .31 B5
Quicks Rd SW19 . . . . .20 B1
Quidhampton RH12 . . . . .115 A1
Quillot The KT12 . . . . .53 F5
Quince Cl SL5 . . . . .29 D5
Quince Dr GU24 . . . . .68 B4
Quincy Rd TW20 . . . . .12 A3
Quinneys GU14 . . . . .85 D1
Quintilis RG12 . . . . .26 F1
Quintin Ave SW20 . . . . .39 F8
Quintin Ct W4 . . . . .7 C7
Quintock House 2 TW9 . . . . . .7 A6
Quinton Cl
Beckenham BR3 . . . . .44 C6
Hackbridge SM6 . . . . .60 B6
Heston TW5 . . . . .4 B7
Quinton Rd KT7 . . . . .37 A1
Quinton St SW18 . . . . .20 C6
Quintrell Cl GU21 . . . . .69 B2

R

Rabbit La KT12 . . . . .54 B3

Rabies Heath Rd
Bletchingley RH1 . . . . .120 F2
Godstone RH1, RH9 . . . . .121 B1
Raby Rd KT3 . . . . .38 D5
Raccoon Way TW4 . . . . .4 C5
Racecourse Rd
Crawley RH6 . . . . .181 F8
Dormansland RH7 . . . . .165 A2
Lingfield RH7 . . . . .165 A2
Racecourse Way RH6 . . . . . . .181 F8
Rachel Ct SM2 . . . . .59 D3
Rackfield GU27 . . . . .207 D7
Rackham Cl RH11 . . . . .201 D4
Rackham Mews SW16 . . . . . . .21 C2
Racks Ct GU1 . . . . .130 D7
Rackstraw Rd GU47 . . . . .45 D2
Racquets Court Hill GU7 . . .150 C6
Rad La Peaslake GU5 . . . . . . .133 D1
Peaslake RH5 . . . . .133 E1
Radbourne Rd SW12 . . . . .21 D7
Radcliff Mews TW12 . . . . .16 C3
Radcliffe Cl GU16 . . . . .86 A7
Radcliffe Gdns SM5 . . . . .59 E3
Radcliffe Rd CR0 . . . . .61 F7
Radcliffe Way RG42 . . . . .26 E8
Radcot Point 2 SE23 . . . . . . .23 D5
Radford Cl GU9 . . . . .125 E5
Radford Rd RH10, RH6 . . . . . .182 C4
Radius Pk TW6 . . . . .3 F3
Radlet Ave SE23 . . . . .23 B6
Radley Cl TW14 . . . . .14 F7
Radley Ct 2 SW16 . . . . .24 C4
Radley Lodge 10 SW19 . . . . .19 D7
Radnor Cl CR4 . . . . .41 E5
Radnor Ct
8 Forest Hill SE23 . . . . .23 D5
Redhill RH1 . . . . .118 E1
Radnor Gdns TW1 . . . . .16 F6
Radnor La
Abinger Common RH5 . . . . . . .155 B7
Ewhurst RH5 . . . . .155 A2
Radnor Rd Bracknell RG12 . . .27 F6
Peaslake GU5, GU6 . . . . .154 E4
Twickenham TW1 . . . . .16 F6
Weybridge KT13 . . . . .53 A7
Radnor Wlk CR0 . . . . .43 E3
Radolphs KT20 . . . . .97 D5
Radstock Way RH1 . . . . .119 D7
Radstone Ct 1 GU22 . . . . .69 F1
Raeburn Ave Surbiton KT5 . . . .38 A3
Raeburn Cl 1 KT1 . . . . .17 C1
Raeburn Ct 1 SW16 . . . . .21 E5
Raeburn Ave Surbiton KT3 . . . .38 B3
Tolworth KT5, KT6 . . . . .38 B3
Raeburn Ct KT1 . . . . .17 D1
Raeburn Way GU47 . . . . .64 D6
RAF Staff Coll RG12 . . . . .27 D5
Rag Hill Cl TN16 . . . . .103 E6
Rag Hill Rd TN16 . . . . .103 E6
Rag Hill Rd TN16 . . . . .103 E6
Raglan Cl Aldershot GU12 . . .105 C1
Frimley GU16 . . . . .86 A8
Reigate RH2 . . . . .118 D3
Raglan Ct CR0, CR2 . . . . .61 A5
Raglan Prec The CR3 . . . . . . .100 E5
Raglan Rd Knaphill GU21 . . . .68 E1
Reigate RH2 . . . . .118 C3
Raglans House RH1 . . . . .118 B4
Ragwort Ct 1 SE26 . . . . .23 B3
Raikes La RH5 . . . . .134 B2
Railey Rd RH10 . . . . .201 E7
Railshead Rd TW1, TW7 . . . . . .6 B3
Railton Rd GU2 . . . . .109 B5
Railway App Chertsey KT16 . .32 F1
East Grinstead RH19 . . . . .185 E1
Frimley GU16 . . . . .86 A7
11 Twickenham TW1 . . . . .17 A8
Wallington SM6 . . . . .60 B5
Railway Cotts CR8 . . . . .79 F6
Railway Rd TW11 . . . . .16 F4
Railway Side SW13, SW14 . . . .7 E4
Railway Terr Egham TW18 . . .12 D3
Feltham TW13, TW14 . . . . .15 A7
Rainbow Ct 3 GU21 . . . . .68 E3
Rainbow Ctr The KT17 . . . . . . .76 E7
Rake La Midford GU8 . . . . .171 A2
Witley GU8 . . . . .170 F7
Rakers Ridge RH12 . . . . .217 D5
Raleigh Ave SM6 . . . . .60 D6
Raleigh Ct Beckenham BR3 . .44 B8
Crawley RH10 . . . . .182 A3
Dulwich SE19 . . . . .22 F3
Staines TW18 . . . . .13 A4
Wallington SM6 . . . . .60 B4
Raleigh Dr Esher KT10 . . . . . . .55 D5
Smallfield RH6 . . . . .162 A3
Tolworth KT5 . . . . .38 C1
Raleigh Gdns CR4 . . . . .40 F6
Raleigh House 1 KT7 . . . . .37 A2
Raleigh Rd
Feltham TW13, TW14 . . . . .14 F5
Penge SE20 . . . . .23 D1
Richmond TW9 . . . . .6 F4
Raleigh Sch The KT24 . . . . . . .92 C2
Raleigh Way Feltham TW13 . . .15 C3
Frimley GU16 . . . . .65 F3
Raleigh Wlk RH10 . . . . .201 E4
Ralliwood Rd KT21 . . . . .96 A8
Ralph Perring Ct BR3 . . . . .44 A5
Ralph Ride RG12 . . . . .27 E2
Rama Cl SW16 . . . . .21 E1
Rambler Cl SW16 . . . . .21 C4
Ramblers Way 17 RH11 . . . .201 B1
Rame Cl SW17 . . . . .21 A3
Ramillis Cl GU11 . . . . .105 E7
Ramin Ct GU1 . . . . .109 C4
Ramornie Cl KT12 . . . . .54 F6
Rams La GU8 . . . . .193 B3

Ramsay Rd GU20 4
Ramsbury Cl RG12 2
Ramsdale Rd SW17 2
Ramsdean House 1 SW15 . . .1
Ramsden Rd Balham SW12 . . .2
Godalming GU7 15
Ramsey Cl Camberley GU15 . . .6
Horley RH6 16
Horsham RH12 2
Ramsey Ct
11 Crawley RH11 20
Croydon CR9 6
Ramsey House SW19 4
Ramsey Pl CR3 10
Ramsey Rd CR7 4
Ramslade Rd RG12 2
Rances La RG40 2
Randal Cres RH2 13
Randall Schofield Ct
RH10 .20
Randalls Cotts KT11 7
Randalls Cres KT22 9
Randalls Park Ave KT22 9
Randalls Park Dr KT22 9
Randalls Rd KT22 9
Randalls Way KT22 9
Randell Cl GU17 6
Randisbourne Gdns SE6 2
Randle Rd TW10 1
Randlesdown Rd SE6 2
Randmore Ct 8 BR3 2
Randolph Cl
Kingston u T KT2 1
Knaphill GU21 6
Oxshott KT11 7
Randolph Dr GU12 8
Randolph Rd KT17 7
Ranelagh Cotts RH6 16
Ranelagh Cres SL5 2
Ranelagh Dr
Bracknell RG12 2
Isleworth TW1 . . . .
Ranelagh Gdns W4 . . . .
Ranelagh Pl KT3 3
Ranelagh Rd RH1 11
Ranelagh Sch RG12 2
Ranfurly Rd SM1 5
Range Ride GU15 6
Range The GU5 15
Range Way GU47 6
Range Villas TW17 3
Range Way TW17 3
Rangefield Prim Sch BR1 2
Rangefield Rd Bromley BR1 2
Catford BR1 2
Rankine Cl GU9 12
Ranmere St SW12 2
Ranmore Ave CR0 6
Ranmore Cl Dorking RH4 13
East Ewell SM2 5
Wotton RH4, RH5 11
Rann House 1 SW14 . . . .
Rannoch Ct 3 KT6 3
Ranyard Cl KT9 5
Rapallo Cl GU14 8
Raphel Dr KT7 3
Rapley Cl GU15 4
Rapley Grn RG12 2
Rapley's Field GU24 8
Rapsley La GU21 6
Rastell Ave SW12 2
Ratcliffe Rd GU14 8
Rathbone House
Crawley RH11 20
6 Wimbledon SW19 1
Rathfern Prim Sch SE23 2
Rathfern Rd SE23, SE6 2
Rathgar Cl RH1 14
Rathlin Rd RH11 20
Raven Ct RH10 20
Raven La RH11 20
Ravendale Rd TW16 3
Ravendene Ct 3 RH10 20
Ravenfield Rd SW17 2
Ravens Cl Bromley BR2 4
Kingston u T KT6 3
Redhill RH1 11
Ravens Wold CR8 8
Ravensbourne 3 TW1 . . . .
Ravensbourne Ave
Bromley BR2, BR3 4
Catford BR2 2
Stanwell TW19 . . . .
Ravensbourne Ct SE6 2
Ravensbourne House BR1 2
Ravensbourne Park Cres
SE6 2
Ravensbourne Pk SE4, SE6 . .2
Ravensbourne Rd
Forest Hill SE23 2
Twickenham TW1 . . . .
Ravensbourne Sta BR3 2
Ravensbury Ave SM4 4
Ravensbury Ct CR4 4
Ravensbury Gr CR4 4
Ravensbury La CR4 4
Ravensbury Rd SW18 2
Ravensbury Terr SW18 2
Ravenscar Lodge 11 SW19 . . .1

nscar Rd Catford BR1 . . . 24 E4
nscott TW16 . . . . 56 F8
nscote Cty Jun Sch
. . . . 66 A3
nscourt TW16 . . . . 34 F8
nscourt Cl GU12 . . . . 106 C3
nscourt Dr RH10 . . . . 217 C3
nscourt Rd Penge BR3 . . . 43 E7
bridge KT13 . . . . 72 CB
nsdale Gdns SE19 . . . . 22 D1
nsdale Rd Ascot SL5 . . . . . 29 A4
. . . . 4 E4
nsfield TW20 . . . . 11 C2
nsfield Gdns KT19 . . . . . . 57 E6
nshaud Cl CR2 . . . . 81 C8
nside KT6 . . . . 37 D4
nsla Rd SW11, SW12 . . . 20 F8
nsmead Rd BR2 . . . . 24 D1
nsroost SE19 . . . . 42 D8
nstone Jun & Inf Schs
. . . . 21 A6
nstone Rd GU15 . . . . 66 D5
nstone St SW12 . . . . 21 A7
nsvierc KT6 . . . . 37 D4
nswood Ave
orth KT6 . . . . 57 A8
it Wickham BR4 . . . . 44 C1
nswood Cl KT11 . . . . 73 D4
nswood Cres BR4 . . . . 44 C1
nswood Ct GU22 . . . . 69 F1
nswood Dr GU15 . . . . 66 A5
nswood Gdns TW7 . . . . . . 5 E6
nswood Rd
nswood Sq
. . . . 21 8B
vdon CR0, CR9 . . . . 61 B7
jins Cl CR22 . . . . 62 F3
linson Rd GU15 . . . . 64 F6
insley Ave CR4 . . . . 40 E4
orth Cl RH10 . . . . 202 C4
Cl Chessington KT9 . . . . . 56 C4
field RH7 . . . . 164 C5
Cnr RH7 . . . . 164 B6
La Blindley Heath RH7 . 163 F7
field RH7 . . . . 164 B6
bridge RH7 . . . . 164 B6
Rd KT8 . . . . 36 B4
nell Ct TW7 . . . . 5 F5
ord Ave SE12 . . . . 24 F6
eigh Ave TW11 . . . . 16 E2
eigh Ct E W11 . . . . 37 F7
eigh Rd SW19 . . . . 39 F8
eigh Rise CR2 . . . . 61 E4
nead Ave CR7 . . . . 42 A4
nead Cl KT22 . . . . 94 F5
nead Way KT22 . . . . 94 F5
mer Wlk RH5 . . . . 161 C4
nond Cl
. . . . 23 C3
. . . . 1 E6
nond Cess GU2 . . . . 129 F8
nond Rd
nkenham BR3 . . . . 43 E5
abledon SW19 . . . . 19 E2
nood Way KT10 . . . . 56 B8
hald House E3 SW16 . . . 21 C5
hers Cl SL3 . . . . 1 C7
hes Park High Sch
. . . . 39 B6
hes Park Sta SW20 . . . . . 39 C7
nesfield SW20 . . . . 39 C6
ce Rd RH4 . . . . 44 C2
nood Cl UB7 . . . . 3 C7
Rd KT21 . . . . 75 D2
dens The SM7 . . . . 78 F3
hard Rd RH1 . . . . 118 F1
ing Rd
ckwater GU17 . . . . 64 B4
nborough GU14 . . . . 85 D1
on SM1 . . . . 59 C5
kingham RG41 . . . . 25 A2
dman Ct E3 SE20 . . . . . . 43 B8
ls Rest La KT20 . . . . 98 A7
land Cl RH1 . . . . 217 D5
pers Cl RH1 . . . . 119 A1
pers Way TW7 . . . . 5 D2
ecca Cl SR3 . . . . 44 A8
overy Sp SM17 . . . . 20 E3
reation Cl GU14 . . . . 64 F1
east Hill SE26 . . . . 23 D4
ldford GU1 . . . . 109 D1
ledge GU10 . . . . 145 E3
reation Way CR4, SW16 . 41 E6
tory Cl Ashstead KT21 . . 95 F8
tcknell RG12 . . . . 27 C5
leet KT14 . . . . 71 E6
hurst GU6 . . . . 175 E5
dalming GU7 . . . . 150 F2
dford GU4 . . . . 110 D3
leton TW17 . . . . 34 A6
ton TW17 . . . . 37 C1
dey RH5 . . . . 177 C3
est Barnes SW20 . . . . 39 C6
tory Cl GU14 . . . . 64 F1
tory Ct Cranford TW5 . . . 4 C5
derstead CR2 . . . . 80 F7
dlington SM6 . . . . 60 C6
tory Gdns BR3 . . . . 44 A8
tory Gn BR3 . . . . 43 F8
tory Gr
ydon CR0, CR9 . . . . 61 B8
npton TW12, TW13 . . . . . 15 F4
tcknell La Ashstead KT21 . 95 F8
tcknell RG12 . . . . 27 B5
ndford RH4 . . . . 116 F3
fleet KT14 . . . . 71 E6
darlwood RH6 . . . . 180 D7

Rectory La continued
Crawley RH11 . . . . 200 F8
Great Bookham KT23 . . . 113 F8
Long Ditton KT6 . . . . 37 C1
Shere GU5 . . . . 133 A4
Streatham SW17 . . . . 21 A3
Titsey TN16 . . . . 103 E4
Wallington SM6 . . . . 60 C6
Windlesham GU20 . . . . 48 C4
Woodmansterne CR5, SM7 . 78 F3
Rectory Orch SW19 . . . . . 19 E4
Rectory Pk CR2 . . . . 80 F8
Rectory Rd Beckenham BR3 . . 44 A8
Cranford TW5 . . . . 4 C5
Farnborough GU14 . . . . . . 85 D4
Lower Kingswood CR5 . . . 98 D2
Sutton SM1 . . . . 59 B7
Wokingham RG40 . . . . 25 C6
Rectory Row RG12 . . . . . . 27 B3
Rectory Sch TW12 . . . . . . 16 A3
Red Admiral St RH12 . . . 217 E5
Red Deer Cl RH3 . . . . 218 B4
Red Gables Cr CR2 . . . . . 61 D1
Red House La
Elstead GU8 . . . . 148 C2
Walton-on-T KT12 . . . . 54 A8
Red House Rd CR0 . . . . . . 41 E4
Red La Claygate KT10 . . . 56 A4
Headley Down GU35 . . . . 187 B7
Limpsfield RH8 . . . . 144 E2
South Holmwood RH5, RH3 . 136 F1
Red Lion Bsns Ctr KT6 . . . 56 F2
Red Lion La Chobham GU24 . 49 E2
Farnham GU9 . . . . 125 B1
Red Lion Rd Chobham GU24 . 49 E2
Surbiton KT6 . . . . 57 A8
Red Lion St TW10 . . . . 6 D2
Red Lodge BR4 . . . . 44 C1
Red Lodge Rd BR3, BR4 . . 44 D2
Red Rd GU18, GU21, GU5 . 67 C7
Red River Ct RH12 . . . . . 217 B5
Redan Gdns GU11 . . . . . . 105 C2
Redan Hill Est GU11 . . . . 105 C2
Redan Rd GU12 . . . . 105 C2
Redbarn Ct CR8 . . . . 80 B8
Redberry Gr SE23, SE26 . . 23 C5
Redcar House SE26 . . . . . . 23 B2
Redcliffe Missionary
Training Coll W4 . . . . 7 B7
Redclose Ave SM4 . . . . . . 40 A4
Redclyffe Terr E2 SM2 . . . 59 A3
Redcote RH4 . . . . 115 D1
Redcourt Pyrford GU22 . . . 70 E4
Woking GU22 . . . . 70 A2
Redcrest Gdns GU15 . . . . 65 F5
Redcroft Wlk GU6 . . . . . . 174 E2
Redding Way GU21 . . . . . . 68 C1
Reddington Cl CR2 . . . . . . 61 D2
Redditch RG12 . . . . 27 D2
Redditch Cl RH11 . . . . 200 E2
Reddons Rd BR3 . . . . 23 E1
Reddown Rd CR5 . . . . 79 D2
Rede Ct KT13 . . . . 53 B7
Redehall Prep Sch RH6 . . 162 B2
Redehall Rd Burstow RH6 . 183 C8
Smallfield RH6 . . . . 162 B2
Redesdale Gdns TW7 . . . . . 6 A7
Redfern Ave TW4, TW14 . . 16 A8
Redfern Rd SE6 . . . . 24 C8
Redford Ave
Horsham RH12 . . . . 217 B4
Thornton Heath CR7 . . . . . 41 F5
Wallington, Clock House CR5 . 79 B4
Wallington, Roundshaw SM6 . 60 E3
Redford Cl TW13 . . . . 14 F6
Redgarth Ct RH19 . . . . . . 185 B3
Redgrave Cl SE25 . . . . 42 F3
Redgrave Dr RH10 . . . . . . 202 D5
Redgrove Ct GU12 . . . . . . 105 F2
Redhall Ct CR3 . . . . 100 D4
Redhearne Fields GU10 . . 167 E2
Redhill Coll RH1 . . . . 140 B8
Redhill Ct SW2 . . . . 22 A6
Redhill Distribution Ctr
RH1 . . . . 161 A8
Redhill Rd KT11 . . . . 72 B5
Redhill Sta RH1 . . . . 119 A2
Redhouse Rd TN16 . . . . . 103 C6
Redkiln Cl RH13 . . . . 217 F4
Redkiln Way RH12, RH13 . 217 F3
Redknap House TW10 . . . . . 6 E2
Redlake La RG40 . . . . 25 F2
Redland Gdns KT8 . . . . . . 35 F5
Redlands Coulsdon CR5 . . 79 E3
Teddington TW11 . . . . 17 A2
Redlands CE Inf Sch The
RH4 . . . . 136 B4
Redlands Cotts RH5 . . . . 136 B1
Redlands Ct BR1 . . . . 24 F1
Redlands Cty Jun Sch The
RH4 . . . . 136 B4
Redlands La
Crondall GU10 . . . . 124 B7
Dorking RH5 . . . . 136 A1
Redlands The BR3 . . . . 44 A4
Redlands Way SW2 . . . . . . 21 F8
Redlane Cotts RH8 . . . . . 123 B2
Redleaves Ave TW15 . . . . 14 B2
Redlees Cl TW7 . . . . 6 A3
Redlin Ct RH1 . . . . 118 F3
Redmayne GU15 . . . . 66 C4
Redroofs Cl BR3 . . . . 44 B8
Redruth House SM2 . . . . . 59 B3
Redshank Ct E SRH11 . . 200 D5
Redstart Cl CR0 . . . . 63 D1
Redstone Hill RH1 . . . . . . 119 A1
Redstone Hollow RH1 . . . 140 A8
Redstone Manor RH1 . . . 119 A1

Redstone Pk RH1 . . . . 119 B1
Redstone Rd RH1 . . . . 140 A8
Redvers Buller Rd GU11 . 105 D7
Redvers Ct CR6 . . . . 81 C1
Redvers Rd Bracknell RG12 . 27 B4
Warlingham CR6 . . . . 81 C1
Redway Cotts GU21 . . . . . . 88 F8
Redway Dr TW2 . . . . 16 C8
Redwing Ave GU7 . . . . . . 150 E8
Redwing Cl Horsham RH13 . 217 F3
Selsdon CR2 . . . . 81 D8
Redwing Gdns KT14 . . . . . 71 B7
Redwing Rise GU4 . . . . . . 110 D3
Redwood TW20 . . . . 32 E7
Redwood Cl Crawley RH10 . 201 E8
Kenley CR8 . . . . 80 C5
Redwood Ct KT6 . . . . 37 D2
Redwood Dr Frimley GU15 . 66 D4
Sunningdale SL5 . . . . 30 B3
Redwood Est TW5 . . . . 4 B8
Redwood Gr GU4 . . . . 131 C3
Redwood Manor GU27 . . 208 C7
Redwood Mount RH1 . . . . 118 E3
Redwood Wlk KT6 . . . . 37 D1
Redwoods Addlestone KT15 . 52 A4
Roehampton SW15 . . . . . . 19 A7
Reed Cl GU11 . . . . 105 D5
Reed Pl GU21, KT14 . . . . . 70 E6
Reed Place Bsns Park
TW17 . . . . 33 F1
Reed's Hill RG12 . . . . 27 B4
Reed's Sch KT11 . . . . 74 E7
Reedham Dr CR8 . . . . 80 A6
Reedham Park Ave CR8 . . 80 A3
Reedham Sta CR8 . . . . 79 F6
Reedings RH11 . . . . 200 D4
Reeds Rd The
Frensham GU10 . . . . 146 E2
Tilford GU10 . . . . 147 A3
Reedsfield Cl TW15 . . . . . . 14 B5
Reedsfield Rd TW15 . . . . . 14 B4
Rees Gdns CR0 . . . . 42 F3
Reeve Ct GU2 . . . . 109 A5
Reeve Rd RH2 . . . . 139 C5
Reeves Cnr CR0, CR9 . . . . 61 B8
Reeves Rd GU12 . . . . 105 C1
Reeves Way RG41 . . . . 25 A4
Regal Cres SM6 . . . . 60 B7
Regal Ct E Guildford GU1 . 109 D1
Z Mitcham CR4 . . . . 40 F6
Regal Dr E RH19 . . . . . . 205 F8
Regalfield Cl GU2 . . . . . . 109 A5
Regan Cl GU2 . . . . 109 B6
Regency Cl Hampton TW12 . 15 F3
Z Penge SE19 . . . . 23 A1
G Surbiton KT6 . . . . 37 F4
Sutton SM1 . . . . 59 B6
Regency Ct KT14 . . . . 70 F6
Regency Gdns KT12 . . . . . 35 D1
Regency Lodge KT13 . . . . 53 E7
Regency Mews
Beckenham BR3 . . . . 44 C8
Isleworth TW7 . . . . 5 F3
Regency Wlk Croydon CR0 . 43 E3
G Richmond TW10 . . . . 6 E2
Regent Cl Cranford TW5 . . . 4 B6
New Haw KT15 . . . . 52 D2
Regent Cres RH1 . . . . 118 F3
Regent Ct Bagshot GU19 . . 47 E2
Guildford GU2 . . . . 109 B3
Regent Lodge E SW2 . . . . 21 F7
Regent Pk KT22 . . . . 75 A1
Regent Pl Croydon CR0 . . . 42 F1
Wimbledon SW19 . . . . 20 C3
Regent Rd KT5 . . . . 38 A4
Regent St W4 . . . . 7 A8
Regent Way GU16 . . . . 66 A1
Regents Cl Crawley RH11 . 201 C2
South Croydon CR2 . . . . . . 61 E4
Whyteleafe CR3 . . . . 80 F1
Regents Ct
L Beckenham BR3 . . . . 24 A1
Bromley BR1 . . . . 24 F1
Weybridge KT13 . . . . 53 B4
Regents Pl
L Kingston u T KT2 . . . . . . 37 E8
Sandhurst GU47 . . . . 64 C8
Regents Wlk SL5 . . . . 29 C2
Regiment Cl GU14 . . . . 84 D3
Regina Coeli RC Prim Sch
CR0 . . . . 61 B3
Regina Rd SE25 . . . . 43 A6
Reginald Ct BR3 . . . . 44 C8
Regis Ct East Bedfont TW14 . 3 D1
Mitcham SW19 . . . . 40 C8
Regnolruf Ct KT12 . . . . . . 35 A2
Reid Ave CR3 . . . . 100 D6
Reid Ct SW14 . . . . 7 C5
Reidonhill Cotts GU21 . . . 68 B1
Reigate Ave SM3, SM4 . . . 40 B1
Reigate Cl RH10 . . . . 182 D1
Reigate Coll RH2 . . . . 118 B1
Reigate Day Hospl RH2 . . 139 A7
Reigate Gram Sch RH1 . . 118 C1
Reigate Heath Cotts RH2 . 117 E1
Reigate Hill GU14 . . . . 85 A6
Reigate Hill Cl KT20 . . . . . 97 E8
Reigate Parish Church
Inf Sch RH2 . . . . 118 B1
Reigate Priory Cty Prim
Sch RH2 . . . . 118 A1
Reigate Rd Banstead KT17 . 77 C4
Betchworth RH3, RH4,
RH2, RH5 . . . . 116 C2
Brockham RH3, RH4, RH2 . . 116 C2
, RH5 . . . . 116 D2
Burgh Heath KT18 . . . . 77 C4
Catford BR1 . . . . 24 F5

Reigate Rd continued
Dorking RH4 . . . . 115 E1
Ewell KT17 . . . . 77 C4
Hookwood RH6 . . . . 160 C4
Leatherhead KT22 . . . . 95 D4
Reigate RH2 . . . . 118 C1
Sidlow RH2, RH6 . . . . 160 C4
Reigate Sch RH1 . . . . 139 C6
Reigate Sch of Art
& Design RH2 . . . . 118 D1
Reigate St Mary's Prep
Sch RH2 . . . . 118 B1
Reigate Sta RH2 . . . . 118 A2
Reigate Way SM6 . . . . 60 E5
Reindorp Cl GU2 . . . . 130 A8
Relko Ct KT19 . . . . 76 D8
Relko Gdns SM1 . . . . 59 D5
Rembrandt Ct KT19 . . . . . . 57 F4
Rembrandt Way KT12 . . . . 54 B8
Rendle Cl CR0, SE25 . . . . . 43 A4
Renfree Way TW17 . . . . 34 A2
Renfrew Ct TW5 . . . . 4 E5
Renfrew Rd Hounslow TW5 . 4 E5
Kingston u T KT2 . . . . 18 C1
Renmans The KT21 . . . . . . 75 F3
Renmuir St SW17 . . . . 20 F2
Rennie Cl TW15 . . . . 13 D5
Rennie Terr RH1 . . . . 140 A8
Renown Cl CR0 . . . . 42 B1
Renshaw House E SW27 . 22 B3
Replingham Rd SW18 . . . . 20 A7
Repton Cl SM1, SM5 . . . . . 59 E5
Repton Ct BR3 . . . . 44 B8
Restmor Way SM5, SM6 . . 60 A8
Restormel Cl TW3 . . . . 5 A2
Restwell Ave GU6 . . . . . . 174 B6
Retreat Rd TW9 . . . . 6 D2
Retreat The
Englefield Green TW20 . . . 11 E3
Mortlake SW14 . . . . 7 E4
North Cheam KT4 . . . . 58 B8
South Norwood CR7 . . . . . 42 D5
Surbiton KT5 . . . . 37 F3
Revell Cl KT22 . . . . 94 B5
Revell Dr KT22 . . . . 94 B5
Revell Rd Cheam SM1 . . . 58 F4
Kingston u T KT1 . . . . 38 B8
Revelstoke Ave GU14 . . . . 85 B6
Revelstoke Rd SW18, SW19 . 20 A6
Revesby Cl GU24 . . . . 67 D6
Revesby Rd SM5 . . . . 40 E3
Rewley Rd SM4 . . . . 40 D3
Rex Ave TW15 . . . . 14 A3
Rex House TW13 . . . . 15 E5
Reynard Cl RH12 . . . . 218 B5
Reynard Dr SE19 . . . . 22 F1
Reynolds Ave KT9 . . . . 56 E3
Reynolds Cl
Carshalton CR4, SM5 . . . . 40 F1
Mitcham CR4, SW19 . . . . . 40 D8
Reynolds Gn GU47 . . . . . . 64 D6
Reynolds Pl Crawley RH11 . 201 C7
E Richmond TW10 . . . . 6 F1
Reynolds Rd
Crawley RH11 . . . . 201 C7
New Malden KT3 . . . . 38 D2
Reynolds Way CR0 . . . . . . 61 E6
Rheingold Way SM6 . . . . . 60 E2
Rhine Banks GU14 . . . . . . 84 D5
Rhodes Cl TW20 . . . . 12 B3
Rhodes Ct KT3 . . . . 12 C3
Rhodes Way RH10 . . . . . . 201 F3
Rhodes-Moorhouse Ct
SM4 . . . . 40 A3
Rhododendron Cl SL5 . . . . 8 F1
Rhododendron Rd GU16 . . 86 B8
Rhododendron Ride
SL4, TW20 . . . . 10 F3
Rhododendron Wlk SL5 . . 8 F1
Rhodrons Ave KT9 . . . . 56 E5
Rialto Rd CR4 . . . . 41 A7
Ribble Pl GU14 . . . . 84 E7
Ribblesdale RH4 . . . . 136 B5
Ribblesdale Rd SW16 . . . . 21 B3
Ricardo Ct GU5 . . . . 151 F5
Ricards Lodge High Sch
SW19 . . . . 19 F3
Ricards Rd SW19 . . . . 19 F3
Rice's Cnr GU4 . . . . 131 A2
Rice's Hill RH19 . . . . 185 E1
Richard Atkins Prim Sch
SW2 . . . . 21 E8
Richard Challoner Sch
KT3 . . . . 38 D2
Richard Thornton House
E SW12 . . . . 40 A7
Richards Cl Ash GU12 . . . 106 A5
Harlington UB3 . . . . 3 D8
Richards Ct BR3 . . . . 43 D8
Richards Field KT19 . . . . . 57 D2
Richardson Ct E RH11 . . 201 B1
Richardson House TW7 . . . 5 F4
Richardson's Lawn Cotts
SL4 . . . . 10 B5
Richbell Cl KT21 . . . . 75 D1
Richens Cl TW3 . . . . 5 D5
Richfield Ct SW2 . . . . 43 F8
Richland Ave CR5 . . . . 79 A5
Richlands Ave KT17 . . . . . 58 A6
Richmond Adult Coll TW9 . 6 D3
Richmond Athletic Gd TW9 . 6 D3
Richmond Ave
Feltham TW14 . . . . 3 E8
Merton SW20 . . . . 39 E8
Richmond Bridge TW1 . . . . 6 D1
Richmond Bridge
Mansions E TW1 . . . . 6 D1

Rav–Rid **275**

Richmond Cl
Biggin Hill TN16 . . . . 103 B8
Epsom KT18 . . . . 76 E5
Farnborough GU14 . . . . . . 84 D3
Fetcham KT23 . . . . 94 C3
Frimley GU16 . . . . 65 F1
Richmond Coll TW10 . . . . 17 E8
Richmond Cres TW18 . . . . 12 F3
Richmond Ct
E Kingston u T KT2 . . . . . 18 A1
Mitcham CR4 . . . . 40 D6
Wimbledon SW20 . . . . 39 B7
Richmond Dr TW17 . . . . . . 34 D3
Richmond Gn CR0 . . . . 60 E7
Richmond Hill TW10 . . . . . 6 E1
Richmond Hill St E SW10 . 6 E1
Richmond House
E Forest Hill SE26 . . . . . . 23 A5
Sandhurst GU47 . . . . 64 E7
Richmond House
(Annexe of Rectory Sch)
TW12 . . . . 15 F3
Richmond Mansions E
TW11 . . . . 6 D1
Richmond Park Rd
Kingston u T KT2 . . . . 17 E1
Mortlake SW14 . . . . 7 D3
Richmond Rd Coulsdon CR5 . 79 B4
Farncombe GU7 GU02 . . . 150 F8
Horsham RH12 . . . . 217 D4
Isleworth TW7 . . . . 6 A4
Kingston u T KT2 . . . . 17 E2
Sandhurst GU47 . . . . 64 E8
Staines TW18 . . . . 13 A2
Thornton Heath CR7 . . . . . 42 B5
Twickenham TW1 . . . . 17 B8
Wallington SM6 . . . . 60 E7
Wimbledon SW20 . . . . 39 B8
Richmond Sq RH19 . . . . . 185 D2
Richmond Sta TW9 . . . . 6 E3
Richmond Upon Thames
Coll TW2 . . . . 16 E8
Richmond Way
East Grinstead RH19 . . . . 205 F8
Fetcham KT23 . . . . 94 C3
Richmondwood SL5 . . . . . . 30 B1
Rickard Cl SW2 . . . . 22 A7
Rickards Cl KT6 . . . . 56 E8
Ricketts Hill Rd TN16 . . . 103 E7
Rickfield RH11 . . . . 201 A5
Rickford Hill GU3 . . . . 88 D1
Rickman Cl RG12 . . . . 27 C3
Rickman Cres KT15 . . . . . 52 B7
Rickman Ct KT15 . . . . 52 B7
Rickman Hill CR5 . . . . 79 B1
Rickman's La RH14 . . . . . 211 F2
Ricksons La KT24 . . . . . . 112 B8
Rickwood RH6 . . . . 161 B4
Rickyard GU2 . . . . 108 D3
Riddens The RH12 . . . . . . 214 A6
Riddings The CR3 . . . . . . 100 F2
Riddlesdown Ave CR8 . . . . 80 C7
Riddlesdown High Sch
. . . . 80 E5
Riddlesdown Rd CR3, CR8 . 80 D5
Riddlesdown Sta CR8 . . . . 80 C6
Ride La GU5 . . . . 153 D7
Ride The RH14 . . . . 212 C2
Ride Way GU5, GU6 . . . . . 154 C1
Riders Way RH9 . . . . 121 C4
Rideway Cl GU15 . . . . 65 B4
Ridge Cl Brockham RH3 . . 137 B5
Woking GU22 . . . . 89 B6
Ridge Ct CR6 . . . . 81 A1
Ridge Gn RH1 . . . . 140 E6
Ridge Green Cl RH1 . . . . . 140 E6
Ridge House E KT1 . . . . . . 18 B1
Ridge Langley CR2 . . . . . . 62 A2
Ridge Moor Cl GU26 . . . . 188 E5
Ridge Mount Rd SL5 . . . . . 30 A1
Ridge Pk CR8, SM6 . . . . . . 60 D1
Ridge Prim Sch SM3 . . . . 39 E1
Ridge Rd Cheam SM3, SM4 . 39 F1
Mitcham CR4 . . . . 21 B1
Ridge The Coulsdon CR5 . . 79 F5
Epsom KT18 . . . . 76 C1
Fetcham KT22 . . . . 94 D3
Limpsfield CR3, CR6 . . . . 102 D2
Surbiton KT5 . . . . 38 A4
Twickenham TW2 . . . . 16 D8
Wallington CR8 . . . . 60 D1
Woking GU22 . . . . 70 B2
Woldingham CR3 . . . . 102 D2
Ridge Way Feltham TW13 . 15 E5
Thorpe GU25 . . . . 31 E4
Ridge Way The CR2 . . . . . . 61 E3
Ridgedale RH10 . . . . 204 B8
Ridgegate Cl RH2 . . . . 118 D3
Ridgehurst Dr RH12 . . . . 216 F1
Ridgelands KT22 . . . . 94 D3
Ridgemead Rd TW20 . . . . 11 B3
Ridgemount Guildford GU2 . 130 B8
Oatlands Park KT13 . . . . . . 53 E8
Ridgemount Ave
Coulsdon CR5 . . . . 79 B2
Croydon CR0 . . . . 62 D8
Ridgemount Cl SE20 . . . . . 23 B1
Ridgemount East GU16 . . . 86 C7
Ridgemount Way RH1 . . . 139 D7
Ridges The GU3 . . . . 130 C4
Ridgeside RH10 . . . . 201 F6
Ridgeway
East Grinstead RH19 . . . . 205 E2
Epsom KT19 . . . . 76 C7

Ridgeway *continued*
Pyrford GU22 .... 71 A4
■ Richmond TW10 .... 6 E1
Walton-on-T KT12 .... 34 F1
Wimbledon SW19, SW20 .... 19 D2
Woking GU21 .... 69 D4
Ridgeway Cl
Cranleigh GU6 .... 175 A3
Dorking RH4 .... 136 A5
Lightwater GU18 .... 67 A8
Oxshott KT22 .... 74 C5
Woking GU21 .... 69 D4
Ridgeway Ct RH1 .... 118 F1
Ridgeway Dr RH4 .... 136 A4
Ridgeway Gdns GU21 ...... 69 D4
Ridgeway Prim Sch CR2 .... 61 E1
Ridgeway Rd Dorking RH4 .. 136 A5
Hounslow TW7 .... 5 E6
Redhill RH1 .... 118 F1
Ridgeway Rd N TW7 .... 5 E7
Ridgeway Sch The GU9 .. 146 C7
Ridgeway The
Bracknell RG12 .... 27 C6
Brookwood GU24 .... 88 A7
Cranleigh GU6 .... 174 F3
Croydon CR0 .... 60 F7
Fetcham KT22 .... 94 D3
Guildford GU1 .... 131 A8
Horley RH6 .... 161 A1
Horsham RH12 .... 217 B4
Lightwater GU18 .... 48 B1
Oxshott KT22 .... 74 C5
Ridgewell Cl SE26 .... 23 F4
Ridgewood Ctr
(Hospl) GU16 .... 66 C3
Ridgley Rd GU8 .... 191 B4
Ridgway Ct SW19 .... 19 D2
Ridgway Gdns SW19 .... 19 D1
Ridgway Hill Rd GU9 .... 146 C8
Ridgway Pl SW19 .... 19 E2
Ridgway Rd Farnham GU9 . 146 C8
Pyrford GU22 .... 70 F4
Ridgway The SM2 .... 59 D4
Riding Hill CR2 .... 81 A6
Riding The Cranleigh GU6 . 174 E4
Sheerwater GU21 .... 70 B5
Ridings The
Addlestone KT15 .... 51 E4
Ashstead KT21 .... 75 D2
Biggin Hill TN16 .... 83 E2
Cobham KT11 .... 74 A2
Crawley RH10 .... 202 D7
East Horsley KT24 .... 92 F2
Epsom KT18 .... 76 F4
Ewell KT17 .... 57 F2
Frimley GU16 .... 66 B3
Kingswood KT20 .... 97 F7
Redhill RH12 .... 118 D3
Send Marsh GU23 .... 91 A4
Sunbury TW16 .... 35 A8
Surbiton KT5 .... 38 A4
Ridlands Gr RH8 .... 123 E5
Ridlands La RH8 .... 123 E5
Ridlands Rise RH8 ...... 123 E4
Ridley Ct SW16 .... 21 E2
Ridley Rd Bromley BR2 ... 44 F6
Merton SW19 .... 20 B1
Warlingham CR6 .... 81 D1
Ridsdale Rd Penge SE20 ... 43 B8
Woking GU21 .... 69 B2
Riesco Dr CR0 .... 62 C4
Rifle Way GU14 .... 84 C3
Rigby Cl CR0, CR9 .... 61 A7
Rigg House ■ SW4 .... 21 E8
Riggindale Rd SW16 ...... 21 D4
Rikkyo Sch in England The
RH14 .... 213 D8
Riley House ■ SW4 ...... 21 DB
Rill Wlk RH19 .... 186 B1
Rillside RH10 .... 202 A3
Rimbault Cl GU11 .... 105 E7
Rinaldo Rd SW12 .... 21 B8
Ring Rd N RH6 .... 182 C8
Ring Rd S RH6 .... 182 C7
Ring The RG12 .... 27 C7
Ringley Ave RH6 .... 161 A2
Ringley Oak RH12 .... 217 F4
Ringley Park Ave RH2 ... 139 D8
Ringley Park Rd RH2 .... 118 C1
Ringley Rd RH12 .... 217 E4
Ringmead Bracknell, Great
Hollands RG12 .... 26 E4
Bracknell, Hanworth RG12 . 27 B2
Ringmore Dr GU4 .... 110 C4
Ringmore Rd KT12 .... 54 C7
Ringmore Rise SE23 ...... 23 B8
Ringstead Rd
Carshalton SM1 .... 59 D5
Lewisham SE6 .... 24 BB
Ringwold Cl BR3 .... 23 E1
Ringwood RG12 .... 26 F2
Ringwood Ave Redhill RH1 118 F4
Thornton Heath CR0, CR9 . 41 E2
Ringwood Cl Ascot SL5 ... 29 B5
Crawley RH10 .... 201 E4
Ringwood Gdns SW15 ..... 19 A7
Ringwood Lodge ■ RH1 .. 119 A4
Ringwood Rd
Blackwater GU17 .... 64 C6
Farnborough GU14 .... 85 C7
Ringwood Way TW12 ..... 16 A4
Ripley Ave TW20 .... 11 E2
Ripley By-Pass
Ockham GU23 .... 91 C4
Ripley GU23 .... 91 C4

Ripley C of E Inf Sch GU23 91 B6
Ripley Cl CR0 .... 63 C4
Ripley Court Sch Rose La
GU23 .... 91 C6
Ripley Ct CR4 .... 40 D7
Ripley Gdns Mortlake SW14 . 7 D4
Sutton SM1 .... 59 C6
Ripley Mouse
■ Kingston u T KT2 ..... 18 B2
Mortlake SW14 .... 7 E4
■ Penge SE26 .... 23 B3
Ripley La Ripley GU23 .... 91 F3
West Horsley KT24, GU23 .. 112 A7
Ripley Rd
East Clandon GU4 .... 111 D6
Hampton TW12 .... 16 A1
Ripley GU23, GU4 .... 111 D7
Riplington Ct SW15 ...... 19 B8
Ripon Cl Frimley GU15 ... 66 D3
Guildford GU2 .... 108 F3
Ripon Gdns KT9 .... 56 D5
Ripon Rd GU14 .... 84 A7
Ripplesmere RG12 .... 27 D5
Ripplesmore Cl GU47 .... 64 B8
Ripston Rd TW15 .... 14 D3
Risborough Dr KT4 ...... 39 A2
Rise Rd SL5 .... 29 F3
Rise The Crawley RH10 .. 202 D6
Crowthorne RG45 .... 45 A5
East Grinstead RH19 ..... 205 F8
East Horsley KT24 .... 92 E1
Ewell KT17 .... 57 F1
South Croydon CR2 .... 62 C2
Tadworth KT20 .... 97 C6
Wokingham RG41 .... 25 A7
Ritchie Cl RH10 .... 202 C2
Ritchie Rd CR0 .... 43 B3
Ritherdon Rd SW17 ...... 21 B6
River Ave KT7 .... 37 A2
River Bank KT7 .... 36 F4
River Crane Way TW13 .. 15 F6
River Ct Kingston u T KT6 . 37 D4
Sheerwater GU21 .... 70 C5
River Gdns Carshalton SM5 . 60 A7
Feltham TW14 .... 4 B2
River Gdns Bsns Ctr TW14 . 4 B3
River Grove Pk BR3 ..... 43 F8
River Hill KT11 .... 73 B4
River House
Forest Hill SE26 .... 23 B5
Mortlake SW13 .... 7 E5
River Island Cl KT22 .... 94 D7
River La Cobham KT11 ... 73 E3
Farnham GU10, GU9 .... 146 E7
Fetcham KT22 .... 94 D6
Leatherhead KT22 .... 94 E7
Richmond TW10 .... 17 D7
Wrecclesham GU10, GU9 . 145 E7
River Mead
Crawley RH11 .... 181 A1
Horsham RH12 .... 217 B1
River Meads Ave
TW13, TW2 .... 16 B5
River Mount KT12 .... 34 F2
River Mount Gdns GU2 .. 130 C6
River Park Ave TW18 ... 12 D4
River Rd TW18 .... 32 F8
River Reach TW11 ...... 17 C3
River View KT15 .... 52 C5
River View Gdns TW1 ... 16 F6
River Way
Twickenham TW13, TW2 .. 16 B6
West Ewell KT19 .... 57 E5
River Wlk KT12 .... 35 A3
Riverbank East Molesey KT8 . 36 B5
Staines TW18 .... 12 F2
Riverbank Way TW8 ...... 6 C8
Riverdale Dorking RH4 ... 115 C3
Wrecclesham GU10 ...... 145 E7
Riverdale Dr
Wandsworth SW18 .... 20 B7
Woking GU22 .... 89 F6
Riverdale Gdns TW1 ...... 6 C2
Riverdale Rd Feltham TW13 . 15 F4
Forest Row RH18 .... 6 C1
Riverdene End KT12 ..... 54 D5
Riverfield Rd TW18 ..... 12 F2
Riverhead Dr SM2 .... 59 B1
Riverholme Dr KT19 ..... 57 E2
Rivermead Byfleet KT14 .. 71 F6
East Molesey KT8 .... 36 C6
Kingston u T KT6 .... 37 D4
Rivermead Cl
New Haw KT15 .... 52 C3
Richmond TW11 .... 17 B3
Rivermead House TW16 .. 35 C6
Rivermead Rd GU15 ..... 65 B2
Rivernook Cl KT12 ...... 35 C4
Riverpark Gdns BR2 ..... 24 D1
Rivers Ct GU21 .... 85 E1
Riversdale Prim Sch
SW18 .... 20 A7
Riversdale Rd KT7 .... 37 A3
Riversdell Cl KT16 ...... 32 F2
Riverside Catford SE6 ... 23 F4
Dorking RH4 .... 115 B3
Egham TW20 .... 12 A5
Forest Row RH18 .... 206 E3
Horley RH6 .... 161 A1
Horsham RH12 .... 217 A2
Oatlands Park TW17 ..... 34 E2
Sunbury TW16 .... 35 D7
Twickenham TW1 .... 17 B7
Wraysbury TW19 .... 11 C8

Riverside Ave
East Molesey KT8 .... 36 D4
Lightwater GU18 .... 67 C8

Riverside Bsns Ctr
Guildford GU1 .... 109 C1
Wandsworth SW18 .... 20 B7
Riverside Bsns Pk
Farnham GU9 .... 125 D3
Merton SW19 .... 40 C8
Riverside Cl
Brookwood GU24 .... 87 F7
Farnborough GU14 .... 84 F5
Hackbridge SM6 .... 60 B7
Kingston u T KT1 .... 37 D5
Staines TW18 .... 32 F8
Riverside Ct Dorking RH4 . 115 D1
Farnham GU9 .... 125 D3
Teddington TW11 .... 17 C3
Riverside Dr Bramley GU5 . 152 A7
Chiswick W4 .... 7 E6
Egham TW18 .... 12 B1
Esher KT10 .... 55 A6
Mitcham CR4 .... 40 E4
Richmond TW10 .... 17 B5
Staines TW18 .... 32 F8
Riverside Gdns
Cobham KT11 .... 73 A6
Old Woking GU22 .... 90 B6
Riverside House SW19 .... 40 C5
Riverside Ind Pk GU9 ... 125 C3
Riverside L Ctr W4 .... 7 E8
Riverside Pk GU9 ...... 125 D3
Riverside Pl TW19 .... 2 D1
Riverside Rd Hersham KT12 . 54 E6
Staines TW18 .... 12 F1
Stanwell TW19 .... 2 A1
Wandsworth SW17, SW19 . 20 C5
Riverside The KT8 ...... 36 D6
Riverside Way GU15 ..... 65 A3
Riverside Wlk Isleworth TW7 . 5 E4
West Wickham BR4 ...... 44 B1
Riverside Yd SW17 ...... 20 B5
Riverview CW17 .... 37 F8
Riverview TW17 .... 34 D2
Riverview Cty Fst Sch KT19 57 D6
Riverview Gr W4 .... 7 B8
Riverview Pk SE6 .... 24 A6
Riverview Rd Chiswick W4 . 7 B8
West Ewell KT19 .... 57 D6
Riverway TW18 .... 33 B8
Riverway Est GU3 ...... 151 C8
Riverwood Ct GU1 ...... 109 C3
Rivett-Drake Rd GU2 .... 109 A5
Rivey Cl KT14 .... 70 F5
Road House Est GU22 .... 90 A7
Roakes Ave KT15 .... 52 B8
Robert Cl KT12 .... 54 B5
Robert Gerard House ■
SE27 .... 22 D4
Robert May Cty Fst Sch
The RH10 .... 201 F4
Robert St CR0, CR9 ...... 61 C7
Robertsbridge Rd SM4 ... 39 D3
Roberts Cl Cheam SM3 ... 58 D3
Stanwell TW19 .... 2 C1
Roberts Ct SE20 .... 43 C8
Roberts House ■ SE27 .. 22 B5
Roberts Rd
Aldershot GU12 .... 105 D1
Sandhurst GU15 .... 65 A6
Roberts Way TW20 ...... 11 C1
Robertsbridge Rd SM5 .. 40 D2
Robertson Ct ■ GU21 ... 68 E1
Robertson House SW17 .. 20 E3
Robertson Way GU12 ... 105 F1
Robin Cl Addlestone KT15 . 52 D5
Ash Vale GU12 .... 106 A6
Crawley RH11 .... 201 C8
East Grinstead RH19 ... 185 F2
Hampton TW12 .... 15 E3
Robin Ct SM6 .... 60 C4
Robin Gdns RH1 .... 119 A3
Robin Gr TW8 .... 6 C8
Robin Hill GU7 .... 150 D7
Robin Hill Dr GU15 ..... 66 A3
Robin Hood Cl
Farnborough GU14 .... 85 A7
Knaphill GU21 .... 68 F1
Robin Hood Cres GU21 .. 68 E2
Robin Hood Inf Sch SM1 . 59 B5
Robin Hood Inf Sch SM1 . 59 A5
Robin Hood Jun Sch SM1 . 59 B5
Robin Hood La
Kingston u T SW15 ...... 18 E4
Sutton SM1 .... 59 B5
Warnham RH12 .... 216 F5
Woking GU4 .... 89 F3
Robin Hood Prim Sch
SW15 .... 18 E3
Robin Hood Rd
Knaphill GU21 .... 68 E2
Knaphill GU21 .... 68 F2
Robin Hood Rdbt SW15 .. 18 E5
Robin Hood Way
(Kingston By Pass)
KT2, SW15, SW20 .... 18 F3
Robin Hood Works GU21 . 68 E2
Robin La GU47 .... 45 C1
Robin Way Guildford GU2 . 109 B5
Staines TW18 .... 12 F5
Robin's Bow GU15 ...... 65 B4
Robin's Ct BR3 .... 44 D7
Robinhood Cl CR4 .... 41 C6
Robinhood La CR4 ...... 41 C6
Robins Ct TW10 .... 6 E2
Robins Dale GU21 .... 68 C2
Robinson Ct ■ TW9 ...... 6 F3
Robinson Rd
Crawley RH11 .... 201 D5
Mitcham SW19 .... 20 E2

Robinsway KT12 .... 54 C6
Robinswood CR 217 F4
Robinwood Pl SW15 ..... 18 D4
Robson Rd SE21, SE27 ... 22 C5
Roby Dr RG12 .... 27 D2
Rochdale ■ SE19 .... 22 E2
Roche Rd SW16 .... 41 F8
Roche Wlk SM4, SM5 .... 40 D3
Rochelle Ct BR3 .... 24 B1
Rochester Ave TW13 .... 14 F6
Rochester Cl SW16 ...... 21 E1
Rochester Ct SE25 ...... 43 A7
Rochester Gdns
Caterham CR3 .... 100 E5
South Croydon CR0 ...... 61 E7
Rochester Par TW13 .... 15 A5
Rochester Rd
Carshalton SM5 .... 59 F6
Egham TW20 .... 12 D2
Rochester Wlk RH2 .... 139 B5
Rochford Way CR0 .... 41 E3
Rock Ave ■ SW14 .... 7 D4
Rock Gdns GU11 .... 104 F1
Rock Hill SE19 .... 22 F4
Rock La GU10 .... 146 A5
Rockbourne Rd SE23 .... 23 D7
Rockdale Dr GU26 ...... 188 D3
Rockery The GU14 ...... 84 E3
Rockfield Cl RH8 .... 122 F4
Rockfield Rd RH8 ...... 122 F5
Rockfield Way ■ GU47 .. 64 D8
Rockhampton Cl ■ SE27 . 22 A4
Rockhampton Rd
South Croydon CR2 ...... 61 E4
West Norwood SE27, SW16 22 A4
Rockingham Cl SW15 ..... 7 F3
Rockingham Ct ■ BR3 ... 24 A1
Rockmount Jun Mix & Inf
Lower Schs SE19 .... 22 D2
Rockmount Jun Mix & Inf
Upper Schs SE19 .... 22 D2
Rocks The RH19 .... 206 D6
Rockshaw Rd
Caterham RH1 .... 119 E8
Merstham RH1 .... 119 E8
Rockwell Gdns SE19 ..... 22 E4
Rocky La RH1, RH2 ..... 119 A6
Rocombe Cres SE23 ...... 23 C8
Rodborough Sch GU8 ... 170 F7
Rodd Est TW17 .... 34 D4
Roden Gdns CR0, SE25 .. 42 E3
Rodenhurst Rd SW4 .... 21 C8
Rodgate La GU27 .... 209 E3
Rodgers House ■ SW4 .. 21 D8
Roding Cl GU6 .... 173 F2
Rodmel Ct GU14 .... 85 E1
Rodmill La SW2 .... 21 E8
Rodney Cl New Malden KT3 38 E4
Thornton Heath CR0 ..... 42 B1
Walton-on-T KT12 .... 35 C1
Rodney Gn ■ KT12 ...... 54 C8
Rodney Pl SW19 .... 40 C8
Rodney Rd Mitcham CR4 . 40 E6
New Malden KT3 .... 38 E4
Twickenham TW4 .... 16 A8
Walton-on-T KT12 .... 54 B8
Roe Way SM6 .... 60 E4
Roebuck Cl Ashstead KT21 . 95 E7
Feltham TW13 .... 15 B4
Horsham RH13 .... 218 B4
Reigate RH2 .... 118 A1
Roebuck Ct ■ KT3 .... 38 E6
Roebuck Rd KT9 .... 57 A5
Roedean Cres SW15 ...... 7 E2
Roedeer Copse GU27 ... 207 E6
Roehampton CE Prim Sch
SW15 .... 19 B8
Roehampton Club Golf
Course SW15 .... 7 F2
Roehampton Gate SW15 ... 7 F2
Roehampton Gate Cty Prim
Sch SW15 .... 7 F2
Roehampton High St
SW15 .... 19 A8
Roehampton La
Putney SW15, SW19 ..... 19 A8
Roehampton SW15, SW19 . 19 A8
Roehampton Vale SW15 .. 18 F5
Roffes La CR3 .... 100 D2
Roffey Cl Horley RH6 ... 160 F3
Purley CR8 .... 80 B1
Roffey Cnr RH12 .... 218 B4
Roffords GU21 .... 69 B2
Roger Simmons Ct KT23 . 94 A3
Rogers Cl Caterham CR3 . 101 B5
Coulsdon CR5, CR8 ...... 100 B7
Rogers La CR6 .... 81 F1
Rogers Mead RH9 ...... 121 B3
Rogosa Rd GU24 .... 67 E6
Rojack Rd SE23 .... 23 D7
Roke Cl Purley CR8 ...... 80 B1
Witley GU8 .... 170 F5
Roke La GU8 .... 170 F5
Roke Lane Cotts GU8 ... 170 F5
Roke Lodge Rd CR8 ..... 80 A2
Roke Prim Sch Purley CR8 . 80 B1
Purley CR8 .... 80 C2
Roke Rd CR8 .... 80 C5

Rokeby Cl RG12 .... 27 E8
Rokeby Ct GU21 .... 68 F2
Rokeby Ho ■ SW12 .... 21 B8
Rokeby Pl SW20 .... 19 B1
Rokeby Sch KT2 .... 18 B1
Rokell House BR3 ....
Rokers La GU8 ....
Roland Ct SE19 ....
Roland Way KT4 ....
Rollesby Rd KT19, KT9 ... ...
Rolleston Rd CR2 ....
Rollit Cres TW3 ....
Roma Read Cl SW15 ....
Roman Cl TW14 ....
Roman House RH2 ....
Roman Ind Est CR0 ....
Roman Rd RH4 ....
Roman Rise SE19 ....
Roman Way Croydon CR0 . ...
Farnham GU9 ....
Thornton Heath CR9 ....
Winkfield RG42 ....
Romana Ct TW18 ....
Romanby Ct RH1 ....
Romanfield Rd SW2 ....
Romanhurst Ave BR2 ....
Romanhurst Gdns
BR2, BR3 ....
Romans Bsns Pk GU9 ....
Romans Ind Pk GU9 ....
Romans Way GU22 ....
Romany Gdns SM3 ....
Romany Prospect SE19 .. ...
Romayne Cl GU14 ....
Rombeny Rd SW17 ....
Romeo Hill RG42 ....
Romeyn Rd SW16 ....
Romley Ct GU9 ....
Rommany Ct SE27 ....
Rommany Rd SE27 ....
Romney Cl Ashford TW15 . ...
Chessington KT9 ....
Romney House RG12 ....
Romney Rd KT3 ....
Romola Rd SE24, SW2 ... ...
Romsey Cl Aldershot GU11 ...
Blackwater GU17 ....
Romulus Ct ■ TW8 ....
Rona Cl RH11 ....
Ronald Cl BR3 ....
Ronald Ross Prim Sch
SW19 ....
Ronelean Rd KT6 ....
Roneo Cnr RH13 ....
Ronson Way KT22 ....
Ronver Rd SE12 ....
Rook La CR3 ....
Rook Way RH12 ....
Rookeries Cl TW13 ....
Rookery Cl KT22 ....
Rookery Dr RH4 ....
Rookery Hill Ashstead KT21 ...
Outwood RH1, RH6 ....
Rookery Rd TW18 ....
Rookery The RH14 ....
Rookery Way KT20 ....
Rookley Cl SM2 ....
Rooks Hill GU5 ....
Rooksmead Rd TW16 ....
Rookside Rd SW17 ....
Rookwood Ave
Roper Way SM6 ....
Sandhurst GU47 ....
Wallington SM6 ....
West Barnes KT3 ....
Rookwood Cl RH1 ....
Rookwood Ct GU2 ....
Rookwood Pk RH12 ....
Roothill La RH3 ....
Roper House ■ SE19, SE21 ...
Roper Way SM6 ....
Ropers Wlk ■ SE24 ....
Rorkes Drift GU16 ....
Rosa Ave TW15 ....
Rosalind Franklin Cl GU2 ...
Rosamond St SE26 ....
Rosamund Cl CR2 ....
Rosamund Rd RH10 ....
Rosary Cl TW3, TW5 ....
Rosary Gdns TW15 ....
Rosary RC Inf Sch TW5 . ...
Rosary RC Jun Sch TW5 ...
Rose Ave Mitcham CR4 .. ...
Morden SM4 ....
Rose Bank Cotts GU22 .. ...
Rose Bushes KT17 ....
Rose Cotts
Eaton Green GU8 ....
Esher KT10 ....
Rose End KT4 ....
Rose Gdns
Farnborough GU14 ....
Feltham TW13 ....
Stanwell TW19 ....
Rose Hill Dorking RH4 .. ...
Sutton SM1, SM4 ....
Rose Hill Pk W SM1 ....
Rose La GU23 ....
Rose St RG40 ....
Rose View KT15 ....
Rose Wlk Purley CR8 ....
Surbiton KT5 ....
West Wickham BR4 ....
Rose Wood GU22 ....
Roseacre RH8 ....
Roseacre Cl TW17 ....
Roseacre Gdns GU4 ....

Rydal Cl Crawley RH11 . . . . . 200 D4
Farnborough GU14 . . . . 84 D3
Frimley GU15 . . . . 66 D5
Sanderstead CR8 . . . . 80 D6
Rydal Dr BR4 . . . . 63 E8
Rydal Gdns
Kingston u T TW15 . . . . 18 E3
Twickenham TW2, TW3 . . . . 5 B1
Rydal Pl GU18 . . . . 67 B8
Rydal Rd SW16 . . . . 21 D4
Rydal Way TW20 . . . . 12 B1
Ryde Cl GU23 . . . . 91 C6
Ryde Ct GU12 . . . . 105 C1
Ryde Heron GU21 . . . . 68 E2
Ryde Lands GU6 . . . . 174 F4
Ryde Pl TW1 . . . . 6 D1
Ryde The TW18 . . . . 33 B8
Ryde Vale Rd SW12 . . . . 21 C6
Ryde's Hill Cres GU2 . . . . . 108 F5
Ryde's Hill Rd GU2, GU3 . . 108 F4
Rydens Ave KT12 . . . . 54 C8
Rydens Cl KT12 . . . . 54 C8
Rydens Gr KT12 . . . . 54 D6
Rydens Pk KT12 . . . . 54 D8
Rydens Rd KT12 . . . . 54 B8
Rydens Sch KT12 . . . . 54 C6
Rydens Way GU22 . . . . 90 A7
Ryder House **5** SW19 . . . 40 B8
Ryders Way RH12 . . . . 217 F7
Rydes Ave GU2 . . . . 108 E3
Rydes Hill Prep Sch GU2 . . 108 F3
Rydon Mews SW19 . . . . 19 C1
Rydon's La CR3, CR5 . . . . . 100 C7
Rydon's Wood Cl
CR3, CR5 . . . . 100 C7
Rye Ash RH10 . . . . 202 A7
Rye Brook Rd KT22 . . . . 75 A4
Rye Cl Farnborough GU14 . . 84 E7
Guildford GU2 . . . . 108 E3
Winkfield RG12 . . . . 27 D8
Rye Ct BR3 . . . . 43 F8
Rye Gr GU20, GU4 . . . . 48 F2
Ryebridge Cl KT22 . . . . 75 A1
Ryebrook Bsns Pk KT22 . . . 95 A7
Ryecotes Mead SE21 . . . . . . 22 E7
Ryecroft Ave TW2 . . . . 16 B7
Ryecroft Dr RH12 . . . . 217 A3
Ryecroft Gdns GU17 . . . . . . 64 E4
Ryecroft Rd SW16 . . . . 22 A2
Ryedale Ct **8** TW12 . . . . . 36 A8
Ryefield Path **7** SW15 . . 19 A7
Ryefield Rd SE19 . . . . 22 C2
Ryehill Ct KT3 . . . . 38 F2
Ryelands Family RH11 . . . 201 A5
Horley RH6 . . . . 161 C4
Ryelands Cl CR3 . . . . 100 E6
Ryelands Ct KT22 . . . . 75 A1
Ryelands Inf Sch SE25 . . . . 43 B4
Ryelands Pl KT13 . . . . 53 E7
Ryemead La RG42, SL4 . . . . 8 C5
Ryersh La RH5 . . . . 178 C8
Ryfold Rd SW19 . . . . 20 A5
Ryland Cl TW13 . . . . 14 F4
Ryland House **11** SW16 . . 21 C3
Rylandes Rd CR2 . . . . 62 B1
Ryle Rd GU9 . . . . 146 B8
Rylston Mews KT12 . . . . 35 A1
Rymer Rd CR0 . . . . 42 E2
Rythe Ct KT7 . . . . 37 A2
Rythe House BR1 . . . . 24 D3
Rythe Rd KT10 . . . . 55 C1
Rythe The KT22 . . . . 55 C1

S

Sabah Ct TW15 . . . . 14 A4
Sable Cl TW4 . . . . 4 C4
Sable Ct **3** KT3 . . . . 38 E4
Sabre Ct GU11 . . . . 104 E2
Sachel Court Rd
GU6 . . . . 193 D3
Sackville Cl RH19 . . . . 185 C3
Sackville Cotts RH1 . . . . . . 120 D1
Sackville Ct **3** RH19 . . . . 205 F8
Sackville Gdns RH19 . . . . . 185 C3
Sackville House **18** SW16 . 21 E5
Sackville La RH19 . . . . 185 C3
Sackville Rd SM2 . . . . 59 A3
Sackville Sch RH19 . . . . . . 186 A1
Sacred Heart Catholic
Prim Sch KT3 . . . . 39 A5
Sacred Heart Coll SL5 . . . . 30 C3
Sacred Heart RC Prim Sch
TW11 . . . . 17 B1
Saddleback Rd GU15 . . . . . . 66 A8
Saddlebrook Pk TW16 . . . . . 14 E1
Saddler Row RH10 . . . . 201 D3
Saddlers Cl GU1 . . . . 110 D2
Saddlers Mews KT1 . . . . 37 C8
Saddlers Scarp GU26 . . . . . 188 A4
Saddlers Way KT18 . . . . 96 D8
Saddlewood GU15 . . . . 65 C4
Sadler Cl CR4 . . . . 40 F7
Sadlers Ride KT8 . . . . 36 C7
Saffron Cl RH11 . . . . 201 A3
Saffron Ct GU14 . . . . 84 C4
Saffron Platt GU2 . . . . 109 A5
Saffron Rd RG12 . . . . 27 B5
Saffron Way KT6 . . . . 37 D1
Sailors La GU8 . . . . 169 A2
Sainfoin Rd SW17 . . . . 21 A6
Sainsbury Ctr The KT16 . . . 33 A2
Sainsbury Rd SE19 . . . . 22 E3
Saint Hill Manor RH19 . . . . 205 C4

Saint Hill Rd RH19 . . . . 205 C5
Saints Cl SE27 . . . . 22 B4
SS Peter & Paul's RC Prim
Sch CR4 . . . . 40 F5
St Agatha's Dr KT2 . . . . 17 F2
St Agatha's Gr CR4, SM5 . . 40 F1
St Agatha's RC Prim Sch
KT2 . . . . 17 F2
St Agatha's RC Sch KT2 . . . 17 F1
St Agnes Rd RH19 . . . . 185 E2
St Aidan's RC Prim Sch
CR5 . . . . 79 C3
St Alban's Gdns TW11 . . . . 17 A3
St Alban's Gr SM5 . . . . 40 E2
St Alban's RC Prim Sch
KT8 . . . . 36 C4
St Alban's Rd RH2 . . . . 118 A3
St Alban's Rdbt GU14 . . . . 105 C7
St Albans Ave
Feltham TW13 . . . . 15 D3
Weybridge KT13 . . . . 53 A7
St Albans Cl GU3 . . . . 108 B2
St Albans House **2** SW16 . 22 A4
St Albans Rd Cheam SM1 . . 58 F6
Kingston u T KT2 . . . . 17 F2
St Amunds Cl SE6 . . . . 24 A4
St Andrew's C of E Fst
& Mid Sch RH10 . . . . 202 A4
St Andrew's Cl
GU9 . . . . 125 B2
Reigate RH2 . . . . 139 B8
Upper Halliford TW17 . . . . 34 D5
Wraysbury TW19 . . . . 11 E8
St Andrew's Ct SW18 . . . . . 20 C6
St Andrew's High Sch CR0 . 61 B6
St Andrew's RC Sch KT22 . . 95 D7
St Andrew's RC Sch The
Grange KT22 . . . . 95 D7
St Andrew's Rd
Coulsdon CR5 . . . . 79 B4
3 Croydon CR0, CR9 . . . 61 C6
Kingston u T KT6 . . . . 37 D3
St Andrew's Sch GU19 . . . . 69 D3
St Andrew's Sq KT6 . . . . . . 37 D3
St Andrew's St Mark's
Sch KT6 . . . . 37 E3
St Andrew's Way GU16 . . . . 85 F7
St Andrew's Wlk KT11 . . . . 73 B4
St Andrews
Bracknell RG12 . . . . 26 E3
Cranleigh GU6 . . . . 174 B4
St Andrews Cl GU21 . . . . . . 69 C2
St Andrews Ct Ascot SL5 . . 29 C4
Chiswick W4 . . . . 7 C6
St Andrews Gdns KT11 . . . . 73 C6
St Andrews RC Prim Sch
SW16 . . . . 21 E3
St Andrews Rd
Carshalton SM5 . . . . 59 E7
Crawley RH11 . . . . 200 D5
St Andrews Way RH8 . . . . . 123 F4
St Ann's Cl KT16 . . . . 32 D3
St Ann's Heath Cty Mid
Sch GU25 . . . . 31 E4
St Ann's Hill SW18 . . . . 20 C8
St Ann's Hill Rd KT16 . . . . . 32 D3
St Ann's Rd KT16 . . . . 32 F3
St Ann's Sch SM4 . . . . 40 B4
St Ann's Way CR2 . . . . 61 B4
St Anne's Ave TW19 . . . . . . 13 D8
St Anne's Dr RH1 . . . . 119 A2
St Anne's Prim Sch TW19 . 13 E8
St Anne's RC Prim Sch
Banstead SM7 . . . . 78 A3
Chertsey KT16 . . . . 33 A1
St Anne's Rd
Crawley RH10 . . . . 182 C2
Godalming GU7 . . . . 151 A5
St Annes Glade GU19 . . . . . 47 D3
St Annes Mount **7** RH1 . 119 A2
St Annes Way RH1 . . . . 119 A2
St Anns Rd SW13 . . . . 7 F6
St Anselm's Ct SW16 . . . . . 21 E3
St Anselm's RC Prim Sch
SW17 . . . . 21 A5
St Anthony's Ct
1 Balham SW12 . . . . . . 21 A8
Upper Tooting SW17 . . . . . 21 A6
St Anthony's Hospl KT14 . . 39 D1
St Anthony's Way TW14 . . . . 3 F3
St Anthonys Cl
Bracknell RG42 . . . . 27 A8
Upper Tooting SW17 . . . . . 20 E6
St Antony's RC Prim Sch
SE20 . . . . 43 B8
St Arvans Cl CR0 . . . . 61 E7
St Aubin Cl RH11 . . . . 200 F2
St Aubyn's Ave
Hounslow TW3, TW4 . . . . . 5 A2
Wimbledon SW19 . . . . 19 F3
St Aubyn's Sch SW19 . . . . . 19 F2
St Aubyn's Rd SE19 . . . . . . 22 F2
St Augustine's Ave
Croydon CR2 . . . . 61 C3
South Croydon CR2 . . . . . . 61 C3
St Augustine's Cl GU12 . . . 105 D1
St Augustine's Rd **3** 43 E7
St Augustine's RC Prim
Sch SE6 . . . . 24 C3
St Austins GU26 . . . . 188 D3
St Barnabas Cl BR3 . . . . 44 C7
St Barnabas Ct RH10 . . . . . 202 C7
St Barnabas' Gdns KT8 . . . 36 A4

St Barnabas Rd
Mitcham CR4 . . . . 21 A1
Sutton SM1 . . . . 59 D5
St Bartholomew CE
Prim Sch GU27 . . . . 208 C7
St Bartholomew's Cl SE26 . 23 C4
St Bartholomew's Ct
GU1 . . . . 130 F7
St Bartholomew's Prim
Sch SE26 . . . . 23 C4
St Bede's C of E Mid Sch
GU3 . . . . 90 D3
St Bede's RC Inf Sch
SW12 . . . . 21 D7
St Bede's Sch RH2 . . . . 118 E4
St Benedict's Cl
Aldershot GU11 . . . . 105 A1
Upper Tooting SW17 . . . . . 21 A3
St Benet's Gr SM4, SM5 . . . 40 C2
St Benets Cl SW17 . . . . 20 E6
St Bernadette RC Jun Mix
Sch SW12 . . . . 21 C8
St Bernadette RC Prim Sch
GU14 . . . . 85 A5
St Bernards CR0 . . . . 61 E7
St Bernards Cl **8** SE27 . . 22 D4
St Boniface Catholic Prim
Sch SW17 . . . . 20 F3
St Brelades Cl RH4 . . . . 136 A5
St Brelades Rd RH11 . . . . . 200 F2
St Catherine's Convent
Girls Prep & Senior Schs
TW1 . . . . 17 A6
St Catherine's Cross
RH1 . . . . 120 F2
St Catherine's Dr GU2 . . . 130 B5
St Catherine's Hill GU2 . . 130 C5
St Catherine's La GU4 . . . 131 D3
St Catherine's RC Mid S
GU5 . . . . 151 F7
St Catherine's RC Prim Sch
SW20 . . . . 39 C4
St Catherine's Sch GU5 . . . 65 C4
St Catherine's Senior Sch
GU5 . . . . 151 F6
St Catherines
Weybridge KT13 . . . . 53 A6
Woking GU21 . . . . 89 C8
St Catherines Bletchingley
Village Cty Prim Sch
RH1 . . . . 120 C2
St Catherines Cl SW17 . . . . 20 E6
St Catherines Ct TW13 . . . . 15 A7
St Catherines Rd
Crawley RH10 . . . . 182 D1
Frimley GU16 . . . . 86 A8
St Cecilia's RC Prim Sch
SM3 . . . . 58 D8
St Chad's RC Prim Sch
SE25 . . . . 42 E4
St Chads Cl KT6 . . . . 37 C2
St Charles Borromeo RC
Prim Sch KT13 . . . . 53 A7
St Charles Pl KT13 . . . . 53 A7
St Christopher's RH7 . . . . . 164 D4
St Christopher's Cl
Haslemere GU27 . . . . 208 A6
Hounslow TW7 . . . . 5 E6
St Christopher's Ct **3**
KT12 . . . . 54 C8
St Christopher's Gn
GU27 . . . . 208 A6
St Christopher's Hospice
SE26 . . . . 23 C3
St Christopher's Mews
SM6 . . . . 60 C5
St Christopher's Rd
2 Farnborough GU14 . . 85 A3
Haslemere GU27 . . . . 208 A6
St Christopher's Sch BR3 . 44 C7
St Christopher's Sch Trust
Ltd KT18 . . . . 76 F6
St Christophers Cl RH12 . . 217 D4
St Christophers Day Hospl
RH12 . . . . 217 D3
St Christophers Gdns
North Ascot SL5 . . . . 28 D8
Thornton Heath CR7 . . . . . 42 A6
St Christophers Pl **1**
GU14 . . . . 85 A3
St Clair Cl Oxted RH8 . . . . 122 D5
Reigate RH2 . . . . 118 C1
St Clair Dr KT4 . . . . 58 B6
St Clair's Rd CR0 . . . . 61 E8
St Claire Cotts RH7 . . . . . . 165 B1
St Clare Bsns Pk TW12 . . . 16 C2
St Clement Rd RH11 . . . . . 200 F2
St Clements Cl GU14 . . . . . . 85 B7
St Clements RC Prim Sch
KT4 . . . . 57 F2
St Cloud Rd SE27 . . . . 22 D4
St Crispin's Sch RG40 . . . . 25 E6
St Crispins Way KT16 . . . . . 51 C2
St Cross Rd Farnham GU9 . 125 C3
Frimley GU16 . . . . 86 B7
St Cuthbert Mayne RC
Prim Sch GU6 . . . . 174 E3
St Cuthbert's Cl CR4 . . . . . . 41 B5
St Cuthbert's RC Prim Sch
TW20 . . . . 11 C1
St Cyprian's St SW17 . . . . . 20 F4
St David's CR5 . . . . 79 F2
St David's Cl
Farnborough GU14 . . . . . . 84 F8
Heath End GU9 . . . . 125 E7
Reigate RH2 . . . . 118 C3
West Wickham BR3, BR4 . . 44 B2
St David's Coll BR4 . . . . 44 C1

St David's Jun Sch TW15 . . 13 F5
St Davids Cl **6** GU12 . . . 105 B1
St Davids Dr TW20 . . . . 11 C1
St Denis Rd SE27 . . . . 22 D4
St Deny's Cl GU21 . . . . 68 D1
St Dominic's Sch GU8 . . . . 171 C1
St Dunstan's C of E Prim
Sch SM1 . . . . 58 E3
St Dunstan's Coll SE6 . . . . . 24 A7
St Dunstan's Hill SM1, SM3 . 58 E4
St Dunstan's La BR3 . . . . . . 44 C4
St Dunstan's RC Prim Sch
GU22 . . . . 70 A2
St Dunstan's Rd
Cranford TW5 . . . . 4 B5
Cranford TW5 . . . . 4 C5
Feltham TW13 . . . . 14 F5
South Norwood SE25 . . . . . 42 F5
St Ebba's Hospl KT19 . . . . . 57 C2
St Edith Cl KT18 . . . . 76 C5
St Edmund Cl RH11 . . . . . . 181 D1
St Edmund's Catholic
Prim Sch TW2 . . . . 16 B8
St Edmund's La TW2 . . . . . . 16 B8
St Edmund's RC Prim Sch
GU7 . . . . 150 F2
St Edmunds Cl SW17 . . . . . 20 E6
St Edmunds Sch GU26 . . . 188 D3
St Edward's Cl RH19 . . . . . 185 C1
St Edwards Cl CR0 . . . . 82 D8
St Elizabeth Dr KT18 . . . . . 76 C5
St Elizabeth's RC Prim Sch
TW10 . . . . 6 F1
St Elphege's RC Prim Sch
SM6 . . . . 60 E4
St Faith's Rd SE24 . . . . 22 B7
St Fillans GU22 . . . . 70 B3
St Fillans Rd SE6 . . . . 24 C6
St Francis Gdns RH10 . . . . 183 C4
St Francis of Assisi RC Sch
RH10 . . . . 201 E4
St Francis RC Prim Sch
RH10 . . . . 200 F6
St Francis RC Sch SL5 . . . . 29 A3
St Francis Wlk RH11 . . . . . 200 E4
St George's Ave GU12 . . . . . 53 C4
St George's Bsns Ctr KT13 . 53 A2
St George's Cl
Farnham GU9 . . . . 126 B6
Weybridge KT13 . . . . 53 A6
St George's Coll KT15 . . . . . 52 D7
St George's Gdns
Epsom KT17 . . . . 76 F5
Horsham RH13 . . . . 217 E4
Tolworth KT6 . . . . 57 B8
St George's Gr SW17 . . . . . 20 D5
St George's Hill Artisan
Golf Club KT13 . . . . 53 C2
St George's Hill Golf
Course KT13 . . . . 53 C2
St George's Hospl SW17 . . 20 D3
St George's Ind Est KT13 . . 53 B1
St George's La SL5 . . . . 29 B5
St George's Lodge KT13 . . . 53 D5
St George's Rd
Aldershot GU11, GU12 . . . 105 B1
Beckenham BR3 . . . . 44 B8
Camberley GU15 . . . . 65 D6
Farnham GU9 . . . . 125 D1
Feltham TW13 . . . . 15 D4
Isleworth TW1 . . . . 6 B2
Kingston u T KT2 . . . . 18 A1
Mitcham CR4 . . . . 41 B6
Richmond TW9 . . . . 6 F4
South Nutfield RH1 . . . . . 140 E1
Wallington SM6 . . . . 60 B5
Weybridge KT13 . . . . 53 D4
Wimbledon SW19 . . . . 19 F2
St George's RC Coll
Addlestone KT15 . . . . 52 C6
Crawley RH10 . . . . 201 D8
East Grinstead RH19 . . . . 185 C3
Weybridge KT13 . . . . 52 D6
St Georges Ind Est GU15 . . 65 B3
St Georges Rd
Addlestone KT15 . . . . 52 C6
Farnham GU10 . . . . 126 B4
St Georges Rd W BR1 . . . . . 24 F1
St German's Rd SE23 . . . . . 23 E7
St Giles C of E Inf Sch
KT21 . . . . 75 F1
St Giles' Sch CR2 . . . . 61 B4
St Gothard Rd SE21, SE27 . 22 D4
St Gregory's RC Inf Sch
GU15 . . . . 65 B6
St Helen's Cres SW16 . . . . . 41 F8
St Helen's Rd SW16 . . . . . . 41 F8
St Helena Terr **20** TW9 . . 6 D2
St Helens KT7 . . . . 37 B3
St Helens Cres GU47 . . . . . 64 B8
St Helier Ave SM4 . . . . 40 C3
St Helier Cl Crawley RH11 . 201 A2
Wokingham RG41 . . . . 25 A5
St Helier Sta SM4 . . . . 40 A3
St Heliers Ave TW3, TW4 . . . 5 A2
St Hilary's Prep Sch GU7 . 150 D3
St Hilda's Ave TW15 . . . . . . 13 E3
St Hilda's Cl
Crawley RH10 . . . . 182 C1

St Hilda's Cl continued
Horley RH6 161
Knaphill GU21 68
St Hildas Cl SW17 20
St Hugh of Lincoln RC
Primary Sch GU21 88
St Hugh's Cl RH10 182
St Hugh's Rd SE20 23
St Hughes Cl SW17 20
St Ignatius RC Fst & Mid
Sch TW16 35
St Ives RH10 202
St Ives Sch GU27 208
St James Ave KT17 77
St James' Ave SM1 59
St James' Ave SM1 125
St James C of E Prim Sch
GU3 148
St James Cl KT18 76
St James' Cl KT3 38
St James Cl GU21 69
St James Ct Ashtead KT21 . 75
Farnham GU9 125
St James' Ct **7** KT1 37
St James Mews KT13 53
St James Rd SM5 59
St James'
Kingston u T KT6 37
Mitcham CR4 21
Purley CR8 80
St James Rd SM1, SM2 . . . 59
St James' Terr GU9 125
St James The Great RC
(Aided) Sch CR7 42
St James Wlk RH11 201
St James's Ave
Beckenham BR3 43
Hampton TW12 16
St James's Cl SW17 20
St James's Cotts **14** TW10 . 6
St James's Dr
Balham SW12, SW17 20
Upper Tooting SW17 20
St James's Lodge **4** CR0 . 42
St James's Pk CR0 42
St James's Rd Croydon CR0 . 42
East Grinstead RH19 185
Hampton TW12 16
Kingston u T KT1 37
Thornton Heath CR0 42
St James's Sch TW2 16
St James's Terr **3** SW12 . 21
St Joan Cl RH11 201
St John Baptist C of E
Prim Sch BR1 24
St John Cl RH13 217
St John Fisher RC Prim
Sch SW20 39
St John Rigby RC Coll
BR4 63
St John The Bapist Sch
GU22 90
St John the Baptist C of
E Jun Sch KT1 17
St John's RH5 136
St John's Ave
Epsom KT17 76
St John's Beamont Prep
Sch TW20 11
St John's Beamont Sch
TW19 11
St John's C of E Fst Sch
GU10 167
St John's CE Jun Sch
CR3 101
St John's CE Prim Sch
CR3 101
St John's CE (VA) Inf Sch
CR3 101
St John's Cl
East Grinstead RH19 185
Guildford GU2 130
Leatherhead KT22 95
St John's Court **2** SE20 . 23
St John's Cotts **1** KT1 . . 37
St John's Cres RH12 217
St John's Ct
Brookwood GU24 87
Farnborough GU14 84
Isleworth TW7 5
St John's Dr SW18 20
St John's Gr Barnes SW13 . . 7
1 Richmond TW9 6
St John's Hill Rd GU21 88
St John's Hill Rd
GU21, GU22 89
St John's Hospl GU7 17
St John's Lye
(Festival Path) GU21 88
St John's Meadow RH7 . . . 163
St John's RC Prim Sch
RH13 217
St John's Rd
Carshalton SM5 . . . .
Crawley RH11 201
Croydon CR0, CR9 61
East Grinstead RH19 185
East Molesey KT8 36
Farnborough GU14 84
Farnham GU9 125
Feltham TW13 15

t John's Rd *continued*
Guildford GU2 130 A8
Isleworth TW7 5 F5
Leatherhead KT22 95 C6
North Ascot SL5 8 F1
Penge SE20 23 C2
Redhill RH1 139 F7
Richmond TW9 6 E3
Sandhurst GU47 64 C7
Sutton SM1 59 B8
Teddington KT1 37 C7
Westcott RH4 135 C6
Wimbledon SW19 19 E2
Woking GU21 69 B2
t John's Rise GU21 89 B8
t John's Sch KT22 95 B6
John's (Shirley) C of E
Prim Sch CR0 62 D7
t John's St GU7 150 F6
t John's Terrace Rd
RH1 139 F7
t Johns Ave KT17 77 A7
t Johns Ct Egham TW20 12 A3
South Godstone RH9 142 F5
Woking GU21 89 A8
Johns Cty Prim Sch
RH1 139 E7
Johns Dr KT12 35 C1
Johns Gr GU9 146 B8
Johns Mews GU21 89 A8
Johns Rd KT3 38 C6
Johns St RG45 45 B4
Johns Way KT16 33 A1
Joseph's Convent
Prep Sch KT8 36 C4
Joseph's RC Coll SW16 22 B2
Joseph's RC Inf Sch
E19 22 C2
Joseph's RC Jun Sch
E19 22 C2
Joseph's RC Prim Sch
Bracknell RG12 27 D7
Dorking RH4 136 A7
Epsom KT18 76 C5
Kingston u T KT1 37 F7
Redhill RH1 118 E2
Joseph's RC Sch GU2 108 F3
Joseph's Rd
GU11, GU12 105 A1
Joseph's Sch GU6 174 F6
Josephs RC Prim Sch
GU11 126 A8
Jude's C of E Sch
W20 11 C2
Jude's Cl TW20 11 C3
Jude's Cotts TW20 11 C3
Jude's Rd TW20 11 C3
Julian's Cl SE27, SW16 22 A4
Julian's Farm Rd
E27, SW16 22 B4
Katharines Rd CR3 101 A2
Kitts Terr SE19 22 E3
Lawrence C of E Mid Sch
T8 36 D5
Lawrence Ct GU24 68 E8
Lawrence Cty Prim Sch
T24 113 D8
Lawrence RC Sch TW13 15 B6
Lawrence Way CR3 100 D4
Lawrences Way RH2 118 A1
Leonard's Gdns TW5 4 E6
Leonard's Rd
aygate KT10 55 F4
roydon CR0, CR9 61 B7
ngston u T KT6 37 D4
ames Ditton KT7 37 A2
indsor SL4 9 D8
Leonard's Sq KT6 37 D4
Leonard's Wlk SW16 21 F1
Leonards C of E Prim
ch SW16 21 D3
Leonards Ct SW14 7 C4
Leonards Cty Inf Sch
13 217 E2
Leonards Dr RH10 202 A4
Leonards Pk RH19 185 E1
Leonards Rd
urgh Heath KT18 97 C8
orsham RH13 218 A1
ortlake SW14 7 C4
Louis Rd SE27 22 D4
Luke's C of E Prim Sch
ngston u T KT2 37 F8
chmond TW9 7 A6
est Norwood SE27 22 C3
Luke's Cl SE25 43 B3
Luke's Hospl GU1 130 F7
Luke's Rd CR3 80 F1
Luke's Sq 9 GU1 130 F8
Lukes Ct GU21 70 C5
Margaret Clitherow RC
rim Sch RG12 26 F2
Margaret's GU1 109 F1
Margaret's Ave
heam SM3 58 E7
ormans Park RH19 185 F6
Margaret's CE Sch
H11 201 B7
Margaret's Ct 9 TW1 6 B1
Margaret's Dr TW1 6 B2
Margaret's Gr TW1 6 A1
Margaret's Rd
ast Grinstead RH19 185 F3
ooley CR5 99 B6
leworth TW1 6 B2
wickenham TW1 6 B2
Margaret's Sta TW1 6 B1
Margarets Ave TW15 14 B3
St Margarets Bsns Ctr 11
TW1 6 B1
St Margarets Ct RH12 216 F7
St Margarets Dr KT18 76 C5
St Mark's C of E Prim Sch
Croydon SE25 43 A5
Farnborough GU14 105 D8
St Mark's Catholic Sch
TW3 5 A4
St Mark's CE Prim Sch
BR2 44 F6
St Mark's CE (VA) Prim
Sch GU7 150 B3
St Mark's Fst Sch CR4 40 F7
St Mark's Hill KT6 37 E3
St Mark's La RH12 217 E6
St Mark's Pl SW19 19 F2
St Mark's Rd
Bracknell RG42 26 C8
Croydon SE25 43 A5
Teddington TW11 17 B1
St Marks Cl GU14 85 C1
St Marks Pl GU9 125 B7
St Marks Rd KT18, KT20 77 C1
St Martha's GU5 154 E8
St Martha's Ave GU22 89 F6
St Martha's Ct GU4 131 B3
St Martin's Ave KT18 76 E5
St Martin's C of E Inf Sch
KT18 76 D4
St Martin's C of E Jun Sch
KT18 76 D4
St Martin's C of E Prim
Sch RH4 136 A8
St Martin's C of E Sch
(Pixham) RH4 115 C1
St Martin's Cl KT17 76 E6
St Martin's Ct
Staines TW15 13 C3
West Norwood SE27 22 B6
St Martin's Way SW17 20 C5
St Martin's Wlk RH4 136 B8
St Martin-in-the-Fields
High Sch SW2 22 A7
St Martins Cl KT24 112 E6
St Martins Ct KT24 112 E6
St Martins Dr KT12 54 C7
St Martins Mews RH4 136 B7
St Mary Ave SM6 60 B7
St Mary Magdalene C of E
Sec Sch TW10 7 A2
St Mary's 4 KT13 53 D7
St Mary's Ave
Beckenham BR2 44 E6
Stanwell TW19 13 D8
Teddington TW11 16 F2
St Mary's C of E Inf Sch
KT22 95 C5
St Mary's C of E Prim Sch
Chessington KT9 56 F4
Long Ditton KT7 37 B1
Winkfield RG42 8 B2
St Mary's C of E Sch
TW19 13 E8
St Mary's CE (Aided) Sch
RH19 185 D2
St Mary's CE controlled
Inf Sch GU8 149 E6
St Mary's CE Jun Sch
RH8 122 E7
St Mary's CE Prim Sch
KT14 71 E6
St Mary's Church Sch
TW1 17 A8
St Mary's Cl
Chessington KT9 56 F3
Ewell KT17 57 F2
Fetcham KT22 94 D4
Oxted RH8 122 E6
Stanwell TW19 13 D8
Sunbury TW16 35 A5
St Mary's Cottage Hospl
TW12 35 F8
St Mary's Cres
Hounslow TW7 5 E7
Stanwell TW19 13 D8
St Mary's Ct
Kingston u T KT3 38 E6
Wallington SM6 60 C6
St Mary's Dr
Crawley RH10 202 B8
East Bedfont TW14 14 C8
St Mary's Gdns
Bagshot GU19 47 E3
Horsham RH12 217 C1
St Mary's Gn TN16 83 C1
St Mary's Gr
Biggin Hill TN16 83 C1
Chiswick W4 7 B8
Richmond TW10, TW9 6 F3
St Mary's High Sch CR0 42 C1
St Mary's Hill SL5 29 C4
St Mary's House RH12 217 C1
St Mary's Mt CR3 100 F3
St Mary's Pl GU9 125 C3
St Mary's RC Inf Sch CR0 42 D1
St Mary's RC Jun Sch
Carshalton SM5 59 F5
Croydon CR0 42 D1
St Mary's RC Prim Sch
Beckenham BR3 24 C1
Chiswick W4 7 E8
Isleworth TW7 6 A4
Merton SW19 20 A1
St Mary's RC Sch TW7 6 A4
St Mary's Rd Ascot SL5 29 B3
Ash Vale GU12 106 A5
Camberley GU15 65 C6
St Mary's Rd *continued*
East Molesey KT8 36 D4
Kingston u T KT6 37 D3
Long Ditton KT6 37 C1
Oatlands Park KT13 53 D6
Reigate RH2 139 B8
South Croydon CR2 61 D2
South Norwood SE25 42 E6
Wimbledon SW19 19 F3
Woking GU21 69 C2
Worcester Park KT4 57 E8
St Mary's Roman Catholic
Inf Sch SM5 59 F6
St Mary's Sch
Ascot SL5 29 B2
Horsham RH12 217 C1
St Mary's & St Peter's
Prim Sch TW11 16 F3
St Mary's Univ Coll TW1 16 F5
St Marys CE (VA) Prim Sch
GU8 191 C4
St Marys Cl GU47 64 C8
St Marys La SL4 8 D5
St Marys Rd KT22 95 B4
St Marys Wlk RH1 120 D2
St Matthew's Ave KT6 37 F1
St Matthew's C of E Prim
Sch RH1 118 F3
St Matthew's CE Fst Sch
SW20 39 A8
St Matthew's CE Prim Sch
KT6 37 E2
St Matthew's Ct TW15 14 A3
St Matthew's Rd RH1 118 F2
St Matthews (C of E) Sch
KT11 73 B1
St Merryn Ct BR3 24 A1
St Michael's Ave GU3 108 C6
St Michael's C of E Prim
Sch RG12 27 A4
St Michael's CE (VA)
Fst Sch RH5 115 C8
St Michael's Cl KT12 54 C8
St Michael's Prim Sch
Forest Hill SE26 23 E4
Wandsworth SW18 19 F8
St Michael's RC Prim Sch
TW15 14 A3
St Michael's Rd
Aldershot GU11, GU12 105 B1
Croydon CR0 42 C1
Farnborough GU14 85 B6
Sheerwater GU21 70 D5
Wallington SM6 60 C4
St Michael's & St Martin's
RC Prim Sch TW4 4 F4
St Michaels C of E Inf Sch
GU11 126 B8
St Michaels C of E Jun Sch
GU11 126 C8
St Michaels Cl KT4 57 F8
St Michaels Cotts RG45 45 C8
St Michaels Ct 1 KT13 53 C5
St Michaels Rd
Ashford TW15 14 A3
Camberley GU15 65 B5
Caterham CR3 100 D5
East Grinstead RH19 185 E2
St Micheal's C of E Sch
SL5 29 D4
St Mildred's Rd GU1 109 F2
St Mildreds Rd SE12, SE6 24 F8
St Monica's Rd KT20 97 F6
St Nazaire Cl TW20 12 C3
St Nicholas Ave KT23 94 B2
St Nicholas C of E Prim
Sch Cranleigh GU6 174 D3
Shepperton TW17 34 B3
St Nicholas Ct RH10 202 C7
St Nicholas Ctr SM1 59 B5
St Nicholas Dr TW17 34 A2
St Nicholas Glebe SW17 21 A2
St Nicholas Hill KT22 95 B5
St Nicholas Rd Sutton SM1 59 B5
Thames Ditton KT7 36 F3
St Nicholas Sch
Croydon CR9 61 A6
Purley CR8 80 A6
St Nicholas Specl Sch
RH1 119 D6
St Nicholas Way SM1 59 B5
St Nicolas Ave GU6 174 E3
St Nicolas CE Inf Sch
GU2 130 C7
St Nicolas Cl GU6 174 E3
St Normans Way KT17 58 A1
St Olave's Cl TW18 12 F1
St Olave's Wlk SW16 41 D7
St Omer Rd GU1 131 A8
St Omer Ridge GU1 131 A8
St Osmund's RC Prim Sch
SW13 7 F6
St Oswald's Rd SW16 42 B8
St Patrick's RC Prim Sch
GU14 85 D4
St Paul's C of E Jun Sch
KT2 18 A1
St Paul's C of E Jun Sch
RG41 25 A6
St Paul's Catholic Sch
TW16 35 A8
St Paul's CE Inf Sch
GU10 127 A7
St Paul's CE Prim Sch
Addlestone KT15 52 A6
Chessington KT9 56 E6
St Paul's CE (VA) Prim Sch
RH4 136 B6
St Paul's Cl
Addlestone KT15 52 A5
Ashford TW15 14 C3
Carshalton SM5 40 E1
Chessington KT9 56 D6
Hounslow TW3, TW4 4 E5
St Paul's Ct TW4 4 E4
St Paul's Gate RG41 25 A6
St Paul's RC Prim Sch
KT7 36 E2
St Paul's Rd Brentford TW8 6 D8
Egham TW18 12 D2
South Norwood CR7 42 C6
St Paul's Rd E RH4, RH5 136 B7
St Paul's Rd W RH4 136 B6
St Pauls C of E Prim Sch
TW8 6 D8
St Pauls' CE Fst Sch
GU10 126 F6
St Pauls Cl GU10 126 F7
St Pauls Rd Richmond TW9 6 F4
Woking GU22 70 B2
St Peter & St Paul CE
Inf Sch CR3 100 A2
St Peter's CE Jun Sch
GU14 85 C4
St Peter's Cl
Old Woking GU22 90 C7
Staines TW18 12 F2
St Peter's Gdns
West Norwood SE27 22 A5
Wrecclesham GU10 145 F6
St Peter's Hospl KT16 51 D7
St Peter's Prim Sch CR2 61 E4
St Peter's RC (Aided) Sch
RH19 185 C1
St Peter's RC Comp
Sch GU1 110 C2
St Peter's RC Prim Sch
KT22 95 C7
St Peter's Rd
Crawley RH11 201 C6
Croydon CR0, CR2 61 D6
East Molesey KT8 36 A5
Isleworth TW1 6 B2
Old Woking GU22 90 B7
St Peter's St CR0, CR2 61 D5
St Peter's Way
Addlestone KT15 51 F6
Addlestone KT15, KT16 51 F7
Chertsey KT15 52 B8
Frimley GU16 85 F7
St Peters CE Inf Sch RH8 122 A2
St Peters CE Prim Sch
GU9 146 A7
St Peters Cl SW17 20 E6
St Peters Ct KT8 36 A5
St Peters Mead GU12 106 B2
St Peters Pk GU11, GU9 125 E8
St Peters Rd KT1 38 A7
St Peters Way UB3 3 D8
St Philip's Ave KT4 58 B8
St Philip's Rd KT6 37 D3
St Philips Sch KT9 56 D4
St Philomena's Sch SM5 59 E5
St Pier's La RH7, TN8 165 B5
St Pinnock Ave TW18 33 A8
St Polycarp's RC Prim Sch
GU9 125 D1
St Richard's with
St Andrew's CE Prim Sch
TW10 17 B5
St Richards Ct TW10 17 B5
St Robert Southwell RC
Sch RH12 218 A6
St Sampson Rd RH11 200 F2
St Saviour's Coll SE27 22 D4
St Saviour's Pl GU1 109 C1
St Saviour's Rd CR0 42 C3
St Stephen's C of E Jun Sch
TW1 6 B1
St Stephen's CE Prim Sch
RH9 142 F6
St Stephen's Cl GU27 207 F6
St Stephen's Cres CR7 42 A6
St Stephen's Gdns TW1 6 C1
St Stephen's Rd TW3, TW4 5 A2
St Stephens Ave KT21 75 E3
St Stephens Cl GU27 208 C7
St Stephens Ct RH9 142 E5
St Swithun's Cl RH19 185 F1
St Teresa's Prep Sch
(Grove House) KT24 113 D7
St Teresa's RC Prim Sch
SM4 40 D3
St Theresa Cl KT18 76 C5
St Theresa's RC Prim Sch
RG40 25 D5
St Theresa's Rd TW14 3 F3
St Thomas' Cl KT6 37 F1
St Thomas Cl GU21 69 C2
St Thomas More RC Sch
KT8 36 C4
St Thomas of Canterbury
RC Mid Sch CR4 41 A6
St Thomas
of Canterbury RC Sch
GU1 110 B1
St Thomas' Rd W4 7 C8
St Thomas Wlk SL3 1 D7
St Thomas's Dr GU4 111 E4
St Thomas's Mews GU1 130 F7
St Vincent Cl
Crawley RH10 202 D5
West Norwood SE27 22 B3
St Vincent Rd
Twickenham TW2 5 C1
Walton-on-T KT12 54 B7
St Wilfrid's RC Sch RH11 201 B5
St William of York RC
Prim Sch SE23 23 E7
St Winifred's RC Prim Sch
SE12 24 F8
St Winifred's Rd
Biggin Hill TN16 83 F1
Teddington TW11 17 B2
St Winifreds CR8 80 C4
Salamanca Pk GU11 104 F3
Salamander Cl KT2 17 C3
Salamander Quay KT1 37 D8
Salbrook Rd RH1 140 A1
Salcombe Dr SM4 39 D1
Salcombe House SE23 23 C6
Salcombe Rd TW15 13 E5
Salcot Cres CR0 63 C1
Salcott Rd CR0 60 F6
Sale Garden Cotts RG40 25 C5
Salehurst Rd RH10 202 E6
Salem Pl CR0, CR9 61 C7
Salerno Cl GU11 105 A2
Sales Ct 7 GU11 105 A1
Salesian Catholic Comp
Sch KT16 51 E8
Salesian Coll GU14 85 D1
Salesian Sch KT16 33 A1
Salesian View GU14 105 E8
Salford Rd SW12, SW2 21 D7
Salfords Cty Prim Sch
RH1 140 A3
Salfords Sta RH1 140 B1
Salfords Way RH1 140 A1
Salisbury Ave SM1, SM2 58 F4
Salisbury Cl
Wokingham RG41 25 A2
Worcester Park KT4 57 F7
Salisbury Gdns SW19 19 E1
Salisbury Gr GU16 86 A3
Salisbury House SW19 19 D5
Salisbury Pl KT14 71 C8
Salisbury Rd Ash GU12 106 A3
Banstead SM7 78 B5
Blackwater GU17 64 C5
Crawley RH10 201 F2
Croydon CR0, SE25 43 A3
Farnborough GU14 85 C3
Feltham TW13 15 C7
Harlington TW6 3 C1
Hounslow TW4 4 C4
Kingston u T KT3 38 D6
Richmond TW9 6 E3
Tyler's Green RH9 121 C4
Wallington SM5 59 F4
Wimbledon SW19 19 E1
Woking GU22 89 E8
Worcester Park KT19, KT4 57 E7
Salisbury Terr GU16 86 A3
Salix Cl TW16 15 B1
Salliesfield TW2 5 D1
Salmons La CR3 100 F7
Salmons La W CR3 100 E7
Salmons Rd
Chessington KT9 56 E4
Effingham KT24 113 C6
Salt Box Rd
Guildford GU3, GU4 109 B6
Worplesdon GU3, GU4 109 B6
Salt La GU8 171 E5
Saltash Cl SM1 58 F6
Saltbox Hill TN16 83 B6
Saltdean Cl RH10 201 D3
Salter House 8 SW16 21 C4
Salter's Hill SE19, SE27 22 D3
Salterford Rd SW17 21 A2
Salterns Rd RH10 202 C3
Saltire Gdns 2 RG42 27 A8
Saltram Rd GU14 85 E2
Salvador SW17 20 F3
Salvation Pl KT22 95 A3
Salvington Rd RH11 200 F3
Salwey Cl RG12 27 B3
Samaritan Cl RH11 200 E4
Samarkand Cl GU15 66 B4
Sambrook Mews SE6 24 B7
Samos Rd SE20 43 B7
Samphire Cl RH11 201 A3
Sampleoak La
Chilworth GU4 131 E2
Wonersh GU4 131 E2
Sampson Bsns Pk GU15 65 B3
Sampson Ct TW17 34 C4
Sampson Pk RG42 26 D8
Sampson's Almshouses
GU9 125 A1
Samuel Cody Sch The
GU14 105 B7
Samuel Ct BR3 44 B6
Samuel Johnson Cl SW16 21 F4
San Carlos App GU11 105 C2
San Feliu Ct RH19 186 B2
Sanctuary Rd TW19, TW6 3 A1
Sanctuary The SM4 40 A3
Sand Hill GU14 85 B7
Sand Hill Ct GU14 85 B7
Sandal Rd KT3 38 E5
Sandalwood GU2 130 B8
Sandalwood Ave KT16 51 E7
Sandalwood Rd TW13 15 B5
Sandbourne Ave SW19 40 B7
Sandcross Cty Sch RH2 138 F6
Sandcross La RH2 139 A5
Sanders Cl TW12 16 C3
Sanders House SW16 21 E2
Sandersfield Rd SM7 78 B4

Sanderstead Cl SW12 . . . . 21 C8
Sanderstead Court Ave
CR2 . . . . 81 A6
Sanderstead Ct CR2 . . . . 81 A7
Sanderstead Hill CR2 . . . . 80 F8
Sanderstead Hts CR2 . . . . 81 A8
Sanderstead Rd CR2 . . . . 61 D2
Sanderstead Sta CR2 . . . . 61 D2
Sandes Pl KT22 . . . . 75 A1
Sandfield Cty Prim Sch
GU1 . . . . 130 D8
Sandfield Gdns CR7 . . . . 42 B6
Sandfield Pl CR7 . . . . 42 C6
Sandfield Rd CR7 . . . . 42 C6
Sandfield Terr GU1 . . . . 130 D8
Sandfields GU23 . . . . 90 D3
Sandford Ct GU11 . . . . 104 F1
Sandford Down RG12 . . . . 27 F4
Sandford Rd
Aldershot GU11 . . . . 104 F1
Heath End GU9 . . . . 125 B7
Sandgate House [14] BR3 . . . . 24 A1
Sandgate La SW17, SW18 . . . 20 E7
Sandhawes Hill RH19 . . . . . . 186 A4
Sandheath Rd GU26 . . . . 188 C7
Sandhill La RH10 . . . . 204 B7
Sandhills CR0, SM6 . . . . 60 D6
Sandhills Ct GU25 . . . . 31 E4
Sandhills La GU25, TW20 . . . 31 E4
Sandhills Meadow TW17 . . . . 34 B2
Sandhills Rd RH2 . . . . 139 A7
Sandhurst Ave KT5 . . . . 38 B2
Sandhurst Cl CR2 . . . . 61 E2
Sandhurst La GU17 . . . . 64 B5
Sandhurst Prim Sch SE6 . . . . 24 E7
Sandhurst Rd Catford SE6 . . 24 E7
Crowthorne RG45 . . . . 45 A1
Wokingham RG40 . . . . 25 E5
Sandhurst Sch GU47 . . . . 45 D1
Sandhurst Sta GU47 . . . . 64 A8
Sandhurst Way CR2 . . . . 61 E3
Sandiford House CR3 . . . . . . 100 E3
Sandiford Rd SM3 . . . . 58 F8
Sandiland Cres BR2 . . . . 63 F8
Sandilands CR0 . . . . 62 A7
Sandlands Gr KT20 . . . . 97 A4
Sandlands Rd KT20 . . . . 97 A3
Sandon Cl KT10 . . . . 36 D1
Sandon House [5] SW2 . . . . . 21 E8
Sandown Ave KT10 . . . . 55 C5
Sandown Cl
Blackwater GU17 . . . . 64 D5
Cranford TW5 . . . . 4 A6
Sandown Cres GU11 . . . . 126 B7
Sandown Ct [2] SM2 . . . . 59 B3
Sandown Dr Frimley GU16 . . 65 E2
Wallington SM5 . . . . 60 A2
Sandown Gate KT10 . . . . 55 D7
Sandown House SE26 . . . . . . 23 A3
Sandown Ind Pk KT10 . . . . . . 55 A8
Sandown Lodge KT18 . . . . . . 76 C5
Sandown Park KT10 . . . . 55 C8
Sandown Rd Coulsdon CR5 . . 79 A3
Croydon SE25 . . . . 43 B4
Esher KT10 . . . . 55 B6
Sandpiper Cl RH11 . . . . 200 D4
Sandpiper Rd Cheam SM1 . . 58 F5
Selsdon CR2 . . . . 81 D8
Sandpit Hall Rd GU24 . . . . 69 A7
Sandpit Heath GU3 . . . . 108 D5
Sandpit Rd Catford BR1 . . . . 24 E3
Redhill RH1 . . . . 139 F8
Sandpits Rd
Richmond TW10 . . . . 17 D6
South Croydon CR0 . . . . 62 D6
Sandra Cl TW3 . . . . 5 B2
Sandra House KT8 . . . . 36 D4
Sandringham Ave SW20 . . . . 39 E7
Sandringham Cl
East Grinstead RH19 . . . . . . 206 A8
Farnborough GU14 . . . . 105 B8
1 Putney SW19 . . . . 19 D7
Pyrford GU22 . . . . 71 A3
Sandringham Ct
Beckenham BR3 . . . . 44 C8
Belmont SM2 . . . . 59 A3
Sandringham Cty Inf Sch
GU16 . . . . 85 F7
Sandringham Dr TW15 . . . . . 13 D4
Sandringham Gdns TW5 . . . . . 4 A6
Sandringham Pk KT11 . . . . . . 74 A2
Sandringham Rd
Crawley RH11 . . . . 201 B2
North Cheam KT4 . . . . 58 A2
Stanwell TW19, TW6 . . . . 2 E7
Thornton Heath CR0 . . . . 42 C4
Sandringham Way GU16 . . . . 85 F6
Sandrock GU27 . . . . 207 F6
Sandrock Hill Rd
Rowledge GU10 . . . . 146 A5
Wrecclesham GU10 . . . . 146 A5
Sandrock Pl CR0 . . . . 62 D6
Sandrock Rd RH4 . . . . 135 B5
Sandroyd Way KT11 . . . . 74 A6
Sands Cl GU10 . . . . 126 D2
Sands Rd Farnham GU10 . . . 126 D2
The Sands GU10 . . . . 126 D2
Sandstone TW9 . . . . 7 A6
Sandways [1] TW9 . . . . 7 A6
Sandy Cl GU22 . . . . 70 C2
Sandy Croft KT17 . . . . 58 C1
Sandy Cross GU10 . . . . 126 F4
Sandy Ct KT11 . . . . 73 F6
Sandy Dr Cobham KT11 . . . . . 73 F6
East Bedfont TW14 . . . . 14 E7

Sandy Hill Rd
Heath End GU9 . . . . 125 B7
Wallington SM6 . . . . 60 C2
Sandy Holt KT11 . . . . 73 F6
Sandy La Albury GU5 . . . . . . 132 D2
Artington GU2, GU3 . . . . 130 B5
Belmont SM2 . . . . 58 E2
Betchworth RH3 . . . . 116 E1
Bletchingley RH1 . . . . 120 C3
Bracknell RG12 . . . . 27 C8
Camberley GU15 . . . . 65 E6
Chobham GU24 . . . . 49 E2
Cobham KT11, KT22 . . . . 74 B7
Crawley Down RH10 . . . . . . 204 A8
East Grinstead RH19 . . . . . . 185 F1
Farnborough GU14 . . . . 84 D7
Farncombe GU7 . . . . 150 D6
Grayswood GU27 . . . . 189 E1
Haslemere GU26, GU27 . . . 207 C7
Haslemere, Nutcombe GU26 188 F2
Kingswood KT20 . . . . 98 A4
Limpsfield RH8 . . . . 123 B7
Mitcham CR4 . . . . 41 A8
Normandy GU3 . . . . 107 D4
North Ascot SL5 . . . . 28 C8
Nutfield RH1 . . . . 119 E1
Oxted RH8 . . . . 122 C6
Pyrford GU22 . . . . 71 A3
Reigate RH2 . . . . 138 B8
Richmond TW10 . . . . 17 D6
Rushmoor GU10 . . . . 168 B5
Sandhurst GU47 . . . . 45 A2
Send GU23 . . . . 90 C4
Shere GU5 . . . . 133 A3
South Nutfield RH1 . . . . 119 E1
Sunningdale SL5 . . . . 30 A4
Teddington KT8, TW11 . . . . . 17 B1
Thorpe GU25 . . . . 31 E5
Walton-on-T KT12 . . . . 35 C3
Woking GU22 . . . . 70 C2
Sandy La S SM6 . . . . 60 D5
Sandy La S SM6 . . . . 60 C2
Sandy Lane Jun Sch RG12 . . 27 C8
Sandy Rd KT15 . . . . 52 A4
Sandy Ride SL5 . . . . 29 E5
Sandy Way Cobham KT11 . . . 74 A7
Croydon CR0 . . . . 62 F7
Walton-on-T KT12 . . . . 34 F1
Woking GU22 . . . . 70 C2
Sandycombe Rd
East Bedfont TW14 . . . . 15 A7
Richmond TW9 . . . . 7 A5
Sandycoombe Rd TW1 . . . . . . 6 C1
Sanger Ave T10 . . . . 38 A6
Sanger Dr GU23 . . . . 90 C4
Sangers Cty Jun Sch
RH6 . . . . 160 F3
Sangers Dr RH6 . . . . 160 F3
Sangley Rd Catford SE6 . . . . 24 C7
South Norwood SE25 . . . . . . 42 E5
Santina Cl GU9 . . . . 125 D8
Sanway Cl KT14 . . . . 71 E5
Sanway Rd KT14 . . . . 71 E5
Sappho Ct GU21 . . . . 68 E3
Sapte Cl GU6 . . . . 175 A3
Saracen Cl CR0 . . . . 42 D3
Sarah House SW15 . . . . 7 F3
Sarah Way GU14 . . . . 85 B4
Sardeson House [13] SW27 . . 22 B3
Sarel Way RH6 . . . . 161 B5
Sargent Cl RH10 . . . . 201 F2
Sarjant Path SW19 . . . . 19 D6
Sark Cl Crawley RH11 . . . . . . 201 A2
Heston TW5 . . . . 5 A7
Sarsby Dr TW19 . . . . 12 A6
Sarsen Ave TW3 . . . . 5 A5
Sarsfeld Rd SW12, SW17 . . . 20 F7
Sarum RG12 . . . . 26 F1
Sarum Cres RG40 . . . . 25 D7
Sarum Gn KT13 . . . . 53 E7
Satellite Bsns Village The
RH1 . . . . 181 E2
Satis Ct KT17 . . . . 76 F8
Saturn Cl RH11 . . . . 200 E4
Saturn Croft RG42 . . . . 8 B2
Saunders Cl RH10 . . . . 202 B7
Saunders Copse GU22 . . . . . 89 B5
Saunders House [11] SW2 . . 22 A8
Saunders La GU22 . . . . 89 B5
Saundersfield House SM7 . . 78 B5
Saunton Ave UB3 . . . . 3 F7
Saunton Gdns [12] GU14 . . . 85 A4
Savernake Way RG12 . . . . 27 F4
Savernake Wlk RH10 . . . . . . 201 F3
Savile Cl New Malden KT3 . . 38 E4
Thames Ditton KT7 . . . . 36 F2
Savile Gdns CR0 . . . . 61 F8
Savill Gardens The TW20 . . 10 F2
Savill Gdns SW20 . . . . 39 A6
Saville Cres TW15 . . . . 14 D2
Saville Gdns GU15 . . . . 66 B5
Saville Rd TW1 . . . . 16 F7
Saville Row BR2 . . . . 44 F1
Savin Lodge SM2 . . . . 59 C3
Savona Cl [3] SW19 . . . . 19 D1
Savona Ct SW20 . . . . 39 D8
Savoy Gr GU17 . . . . 64 D3
Sawkins Cl SW19 . . . . 19 E6
Sawtry Cl SM5 . . . . 40 D2
Sawyer House [15] SE21 . . . . 22 E4
Sawyer's Hill TW10 . . . . 17 F7
Saxby Rd SW2 . . . . 21 E8
Saxby's La RH7 . . . . 164 D5
Saxley RH6 . . . . 161 C4
Saxon Ave TW13 . . . . 15 F6
Saxon Bsns Ctr SW19 . . . . . . 40 C8
Saxon Cl KT6 . . . . 37 D3
Saxon Cres RH12 . . . . 217 B4

Saxon Croft GU9 . . . . 125 C1
Saxon Cty Jun Sch TW17 . . . 34 A4
Saxon Dr RG42 . . . . 27 F8
Saxon House Feltham TW13 . 15 F6
Reigate RH2 . . . . 138 F6
Saxon Rd Ashford TW15 . . . . 14 D2
Bromley BR1 . . . . 24 F1
Crawley RH10 . . . . 202 E5
Thornton Heath CR0, SE25 . . 42 D4
Walton-on-T KT12 . . . . 54 D7
Saxon Way
Harmondsworth UB7 . . . . 2 C8
Reigate RH2 . . . . 117 F2
Saxonbury Ave TW16 . . . . 35 B7
Saxonbury Cl CR4 . . . . 40 D6
Saxonbury Gdns KT6 . . . . 37 C1
Saxons KT20 . . . . 97 D6
Sayer Ct [4] GU21 . . . . 68 E1
Sayer's Wlk TW10 . . . . 17 F8
Sayers House [3] RH19 . . . . 185 C1
Sayers The RH19 . . . . 185 C1
Sayes Court Farm Dr KT15 . . 52 B5
Sayes Court Jun Sch KT15 . . 52 B5
Sayes Ct KT15 . . . . 52 C5
Scaitcliffe Sch SW20 . . . . 11 A5
Scallows Cl RH10 . . . . 202 A7
Scallows Rd RH10 . . . . 202 A7
Scampton Rd TW6 . . . . 2 F1
Scania Wlk RG42 . . . . 8 B2
Scarborough Cl
Belmont SM2 . . . . 77 F8
Biggin Hill TN16 . . . . 83 C1
Scarborough Rd TW6 . . . . 3 C1
Scarbrook Rd CR0, CR9 . . . . 61 C7
Scarlet Oaks GU15 . . . . 65 D3
Scarlet Rd SE6 . . . . 24 E5
Scarlet Cl GU21 . . . . 68 F1
Scarlett's Rd GU11 . . . . 105 A3
Scarlette Manor Wlk [10]
SE24 . . . . 22 A8
Scarth Rd SW13 . . . . 7 F4
Scawen Cl SM5 . . . . 60 A6
Schaffer Ho RH10 . . . . 202 C5
Schiller International Univ
BR4 . . . . 63 D6
Scholars Ct RH10 . . . . 204 A8
Scholars Rd SW12 . . . . 21 C7
Scholars Wlk GU2 . . . . 130 B8
School Cl Bisley GU24 . . . . . . 68 A4
Guildford GU1 . . . . 109 D3
Horsham RH12 . . . . 218 A6
School Cotts GU22 . . . . 89 C5
School Hill
Crowthorne RG45 . . . . 45 D4
Merstham RH1 . . . . 119 C7
Sandhurst GU47 . . . . 45 A1
Seale GU10 . . . . 127 B4
Warnham RH12 . . . . 216 F8
Wrecclesham GU10 . . . . 145 F6
School House La T11 . . . . 17 C1
School Houses GU8 . . . . 172 E4
School La Addlestone KT15 . . 52 A6
Ashurst Wood RH19 . . . . . . 206 E6
Bagshot GU19 . . . . 47 E2
Chiddingfold GU8 . . . . 191 C4
Crondall GU10 . . . . 124 A8
East Clandon GU4 . . . . 111 E4
Egham TW20 . . . . 12 A3
Farnham GU10 . . . . 146 D6
Fetcham KT22 . . . . 94 D5
Forest Row RH18 . . . . 206 F2
Lower Halliford TW17 . . . . . . 34 B2
Mickleham RH5 . . . . 115 C8
Ockham GU23 . . . . 92 B5
Pirbright GU24 . . . . 87 E5
Puttenham GU3 . . . . 128 C4
Shackleford GU8 . . . . 149 F6
Surbiton KT6 . . . . 38 A1
Teddington KT1 . . . . 37 C8
Walton on t H KT20 . . . . 97 A2
West Horsley KT24 . . . . 112 B6
Westcott RH4 . . . . 135 C6
Windlesham GU20 . . . . 48 D4
School Pas [5] KT1 . . . . 37 F7
School Rd Ascot SL5 . . . . 29 B4
Ashford TW15 . . . . 14 B2
East Molesey KT8 . . . . 36 D5
Hampton TW12 . . . . 16 C2
Harmondsworth UB7 . . . . 2 B8
Hascombe GU8 . . . . 172 E4
Hounslow TW3 . . . . 5 C4
Linchmere GU27 . . . . 207 F5
Teddington KT1 . . . . 37 C8
Windlesham GU20 . . . . 48 B5
School Road Ave TW12 . . . . . 16 C2
School Wlk TW16 . . . . 35 A6
Schroder Ct TW20 . . . . 11 B3
Scillonian Rd GU2 . . . . 130 B7
Scilly Isles KT10 . . . . 55 E8
Scizdons Climb GU7 . . . . 150 F4
Scoles Cres SW2 . . . . 22 A7
Scoresdale SE19 . . . . 42 E8
Scory Cl RH11 . . . . 201 A3
Scotia Rd SW2 . . . . 22 A8
Scotland Bridge Rd KT15 . . . 71 A8
Scotland Cl GU12 . . . . 106 A5
Scotland Farm Rd GU12 . . . 106 A5
Scotland Hill
Sandhurst GU47 . . . . 45 A1
Sandhurst GU47 . . . . 64 A8
Scotland La GU27 . . . . 208 C5
Scotlands Cl GU27 . . . . 208 B5
Scotlands Dr GU27 . . . . 208 C5

Scots Cl TW19 . . . . 13 D7
Scotsdale Cl SM2 . . . . 58 E3
Scotshall La CR6 . . . . 82 C4
Scott Cl Guildford GU2 . . . . . 109 A3
Thornton Heath SW16 . . . . . . 41 F8
West Ewell KT19 . . . . 57 C5
Scott Farm Cl KT7 . . . . 37 B1
Scott Gdns TW5 . . . . 4 D7
Scott House TW10 . . . . 17 C6
Scott Rd RH10 . . . . 201 F3
Scott Terr RG12 . . . . 27 E8
Scott Trimmer Way TW3 . . . . . 4 E5
Scott's Ave Ashford TW16 . . . 14 E1
Beckenham BR2 . . . . 44 D7
Scott's Ct GU14 . . . . 85 B7
Scott's Grove Cl GU24 . . . . . . 68 C6
Scott's Grove Rd GU24 . . . . . 68 C6
Scott's Hill RH1, RH6 . . . . . . 162 D5
Scott's La BR2, BR3 . . . . 44 C7
Scott's Way TW16 . . . . 14 E1
Scott-Broadwood CE Inf
Sch The Capel RH5 . . . . 178 D6
Ockley RH5 . . . . 177 D4
Scotts Dr TW12 . . . . 16 B1
Scotts Farm Rd KT19 . . . . 57 C4
Scrooby St [8] SE6 . . . . 24 B8
Scrutton Cl SW12 . . . . 21 D8
Scylla Cres TW6&TW14 . . . . 14 B8
Scylla Pl GU21 . . . . 89 A8
Scylla Rd TW14, TW6 . . . . 3 B1
Seabrook Dr BR4 . . . . 63 E8
Seaford Rd Crawley RH11 . . 201 A2
Stanwell TW19, TW6 . . . . 2 C1
Wokingham RG40 . . . . 25 D6
Seaforth Ave KT3 . . . . 39 B5
Seaforth Gdns KT19 . . . . 57 F5
Seaforth Lodge SW13 . . . . 7 F5
Sealand Rd TW6 . . . . 3 A1
Seale La GU10, GU3 . . . . 126 E4
Seale Rd Elstead GU8 . . . . . 148 B7
The Sands GU8 . . . . 148 B7
Seaman's Gn RH5 . . . . 178 D8
Searchwood Rd CR6 . . . . 81 B1
Searle Ct CR4 . . . . 40 E8
Searle Hill RH2 . . . . 139 A7
Searle Rd GU9 . . . . 146 C8
Searle's View RH12 . . . . 217 E5
Seath House [4] SE26 . . . . . . 23 B3
Seaton Cl Putney SW15 . . . . . 19 B8
Twickenham TW2 . . . . 5 D6
Seaton Dr TW15 . . . . 13 E6
Seaton Rd Camberley GU15 . 65 B5
Mitcham CR4 . . . . 40 E7
Twickenham TW2 . . . . 5 C1
Sebastopol Rd [2] GU11 . . . 105 B2
Second Ave Mortlake SW14 . . 7 E4
Walton-on-T KT12 . . . . 35 B3
Woodham KT15 . . . . 52 B3
Second Cl KT8 . . . . 36 C5
Second Cross Rd TW2 . . . . . . 16 E6
Seddon Ct RH11 . . . . 201 B1
Seddon Rd SM4 . . . . 40 D4
Sedgefield Cl RH10 . . . . 202 C6
Sedgehill Rd SE6 . . . . 24 B3
Sedgehill Sch SE6 . . . . 24 B4
Sedgemoor GU14 . . . . 85 B7
Sedgeway SE6 . . . . 24 F7
Sedgewick Cl RH10 . . . . 202 C6
Sedgewick House [19] SW19 . 19 D6
Sedgewood Cl BR2 . . . . 44 F2
Sedley Ct SE26 . . . . 23 B6
Seebys Oak GU47 . . . . 64 E6
Seeley Dr SE21 . . . . 22 E4
Seely Rd SW17 . . . . 21 A2
Seething Wells Halls Of
Residence KT6 . . . . 37 C3
Seething Wells La KT6 . . . . . . 37 C3
Sefton Cl GU24 . . . . 67 F6
Sefton Rd Croydon CR0 . . . . . 43 B1
West Ewell KT19 . . . . 105 A2
Sefton Lodge [2] TW1 . . . . . . 6 C1
Sefton Rd Croydon CR0 . . . . . 43 A1
Epsom KT19 . . . . 57 C2
Sefton St SW15 . . . . 7 E4
Segrave Cl KT13 . . . . 53 A3
Segsbury Gr RG12 . . . . 27 F5
Sekhon Terr TW13 . . . . 16 A5
Selborne Ave GU11 . . . . 126 C6
Selborne Cl GU17 . . . . 64 C4
Selborne Gdns GU9 . . . . 146 A7
Selborne Rd
Kingston u T KT3 . . . . 38 E7
South Croydon CR0 . . . . 61 F7
Selborne Ave KT15 . . . . 182 D2
Crawley RH10 . . . . 182 D2
Woodham KT15 . . . . 52 B1
Selbourne Rd GU1 . . . . 110 A4
Selbourne Sq RH9 . . . . 121 C5
Selby Cl KT9 . . . . 56 E3
Selby Ct TW2 . . . . 16 A6
Selby Gn SM5 . . . . 40 E2
Selby Rd Ashford TW15 . . . . . 14 C2
Carshalton SM5 . . . . 40 E2
Penge SE20 . . . . 43 A7
Selby Wlk [1] GU21 . . . . 69 B1
Selbys RH7 . . . . 164 D5
Selcroft Rd CR8 . . . . 80 B7
Selham Cl RH11 . . . . 201 A7
Selhurst Cl Putney SW19 . . . . 19 D7
Woking GU21 . . . . 69 F4
Selhurst New Ct SE25 . . . . . . 42 E3
Selhurst New Rd SE25 . . . . . . 42 E3
Selhurst Park SE25 . . . . 42 E3
Selhurst Pl CR0, SE25 . . . . . . 42 E3
Selhurst Rd
South Norwood CR0, SE25 . . 42 E4
Thornton Heath CR0, SE25 . . 42 E4

Selhurst Sta SE25 . . . . 42 E3
Selkirk Rd Twickenham TW2 . 16 C7
Upper Tooting SW17 . . . . 20 E3
Sellar's Hill GU7 . . . . 150 D6
Sellincourt Inf Sch SW17 . . . 20 E1
Sellincourt Jun Sch SW17 . . 20 E1
Sellincourt Rd SW17 . . . . 20 E2
Sellindge Cl BR3 . . . . 23 F1
Selsdon Ave CR2 . . . . 61 D1
Selsdon Cl KT6 . . . . 37 E4
Selsdon Cres CR2 . . . . 62 C1
Selsdon High Sch CR2 . . . . . . 62 D2
Selsdon Park Golf Course
CR2 . . . . 81 E2
Selsdon Park Rd
New Addington CR0, CR2 . . 62 E2
Selsdon CR0, CR2 . . . . 62 C1
South Croydon CR0, CR2 . . . 62 E2
Selsdon Prim Sch CR2 . . . . . 62 C1
Selsdon Rd Croydon CR2 . . . 61 D1
West Norwood SE27 . . . . 22 B5
Woodham KT15 . . . . 71 A8
Selsdon Road Ind Est CR2 . . 61 D1
Selsey Ct [3] RH11 . . . . 201 B2
Selsey Rd RH11 . . . . 201 B2
Selsfield Rd
Turners Hill RH10, RH19 . . 204 E6
West Hoathly RH19 . . . . 204 E4
Seltops Cl GU6 . . . . 174 F1
Selwood Cl TW19 . . . . 2 B1
Selwood Gdns TW19 . . . . 2 B1
Selwood Rd Cheam SM3 . . . . 39 F1
Chessington KT9 . . . . 56 D6
Croydon CR0 . . . . 62 F8
Old Woking GU22 . . . . 90 C6
Selworthy Rd SE23, SE6 . . . . 23 B6
Selwyn Ave TW9 . . . . 6 F4
Selwyn Cl Crawley RH10 . . . 182 D1
Hounslow TW4 . . . . 4 E3
Selwyn Ct [7] TW10 . . . . 6 E2
Selwyn Rd KT3 . . . . 38 D3
Semaphore Rd GU1 . . . . 130 E7
Semley Rd SW16 . . . . 41 E7
Semper Cl GU21 . . . . 68 E2
Send Barns La Send GU23 . . 90 D2
Send Marsh GU23 . . . . 90 D3
Send C of E Fst Sch GU23 . . 90 C4
Send Cl GU23 . . . . 90 C4
Send Hill GU23 . . . . 90 C2
Send Marsh Rd Send GU23 . . 90 D3
Send Rd GU23 . . . . 90 B4
Seneca Rd CR7 . . . . 42 B5
Senga Rd CR4 . . . . 41 D1
Senhouse Rd SM3 . . . . 58 D6
Sequoia Pk RH11 . . . . 201 C1
Serpentine Gn RH1 . . . . 119 D6
Serrin Way RH12 . . . . 217 E5
Service Rd Crawley,
North Terminal RH6 . . . . 181 F8
Crawley,
South Terminal RH6 . . . . . . 182 A8
Servite House
Beckenham BR3 . . . . 43 F8
Dorking RH4 . . . . 115 A1
Knaphill GU21 . . . . 68 E1
Servius Ct [2] TW8 . . . . 6 D7
Setley Way RG12 . . . . 27 F5
Seven Acres SM5 . . . . 59 E7
Seven Arches App KT13 . . . . 53 A3
Seven Hills Cl KT12, KT13 . . 53 E1
Seven Hills Rd KT12, KT13 . . 53 E1
Seven Hills Rd (South)
KT11 . . . . 72 C1
Sevenoaks Cl SM2 . . . . 59 C2
Severn Cl GU47 . . . . 64 E7
Severn Cres SL3 . . . . 1 B8
Severn Dr
Hinchley Wood KT10 . . . . 56 A8
Walton-on-T KT12 . . . . 54 E7
Severn Rd Crawley RH10 . . . 202 B4
Farnborough GU14 . . . . 84 D6
Seward Rd BR3 . . . . 43 D7
Seward Ave KT41 . . . . 25 B6
Sewer's Farm Rd RH5 . . . . . 155 B6
Sewill Cl RH6 . . . . 180 C1
Seychelle Ct BR3 . . . . 24 A1
Seymour Ave
Caterham CR3 . . . . 100 C3
Ewell KT17 . . . . 58 A1
West Barnes SM4 . . . . 39 F2
Seymour Cl KT8 . . . . 36 C4
Seymour Ct GU14 . . . . 66 C3
Seymour Gdns Feltham TW13 . 15 C4
Kingston u T KT5 . . . . 37 F3
Twickenham TW1 . . . . 17 B8
Seymour Mews KT17 . . . . 58 A1
Seymour Pl Croydon SE25 . . . 43 B5
Seymour Rd Carshalton CR4 . 41 A1
Crawley RH11 . . . . 201 B6
East Molesey KT8 . . . . 36 C4
Godalming GU7 . . . . 150 D4
Hampton TW12 . . . . 16 C3
Headley Down GU35 . . . . 187 B6
Teddington KT1 . . . . 37 D8
Wallington SM5 . . . . 60 A4
Wandsworth SW18 . . . . 19 F8
Wimbledon SW19 . . . . 19 E1
Seymour Terr SE20 . . . . 43 B8
Seymour Villas SE20 . . . . 43 B8
Seymour Way TW16 . . . . 14 E1
Shabden Cotts CR5 . . . . 98 F4
Shabden Park CR5 . . . . 99 A4
Shabden Park Hospl CR5 . . . 99 A4
Shackleford Rd
Old Woking GU22 . . . . 90 B6
Shackleford GU8 . . . . 149 E4

 acklegate La TW11 .....16 E4
ackleton Cl SE23 .....23 B6
ackleton Ct
  Dulwich SE21 .....22 D6
  Stanwell TW19 .....2 E1
ackleton Rd RH10 .....201 F3
acksteaad La GU7 .....150 D3
acksdale La GU7 .....150 C3
adbolt Ct KT14 .....57 F8
ady Nook GU9 .....125 B6
adyhanger GU7 .....150 C6
aef Way TW11 .....17 A1
aftesbury Ave TW14 .....4 A1
aftesbury Cl RG12 .....27 D4
aftesbury Cres TW18 .....13 D1
aftesbury Ct
  amborough GU14 .....105 C8
  Fokingham RG40 .....25 D7
aftesbury House SE25 .....43 A3
aftesbury Mount GU17 .....64 D3
aftesbury Rd
  Beckenham BR3 .....43 F7
  isley GU24 .....67 F3
  arshalton SM5 .....40 E2
  Crawley RH10 .....202 D4
  Chertwd TW9 .....6 B4
  oking GU22 .....70 B2
aftesbury Way TW2 .....16 D5
afteswood Ct SW17 .....20 F5
apkroth RH2 .....117 C2
akespeare Ave TW14 .....4 A1
akespeare Gdns GU14 .....84 D5
akespeare Rd KT15 .....52 B6
akespeare Way
  itham TW13 .....15 C4
  inkfield RG42 .....26 E8
albourne Rise GU15 .....65 D5
alden House SW15 .....7 F1
alden Rd GU12 .....126 D8
aldon Dr SM4 .....39 E4
aldon Way KT12 .....54 C7
ale Grn RH1 .....119 D6
alesbrook La RH18 .....206 F1
alford Cty Inf Sch GU4 .....130 E3
alford La GU4 .....130 E4
alford Mill GU4 .....130 E4
alford Rd GU1, GU4 .....130 D5
alford Sta GU4 .....130 E3
alston Villas KT5, KT6 .....37 F3
alstone Rd SW14,TW9 .....7 D4
ambles The GU1 .....130 D7
amrock Cl Fetcham KT22 .....94 D6
  rimley GU16 .....85 F4
amrock House SE26 .....23 A4
amrock Rd CR0 .....41 F3
andys Cl RH12 .....217 A1
anklin Cn GU12 .....105 C1
annon Commercial Ctr
T3 .....39 A5
annon Corner KT3 .....39 A5
annon Ct CR0 .....42 C5
annon Rd RG9 .....24 B2
aron Cl Fetcham KT22 .....94 D6
  osom KT19 .....76 C6
  reat Bookham KT23 .....94 A3
ap Dittan KT16 .....37 C1
aronelle Ct RG40 .....25 A6
arpthorne Cl RH11 .....200 F6
aw Cl Ewell KT17 .....76 F8
attershaw KT16 .....51 C4
  anderstead CR2 .....80 F7
  aw Cres CR2 .....80 F7
  aw Ct CR3 .....100 D6
  aw Dr KT12 .....35 C2
  aw Path BR1 .....24 F5
  aw Rd BR1 .....45 B3
  aw Rd Catford BR1 .....24 E5
atsfield TN16 .....103 C7
  aw Way SM6 .....60 B5
awfield Cty Fst Sch
U12 .....105 A3
awfield La GU12 .....105 A3
awford Rd GU12 .....106 A3
awford Ct KT19 SW15 .....119 A8
awford Rd RH19 .....57 D4
awford La GU16 .....85 F4
awley Cres KT18 .....77 D1
awley Cty Prim Sch
T18 .....77 C1
awley Rd KT18 .....77 C1
aws Rd RH10 .....201 F7
  awson Ct CR0 .....63 C2
  earing De SM4 .....40 C2
  ears Ct TW16 .....14 E1
  earwater Ct 6 RH11 .....200 D5
  earwater Rd SM1 .....58 F5
  een Common Dr
W14,TW10 .....7 A2
  een Gate Gdns SW14 .....7 C3
  een Lawns SW14 .....7 A3
  een Mount Jun Mix & Inf
ch SW14 .....7 C3
  een Pk TW10,TW9 .....6 E3
  een Rd TW10, TW9 .....6 E5
  een Way SM6 .....60 F5
  een Wood SW14 .....7 C2
  eendale Rd TW9 .....6 F3
  eenewood SE26 .....23 B4
  eep Leas KT24 .....112 E2
  eep Walk Mews SW19 ...19 E2
eep Wlk
  angley Vale KT18 .....96 D6
  eigate RH2 .....117 E4
  eepbarn La CR6 .....82 F7
  eepcote Cl TW5 .....4 A7
eepfold Rd GU14 .....108 F4

Sheephatch La GU10 .....147 C6
Sheephouse GU9 .....146 C8
Sheephouse Gn RH5 .....134 F3
Sheephouse La RH5 .....135 A2
Sheephouse Way KT3 .....38 E2
Sheeplands Ave GU1 .....110 C3
Sheeps Ditch Cl TW18 .....13 A1
Sheepwalk Littleton TW17 ...34 A3
  Shepperton TW17 .....33 F3
Sheepwalk La KT15 .....113 A1
Sheerwater Ave KT15 .....70 F7
Sheerwater Bsns Ctr
GU21 .....70 F7
Sheerwater Cotts KT14 .....70 F6
Sheerwater Rd KT14, KT15 ..70 F6
Sheet Street Rd
  Old Windsor SL4 .....10 A7
  Windsor SL4 .....10 A7
Sheet's Heath La GU24 .....48 A7
Sheffield Cl Crawley RH10 .202 B4
  Farnborough GU14 .....84 F4
Sheffield Rd TW14,TW6 .....3 F2
Sheffield Way TW6,TW14 ...3 D2
Shefford Cres RG40 .....25 C6
Shelburne House 9 SW16 .21 C3
Sheldon Cl Crawley RH10 .202 D5
  Penge SE20 .....43 B8
  Reigate RH2 .....139 B8
Sheldon Ct GU1 .....130 F8
Sheldon House TW11 .....17 A2
Sheldon St CR0, CR9 .....61 C7
Sheldrick Cl CR4 .....40 D7
Shelford KT1 .....38 A7
Shelford Rise SE19 .....22 F1
Shelley Ave RG12 .....27 E7
Shelley Cl Coulsdon CR5 ...79 F2
  Crawley RH10 .....202 C8
Shelley Cres TW5 .....4 D5
Shelley Ct Camberley GU15 ..65 C5
  9 Kingston u T KT2 .....17 D4
  West Barnes KT3 .....39 A4
Shelley Dr RH12 .....216 C3
Shelley Rd
  East Grinstead RH19 .....185 D1
  Horsham RH12 .....217 B3
Shelley Way SW17 .....20 G3
Shellwood Dr RH5 .....136 C3
Shellwood Rd RH2, RH3 .....137 E4
Shelly Cl SM7 .....77 E4
Shelly Cty Prim Sch
RH12 .....216 E3
Shellys Ct RH13 .....218 A3
Shelson Ave TW13 .....14 F4
Shelton Ave CR6 .....81 C2
Shelton Cl Guildford GU2 ...109 A6
  Warlingham CR6 .....81 C2
Shelton Rd SW19 .....40 A8
Shelvers Gn KT20 .....97 C6
Shelvers Hill KT20 .....97 B6
Shelvers Spur KT20 .....97 C6
Shelvers Way KT20 .....97 C6
Shene Sec Sch SW14 .....7 E3
Shenley Rd TW5 .....4 E6
Shenstone House SW16 ....21 C3
Shenstone Pk SL5 .....29 E5
Shepherd Cl RH10 .....201 E3
Shepherd's Hill
  Guildford GU2 .....109 A3
  Haslemere GU27 .....208 C6
  Merstham RH1 .....119 C7
Shepherd's Hill Bglws
GU27 .....208 C6
Shepherd's La GU2 .....108 F4
Shepherd's Way GU4 .....130 E4
Shepherds Chase GU19 ....47 E2
Shepherds Cl TW17 .....34 B3
Shepherds Hill RG12 .....27 C8
Shepherds La GU20 .....49 A6
Shepherds Way
  Horsham RH12 .....218 A5
  South Croydon CR2 .....62 D3
  Tilford GU10 .....147 D4
Shepherds' Wlk
KT18 .....96 B7
Shepherds Wlk GU14 .....84 F7
Shepherdsgrove La RH19 .186 F5
Shepley Cl SM5 .....60 A7
Shepley Ct SW16 .....21 C4
Shepley Dr SL5 .....30 D3
Shepley End SL5 .....30 D4
Sheppard Cl KT6 .....37 E5
Sheppard House 6 SW2 ...22 A7
Shepperton Bsns Park
TW17 .....34 C4
Shepperton Court Dr
TW17 .....34 B4
Shepperton Rd
TW17,TW18 .....33 D5
Shepperton Sta TW17 .....34 B4
Shepperton Studios TW17 .33 F6
Sheppey Cl RH11 .....201 C3
Sheraton Cl GU17 .....64 E4
Sheraton Dr KT19 .....76 C6
Sheraton The BR1 .....24 F1
Sheraton Wlk 16 RH11 ..201 B1
Sherborne Cl
  Burgh Heath KT18 .....77 C2
  Poyle SL3 .....1 C6
Sherborne Cres SM5 .....40 E2
Sherborne Ct
  Guildford GU2 .....130 C7
  Penge SE20 .....23 C1
Sherborne Rd Cheam SM3 ..40 A1
  Chessington KT9 .....56 E5
  East Bedfont TW14 .....14 D7
Sherborne GU5 .....132 D5

Sherbourne Ct 2 TW12 ...36 A8
Sherbourne Dr SL5 .....30 D4
Sherbourne Gdns TW17 ....34 E2
Shere Ave KT17, SM2 .....58 C1
Shere CE Inf Sch GU5 .....133 A4
Shere Cl Chessington KT9 ...56 D5
  Dorking RH5 .....136 C3
Shere Ct GU5 .....133 B2
Shere La GU5 .....133 A4
Shere Rd Albury GU4, GU5 ..132 C6
  Ewhurst GU6 .....175 D7
  Shere GU5 .....133 B5
  West Clandon GU4, KT24 .111 B3
  West Horsley KT24 .....112 C4
Sherfield Gdns SW15 .....7 F1
Sheridan Cl
  Aldershot GU11 .....126 A8
  East Grinstead RH19 .....185 C1
Sheridan Ct RH1 .....118 B3
Sheridan Pl Hampton TW12 .36 C8
  Mortlake SW13 .....7 F4
Sheridan Rd Frimley GU16 ..85 D8
  Merton SW19 .....39 F8
  Richmond TW10 .....17 C5
Sheridan Way BR3 .....43 F8
Sheridans Rd KT23 .....94 C1
Sheringdale Prim Sch
SW18 .....19 F7
Sheringham Ave TW12 .....15 F1
Sheringham Rd SE20 .....43 C6
Sherland Rd TW1 .....16 F7
Shermanbury Ct RH12 .....217 D4
Sherringham Ave TW13 ...15 A5
Sherrydon GU6 .....174 F1
Sherwin Cres GU14 .....85 C7
Sherwood Ct KT6 .....56 D8
Sherwood Ave SW16 .....41 D8
Sherwood Cl
  Bracknell RG12 .....28 A7
  Fetcham KT22 .....94 C4
Sherwood Cres RH2 .....139 B5
Sherwood Park Rd
  Mitcham CR4 .....41 D5
  Sutton SM1 .....59 A5
Sherwood Park Sch SM6 ...60 D7
Sherwood Prim Sch CR4 ...41 E5
Sherwood Rd Coulsdon CR5 .79 C3
  Croydon CR0, CR9 .....43 B1
  Hampton TW12 .....16 C3
  Knaphill GU21 .....68 E2
  Merton SW19 .....19 F1
Sherwood Way BR4 .....63 C8
Sherwood Wlk RH10 .....201 F3
Shetland Cl Crawley RH10 .202 E7
  Guildford GU4 .....110 D3
Shewens Rd KT13 .....53 D6
Shey Copse KT22 .....70 C2
Shield Dr TW8 .....6 A8
Shield Rd TW15 .....14 C4
Shifford Path SE23 .....23 D5
Shilburn Way GU21 .....69 A1
Shildon Cl GU15 .....66 D3
Shillinglee Park Golf
  Course GU8 .....210 A4
Shillinglee Rd RH14 .....211 B4
Shimmings The GU1 .....110 A2
Shinners Cl SE25 .....43 A4
Shinwell Wlk 3 RH11 ...201 B1
Ship Alley GU14 .....85 C6
Ship Field Cl TN16 .....103 C6
Ship Hill TN16 .....103 D6
Ship La Farnborough GU14 ...85 C6
  Mortlake SW14 .....7 C5
Ship St RH19 .....205 E8
Ship Yd KT13 .....53 B7
Shipka Rd SW12 .....21 B7
Shiplake Cl SW17 .....20 D4
Shiplake House RG12 .....27 F5
Shipley Bridge La RH10 ...183 A3
Shipley Ct SE20 .....43 A7
Shipley Rd RH11 .....201 A6
Shipleybridge La
RH10,RH6 .....182 F4
Shipman Par SE23 .....23 E6
Shipman Rd SE23 .....23 E6
Shirburn Cl SE23 .....23 C8
Shire Cl GU19 .....47 E2
Shire Ct Aldershot GU11 ...104 E22
  Ewell KT17 .....57 F3
Shire Horse Way TW7 .....5 F4
Shire Par RH10 .....202 D7
Shire Pl RH10 .....202 D7
Shires Cl KT21 .....95 D8
Shires House KT14 .....71 E6
Shires The TW10 .....17 E4
Shirley Ave Belmont SM2 ...58 F1
  Carshalton SM1 .....59 E6
  Coulsdon CR5, CR8 .....100 B8
  Croydon CR5, CR9 .....43 C1
  Redhill RH1 .....139 F4
Shirley Church Rd
  Addington CR0 .....62 E7
  Croydon CR0 .....62 E7
Shirley Cres BR3 .....43 E5
Shirley Ct Guildford GU1 ...130 D8
  Thornton Heath SW16 ...41 F6
Shirley Dr TW3 .....5 C2
Shirley High Sch CR0 .....62 D7
Shirley Hills Rd CR0 .....62 D5
Shirley Hts SM6 .....60 C2
Shirley Hyrst KT13 .....53 D4
Shirley Lodge SE26 .....23 E4
Shirley Oaks Hospl CR0 ...43 C2
Shirley Oaks Rd CR0, CR9 .62 D8

Shirley Park Golf Course
CR0 .....62 C7
Shirley Park Rd CR0 .....43 C1
Shirley Pl GU21 .....68 C2
Shirley Rd
  Croydon CR0, CR9 .....43 B1
  Wallington SM6 .....60 C2
Shirley Way CR0 .....62 F7
Shoe La GU11 .....105 A6
Sholto Rd TW6 .....3 A4
Shop Cl TW10 .....17 D5
Shophouse La GU5 .....153 E7
Shord Hill CR8 .....80 D3
Shore Cl Feltham TW14 .....15 A8
  Hampton TW12 .....15 E3
Shore Gr TW13 .....16 A6
Shore's Rd GU21 .....69 F5
Shoreham Cl CR0 .....43 C3
Shoreham Rd RH10 .....202 C3
Shoreham Rd (E) TW6 .....2 E2
Shoreham Rd (W) TW6 .....2 C2
Shorndean St SE6 .....24 C7
Short Cl RH11 .....201 D8
Short Dale Rd GU11 .....126 C6
Short Gallop RH10 .....202 D7
Short La Longshot RH RH8 .123 B3
  Stanwell TW15, TW19 .....13 F7
Short Rd Chiswick W4 .....7 E8
  Stanwell TW19 .....2 E1
Short St GU11 .....105 A2
Short Way TW2 .....16 C8
Shortacres RH1 .....119 F2
Shortcroft Rd KT17 .....57 F3
Shortfield Rd GU10 .....146 C1
Shortheath Crest GU9 ....145 F6
Shortheath Rd
  Farnham GU9, GU10 .....146 A7
  Wrecclesham GU10, GU9 .146 A7
Shortlands UB3 .....3 D8
Shortlands Gdns BR1, BR2 ..44 E7
Shortlands Gr BR2 .....44 E6
Shortlands Rd
  Beckenham BR2, BR3 .....44 E6
  Kingston u T KT2 .....17 F1
Shortlands Sta BR2 .....44 C2
Shorts Rd SM5 .....59 E5
Shortsfield Cl RH12 .....217 C5
Shortwood Ave TW18 .....13 B5
Shortwood Cty Inf Sch
TW18 .....13 B5
Shottield SM6 .....60 C4
Shottfield Ave SW14 .....7 E3
Shottermill RH12 .....218 A7
Shottermill Cty Fst Sch
GU27 .....207 F7
Shottermill Cty Jun Sch
GU27 .....207 F7
Shottermill Rd GU27 .....207 E5
Shovelstode La KT19 ...206 D8
Shrewsbury Ave SW14 .....7 D3
Shrewsbury Cl KT6 .....56 D8
Shrewsbury House Sch
KT6 .....56 D8
Shrewsbury Rd
  Beckenham BR3 .....43 E6
  Carshalton SM5 .....40 E2
  Harrington TW14, TW6 ....3 D1
  Redhill RH1 .....118 E1
Shrewsbury Wlk 7 TW7 ...6 A4
Shrewton Rd SW17 .....20 F1
Shrivenham Cl GU47 .....64 D8
Shroffold Rd BR1 .....24 E4
Shropshire Cl CR4 .....41 E5
Shrubbery Rd SW16 .....21 E3
Shrubbery The
  Farnborough GU14 .....84 D3
  Surbiton KT6 .....37 E1
Shrubbs Hill GU24 .....49 C2
Shrubbs Hill La SL5 .....30 C3
Shrubbs La GU10 .....145 F4
Shrubland Ct SM7 .....78 A3
Shrubland Gr KT4 .....58 C7
Shrubland Rd SM7 .....78 A3
Shrublands Ave CR0 .....63 A6
Shrublands Cl SE26 .....23 C5
Shrublands Dr GU18 .....67 A8
Shute End RG40, 41 .....25 B6
Shute Rd RG40, 41 .....25 B6
Sibthorp Rd CR4 .....40 F7
Sibton Rd SM5 .....40 E2
Sickle Mill GU27 .....207 F6
Sickle Rd GU27 .....208 A5
Sidbury Cl SL5 .....30 A4
Siddeley Dr TW4 .....4 E4
Siddons Rd
  Croydon CR0, CR9 .....61 B7
  Forest Hill SE23 .....23 E6
Sidings The
  Aldershot GU11 .....105 C3
  Rudgwick RH12 .....214 D7
  Staines TW18 .....13 B4
Sidlaws Rd GU14 .....84 D6
Sidmouth Ave TW7 .....5 E5
Sidney Gdns TW8 .....6 C8
Sidney Rd
  Croydon SE25 .....43 A4
  Penge BR3 .....43 E7
  Staines TW18 .....13 A4
  Twickenham TW1 .....6 B1
  Walton-on-T KT12 .....35 B2
Signal Ct RH7 .....164 E5
Sigrist Sq 4 KT2 .....37 E8
Silbury Ave CR4 .....40 E8
Silchester Ct CR0 .....42 A1
Silchester Dr RH11 .....201 B4
Silkham Rd RH8 .....122 D8
Silkin Wlk 8 RH11 .....201 B1

Silkmore La
  West Horsley KT24 .....92 A2
  West Horsley KT24 .....112 B7
Silo Cl GU7 .....150 E8
Silo Dr GU7 .....150 F8
Silo Rd GU7 .....150 F8
Silver Birch Cl KT15 .....70 E7
Silver Birches Way GU8 ...148 E3
Silver Blades Ice Rink
SW16 .....21 D3
Silver Cl KT20 .....97 E3
Silver Dr GU16 .....66 C3
Silver Hill GU47 .....64 E8
Silver Jubilee Way TW4 .....4 B5
Silver La Purley CR8 .....79 E7
Silver Tree Cl KT12 .....54 A6
Silverdale SE23, SE26 .....23 C4
Silverdale Ave
  Oxshott KT22 .....74 C5
  Walton-on-T KT12, KT13 ..53 F7
Silverdale Cl
  Brockham RH3 .....137 B5
  Cheam SM1 .....58 F6
Silverdale Dr TW16 .....35 B7
Silverglade U9 .....75 C7
Silverhall St TW7 .....6 A4
Silverlea Gdns RH6 .....161 C2
Silverleigh Rd CR7 .....42 A4
Silvermere Ct CR3 .....100 F3
Silvermere Rd 1 SE6 .....24 B8
Silverstone Cl RH1 .....118 F3
Silverton Lodge SE19 .....22 E1
Silverwood Cl
  Beckenham BR3 .....24 A1
  New Addington CR0 .....63 A2
Silverwood Dr GU15 .....66 A3
Silwood RG12 .....26 E1
Silwood Cl SL5 .....29 D7
Silwood Park (Imperial
  Coll) SL5 .....29 F6
Silwood Rd Ascot SL5 .....29 F5
  Sunningdale SL5 .....29 F5
Sim's Cotts KT10 .....55 F4
Simkins Cl RG42 .....8 B2
Simmil Rd KT10 .....55 E5
Simmonds Cl RG42 .....26 E8
Simmonds Cotts GU7 ....150 B4
Simmondstone La GU10 ..167 D2
Simmons Cl KT9 .....56 D8
Simmons Pl TW18 .....12 E3
Simms Cl SM5 .....59 E8
Simon Lodge 31 SW19 ...19 E7
Simone Dr CR8 .....80 C3
Simons Cl KT16 .....51 C4
Simons Wlk TW20 .....11 C1
Simplemarsh Ct KT15 .....52 B6
Simplemarsh Rd KT15 .....52 B6
Simpson Rd
  Richmond TW10 .....17 C4
  Twickenham TW4 .....4 F1
Simpson Way KT6 .....37 C3
Sinclair Cl RH10 .....202 C4
Sinclair Ct
  2 Beckenham BR3 .....24 A1
  2 Croydon CR0 .....61 F8
Sinclair Dr SM2 .....59 B2
Sinclair House SM12 .....22 D7
Sincots Rd RH1 .....118 F1
Sine Cl GU14 .....85 B8
Singlegate Prim Sch
SW19 .....20 D1
Singleton Cl
  Mitcham SW17, SW19 ....20 F1
  Thornton Heath CR0 .....42 C2
Singleton Rd RH12 .....216 D3
Sinhurst Rd GU15 .....65 B4
Sion Ct TW1 .....17 B7
Sion Rd TW1 .....17 B7
Sipson Cl UB7 .....3 A8
Sipson La UB7 .....3 B8
Sipson Rd Harlington UB7 ...3 A7
  Harmondsworth UB7 .....3 A7
Sipson Way UB7 .....3 A7
Sir Cyril Black Way 2
SW19 .....20 A1
Sir William Perkin's
  C of E Sch for Girls KT16 ...32 F1
Sirdar Rd CR4 .....21 A2
Siret Cotts SL5 .....29 C5
Siskin Cl RH12 .....217 E5
Sissinghurst Cl RH10 ....202 D7
Sissinghurst Rd CR0 .....43 A2
Sistova Rd SW12 .....21 B7
Siward Rd SW17 .....20 C5
Six Cross-Roads GU21 ....70 A5
Sixth Cross Rd TW2 .....16 C5
Skeena Hill SW18, SW19 ...19 E8
Skelbrook St SW18 .....20 C6
Skelmersdale Wlk RH11 ..200 E2
Skerne Rd KT2 .....37 D8
Skid Hill La Biggin Hill CR6 ..82 F5
  Fickleholde CR6 .....82 F5
Skiff La RH14 .....213 A1
Skillett Cl 2 CR7 .....42 B5
Skimmington Cotts RH2 .138 D8
Skimpedhill La RG12 .....27 B6
Skinners La Ashstead KT21 ..75 D1
  Chiddingfold GU8 .....191 D5
  Heston TW5 .....4 C6
Skipton Way RH6 .....161 B5
Sky Bsns Pk TW20 .....32 C7
Skyes Dr TW18 .....13 B3
Skylark View RH12 .....217 D7

Skyport Dr UB7 . . . . 2 D7
Skyway 14 Trad Est SL3 . . . . . . 1 F4
Slade Ct KT16 . . . . 51 D4
Slade House TW4 . . . . 4 F1
Slade Rd Ottershaw KT16 . . . . 51 D4
  Pirbright GU24 . . . . 87 D7
Slaidburn Gn RG12 . . . . 27 E2
Slattery Rd TW13 . . . . 15 C7
Slaugham Ct RH11 . . . . 200 F3
Sledmere Ct TW14 . . . . 14 E7
Sleets Rd RH12 . . . . 216 E3
Slim Cl GU11 . . . . 105 E7
Slim Rd GU15 . . . . 65 C7
Slines New Rd CR3, CR6 . . . . . 101 E7
Slines Oak Rd CR3, CR6 . . . . . 102 B6
Slinfold CE Sch RH12 . . . . 215 D4
Slinfold Park (Golf &
  Country Park) RH12 . . . . 215 A2
Slinfold Wlk RH11 . . . . 201 A6
Slip Of Wood GU6 . . . . 174 F4
Slipshatch Rd RH2 . . . . 138 E5
Slipshoe St RH2 . . . . 118 A1
Sloane Hospl BR3 . . . . 44 D8
Sloane Wlk CR0 . . . . 43 F3
Slocock Hill GU21 . . . . 69 C2
Slough La Buckland RH3 . . . . . 117 A3
  Headley KT18 . . . . 96 C2
Sloughbrook Cl RH12 . . . . 217 F6
Slyfield Cl GU1 . . . . 109 E4
Slyfield Gn GU1 . . . . 109 E5
Slyfield Ind Est GU4 . . . . 109 E5
Small's La RH11 . . . . 201 C6
Smallberry Ave TW7 . . . . 5 F5
Smallfield Rd Horley RH6 . . . . 161 D3
  Horne RH6 . . . . 162 E3
Smallmead RH6 . . . . 161 B3
Smalls Hill Rd
  Charlwood RH2, RH6 . . . . 159 C6
  Leigh RH2, RH6 . . . . 159 C6
  Sidlow RH2, RH6 . . . . 159 C6
Smalls Mead RH11 . . . . 201 C6
Smallwood Jun & Inf Schs
  SW17 . . . . 20 D4
Smallwood Rd SW17 . . . . 20 D4
Smart's Heath La GU22 . . . . . . 89 A4
Smart's Heath Rd GU22 . . . . . 89 B5
Smeaton Cl KT9 . . . . 56 D4
Smeaton Rd SW18 . . . . 20 A8
Smith Cl RH10 . . . . 201 D3
Smith Cl GU21 . . . . 70 D6
Smith Rd RH2 . . . . 138 F6
Smith Sq RG12 . . . . 27 D7
Smith St KT5 . . . . 37 F3
Smith's Yd SW18 . . . . 20 C6
Smitham Bottom La
  CR5, CR8 . . . . 79 D7
Smitham Cty Prim Sch
  CR5 . . . . 79 D4
Smitham Downs Rd
  CR5, CR8 . . . . 79 E6
Smitham Prim Sch CR5 . . . . . . 79 C3
Smitham Sta CR5 . . . . 79 E4
Smithbarn RH13 . . . . 218 A2
Smithbarn Cl RH6 . . . . 161 B4
Smithers Cotts RH12 . . . . 214 F7
Smithers House SE20 . . . . 23 D1
Smithers The RH3 . . . . 137 B7
Smithfield La GU35, GU10 . . . 167 A1
Smithwood Ave GU6 . . . . 174 F7
Smithwood Cl SW19 . . . . 19 E6
Smithwood Common Rd
  GU5, GU6 . . . . 174 E7
Smithy Cl KT20 . . . . 97 F1
Smithy La
  Headley Down GU10 . . . . 166 E2
  Lower Kingswood KT20 . . . . . . 97 F1
Smithy's Gn GU20 . . . . 48 D4
Smock Wlk CR0 . . . . 42 C3
Smoke La RH2 . . . . 139 B7
Smokejack Hill RH5 . . . . 196 D7
Smolletts RH19 . . . . 205 C8
Smoothfield TW3 . . . . 5 A3
Smugglers' La RH5 . . . . 197 E7
Smugglers' Way GU10 . . . . . . 126 E1
Snailslynch GU9 . . . . 125 D2
Snatts Hill RH8 . . . . 122 F6
Snelgate Cotts GU4 . . . . 111 D4
Snell Hatch RH11 . . . . 201 B6
Snellings Rd KT12 . . . . 54 C5
Snipe La GU27 . . . . 208 A1
Snow Hill Copthorne RH10 . . 183 F3
  Domewood RH10 . . . . 183 F5
Snow Hill RH10 . . . . 183 F5
Snows Paddock GU20 . . . . 48 B7
Snows Ride GU20 . . . . 48 B6
Snowy Fielder Waye TW7 . . . . . 6 B5
Snoxhall Field GU6 . . . . 174 D2
Soames Wlk KT3 . . . . 38 E8
Soane Cl RH11 . . . . 200 E4
Soho Mills SM6 . . . . 41 B1
Sol-y-vista GU6 . . . . 150 D6

Solartron Rd GU14 . . . . 85 B3
Sole Farm Ave KT23 . . . . 93 F2
Sole Farm Cl KT23 . . . . 93 F3
Sole Farm Rd KT23 . . . . 93 F2
Solecote KT23 . . . . 94 A2
Solent Rd TW6 . . . . 2 F1
Soloms Court Rd CR5, SM7 . . 78 E2
Solway Cl TW4 . . . . 4 E4
Somborne House SW15 . . . . . . 19 A8
Somerfield Cl KT20 . . . . 97 E8
Somergate RH12 . . . . 216 F2
Somers Cl RH2 . . . . 118 A2
Somers Pl **1** Reigate RH2 . . 118 A2
  Streatham SW2 . . . . 21 F8
Somers Rd Reigate RH2 . . . . . 118 A2
  2 Streatham SW2 . . . . 21 F8
Somersbury La
  GU6, RH12 . . . . 195 F7
Somersby Est SE20 . . . . 23 C1
Somerset Ave
  Chessington KT9 . . . . 56 D6
  Wimbledon SW20 . . . . 39 B7
Somerset Cl Epsom KT19 . . . . 57 E2
  Hersham KT12 . . . . 54 B5
  New Malden KT3 . . . . 38 E4
Somerset Ct **3** TW12 . . . . . . 36 A8
Somerset Gdns
  Teddington TW11 . . . . 16 E3
  Thornton Heath SW16 . . . . 41 F6
Somerset House SW19 . . . . 19 E5
Somerset Rd Brentford TW8 . . 6 D8
  Farnborough GU14 . . . . 85 C1
  Kingston u T KT1 . . . . 37 F7
  Reigate RH1 . . . . 139 D7
  Teddington TW11 . . . . 16 E3
  Wimbledon SW19 . . . . 19 D5
Somerset Waye TW5 . . . . 4 E7
Somersway GU4 . . . . 130 E1
Somerton Ave TW9 . . . . 7 B4
Somerton Cl CR8 . . . . 80 A3
Somertons Cl GU2 . . . . 109 A4
Somerville Cl SW16 . . . . 21 D2
Somerville Dr RH10 . . . . 182 C1
Somerville Rd
  Cobham KT11 . . . . 74 A5
  Penge BR3, SE20 . . . . 23 D1
Sondes Farm RH4 . . . . 135 F7
Sondes Place Dr RH4 . . . . 135 F7
Sondes Place Sch RH4 . . . . . 135 F6
Sonia Gdns TW5 . . . . 5 A7
Sonnet Wlk TN16 . . . . 83 C1
Sonning Ct CR0 . . . . 62 F8
Sonning Gdns TW12 . . . . 15 E2
Sonning Rd CR0 . . . . 43 A3
Sonninge Cl GU47 . . . . 64 D8
Soper Dr CR3 . . . . 100 D4
Sopwith Ave KT9 . . . . 56 E5
Sopwith Cl Biggin Hill TN16 . . 83 D3
  Richmond TW10 . . . . 17 F3
Sopwith Dr KT13, KT14 . . . . . . 71 E7
Sopwith Rd TW5 . . . . 4 C7
Sopwith Way KT2 . . . . 37 E8
Sorbie Cl KT13 . . . . 53 D4
Sorrel Bank CR0 . . . . 62 E2
Sorrel Cl Crawley RH11 . . . . . 201 A2
  Farnborough GU14 . . . . 84 C5
  Wokingham RG40 . . . . 25 E8
Sorrel Dr GU18 . . . . 66 F7
Sorrel House TW3 . . . . 5 C6
Sorrel Rd RH12 . . . . 217 E5
Sorrento Rd SM1 . . . . 59 B7
South Albert Rd RH2 . . . . 117 F2
South Atlantic Dr GU11 . . . . 105 C3
South Ave Egham TW20 . . . . . . 12 C2
  Heath End GU9 . . . . 125 D6
  Richmond TW9 . . . . 7 A5
  Wallington SM5 . . . . 60 A3
  Whiteley Village KT12 . . . . 53 E1
South Bank KT6 . . . . 37 E3
South Bank Lodge **2** KT6 . . 37 E3
South Bank Terr **3** KT6 . . . . 37 E3
South Bookham Cty Inf
  Sch KT23 . . . . 114 C8
South Border The CR8 . . . . 79 E8
South Cl Crawley RH10 . . . . . . 201 F7
  Morden SM4 . . . . 40 A3
  Twickenham TW13 . . . . 16 A5
  Woking GU21 . . . . 69 D3
  Wokingham RG40 . . . . 25 D4
South Close Gn RH1, RH2 . . . 119 B6
South Croxted Rd SE21 . . . . . . 22 D4
South Croydon Sta CR2 . . . . . . 61 D5
South Dr
  Banstead SM7 . . . . 78 E6
  Beckenham BR3 . . . . 44 C4
  Belmont SM2 . . . . 58 E2
  Coulsdon CR5 . . . . 79 D4
  Dorking RH5 . . . . 136 C2
  Pirbright GU24 . . . . 87 C6
  Wentworth GU25 . . . . 31 A2
  Wokingham RG40 . . . . 25 C5
South Eden Park Rd
  Beckenham BR3 . . . . 44 B4
  West Wickham BR3 . . . . 44 B4
South End
  Croydon CR0, CR9 . . . . 61 C6
  Great Bookham KT23 . . . . 94 B1
South Farm La GU19 . . . . 48 A2
South Farnborough Cty
  Jun Sch GU14 . . . . 85 D2
South Farnborough Inf
  Sch GU14 . . . . 85 D2
South Farnham Cty Jun
  Sch GU9 . . . . 125 D1
South Gate Ave TW13 . . . . 14 D4
South Gdns SW19 . . . . 20 D1
South Gr Chertsey KT16 . . . . . . 32 F3
  Horsham RH13 . . . . 217 D1

South Hill Godalming GU7 . . . 150 F4
  Guildford GU1 . . . . 130 D7
South Hill Park RG12 . . . . 27 C2
South Hill Rd
  Beckenham BR2 . . . . 44 E5
  Bracknell RG12 . . . . 27 B3
South Holmes Rd RH13 . . . . . 218 B4
South La Ash GU12 . . . . 106 B1
  Kingston u T KT1 . . . . 37 D6
South Lane W KT3 . . . . 38 D3
South La W KT3 . . . . 38 D5
South Lawn Cl GU7 . . . . 150 D6
South Lodge TW7 . . . . 5 C4
South Lodge Ave
  CR4, CR7, SW16 . . . . 41 E5
South Lodge Rd KT12 . . . . 54 B2
South London Coll SE27 . . . . . 22 B4
South Lynn Cres RG12 . . . . 27 B4
South Mead Redhill RH1 . . . . 118 F4
  West Ewell KT19 . . . . 57 F3
South Mead Rd GU11 . . . . 126 B8
South Meadow RG45 . . . . 45 D3
South Merton Sta SW19 . . . . . 39 F6
South Munstead La GU8 . . . . 172 B7
South Norwood Country
  Park SE25 . . . . 43 C5
South Norwood High Sch
  SE25 . . . . 43 A5
South Norwood Hill
  SE19, SE25 . . . . 42 F7
South Norwood Prim Sch
  SE25 . . . . 43 A5
South Oak Rd SW16 . . . . 21 F4
South Par RH6 . . . . 160 F4
South Park Cres SE6 . . . . 24 F7
South Park Dr GU2 . . . . 24 A1
South Park Cty Inf Sch
  RH2 . . . . 139 A6
South Park Gr KT3 . . . . 38 C5
South Park Hill Rd CR2 . . . . . . 61 D6
South Park La RH1 . . . . 142 A7
South Park Rd SW19 . . . . 20 B2
South Pier Rd RH6 . . . . 182 B7
South Pl Surbiton KT5 . . . . 37 F2
  Wokingham RG40 . . . . 25 D6
South Ridge KT13 . . . . 72 B8
South Rise SM5 . . . . 59 E2
South Side GU10 . . . . 126 F7
South St Dorking RH4 . . . . 136 A7
  Epsom KT18 . . . . 76 D5
  Farnborough GU14 . . . . 85 C4
  Godalming GU7 . . . . 150 D4
  Horsham RH12 . . . . 217 C3
  Isleworth TW7 . . . . 6 A4
  Staines TW18 . . . . 12 F3
South Station App RH1 . . . . . 140 F7
South Terr Dorking RH4 . . . . . 136 B6
  Surbiton KT6 . . . . 37 E3
South Vale SE19 . . . . 22 E2
South Vale Rd **4** KT6 . . . . . . 56 E8
South View
  Copthorne RH10 . . . . 183 E3
  Wimbledon SW19 . . . . 19 C2
South View Cl SE19 . . . . 22 C1
South View Ct **5** SW16 . . . . 22 C3
South Way Croydon CR0 . . . . . 62 E7
  Sutton SM5 . . . . 59 C1
South West London Coll
  Streatham SW16 . . . . 21 D5
  Upper Tooting SW17 . . . . 20 E3
South Western Rd TW1 . . . . 6 B1
South Wimbledon Sta
  SW19 . . . . 20 D2
South Wlk Aldershot GU12 . . 105 D2
  Coney Hall BR4 . . . . 63 E7
  Reigate RH2 . . . . 118 A1
South Worple Way SW14 . . . . . 7 D4
Southall La TW5 . . . . 4 B8
Southam House KT15 . . . . 52 B5
Southampton Cl GU17 . . . . 64 C6
Southampton Gdns CR4 . . . . . 41 E4
Southampton Rd TW19, TW6 . . 2 F1
Southampton St GU11 . . . . . . 105 A1
Southbank KT7 . . . . 37 B2
Southborough Cl KT6 . . . . 37 D1
Southborough Rd KT6 . . . . 37 E1
Southborough Sch KT6 . . . . . . 56 E7
Southbridge Pl CR0, CR9 . . . . 61 C6
Southbridge Rd CR0, CR9 . . . . 61 C6
Southbrook RH11 . . . . 201 C1
Southbrook Rd SW16 . . . . 41 E8
Southbury GU2 . . . . 130 C7
Southcote SW19 . . . . 20 D1
Southcote Ave
  Feltham TW13 . . . . 15 A6
  Tolworth KT5 . . . . 38 B2
Southcote Dr GU15 . . . . 66 A5
Southcote Rd Croydon SE25 . . 43 B3
  Merstham RH1 . . . . 119 C6
  South Croydon CR2 . . . . 61 F1
Southcroft TW20 . . . . 11 B3

Southcroft Ave BR4 . . . . 63 C8
Southcroft Rd SW17 . . . . 21 A2
Southdean Gdns SW19 . . . . . . 19 F6
Southdown Cl RH12 . . . . 218 A5
Southdown Rd Carshalton
  SM5 . . . . 60 A3
Southdown Rd
  Hersham KT12 . . . . 54 E6
  Wallington SM5 . . . . 60 A2
  Wimbledon SW20 . . . . 39 D8
  Woldingham CR3 . . . . 101 F5
Southend La Catford SE6 . . . . . 23 F5
  Catford SE6 . . . . 24 B4
  Forest Hill SE26, SE6 . . . . 23 F4
Southend Rd BR3 . . . . 44 A8
Southerland Ct KT13 . . . . 53 C6
Southern Ave
  East Bedfont TW14 . . . . 15 A7
  Salfords RH1 . . . . 140 A1
  South Norwood SE25 . . . . 42 F6
Southern Bglws GU4 . . . . 131 B2
Southern Cotts TW19 . . . . 2 A2
Southern Ind Area RG12 . . . . . 26 F1
Southern Perimeter Rd
  East Bedfont TW6 . . . . 3 B1
  Feltham TW14, TW6 . . . . 3 D2
  Harlington TW14, TW6 . . . . 3 D2
  Stanwell TW19, TW6 . . . . 2 C4
Southern Rd GU15 . . . . 65 C6
Southern Way
  Farnborough GU14 . . . . 84 E3
  Farnham GU9 . . . . 125 C1
Southerns La CR5 . . . . 98 C3
Southey Ct KT23 . . . . 94 B3
Southey Rd SW19 . . . . 20 A1
Southey St SE20 . . . . 23 D1
Southfield Gdns TW1, TW2 . . 16 F4
Southfield Pl KT13 . . . . 53 B3
Southfield Sta SW19 . . . . 19 F1
Southfields KT8 . . . . 36 E3
Southfields Ave SW15 . . . . 14 B2
Southfields Ct SW19 . . . . 19 F7
Southfields Rd CR3 . . . . 102 B3
Southfields Sch SW18 . . . . 20 A7
Southfields Special Sch
  RG40 . . . . 25 D5
Southgate Ave
  Feltham TW13 . . . . 14 D4
  RH10, RH11 . . . . 201 E4
Southgate Cty Fst & Mid
  Sch RH10 . . . . 201 D4
Southgate Dr RH10, RH11 . . 201 E4
Southgate Par RH10, RH11 . . 201 D4
Southgate Rd RH10, RH11 . . 201 E4
Southgate West Cty Fst
  & Mid Schs RH11 . . . . 201 C4
Southholme Cl SE19 . . . . 42 E8
Southland Way TW7 . . . . 5 D2
Southlands
  East Grinstead RH19 . . . . 205 E7
  Horley RH6 . . . . 160 F3
Southlands Ave RH6 . . . . 161 A4
Southlands Cl Ash GU12 . . . . 106 A1
  Coulsdon CR5 . . . . 79 F2
  Wokingham RG40 . . . . 25 D5
Southlands Dr SW19 . . . . 19 D6
Southlands La RH8 . . . . 122 C1
Southlands Rd Ash GU12 . . . . 106 A1
  Wokingham RG40 . . . . 25 D5
Southmead Jun & Inf Sch
  SW19 . . . . 19 E7
Southmont Rd KT10 . . . . 55 E7
Southridge Pl SW20 . . . . 19 D1
Southsea Rd KT1 . . . . 37 E5
Southside Comm SW19 . . . . . . 19 D2
Southview Cl SW17 . . . . 21 A3
Southview Cotts GU10 . . . . . . 146 D1
Southview Ct **6** GU22 . . . . . . 69 E1
Southview Gdns SM6 . . . . 60 C5
Southview Rd Catford BR1 . . . 24 D4
  Headley Down GU35 . . . . 187 B5
  Woldingham CR3 . . . . 102 B3
Southviews CR2 . . . . 62 E2
Southville Cl
  East Bedfont TW14 . . . . 14 E7
  West Ewell KT19 . . . . 57 D2
Southville Cres TW14 . . . . 14 E7
Southville Inf Sch
  TW14 . . . . 14 F7
Southville Rd
  East Bedfont TW14 . . . . 14 E7
  Thames Ditton KT7 . . . . 37 B2
Southwark Cl RH11 . . . . 201 B2
Southwater Cl BR3 . . . . 24 A1
Southway Camberley GU15 . . 65 B4
  Guildford GU2 . . . . 108 F1
  Wallington SM6 . . . . 60 C6
  West Barnes SW20 . . . . 39 D5
Southway Ct GU2 . . . . 108 E1
Southways Pk RH11 . . . . 181 B3
Southwell Park Rd GU15 . . . . . 65 C5
Southwell Rd CR0, CR7 . . . . . . 42 A3
Southwick GU19 . . . . 47 E1
Southwick Cl RH19 . . . . 185 D2
Southwick Ct RG12 . . . . 27 E3
Southwood House KT15 . . . . . 185 D2
Southwold RG12 . . . . 26 E1
Southwood RG40 . . . . 25 D4
Southwood Ave
  Coulsdon CR5 . . . . 79 C4
  Kingston u T KT2, KT3 . . . . 38 B8
  Knaphill GU21 . . . . 68 D1
  Ottershaw KT16 . . . . 51 D5
Southwood Bsns Pk GU14 . . . 84 D4
Southwood Chase GU6 . . . . . 174 F1
Southwood Cl KT4 . . . . 58 D8
Southwood Cres The
  GU14 . . . . 84 D3

Southwood Cty Jnr Sch
  GU14 84
Southwood Dr KT5 38
Southwood Gdns KT10 56
Southwood Golf Course
  GU14 84
Southwood La
  Farnborough GU17 84
  Farnborough,
  Southwood GU14 84
Southwood Rd GU14 84
Sovereign Ct
  East Molesey KT8 35
  3 Richmond TW9 6
Sovereign Dr GU15 66
Sovereign House
  Ashford TW15 13
  Wimbledon SW19 19
Spa Cl SE19 42
Spa Dr KT18 76
Spa Hill CR7, SE19 42
Spa View **6** SW16 21
Space Waye TW14 4
Spalding Rd SW17 21
Sparks Cl TW12 15
Sparrow Cl TW12 15
Sparrow Farm Dr TW14 15
Sparrow Farm Inf Sch
  TW14 15
Sparrow Farm Jun Sch
  TW14 15
Sparrow Farm Rd
  KT17, KT4 58
Sparrow Row GU24 49
Sparrowhawk Cl GU10 124
Sparrows Mead RH1 119
Sparvell Rd GU21 88
Sparvell Way GU15 65
Spats La GU35 187
Speaker's Ct **3** CR0 42
Speart La TW5 4
Speedbird Way UB7 2
Speedwell Cl GU4 110
Speedwell House **5** RH1 . . 119
Speedwell Way RH12 217
Speer Rd KT7 36
Speers Rd RH1 36
Speke Rd CR7 42
Speldhurst Cl BR2 44
Spelthorne Coll TW15 13
Spelthorne Cty Inf
  Sch TW15 14
Spelthorne Gr TW16 14
Spelthorne La TW15, TW17 . . 34
Spelthorne Mus TW18 12
Spelthorne Sports Club
  TW15 14
Spence Ave KT14 71
Spencer Cl Frimley GU16 85
  Langley Vale KT18 96
  Sheerwater GU21 70
Spencer Ct
  Leatherhead KT22 95
  Wimbledon SW20 39
Spencer Gdns
  Englefield Green TW20 11
  Mortlake SW14 7
Spencer Hill Rd SW19 19
Spencer Rd SW18 19
Spencer House
  24 Putney SW19 19
Spencer Mews SE21 22
Spencer Pl CR0 42
Spencer Rd Bracknell RG42 . . 26
  Bromley BR1 24
  Carshalton CR4 41
  Caterham CR3 100
  Chiswick W4 7
  Cobham KT11 73
  East Molesey KT8 36
  Hounslow TW3, TW5, TW7 5
  Mitcham CR4 41
  South Croydon CR2 61
  Twickenham TW2 16
  Wimbledon SW20 39
Spencer Way RH1 140
Spencer's Rd RH12 217
Spencers La RH6 159
Spencers Pl RH12 217
Spencers Rd RH11 201
Spenser Ave KT13 53
Spenser Ct **5** TW10 17
Spiceall GU3 129
Spicer Cl KT12 35
Spicers Field KT22 74
Spices Yd CR0 61
Spiers Way RH6 161
Spindle Way RH10 201
Spindlewood Gdns
  CR0, CR2 61
Spindlewoods KT20 97
Spinis RG12 26
Spinnaker Ct **2** KT1 37
Spinner Gn RG12 27
Spinney Cl Cobham KT11 74
  Crawley Down RH10 204
  Horsham RH12 217
  New Malden KT3 38
  Worcester Park KT4 57
Spinney Dr TW14 14
Spinney Gdns SE19 22
Spinney Hill KT15 51
Spinney La SL4 9
Spinney Oak KT16 51
Spinney The Ascot SL5 29
  Burgh Heath KT18 97
  Cheam SM3 58

Spinney The *continued*
Crawley RH11 ....201 B4
Ripley GU23 ....66 C6
Grayshott GU26 ....188 A4
Great Bookham KT23 .....94 B3
Haslemere GU27 ....208 D8
Horley RH6 ....161 A5
Oxshott KT22 ....74 C7
Purley CR8 ....80 B8
Ripley GU23 ....111 C8
Streatham SW16 ....21 D5
Sunbury TW16 ....35 A8
Spinneycroft KT22 .....74 D4
Spinning Wlk The GU5 .133 A4
Spire Ct ⑫ TW10 ....6 E1
Spital Heath RH4 .....136 C8
Spoil La GU10 ....126 F7
Spokane Cl GU11 ......125 F8
Spook Hill RH5 ....136 B3
Spooner House TW5 .....5 A8
Spooner Wlk SM6 ......60 D8
Spooners Rd RH12 ....218 A4
Sportsbank St SE6 ....24 C8
Spout Hill CR0 ....63 A5
Spout La TW19 ....2 A3
Spout La N TW19 ....2 B3
Spratts Alley KT16 ...51 E4
Spratts La KT15 ......51 E4
Spread Eagle Wlk ② KT18 .76 D6
Spreighton Rd KT8 ....36 B5
Spring Ave TW20 ......11 F2
Spring Bottom La RH1 120 C8
Spring Cnr TW13 ......14 F5
Spring Copse
Copthorne RH10 ....183 C3
East Grinstead RH19 ..185 D3
Spring Cotts KT6 .....37 D4
Spring Ct Ewell KT17 .57 F2
Guildford GU2 ....109 A5
Spring Gdns Ascot SL5 29 B5
Biggin Hill TN16 .....83 C1
Copthorne RH10 ......183 C3
Dorking RH4 ....136 A8
East Molesey KT8 .....36 C5
Farnborough GU14 .....85 A7
Frimley GU15 ....66 A5
Wallington SM6 ....60 C5
Spring Gr Brentford W4 .7 A8
Farncombe GU7 ....150 E8
Fetcham KT22, KT23 ...94 B4
Hampton TW12 ....36 B8
Mitcham CR4 ....41 A8
Spring Grove Cres
TW3, TW5 ....5 C6
Spring Grove Jun & Inf Schs
TW7 ....5 D5
Spring Grove Rd
Hounslow TW3, TW5, TW7 5 C6
Richmond TW10 ....6 F2
Spring Hill SE26 .....23 C4
Wallington SM6 ....60 C5
Spring Hill Wildfowl Park
RH18 ....206 A1
Spring House SW19 ....39 F8
Spring La
Croydon CR0, SE25 ....43 B3
Hale GU9 ....125 A7
Oxted RH8 ....122 D4
Slinfold RH13 ....215 C3
Spring La W GU9 .....125 A6
Spring Meadow
Bracknell RG12 ....27 D8
Forest Row RH18 .....206 F1
Spring Park Ave CR0 ..62 D8
Spring Park Inf Sch CR0 63 A7
Spring Park Jun Sch CR0 63 A7
Spring Park Rd CR0 ...62 D8
Spring Plat RH10 ....202 C6
Spring Plat Ct RH10 .202 C6
Spring Rd TW13 ....14 F5
Spring Rise TW20 .....11 E2
Spring St KT17 ....57 F2
Spring Terr TW10 ......6 E2
Spring Way RH19 .....186 A4
Spring Woods
Sandhurst GU47 ....45 C1
Virginia Water GU25 ..31 B5
Springbank Rd SE13 ..24 D8
Springbourne Ct BR3 .44 C8
Springclose La SM3 ...58 E4
Springcopse Rd RH2 ..139 C7
Springcross Ave GU17 64 D4
Springfarm Rd GU27 .207 E5
Springfield
East Grinstead RH19 .185 D4
Elstead GU8 ....148 D3
Lightwater GU18 ......67 D8
Oxted RH8 ....122 D5
South Norwood SE25 ...43 A6
Springfield Ave
Hampton TW12 ....16 B2
Merton SW20 ....39 F6
Springfield Cl GU21 .69 A1
Merton SW20 ....39 F6
Springfield Cres RH12 217 B2
Springfield Ct
Horsham RH12 ....217 C2
⑥ Kingston u T KT1 ...37 E6
Wallington SM6 ....60 C5
Springfield Cty Prim Schs
TW16 ....34 F7
Springfield Drive KT22 94 F8
Springfield Gdns BR4 63 B8
Springfield Gr TW16 .35 A8
Springfield Hospl SW17 20 E1
Springfield La KT13 ..53 B6
Springfield Meadows
KT13 ....53 B6
Springfield Park Rd
RH12 ....217 B2

Springfield Pl KT3 ...38 C5
Springfield Rd Ash GU12 106 A5
Ashford TW15 ....13 F3
Bracknell RG12 ....26 C8
Brands Hill SL3 ....1 B7
Crawley RH11 ....200 E5
East Ewell KT17 ......58 C1
Frimley GU15 ....66 B5
Guildford GU1 ....109 E1
Horsham RH12 ....217 C2
Kingston u T KT1 .....37 E6
Penge SE26 ....23 B3
South Norwood CR7 ....42 C8
⑥ Teddington TW11 ....17 A3
Twickenham TW2 ....16 A7
Wallington SM6 ....60 C5
Westcott RH4 ....135 C6
Wimbledon SW19 ....20 A3
Springfield Rise SE26 23 B5
Springfield Terr GU5 154 D7
Springfield Way GU8 .148 E3
Springfields Cl KT16 33 B1
Springfields Ct GU1 .109 E1
Springhaven Cl GU1 ..110 A1
Springhaven Cl GU1 ..110 A1
Springhill GU8 ......148 E3
Springhill Ct RG12 ...27 B4
Springhouse CI TN16 .83 C1
Springhurst Cl CR0 ...62 F6
Springlakes Est GU12 105 E3
Springmead Ct GU47 ..45 E1
Springpark Dr BR3 ...44 C6
Springwell Cl SW16 ..22 A4
Springwell Ct TW5 ....4 E5
Springwell Jun & Inf Schs
TW5 ....4 E7
Springwell Rd
Beare Green RH5 .....157 D3
Heston TW5 ....4 D6
Streatham SW16 ....22 A3
Springwood GU8 .....150 A1
Springwood Ct CR2 ...61 E6
Sprint Ind Est KT14 .71 D8
Spruce Dr GU18 ......66 F7
Spruce Pk BR2 ....44 F5
Spruce Rd TN16 ......83 D2
Sprucedale Gdns
South Croydon CR0 ....62 D6
Wallington CR8 ....60 E2
Spur Rd Brentford TW7 6 E7
Feltham TW14 ....4 A3
Spur The GU21 ....68 B1
Spurfield KT8 ....36 B6
Spurgeon Ave SE19 ...42 D8
Spurgeon Cl RH11 ...201 C7
Spurgeon Rd SE19 ....42 D8
Spurgeon's Coll SE25 42 E7
Spurs Ct GU11 ......104 E2
Spy La RH14 ....213 A4
Square Dr GU27 .....208 B1
Square The Bagshot GU19 47 E3
Bracknell RG12 ....27 E5
Crawley RH10 ....201 D6
Guildford GU22 ......129 F7
Harmondsworth TW6 ....2 B8
Lightwater GU18 ......48 C1
Lingfield RH7 ....164 C4
⑫ Richmond TW10 ......6 D2
Rowledge GU10 ......145 E3
Tatsfield TN16 ......103 C2
Wallington SM6 ....60 B5
Weybridge KT13 ....53 C5
Wisley GU23, KT14 ....71 E3
Squarey St SW17 .....20 C4
Squire Cl ⑦ CR0 .....42 E1
Squire's Bridge Rd TW17 34 A5
Squire's Rd TW17 ....34 A5
Squires Bridge Rd KT17 33 F5
Squires Cl RH10 ....204 A8
Squires Ct Chertsey KT16 33 B1
Wimbledon SW19 ....20 A3
Squires Hill La GU10 147 C4
Squires Wlk TW15 ....14 D1
Squirrel Cl Crawley RH11 181 B1
Hounslow TW4 ....4 D4
Sandhurst GU47 ....64 B8
Squirrel Dr SL4 ......9 B7
Squirrel La GU14 ....85 A5
Squirrel Wood KT14 ..70 D4
Squirrel's Way KT18 .76 D4
Squirrels Cl GU7 ...150 E7
Squirrels Ct ⑥ KT4 ..57 F8
Squirrels Gn
Great Bookham KT23 ...94 A4
⑫ Redhill RH1 ....118 F2
Worcester Park KT4 ...58 A8
Stable Cl RH10 .....202 D3
Stable Croft GU19 ...47 D2
Stable Ct GU3 ......101 A5
Stable Mews Reigate RH2 118 A1
West Norwood SE27 ....22 C3
Stables The Cobham KT11 73 B5
Guildford GU1 ....109 D4
Stace Way RH10 .....202 E8
Stacey Ct RH1 ......119 D6
Stacey's Farm Rd GU8 148 D4
Stacey's Mdw GU8 ...148 C4
Stack House RH8 ....122 E5
Stackfield Rd RH11 .200 E5
Staddon Ct BR3 .....43 E5
Staff Coll GU15 .....65 C7
Staff College Rd GU15 65 B6
Staff Rd GU12 ......105 D1
Staffhurst Wood Rd RH8 144 C6
Stafford Cl Caterham CR3 100 F4
Cheam SM3 ....58 E4
Stafford Gdns CR0 ...60 F5
Stafford Lake GU21 ..68 A1
Stafford Pl TW10 ....17 F8

Stafford Rd Caterham CR3 101 A6
Crawley RH11 ....181 B1
Croydon CR0 ....61 A6
Kingston u T KT3 .....38 C6
Wallington SM6 ....60 E4
Stafford Sq ⑥ KT13 ..53 D6
Staffords Pl RH6 ...161 B2
Stag Hill GU2 ......130 A8
Stag La SW15 ....18 F5
Stag Leys KT21 ......95 E7
Stag Leys Cl SM7 ...78 E4
Stagbury Ave CR5 ....78 E1
Stagbury Cl CR5 ....78 E1
Stagbury House CR5 ..98 E8
Stagelands RH11 ...201 C8
Stagelands Ct RH11 201 C8
Stags Way TW7 ....5 F8
Stainash Cres TW18 ..13 B3
Stainash Par TW18 ...13 B3
Stainbank Rd CR4 ....41 B6
Staines Ave SM3 ....58 D8
Staines By-Pass
TW15, TW18 ....13 C3
Staines Central Trad Est
TW18 ....12 E4
Staines La Ct KT16 ..33 A3
Staines Lane Cl KT16 32 F3
Staines Prep Sch The
TW18 ....13 A3
Staines Rd Chertsey KT16 33 A5
East Bedfont TW14 ...14 D8
Feltham TW14, TW3, TW4 4 D2
Hounslow TW14, TW3, TW4 4 D2
Laleham TW18 ....33 B7
Staines TW18 ....33 B7
Twickenham TW13, TW2 16 C6
Wraysbury TW19 ......11 F7
Staines Rd E TW12, TW16 35 C8
Staines Rd W TW15 ...14 D1
Staines Sta TW18 ....13 A3
Stainford Cl TW15 ...14 D3
Stainton Rd SE13 ....24 D8
Stainton Wlk GU21 ...69 C1
Staiths Way KT20 ....97 B7
Stake La GU14 ....85 A3
Stakescorner Rd GU3 130 A2
Stambourne Way
South Norwood SE19 ..22 F1
West Wickham BR4 ....63 C7
Stamford Ave GU16 ..85 F6
Stamford Dr BR2 ....44 F5
Stamford Green Prim Sch
KT19 ....76 B7
Stamford Green Rd KT18 76 B6
Stamford Rd KT12 ...54 D7
Stan Hill RH6 ......180 D8
Stanborough Cl TW12 15 F2
Stanborough Rd TW3, TW7 5 D4
Stanbridge Cl RH11 .200 E6
Standard Rd TW4 .....4 D4
Standen Cl RH19 ....185 A4
Standen (National Trust)
RH19 ....185 E2
Standen Pl RH10 ....218 A7
Standen Rd SW18 ....20 A8
Standinghall La RH10 203 A3
Standlake Point ⑪ SE23 23 D5
Standon La RH5 .....157 C4
Stane Cl SW19 ......20 B1
Stane St Ockley RH5 177 D4
Slinfold RH12, RH13 215 C4
Stane Way KT17 .....58 A1
Stanedge Ct SW16 ...21 E3
Stanford Cl TW12 ...15 F2
Stanford Cotts GU24 67 B1
Stanford Mid Sch SW16 41 D8
Stanford Orch RH12 216 F8
Stanford Prim Sch SW16 41 E8
Stanford Rd SW16 ...41 D8
Stanford Way
Broadbridge Heath RH12 216 D3
Mitcham SW16 ....41 D7
Stanfords The KT17 ..76 F7
Stangate Mansions TW1 16 F5
Stanger Rd SE25 ....43 A5
Stangrave Hall RH9 121 B3
Stanhope Ave BR2 ...44 F1
Stanhope Cotts RH7 164 F3
Stanhope Gr BR3 ....43 F4
Stanhope Heath TW19 2 C1
Stanhope Rd
Camberley GU15 ......64 F4
South Croydon CR0 ...61 E7
Wallington SM5 ......60 A3
Stanier Cl RH10 ...202 B5
Staniland Dr KT13 ..52 F1
Stanley Ave
Beckenham BR2, BR3 ..44 C6
West Barnes KT3 .....39 A4
Stanley Cl Coulsdon CR5 79 F2
Crawley RH10 ....201 E4
Stanley Cotts GU21 .68 D2
Stanley Ct Belmont SM2 59 B3
Wallington SM5 ......60 A3
Stanley Ctr RH10 ..182 A1
Stanley Ctr Inf Sch TW2 16 E4
Stanley Ctr Jun Sch TW2 16 E4
Stanley Dr GU14 ....84 C3
Stanley Gardens Rd TW11 16 E3
Stanley Gdns
Hersham KT12 ....54 C4
Mitcham CR4 ....21 A2
Sanderstead CR2 .....80 E8
Wallington SM6 ......60 C4
Stanley Gr CR0, CR7 .42 A3
Stanley Hill GU24 ...87 C5

Stanley Mansions SW17 20 F6
Stanley Park High Sch
SM5 ....60 A4
Stanley Park Inf Sch SM5 59 F3
Stanley Park Jun Sch SM5 59 F3
Stanley Park Rd SM5, SM6 60 A3
Stanley Rd Ashford TW15 13 E3
Hounslow TW3 ....5 C3
Mitcham CR4 ....21 A1
Morden SM4 ....40 A5
Mortlake SW14 ....7 D3
Sutton SM2 ....59 B3
Teddington TW11, TW12 16 D5
Thornton Heath CR0, CR7 42 A3
Twickenham TW2 ....16 D5
Wallington SM5 ......60 A2
Wimbledon SW19 ....20 A2
Woking GU21 ....69 F2
Wokingham RG40 ......25 E6
Stanley Sq SM5 .....59 F2
Stanley St CR3 ....100 C5
Stanley Tech High Sch
SE25 ....42 F6
Stanley Wlk RH13 ...217 D2
Stanleycroft Cl TW7 5 E6
Stanmore Cl SL5 ....29 A5
Stanmore Gdns
Richmond TW9 ....6 F4
Sutton SM1 ....59 C7
Stanmore Rd TW9 .....6 F4
Stanmore Terr BR3 ..44 A7
Stannet Way SM6 ....60 C6
Stansfield Rd TW4, TW5 4 B5
Stanstead Cl BR2 ...44 F3
Stanstead Gr SE23 ..23 C7
Stanstead Manor SM1 59 A4
Stanstead Rd
Caterham CR3, RH1 ..100 E2
Forest Hill SE23, SE6 23 E7
Stansted Rd TW6 .....2 D7
Stanthorpe Cl SW16 21 E3
Stanthorpe Rd SW16 21 E3
Stanton Ave TW11 ...16 E2
Stanton Cl Cranleigh GU6 174 A3
North Cheam KT4 .....39 D1
Worcester Park KT4 ..57 F8
Stanton Rd Barnes SW13 7 F5
Thornton Heath CR0 ..42 C2
Wimbledon SW20 ......39 D8
Stanton Sq SE6 .....23 F4
Stanton Way SE26, SE6 23 F4
Stanway Sch RH4 ...115 B1
Stanwell Cl TW19 ....2 D1
Stanwell Gdns TW19 2 D1
Stanwell Moor Rd
Harmondsworth TW19,
TW6 ....2 B4
Stanwell New Rd
TW18, TW19 ....13 B4
Stanwell Rd Ashford TW15 13 E4
East Bedfont TW14,
TW19, TW6 ....14 B8
Horton SL3, TW19 ....1 C4
Stanworth Ct TW5 ....5 B7
Stanyhurst SE23 ....23 E7
Staple Hill GU24, KT16 49 F6
Staple La
East Clandon GU4 ...111 E2
Shere GU4 ....132 D6
Staplecross Rd ⑦ RH11 201 A3
Staplefield Cl ⑧ SW2 21 E7
Stapleford Cl
Kingston u T KT1 ....38 A6
Putney SW19 ....19 E8
Staplehurst RG12 ...26 E2
Staplehurst Cl RH2 139 C5
Staplehurst Rd
Reigate RH2 ....139 C5
Sutton SM5 ....59 E3
Stapleton Gdns CR0 .61 A5
Stapleton Rd SW17 ..21 A5
Star and Garter Hill TW10 17 D8
Star Hill Churt GU10 167 D2
Woking GU22 ....89 D8
Star Hill Dr GU10 ..167 D2
Star La Aldershot GU12 105 A1
Hooley CR5 ....99 A6
Star Post Rd GU15 ..65 F8
Star Rd TW7 ....5 D5
Starborough Cotts RH7 185 F7
Starborough Rd TN8 165 E5
Starhurst Sch RH5 .136 C5
Starling Wlk TW12 ..15 E3
Starmead Dr RG40 ...25 E5
Starrock La CR5 ....99 A7
Starrock Rd CR5 ...99 C8
Starwood Cl KT14 ...71 C8
Staten Gdns TW1 ...16 F7
Statham Ct RG42 ...26 E8
Station App
Ash Vale GU12 ......106 A7
Ashford TW15 ....13 F4
Beckenham BR3 ....44 A8
Beckenham, Lower Sydenham
SE6 ....23 F3
Belmont SM2 ....59 A1
Chipstead CR5 ....78 F1
Coulsdon CR5 ....79 D4
⑧ Croydon CR0 ....61 D8
Dorking RH4 ....115 C1
East Horsley KT24 ...92 E1
Epsom KT17, KT19 ....76 D6
Godalming GU7 ......150 D4
Guildford GU1 ......130 C8
Hampton TW12 ....36 A8
Haslemere GU27 .....208 B6
Hinchley Wood KT10 ..55 F7

Station App *continued*
Horley RH6 ....161 B2
⑥ Kingston u T KT1, KT2 38 A8
Leatherhead KT22 ....95 A6
⑥ New Malden KT4 ....39 A1
Oxted RH8 ....122 E6
Purley CR8 ....80 A8
Richmond TW9 ....7 A4
Shalford GU4 ....130 E3
Shepperton TW17 .....34 C4
South Croydon CR2 ...61 D2
Staines TW18 ....13 A3
Streatham SW16 ......21 E5
Sunbury TW16 ....35 A8
⑪ Surbiton KT6 ......37 E3
Sutton SM2 ....59 B1
Tadworth KT20 ......97 C4
Virginia Water GU25 31 D5
West Byfleet KT14 ...71 A7
Weybridge KT13 ......53 A4
Whyteleafe CR3 .....81 A1
Woking GU22 ....69 F2
Worcester Park KT19 58 A5
Station App E RH1 ..139 F7
Station App W RH1 ..139 F7
Station Approach Rd
Chiswick W4 ....7 C7
Coulsdon CR5 ....79 D4
Crawley RH6 ....182 B7
Station Ave Caterham CR3 101 A1
Kingston u T KT3 ....38 E6
Walton-on-T KT12 ....54 A6
West Ewell KT19 .....57 E2
Station Bldgs SW20 .39 C7
Station Cl Hampton TW12 36 B8
Horsham RH13 ....217 D2
Station Cres TW15 ..13 E4
Station Est BR3 ....43 D5
Station Flats SL5 ...30 E7
Station Gdns W4 .....7 C7
Station Hill Ascot SL5 29 A5
Crawley RH10 ....202 B7
⑫ Farnham GU9 ......125 C2
Station Ind Est RG40 25 C6
Station La
Enton Green GU8 ...171 A7
Milford GU8 ....171 A7
Station Par Ashford TW15 13 F4
Chipstead CR5 ....79 E1
East Horsley KT24 ...92 E1
Feltham TW13 ....15 A7
Richmond TW9 ....7 A6
Sunningdale SL5 ....30 A2
⑧ Upper Tooting SW12 21 A7
Virginia Water GU25 31 E4
Station Path TW18 ..12 F3
Station Rd Addlestone KT15 52 D6
Aldershot GU11 .....105 B2
Ashford TW15 ....13 F4
Bagshot GU19 ....47 E4
Barnes SW13 ....7 F5
Belmont SM2 ....59 A1
Betchworth RH3 ....116 E3
Bracknell RG12 .....27 B7
Bramley GU5 ....152 A7
Bromley BR2 ....44 E7
Carshalton SM5 .....59 F6
Chertsey KT16 ......33 A1
Chessington KT9 ....56 E5
Chobham GU24 ....49 E5
Claygate KT10 ......55 E5
Cranleigh GU6 .....195 C3
Crawley RH10, RH11 201 D6
Crawley Down RH10 .204 A1
Croydon CR0 ....42 C1
Dorking RH4 ....136 A8
East Grinstead RH19 185 D1
Egham TW20 ....12 A3
Esher KT10 ....55 D8
Farnborough GU14 ...85 B4
Farncombe GU7 .....150 F7
Forest Row RH18 ...206 F3
Godalming GU7 .....150 D4
Gomshall GU5 ......133 D4
Hampton TW12 ....36 A8
Horley RH6 ....161 B3
Horsham RH13 ......217 D2
Hounslow TW3 ....5 B3
Hydestile GU8 .....171 D6
Kenley CR8 ....80 C5
Kingston u T KT2 ...38 A8
Leatherhead KT22 ...95 A6
Lingfield RH7 .....164 E4
Loxwood RH14 ......213 A3
Merton SM4 ....40 C8
Mersham RH1 ....119 C7
Merton SW19 ....40 C8
Penge SE20 ....23 C1
Redhill RH1 ....118 F2
Rudgwick RH12 ....214 D7
Shackleford GU7 ..149 F3
Shepperton TW17 ...34 C4
South Godstone RH9 142 E5
South Norwood SE25 42 F5
Stoke D'Abernon KT11 73 E3
Sunbury TW16 ......15 A1
Sunningdale SL5 ...30 A4
Teddington TW11 ...17 A3
Teddington, Hampton Wick
KT1 ....37 D8
Thames Ditton KT10 55 A8
Thames Ditton, Weston Green
KT7 ....36 F2
Twickenham TW1 ....16 F8
Warnham RH12 .....217 B8

Station Rd continued
West Barnes KT3 .... 39 B4
West Byfleet KT14 .... 71 A7
West Wickham BR4 .... 44 C1
Whyteleafe CR3 .... 80 F1
Wokingham RG40 .... 25 B6
Woldingham CR3 .... 101 F5
Wraysbury TW19 .... 1 A1
Station Rd E
Ash Vale GU12 .... 106 A7
Oxted RH8 .... 122 E6
Station Rd N
◳ Egham TW20 .... 11 F3
Merstham RH1 .... 119 C7
Station Rd S RH1 .... 119 C7
Station Rd W
Ash Vale GU12 .... 105 F8
Oxted RH8 .... 122 E6
Station Rise SE27 .... 22 B6
Station Row GU4 .... 130 E3
Station Terr RH4 .... 136 A8
Station View GU22 .... 106 A8
Station Way
Crawley SM2, SM3 .... 58 E3
Crawley RH10, RH11 .... 201 D5
Station Yd TW1 .... 17 A8
Staunton Rd K12 .... 17 F1
Staveley Gdns W4 .... 7 D6
Staveley Rd Ashford TW15 ... 14 D7
Chiswick W4 .... 7 D7
Staveley Way GU21 .... 68 E2
Staverton Cl RG40 .... 25 F6
Stavordale Rd SM4, SM5 ...... 40 C2
Stayne End GU25 .... 31 A5
Stayton Rd SM1 .... 59 A7
Steadfast Rd K11 .... 37 D8
Steam Farm La TW14 .... 3 F3
Steel's La K11, K122 .... 74 C5
Steele Rd TW7 .... 6 A3
Steele's Rd GU11 .... 105 B4
Steep Hill Chobham GU24 ..... 49 C3
South Croydon CR0 .... 61 E6
Streatham SW16 .... 21 D5
Steeple Cl SW19 .... 19 E4
Steeple Heights Dr TN16 ..... 83 D2
Steepways GU26 .... 188 B6
Steeres Hill RH12 .... 199 C6
Steerforth Copse GU47 .... 45 E2
Steerforth St SW18 .... 20 C6
Steers La RH10 .... 182 C4
Steers Mead CR4 .... 40 F8
Steetley Ct SM2 .... 59 C3
Steinman Ct TW7 .... 5 F4
Stella Rd SW17 .... 20 F2
Sembridge Rd SE20 .... 43 B7
Stenning Ct K122 .... 95 B5
Stennings The RH19 .... 185 C3
Stepgates K116 .... 33 B2
Stepgates Cl K116 .... 33 B2
Stepgates Prim Sch K116 ..... 33 B2
Stephanie Chase Ct RG40 .... 25 D7
Stephen Cl Crawley RH11 .... 181 D1
Egham TW20 .... 12 C2
Stephen Ct ◳ SW19 .... 19 D7
Stephen Gould Ho GU14 .... 105 B8
Stephendale Rd GU9 .... 125 D4
Stephenson Ct SM2 .... 58 F3
Stephenson Dr RH19 .... 205 F7
Stephenson Pl RH10 .... 202 B6
Stephenson Rd TW4 .... 16 A8
Stephenson Way RH10 .... 202 B6
Stepney Cl RH10 .... 202 C4
Sterling Ave TW17 .... 34 E6
Sterling Bldgs RH12 .... 217 C2
Sterling Pk RH10 .... 182 B3
Sternhold Ave SW12, SW2 ... 21 D6
Sterry Dr Thames Ditton KT7 ... 36 E3
Worcester Park KT19 .... 57 E6
Steucers La SE23 .... 23 E7
Steve Biko La SE6 .... 24 A4
Steve Biko Way TW3 .... 5 A4
Stevenage Rd RH11 .... 200 E3
Stevens Cl Beckenham BR3 .... 23 F1
Epsom K117 .... 76 E6
Hampton TW12 .... 15 F2
Stevens Ct BR3 .... 44 B8
Stevens La K110 .... 56 A4
Stevens Pl CR8 .... 80 B6
Stewart K110 .... 97 D6
Stewart Ave TW17 .... 34 A5
Stewart Cl Hampton TW12 ... 15 E2
Woking GU21 .... 68 F2
Stewart Fleming Prim Sch
SE20 .... 43 C6
Steyning Cl Crawley RH10 ... 201 E8
Purley CR8 .... 80 B3
Steyning Way TW4 .... 4 C1
Strathbrook Rd SW16 .... 21 F1
Stile Gdns GU27 .... 207 F6
Stile House GU4 .... 110 D2
Stile Path TW16 .... 35 A6
Stirling Cl Banstead SM7 .... 77 F3
Crawley RH10 .... 202 C5
Farnborough GU14 .... 85 A3
Frimley GU16 .... 65 E2
Mitcham SW16 .... 41 C8
Stirling Gr TW3 .... 5 C5
Stirling House ⑪ RH1 .... 118 F1
Stirling Rd Guildford GU2 ... 108 E1
Stanwell TW19, TW6 .... 2 A4
Twickenham TW2 .... 16 B8
Stirling Way
East Grinstead RH19 .... 186 B3
Horsham RH13 .... 217 E3
Stirrup Way RH10 .... 202 D7

Stites Hill Rd CR3, CR5 ...... 100 C7
Stoatley Hollow GU27 .... 208 A8
Stoatley House ⑯ SW15 ...... 19 A7
Stoatley Rise GU27 .... 208 A8
Stoats Nest Rd CR5 .... 79 E5
Stoats Nest Village CR5 ...... 79 E4
Stock Hill TN16 .... 83 D2
Stockbridge Dr GU11 .... 126 C6
Stockbury Rd CR0 .... 43 C3
Stockfield RH6 .... 161 B4
Stockfield Rd
Claygate KT18 .... 55 E5
Streatham SW16 .... 21 F5
Stockhams Cl CR2 .... 61 D1
Stocklund Sq GU6 .... 174 D3
Stockport Rd SW16 .... 41 D8
Stocks Cl RH6 .... 161 B2
Stockton Rd RH2 .... 139 A6
Stockwell Ctr RH10 .... 202 A6
Stockwell Rd RH19 .... 205 F8
Stockwell Works RH10 ...... 202 A6
Stockwood Rise GU15 .... 65 F5
Stockwood Way GU9 .... 125 F7
Stocton Cl GU1 .... 109 C2
Stocton Rd GU1 .... 109 C2
Stodart Rd SE20 .... 43 C8
Stofold Cl SW19 .... 19 E8
Stoke Brunswick Sch
RH19 .... 206 E7
Stoke Cl K111 .... 73 F3
Stoke Fields ⑤ GU1 .... 109 D1
Stoke Flds ⑦ GU1 .... 109 D1
Stoke Gr GU1 .... 109 D1
Stoke Hill
(Almshouses) ⑥ GU1 .... 109 D1
Stoke Mews GU1 .... 130 D8
Stoke Park Ct ⑤ GU1 .... 109 D1
Stoke Rd Guildford GU1 ...... 109 D1
Kingston u T K12 .... 18 A1
Stoke D'Abernon KT11 .... 73 E3
Walton-on-T K112 .... 54 C7
Stoke Rd Cotts K122 .... 94 D6
Stokeford Cl ⑤ RG12 .... 27 F4
Stokes Cl RH10 .... 202 C4
Stokes Rd CR0 .... 43 D3
Stokes Ridings K120 .... 97 D4
Stokesby Rd K19 .... 56 F4
Stokesheath Rd K122 .... 74 C8
Stompond La K112 .... 54 A8
Stoms Path SE6 .... 24 A4
Stonards Brow GU5 .... 152 D4
Stondon Pk SE23 .... 23 E8
Stone Cres TW14 .... 14 F8
Stone Hatch GU6 .... 194 A3
Stone House Gdns CR3 ...... 100 F8
Stone Park Ave BR3 .... 44 B5
Stone Pl K14 .... 58 A8
Stone Rd BR2 .... 44 F4
Stone St Aldershot GU12 ..... 126 D8
Croydon CR0, CR9 .... 61 A5
Stone's Rd K117 .... 76 E7
Stonebanks K112 .... 35 A2
Stonebridge Ct
Crawley RH11 .... 201 C2
Horsham RH12 .... 217 A2
Stonebridge Fields GU4 ...... 130 C2
Stonebridge Wharf GU4 ...... 130 D2
Stonecot Cl SM3, SM4 .... 39 E1
Stonecot Hill SM3 .... 39 E1
Stonecourt Cl RH6 .... 161 C3
Stonecroft Way CR0 .... 41 E2
Stonecrop Cl RH11 .... 201 B3
Stonecrop Rd GU1, GU4 ...... 110 C3
Stonedene Cl GU35 .... 187 B4
Stonefield Cl RH10, RH11 .... 201 D5
Stonegate GU15 .... 66 C6
Stonehall Ave BR3 .... 44 B7
Stonehill Cl
Little Bookham KT23 .... 94 A2
Mortlake SW14 .... 7 D2
Stonehill Cres K116 .... 50 E4
Stonehill Pk GU35 .... 187 C4
Stonehill Rd
Chobham GU24, K116 .... 50 D3
Headley Down GU35 .... 187 C4
Lightwater GU18 .... 48 A1
Mortlake SW14 .... 7 C2
Ottershaw GU24, K116 .... 50 D3
Stonehill's Mansions ⑧
SW16 .... 21 E6
Stonehills Ct SE21 .... 22 E5
Stonehouse Rise GU16 .... 65 E1
Stoneleigh Ave K117, K14 .... 58 A2
Stoneleigh
Broadway K117 .... 58 A5
Stoneleigh Cl RH19 .... 185 F1
Stoneleigh Cres K119 .... 57 F1
Stoneleigh Fst Grant
Maintd Sch K17 .... 58 B6
Stoneleigh Lodge ⑫ TW9 .... 6 F6
Stoneleigh Park Ave CR0 .... 43 D3
Stoneleigh Park Rd
K119, K14 .... 58 A3
Stoneleigh Pk K113 .... 53 C4
Stoneleigh Rd
Carshalton SM5 .... 40 E2
The Chart RH6 .... 123 E5
Stoneleigh Sta K119 .... 58 A5
Stonepit Cl GU7 .... 150 C4
Stoners Cl RH6 .... 181 E7
Stones La RH4 .... 135 C6
Stoneswood Rd RH8 .... 123 B5
Stoneworth Ct SE25 .... 43 A3
Stoney Bottom GU26 .... 188 C3
Stoney Brook GU2 .... 108 E2

Stoney Deep TW11 .... 17 A4
Stoney La SE19 .... 22 F2
Stoney Rd RG42 .... 27 A8
Stoneybrook RH12 .... 216 E3
Stoneycroft Cl SE12 .... 24 F8
Stoneycroft Wlk ⑧ RH11 ... 200 D5
Stoneyfield Rd CR5 .... 79 F2
Stoneyland Ct ⑥ TW20 ...... 11 F3
Stoneylands Rd TW20 .... 11 F3
Stony Croft KT21 .... 75 F2
Stony Hill K110 .... 54 F3
Stoop Ct K114 .... 71 B7
Stoop Memorial Ground
TW2 .... 16 E8
Stopham Rd RH10 .... 202 C3
Stormont Way K19 .... 56 C5
Storr's La GU3 .... 88 C3
Storrington Rd CR0 .... 42 F1
Stoughton Ave SM3 .... 58 E5
Stoughton Cl SW15 .... 19 A7
Stoughton Grange Cty Jun
Sch GU2 .... 109 B4
Stoughton Inf Sch GU2 ...... 109 B4
Stoughton Rd GU1, GU2 ...... 109 B3
Stourhead Cl
Farnborough GU14 .... 85 D4
◳ Putney SW19 .... 19 D8
Stourhead Gdns SW20 .... 39 A6
Stourton Ave TW13 .... 15 F4
Stovold's Way GU11 .... 125 F8
Stovolds Hill GU6, GU8 ...... 193 D7
Stowell Ave CR0 .... 63 D2
Stowford Coll SM2 .... 59 C3
Strachan Pl SW19 .... 19 C2
Strachey Ct ◳ RH11 .... 201 B1
Stradford Rd Hounslow TW3 ... 4 F4
Twickenham TW1 .... 17 A8
Straight Rd SL4, TW19 .... 11 C8
Strand Cl Crawley RH10 ..... 202 D4
Langley Vale KT18 .... 96 D8
Strand on the Green Inf Sch
W4 .... 7 A8
Strand on the Green Jun Sch
W4 .... 7 A8
Strand-on-the-Green W4 ..... 7 A8
Stranraer Way ⑪ TW6 .... 2 E1
Stratfield RG12 .... 26 E1
Stratfield House ⑫ GU11 .... 105 A2
Stratford Ct
Farnborough GU14 .... 85 C4
Farnham GU9 .... 125 A3
New Malden KT3 .... 38 D5
Stratford Rd Harlington TW6 ... 3 C2
Thornton Heath CR7 .... 42 B6
Strathavon Cl GU6 .... 174 B7
Strathcona Ave KT24 .... 113 E7
Strathcona Gdns
Knaphill GU21 .... 68 D1
Knaphill GU21 .... 88 C8
Strathdale SW16 .... 21 F3
Strathdon Dr SW17 .... 20 D5
Strathearn Ave
Harlington UB3 .... 3 F7
Twickenham TW2 .... 16 C7
Strathearn Rd Sutton SM1 ... 59 A5
Wimbledon SW19 .... 20 A4
Strathmore Ct CR3 .... 100 E6
Strathmore Rd
Crawley RH11 .... 181 A1
Teddington TW11, TW2 .... 16 E4
Thornton Heath CR0 .... 42 D2
Wimbledon SW19 .... 20 A5
Strathmore Sch TW10 .... 17 D6
Strathville Rd SW18 .... 20 B6
Strathyre Ave CR7, SW16 ... 42 A6
Stratton Ave SM6 .... 60 D2
Stratton Cl Heston TW5 .... 5 A6
Merton SW19 .... 40 A7
Walton-on-T K112 .... 35 C1
Stratton Ct ⑯ SW16 .... 41 E8
Stratton Rd Merton SW19 .... 40 A7
Sunbury TW16 .... 34 F7
Stratton Wlk GU14 .... 85 A7
Strawberry Cl GU24 .... 87 D7
Strawberry Fields GU24 ...... 68 A4
Strawberry Hill Cl TW1 ...... 16 F5
Strawberry Hill Golf
Course TW2 .... 16 E5
Strawberry Hill Rd TW1 ...... 16 F5
Strawberry Hill Sta TW1 ..... 16 F5
Strawberry La SM5 .... 60 A7
Strawberry Rise GU24 .... 68 A4
Strawberry Vale TW1 .... 17 A5
Stream Cl KT14 .... 71 E2
Stream Farm Cl
GU10, GU9 .... 146 D7
Stream Pk RH19 .... 185 B3
Stream Valley Rd GU10 ...... 146 C6
Streatham Cl SW16 .... 21 E6
Streatham Ct SW16 .... 21 E5
Streatham Comm N SW16 ... 21 F3
Streatham Comm S SW16 ... 21 F3
Streatham Common Sta
SW16 .... 21 E3
Streatham Ct SW16 .... 21 E5
Streatham High Rd
SW16, SW2 .... 21 E5
Streatham Hill SW2 .... 21 E7
Streatham Hill & Clapham
High Sch SW2 .... 21 F7
Streatham Hill Sta SW2 ...... 21 F7
Streatham Pl SW2 .... 21 E8
Streatham Rd CR4 .... 41 A8
Streatham St SW16 .... 21 E5
Streatham & Tooting
Adult Inst SW16 .... 21 F6
Streatham Vale SW16 .... 21 D1
Streathbourne Rd SW17 ..... 21 A5

Streatham Wells Prim Sch
SW2 .... 22 A6
Streatleigh Par ④ SW16 ..... 21 E6
Street Hill RH10 .... 202 E5
Street The Ashtead K121 ...... 75 F1
Betchworth RH3 .... 116 E1
Capel RH5 .... 178 D6
Charlwood RH6 .... 180 E7
Compton GU3 .... 129 B2
Dockenfield GU10 .... 166 E6
East Clandon GU4 .... 111 E4
Effingham KT24 .... 113 D8
Ewhurst GU6 .... 175 E5
Fetcham KT22 .... 94 D5
Frensham GU10 .... 167 C7
Plaistow RH14 .... 211 E2
Puttenham GU3 .... 128 C4
Shackleford GU8 .... 149 C8
Shalford GU4 .... 130 E3
Slinfold RH13 .... 215 D4
Thursley GU8 .... 169 C4
Tongham GU10 .... 126 F6
West Clandon GU4 .... 111 B5
West Horsley KT24 .... 112 B6
Wonersh GU5 .... 152 A7
Wrecclesham GU10 .... 145 F6
Streete Court Sch RH9 .... 121 E5
Streeters Cl GU7 .... 151 A6
Streeters La SM6 .... 60 D7
Streetfield GU8 .... 149 C4
Streetfield Rd RH18 .... 215 E3
Streets Heath GU24 .... 67 F7
Stretton Rd Croydon CR0 ..... 42 E2
Richmond TW10 .... 17 C6
Strickland Cl RH11 .... 200 E5
Strickland Row SW18 .... 20 D8
Stringer's Ave GU4 .... 109 D7
Stringhams Copse GU23 ..... 91 A3
Strode House ⑤ SW2 .... 22 A7
Strode St TW20 .... 12 A1
Strode's Coll TW20 .... 11 F3
Strode's Cres TW18 .... 13 C3
Strodes College La TW20 ..... 11 F3
Strood House ⑱ SE20 .... 23 C1
Strood La Warnham RH12 ..... 216 C7
Winkfield SL5 .... 9 C2
Stroud Cres SW15 .... 19 A5
Stroud Green Gdns CR0 ...... 43 C2
Stroud Green Way CR0 .... 43 D3
Stroud La GU5 .... 153 A3
Stroud Rd Croydon SE25 ...... 43 A3
Wimbledon SW19 .... 20 A5
Stroud Way TW15 .... 14 B2
Stroude Rd Egham TW20 ..... 12 A1
Thorpe GU25, TW20 .... 31 E6
Stroudes Cl K114 .... 38 E3
Stroudley Cl RH10 .... 202 B5
Stroudwater Pk K113 .... 53 C4
Strudgate Cl RH10 .... 202 B4
Strudwicks Field GU6 .... 174 F4
Stuart Ave K112 .... 35 C1
Stuart Cl Crawley RH10 ...... 202 D5
Farnborough GU14 .... 85 A5
Stuart Cres Croydon CR0 ..... 62 F7
Reigate RH2 .... 139 A6
Stuart Ct Godalming GU7 ..... 150 E4
⑮ Redhill RH1 .... 119 A2
Stuart Gr TW11 .... 16 E3
Stuart House RG42 .... 26 F8
Stuart Lodge
⑪ Epsom KT18 .... 76 D6
South Norwood SE25 .... 42 E7
Stuart Pl CR4 .... 40 F8
Stuart Rd Reigate RH2 .... 139 A6
Richmond TW10 .... 17 B5
South Norwood CR7 .... 42 C5
Warlingham CR3, CR6 .... 101 C7
Wimbledon SW19 .... 20 A5
Stuart Way
East Grinstead RH19 .... 205 F7
Staines TW18 .... 13 B2
Virginia Water GU25 .... 31 A5
Stubbington House Sch
SL5 .... 29 B1
Stubbs Folly GU47 .... 64 D7
Stubbs La K120 .... 118 A7
Stubbs Moor Rd GU14 .... 84 F5
Stubbs Way SW19 .... 40 D8
Stubfield RH12 .... 217 A3
Stubpond La RH19, RH7 ..... 184 D2
Stubs Cl RH4 .... 136 C5
Stubs Hill RH4, RH5 .... 136 C4
Stubs Ind Site GU12 .... 105 E5
Stucley Rd TW5, TW7 .... 5 F7
Studios Rd TW17 .... 33 F6
Studland Rd Byfleet K114 .... 71 F6
Kingston u T K12 .... 17 F2
Penge SE26 .... 23 D3
Study Prep Sch The SW19 ... 19 C3
Stumblets RH10 .... 202 C7
Stumps Hill La BR3 .... 24 A2
Sturdee Cl GU16 .... 65 E1
Sturges Rd RG40 .... 25 C5
Sturt Ave GU27 .... 207 F5
Sturt Ct GU4 .... 110 C3
Sturt Rd Frimley GU16 .... 85 F5
Haslemere GU27 .... 207 F5
Heath End GU9 .... 125 B7
Sturt's La K120 .... 117 A8
Stychens Cl RH1 .... 120 C2
Stychens La RH1 .... 120 C2
Styles End K123 .... 114 B8
Styles Way BR3 .... 44 C3
Styventon Pl K116 .... 32 F2
Succomb's Hill CR3, CR6 .... 101 B2
Succombs Pl CR6 .... 101 B8
Sudbrook Gdns TW10 .... 17 E5
Sudbrook La TW10 .... 17 E6

Sudbrook Pk (Richmond
Golf Club) TW10 .... 17 E6
Sudbury Gdns CR0 .... 61 E6
Suffield Cl CR2 .... 81 D7
Suffield La
GU3, GU10, GU8 .... 128 B2
Suffield Rd SE20 .... 43 C7
Suffolk Cl Bagshot GU19 ..... 47 E2
Horley RH6 .... 161 A2
Suffolk Ct ⑤ SW16 .... 22 A4
Suffolk Dr GU4 .... 110 B6
Suffolk House
④ Croydon CR0 .... 61 D8
Penge SE20 .... 43 C8
Suffolk Rd Barnes SW13 .... 7 F7
South Norwood SE25 .... 42 F5
Worcester Park KT4 .... 57 F8
Sugden Rd K17 .... 37 B1
Sulina Rd SW2 .... 21 E8
Sulivan Enterprise Ctr 20 E2
Sulivan Prim Sch SW6 .... 20 E3
Sulivan Rd SW6 .... 20 E3
Sullivan Cl
East Molesey KT8 .... 36 B6
Farnborough GU14 .... 85 A4
Sullivan Ct ④ GU9 .... 43 A1
Sullivan Dr RH11 .... 200 E3
Sullivan House Kenley CR8 ... 80 C5
Twickenham TW2 .... 5 D1
Sullivan Rd GU15 .... 65 A5
Sullivans Reach K112 .... 35 A2
Sultan St BR3 .... 43 D7
Summer Ave KT8 .... 36 E4
Summer Gdns
Frimley GU15 .... 66 C5
Thames Ditton KT8 .... 36 E4
Summer Rd
East Molesey KT8 .... 36 D4
Thames Ditton KT7, KT8 .... 36 E4
Summer Trees TW16 .... 35 B8
Summer's Rd GU3, GU7 ..... 151 A8
Summerene Cl SW16 .... 21 C1
Summerfield K121 .... 95 D8
Summerfield La
Long Ditton KT6 .... 56 D8
Rowledge GU10 .... 146 B2
Summerfield St SE12 .... 24 F8
Summerfields Cl K115 .... 51 F5
Summerhayes Cl GU21 ...... 69 E5
Summerhays K111 .... 73 D6
Summerhill Cl GU21 .... 150 D4
Summerhill Way CR4 .... 41 A8
Summerhouse Ave TW5 .... 4 E6
Summerhouse Cl GU7 .... 150 D4
Summerhouse Ct GU26 ..... 188 D3
Summerhouse La UB7 .... 2 D8
Summerhouse Rd GU7 ...... 150 D3
Summerlands GU6 .... 174 E4
Summerlay Cl K120 .... 97 E2
Summerleigh ⑤ K113 .... 53 D4
Summerley St SW18 .... 20 C6
Summerly Ave RH2 .... 118 A2
Summers Cl Belmont SM2 .... 59 A3
Weybridge KT13 .... 72 A6
Summers La GU7 .... 150 A8
Summersbury Dr GU4 .... 130 E5
Summersbury Hall GU4 ...... 130 E5
Summersby Cl GU7 .... 150 F7
Summerset Rd SE27 .... 22 D4
Summersvere Ct RH10 ...... 182 A1
Summerswood Cl CR8 .... 80 D3
Summerville Gdns SM1 ...... 58 F4
Summerwood Rd TW1, TW7 ... 5 F1
Summit Ave GU14 .... 84 C3
Summit Ctr UB7 .... 2 D3
Summit Pl KT13 .... 53 A3
Summit The TW16 .... 15 A8
Summit Way SE19 .... 22 E1
Sumner Cl KT22 .... 94 D3
Sumner Ct GU9 .... 125 C2
Sumner Gdns CR0 .... 42 A1
Sumner Pl K113 .... 52 A5
Sumner Rd Farnham GU9 ..... 125 C2
Thornton Heath CR0 .... 42 B8
Sumner Rd S CR9 .... 42 A1
Sun Alley ⑤ TW9 .... 6 E3
Sun Brow GU27 .... 208 A5
Sun Hill GU22 .... 89 A4
Sun Inn Rd GU8 .... 192 F7
Sun Life Trad Est TW14 .... 4 A3
Sun Ray Est GU47 .... 64 A4
Sunbury Ave SW14 .... 7 D3
Sunbury Court
Island TW16 .... 35 D6
Sunbury Court Rd TW16 ...... 35 C6
Sunbury Cres TW13 .... 14 F4
Sunbury Cross Centre ⑨
TW16 .... 35 A2
Sunbury Ct TW16 .... 35 D6
Sunbury Ct (Con Ctr)
TW16 .... 35 D6
Sunbury Int Bsns Ctr
TW16 .... 34 E6
Sunbury La K112 .... 35 A2
Sunbury Manor Sch TW16 ... 34 F7
Sunbury Rd Cheam SM3 ...... 58 E7
Feltham TW13 .... 14 F4
Sunbury Sta TW16 .... 35 A1
Sunbury Way TW13 .... 15 C2
Suncroft Pl SE26 .... 23 C5
Sundale Ave CR2 .... 62 C2
Sunderland Ct
Dulwich SE22 .... 23 A7
⑪ Stanwell TW19 .... 2 E1
Sunderland Mount SE23 ..... 23 E7
Sunderland Rd SE23 .... 23 E7
Sundew Cl Crawley RH11 .... 201 A2
Lightwater GU18 .... 67 B8

Sundew Cl *continued*
Wokingham RG40 . . . . .25 E7
Sundial Ave SE25 . . . . .42 F6
Sundial Ct KT5 . . . . .57 B8
Sundon Cres GU25 . . . . .31 C4
Sundown Ave CR2 . . . . .80 F8
Sundown Rd TW15 . . . . .14 C3
Sundridge Rd
Croydon CR0, CR9 . . . . .43 A1
Old Woking GU22 . . . . .90 A7
Sunkist Way SM6 . . . . .60 E2
Sunlight Cl SW19 . . . . .20 C2
Sunmead Cl KT22 . . . . .94 F5
Sunmead Rd TW16 . . . . .35 A6
Sunna Gdns TW16 . . . . .35 B7
Sunniholme Ct CR2 . . . . .61 C5
Sunning Ave SL5 . . . . .29 E2
Sunning House Ascot SL5 . . . . . .29 D5
Windlesham GU20 . . . . .48 F8
Sunningdale Ave TW13 . . . . .15 E6
Sunningdale Cl **2** KT6 . . . . .56 E8
Sunningdale Ct
Crawley RH10 . . . . .201 D4
1 Kingston u T KT2 . . . . .18 A1
Sunningdale House CR4 . . . . .40 D7
**Sunningdale Park (Civil
Service Coll)** SL5 . . . . .29 F4
Sunningdale Rd SM1 . . . . .58 F6
Sunningdale Sch SL5 . . . . .29 F3
Sunninghill Cl SL5 . . . . .30 A2
Sunninghill Ct SL5 . . . . .29 D5
Sunninghill Rd SL5 . . . . .29 D5
Sunninghill Lodge SL5 . . . . .29 C7
Sunninghill Rd Ascot SL5 . . . . . .29 D5
Windlesham GU20 . . . . .48 A7
Winkfield SL4, SL5 . . . . .9 E2
Sunningvale Ave TN16 . . . . .83 D3
Sunningvale Cl TN16 . . . . .83 D3
Sunny Ave RH10 . . . . .204 A8
Sunny Bank Croydon SE25 . . . . . .43 A6
Epsom KT18 . . . . .76 C3
Warlingham CR6 . . . . .81 E2
Sunny Down GU8 . . . . .170 E5
Sunny Hill GU8 . . . . .170 E6
Sunny Hill Rd GU1 . . . . .104 D2
Sunny Nook Gdns CR2 . . . . .61 D4
Sunny Rise CR3 . . . . .100 D3
Sunny View Cl GU12 . . . . .105 C1
Sunnybank SL5 . . . . .29 A5
Sunnybank Mews GU22 . . . . . . .106 B3
Sunnybank Rd GU14 . . . . .84 D6
Sunnybank Villas RH1 . . . . .120 F3
Sunnycroft Rd
Croydon SE25 . . . . .43 A6
Hounslow TW3 . . . . .5 B5
Sunnydell La GU10, GU9 . . . . . . .146 A6
Sunnydene Rd CR8 . . . . .80 B6
Sunnydene St SE26 . . . . .23 E4
Sunnydown Boys' Sch
CR3 . . . . .100 F6
Sunnyhill Cl RH10 . . . . .204 A8
Sunnyhill Prim Sch SW16 . . . . . .21 F4
Sunnyhill Rd SW16 . . . . .21 E4
Sunnyhurst Cl SM1 . . . . .59 A7
Sunnymead Crawley RH11 . . .201 D6
Crawley Down RH10 . . . . .204 B8
Sunnymead Ave
CR4, SW16 . . . . .41 D6
Sunnymede Ave
Sutton SM5 . . . . .78 D8
West Ewell KT19 . . . . .57 E3
Sunnyside Knaphill GU21 . . . . . . .88 B1
Walton-on-T KT12 . . . . .35 C4
Wimbledon SW19 . . . . .19 E2
Sunnyside Pl SW19 . . . . .19 E2
Sunnyside Rd
Headley Down GU35 . . . . .187 C4
Teddington TW11 . . . . .16 D4
Sunray Ave KT5 . . . . .57 B8
Sunrise Cl TW13 . . . . .15 F5
Sunset Gdns SE25 . . . . .42 F7
Sunset Rd SW19 . . . . .19 B3
Sunshine Way CR4 . . . . .40 F7
Sunstone Gr RH1 . . . . .119 E6
Sunvale Ave GU27 . . . . .207 D6
Sunvale Cl GU27 . . . . .207 D6
Surbiton Cres KT1, KT6 . . . . .37 E5
Surbiton Ct KT6 . . . . .37 D3
Surbiton Hall Cl KT1 . . . . .37 E5
Surbiton High Sch KT1 . . . . .37 E5
**Surbiton High Jun Sch
for Girls** KT1 . . . . .37 E5
Surbiton Hill Pk KT5 . . . . .38 A4
Surbiton Hill Rd KT6 . . . . .37 E4
Surbiton Hospl KT6 . . . . .37 E3
Surbiton Prep Sch KT6 . . . . .37 E4
Surbiton Rd
Camberley GU15 . . . . .47 A1
Kingston u T KT1 . . . . .37 E5
Surbiton Sta KT6 . . . . .37 E3
Surrey Ave GU15 . . . . .65 A4
Surrey Bsns Pk KT17 . . . . .76 E8
Surrey Gr SM1 . . . . .59 D7
Surrey Heath Mus GU15 . . . . . . .65 D6
Surrey Hills Ave KT20 . . . . .116 C4
Surrey Hills Way KT20 . . . . .116 C5
Surrey Inst of Art & Design
KT17 . . . . .76 E7
Surrey Inst of Art & Tech
KT18 . . . . .76 F6
**Surrey Inst of Art & Design
The** GU9 . . . . .125 B2
Surrey Lane CR2 . . . .
Surrey Lodge KT12 . . . . .54 B5
Surrey Mews SE27 . . . . .22 E4
Surrey Mount SE23 . . . . .23 B7
Surrey Rd BR4 . . . . .44 B1
Surrey Research Pk The
GU2 . . . . .129 D8

Surrey St CR0, CR9 . . . . .61 C7
Surrey Tower **5** SE20 . . . . .23 C1
Surrey Towers KT15 . . . . .52 C5
Surridge Ct GU19 . . . . .47 E2
Surrey Ctr SW17 . . . . .20 E3
Sussex Ave TW7 . . . . .5 E4
Sussex Cl Knaphill GU21 . . . . .68 C1
New Malden KT3 . . . . .38 E5
Reigate RH2 . . . . .139 D8
1 Twickenham TW1 . . . . .6 B1
Sussex Ct Addlestone KT15 . . . . .52 C5
Barnes SW13 . . . . .7 F5
Horsham RH13 . . . . .217 E1
Knaphill GU21 . . . . .68 C2
Sussex Gdns KT9 . . . . .56 D4
Sussex Ho TW9 . . . . .6 F5
Sussex Lodge RH12 . . . . .217 C4
Sussex Manor Bsns Pk
RH10 . . . . .182 A2
Sussex Pl KT3 . . . . .38 E5
Sussex Rd Croydon CR2 . . . . .61 D4
Knaphill GU21 . . . . .68 C1
Mitcham CR4 . . . . .41 E4
New Malden KT3 . . . . .38 E5
South Croydon CR2 . . . . .61 D4
Wallington SM5 . . . . .59 F4
West Wickham BR4 . . . . .44 B1
Sutherland Ave
Biggin Hill TN16 . . . . .83 E1
Guildford GU4 . . . . .109 E7
Hatton TW14 . . . . .4 A4
Sutherland Chase SL5 . . . . .28 F7
Sutherland Dr
Guildford GU1, GU4 . . . . .110 A4
Mitcham SW19 . . . . .40 D8
Sutherland Gdns
Mortlake SW14 . . . . .7 E4
North Cheam KT4 . . . . .39 B1
Sunbury TW16 . . . . .34 F7
Sutherland Gr
Putney SW18, SW19 . . . . .19 F8
Teddington TW11 . . . . .16 E3
Sutherland House TW10 . . . . . . .17 C6
Sutherland Rd Chiswick W4 . . . . .7 E8
Thornton Heath CR0 . . . . .42 A2
Sutton Arc SM1 . . . . .59 B5
Sutton Ave GU21 . . . . .88 E8
Sutton Cl BR3 . . . . .44 B8
Sutton Common Rd
Cheam SM3 . . . . .40 A1
Sutton SM1, SM3 . . . . .59 B8
Sutton Common Sta SM1 . . . . . .59 B8
Sutton Court Rd
Chiswick W4 . . . . .7 C8
Sutton SM1, SM2 . . . . .59 C4
Sutton Courtenay House
SW17 . . . . .20 D4
Sutton Ct Chiswick W4 . . . . .7 C8
East Molesey KT8 . . . . .35 F4
Penge SE19 . . . . .22 F1
Sutton SM2 . . . . .59 C4
Sutton Dene TW3 . . . . .5 B6
Sutton Gdns
Croydon CR0, SE25 . . . . .42 F4
Merstham RH1 . . . . .119 D6
Sutton Gr SM1 . . . . .59 D5
Sutton Gram Sch For Boys
SM1 . . . . .59 C5
Sutton Green Rd GU4 . . . . .89 F1
Sutton Hall TW5 . . . . .5 A7
Sutton High Sch For Girls
SM1 . . . . .59 B4
Sutton Hospl SM1 . . . . .59 B1
Sutton La
Abinger Common RH5 . . . . .155 C8
Banstead SM2, SM7 . . . . .78 B6
Brands Hill SL3 . . . . .1 B8
Hounslow TW3, TW4, TW5 . . . . . .4 F5
Sutton La S W4 . . . . .7 C8
Sutton Lodge GU11 . . . . .109 E1
Sutton Park Rd SM1, SM2 . . . . . .59 B4
Sutton Pl Brands Hill SL3 . . . . . . .1 B8
Peaslake RH5 . . . . .154 F8
Sutton Rd
Camberley GU15 . . . . .47 A1
Heston TW5 . . . . .5 A8
Sutton Sq TW5 . . . . .4 F6
Sutton Sta SM2 . . . . .59 C4
Sutton Way TW5 . . . . .4 F6
Swaby Rd SW17, SW18 . . . . .20 C6
Swaffield Prim Sch SW18 . . . . . .20 C8
Swaffield Rd SW18 . . . . .20 C8
Swail House **8** KT18 . . . . .76 D6
Swain Cl SW16, SW17 . . . . .21 B2
Swain Rd CR7 . . . . .42 C4
Swains Rd
CR4, SW17, SW19 . . . . .20 F1
Swale House **2** RH1 . . . . .119 A3
Swale Rd GU14 . . . . .84 E6
Swaledale RG12 . . . . .27 A4
Swaledale Cl RH11 . . . . .201 C3
Swallands Rd SE6 . . . . .24 A5
Swallow Cl Staines TW18 . . . . . .12 F4
Witley GU8 . . . . .170 E7
Swallow Gdns SW16 . . . . .21 D3
Swallow La RH5 . . . . .136 B1
Swallow Pk KT6 . . . . .56 F7
Swallow Rd RH11 . . . . .201 C8
Swallow Rise GU21 . . . . .68 C2
Swallowdale
New Addington CR0 . . . . .62 D2
Selsdon CR2 . . . . .81 C8
Swallowfield
Dormansland RH7 . . . . .165 A2
Thorpe GU25 . . . . .11 B2
Swallows Ct SE20 . . . . .23 D1
Swallowtail Rd RH12 . . . . .217 E6
Swan Barn Rd GU27 . . . . .208 D6

Swan Cl Croydon CR0 . . . . .42 E2
Feltham TW13 . . . . .15 E4
Swan Ct Guildford GU1 . . . . .109 D3
Leatherhead KT22 . . . . .95 B5
Swan Ctr SW17 . . . . .20 C5
Swan House GU47 . . . . .64 B7
Swan La Charlwood RH6 . . . . . . .180 F7
Guildford GU1 . . . . .130 D7
Sandhurst GU47 . . . . .64 B7
Swan Mill Gdns RH4 . . . . .115 D1
Swan Pl SW13 . . . . .7 F5
Swan Rd TW13 . . . . .15 E4
Swan Sq TW7 . . . . .217 C2
Swan St TW7 . . . . .6 B4
Swan Wlk Horsham RH12 . . . . . .217 C2
Oatlands Park TW17 . . . . .34 E2
Swancote Gn RG12 . . . . .27 B4
Swandrift TW18 . . . . .12 F1
Swann Way RH12 . . . . .216 E3
Swanns Meadow KT23 . . . . .94 A1
Swann Ghyll RH18 . . . . .206 E3
Swansea Rd TW14, TW6 . . . . .3 D1
Swanmore Sch KT12 . . . . .35 C1
Swanton Gdns SW19 . . . . .19 D7
Swanworth La GU5 . . . . .115 B7
Swayne's La GU1 . . . . .110 E1
Swaynesland Rd RH8 . . . . .123 F1
Swaything House SW15 . . . . .7 F1
Swedish Sch SW13 . . . . .7 F8
Sweeps Ditch Cl TW18 . . . . .13 B1
Sweeps La TW20 . . . . .11 F3
Sweet Gr GU5 . . . . .154 E8
Sweetbriar RG45 . . . . .45 A7
Sweetwater Cl GU5 . . . . .152 D4
Sweetwater La
Enton Green GU8 . . . . .171 B2
Shamley Green GU5 . . . . .152 D4
Swievelands Rd TN16 . . . . .83 C1
Swift Ct SM2 . . . . .59 B3
Swift La Crawley RH11 . . . . .201 C8
Windlesham GU19 . . . . .47 F3
Swift Rd Feltham TW13 . . . . .15 E4
Heath End GU9 . . . . .125 C7
Swift's Cl GU10 . . . . .126 B1
Swiftsden Way BR1 . . . . .24 E2
Swinburne Cres CR0 . . . . .43 C3
Swindon Rd Harlington TW6 . . . . .3 C2
Horsham RH12 . . . . .217 B4
Swinfield Cl TW13 . . . . .15 E4
Swingate Rd GU9 . . . . .146 D8
Swinley County Prim Sch
SL5 . . . . .29 A4
Swinley Forest Golf Club
SL5 . . . . .28 F2
Swiss Cl GU10 . . . . .146 A4
Swissland Hill RH19, RH7 . . . . .185 E7
Switchback La
Rowledge GU10 . . . . .145 F4
Rowledge GU10 . . . . .146 A3
Sycamore Ave GU16 . . . . .218 C6
Sycamore Cl
Carshalton SM5 . . . . .59 F6
Crawley RH11 . . . . .181 C1
Feltham TW13 . . . . .15 A5
Fetcham KT22 . . . . .94 F5
Frimley GU16 . . . . .65 E1
Guildford GU4 . . . . .64 B8
Sycamore Ct
Farncombe GU7 . . . . .150 E8
Forest Hill SE26 . . . . .23 C4
Hounslow TW4 . . . . .4 E3
Ottershaw KT16 . . . . .51 C5
8 West Norwood SW16 . . . . . . .22 A3
Sycamore Gr
Kingston u T KT3 . . . . .38 E6
Penge SE20 . . . . .23 A1
Sycamore Lodge **7** TW16 . . . .14 F1
Sycamore Rd
Farnborough GU14 . . . . .85 D2
Guildford GU1 . . . . .109 D1
Wimbledon SW19, SW20 . . . . . . .19 C2
Sycamore Rise
Banstead KT17, SM7 . . . . .77 D5
Bracknell RG12 . . . . .27 D6
Sycamore Way TW11 . . . . .17 C2
Sycamore Wlk
Englefield Green TW20 . . . . .11 B2
Reigate RH2 . . . . .139 C6
Sycamores The
Blackwater GU17 . . . . .64 B5
Farnborough GU14 . . . . .85 D3
Sydenham Ave SE26 . . . . .23 B3
**Sydenham High Sch for
Girls** SE26 . . . . .23 B4
Sydenham Hill SE21, SE22,
SE23, SE26, SE19 . . . . .23 A4
Sydenham Hill Sta SE21 . . . . . . .22 F5
Sydenham House **16** KT6 . . . . .37 D2
Sydenham Ind Est SE26 . . . . .23 F3
Sydenham Park Mansions
SE26 . . . . .23 C5
Sydenham Park Rd
SE23, SE26 . . . . .23 C5
Sydenham Pk SE26 . . . . .23 C5
Sydenham Rd Croydon CR0 . . . . .42 D2
Forest Hill SE26, SE6 . . . . .23 D3
Guildford GU1 . . . . .130 E8
Thornton Heath CR0 . . . . .42 D2

Sydenham Rise SE23 . . . . .23 B6
Sydenham Sch SE26 . . . . .23 B5
Sydenham Sec Sch SE26 . . . . . . .23 B5
Sydenham Sta SE26 . . . . .23 C4
Sydenham Station App
SE26 . . . . .23 C4
Sydmons Ct SE23 . . . . .23 C8
Sydney Ave CR8 . . . . .79 F7
Sydney Cl RG45 . . . . .45 C7
Sydney Cotts KT10 . . . . .55 F4
Sydney Cres TW15 . . . . .14 B2
Sydney Pl GU1 . . . . .130 F8
Sydney Rd
East Bedfont TW14 . . . . .15 A7
Guildford GU1 . . . . .130 F8
Merton SW20 . . . . .39 D7
Richmond TW10, TW9 . . . . .6 E3
Sutton SM1 . . . . .59 A6
Teddington TW11 . . . . .16 F3
Sydney Terr KT10 . . . . .55 F4
Sydney Wood Forest Wlks
GU6 . . . . .193 C2
Sylva Cl **3** SW15 . . . . .19 D8
Sylvan Cl Limpsfield RH8 . . . . . .123 B6
South Croydon CR2 . . . . .62 B1
Woking GU22 . . . . .70 B2
Sylvan Gdns KT6 . . . . .37 D2
Sylvan Hill SE19 . . . . .42 E8
Sylvan Rd Crawley RH10 . . . . . .202 A4
South Norwood SE19 . . . . .42 F8
Sylvan Ridge GU47 . . . . .45 A1
Sylvan Way Coney Hall BR4 . . . . .63 E6
Redhill RH1 . . . . .140 A8
Sylvanus RG12 . . . . .26 F2
Sylvaways Cl GU6 . . . . .175 A3
Sylverdale Rd
Croydon CR0, CR9 . . . . .61 B7
Purley CR8 . . . . .80 B6
Sylvia Cl GU24 . . . . .68 A4
Syon Gate Way
Brentford TW8 . . . . .6 A7
Hounslow TW7, TW8 . . . . .6 A7
Syon Ho & Pk TW8 . . . . .6 C6
Syon La Brentford TW7 . . . . .5 F8
Brentford TW7, TW8 . . . . .6 A8
Hounslow TW7 . . . . .6 A7
Syon Lane Sta TW7 . . . . .6 A7
Syon Park Cotts TW8 . . . . .6 C6
Syon Park Gdns TW7 . . . . .5 F7
Syon Pl GU14 . . . . .85 D4
Sythwood GU21 . . . . .69 B2
Sythwood Cty Prim Sch
GU21 . . . . .69 B3
Szabo Cres GU3 . . . . .107 B1

Tamworth Manor High Sch
. . . . .41 D6
Tamworth Pk CR4 . . . . .41 B6
Tamworth Pl **3** CR0, CR9 . . . . .61 C8
Tamworth Rd CR0, CR9 . . . . .61 C8
Tanbridge House Sch
RH12 . . . . .216 F2
Tanbridge Pk RH12 . . . . .217 B1
Tanbridge Pl RH12 . . . . .217 B1
Tandem Ctr SW19 . . . . .40 D8
Tandridge Ct
Caterham CR3 . . . . .101 A5
Sutton SM2 . . . . .59 B4
Tandridge Gdns CR2 . . . . .81 A6
Tandridge Golf Course
RH9 . . . . .122 B4
Tandridge La
RH7, RH8, RH9 . . . . .143 B4
Tandridge Rd CR6 . . . . .101 B8
Tandridgehill La
Tandridge RH9 . . . . .121 F6
Woldingham RH9 . . . . .121 F6
Tanfield Ct RH12 . . . . .217 B2
Tanfield Rd CR0, CR9 . . . . .61 C6
Tangier Ct GU11 . . . . .104 F2
Tangier Rd Guildford GU1 . . . . . .131 A8
Mortlake TW10 . . . . .7 B4
Tangier Way KT20 . . . . .77 E1
Tangier Wood KT20 . . . . .77 E1
Tangle Oak RH19 . . . . .184 E4
Tanglewood Cl
Longcross KT16 . . . . .50 B7
South Croydon CR0 . . . . .62 C7
Woking GU22 . . . . .70 D3
Tanglewood Ride GU24 . . . . .67 D7
Tanglewood Way TW13 . . . . .15 B5
Tangley Dr RG41 . . . . .25 B4
Tangley Gr SW15 . . . . .18 F8
Tangley La GU3 . . . . .108 F6
Tangley Park Rd TW12 . . . . .15 F3
Tanglyn Ave TW17 . . . . .34 B4
Tangmere Gr KT2 . . . . .17 D3
Tangmere Rd RH11 . . . . .200 F6
Tanhouse La RG41 . . . . .25 A5
Tanhouse Rd RH8 . . . . .122 E3
Tanhurst House **2** SW2 . . . . . . .21 E8
Tanhurst La RH5 . . . . .155 E2
Tank Rd GU15 . . . . .64 F5
Tankerton Rd KT6 . . . . .56 F8
Tankerton Terr CR0 . . . . .41 F3
Tankerville Rd SW16 . . . . .21 E1
Tanner House **1** SW19 . . . . . . .40 C8
Tanner's Ct RH3 . . . . .137 C5
Tanner's Hill RH3 . . . . .137 B8
Tanners Cl KT12 . . . . .35 B3
Tanners Dean KT22 . . . . .95 C5
Tanners La GU27 . . . . .208 C7
Tanners Meadow RH3 . . . . .137 B5
Tanners Yd GU19 . . . . .47 E3
Tannersfield GU4 . . . . .130 C1
Tannery Cl
Beckenham BR3, CR0 . . . . .43 D4
Slinfold RH13 . . . . .215 D3
Tannery Cotts GU5 . . . . .133 C4
Tannery La Send GU23 . . . . .90 E5
Send Marsh GU23 . . . . .90 E5
Shafford GU5 . . . . .151 F8
Tannery The RH1 . . . . .118 F1
Tannsfeld Rd SE26 . . . . .23 D3
Tansy Cl GU4 . . . . .110 C3
Tantallon Rd SW12 . . . . .21 A7
Tanyard Ave RH19 . . . . .206 A8
Tanyard Ct Crawley RH10 . . . . .202 C3
Horsham RH13 . . . . .217 E1
Tanyard Way RH6 . . . . .161 B4
Tapestry Cl SM2 . . . . .59 B3
Taplow Ct CR4 . . . . .40 E5
Tapner's Rd RH2 . . . . .137 F3
Tapping Cl **5** KT2 . . . . .18 A1
Tara Ct BR3 . . . . .44 B7
Tara Pk CR5 . . . . .98 F7
Taragon Cl GU2 . . . . .109 A5
Tarbat Ct **3** GU47 . . . . .64 D8
Target Cl TW14 . . . . .3 E1
Tarham Ct RH6 . . . . .160 E5
Tarleton Gdns SE23 . . . . .23 B7
Tarmac Way UB7 . . . . .2 B7
Tarn Cl GU14 . . . . .84 E2
Tarn Rd GU26 . . . . .188 E3
Tarnbrook Way RG12 . . . . .27 E2
Tarquin House SE26 . . . . .23 A4
Tarragon Cl GU14 . . . . .84 C4
Tarragon Dr GU2 . . . . .109 A5
Tarragon Gr SE26 . . . . .23 D2
Tarrington Cl SW16 . . . . .21 D5
Tartar Hill KT11 . . . . .73 B6
Tartar Rd KT11 . . . . .73 C6
Tasker Cl UB7 . . . . .3 C7
Tasman Ct TW16 . . . . .14 E1
Tatchbury House SW15 . . . . .7 F1
Tate Cl KT22 . . . . .95 C4
Tate Rd SM1 . . . . .59 A5
Tate's Way RH12 . . . . .217 D7
Tatham Ct RH11 . . . . .201 B1
Tatsfield Cty Prim Sch
TN16 . . . . .103 D6
Tatsfield La TN16 . . . . .103 F6
Tattenham Cnr Rd KT18 . . . . .77 A1
Tattenham Corner Rd
KT18 . . . . .77 A1
Tattenham Cres KT18 . . . . .77 B1
Tattenham Gr KT18 . . . . .97 B8
Tattenham Way KT18, KT20 . . . .77 C2

Tattersall Cl RG40 . . . . 25 E5
Taunton Cl
Caterham CR3 . . . . 100 F4
Hounslow TW3 . . . . 5 C5
Wimbledon SW20 . . . . 39 B7
Taunton Cl SM3 . . . . 40 A1
Taunton La CR5 . . . . 100 B8
Tavern Cl SM5 . . . . 40 E2
Tavistock Cl TW18 . . . . 13 D1
Tavistock Cres CR4 . . . . 41 E5
Tavistock Cl **1** CR0 . . . . . . 42 D1
Tavistock Gdns GU14 . . . . . 85 B7
Tavistock Cl CR0 . . . . 42 D2
Tavistock Rd
Beckenham BR2 . . . . 44 F5
Carshalton SM5 . . . . 40 D1
Croydon CR0 . . . . 42 D1
Tavistock Wlk SM5 . . . . 40 D1
Tavy House **3** RH1 . . . . . . 118 F2
Tawfield RG12 . . . . 26 E2
Tawny Cl TW13 . . . . 15 A5
Tay Cl GU14 . . . . 84 E6
Tayben Ave TW2 . . . . 5 E1
Tayles Hill KT17 . . . . 57 F1
Taylor Ave TW9 . . . . 7 B5
Taylor Cl
Hounslow TW3 . . . . 5 C6
Taylor Cl SE20 . . . . 43 C7
Taylor House **10** SW2 . . . . 22 A7
Taylor Rd Aldershot GU11 . . 105 D7
Ashtead KT21 . . . . 75 D2
Mitcham CR4, SW19 . . . . . 20 E1
Wallington SM6 . . . . 60 B5
Taylor Wlk RH11 . . . . 201 C6
Taylor's La SE26 . . . . 23 B4
Taylors Cres GU6 . . . . 174 F3
Taylors Ct TW13 . . . . 15 A6
Taymount Grange SE23 . . . 23 C6
Taymount Rise SE23 . . . . . 23 C6
Taynton Dr RH1 . . . . 119 D6
Teal Cl Horsham RH12 . . . 217 C5
Selsdon CR2 . . . . 81 D8
Teal Ct Dorking RH4 . . . . . 136 A8
Wallington SM6 . . . . 60 C5
Teal Pl SM1 . . . . 58 F5
Tealing Dr KT19 . . . . 57 D6
Teasel Cl Crawley RH11 . . 201 B3
Croydon CR0 . . . . 43 D1
Teazlewood Pk KT22 . . . . . 75 A1
Tebbit Cl RG12 . . . . 27 D7
Tebbs House **14** SW2 . . . 22 A8
Teck Cl TW7 . . . . 6 A5
Tedder Cl KT9 . . . . 56 C5
Tedder Rd CR2 . . . . 62 D2
Teddington Cl KT19 . . . . . . 57 D1
Teddington Memorial Hospl
TW11 . . . . 16 E2
Teddington Park Rd TW11 . 16 F4
Teddington Pk TW11 . . . . . 16 F3
Teddington Sch TW11 . . . . 17 C2
Teddington Sta TW11 . . . . . 17 A2
Tedham La RH9 . . . . 163 B7
Tees Cl GU14 . . . . 84 E6
Teesdale RH11 . . . . 201 C3
Teesdale Gdns
Isleworth TW7 . . . . 6 A6
South Norwood SE25 . . . . . 42 E7
Teevan Cl CR0 . . . . 43 A2
Teevan Rd CR0, CR9 . . . . . 43 A2
Tegg's La GU22 . . . . 70 F3
Tekels Ave GU15 . . . . 65 D4
Tekels Ct GU15 . . . . 65 E4
Tekels Way GU15 . . . . 65 F3
Telconia Cl GU35 . . . . 187 C4
Telegraph La KT10 . . . . 55 F5
Telegraph Rd SW15 . . . . . . 19 B8
Telegraph Track SM5, SM6 . 60 A1
Telfei House **3** SE21 . . . . 22 E4
Telferscot Jun Mix & Inf
Sch SW12 . . . . 21 D7
Telferscot Rd SW12 . . . . . . 21 D7
Telford Ave
Crowthorne RG45 . . . . 45 C8
Streatham SW12, SW2 . . . . 21 E7
Telford Avenue Mansions
SW2 . . . . 21 E7
Telford Cl SE19 . . . . 22 F2
Telford Ct **2** GU1 . . . . . . 130 F8
Telford Ct KT12 . . . . 35 C2
Telford Parade Mansions
SW2 . . . . 21 E7
Telford Pl RH10 . . . . 201 E5
Telford Rd TW4 . . . . 16 A8
Telham Ct **5** RH11 . . . . . 200 F3
Tellisford KT10 . . . . 55 B6
Temperley Rd SW12 . . . . . . 21 A8
Tempest Rd TW20 . . . . 12 C2
Templar Cl GU47 . . . . 64 A8
Templar Ct CR0 . . . . 62 A8
Templar Pl TW12 . . . . 16 A1
Temple Ave CR0 . . . . 62 F7
Temple Bar Rd GU21 . . . . . 88 F8
Temple Cl **3** RH10 . . . . . 202 D5
Temple Cl **10** TW10 . . . . . . 6 E2
Temple Field Cl KT15 . . . . . 52 B4
Temple Gdns SW18 . . . . . . 32 F8
Temple La RH5 . . . . 178 F5
Temple Market KT13 . . . . . 53 B6
Temple Rd Biggin Hill TN16 . 83 D2
Croydon CR0 . . . . 61 D6
Epsom KT19 . . . . 76 D7
Hounslow TW3 . . . . 5 B3
Richmond TW9 . . . . 6 F5
Temple Sheen SW14 . . . . . . 7 C3

Temple Sheen Rd SW14 . . . . 7 C3
Temple Way Bracknell RG42 . 26 E8
Carshalton SM1 . . . . 59 E7
Temple Wood Dr RH1 . . . . 118 F4
Temple's Cl GU10 . . . . 126 C1
Templecombe Mews
GU22 . . . . 70 B3
Templecombe Way SM4 . . . 39 E4
Templecroft TW15 . . . . 14 D2
Templedene BR2 . . . . 44 D7
Templedene Ave TW18 . . . . 13 C2
Templeman Cl CR8 . . . . . . 80 B3
Templemere KT13 . . . . 53 D7
Templeton Cl CR7, SE19 . . 42 D8
Templewood House RH1 . . 118 F4
Ten Acre GU21 . . . . 69 A1
Ten Acre La TW20 . . . . 32 C7
Ten Acres KT22 . . . . 94 D3
Ten Acres Cl GU22 . . . . . . 94 D3
Tenbury Ct SW12 . . . . 21 D7
Tenby Dr SL5 . . . . 29 D4
Tenby Rd GU16 . . . . 86 A8
Tenchley's La
Limpsfield RH8 . . . . 123 D4
The Chart RH8 . . . . 123 E2
Tenham Ave SW2 . . . . 21 D6
Tenniel Cl GU2 . . . . 109 B3
Tennison Cl CR5 . . . . 100 B7
Tennison Rd Croydon SE25 . 42 F4
South Norwood SE25 . . . . . 42 F4
Tennyson Ave
Twickenham TW1 . . . . 16 F7
West Barnes KT3 . . . . 39 B4
Tennyson Cl
Crawley RH10 . . . . 202 B8
Feltham TW14 . . . . 4 A1
Horsham RH12 . . . . 217 E6
Tennyson Ct **8** TW10 . . . . 17 D4
Tennyson Rd
Addlestone KT15 . . . . 52 E6
Ashford TW15 . . . . 13 E3
Hounslow TW3 . . . . 5 C5
Penge SE20 . . . . 23 D1
Wimbledon SW19 . . . . 20 C2
Tennyson Rise RH19 . . . . 205 C8
Tennyson's La
Haslemere GU27 . . . . 208 E4
Lurgashall GU27 . . . . 209 A2
Tennysons GU27 . . . . 208 E4
Tennysons Ridge GU27 . . . 208 E5
Tensing Ct TW19 . . . . 13 E7
Tenterden Gdns CR0 . . . . . 43 A2
Tenterden Rd CR0 . . . . 43 A2
Tern Rd RH11 . . . . 200 D5
Terra Cotta Rd RH9 . . . . . 142 C5
Terrace Gdns SW13 . . . . . . 7 F5
Terrace La TW10 . . . . 6 E1
Terrace Rd KT12 . . . . 35 B3
Terrace The
Addlestone KT15 . . . . 52 E5
Ascot SL5 . . . . 29 D4
Barnes SW13, SW14 . . . . . 7 E5
Camberley GU15 . . . . 65 A5
Crowthorne RG45 . . . . 65 A5
Mortlake SW13, SW14 . . . . 7 E5
Old Woking GU22 . . . . 90 A6
Wokingham RG40 . . . . 25 B6
Terrapin Ct SW17 . . . . 21 B5
Terrapin Rd SW17 . . . . 21 B5
Terrapins KT6 . . . . 37 D2
Terry House SW2 . . . . 22 A7
Terry Rd RH11 . . . . 201 B1
Testard Rd GU2 . . . . 130 C7
Testers Cl RH8 . . . . 123 B3
Teviot Cl GU2 . . . . 109 B4
Tewkesbury Ave SE23 . . . . 23 B8
Tewkesbury Cl KT14 . . . . . . 71 D8
Tewkesbury Rd SM5 . . . . . 40 D1
Thackeray Cl Isleworth TW7 . 6 A5
Wimbledon SW19 . . . . 19 D1
Thackeray Manor SM1 . . . . 59 C5
Thackery Lodge TW14 . . . . . 3 D1
Thakeham Cl SE26 . . . . . . 23 B3
Thames Ave KT16 . . . . 33 A6
Thames Bank SW14 . . . . . . 7 C5
Thames Cl Chertsey KT16 . . 33 C2
East Molesey TW12 . . . . . . 36 B7
Farnborough GU14 . . . . . . 84 E6
Thames Ct KT8 . . . . 36 A6
Thames Ditton Cty Fst Sch
KT7 . . . . 36 F2
Thames Ditton Hospl
Golf Club KT10 . . . . 55 D8
Thames Ditton Hospl KT7 . . 36 F2
Thames Ditton Island KT7 . 37 A4
Thames Ditton Jun Sch
KT7 . . . . 36 F2
Thames Ditton Sta KT7 . . . 36 F2
Thames Eyot **7** TW1 . . . . 17 A7
Thames Haven KT6 . . . . . . 37 D4
Thames Link House **6** TW9 . 6 E3
Thames Mead KT12 . . . . . . 35 A2
Thames Meadow
East Molesey KT8 . . . . 36 A6
Lower Halliford KT12, TW17 . 34 E1
Thames Rd Brentford W4 . . . 7 B8
Chiswick W4 . . . . 7 B8
Thames Side
Kingston u T KT1 . . . . 37 D8
Laleham KT16, TW18 . . . . . 33 C4
Staines TW18 . . . . 12 F2
Thames Ditton KT7 . . . . . . 37 B3
Thames St
East Molesey TW12 . . . . . . 36 B7
Kingston u T KT1, KT2 . . . . 37 D7
Staines TW18 . . . . 12 F3
Sunbury TW16 . . . . 35 B6
Walton-on-T KT12 . . . . 34 F2

Thames St continued
Weybridge KT13 . . . . 53 B7
Thames View House TW12 . 35 A3
Thames Village W4 . . . . 7 C6
Thamesfield Ct TW17 . . . . . 34 C2
Thamesgate TW18 . . . . 33 B8
Thamesgate Cl TW10 . . . . . 17 B4
Thameside TW11 . . . . 17 D1
Thamesmead Sch TW17 . . 34 D3
Thamespoint TW11 . . . . . . 17 D1
Thamesvale Cl TW3 . . . . . . 5 A5
Thanescroft Gdns CR0 . . . . 61 E7
Thanet House **1** SM7 . . . . 22 B5
Thanet Pl CR0 . . . . 61 C6
Tharp Rd SM6 . . . . 60 D5
Thatcher Cl RH10 . . . . 201 D3
Thatchers Cl Horley RH6 . . 161 B5
Horsham RH12 . . . . 217 E4
Thatchers La GU4 . . . . 108 E8
Thatchers Way TW7 . . . . . . 5 D2
Thaxted Pl **7** SW20 . . . . . 19 D1
Thayers Farm Rd BR3 . . . . 43 E8
Theal Cl GU47 . . . . 64 D8
Thelma Gr TW11 . . . . 17 A2
Thelton Ave RH12 . . . . 216 D3
Theobald Rd CR0, CR9 . . . . 61 B8
Theobalds Way GU16 . . . . . 66 C3
Thepps Cl RH1 . . . . 140 F6
Therapia La
Thornton Heath CR0 . . . . . 41 E3
Wallington CR0, CR4 . . . . . 41 D2
Wallington CR0 . . . . 41 D2
Theresa's Wlk CR2 . . . . . . 61 D2
Therfield Sch KT22 . . . . . . 95 A8
Thesiger Rd BR3, SE20 . . . 23 D1
Thetford Cl SE21 . . . . 23 B6
Thetford Rd Ashford TW15 . 13 E5
New Malden KT3 . . . . 38 E3
Thetford Wlk **7** SW20 . . . . 7 A8
Theydon Cl RH10 . . . . 202 A4
Thibet Rd GU47 . . . . 64 C8
Thicket Cres SM1 . . . . 59 C6
Thicket Gr SE20 . . . . 23 A1
Thicket Rd
Penge SE19, SE20 . . . . . . 23 B1
Sutton SM1 . . . . 59 C6
Thickthorne La TW18 . . . . . 13 C1
Third Cl KT8 . . . . 36 C5
Third Cross Rd TW2 . . . . . . 16 D6
Thirlmere Cl
Farnborough GU14 . . . . . . 84 E4
Thorpe Lea TW20 . . . . 12 B1
Thirlmere House TW1 . . . . . 5 F2
Thirlmere Rd
Crawley RH11 . . . . 200 D4
Streatham SW16 . . . . 21 D4
Thirlmere Rise **1** 24 F2
Thirlmere Wlk GU15 . . . . . 66 D4
Thirsk Rd Mitcham CR4 . . . 21 A1
South Norwood SE25 . . . . . 42 D5
Thistle Way RH6 . . . . 162 C3
Thistlecroft Rd KT12 . . . . . 54 C6
Thistledene
Thames Ditton KT7 . . . . . . 36 E3
West Byfleet KT14 . . . . 70 F6
Thistledown Vale RH14 . . . 212 D3
Thistlewood Cres CR0 . . . . 82 D7
Thistleworth Cl TW7 . . . . . . 5 D7
Thistley La GU6 . . . . 174 D3
Thomas Ave CR3 . . . . 100 C6
Thomas Becket Jun Mix
& Inf Sch SE25 . . . . 43 A4
Thomas Bennett Com Coll
RH10 . . . . 201 D3
Thomas Dean Rd SE26 . . . 23 E4
Thomas' La SE6 . . . . 24 A8
Thomas Moore House
RH2 . . . . 118 C1
Thomas More RC High Sch
CR8 . . . . 61 A1
Thomas Pooley Ct KT6 . . . 37 E2
Thomas Rd GU11 . . . . 105 D7
Thomas Wall Cl SM1 . . . . . 59 B5
Thompson Ave TW9 . . . . . . 7 A4
Thompson Cl **14** SM3 . . . . 201 B1
Thompson's La GU24 . . . . . 49 D2
Thompsons Cl GU24 . . . . . 87 D4
Thomson Cres CR0 . . . . . . 42 A1
Thornton Chase GU47 . . . . 64 E6
Thorburn Way SW19 . . . . . 40 D8
Thornhill Gdns KT7 . . . . . . 37 B2
Thornhill Rd KT7 . . . . 37 B2
Thorley Cl KT14 . . . . 71 A5
Thorley Gdns KT14 . . . . . . 71 A5
Thorn Bank GU2 . . . . 130 A7
Thorn Cl GU10 . . . . 145 F4
Thorn Rd GU10 . . . . 146 A5
Thornash Cl GU21 . . . . 69 C4
Thornash Rd GU21 . . . . . . 69 C4
Thornash Way GU21 . . . . . 69 C4
Thornbank Cl TW19 . . . . 2 A2
Thornbury Ave TW7 . . . . . . 5 D7
Thornbury Cl RG45 . . . . . . 45 B5
Thornbury Ct Hounslow TW7 . 5 E7
Whyteleafe CR3 . . . . 100 F7
Thornbury Rd TW7 . . . . 5 D6
Thorncombe St GU5 . . . . . 151 E2
Thorncroft TW20 . . . . 32 B6
Thorncroft Cl CR5 . . . . 100 A8
Thorncroft Rd SM1 . . . . . . 59 B5
Thorndean St SW18 . . . . . 20 C6
Thorndon Gdns KT19 . . . . . 57 E6
Thorndown La GU20 . . . . . 48 D3
Thorndyke Cl RH10 . . . . . 202 D5
Thorne Cl Crowthorne RG45 . 45 A7
Littleton TW15 . . . . 14 C1
Thorne St SW13, SW14 . . . 7 E4

Thorne's Cl BR3 . . . . 44 C6
Thorneloe Gdns CR0, CR9 . 61 B5
Thorneycroft Cl KT12 . . . . . 35 C3
Thornfield Gn GU17 . . . . . . 64 F3
Thornfield Rd SM7 . . . . 78 A2
Thornhill RG12 . . . . 27 E5
Thornhill Ave KT6 . . . . 56 E8
Thornhill Cres GU11 . . . . . 105 C3
Thornhill Rd
Aldershot GU11 . . . . 105 D4
Surbiton KT6 . . . . 56 F8
Thornton Heath CR0 . . . . . 42 C2
Thornhill Way TW17 . . . . . . 34 A4
Thornlaw Rd SE27 . . . . 22 B4
Thornleas Pl KT24 . . . . 92 E1
Thornsbeach Rd SE6 . . . . . 24 C7
Thornsett Pl SE20 . . . . 43 B7
Thornsett Rd Penge SE20 . 43 B7
Wandsworth SW18 . . . . . . 20 B7
Thornsett Terr SE20 . . . . . 43 B7
Thornton Ave
Streatham SW2 . . . . 21 D7
Thornton Heath CR0 . . . . . 41 F3
Thornton Cl Guildford GU2 . 109 A4
Horley RH6 . . . . 160 E3
Thornton Cres CR5 . . . . . 100 A8
Thornton Dene BR3 . . . . . . 44 A7
Thornton Gdns SW12 . . . . 21 D7
Thornton Heath Sta CR7 . . 42 C5
Thornton Hill SW19 . . . . . . 19 E1
Thornton Pl RH6 . . . . 160 F3
Thornton Rd
Carshalton SM5 . . . . 40 D1
Mortlake SW14 . . . . 7 D4
Streatham SW12, SW2 . . . 21 D7
Thornton Heath CR0,
CR7, CR9 . . . . 41 F3
Wimbledon SW19 . . . . 19 D1
Thornton Rd E
Wimbledon SW19 . . . . 19 D2
Wimbledon SW19 . . . . 19 D2
Thornton Row CR7 . . . . . . 42 A4
Thornycroft Ct TW9 . . . . . . 6 F5
Thornyhurst Rd GU16 . . . . 86 A4
Thorold Cl CR0, CR2 . . . . . 62 D1
Thorold House **6** SW2 . . . 21 E8
Thorold Rd GU9 . . . . 125 C3
Thoroughfare The KT20 . . 97 A3
Thorpe By-Pass
KT16, TW20 . . . . 32 B6
Thorpe C of E Fst Sch
TW20 . . . . 32 B6
Thorpe Cl
New Addington CR0 . . . . . . 82 B8
Wokingham RG41 . . . . 25 A3
Thorpe Ind Est TW20 . . . . . 32 C8
Thorpe Ind Pk TW20 . . . . . 32 C8
Thorpe Lea Prim Sch
TW20 . . . . 12 D2
Thorpe Lea Rd
Egham TW20 . . . . 12 C2
Thorpe Lea TW20 . . . . 12 C2
Thorpe Park TW20 . . . . 32 E5
Thorpe Rd Chertsey KT16 . . 32 D4
Egham TW18, TW20 . . . . . 12 D3
Kingston u T KT2 . . . . 17 E1
Thorpes Cl GU2 . . . . 109 A4
Thorpeside Cl TW18, TW20 . 32 E7
Thorpewood Ave
SE23, SE26 . . . . 23 B6
Thorsden Cl GU22 . . . . 89 E8
Thorsden Ct **10** GU22 . . . . 69 E1
Thorsden Way **2** SE19 . . . 22 E3
Thrale Almhouses SW16 . . 21 C3
Thrale Rd SW16 . . . . 21 C3
Three Acres RH12 . . . . . . 217 A1
Three Arch Rd RH1 . . . . . 140 A5
Three Bridges Cty Fst Sch
RH10 . . . . 202 A7
Three Bridges Cty Mid Sch
RH10 . . . . 202 A6
Three Bridges Rd RH10 . . 202 A6
Three Bridges Sta RH10 . . 202 B6
Three Gates GU1 . . . . 110 E3
Three Gates La GU27 . . . . 208 E8
Three Mile Rd GU6, RH5 . 155 A2
Three Pears Rd GU1 . . . . . 110 E1
Three Stiles Rd GU9 . . . . 124 F3
Three Ways GU10 . . . . 166 D6
Threestile Rd RH12 . . . . . 197 F1
Threshfield RG12 . . . . 27 A4
Thriffwood SE23, SE26 . . . 23 D5
Thrift Vale GU4 . . . . 110 D4
Thrigby Rd KT9 . . . . 56 F4
Throat Handpost Cnr The
RG40 . . . . 25 A1
Throwley Rd SM1 . . . . 59 B5
Throwley Way SM1 . . . . . . 59 B5
Thrupp Cl CR4 . . . . 41 B7
Thrupps Ave KT12 . . . . 54 D5
Thrupps La KT12 . . . . 54 D5
Thundery Hill GU10 . . . . . 126 F4
Thurbans Rd GU9 . . . . 146 A7
Thurbarn Rd SE6 . . . . 24 B8
Thurbarns Hill RH5 . . . . . 157 C1
Thurby Rd SE27 . . . . 22 A4
Thurleigh Rd SW11, SW12 . 20 F8
Thurleston Ave SM4 . . . . . 39 E4
Thurlestone Cl TW17 . . . . . 34 C3
Thurlestone Par **7** TW17 . . 34 C3
Thurlestone Rd SE27 . . . . . 22 A5
Thurlow Hill SE21 . . . . 22 C6
Thurlow House **11** SW2 . . . 21 F8
Thurlow Park Rd
Dulwich SE21, SE24 . . . . . 22 C6
West Norwood SE21, SE24 . 22 C6
Thurlow Park Sch SE27 . . . 22 B6

Thurlow Towers SE27 . . . . . 22 A6
Thurlow Wlk GU6 . . . . 174 E1
Thurlton Ct GU21 . . . . 69 E3
Thurnby Ct TW2 . . . . 16 E1
Thurne Way RH12 . . . . . . 214 D6
Thurnham Way KT20 . . . . . 97 C6
Thursby Rd GU21 . . . . 69 A1
Thursley Cres CR0 . . . . 63 D4
Thursley Gdns SW19 . . . . . 19 D7
Thursley House
1 Kingston u T KT2 . . . . . 18 B2
2 Streatham SW2 . . . . . . 21 F8
Thursley Rd
Churt GU10, GU8 . . . . 168 C2
Thursley GU8, GU10 . . . . . 169 B8
Thurso St SW17 . . . . 20 C4
Thurstan Rd SW20 . . . . . . 19 B1
Thurston House BR3 . . . . . 24 B3
Thurza Ct TW7 . . . . 5 F6
Thyme Ct
Farnborough GU14 . . . . . . 84 C4
Guildford GU4 . . . . 110 B4
Tibbet's Cnr SW19 . . . . . . 19 E8
Tibbet's Ride SW19 . . . . . . 19 E7
Tibbets Cl SW19 . . . . 19 D7
Ticehurst Cl RH10 . . . . . . 202 E6
Ticehurst Rd SE23 . . . . . . 23 E6
Tichborne Cl GU17 . . . . . . 64 C6
Tichborne Pl GU12 . . . . . . 126 C2
Tichbourne Cl GU16 . . . . . 65 F3
Tichmarsh KT19 . . . . 57 C1
Tidenham Gdns CR0 . . . . . 61 E7
Tideswell Rd CR0 . . . . 63 A8
Tideway Cl TW10 . . . . 17 C4
Tideway Yd SW13 . . . . 7 E5
Tidwells Lea RG12 . . . . 27 E3
Tiepigs La
Coney Hall BR2, BR4 . . . . . 44 F1
Hayes BR2, BR4 . . . . 44 F1
Tierney Ct **1** CR0 . . . . 61 F7
Tierney Rd SW2 . . . . 21 E7
Tierney Terr SW2 . . . . 21 E7
Tiffin Girls' Sch KT2 . . . . . . 17 F3
Tiffin Sch KT2 . . . . 37 F7
Tilburstow Cotts RH9 . . . . 121 C2
Tilburstow Hill Rd
Blindley Heath RH9 . . . . . 142 C2
South Godstone RH9 . . . . 142 C1
Tile Barn Cl GU14 . . . . . . 85 A4
Tilehouse Rd GU4 . . . . . . 130 E5
Tilehurst La
Betchworth RH3, RH5 . . . . 136 F7
Dorking RH3, RH5 . . . . . . 136 F7
Tilehurst Rd Cheam SM3 . . 58 E4
Wandsworth SW17, SW18 . 20 D7
Tiler's Way RH2 . . . . 139 C5
Tilford Ave CR0 . . . . 63 C3
Tilford Gdns SW19 . . . . . . 19 D7
Tilford House **11** SW2 . . . . 21 F8
Tilford Rd
Beacon Hill GU10, GU26 . . 188 B5
Farnham GU10, GU9 . . . . 146 F7
Hindhead GU10, GU26 . . . 188 B5
Rushmoor GU10 . . . . 168 C5
Tilford GU10 . . . . 147 C6
Tilford St GU10 . . . . 147 C6
Tilgate Comm RH1 . . . . . . 120 C2
Tilgate Dr RH10, RH11 . . . 201 E3
Tilgate Forest Bsns
Ctr RH11 . . . . 201 C1
Tilgate Forest Golf
Course RH10 . . . . 201 D1
Tilgate Forest Recn Ctr
RH10 . . . . 201 D1
Tilgate Par RH10 . . . . 201 E3
Tilgate Pk Ctry Pk RH11 . . 201 E2
Tilgate Pl RH10 . . . . 201 E3
Tilgate Way RH10 . . . . 201 E3
Tilgates Cotts RH1 . . . . . . 120 C2
Tilletts La RH12 . . . . 216 E8
Tilley La KT18 . . . . 96 C1
Tillingbourne Cty Jun Sch
GU4 . . . . 131 B3
Tillingbourne Rd GU4 . . . . 130 E3
Tillingdown Hill CR3 . . . . . 101 A4
Tillingdown La
Caterham CR3 . . . . 101 B1
Woldingham CR3 . . . . 101 B1
Tilman House **8** SW2 . . . . 21 F7
Tilotson Cl RH10 . . . . 202 D5
Tilly's La TW18 . . . . 12 F3
Tilney Ct KT6 . . . . 37 D2
Tilson Gdns SW2, SW4 . . . 21 E8
Tilson House SW2 . . . . 21 E8
Tilt Cl KT11 . . . . 73 E3
Tilt Meadow KT11 . . . . 73 E3
Tilt Rd KT11 . . . . 73 D3
Tithams Corner Rd
GU7, GU7 . . . . 151 C2
Tithams Gn GU7 . . . . 151 B8
Tithview KT11 . . . . 73 C1
Tiltwood Dr RH10 . . . . 204 C3
Timber Bank GU16 . . . . . . 86 A6
Timber Cl
Great Bookham KT23 . . . . 114 C5
Pyrford GU22 . . . . 70 F4
Timber Ct RH12 . . . . 217 C2
Timber Hill KT21 . . . . 95 E8
Timber Hill Rd CR3 . . . . . 101 A3
Timber La CR3 . . . . 101 A3
Timber Pl **15** GU9 . . . . . . 125 B8
Timbercroft KT19 . . . . 57 F5
Timberham Farm Rd
RH6 . . . . 181 D7
Timberham Link RH6 . . . . 181 E8
Timberham Way RH6 . . . . 181 E8
Timberlands **6** RH11 . . . . 201 B1
Timberling Gdns CR2 . . . . 61 D2

Timbermill Ct GU27 .....207 F6
Timberslip Dr SM6 .....60 D2
Timbertop Rd TN16 .....83 C1
Times Sq SM1 .....59 B5
Timline Gn RG12 .....27 F7
Timperley Ct RH1 .....118 E3
Timperley Gdns RH1 .....118 E3
Timsbury Wlk [5] SW15 .....19 A7
Timsway TW18 .....12 F3
Tina Ct SW16 .....22 A5
Tindale Cl CR2 .....80 D8
Tinsey Cl TW20 .....12 B3
Tinsley Gn RH10 .....182 A1
Tinsley Gn RH10 .....182 B4
Tinsley La RH10 .....182 A1
Tinsley La N RH10 .....182 B3
Tinsley La S RH10 .....202 A8
Tintagel Cl KT17 .....76 F5
Tintagel Ct RH13 .....217 D1
Tintagel Dr GU16 .....65 F1
Tintagel Way GU22 .....70 A3
Tintells La KT24 .....112 B7
Tintern Rd SW19 .....20 C2
Tintern Rd Carshalton SM5 .....40 D1
   Crawley RH11 .....201 A4
Tippits Mead RG42 .....26 D8
Tipton Dr CR0 .....61 E6
Tiree Path RH11 .....201 B3
Tirlemont Rd CR2 .....61 C3
Tirrell Rd CR0 .....42 C3
Tisbury Rd SW16 .....41 E7
Titchfield Rd SM5 .....40 D1
Titchfield Wlk SM5 .....40 D2
Titchwell Rd SW18 .....20 D7
Tite Hill TW20 .....11 D3
Tithe Barn Cl KT2 .....37 F8
Tithe Barn The GU4 .....111 D4
Tithe Cl Thorpe GU25 .....31 D3
   Wentworth GU25 .....31 D3
Tithe La TW19 .....1 A1
Tithe Orch RH19 .....184 E4
Tithepit Shaw La CR2, CR6 .....81 B3
Titlarks Hill Rd SL5 .....30 B1
Titmus Dr RH10 .....201 F2
Titsey Cnr RH8 .....123 B7
Titsey Hill CR6, RH8 .....103 B4
Titsey Rd Limpsfield RH8 .....123 B8
   Titsey RH8 .....103 B1
Tiverton Rd TW3 .....5 C5
Tiverton Way
   Chessington KT9 .....56 D5
   Frimley GU16 .....65 F1
Tivoli Rd Hounslow TW4 .....4 E3
   West Norwood SE19, SE27 .....22 C2
Toad La GU17 .....64 E4
Tobias Sch of Art RH19 .....205 E6
Toby Way KT5, KT6 .....57 B8
Todds Cl RH6 .....160 E5
Toftwood Cl RH10 .....202 C5
Toll Bar Ct SM2 .....59 B2
Toll Gdns RG12 .....27 F6
Tolldene Cl GU21 .....68 E2
Tollers La CR5 .....99 F8
Tollgate GU1 .....110 D1
Tollgate Ave RH1 .....139 F4
Tollgate Ct RH1 .....139 F4
Tollgate Dr SE21 .....22 E6
Tollgate Hill RH11 .....201 C1
Tollgate Jun Mix & Inf Sch
   RH1 .....139 F4
Tollgate Rd RH4 .....136 B4
Tollhouse La SM6 .....60 C2
Tolson Ho [2] TW7 .....6 A4
Tolson Rd TW7 .....6 A4
Tolvaddon GU21 .....69 A2
Tolverne Rd SW20 .....39 C8
Tolworth Cl KT6 .....38 B1
Tolworth Girls' Sch KT6 .....56 F7
Tolworth Hospl KT6 .....57 A8
Tolworth Jun Sch KT6 .....57 A8
Tolworth Jun Sch N KT6 .....37 F1
Tolworth Park Rd KT6 .....56 F8
Tolworth Rd KT6 .....56 E8
Tolworth Rise N KT5 .....38 B1
Tolworth Rise S KT5 .....38 B1
Tolworth Sta KT5 .....57 B8
Tolworth Underpass
   KT5, KT6 .....57 B8
Tomlin Cl KT19 .....76 D8
Tomlin Ct KT19 .....76 D8
Tomlins Ave GU16 .....65 F2
Tomlinscote Sch GU16 .....66 A1
Tomlinscote Way GU16 .....66 A2
Tompset's Bank RH18 .....206 F1
Tomtits La RH18 .....206 E1
Tonbridge Cl SM7 .....78 F5
Tonbridge Rd KT12, KT8 .....35 F5
Tonfield Rd SM3 .....39 F1
Tonge Cl BR3 .....44 A4
Tongham Meadows
   GU10 .....126 F7
Tongham Rd
   Aldershot GU12 .....126 D8
   Farnham GU10 .....126 C4
Tonstall Rd Epsom KT19 .....76 D8
   Mitcham CR4 .....41 A7
Tooting Bec Gdns SW16 .....21 D4
Tooting Bec Rd
   Streatham SW16 .....21 B4
   Upper Tooting SW17 .....21 B4
Tooting Bec Sta SW17 .....21 A4
Tooting Broadway SW17 .....20 E3
Tooting Broadway Sta
   SW17 .....20 E3
Tooting Gr SW17 .....20 E3
Tooting High St
   SW17, SW19 .....20 E3
Tooting Mkt SW17 .....20 E3

Tooting Sta SW17 .....20 F2
Tootswood Rd BR2, BR3 .....44 A5
Top Pk BR3 .....44 E4
Topaz House KT14 .....38 D1
Topiary Sq TW9 .....6 F4
Topiary The Ashstead KT21 .....95 E7
   Farnborough GU14 .....84 E3
Toplady Pl GU9 .....125 C7
Topsham Rd SW17 .....21 A4
Tor La KT13 .....72 D8
Tor Rd GU9 .....124 F2
Torcross Dr SE23 .....23 C6
Torin Ct TW20 .....11 C2
Torland Dr KT22 .....74 D6
Tormead Cl SM1 .....59 A4
Tormead Rd GU1 .....109 F1
Toronto Dr RH6 .....162 A3
Torre Wlk SM5 .....40 E1
Torridge Rd Brands Hill SL3 .....1 B8
   Thornton Heath CR7 .....42 B4
Torridon Cl GU21 .....69 B2
Torridon Ind Est SE6 .....24 D6
Torridon Jun Sch SE6 .....24 D6
Torridon Rd SE6, SE23 .....24 D7
Torrington Cl KT10 .....55 C4
Torrington Ct SE26 .....23 A3
Torrington Rd KT10 .....55 C4
Torrington Sq CR0 .....42 D2
Torrington Way SM4 .....40 A3
Torwood La CR3 .....100 F8
Totford La GU10 .....127 E4
Totham Lodge SW20 .....39 B8
Totland Cl GU14 .....85 A6
Tottenham Rd GU7 .....150 E6
Tottenham Wlk GU47 .....45 D1
Totterdown St SW17 .....20 F3
Totton Rd CR7 .....42 A6
Toulouse Cl GU15 .....66 B7
Tournai Cl GU11 .....105 E7
Toutley Rd RG41 .....25 A8
Tovil Cl SE20 .....43 B7
Tower Cl
   East Grinstead RH19 .....185 E2
   Hindhead GU26 .....188 E4
   Horley RH6 .....160 F3
   Penge SE20 .....23 B1
   Woking GU21 .....69 A2
Tower Cotts KT13 .....54 F1
Tower Ct RH19 .....185 E2
Tower Gdns KT10 .....56 A3
Tower Gr KT13 .....53 E8
Tower Hill Dorking RH4 .....136 B5
   Farnborough GU14 .....85 A3
Tower Hill City Prim Sch
   GU14 .....84 F3
Tower Hill Rd RH4 .....136 B5
Tower Hill Rise GU5 .....133 C3
Tower Rd Crawley RH12 .....218 F8
   Hindhead GU26 .....188 E4
   Tadworth KT20 .....97 C4
   Twickenham TW1, TW2 .....16 F5
Tower Rise TW9 .....6 F4
Tower View CR0 .....43 E2
Towerhill GU5 .....133 C3
Towers Pl TW10 .....6 E2
Towers The Kenley CR8 .....80 C4
   [6] Richmond TW9 .....6 F3
Towers Wlk KT13 .....53 B4
Towfield Ct TW13 .....15 F6
Towfield Rd TW13 .....15 F6
Towngate Rd KT11 .....73 E4
Town Barn Rd RH11 .....201 C7
Town End Cl
   Caterham CR3 .....100 E5
   Godalming GU7 .....150 E4
Town End St GU7 .....150 E4
Town Farm Cty Prim Sch
   TW19 .....13 D8
Town Farm Way TW19 .....13 D8
Town Field Way TW7 .....6 A5
Town Hill RH7 .....164 E4
Town La TW19 .....13 D7
Town Mead
   Bletchingley RH1 .....120 D2
   Crawley RH11 .....201 D7
Town Meadow TW8 .....6 D7
Town Quay TW18 .....33 C6
Town Sq Bracknell RG12 .....27 C7
   Camberley GU15 .....65 F2
   [5] Woking GU21 .....69 F2
Town Tree Rd TW15 .....14 A3
Townend CR3 .....100 E5
Townend Ct BR1 .....44 F8
Townfield Ct RH4 .....136 A6
Townfield Rd RH4 .....136 A6
Towngate KT11 .....73 E4
Townmead Rd TW9 .....7 B5
Townsend Cl RG12 .....27 E4
Townsend La GU22 .....90 B6
Townsend Rd TW15 .....13 E3
Townshend Rd TW9 .....6 F3
Townshend Terr TW9 .....6 F3
Townshott Cl KT23 .....94 A1
Townslow La GU23 .....71 C5
Towpath Way CR0, SE25 .....42 F4
Towton Rd SE27 .....22 C6
Toynbee Rd
   Merton SW19, SW20 .....39 E8
   Wimbledon SW19, SW20 .....39 E8
Tracery The SM7 .....78 B4
Tracious Cl GU21 .....69 B3
Traemore Ct SW16 .....22 A5
Trafalgar Ave KT4, SM3, SM4 .....39 D1
Trafalgar Ct
   Cobham KT11 .....73 A6
   Farnham GU9 .....125 C1

Trafalgar Ct continued
   Hounslow TW3 .....4 F4
   West Barnes SW19 .....39 B6
Trafalgar City Inf Sch
   RH12 .....217 B4
Trafalgar Dr KT12 .....54 B7
Trafalgar Inf Sch TW2 .....16 D6
Trafalgar Jun Sch TW2 .....16 D6
Trafalgar Rd
   Horsham RH12 .....217 C4
   Merton SW19 .....20 C1
   Twickenham TW2 .....16 D6
Trafalgar Way
   Camberley GU15 .....64 F4
   Croydon CR0, CR9 .....61 A8
Trafford Rd Frimley GU16 .....85 D8
   Thornton Heath CR7 .....41 F4
Traherne Lodge [3] TW11 .....16 F3
Tramway Path CR4 .....40 E5
Tranmere Ct SM2 .....59 C3
Tranmere Rd
   Twickenham TW2 .....16 B8
   Wandsworth SW17, SW18 .....20 C6
Tranquil Dale RH3 .....116 F3
Transport Ave TW8 .....6 B8
Transport & Road
   Research Laboratory
   RG45 .....45 C7
Trap La RH5 .....176 F2
Traps La KT2, KT3 .....38 E8
Trasher Mead RH4 .....136 C4
Travellers Way TW5 .....4 C5
Travis La GU47 .....64 C7
Treadcroft Dr RH12 .....217 E5
Treadwell Rd KT18 .....76 F4
Treaty Ctr TW3 .....5 B4
Trebor Ave GU9 .....146 D8
Tredenham Cl GU14 .....105 C8
Tredown Rd SE26 .....23 C3
Tredwell Rd SE27 .....22 B4
Tree Ave GU27 .....207 F8
Tree Cl TW10 .....17 D7
Tree Tops CR6 .....81 A1
Tree Tops Ave GU15 .....66 B8
Tree View Cl SE19 .....42 E8
Treebourne Rd TN16 .....83 C1
Treebys Ave GU4 .....109 D7
Treelands RH5 .....136 C4
Treemount Ct KT17 .....76 E6
Treen Ave SW13, SW14 .....7 F4
Trees The GU22 .....90 B8
Treeside Dr GU9 .....125 F4
Treetops RH9 .....142 E6
Treetops Ct CR7 .....42 C4
Treeview RH11 .....201 C7
Treeview Ct [5] RH2 .....118 D1
Treeway RH2 .....118 B4
Trefoil Cl Horsham RH12 .....217 E5
   Wokingham RG40 .....25 E7
Trefusis Ct TW5 .....4 B6
Tregaron Gdns KT3 .....38 E5
Tregarth Pl GU21 .....68 F2
Tregarthen Pl KT22 .....95 C6
Tregolls Dr GU14 .....85 D3
Treherne Par RH2 .....139 B6
Trehern Rd [12] SW14 .....7 D4
Treherne Ct SW17 .....21 A4
Trelawne Dr GU6 .....174 E3
Trelawney Dr KT13 .....53 A4
Treloar Gdns SE19 .....22 D2
Tremaine Rd SE20 .....43 B7
Trematon Pl TW11 .....17 C1
Tremayne Wlk GU15 .....66 C4
Trenance GU21 .....69 A2
Trenchard Cl KT12 .....54 C5
Trenchard St SM4 .....40 A3
Trenear Cl RH13 .....217 E2
Trenham Dr CR6 .....81 C3
Trenholme Cl SE20 .....23 B1
Trenholme Ct CR3 .....101 A4
Trenholme Rd SE20 .....23 B1
Trenholme Terr SE20 .....23 B1
Trent Cl Crawley RH11 .....200 F4
   Farnborough GU14 .....84 E6
Trent Rd SL3 .....1 B8
Trent Way KT4 .....58 C7
Trentham Cres GU22 .....90 A6
Trentham Rd RH1 .....140 A7
Trentham St SW18 .....20 A7
Trenton Cl GU16 .....66 A1
Trereife RH11 .....201 D8
Tresco Cl BR1 .....24 E2
Tresidder House [10] SW4 .....21 D8
Tresillian Way GU21 .....69 B2
Tresta Wlk GU21 .....69 A3
Trevanne Plat RH10 .....202 D7
Trevelyan Rd SW17 .....20 F2
Trevelyan TW13 .....15 A5
Trevellan Ct KT3 .....38 F2
Trevelyan House [6] 16 C1
Trevenna House [3] SE23 .....23 D5
Trevereux Hill RH8 .....123 F4
Treversh Ct BR1 .....44 F8
Trevithick Cl TW14 .....14 F7
Trevor Cl Isleworth TW7 .....5 F2
   Keston BR2 .....44 F2
Trevor Rd SW19 .....19 E1
Trevose Ave KT14 .....70 F5
Trewenna Dr KT9 .....56 D5
Trewince Rd SW20 .....39 C8
Trewint St SW18 .....20 C6
Trewsbury Rd SE26 .....23 D3

Treyford Cl RH11 .....200 F6
Triangle The
   Kingston u T KT3 .....38 C7
   Woking GU21 .....69 C1
Trickett House SM2 .....59 B2
Trident Ind Est SL3 .....1 E4
Trig St RH5 .....178 F8
Trigg's Cl GU22 .....89 D8
Trigg's La GU21, GU22 .....89 D8
Trigo Ct KT19 .....76 D8
Trilby Rd SE23 .....23 D6
Trimmer Ct TW7 .....5 F4
Trimmer Wlk [11] TW8 .....6 E8
Trimmer's Almshouses
   GU9 .....125 A1
Trimmers Cl GU9 .....125 C7
Trimmers Field GU9 .....125 E1
Trimmers Wood GU26 .....188 E6
Trindles Rd RH1 .....140 F7
Tring Ct TW1 .....17 A4
Tringham Cl KT16 .....51 C5
Trinity GU47 .....45 E2
Trinity C of E Sch KT10 .....55 A7
Trinity Cl Crawley RH10 .....202 C8
   Hounslow TW4 .....4 E3
   South Croydon CR2 .....61 E2
   Stanwell TW19 .....2 C1
Trinity Cotts TW9 .....6 F4
Trinity Cres
   Sunningdale SL5 .....30 A4
   Upper Tooting SW17 .....21 A6
Trinity Ct Croydon CR9 .....61 C8
   Forest Hill SE23 .....23 C5
   Thornton Heath SE25 .....42 E3
   Twickenham TW2 .....16 E6
Trinity Fields GU9 .....125 A6
Trinity Mews SE20 .....43 B8
Trinity Par TW3 .....5 B4
Trinity Rd Knaphill GU21 .....68 B1
   Richmond TW9 .....6 F4
   Upper Tooting SW17, SW18 .....20 E7
   Wimbledon SW19 .....20 A2
Trinity Rise SW2, SE24 .....22 B8
Trinity Sch SE19 .....22 E1
Trinity St Mary's (C of E)
   Prim Sch SW12 .....21 A7
Tristram Rd BR1 .....24 F4
Tritton Ave CR0 .....60 E6
Tritton Rd SE21, SE22 .....22 D5
Trittons KT20 .....97 D6
Triumph Cl UB7 .....3 C6
Trodd's La GU1, GU4 .....110 E1
Trojan Way CR0 .....60 F7
Troon Cl RH11 .....200 D5
Troon Ct SL5 .....29 C4
Troston Ct TW18 .....12 F3
Trotsworth Ave GU25 .....31 E5
Trotsworth Ct GU25 .....31 E5
Trotters La GU24 .....69 B7
Trotton Cl RH10 .....202 C3
Trotwood Cl GU47 .....45 E2
Trout Rd GU27 .....207 E6
Troutbeck Wlk GU15 .....66 D3
Trowers Way RH1 .....119 B4
Trowlock Ave TW11 .....17 C2
Trowlock Way TW11 .....17 D2
Troy La TN8 .....144 F4
Troy Rd SE19 .....22 D2
Trumpeters Inn TW9 .....6 D2
Trumpetshill Rd RH2 .....138 B7
Trumps Green Cl GU25 .....31 E4
Trumps Green Ct GU25 .....31 E4
Trumps Green Cty Fst Sch
   GU25 .....31 D3
Trumps Mill La
   Longcross GU25 .....31 F4
   Thorpe GU25 .....31 F4
Trumpsgreen Ave GU25 .....31 D3
Trumpsgreen Rd GU25 .....31 D3
Trundle Mead RH12 .....217 C5
Trunk Rd GU14 .....84 C5
Trunley Heath Rd GU5 .....151 C8
Truslove Rd SE27 .....22 B3
Truss Hill Rd SL5 .....29 C4
Trust Wlk SE21 .....22 B7
Trys Hill KT16 .....51 A8
Trystings Cl KT10 .....56 A4
Tucker Rd KT16 .....51 D4
Tuckers Dr GU6 .....174 B3
Tuckey Gr GU23 .....90 F3
Tudor Ave Hampton TW12 .....16 A1
   North Cheam KT4 .....58 B6
Tudor Circ GU7 .....150 E7
Tudor Cl
   Ashford TW15 .....13 E4
   Banstead SM7 .....77 E4
   Cheam SM3 .....58 E4
   Chessington KT9 .....56 E5
   Cobham KT11 .....73 F6
   Coulsdon CR5 .....99 E7
   Crawley RH10 .....202 D5
   Grayshott GU26 .....188 D2
   Hampton TW12 .....16 C3
   Little Bookham KT23 .....94 A3
   Smallfield RH6 .....162 B3
   Wallington SM6 .....60 C3
   Woking GU22 .....70 A2
Tudor Ct
   Feltham TW13 .....15 C4
   [12] Redhill RH1 .....119 A2
   Stanwell TW19 .....2 E1
   Teddington TW11 .....16 F2

Tudor Dr Kingston u T KT2 .....
   Walton-on-T KT12 .....
   West Barnes SM4 .....
Tudor Gdns
   Mortlake SW13, SW14 .....
   Twickenham TW1 .....
   West Wickham BR4 63
Tudor House
   Bracknell RG12 .....27 B4
   Horsham RH13 .....217 F3
   Weybridge KT13 .....53 A4
Tudor La SL4 .....11 C8
Tudor Pl SW19 .....20 E1
Tudor Prim Sch SM4 .....39 D2
Tudor Rd Ashford TW15 .....14 D2
   Beckenham BR3 .....44 C6
   Croydon CR0, SE25 .....43 B4
   Farncombe GU7 .....150 E7
   Hampton TW12 .....16 A1
   Isleworth TW3 .....5 D3
   Kingston u T KT2 .....18 A1
   Penge SE19 .....22 F1
Tudor Wlk
   Leatherhead KT22 .....94 F7
   [3] Weybridge KT13 .....53 B7
Tudors The BR3 .....44 B7
Tuesley Cnr GU7 .....150 D3
Tuesley La
   Godalming GU7, GU8 .....150 D1
   Milford GU7 .....171 C7
Tufton Gdns KT8 .....36 B7
Tugela Rd CR0 .....42 D3
Tugela St SE6 .....23 F6
Tuggles Plat RH14 .....216 E7
Tulip Cl Croydon CR0 .....43 D1
   Hampton TW12 .....15 F2
Tull St CR4 .....40 F2
Tullett Rd RH10 .....202 B2
Tulse Cl BR3 .....44 C6
Tulse Hill SW2, SE24 .....22 A8
Tulse Hill Sta SE27 .....22 B6
Tulsemere Rd SE21, SE27 .....22 C6
Tulyar Cl KT20 .....97 B7
Tumber St KT18, KT22 .....96 C2
Tumblewood Rd SM7 .....77 E3
Tumbling Bay KT12 .....35 A3
Tummons Gdns SE25 .....42 E7
Tunbridge Ct [8] SE26 .....23 A5
Tunley Rd SW12, SW17 .....21 A6
Tunnel Link Rd TW6 .....3 A2
Tunnel Rd TW6 .....3 B6
Tunnel Rd E TW6 .....3 B6
Tunnmeade RH11 .....200 E5
Tunsgate GU1 .....130 D7
Tunsgate Sq GU1 .....130 D7
Tunstall Ct [17] TW9 .....6 F6
Tunstall Rd CR0 .....42 E1
Tunstall Wlk [9] TW8 .....6 E8
Tunworth Cres SW15 .....7 F1
Tupwood Ct CR3 .....101 A2
Tupwood La CR3 .....101 A1
Tupwood Scrubbs Rd
   CR3, RH9 .....121 A8
Turf Hill Rd GU15 .....65 F8
Turfhouse La GU24 .....49 E2
Turkey Oak Cl SE19 .....42 E8
Turle Rd SW16 .....41 E7
Turnberry RG12 .....26 E2
Turner Ave Mitcham CR4 .....40 F8
   Twickenham TW2 .....16 C5
Turner Cl Biggin Hill TN16 .....83 C7
   Guildford GU1 .....109 F5
Turner Ct
   East Grinstead RH19 .....186 A3
   Godalming GU7 .....150 D4
Turner House RH5 .....157 C4
Turner Lodge [10] SW19 .....19 D7
Turner Pl GU47 .....64 D6
Turner Rd KT3 .....38 D2
Turner's Hill Rd RH19 .....205 B6
Turner Cl TW18 .....13 B3
Turners Hill CE
   (Controlled) Sch RH10 .....204 A3
Turners Hill Rd
   Copthorne RH10 .....183 F2
   Crawley RH10 .....203 C5
   Crawley Down RH10 .....204 A7
   Turners Hill RH10 .....204 B5
Turners La KT12 .....54 B3
Turners Mead GU8 .....191 C3
Turners Meadow Way BR3 .....43 F8
Turners Way CR0, CR9 .....61 A8
Turney Rd SE21 .....22 C8
Turnham Cl GU2 .....130 C5
Turnoak Ave GU22 .....89 E8
Turnoak Cnr GU22 .....89 E8
Turnoak La GU22 .....89 E8
Turnpike La SM1 .....59 C5
Turnpike Link CR0 .....61 E8
Turnpike Pl RH11 .....201 D8
Turnpike Rd RG42 .....26 D7
Turnstone Cl CR0, CR2 .....62 E1
Turnville Cl GU18 .....48 A1
Turpin Rd TW14 .....3 F1
Turpin Way SM6 .....60 B3
Turpins Rise GU20 .....48 B6
Turton Ct RH19 .....185 C3
Turret House KT2 .....17 E2
Turville Ct KT23 .....94 B2
Tuscam Way GU15 .....64 F4
Tushmore Ave RH10, RH11 .....181 E1
Tushmore La RH10, RH11 .....201 E8
Tushmore Rdbt RH11 .....201 D8

287

...40 D2
...40 D1
...84 D3
u BR1 ....44 FJ
Ave Acre Cl KT23 ....93 F3
Twelve Acre Cres GU14 ..84 E5
Twickenham Bridge TW9 ...6 C2
Twickenham Cl CR0 ......60 F7
Twickenham Golf Course
  TW12 ....16 B4
Twickenham Rd
  Feltham TW13 ....15 F5
  Isleworth TW1, TW7 ....6 A4
  Richmond TW1, TW9 .....6 C2
  Teddington TW11 ....17 A4
Twickenham Rugby
  Football Union Ground
  TW2 ....5 E4
Twickenham Sta TW1 ...17 A8
Twickenham Trad Ctr TW1 ..5 F1
Twilley St SW18 ....20 B8
Twining Ave TW2 ......16 D5
Twinoaks KT11 ....74 A6
Twitten La RH19 ......184 E4
Two Oaks KT13 ....53 B6
Two Rivers Sh Ctr TW18 ..12 E4
Two Ways RH14 ....213 A4
Twycross Rd
  Farncombe GU7 ......150 D7
  Wokingham RG40 ....25 E7
Twyford La GU10 ......146 B6
Twyford Par KT6 ....38 A1
Twyford Rd Carshalton SM5 ..40 D1
  Wokingham RG40 ....25 B8
Twyhurst Ct RH19 .....185 D3
Twyne Cl RH11 ....200 F4
Twyner Cl RH6 ....161 D4
Twynersh Ave KT16 ....32 F3
Tybenham Rd SW19 ....40 A6
Tychbourne Dr GU4 ...110 C4
Tydcombe Rd CR6 .....101 D8
Tyers House 1 SW16 ...21 C3
Tylden Way RH12 .....217 F6
Tylecroft Rd SW16 .....41 E7
Tylehost GU2 ....109 A5
Tyler Gdns KT15 ....52 C6
Tyler Rd RH10 ....201 D3
Tylers Cl RH9 ....121 B5
Tylers Path SM5 ....59 F6
Tylney Ave SE19 ....22 F3
Tymperley Ct RH13 ....217 E3
Tynamara KT1 ....37 D5
Tynan Cl TW14 ....15 A7
Tyndalls Estate GU26 ..188 F4
Tyne Cl Crawley RH10 ..202 C5
  Farnborough GU14 .....84 E6
Tynedale Rd RH3 .....137 B5
Tynemouth Rd CR4 .....21 A1
Tynley Gr GU4 ....109 D7
Tynwald House 14 SE26 ..23 A5
Tyrell Ct SM5 ....59 F6
Tyrolean Ct SM7 ....78 B4
Tyrols Rd SE23 ....23 D7
Tyrrell House BR3 .....24 A3
Tyrrell Sq CR4 ....40 E8
Tyrrell's Wood Golf Course
  KT22 ....110 F5
Tyrwhitt Ave GU2 .....109 B5
Tyson Rd SE23 ....23 C8
Tythe The KT12 ....35 B3
Tythebarns La Ripley GU23 ..91 B1
  Send Marsh GU23 ......91 B1
Tytherton RG12 ....27 C7

U

Uckfield Rd CR4 ......41 A8
Udney Park Rd TW11 ...17 A2
Uffington Dr RG12 .....27 E5
Uffington Rd SE27 .....22 A4
Uima Ct SW16 ....21 E4
Ujima House SW16 ....21 C4
Ullathorne Rd SW16 ..21 C4
Ullswater RG12 ....26 E2
Ullswater Ave GU14 ...84 E3
Ullswater Cl Bromley BR1 ..24 E1
  Hale GU9 ....125 A6
  Kingston u T KT2, SW15 ..18 D4
  Lightwater GU18 ......48 B1
Ullswater Cres
  Coulsdon CR5 ....79 E3
  Kingston u T SW15 ....18 D4
Ullswater Rd
  Lightwater GU18 ......48 B1
  West Norwood SE27, SW16 ..22 B6
Ulstan Cl GU4 ....102 A4
Ulster Ct KT13 ....17 D2
Ulverstone Rd SE27 ...22 B6
Ulwyn Ave KT14 ....71 E5
Underhill Cl GU7 .....150 E3
Underhill La GU10 ....146 B7
Underhill Park Rd RH2 ..118 A4
Underhill Rd
  Dulwich SE21, SE22 ...23 B8
  Newdigate RH5 ....158 B1
Undershaw Rd BR1 ....24 F5

Underwood Bracknell RG12 ..26 E3
  New Addington CR0 ....63 C5
Underwood Ave GU12 ..105 F1
Underwood Cl RH10 ...204 B8
Underwood Ct CR3 ....100 F2
Underwood Rd
  Caterham CR3 ....100 E2
  Haslemere GU27 .....208 A5
Undine St SW17 ....20 F3
Unicorn Sch TW9 ......6 F6
Union Cl GU47 ....45 E2
Union Ct 8 KT6 ....37 E4
Union Rd Farnham GU9 ..125 C2
  Frimley GU16 ....86 D8
  Thornton Heath CR0 ...42 C2
Union St Aldershot GU11 ..105 A2
  Farnborough GU14 .....85 B4
  Kingston u T KT1 ......37 D7
  Pirbright GU24 ....87 A6
Union Terr 7 GU11 ...105 A2
Unity Cl New Addington CR0 ..63 B2
  West Norwood SE19, SE27 ..22 C3
Univ of Greenwich The
  SW15 ....19 A8
University Rd SW19 ...20 D2
Unstead La GU5 ......151 C7
Unstead Wood GU3 ...130 C1
Unwin Ave TW14 ....3 D2
Unwin Rd TW7 ....5 E4
Upavon Gdns RG12 ....27 F4
Upchurch Cl SE20 .....23 B1
Updown Hill GU20 .....48 D4
Upfield Horley RH6 ...161 A2
  South Croydon CR0, CR9 ..62 B7
Upfield Cl RH6 ....161 A1
Upfold Cl GU6 ....174 E5
Upfold La GU6 ....174 F5
Upfolds Gn GU4 ......110 C5
Upgrove Manor Way 12
  SE24 ....22 A8
Upland Ct SE23 ....23 C6
Upland Rd Camberley GU15 ..65 D7
  Croydon CR2 ....61 D5
  Dulwich SE21, SE22 ...23 A8
  Sutton SM2 ....59 D3
  Woldingham CR3 .....102 B7
Upland Way KT18 .....77 C1
Uplands
  Ashtead KT21, KT22 ...95 D7
  Beckenham BR3 ....44 A7
  Warlingham CR6 ....81 F1
Uplands Cl
  Haslemere GU27 .....208 D8
  Mortlake SW14 ....7 B3
  Sandhurst GU47 ......64 B8
Uplands Cty Prim Sch
  GU47 ....64 B8
Uplands Rd Farnham GU9 ..125 E1
Uppark Gdns RH12 ...217 F6
Upper Beulah Hill SE19 ..42 E8
Upper Bourne La GU10 ..146 B5
Upper Bourne Vale GU10 ..146 B5
Upper Bridge Rd RH1 ..118 F1
Upper Broadmoor Rd
  RG45 ....45 D5
Upper Butts TW8 ......6 C8
Upper Charles St GU15 ..65 C6
Upper Chobham Rd GU15 ..66 B4
Upper Church La 11 GU9 ..125 B2
Upper College Ride GU15 ..65 E8
Upper Court Rd
  Epsom KT19 ....76 C8
  Woldingham CR3 .....102 A3
Upper Dr TN16 ....83 C1
Upper Dunnymans 6 SM7 ..77 F5
Upper Edgeborough Rd
  GU1 ....130 F8
Upper Elmers End Rd BR3 ..43 F4
Upper Elms Rd GU11 ..105 A1
Upper Fairfield Rd KT22 ..95 B6
Upper Farm L Pk KT20 ..115 F7
Upper Farm Rd KT8 ...35 F5
Upper Forecourt RH6 ..182 B7
Upper Gn E Mitcham CR4 ..40 F6
  Mitcham CR4 ....41 A6
Upper Gn W CR4 ....40 F7
Upper Gordon Rd GU15 ..65 D5
Upper Gr SE25 ....42 F5
Upper Grotto Rd TW1 ..16 F6
Upper Guildown Rd GU2 ..130 C6
Upper Hale Rd GU9 ...125 C6
Upper Halliford Rd
  Upper Halliford TW16 ..34 E5
  Halliford Sta TW16, TW17 ..34 E5
Upper Ham Rd KT2, TW10 ..17 D4
Upper Harestone CR3 ..121 A8
Upper High St KT17 ...76 E6
Upper House La GU5 ..152 F1
Upper Manor Rd
  Farncombe GU7 ......150 F1
  Milford GU8 ....149 F1
Upper Mount GU27 ...189 F1
Upper Mulgrave Rd SM2 ..58 F3
Upper Nursery SL5 ....30 A4
Upper Old Park La GU9 ..125 A5
Upper Park Rd
  Camberley GU15 ....65 D5
  Kingston u T KT2 ......18 A2
Upper Pillory Down SM5 ..79 A7
Upper Pinewood GU12 ..
Upper Queen St GU7 ..150 E4
Upper Rd SM6 ....60 E5

Upper Richmond Rd SW15 ..7 F3
Upper Richmond Rd W
  TW10, SW14, SW15 .....7 B4
Upper Rose Hill RH4 ..136 B6
Upper Sawleywood 3
  SM7 ....77 F5
Upper Selsdon Rd CR2 ..62 A2
Upper Shirley Rd CR0, CR9 ..62 D7
Upper South View GU9 ..125 C3
Upper Springfield GU8 ..148 D3
Upper Sq Forest Row RH18 ..206 E3
  Isleworth TW7 ....6 A4
Upper St GU5 ....133 A4
Upper St Michael's Rd
  GU11 ....126 B8
Upper Stanford Rd CR4 ..87 F1
Upper Sunbury Rd TW12 ..36 A8
Upper Sutton La TW5 ...5 A6
Upper Teddington Rd
  KT1, KT8 ....37 C8
Upper Terr
Upper Tooting
  Independent High Sch
  SW17 ....20 F6
Upper Tooting Park
  Mansions 1 SW17 .....21 A6
Upper Tooting Rd SW17 ..20 F5
Upper Tulse Hill SW2 ..21 F8
Upper Union St 1 GU11 ..105 A2
Upper Union Terr 6
  GU11 ....105 A2
Upper Vann La GU8 ...172 A1
Upper Vernon Rd SM1 ..59 D5
Upper Verran Rd CR3 ...65 D3
Upper Village Rd SL5 ..29 D4
Upper Warlingham Sta
  CR6 ....81 A1
Upper Way GU9 ....146 B8
Upper West St RH2 ...117 F1
Upper Weybourne La
  GU9 ....125 E7
Upper Wlk GU25 ......31 E5
Upper Woodcote Village
  CR8 ....79 D7
Upperton Rd GU2 ....130 C7
Upshire Gdns RG12 ....27 F5
Upshott La GU22 ......70 F2
Upton GU21 ....69 B2
Upton Cl GU14 ....85 A3
Upton Ct Penge SE20 ..23 C1
  4 Wimbledon SW19 ....19 D1
Upton Dene SM2 ......59 B3
Upton Rd Hounslow TW3 ..5 A3
  South Norwood CR7 ....42 D7
Upwood Rd SW16 ......41 E8
Urmston Dr SW19 .....19 E7
Urquhart Ct BR3 ......23 F1
Ursuline Convent Prep Sch
  SW20 ....39 D8
Ursuline Convent Sch
  SW20 ....39 D8
Usherwood Cl KT20 ...116 C4
Uvedale Cl CR0 ....82 D8
Uvedale Cres CR0 .....82 D8
Uvedale Rd RH8 ......122 F5
Uxbridge Rd Feltham TW13 ..15 D6
  Hampton TW12, TW13 ...16 B3
  Kingston u T KT1, KT6 ..37 D4

V

Vachery La GU6 ......194 E7
Vaillant Rd KT13 ......53 C6
Valan Leas BR2 ....44 E6
Vale Cl Coulsdon CR5 ..79 E5
  Farnham GU10 ....146 C4
  Oatlands Park KT13 ...53 D7
  Twickenham TW1 ......17 A3
  Woking GU21 ....69 E3
Vale Cres SW15 ....18 E4
Vale Croft KT10 ....55 F2
Vale Ct KT13 ....53 D7
Vale Dr RH17 ....217 B3
Vale Farm Rd GU21 ....69 E2
Vale House GU21 ......69 E2
Vale Lodge SE23 ......23 C6
Vale Rd Ash Vale GU12 ..106 A5
  Camberley GU15 ....65 A4
  Claygate KT10 ....55 F3
  Mitcham CR4 ....41 D5
  Oatlands Park KT13 ...53 D7
  Sutton SM1 ....59 B6
  Worcester Park KT19, KT4 ..57 F7
Vale Rd N KT6 ....56 E8
Vale Rd S KT6 ....56 E8
Vale The Ashford TW16 ..15 A2
  Coulsdon CR5, CR8 ....79 E5
  Croydon CR0 ....62 D8
  Feltham TW13 ....4 B1
  Heston TW5 ....4 E7
  Sutton SM3 ....59 A5
Valens House 1 SW2 ..22 A7
Valentine Ct SE23 .....23 D6
Valentyne Cl CR0 ......82 E8
Valerie Ct SM2 ....59 B3
Valeswood Rd BR1 ....24 F3
Valewood Rd GU27 ...208 C4
Valley Cres RG41 .....25 A8
Valley Ct CR3 ....101 A5
Valley End C of E Inf Sch
  GU24 ....49 A4
Valley End Rd GU24 ...49 A4
Valley Gardens The TW20 ..30 E7
Valley Gdns SW19 .....20 D1
Valley La GU10 ....146 C7
Valley Mews TW1 .....17 A6
Valley Pl KT6 ....37 E3

Valley Prim Sch BR2 ...44 F7
Valley Prospect 3 SE19 ..22 E2
Valley Rd Beckenham BR2 ..44 E7
  Frimley GU16 ....86 B8
  Kenley CR3, CR8 ....80 D4
  Streatham SW16 ....21 F7
Valley View GU7 ......130 C5
Valley View Biggin Hill TN16 ..83 D1
  Godalming GU7 ....150 D4
Valley View Gdns CR8 ..80 E4
Valley Wlk CR0 ....62 C8
Valleyfield Rd SW16 ...21 F3
Vallis Way KT9 ....56 D6
Valnay St SW17 ....20 F3
Valonus RH1 ....119 B5
Valroy Cl GU15 ....65 D6
Van Dyck Ave KT3 .....38 D2
Vanborough Ct SM2 ...59 C4
Vanbrugh Cl RH11 ...200 E3
Vanbrugh Dr KT12 .....35 C3
Vancouver Cl KT19 ....76 C8
Vancouver Ct RH6 ....162 A3
Vancouver Dr RH11 ...181 D1
Vancouver Rd
  Forest Hill SE23 ......23 E6
  Richmond TW10 ....17 C4
Vanderbilt Rd SW18 ...20 C7
Vandyke RG12 ....27 A3
Vandyke Cl Putney SW15 ..19 D8
  Redhill RH1 ....118 F3
Vanfame Ct KT3 ....38 F6
Vanguard Cl CR0 ......42 B1
Vanguard House
  1 Merton SW19 ....20 C1
  5 Stanmore TW19 ......2 E1
Vanguard Way SM6 ....60 E3
Vann Farm Rd RH5 ...177 E4
Vann La Chiddingfold GU8 ..191 C4
  Hambledon GU8 ....191 D1
Vann Lake RH5 ....177 F4
Vann Lake Rd Ockley RH5 ..177 F3
  Ockley RH5 ....178 A4
Vanners RH10 ....201 E7
Vant Rd SW17 ....20 F3
Vapery La GU24 ....87 D6
Varley Way CR4 ....40 D7
Varna Rd TW12 ....36 B8
Varney Cl GU14 ....84 E5
Varsity Dr TW1, TW7 ...5 F1
Varsity Row SW14 ......7 C5
Vaughan Almshouses
  TW15 ....14 B3
Vaughan Rd KT7 ....37 B2
Vaughan Way RH4 ...136 A7
Vaux Cres KT12 ....54 B3
Vauxhall Gdns CR2 ....61 C4
Veals Mead CR4 ....40 E8
Vectis Gdns SW17 .....21 B2
Vectis Rd SW17 ....21 B2
Vegal Cres TW20 ......11 C3
Vellum Dr SM5 ....60 A7
Venita Manor SE27 ....22 B4
Venner Rd
  Forest Hill SE20, SE26 ..23 C3
  Penge SE20, SE26 ....23 C3
Ventnor Rd SM2 ....59 B3
Ventnor Terr GU12 ...105 C1
Venton Cl GU21 ....69 B2
Verbania Way RH19 ...186 B1
Verdant Ct 18 SE6 .....24 F7
Verdant La SE6 ....24 E7
Verdayne Ave CR0, CR9 ..62 D8
Verdayne Gdns CR6 ...81 C3
Vere Bank SW19 ....19 F7
Vereker Dr TW16 ....35 A6
Vermont Rd
  South Norwood SE19 ..22 E2
  Sutton SM1 ....59 B7
Verney House TW3 .....5 C3
Vernon Ave SW20 .....39 D7
Vernon Cl Horsham RH12 ..218 A4
  Ottershaw KT16 ....51 D4
  West Ewell KT19 ......57 C4
Vernon Ct GU9 ....125 A2
Vernon Dr Caterham CR3 ..100 C5
  North Ascot SL5 ....28 E7
Vernon Rd Feltham TW13 ..14 F6
  Mortlake SW14 ....7 D4
  Sutton SM1 ....59 D5
Vernon Way GU2 ......108 F1
Vernon Wlk KT20 ......97 D7
Verona Dr KT6 ....56 E8
Veronica Gdns CR4, SW16 ..41 C8
Veronica Rd SW17 .....21 B6
Verralls GU22 ....70 B2
Verran Rd Balham SW12 ..21 B8
  Camberley GU15 ....65 D3
Versailles Rd SE20 ....23 A1
Verulam Ave CR8 ......79 C7
Veryan GU21 ....69 A2
Vesey Cl GU14 ....85 A5
Vestris Rd SE23 ....23 D6
Vevers Rd RH2 ....139 C6
Vevey St SE23, SE6 ....23 F6
Vibart Gdns SW2 ......21 F8
Vicarage Ave TW20 ....12 B3
Vicarage Cl
  Farnham GU9 ....146 D7
  Kingswood KT20 ......97 E3
  Lingfield RH7 ....164 D4
  Little Bookham KT23 ..94 A2
Vicarage Cres TW20 ...12 B3
Vicarage Ct
  Beckenham BR3 ....43 E6
  East Bedfont TW14 ....14 C8
  Egham TW20 ....12 B2
  6 Roehampton SW15 ...19 A8

Vicarage Dr
  Beckenham BR3 ....44 A8
  Mortlake SW14 ....7 D2
Vicarage Farm Ct TW5 ..4 F2
Vicarage Farm Rd
  Heston TW3, TW4, TW5 ..4 E6
  Hounslow TW3, TW4, TW5 ..4 E5
Vicarage Fields KT12 ...35 C3
Vicarage Gate GU2 ...130 A7
Vicarage Gdns Ascot SL5 ..29 A4
  Grayshott GU26 ......188 C3
  Mitcham CR4 ....40 E6
  Mortlake SW14 ....7 D2
Vicarage Hill GU10, GU9 ..146 D7
Vicarage House 1 KT1 ..37 E6
Vicarage La Capel RH5 ..178 D6
  Farnham GU9 ....125 E3
  Farnham, Middle
  Bourne GU9 ....146 D7
  Haslemere GU27 .....207 F6
  Heath End GU9 ......125 C7
  Horley RH6 ....160 F4
  Laleham TW18 ....13 A4
  Leatherhead KT22 ....95 B5
  Send GU23 ....90 D1
  Wraysbury TW19 ......11 F1
Vicarage Rd Ashford TW16 ..14 F2
  Bagshot GU19 ....47 C5
  Blackwater GU17 ......64 E4
  Chobham GU24 ....68 E8
  Crawley Down RH10 ...204 A8
  Croydon CR0, CR9 .....61 A7
  Egham TW20 ....12 B3
  Kingston u T KT1, KT2 ..37 D7
  Lingfield RH7 ....164 D4
  Mortlake SW14 ....7 D2
  Stanes TW18 ....12 E4
  Sutton SM1 ....59 B8
  Teddington TW11 ......17 A2
  Teddington, Hampton Wick
  KT1, KT8 ....37 C8
  Twickenham TW2 ....5 C2
  Twickenham, Strawberry Hill
  TW2 ....16 E6
  Woking GU22 ....89 F7
Vicarage Way SL3 ......1 D7
Vicars Oak Rd SE19 ...22 E2
Viceroy Ct CR0 ....42 D3
Viceroy Lodge 8 KT6 ..37 E4
Vickers Ct 3 TW19 .....2 E1
Vickers Dr N KT13 .....52 E6
Vickers Dr S KT13 .....71 E6
Vickers Rd GU12 .....105 D2
Victor Ct RH10 ....182 D1
Victor Rd Penge SE20 ..23 D1
  Teddington TW11 ......16 E4
Victor Seymour Inf
  Sch SM5 ....59 F6
Victoria Almshouses
  3 Redhill RH1 ....119 A4
  1 Reigate RH2 ....118 C1
Victoria Ave
  Camberley GU15 ....65 A4
  East Molesey KT8 .....36 B4
  Hackbridge SM5, SM6 ..60 A7
  Hounslow TW3, TW4, TW5 ..5 A2
  Kingston u T KT6 ......37 D2
  South Croydon CR2 ....61 C2
Victoria Cl
  East Molesey KT8 .....36 A5
  Horley RH6 ....161 A2
  Oatlands Park KT13 ...53 D6
Victoria Cotts 7 TW9 ..7 A6
Victoria Cres Merton SW19 ..40 A8
  West Norwood SE19 ...22 E2
Victoria Ct Bagshot GU19 ..47 E4
  Guildford GU1 ....130 C1
  Horsham RH13 ....217 D2
  Penge SE26 ....23 C4
  Shalford GU4 ....130 E3
Victoria Dr
  Blackwater GU17 ......64 C6
  Putney SW15, SW19 ....19 E1
Victoria Entertainments Ctr
  The GU21 ....69 E2
Victoria Gdns
  Biggin Hill TN16 ....83 C2
  Heston TW5 ....4 F7
Victoria Jun Sch The
  TW13 ....15 E4
Victoria La UB7 ....3 E8
Victoria Lodge SW19 ...18 A2
Victoria Mews SW18 ...20 C7
Victoria Pl 5 Esher KT10 ..55 B6
  Ewell KT17 ....76 E6
  8 Richmond TW9 ....6 E3
Victoria Rd
  Addlestone KT15 ......52 B6
  Aldershot GU11 ......105 A2
  Ascot SL5 ....29 A4
  Coulsdon CR5 ....79 D4
  Cranleigh GU6 ....174 E2
  Crawley RH11 ....201 D5
  Farnborough GU14 ....85 C2
  Farnham GU9 ....125 E4
  Godalming GU7 ......150 E4
  Guildford GU1 ....130 D3
  Horley RH6 ....161 A2
  Kingston u T KT6 ......37 E3
  Kingston u T, Seething Wells
  KT6 ....37 C3
  Knaphill GU21 ....68 E2
  Mitcham SW14 ....20 F2
  Mortlake SW14 ....7 D4
  Oatlands Park KT13 ...53 D7
  Redhill RH1 ....140 A8
  Sandhurst GU47 ......45 A1

toria Rd continued
aines TW18 ....12 E5
ton SM1 ....59 D5
ddington TW11 ....17 A2
ckenham TW1 ....17 B8
king GU22 ....69 F2
oria St
glefield Green TW20 ....11 C2
graham RH13 ....217 D2
oria Terr RH4 ....136 A7
oria Villas TW9 ....6 F3
oria Way
 st Grinstead RH19 ....205 F7
atlands Park KT13 ....53 D7
oking GU21, GU22 ....69 E2
tors Dr TW12 ....12 E2
tory Ave SM4 ....40 C4
tory Bsns Ctr The TW7 ....5 F3
tory Cotts KT24 ....113 E7
tory Park Rd KT15 ....52 C6
tory Rise GU19 ....22 E2
tory Rd Chertsey KT16 ....33 A1
rsham RH12 ....217 B3
erton SW19 ....20 C1
tory Road Mews 5
V19 ....20 C1
nna Ct GU4 ....56 C4
w Cl TN16 ....83 C3
w Terr RH7 ....165 A1
wfield Rd SW18 ....19 F8
gory La GU21 ....69 C4
liant Cl SE26 ....23 A4
ng RG12 ....26 E4
ng Ct TW12 ....36 B8
age Cl 3 KT13 ....53 D7
age Ct SL5 ....29 C4
age Gate TW17 ....34 B4
age Gdns KT17 ....57 F1
age Green Ave TN16 ....83 E2
age Green Way TN16 ....83 E2
age Rd TW20 ....32 C6
age Row SM2 ....59 A3
age St RH5 ....158 B1
lage The SL4 ....10 B5
lage Way Ashford TW15 ....14 A4
eckenham BR3 ....44 A6
understead CR2 ....81 A6
las The RH7 ....163 E8
liers Ave Kingston u T KT5 ....37 F5
wickenham TW2 ....15 F7
liers Ct KT5 ....37 F5
liers Gr SM2 ....58 D2
liers Mead RG41 ....25 A6
liers Rd Hounslow TW7 ....5 E5
ingston u T KT1 ....37 F6
lies Rd RH13 ....43 D7
liers The SL3 ....53 D4
nall Gdns RH12 ....216 D4
ncam Cl TW2 ....16 A8
ncent Ave Sutton SM5 ....78 D8
1 Tolworth KT5 ....38 B1
ncent Cl Chertsey KT16 ....32 E2
oxted RH8 ....122 E7
ltcham KT23 ....94 B4
armondsworth UB7 ....3 A8
orsham RH13 ....217 F2
ncent Dr Dorking RH4 ....136 A6
per Halliford TW17 ....34 E6
ncent House KT3 ....38 F5
ncent La RH4 ....136 A7
ncent Rd Chertsey KT16 ....32 E2
oulsdon CR5 ....79 D2
oydon CR0 ....42 E2
orking RH4 ....136 A7
ounslow TW7 ....5 D6

Violet Gdns CR0 ....61 B5
Violet La CR0 ....61 B5
Violette Szabo House 4
SE27 ....22 D4
Virginia Ave GU25 ....31 C4
Virginia Beeches GU25 ....31 B5
Virginia Cl Ashstead KT21 ....75 D1
Kingston u T KT3 ....38 C5
Laleham TW18 ....33 C6
Weybridge KT13 ....53 C4
Virginia Ct GU25 ....31 D5
Virginia Dr GU25 ....31 C5
Virginia Gdns GU14 ....85 C2
Virginia Pl KT11 ....73 A5
Virginia Rd CR7 ....42 B7
Virginia Water SL5 ....30 E6
Virginia Water Prep Sch
GU25 ....31 A4
Virginia Water Sta GU25 ....31 E4
Viscount Gdns KT14 ....71 E7
Viscount Ind Est SL3 ....1 E4
Viscount Rd TW19 ....13 E7
Viscount Way TW6 ....3 E3
Vivien Cl KT9 ....56 E3
Vivienne Cl Crawley RH11 ....181 D1
Twickenham TW1 ....6 B8
Vivienne House TW18 ....13 A3
Voewood Cl KT3 ....38 F3
Vogan Cl RH2 ....139 B6
Voita Way CR0, CR9 ....41 F1
Voltaire 1 TW9 ....6 F6
Voss Ct SW16 ....21 E2
Vowels Forest Wlk RH19 ....204 E3
Vowels La RH19 ....204 E2
Vulcan Bsns Ctr CR9 ....63 E2
Vulcan Cl Crawley RH11 ....201 C2
Sandhurst GU47 ....64 A7
Wallington SM6 ....60 F3
Vulcan Way
New Addington CR0, CR9 ....63 A1
Sandhurst GU47 ....64 B7

W

Waddington Ave
CR5, CR8 ....100 B8
Waddington Cl
Coulsdon CR5 ....100 B8
Crawley RH11 ....201 A3
Waddington Way
CR7, SE19 ....42 D8
Waddon Cl CR0, CR9 ....61 A7
Waddon Court Rd
CR0, CR9 ....61 A7
Waddon Inf Sch SM6 ....61 A5
Waddon Marsh Way
CR0, CR9 ....41 F1
Waddon New Rd CR0, CR9 ....61 A8
Waddon Park Ave
CR0, CR9 ....61 A7
Waddon Rd CR0, CR9 ....61 A7
Waddon Sta CR0 ....61 A5
Waddon Way CR0, CR2, CR9 ......61 B4
Wade's La TW11 ....17 A2
Wadham Cl Crawley RH10 ....182 C1
Shepperton TW17 ....34 C2
Wadhurst Cl SE20 ....43 B7
Wadlands Brook Rd
RH19 ....185 D5
Wagbullock Rise RG12 ....27 C3
Wagg Cl RH19 ....186 A1
Waggon Cl GU2 ....108 E2
Waggoners Hollow GU19 ....47 E2
Waggoners Way GU26 ....188 A4
Waggoners Wells La
GU26 ....188 A2
Wagtail Cl RH12 ....217 D7
Wagtail Gdns CR2 ....62 E1
Waights Ct KT2 ....37 E8
Wain End RH12 ....217 D5
Wainford Ct SW19 ....19 D7
Wainwright Gr TW7 ....5 D3
Wainwrights RH10 ....201 D3
Waite Davies Rd SE12 ....24 F8
Wakefield Cl KT14 ....71 E7
Wakefield Gdns SE19 ....22 E1
Wakefield House SE22 ....23 B7
Wakefield Rd 9 TW10 ....6 E2
Wakehams Green Dr
RH10 ....182 D1
Wakehurst Dr
RH10, RH11 ....201 D3
Wakehurst Mews RH12 ....216 F1
Wakehurst Path GU21 ....70 C5
Wakelin House SE23 ....23 E8
Wakeling House 6 SE27 ....22 B5
Wakely Cl TN16 ....83 C1
Walburton Rd CR8 ....79 C7
Walbury RH12 ....218 B5
Waldby Ct RH11 ....201 A3
Waldeck Gr SE27 ....22 B5
Waldeck Rd Brentford W4 ....7 A8
South Wimbledon SW4 ....7 C4
Waldeck Terr SW14 ....7 C4
Waldegrave Ct 1 TW11 ....16 F3
Waldegrave Gdns TW1 ....16 F5
Waldegrave Pk TW1 ....16 F4
Waldegrave Rd Penge SE19 ....22 F1
Teddington TW11 ....16 F5
Waldegrave Sch for Girls
TW2 ....16 D5
Waldegrove CR0 ....61 F7
Waldemar Rd SW19 ....20 A2
Walden Cotts GU3 ....107 A3
Walden Gdns CR7, SW16 ....41 F5
Waldens Park Rd GU21 ....69 C3

Waldens Rd GU21 ....69 D2
Waldenshaw Rd SE23 ....23 C7
Waldo Pl SW19 ....20 E1
Waldorf Cl CR2 ....61 B2
Waldorf Hts GU17 ....64 D3
Waldram Cres SE23 ....23 C7
Waldram Park Rd SE23 ....23 D7
Waldram Pl 6 SE23 ....23 C7
Waldron Gdns BR2 ....44 D6
Waldron Hill RG12 ....27 F6
Waldron Rd SW17, SW18 ....20 C6
Waldronhyrst CR0, CR2 ....61 B6
Waldrons The Croydon CR0 ....61 C6
Oxted RH8 ....122 F4
Waldy Rise GU6 ....174 E4
Wales Ave SM5 ....59 E5
Walesbeech RH10 ....202 A5
Waleton Acres SM6 ....60 C4
Waley's La RH5 ....177 C1
Walford Rd RH5 ....136 C3
Walham Rise SW19 ....19 E2
Walk The Ashford TW16 ....14 F7
Tandridge RH8 ....122 A2
Walkden Hall (Hall of
Residence) KT2 ....18 D4
Walker Cl
East Bedfont TW14 ....14 F8
Hampton TW12 ....15 F2
Walker Rd RH10 ....202 C4
Walker's Ridge GU15 ....65 E5
Walkerscroft Mead SE21 ....22 C7
Wakfield Dr KT14 ....71 F7
Walking Bottom GU5 ....154 C6
Wall Hill Rd RH18, RH19 ....206 E5
Wallace Cl Fairlands GU3 ....108 C4
Upper Halliford TW17 ....34 E6
Wallace Cres SM5 ....59 F5
Wallace Fields KT17 ....77 A6
Wallace Fields Cty Inf Sch
KT17 ....77 A6
Wallace Fields Cty Jun Sch
KT17 ....77 A6
Wallace Wlk KT15 ....52 C6
Wallage La RH10 ....203 D6
Wallbrook Bsns Ctr TW4 ....4 B4
Walled Garden The
Loxwood RH14 ....212 F7
Tadworth KT20 ....97 D5
Walled Gdn The
Betchworth RH3 ....137 D8
Sunbury TW16 ....35 B6
Wallgrave Rd TW16 ....14 E6
Wallingford Cl RG12 ....27 E5
Wallington High Sch for
Boys SM6 ....60 B6
Wallington High Sch for
Girls SM6 ....60 B5
Wallington Rd GU15 ....47 A1
Wallington Sq 4 SM6 ....60 C4
Wallington Sta SM6 ....60 B4
Wallis Ct RH10 ....181 D2
Wallis Mews KT22 ....95 A5
Wallis Way RH13 ....218 A3
Wallner Way RG40 ....25 E5
Wallop Sch KT13 ....53 B5
Wallorton Gdns SW14 ....7 D3
Walmer Cl
Crowthorne RG45 ....45 C5
Frimley GU16 ....86 A7
Walmer House 11 SE20 ....43 C7
Walmsley House 8 SW16 ....21 C4
Walnut Cl Aldershot GU11 ....126 A8
Carshalton SM5 ....59 F5
Epsom KT18 ....76 F4
Walnut Ct RH11 ....217 E1
Walnut Dr KT20 ....97 D5
Walnut House SM7 ....77 D5
Walnut La RH11 ....181 B1
Walnut Mews SM2 ....59 C3
Walnut Tree Ave SM4 ....40 B6
Walnut Tree Cl Barnes SW13 ......7 F6
Belmont SM7 ....77 D5
Guildford GU1 ....130 C8
Walnut Tree Gdns GU7 ....150 E7
Walnut Tree La KT14 ....71 D7
Walnut Tree Pk GU1 ....109 C1
Walnut Tree Rd
Brentford TW8 ....6 E8
Charlton TW17 ....34 C7
Heston TW5 ....5 A8
Walpole Ave Chipstead CR5 ....98 F8
Richmond TW9 ....6 F5
Walpole Cres 7 TW11 ....16 F3
Walpole Gdns TW2 ....16 E5
Walpole Pl 2 TW11 ....16 F3
Walpole House 8 GU11 ....105 B2
Walpole Rd
Croydon CR0, CR9 ....61 D8
Mitcham SW19 ....20 D2
Old Windsor SL4 ....11 B8
Surbiton KT6 ....37 E3
Teddington TW11 ....16 F3
Twickenham TW2 ....16 E5
Walsh CE Jun Sch GU12 ....106 A1
Walsh Cres CR0 ....82 E7
Walsh Memorial C of E Inf
Sch GU12 ....105 F1
Walsham Rd TW14 ....15 C7
Walsingham Gdns KT19 ....57 F5
Walsingham Rd
Mitcham CR4 ....40 F4
New Addington CR0 ....63 C1
Walstead House 2 RH10 ....201 D5
Walter Cty Inf Sch RG41 ....25 A6

Walter St 2 KT2 ....37 E8
Walter's Mead KT21 ....75 E2
Walter's Rd SE25 ....42 E5
Waltham Ave GU2 ....109 B5
Waltham Cl GU47 ....45 D1
Waltham Rd
Carshalton SM5 ....40 E1
Caterham CR3 ....101 B5
Walton Ave Cheam SM3 ....58 F7
New Malden KT3 ....38 F5
Walton Bridge Rd
KT12, TW17 ....34 E2
Walton Comm Hospl KT12 ....54 C8
Walton Ct GU21 ....70 A3
Walton Dr Horsham RH13 ....218 C4
North Ascot SL5 ....28 F7
Walton Gdns TW13 ....14 F4
Walton Gn CR0 ....63 C3
Walton Heath RH10 ....202 D8
Walton La
Lower Halliford TW17 ....34 D2
Oatlands Park KT12 ....34 E1
Weybridge KT12, KT13 ....53 C8
Walton Leigh Special
Training Sch KT12 ....53 F6
Walton on the Hill Cty Prim
Sch KT20 ....97 B3
Walton Park La SM5 ....54 D8
Walton Pk KT12 ....54 D8
Walton Rd Ashstead KT18 ....96 C6
East Molesey KT8, KT12 ....36 B5
Walton-on-T KT12/KT13 ....54 C7
Woking GU21 ....70 A3
Walton St KT20 ....97 B3
Walton Terr GU21 ....70 B4
Walton Way CR4 ....41 C5
Wanborough Dr SW15 ....19 B7
Wanborough Hill GU3 ....128 C6
Wanborough La GU6 ....175 A3
Wanborough Sta GU3 ....107 C1
Wandle Bank Merton SW19 ....20 D1
Wallington CR0 ....60 E7
Wandle Cl Ash GU12 ....106 A1
Crawley RH10 ....202 C5
Wandle Court Gdns CR0 ....60 E7
Wandle Ct Wallington CR0 ....60 E7
West Ewell KT19 ....57 C6
Wandle House Catford BR1 ....24 D3
5 Redhill RH1 ....118 F2
Wandsworth SW18 ....20 B8
Wandle Lodge CR0 ....60 E7
Wandle Prim Sch SW18 ....20 B7
Wandle Rd
Croydon CR0, CR9 ....61 C7
Hackbridge SM6 ....60 B8
Morden SM4, SW19 ....40 D4
Upper Tooting SW17 ....20 D6
Wallington CR0 ....60 E7
Wandle Side Croydon CR0 ....60 F7
Hackbridge SM6 ....60 C8
Wandle Tech Pk CR4 ....40 F2
Wandle Trad Est CR4 ....40 F2
Wandle Valley Sch SM5 ....40 E2
Wandle Way Mitcham CR4 ....40 F4
Wandsworth SW18 ....20 C8
Wandsdyke Cl GU16 ....85 F8
Wandsworth Common Sta
SW12 ....21 A8
Wansford Gn GU21 ....68 F2
Wanstraw Gr RG12 ....27 E2
Wantage Cl Bracknell RG12 ....27 E4
Crawley RH10 ....202 C3
Wantage Rd GU47 ....64 B8
Waplings The KT20 ....97 B3
Wapshott Rd TW18 ....12 E3
War Coppice Rd CR3 ....120 D7
War Memorial Homes W4 ....7 D7
War Memorial Hospl SM5 ....59 F4
Warbank Cl CR0 ....63 E1
Warbank Cres CR0 ....63 E1
Warbank La KT2 ....18 F1
Warblers Gn KT11 ....73 F5
Warbleton House 6
RH11 ....200 F3
Warboys App KT2 ....18 B2
Warboys Rd KT2 ....18 B2
Warburton Cl RH19 ....206 A8
Warburton Rd TW2 ....16 B7
Warbury La GU21 ....68 C3
Ward Cl RG40 ....25 D8
Ward La CR6 ....81 D2
Ward St GU1 ....130 D8
Wardle Cl GU19 ....47 E3
Wardley St SW18 ....20 B8
Wardrobe The 3 TW9 ....6 D2
Wards Stone Pk RG12 ....27 E2
Ware Ct SM1 ....58 F6
Wareham Cl TW3 ....5 B3
Wareham Rd RG12 ....27 F4
Warenne Hts RH1 ....139 D7
Warenne Rd KT22 ....94 C5
Warfield Rd Bracknell RG12 ....27 C8
East Bedfont TW14 ....14 E8
Hampton TW12 ....36 B8
Wargrove Dr GU47 ....45 A1
Warham Rd CR0, CR2 ....61 C5
Waring St SE27 ....22 C4
Warkworth Gdns TW7 ....6 A7
Warlingham Cty Sec Sch
CR6 ....81 A3
Warlingham Park Sch
CR6 ....82 A3
Warlingham Rd CR7 ....42 B5
Warttersville Way RH6 ....161 C1
Warminster Gdns SE25 ....43 A7
Warminster Rd SE25 ....43 A7
Warminster Sq SE25 ....43 A7
Warminster Way CR4 ....41 B7

Warner Ave SM3 ....58 E8
Warner Cl Crawley RH10 ....202 C2
Harlington UB3 ....3 D8
Warner Ct SM3 ....58 E8
Warner House BR3 ....24 B2
Warner Rd RH1 ....24 F1
Warners La GU5 ....132 E2
Warnford House SW15 ....7 E1
Warnham CE (Controlled)
Sch RH12 ....216 F8
Warnham Court Rd SM5 ....59 F3
Warnham Ct SM5 ....59 F3
Warnham House 5 SW2 ....21 F8
Warnham Nature Reserve
RH12 ....217 B6
Warnham Rd
Broadbridge Heath RH12 ....216 D4
Crawley RH10 ....202 B4
Horsham RH12 ....217 B5
Warnham Sta RH12 ....217 C8
Warpole Pk KT13 ....53 A3
Warramill Rd GU7 ....151 A5
Warren Ave Belmont SM2 ....58 E1
Bromley BR1 ....24 E1
Mortlake SW14, TW10 ....7 B3
South Croydon CR2 ....62 D3
Warren Cl Esher KT10 ....55 B6
Felbridge RH19 ....184 E3
Sandhurst GU47 ....64 A8
West Norwood SE21 ....22 C8
Warren Cnr GU10 ....124 C7
Warren Ct
5 Beckenham BR3 ....24 A1
2 Croydon CR0 ....42 E1
Weybridge KT13 ....53 A5
Warren Cutting KT2 ....18 D1
Warren Down RG42 ....26 E8
Warren Dr Crawley RH11 ....201 A8
Kingswood KT20 ....98 A4
Warren Dr N KT5, KT6 ....38 B1
Warren Dr S KT5 ....38 C1
Warren Farm Mobile Home
Pk GU23 ....91 B8
Warren Hill KT18 ....76 D3
Warren House Rd RG40 ....25 D8
Warren La Oxshott KT22 ....74 C7
Oxted RH8 ....123 A1
Woking GU22, GU23 ....71 B1
Warren Lodge KT20 ....97 E3
Warren Lodge Dr KT20 ....97 E3
Warren Mead SM7 ....77 C4
Warren Mead Cty Inf Sch
SM7 ....77 D4
Warren Mead Cty Jun Sch
SM7 ....77 D4
Warren Park Rd SM1, SM2 ....59 E4
Warren Pk Kingston u T KT2 ......18 C2
Warlingham CR6 ....81 D1
Warren Rd Ashford TW15 ....14 C1
Banstead KT17, SM7 ....77 E3
Croydon CR0 ....42 E1
Farncombe GU7 ....150 E7
Guildford GU1, GU4 ....131 A8
Kingston u T KT2 ....18 C2
Mitcham SW19 ....20 D2
Purley CR8 ....80 B8
Reigate RH2 ....118 B2
Twickenham TW2 ....5 D1
Woodham KT15 ....52 A1
Warren Rise Frimley GU16 ....65 F3
Kingston u T KT3 ....38 D8
Warren Row SL5 ....28 D7
Warren The
Aldershot GU11 ....104 F1
Ashstead KT21 ....75 D1
East Horsley KT24 ....112 F5
Heath End GU9 ....125 D7
Heston TW5 ....4 F7
Kingswood KT20 ....97 E4
Tatsfield TN16 ....103 D8
Worcester Park KT19, KT4 ....57 E7
Warren Way KT13 ....53 C4
Warren Wood Cl BR2 ....63 F8
Warreners La KT13 ....53 D3
Warren Yard GU1 ....131 A8
Warrington Cl RH11 ....200 E2
Warrington Mews GU11 ....125 D8
Warrington Rd
Croydon CR0, CR9 ....61 B7
21 Richmond TW10 ....6 D2
Warrington Spur SL4 ....11 B8
Warwick 5 RG12 ....27 E2
Warwick Ave Staines TW18 ....13 C2
Warwick Cl SM3 ....32 C8
Warwick Ct
Ash Vale GU12 ....106 A8
Aldershot GU11 ....126 C8
Frimley GU15 ....66 C3
Hampton TW12 ....16 C1
South Holmwood RH5 ....157 C7
Warwick Ct Beckenham BR2 ......44 E7
Weybridge KT13 ....53 A5
Warwick Deeping KT16 ....51 C5
Warwick La 32 C8
Warwick Cl
Ash Vale GU12 ....106 A8

Warwick Rd continued
Ashford TW15 . . . . 13 E3
Coulsdon CR5 . . . . 79 D5
Hounslow TW4 . . . . 4 B4
Kingston u T KT3 . . . . 38 C6
Penge SE20 . . . . 43 B6
Redhill RH1 . . . . 118 F2
South Holmwood RH5 . . . . . . 157 C7
Sutton SM1 . . . . 59 C5
Teddington KT1 . . . . 37 C8
Thames Ditton KT7 . . . . 36 F4
Thornton Heath CR7 . . . . 42 A6
Twickenham TW2 . . . . 5 E1
Warwick Sch The RH1 . . . . 119 A2
Warwick Villas TW20 . . . . . 32 C8
Warwick Wold Rd
Bletchingley RH1 . . . . 120 A7
Caterham RH1 . . . . 120 A7
Warwick's Bench Rd GU1 130 E6
Warwicks Bench GU1 . . . . 130 D6
Wasdale Cl GU47 . . . . 45 D2
Washington Cl RH2 . . . . 118 A3
Washington Ct SW17 . . . . . . 20 F2
Washington Rd
Crawley RH11 . . . . 200 E3
Kingston u T KT1 . . . . 38 A7
North Cheam KT4 . . . . 39 B1
Washpond La CR0 . . . . 82 E2
Wasp Green La RH1 . . . . . . 162 C8
Wassand Cl RH10 . . . . 202 A6
Wastdale Rd SE23 . . . . 23 D7
Watchetts Cty Jun Sch
GU15 . . . . 65 B2
Watchetts Dr GU15 . . . . 65 B2
Watchetts Lake Cl GU15 . . 65 D3
Watchetts Rd GU15 . . . . 65 C4
Watchmoor Pk GU15 . . . . . . 65 A4
Watchmoor Rd GU15 . . . . . . 65 A4
Watchmoor Trade Ctr
GU15 . . . . 65 A3
Watcombe Cotts TW9 . . . . . . 7 A8
Watcombe Rd SE25 . . . . 43 B4
Water La
Abinger Common RH5 . . . . . . 155 B8
Albury GU4, GU5 . . . . 132 B5
Bisley GU24 . . . . 87 E8
Cobham KT11 . . . . 73 F5
Enton Green GU8 . . . . 171 B4
Farnborough GU14 . . . . 85 A7
Farnham GU9 . . . . 125 C2
Kingston u T KT1 . . . . 37 D8
Limpsfield RH8 . . . . 123 A8
Lingfield TN8 . . . . 165 D7
Little Bookham KT23, KT24 . . 93 E1
Richmond TW10, TW9 . . . . 6 D2
South Godstone RH9 . . . . 142 D5
Twickenham TW1 . . . . 17 A7
Wormley GU8 . . . . 171 B4
Water Lea RH10 . . . . 202 A5
Water Mill Way TW13 . . . . . 16 A6
Water Splash La SL5 . . . . . . 29 E8
Water Tower Hill CR0, CR2 . 61 D6
Water View RH6 . . . . 161 C3
Waterbank Rd SE6 . . . . 24 C4
Watercress Way GU21 . . . . . 69 B2
Waterden Cl GU1 . . . . 130 F8
Waterden Rd GU1 . . . . 130 E8
Waterer Gdns KT20 . . . . 77 E1
Waterer House SE6 . . . . 24 C4
Waterers Rise SM6 . . . . 60 D4
Waterers Rise GU6 . . . . 68 D2
Waterfall Cl GU25 . . . . 31 A6
Waterfall Cotts SW19 . . . . . 20 D2
Waterfall Rd SW19 . . . . 20 D2
Waterfall Terr SW17 . . . . 20 E2
Waterfield KT20 . . . . 97 B7
Waterfield Cl RH10 . . . . 217 E3
Waterfield Cty Fst Sch
RH11 . . . . 200 E4
Waterfield Dr CR6 . . . . 101 C8
Waterfield Gdns
Crawley RH11 . . . . 200 E4
South Norwood SE25 . . . . 42 E4
Waterfield Gn KT20 . . . . 97 B7
Waterfields KT22 . . . . 95 B8
Waterford Ct KT11 . . . . 73 E8
Waterford Way RG40 . . . . . . 25 C6
Watergardens The KT2 . . . . 18 C2
Waterham Rd RG12 . . . . 27 B3
Waterhouse Ct █ TW11 . . . 16 F3
Waterhouse La
Bletchingley RH1 . . . . 121 A3
Coulsdon CR8 . . . . 100 C8
Kingswood KT20 . . . . 97 E6
Waterhouse Mead GU47 . . 64 D7
Waterlands La RH1 . . . . 196 E1
Waterloo Cl
Camberley GU15 . . . . 66 B7
East Bedfont TW14 . . . . 14 F7
Waterloo Cres RG40 . . . . . . 25 E4
Waterloo Pl TW9 . . . . 7 A8
Waterloo Rd
Aldershot GU12 . . . . 105 C1
Carshalton SM1 . . . . 59 D5
Crowthorne RG45 . . . . 45 B4
Epsom KT17, KT19 . . . . 76 D6
Wokingham RG40 . . . . 25 F5
Waterlow Rd RH2 . . . . 139 C8
Watermans Bsns Pk The
TW18 . . . . 12 E4
Watermans Ct █ TW8 . . . . . . 6 D8
Watermead
East Bedfont TW14 . . . . 14 F7
Tadworth KT20 . . . . 97 B6
Woking GU21 . . . . 68 F3

Watermead La CR4 . . . . 40 F2
Watermead Rd SE6 . . . . 24 C4
Watermeads High Sch
SM4 . . . . 40 D3
Watermen's Sq █ SE20 . . . 23 C1
Watermill Cl TW10 . . . . 17 C5
Watermill Way SW19 . . . . . . 40 C8
Waterperry La GU24 . . . . 49 F1
Waters Dr TW18 . . . . 12 F4
Waters Rd Catford SE6 . . . . . 24 E5
Kingston u T KT1 . . . . 38 B7
Waters Sq KT1 . . . . 38 B6
Watersedge KT19 . . . . 57 B6
Waterside Beckenham BR3 . . 44 A8
East Grinstead RH19 . . . . 186 B1
Horley RH6 . . . . 161 A5
Waterside Cl Crawley RH11 200 E4
Godalming GU7 . . . . 151 A5
Surbiton KT6 . . . . 56 E8
Waterside Dr KT12 . . . . 35 B4
Waterside La GU7 . . . . 150 C3
Waterside Mews GU1 . . . . . 109 C3
Waterside Rd GU1 . . . . 109 D4
Waterside Trad Est KT15 . . 52 E6
Waterside Way
Wimbledon SW17 . . . . 20 C3
█ Woking GU21 . . . . 69 B1
Waterslade RH1 . . . . 118 E1
Watersmeet Cl GU4 . . . . 110 A6
Watersplash Cl KT1 . . . . 37 E6
Watersplash Rd TW17 . . . . . 34 A5
Waterway Rd Fetcham KT22 95 A5
Leatherhead KT22 . . . . 95 A4
Watery La Chobham GU24 . . 49 D1
Merton SW19, SW20 . . . . 39 F7
Wates Way CR4 . . . . 40 F3
Watford Cl GU1 . . . . 109 F1
Wathen Rd RH4 . . . . 136 B8
Watlings Cl CR0 . . . . 43 E3
Watlington Gr SE26 . . . . 23 E3
Watney Cotts SW14 . . . . 7 C4
Watney Rd SW14 . . . . 7 C4
Watneys Rd CR4 . . . . 41 D4
Watson Ave SM3 . . . . 58 E8
Watson Cl Crawley RH10 . . . 202 C2
Mitcham SW19 . . . . 20 E1
Watson House █ SW2 . . . . . 21 E8
Watson Rd RH4 . . . . 135 C6
Watt's La Tadworth KT20 . . . . 97 D5
Teddington TW11 . . . . 17 A3
Watt's Mead KT20 . . . . 97 D5
Wattenden Prim Sch CR8 . . 80 B3
Wattendon Rd CR8 . . . . 80 B3
Watts Cl KT20 . . . . 97 D5
Watts Lea GU21 . . . . 69 A4
Watts Rd Farnborough GU14 . 84 F5
Thames Ditton KT7 . . . . 37 A2
Wavel Cl █ SW16 . . . . 21 E5
Wavel Pl SE19, SE26 . . . . 22 F4
Wavell Sch The GU11 . . . . . 105 F4
Wavendene Ave TW20 . . . . . 12 C1
Waveney House █ RH1 . . . 118 F1
Waveney Wlk RH10 . . . . 202 B4
Waverleigh Rd GU6 . . . . 174 E1
Waverley RG12 . . . . 26 E4
Waverley Abbey GU9 . . . . . 147 B7
Waverley Abbey CE Jun
Sch GU10 . . . . 147 D5
Waverley Ave Kenley CR8 . . 80 E3
Sutton SM1 . . . . 59 C8
Tolworth KT5 . . . . 38 C3
Twickenham TW2, TW4 . . . . . . 4 F4
Waverley Cl Farnham GU9 . 125 D2
Frimley GU15 . . . . 65 F4
Waverley Ct
Horsham RH12 . . . . 217 B2
█ Woking GU22 . . . . 69 E1
Waverley Dr
Addlestone KT16 . . . . 51 D7
Ash Vale GU12 . . . . 106 A6
Camberley GU15 . . . . 65 F5
Virginia Water GU25 . . . . 31 A5
Waverley Gdns GU12 . . . . . 106 A6
Waverley La
Farnham GU10, GU9 . . . . 147 C8
Farnham, Compton GU9 . . . . 125 E1
Waverley Pl KT22 . . . . 95 B5
Waverley Rd Bagshot GU19 47 C3
Croydon SE25 . . . . 43 B6
Farnborough GU14 . . . . 85 D3
Oxshott KT11, KT22 . . . . 74 B5
Stoneleigh KT17, KT4 . . . . 58 B5
Weybridge KT13 . . . . 53 A5
Waverley Way SM2, SM5 . . . 59 E4
Waverton Rd SW18 . . . . 20 C8
Wavertree Ct █ SW2 . . . . . . 21 E7
Wavertree Rd SW2 . . . . 21 F7
Way The RH2 . . . . 118 D2
Way Way TW5 . . . . 4 A6
Wayland Cl RG12 . . . . 27 F5
Waylands Mead BR3 . . . . . . 44 B8
Waylett Pl SE27 . . . . 22 B5
Wayman Rd GU14 . . . . 84 E8
Waynflete Tower Ave
KT10 . . . . 55 A7
Waynflete Ave CR0, CR9 . . . 61 A7
Waynflete La GU9 . . . . 124 F2
Waynflete St SW18 . . . . 20 C6
Ways End GU15 . . . . 65 E4
Wayside Capel RH5 . . . . 178 D6
Crawley RH11 . . . . 200 E4
Mortlake SW14 . . . . 7 C2
New Addington CR0 . . . . 63 B4
Wayside Ct Hounslow TW7 . . 5 E6
Twickenham TW1 . . . . 6 C1
Woking GU21 . . . . 68 E3
WC Lee's Resthouses
GU20 . . . . 48 D4

Weald CE Prim Sch The
RH5 . . . . 157 D3
Weald Cl GU4 . . . . 130 E3
Weald Day Hospl The
RH11 . . . . 201 C6
Weald Dr RH10 . . . . 202 A4
Weald The RH19 . . . . 185 F4
Weald View Cotts RH5 . . . . 156 D3
Weald Way Caterham CR3 . . 120 E8
Reigate RH2 . . . . 139 C5
Wealdon Cl █ GU2 . . . . 108 F1
Wealdstone Rd SM3 . . . . 58 F8
Weare St Capel RH5 . . . . 178 B4
Ockley RH5 . . . . 177 F1
Weasdale Cl GU21 . . . . 68 F3
Weatherall Cl KT15 . . . . 52 B5
Weatherhill Cl RH6 . . . . 161 F3
Weatherhill Rd RH6 . . . . 162 A4
Weatherill Ct SE25 . . . . 43 B3
Weaver Cl █ RH11 . . . . 200 E5
Weaver Wlk SE27 . . . . 22 B4
Weavers Cl TW7 . . . . 5 E3
Weavers Gdns GU9 . . . . 145 F7
Weavers Yd GU9 . . . . 125 B2
Webb Cl Bagshot GU19 . . . . . 47 C3
Crawley RH11 . . . . 201 B1
Webb Ct RG40 . . . . 25 E8
Webb House TW13 . . . . 15 E5
Webb Rd GU8 . . . . 170 C6
Webster Cl KT11, KT22 . . . . . 74 B5
Websters Cl GU22 . . . . 89 B7
Weddell Rd RH10 . . . . 201 F3
Wedgewood Cl GU22 . . . . 44 F5
Wedgwood Way SE19 . . . . . . 22 C1
Wedgwoods TN16 . . . . 103 C6
Weeks House TW10 . . . . 17 C4
Weighbridge Rd KT15 . . . . . 52 B2
Weighton Rd SE20 . . . . 43 B7
Weihurst Ct SM1 . . . . 59 E5
Weihurst Gdns SM1 . . . . 59 D5
Weir Ave GU14 . . . . 85 A3
Weir Cl GU14 . . . . 85 A3
Weir House █ SW12 . . . . 21 C8
Weir Pl TW18 . . . . 32 E8
Weir Rd Chertsey KT16 . . . . . 33 B2
Streatham SW12 . . . . 21 C8
Walton-on-T KT12 . . . . 35 A3
Wimbledon SW18, SW19 . . . . 20 B5
Weir Wood Resr
(Nature Reserve) RH19 . . . 205 E2
Weirbrook RH10 . . . . 202 A3
Weirbrook RG12 . . . . 26 E4
Welbeck Cl Ewell KT17 . . . . . 58 A3
Farnborough GU14 . . . . 84 F3
New Malden KT3 . . . . 38 F4
Welbeck Rd SM1, SM5 . . . . . 59 D8
Welbeck Wlk SM5 . . . . 40 E1
Welcome Cotts CR3 . . . . 102 A4
Welcome Terr CR3 . . . . 80 F3
Welcomes Rd CR8 . . . . 80 C3
Weldon Cl CR7 . . . . 42 B4
Weldon Dr KT8 . . . . 35 F5
Weldon Way RH1 . . . . 119 D6
Welford Pl SW19 . . . . 19 E4
Welham Rd SW16, SW17 . . . 21 B2
Welhouse Rd SM5 . . . . 59 E8
Well Cl Camberley GU15 . . . . 66 B6
Streatham SW16 . . . . 21 F4
Woking GU21 . . . . 69 C2
Well Farm Rd CR3, CR6 . . . 101 A8
Well House SM7 . . . . 78 B4
Well La Haslemere GU27 . . . 208 D6
Mortlake SW14 . . . . 7 C2
Woking GU21 . . . . 69 C2
Well Path GU21 . . . . 69 C2
Well Way KT18 . . . . 76 A5
Welland Cl SL3 . . . . 1 B8
Wellburn Cl GU47 . . . . 64 B7
Weller Cl RH10 . . . . 202 D5
Weller Dr GU15 . . . . 65 C3
Wellesford Cl SM7 . . . . 77 F2
Wellesley Cl
Ash Vale GU12 . . . . 105 F7
Bagshot GU19 . . . . 47 C3
Wellesley Court Rd █
CR0, CR9 . . . . 61 D8
Wellesley Cres TW2 . . . . 16 E5
Wellesley Ct Cheam SM3 . . . 39 E1
Twickenham TW2 . . . . 16 E5
Wellesley Garden GU9 . . . . 125 C7
Wellesley Gate █ GU12 . . . 105 B1
Wellesley Gr CR0, CR9 . . . . . 61 D8
Wellesley Rd
Aldershot GU11 . . . . 104 E2
Croydon CR0 . . . . 42 C1
Rushmoor GU10 . . . . 168 C6
Sutton SM2 . . . . 59 C4
Twickenham TW2 . . . . 16 E5
Wellfield RH19 . . . . 206 C7
Wellfield Gdns SM5 . . . . 59 E2
Wellfield Rd SW16 . . . . 21 F4
Wellhouse Rd
Beckenham BR3 . . . . 44 A4
Betchworth RH3 . . . . 137 D6
Wellington Ave
Aldershot GU11 . . . . 104 F2
Hounslow TW3, TW4 . . . . 5 A2
North Cheam KT4 . . . . 58 C7
Virginia Water GU25 . . . . 31 B4
Wentworth GU25 . . . . 31 A4
Wellington Cl
Crawley RH10 . . . . 182 E1
Sandhurst GU47 . . . . 64 C8
Walton-on-T KT12 . . . . 34 F1
Wellington Coll RG45 . . . . . . 45 E2
Wellington Cotts KT24 . . . . 112 E6
Wellington Cres KT3 . . . . 38 C6

Wellington Ct
Stanwell TW19 . . . . 13 E8
█ Surbiton KT6 . . . . 37 E3
Teddington TW12 . . . . 16 D3
Wellington Ctr The GU11 . 105 A2
Wellington Dr
Bracknell RG12 . . . . 27 E4
Wallington CR8 . . . . 60 F1
Wellington Gdns
Aldershot GU11 . . . . 104 F1
Teddington TW12, TW2 . . . . . . 16 D4
Wellington La GU9 . . . . 125 D7
Wellington Pl
Cobham KT11 . . . . 73 C7
Farncombe GU7 . . . . 150 E7
Wellington Prim Sch TW3 . . 4 F5
Wellington Rd
Ashford TW15 . . . . 13 E3
Caterham CR3 . . . . 100 C5
Crowthorne RG45 . . . . 45 C4
Hatton TW14 . . . . 4 A3
Horsham RH12, RH13 . . . . . . 217 D2
Sandhurst GU47 . . . . 64 C8
Teddington TW12, TW2 . . . . . . 16 D4
Thornton Heath CR0 . . . . 42 B2
Wimbledon SW19 . . . . 20 A6
Wokingham RG40 . . . . 25 B5
Wellington Rd N TW4 . . . . . . 4 F4
Wellington Rd S TW4 . . . . . . 4 F3
Wellington Rdbt GU11 . . . . 104 E2
Wellington St █ GU11 . . . . 105 A2
Wellington Terr
█ Knaphill GU21 . . . . 68 E1
Sandhurst GU47 . . . . 64 C8
Wellington Town Rd
RH19 . . . . 185 D2
Wellington Way
Byfleet KT13 . . . . 52 F1
Horley RH6 . . . . 160 F5
Weybridge KT13 . . . . 52 F1
Wellingtonia House KT15 . . 52 A5
Wellmeadow Rd SE13, SE6 . 24 E7
Wellow Wlk SM5 . . . . 40 D1
Wells Cl
Great Bookham KT23 . . . . 94 C3
Horsham RH12 . . . . 216 F2
Wells Cotts GU9 . . . . 146 A7
Wells La Ascot SL5 . . . . 29 B5
Normandy GU3 . . . . 107 C4
Wells Lea RH19 . . . . 185 D3
Wells Meadow RH19 . . . . . . 185 D3
Wells Park Ct SE26 . . . . 23 B4
Wells Park Rd SE21, SE26 . . 23 B4
Wells Pl RH1 . . . . 119 B6
Wells Rd Crawley RH10 . . . . 202 C8
Epsom KT18 . . . . 76 B4
Guildford GU4 . . . . 110 C4
Wells The GU27 . . . . 208 C6
Wellside Gdns SW14 . . . . 7 C2
Wellwood Cl
Coulsdon CR5, CR8 . . . . 79 E5
Horsham RH13 . . . . 218 B4
Wellwynds Rd GU6 . . . . 174 E2
Welwyn Ave TW14 . . . . 3 F1
Welwyn Cl RH11 . . . . 200 E2
Wembley Rd TW12 . . . . 36 A8
Wembury Pk RH7 . . . . 163 E1
Wend The CR5 . . . . 79 D5
Wendela Cl GU22 . . . . 69 F1
Wendley Dr KT15 . . . . 51 F1
Wendling Rd SM1, SM5 . . . . 59 D8
Wendover Dr Frimley GU16 . 66 C3
New Malden KT3 . . . . 38 F3
Wendover Pl TW18 . . . . 12 D3
Wendover Rd TW18, TW20 . 12 D3
Wendron Cl █ GU21 . . . . 69 A1
Wendy Cres GU2 . . . . 109 A3
Wenlock Cl RH11 . . . . 201 A4
Wenlock Edge RH4 . . . . 136 C5
Wensleydale RH11 . . . . 201 C3
Wensleydale Dr GU15 . . . . . 66 D5
Wensleydale Gdns TW12 . . 16 B1
Wensleydale Rd TW12 . . . . . 16 B1
Wentland Cl SE6 . . . . 24 D6
Wentland Rd SE6 . . . . 24 D6
Wentworth Ave SL5 . . . . 28 C7
Wentworth Cl
Ash Vale GU12 . . . . 106 A7
Ashford TW15 . . . . 14 B4
Heath End GU9 . . . . 125 F6
Long Ditton KT6 . . . . 56 D8
Morden SM4 . . . . 40 A2
Ripley GU23 . . . . 91 B6
Wentworth Club GU25 . . . . . 31 A4
Wentworth Cres GU12 . . . . 106 A6
Wentworth Ct
█ Kingston u T KT6 . . . . 37 E4
Twickenham TW2 . . . . 16 E5
Wentworth Dr
Crawley RH10 . . . . 202 D7
Wentworth GU25 . . . . 30 F5
Wentworth House KT15 . . . 52 B6
Wentworth Rd CR0 . . . . 42 A2
Wentworth Way
Hamsey Green CR2 . . . . 81 A4
North Ascot SL5 . . . . 28 C7
Werndee Rd SE25 . . . . 43 A5
Wesco Ct GU21 . . . . 70 A3
Wescott Cty Inf Sch RG40 . 25 D6
Wescott Rd RG40 . . . . 25 D6
Wesley Ave TW3 . . . . 4 F5
Wesley Cl Crawley RH11 . . . 200 E3
Horley RH6 . . . . 161 A5
Reigate RH2 . . . . 138 F8
Wesley Pl SL4 . . . . 9 B6
Wesley Pl TW20 . . . . 12 A2
Wessels KT20 . . . . 97 D6
Wessex Ave SW19 . . . . 40 A6

Wessex Cl KT1, KT2 . . . . 38 B7
Wessex Ct █ TW19 . . . . 2 D1
Wessex Pl GU9 . . . . 125 C3
Wessex Rd TW19, TW6 . . . . . . 2 C2
Wesson House █ CR0 . . . . . . 43 A1
West Ashtead Cty Prim Sch
KT21 . . . . 95 D7
West Ave Crawley RH10 . . . . 202 A8
Heath End GU9 . . . . 125 F7
Redhill RH1 . . . . 140 A4
Wallington CR0, SM6 . . . . 60 E5
Whiteley Village KT12, KT13 . . 53 D4
West Bank RH4 . . . . 136 A5
West Barnes La
West Barnes KT3, SW20 . . . . . 39 B5
Wimbledon KT3, SW20 . . . . . . 39 C4
West Byfleet Cty Inf Sch
KT14 . . . . 71 A6
West Byfleet Cty Jun Sch
KT14 . . . . 71 A6
West Ct Ashford TW15 . . . . . . 13 E3
Heath End GU9 . . . . 125 E7
West Cross Ctr TW8 . . . . 6 A8
West Cross Way TW8 . . . . 6 A8
West Croydon Sta CR9 . . . . . 42 C2
West Ct Guildford GU4 . . . . . 110 B4
Hounslow TW7 . . . . 5 A6
West Down KT23 . . . . 114 B8
West Dr Belmont SM2 . . . . . . 58 B4
Burgh Heath KT20 . . . . 77 E1
Streatham SW16, SW17 . . . . . 21 C5
Sutton SM5 . . . . 59 D2
Wentworth GU25 . . . . 31 B5
Woodham KT15 . . . . 52 B2
West Dulwich Sta SE21 . . . . 22 C7
West End Cty Inf Sch
GU11 . . . . 104 F1
West End Gdns KT10 . . . . 54 A6
West End Gr GU9 . . . . 125 A4
West End La
Chiddingfold GU27 . . . . 190 B1
Esher KT10 . . . . 54 A6
Frensham GU10 . . . . 146 B8
Harlington UB7 . . . . 3 C8
West Ewell Cty Inf Sch
KT19 . . . . 57 D3
West Ewell Cty Jun Sch
KT19 . . . . 57 D3
West Farm Ave KT21 . . . . 95 D8
West Farm Cl KT21 . . . . 95 C8
West Farm Dr KT21 . . . . 95 D8
West Flexford La GU3 . . . . . 128 D8
West Gdns Ewell KT17 . . . . . . 57 F2
Mitcham SW19 . . . . 20 E8
West Gr KT12 . . . . 54 B6
West Green Cty Fst Sch
RH11 . . . . 201 C7
West Green Dr RH11 . . . . . . 201 C6
West Hall Rd TW9 . . . . 7 B6
West Heath GU24 . . . . 87 D8
West Heath Rd GU14 . . . . 84 F8
West Hill Biggin Hill BR6 . . . 83 D6
Dormans Park RH19 . . . . 185 E1
East Grinstead RH19 . . . . 205 D8
Elstead GU8 . . . . 148 C4
Epsom KT18, KT19 . . . . 76 C6
Oxted RH8 . . . . 122 D5
Putney SW15 . . . . 19 E8
South Croydon CR2 . . . . 61 D2
Woking GU22 . . . . 89 E8
West Hill Ave KT19 . . . . 76 C6
West Hill Bank RH8 . . . . 122 D5
West Hill Cl
Brookwood GU24 . . . . 88 B6
Elstead GU8 . . . . 148 C4
West Hill Rd
Wandsworth SW18 . . . . 20 A8
Woking GU22 . . . . 89 E8
West Hill Sch KT22 . . . . 95 B4
West Hoathly Rd RH19 . . . . 205 D7
West House Penge SE20 . . . . 23 D1
█ Streatham SW12 . . . . 21 C8
West House Cl SW19 . . . . 19 E7
West La
East Grinstead RH19 . . . . 205 D8
Wotton RH5 . . . . 134 D6
West Leigh RH19 . . . . 205 E8
West Mead KT19 . . . . 57 E4
West Mead Sch RG40 . . . . . . 25 E7
West Meads GU2 . . . . 129 F7
West Middlesex Univ Hospl
TW7 . . . . 6 A5
West Mount GU2 . . . . 130 C7
West Norwood Sta SE27 . . . 22 B5
West Oak BR3 . . . . 44 D7
West Palace Gdns KT13 . . . . 53 B7
West Par RH12 . . . . 217 C2
West Park Ave TW9 . . . . 7 B6
West Park Cl TW5 . . . . 4 F8
West Park Hospl KT19 . . . . . 75 E2
West Park Rd
Domewood RH10 . . . . 183 F4
Epsom KT19 . . . . 75 F2
Horne RH7, RH10 . . . . 184 B8
Richmond TW9 . . . . 7 B6
West Ramp TW6 . . . . 3 A6
West Rd Bracknell RG40 . . . . 26 D7
Camberley GU15 . . . . 65 D5
Chessington KT9 . . . . 56 C5
East Bedfont TW14 . . . . 3 D1
Farnborough GU14 . . . . 85 B8
Guildford GU1 . . . . 130 E8
Kingston u T KT2, KT3 . . . . . . 38 C8
Reigate RH2 . . . . 139 A8
Wentworth GU25 . . . . 31 B5
West Ring GU10 . . . . 126 F7
West Sheen Vale TW9 . . . . 6 F3

...est Side Comm SW19 .....19 C3
...est St Carshalton SM5 ...59 F6
　Crawley RH11 ....201 D5
　Croydon CR0, CR9 ....64 D6
　Dorking RH4 ....136 A7
　Normansland RH7 ....165 A1
　East Grinstead RH19 ....205 E8
　Epsom KT18, KT19 ....76 C6
　Ewell KT17 ....57 F1
...est Street ■ CR0, CR9 ..61 C6
...est Sutton Sta SM1 .....59 A6
...est Temple Sheen SW14 ...7 B2
...est Thames Coll TW7 .....5 E6
...est Thornton Prim Sch
　CR0 ....41 F3
...est View TW14 ....14 C8
...est View Ave GU3 ....80 F1
...est View Rdbt RH19 ....205 E8
...est View Rd
　Headley Down GU5 ......187 C4
　Warlingham CR6 ....101 B8
...est Way Crawley RH10 ..202 A7
　Croydon CR0 ....62 B7
　Cranford TW5 ....4 F6
　Shepperton TW17 ....34 D3
　Winbild RH13 ....215 D3
　Sutton SM2, SM5 ....59 D1
...est Way Gdns CR0 ....62 D8
...est Wickham Sta BR3 ....44 C2
...estacres KT10 ....54 F3
...estbank Rd TW12 ....16 C2
...estborough Cty Prim Sch
　GU2 ....108 F2
...estbourne Ave SM3 .....58 E8
...estbourne Dr SE23 .....23 D6
...estbourne House
　Heston TW5 ....5 A8
　Twickenham TW1 ....17 B8
...estbourne Prim Sch
　SM1 ....59 A7
...estbourne Rd
　Croydon CR0 ....42 F3
　Feltham TW13 ....14 F5
　Penge SE26 ....23 D2
　Sandhurst GU47 ....64 E7
　Sutton SM1 ....59 B5
...estbrook RH18 ....206 E3
...estbrook Ave TW12 .....15 F1
...estbrook Gdns RG12 ....27 D8
...estbrook Hill GU8 ....148 C3
...estbrook Rd
　Godalming GU7 ....150 C5
　South Norwood CR7 ......42 D7
　Staines TW18 ....12 F3

Western Perimeter Rd Rdbt
　TW19 ....2 C2
Western Rd
　Aldershot GU11 ....104 E1
　Bracknell RG12 ....26 F7
　Mitcham CR4, SW19 ......40 E7
　Sutton SM1 ....59 A5
Westfield Ashstead KT21 ...75 F1
　Peaslake RH5 ....154 E8
　Reigate RH2 ....118 A1
Westfield Ave
　Sanderstead CR2, CR8 ...80 E6
　Woking GU22 ....89 E7
Westfield Cl SM1 ....58 F6
Westfield Comm GU22 .....89 E6
Westfield Ct
　Kingston u T KT6 ......37 D4
　New Haw KT15 ....52 D1
Westfield Dr KT23 ....94 B4
Westfield Gr GU22 ....89 E7
Westfield La GU10 ......145 E6
Westfield Par KT15 .....52 D1
Westfield Prim Sch GU22 ..89 E6
Westfield Rd
　Beckenham BR3 ....43 F7
　Camberley GU15 ....65 B3
　Cheam SM1 ....58 F6
　Crawley RH11 ....201 B6
　Guildford GU1 ....109 C5
　Kingston u T KT6 ......37 D4
　Mitcham CR4 ....40 F7
　Thornton Heath CR0, CR9 ..61 B8
　Walton-on-T KT12 ......35 C2
　Woking GU22 ....89 E5
Westfield Way GU22 .....89 E5
Westfields SW13 ....7 F4
Westfields Ave SW13, SW14 ..7 E4
Westfields Sch SW13 .....7 F4
Westgate Rd
　Beckenham BR3 ....44 C8
　Croydon SE25 ....43 B5
Westglade GU14 ....84 D4
Westhall Pk CR6 ....101 C8
Westhall Rd CR6 ....101 B8
Westhay Gdns SW14 ....7 B2
Westhumble St RH5 .....115 B4
Westland Ct ■ GU11 ......2 E1
Westland Dr BR2, BR4 ...63 F8
Westlands RH13 ....217 E3
Westlands Ct
　East Molesey KT8 ......36 E5
　Epsom KT18 ....76 C4
Westlands Way RH8 ....122 D8
Westlea Rd 160 E5
Westlees Cl RH5 ....136 D4
Westleigh Ave CR5 .....79 B3
Westmacott Dr TW14 ....14 F7
Westmark Point ■ SW15 ..19 B7
Westmead
　Farnborough GU14 ......85 B2
　■ Farnham GU9 ....125 B2
　Putney SW15 ....19 B8
　Woking GU21 ....69 B2
Westmead Dr RH1 ......140 A1
Westmead Rd SM1 ....59 D6
Westminster Ave CR7 ....42 B7
Westminster Cl
　East Bedfont TW14 .....15 A7
　Teddington TW11 ....17 A3
Westminster Ct
　Old Woking GU22 ....90 B6
　South Norwood CR7 .....42 C7
Westminster Rd
　Carshalton SM1, SM5 ...59 D8
　Crawley RH10 ....202 C5
Westmont Rd KT10 ......55 E8
Westmore Rd TN16 .....103 C2
Westmoreland Rd
　Barnes SW13 ....7 F6
　Beckenham BR2, BR3 ....44 F5
Westmoreland Terr SE20 ..23 B1
Westmorland Cl
　Epsom KT19 ....57 F6
　■ Twickenham TW1 ......6 B1
Westmorland Ct ■ KT6 ...37 D2
Westmorland Dr GU15 ...66 B6
Westmorland Sq CR4 ....41 E4
Westmorland Way CR4 ...41 E4
Weston Ave
　Addlestone KT15 ....52 B6
　East Molesey KT8 ......35 F5
Weston Cl Coulsdon CR5 ..99 F7
　Farncombe GU7 ....150 E6
Weston Ct Farncombe GU7 .150 E6
　■ Kingston u T KT1 ....37 E6
Weston Fields GU5 ....132 C4
Weston Gdns Hounslow TW7 ..5 E6
　Pyrford GU22 ....70 E3
Weston Gn KT7 ....37 A1
Weston Gr Bagshot GU19 ..47 E2
　Bromley BR1 ....44 F8
Weston Green Prep Sch
　KT7 ....36 E1
Weston Green Rd KT7, KT6 ..36 E1
Weston Lea KT24 ....92 D2
Weston Park
　Kingston u T KT1, KT7 ..37 E1
　Thames Ditton KT7 .....36 E1
Weston Park Cl KT7 ....36 E1
Weston Rd Bromley BR1 ..24 F1
　Ewell KT17 ....57 F2
　Guildford GU2 ....109 A2
　Thames Ditton KT7 ....36 E1
Weston Way GU22 ....70 E3
Westons Cl RH12 ......217 D7
Westover Cl SM2 ....59 B2

Westover Rd SW18 ....20 C8
Westow Hill SE19 ....22 F2
Westow St SE19 ....22 F2
Westpoint 2 A6
Westview ■ GU22 ....69 F1
Westview Cl RH1 ....139 E6
Westville Rd KT7 ....37 A2
Westward Ho GU1 ......110 A2
Westwates Ct RG12 ......27 D8
Westway Caterham CR3 ..100 D5
　Copthorne RH10 ....183 A3
　Crawley RH6 ....182 B7
　Guildford GU2 ....109 A5
　West Barnes KT3, SW20 ..39 C5
　Wormley GU8 ....190 F8
Westway Cl SW20 ....39 B6
Westway Ct CR3 ....100 D4
Westway Gdns RH1 .....119 A4
Westwell Rd SW16 ......21 F2
Westwell Road App SW16 ..21 E2
Westwick Gdns SW4, TW5 ..4 B5
Westwood Ave
　South Norwood SE19 ....42 C8
　Woodham KT15 ....70 F7
Westwood Cl KT10 ......55 C7
Westwood Ct
　■ Forest Hill SE23 ....23 C7
　Guildford GU2 ....108 F2
Westwood Dr SW19 ......19 F3
Westwood Gdns SW13 ....7 F4
Westwood Hill SE19, SE26 ..23 B4
Westwood La
　Flexford GU3 ....107 A2
　Normandy GU3 ....107 A2
　Wanborough GU3 ....128 B2
Westwood Park Cty Prim
　Sch GU2 ....108 E1
Westwood Rd
　Coulsdon CR5 ....79 D1
　Mortlake SW13, SW15 ....7 F4
　Windlesham GU20 ......48 E6
Westwood Sch SE19 .....22 D1
Wetheral Ct SW17 ......20 D4
Wetherby Cl GU14 ......85 C7
Wetherby Gdns GU14 ....85 C1
Wetherby House GU15 ...65 D7
Wetherby Way KT9 ......56 E3
Wettern Cl CR2 ....61 E1
Wetton Pl TW20 ....11 F3
Wexfenne Gdns GU22 ....71 B3
Wexford Rd SW12 ....20 F8
Wey Ave KT16 ....33 A6
Wey Cl Ash GU12 ......106 A1
　Camberley GU15 ....65 D5
　West Byfleet KT14 ....71 B6
Wey Ct Farncombe GU7 ..151 A6
　New Haw KT15 ....52 D2
　West Ewell KT19 ......57 C6
Wey Hill GU27 ....208 B6
Wey House Sch GU5 ....151 E8
Wey Manor Rd KT15 ....52 D2
Wey Rd Godalming GU7 ..151 A5
　Weybridge KT13 ....52 F7
Wey Ret Pk KT14 ......71 F7
Wey View Ct GU1 ......130 C8
Weybank GU23 ....71 E3
Weybank Cl GU9 ......125 C3
Weybarton KT14 ....71 F6
Weybourne Cty Inf Sch
　GU9 ....125 E6
Weybourne Pl CR2 .....61 D1
Weybourne Rd GU11, GU9 ..125 E6
Weybourne St SW18 ....20 C6
Weybridge Bsns Pk KT15 ..52 E6
Weybridge Hospl KT13 ..53 A6
Weybridge House KT13 ..53 D5
Weybridge Pk KT13 ....53 A5
Weybridge Rd
　Addlestone KT15, KT13 ..52 E6
　Thornton Heath CR7 ....42 A5
　Weybridge KT13, KT15 ..52 E6
Weybridge Sta KT13 ...53 A4
Weybrook Dr GU4 .....110 B6
Weycombe Rd GU27 ....208 C8
Weydon Hill Cl GU9 ...146 B8
Weydon Hill Rd GU9 ...146 C8
Weydon La Farnham GU9 ..146 A8
　Wrecclesham GU9 .....145 F8
Weydon Mill La GU9 ..125 B1
Weydon Sch GU9 ......145 F7
Weydown Cl
　Guildford GU2 ....109 A6
　Putney SW19 ....19 E7
Weydown Ct GU27 .....208 B7
Weydown Ind Est GU27 ..208 B7
Weydown La GU2 ......109 A6
Weydown Rd GU27 ....208 B7
Weyfield Prim Sch GU1 ..109 D4
Weylands Pk KT13 .....53 D4
Weylea Ave GU1, GU4 ..110 A4
Weymead Cl KT16 ......33 C1
Weymede KT14 ....71 F7
Weymouth Ct Belmont SM2 ..59 A3
　■ Streatham SW2 ......21 F8
Weyside GU9 ....125 C2
Weyside Cl KT14 ......71 F7
Weyside Gdns GU1 ....109 C3
Weyside Pk GU7 ......151 A5
Weyside Rd GU1 ......109 B3
Weysprings GU27 .....208 A6
Weyvern Pk GU3 ......130 B1
Weyview Cl GU1 ......109 C3
Weywood Cl GU9 ......125 F7
Weywood La GU9 ......125 F7
Whaley Rd RG40 ....25 D8
Wharf Bridge Rd TW7 ...6 B4

Wharf La Send GU23 .....90 C4
　Twickenham TW1 ....17 A7
Wharf Rd Ash GU12 ....106 A4
　Frimley GU16 ....86 A6
　Guildford GU1 ....109 C1
　Wraysbury TW19 ....11 D8
Wharf St GU1 ....130 E4
Wharf Way GU16 ....86 A6
Wharfedale Gdns
　CR7, SW16 ....41 F6
Wharfenden Way GU16 ..85 F3
Wharncliffe Gdns SE25 ..42 E7
Wharncliffe Rd SE25 ...42 E7
Whateley Rd
　Guildford GU22 ....109 B5
　Penge SE20 ....23 D1
Whatley Ave SW20 .....39 E6
Whatley Gn RG12 ......27 B3
Whatman Rd SE23 ......23 D8
Whatmore Cl TW19 ......2 A1
Wheat Knoll CR8 ......80 C3
Wheatash Rd KT15 .....52 B8
Wheatfield Way
　Horley RH6 ....161 C4
　Kingston u T KT1 .....37 E7
Wheathill House SE20 ..43 B7
Wheathill Rd SE20 ....43 B6
Wheatlands TW5 ....5 A8
Wheatlands Rd SW17 ...21 A5
Wheatley GU21 ....68 F1
Wheatley House ■ SW15 ..19 A8
Wheatley Rd TW7 ....5 F4
Wheatley's Ait
　Lower Halliford TW16 ..34 A4
　Sunbury TW16 ....34 A4
Wheatsheaf Cl
　Horsham RH12 ....217 E5
　Ottershaw KT16 ....51 D4
　Woking GU21 ....69 F3
Wheatsheaf La TW18 ...12 F1
Wheatstone Cl
　Crawley RH10 ....182 B3
　Mitcham SW19 ....40 E8
Wheeler Ave RH8 .....122 D6
Wheeler La GU8 ......170 E6
Wheeler Rd RH10 .....202 B4
Wheelers
　Brockham RH3 ....137 C7
　Epsom KT18 ....76 C5
　Smallfield RH6 ....162 B3
Wheelers Way RH19 ...184 E3
Wheelwrights La GU26 .188 A4
Wheelwrights Pl SL3 ...1 C7
Whelan Way SM6 ....60 D7
Wherwell Lodge GU2 ..130 C7
Wherwell Rd GU2 .....130 C7
Whetstone Rd GU14 ...84 D4
Whimbrel Cl CR2, CR8 ..80 D8
Whinfell Cl SW16 .....21 D3
Whins Cl GU15 ....65 B4
Whins Dr GU15 ....65 B4
Whinshill Ct SL5 .....30 A1
Whipley Cl GU4 ......110 B6
Whistler Cl RH10 ....201 F3
Whistler Gr GU47 .....64 D6
Whistley Cl RG12 .....27 E6
Whitby Cl TN16 ....83 D1
Whitby Gdns SM1, SM5 ..59 D8
Whitby Rd SM1, SM5 ...59 D8
Whitchurch Cl GU11 ..126 D6
Whitchurch Ct SW17 ...20 D4
Whitchurch House ■ SE6 ..24 C5
White Acres Rd GU16 ..85 F4
White Beam Way KT20 ..97 A6
White Bridge Cl TW14 ..3 F1
White Bushes RH1 ....140 A4
White City RG45 ......45 D5
White Cottage Cl GU9 .125 D6
White Ct GU2 ....109 A4
White Hart Ct
　Horsham RH12 ....217 C4
　Ripley GU23 ....91 C6
White Hart La
　Mortlake SW14 ....7 E4
　Wood St V GU3 ....108 A2
White Hart Meadows
　GU23 ....91 C6
White Hart Row 33 A2
White Heron Mews TW11 ..16 F2
White Hill Kingswood CR5 ..98 D4
　South Croydon CR2 ...61 D1
　Windlesham GU20 .....48 B4
White Horse Dr KT18 ..76 C5
White Horse La GU23 ..91 C6
White House ■ SW4 ....21 D8
White House Ct BR3 ...44 B8
White House La GU4 ..109 D6
White House Prep Sch
　RG41 ....25 A3
White House Wlk GU9 .125 D7
White Knights Rd KT13 .53 C3
White Knobs Way CR3 .101 A2
White La
　Ash GU10, GU12 ......127 C7
　Guildford GU4 ....131 D7
　Titsey RH8, TN16 ....103 B3
　Tongham GU10, GU12 ..127 C7
White Lodge
　Ashtead KT21 ....95 E7
　South Norwood SE19 ...22 B1
White Lodge Cl SM2 ...59 C3
White Lodge Gdns RH1 .140 A1
White Lodge The Royal
　Ballet Sch SW14 ......7 E1
White Oak Dr BR3 .....44 D7
White Post La GU10 ..146 A4
White Rd GU15 ....64 F6

White Rose La
　Farnham GU9, GU10 ...146 B7
　Old Woking GU22 ......90 A8
　Woking GU22 ....69 F1
White Way KT23 ....94 B1
Whiteham Dr RH2 .....139 B6
Whitebeams Gdns GU14 ..84 C3
Whiteberry Rd RH5 ...156 B7
Whitebines GU9 ......125 D3
Whitecroft Cl BR3 ....44 D5
Whitecroft Way BR3 ...44 D5
Whitefield Ave CR8 ...80 B3
Whitefield House CR8 .80 B3
Whitefoot La BR1, SE6 ..24 D3
Whitefoot Terr BR1 ...24 F5
Whitegate Way KT20 ...97 B7
Whitegates
　Old Woking GU22 ......89 F7
　Whyteleafe CR3 ......101 A8
Whitehall Cres SW19 ..56 D5
Whitehall Dr RH11 ...200 E6
Whitehall Farm La GU25 ..31 E6
Whitehall Gdns W4 ....7 B8
Whitehall La Egham TW20 ..11 F1
　Horton TW19 ....1 A1
　Reigate RH2 ....138 F6
Whitehall Park Rd W4 ..7 B8
Whitehall Pl SM5 .....60 B6
Whitehall Rd CR7 .....42 A4
Whitehead Cl SW18 ...20 C8
Whitehill Cl GU15 ....65 D7
Whitehill La
　Bletchingley RH1 ....120 D6
　Martyr's Green GU23 ..92 C4
Whitehill Pl GU25 ....31 E4
Whitehorse La SE25 ...42 E5
Whitehorse Manor Inf Sch
　CR7 ....42 D5
Whitehorse Manor Jun Sch
　CR7 ....42 D5
Whitehorse Rd
　Horsham RH12 ....218 B6
　South Norwood CR0,
　CR7, SE25 ....42 D3
　Thornton Heath CR0,
　CR7, SE25 ....42 D3
Whitehouse Dr GU1 ...110 B1
Whitelands Coll,
　Roehampton West SW14 ..19 E8
Whitelands Dr SL5 ....28 D8
Whiteley House ■ SW4 ..21 D8
Whiteley House & Hospl
　KT12 ....53 F2
Whiteley Rd SE19 .....22 D3
Whiteleys House TW13 ..16 A5
Whiteleys Way TW13 ..16 A5
Whitelocke Cty Inf Sch
　RG40 ....25 D7
Whitely Hill RH10 ...202 F1
Whitemore Rd GU1 ...109 D5
Whiteoak House TN16 .103 C7
Whiteoaks SM7 ....78 B6
Whitepost Hill RH1 ..118 E1
Whitepost House RH1 .118 E1
Whites Dr BR2 ....44 F2
Whites Rd GU14 ......85 E1
Whitethorn Ave CR5 ...79 B4
Whitethorn Cl GU12 ..106 B1
Whitethorn Cotts GU6 .174 B6
Whitethorn Gdns CR0 .62 A8
Whiteways Ct TW18 ...13 B1
Whiteways End GU10 .126 D4
Whitewood Cotts TN16 .103 C7
Whitewood La RH9 ...163 B7
Whitfield Cl Guildford GU2 ..109 A4
　Haslemere GU27 .....189 C1
Whitfield Ct ■ SE21 ...22 E4
Whitfield Rd GU27 ...189 C1
Whitford Gdns CR4 ....40 F6
Whitgift Ave CR2 .....61 C5
Whitgift Ctr CR0 .....61 C8
Whitgift House CR2 ...61 C5
Whitgift Sch CR2 .....61 C5
Whitgift St CR0, CR9 ..61 C7
Whitgift Wlk RH11 ...201 D3
Whitland Rd SM5 ......40 D1
Whitlet Cl GU9 ......125 B1
Whitlock Dr SW19 .....19 E7
Whitmead Cl CR2 .....61 E4
Whitmead La GU10 ...147 E4
Whitmoor La GU4 .....89 D1
Whitmoor Vale Rd GU26 .188 A5
Whitmore Cl GU47 ....45 D1
Whitmore Gn GU9 ....125 F7
Whitmore La SL5 .....30 A5
Whitmore Rd BR3 .....43 F6
Whitmore Vale
　Grayshott GU26 .....187 F6
　Hindhead GU26 .....187 F6
Whitmore Vale Rd
　Grayshott GU26 .....188 A4
　Headley Down GU10, GU26 .187 E7
Whitmore Way RH6 ...160 E3
Whitmores Cl KT18 ...76 C4
Whitstable Cl BR3 ....43 F8
Whittaker Ave TW10, TW9 ..6 D2
Whittaker Ct KT21 ....75 D2
Whittaker Pl ■ TW10 ...6 D2
Whittaker Rd SM3 ....58 F7
Whitham House SE27 ..22 C3
Whittell Gdns SE26 ...23 C3
Whittingham Ct W4 ....7 E7
Whittington Coll RH19 .185 A4

Whittington Ct SE20 . . . . .43 B7
Whittington Rd N10 . . . . .201 E3
Whittle Cl GU47 . . . . .45 A1
Whittle Cres GU14 . . . . .84 F7
Whittle Rd TW5 . . . . .4 C7
Whittle Rdbt GU14 . . . . .84 C1
Whittle Way RH10 . . . . .182 A3
Whittlebury Cl SM5 . . . . .59 F3
Whitton Dene
  Isleworth TW2, TW3, TW7 . . . .5 D2
  Twickenham TW2, TW7 . . . . . . .5 D2
Whitton Manor Rd TW7 . . . . .5 C1
Whitton Rd Bracknell RG12 . . . . .27 F6
  Hounslow TW3 . . . . .5 B2
  Isleworth TW3 . . . . .5 B2
  Twickenham TW1 . . . . .17 A8
Whitton Sch TW2 . . . . .16 B6
Whitton Sta TW2 . . . . .16 A6
Whitton Waye TW2, TW3 . . . . . . .5 C8
Whitworth Rd
  Crawley RH11 . . . . .181 D2
  South Norwood SE25 . . . . .42 F5
Whopshott Ave GU21 . . . . .69 C3
Whopshott Cl GU21 . . . . .69 C3
Whopshott Dr GU21 . . . . .69 C3
Whynstones Rd SL5 . . . . .29 A4
Whyte Ave GU12 . . . . .126 D7
Whyteacre CR3 . . . . .101 B3
Whytebeam View CR3 . . . . .80 F1
Whytecliffe Rd N CR8 . . . . .80 B8
Whytecliffe Rd S CR8 . . . . .80 B8
Whytecroft TW5 . . . . .4 F7
Whyteleafe Bsns Village
  CR3 .80 F2
Whyteleafe Hill CR3 . . . . .80 F1
Whyteleafe Rd
  Caterham CR3 . . . . .100 F6
  Whyteleafe CR3 . . . . .100 F6
Whyteleafe Sch CR3 . . . . .80 F2
Whyteleafe Sta CR3 . . . . .80 F2
Wick House ■ KT1 . . . . .37 D8
Wick Rd TW20 . . . . .10 F1
Wickers Oake SE19 . . . . .22 F4
Wicket Hill GU10, GU9 . . . . . . .146 A6
Wicket The CR0 . . . . .63 A5
Wickets The TW15 . . . . .13 E4
Wickham Ave
  Cheam KT4, SM3 . . . . .58 C5
  Croydon CR0 . . . . .43 E1
Wickham Chase BR4 . . . . .44 C2
Wickham Ct Horley RH6 . . . . . . .160 F4
  New Malden KT3 . . . . .38 E2
Wickham Court Rd BR4 . . . . .63 C8
Wickham Cres BR4 . . . . .63 C8
Wickham La TW20 . . . . .12 A1
Wickham Rd
  Beckenham BR3 . . . . .44 B6
  Camberley GU15 . . . . .65 E8
  Croydon CR0, CR9 . . . . .62 C8
Wickham Vale RG12 . . . . .26 E3
Wickham Way BR3 . . . . .44 C4
Wickhurst Gdns RH12 . . . . .216 E3
Wickhurst La RH12 . . . . .216 E3
Wickland Ct RH10 . . . . .201 D3
Wicklow Ct SE26 . . . . .23 C3
Wide Way CR4, SW16 . . . . .41 D6
Widgeon Way RH12 . . . . .217 C5
Widmer Ct TW5 . . . . .4 E5
Wiggie La RH1 . . . . .119 A3
Wigley Rd TW13 . . . . .15 D7
Wigmore La RH5 . . . . .157 C1
Wigmore Rd SM5 . . . . .40 E1
Wigmore Wlk SM5 . . . . .59 D8
Wilberforce Cl RH18 . . . . .76 D5
Wilberforce Way
  Bracknell RG12 . . . . .27 A4
  Wimbledon SW19 . . . . .19 D2
Wilbury Ave SM2 . . . . .58 F1
Wilbury Rd GU21 . . . . .69 D2
Wilcot Cl GU24 . . . . .68 A3
Wilcot Gdns GU24 . . . . .68 A3
Wilcox Gdns TW17 . . . . .33 F5
Wilcox Rd Sutton SM1 . . . . .59 B6
  Teddington TW11 . . . . .16 D4
Wild Acres KT14 . . . . .212 D3
Wildacre Cl RH14 . . . . .212 D3
Wildbank Ct ■ GU22 . . . . .69 F1
Wildcroft Dr
  Dorking RH5 . . . . .136 D4
  Wokingham RG40 . . . . .25 A1
Wildcroft Manor SW15 . . . . .19 C8
Wildcroft Rd SW15 . . . . .19 C8
Wildcroft Wood GU8 . . . . .170 D6
Wilde Pl SW18 . . . . .20 D8
Wilde Theatre RG12 . . . . .27 C2
Wilderness Ct GU2 . . . . .129 F7
Wilderness Rd
  Frimley GU16 . . . . .65 E2
  Guildford GU2 . . . . .129 F7
  Oxted RH8 . . . . .122 E5
Wilderness Rise RH19 . . . . .186 A6
Wilderness The
  East Molesey KT8 . . . . .36 C4
  Hampton TW12 . . . . .16 B4
Wilders Cl Frimley GU16 . . . . . . .65 E3
  Woking GU21 . . . . .69 C2
Wilderwick Rd RH19, RH7 . . . . .186 A5
Wildfell Rd SE6 . . . . .24 B8
Wildfield Cl GU3 . . . . .108 B2
Wildgoose Dr RH12 . . . . .216 F3

Wildridings Cty Prim Sch
  RG12 . . . . .27 A5
Wildridings Rd RG12 . . . . .27 A5
Wildridings Sq RG12 . . . . .27 A5
Wildwood Cl
  East Horsley KT24 . . . . .92 F2
  Lewisham SE12 . . . . .24 F8
  Pyrford GU22 . . . . .70 F4
Wildwood Ct CR8 . . . . .80 D4
Wildwood La GU6 . . . . .194 C5
Wilford Rd CR0 . . . . .42 C2
Wilfred Owen Cl SW19 . . . . .20 C2
Wilfred St GU21 . . . . .69 D1
Wilhelmina Ave CR5 . . . . .99 C8
Wilkes Rd ■ TW8 . . . . .6 E8
Wilkins Cl CR4 . . . . .40 E8
Wilkinson Ct
  ⑷ Wandsworth SW11 . . . . . . .201 B1
  Upper Tooting SW17 . . . . .20 D4
Wilkinson House TW7 . . . . .5 A4
Wilks Gdns CR0 . . . . .43 E1
Will Miles Ct ⑥ SW19 . . . . .20 C1
Willats Cl KT16 . . . . .33 A3
Willcocks Cl KT9 . . . . .56 E7
Willems Ave GU11 . . . . .104 F2
Willems Rdbt GU11 . . . . .104 F2
Willerton Lodge ■ KT13 . . . . . . .53 D4
Willett Pl CR7 . . . . .42 A4
Willett Rd CR7 . . . . .42 A4
Willetts RH4 . . . . .136 C1
Willey Broom La CR3 . . . . .100 A2
Willey Farm La CR3 . . . . .100 C1
Willey La CR3 . . . . .100 C1
William Booth Rd SE20 . . . . .43 A8
William Brown Ct SE27 . . . . .22 B6
William Byrd Sch GU17 . . . . .2 D8
William Cobbett Cty Jun
  Sch GU9 . . . . .125 E6
William Evelyn Ct RH5 . . . . .134 F4
William Farthing Cl ■
  GU11 . . . . .105 A2
William Harvey House ■
  SW19 . . . . .19 D7
William Lilly House KT12 . . . . . . .54 C5
William Morris Mid Sch
  CR4 .41 D6
William Morris Way SW6 . . . . . .201 C1
William Rd Caterham CR3 . . . . .100 D5
  Guildford GU1 . . . . .109 C1
  Merton SW19 . . . . .19 E1
  Sutton SM1 . . . . .59 C5
William Russell Ct ⑻ GU21 . . . . .68 E1
William Sim Wood RG42 . . . . .8 B2
William St SM5 . . . . .59 F7
William Wood House SE26 . . . . . .23 C5
Williams Cl
  Addlestone KT15 . . . . .52 B5
  Ewhurst GU6 . . . . .175 E5
Williams House ⑷ SW2 . . . . .22 A7
Williams La Morden SM4 . . . . . . .40 C4
  Mortlake SW14 . . . . .7 C5
Williams Terr CR0 . . . . .61 A4
Williams Way RH10 . . . . .202 B5
Williamson Cl GU27 . . . . .189 F1
Willingham Way KT1 . . . . .38 A7
Willington Cl GU15 . . . . .65 B6
Willington Prep Sch SW19 . . . . . .19 F3
Willis Ave SM2 . . . . .59 E4
Willis Cl KT18 . . . . .76 B5
Willis Rd CR0 . . . . .42 C2
Willows The Cro 62 E8
Willmore End SW19 . . . . .40 B7
Willoughby Ave CR0 . . . . .60 F6
Willoughby Rd
  Bracknell RG12 . . . . .26 F6
  Kingston u T KT2 . . . . .37 F8
  Twickenham TW1 . . . . .6 C2
Willoughbys The SW15 . . . . .7 E3
Willow Ave SW13 . . . . .7 F5
Willow Bank GU22 . . . . .89 F6
Willow Brean RH6 . . . . .160 E5
Willow Cl
  Beare Green RH5 . . . . .157 C4
  Brentford TW8 . . . . .6 C8
  Catford SE6 . . . . .24 F7
  Colnbrook SL3 . . . . .1 C7
  Crawley RH10 . . . . .201 E8
  East Grinstead RH19 . . . . .185 D3
  Mytchett GU16 . . . . .85 E4
  Woodham KT15 . . . . .70 F8
Willow Cnr RH6 . . . . .180 F7
Willow Cotts
  Carshalton CR4 . . . . .40 F2
  Richmond TW9 . . . . .7 A7
Willow Cres GU14 . . . . .84 F5
Willow Ct Ash Vale GU12 . . . . . .106 A7
  Frimley GU16 . . . . .65 D1
  Horley RH6 . . . . .161 B6
  ⑧ Streatham SW16 . . . . .21 F5
  Thornton Heath CR7 . . . . .42 A4
  Wokingham RG41 . . . . .25 B6
Willow Ctr The CR4 . . . . .40 F2
Willow Dr Bracknell RG12 . . . . . .27 C8
  Flexford GU3 . . . . .107 C1
  Send Marsh GU23 . . . . .91 A3
Willow End KT6 . . . . .37 E1
Willow Gdns TW5 . . . . .5 A6
Willow Glade RH2 . . . . .139 B6
Willow Gn GU24 . . . . .68 A6
Willow House ■ TW4 . . . . .4 D4
Willow La Blackwater GU17 . . . . .64 D4
  Guildford GU1 . . . . .110 A2
  Mitcham CR4 . . . . .40 F3
Willow Lodge ⑧ TW16 . . . . .14 F1
Willow Manor SM1 . . . . .58 F6
Willow Mead Dorking RH4 . . . . .136 A8
  ⑧ East Grinstead RH19 . . . . . .205 F8
  Witley GU5 . . . . .170 E5

Willow Mount CR0 . . . . .61 E7
Willow Pk GU12 . . . . .105 F2
Willow Rd Farncombe GU7 . . . . .150 F8
  Horsham RH12 . . . . .218 B5
  Kingston u T KT3 . . . . .38 C5
  Poyle SL3 . . . . .1 E5
  Reigate RH1 . . . . .139 C6
  Wallington SM6 . . . . .60 B3
Willow Ridge RH10 . . . . .204 A3
Willow Tree Cl SW18 . . . . .20 B7
Willow Vale KT23 . . . . .94 B4
Willow View SW19 . . . . .40 D8
Willow Way
  Aldershot GU12 . . . . .126 E8
  East Bedfont SE26 . . . . .23 C5
  Godstone RH9 . . . . .121 B3
  Guildford GU1 . . . . .109 B5
  Heath End GU9 . . . . .125 D6
  Sunbury TW16 . . . . .35 A5
  Twickenham TW2 . . . . .16 B6
  West Byfleet KT14 . . . . .71 C6
  West Ewell KT19 . . . . .57 D4
  Woking GU22 . . . . .89 E7
Willow Wlk Box Hill KT20 . . . . . .116 B5
  Cheam SM1, SM3 . . . . .58 F5
  Chertsey KT16 . . . . .33 B2
  Englefield Green TW20 . . . . . . .11 C3
  Redhill RH1 . . . . .140 B7
Willow Wood Cres SE25 . . . . . . .42 E3
Willowbank Gdns KT20 . . . . .97 B5
Willowbrook Rd TW19 . . . . .13 E6
Willowdene C' 16 C8
Willowfield ⑷ RH11 . . . . .201 D5
Willowhayne Dr KT12 . . . . .35 B2
Willowhayne Gdns KT4 . . . . .58 C6
Willowherb Cl RG40 . . . . .25 E7
Willowmead SW18 . . . . .33 B8
Willowmead Cl GU21 . . . . .69 A3
Willowmere KT10 . . . . .55 C6
Willows Ave SM4 . . . . .40 B4
Willows End GU47 . . . . .64 B8
Willows Path KT18 . . . . .76 B5
Willows The
  Beckenham BR3 . . . . .44 A8
  ⑴ Bracknell RG12 . . . . .27 F5
  Byfleet KT14 . . . . .71 E6
  Chiddingfold GU8 . . . . .191 A4
  Claygate KT10 . . . . .55 E4
  Farnham GU10 . . . . .126 C4
  Guildford, Bushy Hill GU4 . . . .110 D3
  Guildford, Pitch Place GU2 . . .108 F6
  Horsham RH12 . . . . .217 D5
  Lightwater GU18 . . . . .48 C1
  ⑵ Redhill RH1 . . . . .139 F8
  Weybridge KT13 . . . . .53 A7
Willowtree Way SW16 . . . . .42 A8
Wills Cres TW3 . . . . .5 B1
Willson Rd TW20 . . . . .11 B3
Wilmar Gdns BR4 . . . . .44 B1
Wilmer Cl TW10 . . . . .17 C4
Wilmer Cres KT2, TW10 . . . . . . .17 E3
Wilmerhatch La KT18, KT21 . . . .76 B2
Wilmington Ave W4 . . . . .7 D7
Wilmington Cl RH11 . . . . .201 C1
Wilmington Ct SW16 . . . . .21 E1
Wilmot Rd Purley CR8 . . . . .80 A7
  Wallington SM5 . . . . .59 F5
Wilmot Way Banstead SM7 . . . . . .78 A5
  Frimley GU15 . . . . .65 F3
Wilmot's La RH1, RH6 . . . . .162 E5
Wilmots Cl RH2 . . . . .118 C2
Wilna Rd SW18 . . . . .20 C8
Wilson Ave CR4, SW19 . . . . .40 E8
Wilson Cl Crawley RH10 . . . . . . .202 D3
  Croydon CR0 . . . . .61 D5
Wilson Dr KT16 . . . . .51 A6
Wilson Hospl CR4 . . . . .40 E5
Wilson Rd Aldershot GU12 . . . . .105 D1
  Chessington KT9 . . . . .56 F4
  Farnborough GU14 . . . . .84 F3
Wilson Way GU21 . . . . .69 D3
Wilson's Sch SM6 . . . . .60 D4
Wilsons KT20 . . . . .97 D6
Wilsons Rd GU35 . . . . .187 B5
Wilton Cl UB7 . . . . .2 D8
Wilton Cres SW19 . . . . .39 F8
Wilton Ct Farnborough GU14 . . . . .85 D3
  ■ Richmond TW10 . . . . .6 E2
Wilton Gdns
  East Molesey KT8 . . . . .36 A6
  Walton-on-T KT12 . . . . .35 D1
Wilton Gr Merton SW19 . . . . .39 F8
  New Malden KT3 . . . . .38 F3
Wilton Par TW13 . . . . .15 B6
Wilton Pl Beckenham BR3 . . . . . .44 C6
  New Haw KT15 . . . . .52 D2
Wilton Rd Camberley GU15 . . . . . .65 B3
  Hounslow TW4 . . . . .4 D4
  Mitcham SW19 . . . . .20 E1
  Redhill RH1 . . . . .139 F8
Wilton Wlk TW13 . . . . .15 B7
Wiltshire Ave RG45 . . . . .45 B5
Wiltshire Rd CR42 . . . . .25 D7
Wiltshire Gdns TW2 . . . . .16 C7
Wiltshire Rd
  Thornton Heath CR7 . . . . .42 A6
  Wokingham RG40 . . . . .25 C7
Wilverley Cres KT3 . . . . .38 E3
Wilwood Rd RG42 . . . . .26 E8
Wimbart Rd SW2 . . . . .21 F8
Wimbledon Bridge SW19 . . . . . . .19 F2
Wimbledon Chase Mid Sch
  SW20 . . . . .39 E7
Wimbledon Cl
  Camberley GU15 . . . . .46 F1
  ⑵ Wimbledon SW20 . . . . .19 D1

Wimbledon Coll SW19 . . . . .19 D1
Wimbledon Common
  Prep Sch SW19 . . . . .19 D1
Wimbledon High Sch
  SW19 . . . . .19 E2
Wimbledon Hill Rd SW19 . . . . . . .19 E2
Wimbledon House Sch
  SW19 . . . . .40 A8
Wimbledon Lawn Tennis
  Mus SW19 . . . . .19 E5
Wimbledon Park Ct SW19 . . . . . .19 F7
Wimbledon Park Prim Sch
  SW19 . . . . .20 B6
Wimbledon Park Rd
  Putney SW18, SW19 . . . . .19 F7
  Wandsworth SW18, SW19 . . . .19 F7
Wimbledon Park Side
  SW19 . . . . .19 D7
Wimbledon Park Sta
  SW19 . . . . .20 A5
Wimbledon Rd
  Camberley GU15 . . . . .46 F1
  Wandsworth SW17 . . . . .20 C4
Wimbledon Sch of Art
  SW19 . . . . .39 E8
Wimbledon Sch of Art
  Annexe SW19 . . . . .20 A1
Wimbledon Stadium
  SW19 . . . . .20 C5
Wimbledon Stadium
  Bsns Ctr SW17 . . . . .20 B5
Wimblehurst Ct RH12 . . . . .217 C4
Wimblehurst Rd RH12 . . . . .217 C4
Wimbledon Windmill Mus
  SW19 . . . . .19 C6
Wimborne Ave RH1 . . . . .140 A4
Wimborne Cl Epsom KT17 . . . . . .76 E6
  North Cheam KT4 . . . . .39 C1
Wimborne House
  Croydon CR0 . . . . .43 C4
  Upper Tooting SW17 . . . . .21 C5
Wimborne Way BR3 . . . . .43 E5
Wimbourne Ct
  Mitcham SW19 . . . . .20 D1
  South Croydon CR2 . . . . .61 E4
Wimland Hill RH12 . . . . .199 D2
Wimland Rd
  Faygate RH12 . . . . .199 D1
  Rusper RH12 . . . . .199 A4
Wimlands La RH12 . . . . .199 E3
Wimpole Cl ■ KT1 . . . . .38 A7
Wimshurst Cl CR0 . . . . .41 E1
Wincanton Rd SW18 . . . . .19 F8
Winchcombe Rd SM5 . . . . .40 E1
Winchelsey Rise CR2 . . . . .61 F4
Winchendon Rd
  TW11, TW12 . . . . .16 D4
Winchester Ave TW5 . . . . .4 F8
Winchester Cl
  Beckenham BR2 . . . . .44 F6
  Esher KT10 . . . . .55 A7
  Kingston u T KT2 . . . . .18 B1
  Poyle SL3 . . . . .1 E6
Winchester Pk BR2 . . . . .44 F6
Winchester Rd
  Ash GU12 . . . . .106 A3
  Beckenham BR2 . . . . .44 F6
  Crawley RH10 . . . . .201 E2
  Feltham TW13 . . . . .15 E4
  Harlington UB3 . . . . .3 D8
  Rushmoor GU10 . . . . .168 B7
  Twickenham TW1 . . . . .6 B1
  Walton-on-T KT12 . . . . .35 A1
Winchester St SU14 . . . . .105 C8
Winchester Way GU17 . . . . .64 C6
Winchet Wlk CR0 . . . . .43 C3
Winchfield House SW15 . . . . .7 F1
Winchfield Rd SE26 . . . . .23 E3
Winchilsea Cres KT8 . . . . .36 C7
Winchstone Cl TW17 . . . . .33 F5
Windborough Rd SM5 . . . . .60 A3
Windermere Ave
  SM4, SW19 . . . . .40 B6
Windermere Cl
  East Bedfont TW14 . . . . .14 F7
  Farnborough GU14 . . . . .84 E3
  Stanwell TW19 . . . . .13 D6
  Thorpe Lea TW20 . . . . .12 B1
Windermere Ct
  Barnes SW13 . . . . .7 F8
  Purley CR8 . . . . .80 B4
Windermere House TW1 . . . . .5 F1
Windermere Rd
  Coulsdon CR5 . . . . .79 E4
  Croydon CR0 . . . . .42 F1
  Kingston u T SW15 . . . . .18 E3
  Lightwater GU18 . . . . .48 B1
  Mitcham SW16 . . . . .41 D7
  West Wickham BR4 . . . . .63 E8
Windermere Way
  Hale GU9 . . . . .125 A6
  Redhill RH2 . . . . .118 E2
Windermere Wlk GU15 . . . . .66 D5
Windfield KT22 . . . . .95 B5
Windfield Cl SE26 . . . . .23 D4
Windgates GU4 . . . . .110 C4
Windham Ave CR0 . . . . .63 D1
Windham Rd TW9 . . . . .6 F4
Winding Wood Dr GU15 . . . . .66 B3
Windings The CR2 . . . . .80 F8
Windle Cl GU20 . . . . .48 D4
Windlebrook Gn ⑶ RG42 . . . . . . .27 A8
Windlemere Golf Ctr
  GU24 . . . . .48 E6
Windlesham Ct SW20 . . . . .48 C6
Windlesham Gr SW19 . . . . .19 D7
Windlesham House CR4 . . . . .40 D7

Windlesham Rd
  Bracknell RG42 . . . . .26 F8
  Chobham GU24 . . . . .49 C2
  West End GU24 . . . . .67 F7
Windlesham Village Cty Inf
  Sch GU20 . . . . .48 B5
Windley Cl SE23 . . . . .23 C2
Windmill Bridge House
  CR0 . . . . .42 F2
Windmill Bsns Village
  TW16 . . . . .34 F8
Windmill Cl Caterham CR3 . . . . .100 C6
  Charlton TW16 . . . . .14 F1
  Ewell KT17 . . . . .76 F8
  Horley RH6 . . . . .161 A5
  Horsham RH13 . . . . .218 A3
  Long Ditton KT6 . . . . .37 D4
  Windmill Ct RH10 . . . . .201 F8
Windmill Dr
  Headley Down GU35 . . . . .187 B5
  Leatherhead KT22 . . . . .95 D4
  Redhill RH2 . . . . .118 C3
  Windmill End KT17 . . . . .76 F8
  Windmill Field GU20 . . . . .48 A4
  Windmill Gr CR0 . . . . .42 D3
Windmill La
  Ashurst Wood RH19 . . . . .206 E6
  East Grinstead RH19 . . . . .185 D1
  Ewell KT17 . . . . .76 F8
  Thames Ditton KT7 . . . . .37 B2
  Windmill Lodge TW16 . . . . .34 F8
Windmill Rd
  ⑷ Brentford TW8 . . . . .6 D8
  Charlton TW16 . . . . .34 F8
  Hampton TW12 . . . . .16 B3
  Mitcham CR4 . . . . .41 B4
  Roehampton SW19 . . . . .19 A8
  Thornton Heath CR0 . . . . .42 C2
  Windmill Rd W TW16 . . . . .34 F7
  Windmill Rise KT2 . . . . .18 B1
  Windmill Terr TW17 . . . . .34 E2
  Windmill Trad Est TW16 . . . . . . .34 F8
  Windmill Way RH2 . . . . .118 C3
Windrush Cl Bramley GU5 . . . . . .151 F6
  Chiswick W4 . . . . .7 C7
  Crawley RH11 . . . . .200 F3
  Windrush House ⑧ RH1 . . . . . .118 F2
Windrush Hts GU47 . . . . .64 A8
Windrush La SE23 . . . . .23 D5
Winds Ridge GU23 . . . . .90 C2
Windsor Ave Cheam SM3 . . . . . . .58 E7
  East Molesey KT8 . . . . .36 A6
  Merton SW19 . . . . .40 C8
  New Malden KT3 . . . . .38 C4
Windsor Cl Crawley RH11 . . . . . .201 A2
  Guildford GU2 . . . . .129 F7
  West Norwood SE27 . . . . .22 C5
Windsor Cres GU9 . . . . .125 C6
Windsor Ct Ashford TW16 . . . . . .15 A2
  Chobham GU24 . . . . .49 E2
  Horsham RH13 . . . . .217 E2
  South Norwood SE19 . . . . .22 E3
  Windsor Dr TW15 . . . . .13 D3
Windsor Gdns Ash GU12 . . . . . .105 F1
  Wallington CR0 . . . . .60 C7
Windsor Gr SE27 . . . . .22 C4
Windsor Great Pk SL4 . . . . .10 E6
Windsor House RH2 . . . . .139 B6
Windsor Mews Catford SE6 . . . . .24 C7
  Forest Hill SE23 . . . . .23 E7
Windsor Park Rd UB3 . . . . .3 F7
Windsor Pk SW19 . . . . .40 C8
Windsor Pl Chertsey KT16 . . . . . .33 A3
  East Grinstead RH19 . . . . .206 A1
Windsor Rd Ashford TW16 . . . . . .15 A1
  Chobham GU24 . . . . .49 C1
  Cranford TW4, TW5 . . . . .4 A5
  Englefield Green
    TW19, TW20 . . . . .11 D7
  Farnborough GU14 . . . . .85 A4
  Kingston u T KT2 . . . . .17 F1
  North Ascot SL5 . . . . .29 A8
  Richmond TW9 . . . . .7 A5
  South Norwood CR7 . . . . .42 A7
  Teddington TW11 . . . . .16 D3
  Worcester Park KT4 . . . . .58 A8
  Windsor Ride Bracknell SL5 . . . .28 E3
  Sandhurst GU15 . . . . .64 F6
  Windsor St KT16 . . . . .33 A3
Windsor Way
  Aldershot GU11 . . . . .105 B5
  Frimley GU16 . . . . .65 F4
  Woking GU22 . . . . .70 B1
Windsor Wlk
  Walton-on-T KT12 . . . . .35 B1
  Weybridge KT13 . . . . .53 C5
Windways GU8 . . . . .192 A5
Windy Ridge Cl SW19 . . . . .19 D3
Windy Wood GU7 . . . . .150 C2
Windycroft Cl CR5, CR8 . . . . .79 A3
Wyndridge RH11 . . . . .201 C3
Winern Glebe KT14 . . . . .71 A6
Winery La KT1 . . . . .38 A6
Winfield Ct RH5 . . . . .158 A1
Winfield Gr RH5 . . . . .158 A1
Winfrith Rd SW18 . . . . .20 C8
Wingate Cres CR0 . . . . .41 D3
Wingate Ct GU11 . . . . .104 F2
Wingfield Cl KT15 . . . . .52 A1
Wingfield Gdns GU16 . . . . .66 D3
Wingfield Rd KT2 . . . . .18 A1
Wingham House ⑧ SE26 . . . . . . .23 C4
Wingrove Rd SE6 . . . . .24 F6
Wings Cl Hale GU9 . . . . .125 A6
  Sutton SM1 . . . . .59 B6

Woodside continued
Horsham RH13 ....218 B4
Hydestile GU8 ....171 E5
Lower Kingswood KT20 ......117 F7
Sandhurst GU15 ....64 F7
Walton-on-T KT12 ....35 A1
West Horsley KT24 ....92 C1
Wimbledon SW19 ....19 F3
Woodside Ave
Croydon SE25 ....43 B4
Hersham KT12 ....54 B6
Thames Ditton KT10 ....36 E2
Woodside Cl
Caterham CR3 ....100 E3
Chiddingfold GU8 ....191 B4
Knaphill GU21 ....68 D2
Tolworth KT5 ....38 C2
Woodside Cotts GU8 .....148 C3
Woodside Court Rd
CR0, CR9 ....43 A2
Woodside Cres RH6 ....162 A3
Woodside Gn CR0, SE25 ..43 A3
Woodside Gn SW19 ....19 F2
Woodside & Inf Sch
CR0 ....43 A2
Woodside La SL4, SL5 ....9 C3
Woodside Park Est GU7 ..150 F4
Woodside Pk SF75 ....43 B3
Woodside Rd
Beare Green RH5 ....157 D3
Chiddingfold GU8 ....191 B5
Cobham KT11 ....74 A6
Crawley RH10 ....201 F8
Croydon SE25 ....43 B3
Farnborough GU11 ....104 F7
Guildford GU2 ....108 F2
Heath End GU9 ....125 E7
Kingston u T KT2 ....17 E1
Kingston u T KT3 ....38 E7
Purley CR8 ....79 E6
Sutton SM1 ....59 C7
Woodside Way
Croydon CR0 ....43 C3
Redhill RH1 ....140 A3
Redhill RH1 ....140 A8
Streatham CR4 ....41 C8
Virginia Water GU25 ....31 B6
Woodsome Lodge KT13 ...53 C4
Woodspring Rd SW19 ......19 E6
Woodstock
East Grinstead RH19 ....185 C2
West Clandon GU4 ....111 B7
Wokingham RG40 ....25 C6
Woodstock Ave
Cheam SM3, SM4 ....39 F2
Isleworth TW7 ....5 F2
Woodstock Cl
Cranleigh GU6 ....174 F1
Horsham RH12 ....217 D5
Woking GU21 ....70 A3
Woodstock Ct KT17 ....76 D7
Woodstock Gdns BR3 ....24 B1
Woodstock Gr GU7 ....150 E2
Woodstock La N KT6 ....56 C6
Woodstock La S KT10, KT6 ..56 C6
Woodstock Rd
Coulsdon CR5 ....79 B3
Croydon CR0, CR9 ....61 D7
Wallington SM5, SM6 ....60 A6
Woodstock Rise SM3 ....39 F3
Woodstock Way CR4 ....41 C2
Woodstocks GU14 ....85 D6
Woodstone Ave KT17, KT4 ..58 A5
Woodsway KT22 ....74 E5
Woodsyre SE19, SE26 ....22 F4
Woodthorpe Rd
Ashford TW15 ....13 D4
Staines TW15 ....13 D4
Woodvale Ave SE25 ....42 F7
Woodvale Ct SE25 ....42 F5
Woodvale Wlk SE27 ....22 C2
Woodview KT9 ....75 C8
Woodville Cl
Blackwater GU17 ....64 B5
Teddington TW11 ....17 A4
Woodville Gdns KT6 ....37 D2
Woodville Pl CR3 ....100 C5
Woodville Rd
Leatherhead KT22 ....95 B7
Merton SM4 ....40 A5
Richmond TW10 ....17 C5
South Norwood CR7 ....42 D6
Woodville Sch The KT22 ...95 B7
Woodward Cl KT10 ....55 F4
Woodwarde Rd SE22 ....22 F8
Woodwards RH11 ....201 C1
Woodway Camberley GU15 ..65 B5
Guildford GU1 ....110 B2
Woodyard La SE21 ....22 E8
Woodyers Cl GU5 ....152 B7
Wool Rd SW20 ....19 B2
Woolborough Cl RH10 ......201 E7
Woolborough La
Crawley RH10 ....181 F1
Crawley, Three
Bridges RH10 ....202 A8
South Nutfield RH1 ....140 F8
Woolborough Rd RH10 ......201 E7
Woolford Cl RG42 ....8 C1
Woolfords La GU8 ....169 B7
Woolhampton Way RG12 ....27 D4

Woolhams CR3 ....101 A1
Woollards Rd GU12 ....106 B4
Woolmead Rd GU9 ....125 C3
Woolmead The GU9 ....125 C3
Woolmer Hill Rd
GU26, GU27 ....207 D7
Woolmer Hill Sch GU27 ...207 D7
Woolmer View GU26 ....188 D3
Woolsack Way GU7 ....150 F4
Woolstone Rd SE23, SE6 .....23 E6
Woolstone Rd SE23, SE6 .....23 E6
Woosehill La RG41 ....25 A5
Wootton CT KT18 ....76 F3
Wootton Grange GU22 ....89 E8
Worbeck Rd SE20 ....43 C7

Worcester Cl
Croydon CR0 ....63 A8
Farnborough GU14 ....85 B7
Mitcham CR4 ....41 A7
Worcester Ct
Ashford TW15 ....14 B3
Walton-on-T KT12 ....35 C1
Worcester Park KT4 ....57 E7
Worcester Dr TW15 ....14 B3
Worcester Gdns KT4 ....57 E7
Worcester Park Rd KT4 ....57 D7
Worcester Park Sta KT4 ......39 A1
Worcester Rd
Belmont SM2 ....59 B3
Crawley RH10 ....201 E2
Guildford GU2 ....108 F3
Reigate RH2 ....139 B1
Sutton SM2 ....59 B3
Wimbledon SW19 ....19 F3
Wordsworth RG12 ....26 F4
Wordsworth Ave CR8 ....80 D4
Wordsworth Cl RH10 ....202 B8
Wordsworth Dr KT4, SM3 ...58 C5
Wordsworth Mead RH1 .....119 B3
Wordsworth Pl RH12 ....217 E7
Wordsworth Rd
Addlestone KT15 ....52 D6
Hampton TW12, TW13 ....15 F4
Penge SE20 ....43 A8
Wallington SM6 ....60 D4
Wordsworth Rise ⬛ 185 C1
RH19
Works Rd KT15 ....52 B2
Worlds End Hill RG12 ....27 F3
Wormley La GU8 ....171 B1
Worple Ave Isleworth TW7 ....6 A2
Staines TW18 ....13 B1
Wimbledon SW19 ....19 E1
Worple Ct SW19 ....19 E2
Worple Prim Sch TW7 ....6 A3
Worple Rd Epsom KT18 ....76 D6
Epsom KT18 ....76 E5
Isleworth TW7 ....6 A3
Leatherhead KT22 ....95 B4
Staines TW18 ....13 B1
Wimbledon SW19, SW20 ......19 E2
Worple Road Mews SW19 ...19 F2
Worple St SW14 ....7 D4
Worple Way TW10 ....6 E2
Worplesdon City Prim Sch
GU3 ....108 D4
Worplesdon Golf Course
GU22 ....89 E4
Worplesdon Hill
Heath House Rd GU22 ....88 D5
Worplesdon Rd GU2 ....109 A4
Worplesdon Sta GU22 ....89 B3
Worslade Rd SW17 ....20 D4
Worsley Bridge Jun Sch
BR3 ....24 A1
Worsley Bridge Rd
Beckenham BR3, SE6 ....24 A2
Catford SE6 ....23 F3
Worsley House SE23 ....23 B6
Worsley Rd GU16 ....85 E2
Worsted Gn RH1 ....119 D6
Worsted La RH19 ....206 B8
Worth Abbey & Sch
RH10 ....203 B1
Worth Park Ave RH10 ....202 C7
Worth Rd RH10 ....202 C6
Worth Way RH10 ....202 E5
Worthfield Cl KT19 ....57 D3
Worthing Rd Heston TW5 ......4 F8
Horsham RH12 ....217 B1
Worthington Ct CR4 ....41 B6
Worthington
House ⬛ SW2 ....22 A8
Worthington Rd KT6 ....37 F1
Wortley Rd CR0 ....42 A2
Worton Ct TW7 ....5 E3
Worton Gdns TW7 ....5 D5
Worton Hall Est TW7 ....5 E3
Worton Rd TW7 ....5 E4
Worton Way TW3, TW7 ....5 D5
Worton Rd TW7 ....5 E4
Wotton Way SM2 ....58 C1
Wrabness Way TW18 ....33 B8
Wray Cl RH19 ....206 D6
Wray Common Cty Prim
Sch RH2 ....118 D2
Wray Common Rd RH2 .....118 D2
Wray House ⬛ SW2 ....21 E7
Wray La RH2 ....118 F4
Wray Mill House RH2 ....118 E3
Wray Mill Pk RH2 ....118 E3
Wray Park Rd RH2 ....118 C2
Wray Rd SM2 ....58 F2
Wrayfield Ave RH2 ....118 C2
Wrayfield Rd SM3 ....58 D7
Wraylands Dr RH2 ....118 D3
Wraymead Pl RH2 ....118 B2
Wraymill Ct ⬛ RH2 ....118 D1
Wraysbury Cl TW4 ....4 E2

Wraysbury Rd
Staines TW18 ....12 C5
Wraysbury TW19 ....12 C5
Wraysbury Sta TW19 ....1 A1
Wrecclesham Hill GU10 ....145 E5
Wrecclesham Rd
Farnham GU10, GU9 ....145 E8
Wrecclesham GU10, GU9 ....145 F8
Wrekin The GU14 ....85 A1
Wren Cl Horsham RH12 .....217 D7
Selsdon CR2 ....62 D2
Wren Cres KT15 ....52 D5
Wren Ct Ash GU12 ....106 B3
Crawley RH10 ....201 E6
South Croydon CR0 ....61 D6
Wren House ⬛ TW12 ....16 B2
Wren Way GU14 ....84 F7
Wren's Hill KT22 ....74 C4
Wrens Ave TW15 ....14 C4
Wrenthorpe Rd BR1 ....24 E4
Wright Cl RH10 ....202 C2
Wright Gdns TW17 ....34 A4
Wright Rd TW5 ....4 C7
Wright's Row SM5 ....60 B6
Wrighton Cl SM1 ....58 F4
Wrights Rd SE25 ....42 E6
Wriotsley Way KT15 ....52 A4
Wrotham Hill GU8 ....192 E3
Wrotham House BR3 ....23 F1
Wroxham RG12 ....26 F4
Wroxham Wlk RH10 ....202 B4
Wrythe Gn SM5 ....59 F7
Wrythe Green Rd SM5 ....59 F7
Wrythe La SM1, SM5, SM4 ...59 E7
Wyatt Cl TW13 ....15 F7
Wyatt Park Mansions ⬛ 21 E6
SW2
Wyatt Park Rd SW2 ....21 F6
Wyatt Rd TW18 ....13 A3
Wyatt's Almshouses GU7 ..151 A6
Wyatt's Cl GU7 ....151 A6
Wych Elm Rise GU1 ....130 E6
Wych Hill GU22 ....89 C8
Wych Hill La GU22 ....89 E8
Wych Hill Pk GU22 ....89 D8
Wych Hill Rise GU22 ....89 D8
Wych Hill Way GU22 ....89 D8
Wyche Gr CR2 ....61 D2
Wychelm Rd GU18 ....67 C8
Wychwood RH14 ....212 D3
Wychwood Ave
Bracknell RG12 ....27 F5
Thornton Heath CR7 ....42 C6
Wychwood Cl
Aldershot GU12 ....105 F2
Ashford TW16 ....15 A2
Wychwood Pl GU15 ....66 B8
Wychwood Way SE19 ....22 D2
Wycliffe Bldgs GU2 ....130 C7
Wycliffe Ct RH11 ....200 E3
Wycliffe Rd Merton SW19 ...20 B2
Wimbledon SW19 ....20 B2
Wydell Cl SM4 ....39 D3
Wydenhurst Rd CR0, CR9 ...43 B2
Wye Cl TW15 ....14 B4
Wyecliffe Gdns RH1 ....119 C5
Wyeth's Mews KT17 ....76 F6
Wyeth's Rd KT17 ....76 F6
Wyke Ave GU12 ....106 E3
Wyke Bglws GU12 ....106 D3
Wyke Cl TW7 ....5 F8
Wyke Cty Prim Sch The
GU3 ....106 F4
Wyke Green Golf Course
TW7 ....5 F8
Wyke La GU12 ....106 D2
Wyke Rd SW20 ....39 C7
Wykeham Cl GU7 ....3 A8
Wykeham House
Farnborough GU14 ....105 C8
Merton SW19 ....40 A8
Wykeham Rd
Farnham GU9 ....125 C3
Guildford GU1 ....110 D2
Wylam RG12 ....26 F4
Wyleu St SE23 ....23 E8
Wymering Ct GU14 ....85 D3
Wynash Gdns SM5 ....59 E5
Wynbourne Ct SE20 ....43 B7
Wyncote Way CR2 ....62 D2
Wyndham Ave KT11 ....73 A6
Wyndham Cl SM2 ....59 A3
Wyndham Cres
Cranleigh GU6 ....174 A3
Twickenham TW4 ....4 F4
Wyndham Rd
Kingston u T KT2 ....17 F1
Woking GU22 ....69 B1
Wyndham St GU12 ....105 C1
Wyndhams GU22 ....70 B3
Wynell Rd SE23 ....23 E5
Wynfields GU16 ....85 F3
Wynlea Cl RH10 ....204 A8
Wynne Ct ⬛ TW7 ....6 A4
Wynnstow Pk RH8 ....122 F4
Wynsham Way GU18 ....48 B1
Wynton Gdns SE25 ....42 F4
Wynton Gr KT12 ....54 A8
Wyphurst Rd GU6 ....174 E4
Wyresdale RG12 ....27 F2
Wysemead RH6 ....161 C4
Wythegate TW13 ....12 F1

Y

Yaffle Rd KT13 ....53 C1
Yale Cl Hounslow TW4 ....4 F2
Sandhurst GU47 ....45 F2
Yarborough Rd SW19 ....40 D8
Yarbridge Cl SM2 ....59 B1
Yard Mead TW20 ....12 A5
Yarding RG12 ....26 F4
Yardley Cl RH2 ....118 B3
Yardley Ct SM3 ....58 C6
Yarm Cl KT22 ....95 C4
Yarm Court Rd KT22 ....95 C4
Yarm Way KT22 ....95 D4
Yarmouth Cl RH10 ....202 A4
Yarnold Cl RG40 ....25 F7
Yarrow Cl RH12 ....217 E5
Yateley Ct CR8 ....80 C5
Yatesbury Cl GU9 ....145 F7
Yattendon Jun Sch RH6 ....161 A4
Yattendon Rd RH6 ....161 B3
Yaverland Dr GU19 ....47 D2
Ye Market CR0 ....61 D5
Yeats Cl RH1 ....139 C6
Yeend Cl KT8 ....36 A5
Yehudi Menuhin Sch KT11 ..94 A8
Yellowcress Dr GU24 ....68 A3
Yelverton Ct KT23 ....94 A1
Yelverton Lodge TW1 ....17 C8
Yenston Cl SM4 ....40 A3
Yeoman Cl SE27 ....22 B5
Yeoman Ct TW5 ....4 F7
Yeoman Way RH1 ....140 B4
Yeomanry Cl KT17 ....76 F7
Yeomans Cl
Ash GU10, GU12 ....126 F8
Farnborough GU14 ....85 A5
Yeomans Mews TW7 ....5 D2
Yeomans Way GU15 ....65 E5
Yeoveney Cl TW19 ....12 D6
Yeovil Cl GU14 ....85 D1
Yeovil Rd Farnborough GU14 ..85 D1
Sandhurst GU47 ....45 E1
Yeovilton Pl KT2 ....17 C3
Yetminster Rd GU14 ....85 C1
Yew La RH19 ....185 B3
Yew Pl KT13 ....53 F7
Yew Tree Bottom Rd
KT17, KT18 ....77 C2
Yew Tree Cl Chipstead CR5 ...98 F8
Farnborough GU14 ....84 C3
Horley RH6 ....161 A4
New Malden KT4 ....38 E1
Yew Tree Cotts KT10 ....55 D8
Yew Tree Ct SM2 ....59 C3
Yew Tree Dr
Caterham CR3 ....100 F2
Guildford GU1 ....109 C6
Yew Tree Gdns KT18 ....76 E4
Yew Tree House KT4 ....38 E1
Yew Tree La RH2 ....118 B4
Yew Tree Rd
Charlwood RH6 ....180 E7
Dorking RH4 ....115 A1
Witley GU8 ....170 D6
Yew Tree Wlk
Effingham KT24 ....113 D8
Frimley GU16 ....65 F1
Hounslow TW4 ....4 F2
South Croydon CR8 ....61 C1
Yew Trees TW17 ....33 F5
Yewbank Cl CR8 ....80 D4
Yewdale Cl BR1 ....24 E2
Yewens GU8 ....191 B5
Yewlands Cl SM7 ....78 C4
Yewlands Wlk RH11 ....200 D4
Yews The TW15 ....14 B4
Yewtree Rd BR3 ....43 F6
Yewtrees TW20 ....32 C6
Yockley Cl GU15 ....66 D3
Yolland Cl GU9 ....125 C7
York Ave
East Grinstead RH19 ....206 A8
Mortlake SW14 ....7 C2
York Cl Byfleet KT14 ....71 E7
Horsham RH13 ....217 F3
Morden SM4 ....40 B5
York Cres GU11 ....104 F1
York Ct Beckenham BR3 .....44 A8
Kingston u T KT2 ....17 D2
Wallington SM6 ....60 C4
York Hill SE27, SW16 ....22 B5
York House Bracknell RG42 ...26 F8
Forest Hill SE26 ....23 C3
⬛ Kingston u T KT2 ....17 F1
Richmond TW9 ....7 A6
South Norwood SE25 ....42 E5
York Rd Aldershot GU11 ....104 F1
Ash GU12 ....106 A3
Belmont SM1, SM2 ....59 A3
Biggin Hill TN16 ....103 B8
Byfleet KT14 ....71 E7
Camberley GU15 ....65 D7
Crawley RH10 ....201 E2
Farnborough GU14 ....85 C1
Farnham GU9 ....125 C1
Guildford GU1 ....130 D8
Hounslow TW3 ....5 B4
Kingston u T KT2 ....17 F1
⬛ Teddington TW10 ....16 C4
Selsdon CR2 ....62 D1
Teddington TW11 ....16 E4
Thornton Heath CR0 ....42 D2
Weybridge KT13 ....53 C6
Wimbledon SW19 ....20 C2
Woking GU22 ....69 E1

Woolhams CR3 ....101 A1

Z

Zealand Ave UB7 2
Zennor Rd SW12 21
Zermatt Rd CR7 42
Zig Zag Rd Kenley CR8 80
Mickleham KT20, RH4, RH5 ..115
Zinnia Dr GU24 68
Zion Pl CR7 42
Zion Rd CR7, SE25 42
Zodiac Ct CR0 42

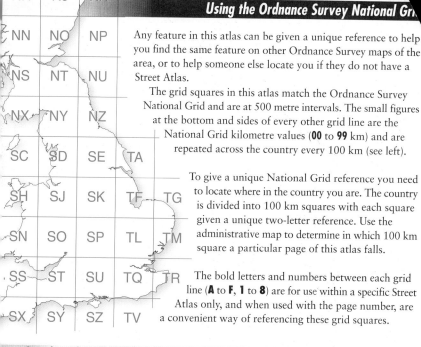

Any feature in this atlas can be given a unique reference to help you find the same feature on other Ordnance Survey maps of the area, or to help someone else locate you if they do not have a Street Atlas.

The grid squares in this atlas match the Ordnance Survey National Grid and are at 500 metre intervals. The small figures at the bottom and sides of every other grid line are the National Grid kilometre values (**00** to **99** km) and are repeated across the country every 100 km (see left).

To give a unique National Grid reference you need to locate where in the country you are. The country is divided into 100 km squares with each square given a unique two-letter reference. Use the administrative map to determine in which 100 km square a particular page of this atlas falls.

The bold letters and numbers between each grid line (**A** to **F**, **1** to **8**) are for use within a specific Street Atlas only, and when used with the page number, are a convenient way of referencing these grid squares.

Example   The railway bridge over DARLEY GREEN RD in grid square B1

Step 1: Identify the two-letter reference, in this example the page is in **SP**

Step 2: Identify the 1 km square in which the railway bridge falls. Use the figures in the southwest corner of this square: Eastings **17**, Northings **74**. This gives a unique reference: **SP 17 74**, accurate to 1 km.

Step 3: To give a more precise reference accurate to 100 m you need to estimate how many tenths along and how many tenths up this 1 km square the feature is (to help with this the 1 km square is divided into four 500 m squares). This makes the bridge about **8** tenths along and about **1** tenth up from the southwest corner.

This gives a unique reference: **SP 178 741**, accurate to 100 m.

Eastings (read from left to right along the bottom) come before Northings (read from bottom to top). If you have trouble remembering say to yourself "Along the hall, THEN up the stairs"!

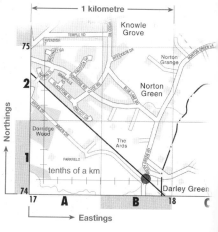

Philip's publish an extensive range of regional an
local street atlases which are ideal for motoring,
business and leisure use. They are widely used by
the emergency services and local authorities
throughout Britain.

Key features include:

◆ Superb county-wide mapping at an extra-large scale of
3½ inches to 1 mile, or 2½ inches to 1 mile in pocket edit

◆ Complete urban and rural coverage, detailing every name
street in town and country

◆ Each atlas available in three handy formats – hardback,
spiral, pocket paperback

'The mapping is very clear...
great in scope and value'
★★★★ **BEST BUY**   **AUTO EXPRESS**

1 Bedfordshire
2 Berkshire
3 Birmingham and
  West Midlands
4 Bristol and Bath
5 Buckinghamshire
6 Cambridgeshire
7 Cardiff, Swansea
  and The Valleys
8 Cheshire
9 County Durham
  and Teesside

10 Derbyshire
11 Edinburgh and
   Central Scotlan
12 North Essex
13 South Essex
14 Glasgow and V
   Central Scotlan
15 Gloucestershire
16 North Hampshi
17 South Hampshi
18 Hertfordshire
19 East Kent
20 West Kent
21 Lancashire
22 Leicestershire
   and Rutland
23 London
24 Greater Manch
25 Merseyside
26 Northamptonsh
27 Nottinghamshi
28 Oxfordshire
29 Staffordshire
30 Surrey
31 East Sussex
32 West Sussex
33 Tyne and Wear
   Northumberlan
34 Warwickshire
35 East Yorkshire
   Northern Lincol
36 North Yorkshire
37 South Yorkshire
38 West Yorkshire

How to order

The Philip's range of street atlases is
available from good retailers or directly from
the publisher by phoning 01933 443863